Inn Place

11th Edition

Published by
Ferrari International Publishing, Inc.
PO Box 37887
Phoenix, AZ 85069 USA
Tel: (602) 863-2408
Fax: (602) 439-3952
E-mail: ferrari@q-net.com

Published
January 1998

Inn Places is a registered trademark of Ferrari International Publishing, Inc.

Ferrari, Marianne
Inn Places 1998

Includes index
ISBN 0-942586-63-8

Copyright © 1998 by Ferrari International Publishing, Inc.

All rights reserved. No part of this book may be reproduced in any form, or by any means, electronic or mechanical, including photocopying, recording, or by any information storage and retrieval system, without the express written permission of the publisher.

Listing of a group, organization or business in Inn Places® does not indicate that the sexual orientation of owners or operators is homosexual, nor that the sexual orientation of any given member of that group or client of that business is homosexual, nor that the organization or business specifically encourages membership or patronage of homosexuals as a group. This book is sold without warranties or guarantees of any kind, express or implied, and the authors and publisher disclaim any liability for loss, damage or injury in connection with it.

Special Sales
Purchases of 10+ copies of any combination of Ferrari Guides can be made at special discounts by businesses and organizations.

Printed in the United States of America

What Is Your Destination?

Big Cities, Like: Atlanta, Boston, Chicago, New York, Philadelphia, Toronto, New Orleans, Los Angeles, San Francisco, San Diego, Milwaukee, Minneapolis/St. Paul, St. Louis, Kansas City, Austin...

Little Cities, Like: Plainfield, Inverness, New Carlisle, Williamston, Milton, Viroqua, Evanston, Fargo, Nauvoo, Wausau, Cave Creek, Woodland Park, Spring City, Porterville...

CARITAS

B&B Network (800) CARITAS
(800) 227-4827 or (312) 857-0801
Bed & Breakfast Accommodations in
Gay Homes Throughout North America

75 E Wacker Dr #3600, Chicago, IL 60601

On the Cover

18-24 James
Cairns, Qld, Australia

Featured on our front cover, this year, is the 18-24 James Hotel and resort in Cairns, Australia. The hotel building surrounds the private, clothing-optional, pool and spa area filled with tropical vegetation. The entire resort was designed and built expressly for gays and lesbians, who flock to Cairns to visit the Great Barrier Reef and Queensland's tropical rainforests. See page 148 for more information about 18-24 James.

FERRARI GUIDES™

CONTENTS

INTRODUCTION
Contents 3
How to Use This Guide 4

COLOR SECTION
Index to Color Section 7
Special Color Section 8

WORLDWIDE LISTINGS

AFRICA
South Africa 33

ASIA
Thailand 37

EUROPE
Belgium 38
Czech Republic 41
Denmark 42
France 43
Germany 56
Greece 61
Iceland 62
Ireland 63
Italy 67
Netherlands 72
Portugal 88
Spain 90
Switzerland 93
UK-England 95
UK-Scotland 127
UK-Wales 130

PACIFIC REGION
Australia 133
New Zealand 159
Fiji Islands 165
French
  Polynesia/Tahiti 165

CANADA
Alberta 166
British Columbia 167
Nova Scotia 178
Ontario 179
Québec 184
Saskatchewan 190

CARIBBEAN
Dutch West Indies 191
Puerto Rico 193
Virgin Islands-BVI 195
Virgin Islands-US 197
West Indies 198

LATIN AMERICA
Costa Rica 201
Mexico 206

UNITED STATES
Alaska 214
Arizona 217
Arkansas 233
California 236
Colorado 292
Connecticut 296
Delaware 297
District of
  Columbia 302
Florida 308
Georgia 345
Hawaii 347
Idaho 370
Illinois 371
Iowa 376
Kentucky 377
Louisiana 378
Maine 388
Maryland 399
Massachusetts 402
Michigan 439
Minnesota 442
Missouri 443
Montana 446
Nevada 447
New Hampshire 448
New Jersey 455
New Mexico 457
New York 470
North Carolina 482
Ohio 488
Oklahoma 489
Oregon 490
Pennsylvania 496
Rhode Island 503
South Carolina 508
South Dakota 510
Tennessee 511
Texas 513
Utah 522
Vermont 524
Virginia 530
Washington 532
West Virginia 546
Wisconsin 546
Wyoming 549

FORMS
The Ferrari Guides™ Order Form 560

INDICES
RV & Camping Index 551
Women's Index 552
Index to Accommodations 554

INN PLACES® 1998

HOW TO USE THIS GUIDE

■ How it Is Organized

This book is organized into the following geographical areas: Africa, Asia, Europe, Pacific Region, Canada, Caribbean, Latin America and United States. Each area is organized alphabetically by country and, within each country, alphabetically by state (or province) and city, or just by city.

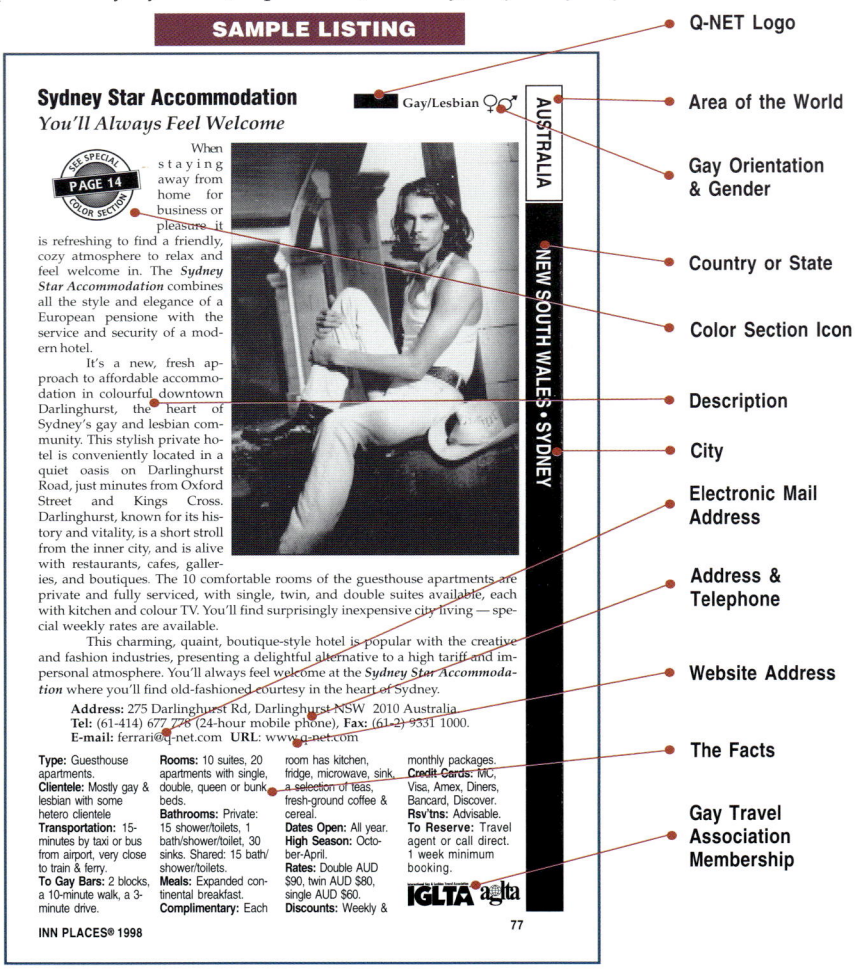

SAMPLE LISTING

- Q-NET Logo
- Area of the World
- Gay Orientation & Gender
- Country or State
- Color Section Icon
- Description
- City
- Electronic Mail Address
- Address & Telephone
- Website Address
- The Facts
- Gay Travel Association Membership

Sydney Star Accommodation
You'll Always Feel Welcome

When staying away from home for business or pleasure it is refreshing to find a friendly, cozy atmosphere to relax and feel welcome in. The *Sydney Star Accommodation* combines all the style and elegance of a European pensione with the service and security of a modern hotel.

It's a new, fresh approach to affordable accommodation in colourful downtown Darlinghurst, the heart of Sydney's gay and lesbian community. This stylish private hotel is conveniently located in a quiet oasis on Darlinghurst Road, just minutes from Oxford Street and Kings Cross. Darlinghurst, known for its history and vitality, is a short stroll from the inner city, and is alive with restaurants, cafes, galleries, and boutiques. The 10 comfortable rooms of the guesthouse apartments are private and fully serviced, with single, twin, and double suites available, each with kitchen and colour TV. You'll find surprisingly inexpensive city living — special weekly rates are available.

This charming, quaint, boutique-style hotel is popular with the creative and fashion industries, presenting a delightful alternative to a high tariff and impersonal atmosphere. You'll always feel welcome at the *Sydney Star Accommodation* where you'll find old-fashioned courtesy in the heart of Sydney.

Address: 275 Darlinghurst Rd, Darlinghurst NSW 2010 Australia.
Tel: (61-414) 677 776 (24-hour mobile phone), **Fax:** (61-2) 9331 1000.
E-mail: ferrari@q-net.com **URL:** www.q-net.com

Type: Guesthouse apartments.
Clientele: Mostly gay & lesbian with some hetero clientele
Transportation: 15-minutes by taxi or bus from airport, very close to train & ferry.
To Gay Bars: 2 blocks, a 10-minute walk, 3-minute drive.

Rooms: 10 suites, 20 apartments with single, double, queen or bunk beds.
Bathrooms: Private:
15 shower/toilets, 1 bath/shower/toilet, 30 sinks. Shared: 15 bath/shower/toilets.
Meals: Expanded continental breakfast.
Complimentary: Each

room has kitchen, fridge, microwave, sink, a selection of teas, fresh-ground coffee & cereal.
Dates Open: All year.
High Season: October-April.
Rates: Double AUD $90, twin AUD $80, single AUD $60.
Discounts: Weekly &

monthly packages.
Credit Cards: MC, Visa, Amex, Diners, Bancard, Discover.
Rsv'tns: Advisable.
To Reserve: Travel agent or call direct. 1 week minimum booking.

IGLTA agIta

INN PLACES® 1998

77

■ Type of Accommodations

Until hospitality professionals agree on standardized definitions of the terms "B&B," "inn" and "guesthouse," *Inn Places*® continues to honor the terminology chosen by each innkeeper.

4   FERRARI GUIDES™

■ Gay Orientation & Gender
At the top right corner of each listing is the answer to the perennial first question, "How gay is it and is it for men or women?" The range of possible answers, and what they mean, is given below. In describing clientele, these answers employ both words and the symbols for male ♂ and female ♀.

        Men ♂   Gay male clientele
      Women ♀   Female clientele
   Gay/Lesbian ♂   Mostly gay men
   Gay/Lesbian ♀   Mostly gay women
   Gay/Lesbian ♀♂   Gay men and women about 50/50
   Gay-Friendly ♀♂ } Mostly straight (non-gay) clientele with a gay and
   Gay-Owned ♀♂ } lesbian following, or a place that welcomes gay
                   and lesbian customers
   Gay-Friendly ♀ } Mostly straight (non-gay) clientele with a gay female
   Gay-Owned ♀ } following
   Gay-Friendly ♂ } Mostly straight (non-gay) clientele with a gay male
   Gay-Owned ♂ } following
   Gay-Friendly 50/50 } Half gay and half straight (Symbols indicate gay
   Gay-Owned 50/50 } male ♂ or lesbian ♀ predominance)

■ Q-NET Logo
Placement of the "q-net" logo next to an entry signifies that a detailed entry with color photography appears on the Ferrari Internet sites. **Q-net** is a gay-lesbian site containing comprehensive accommodations and tours listings.

■ Member AGLTA, IGLTA, NZGLTA
AGLTA is the Australian Gay & Lesbian Travel Association. IGTA is the International Gay & Lesbian Travel Association. NZGLTA is New Zealand's organization

■ Description
A description of the inn's architecture, ambiance, decor, amenities and services helps you to decide which inn to choose. Information is frequently also given on local activities.

■ Addresses
Some businesses do not list their addresses. Others list mailing addresses only. Some have deleted their zip codes to indicate they do not wish to receive advertising solicitations from other publications using this book as a lead list.

■ Telephones
Inside the US, area codes appear within parentheses. Outside the US, both country and city codes are used. For example, "Country: Netherlands, City: Amsterdam" is expressed by "(31-20)" followed by the phone number. When calling between two cities which are both within a country's boundaries (except in the US), always drop the country code and add a zero in front of the city code. Some countries are now dropping the city code and increasing phone numbers to 9 digits.

■ Telephones Are Changing
Watch the space just under city headings for notices of changes taking place.

■ All the Facts
Up to 32 facts may be included in a given listing. Variations in the length of listings are determined by the amount of information supplied to us by each establishment.

■ **Type** - Defines the kind of establishment (bed & breakfast, hotel, resort, etc.), and indicates whether restaurants, bars or shops are on the premises.

■ **Clientele** - A more specific and detailed description than provided in the gay orientation & gender line.

■ **Transportation** - Tells you if airport/bus pickup is provided and, if not, the best mode of transport is indicated.

■ **To Gay Bars** - The distance from your lodgings to the nearest gay or lesbian bar(s).

■ **Rooms** - The number and kind of accommodations provided. A cottage or cabin is an accommodation in a freestanding building. A bunkroom is a large room in which beds can be rented singly at a reduced rate. Bed sizes are also indicated.

■ **Bathrooms** - The number and type of private bathrooms and shared bathrooms.

■ **Campsites** - The number and kind of sites provided. Full RV hookups have both electric and sewer unless otherwise noted.

■ **Meals** - Describes meals included with room rate and those available at extra charge. Full breakfast includes meat, eggs and breads with coffee, tea, etc. Continental breakfast consists of breads and jams with coffee, tea, etc.

■ **Vegetarian Food** - Availability indicated.

■ **Complimentary** - Any complimentary foods, beverages or amenities.

■ **Dates Open** - Actual dates, if not open all year.

■ **High Season** - Annual season of high occupancy rate.

■ **Rates** - The range of rates, from lowest to highest, is given. Note: Rates are subject to change at any time and travelers should always request current rates when making reservations.

■ **Discounts** - Amounts and conditions.

■ **Credit Cards** - Lists cards accepted (MC=MasterCard, Amex=American Express). Access is MC in Europe. Bancard is British and Australian.

■ **Reservations** - Tells if required and how far in advance.

■ **Reserve Through** - How to make reservations.

■ **Minimum Stay** - If required, indicates how long.

■ **Parking** - Availability and type.

■ **In-Room** - Facilities provided INSIDE your room (TV, phone, AC, etc).

■ **On-Premises** - Facilities not provided inside your room, but available on the premises.

■ **Exercise/Health** - Availability of facilities such as hot tub, gym, sauna, steam, massage, weights.

■ **Swimming** - Availability, type, location.

■ **Sunbathing** - Areas described.

■ **Nudity** - Indicates if permitted and where.

■ **Smoking** - Restrictions, if any, are noted and availability of non - smokers' rooms is indicated.

■ **Pets** - Indicates if permitted, and restrictions are described.

■ **Handicap Access** - Indicates if accessible, and limitations are described.

■ **Children** - Preferences described.

■ **Languages** - All languages spoken by staff.

■ **Your host** - Name(s) of innkeeper(s).

Travel Safety - Constantly changing political and social situations in every nation can increase or decrease the risks of visiting any given destination without warning. This book does not include specific information about health and safety risks that readers may encounter in the places described herein. Travelers should always be mindful of their health and safety when traveling or staying in unfamiliar places.

■ **Advertisements** - The author, editor, and publisher of this book are not responsible for the contents of advertisements that appear in this book and make no endorsements or guarantees about their accuracy.

■ **We Welcome Reader Comments** - Specific information described in the listings, articles and other materials in this book may change without the knowledge of the author, editor and publisher, and the author, editor, and publisher cannot be responsible for the accuracy and completeness of such information or advice. We welcome all information sent to us by readers. We will consider your comments and suggestions in updating the next issue. Information on new areas, not yet covered, are especially valued.

INDEX

Inns Featured in the Color Section

Australia
- New South Wales, Sydney
  - Medusa Hotel 8
  - Sullivans Hotel 9

Canada
- Montreal, Quebec
  - La Conciergerie Guest House 9

Caribbean
- Dutch West Indies, Saba
  - Captain's Quarters 10
- Virgin Islands - BVI, Cooper Island
  - Cooper Island Beach Club 11

United States
- Arizona, Phoenix
  - Casa De Mis Padres 12-13
- Arizona, Tucson
  - Tortuga Roja Bed & Breakfast 14
- California, Laguna Beach
  - Casa Laguna B&B Inn 15
- California, Lake Tahoe Area
  - Lakeside B 'n B 16
- California, Palm Springs
  - La Posada de Las Palmas 16
  - Santiago Resort 17
- California, Russian River
  - Applewood Inn and Restaurant 17
  - Fern Falls 18
- California, San Francisco
  - Inn On Castro 18
  - Lombard Central,
    - A Super 8 Hotel, The 19
  - Renoir Hotel 19
  - Villa, The 20

- District of Columbia, Washington
  - Morrison House 21
- Florida, Key West
  - Rainbow House 22
- Maine, Ogunquit
  - Admiral's Inn & Guesthouse 23
  - THE INN at Two Village Square 23
- Massachusetts, Provincetown
  - Admiral's Landing Guest House 24
  - Beaconlight Guest House 24
  - Boatslip Beach Club 25
  - Tucker Inn at Twelve Center, The 25
- New Jersey, Atlantic City
  - Surfside Resort Hotel 26
- New Mexico, Santa Fe
  - Inn of the Turquoise Bear 27
- New Mexico, Taos
  - Ruby Slipper, The 28
- Texas, Austin
  - Ziller House 28
- Vermont, Andover
  - Inn at Highview, The 29
- Vermont, Stowe
  - Fitch Hill Inn 29
- Washington, Lopez Island
  - Inn At Swifts Bay 30
- Washington, Seattle
  - Gaslight Inn 31
- Washington, Port Townsend
  - Ravenscroft Inn 32
- Wisconsin, Sturgeon Bay
  - Chanticleer Guesthouse 32

Medusa Hotel

Unconventional, Yet Enthralling. Luscious Design with Urban Chic. Medusa — No Stone Unturned

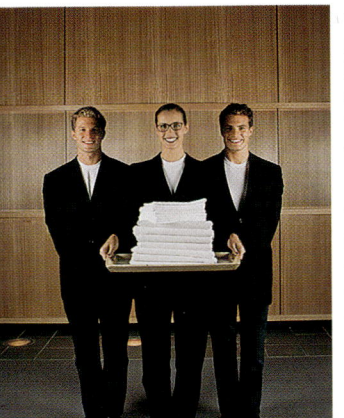

Medusa's innate elegance turns heads with a vibrant blend of the historic and the modern. The eye of Medusa is focused on indulgence: Enormous beds, natural fibre linen, organic toiletries and sumptuous evening chocolates are a few hedonistic examples.

Decadent, Yet Delightful...

Bold splashes of vivid colour invite exploration — such as the dappled light dancing, like snakes, from the reflection pool. Lighting is angled for maximum flattery. The place screams romance and glamour. Outside the door is a gourmet and cafe metropolis. Around the corner is fabulous Oxford Street. Medusa is conveniently located in the midst of Darlinghurst, Sydney's new focal point.

Floating Interiors...

The 18 individually-designed studios of this unique luxury hotel challenge those who dare to be a little different. This is no ordinary hotel. Medusa's effortless interior elegance floats in space, while accommodating state-of-the-art facilities.

Spirit of Medusa...

Service that evokes personality, performance and sleek sophistication. Our lively team of people are alert and care for your needs. Guest comfort and privacy is top priority.

Cutting-edge interiors... Located in the epicentre of Darlinghurst... Walking distance to the central business district and harbour... 24-hour reception and service... State-of-the-art security, including room safe... Cable television, video and hi-fi in your room... Climate control air conditioning... International dial telephone with modem... Business and internet facilities... Kitchenette and marbled bathroom ensuite... Courtyard and reflection pool

Address: 267 Darlinghurst Rd, Darlinghurst, Sydney, NSW 2010 Australia.
Tel: (61-2) 9331 1000, **Fax:** (61-2) 9380 4901.
E-mail: info@medusa.com.au **URL:** www.medusa.com.au

For complete details, see page 142

FERRARI GUIDES™

Sullivans Hotel

Q-NET Gay-Friendly ♀♂

Do Sydney — Stay Sullivans
   Sullivans, a small, stylish hotel, offers great value, a delightful garden courtyard and an intimate atmosphere. Included among the amenities to be enjoyed are all private baths, direct-dial telephones, air conditioning and colour TV. Breakfast is served daily in our breakfast cafe, and for guests with cars, there is ample covered parking available. Conveniently situated in central Paddington, *Sullivans* is close to all of Oxford Street's major attractions, including excellent shops, restaurants, cafes, cinemas and art galleries. For those guests who are sunworshippers, buses leave from outside the hotel to take you to Bondi and Bronte beaches.

Address: 21 Oxford St, Paddington, Sydney, NSW 2021 Australia.
Tel: (61-2) 9361 0211, **Fax:** (61-2) 9360 3735.

For complete details, see page 144

La Conciergerie Guest House

Q-NET Gay/Lesbian ♂

Your Resort in the City!
   La Conciergerie is Montréal's premier guest house. Since our opening in 1985, we have gained an ever-growing popularity among travelers from Canada, the United States, Europe and Australia, winning the 1995 Out & About Editor's Choice Award.
   The beautiful Victorian home, built in 1885, offers 17 air-conditioned rooms with queen-sized beds and duvet comforters. A complimentary European breakfast is served either in the breakfast room or on an outdoor terrace.
   The house is within walking distance of most major points of interest, including downtown shopping, Old Montréal, rue St.-Denis, rue Ste.-Catherine, and the East Village, with its many gay shops, restaurants and bars. We're two blocks from the Metro (subway) and there is plenty of on-street parking for those who drive.

Address: 1019 rue St.-Hubert, Montréal, QC H2L 3Y3 Canada.
Tel: (514) 289-9297, **Fax:** (514) 289-0845.
URL: http://www.gaibec.com

For complete details, see page 186

INN PLACES® 1998

Captain's Quarters

Q-NET Gay-Friendly ♀♂

The Unspoiled Queen of the Caribbean

Orchids, tree frogs, crested hummingbirds, sea turtles, hot springs, snorkeling... Enjoy all of this when you stay at *Captain's Quarters*. This 16-room Victorian guesthouse (which has hosted royalty, celebrities, and adventurous travelers for more than 30 years) is set in a tropical paradise, a short 10-minute flight from St. Maarten. Rooms feature antique and four-poster beds, many with elegant canopies. From the balconies and patios are stunning views of the Caribbean and mountain scenery. Enjoy the garden dining pavilion, cliffside pool/bar, and some of the friendliest people in the Caribbean.

Saba is a storybook setting of Dutch gingerbread villages that date from the 1850s. Originally settled by pirates and sea captains as a safe haven for their families, "The Rock" was accessible only by footpaths and thousands of steps until "the Road that Couldn't be Built" was handcrafted in the 1950s. Saba will remind you of Switzerland with palm trees! World-class scuba diving, well-marked hiking trails, a pristine rainforest, and spectacular views at every turn make Saba unforgettable.

Note: Saba has no beaches. All swimming is from rocks, boats, tidal pools, and hotel swimming pools. However, since you have to fly through St. Maarten anyway, spend a few days there and enjoy some of the best beaches in the world. Then visit us — just minutes away.

Address: Windwardside, Saba Netherlands Antilles.
Tel: (5994) 62201, (800) 446-3010
Fax: (5994) 62377.
E-mail: SabaCQ@megatropic.com

IGLTA

For complete details, see page 192

FERRARI GUIDES™

Cooper Island Beach Club
A Casual Caribbean Beachfront Resort

Gay-Friendly ♀♂

Cooper Island Beach Club is a small resort on a 1 1/2-mile by 1/2-mile island, where there are no roads, nightclubs, malls or fast-food outlets. Apart from the Beach Club and its staff, there is one local family, five holiday houses and many goats on the island. Our beachfront restaurant and bar offer one of the best sunset views in the islands. Sheltered from the sun, you can enjoy a cool drink with the Caribbean Sea lapping the sand only a few feet away. In addition, we have built a reputation for serving quality meals in an informal setting, at a reasonable price.

Photo by Jim & Odile Scheiner

Our twelve guest rooms were built in 1992 and 1996, and have an open-plan bedroom/living room/kitchen, plus balcony, bathroom, a shower that is almost outdoors, and a magnificent view of the Sir Francis Drake channel and several other islands. They are all on the beach, just a few steps from the warm, clear ocean where there is wonderful snorkelling.

Your principal activities on Cooper Island will consist of sunbathing, swimming, reading, writing, enjoying relaxing meals in the restaurant and conversation in the bar. If you wish to be more active, you can hike around the island (it's too small to get lost!), and we can arrange day sails and boat trips to other islands. For the SCUBA diver, novice or experienced, we have a fully equipped PADI dive shop on the property where we offer basic and advanced SCUBA instruction, and can take you on a variety of dive tours, including the wreck of the RMS Rhone, a Royal Mail steamship sunk in 1867, which is only 15 minutes by boat from our dock. **Guest Comment:** "There are not enough words to do justice to the immense beauty, tranquility and serenity to be found here."

Address: Cooper Island, British VI
USA office: PO Box 512, Turners Falls, MA 01376
Tel: (413) 863-3162, (800) 542-4624 (USA office), **Fax:** (413) 863-3662.
E-mail: info@cooper-island.com **URL:** http://www.cooper-island.com

Type: Beach resort with restaurant, bar, & scuba dive shop.
Clientele: Mainly straight with gay & lesbian following
Transportation: Pick up from ferry dock, no charge on scheduled trips.
Rooms: 12 rooms with queen beds.

Bathrooms: All private shower/toilets.
Vegetarian: Avail. for lunch & dinner with prior notice.
Dates Open: All year.
High Season: December 15th to April 15th.
Rates: Per night for 2: US $95 (Jun 1-Oct 30); US $155

(Dec 15-Apr 15); US $115 (Apr 15-May 31 & Nov 1-Dec 14). Meal and/or dive packages available.
Discounts: Weekly discounts available.
Credit Cards: MC, Visa, with 5% handling charge.

Rsv'tns: Required.
To Reserve: Travel agent or call direct.
Parking: Boat moorings available.
In-Room: Ceiling fans, kitchen, refrigerator & maid service.

For complete details, see page 195

Casa De Mis Padres

Q-NET Gay-Owned & -Operated ♀♂

Your Oasis in the Desert

Guests who seek an intimate Southwest atmosphere in the spirit and style of Arizona need look no further — *Casa De Mis Padres* is your oasis in the desert. This private and exclusive retreat was originally built in 1950, expanded in 1980, and restored in 1995. The 8000-square-foot Santa Barbara-style home is surrounded by mature palm trees, fragrant citrus, and lawn areas for year-round outdoor recreation such as croquet or badminton. Mexican paved patios and fireplaces embrace the pool, which is heated in winter. During the lazy summer months, relax poolside under a blanket of refreshingly cool mist as you take in the warm southern sun. You may enjoy an expanded continental breakfast and cocktail hour each day in the main residence or, weather permitting, poolside, served by your warm and responsive hosts.

Impeccable decor and fine art are only part of your experience. Great care and attention to detail have been given to our two unique resort-style accommodations. The *Pool Casita* has two king suites and is set up for longer stays for couples traveling together. There is also a full kitchen with separate dining and living rooms open to the pool patio, bar-be-cue and outside wet bar.

FERRARI GUIDES™

ARIZONA • PHOENIX

The three-room *Library Suite* features a home theatre system and an extensive collection of books and magazines. We are minutes away from golf, tennis, shopping and fine dining of Old Town Scottsdale. Arrive as a guest and leave as a friend who is already looking forward to coming home again.

Address: 5965 E Orange Blossom Ln
Phoenix, AZ 85287
Tel: (602) 675-0247
Fax: (602) 675-9476.
E-mail: casadmp@aol.com

Type: Bed & breakfast in a private home.
Clientele: Mostly men with women welcome, straight-friendly
Transportation: Car or a short taxi drive.
To Gay Bars: 2 miles, a 5 min drive.
Rooms: 2 suites, 1 cottage with king beds.
Bathrooms: All private: 1 bath/shower/toilet, 2 shower/toilets.

Meals: Expanded continental breakfast.
Vegetarian: Always available, no meat served.
Complimentary: Welcome champagne tray with snacks, evening cocktail hour, in-room tea & coffees.
Dates Open: All year.
High Season: Late Oct-May.
Rates: $150-$250.
Discounts: 5 nights or more 10% off.
Credit Cards: MC, Visa, Amex, Discover.

Rsv'tns: Required.
To Reserve: Travel agent or call direct.
Minimum Stay: 2 nights. 3 nights on holiday weekends.
Parking: Ample free off-street parking.
In-Room: Telephone, AC, ceiling fans, color cable TV, VCR, coffee & tea-making facilities, maid service. Cottage has kitchen. Library suite has refrigerator.
On-Premises: Video tape library.

Swimming: Pool on premises, heated in winter.
Sunbathing: Poolside & on patio.
Smoking: Permitted outside. All non-smoking rooms.
Pets: Not permitted.
Handicap Access: No.
Children: No, not set up for children.
Languages: English.
Your Host: Brian.

See also page 219

INN PLACES® 1998

Tortuga Roja Bed & Breakfast

Q-NET Gay/Lesbian ♀♂

Come, Share Our Mountain Views

Tortuga Roja Bed & Breakfast is a 4-acre cozy retreat at the base of the Santa Catalinas, whose windows look out on an open landscape of natural high-desert vegetation. A bicycle and running path along the Rillito River right behind our house can be followed for four miles on either side. Our location is close to upscale shopping and dining and numerous hiking trails. It's an easy drive to the university, local bars and most tourist attractions. Some of our accommodations have fireplaces and kitchens.

Address: 2800 E River Rd, Tucson, AZ 85718
Tel: (520) 577-6822, (800) 467-6822.

Type: Bed & breakfast.
Clientele: Good mix of gays & lesbians
Transportation: Car is best.
To Gay Bars: 10-minute drive.
Rooms: 2 rooms & 1 cottage with queen beds.
Bathrooms: All private.
Meals: Expanded continental breakfast.

Dates Open: All year.
High Season: September-May.
Rates: Please call for rates.
Discounts: For weekly & monthly stays.
Credit Cards: Discover, MC, Visa.
Rsv'tns: Often essential.
To Reserve: Travel agent or call direct.

Minimum Stay: 2 nights on holiday weekends.
Parking: Ample free off-street parking.
In-Room: Color TV, VCR, AC, ceiling fan, radio & telephone. Cottage has kitchen.
On-Premises: Laundry facilities & kitchen privileges.
Swimming: Pool & hot tub on premises.

Sunbathing: At poolside & on the patio.
Nudity: Permitted poolside & in hot tub.
Smoking: Permitted outdoors only.
Pets: Not permitted.
Handicap Access: Limited. Not wheelchair accessible.
Children: Permitted in guest cottage only.
Languages: English.

IGLTA

See also page 232

FERRARI GUIDES™

Casa Laguna
Bed & Breakfast Inn

Q-NET Gay-Friendly ♀♂

Sun, Sand & Sea

Casa Laguna is a unique, 20-room country inn on a terraced hillside, overlooking the Pacific Ocean. Its towering palms hover over meandering paths and flower-splashed patios, swimming pool, aviary and fountains, making this intimate, mission-style inn a visual delight. Many rooms and suites have sweeping views. A cottage, set on its own, has private garden, sun decks and ocean views. The mission house, itself, has two bedrooms and two fireplaces. Laguna Beach combines art, seaside casualness and colorful landscapes for an ideal retreat.

Address: 2510 South Coast Hwy, Laguna Beach, CA 92651
Tel: (714) 494-2996, (800) 233-0449, Fax: (714) 494-5009.

Type: Bed & breakfast inn.
Clientele: Mostly straight clientele with a gay & lesbian following
Transportation: Car is best. Jitney service from Orange County Airport, about $20.
To Gay Bars: One mile to nearest one. There are others in Laguna Beach.
Rooms: 15 rooms, 4 suites & 2 cottages. Single, double or king beds.
Bathrooms: All private shower/toilets.

Meals: Expanded continental breakfast.
Vegetarian: Fruit, cereals & breads available at breakfast.
Complimentary: Wine, cheese, snacks, tea & coffee are served each afternoon in the library.
Dates Open: All year.
High Season: July until Labor Day.
Rates: Winter $79-$175, summer $90-$225.
Discounts: Winter & mid-week discounts.

Credit Cards: MC, Visa, Amex, Diners, Bancard, Eurocard & Discover.
Rsv'tns: Required, but walk-ins accepted.
To Reserve: Travel agent or call direct.
Minimum Stay: Only on national holidays.
Parking: Ample free off-street parking.
In-Room: Color cable TV, telephone, ceiling fans & maid service. Some rooms with refrigerators. Kitchens in the 4 suites & 2 private homes.

On-Premises: Meeting rooms & TV lounge/library.
Swimming: Pool.
Sunbathing: At poolside, on the patio & common sun decks.
Smoking: Permitted. Non-smoking rooms available.
Pets: Small pets permitted with prior arrangements.
Handicap Access: No.
Children: Permitted, but must be attended by an adult at all times.
Languages: English, Spanish.

See also page 239

INN PLACES® 1998 15

Lakeside B 'n B Tahoe

Gay/Lesbian ♀♂

Romantic, Exciting, Right on the Water!

Lakeside B 'n B Tahoe, a private home smack-dab on the water, has antiques, plants and magnificent views of Lake Tahoe and mountains from all three guest rooms. There is a steam room, Jacuzzi, grand piano, fireplace, library, lakeside deck and parklike grounds. Fresh-baked bread and gargantuan gourmet breakfasts are served from a printed, personalized menu with many choices. Fabulous skiing in winter, swimming, boating and nude sunbathing in summer, and 24-hour Nevada gaming action are minutes away. On the quiet Nevada side of North Lake Tahoe, the B&B is 4 hours from San Francisco and 45 minutes from Reno.

Address: Box 1756, Crystal Bay, NV 89402
Tel: (702) 831-8281, **Fax:** (702) 831-7FAX (7329).
E-mail: TahoeBnB@aol.com

For complete details, see page 243

La Posada de Las Palmas

Gay-Owned & -Operated ♂

Return in Style to Old Palm Springs

Desert home of many Hollywood stars, the Las Palmas area of Palm Springs is also home to **La Posada de Las Palmas,** an Old Palm Springs-style hotel reflecting the area's Spanish Colonial, Mediterranean and Old California heritage. Nine studios and rooms surround a large pool and landscaped patio and, thanks to nearby Mt. Jacinto, many have dramatic mountain views. All studios and suites have direct-dial phones, color TV, coffee-makers, refrigerators and most have full kitchens. Continental breakfast is served poolside or in the comfortable reception area. Private and quiet, we're walking distance to restaurants, bars, shopping, and the center of Palm Springs village.

Address: 120 W. Vereda Sur,
Palm Springs, CA 92262
Tel: (760) 323-1402, (888) 411-4949,
Fax: (760) 416-3337.

For complete details, see page 259

FERRARI GUIDES™

Santiago Resort

Men ♂

Palm Springs' Most Spectacular Private Men's Resort

We're winners of Out & About's 1997 Editor's Choice Award for "exceptionally notable & distinctive gay lodging...a men's guesthouse that reflects stylish sophistication," and *Genre Magazine* says we're "...one of Palm Spring's most refined gay resorts," voting us "the most elegant men's guesthouse." Exotically landscaped, secluded grounds provide a peaceful enclave for the discriminating traveller. Enjoy magnificent mountain views from our terrace level, while an oversized diving pool, a 12-man spa and an outdoor cooling mist system complete the setting. Our poolside, courtyard or terrace suites and studios, featuring king-sized beds with feather duvet covers, superior quality towels and linens and shower massages, set the *Santiago's* standard of excellence and luxury. And clothing is forever optional...

Address: 650 San Lorenzo Rd, Palm Springs, CA 92264-8108
Tel: (760) 322-1230, (800) 710-7729, **Fax:** (760) 416-0347.
E-mail: santiagops@earthlink.net
URL: www.prinet.com/santiago

For complete details, see page 261

CALIFORNIA • PALM SPRINGS

Applewood Inn and Restaurant

Q-NET Gay-Friendly ♀♂

Russian River's Preeminent B&B

Once a mission-style retreat in the redwoods, *Applewood* has been transformed into an elegant country inn and restaurant that has become the darling of food critics and editors steering their readers to romantic getaways. "If you can't spend the night — *Applewood* is truly one of the finest inns in the wine country — dinner is the next best excuse for a visit," noted *The Press Democrat* in August, 1997. The beauty of the redwoods, apple trees and vineyards...the relaxing pool and Jacuzzi...the stylish rooms with European down comforters...the pleasure of sitting by the fire or reading in the library...the marvelous food in a firelit dining room...your willing hosts and two tail-wagging dogs...all await your arrival at this contemporary Eden.

Address: 13555 Hwy 116, Guerneville, CA 95446
Tel: (707) 869-9093, (800) 555-8509. **E-mail:** stay@applewoodinn.com
URL: http://applewoodinn.com

For complete details, see page 264

RUSSIAN RIVER

INN PLACES® 1998

Fern Falls

Q-NET Gay/Lesbian ♀♂

Romance Amidst the Redwoods

Fern Falls is a hillside habitat in a captivating canyon of Cazadero, whose cascading creeks merge with the languid waters of the Russian River. The custom-designed curved deck of the main house looks over the creek and ravine, and an ozonator spa sits above the waterfall on a hill nestled below a giant boulder amidst beautiful gardens.

Nearby you can try wine tasting at the Korbel Winery, horseback riding, a soothing enzyme bath and massage at Osmosis, canoeing on the Russian River, or hiking in the redwood forests.

Address: 5701 Austin Creek Rd, PO Box 228, Cazadero, CA 95421
Tel: (707) 632-6108, **Fax:** (707) 632-6216.

For complete details, see page 265

Inn On Castro

Q-NET Gay/Lesbian ♀♂

The innkeepers invite you into a colorful and comfortable environment filled with modern art and exotic plants. All rooms vary in size and have private baths. Meet fellow travelers from all over the world for a memorable breakfast. The *Inn On Castro's* location is unique, just 100 yards north of the intersection of Market and Castro, where you are in a quiet neighborhood, yet only a stone's throw away from the Castro Theater, plus dozens of bars, restaurants and shops. With the *Underground* almost virtually adjacent to the *Inn,* big-name store shopping and cable car, etc. are just a few minutes away. There is literally something for everyone.

Address: 321 Castro St,
San Francisco, CA 94114
Tel: (415) 861-0321.

For complete details, see page 282

18

FERRARI GUIDES™

The Lombard Central, A Super 8 Hotel

Gay-Friendly ♀♂

Old-World Charm and Today's Hospitality

The **Lombard Central**, reminiscent of old San Francisco with an intimate lobby featuring marble floors, etched glass, mahogany columns, and a grand piano, offers guests old-world charm and Super 8 hospitality. At the 100-room hotel, you'll find the attention to detail and personal service exceptional. From making reservations at the hotel's famous Faces Cafe Restaurant to arranging special tours of the city and beyond, the staff is eager to make your stay perfect. We are conveniently located in the heart of downtown San Francisco's performing arts and civic center district, and are only five blocks from the famous cable cars.

Address: 1015 Geary Blvd,
San Francisco, CA 94109
Tel: (415) 673-5232, (800) 777-3210,
Fax: (415) 885-2802.

For complete details, see page 283

Renoir Hotel

Gay-Friendly ♀♂

San Francisco's Newest First Class Downtown Hotel

The **Renoir Hotel** is a newly-renovated historical landmark building, just three blocks from Folsom Street, Polk Street, and three subway stations from the Castro. It is the best bargain in downtown San Francisco, providing charming European ambiance with classical music throughout. The ornate interior includes an original Renard in the reception area and Renoir prints placed tastefully throughout the hotel. The Royal Delight Restaurant serves breakfast, lunch and dinner. Also available are the lounge and lobby cafe and room service. *Inn Places* discount to $79 available most dates.

Address: 45 McAllister St,
San Francisco, CA 94102
Tel: (415) 626-5200, (800) 576-3388, **Fax:** (415) 626-0916
URL: www.renoirhotel.com

For complete details, see page 285

INN PLACES® 1998

The Villa

Gay/Lesbian ♀♂

Spectacular Views of San Francisco

The Villa is the flagship guesthouse of San Francisco Views rental services. Located atop one of the Castro's legendary hills, we offer magnificent views of the city from our double rooms and suites. Guests have the use of our fireplace lounge, complete kitchen and dining area overlooking our decks and swimming pool. Suites are equipped with TV, VCR and telephone with answering machine. We are minutes from the financial and shopping districts of downtown San Francisco, three blocks from the heart of the Castro and are open all year. Short- or long-term rentals available.

Address: 379 Collingwood, San Francisco, CA 94114
Tel: (415) 282-1367, (800) 358-0123,
Fax: (415) 821-3995.
E-mail: sfviews@aol.com

Type: Guesthouse.
Clientele: Good mix of gays & lesbians
Transportation: Easily accessible by car, or shuttle from airport.
To Gay Bars: 3 blocks or a 5-minute walk.
Rooms: 4 rooms, 3 suites & 4 apartments with single, double, queen or king beds.
Bathrooms: Rooms: private & shared. Apartments have private baths.

Meals: Continental breakfast.
Vegetarian: Restaurants nearby.
Dates Open: All year.
High Season: Summer & Fall.
Rates: Daily from $80, weekly $500, monthly rates available.
Discounts: Please inquire.
Credit Cards: MC, Visa, Amex.

Rsv tns: Recommended.
To Reserve: Call direct.
Minimum Stay: 2 days.
Parking: Free off-street & on-street parking.
In-Room: Color cable TV, VCR, telephone, kitchen, refrigerator & maid service.
On-Premises: TV lounge, laundry facilities & shared kitchen on each floor.
Swimming: Pool on premises, ocean nearby.

Sunbathing: At poolside & on common sun decks.
Smoking: Permitted inside the rooms. Non-smoking rooms available upon request.
Pets: Not permitted.
Handicap Access: No.
Children: Permitted, but not especially welcome.
Languages: English & Spanish.

See also page 287

Morrison House

Q-NET Gay-Friendly ♂

The Romance of Old Europe, The Charm of Early America

Designed and staffed with the utmost care, *Morrison House* blends the romance of Old Europe with the charm of Early America. Elegantly decorated with authentic Federal Period reproductions, we offer gracious hospitality and uncompromising service. Designed after the grand manors of the Federal Period, our guestrooms evoke the traditional elegance of late-eighteenth century Alexandria with their four-poster mahogany beds, brass chandeliers and sconces, and decorative fireplaces. *Morrison House* is centrally located in historic Old Town Alexandria, just minutes from Washington, DC and Washington International Airport. We're a Mobil four-star and AAA four-diamond hotel.

Address: 116 South Alfred Street, Alexandria, VA
Tel: (703) 838-8000, (800) 367-0800,
Fax: (703) 548-2489.

Type: Inn & hotel with restaurant & bar.
Clientele: Mostly straight clientele with a gay male following
Transportation: Taxi from National Airport. 7 blocks from metro station.
To Gay Bars: 7 miles, a 15 min drive.
Rooms: 42 rooms, 3 suites with single, queen or king beds.
Bathrooms: 45 private bath/shower/toilets.
Meals: Continental breakfast.
Vegetarian: Can be accommodated at all times.
Complimentary: Tea & coffee in mornings, turn-down "treat" (cookies).
Dates Open: All year.
High Season: Apr-Jun & Sept-Nov.
Rates: Jan-Feb & Jul-Aug: $125-$295/nt, Mar-Jun & Sept-Dec: $185-$295/nt.
Credit Cards: MC, Visa, Amex, Diners.
Rsv'tns: Required.

To Reserve: Travel agent or call direct.
Parking: Ample, pay covered parking. Valet parking.
In-Room: Telephone, AC, color cable TV, maid & room service.

On-Premises: Meeting rooms, 2 restaurants.
Exercise/Health: Gym nearby.
Smoking: Permitted in the grill. Smoking & non-smoking rooms available.

Pets: Not permitted.
Handicap Access: Yes, elevator.
Children: Welcome.
Languages: English, Spanish, Japanese, Ethiopian, Arabic, Italian, French.

See also page 305

DISTRICT OF COLUMBIA • WASHINGTON

Rainbow House

Q-NET Women ♀

Welcome to Paradise - We've Expanded!

*2 Hot Tubs!
2 Swimming Pools!
38 Rooms &
Suites!*

At the *Rainbow House*, we have everything from a standard room to a deluxe suite. All of our rooms have queen-sized beds, color TV, telephones, air conditioning, as well as Bahama fans and, of course, private bath. We serve an expanded continental breakfast poolside every morning. Enjoy it in our air conditioned pavilion or poolside. It's complimentary to our guests and a wonderful social setting. After breakfast, lounge on one of the sunbathing decks, or sit in the shade while you read a book with the gentle island breezes rustling the palm trees above.

As relaxing and comfortable as the guesthouse is, you may want to venture out to have fun. We can take care of that, too. We have a full-time concierge to help with snorkeling, scuba, kayaking, parasailing, bike trails, beaches, and, of course, Key West's many different restaurants. Just turn the corner of our street, and start your shopping exodus. Duval Street has everything you can imagine, from art galleries to T-shirts, from jewelers to sushi bars.

Of course, while you're in Key West, you'll have to experience one of our fabulous sunsets. They light up the sky and they're always memorable. And why not watch the sunset from Mallory Square, where you'll see jugglers, sword swallowers, tightrope walkers and characters that'll make you say "Only in Key West!"

There's plenty of nightlife, from rock-and-roll to disco, from piano bars to jazz, all within walking distance. As a matter of fact, most of our guests park their cars and leisurely stroll the streets of Old Town Key West. Whatever your vacation needs are...peace and quiet, the laid-back life, sun and fun, romantic or rejuvenating...pamper yourself with the special atmosphere we've created for you at the *Rainbow House*.

Address: 525 United St, Key West, FL 33040
Tel: (305) 292-1450, (800) 74-WOMYN (800 749-6696).

Type: Bed & breakfast guesthouse.
Clientele: Women only
To Gay Bars: 5-minute walk to gay/lesbian bars.
Rooms: 38 rooms & suites.
Bathrooms: All private.
Meals: Expanded continental breakfast.
Dates Open: All year.

High Season: Jan-Apr.
Rates: $69-$189.
Credit Cards: MC, Visa, Discover, Preferred, Amex.
Rsv'tns: Strongly recommended.
To Reserve: Call direct or travel agent.
Minimum Stay: During holidays.

Parking: On-street parking.
In-Room: Maid service, color TV, phones, AC. Kitchens available.
Exercise/Health: Jacuzzi.
Swimming: 2 pools or 1 block to ocean.
Sunbathing: At poolside, on private sun decks or on ocean beach.

Nudity: Permitted at poolside.
Pets: Not permitted.
Handicap Access: One unit available.
Children: Not permitted.
Your Host: Marion.

IGLTA

See also page 331

FERRARI GUIDES™

Admiral's Inn & Guesthouse

Q-NET Gay-Owned

Unique in Ogunquit...

The Admiral's Inn is located 65 miles north of Boston in Ogunquit, Maine. Our spacious grounds are within walking distance of the beach and all other village pleasures, and the privacy of our backyard pool is perfect for enjoying a morning or late-night swim, or a quiet afternoon retreat. We are unique in that we offer not only traditional guesthouse accommodations, but also efficiency and motel rooms with refrigerators and private baths. All rooms are air-conditioned and have electic heat and television. *Admiral's Inn* is gay-owned and -operated.

Address: #70 US Rt. 1, PO Box 2241, Ogunquit, ME 03907
Tel: (207) 646-7093.

For complete details, see page 392

THE INN at Two Village Square

Q-NET Gay/Lesbian

Ogunquit, Maine — The Quiet Alternative

Overlooking Ogunquit Square and the Atlantic Ocean, **THE INN** is an 1886 Victorian home perched on a hillside amidst towering trees. Our heated pool, hot tub and extensive decks provide views far to sea. Our atmoshpere is congenial and relaxed. Deluxe continental breakfast is served in our wicker-filled dining room, and guest rooms have color TV, ceiling fans and air conditioning. You are invited to join our Saturday get-acquainted party, Tuesday poolside barbeque and reserved seating at Ogunquit's Playhouse. Make our "home on the hill" YOUR home in Ogunquit.

Address: 135 US Rte 1, PO Box 864, Ogunquit, ME 03907
Tel: (207) 646-5779, **Fax:** (207) 646-6797.
E-mail: theinntvs@aol.com
URL: http://www.q-net/theinntvs

For complete details, see page 394

Admiral's Landing Guest House

Gay/Lesbian ♀♂

You've Been Waiting a Long Time to Get Away

Admiral's Landing Guest House... One block from the bay beach, shops and restaurants, offering spacious rooms with private baths, parking and a friendly, social atmosphere. Provincetown has miles of sandy beaches and dunes, wonderful shops and restaurants. This is the perfect place to truly relax and be yourself. Call or write for photo brochure, or visit our web site.

Address: 158 Bradford St, Provincetown, MA 02657
Tel: (800) 934-0925, (508) 487-9665,
Fax: (508) 487-4437.
E-mail: adm158@capecod.net
URL: http://www.ptown.com/ptown/admiralslanding/

For complete details, see page 410

The Beaconlight Guest House

Q-NET Gay/Lesbian ♀♂

"The Kind of House We Wished We Lived In"

Awaken to the aroma of freshly-brewed coffee and home-baked cakes and breads. Relax in the English country house charm of our elegant bedrooms and spacious drawing rooms, complete with open fire, grand piano, and antique furnishings. Multi-level sun decks provide panoramic views of Provincetown. *Beaconlight's* exceptional reputation for pampered comfort and caring service has grown by the word of mouth of our many returning guests. We truly become your home away from home! "The kind of house we wished we lived in. Exceptional 5-Palms Award 1997" — Out & About.

Address: 12 Winthrop St, Provincetown, MA 02657
Tel: (508) 487-9603 **(Tel/Fax)**, (800) 696-9603.
E-mail: beaconlite@capecod.net
URL: www.capecod.net/beaconlight/

For complete details, see page 413

FERRARI GUIDES™

Boatslip Beach Club

Gay/Lesbian ♀♂

Simply the Best for Over 25 Years!

The *Boatslip Beach Club*, beginning its 30th season, is a 45-room contemporary resort on Provincetown Harbor. Thirty-three rooms have glass doors opening onto private balconies overlooking our fabulous deck, pool, private beach and the bay. All rooms have either one queen or two double beds, private baths, direct-dial phones and color cable TV. Off-street parking, morning coffee, admission to Tea Dance and sun cots are all complimentary. We offer a full-service restaurant, poolside grille and raw bar and evening entertainment. Call or write your hosts: *Peter Simpson and Jim Carlino* for further information....*YOU OWE IT TO YOURSELF!!!.*

Address: 161 Commercial St Box 393, Provincetown, MA 02657
Tel: (800) 451-SLIP (7547), (508) 487-1669, **Fax:** (508) 487-6021.
E-mail: boatslip@provincetown.com
URL: www.provincetown.com/boatslip

For complete details, see page 414

The Tucker Inn at Twelve Center

Q-NET Gay/Lesbian ♀♂

A Romantic Country Inn by the Sea

The *Tucker Inn at Twelve Center,* originally a sea captain's home, pays tribute to Provincetown's history and Captain Miles B. Tucker's tradition of gracious hospitality. There are eight spacious, antique-filled rooms, most with queen-sized beds and private baths, and one fully equipped cottage. The inn is located on a quiet side street in the heart of Provincetown. A complimentary expanded continental breakfast is served daily in the comfortable living room or on a private tree-shaded patio. There is ample on-site parking.

Address: 12 Center St, Provincetown, MA 02657
Tel: (508) 487-0381, **Fax:** (508) 487-6236.
URL: http://www.provincetown.com/tucker

For complete details, see page 436

INN PLACES® 1998

Surfside Resort Hotel

Gay/Lesbian ♂

A Complete Gay Destination in Atlantic City

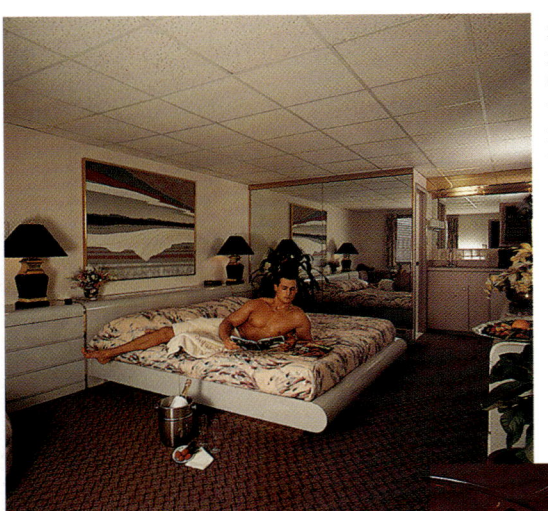

The Surfside Resort Hotel is a complete destination right in the heart of Atlantic City. Our boutique-style hotel features 50 individually decorated rooms offering accommodations from single to king beds; from affordable to deluxe. Our expansive pool and sun deck are surrounded on all sides to form a private space for your relaxation and enjoyment. You can sun yourself all day by our heated swimming pool with the convenience of cool drinks from the bar and snacks to dinner from the grill. Our current expansion has doubled the size of the hotel and added a grand new lobby, complete with a fireplace and continental breakfast bar. The hotel now offers phones in every room and electronic locks that use magnetic stripe cards in place of keys.

Always a popular destination, there's something happening 24 hours a day, 365 days a year in Atlantic City. Enjoy the world-famous beach and boardwalk. Dine in world-class restaurants and incredible all-you-can-eat buffets. Test your luck gambling at Atlantic City's famous casinos. See the biggest names in entertainment, plus cabarets and review shows. STUDIO SIX, New Jersey's hottest dance club specializing in the very best dance music and featuring a dazzling light, sound and video spectacular, is right next door. Doors open at 10 pm and don't close until dawn. The Brass Rail Tavern is open 24 hours, offering draft beer and friendly atmosphere. The Surfside Sun Deck bar is open seasonally. Enjoy a cool drink while catching some sun, or gaze at the stars at night. The Surfside Grill and the Brass Rail Grill offer breakfast, lunch, dinner and snacks. There's something for everyone, and there's always something to do. We're 1-1/2 blocks from the beach and boardwalk, and 1/2 block from the Sands, Ballys and Claridge casinos.

Address: 10-18 S. Mt. Vernon Avenue, Atlantic City, NJ 08401
Tel: (609) 347-SURF (7873), (888) 277-SURF (7873).

IGLTA

For complete details, see page 455

FERRARI GUIDES™

Inn of the Turquoise Bear

Q-NET Gay/Lesbian ♀♂

Where the Action Is... Stay Gay in Santa Fe!

The *Inn of the Turquoise Bear* occupies the home of Witter Bynner (1881-1968), a prominent gay citizen of Santa Fe, active in cultural and political affairs. A noted poet, essayist and translator, Bynner was a staunch advocate of human rights (supporting the suffrage movement and the rights of Native Americans and other minorities) and a vocal opponent of censorship.

Bynner's rambling adobe villa, built in Spanish-Pueblo Revival style from a core of rooms dating to the mid 1800's, is one of Santa Fe's most important historic estates. With its signature portico, tall pines, magnificent rock terraces, meandering paths, and flower gardens, the inn offers guests a romantic retreat close to the center of Santa Fe. As the only gay-oriented bed & breakfast in downtown Santa Fe, the *Turquoise Bear* is the perfect choice for both couples and individuals traveling alone.

Bynner and Robert Hunt, his lover of more than 30 years, were famous for the riotous parties they hosted in this house, referred to by Ansel Adams, a frequent visitor, as "Bynner's Bashes." Their home was the gathering place for the creative and fun-loving elite of Santa Fe and guests from around the world. Their celebrity guests included D.H. & Frieda Lawrence, Igor Stravinsky, Willa Cather, Errol Flynn, Martha Graham, Christopher Isherwood, Georgia O'Keeffe, Rita Hayworth, Thornton Wilder, Robert Frost — and many others.

Ralph and Robert, the new owners of the Witter Bynner Estate, reside on the property. Their goals are to rekindle the spirit of excitement, creativity, freedom and hospitality for which this remarkable home was renowned; to protect, restore and extend the legacy of its famous gay creator; and to provide their guests with the experience of a unique setting that captures the essence of traditional Santa Fe. Whether you are coming to New Mexico for the opera, the art scene, the museums, skiing, hiking, exploring Native American and Hispanic cultures, or just to relax away from it all, the *Inn of the Turquoise Bear* is the place to stay in Santa Fe. Robert and Ralph look forward to the privilege of serving as your hosts during your visit.

Address: 342 E Buena Vista Street, Santa Fe, NM 87501 **Tel:** (505) 983-0798, (800) 396-4104, **Fax:** (505) 988-4398. **E-mail:** bluebear@roadrunner.com

Type: Bed & breakfast inn.
Clientele: 70% gay & lesbian and 30% straight clientele
Transportation: Car is best, shuttle bus from Albuquerque airport.

To Gay Bars: 8 blocks, 1 mile, a 15 min walk, a 2 min drive.
Rooms: 9 rooms, 2 suites with double, queen or king beds.

Bathrooms: Private: 1 bath/toilet, 4 shower/toilets, 4 bath/shower/toilets. Shared: 1 shower only.

Meals: Expanded continental breakfast.

IGLTA

For complete details, see page 466

INN PLACES® 1998 27

The Ruby Slipper

Q-NET Gay/Lesbian ♀♂

A Perfect Balance of Privacy & Personal Attention

At **The Ruby Slipper,** our guest rooms, individually decorated with handmade furniture, have private baths and fireplace or woodstove. Breakfast specialties include scrumptious breakfast burritos, omelettes and banana pancakes. Our lovely grounds are complete with an outdoor hot tub. A vacation in Taos might include hiking, horseback riding, world-class skiing, gallery viewing, shopping or visiting Taos Pueblo. *The Ruby Slipper* is Northern New Mexico's most popular and relaxing gay-friendly bed and breakfast. Come see what everybody's talking about!

Address: PO Box 2069, Taos, NM 87571
Tel: (505) 758-0613.

For complete details, see page 469

Ziller House

Q-NET Gay-Owned 50/50 ♀♂

An Exclusive Alternative to Austin's Premium Hotels

This exquisitely renovated 1930s Mediterranean-style estate is nestled among giant oaks on a secluded bluff above the south shore of Town Lake. Private, yet centrally located, *Ziller House* evokes the feeling of an Italianate villa of the '30s with a blend of antique and contemporary appointments. Five large bedrooms offer elegant alternatives to Austin's premium hotels. Enjoy a game of pool in the oak-paneled billards room, or, after a jog along the neighborhood hike-and-bike trail, relax in the natural-stone swimming pool and spa with views of Austin's skyline. Austin's live music and entertainment district, gay bars, restaurants and shopping are minutes away.

Address: 800 Edgecliff Terrace, Austin, TX 78704
Tel: (512) 462-0100, (800) 949-5446, **Fax:** (512) 462-9166.

For complete details, see page 515

FERRARI GUIDES™

The Inn at HighView

Q-NET Gay-Friendly ♀♂

Vermont the Way You Always Dreamed It Would Be...

...but the way you've never found it, until now. Everyone who arrives at *The Inn at HighView* has the same breathless reaction to the serenity of the surrounding hills. The inn's hilltop location offers incredible peace, tranquility and seclusion, yet is convenient to all the activities that bring you to Vermont, such as skiing, golf, tennis and antiquing. Ski cross-country or hike our 72 acres. Swim in our unique rock garden pool. Enjoy our gourmet dinner, relax by a blazing fire, snuggle under a down comforter in a canopy bed, or gaze 50 miles over pristine mountains.

Address: RR 1, Box 201A, East Hill Road, Andover, VT 05143
Tel: (802) 875-2724, **Fax:** (802) 875-4021.
E-mail: hiview@aol.com

For complete details, see page 524

Fitch Hill Inn

Gay-Friendly ♀♂

Elegant, But Not Stuffy

Historic *Fitch Hill Inn*, c. 1797, occupies a hill overlooking the magnificent Green Mountains. Its location, central to Vermont's all-season vacation country, offers a special opportunity to enjoy the true Vermont experience. This is the town in which Charles Kuralt said he would like to settle. Antique-decorated guest rooms all have spectacular views. Breakfasts and, by arrangement, gourmet dinners, are prepared by the innkeeper. The library has video tapes, books, and an atmosphere of comfort and ease. The newly-renovated 18th century living room is wonderful for music, reading, and sitting by the fireside.

Address: RR 2 Box 1879, Fitch Hill Rd, Hyde Park, VT 05655
Tel: (802) 888-3834, (800) 639-2903, **Fax:** (802) 888-7589.

For complete details, see page 527

INN PLACES® 1998

Inn At Swifts Bay

Gay-Owned ♀♂

A Small Inn with a National Reputation

Since 1988, *The Inn At Swifts Bay* has gained national recognition as one of the finest accommodations in the beautiful San Juan Islands of Washington State. This elegant country home sits on three wooded acres with a private beach nearby. The inn has five quiet and romantic guest rooms, three with private baths and fireplaces. The living room also has a fireplace and the den has over 300 videos to choose from. After a workout and sauna in the exercise studio, relax in the hot tub located at the edge of the woods — we provide robes and slippers. Here's what others say about the inn."The most memorable part of the trip...a stay at Inn At Swifts Bay...the setting is beautiful and serene, the accommodations excellent, and the food of gourmet quality!" — *San Francisco Sunday Chronicle-Examiner* "Stateroom elegant." — *Vogue*"

Entrust yourself to the warm hospitality of the Inn At Swifts Bay. In the morning, one of the greatest pleasures of your stay awaits, a breakfast that is famous island-wide!" — *Brides Magazine*"

Those who appreciate luxury and superb cuisine will find the Inn At Swifts Bay to their liking. The Tudor-style inn is classy, stylish and oh, so comfortable...a breakfast that is nothing short of sensational!" — *West Coast Bed & Breakfast Guide*

Inn Places Reader Commment: "The inn is impeccably and tastefully decorated. Everything is done with warmth and quality. All of your needs and desires are met before you know what you want. The inn has a sense of class I have dreamed about, but have never found."

Address: Lopez Island, WA 98261 **Tel:** (360) 468-3636, **Fax:** (360) 468-3637.
E-mail: inn@swiftsbay.com **URL:** www.swiftsbay.com

Type: Bed & breakfast inn.
Clientele: Mostly straight clientele with a gay/lesbian following
Transportation: By car ferry from Anacortes or daily plane from Seattle or Anacortes. Pick up from airport, ferry dock, or marina.
To Gay Bars: Drive 1 hr to Bellingham or Everett. 1-1/2 hrs to Seattle bars.
Rooms: 2 rooms, 3 suites with queen beds.

Bathrooms: 3 private shower/toilets & 1 shared bath/shower/toilet.
Meals: Full gourmet breakfast.
Vegetarian: Dietary restrictions accommodated.
Complimentary: Sherry in living room. Fridge with mineral waters, microwave popcorn, tea & apples.
Dates Open: All year.
High Season: May-Oct.
Rates: $95-$175.

Credit Cards: MC, Visa, Discover, Amex.
Rsv'tns: Preferred.
To Reserve: Travel agent or call direct.
Minimum Stay: Only on holiday weekends.
Parking: Ample free off-street parking.
In-Room: Maid service. Room 5 has TV, VCR & stereo.

On-Premises: Telephone in library, VCR with film library, fax, refrigerator with ice & mineral water.
Exercise/Health: Hot tub & massage (by appointment only), exercise studio & sauna
Swimming: Ocean or lake (very cold!).

IGLTA

For complete details, see page 535

FERRARI GUIDES™

Gaslight Inn

Q-NET Gay/Lesbian ♀♂

Welcome to *Gaslight Inn,* a Seattle four-square house built in 1906. In restoring the inn, we have brought out the home's original turn-of-the-century ambiance and warmth, while keeping in mind the additional conveniences and contemporary style needed by travelers in the nineties. The interior is appointed in exacting detail, with strikingly rich, dark colors, oak paneling, and an enormous entryway and staircase.

Gaslight Inn's comfortable and unique rooms and suites are furnished with quality double or queen-sized beds, refrigerator and television. Additional features for your special needs, such as private bath and phone service, are available in some rooms. Some rooms also have decks with fabulous views or fireplaces. The living room, with its large oak fireplace, is always an inviting room, as is the library. Through the late spring and summer, we encourage you to relax and unwind at poolside with a glass of wine after a long, busy day. This private, in-ground, heated pool with several decks and interesting plant arrangements, is found at the back of the inn.

Gaslight Inn is convenient to central Seattle's every attraction: Volunteer Park, City Center, and to a plethora of gay and lesbian bars, restaurants and retail stores in the Broadway district. All of us at *Gaslight Inn* send you a warm advance welcome to Seattle.

Address: 1727 15th Ave, Seattle, WA 98122
Tel: (206) 325-3654,
Fax: (206) 328-4803.
E-mail: innkeepr@gaslight-inn.com
URL: www.gaslight-inn.com

Type: Guesthouse.
Clientele: Mostly gay/lesbian with some straight clientele
Transportation: Shuttle Express from airport $15. (206) 286-4800 to reserve ride.
To Gay Bars: 2 blocks to men's bars, 3 blocks to women's bars.
Rooms: 9 doubles, 7 suites.
Bathrooms: 11 private, others share.

Meals: Expanded continental breakfast.
Complimentary: Coffee, tea & juices, fresh fruit, pastries.
Dates Open: All year.
High Season: Summer.
Rates: $68-$158.
Credit Cards: MC, Visa, Amex.
Rsv'tns: Recommended at least 2 weeks in advance.
To Reserve: Call direct.

Minimum Stay: 2 days on weekends, 3 days on holidays.
Parking: Ample on-street & off-street parking.
In-Room: Color TV, maid service & refrigerator.
On-Premises: Meeting rooms, living room, library,

public telephone.
Swimming: Seasonal heated pool.
Sunbathing: On private or common sun decks or at poolside.
Smoking: Permitted on decks & porches only.
Pets: Not permitted.

For complete details, see page 543

Ravenscroft Inn

Gay-Friendly ♀♂

Take a Short Trip to Far Away...
One of the most romantic hideaways in the Pacific Northwest is located high on a bluff overlooking historic Port Townsend, the Olympic Peninsula's Victorian seaport. The **Ravenscroft Inn** is noted for its colonial style, a replication of a historic Charleston single house. The Inn offers a unique combination of colonial hospitality, mixed with a casual air that spells comfort to its guests. The hosts take great pleasure in looking after their guests' special requests, whether it's dinner, theatre, concert reservations, or arranging for flowers or champagne, all are carried out with ease and alacrity. While staying at the **Ravenscroft Inn,** you can explore the Olympic National Park, walk the seven mile sand spit at Dungeness or hike through North America's only rainforest. Port Townsend and its environs meets all your vacation requirements offering scenic beauty, theatre, unparalleled dining, boating, biking, fishing, kayaking and hiking. Top this off with a delectable breakfast and fresh roasted gourmet coffee, served each morning. **Guest Comment:** "There was never a detail left unattended."

Address: 533 Quincy St, Port Townsend, WA 98368
Tel: (360) 385-2784, (800) 782-2691, **Fax:** (360) 385-6724.   *For complete details, see page 539*

Chanticleer Guesthouse

Q-NET Gay-Friendly 50/50 ♀♂

A Romantic Country Inn Nestled Among the Orchards of Door County
Welcome to the *Chanticleer,* situated on 30 private acres in picturesque Door County, WI. With over 250 miles of shoreline, 12 lighthouses, 5 state parks and countless antique and gift shops, you're not far from unlimited fun and adventure.

The *Chanticleer's* majestic maples and delicate fields of wild flowers are a grand sight as you stroll on our nature trail. After your walk, tour our beautiful gardens, lounge poolside or relax on your private terrace overlooking the *Chanticleer's* serene countryside. All deluxe suites include double whirlpools, fireplaces and breakfast delivered to your room.

Address: 4072 Cherry Rd, Sturgeon Bay, WI 54235
Tel: (920) 746-0334.

For complete details, see page 548

FERRARI GUIDES™

The Owl and the Pussycat

Lesbian-Owned & -Operated ♀

Come Dance by the Light of the Moon — E. Lear, 1812-1888

The **Owl and the Pussycat** is nestled in the Noordhoek Valley, surrounded by Chapman's Peak and the Silvermine mountain range, just five minutes from both the Indian and Atlantic Ocean. Here, you find yourself immersed in Cape Town's natural beauty with breathtaking beaches, mountain walks, picnic spots and scenic drives. And, if the mood takes you, you're a mere 30 minutes from the buzz of city life and the famous Waterfront. We offer a cosy, friendly atmosphere, so relax and enjoy a taste of South Africa with sunset braais (barbecues) with your hosts. Our wish is to make you feel comfortable and totally spoiled in our "home-from-home," yet "away-from-it-all" environment. TO OPEN DECEMBER 10, 1997.

Address: 56 Jefferson Rd, Milkwood Park, Noordhoek, Cape Town 7975 South Africa.
Tel: (27-21) 785 2454 (Tel/Fax).

Type: Bed & breakfast guesthouse with bar.
Clientele: Women only
Transportation: Car is best. Pick up from airport R70, from nearest train station R10.
To Gay Bars: A 30 min drive to gay bars.
Rooms: 3 rooms with single, double or queen beds.

Bathrooms: 1 private shower/toilet, 1 shared bath/shower/toilet.
Meals: Cont. breakfast.
Vegetarian: Available on request.
Complimentary: Tea & coffee on request.
Dates Open: All year.
Rates: Single: R150 per person; Sharing: R175 per person.

Credit Cards: MC, Visa.
Rsv'tns: Required.
To Reserve: Call direct.
Parking: Ample free off-street parking.
In-Room: Room & laundry service.
On-Premises: TV lounge.
Swimming: Nearby ocean.
Sunbathing: At beach, on patio & in garden.

Smoking: Permitted in TV lounge only. All bedrooms must be smoke-free.
Pets: Not permitted.
Handicap Access: No.
Children: No.
Languages: English & Afrikaans.
Your Host: Paula & Vanessa.

Bliss Flatlits

Lesbian-Owned 50/50 ♀♂

Welcome to Paradise

Privacy is the key word at **Bliss Flatlits**, comfortable, well-appointed units situated on the premises of our home — close to all amenities and with stunning views of the lagoon. Your hostesses have lived in this area for many years and are here to advise and guide you, thus making your stay that much better. The town of Knysna, situated around a lagoon fed by the warm Indian Ocean, is located in the heart of the Garden Route, an area extending from Cape Town to Port Elizabeth. Knysna is arrived at via "The Heads," two large sandstone cliffs guarding the exit of the lagoon into the sea. We have beautiful beaches, ideal for swimming and surfing, scenic drives, the largest indigenous forest in South Africa, an elephant park, oyster farm, art galleries, shopping and much, much more! Many eateries can also be enjoyed — feel at home in Mike's Can-De-Light Bistro, enjoy an evening with Mario and Duke at The Gekko Bar, or sample light lunches at The Old Jail where Brigit's ready smile and delicious delights will satisfy your tum. Knysna is beautiful, varied and unforgettable... See you here!

Address: 12 Faure Street, West Hill, Knysna, on the Cape 6570 South Africa.
Tel: (27-445) 24569 (Tel/Fax).

Type: 2 self-catering cottages.
Clientele: 50% gay & lesbian & 50% hetero clientele
Transportation: Car. Free pick up from bus, charge for pick up from airport (a 45 min drive).

Rooms: 2 cottages with twin or double beds.

continued next page

INN PLACES® 1998

Bathrooms: Private shower/toilets.
Meals: Full, continental or expanded breakfast. Basket provided at extra cost.
Vegetarian: Vegetarians catered for at most food outlets.
Complimentary: Tea & coffee.
Dates Open: All year.
High Season: Dec-Mar.
Rates: Per person: low R100, high R200.
Credit Cards: Visa, MC.
Rsv'tns: Highly recommended in high season.
To Reserve: Call direct.
Minimum Stay: 2 nights.
Parking: Adequate free off-street parking. 1 covered garage.
In-Room: Color TV, kitchenette, refrigerator, coffee & tea-making facilities, maid service. Laundry service by arrangement.
Exercise/Health: Nearby gym, weights, sauna, massage.
Swimming: Nearby ocean & lake.
Sunbathing: At beach.
Nudity: We don't mind.
Smoking: No limits.
Pets: Not permitted.
Handicap Access: No.
Children: Not as a rule (18 yrs & over only).
Languages: English, Afrikaans.
Your Host: Noreen & Grace.

The Cottages   Gay-Friendly ♀♂

Come Share Our Paradise

Treat yourself to the most "Out of Africa" experience in individually decorated stone & thatch cottages, some with their own catering facilities and glorious views. *The Cottages* (AD 1905) are set on the Observatory Ridge, a 10-minute drive east of the city and business centres and close to the airport, bars, restaurants and nightlife. Other wonderful facilities include a hiking trail, rock pool, a verdant English garden and unlimited tranquility (at no extra charge!) We look forward to welcoming you to a Johannesburg you never knew existed!

Address: 30 Gill St, Observatory, Johannesburg 2198 South Africa.
Tel: (27-11) 487 2829, **Fax:** (27-11) 487 2404.

Type: Guesthouse.
Clientele: Mostly hetero with 15% gay & lesbian clientele
Transportation: Car is best. Pick up from airport or train R100.
To Gay Bars: 6 blocks, a 10-15 minute walk.
Rooms: 13 cottages with single or double beds.
Bathrooms: Private.
Meals: Full breakfast. Dinners on request.
Vegetarian: Available on request.
Complimentary: Tea- & coffee-making facilities with tea, coffee & sugar provided.
Dates Open: All year.
High Season: All year, quiet Christmas period.
Rates: Single R255-R275, double R320-R400.
Discounts: 7 or more days, less 5%. Monthly, less 10%.
Credit Cards: MC, Visa, Amex, Diners.
Rsv'tns: Advisable.
To Reserve: Travel agent or call direct.
Parking: Ample free parking.
In-Room: Coffee/tea-making facilities, color TV, phone, laundry & maid service. Laundry service in 5 units, refrigerator in 5 units, color cable TV in 4 units.
On-Premises: Fax, small conference centre (14 people).
Exercise/Health: Trampoline, hiking trail adjacent.
Swimming: Pool on premises.
Sunbathing: Poolside & on patio.
Smoking: Not permitted in dining room.
Pets: Not permitted.
Handicap Access: Very hilly terrain, difficult access for the handicapped.
Children: Welcome.
Languages: English, Afrikaans, Italian, German.
Your Host: John & Sonja.

Shangri-La Country Lodge   Gay-Friendly ♀♂

Luxury Thatched Rondavels in the Waterberg Mountain Foothills

Shangri-La Country Lodge, near Nylstroom in the Northern Province, is an idyllic retreat offering the comfort, style and intimacy of days gone by. Such is the atmosphere of warmth and generosity created by the hosts and staff that you will feel like both a guest and a friend in their home. Nestling cosily in dense bushveld in the foothills of the Waterberg mountain range, *Shangri-La* lives up to its mythical name. Mild winters and sub-tropical summers invite you to relax and unwind all the year round in a true haven of peace and tranquility. A select number of guests are accommodated in luxury thatched rondavels, each with en suite bathroom. An atmosphere of "olde-world charm" and gracious living is created by the antique decor, country-style handmade quilts and festoon blinds.

Address: Eersbewoond Rd, PO Box 262, Nylstroom 0510 South Africa.
Tel: (27-14) 717 53 81, **Fax:** (27-14) 717 31 88.

Type: Country lodge with restaurant & bar, 1 hour north of Pretoria. **Clientele:** Mostly hetero clientele with a gay/lesbian following **Transportation:** Pick up from airport. **To Gay Bars:** A 60-minute drive. **Rooms:** 34 rooms with single or double beds. **Bathrooms:** All private bath/toilets.	**Meals:** Buffet breakfast, dinner. **Vegetarian:** Available on request. **Complimentary:** Tea & coffee. **Dates Open:** All year. **High Season:** Apr, Jul, Oct, Dec. **Credit Cards:** Diners, VISA. **Rsv'tns:** Required. **To Reserve:** Travel agent or call direct.	**Parking:** Adequate free parking. **In-Room:** AC, color TV, telephone, coffee/tea-making facilities, maid, room & laundry service. **On-Premises:** Meeting rooms, laundry facilities. **Exercise/Health:** Tennis court. Nearby gym, weights, Jacuzzi, sauna, steam, massage.	**Swimming:** Pool on premises. Nearby pool, river, lake, hydro health hot water spa. **Sunbathing:** At poolside. **Smoking:** Permitted. **Pets:** Not permitted. **Handicap Access:** Yes. **Children:** Welcome. **Languages:** Afrikaans, English. **Your Host:** Lieben.

Noupoort Guest Farm
Gay-Owned ♀♂

Noupoort Guest Farm is only 1-1/2 hours' drive from Cape Town on the western slopes of the Piketberg mountains, a little-known paradise set amongst spectacular rock formations. If you can appreciate crisp mountain air, scenic walks in unspoilt splendor, wholesome country fare, outdoor activity, star-filled skies, and an open hearth in the evenings, make *Noupoort Guest Farm* your country getaway. It is ideal for that relaxing break you deserve, whether you choose to be indulged and catered for, or simply prefer to self-cater in the privacy of your own country cottage. Gay theatre weekends with cabaret take place here four times a year.

Address: PO Box 101, Piketberg 7320 South Africa.
Tel: (27-0261) 5754, **Fax:** (27-0261) 5834. **E-mail:** noupoort@mickey.iaccess.za

Type: Mountain retreat on a guest farm. **Clientele:** Mostly hetero clientele with 25% gay & lesbian clientele in-season **Transportation:** Car is best. Daily bus service from Cape Town to Piketberg. Nominal charge for pick up at Piketberg. **Rooms:** 14 rooms in 10 cottages with single, 3/4 or queen beds. 9 new suites. **Bathrooms:** All private.	**Vegetarian:** Available with prior notice. **Dates Open:** All year. **Rates:** R260-R290 pp, sharing dinner or bed & breakfast. **Discounts:** Group bookings encouraged. **Credit Cards:** MC, Visa, Amex, Diners. **Rsv'tns:** Required. **To Reserve:** Call direct. **Parking:** Ample free off-street parking.	**In-Room:** Dining room, fireplace, kitchen, refrigerator, coffee/tea-making facilities & private braai. 9 new suites with mountain views, fireplaces & sleeping lofts. **On-Premises:** Conference room with flipcharts, projector, VCR & monitor, TV lounge. BBQ & sun deck. Full-service bar, pool table. **Exercise/Health:** Sauna & basic work-out gym, Jacuzzi & weights.	**Swimming:** Pool on premises. **Sunbathing:** At poolside, on patio & common sun decks. **Nudity:** Permitted on special weekends. **Pets:** Not permitted. **Children:** No children under 12 years of age. **Languages:** English, Afrikaans, Xhosa. **Your Host:** Brent.

INN PLACES® 1998

Elephant Springs Hotel

Gay-Friendly ♀♂

Enjoy 365 Days of Sunshine

The days of the old African hunters and explorers live again in Warmbaths, the recreation and fun capital of the Northern Province, less than 90 minutes' drive from Johannesburg. The *Elephant Springs Hotel and Cabanas* commemorates the discovery over a century ago of a veritable graveyard of animal bones and elephant tusks in the marshland surrounding the famous Hetbad Mineral Spring. Forty large bedrooms, all with en suite bathrooms, TV, telephone, as well as tea- and coffee-making facilities, surround a lawn courtyard with its sparkling swimming pool. All rooms are newly decorated and have ceiling fans, and some have air conditioning. A delicious range of South African traditional dishes is served in the Lion & Elephant Restaurant. The wine list is excellent, and the atmosphere is warm and friendly.

A valuable feature of the entertainment area is its capacity to offer a variety of theme evenings, especially for groups using the *Elephant Springs* conference facilities. The main conference rooms seats up to 150 delegates and boasts a full range of conference equipment. Several breakaway rooms are available, as well as a comfortable lounge area and colonial open verandah, graced with fine antique pieces. The world-famous Aventura Resort and Hot Springs is only a two-minute walk away, and offers a Hydro Spa, fully equipped gym, beauty salon, specialised therapeutic massage facilities and a host of outdoor activities.

Address: 31 Sutter St, Warmbaths 0480 South Africa.
Tel: (27-14) 736 21 01, **Fax:** (27-14) 736 35 86.

Type: Bed & breakfast with restaurant & bar, 90 minutes from Johannesburg, 60 minutes from Pretoria.
Clientele: Mostly hetero clientele with a gay/lesbian following
Transportation: Car is best. Pick up from airport.
To Gay Bars: A 60-minute drive.
Rooms: 40 rooms or apartments with single or double beds.

Bathrooms: All private bath/toilets.
Meals: Full breakfast.
Vegetarian: Available upon request.
Complimentary: Tea & coffee available in rooms.
Dates Open: All year.
High Season: Apr, Jul, Oct, Dec.
Rates: R144-R200 per person, sharing.
Credit Cards: Diners, Visa, Amex.
Rsv'tns: Required.

To Reserve: Travel agent or call direct.
Parking: Adequate free parking.
In-Room: AC, ceiling fans, color TV, telephone, coffee/tea-making facilities, room, maid & laundry service.
On-Premises: Meeting rooms, laundry facilities. Discount tickets to Aventura Resort & Hot Springs.
Exercise/Health: Nearby gym, weights, Jacuzzi, sauna, steam, massage.

Swimming: Pool on premises. Nearby pool, river, lake, health hydro hot water spa.
Sunbathing: At poolside.
Smoking: Permitted. No non-smoking rooms available.
Pets: Not permitted.
Handicap Access: Yes.
Children: Welcome.
Languages: Afrikaans, English.
Your Host: George & Johan.

Lotus Hotel

Q-NET Gay/Lesbian ♂

The Center of Gay Chiang Mai

Nightly, the street in front of the *Lotus Hotel* becomes the lively center of gay Chiang Mai. Across from the hotel is the largest and most popular gay club in town — The Adams Apple Club. Four floors of gay entertainment include a restaurant serving Western and Thai dishes, a reading lounge, a gift shop, private rooms with traditional Thai massage, a showplace with 40 go-go dancers swaying to the latest pop music, and a karaoke facility. The gay *Lotus Hotel* in Chiang Mai is perfectly located in the busiest district with easy access to local Thai markets, shopping centers, movie theaters, banks, and post offices.

A popular feature of the hotel is a tropical garden with its very busy Bamboo Bar that sells inexpensive drinks. Deep in the garden there is a Thai Sala where customers can relax amidst lush vegetation, have a soothing Thai massage, or just relax and watch Thai boys pump up their muscles. All the rooms have en suite bathrooms and are equipped with air conditioning, mini bar, stereo, cable TV, and VCR. Amenities are of top quality: therapeutic mattresses, soft pillows, and cotton linens. The hotel also: serves meals at any time to your room or the terrace, has laundry service, rents cars, offers guided tours around Chiang Mai, confirms tickets and reservations, has a video and book library, and, best of all, has a very friendly staff.

Address: 2/25 Soi Viangbua, Tambol Chang-Phuk, Amphur Muang, Chiang Mai 50300 Thailand.
Tel: (66-53) 215 376, 215 462, **Fax:** (66-53) 221 340.
E-mail: mohamad@loxinfo.co.th

Type: Gay-owned hotel with bar, restaurant, kiosk shops, drag & boys show, karaoke, massage.
Clientele: Mostly men with women welcome & some gay-friendly hetero clientele
Transportation: Pick up from airport, bus, train station. Taxi 120 baht.
To Gay Bars: Opposite hotel.
Rooms: 6 rooms with king & queen beds & 3 suites.

Bathrooms: All private.
Vegetarian: Available on restaurant menu.
Complimentary: Fruit for regular customers.
Dates Open: All year.
High Season: Nov-Apr 15 & Aug.
Rates: High season 750-1650 Baht.
Discounts: 20% in low season or for stays over one month.

Credit Cards: MC, Visa.
Rsv'tns: Required.
To Reserve: Travel agent or call direct.
Parking: Limited free parking.
In-Room: Color TV, video tape library, AC, phone, refrigerator, maid, room & laundry service. VCR in suite, cable TV.
On-Premises: Bar, terrace & garden.

Exercise/Health: Outdoor gym.
Sunbathing: Private sun decks in the garden.
Smoking: Permitted without restrictions.
Pets: Not permitted.
Handicap Access: No.
Children: Not permitted.
Languages: Thai, English, French & Arabic.

ASIA
THAILAND • CHIANG MAI

Kris's Antwerp Women's B&B

Women ♀

Antwerp is so strategically located that your stay here will never be boring. Just get up and go to Brussels, Amsterdam or even Paris. Many interesting places are within an hour to three hours' drive or train from here. As an alternative to run-of-the-mill hotels, your host, Kris, offers you your own bedroom in a big, two-story Art Deco-style country house with garden. It's close to the city center, and there are cafes, restaurants and cultural activities nearby. As an alternative to staying in the city, your host, Kris, also offers a room in a two-story house in the nearby suburban countryside where there is also a lot to do.

Address: Dolfijnstraat 69, Antwerp 2018 Belgium.
Tel: (32-3) 271 0613 or (32-3) 322 9370.

Type: Bed & breakfast in the city, or a room in a country home.
Clientele: Women only
Transportation: Airport bus or train. Free pick up from bus or train.
Rooms: 1 room with double bed.

Bathrooms: Shared: 1bath/shower/toilet, 2 WCs.
Meals: Full breakfast.
Complimentary: Tea in room.
Dates Open: Normally all year.
Rates: BEF 700-BEF 800.
Rsv'tns: Required.
To Reserve: Call direct.

Parking: Adequate on-street parking.
In-Room: Coffee/tea-making facilities, VCR.
On-Premises: TV lounge, garden.
Sunbathing: In garden.
Smoking: Not permitted in rooms.
Pets: Not permitted.

Handicap Access: No.
Children: No.
Languages: Dutch, French, English, German, Russian, Polish.
Your Host: Kris Kowalski.

Bungalow 't Staaksken

Gay/Lesbian ♀♂

A Flemish Cottage in the Heart of the Meetjesland Creek Area, Where Time Stands Still...

The willow-lined canals, lush green pastures and extensive soft, sandy dunes of Flanders need no introduction; their beauty has been captured for centuries by some of the world's greatest artists. The Meetjesland, however, is known only to a discerning few, yet it has much to offer anyone seeking peace and quiet. It is one of those rare corners of Western Europe where time has virtually stood still and man has barely changed the face of nature. Today, it is a land of creeks and polders, tall fields of maize, "sleeping" dikes and old smugglers routes in the north and woodlands in the south which contain beautiful castles and castle farms. The terrain is ideal for cycling, walking, relaxing and fishing.

Bungalow 't Staaksken, our country bungalow, is situated atop an old dike, 2 kilometres from the gastronomic village of Assenede. With a population of 7,000, Assenede is one of the oldest villages in Flanders and enjoys the distinction of having many restaurants of international repute. In particular, we can recommend the restaurant Den Hoek with its creative dinners, beautiful art interior and green surroundings with creeks and dikes. We offer you a free appetizer when you dine at Edward's place. After dinner, you are welcome to spend the rest of the evening at his brother Marius' artcafe, Cafe Passe, where we offer you, free, one of the good Belgian beers.

Assenede is on the Belgium/Netherlands border, only 20-45 minutes from the towns of Ghent to the south, Brugges (the Venice of the North) to the west, and Antwerp (Belgium's premier gay city) to the east. Also easily accessible are the cities of Brussels and Middelburg (Netherlands). The resort town of Knokke, on the Nordsee coast, is a 30-minute drive. There are also very good connections by car or train (Eurostar/TGV/Thalys) to Paris, London, Amsterdam and Cologne.

Bungalow 't Staaksken has furniture in the Flemish style and sleeps up to five guests in one single and two double rooms. From the sitting room/terrace a panoramic view encompasses the garden, lake and surrounding fields and pasture land. At the house, free bicycles are provided for guests. Flanders is also known for its year-round art and music fesitvals. Activities in the Assenede area include tennis, bowling, golf, sailing, surfing, cable gliding and free guided walks with your host, Jan. *Bungalow 't Staaksken* is rated 4 Shamrocks. Colour brochure on request.

Address: Staakstraat 136/138A, Assenede 9960 Belgium.
Tel: (32-9) 344 0954 (Tel/Fax).

Type: Bed & breakfast & self-catering, 4-shamrock-rated bungalow.
Clientele: Mostly gay & lesbian with hetero clientele welcome
Transportation: Car is best. Free pick up from train & bus. Pick up from Zeebrugge & Breskens (Holland) ferry dock, 400 BF.
To Gay Bars: 2 miles. A 20-min drive to Ghent, 35-min drive to Antwerp.
Rooms: 3 rooms & self-catering bungalow. Single & double beds.
Bathrooms: 1 bath/shower/toilet & 1 shared toilet.
Meals: Full Flemish breakfast in B&B. Bungalow self-catering. Dinner on request (Belgian & Mauritian specialties).

Vegetarian: Available 1 mile away.
Complimentary: Tea & coffee on arrival with Belgian chocolates & cakes, flowers.
Dates Open: All year.
High Season: Jul-Aug, Christmas & New Year.
Rates: Bungalow: Low: 9,000-10,500 BF/wk, 4,500 BF (2n)/wknd, 7,000 BF (4n) midweek; High: 15,000 BF/wk. B&B: 1,250 BF (1 person), 1,800 BF (2 people). Extra person 750 BF.
Discounts: Bungalow: 5% off on 2 weeks or more low season. 10% to ECMC, IPA & police & army unit members, also mention Inn Places.
Rsv'tns: Required.

To Reserve: Call, fax or mail direct.
Minimum Stay: 2 nights.
Parking: Adequate free covered parking.
In-Room: Bungalow: color cable TV, radio/CD, well-appointed kitchen, VCR on request, laundry service, tourist info.
On-Premises: Meeting & dining room, TV lounge, BBQ, fax, large garden.
Exercise/Health: Nearby gym, weights, Jacuzzi, sauna, steam & massage.
Swimming: Lake & pond on premises. Nearby tropical in- & outdoor pool. 30km to Nordsee coast.
Sunbathing: On private sun decks or in the garden.

Nudity: Permitted on sun terraces, in garden w/discretion & at nude beaches (Paulinapolder 10km, Nordsee 30km).
Smoking: Permitted outside only, not in house.
Pets: No.
Handicap Access: Yes.
Children: No. Permitted only on special request when there are no other guests.
Languages: Dutch, English, French, German, Creole, some Danish.
Your Host: Jan & Margaret.

New Hotel de Lives

Q-NET Gay/Lesbian ♀♂

A 3-Star Manor with Maximum Comfort, Privacy & Convenience

A stylish hotel manor dating from the 19th century, *New Hotel de Lives* has been completely renovated. The hotel's atmosphere is pleasant and homey, and guests are offered the same modern conveniences and services found in first-class hotels. In a natural setting, close to the banks of the river Meuse, our manor is just in front of the rocks of Marche-les-Dames. We are located in the town of Lives-Sur-Meuse, which is only a few kilometers away from many cities popular with tourists, such as Namur-Namen, Jambes, Andenne, Huy and Ciney. If you come to us by car via highway E-411 (Brussels-Namur-Luxemburg), take exit number 15 (Loyers) in the direction of Andenne (N-90). The manor is situated four kilometers further on, on the right-hand side of the road.

Address: Chaussée de Liège 1178, NamurLives-Sur-Meuse B-5101 Belgium.
Tel: (32-81) 58 05 13, **Fax:** (32-81) 58 15 77. **E-mail:** Francis40@infonie.be
URL: http://www.ciger.be/hotels/lives/index.html

Type: Bed & breakfast hotel with restaurant & bar with snacks.
Clientele: Gay & lesbian. Good mix of men & women
Transportation: Car is best. Namur train station, then bus #12 which stops in front of hotel. Free pick up from bus & Namur train & airport.
To Gay Bars: 4 miles, a 5 min drive.
Rooms: 8 rooms, 2 suites with single, double or king beds.
Bathrooms: All private bath/shower/toilet/sink.

Meals: Buffet breakfast.
Vegetarian: Must be requested at time of reservation.
Complimentary: Snacks in restaurant, dining room or in rooms.
Dates Open: All year.
High Season: Jun-Sept.
Rates: BF 2200-BF 4300. Children: up to 3 yrs of age, free; 3 yrs & over BF 700.
Discounts: Please inquire.
Credit Cards: MC, Visa, Amex, Diners, Eurocard.
Rsv'tns: Required.

To Reserve: Travel agent or call direct.
Parking: Ample free parking.
In-Room: Telephone, color cable TV, maid, room & laundry service. VCR on request.
On-Premises: Meeting rooms, TV lounge, laundry facilities, computer, fax, copy machine, printer-video, screen.
Exercise/Health: Nearby gym, tennis, horseback riding, 4X4, canoe.

Swimming: Nearby pool, river, lake.
Sunbathing: On patio & in private garden.
Smoking: Permitted, non-smoking rooms available.
Pets: Permitted, BF 250 extra per pet.
Handicap Access: Yes.
Children: Welcome. We have 3 extra-special beds for children.
Languages: Flemish, French, German, English, Japanese, Italian, Spanish.
Your Host: Sir Francis.

Penzion David Hotel
Gay/Lesbian ♀♂

Penzion David is a 1920's bourgeois house built on a slope next to a green hill area. The last owner was a pop singer. The house has been beautifully renovated with many modern features, including a terrace, a garden, a sauna and a restaurant and bar. The staff is friendly. All rooms have private baths, telephone, satellite TV and clock radio. The main tourist attractions of Prague can be easily reached by tram or metro (yellow line "B", metro station Radlicka) which is a five-minute walk from the hotel.

Address: Holubova 5, Praha 5 150 000 Czech Republic.
Tel: (420-2) 900 11 293 or 294, **Fax:** (420-2) 549 820.

Type: Hotel with restaurant, sauna & bar.
Clientele: Mostly gay & lesbian with some hetero clientele
Transportation: Tram #14 to Laurová terminal, then 2-min walk. Or yellow metro line B, Radlicka station, then a 5 min walk.
To Gay Bars: On the premises.

Rooms: 6 suites with double beds, additional single beds available.
Bathrooms: All en suite shower/toilets.
Meals: Expanded continental breakfast.
Vegetarian: Available upon request.
Dates Open: All year.
Rates: DM 80-DM 120 (CZK 1360-2040) per person per night.

Credit Cards: Visa, Amex, MC.
Rsv'tns: Recommended.
To Reserve: Call or fax direct.
Parking: Ample on-street parking.
In-Room: Maid service, colour cable TV & telephone.
On-Premises: Restaurant, bar, terrace & garden.

Exercise/Health: Sauna.
Swimming: 10-minute walk to municipal swimming pool.
Sunbathing: In the garden.
Smoking: Permitted.
Pets: Permitted.
Handicap Access: No.
Children: Permitted.
Languages: Czech, German & English.

Prague Home Stay
Gay/Lesbian ♀♂

Prague Home Stay offers inexpensive rooms, not only at the above address, but even in a number of other rooms in the homes of our friends, members of Lambda Prague. Our own rooms provide quiet rest in a residential area, within easy 24-hour reach by tram of all parts of the city. The city, itself, is miraculous, with impressive architecture and historical monuments, hidden beauties and even ghosts. Your hosts will take the time to talk with guests and help them get to know this fascinating city.

Address: Pod Kotlárkou 14, Prague 5 150 000 Czech Republic.
Tel: (420-2) 527 388. Phone may be altered in 1998, for information, call (420-2) 5721 0862.

Type: Lodging & kitchen privileges in a private home.
Clientele: Mostly gay & lesbian with some hetero clientele
Transportation: Metro B (Yellow Line) to station Andel, then 5 stops by trams No 4,7,9, stop Kotlárka.
To Gay Bars: 10-20 minutes by municipal transport or car.

Rooms: 1 single, 2 doubles with single beds & 1 suite with double bed.
Bathrooms: 2 rooms share 1 bath.
Complimentary: Tea & coffee.
Dates Open: All year.
Rates: USD $20-$34 per person, per night (CZK 600-1100).

Rsv'tns: Required by telephone.
To Reserve: Call direct.
Minimum Stay: 2 nights.
Parking: Ample on-street parking. Room for 1 car on premises.
In-Room: Telephone upon request.
On-Premises: Kitchen privileges for 2 rooms.

Sunbathing: At the swimming pool.
Smoking: Permitted.
Pets: Not permitted.
Handicap Access: No.
Children: Not permitted.
Languages: Czech, Slovak, English, German, Russian & Polish.

INN PLACES® 1998

Hotel Windsor

Gay/Lesbian ♀♂

Reasonable Accommodations Near the Central Station

Hotel Windsor offers centrally located and immaculately clean accommodations at prices reasonable for Denmark! You can walk to the gay bars and you can bring back friends, even to breakfast. Certain floors are designated for men only and have a somewhat bath house atmosphere. The hotel is accessed by a stairway, so be prepared to climb steps. We have cable TV in all rooms, both telephone and fax service are in reception, and guests have their own keys. Our staff is ready to help you with information about sightseeing, of which Tivoli Garden is the most spectacular example, with many restaurants, free shows, and an amusement park.

Address: Frederiksborggade 30, Kobenhavn 1360 Denmark.
Tel: (45) 33 11 08 30, **Telefax:** (45) 33 11 63 87.
E-mail: hotelwindsor@inet.uni2.dk **URL:** www.hotelwindsor.dk

Type: Hotel.
Clientele: Exclusively for gays and their friends
Transportation: Airport bus to central station, then bus or taxi.
To Gay Bars: 5-minute walk to men's bar, 10-minute walk to women's.
Rooms: 10 singles, 10 doubles, 1 triple, 1 quad, 1 apartment.
Bathrooms: All shared. Sinks in rooms.

Meals: Continental breakfast.
Vegetarian: We can recommend vegetarian restaurant.
Dates Open: All year.
High Season: Mid May-early Oct.
Rates: Single Dkr 325.00-500.00, double Dkr 500-600.
Credit Cards: MC, Visa, Eurocard.
Rsv'tns: Required, especially in high season.

To Reserve: Call direct.
Parking: Ample off-street pay parking, some free on-street after 6 PM.
In-Room: Maid service, laundry service, cable color TV & refrigerator.
On-Premises: TV lounge, public telephones.
Swimming: Public pool nearby, nude beach accessible by train.
Sunbathing: 2-minute walk to sunbathing area.

Nudity: Permitted on men-only floor.
Smoking: Permitted without restrictions.
Pets: Not permitted.
Handicap Access: No! Many stairs!
Children: Permitted.
Languages: Danish, English, Norwegian, Swedish, German, French, Italian.
Your Host: John.

Finns Hotel Pension

Gay/Lesbian ♀♂

Finns Hotel Pension is a beautiful old wood house decorated in the old style. It's a great place to stay for a holiday in this very special corner of Denmark, the most famous holiday place in the country. Enjoy the sun drenched beaches, lovely scenery, and outstanding local museums. The owner is gay and promotes a relaxed atmosphere for gay people.

Address: Ostre Strandvej 63, Skagen 9990 Denmark.
Tel: (45) 98 45 01 55.

Type: Hotel with restaurant for guests.
Clientele: Mostly gay & lesbian with some hetero clientele
Transportation: Car or train is best. Free pick up from train.
Rooms: 6 rooms with single or double beds.
Bathrooms: Sinks in rooms. 2 rooms with private WC. Shared: 2 full baths, 1 shower & 1 WC.
Meals: Expanded cont. breakfast. Optional lunch & dinner.

Vegetarian: Available if ordered before arrival.
Dates Open: All year. If visiting in winter, call first, could be closed during some part of winter months.
High Season: May 1-Aug 31.
Rates: High season: single Dkr 325-475, double Dkr 575-725. Low season: single Dkr 300-425, double Dkr 525-675.
Discounts: 10% for stays of 3+ days, 15% for stays of 7+ days.
Rsv'tns: Required.

To Reserve: Call direct.
Parking: Limited free off-street parking.
In-Room: Radio & room service.
On-Premises: Garden, library, lounge, telephone, & laundry facilities.
Exercise/Health: Small weights.
Swimming: Public pool 1 km. Ocean beach nearby.
Sunbathing: At the beach or in the garden.

Nudity: Permitted at the beach.
Smoking: Permitted. No non-smoking rooms available.
Pets: Permitted.
Handicap Access: No. Stairs to rooms.
Children: Permitted, but maximum of 2.
Languages: Danish, English, German, & Swedish.
Your Host: Finn.

IGLTA

Mas La Bonoty Hotel & Restaurant

Q-NET Gay-Owned & -Operated ♀♂

A 17th-Century Farmhouse in the Heart of Provence

In the heart Provence, 20 kilometres from Avignon, in a region rich in history and scenic beauty is *Mas La Bonoty*, an elegantly restored Provençal farmhouse dating from the 17th century. The bedrooms have ensuite bath or shower rooms with WC, television and tea- and coffee-making facilities. The hotel is situated on over two acres of private landscaped gardens featuring lavender and olive trees, and has its own pool, as well. The comfort, tranquility, sophisticated Provençal cuisine and the carefully selected wine list found here will ensure a memorable stay. Lunch can be served under the shade of pine trees and dinner on the terraces surrounding the pool.

Pernes Les Fontaines, not far from Mont Ventoux, is a medieval town with 36 fountains and numerous ramparts, monuments and churches. Within easy reach of *Mas La Bonoty* are the famous vineyards of Côtes du Rhône, Châteauneuf du Pape and Tavel, as well as the excellent "vins du pays" such as Côtes de Ventoux and Côtes de Luberon. Many vinyards are pleased to arrange wine tastings. Day excursions can include Aix en Provence, the Mediterranean coast and many other well-known attractions throughout Provence. The area is also internationally renowned for its diverse cultural activities, among which are the celebrated Avignon Festival and opera in the magnificent Roman arenas at Orange and Nîmes. Sporting activities such as golf, tennis and horseriding are also available nearby.

Address: Chemin de la Boniaty, Pernes Les Fontaines 84210 France.
Tel: (33) 490 616 109, **Fax:** (33) 490 613 514.

Type: Hotel with restaurant, 20 km from Avignon.
Clientele: Mostly hetero clientele with a gay/lesbian following
Transportation: Car is best. Nearest airports in Avignon or Marseille.
To Gay Bars: 14 miles, a 30 min drive.
Rooms: 8 rooms with single or double beds.
Bathrooms: 8 private bath/shower/toilets.

Meals: Expanded continental breakfast 45FF.
Vegetarian: Available, please advise in advance.
Complimentary: Welcome cocktail. Tea & coffee in rooms.
Dates Open: Closed Jan & Feb.
High Season: June-Sept.
Rates: 300FF-400FF per night for 2 persons.
Credit Cards: MC, Visa, Amex, Eurocard.

Rsv'tns: Required.
To Reserve: Travel agent or call direct.
Parking: Ample free, private off-street parking.
In-Room: Telephone, color TV, coffee & tea-making facilities, maid service.
On-Premises: TV lounge, fax.
Exercise/Health: Nearby gym, weights.

Swimming: Pool on premises. Ocean nearby.
Sunbathing: Poolside.
Smoking: Permitted, no restrictions.
Pets: Small dogs permitted by arrangement.
Handicap Access: No.
Children: No.
Languages: French, English.
Your Host: Peter & Richard.

INN PLACES® 1998　　　　　　　　　　　　　　　　　　　　　　　　　　　　　43

Chez Jacqueline
Women ♀

Jaqueline Boudillet offers her quiet, rural home as a bed and breakfast for women only. Here you can enjoy the peaceful countryside, visit many nearby touristic areas or simply stay at home. The home has a women's library, a lovely garden and musical instruments which guests are free to play. Guests are encouraged to take advantage of activities including swimming, riding, walking through forests, by the lakes or the sea-side.

Address: c/o Jacqueline Boudillet, La Croix Cadio, St Donant, Brittany 22800 France.
Tel: June through Sept: (33-2) 96 73 81 22, Oct-May: Paris (33-1) 47 39 94 54.

Type: Bed & breakfast in a big country house in Brittany.
Clientele: Women only
Transportation: Car is best.
Rooms: 3 doubles.
Bathrooms: 2 shared.

Meals: FF 20 for continental breakfast.
Dates Open: Jun-Sep, sometimes May. Use mail address above. Rest of year, use Paris addr.
Rates: Room FF 200.00.

Rsv'tns: Required. Call ahead. Oct-May in Paris: 6, rue du Port, 92110 Clichy, (1) 47 39 94 54.
To Reserve: Call direct.
Parking: Ample free off-street parking.
On-Premises: TV room.
Swimming: Ocean beach 20 minutes by car.

Sunbathing: In the garden.
Smoking: Permitted.
Pets: Only dogs who love cats are permitted.
Handicap Access: 1 bedroom is on ground floor.
Children: Not permitted.
Languages: French, English & some German.

Hotel de France
Lesbian-Owned & -Operated ♀⚥

In the Heart of Brittany...

Visitors to the city of Vannes will be charmed by its ancient streets, ramparts and beautiful gardens landscaped "a la française." This busy port city is also a center for sailing excursions in the Gulf of Morbihan with its over 300 islands, as well as to the Iles au Moines, Iles d'Arz and Belle-ile further out in the Atlantic. Vannes is an ideal home base from which to explore the surrounding countryside of Brittany, including the megalithic monument Carnac and various fortifications, chateaux and manor houses built by the Dukes of Brittany or their vassals. *Hotel de France* offers 25 extremely well-appointed rooms in quiet surroundings, where helpful service and a warm welcome await. The hotel, with its patio and flower garden, is situated between the train station and the Conference Centre.

Address: 57 Avenue Victor Hugo, Vannes 56000 France.
Tel: (33-2) 97 47 27 57, **Fax:** (33-2) 97 42 59 17.

Type: Hotel with bar.
Clientele: Mostly hetero clientele with a gay & lesbian following
Transportation: Near train station (TGV train from Paris to Vannes), inquire about pick up service.
To Gay Bars: A 15 min drive.
Rooms: 25 rooms with single or double beds.

Bathrooms: Private: 2 bath/toilets, 19 shower/toilets, 4 sink only. Shared: 2 shower only, 3 WC only.
Meals: Continental breakfast.
Complimentary: All drinks.
Dates Open: Closed Dec 25-Jan 15.
High Season: May-Sept.
Rates: For 2 persons: summer FF 295-FF 320, winter FF 170-FF 260.

Discounts: 20% on weekends during low season.
Credit Cards: Eurocard, Visa, Amex.
Rsv'tns: Required.
To Reserve: Travel agent or call direct.
Parking: Adequate free on- & off-street parking.
In-Room: Telephone, color satellite TV, refrigerator, room service.

Swimming: Nearby pool & ocean.
Sunbathing: On patio.
Smoking: Permitted.
Pets: Small pets permitted, but not in breakfast room.
Handicap Access: No.
Languages: French, English, Spanish.

La Salamandre

Q-NET Gay-Owned ♀♂

18th-Century Home in the Wine Country of Burgundy

Passing through the hilly region of Burgundy, you'll find *La Salamandre*, our beautifully decorated 18th-century home surrounded by a large park-like area populated with old trees. Without sacrificing the charm of the past, we have completely renovated the house to the standards of modern comfort. The atmosphere of the surrounding vineyards and hills turns a simple country walk or bike ride into a memorable visual experience, especially for city folk whose eyes crave distances and panoramas. The Chateau de Cormatin (17th century), only a dozen kilometers away, is a striking example of the architecture of the time. And the area abounds with equestrian centers and scenic places to ride.

At the end of an active day, guests enjoy gathering for a good meal in a warm convivial atmosphere. Wine to accompany your meal can be purchased from our wine list, which is small, but includes a variety of good wines. After dinner, guests can repare to the salon whose corner library and fireplace set the tone for relaxation.

Address: Au Bourg, Salornay sur Guye 71250 France.
Tel: (33) 385 59 91 56, **Fax:** (33) 385 59 91 67.

Type: Guesthouse. Town of Salornay is close to the cities of Mâcon, Dijon & Lyon & is a short drive NE of the town of Cluny.
Clientele: Mostly hetero clientele with a gay & lesbian following
Transportation: Car is best. Train (TGV) from Paris to Mâcon Loché station, then bus or taxi. Free pick up from train upon request.
To Gay Bars: 18 miles (30 min drive) to gay disco. 1-1/2 hrs to Lyon gay bars & activities.

Rooms: 4 rooms, 1 suite with single or double beds.
Bathrooms: Private: 2 bath/toilets, 3 shower/toilets.
Meals: Expanded continental breakfast included in rate. Three-course dinner for guests FF 120.
Vegetarian: Available if requested in advance.
Complimentary: Chocolates on pillow.
Dates Open: All year.
High Season: July-September.

Rates: Single FF 270, double FF 390, suite FF 490 (for 2-3 persons).
Discounts: From 4 nights, 10% discount on above rates.
Credit Cards: MC, Visa, Eurocard.
Rsv'tns: Recommended in high season & on weekends.
To Reserve: Call direct.
Parking: Ample free off-street parking.
In-Room: Telephone, maid service.

On-Premises: TV lounge, meeting rooms.
Exercise/Health: Bicycle on premises. Nearby golf, horse riding, fishing.
Swimming: At nearby river & lake.
Smoking: Permitted in lounge. All rooms are non-smoking.
Pets: Not permitted.
Handicap Access: No.
Children: Welcome.
Languages: French, English, German, Italian.
Your Host: Guy & Jean-Pierre.

EUROPE

FRANCE • BURGUNDY REGION

INN PLACES® 1998　　　　　　　　　　　　　　　　　　　　　　　　　　　　45

Touring Hotel
Gay-Friendly ♀♂

Your Breakfast Free When You Mention Inn Places

Located in the heart of Cannes, the *Touring Hotel* is just five minutes from the sea and magnificent beaches of the Côte d'Azur. For your comfort, amenities include private baths, colour TV, direct dial telephones and minibar in every room. There is an elevator and TV lounge on the premises. Our reception staff is always on hand to offer you a warm welcome to our beautiful city.

Address: 11 rue Hoche, Cannes 06400 France.
Tel: (33-4) 93 38 34 40, Fax: (33-4) 93 38 73 34.

Type: Hotel.
Clientele: Mostly hetero with a 30% gay & lesbian following
Transportation: Take bus from airport.
To Gay Bars: 2 minutes.
Rooms: 24 doubles & 6 triples.
Bathrooms: All private.

Meals: Continental breakfast FF 38.
Complimentary: Minibars in rooms.
Dates Open: All year.
High Season: Apr-Oct.
Rates: FF 280-FF 450.
Credit Cards: MC, Visa, Amex, Diners.
Rsv'tns: Required.

To Reserve: Travel agent or call direct.
Parking: Limited off-street covered pay parking, 50,00 FF per day.
In-Room: Color TV, telephone, mini bar, maid & laundry service.
On-Premises: TV lounge.

Swimming: 3 min from beach, 10 min to nude beach.
Sunbathing: On the beach.
Pets: Permitted.
Handicap Access: No.
Children: Welcome.
Languages: French, English, German.
Your Host: Didier.

La Dordogne Camping de Femmes
Women ♀

For those who have never seen the countryside of France, staying at *La Dordogne Camping de Femmes* is a special experience. In addition to the camaraderie with other women from many countries, you can bicycle or hike through the rolling, green countryside, or explore the fascinating caves and ancient castles nearby. Most accommodations consist of tent sites. There are also five caravans, which can be rented, and a bungalow tent, which is furnished, has a kitchen, etc., and accommodates two people. There are two bars on the premises, one for smokers and one for non-smokers. Wild womyn don't get the blues. They go to a women's campground for Dutch hospitality with a French accent.

Address: St.-Aubin de Nabirat, Domme 24250 France.
Tel: (33-5) 53 28 50 28.

Type: Campground.
Clientele: Women only
Transportation: 8 km from railway station, taxis available.
To Gay Bars: 2 hrs by car to Toulouse.
Campsites: 20 tent sites, 4 electric, 5 caravans (campers), 2 toilets, 2 hot & 1 cold shower, laundry facilities, 2 bars, library.

Vegetarian: Always.
Complimentary: Snack bar on the campground.
Dates Open: May-Sept.
High Season: Jul-Aug.
Rates: FF 45.00 per day per woman for tent sites. Caravan with electric, FF 1200 per week for 2 persons.
Rsv'tns: Required.
To Reserve: Call direct.

Parking: Off-street private parking.
On-Premises: Meeting rooms, TV lounge, laundry facilities for guests.
Exercise/Health: Tennis, volleyball, pingpong hall, jeu de boule on the premises, nearby canoeing, riding, walking & bicycle trips.
Swimming: At pool on premises.

Sunbathing: At poolside & tent sites.
Nudity: Topless only.
Smoking: Permitted outdoors & in one of the bars.
Pets: Permitted.
Children: Only girls over 14 years old.
Languages: Dutch, German, French, English.
Your Host: Joan & Marion.

FERRARI GUIDES™

Private Chateau Accommodations

Q-NET Gay ♂

What's the Point of Being in an Area with 850 Chateaux, if 99% are Private?

Stay in one of our selected private chateaux (not a chateau hotel) in a 10th-century room or rent half of an 18th-century chateau on its 800-acres. Or enjoy a 15th-century monastery in a sea of sunflowers. All are hosted by local aristocracy who will explain to you the ins-and-outs of the region, as well as the gossip of the past 900 years.

Also available: Tours including private openings of chateaux and truffle lunches at a truffle-producing chateau surrounded by truffle oak trees. Tours can be done in your own car or that of your host, which means you do not need to rent a car. You will be collected at your bullet train (it's only one hour and a half traveling time from Paris). Find out why kings chose the Loire Valley for their secondary homes. We also offer accommodations in Paris, New York City, London and South Beach, Miami.

Address: Contact: NY B&B Reservation Center, in New York, USA.
Tel: (212) 977-3512.

INN PLACES® 1998

47

Hotel Central Marais
Gay/Lesbian ♂

In the Middle of Everything

    Hotel Central Marais is a small, exclusively gay hotel in the Marais, the old, aristocratic, historic quarter of central Paris. Surrounded by the principal gay bars and restaurants, it is a 5-minute walk from Notre Dame, La Bastille and Les Halles. The 17th-century hotel has been carefully restored to enhance the charm of its old-world character, while providing modern conveniences. Accommodations consist of two double-bedded rooms per floor, with a bathroom off the short lobby between. A small, communal salon is available to guests on the first floor. Guests are substantially on their own, with limited guest services. On the ground floor is the famous Belle Epoque bar, *Bar Hotel Central*, a popular gay rendezvous. Available in the building opposite is a 2-room apartment with kitchenette, bath and small balcony. We speak English and French. A bientôt — Maurice

    NOTE: Hotel entry with intercom at 2, rue Ste. Croix de la Bretonnerie (corner building).

Address: 33, rue Vieille-du-Temple (Enter: 2, rue Ste, Croix de la Bretonnerie), Paris 75004 France.
Tel: (33-1) 48 87 56 08, **Fax:** (33-1) 42 77 06 27.

Type: Hotel above a popular men's bar & 2-room apartment across street.
Clientele: Mostly men with women welcome
Transportation: From: CDG airport Bus Train (RER); Orly airport ORLY VAL (RER) to Chatelet Les Halles Sta, exit Centre Georges Pompidou.
To Gay Bars: On the premises or 12 gay bars within 10 minutes walk.

Rooms: 7 rooms with double beds.
Bathrooms: One shared bath per floor, private bath 5th floor (no lift).
Meals: Continental breakfast 35 FF per day, available 8:30-13:00.
Dates Open: All year.
High Season: All year.
Rates: Hotel: FF 400 single, FF 485 double. Apt: FF 595 (1-2 people), FF 720 (3-4 people).

Credit Cards: MC, Visa & Eurocard.
Rsv'tns: Required.
To Reserve: Call direct.
Minimum Stay: Apartment: 3 days.
Parking: Parking is difficult. Parking garage under Hotel de Ville.
In-Room: Maid service & telephone.
On-Premises: TV lounge, meeting room & gay bar.

Exercise/Health: Gym, weights, Jacuzzi, sauna, steam & massage all available nearby.
Swimming: At nearby pool.
Sunbathing: By the river.
Smoking: Permitted.
Pets: Not permitted.
Handicap Access: No.
Children: Not permitted.
Languages: French & English.

IGLTA

Hotel des Nations
Gay-Friendly ♀♂

In the Heart of Paris' Quartier Latin, Near the Gay Nightlife of the Marais

    Dance all night, walk along the Seine, get up early or stay up late to see the sun rise over Notre Dame. You're in the Latin Quarter, smack in the center of Paris, yet in a neighborhood of overarching trees, cafe society, the Pantheon and the Sorbonne. It's a neighborhood that is very close to the gay nightlife of the Marais, yet free of the frenetic pace of the center city. At *Hotel des Nations*, we endeavor to set a peaceful mood of soft lights, warmth and friendliness that will put you right at ease. In your room, you will find all the convenience of modern decor and amenities, such as direct-dial phone, radio, TV and individual safes. You'll find the bar a congenial meeting place for business encounters and the lounge, with its pleasant hearthside, a cozy nook for evenings of relaxation.

Address: 54 rue Monge, Paris 75005 France.
Tel: (33-1) 43 26 45 24,
Fax: (33-1) 46 34 00 13.
URL: http://www.hotel.co.uk/helan

Type: Hotel.
Clientele: Mostly hetero clientele with a 10% gay/lesbian following
Transportation: Metro Place Monge & Cardinal Lemoine.
To Gay Bars: 1 mile, 10-minutes by metro.
Rooms: 38 rooms with single & double beds.
Bathrooms: Private: 20 bath/toilets, 18 shower/toilets.
Vegetarian: Vegetarian restaurant nearby.
Dates Open: All year.
High Season: May-June, Sept-Oct.
Rates: Double 560 FF-630 FF.
Discounts: 15% for seniors.
Credit Cards: MC, Visa, Amex, Diners, Eurocard, JCB.
Rsv'tns: Required.
To Reserve: Travel agent or call direct. Sabre CN 29594, Galileo CN 70816, Amadeus CN PARDES, Worldspan CN DESNA.
Parking: On-street public pay parking.
In-Room: Color cable TV, VCR, maid service.
Smoking: Permitted. Non-smoking rooms available.
Pets: Permitted.
Handicap Access: No.
Children: Welcome.
Languages: French, English, Brazilian Portuguese, Spanish, Italian.
Your Host: Bernard.

Hotel Louxor

Gay-Friendly 50/50 ♀♂

We are a 2-Star Hotel

In a peaceful street, close to the northern and eastern railway stations and a few minutes from the main boulevards, department stores and entertainment centres of Paris, you will find the *Hotel Louxor,* a charming building, constructed at the turn of the century. You'll enjoy your intimate, individualized room and the quiet lounge where breakfast is served. You'll also appreciate the restful surroundings in the reading lounge. Here is a hotel which has not lost the human touch and where you will feel at home.

Address: 4 rue Taylor, Paris 75010 France.
Tel: (33-1) 42 08 23 91, **Fax:** (33-1) 42 08 03 30.

Type: Hotel.
Clientele: 50% gay & lesbian & 50% hetero clientele
Transportation: Subway, bus or taxi.
To Gay Bars: 6 blocks to gay bars or a 10-min walk.
Rooms: 30 rooms with single or double beds.
Bathrooms: All private shower/toilets.
Meals: Breakfast FF25.
Dates Open: All year except Feb.
Rates: Single FF 250-280, double FF 320, double with 2 beds FF 260, 3 beds FF 390.
Credit Cards: MC, Visa & Eurocard.
Rsv'tns: Required by fax with credit card number as guarantee.
To Reserve: Travel agent or call direct.
Parking: Off-street parking.
In-Room: Cable color TV, direct-dial telephone, quiet lounge & reading lounge.
Smoking: Permitted without restrictions in the room. No public smoking sections.
Pets: Not permitted.
Handicap Access: No.
Children: No.
Languages: French, English, Brazilian Portuguese.

Private Paris Accommodations

Q-NET Gay ♂

Your Home in Paris

Next time you're in Paris, why not rent a charming studio apartment in an 18th-century building on the pedestrian Rue Bourbon le Chateau (behind the church of St. Germain) in the heart of the Left Bank St. Germain des Pres? Its convenient location makes it easy to walk to just about anywhere in Central Paris. To help you get accustomed to the area, the trilingual owner is happy to show you around the neighborhood. You are just a few blocks from Café de Flor and Les Deux Magots. Around the corner is the Place Furstemberg, and a six-day-a-week open-air market is down the street, convenient for food and flower shopping. The photo shown is a view from one of our apartments. We also have another accommodation with views of the Eiffel Tower and Paris.

The studio apartment has been entirely rebuilt with a modern bath and kitchen and has parquet floors and high-beamed ceilings. It is furnished with a mixture of contemporary and antique furniture with a king-sized bed and double pullout sofa. Guests will also find a TV (with English cable) and a telephone. Two tall windows face the street on the second floor. We also offer accommodations in the Loire Valley, New York, London and South Beach, Miami. Call to make reservations.

Address: Contact: NY B&B Reservation Center, in New York, USA.
Tel: (212) 977-3512.

Type: Private apartment in St. Germain des Pres on Left Bank.
Clientele: Gay
Transportation: Metro or taxi.
To Gay Bars: Walking distance to many.
Rooms: 1 studio apartment.

Bathrooms: Private shower/toilet.
Rates: US $150-US $200 per night.
Credit Cards: Amex.
Rsv'tns: Required.
To Reserve: Travel agent or call direct.

Minimum Stay: 4 days.
Parking: On-street parking or parking in paid public garage.
In-Room: Color cable TV, telephone, kitchenette, refrigerator & weekly maid service.

Swimming: 10-minute walk to floating pool on the Seine.
Smoking: Permitted.
Pets: Inquire.
Handicap Access: No.
Children: Welcome.
Languages: French, English, Spanish & Italian.

Hilltop Cantegrive Farmhouses

Gay-Friendly ♀

A Tranquil Hideaway in Foie Gras, Chateaux and Wine Country

Perched on a hilltop in 50 private acres, **Cantegrive** is a 17th-century Perigordian country estate, 75 miles east of Bordeaux and 18 miles east of Bergerac on the Dordogne River. Our thick stone walls of local yellow sandstone have stood for centuries, supporting massive oak beams and a dizzyingly steep gabled roof of handcrafted tiles — admire their golden beauty as you relax with a glass of Bergerac wine.

The Dordogne/Perigord region is French countryside at its best. This is Eleanor of Aquitane country where troubadours sang in fairy tale castles. Later, this peaceful area became the site of centuries of bitter warfare between French and English kings. Medieval castles and fortified bastide villages still bear testimony to those fierce times. Even earlier, prehistoric man settled here which is evidenced by many caves with their fascinating wall paintings and sculpture.

Amid all these traces of earlier times, today's visitor can also enjoy canoeing, biking, horseback riding, tennis — a cornucopia of outdoor activity! And, do not forget that France, food and wine go together. Village markets abound with fresh local produce, cheeses, foie gras and wines. Cozy restaurants dot the countryside, offering local fare at prices kind to your wallet. For quieter moments, stroll or jog on our forest trails. Or, relax and enjoy your spacious house, nicely furnished in antique and wicker. On warm evenings, admire the magnificent sunsets from your own terrace, or take the chill off cool seasons in front of your natural stone fireplace.

Address: Bidot Haut, St. Avit Sénieur (Bergerac) 24 440 France.
Tel: (33-5) 53 22 01 94, **Fax:** (33-5) 53 27 87 85.

Type: 2 self-catering houses.
Clientele: Mostly hetero clientele with a gay female following
Transportation: Car essential. Airports at Bordeaux & Bergerac. Free pick up from train in Bergerac.
To Gay Bars: 45 miles (1 hr) north to Perigueux or 2 hrs to Bordeaux.
Rooms: 2- & 3-bedroom houses with single, double or queen beds.

Bathrooms: Private, tiled with tub & shower.
Meals: Self-catering cottages.
Vegetarian: Ample supply of fresh local seasonal produce. Available upon request at local restaurants.
Complimentary: Welcome wine on arrival. Figs & plums in season from own trees. Firewood in season from own forests.
Dates Open: All year.
High Season: July-August.

Rates: Houses per week: 2-bedroom US $450-US $700, 3-bedroom US $900-US $1200.
Discounts: For long-term & off-season, on request.
Rsv'tns: Necessary with deposit.
To Reserve: Directly.
Minimum Stay: 1 week, Saturday-Saturday.
Parking: Plenty of space on-site for parking.
In-Room: Each house has Satellite TV, fireplace, dishwasher, microwave, refrigerator/freezer, oven, linen & towels.

On-Premises: Laundry facilities, Weber grill for each house. Central oil heat, fax.
Exercise/Health: Petanque, badminton.
Swimming: 20 x 50 ft. pool.
Sunbathing: At pool, or as you like on property.
Smoking: Preferably outdoors.
Pets: No.
Handicap Access: No.
Children: Permitted if well-behaved.
Languages: French, English, German, Finnish, Swedish.
Your Host: Joan.

EUROPE • FRANCE • SOUTHWEST FRANCE - RURAL

Mondès

Women ♀

A Women's Inn in France's Armagnac Region

Here, in the heart of the Gasgogne with its medieval castles and churches, with its fields of sunflowers and its grapevines from which the famous Armagnac is made, is *Mondès*. The two structures, an old country house made of natural stone, and a newly built cosy cottage nearby, are surrounded by eight hectares of land where sheep and two donkeys live next to ducks, chickens, cats and dogs. Our organic garden provides gourmet vegetarian meals. At the lower end of our land, we have built a pond with an island and sand beach for swimming and relaxing. Next to it is our shady campsite. You may want to play ping-pong, volleyball, badminton, or bike around the lovely countryside. Take sightseeing trips to historical places or nearby cities, the Atlantic Ocean, or pass the day in the Pyrenees. Perhaps you might like to meet women from other vacation houses at their women's discos, or in the cafe Le Divan on Thursdays after the market in Eauze.

Address: Courrensan, Gondrin 32330 France.
Tel: (33-5) 62 06 59 05 (Tel/Fax). In France dial: 0562 06 59 05.

Type: Inn, cottage & campsite.
Clientele: Women only
Transportation: Car is best, train to Agen + bus to Gondrin.
To Gay Bars: Jul-Aug women-only discos 3 times/wk in various vacation houses & at Bagdam Cafe in Toulouse, 120km.
Rooms: 4 doubles. Cottage with 2 double beds, kitchen, veranda.
Bathrooms: Private in cottage. 2 shared in inn & on campsite.
Campsites: 20 tent sites without cars, 3 powered sites for caravans.
Meals: Full breakfast buffet & gourmet vegetarian dinners.
Vegetarian: Mostly organic vegetarian. Organic lamb from own farm occasionally.
Dates Open: All year.
High Season: Jul 1-Sept 14, Easter & Christmas.
Rates: Per person: FF 190 room, breakfast & dinner. FF 45 camping, FF 155 camping, breakfast & dinner. Cottage: FF 300 per day.
Discounts: Inquire for groups. Children aged 4-10 50%. Reduced rates for pre- & post-season.
Rsv'tns: Required.
To Reserve: Call direct.
Minimum Stay: 3 days.
Parking: Adequate parking on own land.
On-Premises: Meeting room.
Exercise/Health: Bicycles, volleyball, badminton, ping-pong & swimming. Horseriding & tennis nearby.
Swimming: In lake on private ground.
Sunbathing: Everywhere.
Nudity: Permitted around the lake.
Smoking: Permitted everywhere except in bedrooms.
Pets: Not permitted.
Handicap Access: Yes.
Children: Welcome. Males up to 8 years old.
Languages: French, German & English.
Your Host: Dorothee & Monika.

Pitau

Gay-Owned & -Operated ♀♂

A Country House for Gay & Lesbians in the Heart of Gascony

Nearly undisturbed by mass tourism, this area in Gascony is rich in vineyards, luminous fields of sunflowers, deep forests and lush meadows which cover the soft, hilly landscape. Typical stone houses, some dating from the time of the French Revolution, fit beautifully into the picturesque scenery and have their own rich history to tell. Six miles south of the town of Condom, in the heart of Gascony, **Pitau** is situated on a hill with beautiful panoramic views of the countryside below. In the wintertime, you can sometimes see as far as the Pyrenees mountains. Our country home, built of stone, was constructed in 1798 during the French Revolution. Its 35 acres of arable land and 10 acres of forest and meadows make it a very inviting retreat. Indeed, what could be more wonderful than stepping out onto the sunny terrace after waking up, taking a deep breath and welcoming the new day in such surroundings?

We offer several choices of accommodation for your **Pitau** holiday, including single or double rooms with or without half-board (breakfast and dinner), B&B (minimum stay of three days), or camping. One of the day's high points is the shared evening meal, rounding off the day with a delicious three-course French or international menu (vegetarian, if desired). This enjoyable event often allows for interesting conversations. We are often asked if living in the country isn't really quite boring. In answer, all we have to do is list the area's myriad activities which include hiking the picturesque pilgrimage routes of St. Jaques de Compostella, cycling (bicycles can be hired in the nearest village) and visiting the area's charming medieval villages and chateaux. Visit the typical markets of Gascony which are famous for their liveliness and colour, enjoy the nearby open-air swimming pool in Gondrin, take day trips to the Pyrenees or the Atlantic Ocean... and don't forget to ask about the many local festivals, exhibitions and the midnight markets. Your hosts Henry and Michael, along with their daughter, Yvonne, have lived here for the past decade. They share their home with three dogs, six cats, a proud rooster, hens and ducks.

Address: Lagraulet du Gers, Gondrin 32330 France.
Tel: (33-5) 62 29 15 08 (Tel/Fax).

Type: Guesthouse & campground.
Clientele: Mostly gay & lesbian with some hetero clientele

Transportation: Car is best. Free pick up from Toulouse airport, Gondrin bus, Auch & Agen train.
To Gay Bars: 2 hours to Toulouse gay & lesbian bars.

Rooms: 3 rooms with single or double beds.
Bathrooms: Shared: 1 bath/shower/toilet, 1 WC only.

Campsites: 5 tent sites. 1 bathroom w/ bathtub, sink, bidet, 1WC & 1WC w/ sink.
Meals: Continental breakfast.

continued next page

Dates Open: All year.
High Season: Apr-May & Sept-Oct.
Rates: B&B: FF 183 with breakfast & dinner. Camping: FF 45 (with breakfast & dinner, FF150).
Discounts: 50% discount for children ages 4-10.
Rsv'tns: Required.
Minimum Stay: 3 days.
Parking: Adequate free on-site parking.
On-Premises: Meeting room, laundry facilities.
Swimming: Nearby pool & lake.
Sunbathing: On veranda & in meadows.
Smoking: Please inquire.
Pets: Not permitted.
Handicap Access: No.
Children: Welcome.
Languages: French, German, English, Chinese.
Your Host: Michael & Henry.

Roussa
Women ♀

Come and Fall in Love

Roussa is a 200-year-old renovated farmhouse with a beautiful, big garden, German-run, but international in atmosphere and clientele. You will find all holiday activities nearby, but no mass tourism. Come, and fall in love with the vineyards and the fields of sunflowers and corn which surround us. You'll enjoy discovering charming small towns and marketplaces and exploring musketeer castles, medieval fortifications and Roman ruins. Terribly tempting dining specialties await you in Gascony, including famous wines. You can get in touch with a lesbian network through *Roussa*, making interesting contacts along the way. By the way, at *Roussa*, you can rent a beautiful conference room and organize, or participate in, group activities of all sorts. Ask about our program. Gabriele and Monika, with their pets (cats, hens, sheep), wish you a warm welcome.

Address: Courrensan, Gondrin 32330 France.
Tel: (33-5) 62 06 58 96, **Fax:** (33-5) 62 64 45 34.

Type: Guesthouse & camping.
Clientele: Women only
Transportation: Car recommended. Pick up service from bus or train station.
Rooms: 7 rooms with single & double beds.
Bathrooms: 2 shared bath/shower/toilets & 3 shared WCs.
Campsites: Space for 10 tents in garden.
Meals: Generous breakfast & vegetarian dinner.
Vegetarian: Always.
Dates Open: All year except Nov.
High Season: Apr, Jul-Sept.
Rates: Per person: FF 170 high season, FF 150 off season. Camping FF 30 without meals.
Discounts: Call for details.
Rsv'tns: Call for reservations.
To Reserve: Call direct.
Minimum Stay: 2 nights.
Parking: Adequate free off-street parking.
On-Premises: TV lounge, meeting rooms, laundry service.
Exercise/Health: Bicycles to rent on premises. Horseback riding & tennis nearby.
Swimming: 4km to nearby pool in town. 3km to lake for women only.
Sunbathing: In the garden.
Smoking: Permitted.
Pets: Dogs permitted, if they don't eat our cats.
Handicap Access: No.
Children: Welcome, boys only to age 10.
Languages: German, French, English.
Your Host: Gabriele, Monika.

Saouis
Women ♀

Surrounded by vineyards, fields and woods, *Saouis* is situated 80 km from the Pyrenees and 120 km from the Atlantic Coast. For 7 years, women from many different countries have spent their holidays here in this beautiful, tranquil spot, spoiling themselves with the sun, fresh air and fine cuisine. The house has 5 double rooms and plenty of space outdoors for tent camping. For women interested in outdoor activities, we have a 6x14-meter swimming pool on premises, and a paved tennis court 1-1/2 km, from the house. Horseback riding is one km. away. For women who have come without cars, transportation is available, for a fee, to the Pyrenees or the Atlantic Coast. It is also possible, without leaving the farm, to find quiet corners for peaceful solitude, sunbathing, reading and relaxing. If you appreciate good, healthy food, you will not be disappointed with the dishes we prepare! Reservations are required in advance.

Address: Cravencères, Nogaro 32110 France.
Tel: (33-5) 62 08 56 06.

Type: Guesthouse.
Clientele: Women only
Transportation: Car is best. Pick up from bus in Manciet (near Mont-de-Marsan).
To Gay Bars: 150 km Toulouse Bagdam Cafe, & Bordeaux.
Rooms: 5 doubles.
Bathrooms: 2 shared hot showers & 2 WCs.
Campsites: 10 tent sites, 2 hot showers, 1 cold shower, & 2 WCs.
Meals: Expanded continental breakfast and dinner.
Vegetarian: Mainly vegetarian meals, but also seafood & meat dishes.
Complimentary: Cocktails, "floc" (a regional specialty), & pousse rapier.
Dates Open: Mar-Oct.
High Season: July-Aug.
Rates: Rooms FF 175, camping FF 45, with breakfast & dinner FF 145.
Rsv'tns: Recommended in July & Aug.
To Reserve: Call direct.
Minimum Stay: 3-day minimum for rooms.
Parking: Adequate, free parking.
Swimming: At lake 5 km away. 6x14-meter swimming pool on premises.
Sunbathing: In the garden.
Nudity: Permitted.
Smoking: Permitted.
Pets: Permitted.
Handicap Access: No.
Children: Permitted, but boys to age 10 only.
Languages: French, German, & English.
Your Host: Dagmar.

Villa Roumégous

Q-NET Lesbian-Owned & -Operated ♀♂

The Real Charm of a Simple Life

A comfortable house with plenty of character, *Villa Roumégous* is set in the middle of a park, beside the river Aveyron. For those of you who dream of calm, walks beside the river, bicycling, canoeing, horse riding, speleology, tennis or swimming, St. Antonin Noble de Val and its surrounding areas must be visited. The town is situated at the foot of high cliffs in the heart of the valley of Aveyron. A medieval site of Gothic and Roman art, nearby are rustic villages, castles, abbeys and churches. There are many magnificent natural sights of striking beauty and nature lovers will find the area rich in flora and fauna.

Michou and Jane have lovingly restored part of their large house to enable you to relax and enjoy your holiday in this beautiful setting. They are available to guide you in your choice of activity or eating place. We're only one hour from the Toulouse-Blagnac airport, and half an hour from the Montauban station, at which the high-speed train from Paris stops. You can be sure that you will find genuine hospitality when you arrive at *Villa Roumégous*.

Address: St. Antonin Noble Val 82140 France.
Tel: (33-5) 63 30 60 55 (Tel/Fax). **E-mail:** jlovell@ilink.fr

Type: Holiday home (gîte).
Clientele: Mostly gay & lesbian with some hetero clientele
Transportation: Air, then car.
To Gay Bars: 60 kilometers.
Rooms: 5 rooms with single or double beds.
Bathrooms: Shared: 5 showers only, 2 WCs only.
Meals: Continental breakfast.
Dates Open: All year.
High Season: Apr-Oct.
Rates: 290 FF for 2 people.
Rsv'tns: Required.
To Reserve: Call direct.
Minimum Stay: Required.
Parking: Ample, free off-street parking.
In-Room: Color TV, kitchen, refrigerator, coffee & tea-making facilities, laundry service.
On-Premises: TV lounge, laundry facilities, terrace garden, BBQ.
Swimming: River on premises. Pool nearby.
Sunbathing: On patio, in garden.
Smoking: Permitted in rooms & in garden.
Pets: Not permitted.
Handicap Access: No.
Children: No.
Languages: French, English.
Your Host: Micheline & Jane.

ARCO Hotel — Norddeutscher Hof

Gay-Friendly 50/50 ♀♂

The New ARCO Hotel

In January, 1996, the *ARCO* reopened on a quiet sidestreet two blocks from the central Wittenbergplatz. The pleasant, safe neighbourhood, right in the gay area, offers a wide range of restaurants, bars, shops and cafés. The 21 renovated rooms (most on the ground and first floors) all have telephones, safes, TV, radio, alarm clock and most have a private bath or shower. The helpful *ARCO* staff is especially proud of the terrace and the quiet, shady garden and is looking forward to welcoming you in its new environment.

Address: Geisbergstr. 30, Berlin 10777 Germany.
Tel: (49-30) 218 21 28, **Fax:** (49-30) 211 33 87.

Type: Hotel/pension.
Clientele: 50% gay & lesbian & 50% hetero clientele
Transportation: 5-minute walk from Wittenbergplatz U-bahn station. 3 U-bahn lines & several bus stops nearby.
To Gay Bars: 2-8 minute walk.
Rooms: 14 double rooms, 7 single rooms, 1 apartment.

Bathrooms: 14 private, 7 shared.
Meals: Breakfast buffet.
Dates Open: All year.
Rates: Singles DM 75-DM 140, doubles DM 120-DM 175.
Credit Cards: MC, Visa, Amex, Diners.
Rsv'tns: Preferred.
To Reserve: Call direct.

Parking: On the street or in nearby garage.
In-Room: Maid service, phone, safe, TV, radio, alarm clock.
On-Premises: Small lounge, terrace, garden.
Exercise/Health: Gym nearby.
Swimming: Lake nearby.
Sunbathing: At the lake or in the park.

Nudity: Permitted in park or at the lake.
Smoking: Permitted.
Pets: Permitted.
Handicap Access: Yes. Please inquire.
Children: Permitted.
Languages: German, English, French, Spanish, Portuguese.
Your Host: Jacques & Rolf.

Artemisia, Women Only Hotel

Women ♀

Artemisia, the hotel for women only, is located just minutes from the Kurfürstendamm, Berlin's most exciting avenue. Renovated and redecorated in soothing pastels, our hotel offers rooms with modern furniture, telephones and spacious, private bathrooms. *Artemisia's* special features also include a sun deck with an impressive view of Berlin. At *Artemisia,* travelling women find complete comfort and convenience. If you come to Berlin, for business or pleasure, *Artemisia's* personal, woman-identified atmosphere will make your stay a memorable experience.

Address: Brandenburgischestrasse 18, Berlin 10707 Germany.
Tel: (49-30) 873 89 05, or 873 63 73, **Fax:** (49-30) 861 86 53.

Type: Hotel with bar.
Clientele: Women only
Transportation: Taxi or U-bahn: Konstanzerstrasse, airport bus to Adenauerplatz.
To Gay Bars: 10-minute drive to women's bars.
Rooms: 7 rooms & 1 suite with single or double beds.
Bathrooms: 1 private bath/toilet & 7 private shower/toilets.

Meals: Lavish buffet-style breakfast with eggs, cereal, fruits, vegetables, yogurt, cheeses & meats, jams, etc.
Vegetarian: Buffet breakfast has a variety of items to please everyone.
Complimentary: Bar with room service.
Dates Open: All year.
Rates: Single 99.00-149.00 DM, double 169.00-220.00 DM.

Discounts: On stays exceeding 1 week (7 nights).
Credit Cards: MC, Visa, Amex, Eurocard & Diners.
Rsv'tns: Recommended!
To Reserve: Call direct.
Parking: Adequate free on-street parking.
In-Room: Maid & laundry service, telephone, heat. In suite only: color cable TV.
On-Premises: Meeting rooms, TV lounge, cocktail lounge, women's art displays.

Sunbathing: On common sun deck.
Smoking: Permitted without restriction except during breakfast (no smoking).
Pets: Not permitted.
Handicap Access: No.
Children: Permitted, but males only up to 14 yrs.
Languages: German, English, Italian & French.

Pension Niebuhr
Gay-Owned 50/50 ♂

Willkommen, Bienvenue, Welcome

Pension Niebuhr follows an old Berlin tradition: You are accommodated in a house built in the beginning of this century, with converted former apartments, so you'll get a feeling of privacy. Rooms are typically spacious, with high ceilings. All have been newly furnished during the last two years and don't look like most hotel rooms. The interior is modern and decorated with paintings by young Berlin artists. Seven of the 12 rooms have private bathrooms, cable TV, telephone and clock/radio. The other five have sinks with hot water and a shared shower and toilet on the same floor. As a special free service, an extended breakfast is served in the room any time after 7 a.m.

In the well-known district of Berlin-Charlottenburg, *Pension Niebuhr* is centrally located, yet in a quiet neighborhood. Kurfürstendamm, the popular main street for shopping and strolling, is within a three-minute walk. The S-Bahn-station Savignyplatz is about 200 meters from us. From there it's just one station to Zoologischer Garten, the former main station of West Berlin. The surrounding area offers a wide choice of international restaurants with their typical cuisine, several little galleries, bars and antique shops. A VERY IMPORTANT NOTE: THIS IS CONSIDERED A SAFE AREA.

Willi, the friendly host, is always glad to take the time to chat and share information about this great city.

Address: Niebuhrstr 74, Berlin 10629 Germany.
Tel: (49-30) 324 95 95 or 324 95 96, **Fax:** (49-30) 324 80 21.

Type: Pension.
Clientele: 50% hetero with a gay male following
Transportation: Bus (NR 109) from airport to Bleibtreustr, then 3-minute walk. From Zoo station, S-Bahn to Savignyplatz.
To Gay Bars: About 10 minutes by bus to gay bar area or 5-min walk to nearest bar.
Rooms: 12 rooms.
Bathrooms: 7 private showers/toilets, 5 rooms share.

Meals: Expanded continental breakfast.
Vegetarian: Vegetarian breakfast by request. Restaurants also offer vegetarian food.
Complimentary: Coffee, tea, juices, sparkling wine, coke & mineral water.
Dates Open: All year.
Rates: Single DM 95,00-DM 140,00. Double DM 125,00-DM 170,00.
Discounts: On stays exceeding 7 nights. Winter rates from Nov-Feb.

Credit Cards: MC, VISA, Amex & Eurocard.
Rsv'tns: Required.
To Reserve: Call direct.
Parking: Limited on-street parking, DM 5 per day. Empty spaces hard to find.
In-Room: Color cable TV, telephone, maid & room service.
On-Premises: Fax machine.
Exercise/Health: Nearby gym, sauna & massage.
Swimming: Pool & lake 1 km away.

Sunbathing: At the park or lake.
Nudity: Permitted at the lake or partly common pool.
Smoking: Permitted without restrictions.
Pets: Permitted.
Handicap Access: No.
Children: Not especially welcome.
Languages: German & English.
Your Host: Willi.

Hotel Acon
Gay-Friendly 50/50 ♀♂

Our Staff Will Make You Feel at Home

Hotel Acon, a three-star hotel located in the centre of town, is just a short walk to Central Station, several international restaurants, and plenty of shopping. A 15-minute walk from the hotel is the Altstadt, which is known as the longest bar in the world, with its hundreds of bars, discos, and restaurants. Düsseldorf offers sightseers many attractions. Visit sea lions, piranhas, penguins and crocodiles at the Aqua Zoo, spend a day at the Kunsthalle art museum or the Goethe museum, or cheer on the ice hockey team, which has won five of the last six playoffs. For your convenience, all rooms have private bath and each of our rooms has a direct-

continued next page

INN PLACES® 1998

dial telephone and cable TV. Our complimentary English breakfast will get you off to a good start each morning. Please keep in mind that we are usually booked during every exhibition, so it is imperative that you make your reservations early.

Address: Mintropstrasse 23, Düsseldorf 40215 Germany.
Tel: (49-211) 37 70 20, **Fax:** (49-211) 37 70 31.

Type: Hotel with bistro/bar.
Clientele: 50% hetero & 50% gay & lesbian clientele
To Gay Bars: 5-minute walk to gay/lesbian bars.
Rooms: 24 rooms.
Bathrooms: All private bathrooms with shower & WC.

Meals: Expanded continental breakfast.
Dates Open: All year.
Rates: Single DM 115-DM 245, double/twin DM 165-DM 345, 3-beds DM 195-DM 375.
Discounts: Ask about special weekend rates.

Credit Cards: MC, Visa, Amex, Diners, Eurocard.
Rsv'tns: Required.
To Reserve: Travel agent or call direct.
Parking: Parking garage, DM 12 per car, per night.
In-Room: Telephone, color TV, maid service.

Smoking: Permitted without restrictions. Some special non-smoking rooms available.
Pets: Permitted.
Children: OK.
Languages: German, English.

Künstler-Pension Sarah Petersen   Gay/Lesbian ♀♂
The Artist Pension

In early summer, 1998, the *Künstler-Pension Sarah Peterson* will re-occupy its original location in the newly-restored, early 19th-century building at Lange Reihe 50, just down the street from its 1997 temporary quarters at Lange Reihe 88. The official re-opening will be accompanied by a series of art exhibitions, house concerts and lots of public attention.

The German word "Künstler" means "artist," and the *Künstler-Pension Sarah Petersen* carries on the tradition of the famous European artist pensions of the '20s and '30s, in this venerable, early 19th-century home. Sarah says, "Writers, actors musicians, fashions designers, and all people who like the special atmosphere of a small, familiar hotel, are part of the good spirit our little guest house has to offer." Sarah's guests are always pleased by the variety of museums, coffee houses, small stores, restaurants and gay bars in the area surrounding the hotel. A five-minute walk will also take you to the large, city lake, Alster, which is overlooked by parks and cafes.

Extensive restoration work (1.3 million d-marks), which took place throughout 1997 and into 1998, have transformed Sarah's place into a historical landmark. The new hotel exhibits beautifully-restored and rare early 19th-century architecture and creative furnishings. Its newly-renovated rooms combine the comfort of "upper middle class standards," as Sarah says, "with the charm of the antique interior." They are well-appointed with all the modern conveniences, such as in-room telephone, fax, answering machine and mini fridge with drinks. The Lange

Reihe 88 building, which was occupied by the hotel during renovations, will continue to serve as guest quarters for long-term visitors.

Address: Lange Reihe 88 (moving back to newly restored location, in early summer, '98 at Lange Reihe 50, call for exact date), Hamburg 20099 Germany. **Tel:** (49-40) 24 98 26 (Tel/Fax).

Type: Guesthouse with small picturesque hotel bar.
Clientele: Good mix of gay men & women with 30% straight clientele
Transportation: Airport bus to Hauptbahnhof.
To Gay Bars: 1/2 block or 4 minutes by foot.
Rooms: 8 rooms.
Bathrooms: All private showers or complete bathrooms.
Meals: Expanded (meatless) continental breakfast.
Vegetarian: Breakfast. Several restaurants & coffeehouses nearby serve vegetarian food.
Complimentary: Tea, coffee, juices, beer, wine & champagne.
Dates Open: All year.
High Season: July-Sept.
Rates: Single DM 79, double DM 98-DM 160, triple DM 140, apartment DM 180.
Credit Cards: Eurocard.
Rsv'tns: Required with deposit.
To Reserve: Call direct, fax or write.
Parking: Free on-street parking, parking house around the corner.
In-Room: Color TV, room service. Some rooms have telephone, fax, answering machine & mini fridge with drinks.
On-Premises: House bar for guests & friends.
Swimming: 10-minute walk to indoor public pool.
Sunbathing: 5 minutes to Lake Alster.
Smoking: Permitted without restrictions.
Pets: Inquire.
Handicap Access: No.
Children: Permitted.
Languages: German & English.

Berkhöfel

Lesbian-Owned & -Operated ♀

Along the Lower Rhine in Beautiful Westphalia

In the midst of pastures, orchards and fields, near the lower Rhine and the border between Germany and The Netherlands is *Berkhöfel*. Restored in 1994, our farmhouse offers bright, clean and welcoming guestrooms, meeting rooms, a livingroom and a dining hall where all-vegetarian meals are served. From the dining room, doors open out onto the sun-terrace and patio with deck chairs. The area has many manors and beautiful little museums and the wide, flat landscape is ideal for bicycle trips. *Berkhöfel* is a one hour's drive from Düsseldorf, 30 minutes from Nijmegen in The Netherlands and 1-1/2 hours from Amsterdam.

Address: Uedemer Str. 196, Bedburg-Hau 47551 Germany.
Tel: (49-2823) 29749.

Type: Guesthouse.
Clientele: Mostly women with men welcome
Transportation: Car is best, or train to Goch or Emmerich. Free pick up from train & Düsseldorf airport.
To Gay Bars: 10 min drive to "Le Journal" bar in Kleve, 30 min drive to Nijmegen, Netherlands gay bars.
Rooms: 12 rooms with single beds.
Bathrooms: Shared: 5 showers only, 6 WCs only.
Meals: Full breakfast, supper, dinner.
Vegetarian: All meals are vegetarian.
Complimentary: Tea & coffee.
Dates Open: All year.
Rates: DM 39.50-DM 102.
Rsv'tns: Appreciated, if possible. Guests without reservations welcome if rooms are available.
To Reserve: Call direct.
Parking: Adequate free off-street parking in our court.
In-Room: Maid service.
On-Premises: Meeting rooms, CD player, tape library.
Exercise/Health: Nearby gym, sauna, massage, golf.
Swimming: Nearby pool & lake.
Sunbathing: On patio.
Nudity: Permitted on patio.
Smoking: Permitted only in smoking room.
Pets: Not permitted.
Handicap Access: No.
Children: Please inquire. Playground, child's chair & bed.
Languages: German, English & Dutch.
Your Host: Brigitte & Barbara.

Frauenferienhof Ostfriesland

Women ♀

Ride Horses on the Moors... Indulge in a Massage... Dream by the Fireplace...

On the windswept plains not far from the North Sea, we have established a place for women, for us and for our animals, and a place for you to enjoy an un-

continued next page

usual vacation amongst other women from many places. *Frauenferienhof Ostfriesland* means "A place for women to vacation in Ostfriesland." You can have as active or as meditative a vacation as you like. You can bicycle or ride Icelandic horses over the lowlands and through the moors, meadows and woods. Or you can relax under the broad skies of Ostfriesland and repose in our garden, relax in the sauna or just dream by the fireplace. When you feel like it, you can join other women in lively conversation, games or dancing, or indulge yourself in a Reflexology treatment or massage. We also offer courses and programs, whose subjects change from year to year. We provide food which is mainly organically grown. As a rule, guests do their own cooking.

Address: Zum Lengener Meer 2, Friedeburg-Bentstreek 26446 Germany.
Tel: (49-4956) 4956 (Tel/Fax).

Type: Women's retreat with courses & program.
Clientele: Women only
Transportation: Pick up from bus, train.
Rooms: 2 singles, 2 doubles, 2 with 3 beds.
Bathrooms: 2 shared.

Meals: All meals included.
Vegetarian: Only vegetarian.
Dates Open: All year.
Rates: DM 50 per day (meals included), not including course.
Rsv'tns: Required.

On-Premises: Meeting rooms.
Exercise/Health: Sauna.
Swimming: At nearby lake (10km).
Nudity: Permitted in the garden.

Smoking: Permitted in the designated living room only.
Pets: Not permitted.
Handicap Access: Yes.
Children: Permitted, boys under 10 years old only.
Languages: German, English.

Hotel Sonnenhof

Men ♂

Fantastic Days and Hot Nights for Gay Men

Hotel Sonnenhof is the largest exclusively gay vacation and weekend getaway in Germany. Here, within our house and grounds, like-minded gay men relax in an atmosphere both uninhibited and discreet. Nudism? No problem! In this clothing-optional environment, each person can enjoy the sun — dressed or undressed — as he pleases. You'll find us north of Munich, about midway between Nürnberg and Bayreuth.

The 3-story main house has common rooms where guests dine and socialize, a late-night disco bar, as well as a TV lounge with video and games. Guest rooms are well-furnished, some with private bath and balconies. Our round swimming pool (8-meter in diameter) has an area of 650 square meters and is unequaled in the German gay scene. In winter, cross-country and downhill skiing are popular. Nearby castles and limestone caves make for interesting side trips at all times of the year. Canoeing, riding and tennis are also available. Gay events held at *Hotel Sonnenhof* throughout the year include showtime with Miss Mara, a drag extravaganza, the election of Mr. Sonnenhof, and various drag and strip show events.

Address: Ittling 36, Simmelsdorf 91245 Germany.
Tel: (49-9155) 7233, **Fax:** (49-9155) 7278. **E-mail:** SONNENHOF.HOTEL@t-online.de **URL:** http://ourworld.compuserve.com/homepages/GAY_HOTEL/

Type: Hotel with disco/bar.
Clientele: Men only
Transportation: Car is best. Pick up from train station. (Simmelsdorf free, Lauf/Peg DM 30,00.)
To Gay Bars: 45 miles or a 40-minute drive.
Rooms: 20 rooms & 1 apartment with single or double beds.

Bathrooms: Private: 3 shower/toilet, 17 sink only.
Meals: Buffet breakfast, dinner.
Complimentary: Tea, coffee, cake, ice, snacks.
Dates Open: Closed in January. Call for details.
High Season: May-September, December.
Rates: Single DM 65,00 to DM 70,00. Double DM 130,00 to DM 170,00.
Discounts: Varies per season. Please inquire.
Rsv'tns: Required.
To Reserve: Call direct.
Parking: Free off-street parking.
On-Premises: TV lounge, reading room & disco bar.
Exercise/Health: Sauna in Nuremberg. Skiing nearby.

Swimming: Pool outside premises.
Sunbathing: At poolside.
Nudity: Permitted at poolside & in bar (not in dining area).
Smoking: Permitted.
Pets: Permitted.
Handicap Access: No.
Children: Not permitted.
Languages: German, English.

Hotel Elysium

Q-NET Gay/Lesbian ♀♂

The Most IN Island in the Mediterranean

EUROPE

GREECE • MYKONOS

You are captivated at first glance by the ever-changing patterns of blue and white on the walls, the narrow streets and the wonderful, sandy beaches, with waters in all shades of blue. Such intensive contrasts in colour, and such harmonious shapes, can be found on no other island. Mykonos is a place where sun, sea and entertainment come together in a superb, natural setting, to create the perfect atmosphere for your holiday. And, you'll find *Hotel Elysium* the perfect environment in which to enjoy it.

The hotel was built in a traditional Mykonian architectural style in 1989 and offers panoramic views of Mykonos Old Town and the ocean. Each of the hotel's 42 rooms and three suites have ceiling fans, hairdryers, direct-dial phones, stereo music, refrigerator, safe box and color satellite TV. For relaxation and fitness there is a swimming pool, Jacuzzi, and a fully-equipped fitness center with sauna. The breakfast is American Buffet. Other features of *Hotel Elysium* include a snack-bar, living room, TV lounge, pool bar, private parking, guest laundry facilities and beach towels. All facilities into *Hotel Elysium* are free of charge.

Address: School of Fine Arts, Mykonos Town, Mykonos 84600 Greece.
Tel: (30-289) 23952, 24210, 24684, **Fax:** (30-289) 23747.

Type: Hotel with rest. & bar.
Clientele: Mostly gay with some straight clientele
Transportation: Car is best, free hotel bus pick up from airport or port.
To Gay Bars: 2 min. walk.
Rooms: 43 rooms & 3 apartments with single, double or king beds.
Bathrooms: All private.
Meals: American buffet breakfast.

Complimentary: Juices.
Dates Open: April to November.
High Season: July 1 through September 15.
Rates: Doubles 26,000-34,000 drachmas, suites 43,000-48,000 drachmas, depending on season.
Discounts: 5% for stays of a week or more.
Credit Cards: VISA, Amex, Diners & Eurocard.

Rsv'tns: Required.
To Reserve: Travel agent or call direct.
Parking: Free off-street parking.
In-Room: Color TV, telephone, hair dryer, refrigerator, maid & laundry service.
On-Premises: TV lounge, meeting rooms.
Exercise/Health: Jacuzzi, sauna, gym, weights.
Swimming: Pool on premises, nearby ocean beach.
Sunbathing: At poolside.
Nudity: Permitted poolside.
Smoking: Permitted.
Pets: Permitted.
Children: Not permitted.
Languages: Greek, English, French, Italian & Spanish.

IGLTA

Villa Konstantin

Gay/Lesbian ♀♂

A Peaceful Oasis Near the Heart of Mykonos

Villa Konstantin is situated 700m from the town of Mykonos, offering panoramic sea views and peaceful tranquility just a ten-minute walk from the nightlife. All the studios and apartments have large patios, wonderful sea views, private entrances, and accommodate from two to six people. *Villa Konstantin* is perfect for people who want to be somewhere quiet and beautiful yet near the pulse of the city. We look forward to meeting you.

Address: Mykonos 84600 Greece.
Tel: (30-289) 25824/26204, (30-289) 23461, **Fax:** (30-289) 26205.

Type: Studios & apartments.
Clientele: Mostly gay & lesbian with some straight clientele
Transportation: Car is best, or Moto Bike. Free pick up from ferry dock.
To Gay Bars: A 10-minute walk or 2-minute drive.

Rooms: 5 rooms & 5 apartments with single or double beds.
Bathrooms: All private shower/toilets.
Vegetarian: Available in town, a ten-minute walk.
Dates Open: April-October.
High Season: July-August.
Rates: 8,000 -35,000 DR.
Discounts: Large groups & stays of over 8 days.

Credit Cards: MC & VISA.
Rsv'tns: Required.
To Reserve: Call direct.
Minimum Stay: 4 nights.
Parking: Limited free parking.
In-Room: Kitchen, refrigerator, coffee/tea-making facilities & maid service.
On-Premises: Laundry facilities & bar.

Swimming: Nearby pool & ocean.
Sunbathing: On patio, private sun decks & at poolside.
Nudity: Permitted.
Pets: Permitted.
Handicap Access: No.
Children: Welcome.
Languages: Greek, English, Italian.
Your Host: Sharon.

Room With a View

Gay/Lesbian ♀♂

Panoramic Rooftop Apartments in Iceland

Haven't you always wanted to visit Iceland and stay for a few days — or perhaps a few weeks? If so, make your stay a memorable one and rent an apartment in downtown Reykjavík. Ideal for long stays, *Room With a View's* luxurious, fully furnished apartments have separate bedroom, TV, stereo equipment, laundry facilities, kitchen, and Jacuzzi. Inspiring panoramic views of the city, sea, mountains and midnight sun can be seen from each apartment's large balcony. Downstairs we have added a coffee shop which is open daily 9am-10pm.

Address: Laugavegur 18, 6th floor, Reykjavik 101 Iceland.
Tel: (354) 552 7262 (Tel/Fax). **E-mail:** arnike@mm.is

Type: Rental apartments with bookshop & coffee shop on premises.
Clientele: Mostly gay & lesbian with some hetero clientele.

Transportation: Bus from airport to town terminal, then bus, taxi or walking.
To Gay Bars: Next door to apartments.

Rooms: Two 1-bedroom apartments with queen beds, sleep 1-4 persons.
Bathrooms: Private bath/shower/toilets.
Dates Open: All year.

High Season: May-August.
Rates: US $63.
Discounts: Please inquire.
Credit Cards: MC, VISA, Amex, Eurocard.
Rsv'tns: Recommended.

To Reserve: Travel agent or call direct.
Minimum Stay: 3 days.
Parking: Ample on-street parking.
In-Room: Fully furnished, color TV, kitchen, coffee/tea-making facilities, refrigerator, laundry facilities.
On-Premises: Laundry facilities, video tape library.
Exercise/Health: Jacuzzi, steam.
Swimming: Nearby pool.
Sunbathing: On roof.
Nudity: Permitted on roof.
Smoking: Permitted on balcony.
Pets: Not permitted.
Handicap Access: There is an elevator.
Children: Welcome.
Languages: Icelandic, English, Danish.
Your Host: Arni.

Amazonia
Women ♀

The Welcome of Amazonia and Ireland Make an Unforgettable Vacation

From the hilltop windows of *Amazonia* you can look upon the beautiful, rolling, green hills of Ireland and the Atlantic Ocean. The beach is at the bottom of the hill and is very safe for swimming and sports. The walks to the nearby pubs afford marvelous views of the ocean rolling in along the rocky coastline. We have bikes, canoes, body boards, tennis racquets and golf clubs free for the guests' use and we can arrange horseback riding for you. Breakfast, which is either vegetarian or a full Irish fry, is served from 9:00 until 12:00 and you can eat as much or as little as you like! There is free tea and coffee all day. We prepare excellent vegetarian evening meals (optional) with lots of homemade wine and beer. We want you to feel at home and enjoy our Irish hospitality.

Address: Coast Road, Fountainstown, Myrtleville, Cork Ireland.
Tel: (353-21) 831 115.

Type: Bed & breakfast guesthouse with campsites.
Clientele: Women only
Transportation: Car or bus from Cork city. Pick up from arrival point in Cork city (airport, ferry dock) £5.00.
To Gay Bars: 10 miles or 30 minutes by car.
Rooms: 1 log cabin, 3 rooms with single, twin or queen beds & a house tent with double bed.
Bathrooms: Private & shared.
Campsites: 3 tent sites with breakfast in the main house.
Meals: Full breakfast served until 12:00. Optional vegetarian evening meal, including homemade wine & beer, for £12 extra.
Vegetarian: As breakfast option or excellent evening meal.
Complimentary: Tea or coffee all day.
Dates Open: All year except Christmas.
High Season: May-September.
Rates: Cabins & rooms £15-£20 per woman, house tent £10/woman. Camping £4 per tent + £6 per woman (includes breakfast & use of house).
Discounts: 50% off for children under 10 years.
Rsv'tns: Required during high season.
To Reserve: Call direct.
Parking: Ample off-street free parking.
In-Room: Room service.
On-Premises: TV lounge, library & laundry service.
Exercise/Health: Kayaks, bicycles, wind surfers, snorkeling equipment. Nearby tennis club, horse riding arranged.
Swimming: In nearby ocean or river.
Sunbathing: On the patio or in the garden.
Nudity: Permitted in the garden.
Smoking: Limited to garden.
Pets: Permitted. We have dogs & cats.
Handicap Access: Yes. Bungalow allows reasonable wheelchair access.
Children: Welcomed.
Languages: English, French.
Your Host: Penny & Aine.

Dunsany Bed & Breakfast

Gay/Lesbian ♀♂

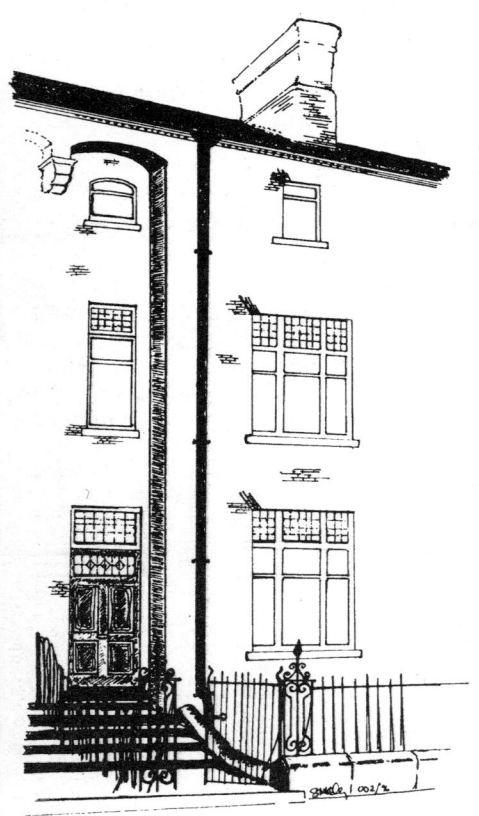

A Friendly Welcome is Assured — Visit Once and You'll Want to Return

Dunsany Bed & Breakfast assures you of a warm Irish welcome. This delightful Victorian house with its period features has been lovingly maintained by its owners. A haven in a bustling city, the house is situated in a quiet cul-de-sac with a bowling green to the front and fields behind, truly a country-like setting. We offer you a full Irish breakfast (or a vegetarian version, if you prefer) to sustain you on your travels, and tea and coffee are available all day. Dublin city has many attractions for the visitor, including cultural, historical and, of course, social! The city and its sights are easily accessible by bus, car, taxi, or on foot. Dublin is also renowned for easy access to sea, mountains and countryside — well worth a visit!

Address: 7 Gracepark Gardens, Drumcondra, Dublin 9 Ireland.
Tel: (353-1) 857 1362,
Mobile: (353-88) 695 051.

Type: Bed & breakfast.
Clientele: 70% gay & lesbian clientele
Transportation: Airport bus 41 to Drumcondra, or taxi from airport (about £8), excellent bus service from city centre.
To Gay Bars: 2 miles, a 25 minute walk, a 10 minute drive.

Rooms: 4 rooms with single or double beds.
Bathrooms: 2 private, others share.
Meals: Full Irish breakfast.
Vegetarian: Vegetarian breakfast available. Vegetarians catered for nearby (5 min walk) or in city centre (2 miles).
Complimentary: Tea & coffee.

Dates Open: All year. Closed Dec 24-26.
High Season: Jun-Aug.
Rates: £23-£25 per person, no single supplement.
Rsv'tns: Required.
To Reserve: Call direct.
Parking: Ample free on-street parking.
On-Premises: TV lounge.

Smoking: Permitted in TV lounge only.
Pets: Permitted.
Handicap Access: No.
Children: Permitted.
Languages: English, French.
Your Host: Anne & Maureen.

Fairfield Lodge

Gay/Lesbian ♀♂

Our luxury double studio apartment, *Fairfield Lodge,* is set in a glorious award-winning garden and is designed to provide all of the peace and tranquility that you would expect in Ireland. It is within easy reach of our bustling city, only 15 minutes by car from Dublin's city centre. For your convenience, there is also a bus stop outside the gate which takes you into Dublin every seven minutes. The studio is newly decorated and furnished to the highest standards. It is totally self-contained with secured parking.

Address: Monkstown Ave, MonkstownCounty Dublin Ireland.
Tel: (353-1) 280 3912 (Tel/Fax). **E-mail:** JSB@Indigo.ie

Type: Studio apartment for 2 with own entrance.
Clientele: Gay & lesbian
Transportation: Bus stop outside the gate, but car is handy. Pick up from airport & train £10.
To Gay Bars: 20 min drive into city center.
Rooms: 1 studio apartment with double bed.

Bathrooms: Private.
Meals: Breakfast food items supplied in studio's kitchen.
Complimentary: Tea & coffee.
Dates Open: All year.
High Season: May-Sept.
Rates: £40 per night, but vary depending on no. of nights. Single supplement on request.

Discounts: Inquire during off season (Oct-end of April).
Rsv'tns: Required.
To Reserve: Travel agent or call direct.
Parking: Adequate free off-street parking, locked up at night.
In-Room: Color TV, VCR on request, telephone, refrigerator, kitchen, maid service, coffee & tea-making facilities.
Sunbathing: In garden, weather permitting.
Smoking: Permitted.
Pets: Not permitted.
Handicap Access: No.
Children: No.
Languages: English, French, German, Italian.
Your Host: John.

Frankies Guesthouse

Q-NET Gay/Lesbian ♂

Céad Mile Fáilte — A Million Welcomes

Established in 1989 in a mews-style building over 100 years old, *Frankies* offers year-round accommodations exclusively for gays. Dublin has an expanding gay scene, which offers a variety of venues for those looking for adventure, and *Frankies* is located close to the bars, clubs and saunas. Our beautiful south-facing roof terrace & sun deck is surrounded with tropical potted plants and is a good place to relax after a day of sightseeing. We have recently added a sauna and a bar on premises for our guests to enjoy. Dublin is a capital city of many charms and delights. From magnificent Dublin Castle and the supreme architecture of the city's cathedrals, to Phoenix Park (the largest enclosed park in Europe), the choice is endless.

Travellers wishing to tour outside Dublin will find breathtaking scenery along the coast road which leads to sandy beaches and sand dunes, well worth the trip for those who enjoy the smell of the sea and a sense of freedom. You'll be glad you visited Ireland, a country renowned for its hospitality and friendliness. We are planning to open a place in Athens, Greece. Please contact us here in Dublin for more details.

Address: 8 Camden Place, Dublin 2 Ireland.
Tel: Reservations: (353-1) 478 3087 (Tel/Fax) or (353-1) 475 2182.

Type: Guesthouse with bar.
Clientele: Mostly men with women welcome

Transportation: Airport bus to city bus sta., taxi from bus sta. approx £3. Taxi from airport approx £10.

To Gay Bars: 8 minutes walking.
Rooms: 12 rooms with single or double beds & an apartment in town.

Bathrooms: 5 en suite. Shared: 2 bath/shower/toilets, 1 WC. All have hand wash basin.

continued next page

Meals: Full Irish breakfast.
Vegetarian: Available on request.
Complimentary: Tea & coffee.
Dates Open: All year.
High Season: July, August, & September.

Rates: Singles £21.00-£31.00. Doubles from £48.00-£58.00.
Discounts: On extended stays.
Credit Cards: MC, Visa, Amex, Eurocard.
Rsv'tns: Required.

To Reserve: Call direct.
Parking: Ample, free on-street parking.
In-Room: Color TV & maid service.
On-Premises: TV lounge.
Exercise/Health: Sauna.
Sunbathing: On the roof terrace.

Smoking: Permitted without restrictions.
Pets: Not permitted. We have our own dogs.
Handicap Access: Yes, some ground floor rooms.
Children: Not permitted.
Languages: English, Chinese & Malay.
Your Host: Joe & Frankie.

Stoneybroke House   Gay/Lesbian ♀♂

Experience the Garden of Ireland in an Irish Country Home

Stoneybroke House is an Irish Country House in County Wicklow, the Garden of Ireland, situated 1-1/2 miles from the historic town of Tinahely, and approximately 60 miles south of Dublin. The original house is more than 200 years old and has recently been extended and refurbished. It enjoys spectacular views across the local river and on across the valley and surrounding hills. Emphasis is on your comfort and relaxation coupled with high-quality food, lovingly prepared in our own kitchen. Our menu features eight entrees, including Wicklow leg of lamb butterfly-style and marinated in olive oil, garlic, rosemary and lemon juice; Wicklow sirloin steak served with a mushroom and red wine sauce; Chicken breast a la Stoneybroke with a whole grain mustard, white wine & cream sauce, garnished and stuffed with olives; Salmon steak with a traditional Hollandaise sauce; and for vegetarians, a special vegetable Kiev. The house specialty is crispy roast duck with orange brandy sauce. We look forward to your visit. You are assured a warm welcome and, upon your departure, we hope that you leave us as new-found friends.

Address: Ballinamanogue, Tinahely, Co. Wicklow Ireland.
Tel: (353-402) 38236.

Type: Inn with restaurant & wine bar.
Clientele: Gay & lesbian. Good mix of men & women
Transportation: Car is best. Dublin airport limousine. Limousine hire service available. Pick up £70 one way.
Rooms: 4 rooms with single or double beds.
Bathrooms: 2 private with bath or shower, others share.

Meals: Full breakfast, dinner.
Vegetarian: Available if requested at time of booking.
Complimentary: Tea & coffee on arrival. Biscuits in room.
Dates Open: All year.
High Season: June-September.
Rates: £35-£50.
Discounts: 1 night free in 7. Weekend & mid-week discount packages.

Credit Cards: MC, Visa, Amex, Eurocard.
Rsv'tns: Required.
To Reserve: Call direct.
Minimum Stay: 2 nights.
Parking: Ample free off-street parking.
In-Room: Colour TV, coffee & tea-making facilities, hair dryer, clock radio, bathrobes, room, maid & laundry service.
On-Premises: TV lounge, restaurant & wine bar.

Sunbathing: On private & common sun decks, on patio, in gardens.
Nudity: Permitted in house.
Smoking: No restrictions. Non-smoking rooms available.
Pets: Not permitted.
Handicap Access: No.
Children: No.
Languages: English.
Your Host: Richard & Liam.

La Filanda Guesthouse

Q-NET Women ♀

A Woman's Cultural Center and Guesthouse

This romantic Italian villa, surrounded by a huge wild garden, imposing old trees, and the lovely hills of the Piemonte region, was created by female artists. The ancient city of Acqui Terme, famous for its thermal baths and traffic-free center, is within walking distance, while Genova, Milan and the Mediterranean Sea are 40 miles away (a one-hour drive). Piemonte is well-known for its superb cuisine and high-class wines, such as Barolo and Barbaresco — a gourmet's delight! At *La Filanda* we organize a yearly workshop program along diverse cultural lines. We hope to see you soon.

Address: Reg. Montagnola No. 4, Acqui Terme 15011 Italy.
Tel: (39-144) 32 39 56 (Tel/Fax).

Type: Guesthouse & cultural center with music room & workshops.
Clientele: Women only
Transportation: Train from Genova to Acqui Terme (1 hour), then taxi. Pick up from train 10,000 lire.
To Gay Bars: 40 miles, 1-hour drive to Genova, Milan or Turin gay bars.
Rooms: 7 rooms with single or double beds.
Bathrooms: Shared: 2 bath/shower/toilets, 2 showers only, 2 WCs only.
Vegetarian: Restaurants in town have vegetarian dishes.
Dates Open: Mar-Oct. Open in winter during special periods, on request.
High Season: June-Sept.
Rates: Double 45,000 LI, single 60,000 LI (35 Sfr-55 Sfr).
Discounts: Special group rates.
Rsv'tns: Required.
To Reserve: Call direct.
Parking: Free parking.
On-Premises: 2 fully equipped kitchens, living rooms, video library, books, music/cassettes.
Exercise/Health: Health center nearby with fango & massage.
Swimming: Pool & river nearby.
Sunbathing: In garden & on terrace.
Nudity: Permitted in garden.
Smoking: Permitted, but preferably outside.
Pets: Permitted if well-behaved.
Handicap Access: No.
Children: Welcome. Boy children welcome up to 10 years of age.
Languages: Italian, German, English, French.
Your Host: Regula, Sibylla.

Morandi alla Crocetta

Gay-Friendly ♀♂

The Special Feeling of a Genteel Tuscan Home

In the quiet, distinguished atmosphere of a former convent, *Morandi alla Crocetta* follows an ancient tradition of hospitality. Its location is close to every point of artistic and cultural interest, such as the Statue of David, the Archaeological Museum and the Academy of Fine Arts. This is a hotel for those seeking a small and comfortable place filled with character and charm, in the city centre and yet away from the typical tourist establishments.

Address: Via Laura 50, Firenze 50121 Italy.
Tel: (39-55) 2344747, **Fax:** (39-55) 2480954.
E-mail: Hotel.Morandi@dada.it
URL: www.dada.it/Hotel.Morandi

Type: Guesthouse.
Clientele: Mostly straight clientele with a gay & lesbian following
Transportation: Taxi from airport US $15. From train station $7.00.
To Gay Bars: 2 blocks to gay/lesbian bars.
Rooms: 10 rooms.
Bathrooms: All private.
Meals: Continental breakfast 18.000 Lire per person.
Dates Open: All year.
High Season: Easter, Apr-May, Sept-Oct.
Rates: 120.000-250.000 Lire if booked direct.
Credit Cards: MC, Visa, Amex, Diners, Access, Eurocard.
Rsv'tns: Recommended. Fax or phone O.K.
To Reserve: Call direct or travel agent.
Parking: Garage nearby & nearby on-street parking.
In-Room: Maid & room service, color satellite TV, telephone, AC, mini-bar refrigerator & laundry service.
Exercise/Health: Nearby gym & weights.
Smoking: Permitted without restrictions.
Pets: Permitted if small and well-behaved.
Handicap Access: No.
Children: Permitted.
Languages: Italian, English, & limited French & German.

INN PLACES® 1998

Casa Scala

Q-NET Women ♀

An Italian Home on a Picturesque Island

Picture Elba Island, covered with lush vegetation such as wild rosemary, anise, blackberries, grapes (small, family-owned vineyards), cactus, and trees as varied as apricot, lemon, almond, pine, fir, eucalyptus, cypress, and palm. Amidst this splendor is *Casa Scala*. This small, Italian house with four apartments and two sun terraces is surrounded by a garden with trees and flowers and has a view of some of the many tree-covered hills. The nearby hills are a brilliant red, due to iron-rich land. Abandoned mine sites are cluttered with stones and rocks waiting to be scooped up by hand. *Casa Scala* is just a few minutes by bike (available for the duration of your stay for a small fee) from one of the sandy beaches. Boating excursions to some of the caverns (accessible only by sea) are also available.

Address: Loc. Filetto No 9, Marina di Campo, Isola d'Elba 57034 Italy.
Tel: (39-565) 977 777, Fax: (39-565) 977 770.

Type: Cottage with workshops available.
Clientele: Women only
Transportation: Car is best or train from Florence to Elba, pick up from bus station Marina di Campo.
Rooms: 4 apartments with single beds.
Bathrooms: Each apartment has its own bath.
Meals: Continental breakfast with workshop.

Dates Open: March-October.
High Season: July-August.
Rates: DM 1,000 for two-week workshop (includes accommodations & breakfast), or DM 35-DM 40 per night (35,000-40,000 Lire).
Credit Cards: Eurocheck.
Rsv'tns: Required.
To Reserve: Call direct.
Minimum Stay: One week in general. Single days for women from overseas.

Parking: Adequate free off-street parking.
In-Room: VCR, video tape library, kitchen, refrigerator, coffee & tea-making facilities.
On-Premises: Meeting rooms, garden.
Swimming: Nearby ocean beach.
Sunbathing: In the garden, on the beach.

Nudity: Permitted in the garden.
Smoking: Permitted.
Pets: Not permitted.
Handicap Access: No.
Children: Boys not permitted after 10 years of age.
Languages: German, Italian, English.
Your Host: Marianne & Elvira.

Hotel Celeste Residence

Gay-Friendly ♀♂

Hotel Celeste Residence consists of three two-story sections. The ground floor is raised above street level, and is accessible via an outside stairway. (So the location is not handicap-accessible.) Guests occupy their own private apartments, graced by an interior garden and by terraces with panoramic views. The hotel is just 20 meters from the nearest busstop and 200 meters from the beach and from the Chiaiolella, Prócida's fishing harbor, where there are numerous restaurants and shops. Prócida is easily reached from Naples Airport by taxi, bus or the ferry, which accommodates vehicles. The ferry ride takes just an hour and gives visitors a mini-cruise of the gulf. If you're driving, take the Napoli cittá/Piazza Municipio exit and proceed to the Molo Beverello city sea terminal. On arrival at the port of Prócida, you can reach the hotel by bus (line 1.1, which stops just a few meters from the hotel). The hotel advises visitors not to come by car, as the streets are very narrow and it is necessary to know the island very well to get around successfully. Also, the entire island becomes a pedestrian-only area in the evening hours, with all private vehicle traffic banned.

Prócida is an enchanting island of volcanic origin. It is the smallest of the three islands in the Gulf of Naples, and the closest one to the mainland. The island is renowned for its fresh fish, which can still be purchased directly from the fishermen, for wine. Above all, the island is known for its climate, which is moderated by the sea, and for the typically Mediterranean architecture of its houses, painted in pastel colors and dating back to medieval times. Similar constructions are today visible only in Spain and Tunisia.

A little further on, is the tiny island of Vivara. Connected by a bridge which unites two arms of one of the many volcanic craters, of which the island is made. Visits are possible, with permission, for the island is a protected natural park containing archaeological remains from the Mycenaean era. This ancient hunting reserve of the Bourbons remains a protected nature area and is a stopping point for many migrating birds. Swimming, boating and scuba diving are possible along the rocky shore near the bridge connecting Prócida to the little island. *Hotel Celeste Residence* is happy to arrange a variety of excursions, including boat excursions, trips to the island of Vivara, courses in underwater photography, guided scuba tours of the submerged city and nighttime dives.

Address: Via Rivoli 6, Isola di Prócida Napoli 80079 Italy.
Tel: (39-81) 896 7748, Fax: (39-81) 896 7670.
E-mail: procida@mbox.vol.it

Type: Hotel with restaurant & bar.
Clientele: Mostly hetero clientele
Transportation: Ferry from Naples. Pick up from ferry dock 15,000 Lire.
Rooms: 7 rooms, 3 suites, 10 apartments with double beds.

Bathrooms: 20 private bath/shower/toilets. Showers in the garden under lemon trees.
Meals: Buffet breakfast, supper.
Vegetarian: On request.
Dates Open: All year.
High Season: Jul-Aug.
Rates: 80,000-120,000 Lire.
Discounts: Please inquire.
Rsv'tns: Required.

To Reserve: Travel agent or call direct.
Minimum Stay: 2 weeks during high season.
Parking: Adequate on-street pay parking.
In-Room: Telephone, kitchen, refrigerator, coffee & tea-making facilities, maid, room & laundry service.
On-Premises: Laundry facilities.

Swimming: Ocean nearby.
Sunbathing: On roof, private & common sun decks, patio & at beach.
Pets: Permitted.
Handicap Access: No.
Children: Welcome.
Languages: Italian, English, French, Spanish.
Your Host: Giacinto & Concetta.

Hotel Scalinata di Spagna

Gay-Friendly ♀♂

Hotel Scalinata di Spagna has one of the best possible locations, right in the center of Rome and at the top of the famous Spanish Steps. At the foot of the steps is American Express's central office and in the surrounding streets, some of the most famous stores and finest restaurants in the world. Each room has private bath, air conditioning, telephone, security box, and a TV. Breakfast is served on the terrace overlooking all of Rome. Parking is nearby.

Address: Piazza Trinità dei Monti 17, Roma 00187 Italy.
Tel: Bookings: (39-6) 679 3006 or 699 40896, Fax: (39-6) 699 40598.

Type: Bed & breakfast with roof garden.
Clientele: Mostly straight clientele with a 20%-30% gay/lesbian following
Transportation: Taxi or Metro to Piazza di Spagna.
To Gay Bars: 5-minute walk to gay bar.
Rooms: 2 singles, 12 doubles, 3 triples.
Bathrooms: All private.
Meals: Expanded continental breakfast.

Complimentary: Tea, coffee, juices, candy on pillow.
Dates Open: All year.
High Season: June-October, except August.
Rates: Single LI 250,000-LI 350,000, double LI 300,000-LI 380,000.
Credit Cards: MC, Visa, Amex.
Rsv'tns: Required, two months in advance or at last moment.

To Reserve: Call direct.
Parking: 35,000 LI/day or on street, a 5-minute walk.
In-Room: Mini bar, radio, AC, TV, telephone, safe deposit box, and maid, room & laundry service.
On-Premises: TV lounge, public telephone.
Exercise/Health: Convenient to Borghese Garden for jogging. Steam, sauna, Jacuzzi, gym, 5 min away at Villa Borghese.

Swimming: Ocean beaches 20 miles by train.
Sunbathing: On beach or roof deck.
Smoking: Permitted without restrictions.
Pets: Permitted.
Handicap Access: Yes.
Children: Permitted.
Languages: Italian, English, Spanish, French, German.

INN PLACES® 1998   69

Hotel Villa Schuler

Gay-Friendly ♀♂

History & Tradition, Comfort & Romance

Family-owned *Hotel Villa Schuler* was converted from a Sicilian villa to a hotel in 1905. In recent years the hotel has been extensively refurbished, emphasizing its original elegance, charm and atmosphere. Superbly situated above the Ionian Sea, its unique location offers stupendous views of snow-capped Mount Etna and the Bay of Naxos. Its central position, next to the delightful Botanical Gardens and tennis courts, is just 2 minutes from Taormina's famous traffic-free Corso Umberto. The ancient Greco-Roman theater and the cable-car to the beaches are just a 10-minute walk away.

The hotel is surrounded by its own extensive, shady, terraced gardens, where the fragrance of jasmine and bougainvillaea blossoms blend soothingly, enhancing the comfortable, romantic surroundings. Rooms are spacious, each with private bath/shower, WC, orthopaedic beds and mattresses, direct-dial telephone and electronic safe. Most have balcony/terrace or loggia and seaview. Other amenities include a roof terrace solarium, the palm terrace pavilion, dining and TV rooms (color satellite), small library, piano, 24-hour bar and room service, laundry, parking, garages and central heating. You have the choice of having breakfast served à la carte, in your room, in the dining room or on the panoramic palm terrace overlooking the entire coastline. Tennis courts nearby. Regular shuttle-service to the beaches (May-Oct). Multilingual staff.

Address: Via Roma 17, Taormina/Sicily 98039 Italy.
Tel: (39-942) 23481, **Fax:** (39-942) 23522.
E-mail: schuler@tao.it **URL:** http://www.cys.it/schuler

Type: Bed & breakfast hotel & bar.
Clientele: Mainly hetero clientele with a gay & lesbian following
Transportation: Airport bus to Taormina, or pick up from airport by arrangement LIT 95.000, taxi from train LIT 20.000.
To Gay Bars: 5-minute walk.
Rooms: 26 rooms, 1 suite & 4 apartments with single or double beds.

Bathrooms: Private: 8 bath/toilets, 15 shower/toilets, 3 sinks. 1 shared bath.
Meals: Expanded continental breakfast à la carte.
Vegetarian: Restaurants nearby.
Dates Open: Mar 7-Nov 15, 1998
High Season: Easter, August.
Rates: LIT 58,000-LIT 72,500 per person for B&B.
Credit Cards: MC, VISA, Amex, Eurocard, Diners.

Rsv'tns: Recommended, by FAX or e-mail if possible.
To Reserve: Travel agent or call direct.
Parking: Private parking LIT 5,000 per day, garage LIT 15,000 per day (reservable).
In-Room: Maid & room service, telephone, safe, laundry service.
On-Premises: TV lounge with satellite TV, meeting rooms, laundry facilities, solarium, exotic garden, furnished terraces.

Exercise/Health: Nearby gym, weights, sauna & massage.
Swimming: At nearby ocean beach, shuttle service available.
Sunbathing: On the roof terrace or at nearby beach.
Smoking: Permitted without restrictions.
Pets: Not permitted.
Handicap Access: No.
Children: Welcomed.
Languages: Italian, English, German, French, Spanish & Belgian.

Priello Bed & Breakfast

Gay & Lesbian ♀♂

An Unforgettable Vacation in Tuscany

Starting with our winding mountain road, you'll realize that **Priello** is not your everyday guesthouse. Nestled high in the mountains overlooking green Tuscan countryside, you'll find our fifty-acre working farm. Formerly a monastery, our 16th-century farm house has been fully and beautifully restored. You can choose between three guestrooms in the main farm house and two mini-apartments with independent entrance and kitchen facilities. Start your day with a full country breakfast, including fresh milk (milked by you!), freshly gathered eggs, homemade yoghurt, biscuits or muffins topped with homemade jam, juice, coffee, cereal and seasonal fruit.

Join us for a group dinner, or try one of the fantastic local restaurants and meet us afterwards for a glass of wine by the fireplace. Saddle up the horses for a sunset ride through the mountains, help chase the cow out of the sunflowers, look for chicken eggs or milk a sheep and help make cheese. With views spreading out over thirty miles of mountain peaks and lush valleys, you can spend your days relaxing in absolute quiet or lending a hand with the farm work — a helping hand is always welcome!

This is a perfect place for bird watching, star gazing or touring the hill town monasteries or castles. For guests who are interested in history and art, the towns of Caprese Michelangelo (the birthplace of Michelangelo), Sansepolcro (hometown of Piero della Francesca), Perugia and Urbino, as well as many other interesting and beautiful places in Tuscany, Umbria and Marche are all within a half-hour's drive. However you spend it, you time here will be filled with unique experiences, great memories of fun time and new friends.

Address: Caprese Michelangelo Arezzo 52033 Italy.
Tel: (39-575) 791 218 (Tel/Fax). **E-mail:** a.voglino@agora.stm.it

Type: Bed & breakfast, 1-1/2 hours east of Florence, 1-1/2 hours west of Rimini.
Clientele: Mostly gay & lesbian with some hetero clientele
Transportation: Car is best. Inquire about charge for pick up from train or bus.
To Gay Bars: 1-1/2 hours from Florence, Bologna & Rimini gay bars.
Rooms: 3 rooms, 2 apartments with queen beds.
Bathrooms: Private: 1 bath/shower/toilet, 2 shower/toilets. Shared: 1 bath/shower/toilet.
Meals: Full breakfast.
Vegetarian: We have a large organic garden free for the picking.
Complimentary: Afternoon wine & cheese, homemade ice cream & after-dinner liquers, organic garden, chicken eggs, fresh cow milk.
Dates Open: All year.
High Season: Easter thru Oct.
Rates: Lire 100,000-Lire 125,000 per room.

Discounts: Discounts for lengthy stays.
Credit Cards: MC, Diners, Visa, Amex.
Rsv'tns: Required.
To Reserve: Travel agent or call direct.
Minimum Stay: 3 days in apartments.
Parking: Ample free parking. We have a mile-long mountain driveway.
On-Premises: Meeting rooms, TV lounge, laundry facilities, e-mail, fax, copier, printer phone, video tape library.
Exercise/Health: Jacuzzi, horseback riding.
Swimming: River nearby.
Sunbathing: On patio & hillsides.
Nudity: Permitted.
Smoking: Permitted outside only. Non-smoking rooms available.
Pets: Not permitted.
Handicap Access: No, lots of steps.
Children: Welcome.
Languages: Italian, English, French.
Your Host: Brent, Alex, Carol.

EUROPE

ITALY • TUSCANY - RURAL

INN PLACES® 1998

Amsterdam House BV

Q-NET Gay-Friendly ♀♂

A Luxurious Apartment or Houseboat for the Price of a Hotel Room

If you need excellent business or tourist accommodations in Amsterdam, call *Amsterdam House*, in the heart of the gay center, available for long- and short-term rentals. We're the gay-friendliest hotel in the city center, offering canal views and gourmet breakfast, and we're situated close to the main railway station and other major transport intersections. All of our apartments and houseboats are spacious, with luxuriously furnished rooms, fully equipped kitchens and bathrooms, direct telephone, hi-fi set and TV. A fax, answering machine, and photocopier are available on request, as is secretarial service. Of course, all apartments and houseboats are provided with bed linen and towels, and maid service is included. Some apartments have a sauna and a grand piano and most of the apartments overlook the picturesque Amsterdam canals. All houseboats are comfortably heated. Your stay will be unforgettable and something special when you stay in the "Venice of the North."

For easy access to the Amsterdam International Airport, the business and commercial sections of town, and the other downtown amenities offered by one of Europe's greatest capitals, stay in one of the apartments or houseboats offered by *Amsterdam House*.

Address: Amstel 176a,
Amsterdam 1017 AE Netherlands.
Tel: (31-20) 62 62 577, Fax: (31-20) 62 62 987,
USA: (904) 677-5370, (800) 618-1008,
Fax: (904) 672-6659.

Type: Apartment hotel.
Clientele: Mostly hetero with a gay & lesbian following
To Gay Bars: Some apartments are steps away & most are only 1 minute away.
Rooms: 35 apartments & 10 houseboats.
Bathrooms: All private.
Meals: Gourmet breakfast included.

Dates Open: All year.
High Season: June-September.
Rates: From Hfl 145.
Discounts: Long stays.
Credit Cards: MC, Visa, Amex, Diners.
Rsv'tns: Preferred.
To Reserve: Travel agent or call direct.
Parking: Adequate on-street parking, depending on traffic.

In-Room: Color TV, telephone, kitchen, refrigerator, maid & laundry service.
On-Premises: Meeting rooms & laundry facilities. Some houseboats have terraces.
Exercise/Health: Many exercise facilities in the neighborhood.
Sunbathing: At the beach.

Smoking: Permitted. Non-smoking rooms available.
Pets: Permitted.
Handicap Access: Some accommodations are accessible.
Children: Permitted.
Languages: Dutch, German, Spanish, English, French.
Your Host: Willemina & Cyril.

Amsterdam Toff's

Gay-Friendly 50/50 ♀♂

Your Holiday Home in Amsterdam

Amsterdam Toff's are self-contained, self-catering, serviced apartments in an area known as "De Pijp," overlooking the Boerenwetering canal and situated close to museums and art galleries. This is the real Amsterdam, the Amsterdam that the tourist does not normally see, yet it is only 15 minutes' walk from the Leidseplein. These 100-year-old buildings were rebuilt in 1990, and their interiors have been completely renovated with modern comforts in mind. Each apartment is outfitted with color TV, a fully-equipped kitchen and bathroom. *Amsterdam Toff's* are listed and recommended by both the Amsterdam Tourist Board and the Netherlands Reservations Centre. Our guests frequently make comments, such as, "What luck to get this place." "Fantastic—a very nice apartment." "Much better than a hotel stay." Next time you're in Amsterdam, try staying in *Amsterdam Toff's* , where you can relax and be truly comfortable and on your own.

Address: Ruysdaelkade 167, Amsterdam 1072 AS Netherlands.
Tel: (31-20) 67 38 529, **Fax:** (31-20) 66 49 479.

Type: Self-catering apartments with maid service.
Clientele: 50% gay & lesbian & 50% straight clientele
Transportation: Train from airport to central station, then Tram 24 or taxi.
To Gay Bars: 10 minutes by taxi to main gay/lesbian areas.
Rooms: 4 apartments with single or double beds & 1 bed/settee.

Bathrooms: All private bath/shower/WCs.
Dates Open: All year.
High Season: April through August.
Rates: Hfl 175/night, Hfl 950/week, Hfl 2,800/month (prices include city tourist tax). Special off season rates available.
Discounts: 5% discount for cash.
Credit Cards: MC, Visa, Amex & Eurocard. 5% surcharge for credit cards.

Rsv'tns: Deposit or credit card number for all reservations.
To Reserve: Travel agent, but prefer to deal direct.
Minimum Stay: 3 days.
Parking: Limited on-street parking. Pay parking.
In-Room: Color cable TV, telephone, kitchen, refrigerator, coffee & tea-making facilities. VCR on request.
On-Premises: Pay phone.
Swimming: Short train ride to ocean beach. Municipal pool nearby.

Nudity: Nudist beaches 30 minutes out of town at Zandvoort.
Smoking: Permitted without restrictions.
Pets: Not permitted.
Handicap Access: No, because of steep stairway.
Children: Welcome.
Languages: Dutch, English, German, & basic French.
Your Host: Russell & Trevor.

Anco Hotel-Bar

Q-NET Men ♂

Welcoming Leathermen from all over the World

The *ANCO* is a gay-owned and -operated hotel-bar that welcomes leathermen from all over the world. It is located in a historic canal building which dates from 1640, and is situated between the leather district (Warmoesstraat) and Amsterdam's famous red light district. The Central Railway Station is just a short walk from the hotel.

Address: Oudezijds Voorburgwal 55, Amsterdam 1012 EJ Netherlands.
Tel: (31-20) 624 11 26, **Fax:** (31-20) 620 52 75. **E-mail:** lira@xs4all.nl

Type: Hotel & bar for leathermen.
Clientele: Men only
Transportation: Train from airport to central station, then taxi or 5-minute walk.
To Gay Bars: On premises, open from 10am-10pm. 2-minute walk to other gay bars.
Rooms: 11 rooms, 2 dormitories & 1 suite with private bath.
Bathrooms: Private: 14 sinks. Shared bath/shower/toilet on each floor.

Meals: Expanded continental breakfast.
Dates Open: All year.
High Season: July 1-Sept 30.
Rates: HFL 70.00-140.00. With private bath & TV HFL 200.00.
Credit Cards: All major cards accepted.
Rsv'tns: Required at least 4 weeks in advance in high season.
To Reserve: Call or fax direct.
Minimum Stay: 3 nights during high season.
In-Room: Maid service, color cable TV, 24hr gay video.

On-Premises: Meeting room, gay bar.
Swimming: 20 miles to nude beach & lakeside Amsterdam.
Sunbathing: At the beach.
Nudity: Permitted. 30-minute train ride to nude beach.
Smoking: Permitted without restrictions.
Pets: Not permitted.
Handicap Access: No.
Children: Not permitted.
Languages: Dutch, English, German, Italian & French.
Your Host: Kees.

Black Tulip Guesthouse

Q-NET Men Only ♂

Europe's Only 3-Star Hotel Specifically Designed for Leathermen

Black Tulip Guesthouse is Europe's classiest hotel catering to leather guys. Newly opened in a 16th-century building on a central Amsterdam canal, this three-star hotel is minutes from the railway station, the leather district, restaurants and shops. The rooms, all different, share a high standard of comfort. They are equipped with a floor-heated bathroom, large, two-seater bathtubs and high-pressure showers. Some rooms have a wonderful canal view and all have typical Dutch wooden-beamed ceilings. One room has a period mantelpiece, two contain a bathtub spa system. Rooms, decor, marble entrance hallway and other communal spaces reflect style and sophistication. Facilities include a breakfast/lounge area with a small patio where newspapers, books and magazines can be browsed, local tourist information can be consulted, and where friends can be made among fellow travellers.

Particular attention has been paid to noise insulation between rooms. Some rooms contain a metal cage, and the largest has a built-in play area with various fun pieces of equipment. Each room has strategically located bondage hooks, a sling and hygienically sealed douche hoses/nozzles. VCR tapes are available, in addition to the adult channel. Boots can be rented. A separate darkroom area can be used by all, or rented for private use by a guest. Guests carry their own house key, adding to their privacy, and there is no charge, other than for breakfast, for someone you bring home for the night. Prior reservations are essential, as Amsterdam's status as the Gay Capital of Europe is reflected by gay events throughout the year. These events include monthly leather parties in town, which traditionally attract many from outside the local community. The entire hotel can also be rented to hold group meetings, and the lounge area easily converts into a space for workshops and seminars.

Address: Geldersekade 16, Amsterdam 1012 BH Netherlands.
Tel: (31-20) 427 0933, **Fax:** (31-20) 624 4281.

Type: Guesthouse with playroom.
Clientele: Gay men only
Transportation: Direct airport train to cent. Amsterdam, then 3 min walk.
To Gay Bars: 2 blocks, 1/2 mile, a 5 min walk.
Rooms: 9 rooms with single or double beds.
Bathrooms: Private: 8 bath/shower/toilets, 1 shower/toilet.
Meals: Buffet break. till 2pm.
Vegetarian: Vegetarian breakfast available, many vegetarian restaurants in neighborhood.
Complimentary: Tea & coffee-making facilities, welcome drinks.
Dates Open: All year.
Rates: HFL 190-HFL 350.
Discounts: For motorcycle boys & for single occupancy in a double room.
Credit Cards: MC, Visa, Amex, Diners, Eurocard.
Rsv'tns: Required.
Parking: Adequate on-street pay parking. Parking garages in neighborhood.
In-Room: Direct-dial phone, voice mail, color cable TV, radio, VCR, refrig. minibar, coffee & tea-making facilities, safe deposit box, computer connections, maid serv.
On-Premises: Meeting rooms, fax, voice mail, computer connections, video tape library.
Exercise/Health: Jacuzzi. Nearby gym, weights, Jacuzzi, sauna, steam, massage.
Swimming: Nearby pool, ocean, lake.
Sunbathing: 30 min train ride to beach.
Nudity: Permitted in playroom.
Smoking: Permitted everywhere. Non-smoking rooms available on request.
Pets: Not permitted.
Handicap Access: 2 rms, lobby, breakfast & lounge area all on ground floor.
Languages: Dutch, English, German, French, Spanish.

IGLTA

INN PLACES® 1998

C&G Bed & Breakfast House

Gay/Lesbian ♂

Finest Hospitality in the Heart of Amsterdam,
WITH CANAL VIEW!

Our two modern houses, built in May, 1997, form a private enclave in the beautiful Iordaan residential quarter of Amsterdam. We offer you great rates in this unique accommodation in the world's gayest city. The gay owners proudly offer to share with you the comfort of these well-furnished houses. Our deluxe rooms, SOME WITH CANAL VIEW, and some with antique decor, each have their own distinctive style and the shared bath/toilets are modern and immaculately clean. Each house has a cozy living room and dinning room area with cable TV. Complimentary continental breakfast is served here each morning and coffee and tea facilities are available all day. Here, also, is the telephone, where you can receive calls from anywhere and place local calls as necessary.

The *C&G Bed & Breakfast House* accommodations are so centrally located that you can walk to the museums, the Royal Palace, the major department stores and, of course, Amsterdam's famous gay bars. Intimate restaurants and cafes and shops of all kinds abound in the streets of the surrounding neighborhood. In summertime, guests can use the roof garden at the top of each house for sunning and socializing with other guests. Your hosts are longtime residents of Amsterdam who can advise you on getting around the city and tell you what to expect of various gay venues. For any further information, please contact us. We will be very pleased to inform you about our very nice houses! Please remember, we must know your arrival time in advance.

Address: 2nd Leliedwarsstraat 4, PO Box 15889, Amsterdam 1001 NJ Netherlands.
Tel: (31-20) 422 7996 or (31-20) 5300 8800.
Mobile: (31-20) 653 713452 (for calls within Amsterdam, dial "0" before the "6").

Type: Private housing sharing living space with gay owners.
Clientele: Mostly men but women are welcome
To Gay Bars: A 5 to 8 minute walk to gay bars.
Rooms: Rooms with single or double beds.
Bathrooms: Shared baths, showers, toilets.

Meals: Self-service continental breakfast.
Dates Open: All year.
Rates: Hfl 120 single, Hfl 140 double.
Credit Cards: Accepted only for using pre-reservation.
Rsv'tns: Required.
To Reserve: Call direct.

Minimum Stay: 2 days & nights.
Parking: On-street parking.
In-Room: Telephone, color cable TV, kitchen, refrigerator, coffee & tea-making facilities. Maid & laundry service on request.
On-Premises: Roof garden.
Swimming: Pool & ocean nearby.

Sunbathing: On roof.
Smoking: Permitted throughout house.
Pets: Not permitted.
Handicap Access: No.
Children: No.
Languages: Dutch, English, Spanish, French, Italian, Portuguese, German.

Centre Apartments Amsterdam

Gay/Lesbian ♀♂

Apartments and Studios Smack Dab in the Middle of Amsterdam

For a weekend or holiday, the comfort, convenience and affordability of *Centre Apartments Amsterdam* is unsurpassed. You will find complete quiet and privacy while being located immediately adjacent to Centraal Station, the city's transportation hub; Damrak; Dam Square; some of the city's busiest shopping streets; and the Warmoesstraat, Amsterdam's most famous gay district.

Fourteen apartments and studios are new, some within restored old houses. They are spotlessly clean, fully furnished, and provide a home-away-from-home atmosphere. Guests can choose between two- or three-room apartments accommodating a maximum of four persons or studios for three. The apartments are furnished with one large double bed and a single bed. The accommodations include TV/stereo tower, tape deck **or** CD player. A VCR is for rent in the apartments. The modern kitchens are fully equipped and the bathrooms are spacious, modern, and immaculate. Double-glazed windows ensure quiet. Pets are not allowed, and the units are not suitable for children.

Nearby you can find the Albert Heijn supermarket; neighborhood shops for baked goods, coffee and tea, and flowers; restaurants; bars; coffee shops; the Dam; the Royal Palace; and Madame Tussaud's. Next door is the unique Amstelkring, a 17th-century canal house famous for its clandestine Roman Catholic church and authentic period rooms. At one end of the street is the famous red-light district, while at the other end are the city's legendary leather bars. The proprietors speak English, Spanish, Italian, German, Portuguese, and French and accept all credit cards, but prefer cash. Our rates are as follows: Apartment: Hfl 225; Studio: Hfl 190. **We must know your arrival time in advance.**

Address: Heintje Hoekssteeg 27, PO Box 15889,
Amsterdam 1001 NJ Netherlands.
Tel: (31-20) 627 25 03, **Fax:** (31-20) 625 11 08.
Mobile: (31-20) 653 713452 (for calls within Amsterdam, dial "0" before the "6").

EUROPE — AMSTERDAM • NETHERLANDS

Chico Guest House
Gay/Lesbian ♂

Address: Sint Willibrordusstraat 77, Amsterdam 1073 VA Netherlands.
Tel: (31-20) 675 4241.

Type: Guesthouse.
Clientele: Mostly men with women welcome
To Gay Bars: 15 minutes walking, 3 minutes by tram.
Rooms: 3 rooms & 2 apartments with single & double beds.
Bathrooms: Rooms share baths on landing. Apartments have private baths.
Complimentary: Coffee & tea.
Dates Open: All year.
Rates: Hfl 40-Hfl 80 per person per night.
Rsv'tns: Required.
To Reserve: Call direct.
Parking: Limited on-street parking.
In-Room: Clean towels daily, bed linen every 3-4 days.
Smoking: Permitted without restrictions.
Pets: Not permitted.
Handicap Access: No.
Children: We prefer not.
Languages: Dutch, German, English, a little French.
Your Host: Herman.

Hotel Aero
Gay/Lesbian ♂

Hotel Aero is conveniently located in the heart of Amsterdam. All rooms have been converted to satisfy modern tastes and are provided with every comfort and convenience. Most rooms have telephones and TV with VCR. Our Tavern de Pul, with its inviting Dutch atmosphere, is a place where everyone drops in and feels in his element.

Address: Kerkstraat 49, Amsterdam-C 1017 GB Netherlands.
Tel: (31-20) 622 77 28, **Fax:** (31-20) 638 8531.

Type: Hotel with bar & gay-sex shop downstairs.
Clientele: Mostly men with women welcome
Transportation: Taxi or trams or walking.
To Gay Bars: All within walking distance & many on the same street.
Rooms: 4 singles, 12 doubles.
Bathrooms: 11 private, others shared.
Meals: Full breakfast.
Dates Open: All year.
Rates: Hfl 120-Hfl 145.
Credit Cards: MC, Visa, Amex, Eurocard.
Rsv'tns: Required two weeks in advance.
To Reserve: Call direct.
Parking: Off- & on-street parking available.
In-Room: Color TV, telephone & VCR in most rooms.
Swimming: Ocean & lake beaches nearby.
Nudity: 30-minute train ride to nude beach.
Smoking: Permitted without restrictions.
Pets: All permitted.
Handicap Access: No.
Children: Not permitted.
Languages: Dutch, English, Spanish, French, German.
Your Host: Pedro.

Hotel New York

Gay/Lesbian ♂

Right in the Heart of Amsterdam

Hotel New York is located on one of Amsterdam's most beautiful canals and overlooks the famous Milkmaid's Bridge. Our newly renovated hotel occupies three historic 17th-century houses, joined together into a 20-room complex. All rooms are centrally heated and single rooms are furnished with double beds. The comfort of all private baths makes *Hotel New York* especially popular with American travelers. Each room has a private shower and/or toilet, and some rooms have either a bath/toilet combination or a full luxurious bathroom.

Guests are provided with their own private entrance key so that they may come and go as they please... undisturbed... at any hour of the day or night. A full Dutch breakfast is served in our hotel lounge area every morning from 8:00 am untill 11:00 am (for those late risers). There is no extra charge for breakfast, as it is included in the price of your room. At *Hotel New York* you are situated in the center of the city, within easy walking distance of gay bars, restaurants, shopping and most sightseeing attractions. Central Station with the direct airport-train is a quick five minutes away.

Address: Herengracht 13, Amsterdam 1015-BA Netherlands.
Tel: (31-20) 624 30 66, **Fax:** (31-20) 620 32 30.

Type: Bed & breakfast hotel with cocktail lounge & bar.
Clientele: Mostly men with women welcome
Transportation: Direct airport-train to central station.
To Gay Bars: 5 minutes by foot.
Rooms: 20 rooms with single, double, queen or king beds.
Bathrooms: All private.

Meals: Dutch breakfast.
Dates Open: All year.
High Season: April-November.
Rates: HFL 150.00-HFL 250.00.
Credit Cards: MC, Visa, Amex, Diners, Eurocard.
Rsv'tns: Required.
To Reserve: Call direct.
Parking: Adequate off-street covered pay parking.

In-Room: Color TV, direct-dial telephone, refrigerator, hair dryer, maid, room & laundry service.
On-Premises: TV lounge, laundry facilities.
Exercise/Health: Gym, weights, sauna & steam.
Swimming: Ocean or nearby pool.
Sunbathing: On the patio & beach.
Nudity: 30-minute train ride to nude beach.

Smoking: Permitted.
Pets: Permitted with prior permission.
Handicap Access: No.
Children: Not especially welcome.
Languages: Dutch, English, French, Portuguese, Spanish, German, Italian & Friesian.
Your Host: Arno.

INN PLACES® 1998   79

Hotel Orfeo
Men ♂

Orfeo is a mostly-male guesthouse in the centre of the city, two minutes walking distance from gay activities, museums, shopping mall, restaurants, and casino. All guests get their own keys and can come and go as they please. There is a fully-licensed bar on the hotel premises. Travellers from North or South America ALWAYS arrive in the early morning on the day after departure, and may wish to consider reserving a room from the previous day onwards, so that they can occupy their room immediately upon arrival. Reservations can be made by phone or mail.

Address: Leidsekruisstraat 14, Amsterdam 1017 RH Netherlands.
Tel: (31-20) 623 1347, Confirmation only: **Fax:** (31-20) 620 2348.

Type: Bed & breakfast with bar.
Clientele: 99% men
Transportation: From the airport take a taxi or train to Central Station. From Central Station take a taxi or tram no. 1, 2, or 5.
To Gay Bars: 5-minute walk to gay & lesbian bars.
Rooms: 24 rooms, singles, doubles, triples, some rooms are like studio apts.
Bathrooms: 7 private, others share.
Meals: Full breakfast.
Dates Open: All year.
High Season: April 1st-November 15th.
Rates: Hfl 75-198 with guaranteed reservation. NO refund on first night.
Credit Cards: All major credit cards.
Rsv'tns: Required in high season one month in advance.
To Reserve: Call direct.
Minimum Stay: 4 nights in high season.
Parking: Covered off-street pay parking at Prinsengracht.
In-Room: Personal safe, room and laundry service. Direct calling system.
On-Premises: TV Lounge, laundry facilities & public telephone.
Exercise/Health: Sauna.
Nudity: 30-minute train ride to nude beach.
Smoking: Permitted without restrictions.
Handicap Access: No.
Languages: Dutch, Spanish, French, German, Italian, Hebrew & English.
Your Host: Avi & Peter.

Hotel the Golden Bear
Q-NET Gay-Lesbian ♀♂

In the Center of Amsterdam

Hotel the Golden Bear (formerly Hotel Unique), Amsterdam's first exclusively gay-hotel, has been welcoming gay visitors since 1948. Rooms in our 1737 building are comfortable, some with private facilities, others sharing a bathroom on the corridor. Our rooms also have direct-dial telephones, central heating and wash basins. Colour cable TV is available. A free, extended Dutch breakfast is served in the cozy lounge area of the hotel's bar. On Sundays, enjoy our special champagne breakfast. And... you get your own front door key. We're situated in the very centre of Amsterdam, close to all gay bars, clubs and saunas. The main cultural attractions, galleries, museums, etc. are also within easy walking distance. We will be happy to give you any information you need during your stay.

Address: Kerkstraat 37, Amsterdam 1017 GB Netherlands.
Tel: (31-20) 624 47 85, Fax: (31-20) 627 0164. **E-mail:** goldbear@xs4all.nl
URL: http://www.xs4all.nl/~goldbear

Type: Hotel.
Clientele: Mostly men with women welcome
Transportation: Train from airport to Central Station then Tram 1, 2 or 5 get off at Prinsengracht.
To Gay Bars: Gay bar down the street.
Rooms: 17 rooms with single/twin, double or king beds.
Bathrooms: 2 private, others share.
Meals: Expanded continental breakfast.
Vegetarian: Vegetarian breakfast possible. Vegetarian restaurants in neighbourhood.
Complimentary: Champagne breakfast on Sundays. Coffee & tea, various alcoholic & non-alcoholic beverages available.
Dates Open: All year.
High Season: Jul-Sept.
Rates: Hfl 85-Hfl 195.
Discounts: Possible for longer stays.
Credit Cards: Visa, MC, Amex, Diners.
Rsv'tns: Please inquire.
To Reserve: Call direct.
Parking: Paid parking on street & in nearby private garage.
In-Room: Color cable TV, VCR, telephone, coffee- & tea-making facilities, safe.
Exercise/Health: Gay night sauna down the street.
Swimming: In nearby pool & ocean.
Sunbathing: At the beach.
Smoking: Permitted, no non-smoking rooms available.
Pets: Not permitted.
Handicap Access: No.
Children: Very young children not welcomed.
Languages: Dutch, German, English, Spanish & French.
Your Host: Theo.

Hotel "The Village"

Gay-Owned 50/50 ♀♂

You Don't Need an Expensive Taxi

Situated on the Kerkstraat, Amsterdam's gayest street, *Hotel "The Village"* places you right in the middle of what's happening. This is where you want to be: in the center of town within easy reach of nightlife, restaurants, museums and other attractions. The hotel has 2-, 3- and 4-person rooms with shower and bathroom and there is a café on the premises. You get your own key to the front door.

Address: 25 Kerkstraat, Amsterdam 1017 GA Netherlands.
Tel: (31-20) 626 9746, **Fax:** (31-20) 625 4081.

Type: Hotel with bar for residents, café downstairs.
Clientele: 50% gay & 50% straight clientele
Transportation: Tram 1, 2 & 5 from central station.

To Gay Bars: Close to all gay/lesbian bars.
Rooms: 10 rooms for 1-5 people & 2 apartments. Guests receive their own front door key.
Bathrooms: All private.
Meals: Dutch breakfast.

Dates Open: All year.
Rates: Summer Hfl 125, winter Hfl 120.
To Reserve: Call direct.
In-Room: The larger rooms have sofas, tables & easy chairs. All rooms have refrigerators & colour TVs.

Nudity: Short train ride to nude beach.
Smoking: Permitted without restrictions.
Pets: Not permitted.
Languages: Dutch & English.

Hotel Wilhelmina

Gay-Friendly ♀♂

Hotel Wilhelmina is centrally located in the heart of Amsterdam's shopping and cultural centre, convenient to museums, the concert hall, Vondel Park, the World Trade Centre and the Central Station. Schiphol Amsterdam Airport is a 10-minute drive away. The hotel is recommended in the Michelin Hotel Guide, the Amsterdam Tourist Office, most European automobile clubs and airlines. The efficient management, inspired by great hospitality, will do all to enhance the pleasure and comfort of your stay. Breakfast is served in the hotel, and an enormous variety of restaurants can be found in the vicinity.

Address: Koninginne Weg 167-169, Amsterdam 1075 CN Netherlands.
Tel: (31-20) 662 5267, **Fax:** (31-20) 679 2296, **Telex:** WILHL NL.
E-mail: wilhlhtl@euronet.nl

Type: Hotel.
Clientele: Mostly straight clientele with a gay & lesbian following
Transportation: Trams 2 & 16 to Valeriusplein.
To Gay Bars: 1 km to Kerkstraat gay bars.
Rooms: 19 rooms with single or double beds.

Bathrooms: 14 private, others share.
Meals: Full Dutch breakfast buffet.
Vegetarian: Vegetarian breakfast. Vegetarian restaurants nearby.
Dates Open: All year.
High Season: Mar-Nov.
Rates: Single Hfl 85-Hfl 165; double Hfl 145-Hfl 195.

Discounts: Please inquire.
Credit Cards: Most major credit cards.
Rsv'tns: Required.
To Reserve: Call direct.
Parking: Adequate free on-street parking.
In-Room: Maid, room & laundry service, color cable TV, direct-dial telephone.
On-Premises: Private dining rooms, TV lounge & bicycle storage.
Sunbathing: On the patio.
Smoking: Not permitted in dining room, lounge, toilets, or passageways.
Pets: Not permitted.
Handicap Access: No.
Children: Permitted.
Languages: Dutch, German & English.

INN PLACES® 1998   81

Liliane's Home — Guesthouse for Women Only Women ♀

Small, Comfortable & Personal

Liliane's Home is located in a renovated manor in the stately Plantagebuurt and provides short- or extended-stay women-only lodging in the heart of Amsterdam. Public transportation access is excellent. Your room will be on one of two floors located directly above the owner's own home. This intimate arrangement ensures personal attention in a warm and comfortable environment. Common rooms include living room, kitchen and bath facilities.

This combination of central location and comfortable, intimate, personal service, provides all the necessary ingredients for a pleasant and successful visit to Amsterdam. Public transportation access is excellent. The bus, tram and metro all stop at the door, and transportation to and from Schiphol Airport is optimal. Downtown cultural centers, movies, galleries and a variety of nightlife are all within walking distance.

Address: Sarphatistraat 119, Amsterdam 1018 GB Netherlands.
Tel: (31-20) 627 4006 (Tel/Fax).

Type: Guesthouse.
Clientele: Women only
Transportation: From Schiphol Airport, train to Central Station, then subway to Weesperplein or tram 6, 7, 10. Pick up, Hfl 45.
To Gay Bars: 2 blocks or a 10-minute walk.
Rooms: 5 rooms & 2 apartments with single or double beds.

Bathrooms: 4 private sinks only. Shared: 2 bathtub, 4 shower & 4 WC only. Apartments have private bath.
Meals: Breakfast included.
Vegetarian: Vegetarian restaurants nearby.
Complimentary: Tea & coffee. Soft drinks & beer, Hfl 2.
Dates Open: All year.
Rates: Per room: Hfl 65-70 1 person, Hfl 120 2 people, Hfl 155-170 3 people. Apts: Hfl 165-175 2 people, Hfl 200-210 3 people, Hfl 240 4 people.

Discounts: 5% for longer than 7 days.
Rsv'tns: Required.
To Reserve: Call direct.
Minimum Stay: 2 days.
Parking: Limited on-street pay parking. Covered private parking, 1 car Hfl 25/day.
In-Room: Color cable TV, coffee/tea-making facilities, maid & laundry service. Apartments have kitchen & balcony.
On-Premises: Meeting rooms, garage, big living room & kitchen.

Exercise/Health: Massage. Nearby gym, weights, sauna, steam & massage.
Sunbathing: On the patio & balcony.
Smoking: Permitted in living room. Sleeping rooms are non-smoking!
Pets: Not permitted.
Handicap Access: No.
Children: Not especially welcome.
Languages: Dutch, English & German.
Your Host: Liliane.

Maes B&B

Q-NET Gay/Lesbian ♀♂

Maes B&B's recently renovated 19th-century home has quaint, comfortable guestrooms decorated in the style of that period, with the accent on cozy homelike ambiance. Awaken to fresh croissants, just part of the extended continental breakfast served. Our small shopping street is located between two canals and is near the Anne Frank house, Homomonument, open-air markets, as well as all nightlife and all public transport. Numerous restaurants and cafes are within easy walking distance.

Address: Herenstraat 26, Amsterdam 1015 CB Netherlands.
Tel: (31-20) 427 5156,
Fax: (31-20) 427 5166.
E-mail: maesbb94@xs4all.nl
URL: http://www.xs4all.nl/~maesbb94/

Type: Bed & breakfast.
Clientele: Mostly gay & lesbian with some hetero clientele
Transportation: Taxi from airport or train station. Or from central station, take trams #1, 2, 5, 13, or 17 to 2nd stop. From there, turn onto Korte Lijnbaanssteeg & continue over 2 bridges to Herenstraat.
To Gay Bars: 5-10 minute walk at most.
Rooms: 3 rooms with single, twin or king beds.
Bathrooms: 3 ensuite.
Meals: Expanded continental breakfast.
Complimentary: Tea & coffee available from guest pantry all day.
Dates Open: All year.
High Season: April-October.
Rates: Hfl 95.00-Hfl 155.00.
Discounts: On stays of 7 or more nights.
Credit Cards: MC, Eurocard, Amex, Visa, Diners.
Rsv'tns: Required.
To Reserve: Call or e-mail direct.
Minimum Stay: 2 nights on weekends.
Parking: Paid parking (parking meters).
On-Premises: Laundry facilities & guest pantry with refrigerator & coffee/tea-making facilities. Telephone & fax services.
Exercise/Health: Nearby gym, weights, Jacuzzi, sauna, steam & massage.
Swimming: In nearby North Sea & city swimming pools.
Sunbathing: On the beach or in the parks.
Nudity: Permitted at the beach & in some parks.
Smoking: Restricted to some rooms.
Pets: Not permitted.
Handicap Access: No.
Children: Welcome.
Languages: Dutch, English, Russian, some French & German.
Your Host: Ken & Vladimir.

INN PLACES® 1998

Riverside Apartments

Gay-Friendly 50/50 ♀♂

A Wide Variety of Accommodations in Central Amsterdam and Beyond

Riverside Apartments offers both short-term and long-term rentals, with most short-term accommodations within walking distance of most gay bars and discos. For those staying for six months or longer, apartments and houses are available along the canals, in the suburbs and in surrounding towns. Rates vary from Fl. 1,000 to Fl. 1,750 per week for single or double occupancy during low season, and from Fl. 1,500 to Fl. 2,000 during high season. Daily rates are available on request and require a minimum stay of four days. The rates for a stay of six months or more depend on the type of accommodation required, as well as its location. Monthly rates vary from Fl. 2,000 to Fl. 5,000 and, in most cases, a deposit of one or two month's rent is required.

Singles, doubles and larger parties can also be accommodated in hotels, apartments and houses. All accommodations have private facilities, cable TV, refrigerator and coffee- and tea-making facilities. Some have fax, answering machines and minibars, and most have private kitchens, telephones and VCRs. In some cases breakfast is included in the rate. As a rule, all major credit cards are accepted. Parking is difficult in the center of the city and is expensive. Maid service is available and varies with the accommodation. It is sometimes included on a daily basis, sometimes two or three times a week, and some accommodations are serviced only before checking in and after checking out. In most cases, pets are not allowed and smoking is permitted. Although most places are not handicap-accessible, there are some which are accessible and which do allow pets. Children are not especially welcomed in most short-term rentals. The owner, Jerry, speaks Dutch, English, German and French. Please call direct.

Address: Weteringschans 187 E, Amsterdam 1017 XE Netherlands.
Tel: (31-20) 627 9797, **Fax:** (31-20) 627 9858.
E-mail: geuje@worldonline.nl

Rubens Bed & Breakfast

Q·NET Gay-Friendly 50/50 ♀♂

Welcome to a Nice Private Home in Amsterdam

Situated in a private apartment, *Rubens B&B* is conveniently located in a 1930s residential neighbourhood in the city centre. Its two rooms share a small state-of-the-art, 1920s-style bathroom with shower and an unusual Roman touch — a heated floor. The larger of the two rooms is appointed with original French Art Deco furniture. The Frisian Room is currently decorated in contemporary style, but will be converted to traditional Frisian style in the near future. The bed & breakfast's recent renovation restored its original style with modern comforts such as central heating. Both rooms open up to a balcony with morning sun.

Rubens B&B is within walking distance (or a few tram stops) from the major museums and tourist attractions. The upscale shopping street Beethovenstraat is very close by, as is the exhuberant Amsterdam nightlife. The neighbourhood was designed in the 1930s as part of the "Plan Amsterdam Zuid" by the famous architect and town planner, Berlage. The architectural style is called "Amsterdamse School."

Rubens B&B is owned and operated by two Dutch guys: Tjeerd Visser, born in Friesland, who works for the international branch of the Dutch Postal organisation, and Franklin Wollring, an Amsterdam local who is a purser for KLM Royal Dutch Airlines.

Address: Rubensstraat 38bv, Amsterdam 1077 MS Netherlands.
Tel: (31-20) 662 9187 (tel/fax).
E-mail: rubensbb@xs4all.nl
URL: http://www.xs4all.nl/~rubensbb

Type: Bed & breakfast.
Clientele: 50% gay & lesbian & 50% hetero clientele
Transportation: From airport: taxi or train to Station Zuid/WTC, then tram 5 to Beethovenstraat. From Central Stn: tram 5 to Beethovenstraat.
To Gay Bars: 10 minutes by car, 15 min by tram.
Rooms: 2 rooms with queen beds.

Bathrooms: 1 private sink, 1 shared shower/toilet, 1 shared toilet/WC only.
Meals: Expanded continental breakfast.
Complimentary: Tea, coffee, cookies.
Dates Open: All year.
Rates: Per room, per night: Art Deco room Hfl 135; Frisian room Hfl 100.
Discounts: 10% on stays of 1 week or longer.
Credit Cards: MC, Visa, Amex, Diners, Eurocard.
Rsv'tns: Required.

To Reserve: Call, fax or e-mail direct.
Minimum Stay: 2 nights on weekends.
Parking: Adequate on-street pay parking. Free parking during evenings & Sundays.
In-Room: Maid service.
On-Premises: Telephone, fax, laundry facilities.
Exercise/Health: Nearby Jacuzzi, sauna, gym, weights, steam, massage.
Swimming: At nearby pool, lake & in the Northsea.

Sunbathing: At beach & in parks.
Nudity: Permitted at beach & in some parks.
Smoking: No smoking permitted anywhere on the premises.
Pets: Not permitted.
Handicap Access: No.
Children: No.
Languages: Dutch, English, French, German, Spanish, Frisian.
Your Host: Tjeerd & Franklin.

IGLTA

EUROPE • NETHERLANDS • AMSTERDAM

INN PLACES® 1998

Singel Suite — The Bed & Breakfast Suites

Q-NET Gay-Friendly ♀♂

Overlooking One of the Prettiest Canals in the Heart of Amsterdam

The *Singel Suites* are on the first and second floors of a classic Amsterdam *grachtenpand* house. Both overlook one of the prettiest canals in the heart of Amsterdam. It is in this area where, gay or straight, Amsterdam's rich and famous live. The apartments have a separate living room and bedroom. The first-floor apartment has a Jacuzzi-bath bathroom next to the private patio, and both apartments overlook the canal and Amsterdam bridges. Although the *Singel Suite* has preserved its original 17th-century style, it has luxury, modern comfort, and more. Surrounded by culture, canals, and antique shops, the famous Spui, Rembrandtsplein, Leidseplein, cinemas, museums and the flowermarket are close by. We are also near the city's most well-known clubs & restaurants, among them the gay bars and discos of Reguliersdwarsstraat. Guests at *Singel Suite* will find something better than the average hotel. They will find luxury, comfort and privacy.

Address: Singel 420, Amsterdam 1016 AK Netherlands.
Tel: (31-20) 625 8673,
Fax: (31-20) 625 8097.

Type: Bed & breakfast apartment suite.
Clientele: We don't question our guests' orientation
Transportation: Train from airport to Central Station, then trams 1, 2, or 5 (a 10-minute ride) to Koningsplein, or taxi direct.
To Gay Bars: 1 block or a 2-minute walk.
Rooms: 2 apartments with king & extra bed.
Bathrooms: Private full baths.
Meals: Expanded continental breakfast in Suite.
Vegetarian: Available nearby.
Complimentary: Coffee & tea.
Dates Open: All year.
Rates: Hfl 250-Hfl 275 for 2 persons.
Discounts: Weekly rates, 3 day weekend.
Credit Cards: MC, Visa, Amex, Diners, Eurocard.
Rsv'tns: Preferred.
To Reserve: Fax or call direct.
Minimum Stay: Depends on time of arrival. If in the morning, 2 days.
Parking: Limited on-street pay parking. Best to park in parking garage.
In-Room: Color cable TV, VCR, video tape & international libraries, direct-dial phone, refrigerator, bathrobes, bathing salts, free coffee/tea-making & limited kitchen facilities & maid service.
On-Premises: Fax. Car rental service available from Singel Suite.
Exercise/Health: Jacuzzi on premises. Nearby gym, weights, Jacuzzi, sauna, steam & massage. 45 minutes to lakes & rental boats.
Swimming: Nearby pool. 30 minutes to ocean, 20 minutes to lake.
Sunbathing: At nearby pool, 30 mins to beach or lakes, 10 mins to Vondelpark.
Nudity: 15-20 minutes to nude area.
Smoking: Permitted.
Pets: Small pets permitted with deposit.
Handicap Access: No.
Children: Welcome.
Languages: Dutch, French, English & German.
Your Host: Anthony & Jacqueline.

Sunhead of 1617

Q-NET Gay/Lesbian ♀♂

The GENEROUS Dutch Treat!

Located in one of the oldest listed canal houses of rustic Amsterdam, this small and friendly bed-and-delicious-breakfast offers the best value for your money. *Sunhead's* very central, yet quiet, location is a five-minute walk from Central Station and virtually all the city's historical, cultural and gay amenities such as the Anne Frank House, the Homo monument, the Royal Palace, several historical churches and synagogues, the "Begijn" courtyard, the Theater museum and the Warmoesstraat and Regulierdwarsstraat gay district. Our area is famous for its boutiques, good restaurants and cafés.

The third-floor rooms overlook Amsterdam's loveliest canal and gabled roofs. Each room has vaulted ceilings, Japanese-inspired decor, skylighting, a modern toilet and shower, cable TV, a VCR, a fridge, coffee/tea-making facilities, daily maid service and fresh flowers and plants galore! This 17th-century house has no elevator, so expect to use the stairs. Full breakfast is served in the privacy of your own room or in the dining room from 8:30 a.m. till late, and optional dinner is served upon request. Other amenities include in-house pay phone, fax and IBM PC. Guests also have access to the city center's best equipped gym with licensed trainer (US $10 per visit).

Address: Herengracht 152, Amsterdam 1016 BN Netherlands.
Tel: (31-20) 626 1809, **Fax:** (31-20) 626 1823. **E-mail:** sunhead@xs4all.nl

Type: Bed & breakfast.
Clientele: Mostly gay & lesbian with some hetero clientele
Transportation: Pick up from airport Hfl 35.00. Pick up from train Hfl 10.00.
To Gay Bars: 4 blocks or a 5-minute walk.
Rooms: 2 rooms & 1 apt. with single or double beds.
Bathrooms: All private.
Meals: Full breakfast.
Vegetarian: Available upon request. Many vegetarian restaurants & cafes nearby.

Complimentary: Welcome fruit basket & bottle of house wine. Tea & coffee.
Dates Open: All year.
High Season: July, August & December.
Rates: Hfl 145-135 per room for 2. Hfl 105 per room for single. Self-catering apartment for 2: Hfl 185 (Hfl 40 per extra person, maximum 5 people).
Discounts: 5% for cash.
Credit Cards: MC, Visa, Amex, Diners, JCB, Eurocard.

Rsv'tns: Advisable.
To Reserve: Travel agent or call direct.
Minimum Stay: 2 days on weekends.
Parking: Adequate on-street pay parking. Free evenings & Sundays.
In-Room: Color cable TV, VCR, telephone, fans, refrigerator, coffee/tea-making facilities, maid & laundry service.
On-Premises: Fax machine.

Exercise/Health: Nearby gym, weights, Jacuzzi, sauna, steam & massage.
Swimming: Nearby pool, ocean & lake.
Sunbathing: In the park.
Smoking: Permitted in some rooms.
Pets: Not permitted.
Handicap Access: No.
Children: Welcome.
Languages: Dutch, English, Tagalog, Cebuano, French & German.
Your Host: Carlos & Roelf-Jan.

EUROPE • NETHERLANDS • AMSTERDAM

INN PLACES® 1998

Westend Hotel & Cosmo Bar
Gay/Lesbian ♂

Located on Kerkstraat, site of one of the heaviest concentrations of gay nightlife in Amsterdam, the *Westend* offers you comfortable rooms with shared showers, very centrally located to all gay bars and tourist attractions. Right downstairs from your room is an assortment of gay nightlife, interesting cafes, a gay video shop, and even a night sauna.

Address: Kerkstraat 42, Amsterdam 1017 GM Netherlands.
Tel: (31-20) 624 80 74, **Fax:** (31-20) 622 99 97.

Type: Bed & breakfast with bar.
Clientele: Mostly men with women welcome
Transportation: Train to Central Station, then taxi or tram line 1, 2 or 5.
To Gay Bars: Men's bars & sauna on the same & next block.
Rooms: 5 doubles also available for single use.

Bathrooms: 2 shared toilets & 2 shared showers.
Dates Open: All year.
High Season: July, August, September.
Rates: Single Hfl 85.00. Room with double bed Hfl 120.00. Twin bedded room Hfl 140.00. Triple Hfl 180.00.
Credit Cards: MC, Visa, Amex, Diners & Eurocard.

Rsv'tns: Required 2 weeks in advance.
To Reserve: Call direct.
Parking: Limited on-street parking with meters. 15-min walk to guarded parking.
In-Room: Color cable TV with CNN, maid service, telephone, refrigerator & coffee & tea-making facilities.
Sunbathing: On beach 1/2 hour away.

Nudity: 30-minute train ride to nude beach.
Smoking: Permitted without restrictions.
Pets: Small pets permitted.
Handicap Access: No.
Children: Not permitted.
Languages: Dutch, English, French & German.
Your Host: Herman.

Casa Amigos
Men ♂

An Intimate Guesthouse in the Algarve

In two acres of gardens surrounded by orange and lemon groves with mountain views, you can't help but relax. *Casa Amigos,* an exclusive gay guesthouse, is situated just 12 miles inland from the main resort of Albufeira, 35 minutes from Faro International Airport, three hours from Lisbon, and two hours from the Spanish city of Seville. Local Portuguese restaurants are nearby and the guesthouse is only 15 minutes from the nearest gay beach and clubs of Albufeira. All rooms lead directly onto the pool terrace.

Address: Larga Vista, Foral, S.B. Messiness, Algarve 8357 Portugal.
Tel: (351-82) 576597, **Fax:** (351-82) 576090, **or London tel:** (44-181) 743 7417.

Type: Bed & breakfast guesthouse with bar.
Clientele: Men only
Transportation: Pick up arranged.
To Gay Bars: 15-minute drive to bar.
Rooms: 3 rooms & 1 suite with single & double beds.
Bathrooms: All en suite.
Meals: Expanded continental breakfast. Evening meals & BBQ by arrangement.

Vegetarian: Available upon request.
Complimentary: Welcoming cocktail, tea & coffee in rooms.
Dates Open: Apr-Oct.
High Season: May-Oct.
Rates: Shared: 10.000-13.200; Single: 7500-9900.
Rsv'tns: Required.
To Reserve: Travel agent or call direct.
Parking: Ample free, own car park.

In-Room: Color TV & maid service.
On-Premises: Meeting rooms, TV lounge, poolside bar & food services.
Exercise/Health: Weights on premises. Nearby gym, weights, Jacuzzi, sauna & steam.
Swimming: Pool on premises. 15-minute drive to ocean.
Sunbathing: At poolside, on patio, roof & at the beach.

Nudity: Permitted at poolside & at gay beach (20-minute drive).
Smoking: Permitted.
Pets: Not permitted.
Handicap Access: 2 ground floor rooms.
Children: Not permitted under 18 years.
Languages: English, Portuguese & a little German.
Your Host: Roy.

Casa Marhaba

Gay/Lesbian ♂

"Marhaba" Means "Welcome" - We Mean to Make You Just That

Casa Marhaba is set on one acre in a pleasant rural area, 1 km from the nearest beach, 5 km from Carvoeiro and Lagoa, and 50 km west of Faro International Airport. All five of our double rooms have en suite bathrooms with showers. We serve a substantial continental breakfast on the poolside terrace and picnic lunches and pub-style snacks are available to order. Barbecue by the pool or enjoy the TV lounge with satellite TV and video facilities.

The Algarve region provides a perfect mix of contrasts: unspoiled countryside with miles of beaches, quaint and historical villages with lively towns and resorts, deep sea fishing and coastal boat trips, and great restaurants offering a wide range of cuisine. We will be delighted to recommend restaurants, beaches, and bars or help you with any other aspect of your holiday.

Address: Rua de Benagil, Alfanzina, Lagoa 8400 Portugal.
Tel: (351-82) 358720 (Tel/Fax).

Type: Bed & breakfast guesthouse with bar.
Clientele: Mostly men with women welcome
Transportation: Faro Airport, then rental car. Pick up can be arranged for a fee.
To Gay Bars: 10 miles or a 15-minute drive.
Rooms: 5 rooms with single or double beds.
Bathrooms: 5 private shower/toilets.
Meals: Expanded continental breakfast.
Vegetarian: Available upon advanced request. Vegetarian food nearby.
Complimentary: Welcome cocktail.
Dates Open: April thru October.
High Season: April thru October.
Rates: Single: £160 per week, £30 per night. Double: £199 per week, £36 per night.
Rsv'tns: Required.
To Reserve: Call direct.
Parking: Ample free off-street parking.
In-Room: Maid & laundry service.
On-Premises: TV lounge with satellite TV & video facilities.
Swimming: Pool on premises, ocean nearby.
Sunbathing: At poolside, on patio & private sun decks.
Nudity: Permitted on special sun deck poolside.
Smoking: Permitted throughout.
Pets: Not permitted.
Handicap Access: No.
Children: Not especially welcome.
Languages: English & French.
Your Host: Tony & Sam.

Casa Pequena

Q-NET Gay/Lesbian ♂

All the Comforts of Home...

Situated in 1100 square metres of gardens on a hillside overlooking the village and beach of Praia da Luz, *Casa Pequena* is, first and foremost, our home. As such, you will find it comfortable and well-furnished with the usual amenities, including TV, video, audio equipment and a good library of books, all available to our guests. We have two guest rooms, each with adjacent bath/shower and we provide all linens, towels and beach towels. We also have a swimming pool, hot tub, extensive terraces and sun-beds. If you want to explore, we can advise you where to visit and explain the eccentricities of gay nightlife in Portugal. You will have your own key so you can come and go as you please.

Address: Apartado 133, Praia da Luz, Lagos, Algarve 8600 Portugal.
Tel: (351-82) 789068 (24-hr tel/fax). **E-mail:** mop02352@mail.telepac.pt

Type: Guesthouse with honour bar.
Clientele: Mostly gay men with women welcome
Transportation: Car is best. Pick up from airport, train, bus. 5,000 escudos from Faro. Free from Lagos.
To Gay Bars: 5 km or 10 minutes by car.
Rooms: 2 rooms with single or double bed.
Bathrooms: Private adjacent to room: 1 shower/toilet, 1 bath/shower/toilet.
Meals: Expanded continental breakfast. Other meals can be provided at reasonable cost.
Vegetarian: Available upon request. Most restaurants have non-meat dishes.
Complimentary: Tea & coffee.

continued next page

Dates Open: All year.
High Season: April/May-end of October.
Rates: 6000 escudos per night single. 9,000 escudos per night double.
Discounts: 10% if both rooms booked by same party (4 persons).
Rsv'tns: Required.
To Reserve: Call direct.
Minimum Stay: 3 nights minimum charge though you can stay for fewer nights.
Parking: Ample free off-street parking.
On-Premises: TV lounge. Entire house is available for guests.
Exercise/Health: Jacuzzi on premises. Nearby hotel/sports centre with gym, weights, Jacuzzi, sauna, steam & massage.
Swimming: Swimming pool on premises, ocean nearby.
Sunbathing: At poolside, on common sun decks & at nearby beaches (some nude & gay).
Nudity: Permitted wherever guests feel comfortable.
Smoking: Permitted everywhere except in bedrooms.
Pets: Not permitted. 2 resident cats & 1 dog.
Handicap Access: No.
Children: By special arrangement.
Languages: Portuguese, English, French.
Your Host: Jim & Geoff.

Casa Alexio

Men ♂

On top of a rise above the bay of Talamanca is placed the very private gayhouse called *Casa Alexio*, far away from any road noise, but only 3 minutes by car to town. From the breakfast terrace, one has a wonderful view over Ibiza Town, the harbor and the sea reaching to the neighboring island of Formentera. A pool with bar, terraces and a comfortable living room with cable TV add to your comfort. The beach is a five-minute walk.

Address: Barrio Ses Torres 16, Jesús, Ibiza 07819 Spain.
Tel: (34-71) 31 42 49,
Fax: (34-71) 31 26 19.
E-mail: alexio@alexio.com

Type: Gayhouse with 24 hr self-service poolside bar.
Clientele: Men only
Transportation: Free pick up service or taxi from airport.
To Gay Bars: 1.7 miles or 3 minutes by car.
Rooms: 15 rooms with king beds.
Bathrooms: All private bathrooms.
Dates Open: All year.
High Season: April through October.
Discounts: Special off-season rates.
Credit Cards: Visa, MC, Amex, Eurocard.
Rsv'tns: Required.
To Reserve: Travel agent or call direct.
Parking: Free off-street parking.
In-Room: Satellite TV, AC, maid and laundry service.
On-Premises: TV lounge, meeting rooms, laundry facilities.
Exercise/Health: Whirlpool. Workout possibilities in pool area.
Swimming: Pool, ocean beach next door.
Sunbathing: At poolside or on beach.
Nudity: Permitted at the pool. Nude beach nearby.
Smoking: Permitted without restrictions.
Pets: Not permitted.
Children: Not permitted.
Languages: Spanish, English, German, French, Italian, Portuguese.

Hotel Rosamar

Gay-Friendly ♀♂

Relax and Just Do Nothing

The *Hotel Rosamar*, privately owned and recently refurbished, offers comfortable accommodation together with a friendly bar and a large, attractive garden terrace. All rooms have private bathrooms and terraces. It has a very easy, relaxed atmosphere. The hotel is situated in the midst of Palma's night life area with all the gay bars and discos situated on the same street and within walking distance of the hotel. There is also a small, interesting beach a ten-minute walk away. Mallorca is the largest of the Balearic Islands off the eastern coast of Spain. It is extremely beautiful with many changes of landscape and one of the most stunning beaches in Europe. Chopin, George Sand, Robert Graves, and now Michael Douglas are some of the people who have made their homes here.

Address: Avenida Joan Miro 74, Palma de Mallorca 07015 Spain.
Tel: (34-71) 732723, Fax: (34-71) 283828.
E-mail: rosamar@ocea.es

Type: Hotel with bar.
Clientele: Mostly hetero with a gay & lesbian following
Transportation: Airport bus to Plaza España, then taxi. Or taxi direct from airport. Hire car best for sightseeing.
To Gay Bars: All the present gay bars are located on the same street as the hotel.
Rooms: 40 rooms with single or double beds.
Bathrooms: All en suite.

Meals: Continental breakfast.
Vegetarian: 2 or 3 restaurants in Palma city 10 minutes away.
Dates Open: Mar 20-Jan 8.
High Season: Jul-Sept.
Rates: Per night per room: Double Pta 4,950-Pta 5,450, single Pta 4,200-Pta 4,700.
Credit Cards: MC, Visa, Eurocard.
Rsv'tns: Required.
To Reserve: Travel agent or call direct.

Parking: Ample free off-street parking.
In-Room: Telephone, towels changed daily, most rooms with balconies.
On-Premises: Terrace, sun deck, meeting rooms & TV lounge.
Exercise/Health: Sauna 50 metres away.
Swimming: In nearby ocean.
Sunbathing: On common sun deck.

Nudity: Permitted on the sun deck at the discretion of other guests.
Smoking: Permitted.
Pets: Not permitted.
Handicap Access: No.
Children: Permitted only if WELL-controlled, otherwise NO!!!
Languages: Spanish, English, German, Italian, French.
Your Host: Bill & Basilio.

IGLTA

Hotel Romàntic i La Renaixença

Gay/Lesbian ♀♂

Two Lovely Hotels in the Center of Sitges

Hotel Romàntic & Hotel Renaixença are in the center of Sitges, a resort town with a long tradition as a vacation spot and center for culture. *Hotel Romàntic's* spacious garden is open daily, with snack and drink service. Occupying three adjacent townhouses, its rooms have baths, period furniture and many have terraces overlooking the garden. *Hotel Renaixença's* 16 nicely decorated rooms have private bath and WC. There is easy access, by foot, to the beach, shopping and nightlife. Nearby transportation services places as diverse as Port Aventura and the city of Barcelona.

Address: Carrer de Sant Isidre 33, Sitges 08870 Spain.
Tel: (34-3) 894 8375, **Fax:** (34-3) 894 8167.

Type: Bed & breakfast hotel with bar & solarium.
Clientele: Mostly gay & lesbian with some hetero clientele
Transportation: From Barcelona aiport, train to El Prat de Llobregat then train to Sitges. Taxi.
To Gay Bars: Centrally-located to all gay bars.
Rooms: 85 rooms with single or double beds.
Bathrooms: All private.
Meals: Continental breakfast, buffet breakfast.
Dates Open: La Renaixença all year. Hotel Romàntic Mar 15-Oct 19.
Rates: 6,600 Pts-12,000 Pts plus VAT.
Credit Cards: Visa, Amex, Diners, Eurocard.
Rsv'tns: Required, but call-ins welcome.
To Reserve: Call direct.
Minimum Stay: 1 day.
Parking: Off-street public pay parking.
In-Room: Telephone & maid service. Top rooms have ceiling fans.
On-Premises: Meeting rooms, TV lounge & solarium.
Swimming: Ocean beach and swimming pool nearby.
Sunbathing: On roof, private & common sun decks.
Nudity: 1/2 hr walk to nudist beach.
Smoking: Permitted without restrictions.
Pets: Permitted.
Children: Welcome.
Languages: Catalan, Spanish, English, French & Italian.
Your Host: José Manuel.

White Horse Hotel

Gay-Owned ♀♂

The White Horse is a small hotel in the center of Basel. The hotel's modern atmosphere is reflected in each room, as well as in the especially welcoming breakfast room. Its huge two-storey glass panel window admits ample sunlight, brightening up this always pleasant morning space. Our continental breakfast, much more than the usual, spoils our guests with a buffet area brimming with a variety of fresh bread, yoghurts, fresh fruit, etc.

All our rooms have a shower, WC, television and telephone. Our rates include service, taxes and a Swiss breakfast buffet. The bar is open to everybody, especially our guests, and in the summer, the courtyard is used for relaxing and enjoying drinks until late at night. You can take nice long walks along the river Rhine, only one block away. We look forward to welcoming you the next time you visit Switzerland.

WHITE HORSE

Address: Webergasse 23, Basel 4005 Switzerland.
Tel: (41-61) 691 57 57, **Fax:** (41-61) 691 57 25.

Type: Hotel with a bar for residents.
Clientele: Mostly straight clientele with a gay & lesbian following (20%-50%)
Transportation: Airport bus to central station, then taxi, or direct streetcar #8 to "Rheingasse."
To Gay Bars: 5-minute walk to gay/lesbian bar.

Rooms: 5 singles, 5 doubles, 6 have queen beds.
Bathrooms: All private showers & toilets.
Meals: Expanded continental breakfast buffet.
Dates Open: All year.
Rates: Single SF 95.00-125.00, double & queen SF 125.00-185.00.

Discounts: 10% to guests who mention Inn Places.
Credit Cards: Visa, Eurocard, Diners.
Rsv'tns: Required 2 wks in advance.
To Reserve: Call direct.
Parking: Nearby free on-street parking.
In-Room: Telephone, color cable TV.

On-Premises: Public telephone, shoeshine & cigarette machines.
Smoking: Permitted without restrictions.
Pets: Limited (1 dog or cat).
Handicap Access: No.
Children: Permitted.
Languages: German, French, English, Spanish, Italian.
Your Host: Claude & Max.

EUROPE

SWITZERLAND • BASEL

INN PLACES® 1998

Hotel Goldenes Schwert

Gay/Lesbian ♀♂

Switzerland's Only Truly Gay Hotel

The relaxed and informal atmoshpere of *Hotel Goldenes Schwert* radiates from the front desk to each of the guestrooms. Located in the heart of the Old Town, near the financial district and just two minutes from the famous Bahnhofstrasse shops, the hotel offers the charm and warmth of a quality hotel. There are 25 large rooms and three suites, and single rooms have French beds. All rooms have private bath, hair dryer & cosmetic box, color TV, VCR, direct-dial phone. Some rooms have attractive balconies. The popular one-and-only T&M gay disco is on premises, and other gay venues are a short walk away.

Address: Marktgasse 14,
Zürich 8001 Switzerland.
Tel: (41-1) 266 1818,
Fax: (41-1) 266 1888.
E-mail: hotel@gaybar.ch
URL: http://www.gaybar.ch/hotel

Type: Hotel with bar & disco.
Clientele: Mostly gay & lesbian with some hetero clientele
Transportation: Airport hotel bus on request, or taxi. 12 km from airport.
To Gay Bars: T&M disco on premises, others a 2 min walk.
Rooms: 22 rooms, 3 suites, 5 theme rooms with single or double beds.
Bathrooms: All private bath/toilets.
Meals: Continental breakfast Sfr 9.50.
Dates Open: All year.
High Season: May-September.
Rates: Single Sfr 99; Double Sfr 130-150; Suites Sfr 290-320.
Discounts: 20% after 4 days.

Credit Cards: MC, Visa, Amex, Diners, Eurocard.
Rsv'tns: Required.
To Reserve: Travel agent or call direct.
Parking: Adequate on-street pay parking.
In-Room: Maid & laundry service, telephone, color cable TV, VCR.
Exercise/Health: Nearby gym, Jacuzzi, sauna, steam, massage.
Swimming: Lake.
Sunbathing: At beach.
Smoking: Permitted everywhere. No non-smoking rooms available.
Pets: Permitted.
Handicap Access: No.
Children: No.
Languages: German, English, French.
Your Host: Thomas.

FERRARI GUIDES™

The Lodge and The Keep

An Englishman's Home is His Castle

Men ♂

It is said that an "Englishman's home is his castle," but this Englishman's Castle is his Home! The buildings, Banwell Castle and *The Lodge*, are set in 21 acres of grounds and gardens, with fine views to The Mendips and The Welsh Hills. Completed in 1847, Banwell Castle is of historical and architectural interest. *The Lodge* is a charming Victorian Gate House Lodge, full of Olde World charm and atmosphere. It is peaceful, romantic and intimate, for those very special occasions, either weekend or mid-week breaks. Also of interest is Banwell Village, a pleasant rural Somerset Village, with 4 pubs and a selection of shops. Visitors will take pleasure in strolling through the older parts of the village which have buildings dating back to the 17th century.

Address: Banwell Castle, Banwell, Avon BS24 6NX England.
Tel: (44-1934) 823 122, **Fax:** (44-1934) 823 946.

Type: Bed & breakfast with The Keep restaurant.
Clientele: Mostly men with women welcome
Transportation: Car is best, free pick up from bus or train.
To Gay Bars: 20 minutes by car.
Rooms: 4 doubles/singles.
Bathrooms: All private.

Meals: Full English breakfast.
Vegetarian: Always available.
Complimentary: Fresh fruit, tea, coffee.
Dates Open: All year.
High Season: July, August, September.
Rates: £25.00 per person per night.

Discounts: 10% for 2 or more nights.
Rsv'tns: Required.
To Reserve: Call direct.
Parking: Ample off-street parking.
In-Room: Color TV, laundry service, maid & room service.
On-Premises: TV lounge.

Swimming: Five miles to pool or ocean beach.
Sunbathing: On roof.
Smoking: Permitted in TV lounge.
Pets: Permitted by prior arrangement.
Handicap Access: No.
Children: Not permitted.
Languages: English.
Your Host: Chris.

The Kennard Hotel

Q-NET Gay-Owned ♀♂

A Georgian Town House of Charm and Character

Staying at *The Kennard Hotel* gives you a chance to discover and enjoy a true Georgian Town House. Now restored to a charming small hotel with its own special character, it was originally built in 1794 during Bath's grand era of elegance and prosperity. Each of its 13 bedrooms are thoughtfully and individually fur-

continued next page

nished for your comfort. The original Georgian kitchen, now a delightful garden-style bistro, is the setting for a full choice of English or continental breakfasts. Quietly situated in Henrietta Street, its city centre location is ideal — just over Pulteney Bridge, only minutes from the Abbey and Roman Baths and with easy access from London or the Station.

Address: 11 Henrietta Street, Bath, Avon BA2 6LL England.
Tel: (44-1225) 310472, **Fax:** (44-1225) 460054. **E-mail:** kennard@dircon.co.uk

Type: Bed & breakfast hotel.
Clientele: Mostly hetero with a gay & lesbian following
To Gay Bars: 5-minute walk.
Rooms: 10 doubles & 2 singles.

Bathrooms: 10 private, others share.
Meals: Full English breakfast.
Vegetarian: Available upon request.
Complimentary: Coffee & tea-making facilities in room.

Dates Open: All year.
Rates: £68-£88.
Credit Cards: MC, Visa, Amex, Diners.
Rsv'tns: Required.
To Reserve: Call, fax or e-mail direct.
Parking: On-street parking.

In-Room: Colour TV, direct-dial phone, hair dryers, tea & coffee.
Smoking: Non smoking.
Children: Not permitted.
Languages: English.

Leigh House
Gay-Owned & -Operated ♀♂

Log Fires, History & Home Cooking... England at its Best

Deep in the heart of the West Country lies the beautiful historic town of Bradford-on-Avon, set on a hillside with a winding river at its base and terraces of weavers' cottages and grand merchants' houses. The town dates from its 7th-century Saxon church, 14th-century tithe barn, and medieval bridge with pilgrims' chapel (later used as a lock-up cell), to the woollen trade of the 18th century. It is here, in this town rich in tradition, that you will find the beautiful 16th-century farmhouse called *Leigh House*. It was one of four farms granted by Queen Elizabeth I to the only man she cared to marry, Robert Dudley, Earl of Leicester, in 1574 and sits in six acres with the unusual feature of a collection of rare-breed animals and fowl. Each room has individual, tasteful style with views to the hills or overlooking the walled garden. There is a converted 16th-century bakehouse available for bed and breakfast or self catering up to seven people. In the sitting room, with its beamed ceiling and old tiled floor, are an open-hearth fireplace, bread oven, and a separate smoking oven. Enjoy fresh home-cooked meals served at a long chestnut table on a flagstone floor, glowing with dark woods and candles, complimented by rustic country furniture and low beams.

Enjoy surrounding rivers, canals and countryside, with walks, cycle rides, canoes and narrowboats, or visit nearby Bath City with its grand Georgian buildings, museums, attractive shops and famous Roman Baths. There is a main railway link for Bath, London, Plymouth and the Midlands. Visit National Trust properties, gardens, moated manor house, open-air plays, concerts, local villages and abbeys used for television and film dramas, tropical bird gardens, woodland parks, underground quarries, and the American Museum. See the famous sites of Stonehenge, the Avebury ancient stone circle, castles, cathedrals, the Cotswolds, Tetbury (Prince Charles's home), ancient docks, market towns, antique shops, Wells and Glastonbury Tor, and Longleat House Safari Park.

Address: Leigh Road West, Bradford-on-Avon Wiltshire BA15 2RB England.
Tel: (44-1225) 867835.

Type: Bed & breakfast cottage guesthouse with restaurant.
Clientele: Mostly gay & lesbian with some hetero clientele
Transportation: Car is best. Free pick up from train.
To Gay Bars: 8 miles to gay bars.
Rooms: 3 rooms, 1 cottage with single, double or king beds.

Bathrooms: 2 private bath/shower/toilets, 1 private bath/toilet.
Meals: Full breakfast.
Vegetarian: Special diets catered for, please inform when booking.
Complimentary: Tea & coffee any time, wine with meals.
Dates Open: All year.
High Season: Jun-Aug & Christmas.

Rates: £24-£30 per person.
Discounts: 10% for 3 or more nights B&B, reductions for self-catering & groups/house parties.
Rsv'tns: Required.
To Reserve: Call direct.
Parking: Ample free off-street parking.
On-Premises: TV lounge, video tape library.
Swimming: Pool nearby.
Sunbathing: On patio.

Smoking: Permitted in guest lounge. All bedrooms are non-smoking.
Pets: Permitted with advance notice when booking.
Handicap Access: Yes. Cottage has ground-floor bedroom & bath.
Children: Not heavily encouraged.
Languages: English.
Your Host: Alan & Peter.

The Fountain Inn
Gay/Lesbian ♂

Built as a traditional Victorian public house, *The Fountain Inn* retains much of its original character. With guest accommodations refurbished to the highest standards, *The Fountain Inn* offers its guests a warm and welcoming stay. All rooms are en suite or have separate, private toilet and tea- and coffee-making facilities, telephone, central heating and colour TV with satellite movie channel and in-house video channel. Guest keys give 24-hour access.

The Fountain Inn's very popular, ground-floor gay bar is only a 5- to 10-minute walk from the other gay bars and clubs, the main railway station and Birmingham's shopping and entertainment areas. Birmingham is known as the "Second City" (London being the first!), and is at the heart of the motorway network, with London approximately 1-1/2-hour's drive away and "Shakespeare country" only a half-hour's drive. Birmingham now boasts one of the largest conference centers, exhibition centers and international airports in Europe.

Address: 102 Wrentham St, Birmingham, West Midlands B5 6QL England.
Tel: (44-121) 622 1452, **Fax:** (44-121) 622 5387.
In USA call (407) 994-3558, Fax: (407) 994-3634.

Type: Guesthouse inn. Our bar has pub food & is open evenings & Sat & Sun days.
Clientele: Mostly men with women welcome
Transportation: Car, 5-min taxi ride from railway station (£2), taxi from Birmingham International Airport approx £12.
To Gay Bars: Five min walk to nearest bars & discos.

Rooms: 5 rooms with single or double beds.
Bathrooms: All private.
Meals: Full English breakfast. Continental breakfast served in bedroom.
Vegetarian: Available on request before arrival.
Complimentary: Tea/coffee making facilities & biscuits.
Dates Open: All year.
Rates: £30.00-£40.00 per night.

Discounts: 10% for 3 nights & over, if booked direct.
Credit Cards: MC, Visa.
Rsv'tns: Required.
To Reserve: Call direct.
Parking: Free off-street parking for 5 cars, on-street pay parking, free weekends.
In-Room: Color TV with in-house, non-porn video channel, movie channel via satellite, telephone, coffee/tea-making facilities & maid service.
On-Premises: Meeting rooms.
Smoking: Permitted.
Pets: Not permitted.
Handicap Access: No.
Children: Not permitted.
Languages: English.
Your Host: Erick or Wayne.

Edward Hotel

Gay-Owned & -Operated ♀♂

When visiting Blackpool, stay at the *Edward Hotel* and let Ian and Alec look after your needs. The hotel is situated within easy walking distance to all of Blackpool's gay bars and makes an ideal home base from which to explore not only Blackpool, but the Northwest of England as well. All rooms have tea- & coffee-making facilities, colour television, heating, washbasin and some rooms have private facilities. Maid service is available on request. Room prices include breakfast, and discounts are available for group bookings and on stays more than four days. Member: B.A.G.S.

Address: 27 Dickson Road, Blackpool FY1 2AT England.
Tel: (44-1253) 24271.

Type: Bed & breakfast hotel with bar.
Clientele: Gay & lesbian. Good mix of men & women.
Transportation: Train to Blackpool, then 1 min walk.
To Gay Bars: 2 min walk to Pepe's, Basics, Flying Handbag & Flamingo.
Rooms: 10 rooms with single, double or king beds.
Bathrooms: Private: 3 shower/toilets, 7 sinks only. Shared: 2 showers only, 3 WCs only.

Meals: Full breakfast.
Vegetarian: Must be ordered on arrival.
Complimentary: Tea, coffee in all rooms.
Dates Open: All year.
High Season: Jul-Oct.
Rates: Per person: single room £15-£25, double/twin room: £12-£25.
Discounts: Up to 25% for longer stays.
Credit Cards: MC, Visa.
To Reserve: Call direct.

Minimum Stay: Required Sept-Oct & all bank holidays.
Parking: Limited pay parking. Large car park 2 blocks behind hotel.
In-Room: Colour TV, coffee & tea-making facilities.
On-Premises: Meeting rooms, TV lounge, video tape library.
Exercise/Health: Nearby gym, weights, Jacuzzi, sauna, steam, massage.

Swimming: Nearby pool, ocean.
Sunbathing: At beach.
Smoking: Permitted in all areas. Non-smoking rooms available.
Pets: Permitted by appointment.
Handicap Access: No.
Children: No.
Languages: English, very little Spanish.
Your Host: Ian & Alec.

Kingsmead Guest House

Gay-Owned 50/50 ♀♂

The World Will Always be Welcome

The *Kingsmead Guest House* offers clean and comfortable rooms at reasonable prices. The gay pubs, clubs, cafes and sauna of Blackpool are a short five-minute walk from us, and we provide guests with complimentary concessions to the Flamingo, one of Europe's largest gay clubs (open seven days a week). Our resident I.H.B.C.-qualified masseur is on hand to relieve stress at special discount rates for guests. Free maps detailing the area's gay attractions are available on request.

Address: 58 Lord St, Blackpool FY1 2BJ England.
Tel: (44-1253) 24496, **Fax:** (44-1253) 292 634.
E-mail: evanswarburton@msn.com

Type: Bed & breakfast guesthouse.
Clientele: 50% gay & lesbian & 50% hetero clientele
Transportation: Bus or train to Blackpool, then by foot or taxi. Free pick up from train.
To Gay Bars: A 5 min walk or a 2 min drive.
Rooms: 11 rooms with single or double beds.

Bathrooms: Private: 11 sinks only. Shared: 2 showers only, 2 WCs only.
Meals: Full breakfast. Dinner optional.
Vegetarian: Available.
Complimentary: Tea & coffee in all rooms.
Dates Open: All year.
High Season: Sept-Oct.
Rates: £12-£18. Special rates for weekly, Easter & New Year.

Discounts: 10% discount for Body Positive & Unison Union for 3 days or more.
Rsv'tns: Required.
To Reserve: Call direct.
Parking: Limited on-street parking.
In-Room: Coffee & tea-making facilities, maid service.
On-Premises: TV lounge.
Exercise/Health: Massage. Nearby gym, weights,

Jacuzzi, sauna, steam.
Swimming: Pool & ocean nearby.
Sunbathing: At beach.
Smoking: Permitted everywhere.
Pets: No.
Handicap Access: No.
Children: No.
Languages: English.
Your Host: Bill & John.

The Primrose Hotel

Gay-Owned ♀♂

The Warmest Welcome in Town

Primrose Hotel is ideally situated close to North Station, a 5-minute walk from the town centre, promenade and theatres. The hotel is run by resident proprietors, whose main concern is your comfort and enjoyment. No effort is spared to make your holiday a happy one. Rooms feature modern furniture, comfortable beds, tea-making facilities, shaver and power point. Our lounge bar has McEwans on draught. You will find this charming, small hotel spotlessly clean. Nothing is too much trouble to ensure that your stay is a happy one. Just relax, you are in good hands and nobody does it better!

Address: 16 Lord St, Blackpool, Lancashire FY1 2BD England.
Tel: (44-1253) 22488.

Type: Hotel with bar.
Clientele: 60% gay/lesbian with all exclusively gay bank holidays, including New Year, Easter
Transportation: Rail or motor car or coach.
To Gay Bars: 2-minute walk to gay/lesbian bars.
Rooms: 6 doubles, 2 triples, 1 quad, 1 twin.
Bathrooms: 2 shared, 2 private.
Meals: Continental breakfast or full English breakfast.

Vegetarian: Upon request.
Complimentary: Concessionary pass to the Flamingo night club, tea, coffee.
Dates Open: All year.
High Season: September 2nd-November 5th.
Rates: Singles, £13.00-£18.00, doubles, £22.00-£36.00.
Discounts: For senior citizens, stays over 3 nights, weekly stays.

Rsv'tns: Advisable.
To Reserve: Write for information.
Parking: Limited free on-street parking, 2-minute walk to car park.
In-Room: Maid, room & laundry service, tea/coffee making facilities, late keys.
On-Premises: TV lounge, masseur.
Exercise/Health: Weights, Massage.
Swimming: Excellent indoor pool nearby, ocean beach.

Sunbathing: On the beach.
Smoking: Permitted without restrictions.
Pets: Small dogs only permitted in owner's room.
Handicap Access: No, we have no ground-floor rooms.
Children: Over 5 years preferred.
Languages: English, limited French.
Your Host: Barry & Chris.

Beech Crescent

Gay-Owned & -Operated ♂

Quality Accommodation for Discerning Guests

Relax in the comfort of *Beech Crescent*, a stylish 1900's residence in the prestigious conservation area of Branksome Park. Spacious, tastefully furnished bedrooms offer a full array of comforts, and guests have their own bedroom and front door keys to allow for complete freedom. Hearty English breakfasts are served in our open-aspect dining room which looks directly onto the colourful patio and garden. Locally, there are many areas of unspoilt beauty to explore. Pleasant, tree-lined walks take you to the beach and from there, along the promenade into Bournemouth or Poole where there are shopping arcades, restaurants, theatres and entertainment spots.

Address: Branksome Park, Poole, England.
Tel: (44-1202) 762092 (Tel/Fax).

continued next page

INN PLACES® 1998 99

Type: Guesthouse.
Clientele: Mostly men with women welcome
Transportation: Car is best, train or bus to Bournemouth, then taxi. Free pick up from Bournemouth train or bus.
To Gay Bars: 2 miles, a 30 min walk, a 10 min drive.
Rooms: 4 rooms with single or double beds.
Bathrooms: Private: 1 bath/shower/toilet, 3 shower/toilets. 1 shared WC only.
Meals: Full or continental breakfast.
Vegetarian: Always available.
Complimentary: Tea, coffee, cold drinks, biscuits on arrival.
Dates Open: All year, except Christmas & New Year.
High Season: May-Oct.
Rates: £25 per person, per night.
Rsv'tns: Required.
To Reserve: Call direct.
Parking: Ample, free on- & off-street parking.
In-Room: Color TV, hot chocolate, coffee & tea-making facilities, radio alarms, hair dryer, mineral water.
On-Premises: Meeting rooms, lounge, dining room for breakfast, book library, private garden.
Exercise/Health: Gym, weights, Jacuzzi, sauna, steam, massage.
Swimming: Nearby pool & ocean.
Sunbathing: On patio & at beach.
Smoking: Permitted everywhere, except dining room.
Pets: Permitted by arrangement. Not permitted in public rooms.
Handicap Access: No.
Children: No.
Languages: English.
Your Host: Keith & Frank.

The Creffield   Gay/Lesbian ♂

Exclusively Gay Hotel With the Air of a Country Home

A well-appointed red-brick, late Edwardian house, *The Creffield* was originally built as a rich man's family summer home. It stands on its own grounds with a car park to the fore and a large private garden to the rear. All of the bedrooms are en-suite and the single rooms aren't single rooms at all, but small doubles. Our two largest bedrooms have four-poster beds. Breakfast is served either in the conservatory or outside on the patio. It is an easy walk from *The Creffield* to all of Bournemouth's main venues. If, like the hotel's owner, you have a car, like a drink, but don't much relish the thought of walking your feet off, then this is the place for you. Park your car in the free car park and five licensed venues are a hop, skip and a jump away (no taxis necessary).

Address: 7 Cambridge Road, Bournemouth BH2 6AE England.
Tel: (44-1202) 317 900.

Type: Bed & breakfast guesthouse with bar for residents on premises.
Clientele: Mostly men with women welcome
Transportation: Car, train from London, taxi.
To Gay Bars: A 2 minute walk to gay bars.
Rooms: 9 rooms with singles or doubles. 2 rooms have 4-poster beds.
Bathrooms: All private shower/toilets.
Meals: Full English breakfast.
Vegetarian: Always available.
Complimentary: Tea & coffee. Courtesy trays in each room.
Dates Open: All year.
High Season: June-September.
Rates: Single £30; Double £45-£48; 4-poster £50-£54.
Discounts: 10% on stays of 7 or more nights.
To Reserve: Call direct.
Minimum Stay: Two nights during high season.
Parking: Adequate free, well-lit off-street parking.
In-Room: Color TV, coffee & tea-making facilities, maid service.
On-Premises: Meeting room, TV lounge, full central heating, large private garden.
Exercise/Health: Nearby gym, sauna, steam.
Swimming: Pool & ocean nearby.
Sunbathing: On patio.
Smoking: Permitted in rooms, bar & smoking room. There is a non-smoking "dry" lounge.
Pets: Permitted. Must be kept on a lead.
Handicap Access: No.
Children: Absolutely not.
Languages: English.
Your Host: Roger.

Leicester Grange

Men ♂

Quality Accommodation Close to the Sea

Relax in the stylish comfort of *Leicester Grange,* a 1920's residence set high in an acre of grounds within the prestigious area of Branksome Park. The property has fine views of Branksome Chine, a conservation area, through which there are pleasant tree-lined walks to the beach and from there along the promenade into Bournemouth. The unspoiled beauty of Shell Bay, Poole Harbour and its islands, and the beach at Studland via the ferry at Sandbanks Peninsular are within easy reach.

Leicester Grange provides the discerning guest with quality accommodation in the most pleasant surroundings. Two standards of rooms are available — luxury with ensuite bath or shower room and rooms sharing a bathroom between two. You will be served complimentary tea or coffee on arrival. Early morning tea or coffee followed by a super continental breakfast served in the comfort of your room starts the day.

There is time to relax here, to savour your well-earned break, or prepare for a business meeting in the day ahead. Whatever time of year you choose to stay, you will appreciate the superb position of the B&B, the stylish comfort of its rooms, and the attentive staff. *Leicester Grange* is an ideal base from which to enjoy the contrasting scenery from the coast and beaches to the ever-changing beauty of the New Forest. For sporty types, there are many local facilities and a number of parks and gardens for those who enjoy more leisurely activities. Shopping arcades and a number of theatres, restaurants, and entertainment spots are in and around the Bournemouth and Poole area.

Address: Bournemouth/Poole   England.
Tel: (44-1202) 760278.

Type: Bed & breakfast in a large, private house.
Clientele: Men only
Transportation: Best to have own car. Good local taxi service.
To Gay Bars: 5 minutes by car to town center.
Rooms: 3 rooms with double beds.
Bathrooms: 2 en suite & 1 shared.
Meals: Expanded continental breakfast.
Complimentary: Tea or coffee when you arrive. Water & mints each day in room.
Dates Open: All year except Christmas week. Phone to confirm.
High Season: July, August, & September.
Rates: En suite, £25.00-£30.00 per person per night. Shared bath, £20.00-£25.00 per person per night.
Discounts: Each 7th consecutive night at no charge.
Credit Cards: MC, Visa.
Rsv'tns: Required. Can be made by telephone with credit card.
To Reserve: Call direct.
Minimum Stay: 2 days required on bank holidays only.
Parking: Ample parking at top of the drive.
In-Room: Color TV, maid service.
Swimming: Public pool 10 minutes by car. Beach 5 minutes by car or 15 minute walk.
Sunbathing: On part of the grounds or at the beach.
Nudity: Permitted at the beach with care. Ask for details.
Smoking: Permitted.
Pets: Not permitted.
Handicap Access: No. Too many steps.
Children: Not permitted.
Languages: English.
Your Host: Chris.

Alpha Lodge Private Hotel

Gay/Lesbian ♂

THE Gay Hotel for Single People

As Brighton's longest established exclusively gay hotel (since 1980), *Alpha Lodge* welcomes gay men and women year round. We are situated in a pleasant Regency square, overlooking the Victorian Palace Pier, a few yards from the beach and most gay clubs. Local gay saunas and nude bathing beaches are nearby. Our well-appointed, intimate hotel, originally built in the early 1800's, is run by Derrick and Charles, both of whom are actively gay. It is run as a continuous house party.

continued next page

Five rooms have double beds, each with its own private shower. The remainder, with single beds, are both with and without private showers. All rooms have colour TV, radio/alarm clocks, intercom and hot drink facilities, and, of course, self-controlled central heating. There are adequate public showers, toilets, a bathroom and a cosy lounge with an open fire and colour TV. Our full English breakfast is renowned. The Steine Room Suite, consists of Turkish Bath, rest area with an open fire and colour TV, shower area, hair dryer, toilet and lockers. Towels and wraps are provided, and the facility is free to residents Wednesday, Friday and Saturday for 1-1/2 hours in early evening.

All guests have front door keys, and there are no petty restrictions. Friends may be brought in at all times. There is a safe for valuables (free). Everything is geared to make one's stay comfortable and relaxing. A full fire certificate has been issued. A map of Gay Brighton, a privilege card for entry to the gay clubs, and a welcoming drink upon arrival are all provided as part of the basic charge for the room. We are not licensed, but alcoholic drinks may be brought into the hotel, where ice and mixers are available 24 hours a day. We look forward to your joining us.

Address: 19 New Steine, Brighton, E Sussex BN2 1PD England.
Tel: (44-1273) 609 632, **Fax:** (44-1273) 690 264.

Type: Guesthouse with a steam-room suite.
Clientele: Mostly men with women welcome. Exclusively gay
Transportation: Take taxi or No. 7 minibus from the station.
To Gay Bars: 2-minute walk to gay & lesbian bars.
Rooms: 10 rooms with single & double beds.
Bathrooms: 1 shared bath, 7 showers (2 shared) & 5 shared toilets.
Meals: Full English breakfast. Cold soft drinks at low cost 24 hours.
Vegetarian: Available with overnight notice.

Complimentary: Coffee, tea, soft drink on arrival. Unlimited hot drinks in the rooms.
Dates Open: All year. Closed in Jan for vacation.
High Season: July, Aug & Bank Holidays, mid-season May/June & Sept/Oct.
Rates: Low season: £21-£42 per room; mid-season: £23-£46; high season: £24-£48. Bank holidays £25-£50.
Discounts: Stay 6 nights & get 1 night free to all & 10% to members of gay groups.
Credit Cards: MC, Visa, Amex, Eurocard.

Rsv'tns: Recommended in summer 10 days in advance.
To Reserve: Travel agent or call direct.
Minimum Stay: One night. Longer stays on bank holidays.
Parking: Free & pay parking on the street at or near the hotel.
In-Room: Color TV, beverage-making facilities, radio/alarm clock & intercom in all rooms. Room service for continental breakfast.
On-Premises: TV lounge, public telephone, meeting

rooms & refrigerator for cold sodas.
Exercise/Health: Steam room (free on Wed., Fri. and Sat. evenings).
Swimming: Pool, ocean beach nearby.
Sunbathing: On the beach.
Nudity: 10-minute walk to public nudist beach.
Smoking: Permitted without restrictions.
Pets: Not permitted.
Handicap Access: No.
Children: Not permitted.
Languages: English.
Your Host: Derrick & Charles.

Bannings Guest House
Gay-Owned & -Operated ♀

Run by two gay men who enjoy entertaining and providing a safe environment for women, *Bannings Guest House* is highly recommended by the Official Tourist Authorities and Motoring Organizations (we were awarded 3 Qs for Quality). Our Regency house is in the heart of Brighton's extensive gay area, minutes from pubs, clubs, bookshops and restaurants. All rooms are immaculately clean and have showers, and en-suite rooms are also available. Other amenities offered are complimentary tea and coffee, as well as TV and radio alarms. A full English, vegetarian/vegan breakfast is included and ironing facilities are available.

Address: 14 Upper Rock Gardens, Brighton BN2 1QE England.
Tel: (44-1273) 681403.

Type: Guesthouse.
Clientele: Women-only
Transportation: Taxi from Brighton Station.

To Gay Bars: 1 block, a 5 min walk.
Rooms: 6 rooms with single or double beds.

Bathrooms: Private & shared. All rooms have shower.
Meals: Full breakfast.

Vegetarian: Breakfast is vegetarian.
Complimentary: Tea & coffee in rooms.

Dates Open: Feb-Nov.
High Season: Apr-Oct.
Rates: £35-£48.
Credit Cards: MC, Visa, Diners, Eurocard, Amex.

Rsv'tns: Required.
To Reserve: Call direct.
Minimum Stay: 2 nights on weekends.

Parking: Adequate on-street parking.
In-Room: Color TV, coffee & tea-making facilities.
Swimming: Ocean nearby.
Sunbathing: On beach.

Smoking: Please inquire.
Pets: Not permitted.
Handicap Access: No.
Children: No.
Languages: English.
Your Host: Geoff & Steve.

Barrington's Private Hotel
Gay-Friendly 50/50 ♀♂

Luxury rooms, all with direct-dial telephones, and a full English breakfast enhance your stay at *Barrington's Private Hotel*. Most rooms in this Regency Building overlook the Royal Pavilion and Pavilion Gardens. Our fully licensed bar and lounge are open to the public, and an enclosed patio garden is just off the bar. Four-course dinners can be prepared to order at £7.95. Brighton's gay scene is one of the busiest in England, and we are only two minutes from Revenge nightclub.

Address: 76 Grand Parade, Brighton BN2 2JA England.
Tel: (44-1273) 604 182.

Type: Hotel with licensed lounge bar.
Clientele: 50% gay & lesbian & 50% hetero clientele
Rooms: Luxury rooms with double & twin beds.
Bathrooms: Private showers, shared bath, 1 private bath.
Meals: Full English breakfast.
High Season: June-September.
Rates: £18-£24 per person.

To Reserve: Call direct.
Parking: Free parking behind hotel
In-Room: Remote control colour TV, radios & intercom, direct-dial telephone.
Swimming: 2-minute walk to ocean.

Smoking: Permitted.
Pets: Small pets permitted.
Handicap Access: No.
Children: Permitted over 5 years of age.
Languages: English.
Your Host: Barry.

Catnaps Private Guest House
Gay/Lesbian ♂

Catnaps is situated close to the sea, about 8 minutes' walk from the Royal Pavilion, unique to Brighton and actually the historical reason for the growth of the town in the 18th-19th centuries. We aim for a family atmosphere and we like guests to feel welcome. All rooms have hot and cold water and are centrally heated. Showers and toilets are in a separate area of the house and are easily reached from the bedrooms. Guests have their own keys to the house.

Address: 21 Atlingworth St, Brighton, E Sussex BN2 1PL England.
Tel: (44-1273) 685 193, **Fax:** (44-1273) 622 026.

Type: Guesthouse.
Clientele: Mostly men with women welcome
Transportation: Taxi or bus from station.
To Gay Bars: 5-minute walk to gay & lesbian bars.
Rooms: 7 rooms.
Bathrooms: Shared baths & toilets. 2 rooms have private showers, all have sinks.
Meals: Full English breakfast.

Complimentary: Tea & coffee upon arrival.
Dates Open: All year.
High Season: June-August.
Rates: Single £19 for 1 night. Double £36 twin. Double £36 for a night with shower, £34 without shower.
Discounts: On longer stays.
Rsv'tns: Preferred.
To Reserve: Call direct.

Parking: Adequate free on-street parking.
In-Room: Tea or coffee delivered to room.
On-Premises: TV lounge & public telephone.
Swimming: Pool & ocean beach are nearby.
Sunbathing: On the beach.
Nudity: 5-minute walk to nude beach.
Smoking: Permitted without restrictions.

Pets: Permitted with prior arrangement. Owner responsible for pets.
Handicap Access: No.
Children: Not normally, but open to requests.
Languages: English, limited French.
Your Host: Malcolm & Charlie.

EUROPE • UK - ENGLAND • BRIGHTON

Coward's Guest House

Men ♂

Coward's Guest House is a Regency-style guesthouse in the heart of Brighton's gay area, five minutes' walk from gay bars and clubs. Brighton is a very gay town with a lively gay nightlife. The town is known for its Regency architecture and for The Pavilion, a winter palace which was built by the Prince Regent. The train from London takes only 50 minutes, making Brighton an easy commute to London's tourist attractions.

Address: 12 Upper Rock Gardens, Brighton BN2 1QE England.
Tel: (44-1273) 692677.

Type: Guesthouse.
Clientele: Men only
Transportation: Brighton Station, then taxi.
To Gay Bars: Many gay pubs & clubs within 5 min walk.
Rooms: 2 singles, 4 doubles & 2 triples with single & double beds.
Bathrooms: 4 en suite. All rooms have showers.
Meals: Full English or vegetarian breakfast.
Vegetarian: Anytime.
Complimentary: Tea & coffee in all rooms.
Dates Open: All year.
High Season: April thru October.
Rates: Summer: double £42-£55, single £25-£27.
Winter: double £38-£50, single £23-£25.
Credit Cards: Visa, Access.
Rsv'tns: Required.
To Reserve: Call direct.
Parking: Free on-street parking.
In-Room: Color TV, tea & coffee.
Swimming: At nearby sea, a 5 min walk.
Sunbathing: On the beach.
Nudity: Permitted on nude beach 5 min from inn.
Smoking: Permitted.
Pets: Not permitted.
Handicap Access: No.
Children: Not permitted.
Languages: English.
Your Host: Gerry & Cyril.

George IV Hotel

Gay/Lesbian ♀♂

Our Welcome is Warm Throughout the Year

Only 100 yards from the sea, Brighton's *George IV Hotel* offers comfortable accommodation in a beautiful five-floor Regency building. Our small, gay-run motel is situated in the city centre, a five-minute walk to the gay bars and nightclubs. In addition, we have a licenced bar on premises for residents and their friends. We also maintain a connection with the gay-friendly Sussex Arts Club, which has a licenced restaurant and further accommodation. All of our rooms have single or queen-sized beds, full ensuite baths, colour television and telephone, as well as tea- & coffee-making facilities. Our rates range from £25 for a single room to £70 for a double room with a sea view. From Gatwick Airport it is a short 20-minute train ride to Brighton. Genuine guest comments about our room with a sea view include "A handsome house in which to lodge a friend." "The seafront at the garden's end." "Perfect views of an historic pier." "The welcome is warm throughout the year."

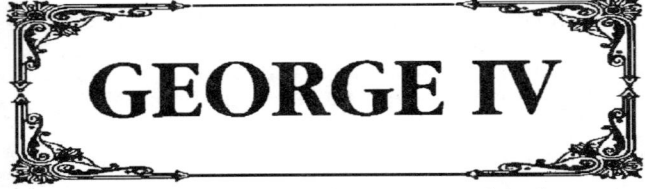

Address: 34 Regency Square, Brighton BN1 2FJ England.
Tel: (44-1273) 321 196.

Type: Hotel with bar for residents & their friends.
Clientele: 60% gay & lesbian & 40% hetero clientele
Transportation: 20 min from Gatwick Airport on train.
To Gay Bars: A 5 min walk to gay bars.
Rooms: 8 rooms with single or double beds.
Bathrooms: All private.
Meals: Continental breakfast included. Full English breakfast £3.95.
Complimentary: Tea & coffee tray in room.
Dates Open: All year.
High Season: Apr-Nov.
Rates: Single: £25 single. Double: with sea view £70, without sea view £50.
Discounts: 10% on stays of 7 nights or more.
Credit Cards: MC, Visa, Diners, Eurocard, Electron, Amex.
Rsv'tns: Better to book ahead.

To Reserve: Call direct.
Parking: Ample on-street pay parking. Underground car park next to hotel.
In-Room: Color TV, telephone, coffee & tea-making facilities.
On-Premises: Lounge.
Exercise/Health: Nearby gym.
Swimming: 100 yards to the sea.
Smoking: Permitted.
Pets: Not permitted.
Handicap Access: No.
Children: Welcome.
Languages: English.
Your Host: Brian.

Hudsons Guest House
Gay/Lesbian ♀♂

Hudsons is an early 19th century gentleman's residence, which has been skillfully converted to an exclusively gay guest house. Concealed behind louvered doors in each room, are shower and washbasin, wardrobes and tea- and coffee-making facilities. All rooms also have colour TV, and some have sofas. Also of high standard is the decor, which was coordinated by Next Interiors. Devonshire Place is a quiet road in the middle of Brighton's gay village, so clubs and bars are only a five-minute walk from our door. Also nearby are the Royal Pavilion, the sea, beaches, the pier and the town centre. *Hudsons* is the only gay hotel inspected by, and whose standards are approved by, the Tourist Authority. The quality and warmth of *Hudsons* has established it in the fine tradition of English hospitality. We promise to do our best to make sure you go away wishing the next visit were tomorrow.

Address: 22 Devonshire Place, Brighton, E Sussex BN2 1QA England.
Tel: (44-1273) 683 642, **Fax:** (44-1273) 696 088.

Type: Guesthouse.
Clientele: Good mix of gay men & women
Transportation: Train to Brighton Station then taxi or No. 7 bus.
To Gay Bars: Within easy walking distance (2 mins) of all gay bars.
Rooms: 9 rooms with single, queen or king beds.
Bathrooms: All have private showers, 4 have shower/toilet en suite.
Meals: Proper English breakfast in dining room with homemade preserves.
Vegetarian: Just ask, one of us is vegetarian! Superb vegetarian restaurants nearby.
Complimentary: Tea, coffee, sherry, juice, biscuits & free Brighton map at check-in, concessions to clubs.
Dates Open: All year.
Rates: Single £24.00-£28.00, double £38.00-£48.00 (includes breakfast for two).
Discounts: Mid-week, extended stay.
Credit Cards: MC, Visa, Amex.
Rsv'tns: A good idea, but not always necessary.
To Reserve: Travel agent or call direct.
Minimum Stay: Bank holidays or weekends.
Parking: On-street parking nearby.
In-Room: Washbasins, private shower, tea-making facilities, colour TV, central heating, telephone, laundry service, maid service.
On-Premises: Guests lounge.
Exercise/Health: Nearby gym, weights, Jacuzzi, sauna, steam, massage.
Swimming: At nearby ocean beach & pool.
Sunbathing: Patio and nearby beach.
Nudity: Permitted at nearby beach (10 mins).
Smoking: Not permitted in dining room or in some bedrooms.
Pets: Not permitted.
Handicap Access: No.
Children: Not permitted.
Languages: English, some French, German.
Your Host: Frank & Graham.

Shalimar Hotel
Gay/Lesbian ♂

Undisputedly: Brighton's Most Centrally Located Hotel for Clubs and Bars

Shalimar, under the personal supervision of your internationally known hosts, Kevin and Lawrence, offers tastefully decorated rooms with color TV, vanity units and shaving points. Front rooms have sea views. Deluxe rooms have full bath, fridge and a private balcony overlooking the sea and pier. Not to be missed is our Victoria Suite, complete with four-poster bed. An excellently cooked breakfast is included. A free map gives you the locations of gay bars and clubs, and a privilege pass for entry to clubs is also provided. We now have a full residents' bar, the Backroom Bar, which is proving very popular and is a fun place to meet other

continued next page

guests. Send for our brochure. You will not be disappointed. Special discount on presentation of Inn Places. Fax us at any time, don't worry about the time difference.

Address: 23 Broad St, Marine Parade, Brighton, Sussex BN2 1TJ England.
Tel: (44-1273) 605 316 (Tel/Fax).

Type: Hotel with backroom resident's bar.
Clientele: Mostly men with women welcome
Transportation: Car, taxi or bus. Nearest airport London Gatwick, then 1/2 hour by train to Brighton.
To Gay Bars: 2 minutes by foot.
Rooms: 11 rooms with single, double or queen beds.
Bathrooms: 7 private & 3 private showers only. Shared: 1 full bath, 1 WC.

Meals: Full breakfast.
Vegetarian: Available upon request.
Complimentary: Tea, coffee in rooms.
Dates Open: All year.
High Season: Apr-Oct.
Rates: £36-£52 for two people.
Discounts: 10% on stays of 1 week or longer.
Credit Cards: MC, Visa, Amex, Diners, Eurocard, JCB.
Rsv'tns: Preferred.

To Reserve: Travel agent or call direct.
Minimum Stay: 3 days during bank holidays only.
Parking: Adequate on-street parking.
In-Room: Colour TV, telephone, coffee & tea-making facilities & room service. Deluxe rooms with refrigerators.
On-Premises: Backroom bar, fun bar.
Exercise/Health: Nearby gym, weights, Jacuzzi, sauna, steam, massage.

Swimming: Nearby pool. 2 minutes to the beach.
Sunbathing: On beach.
Nudity: 10 minutes to nude beach.
Smoking: Permitted except in dining room, non-smokers' rooms available.
Pets: Not permitted.
Handicap Access: No.
Children: Not permitted.
Languages: English.
Your Host: Kevin & Lawrence.

Sinclairs Guest House   Gay/Lesbian ♂

Exclusively Gay

Sinclairs is a historically listed building located within minutes of the major Brighton gay area, the famous Regency Pavilion and the sea. All bedrooms have color TV, alarm clock radios, free tea- and coffee-making facilities and central heating. Some have refrigerators and en-suite facilities. A full English breakfast is served till late in the morning, and a continental one till midday. *Sinclairs* is exclusively gay and provides a detailed, up-to-date map of the gay area. The garden is available in summer for relaxing in the sun. All guests have room and front door keys, and friends of guests are welcome.

Address: 23 Upper Rock Gardens, Brighton BN2 1QE England.
Tel: (44-1273) 600 006 (Tel/Fax) and (44-1831) 248 361.

Type: Bed & breakfast guest house.
Clientele: Mostly men with women welcome
Transportation: Train to Brighton station, then taxi.
To Gay Bars: 5-minute walk to nearest gay bar or club.
Rooms: 5 rooms & 1 suite with single or double beds.

Bathrooms: 3 en suite, 3 sinks only, 1 shared WC, & 2 shared bath/shower/toilet.
Meals: Full breakfast.
Vegetarian: Upon request with no extra charge.
Complimentary: Tea & coffee in room.
Dates Open: All year.
High Season: July-September.

Rates: £16.00-£21.50 per person.
Credit Cards: MC, VISA & Eurocard.
Rsv'tns: Preferred.
To Reserve: Call direct.
Parking: Adequate on-street parking.
In-Room: Color TV, fridge, hair dryer, clock radios, coffee/tea-making facilities.
On-Premises: Lounge.

Swimming: Ocean beach.
Sunbathing: On beach & in garden.
Nudity: Permitted on the public beach.
Smoking: Permitted without restrictions.
Pets: Not permitted.
Handicap Access: No.
Children: Not permitted.
Languages: English.

The White House Hotel

Gay-Owned 50/50 ♀♂

The White House is a privately owned, gay-run, 150-year-old Regency hotel situated in the Kemp Town area of Brighton. We're just 150 metres from the seafront and a half a mile from all of the town's main attractions, including the main shopping centre and famous lanes, the Royal Pavilion, theatres, the Palace Pier and Brighton Conference Centres. Brighton's gay village, with its many pubs, clubs, shops and restaurants is a quick four-minute walk from us. The nudist beach, complete with cruising area, is only a two minute's walk away.

Address: 6 Bedford St, Brighton, East Sussex BN2 1AN England.
Tel: (44-1273) 626266 (Tel/Fax).

Type: Bed & breakfast hotel.
Clientele: 50% gay & lesbian & 50% hetero clientele
Transportation: Car or taxi from Brighton train station.
To Gay Bars: 2 blocks, a 3 min walk.
Rooms: 9 rooms with single or double beds.
Bathrooms: Private: 7 bath/shower/toilets, 2 shower/washbasins only. Shared: 1 WC only.
Meals: Full breakfast.
Vegetarian: Vegetarian breakfast available.
Complimentary: Tea & coffee.
Dates Open: All year.
High Season: May-Sept.
Rates: Per person: winter £20-£24; summer £20-£27; double rooms £40.
Discounts: 10% on stays of 7 or more nights.
Credit Cards: MC, Visa.
Rsv'tns: Required.
To Reserve: Call direct.
Parking: Limited free on-street parking.
In-Room: Color TV, coffee & tea-making facilities, maid service.
On-Premises: Meeting rooms, fax.
Exercise/Health: Nearby gym, weights, Jacuzzi, sauna, steam, massage.
Swimming: Nearby ocean.
Sunbathing: On roof & at beach.
Smoking: Permitted in rooms only. Non-smoking rooms available.
Pets: Not permitted.
Handicap Access: No.
Children: No.
Languages: English.
Your Host: Shane & Antony.

Penryn House

Gay-Friendly 50/50 ♀♂

A Picturesque Cornish Seaside Getaway

Polperro is probably the most photographed and painted Cornish fishing village with its whitewashed fishermen's cottages and colourful fishing fleet bobbing in the harbour. It is conveniently located for British Rail and is easily accessible by car, just 30 minutes from the city of Plymouth. *Penryn House* is set in its own grounds a short seven-minute walk to the picturesque harbour. Ensuite rooms are comfortably furnished, centrally heated, and the candlelit restaurant offers excellent cuisine using the best of local seafood and produce. Parking is available on the grounds. Ask about our Gay Murder Mystery Weekends and women-only holidays.

Address: The Coombes, Polperro, Cornwall PL13 2RQ England.
Tel: (44-1503) 272 157.

continued next page

Type: Hotel with restaurant & bar.
Clientele: 50% gay & lesbian & 50% hetero clientele
Transportation: Train to nearby town of Looe.
To Gay Bars: 40 minutes to gay bars.
Rooms: 10 doubles, 2 twins.
Bathrooms: 12 ensuite.
Meals: Full English breakfast & dinner.
Vegetarian: Always available.
Complimentary: Tea & coffee in rooms.
Dates Open: All year.
High Season: Jul-Aug.
Rates: £28 per person, per night (£56 per room) high season.
Discounts: Low & mid-season discounts available.
Credit Cards: Visa, MC, Amex.
Rsv'tns: Recommended during high season.
To Reserve: Phone or fax direct.
Parking: Parking on grounds.
In-Room: Television, telephone, alarm clock, courtesy tray, hair dryers, radio.
On-Premises: Bar, restaurant, log fires in cooler months.
Swimming: Nearby pool & beach.
Sunbathing: At nearby beach.
Smoking: Permitted in bar.
Pets: Welcome.
Handicap Access: No.
Your Host: Christine & Isa.

Rosehill in the Fern   Gay/Lesbian ♀♂

Cornwall is a beautiful, rural part of England, with fabulous beaches, cliffs and a warm climate (by British standards!). *Rosehill in the Fern* is about 8 miles from Truro, the small city which is the main town in Cornwall, with its magnificent cathedral built out of Cornish granite. We are also about 8 miles from the village of Portreath, where there is a thriving gay club. The spectacular north Cornish coast, with its golden beach and breathtaking cliffs, is only five minutes by car. Our house is a very attractive eighteenth-century country house set in two acres of garden and woodland. The property is secluded but conveniently located for all that Cornwall has to offer, and is ideal for either a quiet "get away from it all" break, or a more energetic touring holiday.

The interior of the house is quietly and tastefully decorated and furnished, the emphasis being on country-house-style comfort, where guests are able to enjoy privacy or each other's company by choice. We have a large drawing room and dining room. Each bedroom is spacious and comfortably furnished with double or twin beds. Our two principal rooms have access through French windows to their own private patio with room to sit outside. The en suite bathrooms are appointed to a very high standard with bath, shower, wash basin and WC. Guests are given a front door key and are encouraged to come and go as they wish. We aim to provide a high standard of comfort and good home cooking in order to ensure that our guests feel welcome and at home.

Address: Roseworthy, Camborne, Cornwall TR14 0DU England.
Tel: (44-1209) 712 573.

Type: Guesthouse (private hotel).
Clientele: Mainly gay & lesbian with some hetero clientele
Transportation: Car is best. Pick up airport, train, bus or ferry dock.
To Gay Bars: 10 miles to Perranporth.
Rooms: 3 rooms with single or double beds.
Bathrooms: All private.
Meals: Full English breakfast.
Vegetarian: We cater to special dietary needs with advance notice.
Dates Open: All year.
High Season: Apr-Sept.
Rates: £25.00 per person per night in high season, £20.00 during off season.
Discounts: Weekly and fortnightly rates.
Rsv'tns: Greatly appreciated.
To Reserve: Call direct.
Parking: Ample free off-street parking.
In-Room: Color TV, coffee & tea-making facilities.
On-Premises: TV lounge & meeting rooms.
Exercise/Health: Nearby gymnasium and leisure centre.
Swimming: At nearby full-sized heated pool or ocean.
Sunbathing: On the patio, lawn & at the beach.
Smoking: Permitted in public rooms, discouraged in sleeping rooms.
Pets: Dogs welcome by arrangement.
Handicap Access: Not equipped for severe disabilities.
Children: Not permitted.
Languages: English.
Your Host: Barry.

Woodbine Villa
Gay/Lesbian ♂

Woodbine Villa is a grade II listed 18th century former farmhouse in the centre of the pretty Georgian village of Grampound. The house is furnished with antiques. Your spacious bedroom may have a Victorian brass bed, mahogany half-tester, or even a genuine regency four-poster. Our British breakfast is substantial. The grill includes Cornish hogs pudding, even Kedgeree, if you fancy it! Quality fresh-cooked evening meals can be provided. I'll even throw in a complimentary decanter of wine (not literally). The sauna will be open some nights for both guests and non-residents. All in all, spectacular scenery, fine beaches, pleasant weather, verdant countryside, pleasant walks and masses of historic houses, gardens and interesting places to visit make Cornwall a must on any trip to the U.K. I hope to welcome you as a house guest and I intend to offer true Cornish hospitality and would wish to make your stay with me both pleasant and memorable.

Address: Fore St, Grampound, near Truro, Cornwall TR2 4QP England.
Tel: (44-1726) 882 005.

Type: Bed & breakfast in a private home with sauna open to guests & non-residents.
Clientele: Mostly men with women welcome
Transportation: Coaches from Victoria Stn. & Heathrow to Grampound stop 200 yrds from house, but car is best.
To Gay Bars: 20-40 miles.
Rooms: 4 rooms with double or king beds.
Bathrooms: 1 shared shower, 1 shared bath/shower/toilet & 1 shared toilet.
Meals: Full English breakfast.
Vegetarian: Available with 24 hour notice for evening meal. 2 restaurants in village.
Complimentary: Choice of teas & coffees.
Dates Open: All year.
High Season: May-Oct.
Rates: £20-£25 for singles, £36-£42 for doubles.
Discounts: 10% to Bears Club members, anyone making a return visit, P.W.A.
Rsv'tns: Advisable.
To Reserve: Call direct.
Minimum Stay: Additional charge for 1-night stays.
Parking: Free, limited off-street parking, free on-street parking.
In-Room: Maid service.
On-Premises: TV, VCR, log fireplace in drawing room.
Exercise/Health: Sauna.
Swimming: A few miles to sea beaches.
Sunbathing: On beach or in garden.
Nudity: 7 miles to nude beach.
Smoking: Permitted outdoors only.
Pets: Not permitted.
Handicap Access: No.
Children: Not permitted.
Languages: English, limited French.
Your Host: Mike.

Crestow House
Gay-Friendly ♀♂

English Victorian Stone Country House in a Picturesque Cotswold Village

Crestow House was built in 1870 out of Cotswold sandstone by a local wool merchant. The generously-sized rooms and 12 foot ceilings speak of the affluence this region once knew. Stow is on the Fosse Way, the old wool route built at the time of the Roman occupation. The concluding battles of the English Civil War took place in the fields outside Stow. The town still preserves its Mediaeval stocks and has one of the oldest pubs in Britain. The wool trade has since given way to the antiques business, with Stow having about 20 antique dealers. There is also a twice-yearly horse trading fair (mid

continued next page

INN PLACES® 1998

May and October) where gypsies from England and Ireland trade their ponies. The area is filled with castles and stately homes with formal, world-renowned gardens and is also known for its high quality food. We would be glad to recommend some of our fine local restaurants or cook for you if you let us know in the morning that you would like to eat with us that evening. Stow is about a 2-hour drive from London (1-1/4-hour train ride from Paddington Station), 20 minutes north of Oxford and 15 minutes south of Stratford-on-Avon, home of the Royal Shakespeare Company.

Crestow House is three-storied with a large conservatory, living room, dining room, large country breakfast room and back veranda, with some of the best views and sunsets in Britain. The house has a large walled back garden with heated swimming pool. The middle floor consists of four double bedrooms with en suite bathroom/toilets, antique furnishings, English country decor and modern double beds. The floor-to-ceiling windows make the best of the beautiful countryside that surrounds the house. The owners live on the upper floor.

Address: Stow-on-the-Wold, Gloucestershire GL54 1JY England.
Tel: (44-1451) 830 969, **Fax:** (44-1451) 832 129.
E-mail: 100620.773@compuserve.com

Type: Bed & breakfast country manor house.
Clientele: Mostly straight with a gay & lesbian following
Transportation: Car is best. Train service available from London's Paddington Station to Moreton-In-Marsh.
To Gay Bars: 15 miles or 35 minutes by car.
Rooms: 4 rooms with double or king (2 twin) beds.
Bathrooms: All en suite.
Meals: Expanded continental breakfast.
Vegetarian: Available upon prior request. 5-minute walk to restaurant.
Complimentary: Tea or coffee on arrival, pre-dinner sherry.
Dates Open: All year except Jan.
High Season: June-Sept.
Rates: £34 per person. Single suppplement add £10 per person.
Discounts: For 2 nights or longer.
Credit Cards: MC, Visa.
Rsv'tns: Preferred.
To Reserve: Call direct.
Parking: Free off-street parking.
In-Room: Color TV, laundry service.
On-Premises: Laundry facilities. Can send/receive fax.
Exercise/Health: Sauna & fitness equipment on premises.
Swimming: Pool on premises.
Sunbathing: At poolside.
Smoking: Not permitted.
Pets: Not permitted.
Handicap Access: No.
Children: Not especially welcome.
Languages: English, Spanish, Italian & German.
Your Host: Frank & Jorge.

Hodgkinson's Hotel & Restaurant

Gay-Owned 50/50 ♀♂

Hodgkinson's Hotel and Restaurant, built over 200 years ago, was purchased in run-down condition by Malcolm and Nigel and has been undergoing renovations ever since. Current restoration projects include the 1/4-acre of terraced gardens, affording fine views of the valley. The main project, however, is the opening of the caves which have been used as cellars until recent times. They form part of the labyrinth which runs through the hillside, supposedly dating back to Roman times. Malcolm's hairdressing salon, Redken-appointed, is now well-established, used by the local community & hotel guests.

Address: South Parade, Matlock Bath, Derbyshire DE4 3NR England.
Tel: (44-1629) 582 170, **Fax:** (44-1629) 584 891.

Type: Hotel and hairdressing salon.
Clientele: 50% gay & lesbian & 50% hetero clientele
Transportation: Car is best, free pick up from train.
To Gay Bars: 3/4 hour to Derby, Nottingham, Sheffield.
Rooms: 6 doubles, 1 single.
Bathrooms: All private shower & toilet en suite.
Meals: Full English breakfast.
Vegetarian: Available to order.
Complimentary: Tea & coffee in rooms.
Dates Open: All year.
Rates: £60.00-£90.00 double, £30.00-£35.00 single.
Discounts: For special breaks & 2-night weekends.
Credit Cards: MC, Visa, Amex, Access.
Rsv'tns: Recommended.
To Reserve: Travel agent or call direct.
Parking: Adequate off-street parking.

FERRARI GUIDES™

In-Room: Color TV, telephone, room & laundry service, tea & coffee-making facilities.

On-Premises: Meeting rooms.
Swimming: 2 miles to public pool.

Smoking: Permitted except in dining room.
Pets: Permitted, but not in dining room.
Handicap Access: No.

Children: Permitted.
Languages: English.
Your Host: Malcolm & Nigel.

Mayfair Hotel & Ye Olde Cottage Inne
Gay/Lesbian ♀♂

Spend a Glorious Holiday in the Devon Countryside

The *Mayfair Hotel* enjoys stunning views of the North Devon coast and is perfectly situated for the National Trust Coastal Path, Exmoor, and glorious beaches. Decorated to a high standard by its friendly owners, you are assured of a comfortable stay. *Ye Olde Cottage Inne* is only five minutes away. Set in a beautiful wooded valley by the River Lyn and recently refurbished, the gay-friendly 14th-century inn and pub is the perfect spot for enjoying the National Trust countryside and a pleasant drink or meal.

Address: Lynway, Lynton, North Devon EX35 6AY England.
Tel: (44-1598) 753 227.

Type: Hotel inn with restaurant & bar.
Clientele: 70% gay & lesbian with a hetero following
Transportation: Car is best.
Rooms: 9 rooms with single or double beds.
Bathrooms: 9 private bath/toilets.

Meals: Full English breakfast.
Vegetarian: Available on request at pub.
Complimentary: Tea, coffee.
Dates Open: All year.
High Season: July-September.
Rates: £25 per person, per night.

Credit Cards: Visa, MC.
Rsv'tns: Required, but please ring for possible vacancies.
To Reserve: Call direct.
Parking: Ample off-street parking.
In-Room: Color TV, coffee/tea-making facilities, room service.

On-Premises: TV lounge.
Swimming: 2 miles to beaches.
Smoking: Permitted in rooms, but not in dining room.
Pets: Not permitted.
Handicap Access: No.
Children: No.

The Sunridge Hotel
Q-NET Gay-Owned & -Operated ♀♂

A Small Hotel of Unusual Charm

The Sunridge Hotel, an 1877 townhouse hotel, offers a warm welcome, friendly service and quiet informality. Tastefully furnished and modernised, it includes the essentials for a comfortable stay — ensuite bath or shower, colour television, clock radio, direct-dial telephone, hairdryer and tea- and coffee-making facilities. Dinner is served in our Orchid Restaurant. Elegant without being formal, traditional home-cooked dishes are prepared, using fresh local produce accompanied by fine wines and ports from our cellar. Shaftesbury, a thriving market town, has an extensive

continued next page

history dating to Saxon times, and its hilltop position affords magnificent views over Blackmore Vale. Notable local features include the Abbey Ruins and, particularly Golden Hill, famous for its steep cobbles and charming cottages. Within easy reach of the town are ancient historical sites, such as Stonehenge and Avebury, and the beautiful cathedrals of Salisbury and Wells.

Address: Bleke Street, Shaftesbury, Dorset SP7 8AW England.
Tel: (44-1747) 853 130, **Fax:** (44-1747) 852 139.

Type: Hotel with restaurant.
Clientele: Mostly hetero with a gay/lesbian following
Transportation: Car is best. Pick up from train about £10.
To Gay Bars: 30 miles to Bournemouth gay bars, a 1 hour drive.
Rooms: 9 rooms with single or double beds.

Bathrooms: All private.
Meals: Full breakfast.
Vegetarian: Available anytime.
Complimentary: Beverage trays in rooms.
Dates Open: Feb-Dec.
High Season: Jun-Sept.
Rates: Per person: low season £30-£35, high season £33-£38.

Discounts: 10% for 2 or more nights B&B.
Credit Cards: MC, Visa, Amex, Diners.
To Reserve: Travel agent or call direct.
Parking: Limited free parking.
In-Room: Telephone, color TV, coffee & tea-making facilities.

On-Premises: Bar.
Exercise/Health: Nearby sauna.
Swimming: Pool nearby.
Smoking: Permitted in bar. Non-smoking rooms available.
Pets: Not permitted.
Handicap Access: No.
Children: No.

The Edgecliffe Hotel

Gay-Owned ♀♂

Always a Warm Welcome

Minutes from the famous cliff top walk, the *Edgecliffe* is a charming and comfortable, well-run hotel with an enviable reputation for its first-class food and relaxed, friendly atmosphere. From the moment you enter, you know you are in a hotel that cares about its guests and as a result, a non-smoking regime has been adopted. The hotel is fully centrally heated and guests have their own bedroom and front door keys to allow complete freedom. Our tastefully decorated bedrooms are light, spacious and airy. Most are en-suite and each offers a full array of comforts including shaver socket, hair dryer, colour TV — and beautiful views. Enjoy a hearty breakfast to start the day or savour our expertly cooked five-course evening dinner. We offer a choice of menus to suit every palatte, including vegetarian. Sunny Shanklin is an ideal holiday destination with its picturesque old village, history, entertainment and easy access to wonderful walking country. We have maps and guidebooks, as well as walking itineraries for you. Our aim is to ensure that the *Edgecliffe Hotel* offers all that you seek to make your stay a memorable one.

Address: 7 Clarence Gardens, Shanklin, Isle of Wight PO3 6HA England.
Tel: (44-1983) 866 199 (Tel/Fax).

Type: Hotel with bar & small fitness room.
Clientele: Mostly hetero with 33% gay & lesbian clientele
Transportation: Ferries cross to the island from Portsmouth & Southampton, then train or bus to Shanklin.
To Gay Bars: No gay bars here.
Rooms: 10 rooms with single, queen or bunk beds.
Bathrooms: Private: 4 shower/toilets, 2 bath/toilet/

shower, 6 sinks only. Shared: 1 bath/shower/toilet, 2 WCs only.
Meals: Full breakfast, dinner.
Vegetarian: We offer a full vegetarian choice at breakfast & dinner.
Complimentary: Full range of beverages in rooms, with biscuits.
Dates Open: All year.
High Season: July-August.
Rates: Low £15.00-£19.00, mid £16.00-£22.00, high £18.50-£26.50.

Discounts: Group bookings 5%-10%.
Credit Cards: MC, Visa, Amex, Diners, Eurocard.
Rsv'tns: Required.
To Reserve: Travel agent or call direct.
Parking: Adequate on-street parking.
In-Room: Colour TV, coffee & tea-making facilities, maid service.
On-Premises: Video tape library, TV lounge.

Exercise/Health: Gym, weights. Nearby gym, weights, Jacuzzi, sauna, steam, massage.
Swimming: Nearby pool & ocean.
Sunbathing: On patio.
Smoking: We are a non-smoking establishment.
Pets: Not permitted.
Handicap Access: No.
Children: Welcome.
Languages: English, some French & German.
Your Host: Gary & John.

Ridge Cottage

Woman-Owned & -Operated ♀

"The Isle is Full of Noises, Sounds & Sweet Airs, That Give Delight & Hurt Not"

Our stone-built cottage on the edge of the village of Shorwell, in the beautiful southwest of the Isle of Wight, is surrounded by peaceful downland, 1-1/2 miles from the coast. A network of country lanes and footpaths over downland and along the coast make *Ridge Cottage* an ideal location for a walking or cycling holiday. We are also well situated for water or adventure sports — one of the highlights of the year is the Cowes Sailing Regatta. If, perhaps, you'd prefer a quiet place to read, think or be with a friend, we have a wide range of books and a pleasant garden which you are welcome to use. Sites of historical interest include manor houses, castles and old villages, and most nights of the week a variety of live music is performed at local pubs.

Address: Sandy Way, Shorwell, Isle of Wight PO30 3LN England.
Tel: (44-1983) 740 980.

Type: Bed & breakfast.
Clientele: Women only
Transportation: Car, train or ferry. Pick up from ferry dock £6.
To Gay Bars: 10 miles (1/2 hour drive) to lesbian bar, 1 hour (including ferry) to Southampton restaurants, bars, discos.
Rooms: 2 rooms with double beds.

Bathrooms: 1 private bath/shower/toilet, 1 shared bath/shower/toilet.
Meals: Full or continental breakfast. Supper on request.
Vegetarian: Always available if requested.
Complimentary: Tea & coffee in rooms.
Dates Open: All year.
High Season: Aug.
Rates: £18 all year.

To Reserve: Call direct.
Parking: Ample free on-street parking.
In-Room: Color TV, coffee & tea-making facilities.
On-Premises: Garden, dining room, sitting room with log fire.
Exercise/Health: Massage.
Swimming: Nearby pool, ocean. Many good beaches.

Sunbathing: At beach & in garden.
Nudity: Nudist beach nearby.
Smoking: Permitted downstairs. Non-smoking rooms available.
Pets: Not permitted.
Handicap Access: No.
Children: No.
Languages: English, Spanish, French.

Holly Park House

In the Heart of the English Lake District

Gay-Owned & -Operated ♀♂

Holly Park House, an elegant Lakeland stonebuilt house, has been tastefully modernised and furnished to a high standard, providing our guests with a comfortable base from which to explore England's beautiful Lake District countryside. Situated in a quiet area only a five-minute walk from the railway and bus station, it is an ideal starting point for tours to famous areas of natural beauty such as the Langdales, Tarn Hows, Grasmere or Hawkshead. Our guesthouse is just one mile from the bustling town of Bowness and Lake Windermere, itself.

Address: 1 Park Rd, Windermere, Cumbria LA23 2AW England.
Tel: (44-15394) 42107, **Fax:** (44-15394) 48997.

Type: Guesthouse with bar.
Clientele: Mostly hetero clientele with a gay/lesbian following
Transportation: Car or train. Free pick up from train or bus.
Rooms: 6 rooms with single or double beds.
Bathrooms: Private: 1 bath/shower/toilet, 5 shower/toilets.

Meals: Full breakfast.
Vegetarian: Available, if ordered.
Complimentary: Tea, coffee. Sweets in room.
Dates Open: All year.
High Season: Easter to end of Oct.
Rates: Summer £18-£30; winter £18-£28.
Credit Cards: MC, Visa, Amex, Diners.

Rsv'tns: Not always.
To Reserve: Call direct.
Parking: Adequate, free off-street parking.
In-Room: Color TV, coffee & tea-making facilities, maid service.
On-Premises: TV lounge.
Exercise/Health: Nearby walking, climbing, fishing, boating, golf.
Swimming: Nearby pool & lake.

Smoking: Permitted in some bedrooms & lounge. Non-smoking rooms available.
Pets: Permitted by arrangement.
Handicap Access: No.
Children: Not especially welcome, but we do sometimes have them.
Languages: English.
Your Host: Roger & James.

Bromptons Guesthouse

Q-NET Gay-Owned & -Operated ♂

Accommodations in the Centre of Gay London

Experience the ever-growing, lively, fun gay scene from *Bromptons Guesthouse*, in the heart of Earls Court gay village, London. Guests are within 250 yards walking distance of all Earls Court nightlife, restaurants, shopping, and close enough to experience London's history, theatre, and many galleries. Access to London's airports, all within easy reach, is made even more convenient with our airport pick-up and drop-off service.

Bromptons is personally run by owners Peter and Jeremy, and guesthouse manager, Patrick, who are pleased to offer expert advice on how to get the best out of your London vacation. The guesthouse's spacious, clean, well-decorated rooms all have a double bed (including singles), colour TV, direct-dial phones, coffee- and tea-making facilities, and iron/ironing boards. We provide up-to-date magazines and maps in each room for your personal use, which give all the latest information about what's happening on London's vibrant gay scene.

Our proximity to Earls Court underground station makes travelling within London extremely easy, and we are on a direct tube (subway) line with Heathrow Airport. For longer stays we offer a discount of one night per week, and we'll be pleased to quote for very long visits. Come to London at any time of the year — there is always plenty to do and see. We are busy throughout the year, and an early reservation is recommended.

Address: PO Box 629, London SW5 9XF England.
Tel: (44-171) 373 6559, **Fax:** (44-171) 370 3583.
E-mail: brompton@dircon.co.uk

Type: Guesthouse.
Clientele: Exclusively gay. Mostly men
Transportation: From Heathrow: tube to Earls Court. From Gatwick: Express train to Victoria, then tube to Earls Court.
To Gay Bars: 250 yards.
Rooms: 10 (for single or double occupancy).

Bathrooms: 5 private, others share.
Dates Open: All year.
Rates: Guesthouse: £45-£75.
Discounts: 10% for cash payment. Guesthouse: weekly rate, pay for 6 nights.
Credit Cards: MC, VISA, Amex.

Rsv'tns: Required.
To Reserve: Call direct.
Parking: Off-street parking (but not recommended in Central London).
In-Room: Daily maid service, TV, phones, coffee & tea-making facilities, irons & hairdryers.
Exercise/Health: Nearby gym.

Sunbathing: At Hyde Park.
Smoking: Permitted without restrictions.
Pets: Not permitted.
Handicap Access: No.
Children: Not permitted.
Languages: English & Hebrew.
Your Host: Peter, Jeremy & Patrick.

The New York Hotel

Gay/Lesbian ♂

The New York Hotel is London's newest and most luxurious gay hotel, situated in the heart of London's gay scene, ideally located for the many local gay bars, clubs, shops and activities in the Earl's Court area. The hotel offers a luxury lounge, beautiful private rear garden and licensed bar facilities. Guests have 24-hour access to our Jacuzzi and sauna. Our 14 spacious and well-decorated single, double, or twin rooms all have 24-hour room service, en suite bathrooms equipped with high-powered showers and hairdryers, colour TV, direct dial tele-

continued next page

phones, coffee-making facilities, trouser press and iron. If you are looking for a wonderful time in London, then *The New York Hotel* is for you!

Address: 32 Philbeach Gardens, Earls Court, London SW5 9EB England.
Tel: (44-171) 244 6884, **Fax:** (44-171) 370 4961.

Type: Hotel.
Clientele: 90% gay men & 10% women
Transportation: Tube or taxi.
To Gay Bars: 2 blocks or 3-5 min walk to several.
Rooms: 5 singles, 9 doubles.
Bathrooms: 13 private, 2 shared.
Meals: Expanded continental breakfast.

Complimentary: Tea & coffee in room.
Dates Open: All year, except 3 days during Christmas.
High Season: May-Dec.
Rates: £50-£90.
Credit Cards: MC, Visa, Amex, Access, Eurocard.
Rsv'tns: Required.
To Reserve: Call direct.
Minimum Stay: Required

on holiday weekends.
Parking: Paid parking up the street for £12 a day (24-hr access).
In-Room: Color cable TV with remote, telephone, maid & room service.
On-Premises: TV lounge.
Exercise/Health: Jacuzzi & sauna with shower area.
Swimming: At nearby pool.
Sunbathing: Hotel garden

or 1 hr on train to beach at Brighton.
Nudity: 1 hour to Brighton Beach.
Smoking: Permitted, non-smoking rooms available.
Pets: Not permitted.
Handicap Access: No.
Children: Not permitted.
Languages: English, Spanish, French, Welsh, German.

Number Seven Guesthouse

Q-NET Gay/Lesbian ♀♂

Voted Best UK Gay Hotel

A warm welcome awaits you at *Number Seven*, voted Best UK Gay Hotel, where we're setting the standard for others to follow. This elegant Victorian townhouse, with private parking, is situated in a quiet tree-lined avenue in Brixton, a "funky" cosmopolitan neighborhood, just south of the centre, buzzing with the vitality of 44 different cultures. Just a short walk from The Fridge (voted Best London Gay Club) and Sub-Station South, one of London's favourite gay dance clubs, we're within easy reach of a variety of gay bars and clubs. We have good connections with all London airports and rail termini, including EuroStar trains direct to Paris and Brussels.

The guesthouse is tastefully decorated with striking colours and antique pine furnishings and maintains many original features. All rooms have modern facilities, including private bathroom, direct-dial telephone, ceiling fan, colour TV, tea and coffee, hair dryer, central heating and fridge mini-bar. Our variety of rooms cater for most travellers, from the single person on a budget to our larger deluxe rooms for those who require something more special. The Honeymoon Suite with a queen-sized bed and large bathroom with corner-bath is very popular. Breakfast is served in the conservatory overlooking our enchanting private, walled garden;

with a background of classical music we offer freshly-pressed coffee and a selection of teas served in the pot, to accompany our expanded continental breakfast.

Your gay hosts, John and Paul, will provide you with good orientation and information on London's gay scene, theaters and major attractions. You will have your own keys so you can come and go as you please - check-in is by prior arrangement. Business or vacation, a warm welcome awaits you on your next visit to London. For up-to-date information, visit our website at http://www.no7.com.

Address: 7 Josephine Ave, London SW2 2JU England.
Tel: (44-181) 674 1880, **Fax:** (44-181) 671 6032.
E-mail: hotel@no7.com **URL:** http://www.no7.com

Type: Bed & breakfast guesthouse.
Clientele: Gay & lesbian. Good mix of men & women
Transportation: Main line train, tube, bus, car, or taxi from London airports, intercity train stns; pick ups cost petrol plus time.
To Gay Bars: 4 min walk or 4 min by tube to a variety of gay & lesbian bars & clubs.
Rooms: 8 rooms with single, twin, double, triple or queen beds.
Bathrooms: 4 en suite bath/shower/toilets & 4 en suite shower/toilets.

Meals: Full, buffet, continental or expanded continental breakfasts included in room rate.
Vegetarian: Vegetarian breakfast always available. Good local vegetarian restaurants.
Complimentary: Tea & coffee on arrival & in rooms.
Dates Open: All year.
Rates: £49-£99.
Credit Cards: MC, VISA.
Rsv'tns: Required. Preferred credit card booking.
To Reserve: Call direct.
Minimum Stay: 2 nights weekends & other holidays.
Parking: Ample easy off-street free parking in front of guesthouse.
In-Room: Clock/radio, remote CTV w/video & satellite link, direct-dial telephone, ceiling fans, tea/coffee-making facilities, Bahama fans, hair dryer, maid & laundry service. Iron & ironing board upon request.
On-Premises: Pay phone, dining room with maps & guides, conservatory, private walled garden, photo copier, fax machine, message service.
Exercise/Health: Weights, rowing machine, situp bench available upon request. Recreation centre & park nearby.
Swimming: 2 pools 1/2 mile away.
Sunbathing: In front & back gardens.
Smoking: Permitted without restrictions in bedrooms.
Pets: Not permitted.
Handicap Access: No. 3 steps to front door, no wide doorways.
Children: Not permitted.
Languages: English, British Sign Language.
Your Host: Paul & John.

IGLTA

Private London Accommodations Gay ♂

Stay in Central London at a Reasonable Price

Having started out as the host of a bed and breakfast in Manhattan (New York City), I know that potential guests appreciate getting a clear and honest description of the accommodations and of the surrounding neighborhood before they book. I know they appreciate dealing with a person who is not only interested in booking once, but looking down the road for repeat business.

Private London Accommodations offers a wide variety of bed and breakfast accommodations in central London at reasonable prices. We also have private studios and apartments for people who wish to be on their own. These unhosted fa-

continued next page

Stay in Central London at a Reasonable Price

cilities are available by the night, and some also by the month. Our clients are not only tourists, but corporations who are trying to cut down on their corporate travel expenses. Our hosts are Londoners who make their guest rooms or apartments available for paying guests. Our hosted accommodations include continental breakfast.

All accommodations are personally inspected. I turn down an average of seven out of ten inquiries to join our center, although many have been doing bed and breakfast for years. I prefer to turn down a property, rather than to place someone in an accommodation that is not satisfactory. Aside from finding the most appropriate accommodations for our guests, we try to enhance their stay in London by assisting in every way possible. We also offer accommodations in Paris, the Loire Valley, New York City and South Beach, Miami.

Photo courtesy of the British Tourist Authority

Type: Bed & breakfast & apartments.
Clientele: Gay
Transportation: Taxi is best.
Bathrooms: Most are private, but some are shared.
Meals: Continental breakfast at hosted accommodations.
Complimentary: Tea & coffee.
Dates Open: All year.

Address: Contact: NY B&B Reservation Center, in New York, USA.
Tel: (212) 977-3512.
Rates: Inquire.
Rsv'tns: Required.
To Reserve: Call direct.
Minimum Stay: 2 days.
In-Room: Color TV, telephone, kitchen & refrigerator in hosted facilities.
Smoking: By request.
Children: Permitted.
Languages: English, Spanish & French.

Soho Guestrooms

Q-NET Gay-Owned & -Operated ♀♂

Deluxe Guestrooms, Suite & Apartment in the Heart of the West End

Your host, James, welcomes you to an extraordinary stay at two premier apartments, uniquely located in the very heart of London, next to the city's most infamous landmark — the enormous Centrepoint tower building. Situated at the junctions of Oxford Street, Charing Cross Road, Tottenham Court Road and New Oxford Street, the apartments overlook Soho and Covent Garden, offer-

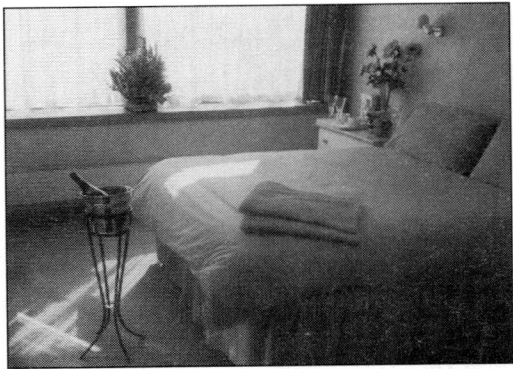

FERRARI GUIDES™

ing wonderful panoramic views of the capital, including the Post Office Tower. *Soho Guestrooms'* ideal location places you within walking distance of everything from cafes, bars and nightclubs to museums, art galleries and restaurants. Numerous tourist attractions, royal palaces and parks, famous landmarks, exclusive shopping areas, the red-light district and the excitement of the West End's theatreland are also just a walk away. And if you want to stay in shape while on holiday, there are gyms, saunas, leisure facilities and indoor and outdoor public swimming pools a quick one-minute walk from us. Our central location offers you the opportunity to travel in any direction without having to go too far to travel back "home." You will find that our prices are amazingly reasonable when compared to central hotels of a similar standard. In fact, many guests tell us that our facilities are superior!

Accommodations at *Soho Guestrooms* are bright, spacious and inviting with modern decor and quality furnishings. You have your choice of staying in a double guestroom, or having a one-bedroom suite or two-bedroom apartment with a kitchen, lounge and spacious balcony. The apartment also features a giant 33-inch surround-sound TV and VCR, plus a room that functions as a swish meeting room, dining room and additional bedroom with two pull-out futon sleepers. Check-in is from 2 p.m. and check-out time is 11 a.m., though special arrangements can be made, if necessary. If you plan to arrive earlier, we can store your luggage safely until your room is ready. A personal visit beats any description, so for your next trip to London, be sure to come to the most central apartments and have a simply wonderful stay!

Tel: Reservations: (44-973) 167 103. Ansaphone/Fax: (44-171) 497 7010.

Type: Guesthouse & apartment.
Clientele: Mostly gay & lesbian with some hetero clientele
Transportation: Tottenham Court Road nearest tube station.
To Gay Bars: Right outside.
Rooms: 3 double rooms, 1 double-BR suite (can sleep 2 extra on futons), 1 2-bed apartment.
Bathrooms: Private & shared, good-sized baths with modern powershowers.
Meals: Free daily provisions for self-serve breakfast, cereals, toast, spreads, etc.
Complimentary: Wine or champagne on arrival, fruit basket in room, chocolates on pillow, 24-hr tea, coffee & soft drinks. Laundry facilities, maps, local magazines & newspapers.
Dates Open: All year.
High Season: All year.
Rates: Single or double occupancy: rooms £79, suite £149/night. Apartment: please inquire.
Discounts: Call for special offers.
Credit Cards: MC, Visa.
Rsv'tns: Recommended 1 month ahead for weekly & weekend stays. Deposits or full payment required.
To Reserve: Call direct.
Minimum Stay: Required at times, inquire (2 nights weekends, 3 nights holiday weekends).
Parking: Free street parking behind bldg 20:30-08:00 or use meters. Nearest NCP: Museum St, off Drury Ln.
In-Room: Colour TV, alarm-clock radio, oversized towels, mirrored wardrobe, safe-cabinet. Suite has lounge/dining room, balcony & kitchen with fridge, dishwasher, microwave, utensils. Own keys.
On-Premises: Phone, fax, business services, grocery & drinks shopping service, 2 lifts, free laundry facilities, steam iron/board, hairdryer.
Exercise/Health: 1 min to gym & saunas.
Swimming: 1 min to indoor & outdoor public pools.
Sunbathing: At public pool or on balcony with suite rental.
Smoking: Not permitted on premises.
Pets: Not permitted.
Handicap Access: No.
Children: By prior arrangement.
Languages: English.
Your Host: James.

INN PLACES® 1998 119

Carlton Hotel
Gay/Lesbian ♀♂

The *Carlton Hotel* is situated in a residential area of Victorian homes, many of which have been converted into apartments. The hotel, comprised of two early 18th-century Victorian houses, features a bar/TV lounge and a function room. A bus stop across the road provides easy access to the city center, 1-1/2 miles away. Our full English breakfast offers a choice of thirteen cereals, seven jams (including rhubarb, gooseberry, ginger jam and lime and lemon curd), all homemade, as well as fresh fruit, whole grain toast, sausage, bacon, mushrooms, beans, tomatos and eggs. Vegetarian breakfast is always available and includes Linda McCartney's vegetarian sausage.

Address: 153 Upper Chorlton Rd, Whalley Range,
Manchester M16 7SH England.
Tel: (44-161) 881 4635.

Type: Hotel located above gay men's sauna (separate entrance).
Clientele: Good mix of gay men & women.
To Gay Bars: 1-1/2 miles to gay bars.
Rooms: 15 rooms with single, double or queen beds.
Bathrooms: 4 private bath/ shower/toilets, others share.
Meals: Breakfast.
Complimentary: Tea & coffee in rooms.
Dates Open: All year.
Rates: £25 single, £35 twin or double, £40 twin or double ensuite.
Discounts: On long stays.
Credit Cards: MC, Visa.
Rsv'tns: Recommended.
To Reserve: Call direct.
Parking: Ample off-street parking.
In-Room: Color TV, coffee & tea-making facilities, maid service.
On-Premises: TV lounge/ bar for clients.
Exercise/Health: Weights,
Jacuzzi, sauna & steam at men-only Stallion sauna complex downstairs.
Smoking: Permitted.
Pets: Permitted.
Handicap Access: No.
Children: No.
Languages: English, Spanish.
Your Host: David & Chris.

Cheviot View Guest House
Gay/Lesbian ♀♂

Anywhere Else is a Compromise

One of England's most highly recommended gay guesthouses, *Cheviot View Guest House* offers exceptional standards of service and comfort. Indulge yourself in luxury! Linden, of *APN Magazine* called it "...the best gay guest house I've ever stayed in..." *Northern Scene* called it "One of the best gay hotels in England." Here, you can enjoy Newcastle's sparkling and exciting nightlife, explore the coast and the magnificence of Northumbria. Our brochure gives details of champagne weekends, mini-breaks and day trips in our chauffeur-driven Daimler Sovereign. Member of the British Hospitality Association.

Address: 194 Station Rd, Wallsend, Newcastle NE28 8RD England.
Tel: (44-191) 262 0125, **mobile:** (0378) 863 469,
Fax: (44-191) 262 2626.

Type: Guesthouse with residents' cocktail bar.
Clientele: Gay men & women, about 50/50
Transportation: Metro from city centre (10 minutes) is best.
To Gay Bars: 10 minutes by car or metro.
Rooms: 5 rooms with single, double or king beds.
Bathrooms: Private: 1 bath/toilet, 1 shower/toilet.
Shared: 1 bath/shower/toilet.
Meals: Full English breakfast.
Vegetarian: Available at breakfast.
Complimentary: Tea, coffee, biscuits & orange juice in rooms, mnts on pillows. Free entry to all gay clubs.
Dates Open: All year.
Rates: £18.00-£50.00.
Discounts: For stays of 5 nights or more.
Credit Cards: All major credit & debit cards & Amex.
Rsv'tns: Recommended.
To Reserve: Call direct.
Parking: Ample free off-street parking.
In-Room: Exceptional standards of service & comfort. Color TV, telephone, hair dryer, razor points, radio/ alarm clock, coffee/tea-making facilities, room service.
On-Premises: Drawing room & Empire Lounge, laundry facilities.
Swimming: Nearby pool & ocean beach.
Sunbathing: At the beach.
Smoking: Permitted in cocktail bar. Drawing room & all bedrooms are non-smoking.
Pets: Small dogs permitted.
Handicap Access: Yes. Please check for full details.
Children: Permitted.
Languages: English & French.
Your Host: Colin & Scott.

Stratford Lodge

Gay/Lesbian ♀♂

Quality Accommodation & Friendly Atmosphere, Exclusively for Gay & Lesbian Guests

Situated in a tree-lined crescent, **Stratford Lodge** is a mid-Victorian property only minutes from the amenities of the city centre. Throughout its refurbishment, every effort has been made to retain its original features and character and to present them in a tasteful and comfortable light. We provide quality accommodations, contemporary and antique furnishings, easy parking and a friendly atmosphere exclusively for gay and lesbian guests. Our double and king rooms are of comfortable proportions. All rooms have colour satellite TV, and a tea and coffee tray. Continental breakfast is served in your room. New to our B&B is a French-style room with canopy, a master bedroom with a king-sized four-poster bed and a Victorian-style room with brass bed, open fireplace and Victorian antique furnishings. Our 300-ft gardens running down to Jesmond Vale are a combination of terraced patios, meadow with pond and woodland.

Address: 8 Stratford Grove Terrace, Heaton, Newcastle upon Tyne NE6 5BA England.
Tel: (44-191) 265 6395, **mobile:** (44-831) 879182.

Type: Bed & breakfast.
Clientele: Gay & lesbian. Good mix of men & women
Transportation: Metro from airport, then taxi, or taxi from British Rail Station.
To Gay Bars: 1 mile or a 20-minute walk or 5-minute drive.
Rooms: 6 rooms with single, double or king bed.
Bathrooms: 1 bathroom per floor.
Meals: Expanded continental breakfast.
Vegetarian: Vegetarian continental breakfast available. Vegetarian restaurants in city.
Complimentary: Tea & coffee tray in each room. Free entry into local gay clubs, discount at gay sauna.
Dates Open: All year.
Rates: £19.00-£48.00.
Discounts: Special business rates available & student discounts.
Credit Cards: Visa, MC, Switch.
Rsv'tns: Required.
To Reserve: Call direct.
Parking: Ample on-street parking.
In-Room: Color satellite TV, tea/coffee making facilities & laundry service.
On-Premises: TV lounge with satellite TV.
Exercise/Health: Traditional Swedish massage, aromatherapy massage & sauna on premises. Nearby gym, weights, Jacuzzi & steam. Discount to new gay sauna.
Swimming: 1/4 mile to pool, 3 miles to ocean.
Sunbathing: On patio & beach.
Nudity: Permitted in sauna.
Smoking: Permitted except for sauna area.
Pets: Not permitted.
Handicap Access: No.
Children: Not especially welcome.
Languages: English, Cantonese, Mandarin, some French.
Your Host: David.

Briars

Gay/Lesbian ♀♂

Situated by the River Yare in the village of Reedham, **Briars** is in the heart of the Norfolk Broads area of England. We are midway between the fine city of Norwich and the seaside town of Great Yarmouth, and about six miles south of the market town of Acle. Overlooking the river and marshes, our first-floor conservatory and balcony offer superb sweeping views. We have three clean double rooms, each tastefully furnished in a traditional cottage style. The tea shop on our ground floor serves light meals — and our superb cream teas are reputed to be the best north of Devonshire!

Address: Riverside, Reedham, Norwich NR13 3TF England.
Tel: (44-1493) 700054 (Tel/Fax).

Type: Guesthouse with restaurant & hairdresser.
Clientele: Mostly gay & lesbian with some hetero clientele
Transportation: Car is best. Free pick up from Reedham train stn. Pick up from Norwich airport, £15.
To Gay Bars: 12 miles, a 15 min drive.
Rooms: 3 rooms with double beds.
Bathrooms: Private: 2 shower/toilets, 1 bath/toilet/shower.
Meals: Full breakfast.
Vegetarian: Vegetarian breakfast always available.

continued next page

Walking distance to vegetarian lunch & dinner.
Complimentary: Coffee, tea, biscuits, sweets on pillow.
Dates Open: All year.
High Season: May-Sept.
Rates: £45 all year, double room.

Credit Cards: MC, Eurocard, Visa.
Rsv'tns: Required.
To Reserve: Call direct.
Parking: Ample, free off-street parking.
In-Room: Colour TV, VCR, coffee & tea-making facilities.

On-Premises: TV lounge, video tape library.
Sunbathing: On patio & on common sun decks.
Smoking: No smoking in eating area.
Pets: Small pets permitted by arrangement.

Handicap Access: 1st floor rooms with stair access only, help will be given to handicapped persons.
Children: No.
Languages: English.
Your Host: Alan & Alan.

Warham Old Post Office Cottage Gay-Owned ♀♂

Bed & Breakfast Tranquility in North Norfolk

Warham Old Post Office Cottage offers a perfect setting for a quiet break in the country. It has many exposed beams and other period features, as well as home comforts. All rooms have wash basins, wardrobes, and tea/coffee making facilities. The common lounge has an inglenook fireplace, comfortable seating, and a colour TV. The village pub, Three Horseshoes, is adjacent to the cottage. Home cooking is the speciality for lunches and evening meals. Beaches and many attractions are nearby.

Address: c/o Three Horseshoes Free House,
In Warham near Wells-next-the-Sea NR23 1NL England.
Tel: (44-1328) 710 547.

Type: Bed & breakfast inn with restaurant & bar.
Clientele: Mainly straight with 20% gay & lesbian clientele
Transportation: Car is best.
To Gay Bars: In Norwich, 1 hr by car.
Rooms: 2 singles, 3 doubles.
Bathrooms: 1 ensuite, others share.

Meals: Full English breakfast.
Vegetarian: Available at all times.
Complimentary: Tea & coffee in rooms.
Dates Open: All year.
High Season: Easter-September.
Rates: £22.00 per person, per night.
Discounts: Inquire.

Rsv'tns: Not always required.
To Reserve: Call direct.
Parking: Ample free off-street parking.
In-Room: Tea & coffee-making facilities, maid & laundry service.
On-Premises: TV lounge, meeting rooms.
Swimming: 1 mile to ocean beach.

Sunbathing: At nearby ocean beach.
Nudity: Nude beach 1 mile.
Smoking: Permitted in public rooms only, all bedrooms are non-smoking.
Pets: Permitted by prior arrangement.
Handicap Access: No.
Children: Not permitted.
Languages: English.
Your Host: Ian & Mac.

Bathley Guest House Gay/Lesbian ♂

Bathley Guest House is an exclusively gay bed & breakfast two minutes from the city's gay life. Conveniences include late keys and no restrictions, tea making facilities in all rooms, weekly rates on request. Concessions for admission to gay bars and sauna are available to our guests. Special midweek breaks are also available and women are welcome. Just 10 minutes' walk from our house is the Nottingham Castle, where the sheriff of Nottingham lived. Sherwood Forest is only 20 minutes by car. There, you can view the Major Oak, Robin Hood's hiding place. In Nottingham is Britain's oldest inn, Trip to Jerusalem, built in 1650.

Address: 101 Bathley St, Trent Bridge, Nottingham NG2 2EE England.
Tel: (44-115) 9862 463.

Type: B & B guesthouse with bar for residents.
Clientele: Mostly men with women welcome
To Gay Bars: 2 minutes

from gay bars.
Rooms: 8 rooms with single & double beds.
Bathrooms: 2 shared.

Meals: Full English breakfast.
Complimentary: Concessions to local gay clubs & gay & lesbian sauna.

Dates Open: All year.
Rates: Single £18.00, double £32.00, twin rooms £30.00.

FERRARI GUIDES™

Discounts: Special midweek rates.
To Reserve: Travel agent or call direct.
Parking: Ample free on-street parking.
In-Room: Tea/coffee making facilities.
On-Premises: TV lounge.
Smoking: Permitted only in lounge.
Pets: Welcome.
Handicap Access: No.
Children: Gay parents with children welcome.
Languages: English.
Your Host: Keith & Jeff.

Bales Mead
Gay-Friendly 50/50 ♀♂

The Ritz in Miniature

Bales Mead is a small, elegant Edwardian country house, offering superb, luxurious accommodation in an outstanding setting. The peaceful location has magnificent panoramic views of both the sea and the rolling countryside of Exmoor. All three double bedrooms are exquisitely furnished, offering every modern comfort and facility. Breakfast is served in the elegant dining room or *al fresco* in the summer, weather permitting. *Bales Mead* provides an excellent base for walking or touring Exmoor and the North Devon Coast.

Address: West Porlock, Somerset TA24 8NX England.
Tel: (44-1643) 862565.

Type: Country house bed & breakfast.
Clientele: 50% gay & lesbian & 50% hetero clientele
Transportation: Car is best, train from London to Taunton then bus to Porlock is possible.
To Gay Bars: 1-1/2 hours.
Rooms: 3 doubles.
Bathrooms: 2 private baths, others share.

Meals: Expanded continental or full English breakfast.
Vegetarian: Always available.
Complimentary: Tea, coffee & hot chocolate making facilities, mineral water, mints & toffees.
Dates Open: All year except Xmas & New Years.
High Season: May-Oct.
Rates: From £26.00.
Rsv'tns: Recommended.

To Reserve: Call direct.
Parking: Parking available for 6 cars in private drive in front of house.
In-Room: Color TV, radio alarm clocks, hairdryers, & tea & coffee makers.
On-Premises: Central heating & log fire in winter. Lounge & dining room for breakfast. Private gardens available for sitting & relaxing.

Swimming: Nearby pool & ocean beach.
Sunbathing: At the beach.
Smoking: Not permitted.
Pets: Not permitted.
Handicap Access: No.
Children: Not permitted.
Languages: English, French, Spanish, & German.
Your Host: Stephen & Peter.

Cliff House Hotel at the Beach
Q-NET Gay/Lesbian ♀♂

England's First and Foremost Gay Hotel

Originally a millionaire's home, *Cliff House,* celebrating its 25th year, is an exclusive, luxury hotel with a secluded garden at sea's edge. Here one can view the sea from the terrace that fronts the comfortable bar lounge. This gracious house has the elegance of a bygone age with the advantages of modern amenities. All bedrooms have a bathroom en suite. Full central heating warms us in cooler months, which are so delightful in this beautiful part of the country. There are ample parking facilities. Old friends meet, and newfound friends are made, and no one ever wants to leave. A visit to England is not the same unless you visit *Cliff House.*

Address: St. Marks Rd, Meadfoot Beach, Torquay TQ1 2EH England.
Tel: (44-1803) 294 656, Fax: (44-1803) 211 983.

Type: Hotel with restaurant & bar.
Clientele: Good mix of gay men & women
Transportation: Train or bus from London. Pick up from train.

To Gay Bars: A 5-minute walk or 2-minute drive.
Rooms: 16 rooms with single or double beds.
Bathrooms: All private bath/toilets.
Meals: Full Eng. breakfast.

Vegetarian: With prior arrangement.
Complimentary: Tea & coffee in room.
Dates Open: All year.
High Season: Easter, June-Oct and Christmas.

Rates: £21-£26. Accounts subject to V.A.T.
Discounts: Party discounts.
Credit Cards: MC, VISA, Access & Switch.

continued next page

INN PLACES® 1998   123

Rsv'tns: Required during high season.
To Reserve: Call direct.
Parking: Ample on- and off-street parking.
In-Room: Color TV, coffee & tea-making facilities & room service.
On-Premises: TV lounge, bar & public telephone.
Exercise/Health: Steam room, Jacuzzi, massage and gym.
Swimming: Ocean beach.
Sunbathing: On the beach, sun deck or in the secluded garden.
Nudity: Permitted in the secluded garden.
Smoking: Permitted without restrictions.
Pets: Dogs are permitted, but not in public rooms.
Handicap Access: Yes, 2 rooms.
Children: Not permitted.
Languages: English.
Your Host: Alan & Robbie.

Ravenswood Hotel

Gay-Owned ♀♂

Ravenswood is a friendly hotel overlooking Torwood Gardens. Bedrooms are attractive, well-appointed and equipped with hot and cold water, shaver points, colour TV and tea-making facilities. Some have private bathroom or shower. Rates include breakfast, and the licensed restaurant is available for lunch and dinner. Free parking is nearby. We're 350 yards from the harbour, main shopping centre and entertainment. A pleasant walk takes you to popular beaches.

Address: 535 Babbacombe Rd, Torquay, South Devon TQ1 1HQ England.
Tel: (44-1803) 292 900 (Tel/Fax).

Type: Hotel with residents' bar & public restaurant.
Clientele: Mostly hetero clientele with a 20% gay/lesbian following
To Gay Bars: 4-min. walk to gay/lesbian bars.
Rooms: 12 doubles.
Bathrooms: 9 private, others share.
Meals: Full English breakfast. Dinner optional.
Vegetarian: Available upon request that morning.
Complimentary: Tea & coffee in rooms.
Dates Open: All year.
High Season: Summer.
Rates: £15.00-£21.00 per person.
Credit Cards: MC, Visa, Access, Eurocard, Diners.
Rsv'tns: Required.
To Reserve: Call direct.
Parking: Free car park.
In-Room: Maid service, colour cable TV, telephone, wash basin, tea & coffee makers, & late-night keys.
On-Premises: TV lounge with video & tape library.
Swimming: 5-minute walk to ocean beach. 20-minute walk to nude beach.
Sunbathing: On beach.
Smoking: Permitted without restrictions.
Pets: Permitted if well supervised.
Handicap Access: No.
Children: Permitted.
Languages: English, Deaf Sign Language.

Red Squirrel Lodge

Gay-Owned ♀♂

The English Tourist Board Rated Us Three Crowns!

A superb Victorian villa, **Red Squirrel Lodge** is in a quiet, peaceful area surrounded by spacious gardens. We are located near shops, buses and railway station, yet are only 200 yards from Torquay's finest beach. It is most beautifully furnished and has been established as a distinctive hotel for many years. You will be welcomed by resident proprietors John and David. A courtesy car from the bus and railway station is available.

Address: Chelston Rd, Torquay TQ2 6PU England.
Tel: (44-1803) 605 496, **Fax:** (44-1803) 690 170.
E-mail: squirrel@mail.zynet.co.uk

Type: Hotel with bar for residents.
Clientele: Mainly hetero clientele with a 20% gay & lesbian following
Transportation: Car is best, or train from London Paddington Stn. Free pick up from bus or train.
To Gay Bars: 5 minutes by car.
Rooms: 14 rooms with single, double & queen beds.
Bathrooms: All private.
Meals: Full English breakfast. Optional dinner extra charge.
Vegetarian: Available with 24 hour notice.
Complimentary: Tea & coffee-making facilities in rooms. Tea, coffee, & soft drink upon arrival.
Dates Open: All year.
Rates: £20.00 per person low season, £30.00 per person high season.
Discounts: For 2 or more nights in low season.
Credit Cards: MC, Visa, Amex.
Rsv'tns: Required with deposit.
To Reserve: UK travel agent or call direct.
Minimum Stay: 3 nights high season (July-Aug).
Parking: Space for 10 cars & easy on-street parking.
In-Room: Color TV, coffee & tea-making facilities, hair dryers, shoe cleaners, maid service.

On-Premises: TV lounge, pay phone, & separate bar for residents & friends.
Exercise/Health: Sport & leisure center with gym, sauna & Jacuzzi nearby.

Swimming: At nearby pool, ocean 250 yards, easy walk to 7 or 8 beaches.
Sunbathing: In extensive gardens.

Nudity: Permitted on nude beach 3 miles away.
Smoking: Permitted except in dining room.
Pets: Permitted except in dining room, bar & lounge.

Handicap Access: Yes. 3 ground floor rooms, 1 single is adapted.
Children: Not permitted.
Languages: English.
Your Host: John & David.

Ellesmere House
Gay/Lesbian ♂

A Friendly Welcome to the Heart of England

Ellesmere House is an elegant, early Victorian town residence with spacious rooms furnished in antiques. It has been modernized to a high standard of comfortable accommodation and is situated in a quiet, tree-lined avenue within walking distance of all the facilities of this attractive regency town. Shakespeare's Stratford, The Castles at Warwick and Kenilworth are all within easy reach.

Address: 36 Binswood Ave, Royal Leamington Spa, Warwickshire CV32 5SQ England.
Tel: (44-1926) 424 618.

Type: Bed & breakfast homestay.
Clientele: Mostly men with women welcome
Transportation: Own vehicle is best, but train, bus OK.
To Gay Bars: Warwick gay bar 3 miles, Leamington club 1/4 mile.
Rooms: 3 rooms with single or double beds.
Bathrooms: 2 private bath/toilets & 1 private shower/toilet.
Meals: Full English breakfast.

Dates Open: All year.
Rates: £28.00-£40.00.
Rsv'tns: Required.
To Reserve: Call direct.
Parking: Adequate, free on-street parking.
In-Room: Color TV.
Sunbathing: In garden.
Smoking: Not encouraged.

Pets: Not permitted.
Handicap Access: No.
Children: Not permitted.
Languages: English, Spanish, limited French, Italian.
Your Host: Francisco & Colin.

Bull Lodge
Gay-Friendly ♀♂

"The History of York is the History of England"

Bull Lodge is a modern, detached residence on a quiet side street, three quarters of a mile from the city centre and close to the University and Barbican Leisure Centre. We're on a bus route and have private, enclosed parking. Single, twin, or double bedrooms are available. Twins and doubles can be with or without private shower and toilet. All rooms have tea & coffee facilities, colour TV, clock-radio, and direct-dial telephones. A full-choice English breakfast is served, evening meals can be ordered, and snacks and drinks are available.

York can be busy all year, so booking ahead is always a good idea. In the winter, weekends are usually busy, and June through October is busy almost every day. Allow at least two days to enjoy this beautiful city and its many sights and attractions. York is also an excellent base to explore the surrounding countryside, the moors and the dales, to visit Castle Howard of "Brideshead Revisited" fame, or nearby Bronte country. If you're touring the U.K., relax for a few days here, between the busy cities of Edinburgh and London.

Address: 37 Bull Lane, Lawrence St, York YO1 3EN England.
Tel: (44-1904) 415522 (Tel/Fax).

Type: Guesthouse.
Clientele: Mostly straight clientele with a gay/lesbian following
Transportation: Convenient direct bus from train/bus stations. Pick up by prior arrangement if minimum 2 night advance booking.
To Gay Bars: 1 mile.
Rooms: 1 single, 6 doubles, 1 twin.
Bathrooms: 3 private, 2 shared. Ground floor with private suitable for disabled.
Meals: Full English breakfast. Evening meal additional charge (low season only).
Complimentary: Tea & coffee.

continued next page

Dates Open: End January to mid-December.
High Season: June thru October.
Rates: 1998: summer £17-£21; winter £15-£18.
Discounts: £1 per person per night for more than 4 nights. Off-season breaks.
Rsv'tns: Recommended for weekends & summer period.
To Reserve: Travel agent or call direct.
Parking: Private enclosed parking. Garage for motorbikes & bicycles.
In-Room: Color TV, tea/coffee makers, radio alarm clocks, hot & cold water, maid service, telephone.
On-Premises: Non-smoking TV lounge with books & games.
Swimming: 10-minute walk to Barbican pool & leisure centre.
Smoking: Permitted except in lounge & dining room.
Pets: Permitted.
Handicap Access: Yes, ground floor en suite double room.
Children: Permitted, minimum age 3 years.
Languages: English.
Your Host: Roy & Dennis.

Interludes

Gay-Friendly 50/50 ♀♂

Little "Scene," But Great Scenery

Interludes is an elegant Georgian townhouse with sea views, peacefully situated in a conservation area, yet close to beach, town centre, theatres, castle, etc. The hotel is licensed, and, because of our connections with the Stephen Joseph Theatre (artistic director Alan Ayckbourn), has a theatrical theme. The bedrooms are well equipped. *Interludes* is informal, friendly and most relaxing. Scarborough is an attractive resort, and is an ideal centre for exploring the nearby North Yorkshire Moors National Park and the historical towns of York and Whitby.

Address: 32 Princess St, Old Town, Scarborough, North Yorkshire Y011 1QR England.
Tel: (44-1723) 360 513, **Fax:** (44-1723) 368 597.

Type: Hotel.
Clientele: 50% gay & lesbian & 50% hetero clientele
Transportation: Car, bus or train (rail link to Manchester Airport).
Rooms: 5 rooms with twin, king & four poster beds.
Bathrooms: 4 en suite, 1 with sink & adjacent shower & toilet.
Meals: Full breakfast. 4 course dinner available at additional cost.
Vegetarian: Available with prior notification.
Complimentary: Tea, coffee, chocolate, juice, etc.
Dates Open: All year.
High Season: July-September.
Rates: £46 standard, £52 superior per double room.
Discounts: Single occupancy, 5%-15% groups of 7 or more, special pckg with Stephen Joseph Theatre. 12-1/2% for 7 or more days, 5% 4-6 days.
Credit Cards: MC, Visa.
Rsv'tns: Wise to confirm availability.
To Reserve: Call direct.
Minimum Stay: Required public holiday weekends.
Parking: Adequate free on-street parking, limited during high season.
In-Room: Color TV, coffee & tea-making facilities & maid service.
On-Premises: Laundry facilities.
Swimming: Nearby pool & ocean beach.
Sunbathing: On the patio, at the beach.
Nudity: 20 miles to unofficial public nude beach.
Smoking: Permitted in lounge & outside. All bedrooms are non-smoking.
Pets: Not permitted.
Handicap Access: No.
Children: Not permitted.
Languages: English.
Your Host: Bob & Ian.

Auchendean Lodge Hotel

Gay-Friendly ♀♂

We are more a home than a hotel. So, come and relax in the Scottish Highlands in our Edwardian hunting lodge. *Auchendean Lodge Hotel* is an elegant, comfortable country hotel furnished with antiques and fine paintings. When you stay here, plan on enjoying interesting, award-winning food, good wines and malt whiskies, spectacular views of Spey and the Cairngorm Mountains, walking, fishing, golfing and skiing. Our hotel is set in a magnificent garden on the edge of 200 acres of mature forest. Call Ian or Eric for a brochure. Although our clientele is not exclusively gay, you will be warmly welcomed.

Reader's Comment: "The Scottish dinners were superb. The hosts were very friendly and welcomed us warmly. The other guests, while not gay, were friendly and very nice. I would recommend this hotel without reservation, but plan on TWO nights. One night will make you want another." — *Richard H., St. Louis, MO*

Address: Dulnain Bridge near Grantown-on-Spey, Inverness-Shire PH26 3LU Scotland.
Tel: (44-1479) 851 347 (Tel/Fax).

Type: Inn with restaurant.
Clientele: Mostly hetero with a gay & lesbian following
Transportation: Car is best.
To Gay Bars: 2 hrs by car.
Rooms: 8 rooms with single, double or queen beds.
Bathrooms: Private: 5 bath/- or shower/toilets, 3 sinks. Shared: 1 shower & 2 WC.
Meals: Full breakfast with dinner optional at £25 (book in advance).
Vegetarian: Available with advance notice.
Complimentary: Tea, coffee, biscuits.
Dates Open: All year.
High Season: Easter thru early October, Xmas & New Year.
Rates: B&B, summer £23.00-£49.00, winter £17.50-£36.00; B&B + dinner, add £24.00.
Discounts: 10% for 3 days or more on dinner, bed & breakfast rates.
Credit Cards: MC, Visa, Amex, Diners. Commission charged.
Rsv'tns: Recommended.
To Reserve: Call direct.
Parking: Ample free off-street parking.
In-Room: Color TV, coffee & tea-making facilities, room & laundry service.
Exercise/Health: Walking, fishing, golfing, skiing, jogging (with Ian).
Swimming: Nearby pool, river, lake.
Sunbathing: In adjacent woods.
Nudity: Permitted in adjacent woods.
Smoking: Permitted in bedrooms & 1 lounge.
Pets: Permitted. Large gardens & woods attached to premises.
Handicap Access: Yes, restaurant. Flight of steps to bedrooms.
Children: Permitted.
Languages: English, French.
Your Host: Ian & Eric.

The Amaryllis Guest House

Gay/Lesbian ♀♂

Lesbian-owned and -run, *The Amaryllis Guest House* is a newly refurbished Georgian Town House, centrally located and within walking distance of the city centre. Late breakfast is available for those who enjoy Edinburgh's great gay nightlife.

Address: 21 Upper Gilmore Place, Edinburgh EH3 9NL Scotland.
Tel: (44-131) 229 3293 (Tel/Fax).

continued next page

EUROPE

Type: Guesthouse.
Clientele: Mainly gay & lesbian with some hetero clientele
To Gay Bars: 10 minutes by taxi or bus.
Rooms: 1 double, 1 twin, 3 family, 2 en-suite.

Bathrooms: 2 shared baths.
Meals: Full breakfast. Early or late trays are always available.
Vegetarian: Available on request.
Complimentary: Tea & coffee.

Dates Open: All year.
High Season: June-October.
Rates: £15-£28 per person.
Credit Cards: Visa, Access, MC.
To Reserve: Call direct.
Parking: Adequate on-steet parking at night. Limited on-

street parking by day. Some private parking.
In-Room: TV, coffee & tea-making facilities.
Smoking: Permitted in all rooms.
Pets: Not permitted.
Children: Permitted.
Languages: English.

Aries Guest House

Q-NET Gay/Lesbian ♀♂

Capital Accommodation, Superb Value

A friendly Scottish welcome is assured to all guests who stay at the *Aries Guest House*. Lesbian-run and -owned, the guesthouse is centrally located in Edinburgh, within minutes of Princes Street, the castle, Old Town, theatres, shops, cinemas, clubs and gay nightlife.

Address: 5 Upper Gilmore Place, Edinburgh EH3 9NW Scotland.
Tel: (44-131) 229 4669.

Type: Bed & breakfast guesthouse.
Clientele: Mostly gay & lesbian with some hetero clientele
Transportation: Taxi, bus or car.
To Gay Bars: 15-minute walk, 5-minute drive.
Rooms: 5 rooms with single, double or king beds.
Bathrooms: Private &

shared.
Meals: Full Scottish breakfast, early/late trays available on request.
Vegetarian: Available on request.
Complimentary: Tea & coffee.
Dates Open: All year.
High Season: June-Oct.
Rates: £13-£22.
Discounts: Child discounts 30%.

Credit Cards: Yes.
Rsv'tns: Required.
To Reserve: Call direct.
Parking: Adequate on-street parking at night. Limited pay parking during day.
In-Room: Color TV, coffee/tea-making facilities, maid service.
On-Premises: TV lounge.
Exercise/Health: Nearby

gym, weights, Jacuzzi, sauna, massage.
Swimming: Pool nearby.
Sunbathing: In city parks.
Smoking: Permitted in all rooms.
Pets: Permitted.
Handicap Access: Ground-floor rooms accessible.
Children: Welcome.
Languages: English.
Your Host: Stella.

The Armadillo Guest House

Gay/Lesbian ♀♂

The Armadillo Guest House, highly commended by the Tourist Board of Scotland, is newly refurbished throughout to an excellent standard and provides a friendly, warm atmosphere. We have maps and full information on gay and happy life here in Scotland. Come and join in the fun of "Tartan Kilt" country, only at *The Armadillo*.

Address: 12 Gilmore Place, Edinburgh EH3 9NQ Scotland.
Tel: (44-131) 229 6457.

Type: Guesthouse.
Clientele: Mostly gay & lesbian with some hetero clientele
Transportation: Bus, taxi.
To Gay Bars: A 20-minute walk or 5-minute drive.
Rooms: 6 rooms with single or double beds.

Bathrooms: Shared: 3 bath/shower/toilets, 3 WCs, 3 showers & 1 bathtub.
Meals: Full breakfast. Late breakfast also available.
Vegetarian: Always available to guests.
Complimentary: Tea, coffee & set-up service.

Dates Open: All year.
High Season: July through October.
Rates: Double/twin £15-£25. Single £18-£28.
Discounts: For longer stays.
Rsv'tns: Required.
To Reserve: Call direct.
Parking: Limited off-street

& on-street parking.
In-Room: Color TV, telephone, coffee/tea-making facilities, room, maid & laundry service.
On-Premises: Laundry facilities.
Pets: Permitted.
Handicap Access: No.
Languages: English.

Mansfield House

Gay/Lesbian ♀♂

The True Spirit of Edinburgh's Georgian Era

Step through the doors of **Mansfield House** into a house that has been lovingly restored to its former Georgian grandeur. Original period features and elegant antiques combine with traditional fabrics and wall coverings to create accommodation of the highest quality. Ideally located in the heart of the city we're considered to be THE place to stay in Edinburgh. The hotel is two minutes from Princes Street and within easy walking distance of many of Edinburgh's popular sights. Local gay clubs, bars, discos, restaurants and shops are also nearby.

Address: 57 Dublin St, Edinburgh EH3 6NL Scotland.
Tel: (44-131) 556 7980 (Tel/Fax).

Type: Guesthouse.
Clientele: Good mix of gays & lesbians
Rooms: 5 rooms with double beds.
Bathrooms: 1 en suite with shower, bidet. Four rooms share 1 toilet & shower.
Meals: Continental breakfast available at breakfast bar.
Complimentary: Tea, coffee in room.
Dates Open: All year.
High Season: June-Sept.
Rates: £30-£50. En suite: £40-£55.
Credit Cards: Inquire.
Rsv'tns: Required.
To Reserve: Travel agent or call direct.
Parking: Limited off-street parking.
In-Room: Color TV, maid service, & ceiling fans in most rooms, private refrigerator in some rooms.
On-Premises: Public pay phone.
Smoking: Permitted.
Pets: Not permitted.
Handicap Access: No.
Children: Not permitted.
Languages: English.

Regis House

Gay-Friendly 50/50 ♀♂

Regis House is situated on a residential street near the city centre, five minutes from Princess Street. We provide comfortable guest lodgings and guests have their own keys.

Address: 57 Gilmore Place, Edinburgh EH3 9NT Scotland.
Tel: (44-131) 229 4057.

Type: Guesthouse.
Clientele: 50% gay & lesbian & 50% hetero clientele
To Gay Bars: 5 minutes to French Connection, Blue Oyster.
Rooms: 6 doubles.
Bathrooms: 1 en suite, others share.
Meals: Scottish breakfast Mon-Fri, continental Sat & Sun.
Complimentary: Tea, coffee.
Dates Open: All year.
High Season: Aug-Sept.
Rates: £20 per person.
Credit Cards: MC, Visa, Amex, Access.
Rsv'tns: Required.
To Reserve: Call direct.
Parking: Adequate on-street parking.
In-Room: Color TV, maid service.
Smoking: Permitted.
Pets: Not permitted.
Handicap Access: No.
Children: Permitted.
Languages: English, German.

Ardmory House Hotel

Gay-Owned ♂

Fall in Love With This Restful Scottish Hotel

Golf, fishing, birdwatching, and walking are restful and relaxing pastimes for guests on the Isle of Bute, approximately 60 minutes from Glasgow and 30 minutes on the ferry from Wemyss Bay. **Ardmory House Hotel** sits in its own grounds on a hill overlooking Rothesay Bay, commanding an outstanding view over the Bay, Firth of Clyde, and Loch Striven. Although the hotel's clientele is not exclusively gay, gays are warmly welcomed. Contact Donald or Bill for a brochure.

Address: Ardmory Road, Ardbeg, Isle of Bute PA20 0PG Scotland.
Tel: (44-1700) 502 346, **Fax:** (44-1700) 505 596.
E-mail: Ardmory.House.Hotel@DIAL.PIPEX.COM

continued next page

Type: Hotel with restaurant & bar.
Clientele: Mostly hetero with a gay male following
Transportation: Car is best, or rail from Glasgow, ferry, taxi.
To Gay Bars: 1-1/2 hours to gay bars.
Rooms: 5 rooms with single or double beds.
Bathrooms: All private: 3 shower/toilets, 2 bath/shower/toilets.
Meals: Full breakfast. Bar lunches & dinner optional.
Vegetarian: Available at breakfast, dinner or bar meal.
Complimentary: Tea, coffee, fruit basket & quarter bottle of wine in all rooms.
Dates Open: All year.
High Season: July-August.
Rates: B&B: single £35, double £60. Dinner B&B: single £50, double £90.
Discounts: Dinner B&B: 10% on stays of 3 or more days.
Credit Cards: MC, Visa, Amex, Diners.
Rsv'tns: Required.
To Reserve: Travel agent or call direct.
Parking: Ample free off-street parking.
In-Room: Colour TV, telephone, coffee/tea-making facilities, maid & room service, limited laundry service.
On-Premises: Laundry facilities.
Swimming: Nearby pool & ocean.
Sunbathing: In garden.
Smoking: Not permitted in bedrooms or restaurant.
Pets: Permitted.
Handicap Access: Please inquire.
Children: No.
Languages: English.
Your Host: Donald & Bill.

Apple Cottage
Women ♀

Apple Cottage, situated in an area of outstanding natural beauty, is a semi-detached, self-contained, stone cottage that is more than 200 years old. The living area of this clean and cozy 1-bedroom accommodation, has an exposed painted stone wall with an open fire range, color television and fitted wool carpet and rugs. The fully-equipped kitchen includes an electric cooker and small fridge. Patio doors lead to a small, furnished patio area which overlooks a large, enclosed garden. The upstairs bedroom is furnished with antiques and has a velux window for extra light. From the front of the cottage are views of a wide grazing common with the Black Mountain as a backdrop. It is 2 miles to the Brecon Beacons National Park, about 10 miles to the Vale of Neath, known for magnificent and abundant waterfalls and 13 miles to Swansea City.

Tel: (44-1269) 824072.

Type: Self-contained stone cottage with kitchen.
Clientele: Mostly women with men welcome
Transportation: Bus, taxi.
To Gay Bars: 30-min drive to Swansea gay bars.
Rooms: 1 bedroom with 1 double & 1 single bed.
Bathrooms: Private shower/toilet with pine wash stand.
Vegetarian: Available.
Dates Open: All year.
High Season: Jun 11-Sep 24, Easter, Christmas & New Year.
Rates: High season: £135-£150 per week. Off-season £120 per week. £25 per night.
Rsv'tns: Required, with deposit. Balance paid immediately on arrival.
To Reserve: Call direct.
Minimum Stay: 2 nights.
Parking: Off-street parking.
In-Room: Fully-equipped kitchen, color TV, open fire range, oil central heat, hot water, linens, thermostatically-controlled shower.
On-Premises: Large enclosed garden.
Exercise/Health: Horseback riding, water sports, climbing, walking & swimming.
Swimming: On coast, in rivers.
Sunbathing: In garden.
Smoking: Permitted.
Pets: Permitted.
Handicap Access: Yes.
Children: Yes.
Languages: English.

Tybesta Tolfrue
Gay/Lesbian ♀♂

In the Heart of Brecon Beacons National Park

Hosts Richard and Steve warmly welcome travellers to their listed 18th-century townhouse. Ideally situated in the town of Brecon, 45 miles north of Cardiff, *Tybesta Tolfrue's* location offers ample opportunity for guests to go walking, pony trekking, cycling, sailing, or to simply relax. The attractive bedrooms are standard to full en suite, and offer amenities such as a full breakfast, in-room tea- and coffee-making facilities and colour TV.

Address: Brecon, Wales.
Tel: (44-1874) 611 115.

Type: Bed & breakfast. **Clientele:** Gay & lesbian. Good mix of men & women **Transportation:** Car is best. Nat'l Express Coach Network or rail to Merthyr Tydfil, then local bus service. **To Gay Bars:** 45 miles to Cardiff, a 45-60 minute drive. **Rooms:** 4 rooms with single or double beds. **Bathrooms:** 2 ensuite, 1 shared. **Meals:** Full English or vegetarian breakfast. **Vegetarian:** Vegetarian breakfast on request. Available locally for lunch & dinner. **Complimentary:** Tea, coffee in rooms. **Dates Open:** All year. **High Season:** July & August. **Rates:** £17.50-£19.50 per person per night. **Rsv'tns:** Required when possible. Deposit preferred. **To Reserve:** Call direct. **Minimum Stay:** Required over bank holiday periods. **Parking:** Ample free off- & on-street parking. **In-Room:** Colour TV, coffee/tea-making facilities, maid service. **On-Premises:** TV lounge. **Exercise/Health:** 1 mile to in-town gym with weights, Jacuzzi, sauna & steam. **Swimming:** 1 mile to pool. **Smoking:** Permitted anywhere with care. **Pets:** Permitted by prior arrangement. **Handicap Access:** No. **Children:** No. **Languages:** English. **Your Host:** Richard & Steve.

Courtfield Hotel
Gay-Friendly ♀♂

The *Courtfield Hotel* is a tastefully-decorated hotel close to Cardiff Castle and the city centre. Our setting is a wide and tree-lined avenue with stately homes and buildings. Our hotel, restaurant and bar have a mixed clientele. Gay bars are just 10 minutes away. Guests have their own keys.

Address: 101 Cathedral Rd, Cardiff CF1 9PH Wales.
Tel: (44-1222) 227 701 (Tel/Fax).

Type: Hotel with restaurant & bar. **Clientele:** Mostly straight clientele with a gay & lesbian following **Transportation:** Cardiff (Wales) airport, then taxi to city. **To Gay Bars:** 10 minutes to gay bars. **Rooms:** 16 rooms with single & double beds. **Bathrooms:** 4 private shower/toilets. Shared: 2 bath/shower/toilets, 1 WC. **Meals:** Full Welsh breakfast. **Vegetarian:** Vegetarians catered for. **Complimentary:** Tea & coffee facilities in rooms. **Dates Open:** All year. **Rates:** Single £20-£30, double £35-£45. **Discounts:** 10% on long-term stays. **Credit Cards:** MC, Visa, Amex, Access, Diners, Eurocard. **Rsv'tns:** Required 1 week in advance. **To Reserve:** Travel agent or call direct. **Parking:** On-street parking. **In-Room:** Maid & room service, color TV, telephone, tea making facilities & clock radio. **On-Premises:** Meeting rooms. **Swimming:** Pool nearby. **Smoking:** Permitted without restrictions. **Pets:** Permitted by prior arrangement. **Handicap Access:** No. **Children:** Permitted. **Languages:** English, Dutch, German & French.

Dewis Cyfarfod
Women ♀

Women's Guesthouse with Art Courses

Dewis Cyfarfod is a small, friendly, licensed women's guesthouse offering a warm welcome and a high standard of service. The house is set in an elevated position on five acres of woodland overlooking the River Dee in the Snowdonia National Park three miles from Bala and the largest natural lake in Wales. There are excellent facilities locally for many outdoor sports with equipment for hire and tuition available. Art tuition and residential courses in drawing, painting and sculpture are available at *Dewis Cyfarfod.*

Address: Llandderfel, near Bala, Gwynedd LL23 7DR Wales.
Tel: (44-1678) 530 243.

Type: Licensed guesthouse with art courses. **Clientele:** Women only **Transportation:** Car is best. **To Gay Bars:** 40 miles. **Rooms:** 2 rooms with single or double beds. **Bathrooms:** 2 ensuite shower/toilet. **Meals:** Full or continental breakfast. **Vegetarian:** With prior notice. **Complimentary:** Tea & coffee. **Dates Open:** All year. **Rates:** £16-£18. **Rsv'tns:** Required. **To Reserve:** Call direct. **Parking:** Ample free off-street parking. **In-Room:** TV, tea & coffee-making facilities. **On-Premises:** Small bar lounge.

continued next page

Exercise/Health: Nearby weights, sauna & massage.
Swimming: 3 miles to swimming pool & lake.
Sunbathing: Anywhere on our 5 acres.
Nudity: Anywhere on our 5 acres.
Smoking: Permitted anywhere. One non-smoking sleeping room.
Pets: Not permitted.
Handicap Access: Partially. Ground-floor rooms.
Children: Not especially welcome.
Languages: English, French, Spanish, German.

Pennant Hall

Gay/Lesbian ♂

Where the Spectacular Welsh Mountains Meet the Sea

Pennant Hall is a period building set in its own floodlit grounds overlooking the sea. The village nestles between two headlands at the foot of the Snowdonia National Park with Mount Snowdon as its centrepiece. A warm and friendly welcome awaits our guests, all of whom are gay and are predominantly men. This ten-bedroom hotel is elegantly appointed with a bar, restaurant and large sauna suite. These are open to non-residents, thus ensuring a convivial atmosphere. When in the U.K., a visit to North Wales is a must. With its own language, culture, historic castles, mountains and spectacular scenery, you will be captivated by its mystery and sense of adventure. At the heart of all this, *Pennant Hall* awaits.

Address: Beach Road, Penmaenmawr Conwy LL34 6AY North Wales.
Tel: (44-1492) 622 878.

Type: Hotel with restaurant & bar.
Clientele: Mostly men with women welcome
Transportation: Car is best. Train, then taxi (a 2-min walk). Free pick up from train.
To Gay Bars: 6 miles, a 10-minute drive.
Rooms: 10 rooms with single or double beds.
Bathrooms: 10 private shower/toilets.
Meals: Expanded continental breakfast.
Vegetarian: Vegetarian menu available.
Complimentary: Tea & coffee in rooms.
Dates Open: All year.
High Season: June-September.
Rates: £25 all year.
Credit Cards: MC, Visa.
Rsv'tns: Required.
To Reserve: Travel agent or call direct.
Parking: Ample free off-street parking.
In-Room: Colour TV, coffee & tea-making facilities.
On-Premises: TV lounge.
Exercise/Health: Jacuzzi, sauna, steam, sun room.
Swimming: Ocean nearby.
Sunbathing: On private sun decks, patio & at beach.
Nudity: Permitted in sun terrace & sauna area.
Smoking: Permitted in bar. Inquire about non-smoking area.
Pets: Small dogs permitted.
Handicap Access: No.
Children: No.
Languages: English, Welsh.
Your Host: Terry.

Tara Country Retreat

Q-NET Gay/Lesbian ♀♂

Australia's Most Popular Country Gay Guesthouse

At *Tara Country Retreat* we especially welcome overseas guests, and are happy to take them on a tour of the surrounding tourist spots and koala and kangaroo parks. *Tara* is a convenient stop-off for travel between Sydney, Canberra and Melbourne. Facilities include swimming pool, spa, game room, TV and video. We can arrange for tennis, canoeing and guided bushwalks. *Tara* is only 9 km from historic Berry, famous for fine restaurants and antique shops. It's 15 minutes from Seven Mile Beach and adjoins the nature reserve and rainforests of the Kangaroo Valley.

Address: 219 Wattamolla Rd, Berry NSW 2535 Australia.
Tel: (61-2) 4464 1472, **Fax:** (61-2) 4464 2265.
E-mail: rods@ozemail.com.au
URL: http://www.ozemail.com.au/~rods

Type: Guesthouse & campground with restaurant, bar & a variety of village shops.
Clientele: Good mix of gay men & women
Transportation: Car is best. Free pick up from train or bus, AUD $75 for pick up from airport.
To Gay Bars: Nearest bars are in Sydney, Canberra, or Wollongong. 50 miles or 1 hour.
Rooms: 6 rooms with single or queen beds.
Bathrooms: 2 shared showers & 2 shared WCs.
Campsites: 10 tent sites with use of guesthouse facilities. 2 RV parking sites.
Meals: Full country breakfast, other meals at extra charge.
Vegetarian: Available upon request.
Complimentary: Tea & coffee, wine with meals.
Dates Open: All year.
High Season: December & January.
Rates: AUD $50-AUD $120, campsites AUD $10.
Discounts: For midweek stays.
Credit Cards: MC, Visa, Amex, Bancard, Diners.
Rsv'tns: Recommended.
To Reserve: Travel agent or call direct.
Parking: Ample free off-street parking.
In-Room: Coffee & tea-making facilities.
On-Premises: TV lounge, meeting rooms & laundry facilities.
Exercise/Health: Jacuzzi, weights, massage, gym.
Swimming: Pool on premises, nearby swimming holes & river. 15-minute drive to ocean.
Sunbathing: At pool or riverside, on ocean beach.
Nudity: Permitted in pool area & Jacuzzi at discretion of other guests.
Smoking: Permitted without restrictions.
Pets: Dogs & cats permitted.
Handicap Access: Yes.
Children: No.
Languages: English.
Your Host: Rod & Jason.

IGLTA aglta

The Hill Nudist Retreat
"The Gem of New England"

Men ♂

AUSTRALIA • **BINGARA • NEW SOUTH WALES**

The Hill, a property of 2,565 acres, is located 20 km from the town of Bingara at the end of Kiora Road, off Narrabri Road. This hilly land is a painter's delight, with its high lookouts, wide variety of flora and fauna, as well as splendid views of both the Horton and Bingara valleys. Four-wheel drive access is available to most of the property. The homestead is a turn-of-the-century timber house with four bedrooms, three of which are available to guests. Many farm animals live here, and visitors to *The Hill* will be able to see general farm activities, including working sheep dogs. Many off-farm attractions and places to visit, all less than two hours away, include fishing, sports, gold panning & gem fossicking and goldfield tours.

Address: "The Hill" Homestead, Bingara NSW 2404 Australia.
Tel: (61-267) 24 1686, **Fax:** (61-267) 24 1381, **Mobile:** 017 115 147.

Type: Country camping retreat: 100 acres clothing-optional, 2400 acres clothed access.
Clientele: Men only
Transportation: Car is best. From Sydney, 4 hrs by train to Bingara. Pick up from train.
Rooms: 3 rooms with double & single beds.
Bathrooms: Private & shared.
Campsites: Tents, campers, caravans. Campers share inside bath.

Meals: B&B or full board.
Vegetarian: Available, if advised with booking.
Complimentary: Morning & afternoon tea, coffee & biscuits. Wine with evening meal.
Dates Open: All year.
High Season: Sept-May.
Rates: In-house, B&B, AUD $50. 4-berth caravan AUD $30 per day. Camping $8/day, per person.
Discounts: After 5 days.
Credit Cards: Amex, Diners, MC, Visa, B/C.

Rsv'tns: Required.
To Reserve: Direct or by travel agent.
Minimum Stay: 1 night.
Parking: Unlimited.
In-Room: Telephone, ceiling fans, electric blankets.
On-Premises: TV, video, books, magazines.
Exercise/Health: Sauna room, volleyball & tennis courts, table tennis, badminton, billiards/pool/snooker table, cards.
Swimming: In pool.

Sunbathing: Poolside or on lawn.
Nudity: Permitted on home 100 acres.
Smoking: Permitted outside, not in house.
Pets: Welcome, but not in house. Many & varied pets on premises.
Handicap Access: We can help.
Children: No. Not with nudist guests.
Languages: English.
Your Host: Norman.

aglta

Bygone Beautys Cottages

Q-NET Gay-Friendly ♀♂

From Pure Relaxation to Total Indulgence

From modest mountain cottages to executive residences, from romantic settings for two to cottages designed for 10 people or more, *Bygone Beautys Cottages* has a range of fully self-contained accommodations set in beautiful gardens in the heart of the Blue Mountains. The cottages are conveniently located to the sights of the Blue Mountains and to many recreational activities available in the area.

On arrival, guests will find chocolates and fresh flowers greeting them in each of the fully self-equipped cottages. The kitchens are stocked with ingredients for a traditional Aussie breakfast of bacon, eggs, tomatoes, bread, cereals, oranges for juice, and fresh fruit. The bathrooms, some with spas, have a generous supply of fluffy towels and bath toiletries. Most of the cottages have central heating and, for that extra mountain atmosphere, a burning log fire in the living room. The *Bygone Beautys* tearooms serve delicious complimentary Devonshire tea to guests at any time during their stay.

Address: 20-22 Grose St, Leura NSW 2780 Australia.
Tel: (61-47) 84 3117, (61-47) 84 3108, **Fax:** (61-47) 84 3078.

Type: Bed & breakfast cottages with restaurant & bric-a-brac & craft shop.
Clientele: Mostly hetero clientele with a gay & lesbian following
Transportation: Car or train, then taxi.
To Gay Bars: 55 km, an hour by car.
Rooms: 16 cottages with double, queen or king beds.
Bathrooms: All private.

Meals: Full breakfast.
Vegetarian: Available upon request.
Complimentary: Devonshire tea, chocolates, coffee, tea, milk.
Dates Open: All year.
High Season: June-Sept.
Rates: Per person per night from AUD $60-AUD $100.
Discounts: For groups, extended periods of stay, children.

Credit Cards: Amex, Visa, MC.
Rsv'tns: Required.
To Reserve: Call direct.
Minimum Stay: Required.
Parking: Ample free off-street parking.
In-Room: Color TV, VCR, kitchen, refrigerator, coffee/tea-making facilities & laundry service.
Exercise/Health: Tennis court & Jacuzzi on one property, bushwalking, abseiling, rock climbing.
Sunbathing: In the garden.
Smoking: Permitted in all areas.
Pets: Not permitted.
Handicap Access: Yes.
Children: Welcome.
Languages: English.

agta

INN PLACES® 1998

Santa Fe Luxury Bed & Breakfast
Gay-Owned ♀♂

Santa Fe is not only the romance of Santa Fe, but the irresistible appeal of its lifestyle...a casual elegance.

Tucked away in a secluded valley just 10 minutes north of Coffs Harbour and only 2 minutes from beautiful Sapphire Beach, discover this unique peaceful retreat set in 5 acres of subtropical gardens, waterfalls and natural bushland. Take a stroll through the gardens, feed the Koi fish or relax around the large salt water pool that is set in terraced lawns and gardens. Enjoy a log fire, the adobe BBQ area and healthy breakfasts served on the deck.

Address: The Mountain Way, Coffs Harbour NSW 2450 Australia.
Tel: (61-66) 537 700, Fax: (61-66) 537 050.

Type: Bed & breakfast.
Clientele: Gay-friendly
Transportation: Free pick up from airport & train.
Rooms: 3 rooms with single, queen or king beds.
Bathrooms: 3 private shower/toilets.
Meals: Full breakfast.
Vegetarian: Available upon request.

Complimentary: Tea & coffee.
Dates Open: All year.
High Season: Nov, Dec, Jan, Feb.
Rates: Winter (May-Sept) AUD $125. Summer (Oct-Apr) AUD $145.
Credit Cards: MC, Visa, Bankcard, Amex, Diners.
Rsv'tns: Required.
To Reserve: Call direct.

Parking: Ample free off-street parking.
In-Room: Color TV, VCR, video tape library, ceiling fans, coffee/tea-making facilities & room service.
On-Premises: TV lounge & laundry facilities.
Swimming: Pool & spa jet on premises. Nearby ocean, 5 minutes to gay beach.
Sunbathing: At poolside, on common & private sun decks and at the beach.
Smoking: Permitted outside only.
Pets: Not permitted.
Handicap Access: No.
Children: Not especially welcome.
Languages: English.
Your Host: Sharon, Ben & Alan.

Brickfield Hill Bed & Breakfast Inn
Gay/Lesbian ♀♂

Quality Service and Understated Elegance in Sydney's Gay District

Located in a residential part of the gay district, the inn has been restored to reflect its 1880's character with rugs and runners throughout, antique furniture and an inviting Victorian colour scheme. Guests comment that just arriving at *Brickfield Hill* is a feast for the senses and a relief from the hustle and bustle of Oxford Street, just a few blocks away. The inn is located in a quiet street, fifteen minutes from the airport and five minutes to downtown. In 1886, Mrs. Lydia King established a boarding house at *Brickfield Hill* where she cared for her guests personally. Today, your hosts maintian her time-honoured traditions.

Address: 403 Riley St, Surry Hills, Sydney NSW 2010 Australia.
Tel: (61-2) 9211 4886,
Fax: (61-2) 9212 2556.
E-mail: fields@zip.com.au

Type: Bed & breakfast inn.
Clientele: Mostly gay & lesbian with some hetero clientele
Transportation: Taxi or city shuttle direct from Sydney Airport, or airport bus to Central Station, then taxi or walk.
To Gay Bars: 3 blocks to Oxford St (The Golden Mile), an 8 minute walk, a 1 minute drive.
Rooms: 4 rooms with double or queen beds.
Bathrooms: Private: 1 bath/toilet, Shared: 1 bath/shower/toilet.
Meals: Expanded continental breakfast.
Vegetarian: Vegetarians are catered for. Good neighbourhood restaurants also have vegetarian food.
Complimentary: Tea & coffee.
Dates Open: All year.
High Season: Feb-Mar.
Rates: AUD $80-AUD $130.
Discounts: 7th night complimentary.
Credit Cards: MC, Visa.
Rsv'tns: Required.
To Reserve: Travel agent or call direct.
Parking: Limited on- & off-street parking. If parking is needed, please reserve a parking space when booking your room.
In-Room: Colour TV, maid service.
On-Premises: Meeting rooms, fax & limited word processing service, refreshments.
Exercise/Health: Nearby gym, weights, Jacuzzi, sauna, steam, massage.
Swimming: Pool, ocean & harbour nearby.
Sunbathing: Some rooms have private verandahs.
Smoking: The inn is completely non-smoking.
Pets: Not permitted.
Handicap Access: No.
Children: No.
Languages: English, Japanese, French, German, Italian.
Your Host: Ivano & David.

IGLTA

Dorchester Inn
Gay-Operated ♀♂

Comfort, Charm and a Perfect Location

Built in 1886, *The Dorchester Inn* offers all the comfort and convenience of modern accommodation, while still retaining its unique charm and decor of yesteryear. Recently, tastefully refurbished to enhance its Colonial atmosphere, the hotel is a delightfully small "home away from home." Our well-appointed one- and two-bedroom and studio apartments each contain a fully equipped kitchen, private bathroom, air conditioning, direct-dial telephone, colour television and in-house movies. Ideally located, we're close to public transport, and are just a few minutes' walking distance to popular sightseeing and nightlife spots. Our hotel is a prime place to stay in Sydney for access to city shopping, beaches, the harbour and much more.

Address: 38 Macleay St, Potts Point, Sydney NSW 2011 Australia.
Tel: (61-2) 9358 2200, **Fax:** (61-2) 9357 7579.

Type: Guesthouse inn.
Clientele: Mostly gay & lesbian with some hetero clientele
Transportation: Airport bus AUD $6.
To Gay Bars: 3 blocks, 1/2 mile, a 7 min walk, a 2 min drive.
Rooms: 14 apartments with single, queen or king beds.
Bathrooms: Private: 2 bath/shower/toilets, 12 shower/toilets.
Vegetarian: Available nearby.
Complimentary: Tea & coffee.
Dates Open: All year.
High Season: Late Dec-Mar.
Rates: Single AUD $88-AUD $160, double AUD $98-AUD $180.
Discounts: Inquire.
Credit Cards: MC, Visa, Amex, Diners, Bancard.
Rsv'tns: Required.
To Reserve: Travel agent or call direct.
Parking: Ample off-street covered parking.
In-Room: Telephone, AC, color TV, VCR, kitchen, refrigerator, coffee & tea-making facilities, maid & laundry service.
On-Premises: Video tape library.
Exercise/Health: Nearby gym, weights, Jacuzzi, sauna, steam, massage.
Swimming: Nearby pool & ocean.
Pets: Not permitted.
Handicap Access: No.
Children: No.
Languages: Australian.
Your Host: Roy

IGLTA aglta

Furama Hotel Central
Gay-Friendly ♀♂

Featuring 270 luxurious rooms, this modern Australian-style hotel offers complete privacy and convenience in a comfortable and relaxing environment. Situated in the heart of Sydney's gay area, *Furama Hotel Central's* spacious and well-appointed rooms feature many amenities, including colour TV, reverse cycle air-conditioning, direct-dial ISD/STD telephones, executive desks, computer/mo-

continued next page

AUSTRALIA • SYDNEY • NEW SOUTH WALES

dem ports, mini bars, 24-hour room service, and more. An à la carte restaurant featuring modern Australian cuisine and an inner-city-style cafe with extensive wine and food selections are on premises. We are minutes from the city centre, a step away from Central Railway Station, and a short stroll to Darling Harbour, the gay bars and clubs of Oxford Street, theatres, cinemas, and 3kms from Sydney's most beautiful beaches.

Address: 28 Albion St, Surry Hills, Sydney NSW 2010 Australia.
Tel: (61-2) 9281 0333, Fax: (61-2) 9281 0222.

Type: Hotel with restaurant & bar.
Clientele: Mostly hetero with a gay & lesbian following
Transportation: Airport bus to hotel or taxi.
To Gay Bars: 2 blocks, 10 min walk, 3 min drive.
Rooms: 270 rooms with single, twin or double beds.
Bathrooms: All private bath/toilet/showers.
Meals: Buffet breakfast.

Vegetarian: Vegetarian options on menu at restaurants.
Complimentary: Tea & coffee facilities in rooms.
Dates Open: All year.
Rates: AUD $165.
Credit Cards: Visa, Diners, Amex, MC.
Rsv'tns: Required.
To Reserve: Travel agent or call direct.
Parking: Ample off-street pay, covered parking.
In-Room: Color TV, telephone, AC, coffee & tea-making facilities, refrigerator, maid, room & laundry service.
On-Premises: Meeting rooms, business services.
Exercise/Health: Spa, sauna, gym, weights.
Swimming: 20-metre indoor heated lap pool on premises.

Sunbathing: Poolside & on common sun decks.
Smoking: Permitted in rooms only. Non-smoking rooms available.
Pets: Not permitted.
Handicap Access: Yes.
Children: Welcome.
Languages: English.
Your Host: Bruce.

agta

Furama Hotel Darling Harbour Gay-Friendly ♀♂

Affordable Luxury!

Furama Hotel Darling Harbour is ideally situated opposite the Sydney Entertainment Centre, next to Chinatown and is at the gateway to Sydney's famous Darling Harbour Convention and shopping complexes. It is just a short walk from the hotel to the monorail, major theatre's, cinemas, main department stores, the business district and other major tourist attractions. This international-standard hotel is partly located in a historic woolstore. Its Executive Suites and Deluxe and Superior Rooms offer a wide range of amenities from complimentary toiletries to express check out. Experience the atmosphere of a turn-of-the-century coffee and spices mill at Shipley's restaurant. It offers fresh, modern cuisine and features a great range of Hunter Valley wines.

Address: 68 Harbour Street, Darling Harbour, Sydney NSW 2000 Australia.
Tel: (61-2) 9281 0400, Fax: (61-2) 9281 1212.

Type: Hotel with restaurant.
Clientele: Mostly hetero with a gay & lesbian following
Transportation: Airport bus to Furama, or taxi or car.
To Gay Bars: 4 blocks, 1/2 mile, a 15 min walk, a 3 min drive.
Rooms: 236 rooms, 14 suites with single or queen beds.

Bathrooms: All private bath/toilet/showers.
Vegetarian: Vegetarian menu options in hotel restaurants.
Complimentary: Tea & coffee facilities.
Dates Open: All year.
Rates: AUD $165.
Credit Cards: Visa, Diners, Amex, MC.
Rsv'tns: Required.

To Reserve: Travel agent or call direct.
Parking: Ample off-street pay, covered parking.
In-Room: Color TV, telephone, AC, coffee & tea-making facilities, refrigerator, maid, room & laundry service.
On-Premises: Meeting rooms, business services.

Exercise/Health: Gym, sauna, spa.
Smoking: Permitted in rooms. No non-smoking rooms available.
Pets: Not permitted.
Handicap Access: Yes.
Children: Welcome.
Languages: English.
Your Host: Bruce.

FERRARI GUIDES™

Governors on Fitzroy B&B

Gay/Lesbian ♀♂

An Australian B&B in the Heart of Sydney

Whether traveling for pleasure or business, *Governors on Fitzroy B&B Guesthouse* will be your home in Sydney. Our quiet location is a sanctuary from the busy city of Sydney, yet conveniently just half a mile from the city centre. The B&B was established in 1987, with refurbishment of an 1863 terrace-style house. Six guest rooms provide comfortable, private accommodation and a full American-style breakfast is served each morning. Our private garden, lounge and TV rooms are available for guest use. Your hosts live on the property and are available for travel information and tips on making your stay in Sydney the best!

Address: 64 Fitzroy St, Surry Hills NSW 2010 Australia.
Tel: (61-2) 9331 4652, **Fax:** (61-2) 9361-5094.
E-mail: governor@zip.com.au

Type: Bed & breakfast.
Clientele: Good mix of gays & lesbians
Transportation: Taxi from airport approximately AUD $15.
To Gay Bars: 2 blocks to men's/women's bars.
Rooms: 6 rooms with double & queen beds.
Bathrooms: 5 private sinks, 2 shared bath/shower/toilets & 2 shared toilets.

Meals: Full American-style breakfast.
Vegetarian: Upon request.
Complimentary: Coffee, tea available 24 hours.
Dates Open: All year.
High Season: February-March, during Gay & Lesbian Mardi Gras.
Rates: Single AUD $80, double AUD $100.
Discounts: 7 nights for price of 6 nights.
Credit Cards: MC, Visa, Amex, Diners Club.

Rsv'tns: Recommended.
To Reserve: Call direct.
Minimum Stay: 5 nights during Mardi Gras.
Parking: Limited on-street parking.
In-Room: Maid service.
On-Premises: Meeting rooms, telephone, fax, piano, library, TV lounge, private garden.
Exercise/Health: Spa on premises. Nearby gym, sauna & massage.

Swimming: 20-min drive to ocean.
Sunbathing: On common sun decks or ocean beach.
Nudity: Permitted in spa area.
Smoking: Permitted, but not in bedrooms.
Pets: Not permitted.
Handicap Access: No.
Children: Not permitted.
Languages: English.

IGLTA

AUSTRALIA • NEW SOUTH WALES • SYDNEY

Helen's Hideaway

Lesbian-Owned & -Operated ♀

A Hideaway Downunder Exclusively for Women

Picture a comfortable, secure haven, exclusively for women, in a quiet, leafy cul-de-sac in the heart of Sydney and you'll be picturing *Helen's Hideaway*. This charming accommodation offers individually decorated rooms in a friendly, relaxed atmosphere, perfect for recovering from the rigours of sightseeing, shopping or business. Enjoy breakfast in the sun-filled atrium or the elegant dining room, recline with a good book on the roof terrace, or watch television in the cosy sitting room. This hideaway is surrounded by restaurants, galleries, cafes and shops, but is far from inner-city noise and traffic. Your hosts offer a wealth of local knowledge and first-hand information to make your stay even more enjoyable.

Address: PO Box 113, Darlinghurst NSW 2010 Australia.
Tel: (61-2) 9360 1678, **Fax:** (61-2) 9360 4865.

Type: Bed & breakfast guesthouse.
Clientele: Women only
Transportation: 15 min by taxi or bus from airport, all public transport nearby.
To Gay Bars: 2 blocks, a 5-min walk, a 2-min drive.
Rooms: 5 rooms with double or queen beds.
Bathrooms: Shared: 1 bathtub only, 2 showers only, 3 WCs only.

Meals: Buffet breakfast.
Vegetarian: Breakfast suitable for vegetarians, vegetarian restaurants & cafes nearby.
Complimentary: Tea & coffee 24 hours.
Dates Open: All year.
Rates: AUD $75-AUD $90.
Rsv'tns: Required.
To Reserve: Travel agent or call direct.
Minimum Stay: Required

during long weekends & Mardi Gras only.
Parking: Ample on-street parking.
In-Room: Maid service.
On-Premises: Meeting rooms, TV lounge.
Exercise/Health: Nearby gym, weights, Jacuzzi, sauna, steam, massage, cycling.
Swimming: Nearby pool,

ocean.
Sunbathing: On common sun decks, at beach.
Smoking: Permitted outdoors only.
Pets: Not permitted.
Handicap Access: No.
Children: No.
Languages: English, French, Japanese.
Your Host: Helen & Anni.

Manor House Boutique Hotel

Gay/Lesbian ♂

The Ultimate in Gay Boutique Hotels

The *Manor House*, built circa 1850, was the original residence of the first Lord Mayor of Sydney. Now totally refurbished and renovated to its former glory, it is one of Sydney's finest boutique hotels. This two-story terrace mansion features ornate ceilings, cornices and chandeliers, along with extensive balconies, lead light windows and a polished timber staircase. There are 19 boutique accommodation rooms, a fully licensed restaurant and bar, a heated outdoor spa pool and cabana. *The Manor House* is situated in one of Sydney's premier entertainment districts, only 300 metres from Oxford Street which is internationally renowned for its abundance of restaurants, bars and night clubs.

Address: 86 Flinders St, Darlinghurst, Sydney NSW 2010 Australia.
Tel: (61-2) 9380 6633, **Fax:** (61-2) 9380 5016.

Type: Hotel with restaurant & bar.
Clientele: Mostly men with women welcome
Transportation: Taxi or car.
To Gay Bars: Gay bar across the street.
Rooms: 19 rooms with single, queen or king beds.
Bathrooms: All private.
Meals: Continental buffet breakfast.
Vegetarian: An abundance of restaurants for vegetarians only 2 mins away.
Complimentary: Tea & coffee.
Dates Open: All year.
High Season: Feb & Oct.
Rates: Low season AUD $100-$200, high season AUD $150-$250, +10% tax.

Credit Cards: MC, Visa, Amex, Diners, Bancard.
Rsv'tns: Usually required.
To Reserve: Travel agent or call direct.
Minimum Stay: 1 week minimum required during high season.
Parking: Limited off-street parking.
In-Room: Color TV, VCR, telephone, coffee & tea-making facilities, refrigerator, electronic safe, hair dryers. AC in deluxe & superior rooms.
On-Premises: Video tape library.
Exercise/Health: Nearby gym.
Swimming: Pool, ocean nearby.

Sunbathing: Poolside & at beach.
Smoking: Permitted.
Pets: Not permitted.
Handicap Access: No.
Children: No.
Languages: English, Chinese.
Your Host: Tom & Korey.

IGLTA aglta

Medina Executive Apartments   Gay-friendly ♀♂
Your Oasis of Luxury in the Middle of the City

Four-star *Medina Executive Apartments* is an ideal alternative for business executives, offering a range of competitively-priced one- and two-bedroom apartments in the heart of Sydney. Emphasising the needs of business people, we provide comfortable and spacious settings in which to relax and wind down. Apartments include fully-equipped kitchen and laundry facilities, direct-dial STD/ISD telephone, fax and a full range of business services. Many apartments offer wonderful city views and all feature ensuite bathrooms in each bedroom, enabling business people to share an apartment and cut costs.

Our valet service can order in grocery and liquor supplies and will also pre-order food and beverages prior to guests' arrival. A charge-back facility enables guests to dine at any of 13 restaurants in the vicinity. Our full residential conference facilities cater for groups up to 130 people. We provide standard conferencing equipment, including secretarial, typing, fax and photocopying, available on request. Facilities include a large outdoor pool and BBQ area, a fully-equipped gym with spa, sauna and a rooftop tennis court.

Address: 359 Crown St, Surry Hills, Sydney NSW 2010 Australia.
Tel: (61-2) 9360 6666, **Fax:** (61-2) 9361 5965.
E-mail: medina@s055.aone.net.au

Type: 4-star serviced apartments with restaurant.
Clientele: Mostly hetero with a gay & lesbian following
Transportation: Taxi (AUD $30), or airport bus to Wynyard then taxi.
To Gay Bars: 1 block, a 10-min walk.
Rooms: 84 apartments with single, double or queen beds.
Bathrooms: All private.

continued next page

Vegetarian: Available in restaurant on premises.
Dates Open: All year.
High Season: Sydney Gay Mardi Gras (Jan/Feb).
Rates: Apartments: 1-bedroom AUD $195-210; 2-bedroom AUD $240-260.
Credit Cards: MC, Visa, Amex, Diners.

Rsv'tns: Required.
To Reserve: Travel agent or call direct.
Parking: Ample free underground parking with security.
In-Room: Telephone, color TV, VCR, AC, kitchen with microwave, refrigerator, coffee & tea-making facilities,

maid & laundry service.
On-Premises: Meeting rooms, business services.
Exercise/Health: Gym, weights, Jacuzzi, sauna, massage, tennis, beauty/massage/health parlor.
Swimming: Pool on premises.
Sunbathing: Poolside and

on rooftop tennis court.
Smoking: Permitted without restriction. Non-smoking rooms available.
Pets: Not permitted.
Handicap Access: Yes.
Children: Welcomed.
Languages: English, Chinese, Malay.
Your Host: Craig.

Medusa Hotel

SEE SPECIAL PAGE 8 COLOR SECTION

Unconventional, Yet Enthralling...
Luscious Design with Urban Chic.
Medusa — No Stone Unturned...

Medusa's innate elegance turns heads with a vibrant blend of the historic and the modern. The eye of Medusa is focused on indulgence: Enormous beds, natural fibre linen, organic toiletries and sumptuous evening chocolates are a few hedonistic examples.

Decadent, Yet Delightful...

Bold splashes of vivid colour invite exploration — such as the dappled light dancing, like snakes, from the reflection pool. Lighting is angled for maximum flattery. The place screams romance and glamour. Outside the door is a gourmet and cafe metropolis. Around the corner is fabulous Oxford Street. Medusa is conveniently located in the midst of Darlinghurst, Sydney's new focal point.

Floating Interiors...

The 18 individually-designed studios of this unique luxury hotel challenge those who dare to be a little different. This is no ordinary hotel. Medusa's effortless interior elegance floats in space, while accommodating state-of-the-art facilities.

Spirit of Medusa...

Service that evokes personality, performance and sleek sophistication. Our lively team of people are alert and care for your needs. Guest comfort and privacy is top priority.

- Cutting-edge interiors
- Located in the epicentre of Darlinghurst
- Walking distance to the central business district and harbour
- 24-hour reception and service
- State-of-the-art security, including room safe
- Cable television, video and hi-fi in your room
- Climate control air conditioning
- International dial telephone with modem
- Business and internet facilities
- Kitchenette and marbled bathroom ensuite
- Courtyard and reflection pool

Address: 267 Darlinghurst Rd, Darlinghurst, Sydney NSW 2010 Australia.
Tel: (61-2) 9331 1000, **Fax:** (61-2) 9380 6901.
E-mail: info@medusa.com.au **URL:** www.medusa.com.au

Type: Luxury hotel.
To Gay Bars: Around corner from Oxford St.
Rooms: 18 studios
Bathrooms: All private.
Complimentary: Organic

toiletries, evening chocolates
Rates: Per room, per night: standard AUD $170, deluxe: AUD $195, grand: AUD $265. Plus 10% bed tax. Subject to change w/o notice.

To Reserve: Travel agent or call direct. Apollo & Galileo: SB86862, Sabre: SB40785, Amadeus & System One: SBSYD689.
In-Room: International-dial phone with moden, climate-control AC, cable TV, video, hi-fi, room safe, kitchenette.
On-Premises: 24-hour reception & service, business & internet facilities, courtyard & reflection pool.

Park Lodge Hotel

Gay-Owned 50/50 ♀♂

The Olympic City's Best Value and Friendliest People

Old-world charm describes **Park Lodge Hotel**, a Victorian-style boutique hotel built in 1880, situated opposite Sydney's spacious Moore Park and Royal Agriculture Society Showground. The hotel is only 10 minutes from both of Sydney's airports and is in the heart of Sydney's gay area, only a short bus ride from the city centre, the beautiful harbour, and renowned ocean beaches. The hotel has 20 rooms, most with en suite facilities, and a delightful courtyard oasis in the bustling city environment. Enjoy continental breakfast in the quaint breakfast room or sunny courtyard. Of course, the numerous nearby Oxford Street restaurants are renowned for offering inexpensive, top-quality cuisine.

Address: 747 South Dowling St, Moore Park, SydneyNSW 2016 Australia.
Tel: (61-2) 9318 2393, **Fax:** (61-2) 9318 2513.
E-mail: pklodge@geko.net.au **URL:** http://www.geko.net.au/~pklodge/

Type: Hotel.
Clientele: 50% gay & lesbian & 50% hetero clientele
Transportation: Taxi (about AUD $15).
To Gay Bars: 3 blocks, a 15-min walk, a 5-min drive.
Rooms: 20 rooms with single, double, queen, king or bunk beds.
Bathrooms: 18 private bath/toilets, 2 shared bath/toilets.
Meals: Continental breakfast.
Vegetarian: Non-meat selections at breakfast.

Complimentary: In-room tea & coffee.
Dates Open: All year.
High Season: Sydney Gay & Lesbian Mardi Gras (Feb-Mar).
Rates: Low season (winter) AUD $70-AUD $110, high season (summer) AUD $80-AUD $120.
Discounts: On longer stays & referrals.
Credit Cards: MC, Visa, Amex, Diners, Bancard, EFTPOS.
Rsv'tns: Required during high season.

To Reserve: Travel agent or call direct.
Parking: Limited on-street parking.
In-Room: Color TV, VCR rental, ironing facilities, telephone, refrigerator, pay laundromat, coffee/tea-making facilities, maid service.
On-Premises: Courtyard, laundry facilities, video tape library.
Exercise/Health: Massage by appointment. Nearby gym, weights, Jacuzzi, sauna, steam, massage.

Swimming: Nearby pool, ocean.
Sunbathing: At beach & in courtyard.
Smoking: Permitted in room & outside areas.
Pets: Considered on request.
Handicap Access: Ground-floor room.
Children: Welcome, but no extra provisions other than beds, cots & interconnecting rooms.
Languages: English.

IGLTA aglta

Sullivans Hotel

Q-NET Gay-Friendly ♀♂

SEE SPECIAL PAGE 9 COLOR SECTION

Do Sydney — Stay Sullivans

Sullivans, a small, stylish hotel, offers great value, a delightful garden courtyard and an intimate atmosphere. Included among the amenities to be enjoyed are all private baths, direct-dial telephones, air conditioning and colour TV. Breakfast is served daily in our breakfast cafe, and for guests with cars, there is ample covered parking available. Conveniently situated in central Paddington, *Sullivans* is close to all of Oxford Street's major attractions, including excellent shops, restaurants, cafes, cinemas and art galleries. For those guests who are sunworshippers, buses leave from outside the hotel to take you to Bondi and Bronte beaches.

Address: 21 Oxford St, Paddington, Sydney NSW 2021 Australia.
Tel: (61-2) 9361 0211, **Fax:** (61-2) 9360 3735.

Type: Hotel with breakfast cafe.
Clientele: Mostly hetero with a gay & lesbian following
Transportation: Airport bus or taxi to door.
To Gay Bars: 1 block or a 2-minute walk.
Rooms: 66 rooms with single or queen beds.
Bathrooms: All private.
Vegetarian: Healthy vegetarian breakfast available & several vegetarian restaurants nearby.
Complimentary: Evening chocolates, tea & coffee in room.
Dates Open: All year.
High Season: Summer and Mardi Gras (early March).
Rates: AUD $116 per room all year (except Mardi Gras).
Discounts: Weekly discounts, 10%.
Credit Cards: MC, Visa, Amex, Diners, Bancard, Eurocard.
To Reserve: Travel agent or call direct.
Minimum Stay: 5 nights during Mardi Gras.
Parking: Ample free covered parking.
In-Room: Colour TV, AC, telephone, tea/coffee-making facilities, refrigerator.
On-Premises: Laundry facilities, typing, fax & photocopying.
Exercise/Health: Guest bicycles. Nearby gym, weights, Jacuzzi, sauna, steam & massage.
Swimming: Pool on premises. Ocean nearby.
Sunbathing: At poolside.
Smoking: Permitted in rooms.
Pets: Not permitted.
Handicap Access: No.
Children: Welcome. Family rooms available.
Languages: English, American, Greek, Japanese.
Your Host: Peter.

Sydney Star Accommodation
You'll Always Feel Welcome

Q-NET Gay/Lesbian

AUSTRALIA — NEW SOUTH WALES • SYDNEY

When staying away from home for business or pleasure it is refreshing to find a friendly, cozy atmosphere to relax and feel welcome in. The *Sydney Star Accommodation* combines all the style and elegance of a European pensione with the service and security of a modern hotel.

It's a new, fresh approach to affordable accommodation in colourful downtown Darlinghurst, the heart of Sydney's gay and lesbian community. This stylish private hotel is conveniently located in a quiet oasis on Darlinghurst Road, just minutes from Oxford Street and Kings Cross. Darlinghurst, known for its history and vitality, is a short stroll from the inner city, and is alive with restaurants, cafes, galleries, and boutiques. The 10 comfortable rooms of the guesthouse apartments are private and fully serviced, with single, twin, and double suites available, each with kitchen and colour TV. You'll find surprisingly inexpensive city living — special weekly rates are available.

This charming, quaint, boutique-style hotel is popular with the creative and fashion industries, presenting a delightful alternative to a high tariff and impersonal atmosphere. You'll always feel welcome at the *Sydney Star Accommodation* where you'll find old-fashioned courtesy in the heart of Sydney.

Address: 275 Darlinghurst Rd, Darlinghurst NSW 2010 Australia.
Tel: (61-414) 677 778 (24-hour mobile phone), **Fax:** (61-2) 9331 1000.

Type: Guesthouse apartments.
Clientele: Mostly gay & lesbian with some hetero clientele
Transportation: 15-minutes by taxi or bus from airport, very close to train & ferry.
To Gay Bars: 2 blocks, a 10-minute walk, a 3-minute drive.
Rooms: 10 suites, 20 apartments with single, double, queen or bunk beds.
Bathrooms: Private: 15 shower/toilets, 1 bath/shower/toilet, 30 sinks. Shared: 15 bath/shower/toilets.
Meals: Expanded continental breakfast.
Complimentary: Each room has kitchen, fridge, microwave, sink, a selection of teas, fresh-ground coffee & cereal.
Dates Open: All year.
High Season: October-April.
Rates: Double AUD $90, twin AUD $80, single AUD $60.
Discounts: Weekly & monthly packages.
Credit Cards: MC, Visa, Amex, Diners, Bancard, Discover.
Rsv'tns: Advisable.
To Reserve: Travel agent or call direct. 1 week minimum booking.
Minimum Stay: Inquire.
Parking: Ample on- & off-street parking.
In-Room: Color TV, telephone, refrigerator, kitchen, coffee/tea-making facilities.
Exercise/Health: Nearby gym, weights, Jacuzzi, sauna, steam, massage.
Swimming: Nearby pool, ocean, beautiful beaches.
Sunbathing: At beach.
Smoking: Permitted on balcony & in courtyard, not encouraged in rooms.
Pets: Not permitted.
Handicap Access: No.
Children: No.
Languages: Australian English, Dutch, French, German.
Your Host: Robert.

IGLTA agta

INN PLACES® 1998

Victoria Court Sydney

Q-NET Gay-Friendly ♀♂

Victorian Charm in the Heart of Sydney

The focal point of *Victoria Court* is the verdant courtyard conservatory where, to the accompaniment of twittering free-flying birds, guests can enjoy their breakfast. *Victoria Court* is comprised of two elegant Victorian terrace houses, built in 1881, that were restored and modernised. Here in an informal atmosphere, amidst Victorian charm, guests are offered friendly and personalised service.

Not unexpectedly, no two rooms are alike: most have marble fireplaces, some have balconies that offer views over National Trust classified Victoria Street, and others feature patios. For romantics there are even some rooms with four-poster beds. Guests can relax and read the daily papers or browse through books in the fireplaced lounge. All rooms have en suite bathrooms, hairdryers, air conditioning, coffee- and tea-making facilities, colour televisions, AM/FM radios, and direct-dial telephones for local and international calls.

The historic boutique hotel is centrally located on a quiet, leafy street in lively Potts Point, the heart of Sydney's gastronomic scene. The hotel is an ideal base from which to explore Sydney. It is within minutes of the Opera House, Oxford Street, the Central Business District with its superb shopping, the Harbour, Chinatown, and beaches. In the immediate vicinity are some of Sydney's most renowned restaurants and clubs, as well as innumerable others with menus priced to suit all pockets. The wide variety of cuisines includes Australian, Italian, French, Thai, Chinese, Japanese, and Indian, to name but a few. Public transport, car rental, travel agencies, and banks are within easy reach. An airport shuttle bus operates to and from the hotel, while, for those with their own transport, security parking is available. E-mail: vicsyd@ozemail.com.au(fe)

Address: 122 Victoria Street, Sydney-Potts Point NSW 2011 Australia.
Tel: (61-2) 9357 3200, **Fax:** (61-2) 9357 7606. Toll-free in Australia: (1800) 63 05 05.
E-mail: vicsyd@ozemail.com.au(qn) **URL:** www.VictoriaCout.com.au

Type: Bed & breakfast hotel.
Clientele: Mostly hetero clientele with a gay/lesbian following.
Transportation: Taxi, airport bus, train or bus.
To Gay Bars: 1 block, a 5-minute walk.
Rooms: 25 rooms with single, queen or king beds.
Bathrooms: All private.
Meals: Buffet breakfast.

Vegetarian: Vegetarian restaurants nearby.
Complimentary: Coffee, tea.
Dates Open: All year.
High Season: Oct-Mar.
Rates: AUD $75-AUD $250.
Discounts: Long-term & corporate rates.
Credit Cards: MC, Visa, Amex, Diners, Bancard, Eurocard.

Rsv'tns: Recommended.
To Reserve: Travel agent or call direct.
Parking: Limited covered parking.
In-Room: AC, telephone, colour TV, refrigerator, coffee/tea-making facilities, ceiling fans, laundry & maid service.
Exercise/Health: Nearby gym with weights, Jacuzzi, sauna, steam, massage.

Swimming: Nearby pool, ocean, river.
Sunbathing: At beach.
Smoking: Permitted in rooms. Non-smoking rooms available.
Pets: Not permitted.
Handicap Access: Yes.
Children: No.
Languages: English, German, French, Spanish.

Edward Lodge

Gay/Lesbian ♂

Brisbane's Finest Gay Accommodation

Edward Lodge was built in the 1920s in a tudor style. The rooms are all large, comfortably furnished and serviced each day. The lounge/breakfast room opens onto the courtyard where a generous complimentary continental breakfast is served until 10 am. Amenities also include 24-hour tea/coffee-making facilities and a spa. *Edward Lodge*, located in the cosmopolitan Brisbane suburb of New Farm, is close to gay venues, cafes and restaurants, and a range of shopping, transportation and entertainment facilities. A stay at *Edward Lodge* is a relaxing and friendly experience.

Address: 75 Sydney St, New Farm, Brisbane QLD 4005 Australia.
Tel: (61-7) 3254 1078, **Fax:** (61-7) 3254 1062.

Type: Bed & breakfast guesthouse.
Clientele: Mostly men with women welcome
Transportation: Bus, ferry or taxi.
To Gay Bars: 2 km.
Rooms: 8 rooms with twin or queen beds.
Bathrooms: 8 private shower/toilets.

Meals: Expanded continental breakfast.
Complimentary: Tea, coffee.
Dates Open: All year.
High Season: Mid year.
Rates: Single AUD $65, double AUD $75.
Credit Cards: MC, Visa, Bancard, Diners, Amex.
Rsv'tns: Recommended.

To Reserve: Travel agent or call direct.
Parking: Ample on-street parking.
In-Room: Telephone, ceiling fans, color TV, VCR, refrigerator, laundry service.
On-Premises: TV lounge, video tape library.
Exercise/Health: Jacuzzi. Nearby gym.

Swimming: Nearby pool.
Nudity: Permitted in Jacuzzi.
Smoking: Permitted outside only.
Pets: Not permitted.
Handicap Access: No.
Children: Not permitted.
Languages: English.
Your Host: Gary & Grant.

aglta

Mengyuan

Gay/Lesbian ♀♂

Dreaming Down Under

Escape from the big city to *Mengyuan*, a tranquil hideaway with cool, relaxing verandahs, well-appointed bedrooms and BBQ. Night skies reveal more stars than can be imagined, and while watching the passage of meteors across the sky, one could be forgiven for forgetting that the rest of the world still actually exists. Our large ranch-style home is about 40 minutes inland from Bundaberg (north of Brisbane) and the coast, yet within easy reach of local attractions including whale watching, turtle rookeries and the Great Barrier Reef.

Address: Lot 24, Woodswallow Dr, MS 882, Gin Gin QLD 4671 Australia.
Tel: (61-71) 573 024, **Fax:** (61-71) 573 025.
E-mail: fod@ozemail.com.au

Type: Bed & breakfast guesthouse.
Clientele: Mostly gay & lesbian with some hetero clientele
Transportation: Car is best. Free pick up from Bundaberg airport, bus, train.
To Gay Bars: 40 mins by car.
Rooms: 4 rooms with queen beds.

Bathrooms: Shared.
Meals: Continental breakfast. 3-course evening meal available.
Vegetarian: Available by request.
Complimentary: Tea & coffee 24 hrs.
Dates Open: All year.
Rates: Mon-Thurs AUD $70, Fri-Sun AUD $80.
Discounts: For tertiary students, artists, retirees, etc.

Rsv'tns: Required.
To Reserve: Call direct.
Parking: Ample free off-street parking.
In-Room: Colour TV.
On-Premises: TV lounge, video tape library, laundry facilities.
Swimming: Ocean nearby.
Sunbathing: On patio, at beach.
Smoking: Permitted outside.

Pets: Permitted.
Handicap Access: No.
Children: Welcomed.
Languages: English, Mandarin Chinese, Hokkien, Bahasa Malaysia.
Your Host: Kim & Kay Hock.

IGLTA

AUSTRALIA • QUEENSLAND • BRISBANE • BUNDABERG

INN PLACES® 1998

AUSTRALIA • CAIRNS • QUEENSLAND

Eighteen Twenty-Four James

Q-NET Gay/Lesbian ♂

Bring Your Body to where Summer Never Ends...

Gay-owned and -operated *18-24 James* in Cairns, Australia, has been designed by gay people, exclusively for gay people. This plantation-style hotel, set in tropical rainforest gardens, is located five minutes from Cairns International Airport and is a 20-minute walk along the Esplanade to the city centre.

18-24 James consists of 26 rooms on two levels, with facilities which have been architecturally designed around the central pool and spa for a completely private, clothing-optional area. Bring your body to where summer never ends...peel off around our pool, or pump it up in our gym and sweat it out in our sauna. All guestrooms have ensuite baths, king-sized beds, television with free, in-house movies, clock radio, direct-dial telephone, refrigerator and tea- and coffee-making facilities. As a further convenience, the hotel also provides guest laundry facilities and free airport transfers. Mornings, luxuriate while a complimentary tropical breakfast is served to you poolside. There is a licensed, indoor/outdoor restaurant and bar on premises with outdoor poolside dining available.

Our tour desk can arrange your gay-only tours to the Great Barrier Reef, World Heritage-listed rainforests and, for the more adventurous, white water rafting trips. A local bus which runs every 20 minutes will take visitors to the unofficial gay/nude beach, Buchan Point, and offers a good opportunity to see the beach suburbs of Cairns. Guests wanting an exciting and varied nightlife will not be disappointed by the city's many restaurants, nightclubs and casino. But then, you may never want to leave the hotel...

Address: 18-24 James St, Cairns QLD 4870 Australia.
Tel: (61-70) 514 644, **Fax:** (61-70) 510 103. **E-mail:** 18_24james@internetnorth.com.au. **URL:** http://www.eagles.bbs.net.au/james

Type: Plantation-style hotel with restaurant & bar.
Clientele: Mostly men with women welcome
Transportation: Free pickup from airport, bus & train. Complimentary airport transfers.
To Gay Bars: 1 mile, a 5-minute drive.
Rooms: 26 rooms with king & single beds.
Bathrooms: All private shower/toilets.

Meals: Poolside tropical breakfast.
Vegetarian: Please inquire.
Complimentary: Tea & coffee in room.
Dates Open: All year.
Rates: AUD $55-AUD $95.
Credit Cards: MC, Visa, Amex, Diners, Bancard.
Rsv'tns: Required.
To Reserve: Travel agent or call direct.
Parking: Ample off-street parking.

In-Room: AC, ceiling fans, color TV with free in-house movies, direct-dial telephone, clock radio, refrigerator, coffee/tea-making facilities, maid service.
On-Premises: Laundry facilities, meeting rooms, tour booking desk, hire cars.
Exercise/Health: Gym, weights, Jacuzzi, sauna, massage. Nearby gym, weights, Jacuzzi, sauna, massage.

Swimming: Pool on premises. Nearby pool, ocean, river, lake.
Sunbathing: Poolside.
Nudity: Permitted poolside.
Smoking: Permitted.
Pets: Not permitted.
Handicap Access: Yes.
Children: Not especially welcomed.
Languages: English, Dutch.
Your Host: Keith & Peter.

agla

FERRARI GUIDES™

Lugger Bay Beach Resort

Gay-Operated ♀♂

Rainforest Beach Houses 1-1/2 Hours South of Cairns

    Lugger Bay is a purpose-built, quality retreat situated in the rainforest above three beautiful beaches. This luxury boutique retreat consists of pole-style tree houses designed to compliment the environment whilst still capturing the fabulous rainforest and sea views. You can have all the fun you want or just relax in this truly magical setting of rainforest and Great Barrier Reef. Many adventure tours can be accessed from Lugger Bay, Mission Beach, via Carins, including breathtaking coral and marine life tours. *Lugger Bay* offers many services to pamper your every whim — from massage, a gym and hairdressing to a personal guide. We look forward to giving you our personal attention.

    Address: Explorers Drive, South Mission Beach (via Cairns) QLD 4852 Australia.
    Tel: (61-740) 688 400, **Fax:** (61-740) 688 586.
    E-mail: lugger@ozemail.com.au **URL:** http://www.ozemail.com.au/~lugger

Type: Boutique retreat.
Clientele: Gay & lesbian. Good mix of men & women
Transportation: Car or airport bus transfer.
To Gay Bars: Gay bar on premises.
Rooms: Rooms, suites, apartments & cottages with single, double, queen, king or bunk beds.
Bathrooms: Private: 4 bath/toilet/showers, 6 shower/toilets. Shared: 2 bath/shower/toilets, 2 WCs only.
Vegetarian: Available nearby.
Complimentary: Arrival drink, random pool & bar prizes on special occasions.
Dates Open: All year.
High Season: Dec-Mar.
Rates: AUD $55-AUD $650.
Discounts: 10%-45% on long stays (7-30 days).
Credit Cards: MC, Visa, Amex Diners
Rsv'tns: Required.
To Reserve: Travel agent or call direct.
Parking: Adequate free off-street parking.
In-Room: Telephone, ceiling fans, color TV, VCR, refrigerator, coffee & tea-making facilities, maid service.
On-Premises: Meeting rooms, TV lounge, video tape library.
Exercise/Health: Gym, weights, massage.
Swimming: Pool & ocean on premises.
Sunbathing: Poolside, on private sun decks & at beach.
Nudity: Permitted throughout resort.
Smoking: Permitted. No non-smoking rooms available.
Pets: Permitted, must be by prior arrangement.
Handicap Access: No.
Children: No.
Languages: English.

aglta

Turtle Cove Resort Cairns

Q-NET Gay/Lesbian ♀♂

Turtle Cove is Gay Heaven

    Once you get to *Turtle Cove* you'll soon know why it's one of the world's most popular gay resorts. Just 30 minutes from Cairns International Airport by one of our coaches, your choice of accommodation is a garden cabin, one of our elevated oceanview terraces, or a 5-star beachfront room with only lawn, sand and the odd palm tree between you and the Coral Sea. All rooms feature queen and single beds, en suite bathrooms, airconditioning, ceiling fans, television with in-house video, radio, phones, refrigerator and tea- and coffee-making facilities. The resort features a fully stocked cocktail bar open from early to late, and a licensed restaurant serving great tropical food. Complimentary breakfasts are served on the terrace, and lunch and dinner are available by the pool and under the stars.

continued next page

Without a doubt, the highlight of *Turtle Cove* is our exclusively gay and totally private beach. With the backdrop of tropical rainforest, it has one of the best locations in the world, gay or straight. It's ideal for sunning, relaxing under an umbrella, swimming, or cruising. You'll share it with fellow guests, visiting locals and, if you are lucky, one of the large turtles which nest there each year.

Other facilities include a large pool above the beach, two Jacuzzis, extensive tropical gardens and lawns, rental cars, a resort shop, tour desk, mini-gym and all-gay trips to the world heritage rainforests, as well as the Great Barrier Reef. The Reef is a wonder of the world and we visit it twice a week, in all-gay company, on a luxury boat for snorkeling and diving. Our location is private, but many restaurants, bars and clubs are within 30 minutes of the resort. When considering Australia, we invite you to include *Turtle Cove*. We look forward to making it the highlight of your vacation downunder.

Address: Captain Cook Hwy, PO Box 158, Smithfield,
Cairns Far North QLD 4878 Australia.
Tel: (61-70) 591 800, **Fax:** (61-70) 591 969.
E-mail: turtlecove@iig.com.au **URL:** http://www.iig.com.au/turtle_cove/

Type: Beachfront resort with full-service restaurant, bar & resort shop.
Clientele: Good mix of men & women
Transportation: Bus from airport passes by our front door. Pick up from airport, RR or bus station, city hotel.
To Gay Bars: 35 minutes to Cairns gay bar. Bus from resort Sat nights.
Rooms: 27 rooms with single, double or queen beds.
Bathrooms: All rooms have private showers & toilets.

Meals: Tropical & continental buffet breakfast.
Vegetarian: Available in our restaurant.
Complimentary: Tea & coffee in rooms, airport transfers, welcome drink on arrival.
Dates Open: All year.
Rates: AUD $110-AUD $220.
Discounts: For most of year: stay 7, pay for 6.
Credit Cards: MC, Visa, Amex, Diners, Bankcard.
Rsv'tns: Suggested.
To Reserve: Travel agent or call direct.

Parking: Ample free off-street covered parking.
In-Room: Colour TV, AC, refrigerator, telephone, ceiling fans, coffee/tea-making facilities, room & maid service. Rooms serviced daily. In-house video, video tape library.
On-Premises: Meeting rooms, private dining rooms & laundry facilities.
Exercise/Health: Jacuzzi, massage, beach equipment, volleyball, gym & weights.
Swimming: Pool, beachfront & river swimming hole on premises.
Sunbathing: At poolside, on our patio, common sun decks & on the beach.
Nudity: Permitted poolside & on the beach.
Smoking: Permitted without restrictions.
Pets: Not permitted.
Handicap Access: Yes. Mostly single story with minimal steps.
Children: Not permitted.
Languages: English, Dutch, German & French.
Your Host: Bert & Michael.

IGLTA agta

Witchencroft

Q-NET Women ♀

Welcome to *Witchencroft*, two very private and comfortable self-contained units for women only. Relax and enjoy a nature-based holiday in five acres of gardens on the Atherton Tablelands. We specialise in 4WD and bushwalking tours to suit your individual interests. This is an ideal base from which to escape the tourism of Cairns and explore a great diversity of nature, including the World Heritage tropical rainforest. There is all-year-round fine weather within an hour of *Witchencroft!* Your host is a fourth generation north Queenslander, and a great source of local information.

Address: Write: Jenny Maclean, PO Box 685, Atherton QLD 4883 Australia.
Tel: (61-740) 912 683 (Tel/Fax). **E-mail:** jj@bushnet.qld.edu.au

Type: Guesthouse on a 5-acre organic farm.
Clientele: Women only
Transportation: Free pickup from Atherton, bus from Cairns daily.
To Gay Bars: 90 kms to Cairns.

Rooms: 2 apartments with double beds.
Bathrooms: All private shower/toilets.
Campsites: Tent sites, powered sites.
Meals: Self-cater or enjoy

our vegetarian cuisine.
Vegetarian: Vegetarian, vegan.
Complimentary: Tea, coffee & milk.
Dates Open: All year.
High Season: July, August.

Rates: Single US $50, double US $70.
Discounts: Garden work exchange.
Rsv'tns: Required.
To Reserve: Call direct.

FERRARI GUIDES™

Min. Stay: Two nights.
Parking: Ample parking.
In-Room: Color TV, ceiling fans, kitchen, refrigerator, coffee & tea-making facilities.

Exercise/Health: Bushwalks.
Swimming: 10 minutes to rivers & lakes.
Sunbathing: In the garden.

Nudity: Permitted.
Smoking: Permitted outdoors.
Pets: Permitted with restrictions because of resident livestock.

Handicap Access: Yes.
Children: Permitted.
Languages: English, some French & German.

The Lakes Holiday Apartments

Men & Women ♂

The Lakes is a small, luxurious resort with ten holiday apartments. The apartments are comprised of nine two- and three-bedroom apartments and, because the resort is north-facing, there are beautiful views of Noosa and the tranquil river. Landscaped gardens surround a large swimming pool and BBQ, and there is also undercover parking. *The Lakes* is conveniently located just 150 metres from beaches, restaurants, shopping centres and fishing spots.

Address: 1/273 Weyba Rd, Noosaville QLD 4566 Australia.
Tel: (61-7) 5449 8605.

Type: Holiday resort.
Clientele: Men & women
Transportation: Bus stop nearby.
To Gay Bars: 5 min by car to Hasting Street.
Rooms: 9 2- & 3-bedroom apartments.
Complimentary: Tea & coffee.

Dates Open: All year.
Rates: Low season: single from AUD $52. High season: from AUD $120.
Discounts: AUD $294 per week on stays of over 28 days.
Credit Cards: Visa, MC.
Rsv'tns: Required.
To Reserve: Call direct.

Parking: Lots of covered parking.
In-Room: Ceiling fans.
Exercise/Health: Nude running group runs weekdays in early morning.
Swimming: Large swimming pool on premises, ocean beach nearby.

Sunbathing: In pool area or on own patio.
Nudity: Nudist-friendly.
Smoking: Permitted.
Pets: Not permitted.
Handicap Access: No.
Children: Permitted.
Languages: English.
Your Host: David.

Noosa Cove

Gay/Lesbian ♂

The Gay Beach Resort Capital of Australia

You'll be met at the airport or terminal by our Mercedes Benz, then whisked to *Noosa Cove,* a resort set in the most up-market, sought-after location in Noosa near Australia's best beach. Our location overlooking Noosa's fabulous national park, provides access to many natural coves and beaches, including the famous gay naturist beach, Alexandria Bay. Guests can indulge in physical activities, such as bushwalking, surfing, windsurfing, waterskiing, boating, fishing, sailing and swimming, or just enjoy sun-baking by the private pool. Apartments in a subtropical garden and pool setting have two bedrooms, sunny balcony, kitchen and colour TV with remote in the main bedroom. The gay nightclub and restaurant are situated 2 minutes' walk from your apartment. We're about a 1-1/2 hour drive just north of Brisbane.

Address: 82 Upper Hastings St, Noosa QLD 4567 Australia.
Tel: (61-7) 5449 2668, **Fax:** (61-7) 5447 5373.

Type: Holiday apartments & guesthouse.
Clientele: Mostly men with women welcome
Transportation: Pick up from airport & bus.
To Gay Bars: 1 block or 400 yards. 3 minutes by foot or 1 minute by car.
Rooms: 3 spacious, fully

self-contained apartments & 1-bedroom studio unit with queen beds.
Bathrooms: All private.
Meals: 3 min walk to 50 beachfront restaurants.
Vegetarian: 3 min walk to 50 beachfront restaurants.
Complimentary: Tea & coffee.

Dates Open: All year.
High Season: 1st 2 wks of Jan. & school/public holidays.
Rates: High season, AUD $100-AUD $140 per night. Low season AUD $80-AUD $95 per night. Guesthouse AUD $60 per night.
Credit Cards: Visa, Amex, MC.

Rsv'tns: Recommended.
To Reserve: Travel agent or call direct.
Parking: Ample free off-street covered parking.
In-Room: Color TV, VCR, telephone, ceiling fans, coffee & tea-making facilities, kitchen, refrigerator & laun-

continued next page

INN PLACES® 1998   151

dry service.
Exercise/Health: Gym & weights on premises. Nearby gym, weights, Jacuzzi/spa, sauna & massage.
Swimming: Pool in apartment complex. Nearby ocean & river.
Sunbathing: At poolside, on private sun decks, or at the beach.
Nudity: Permitted at poolside or at the beach.
Smoking: Permitted outside of rooms.
Pets: Not permitted.
Handicap Access: 1 apartment on ground level.
Children: Not permitted.
Languages: English.
Your Host: Alan.

Sandy's on the Strand
Gay-Owned & -Operated ♀♂

Townsville's Only Gay Bed & Breakfast

Sandy's, Townsville's only gay bed and breakfast, is situated on the beachfront, offering picturesque views across Cleveland Bay to Magnetic Island. Our accommodations include air-conditioned bedrooms with queen-sized beds, ensuite bathrooms and your own balcony. We are centrally located, within walking distance to the city centre, casino, rock pool, marine wonderland and many other attractions. If you wish to travel further afield, *Sandy's* can offer motor scooters for your exclusive use. Guests can swim at the safe beach across the road, the rock pool, or try the salt-water pool on premises. Hosts, Peter and Robert will go out of their way to make your stay enjoyable.

Address: PO Box 193, Townsville QLD 4810 Australia.
Tel: (61-07) 4772 1193 (Tel/Fax).

Type: Bed & breakfast.
Clientele: Gay & lesbian. Good mix of men & women
Transportation: Car is best. Free pick up from airport, train & bus.
To Gay Bars: 2 miles, a 20 min walk, a 5 min drive.
Rooms: 2 rooms with queen beds.
Bathrooms: 1 private bath/ shower/toilet, 1 shared bath/shower/toilet.
Meals: Continental breakfast.
Vegetarian: Available in nearby cafes & restaurants.
Complimentary: Hot or cold drinks & nibbles.
Dates Open: All year.
Rates: AUD $55-$65.
Rsv'tns: Required. Bookings are essential.
To Reserve: Call direct.
Parking: Ample, free off-street parking.
In-Room: Telephone, AC, ceiling fans, color TV, VCR.
On-Premises: TV lounge, laundry facilities.
Exercise/Health: Nearby gym, weights, massage.
Swimming: Pool. Ocean nearby.
Sunbathing: Poolside & on patio.
Smoking: Permitted outside & on patio.
Pets: Not permitted.
Handicap Access: No.
Children: No.
Languages: English.
Your Host: Peter & Robert.

Greenways Apartments
Gay/Lesbian ♀♂

Adelaide, our state capital, features traditional stone architecture and wide encircling parklands. This elegant city is situated near one of the world's most famous winegrowing districts, and its residents are relaxed and friendly. These features, combined with the picturesque backdrop of the Adelaide Hills, give Adelaide an atmosphere found nowhere else in Australia. South Australia was the first Australian state to legalize homosexuality. *Greenways* provides excellent, comparatively cheap accommodations in fully furnished, self-contained private apartments. It is situated near city center and gay venues. Hosts are gay-friendly and are willing to assist with local information and they especially welcome international travelers.

Address: 45 King William Rd, North Adelaide SA 5006 Australia.
Tel: (61-8) 8267 5903, Fax: (61-8) 8267 1790.

Type: Holiday apartments.
Clientele: Gay & lesbian, straight-friendly
Transportation: Taxi best from airport, bus or train station.
To Gay Bars: 1 mile to gay/lesbian bars.
Rooms: 25 apartments with single or double beds.
Bathrooms: All private.
Dates Open: All year.
Rates: 1-bdrm AUD $67, 2-bdrm AUD $95 & up,
3-bdrm AUD $135 & up.
Discounts: AUD $5/night on stays of 4 nights or longer (private bookings only).
Credit Cards: MC, Visa, Bancard, Diners, Amex.
Rsv'tns: Required 1 month in advance, we're very popular.
To Reserve: Travel agent or call direct.
Minimum Stay: 3 days.

FERRARI GUIDES™

Parking: Ample free off-street parking.
In-Room: Telephone, kitchenette, refrigerator, weekly maid service, AC/heat, color TV.
On-Premises: Coin-operated laundry facilities.
Exercise/Health: Public gym, spa & sauna 3/4 mi.
Swimming: Public pool 3/4 mile, ocean 15 miles.
Sunbathing: At public pool, on ocean beach (nude beach 1 hour).
Smoking: We prefer that you smoke outside only.
Pets: Not permitted.
Handicap Access: No.
Children: Permitted.
Languages: English.
Your Host: Brenton, Simon & Keith.

agta

Rochdale

Gay/Lesbian ♀♂

One of Adelaide's Special Secrets!

Adelaide's only accommodation provider for gay men and women, **Rochdale** is a private, traditional bed and breakfast. The residence is a typical late '20's Adelaide residence, with spacious, well-appointed rooms and an air of understated elegance. Wood panelling is used extensively throughout the formal living areas and open fires warm the study, lounge and one of the guest rooms. The gardens provide areas suited to quiet, secluded relaxing, reading and alfresco dining. We are within strolling distance of shopping and restaurants, conveniently located for easy access to the city and Adelaide Hills and serviced with public transport.

Address: 349 Glen Osmond Rd, Glen Osmond SA 5064 Australia.
Tel: (61-8) 8379 7498, **Fax:** (61-8) 8379 2483. **E-mail:** jonespk@ozemail.com.au

Type: Bed & breakfast.
Clientele: Gay & lesbian preferred accommodation
Transportation: Car or public transport from city centre. Free pick up (by arrangement only) from airport, bus or train.
To Gay Bars: 7 minutes by car.
Rooms: 3 rooms with queen or double beds.
Bathrooms: 3 private shower/toilets.
Meals: Full cooked breakfast. 3-course gourmet dinner & luncheon picnic hamper available at additional cost with prior arrangement.
Vegetarian: Available with prior arrangement.
Complimentary: Morning or afternoon tea upon arrival, tea & coffee, Port in rooms.
Dates Open: All year.
Rates: From AUD $70 single, AUD $90 double, dinner B&B AUD $180 minimum 2 persons.
Credit Cards: MC, Visa, Amex, Diners, Australian Bankcard.
Rsv'tns: Required.
To Reserve: Travel agent or call direct.
Parking: Limited free off-street parking.
On-Premises: TV lounge, meeting rooms.
Exercise/Health: Nearby gym, weights, Jacuzzi, sauna, steam & massage.
Swimming: Enclosed swimming pool on premises.
Sunbathing: On the patio, in garden.
Nudity: Permitted in private garden. 1 hour to nude beach.
Smoking: Permitted outside only.
Pets: Not permitted.
Handicap Access: One bathroom is accessible.
Children: Adult-oriented accommodation.
Languages: English.
Your Host: Peter & Brian.

agta

Corinda's Cottages

Gay Hosts 50/50 ♀♂

Awaken to the Sound of Birdsong!

Overlooking a cobbled courtyard are the converted coach-house and servant's quarters of *Corinda*, an award-winning National Trust Classified property in the heart of Hobart. Its historic outbuildings are now delightful gay-owned, self-contained cottages. *Corinda's* gardens are a real delight. Lime trees and hedges of box and yew create formal enclosed areas, each with its own colour scheme. Though only a five-minute stroll from Sullivans Cove, the property has a real "country" feel as it adjoins the Queens Domain, a large park teaming with birdlife.

Address: 17 Glebe St, Glebe, Hobart TAS Australia.
Tel: (61-03) 62 34 1590, **Fax:** (61-03) 62 34 2744.

Type: Self-contained cottages.
Clientele: 50% gay & lesbian & 50% straight clientele
Transportation: Car is best.
To Gay Bars: 1 mile, a 15-min walk, a 5-min drive.
Rooms: 3 cottages with single, double or queen beds.

continued next page

INN PLACES® 1998

Bathrooms: Private: 1 shower/toilet, 1 bath/shower/toilet, 1 spa/shower/toilet.
Meals: Expanded continental breakfast.
Vegetarian: Vegetarian restaurants nearby.
Complimentary: Tea, coffee, decaf, fruit juice, range of condiments, fudge.
Dates Open: All year.
High Season: Jan-Feb.
Rates: AUS $150 per cottage (2 persons), all year. Spa cottage AUS $170.
Discounts: 20% to readers of Ferrari Guides if booked directly with owners.
Credit Cards: Visa, Bancard.
Rsv'tns: Required.
To Reserve: Travel agent or call direct.
Parking: Ample, free, on- & off-street parking.
In-Room: Color TV, refrigerator, kitchen, coffee & tea-making facilities, maid & laundry service.
On-Premises: Laundry facilities & use of phone/fax.
Exercise/Health: Nearby gym, weights, Jacuzzi, sauna, steam, massage.
Swimming: Nearby pool, ocean & river.
Sunbathing: At beach & in garden.
Smoking: Permitted anywhere. Non-smoking rooms available.
Pets: Not permitted.
Handicap Access: No.
Children: No children under 12.
Languages: English, Dutch.
Your Host: Wilmar & Matthew.

aglta

Brickfields Terrace

Gay-Friendly ♀♂

Part of Tasmania's Heritage

Spoil yourself with the elegance and comfort of 4-1/2 star Victorian townhouses (circa 1889) that overlook century-old elm trees and park land in the heart of Launceston. Two terraces offer spacious warm rooms filled with freshly picked flowers and potpourri. Beautiful decorative touches and charming antique furniture lend an air of sophistication. Share a crackling log fire during the crisp winter evenings, browse through a wonderful array of magazines, and feast on delicious handmade fudge. Your exclusive occupancy ensures complete privacy. Whether you are looking for a romantic retreat or simply a chance to relax with friends, *Brickfields Terrace* is the perfect choice.

Address: 64 & 68 Margaret St, Launceston TAS 7250 Australia.
Tel: (61-03) 6330 1753, **Fax:** (61-03) 6330 2334.

Type: Historic terraces.
Clientele: Mostly hetero with a gay/lesbian following
Transportation: Car, airport bus to front door, taxi.
To Gay Bars: A 15-minute walk, a 5-minute drive (limited venues).
Rooms: 2 cottages with single or queen beds.
Bathrooms: All private.
Meals: Expanded continental breakfast.
Vegetarian: Available in nearby restaurant on request.
Complimentary: Tea, coffee, handmade Tasmanian fudge, champagne for special occasions.
Dates Open: All year.
High Season: Jan-April.
Rates: AUD $140-AUD $208.
Discounts: Seasonal discounts available on application.
Credit Cards: MC, Visa, Bankcard.
Rsv'tns: Required.
To Reserve: Travel agent or call direct.
Parking: Ample free on- & off-street parking.
In-Room: Colour TV, telephone, refrigerator, fully equipped kitchen, open fire, games, magazines, books, radio, lunch & dinner room service.
On-Premises: Laundry facilities. Coffee/tea-making facilities in the terrace.
Exercise/Health: Nearby gym with weights, sauna, steam, massage.
Swimming: Nearby pool & river.
Smoking: Permitted outside only. Terraces are smoke-free.
Pets: Not permitted.
Handicap Access: No.
Children: Welcome.
Languages: English.
Your Host: Sarah.

The Balconies

Gay/Lesbian ♀♂

Relax on the Balconies and Enjoy the View of Beautiful Lake Daylesford

Your hosts, Geof and Theo invite you to experience their hospitality midst the picturesque surroundings of Daylesford, Australia's largest gay-populated country town, and Hepburn Springs. Here, in the heart of the mineral springs and central goldfields, gays and lesbians have been building a base of gay businesses and properties since 1992. Established in that same year, and one of the first gay properties here, *The Balconies* is set in three acres with views of Lake Daylesford. Guests enjoy a heated indoor pool and spa or a stroll around beautiful Lake Daylesford after breakfast. Some prefer to sit on the balcony and watch the ducks. Remember to bring bottles to take home some mineral water, and bread to feed the ducks.

Address: 35 Perrins St, Daylesford VIC 3460 Australia.
Tel: (61-3) 53 48 1322 (Tel/Fax).
URL: http://www.spacountry.net.au/balconys

Type: Bed & breakfast with in-house dinner.
Clientele: Good mix of gays & lesbians
Transportation: Car, train & bus. Free pick up from train & bus.
Rooms: 5 rooms with single or queen beds.
Bathrooms: 2 private shower/toilets. Others share.
Meals: Continental or cooked breakfast.
Vegetarian: Can be arranged.
Complimentary: Tea, coffee & cake.
Dates Open: All year.
Rates: AUD $75-$135.
Discounts: Mid-week Sun to Thur.
Credit Cards: MC, Visa & Bancard.
Rsv'tns: Required.
To Reserve: Travel agent or call direct.
Parking: Free off-street parking.
On-Premises: TV lounge, video library, coffee & tea-making facilities & laundry facilities.
Exercise/Health: Jacuzzi on premises, nearby massage.
Swimming: Heated indoor pool on premises. Nearby pool, river & lake.
Sunbathing: On the patio.
Nudity: Permitted in indoor pool room.
Smoking: Permitted in games room or on balconies. All bedrooms are non-smoking.
Pets: Not permitted.
Handicap Access: Yes.
Children: Not especially welcome.
Languages: English, Greek & Italian.
Your Host: Theo & Geof.

One Sixty-Three Drummond Street

Gay/Lesbian ♀♂

You Will be Pleasantly Surprised

163 Drummond Street comprises two magnificent Victorian mansions, authentically renovated, retaining all their original features including marble fireplaces, tiled entrance halls with Persian runners and winding cedar staircases. A 19th-century elegance together with 20th-century comforts and amenities distinguishes this guesthouse. The atmosphere is warm; one where friends, newcomers

continued next page

and their guests can relax in the communal living and dining areas furnished with antiques and artwork. We are committed to informality and generosity with 24-hour access to all facilities. *163 & 169* are located two minutes away from Melbourne's famous Italian restaurant Mecca, Lygon Street, the theaters, Chinatown and the central business center. We overlook the majestic gardens and The Exhibition Building.

Address: 163 Drummond Street, Carlton, Melbourne VIC 3053 Australia.
Tel: (61-3) 9663 3081, **Fax:** (61-3) 9663 6500.

Type: Bed & breakfast guesthouse.
Clientele: Good mix of gays & lesbians
Transportation: Taxi from airport (approx. AUD $22). Shuttle pick up from "163."
To Gay Bars: A 20-minute walk or 5-minute drive.
Rooms: 11 rooms with single, double, queen or king beds.
Bathrooms: 4 ensuite bathrooms, 4 private sinks only. 2 shared bath/shower/toilets, 1 shared WC only.
Meals: Expanded continental breakfast, tea or coffee is 24 hours, self-service.
Vegetarian: 5-minute walk to a vegetarian restaurant.
Complimentary: Beverages, self-service 24 hours in dining room. Confectionery, biscuits & fruit.
Dates Open: All year.
High Season: Summer & autumn.
Rates: AUD $45-$105.
Discounts: Weekly rates.
Credit Cards: MC, Visa & Bancard.
Rsv'tns: Required.
To Reserve: Travel agent or call direct.
Parking: Adequate off-street parking, covered car park.
In-Room: Color TV, ceiling fans, AC.
On-Premises: TV lounge & laundry facilities.
Exercise/Health: Nearby gym, weights, Jacuzzi, sauna, steam & massage.
Swimming: Nearby pool.
Sunbathing: On the patio.
Smoking: Permitted in courtyard gardens & balconies.
Pets: Not permitted.
Handicap Access: No.
Children: Not especially welcome.
Languages: English.
Your Host: Ian.

Palm Court Bed & Breakfast

Q-NET Gay/Lesbian ♂

Melbourne's Best-Kept Secret

Palm Court B&B is a gracious boutique accommodation offering a friendly atmosphere in a non-smoking environment. The house has been restored to its former glory with relaxed living areas and large bedrooms, ensuring the most intimate and cosy environment for holiday guests. Bedrooms are spacious doubles with television, electric blankets and all of the comforts of home. The landscaped gardened courtyards provide a pleasant outdoor retreat.

Address: 22 Grattan Place, Richmond, Melbourne VIC 3121 Australia.
Tel: (61-3) 9427 7365 (Tel/Fax), **Mobile:** (0419) 777 850.

Type: Bed & breakfast.
Clientele: Mostly men with women welcome
Transportation: Airport bus to city, then taxi.
To Gay Bars: 1 mile, a 15 minute walk, a 5 minute drive.
Rooms: 4 rooms with single or double beds.
Bathrooms: Shared.
Meals: Expanded continental breakfast.
Vegetarian: Vegetarian restaurants a short walk away.
Complimentary: Tea, coffee, biscuits.
Dates Open: All year.
High Season: Sept-Apr.
Rates: AUD $50-AUD $80.
Credit Cards: Visa, MC.
Rsv'tns: Advised.
To Reserve: Travel agent or call direct.
Parking: Adequate on-street parking.
In-Room: Color TV, electric blankets.
On-Premises: TV lounge, video tape library, laundry facilities.
Swimming: Pool & ocean nearby.
Sunbathing: On patio.
Smoking: Non-smoking accommodation. Permitted in gardens only.
Pets: Not permitted.
Handicap Access: No.
Children: No.
Languages: English, Thai.
Your Host: Trevor & Mac.

Cape Schanck Lodge Bed & Breakfast

Gay-Owned & -Operated ♀♂

Australian Hospitality, Friendly & Discrete!

Located on the rugged southern tip of the Mornington Peninsula, *Cape Schanck Lodge Bed & Breakfast* is a large, modern ranch-style home, close to the lighthouse and spectacular coastal walks. It is adjacent to a scenic golf course and close to horse riding, vineyards, galleries, surf and bay beaches, and is an easy 88 kilometre drive from Melbourne. Service is typically Australian — friendly and, yes, discrete. The ambiance is relaxing and according to some, "quirky." Silver-service dinner by candlelight is available, and a gourmet breakfast (inclusive) is served at your leisure in the breakfast area overlooking the courtyard.

Address: 134 Cape Schanck Rd, Cape Schanck VIC Australia.
Tel: (61-3) 5988 6395 (Tel/Fax). **E-mail:** graem@alphalink.com.au

Type: Bed & breakfast.
Clientele: Mostly straight clientele with a gay & lesbian following
Transportation: Cas is essential.
To Gay Bars: 88km, 1-1/2 hour drive to gay bars.
Rooms: 2 suites with queen beds.
Bathrooms: 2 private shower/toilets
Meals: Full breakfast.
Vegetarian: Available by arrangement & nearby.
Complimentary: Cappuccino, espresso, tea & cake on arrival. Pre-dinner cocktails, chocolates in room.
Dates Open: All year.
High Season: Dec-Mar.
Rates: AUD 80 single, AUD 110 double.
Discounts: Extended stay, 10% after 2 days.
Credit Cards: MC, Visa, Bancard.
Rsv'tns: Required.
To Reserve: Travel agent or call direct.
Minimum Stay: Required on long weekends.
Parking: Ample free off-street parking.
In-Room: Telephone, pedestal fans, color TV, VCR, refrigerator, coffee & tea-making facilities.
On-Premises: Video tape library, laundry facilities.
Exercise/Health: Sauna & masage.
Swimming: Pool on premises. Nearby ocean.
Sunbathing: Poolside & at beach.
Smoking: No smoking inside house.
Pets: Not permitted.
Handicap Access: No.
Children: No.
Languages: English, German, some Italian.
Your Host: Graeme & Edward.

The Lawley on Guildford
Gay/Lesbian ♀♂

The Ultimate Address When in Perth

Australian hospitality surrounds *The Lawley on Guildford*, a 1920's two-storey residence, located in one of Perth's older established city areas. The B&B has three large bedrooms, a cozy guest lounge with log fire, high ceilings, leadlight windows, a large dining room, wood paneling, an enclosed conservatory, and private garden spaces with grass tennis court. Guests are only minutes (by train or taxi) to the heart of the city and all Northbridge venues. *The Lawley* is the place to stay for warm, friendly hospitality when in Perth.

Address: 72 Guildford Rd, Mount Lawley WA 6050 Australia.
Tel: (61-8) 9272 5501 (Tel/Fax), mobile (61-41) 299 5178.

Type: Bed & breakfast.
Clientele: Exclusively gay & lesbian
Transportation: Taxi from airport. Free pickup from airport.
To Gay Bars: 2-1/2 miles, a 7-minute drive.
Rooms: 3 rooms with double or queen beds.
Bathrooms: 1 private bath/shower/toilet, 2 private shower/WC only.
Meals: Expanded continental breakfast.
Vegetarian: Available at cafes & restaurants, a 20-minute walk.
Complimentary: Chocolates, water jug set up, tea & coffee.
Dates Open: All year.
High Season: September-March.
Rates: AUD $55-AUD $80.
Discounts: Weekly rates.
Credit Cards: MC, VISA.
Rsv'tns: Required.
To Reserve: Travel agent or call direct.
Parking: Adequate off-street parking.
In-Room: Colour TV, AC, maid service.

continued next page

INN PLACES® 1998

On-Premises: Meeting rooms, TV lounge, public phone, laundry facilities, guest refrigerator, all-day coffee/tea-making facilities. **Exercise/Health:** Weights, Jacuzzi, grass tennis court, bicycles for hire on premises. Nearby sauna, steam & massage. **Swimming:** River nearby. **Sunbathing:** On patio & in private gardens on premises. **Smoking:** Permitted in enclosed conservatory smoking area. All rooms non-smoking. **Pets:** Not permitted. **Handicap Access:** No. **Children:** No. **Languages:** English. **Your Host:** Ian.

Swanbourne Guest House

Gay/Lesbian ♂

Your Tranquil Retreat Between City and Surf

This four-star RAC-rated private residence, ten minutes outside central Perth, is set in lush gardens overlooking trees and Australian flora. A rear patio offers privacy for nude sunbathing. Golf, tennis and swimming pool are within walking distance — you can make the gay beach in 2 minutes. Claremont's yuppie, cosmopolitan atmosphere, restaurants, bars and shops, all top class, are also close by. The *Swanbourne's* cool, Mediterranean interior and large, exquisitely appointed rooms make it a perfect haven from stressful, hectic city living, whilst offering all the amenities and activities a cosmopolitan city has to offer.

Perth, perched on the edge of the Indian Ocean, has superb beaches which stretch for miles at a time. The coastline offers breathtaking views and beautiful swimming locations. With temperatures generally over the thirties, centigrade, a comfortable dry heat and gusty cooling afternoon breezes make Perth a watersports-lover's paradise. Scub diving, sailing, water skiing, windsurfing, parasailing and surfing on both the ocean and the river are favourites among the locals and are readily available for all to try. With all the amenities of a cosmopolitan city, Perth also has on offer a wide variety of restaurants — seafood, Italian, French, Greek, Chinese and Japanese — a variety of boutiques and great food halls selling the best local produce and seafood. Ten kilometres to the south of *Swanbourne* stands Freemantle, an old sailing port which has been converted into bustling outdoor markets and promenades. Ten kilometres to the north, adjacent to the city centre, is Northbridge, an exciting night spot which caters to every taste — family restaurants, bars, nightclubs and cabarets. For those wishing to venture further afield, the possibilities are endless. Visit Margaret River with its world-renowned wineries, the Karri forests and spectacular coastlines, or feed the world-famous Monkey Mia dolphins in their natural environment. Drive inland and witness Australia's barren, arresting outback, or make a trip to Rottnest, an exotic island located 26 kilometres off the mainland.

Address: 5 Myera St, Swanbourne, Perth WA 6010 Australia.
Tel: (61-9) 383 1981, mobile (041) 893 2994, **Fax:** (61-9) 385 4595.
URL: www.ozemail.com.au/~ksetra/sgh.html

Type: Bed & breakfast guesthouse.
Clientele: Mostly gay men with gay women welcome
Transportation: Airport bus to Perth, then taxi. Free pick up from train or bus.
To Gay Bars: 4 miles or 10 minutes by car.
Rooms: 4 rooms, 3 suites with single, double, queen beds or king.
Bathrooms: 3 private. Shared: 2 bathtubs, 2 showers & 1 full bath.
Meals: Continental breakfast with eggs & fresh fruit when in season.
Vegetarian: Vegetarian food nearby.
Complimentary: Tea, coffee, mints on pillows & fresh flowers daily.
Dates Open: All year.
High Season: Nov-Apr.
Rates: AUD $55-AUD $95.
Discounts: One day free for weekly stays.
Credit Cards: MC, Visa, Bancard.
Rsv'tns: Required.
To Reserve: Call direct.
Minimum Stay: 2 nights.
Parking: Ample free off-street covered parking.
In-Room: Color cable TV, VCR, video tape library, telephone, ceiling fans, kitchen, refrigerator, coffee & tea-making facilities, room & laundry service.
On-Premises: Meeting rooms, TV lounge, laundry facilities, courtyard with BBQ. Cars for hire.
Exercise/Health: Gym, weights on premises. Nearby Jacuzzi, sauna, steam & massage.
Swimming: Nearby pool, ocean, river, lake & beach.
Sunbathing: On private & common sun decks, patio, lawn or at the beach. Gay nude beach 2 km.
Nudity: Permitted on back patio.
Smoking: Permitted outside.
Pets: Not permitted.
Handicap Access: No.
Children: Not especially welcome.
Languages: English.
Your Host: Ralph.

aglta

Aspen Lodge
Gay-Friendly ♀♂

A Tranquil Little Oasis in the Heart of the City, Where Everyone is Welcome

Traditionally known as the "Pink Palace" this colourful landmark is not an exclusive gay residence. Just a quiet, friendly house where gays, lesbians and other folks, both young and old, enjoy budget bed and breakfast hospitality in central Auckland. In our reading room we keep the local gay & lesbian newspaper, as well as books on gay accommodation and travel in NZ. Our gay night manager and his partner will do their best to provide additional information on gay nightlife and activities.

Aspen Lodge is an older-style guesthouse opposite a beautiful park, yet we're only minutes walking distance from Queen Street, restaurants, railway station, ferry and bus terminals. A healthy "all you can eat" breakfast is included in the tariff, and beverage making facilities are provided free in the TV lounge at any time. Additionally, our friendly team are happy to arrange rental cars, camper vans and sightseeing trips. We don't provide frills, but we do provide clean, comfortable, budget accommodation at a great location with good, old-fashioned Kiwi hospitality.

Address: 62 Emily Place, Auckland North Island New Zealand.
Tel: (64-9) 379 6698, **Fax:** (64-9) 377 7625. **E-mail:** aspenlodge@xtra.co.nz

Type: Bed & breakfast.
Clientele: Mostly hetero with 20% gay & lesbian clientele
Transportation: Supershuttle from airport to door NZ $10 per person.
To Gay Bars: 5-minute walk to gay bar & sauna.
Rooms: 14 singles, 6 doubles (1 dbl bed) & 6 twins (2 single beds).
Bathrooms: 5 shared showers & 6 shared toilets.
Meals: Continental breakfast.
Vegetarian: 5-minute walk.
Complimentary: Tea & coffee.
Dates Open: All year.
High Season: November-May.
Rates: Single NZ $49, twin NZ $69.
Discounts: Winter, May 1-Sept 30. Yearly winter specials available.
Credit Cards: MC, Visa, Amex, Diners, JBC.
Rsv'tns: Required, especially in high season.
To Reserve: Travel agent or call direct.
Parking: Limited on-street pay parking. 1st come, first served.
In-Room: Maid service.
On-Premises: TV lounge, laundry facilities, public telephones.
Exercise/Health: 5 min to nearby gym, weights, sauna, steam, massage.
Swimming: 5 min to nearby pool.
Sunbathing: On the patio.
Smoking: Permitted in designated areas only, rooms are non-smoking.
Pets: Not permitted.
Handicap Access: No.
Children: Permitted.
Languages: English, Dutch, German, French.
Your Host: Sarah & Phillip.

Park Central The Darlinghurst
Gay-Owned & -Operated ♀♂

Apartment Freedom & Hotel Service Come Together

Charming and elegant, **Park Central The Darlinghurst** combines the advantages of staying in a hotel in the centre of the city with the privacy, pleasure and convenience of your own modern apartment. We look after you with traditional hotel service whenever you require it, while leaving you free to choose the level of "hotel" care you desire... as self-contained or as pampered as you wish. And we make sure you really can enjoy the best of both worlds at a very reasonable price. Our Deco-style apartment hotel features sweeping ocean views and is a quick stroll from the city centre and the water's edge. Auckland is New Zealand's most vibrant, bustling and multi-cultural city. Every city attraction is here — all set against the backdrop of Waitemata Harbour.

Address: 52 Eden Crescent, Auckland City 1001 New Zealand.
Tel: (64-9) 366 3260, (0800) 944 400, **Fax:** (64-9) 366-3269.
E-mail: darlinghurst@parkcentral.co.nz

Type: Apartment hotel.
Clientele: Mostly hetero with a gay/lesbian following
Transportation: Airport shuttle or taxi. Pick up from airport NZ $67.
To Gay Bars: 1 mile, a 20 min walk, a 5 min drive.
Rooms: 41 apartments with single or queen beds.
Bathrooms: 41 private shower/toilets.

Vegetarian: Available.
Complimentary: Tea & coffee.
Dates Open: All year.
High Season: Nov-Mar.
Rates: NZ $175-NZ $235.
Discounts: Weekend, corporate, senior citizen.
Credit Cards: MC, Visa, Amex, Diners.
Rsv'tns: Required.
To Reserve: Travel agent or call direct.

Parking: Adequate free, covered off-street parking (request when reserving).
In-Room: Telephone, color cable TV, kitchen, refrigerator, coffee & tea-making facilities, maid, room & laundry service.
On-Premises: Secretarial, fax, photocopy services, equipment & computer hire.
Exercise/Health: Massage. Nearby gym, weights,

Jacuzzi, sauna, steam, massage.
Swimming: Nearby pool & ocean.
Sunbathing: At beach.
Smoking: Non-smoking apartments available.
Pets: Not permitted.
Handicap Access: No.
Children: Welcome.
Languages: English.

Orongo Bay Homestead
Gay-Friendly 50/50 ♀♂

Reserve a "Peace" of Paradise

Orongo Bay Homestead offers historic charm and fine cuisine on the coast in the Bay of Islands. This historic First American Consulate (c. 1863) is now an exclusive, lovingly restored retreat with natural spring water. Sequestered in 17 private acres of bush, lake and lawns, there are sweeping views over a tranquil bush-framed bay towards New Zealand's birthplace. Just a 50-minute flight from Auckland, the **Homestead** is central to yachting, gentle walks, sea-kayaking, vintage aircraft flightseeing, unspoiled beaches and world-record game fishing. The many amenities and features found here include attentive service, wood-panelled ceilings, private bathrooms, natural wool bedding, fluffy bathrobes, complimentary natural skin-care creams and a dry Finnish sauna. Maori co-hosts Chris Swannell and *Foodwriters'* award-winner chef Michael Hooper, feature health-conscious, luxurious cuisine from ocean, farm, organic gardens and exotic orchard, plus a fabulous "champagne brunch." Oysters are served live, harvested from the bay just before dinner.

Address: Aucks Road, RD1, Russell, Bay of Islands New Zealand.
Tel: (64-9) 403 7527, **Fax:** (64-9) 403 7675. **E-mail:** orongo.bay@clear.net.nz

Type: Guesthouse with dining room & historic wine cellar.

Clientele: 50% gay & lesbian & 50% hetero clientele
Transportation: Car or 50-

min flight from Auckland. Inquire about fee for pick up from airport, ferry dock &

Rolls Royce limo service from airport (35 mins).

Rooms: 2 rooms & 2 suites with single, queen or king beds.
Bathrooms: All private.
Meals: Full breakfast with champagne. Property is organic & pesticide-free, free-range hens.
Vegetarian: By arrangement vegetarian & all dietary requirements are welcome (low-fat, low-cholesterol, etc).
Complimentary: Chocolate chunk cookies, fresh tea & coffee, fresh herbal tisanes, homemade cognac truffles, spring water.
Dates Open: All year.
High Season: Dec 1-April 30.
Rates: Per person: winter NZ $135-185 per person, summer NZ $135-$225, includes champagne brunch.
Discounts: 10% "family" discount during low season, advance payment.
Credit Cards: MC, Diners, Visa, Amex.
Rsv'tns: Essential.
To Reserve: Travel agent or call direct.
Parking: Ample free off-street parking.
In-Room: Maid & laundry service. Suites have coffee & tea-making facilities & refrigerator.
On-Premises: TV lounge, meeting rooms.
Exercise/Health: Sauna, massage. Nearby bush walks, tennis, golf, sailing, game fishing.
Swimming: Ocean, diving nearby.
Sunbathing: On hills & fields of estate, on patio, private & common sun decks, at beach.
Smoking: Permitted on covered verandahs. House is smoke-free.
Pets: Not permitted.
Handicap Access: Yes.
Children: No. Inquire if booking all 4 rooms.
Languages: English, some Danish, Maori & French.
Your Host: Michael & Chris.

Troutbeck

Gay/Lesbian ♂

Gay Homestay with Trout Fishing from the Garden's Edge

Troutbeck lies five kilometres from Rotorua on a half-acre of landscaped garden on the banks of the Waiteti Stream, by its outlet into Lake Rotorua. Right from the banks of the stream at the foot of our garden, guests can fly fish for Rainbow or Brown trout from December to May, or troll Lake Rotorua using our dinghy and private landing ramp. *Troutbeck* is the first Lockwood house built in New Zealand in 1953 of Californian redwood, a prototype of many in the country, all renowned for their quality wooden construction and open-plan design. We're close to the thermal areas and Maori culture. Golf courses are nearby.

Address: 16 Egmont Rd, PO Box 242, Ngongotaha, Rotorua New Zealand.
Tel: (64-7) 357 4795, Fax: (64-7) 357 4780.
E-mail: troutbeck@xtra.co.nz URL: http://nz.com/webnz/troutbeck

Type: Homestay.
Clientele: Mostly men with women welcome
Transportation: Car is best. Will pick up from airport, train or bus.
Rooms: 3 rooms with king or queen beds.
Bathrooms: 2 shared baths.
Meals: Full breakfast. Optional lunch & dinner with wine.
Vegetarian: Available on request.
Complimentary: Tea & coffee.
Dates Open: All year.
High Season: December-April.
Rates: Single NZ $50, double NZ $70.
Credit Cards: MC, Visa, Amex, Bancard.
Rsv'tns: Preferred.
To Reserve: Travel agent or call direct.
Parking: Adequate free off-street parking.
In-Room: Refrigerator, maid, room & laundry service.
On-Premises: TV lounge with VCR, laundry facilities.
Exercise/Health: Nearby gym.
Swimming: At nearby lake.
Sunbathing: On private 1/2 acre of land.
Nudity: Permitted while sunning in private garden.
Smoking: We prefer no smoking.
Pets: We prefer no pets.
Handicap Access: Yes, there are no steps.
Children: No.
Languages: English, Tongan.
Your Host: Ken & Tali.

Te Puru Coast View Lodge

Gay-Friendly ♀♂

High-Quality, Full-Service Accommodation on the Western Coromandel Coastline

With an emphasis on high quality and personal service, *Te Puru Coast View Lodge* offers full-service accommodation for travellers seeking a moderately priced New Zealand lodge experience. This stunning scenic hideaway, 15 minutes north of the town of Thames, overlooks the small seaside village of Te Puru and is situated on one of the largest recorded prehistoric Maori archaeological sites in the

continued next page

region. The distinctive, well-appointed guestrooms feature handcrafted furniture and furnishings throughout. Our fully-licensed, award-winning in-house restaurant specialises in superb New Zealand and Coromandel cuisine, with an a la carte menu that includes New Zealand lamb, Coromandel mussels and fine New Zealand wines.

Address: 468 Thames Coast Road,
Te Puru Coromandel Peninsula New Zealand.
Tel: (64-7) 868 2326, **Fax:** (64-7) 868 2376.
URL: 100036.2460@compuserve.com

Type: Small hotel, inn, lodge with fully licensed restaurant.
Clientele: Mostly hetero clientele with a gay/lesbian following
Transportation: Car is best. Free pick up from bus.
To Gay Bars: 1-1/2 hours to Auckland gay bars.
Rooms: 4 rooms with double, queen or king beds.
Bathrooms: Private bath/shower/toilets & private shower/toilets.

Vegetarian: A la carte menu includes vegetarian dishes.
Complimentary: Tea, coffee, cookies in room. After-dinner mints, liqueurs in restaurant or room.
Dates Open: All year.
High Season: Late Oct-early Apr.
Rates: NZ$ 110 (single) to NZ$ 150 (double).
Discounts: On pre-booked, all-inclusive packages (eg: dinner/B&B) P.O.A.

Credit Cards: MC, Visa, Amex.
Rsv'tns: Preferred, especially during high season.
To Reserve: Travel agent or call direct.
Parking: Ample, free, off-street parking.
In-Room: Ceiling fans, color TV, coffee & tea-making facilities, maid & laundry service, limited room service.
On-Premises: TV lounge, video tape & book libraries, telephone/fax, PC.

Swimming: Nearby ocean, river.
Sunbathing: At beach.
Smoking: Non-smoking premises. Permitted in outdoor areas, patios, etc.
Pets: Not permitted.
Handicap Access: Yes, rails in bathroom, wide doors, wet area shower & raised WCs, queen-sized double room w/ active pusher.
Children: No.
Languages: English.
Your Host: Pam & Sam.

The Mermaid

Q-NET Women ♀

The Mermaid, a turn-of-the-century character building, is situated in Wellington's inner city Aro Valley, an historic area with picturesque Victorian Villas. The four individually decorated rooms all have views, either of the tree-lined garden or of the surrounding hillsides. One room has private facilities, while the others share a bathroom with tub and shower. All have luxurious robes, towels and fragrant soaps for your extra comfort. We're minutes from Wellington's downtown cafes, university shops, theatres, the nearest gay bar and the stunningly picturesque waterfront. Owner, Francesca, is happy to share her knowledge of restaurants, theater, events and how to network the New Zealand women's scene to make your stay completely personalised and memorable.

Address: 1 Epuni St, Aro Valley, Wellington New Zealand.
Tel: (64-4) 384 4511 (Tel/Fax). **E-mail:** mermaid@sans.vuw.ac.nz

Type: Guesthouse.
Clientele: Women only
Transportation: Airport shuttle, bus from railway station to Aro Valley. Pickup from airport, NZ$10 per person.
To Gay Bars: 5 blocks, a 15 minute walk, a 5 minute drive.
Rooms: 4 rooms with single, double or queen beds.

Bathrooms: 1 private shower/toilet, 1 shared bath/shower bath.
Meals: Buffet breakfast.
Vegetarian: Restaurant nearby.
Complimentary: Tea, coffee, wine on arrival, fresh fruit.
Dates Open: All year.
High Season: Dec-Jan.
Rates: NZ$68-NZ$120.
Discounts: 10% on stays of over 1 week.

Credit Cards: MC, Visa, Amex.
Rsv'tns: Required.
To Reserve: Call direct or e-mail.
Parking: Adequate off-street parking.
In-Room: Television, VCR, coffee/tea-making facilities.
On-Premises: Pool table, library, telephone.
Exercise/Health: Massage by appointment. Nearby gym, Jacuzzi, massage.

Swimming: Nearby pool & ocean.
Sunbathing: On common sun decks, on patio.
Smoking: Permitted outside.
Pets: Not permitted.
Handicap Access: No.
Children: Welcome.
Languages: English, Greek.
Your Host: Francesca.

Bushline Lodge

Q-NET Women ♀

Breath-of-Fresh-Air Vacations

    Bushline Lodge, across the main divide on the West Coast of New Zealand, is the ideal retreat for women seeking time out in a women's space and ambiance. This unique lodge is situated in a spectacular area. Easily accessible by car from the lodge are snow-capped mountains, Alpine herb fields, mountain and coastal rainforest, sea stacks and blowholes, limestone caves, bush-fringed lakes, advancing glaciers, and lagoons. The area is ideal for bushwalkers and bird lovers. For the daring, there is caving, cave rafting and tubing; for the angler, year-round world-class trout fishing; and for those who like to delve into the past, historic trails and gold panning. A naturally different hot spot.

    Address: c/o Bushwise Women, PO Box 28010, Christchurch New Zealand.
    Tel: (64-3) 332 4952 (Tel/Fax), (64-3) 738 0077, or mobile: (64-3) 25 360 926.
    E-mail: bushwise@bushwise.co.nz **URL:** http://www.bushwise.co.nz

Type: Bed & breakfast.
Clientele: Women only
Transportation: Car, shuttle bus or Tranz Alpine railway. Free pick up from train.
Rooms: 3 rooms with single or double beds.
Bathrooms: Private & shared.
Meals: Expanded continental breakfast, dinner, supper.
Vegetarian: Vegetarian menu.
Complimentary: Pre-dinner drinks & hors d'oeuvres, tea & coffee.
Dates Open: All year.
High Season: Dec-Feb.
Rates: B&B: double NZ$ 85, single NZ$ 50. Full accommodation: double NZ$ 125, single NZ$ 70.
Credit Cards: Visa, MC.
Rsv'tns: Required.
To Reserve: Call direct.
Parking: Ample free off-street parking.
On-Premises: Library, laundry facilities, musical instruments.
Sunbathing: On common sun decks, at beach, lakeside.
Smoking: Permitted outside.
Pets: Not permitted.
Handicap Access: No.
Children: No.
Languages: English.
Your Host: Joy.

Rainbow House

Gay/Lesbian ♂

Where Comfort is Affordable & Diversity is Appreciated

    Rainbow House is only 10 minutes from two gay bars, three cruise clubs and many excellent restaurants in downtown Christchurch. Our park-like hillside location offers marvelous views of the city. The spacious sleeping quarters feature queen-sized beds and, for your private enjoyment, there is also a garden spa pool on premises. Great, all-inclusive breakfasts are prepared each morning and you'll appreciate our friendly, unobtrusive service. Beaches, skifields and city sights are all cose by. Please e-mail us for more information about the inn, Christchurch and New Zealand.

    Address: 9 The Crescent, Christchurch 8002 New Zealand.
    Tel: (64-3) 337 1438, **Fax:** (64-3) 337 1496.
    E-mail: mfraser.rainbowhouse@clear.net.nz

Type: Bed & breakfast guesthouse inn.
Clientele: Mostly men with women welcome
Transportation: Car. Pick up from airport (NZ$ 12), bus, train. Free ride to city & return 10:30am-11pm.
To Gay Bars: 3 miles, an 8 min drive, a 30 min walk.
Rooms: 4 rooms with single or queen beds.
Bathrooms: Shared: 1 bath/shower/toilet, 1 bathtub only, 1 shower only.
Meals: Full breakfast.
Vegetarian: Request when booking. Vegetarian restaurants nearby.
Complimentary: Tea, coffee, soda.
Dates Open: All year.
High Season: Nov-Mar.
Rates: NZ$ 38-NZ$ 58.
Rsv'tns: Required.
To Reserve: Travel agent or call direct.
Parking: Adequate free off-street parking.
In-Room: Maid & laundry service.
On-Premises: TV lounge, video tape library, meeting rooms, laundry facilities, E-mail.
Exercise/Health: Nearby gym, weights, Jacuzzi, sauna, steam, massage.
Swimming: Nearby pool, ocean.
Sunbathing: On common sun decks.
Nudity: Permitted on sun decks.
Smoking: No smoking inside.
Pets: No pets.
Handicap Access: No, some steps.
Children: No.
Languages: English.
Your Host: Martin & Robbie.

Te Puna Wai Lodge

Gay-Owned 50/50 ♀♂*

"'Tis Distance Lends Enchantment to the View & Robes the Mountains in its Azure Hue" — Alexander Pope

Te Puna Wai Lodge is a restored early Victorian villa, once the home of noted New Zealand photographer William Tyree. Set in the magnificent Port Hills, views are unsurpassed, encompassing the whole sweep of Tasman Bay, with mountains to the west, snow-clad in winter. The home provides a well-designed living area, sunny verandas and a private garden, with all guestrooms having luxuriously appointed marble ensuite bathrooms and central heating. Our sumptuous breakfasts include a variety of fresh juices, fruit, fine coffees and teas, and local produce. Excellent waterfront restaurants are a five-minute walk away, and the town centre is a short five-minute drive from us. We fly the rainbow flag, as well as the country flag of our visiting guests.

Address: 24 Richardson Street, Nelson 7001 New Zealand.
Tel: (64-3) 548 7621 (Tel/Fax).

Type: Bed & breakfast.
Clientele: 50% gay & lesbian & 50% hetero clientele
Transportation: Car or taxi is best. Free pick up from airport or bus.
Rooms: 3 suites with double or queen beds.
Bathrooms: Private: 1 bath/shower/toilet, 2 shower/toilets.
Meals: Expanded continental breakfast.
Vegetarian: Available upon request & nearby.
Complimentary: Tea, coffee, juices, water.
Dates Open: All year.
High Season: Dec-Mar.
Rates: NZ$ 115-NZ$ 125 single, NZ$ 125-NZ$ 145 double.
Discounts: For longer stays.
Credit Cards: MC, Visa, Amex, Diners, Bancard.
Rsv'tns: Required.
To Reserve: Travel agent or call direct.
Parking: Adequate free on- & off-street parking.
In-Room: Telephone, color TV, room & laundry service.
On-Premises: Laundry facilities.
Exercise/Health: Nearby gym, weights, Jacuzzi, sauna, massage.
Swimming: Nearby pool, ocean, river, lake.
Sunbathing: On private sun decks, patio & at beach.
Nudity: Permitted at nudist beaches, secluded beaches & bays.
Smoking: Permitted, but preferably on verandas & patios.
Pets: Permitted.
Handicap Access: No.
Children: Welcome.
Languages: English, Polish, German, Spanish, French, Portuguese, Danish.
Your Host: Richard, Szczepan.

The West's Motor Inn

Gay-Friendly ⚥

The Best in the West

Situated in Martintar, ***The West's Motor Inn*** is located between Nadi International Airport and Nadi Town, a ten-minute drive from each. The hotel's recent refurbishing has resulted in a convenient and affordable accommodation for tourists, families and businesspeople. Room amenities include air conditioning, ceiling fans, telephones and radio alarm clocks. Drinks and meals can be enjoyed in our covered, open-air bar, lounge and cafe-style restaurant. Inside, there is also an air-conditioned piano bar. Cool off in our large swimming pool which meanders around a superb mango tree. Accessible to public transport, a bus stop is just outside the hotel entrance and taxi service is available twenty-four hours.

Address: Martintar, Nadi Fiji.
Tel: (679) 720 044, **Fax:** (679) 720 071.

Type: Hotel, motor inn with restaurant, bar, piano bar & gift shop.
Clientele: Mostly hetero clientele with a gay/lesbian following
Transportation: Courtesy airport shuttle. Free pick up from airport.
Rooms: 62 rooms with single or double beds.
Bathrooms: Private & shared.
Vegetarian: Available.
Complimentary: Tea & coffee.
Dates Open: All year.
High Season: May-Sept.
Rates: Fijian$ 44-$ 129, extra person Fijian$ 20.
Rsv'tns: Required.
To Reserve: Travel agent or call direct.
Parking: Ample free off-street parking.
In-Room: AC, ceiling fans, phone, color TV, radio/alarm clock, refrigerator, coffee & tea-making facilities, maid & room service.
On-Premises: Meeting rooms, fax, typing, valet.
Exercise/Health: Nearby gym, weights.
Swimming: Pool on premises.
Sunbathing: Poolside.
Smoking: Permitted. Non-smoking rooms available on request.
Pets: Not permitted.
Handicap Access: No.
Children: Welcome. Restaurant has special menu & drinks.
Languages: English, Fijian, Indian.
Your Host: Peter & Dave.

Residence Linareva

Gay-Friendly 50/50 ⚥

Just What you Need!

Here, at the foot of lush, green hills, on the shores of a lagoon, we have created an environment of tropical ease for gay, lesbian and other visitors from far away. Each of the typical Tahitian grass bungalows at ***Residence Linareva*** has its own character. Special care has been taken in decorating them with traditional crafts. Also enjoy the most exquisite French cuisine in the unique surroundings of our floating pub-restaurant and over-water terrasse. Charmingly converted from a former inter-island trading boat, this small, but delightful, floating restaurant specializes in fresh local seafood with a definite European flair and provides a romantic setting for cocktails at sunset.

Address: PO Box 1, Haapiti, Moorea French Polynesia.
Tel: (689) 56 15 35 (Tel/Fax).

Type: Residence with floating bar-restaurant.
Clientele: 50% gay & lesbian & 50% hetero clientele
Transportation: From Moorea airport, taxi or rental car. From dock, bus or rental car. Rental cars & scooters available.
To Gay Bars: A 5-minute drive.
Rooms: 3 rooms, 1 suite & 1 bungalow with king beds.
Bathrooms: All private shower & toilet.
Dates Open: All year.
Rates: 7,200-15,600 Pacific Francs.
Discounts: 25% for stays of at least 7 nights.
Credit Cards: MC, Visa, Amex.
Rsv'tns: Required.
To Reserve: Travel agent or call direct.
Parking: Free parking.
In-Room: Color TV, ceiling fans, kitchen, refrigerator, coffee/tea-making facilities & maid service.
Exercise/Health: Bicycles, outrigger canoes, masks, snorkels.
Swimming: At deep water spot at end of pier or at nearby sand beaches.
Sunbathing: On private sun decks & beach.
Nudity: Permitted in garden & on raft.
Pets: Not permitted.
Handicap Access: No.
Children: Not especially welcome.
Languages: French, English & Italian.

CANADA · CALGARY · ALBERTA

Calgary Westways Guest House
Q-NET Gay/Lesbian ♂

Alberta's First, Calgary's Leading Gay-owned B&B

Westways is a 1914 Heritage home, offering four tastefully-appointed bedrooms with private baths. After an active day, guests can relax in a hot tub or on the secluded deck. Each morning offers a choice of a traditional English, Canadian or health-conscious breakfast prepared by an award-winning chef and served in an Edwardian dining room. While bus and tram stops are nearby, we're just a ten-minute walk to bars and restaurants, and twenty minutes' walking to downtown. **GUEST COMMENT:**"*Very helpful host, quiet location, excellent breakfast, comfortable.*" E.S., Milan, Italy.

Address: 216 25th Ave SW, Calgary, AB T2S 0L1 Canada.
Tel: (403) 229-1758, **Fax:** (403) 228-6265.
E-mail: calgary@westways.ab.ca **URL:** http://www.westways.ab.ca

Type: Bed & breakfast.
Clientele: Mostly men with women welcome
Transportation: Near rapid transport & bus. Pick up from airport CDN $12.
To Gay Bars: 10-min. walk.
Rooms: 4 rooms with double or queen beds.
Bathrooms: All private, ensuite.
Meals: Full cooked breakfast.

Vegetarian: Available.
Complimentary: Tea & coffee in kitchen. Fresh fruit.
Dates Open: All year.
High Season: June-July.
Rates: CDN $60-$100 double, CDN $40-$80 single.
Discounts: Weekly rates.
Credit Cards: MC, Visa, Amex.
Rsv'tns: Required.

To Reserve: Travel agent or call direct.
Parking: Ample free off-street & on-street parking.
In-Room: Ceiling fans, telephone, cable colour TV, maid & laundry service.
On-Premises: TV lounge & laundry facilities.
Exercise/Health: Outdoor hot tub, gym, weights, indoor running track, squash. 10 min walk to sports centre.

Swimming: Pool in nearby sports arena.
Sunbathing: On deck or in park across the lane.
Smoking: Permitted in kitchen, on porch & by hot tub.
Pets: Permitted.
Handicap Access: No.
Children: Not especially welcome.
Languages: English.
Your Host: Jonathon.

The Foxwood Bed & Breakfast
Gay/Lesbian ♀♂

Western Hospitality in the Heart of Calgary

The beautifully restored *Foxwood* is a charming 1910 Edwardian home in the heart of Calgary, offering three different sleeping rooms, each with its own style and antique decor. Plush pillow-top queen-sized beds are accented with fine linens, a luxurious down comforter and soft pillows. Awake rested and treat yourself to a delicious home-made Canadian full breakfast, complete with special "home-baked goods" hot from the oven. Loated in the historic area of Calgary known as "Uptown 17," we're close to a variety of unique shops, restaurants, galleries and local clubs for dancing or live jazz.

Address: 1725-12 Street SW, Calgary, AB T2T 3N1 Canada.
Tel: (403) 244-6693.

Type: Bed & breakfast.
Clientele: Mostly gay & lesbian with some cool straight clientele
Transportation: Car, airport pick up, taxi. Pick up from airport CDN $15, from bus CDN $6.
To Gay Bars: 10 blocks, a 15 minute walk, a 5 minute drive.
Rooms: 3 rooms with queen beds.
Bathrooms: Rooms with shared 1/2 bath: sink, toilet & shared master bath: sink, toilet & dual shower.
Meals: Full home-baked breakfast (changes daily).
Vegetarian: Available with advance notice, when making reservation.
Complimentary: Coffee, tea, snacks, ice, before-bed mints or chocolates.
Dates Open: All year.
High Season: Jun-Sept.
Rates: Low season (Oct-May): CDN $55-CDN $70; high season (Jun-Sept) CDN $65-CDN $80.
Discounts: 10% off 7+ days (weekly).
Credit Cards: MC, Visa.
Rsv'tns: Required.
To Reserve: Call direct.
Minimum Stay: 2 nights on holiday weekends.
Parking: Adequate free on-street parking. Winter plug-ins available.
In-Room: Color cable TV, homemade robes, blow dryers, slippers. One room has private deck.
On-Premises: TV lounge, video tape library, verandah, deck, English garden, laundry facilities.
Exercise/Health: Nearby gym, Jacuzzi, massage & tanning.
Swimming: Nearby pool & river.
Sunbathing: On patio.
Smoking: Permitted on outside patio & porches only.
Pets: Not permitted.
Handicap Access: No.
Children: No.
Languages: English.
Your Host: Brent & Devon.

Fernie Westways Guest House

Q-NET Gay-Owned & -Operated

In Beautiful Elk Valley, South of Banff & Radium Hot Springs

Westways is known for offering comfort, elegance and a warm, friendly ambiance. Our 1908 Heritage home with its high ceilings and hardwood floors, presents three spacious bedrooms, one with a king-sized bed and private bathroom, and two with queen-sized beds and shared bathroom. Relax in the hot tub and take in views of the Rocky Mountains, or simply curl up in front of the wood-burning fireplace. A full breakfast, prepared by your European-trained host, is served in the elegant dining room. *Fernie Westways Guest House* is five minutes from Fernie Snow Valley Ski Resort and within walking distance to shops. Quiet and down-to-earth, Fernie is a refreshing alternative to the busier Rocky Mountain resorts.

Address: Box 658, 202-4a Avenue, Fernie, BC V0B 1M0 Canada.
Tel: (250) 423-3058, **Fax:** (250) 423-3059.
E-mail: fernie@westways.ab.ca

Type: Bed & breakfast guesthouse.
Clientele: Mostly gay & lesbian with some hetero clientele
Transportation: Car is best or Greyhound bus. Free pick up from bus.
To Gay Bars: 3 hour drive to Calgary gay bars.
Rooms: 4 rooms with double, queen or king beds.
Bathrooms: Private: 1 bath/shower/toilet, 1 shower/toilet. Shared: 2 bath/shower/toilets. More bathrooms planned.
Meals: Full breakfast.
Vegetarian: Breakfast is vegetarian. Vegetarian food nearby.
Complimentary: Tea & coffee.
Dates Open: All year.
High Season: Dec-Apr.
Rates: Summer: CDN $45-CDN $75, winter: CDN $50-CDN $90.
Discounts: Weekly & monthly.
Credit Cards: MC, Visa, Amex.
Rsv'tns: Required.
To Reserve: Travel agent or call direct.
Parking: Amle covered on- & off-street parking.

continued next page

In-Room: Color cable TV, maid service.
On-Premises: Meeting rooms, TV lounge, video tape library, home theatre, laundry facilities. Storage available in garage.
Exercise/Health: Jacuzzi. Nearby gym, weights.
Swimming: Nearby pool & river.
Sunbathing: On common sun decks & patio.
Smoking: Permitted on deck & porch. Non-smoking rooms available.
Pets: Permitted.
Handicap Access: No.
Children: Are not refused.
Languages: English, French.
Your Host: Jonathon & Peter.

Green Rose at Scott Point
Gay-Friendly 50/50 ♀♂

Green Rose at Scott Point is a charming suite in a West Coast waterfront cottage, with views facing south toward the other Gulf Islands and the San Juans. Enjoy the privacy of your deck just above the tideline, read by the fireplace, watch the seals, otters and birdlife, or walk the point. The suite, with its decor of crisp whites, model boats and old pine, consists of a sitting room, bedroom, bathroom and a small kitchenette. Completing the scene is the sound of water lapping against the shore. The *Green Rose* is ten minutes from the town of Ganges and minutes from the Long Harbor ferry terminal.

Address: 388 Scott Point Dr, Salt Spring Island, BC V8K 2R2 Canada.
Tel: (250) 537-9927.

Type: Private suite with kitchenette.
Clientele: 50% gay & lesbian & 50% straight clientele
Transportation: Ferry from Vancouver or Victoria.
Rooms: 1 self-contained suite.
Bathrooms: Private bath/shower/toilet.
Complimentary: Coffee, fruit, muffins in room.
Dates Open: All year.
High Season: Jun-Sept.
Rates: CDN $125.
Discounts: Weekly rates available.
Credit Cards: MC, Visa.
Rsv'tns: Recommended.
To Reserve: Call direct.
Minimum Stay: 2 nights.
Parking: Ample off-street parking.
Swimming: Ocean or nearby lakes.
Smoking: Permitted outside only.
Pets: Not permitted.
Handicap Access: No.
Children: No.
Languages: English.
Your Host: Tom & Ron.

Summerhill Guest House
Gay-Friendly 50/50 ♀♂

Island Living at Its Best

At water's edge, *Summerhill* evokes peace and serenity. Tasteful and understated, the guest rooms overlook either magnificent Sansum Narrows or pastoral meadows. All have private baths, cozy duvets and excellent bedside reading lamps. Relax by the fire in the spacious oceanside sitting room or escape to sun-drenched decks and watch the eagles glide by. Tantalizing breakfasts are served overlooking the sea. While on Salt Spring, explore nature or browse the numerous shops and galleries in the village. Connections from Vancouver and Seattle.

Address: 209 Chu-An Drive, Salt Spring Island, BC V8K 1H9 Canada.
Tel: (250) 537-2727, **Fax:** (250) 537-4301. **E-mail:** summerhill@saltspring.com

Type: Bed & breakfast.
Clientele: 50% gay & lesbian & 50% straight clientele
Transportation: Ferry (walk-on or with car) or float plane. Free pick up from ferry dock or float plane dock.
Rooms: 3 rooms with twin or queen beds.

Bathrooms: 1 private shower/toilet & 2 private bath/toilet/showers.
Meals: Full breakfast.
Vegetarian: Available upon request. Vegetarian food & restaurant nearby.
Complimentary: Welcoming wine, beer, coffee, tea, juice. Room snacks.
Dates Open: All year.

High Season: May-September.
Rates: CDN $90-$120.
Credit Cards: MC, Visa.
Rsv'tns: Recommended.
To Reserve: Call direct.
Parking: Ample free off-street parking.
On-Premises: Sitting & dining rooms, fireplace & guest refrigerator.
Exercise/Health: Nearby gym, weights & massage.
Swimming: Nearby ocean & lake access.
Sunbathing: Common sun decks & at the beach.
Smoking: Permitted outside.
Pets: Not permitted.
Handicap Access: No.
Children: Adults only.
Languages: English.
Your Host: Michael & Paul.

The West Wind Guest House

Q-NET Gay/Lesbian ♀♂

A Fine West Coast Experience in Any Season

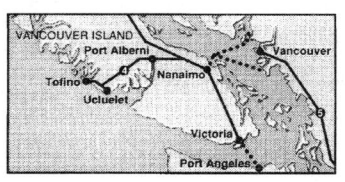

In this area of pounding surf and wind-swept shores is *The West Wind*, situated on two acres of wooded privacy. Tofino is a year-round destination for beachcombers and storm watchers alike. You can go whale watching, kayaking, and hiking and enjoy the beauty of endless beaches and ancient rainforest. The West Coast ambiance of the guesthouse includes feather beds, goose down duvets, antique furnishings, tranquil gardens and expansive sun decks. Fine restaurants, grocery stores, pubs, and galleries are nearby.

Address: 1321 Pacific Rim Hwy, Mail: Box 436, Tofino, BC V0R 2Z0 Canada.
Tel: (250) 725-2224, **Fax:** (250) 725-2212. **E-mail:** Westwind@island.net

Type: Private cottage & suite.
Clientele: Good mix of gays & lesbians
Transportation: Car is best. Complimentary aioprt or bus pick up/drop off.
Rooms: 1 cottage, 1 suite.
Bathrooms: Private baths.
Meals: Breakfast tray served to suite.
Complimentary: Coffee, teas, fruit basket.
Dates Open: All year.

High Season: May-Sept.
Rates: Winter CDN $60-$110 double, summer CDN $95-$185 dbl (addt'l person CDN $20).
Discounts: On extended stays in low season.
Credit Cards: MC, Visa, Amex.
Rsv'tns: Required.
To Reserve: Travel agent or call direct.
Parking: Private covered parking.

In-Room: VCR, video tape library, refrigerator, coffee/tea-making facilities, ceiling fans. Kitchen in cottage.
On-Premises: Video library, laundry facilities, phone.
Exercise/Health: Hot tub, gym, mountain bikes for loan, hiking, beachcombing, kayaking, canoeing, golfing, surfing.
Swimming: 5 minute-walk to ocean & beaches.

Sunbathing: On private sun decks, private garden & at the beach.
Nudity: Clothing optional with discretion. Nude sunbathing in private garden, sun decks & hot tub.
Smoking: Permitted on outdoor deck areas only.
Pets: Sorry, not permitted. Cats in residence.
Handicap Access: No.
Children: Permitted.

Colibri Bed & Breakfast
Gay/Lesbian ♀♂

Calm in the City Centre

Our warm welcome will make you feel right at home here while you discover the city, or yourself. We provide you with plenty of insider information so you can shop till you drop or take time for your inner self. *Colibri* is in the heart of the gay West End of beautiful Vancouver, just blocks to scenic beaches, hectares of forest, and kilometres of oceanside promenade. Come, be yourself with us. A European-style bed and breakfast for those who value a sense of home while on the road.

Address: 1101 Thurlow St, Vancouver, BC V6E 1W9 Canada.
Tel: (604) 689-5100, **Fax:** (604) 682-3925. **E-mail:** smokry@ibm.net

Type: Bed & breakfast.
Clientele: Mostly gay & lesbian with some hetero clientele
Transportation: Airport bus to Century Plaza, then walk 1 block west.
To Gay Bars: 2 blocks.
Rooms: 5 rooms with single, double, queen or king beds.
Bathrooms: 2 shared bath/shower/toilets.
Meals: High season: full breakfast. Low season: continental breakfast.

Vegetarian: By arrangement on arrival.
Restaurants nearby (1-1/2 blocks).
Complimentary: Beverage on arrival. In summer fresh Belgian chocolates on pillows at turn-down.
Dates Open: All year.
High Season: May-October.
Rates: May-Oct CDN $125-$150. Nov-May CDN $55-$95.
Discounts: By arrangement on long stays in low season.

Credit Cards: MC, Visa, Amex.
Rsv'tns: Highly recommended.
To Reserve: Call/fax direct.
Minimum Stay: 2 days in high season.
Parking: Available.
In-Room: Maid & laundry service.
Exercise/Health: Nearby gym, weights, Jacuzzi, sauna, steam & massage.
Swimming: At Olympic-sized heated indoor pool 4 blocks away or nearby ocean.

Sunbathing: On common sun decks & at the beach.
Nudity: Nude beach 20 minutes by bus.
Smoking: Permitted on front & back decks & on room balconies.
Pets: Not permitted. 2 resident cats.
Handicap Access: Regrettably not.
Children: No.
Languages: English, French & Spanish.

Columbia Cottage Guest House
Gay-Friendly ♀♀♂

A Tranquil Oasis in the City with Fabulous Gourmet Breakfasts

On a tree-lined street, featuring an English country garden with a fountain flowing into the fish pond covered with waterlilies, *Columbia Cottage* offers peace and tranquility. Our breakfasts are fabulous — perhaps a baked apple, basted eggs with mango salsa, English scones, fresh orange juice, or those wonderful BC berries with crême-Anglaise. We're a five-minute drive to gay clubs downtown or to Q.E. Park for a romantic evening stroll to watch the sunset. Vancouver offers many attractions, so plan to stay a few days for complete satisfaction.

Address: 205 West 14th Ave, Vancouver, BC Canada.
Tel: (604) 874-5287, **Fax:** (604) 879-4547.
E-mail: goobles@msn.com **URL:** http://www.novamart.com/columbia

Type: Bed & breakfast.
Clientele: 20% gay & lesbian & 80% hetero clientele
Transportation: Car or cab. 15 minutes from international airport.
To Gay Bars: 5-minute drive to Vancouver's gay clubs.
Rooms: 4 double rooms &

1 garden suite with single, double, queen or king beds.
Bathrooms: All private.
Meals: Full gourmet breakfast.
Vegetarian: Available, as well as other special diets, if requested at time of booking.
Complimentary: Robes,

slippers, coffee, tea, sherry & local calls.
Dates Open: All year.
High Season: May-October.
Rates: Summer single CDN $100-$135, double CDN $125-$160. Winter single CDN $85, double CDN $105.

Discounts: For extended stays, business traveler.
Credit Cards: MC, Visa.
Rsv'tns: Recommended.
To Reserve: Call direct.
Parking: Ample free parking.
In-Room: Maid & laundry service, telephone, refrigerator, kitchen, coffee/

tea-making facilities.
On-Premises: Private dining room, enclosed garden.
Exercise/Health: Nearby gym, massage.
Swimming: 10 minutes

from most beaches. Walk to nearby pool.
Sunbathing: On the patio, at the beach.
Nudity: 15-minute drive to nude beaches.

Smoking: Permitted outside only.
Pets: Not permitted.
Handicap Access: No.
Children: Permitted over 8 years old.

Languages: English, German.
Your Host: Alisdair & Susanne.

Hawks Avenue Bed & Breakfast

Q-NET Women ♀

A Quiet and Comfortable Women's Bed & Breakfast

A bright and spacious room awaits you at *Hawks Avenue Bed & Breakfast*. Our heritage three-level townhouse is in Vancouver's Strathcona neighbourhood, a section of town rich in character and colour. We're ten minutes from downtown restaurants, shopping, theatres, clubs and galleries, as well as historic Gastown, Chinatown and Commercial Drive — renowned for its coffee bars and alternative atmosphere. Your room opens onto two decks, one of which overlooks a small park, and has a queen-sized bed, colour TV, telephone and a private half bathroom. We serve an expanded continental breakfast. There is ample street parking and non-smokers are preferred.

Address: 734 Hawks Avenue, Vancouver, BC V6A 3J3 Canada.
Tel: (604) 253-0989.

Type: Bed & breakfast.
Clientele: Women only
Transportation: Car, taxi from airport, or airport bus to downtown, then taxi.
To Gay Bars: 10 blocks, 1 mile, a 20 minute walk, a 5 minute drive.
Rooms: 1 room with queen bed.
Bathrooms: Private sink & toilet. Shared bath/shower/toilet.

Meals: Expanded continental breakfast.
Vegetarian: Available. Vegetarian restaurant & organic grocery are nearby.
Dates Open: All year.
High Season: May-Sept.
Rates: Summer: single CDN $75, double CDN $85. Winter: single CDN $65, double CDN $75.
Discounts: 10% on stays of over 2 nights.

Rsv'tns: Required.
To Reserve: Call direct.
Parking: Ample free on-street parking.
In-Room: Color cable TV, telephone.
Exercise/Health: Nearby gym, weights, Jacuzzi, sauna, steam, massage.
Swimming: Nearby pool, ocean.

Sunbathing: On private sun decks, at beach.
Smoking: Permitted outside. Entire house is non-smoking.
Pets: Not permitted, resident cat & Burmese Mtn. dog.
Handicap Access: No.
Children: Yes.
Languages: English.
Your Host: Louise.

Nelson House

Q-NET Gay/Lesbian ♀♂

No Boring Old B&B!

Nelson House is a large, 1907 Edwardian on a quiet, residential street, only minutes' walk from the business district, shopping, entertainment, Stanley Park and the beaches. Glowing fireplaces and the wagging tail of a Springer Spaniel ensure a warm welcome. Every spacious corner guestroom suggests a different travel itinerary. Will it be Sailor's, Vienna, Klondyke or Holly-

continued next page

INN PLACES® 1998

wood? The third-floor studio suite, with Far Eastern ambiance, a fireplace, deck, kitchen and Jacuzzi ensuite, is especially appealing. We are often complimented on our breakfast food, fun and conversation. Visit awhile. After all, Vancouver is right at your doorstep.

Address: 977 Broughton St, Vancouver, BC V6G 2A4 Canada.
Tel: (604) 684-9793, Fax: (604) 684-4141.

Type: Bed & breakfast.
Clientele: Mostly gay & lesbian with some hetero clientele
Transportation: By car or airport bus to Landmark Hotel, walk or taxi remaining 2 blocks.
To Gay Bars: Four blocks.
Rooms: 5 rooms & 1 suite with double or queen beds.
Bathrooms: 4 private (1 with Jacuzzi), 1 shared. Guestrooms have wash basins.
Meals: Full breakfast.
Vegetarian: Available upon request, prior notice appreciated. Plenty of veggies nearby.
Complimentary: 2 kitchenettes stocked with tea & coffee.
Dates Open: All year, except Christmas thru New Year.
High Season: May thru mid-Oct.
Rates: Low season CDN $58-$120, high season CDN $78-$165.
Discounts: Available by week in low season.
Credit Cards: MC, Visa.
Rsv'tns: Required.
To Reserve: Travel agent or call direct.
Minimum Stay: 2 nights on holiday weekends only.
Parking: Ample free off-street parking.
In-Room: Maid service, some rooms with kitchens, some refrigerators. Studio has cable colour TV.
On-Premises: TV lounge, VCR, stereo, house telephone, complimentary storage of bicycles & bags.
Exercise/Health: Massage. Nearby gym, weights, Jacuzzi, sauna, steam & massage.
Swimming: Five- to ten-minute walk to ocean beach.
Sunbathing: On beach or private sun decks.
Nudity: Directions available to excellent clothing-optional beaches.
Smoking: Permitted on front porch or in garden.
Pets: Not permitted.
Handicap Access: No.
Children: Permitted by prior arrangement, 12 or older only.
Languages: English & French.
Your Host: David & O'Neal.

IGLTA

"O Canada" House

Gay-Friendly ♀♂

The Home of Canada's National Anthem

"O Canada" House offers the ultimate in old-world charm and hospitality in a beautifully restored 1897 Victorian home. The restoration of our historic home has resulted in the enhancement of the home's original late-Victorian ambiance, charm and warmth, while providing many additional conveniences needed by travellers in the '90s. The home is large enough to ensure maximum privacy and comfort. Its spacious main floor contains a large entry hall with open staircase, front and rear parlors with fireplaces, and, of course, a large dining room with a serving pantry stocked with goodies. The Common Room, furnished with museum-quality lighting, furniture and artwork from the Victorian and Edwardian eras, offers many opportunities for recreation in its beautiful surroundings. Our wraparound

porch looks out into an English garden.

Each of our five large bedrooms are decorated in a late Victorian style and have comfortable sitting areas, as well as many of today's conveniences. Designer linens, television, VCR, refrigerator and telephone blend discreetly into the decor of your room. Mornings, you are sure to enjoy our gourmet breakfasts which are served in the dining room or, if you prefer, in the privacy of your room or on the front porch. Complimentary sherry is served in the front parlor at 5 pm. Located in a quiet downtown neighbourhood, *"O Canada" House* is a short walking distance to all of the best bars, restaurants and shopping in Vancouver. Our concierge service specializes in setting up itineraries and making reservations to ensure that you will maximize your stay in our beautiful city. Your hosts, Mike and Jim, invite you to enjoy the quiet, late-Victorian ambiance of this historic home, where our national anthem, "O Canada" was written in 1909.

Address: 1114 Barclay St, Vancouver, BC V6E 1H1 Canada.
Tel: (604) 688-0555, **Fax:** (604) 488-0556.
URL: http://www.bbcanada.com/919.html

Type: Bed & breakfast.
Clientele: Mostly straight with a gay & lesbian following
Transportation: Car is best, taxi, airport shuttle bus.
To Gay Bars: 3 blocks, a 5 minute walk, a 3 minute drive.
Rooms: 5 rooms with king or queen beds.
Bathrooms: Private: 4 shower/toilets, 1 bath/toilet/shower.
Meals: Full breakfast.

Vegetarian: Available nearby.
Complimentary: Sherry in front parlor in late afternoon. Mints on pillows, cookies in room. Available 24 hrs: snacks, fruit juices, pop, coffee, tea.
Dates Open: All year.
High Season: May-October.
Rates: High season: CDN $150-CDN $195. Low season CDN $125-CDN $160.
Discounts: For extended stays, singles, AAA members.

Credit Cards: MC, Visa.
Rsv'tns: Required.
To Reserve: Travel agent or call direct.
Minimum Stay: 2 days on weekends.
Parking: Adequate free off-street parking.
In-Room: Color cable TV, VCR, telephone, refrigerator, maid service.
On-Premises: Meeting rooms, TV lounge, video tape library, fax. Front & rear parlors have fireplaces.
Exercise/Health: Nearby gym, weights, Jacuzzi, sauna, steam, massage.
Swimming: Nearby pool, ocean, short walk to beaches.
Sunbathing: At beach.
Smoking: Permitted on front porch.
Pets: Not permitted.
Handicap Access: No.
Children: Children ages 12 & over welcome.
Languages: English.
Your Host: Mike & Jim.

Royal Hotel

Q-NET Gay/Lesbian ♀♂

Vancouver's Gay Hotel & Pub

In this European-style, downtown Vancouver hotel, accommodations are the cleanest and most reasonably priced on the strip, and our staff is friendly. The *Royal Hotel* was constructed in 1912. Its exterior is accented with flower-filled window boxes. Contemporary interior furnishings create a comfortable atmosphere. The hotel bar, recently renovated, is a popular gay night spot.

Address: 1025 Granville St, Vancouver, BC V6Z 1L4 Canada.
Tel: (604) 685-5335, **Fax:** (604) 685-5351.

Type: Hotel with gay bar.
Clientele: Gay & lesbian. Good mix of men & women
Transportation: Car is best or taxi from transport terminals.
To Gay Bars: Gay bar on premises with live bands.

Rooms: 90 rooms.
Bathrooms: 25 private. Others share.
Meals: Continental breakfast in 1998.
Dates Open: All year.
High Season: May-Oct.
Rates: From CDN $60/night.

Credit Cards: Visa, MC.
To Reserve: Call direct.
Parking: Adequate on-street parking.
In-Room: Color TV, telephone & maid service.
Swimming: Ocean beach.
Sunbathing: At nearby ocean beach.

Smoking: Non-smoking rooms available.
Pets: Not Permitted.
Handicap Access: No.
Children: Permitted.
Languages: English, Hungarian, Chinese & Polish.

Rural Roots Bed and Breakfast

Gay/Lesbian ♀♂

Luxurious, Affordable, Country Setting at Vancouver's Doorstep

Less than one hour from Vancouver, Canada, and two hours from Seattle, **Rural Roots** is a luxury, country B&B on ten parklike acres with gardens, an orchard, rolling pastures, grazing cows and a small forest. Relax in the hot tub, breakfast in a Victorian conservatory and lounge on the sun decks. Let us be your "getaway" from the city or, when touring, make us your base for Vancouver and the many recreational opportunities of the Pacific Northwest. After a busy day, return to the relaxed pace of **Rural Roots** to enjoy the best of both worlds, rural and urban.

Address: 4939 Ross Road, Vancouver-Mt. Lehman, BC V4X 1Z3 Canada.
Tel: (604) 856-2380, **Fax:** (604) 857-2380. **E-mail:** rroots@uniserve.com
URL: http://cimarron.net/canada/bc/rdrr/html

Type: Bed & breakfast.
Clientele: Gay & lesbian. Good mix of men & women
Transportation: Car is best.
To Gay Bars: 33 miles or an hour drive to Vancouver gay bars.
Rooms: 4 rooms with twin, double, queen or king beds.
Bathrooms: 3 private bath/toilets, 1 shared shower/toilet.

Meals: Full breakfast.
Vegetarian: Available upon request. Vegetarian restaurants nearby.
Complimentary: Tea, coffee & soft drinks.
Dates Open: All year.
Rates: CDN $55-$95.
Rsv'tns: Required.
To Reserve: Call direct.
Parking: Ample free parking.
In-Room: Color TV.

On-Premises: TV lounge, guest kitchen, laundry facilities.
Exercise/Health: Jacuzzi. Recreation centre 20 minutes away, exercise equipment.
Swimming: Pool at recreation centre, 60 minutes to ocean.
Sunbathing: On common sun decks.

Nudity: Permitted in hot tub area.
Smoking: Permitted outdoors only.
Pets: Permitted. Kennelled at night.
Handicap Access: No.
Children: Not especially welcome.
Languages: English, French & Spanish.
Your Host: Jim & Len.

Claddagh House Bed & Breakfast

Gay/Lesbian ♀♂

Savor the Comfort, Diversity & Joy

A warm welcome awaits you in our 1913 heritage home. At **Claddagh House B&B**, you can step back from the pressures of everyday life and give yourself up to the relaxation and charm of an authentic Irish B&B experience. Expect cheerful hospitality and attention to your comfort. Enjoy a quiet time or conversation with new friends on the front porch or balcony, or perhaps an evening in front of a fire. For significant occasions, enhance your experience with our *Celebrations Package*. Two-night *Island Escape Packages* include your choice of relaxation treatments. **Reader's Comment:** "Our every need seemed anticipated and no comfort was spared... Once in awhile there is a treasure that should be experienced. This is it." — Danit C. & Judy F., Eugene, OR. "Superb hosts." — Olivier G. & Joe B., Victoria, BC.

Address: 1761 Lee Ave, Victoria, BC V8R 4W7 Canada.
Tel: (250) 370-2816, **Fax:** (250) 592-0228.

Type: Bed & breakfast.
Clientele: Mostly gay & lesbian with some hetero clientele
Transportation: Easy access to city by car, bus, bicycle, taxi, tour companies.
To Gay Bars: 8 min by car to gay & lesbian bars.
Rooms: 4 rooms with double, queen or king beds.
Bathrooms: 3 private bath/toilet and 1 shared bath/shower/toilet.
Meals: Hearty breakfast from homemade & home-grown foods.
Vegetarian: Lacto-ovo vegetarian always available.
Complimentary: Tea, coffee, cookies & Irish Milsèan confectionery.
Dates Open: All year.
High Season: May through September.
Rates: CDN $65-$125 for two, CDN $50-$100 for one.
Discounts: 7th consecutive night free. Frequent-sleeper discounts for return guests.
Credit Cards: MC & VISA.
Rsv'tns: Recommended & preferred.
To Reserve: Travel agent or call direct.
Minimum Stay: 2 nights on holiday weekends.
Parking: Ample free on-street parking.
In-Room: Coffee & tea-making facilities.
On-Premises: TV lounge, laundry facilities, front porch, garden & fireplace.
Exercise/Health: Health & recreation centre & bicycle rental 1 block. Massage, reflexology & aromatherapy with advance notice.
Swimming: Pool 1 block, ocean beach 5-min drive.
Sunbathing: At ocean beach or in garden.
Smoking: Permitted outdoors.
Pets: Pets by arrangement. Resident cat, Polly, has private quarters.
Handicap Access: No.
Children: Welcome.
Languages: English.
Your Host: Maggie.

Oak Bay Guest House

Gay-Friendly ♀♂

At this classic inn, established since 1922, we have your comfort and pleasure at heart. Guests at *Oak Bay Guest House* enjoy the peaceful location, scenic walks a block from the ocean, and the beautiful gardens that surround. All eleven rooms have private bathrooms. There are two sitting rooms decorated with antiques, a library and gas fireplace. We are frequently complimented on our home-cooked breakfast. Golf, village shopping, fine dining and a city bus tour are accessible from our location, just minutes from downtown. Come, and enjoy.

Address: 1052 Newport Ave, Victoria, BC V8S 5E3 Canada.
Tel: (250) 598-3812, (800) 575-3812, **Fax:** (250) 598-0369.
E-mail: OakBay@beds-breakfasts.com
URL: http://beds-breakfasts.com/OakBay

Type: Inn.
Clientele: Mostly straight clientele with a gay & lesbian following
Transportation: Car is best. Bus stop right outside.
To Gay Bars: 2 miles or 10 mins by car.
Rooms: 11 rooms with single or queen beds.
Bathrooms: All private bath/toilets.
Meals: Full breakfast.
Vegetarian: Available upon request.
Complimentary: Tea & coffee.
Dates Open: All year.
High Season: Jun-Sept.
Rates: CDN $65-$120 winter, CDN $120-$165 summer.
Credit Cards: MC, Visa, Amex.
Rsv'tns: Required.
To Reserve: Call direct.
Parking: Ample free off-street & on-street parking.
On-Premises: TV lounge, coffee & tea-making facilities in guest lounge.
Swimming: Nearby pool, lake & ocean beach.
Sunbathing: On the beach.
Smoking: Non-smoking guesthouse.
Pets: Not permitted.
Handicap Access: No.
Children: Not permitted.
Languages: English.

Ocean Wilderness

Q-NET Gay-Friendly

An Elegant Jewel in a Wilderness Setting

Ocean Wilderness features nine guest rooms on five forested acres of oceanfront with breathtaking view of forests, the Straits of Juan de Fuca and the Olympic Mountains. Guestrooms are large and beautifully decorated, with private baths and bed canopies. A silver service of coffee is delivered to your door as a gentle wake-up call. Home baking makes breakfast a special treat. The hot tub, in a Japanese gazebo, is popular with weary vacationers. Book your time for a private soak. Several rooms have private soak tubs for two, overlooking the ocean.

Address: 109 West Coast Rd RR#2, Sooke, BC V0S 1N0 Canada.
Tel: (250) 646-2116, (800) 323-2116, **Fax:** (250) 646-2317.
E-mail: ocean@sookenet.com **URL:** www.sookenet.com/ocean

Type: Bed & breakfast inn with gift shop.
Clientele: Mostly straight with gay/lesbian following
Transportation: Car is best.
To Gay Bars: 30 miles.
Rooms: 9 rooms with single, queen or king beds.
Bathrooms: All private.
Meals: Full breakfast.
Vegetarian: Available with prior notification or upon arrival.
Complimentary: Wake up coffee to your door on silver service, 24-hr beverage station.
Dates Open: All year.
High Season: May-Oct.
Rates: Summer (June 1-Sept 30) CDN $85-$175, winter (Oct 1-May 30) CDN $65-$140.
Discounts: Winter rates + 3 nights for the price of 2.
Credit Cards: MC, Visa.
Rsv'tns: Required in season.
To Reserve: Travel agent or call direct.
Parking: Off-street parking.
In-Room: Room service, telephone, refrigerator, maid service.
On-Premises: Beach, wilderness, wildlife, landscaped gardens, winter retreats, rainforest rejuvenation, motivational makeovers.
Exercise/Health: Gazebo hot tub overlooking ocean, massage, mud treatment, tai chi, seaweed wraps, meditation.
Swimming: Ocean beach & river.
Sunbathing: On beach, patio, private sun decks.
Nudity: Permitted on private sun decks.
Smoking: Permitted outdoors only, all rooms non-smoking.
Pets: Permitted by prior arrangement.
Handicap Access: Yes, 1 room.
Children: Permitted occasionally, please inquire. Must be adult oriented.
Languages: English.

The Weekender Bed & Breakfast

Gay/Lesbian

A Seaside Bed & Breakfast

Weekender Bed & Breakfast is located just steps from the ocean, along Victoria's scenic drive. Our location is but a short distance from Beacon Hill Park, Cook Street Village, Fairfield Shopping Plaza, local restaurants, nightlife and most tourist attractions. The inn's spacious, bright rooms all have private baths. The deluxe suite has ocean views and a private sun deck.

Address: 10 Eberts St, Victoria, BC V8S 5L6 Canada.
Tel: (250) 389-1688.

Type: Bed & Breakfast.
Clientele: Mostly gay & lesbian with some hetero clientele
Transportation: Car is best. Taxi from city centre, about $9.00.
To Gay Bars: 2 miles or 30 minutes by foot, 5 minutes by car.
Rooms: 3 rooms with queen beds.
Bathrooms: 3 private bath/toilets.
Meals: Expanded continental breakfast.
Vegetarian: Always available.
Complimentary: Complimentary beverage on check-in. Fresh fruit always available.
Dates Open: Full time.
High Season: Mid-May to mid-October.
Rates: High season CDN $89-105. Low season CDN $72-$84.
Credit Cards: MC, Visa.
Rsv'tns: Recommended & preferred.
To Reserve: Call direct.
Minimum Stay: 2 nights on holiday weekends & special events days.
Parking: Ample on-street parking.
In-Room: Maid service.
Exercise/Health: Massage. Nearby YMCA & YWCA.
Sunbathing: On private sun decks.
Smoking: Permitted outdoors only.
Pets: Not permitted.
Handicap Access: No.
Children: Not especially welcomed.
Languages: English.
Your Host: Michael.

The Beach House

Gay-Friendly 50/50 ♀♂

A Tranquil Mountain Lakefront Retreat Minutes from Natural Hot Springs

The Beach House is beautifully renovated and has outstanding views, delicious breakfasts and gracious hospitality. Explore the private beach and, as you take in the serene beauty of the Kootenays, plan your activities such as guided hiking, horseback excursions, cycling or fishing. Walk in the forests, go mountain biking or do nothing at all! To finish off the day, relax in the underground cave hot springs a few minutes away. Appropriate for adults seeking a rejuvenating getaway. Heterosexual friendly.

Address: PO Box 1375, Kaslo, BC V0G 1M0 Canada.
Tel: (250) 353-7676, **Fax:** (250) 879-4547.
E-mail: rdwilson@nel.auracom.com

Type: Bed & breakfast.
Clientele: 50% gay & lesbian & 50% straight clientele
Transportation: Car. 1-1/2 hours from Castlegar Airport.
Rooms: 3 rooms with double, queen or single beds.
Bathrooms: 3 baths, private or shared.
Meals: Full gourmet breakfast.
Vegetarian: Available, as well as other special diets, if requested at time of booking.
Complimentary: Coffee, tea & cookies.
Dates Open: June-Sept.
High Season: June-Sept.
Rates: CDN $50 single, CDN $65 double.
Discounts: On extended stays.
Rsv'tns: Recommended.
To Reserve: Call direct.
Parking: Ample free off-street parking.
In-Room: Maid service.
Exercise/Health: Massage & natural hot springs nearby.
Swimming: Cold-water lake with private beach on premises. Nearby pool & lake.
Sunbathing: On common sun decks & private beach.
Nudity: Yes, with courtesy to other guests.
Smoking: Permitted outside.
Pets: Not permitted.
Handicap Access: No.
Children: Not especially welcome.
Languages: English, little French.
Your Host: Robert.

CANADA — WHISTLER • BRITISH COLUMBIA

The Whistler Retreat
Whistler's Favorite Gay & Lesbian B&B

Q-NET Gay/Lesbian

Discovering *The Whistler Retreat*, brings downhill and cross-country skiing, snowshoeing, snowmobiling, hiking, mountain biking, swimming, sunbathing, golf, tennis, canoeing, and horseback riding to your doorstep. This spacious alpine home, located just five minutes north of Whistler Village, has spectacular mountain views, three fireplaces, queen-sized beds, an outdoor Jacuzzi, a sauna, and a pool table. Whistler, a world-renowned mountain resort, has been rated one of the best places in the world to ski by *Snow Country Magazine* and *SKI Magazine*.

Address: 8561 Drifter Way, Whistler, BC V0N 1B8 Canada.
Tel: (604) 938-9245 (Tel/Fax). **E-mail:** whistler@axionet.com

Type: Bed & breakfast.
Clientele: Gay & lesbian. Good mix of men & women
Transportation: Car is best.
To Gay Bars: 70 miles to Vancouver bars.
Rooms: 3 rooms with queen beds.
Bathrooms: 2 shared bath/shower/toilets.
Meals: Full breakfast.
Vegetarian: Available on request.

Dates Open: All year.
High Season: December-March.
Rates: Low season: single CDN $65, double CDN $79. High season: single CDN $85, double CDN $99.
Discounts: 10% on stays of 3 or more nights.
Credit Cards: MC, Visa.
Rsv'tns: Recommended.
To Reserve: Travel agent or call direct.

Parking: Ample free off-steet parking.
In-Room: Maid service.
On-Premises: TV lounge, video tape library, pool table, laundry facilities.
Exercise/Health: Jacuzzi, sauna. Nearby gym, weights, Jacuzzi, sauna, steam, massage, squash & tennis courts, ice skating.
Swimming: Nearby pool, lake.

Sunbathing: On common sun decks, at beach.
Nudity: Permitted in sauna & Jacuzzi. Nude sunbathing at nearby beach.
Smoking: Permitted except in bedrooms.
Pets: Not permitted.
Handicap Access: No.
Children: No.
Languages: English.

IGLTA

PEGGY'S COVE • NOVA SCOTIA

The Old Fisher House B&B
Where the Sea Surrounds You & Paddy's Head Lighthouse Beckons

Gay/Lesbian

Located in a traditional fishing village surrounded by the sea, the 125-year-old *Old Fisher House B&B* offers a quiet, restful retreat from everyday life. It is situated in a well-protected cove with plenty of fresh sea air and sun. Much of the original charm and character has been maintained in this lovely, renovated house and the carefully kept grounds reflect the rustic nature of its original use as a fisherman's home. Our guestrooms have a maritime flavour with either oceanfront or lighthouse views. Breakfasts are European or Canadian-style and afternoon treats of European cakes, baked fresh daily, will often be available and delivered to your room on request.

FERRARI GUIDES™

Address: 204 Paddy's Head Road, RR 1, Box 1527, Indian Harbour, NS B0J 3J0 Canada.
Tel: (902) 823-2228 (Tel/Fax).

Type: Bed & breakfast, 40 min drive from Halifax.
Clientele: Mostly gay & lesbian with some hetero clientele
Transportation: Car is best. Pick up by car CDN $40 from airport, train, bus.
To Gay Bars: 30 miles, a 45 min drive.
Rooms: 3 rooms with queen beds.
Bathrooms: 1 shared bath.
Meals: Full breakfast.
Vegetarian: Advise us in advance & we'll prepare it.
Complimentary: Cappuccino & homemade German cakes & cookies.
Dates Open: May 15-Oct 15.
High Season: June-Sept.
Rates: CDN $60-CDN $85 (extra person CDN $15).
Discounts: Stay 6 days, get 7th day free.
Credit Cards: Visa.
Rsv'tns: Required.
To Reserve: Call direct.
Parking: Limited free parking.
On-Premises: Library, fax.
Swimming: Ocean on premises. Nearby ocean & lake.
Sunbathing: On private & common sun decks, at beach.
Smoking: Not permitted. Non-smoking rooms available.
Handicap Access: No.
Languages: English, German.

Cedars Tent & Trailer Park
Gay/Lesbian ♀♂

Experience The Cedars

Cedars Tent & Trailer Park is the only mixed campground in Ontario. We've been in business for twelve years, building and improving each year. Come visit us on our 130 green Ontario acres.

Address: PO Box 195, Millgrove, ON L0R 1V0 Canada.
Tel: (905) 659-7342 or 659-3655.

Type: Campground with rental trailers, clubhouse, restaurant & bar.
Clientele: Good mix of gay men & women
Transportation: Car is best.
To Gay Bars: 5 miles to gay bars.
Bathrooms: Shower & toilet building plus outhouses throughout.
Campsites: 600 campsites with shared shower facilities.
Meals: Full-service restaurant on premises.
Dates Open: April 1-Sept 30.
Rates: CDN $13.50 per person per day.
To Reserve: Call direct.
Parking: Ample free parking.
On-Premises: Clubhouse, bar, dance floor & game rooms.
Exercise/Health: Recreational area.
Swimming: Pool.
Sunbathing: At poolside.
Smoking: Permitted without restrictions.
Pets: Permitted. Must be on a leash.
Handicap Access: Yes.
Children: Welcome. Children under 12 free, parent responsible.
Languages: English & French.

Danner House Bed & Breakfast
Gay-Owned & -Operated ♀♂

Combine Historical Values with Modern Comfort & Convenience

This solid stone residence was used as a barracks during the War of 1812 and, later, during the MacKenzie Rebellion and the Fenian Raids of the 1830s. Its two large bedrooms offer river views and comfortable beds — either a queen-sized goose-down bed or an Edwardian-style, hand-carved double bed. The common area features a large colonial fireplace and its own exceptional view of the mighty Niagara River. The *Danner House Bed & Breakfast* is located minutes away from famous Niagara Falls, Casino Niagara, and is a short ten-minute drive from Buffalo, NY.

Address: 12549 Niagara River Parkway, Niagara Falls, ON L2E 6S6 Canada.
Tel: (905) 295-5166, Fax: (905) 295-0202.
E-mail: comniag@vaxxine.com
URL: http://www.vaxxine.com/danner

continued next page

CANADA — NIAGARA FALLS • ONTARIO

Type: Bed & breakfast.
Clientele: Gay & lesbian. Good mix of men & women
Transportation: Car.
To Gay Bars: 15 min drive to Buffalo, NY gay bars.
Rooms: 2 rooms with queen beds.
Bathrooms: 2 private bath/shower/toilets.
Meals: Full breakfast.
Vegetarian: Available on request.
Complimentary: Tea, coffee, juices & soft drinks.
Dates Open: All year.
Rates: CDN $85 per room, per night.
Credit Cards: MC, Visa.
Rsv'tns: Required.
To Reserve: Call direct.
Parking: Ample free parking.
In-Room: AC, ceiling fans, maid, room & laundry service.
On-Premises: TV lounge, boat launching & docking facilities.
Exercise/Health: Hike, bike & roller blade on nearby 30km recreational trail. Nearby gym, weights, Jacuzzi, sauna, steam, massage.
Swimming: Nearby river & lake.
Sunbathing: At beach.
Smoking: No smoking permitted in home.
Pets: Not permitted.
Handicap Access: No.
Children: No.
Languages: English & French.

Fairbanks House Bed & Breakfast
Gay-Owned 50/50 ♀♂

Our location right on the Niagara River lets you walk, in just ten minutes, to the Niagara Falls viewpoint and to Canada's largest casino. All Niagara tourist attractions and restaurants are close by. Though we're in the midst of the tourist area, our half acre of land overlooking the river helps make our gracious Victorian home a romantic hideaway. All four guest rooms at *Fairbanks House Bed & Breakfast* are furnished in antiques and have private baths, and a separate, private living room is reserved for our guests' use. Full breakfast with silver and crystal service, and free picnic baskets for your outings are included.

Address: 4965 River Rd, Niagara Falls, ON L2E 3G6 Canada.
Tel: (905) 371-3716. **E-mail:** FBH@mergetel.com

Type: Bed & breakfast.
Clientele: 50% gay & lesbian & 50% straight clientele
To Gay Bars: 20 min drive to gay bars in Buffalo, NY.
Rooms: 4 rooms with double or queen beds.
Bathrooms: All private.
Campsites: RV parking only.
Meals: Full breakfast with silver & crystal.
Vegetarian: Vegetarian restaurant a 20 min walk.
Complimentary: Coffee, tea, juice. Free picnic baskets.
Dates Open: All year.
High Season: Apr-Oct 31.
Rates: CDN $100 per night.
Discounts: No tax charged.
Credit Cards: MC.
Rsv'tns: Required.
To Reserve: Call direct.
Minimum Stay: 2 days on weekends in Jul & Aug.
Parking: Ample, free, off-street parking.
In-Room: AC, color TV, VCR, maid service. 1 room has refrigerator.
On-Premises: Meeting rooms, video tape library, laundry facilities. Special living room for guests' use.
Swimming: Nearby lake at Dufferin Island.
Sunbathing: On common sun decks.
Smoking: Permitted outdoors.
Pets: Not permitted.
Handicap Access: No.
Children: Welcome.
Languages: English.
Your Host: Darlene & Coral.

Burnside — STRATFORD
Gay-Friendly 50/50 ♀♂

Burnside is an ancestral, turn-of-the-century home featuring many family heirlooms and antiques, redecorated in light, airy colors. Our host is a horticultural instructor and an authority on local and Canadian geneology. Relax amid flowers and herbs in the gardens overlooking Lake Victoria. We are a mere 12 minutes' walk from the Stratford, Avon and Tom Patterson theatres and a short walk from interesting shops and good restaurants. Nearby is the Avon Trail, part of a network of trails enabling one to walk from London, Ontario to Niagara Falls. We will pick up guests at the train or bus stations.

Address: 139 William St, Stratford, ON N5A 4X9 Canada.
Tel: (519) 271-7076, **Fax:** (519) 271-0265

Type: Bed & breakfast.
Clientele: 50% gay & lesbian & 50% hetero clientele
Transportation: Car is best. Free pick up from train & bus station. Use Stratford Airporter from airport to our front door.
To Gay Bars: 5-minute walk to gay/lesbian bar (Down the Street Bar & Cafe).
Rooms: 4 rooms with single/twin, double or king beds.
Bathrooms: Shared: 1 full bath, 2 bathtubs, 2 showers & 1 toilet room.
Meals: Full or expanded continental breakfast.

FERRARI GUIDES™

Vegetarian: Cater to special diets.
Complimentary: Ice provided.
Dates Open: All year.
High Season: July & August.
Rates: Student CDN $25, single CDN $50, twin & double CDN $65, king CDN $70.
Discounts: For stays of over 3 nights.
Rsv'tns: Preferred.
To Reserve: Call direct.
Minimum Stay: 2 nights on July & August weekends.
Parking: Adequate free off-street parking.
In-Room: Central AC/heat, refrigerator.
On-Premises: Private dining room, TV lounge with color cable TV, VCR & limited video tape library, & spacious gardens.
Exercise/Health: Whirlpool tub & massage.
Swimming: Lions Club pool 1/2 block, YMCA pool 3 blocks.
Sunbathing: At Grand Bend Beach & Shakespeare Conservation Park.
Nudity: Permitted on lower level.
Smoking: Permitted outside.
Pets: Not permitted.
Handicap Access: No.
Children: Permitted but not encouraged during festival season (May-Oct).
Languages: English, limited French.
Your Host: Les.

Banting House
Gay-Owned & -Operated ♀♂

A Welcome Respite from the Urban Bustle

A gracious 1900s Edwardian house, **Banting House** is named after its most famous inhabitant, the co-developer of insulin, Frederick Grant Banting. Carefully restored to its original splendour, the home features a winding three-story oak staircase and stained-glass windows. The spacious, secluded garden with century-old trees and fountains is a welcome respite from the urban bustle. Guests will appreciate the dozens of restaurants, bars and dance clubs to be found in the gay and lesbian village, just two blocks away, as well as the many museums and theatres also within walking distance.

Address: 73 Homewood Ave, Toronto, ON M4Y 2K1 Canada.
Tel: (416) 924-1458, **Fax:** (416) 924-3304.
E-mail: bantinghs@aol.com **URL:** www.bbcanada.com/1960.html

Type: Bed & breakfast.
Clientele: Mostly gay & lesbian with some hetero clientele
Transportation: Airport bus to front door. Pick up from airport CDN $21.
To Gay Bars: 2 blocks, a 5 min walk.
Rooms: 4 rooms with double beds.
Bathrooms: 2 shared bath/shower/toilets.
Meals: Expanded continental breakfast.
Vegetarian: Available upon request & at most local restaurants.
Complimentary: Tea & coffee all day. Other food & drink available upon request.
Dates Open: All year.
High Season: May-Sept.
Rates: CDN $60-CDN $80 per night.
Discounts: Inquire about group rates, cash & time of stay discounts.
Credit Cards: MC, Visa.
Rsv'tns: Required.
To Reserve: Travel agents or call direct.
Minimum Stay: Usually required in high season.
Parking: Ample free off-street parking.
In-Room: AC, color cable TV, maid service. 1 kitchen for each 2 rooms.
On-Premises: Laundry facilities.
Sunbathing: On patio.
Smoking: Permitted in designated areas in house only.
Pets: Permitted.
Handicap Access: No.
Children: Welcome under parental supervision.
Languages: English, French.
Your Host: Paul & Maurice.

Catnaps 1892 Downtown Guesthouse
Q-NET Gay/Lesbian ♀♂

Toronto's Purrfect Place to Be

Stay at *Catnaps* — voted Toronto's Best B&B. Our home, located right downtown, is the oldest Toronto gay and lesbian guesthouse. Each room has a different personality, and all are cozy and comfortable. We're close to 24-hour public transportation, and guests have use of kitchen and laundry facilities. Relax in a casual, informal atmosphere just steps from all Toronto has to offer...theatre, nightlife, shopping, world-famous tourist attractions. Next time you're passing through, stay with us and help us celebrate 17 years.

Address: 246 Sherbourne St, Toronto, ON M5A 2S1 Canada.
Tel: (416) 968-2323, **Reservations:** (800) 205-3694, **Fax:** (416) 413-0485.
E-mail: catnaps@onramp.ca

continued next page

CANADA — TORONTO · ONTARIO

Type: Bed & breakfast guesthouse.
Clientele: Good mix of gay men & women
To Gay Bars: 2 blocks or 1/4 mile. 5 minutes by foot.
Rooms: 9 rooms.
Bathrooms: 1 private toilet only, 2 shared bath/shower/toilets.
Meals: Expanded continental breakfast with fresh-baked goods.
Vegetarian: Readily available.
Complimentary: Coffee & tea all day.
Dates Open: All year.
High Season: May through September (Victoria Day through Labour Day).
Rates: Rooms CDN $45-$65.
Discounts: Off-season weekly & monthly rates.
Credit Cards: MC, Visa.
Rsv'tns: Recommended.
To Reserve: Call direct.
Minimum Stay: 2 nights on holiday weekends.
Parking: Adequate off-street parking, CDN $5 per night.
In-Room: Color cable TV, AC, clock radios, ceiling fans & maid service.
On-Premises: Laundry facilities, kitchen, tourist information, courtesy phone.
Exercise/Health: Gym, weights, sauna, steam, massage & Jacuzzi nearby.
Swimming: Lake Ontario (Toronto Islands), YMCA & other clubs nearby.
Sunbathing: On beach at Toronto Islands and on house sun decks (private & common).
Smoking: Permitted in some guest rooms, kitchen, garden & decks.
Pets: No.
Handicap Access: No.
Children: Welcomed, some restrictions. Reservations required.
Languages: English, French & German.

Divine Lake Nature's Sport & Spa Resort
Gay-Friendly ♀♂

Gay-friendly *Divine Lake* is in Muskoka amid 86 acres of lovely nature 2 hours north of Toronto. Cottages and chalets with fireplaces and kitchenettes are available. There are two lounges, a bar, a restaurant, heated pool, hot tub, Finnish sauna, tennis court, table-tennis, pool table, TV-video room, and conference rooms. Our restaurant features a great menu and is open for breakfast, lunch and dinner Outdoor activities include boating, windsurfing, fishing, hiking on breathtaking trails, cross-country skiing, and motorboat tours. Stay with us at *Divine Lake Nature's Sport & Spa Resort*, in Canada.

Address: Port Sydney, ON P0B 1LO Canada.
Tel: (705) 385-1212, **Fax:** (705) 385-1283.
Information & reservations (Canada & USA): (800) 263-6600.
E-mail: divinelk@vianet.on.ca **URL:** www.divinelake.com

Type: Resort with restaurant, bar, shops.
Clientele: Gay & straight clientele
Transportation: Coach from Toronto Int'l Airport, or bus or train from Toronto to Port Sydney.
To Gay Bars: In Toronto, a 2-hour drive.
Rooms: 10 cottages, 9 chalets.
Bathrooms: All private.
Meals: Full or continental breakfast, dinner.
Vegetarian: Available on request when booking.
Dates Open: All year.
High Season: June thru October.
Rates: From CDN $139/night for a cottage (max 2 guests).
Discounts: Special packages available.
Credit Cards: MC, Visa & Amex.
Rsv'tns: Required.
To Reserve: Travel agent or call direct.
Parking: Ample free parking.
In-Room: Fireplace, color TV, VCR, kitchen, refrigerator, maid service.
On-Premises: Meeting rooms, TV lounge, laundry facilities for guests.
Exercise/Health: Health spa with steam/herb sauna, massage, mudpacks, gym, tennis court. Spa packages available.
Swimming: Heated pool on premises, lake.
Sunbathing: Poolside, on sun deck, at the beach.
Smoking: In designated dining room area, lounge; non-smoking rooms available.
Pets: Not permitted.
Handicap Access: Yes, bathroom.
Languages: French, English, German.

IGLTA

The House on McGill
Gay-Owned & -Operated ♀♂

Affordable Luxury

The dour Victorians are long-gone from *The House on McGill* (circa 1892), and have been replaced by a friendly, tolerant mix of people. Quiet, shady McGill Street is close to the bustle of downtown Toronto, the busy Gay Village and the vibrant theatre district. Explore this exciting city by foot, on Toronto's excellent transit system, or borrow a bicycle. Come home to lovingly restored, modernized and peaceful surroundings with many amenities to enjoy and hosts who are interested in your explorations.

Address: 110 McGill St, Toronto, ON M5B 1H6 Canada.
Tel: (416) 351-1503 (Tel/Fax). For fax, call ahead to alert computer.

Type: Bed & breakfast.
Clientele: Mostly gay & lesbian with some hetero clientele
Transportation: Private B&B limo service, taxi.
To Gay Bars: 1 block.
Rooms: 3 rooms with double or queen beds.
Bathrooms: Private: 1 sink only. Shared: 1 bath/shower/toilet.
Meals: Expanded continental breakfast.

Vegetarian: Upon special request. Many restaurants nearby.
Complimentary: Fresh fruit, coffee, tea, hot chocolate, herbal teas.
Dates Open: All year.
High Season: May 1-Sept 30.
Rates: CDN $50-CDN $85.
Discounts: 10% on stays over 7 days, 20% over 14 days.
Credit Cards: MC.

Rsv'tns: Required. Walk-ins allowed.
To Reserve: Travel agent or call direct.
Parking: Ample pay parking.
In-Room: AC, maid & laundry service.
On-Premises: TV lounge, video tape library, fax, internet, e-mail, computer services, free local calls.
Exercise/Health: Bicycle loan. Nearby gym, weights, Jacuzzi, sauna, steam, massage.
Swimming: Nearby pool & lake.
Sunbathing: On roof.
Smoking: Permitted on front porch.
Pets: Not permitted.
Handicap Access: No.
Children: No.
Languages: English, Australian & French.
Your Host: Dave & Adam.

Ten Cawthra Square B&B & Cawthra Square Guesthouse

Q-NET Gay/Lesbian

Living in Style

Our elegant Edwardian or Victorian homes are beautiful retreats in the heart of Toronto's vibrant gay village. Relax in front parlours, with fireplaces and grand pianos, and enjoy views of tree-shaded streets or our back gardens. *Ten Cawthra Square B&B & Cawthra Square Guesthouse* offer spacious guest rooms with private terraces and breakfasts served in country-style kitchens or formal dining rooms. Toronto's attractions are easily accessible via the nearby subway and, across the adjacent park, are shops, restaurants, cafes & nightclubs. Toronto's best theatres and museums are also at your doorstep.

Address: 10 Cawthra Square, Toronto, ON M4Y 1K8 Canada.
Tel: (416) 966-3074, (800) 259-5474, **Fax:** (416) 966-4494.
E-mail: host@cawthra.com **URL:** http://www.cawthra.com

Type: Bed & breakfast & guesthouse.
Clientele: Mostly gay & lesbian with some straight clientele
Transportation: Airport bus to subway. Readily accessible by all means of transportation. Reduced rate limo.
To Gay Bars: 1 blocks, a 2-min walk.
Rooms: 3 + 12 rooms with double or queen beds.

Bathrooms: Shared; mostly 2 rooms/bath, some ensuites.
Meals: Expanded continental or full breakfast option.
Vegetarian: Generally. Excellent vegetarian restaurants & supplies within a few blocks.
Complimentary: Sherry, Port, tea & coffee, mints.
Dates Open: All year.

continued next page

CANADA

High Season: All year.
Rates: CDN $79-CDN $150.
Discounts: Please inquire.
Credit Cards: MC, Visa, Amex, Diners Club.
Rsv'tns: Credit card required (MC or Visa) for reservation deposit to guarantee.
To Reserve: Call direct or travel agent.
Minimum Stay: Depending on availability.
Parking: Ample parking available.
In-Room: Color TV, VCR, phones with voice mail, ceiling fans, AC, laundry service.
On-Premises: Meeting rooms, business service (complete home office: access to Internet, fax, PC, copier, etc.), laundry facilities.
Exercise/Health: Jacuzzi & massage services available. Complimentary access to nearby gym with weights, sauna, steam, massage, cycling & running trails.
Swimming: Nearby pools & lake.
Sunbathing: On private & common sun decks, patio.
Nudity: On private decks.
Smoking: Strictly non-smoking inside. Permitted outdoors (w/ doors closed).
Pets: Permitted if socialized & restricted. There are house dogs on premises. Not in rooms.
Handicap Access: Inquire.
Children: No.
Languages: English, French, Spanish, Italian, ASL.
Your Host: Frank & Ric.

IGLTA

TORONTO • ONTARIO

Winchester Guest House
(formerly Sapho's Choice)

Q-NET Gay/Lesbian ♀♂

This 1920's home has been renovated to its original charm. All common areas and rooms contain period pieces consisting of Art Deco and Victorian antiques. Other amenities include a complete gay library, parking and a relaxing hot tub in the midst of our beautifully sculptured garden. *Winchester Guest House* is minutes from Toronto's foremost gay bars.

Address: 35 Winchester, Toronto, ON M4X 1A6 Canada.
Tel: (416) 929-7949 (Tel/Fax).

Type: Guesthouse.
Clientele: Gay & lesbian. Good mix of men & women
Transportation: Taxi, bus, & subway.
To Gay Bars: 5 minutes to gay/lesbian bar.
Rooms: 3 triples & 1 apartment.
Bathrooms: 1 en suite & 2 shared.
Meals: Expanded continental breakfast.
Vegetarian: Upon request.
Complimentary: Flowers, mints, coffee, tea, & juice.
Dates Open: All year.
High Season: Summer (May-Oct).
Rates: CDN $65-CDN $100 (tax included).
Discounts: For 1-week stay.
Credit Cards: MC, Visa, Amex.
Rsv'tns: Required.
To Reserve: Call direct.
Parking: On-site parking.
In-Room: Color TV, maid service, room service & laundry service.
On-Premises: TV lounge & laundry facilities.
Exercise/Health: Jacuzzi & massage.
Swimming: At the lake.
Sunbathing: On common sun decks.
Smoking: Permitted. Non-smoking rooms available.
Pets: No.
Handicap Access: No.
Children: No.
Languages: English.
Your Host: Rae & Debbie.

MONTREAL • QUEBEC

Aux Berges
Canada's Finest All Male Hotel

Men ♂

From the time *Aux Berges* was founded in 1967, it has acquired an atmosphere which is relatively unique among establishments having a constant flow of guests. The fact that they are from various countries and backgrounds certainly helps to make their stay with us a most pleasant

FERRARI GUIDES™

and memorable experience. We regard ourselves as a large family, and would gladly welcome you to join us. Our staff are always ready to help you with any problems you might have during your stay in Montréal.

Address: 1070 rue Mackay, Montréal, QC H3G 2H1 Canada.
Tel: (514) 938-9393, (800) 668-6253.

Type: Hotel.
Clientele: Men only
Transportation: Airport bus to Sheraton Center Hotel, then 5-minute walk, or taxi directly from airport CDN $25.
To Gay Bars: 1 block to gay bar.
Rooms: 42 rooms with double beds.
Bathrooms: 29 private, 13 shared.

Meals: Continental breakfast.
Dates Open: All year.
High Season: May-October.
Rates: CDN $65-CDN $100.
Discounts: On 7-day stay, 2 days free (good Nov-Mar.).
Credit Cards: MC, Visa, Amex, Diners Club, En Route & Discover.
Rsv'tns: Recommended.

To Reserve: Travel agent or call direct.
Parking: Adequate on- & off-street parking.
In-Room: Color TV with video, in-house movies, AC, telephone, laundry & maid service.
On-Premises: Kitchen facilities, TV lounge, snack bar.
Exercise/Health: Jacuzzi, dry & steam saunas.
Swimming: Pool & lake nearby.

Sunbathing: On private sun deck & terrace.
Nudity: Permitted on the sun deck, terrace & sauna area.
Smoking: Permitted without restrictions.
Pets: Small pets permitted.
Handicap Access: No.
Children: Not permitted.
Languages: French, English, German & Spanish.
Your Host: Serge & Christian.

Château Cherrier B&B

Gay/Lesbian ♀♂

Château Cherrier is a magnificent Tudor building decorated throughout with authentic period furniture. Large original oils of the same period adorn the sitting room and entry. Our strategic location near the gay village, restaurants, boutiques and nightlife, is further enhanced by a private parking lot, a rarity in the area. Leo and Jacques invite you to experience Montréal.

Address: 550 rue Cherrier, Montréal, QC H2L 1H3 Canada.
Tel: (514) 844-0055, (800) 816-0055,
Fax: (514) 844-8438.
E-mail: chateau.cherrier@sympatico.ca

Type: Bed & breakfast in a private home.
Clientele: Mainly gay/lesbian with some hetero clientele
Transportation: Taxi from airport 20 minutes. Limousine service (flat rate charge).
To Gay Bars: 4 blks to rue Ste-Catherine gay bars.
Rooms: 8 rooms with double & twin beds & a fourfold.
Bathrooms: 1 private bath/toilet/shower, 2 shared showers & 4 shared toilets.

Meals: Full breakfast prepared by Chef Leo.
Complimentary: Ice cubes.
Dates Open: April 1-November 30.
Rates: CDN $50-$75+.
Credit Cards: MC, Visa, Amex.
Rsv'tns: Required.
To Reserve: Travel agent or call direct. TAC 15%.
Minimum Stay: 3 nights long weekends or grand event.
Parking: Free private valet parking.

In-Room: AC, fan, color cable TV and maid service.
On-Premises: 2 living rooms, laundry service on long stays, shared refrigerator, safety box.
Smoking: Permitted in lounge only, not in rooms.
Languages: French, English, Spanish.

Gingerbread House Bed & Breakfast
Q-NET Gay-Owned & -Operated ♂

Turn-of-the-Century Charm in Downtown Montreal

Listed in Montréal's inventory of homes of architectural interest, the **Gingerbread House Bed & Breakfast** takes its name from the gingerbread ornamenting on the exterior and interior of the house. Built before the end of the last century, the bed & breakfast has been totally renovated. Two tastefully decorated rooms, in a smoke-free environment, are comfortably furnished with a double bed and share a bath, complete with amenities. Enjoy breakfast at your leisure while chatting with other guests, watching television, listening to music or planning your busy day in Montréal.

Address: 1628 St. Christophe, Montreal, QC H2L 3W8 Canada.
Tel: (514) 597-2804, **Fax:** (514) 526-4636. **E-mail:** gingerbreadhouse@gai.com

Type: Bed & breakfast.
Clientele: Mostly men with women welcome
Transportation: Near central bus station & metro.
To Gay Bars: 2 blocks, a 5 min walk.
Rooms: 2 rooms with double beds.
Bathrooms: Shared shower/toilet.
Meals: Expanded continental breakfast.

Vegetarian: Available on request, with prior notice. 5 min walk to vegetarian restaurant.
Dates Open: All year.
High Season: Apr thru beginning Nov.
Rates: Summer CDN $45-CDN $60, winter CDN $35-CDN 50.
Discounts: 10% for card-out member. 7th night free.
Credit Cards: MC, Visa, Amex.

Rsv'tns: Required.
To Reserve: Travel agent or call direct.
Minimum Stay: Required on long weekends only.
Parking: Notify us if coming by car. Adequate on-street parking.
In-Room: Color cable TV.
On-Premises: TV lounge, laundry facilities, internet access.
Exercise/Health: Nearby gym, weights, Jacuzzi, sauna, steam, massage.
Swimming: Nearby pool in summer only.
Smoking: No smoking allowed.
Pets: Not permitted.
Handicap Access: No.
Children: No.
Languages: English, French, Hebrew.
Your Host: Yves & Ephraim.

La Conciergerie Guest House
Q-NET Gay/Lesbian ♂

SEE SPECIAL PAGE 9 COLOR SECTION

Your Resort in the City!

La Conciergerie is Montréal's premier guest house. Since our opening in 1985, we have gained an ever-growing popularity among travelers from Canada, the United States, Europe and Australia, winning the 1995 Out & About Editor's Choice Award.

The beautiful Victorian home, built in 1885, offers 17 air-conditioned rooms with queen-sized beds and duvet comforters. A complimentary European breakfast is served either in the breakfast room or on an outdoor terrace. The house is within walking distance of most major points of interest, including downtown shopping, Old Montréal, rue St.-Denis, rue Ste.-Catherine, and the East Village, with its many gay shops, restaurants and bars. We're two blocks from the Metro (subway) and there is plenty of on-street parking for those who drive.

Address: 1019 rue St.-Hubert, Montréal, QC H2L 3Y3 Canada.
Tel: (514) 289-9297, **Fax:** (514) 289-0845.
URL: http://www.gaibec.com

Type: Bed & breakfast.
Clientele: Mostly men with women welcome
Transportation: Airport bus to Voyageur Bus Station, then walk, or taxi directly for CDN $25. Take a cab if arriving by train.
To Gay Bars: 2 blocks to men's & women's bars.
Rooms: 17 rooms with queen beds.
Bathrooms: 9 private. Shared: 1 bathtub, 3 showers, 3 toilets, 1 full bath.
Meals: Expanded continental breakfast.
Vegetarian: Bring your own. Vegetarian restaurants nearby.
Dates Open: All year.
High Season: April-December.
Rates: High season CDN $72-$135, low season CDN $52-$110.
Discounts: On 7-day stays in off-season.
Credit Cards: MC, Visa, Amex & Diners.
Rsv'tns: Recommended.
To Reserve: Call direct.
Minimum Stay: 3 nights on long weekends.
Parking: Ample free on-street parking.
In-Room: Maid service & AC.
On-Premises: Meeting rooms, TV lounge, public telephone, central AC/heat, laundry facilities, private terrace, gardens, & kitchen privileges.
Exercise/Health: Jacuzzi & small gym on premises. Massage by appointment only.
Swimming: At nearby pool.
Sunbathing: On common sun deck & roof.
Nudity: Permitted on roof & Jacuzzi.
Smoking: Permitted, except in bedrooms.
Pets: Permitted with prior notice.
Handicap Access: No.
Children: Not permitted.
Languages: French & English.
Your Host: Luc & Michael.

IGLTA

La Douillette
Women ♀

Love to Travel, but Hate to Leave Home & Cat? Borrow Mine!

La Douillette is a private home with small garden, purring cat and wonderful cuisine. The house, furnished with antiques, conveys a feeling of tranquility. Each room is supplied with local maps and information about current events, to help you enjoy this great city of Montréal to the fullest. I will also be pleased to advise you in any way that will help you enjoy your stay. In summer, relax and enjoy a home-cooked breakfast in our flower garden. Bienvenue à toutes! *Micheline*

Address: 7235 de Lorimier St, Montréal, QC H2E 2N9 Canada.
Tel: (514) 376-2183.

Type: Bed & breakfast.
Clientele: Women only
Transportation: Pickup from airport when possible, CDN $15.00. Bus from airport to Bonaventure Subway Stn, then to Fabre Stn.
To Gay Bars: 15 minutes by car or metro.
Rooms: 3 rooms with double or queen beds.
Bathrooms: 1 shared bath/shower/toilet.
Meals: Full breakfast.
Vegetarian: Available at all times.
Complimentary: Juices, tea, coffee & chocolates.
Dates Open: All year.
High Season: Spring, summer & autumn.
Rates: CDN $40-$60.
Rsv'tns: Recommended.
To Reserve: Call direct.
Parking: Ample on-street parking.
In-Room: Ceiling fans.
On-Premises: TV/stereo lounge.
Swimming: At free nearby pool or river.
Smoking: Permitted with some restrictions.
Pets: Not permitted.
Handicap Access: No.
Children: Permitted with restrictions.
Languages: French, English, Spanish & German.
Your Host: Micheline.

Le St. Christophe Bed & Breakfast

An Unexpected Canadian Treat

Men ♂

A Montreal-style townhouse built in 1875, *Le St-Christophe* is now fully restored to offer guests all the modern luxuries while maintaining the charm of the past. For more than ten years we have collected and filled our inn with antiques and memorabilia to enchant and delight you. There is always something new to discover at *Le St-Christophe*. We offer five spacious guest rooms: The Library, The French Canadian, The Sunrise, The Gallery and The China Room, each decorated in a different theme. Some have their own private baths, others share bathrooms, and all have color TVs and VCRs. There are two common rooms for your enjoyment. The first one is a great place for relaxing, reading or just socializing. It houses our collection of sailing ships reminiscent of the type Captain Jacques St-Pierre, the original owner of the house, once sailed. The second common room, also a nice place in which to spend some time, has a working fireplace, a small library of gay reading materials and a four-man Jacuzzi.

As one of your day's highlights, a full breakfast is served each morning from 9:00 am to 11:00 am either in our dining room. Seated at your own table, you can expect eggs Benedict, omelets, or Stephen's famous French toast. We also offer our guests the use of our very private rooftop sun deck, where you will find sun all day and a million stars at night. Clothing is optional, of course. *Le St-Christophe* is located in the East end of Montreal in the area known as the gay village. It is one block from Ste-Catharine St., where all of the gay bars and restaurants are situated, and is within walking distance of places like Old Montreal, rue St-Denis and China Town.

Address: 1597 St.-Christophe, Montréal, QC H2L 3W7 Canada.
Tel: (514) 527-7836, **Fax:** (514) 526-6488. **URL:** www.lebab.com/stchristophe

Type: Bed & breakfast guesthouse with full breakfast.
Clientele: Men only
Transportation: Airport bus to Voyageur bus station. Walk one block. Take metro to Berri if arriving by train.
To Gay Bars: 1 block.
Rooms: 5 rooms with double beds.
Bathrooms: 2 private shower/toilets, 1 private sink. 2 shared full baths.
Meals: Full breakfast.
Vegetarian: Available by pre-arrangement.
Complimentary: Fruits, coffee & tea.
Dates Open: All year.
High Season: May-Dec.
Rates: CDN $50-$79. High season CDN $60-$89.
Discounts: On 7-day stays in off season.
Credit Cards: MC, Visa.
Rsv'tns: Required.
To Reserve: Call direct.
Minimum Stay: 3 nights on long weekends.
Parking: Ample, free on-street parking.
In-Room: Color TV & VCR with video tapes, ceiling fans, maid service.
On-Premises: 2 lounges, private dining room, laundry service, working fireplace, breakfast deck.
Exercise/Health: Jacuzzi.
Swimming: Nearby pool.
Sunbathing: On private sun decks.
Nudity: Permitted.
Smoking: Permitted without restrictions.
Pets: No.
Handicap Access: No.
Children: Not permitted.
Languages: French & English.
Your Host: Stephen.

Le Traversin

A Charming Place For Charming Men

Gay-Owned & -Operated ♂

Le Traversin, a new bed and breakfast for men in Montreal, is situated in the heart of the "Chic Plateau Mont-Royal" near the terraces, restaurants and theatres of St-Denis street, and within walking distance of the village. This completely restored and modernized house with its uniquely French atmosphere, features a large dining room where you'll enjoy an elaborate continental breakfast and a living room that is perfect for socializing with other guests. Our five huge, comfortable bedrooms have feather duvets and pillows, television, bathrobes, slippers and more, and some have private bath.

Address: 4124 St-Hubert, Montréal, QC H2L 4A8 Canada.
Tel: (514) 597-1546, **Fax:** (514) 597-0818.
E-mail: travrsin@colba.net **URL:** www.homeniscience.com/le_traversin

Type: Bed & breakfast.
Clientele: Men only
Transportation: Airport bus to Berri Station, then taxi or metro Mt-Royal. 5 min walk to metro.
To Gay Bars: A 30 min walk, a 5 min drive.
Rooms: 5 rooms with single, double or queen beds.
Bathrooms: Private: 1 shower/toilet. Shared: 2 bath/shower/toilets, 1 WC only.
Meals: Expanded continental breakfast.
Vegetarian: Breakfast is mostly vegetarian.
Complimentary: Tea & coffee, chips, chocolate on pillows.
Dates Open: All year.
Rates: CDN $60-CDN $100.
Credit Cards: Visa.
Rsv'tns: Suggested.
To Reserve: Travel agent or call direct.
Parking: Adequate on-street parking.
In-Room: Ceiling fans, color TV, room service, bathrobes, slippers.
On-Premises: Meeting rooms, TV lounge, laundry facilities, fax, e-mail.
Exercise/Health: Jacuzzi.
Sunbathing: On common sun decks.
Nudity: Permitted in secluded garden.
Smoking: Non-smoking only.
Pets: Not permitted.
Handicap Access: No.
Children: No.
Languages: French, English, Spanish.
Your Host: Jean & Sylvain.

Pension Vallières

We Welcome You to Montréal!

Women ♀

We extend a warm welcome to guests at *Pension Vallières*, our cozy, quiet home in Montréal. The house is decorated in an "Art Deco" style and we offer two choices of accommodation. We have a bedroom with queen-sized bed, as well as a fully-equipped studio with a private entrance. Amenities in the studio include kitchenette, private bath, pool table, color cable TV and a stereo. You may choose from a variety of hearty breakfasts, which, if you like, we will serve in your room. To help make the most of your stay in Montréal, your hostess, Lucille, is available to take you on a sightseeing tour of this beautiful city.

Address: 6562, Delorimier St, Montréal, QC H2G 2P6 Canada.
Tel: (514) 729-9552.

Type: Bed & breakfast.
Clientele: 95% women, men welcome
Transportation: Pick up from airport, train (CDN $25-$35), bus. #18 bus from airport to Bonaventure Subway Sta, then to Beaubien Station
To Gay Bars: 10 minutes by Métro.
Rooms: 1 room & 1 bachelor studio (private bath) with double or queen bed.
Bathrooms: 1 private bath/shower/toilet & 1 shared bath/shower/toilet.
Meals: Full breakfast.
Vegetarian: 5-minute walk to vegetarian food store.
Complimentary: Tea, herbal tea, coffee & juice.
Dates Open: All year.
High Season: Spring, summer, autumn.
Rates: 1 person CDN $50, 2 people CDN $60, each addt'l person CDN $15.
Discounts: 10% for stays of over 8 nights.
Rsv'tns: Required.
To Reserve: Call direct.
Parking: Ample on-street parking.
In-Room: Ceiling fan, coffee/tea-making facilities, room & maid service. Studio has color cable TV, kitchen.
On-Premises: Pool table, stereo & laundry facilities.
Sunbathing: Beach on Notre Dame islands.
Smoking: Permitted without restriction.
Pets: Not permitted.
Handicap Access: No.
Children: Permitted.
Languages: French & English.
Your Host: Lucille.

Le Coureur des Bois
Gay/Lesbian ♀♂

Le Coureur des Bois is located in a historic stone house typical of the early French Canadian period. Well-maintained, the interior of the house is modern. Seven guest rooms, each with its own character, are simply furnished with emphasis on cleanliness and comfort. None of our rooms have private bath, but with 3 full baths to 7 rooms, we've yet to have anyone complain. Fresh fruit, croissants, rolls, muffins, cheeses, cereals and coffee make up the continental breakfast. What distinguishes us from the competition is our unique location within the walled city and the famous *Coureur des Bois* hospitality.

Address: 15 rue Ste.-Ursule, Québec, QC G1R 4C7 Canada.
Tel: (418) 692-1117, (800) 269-6414.

Type: Guesthouse.
Clientele: Good mix of gay men & women
Transportation: Taxi from airport or train.
To Gay Bars: 6-minute walk to gay/lesbian bars.
Rooms: 7 rooms with double or queen beds.
Bathrooms: 3 shared.
Meals: Our continental breakfast is a hearty combination of croissants, muffins, sweet breads, fruit dishes, cereals & assorted beverages.
Vegetarian: Available with advance notice.
Dates Open: All year.
High Season: April-November.
Rates: CDN $42-$92.
Credit Cards: MC, VISA, Amex & Diners.
Rsv'tns: Recommended.
To Reserve: Travel agent or call direct.
Parking: 4-minute walk to underground parking for CDN $6 per day.
In-Room: Maid service.
On-Premises: TV lounge, outdoor terrace, & fridge in lounge.
Swimming: River & lake 15 minutes by car.
Sunbathing: On the terrace.
Smoking: Permitted, but not in bedrooms.
Pets: Permitted by prior arrangement.
Handicap Access: No.
Children: Not permitted.
Languages: French & English.
Your Host: Jean Paul & Mark.

Spring Valley Guest Ranch
Gay-Owned 50/50 ♀♂

Enjoy bed and breakfast at *Spring Valley Guest Ranch* in a cozy 3-story, 1913-era home where the home-cooked meals are prepared in "The Country" Tearoom. The tearoom specializes in croissants and serves three meals daily. For a different experience, you can stay in a log cabin. Wood, water and outdoor washrooms are furnished. Activities include horseback riding, lawn games and hiking. The area is excellent for naturalists, photographers, historians, hikers or anyone who can appreciate silence and solitude. Our large meeting hall accommodates 100 guests and is ideal for reunions and meetings.

Address: Box 10, Ravenscrag, SK S0N 0T0 Canada.
Tel: (306) 295-4124.

Type: Bed & breakfast & campground with restaurant.
Clientele: 50% gay & lesbian & 50% straight clientele
Transportation: Private auto best.
To Gay Bars: No gay bars in area.
Rooms: 4 doubles in house. 2 doubles in log cabin.
Bathrooms: 1 shared in house. Outdoor facilities for cabin.
Campsites: Unlimited space for tents, trailers, RV's but no water or electrical hook-ups.
Meals: Full breakfast for B&B guests.
Vegetarian: Fresh vegetables available, no special dishes cooked.
Dates Open: All year.
High Season: July-August.
Rates: Log cabin & house: single CDN $35, double CDN $55.
Discounts: Group discounts for wilderness camp.
Credit Cards: MC.
Rsv'tns: Required one week in advance.
To Reserve: Call direct.
Parking: Ample free parking.
In-Room: Maid service, room service.
On-Premises: Laundry facilities, public telephone, TV lounge, refrigerator.
Exercise/Health: Horseback riding on the ranch.
Sunbathing: On lawn.
Smoking: Permitted in TV lounge and restaurant.
Pets: Permitted, except in restaurant & kitchen.
Handicap Access: No.
Children: Permitted but no cribs or facilities for infants.
Languages: English.
Your Host: Jim.

Ocean View Villas

Q-NET Gay/Lesbian

Your Invitation to Paradise

Exclusive and intimate, warm and alive, *Ocean View Villas* is our little corner of paradise and we'd like to share it with you. Arid and pristine, the island of Bonaire is in the southern Caribbean, 50 miles north of Venezuela and well below the hurricane belt. Wild goats and donkeys roam the flat terrain making quick meals of any accessible greenery. Bonaire's spartan landscapes contrast sharply with its spectacular underwater world teeming with exotic creatures. Maintained through a rigorous program of conservation, the surrounding coral reefs have made Bonaire a favorite destination for scuba divers and snorkelers. The constant easterly blowing tradewinds cool Bonaire's sunny days and make it a windsurfing and sailing mecca.

Bonaire's 13,000 inhabitants are outnumbered by its flamingos. Unencumbered by such annoyances as traffic lights or the daily stress of more developed locales, Bonaireans are known as the friendliest people in the Caribbean. The native population is of predominantly African descent with a rich infusion of Dutch and Portuguese cultures; but everyone speaks English. As your hosts, we pay personal attention to every detail. Our award-winning home includes our residence and rental apartments as well. It is one of the very few designated gay-owned and -operated vacation homes in the Caribbean.

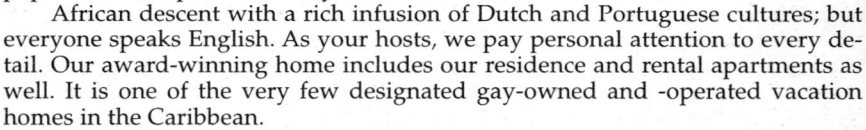

After having morning coffee on your private patio, pack up your dive and snorkeling gear for a trip to nearby Pink Beach or the wreck of the Hilma Hooker. After your dive, stop by the seaside markets in town for a basketful of the freshest fruits, vegetables, and fish. Have a nice lunch in your apartment, then take a siesta (everyone else does from noon until 2 p.m.). Upon waking, drive or bicycle south to the salt ponds where Bonaire's flamingos nest, walk to Bachelor's Beach, or visit one of the historic sites on the north end of the island. At the end of the day, you may want to sit in the courtyard and swap fish tales with the other guests or enjoy a sunset drink. Or you can choose to do nothing...it's your vacation!

Address: Kaya Statius Van Eps 6, Bonaire, Netherlands Antilles.
Tel:/Fax: (599-7) 4309.

Type: Apartments.
Clientele: Mostly gay & lesbian with some hetero clientele
Transportation: All guests are picked up at no charge from airport.
To Gay Bars: No gay bars on the island.
Rooms: 3 apartments.
Bathrooms: All private baths.
Vegetarian: Most restaurants have a vegetarian menu.
Dates Open: All year.
Rates: US $80-US $140.
Discounts: For groups, multi-unit rentals & long-term stays.
Credit Cards: MC, Visa.
Rsv'tns: Required.
To Reserve: Call direct.
Parking: Ample free uncovered off-street parking.
In-Room: Color TV, AC, kitchen, refrigerator, maid & laundry service.
Swimming: 300 feet to ocean beach.
Sunbathing: Each unit has a private yard. At nearby ocean beach.
Nudity: Permitted in & around your unit.
Smoking: No rules.
Pets: Not permitted.
Handicap Access: No.
Children: No.
Languages: English, Papiamentu, Dutch, Spanish.
Your Host: Tim & John.

Captain's Quarters

Q-NET Gay-Friendly ♀♂

The Unspoiled Queen of the Caribbean

SEE SPECIAL PAGE 10 COLOR SECTION

Orchids, tree frogs, crested hummingbirds, sea turtles, hot springs, snorkeling... Enjoy all of this when you stay at *Captain's Quarters*. This 16-room Victorian guesthouse (which has hosted royalty, celebrities, and adventurous travelers for more than 30 years) is set in a tropical paradise, a short 10-minute flight from St. Maarten. Rooms feature antique and four-poster beds, many with elegant canopies. From the balconies and patios are stunning views of the Caribbean and mountain scenery. Enjoy the garden dining pavilion, cliffside pool/bar, and some of the friendliest people in the Caribbean.

Saba is a storybook setting of Dutch gingerbread villages that date from the 1850s. Originally settled by pirates and sea captains as a safe haven for their families, "The Rock" was accessible only by footpaths and thousands of steps until "the Road that Couldn't be Built" was handcrafted in the 1950s. Saba will remind you of Switzerland with palm trees! World-class scuba diving, well-marked hiking trails, a pristine rainforest, and spectacular views at every turn make Saba unforgettable.

Note: Saba has no beaches. All swimming is from rocks, boats, tidal pools, and hotel swimming pools. However, since you have to fly through St. Maarten anyway, spend a few days there and enjoy some of the best beaches in the world. Then visit us — just minutes away.

Address: Windwardside, Saba Netherlands Antilles.
Tel: (5994) 62201, (800) 446-3010, **Fax:** (5994) 62577.
E-mail: SabaCQ@megatropic.com **URL:** http://saba-online.com

Type: Hotel with restaurant & bar.
Clientele: Mostly straight clientele with a gay & lesbian following
Transportation: 10-minute flight from St. Maarten, on Wiriair (Wm). Airport transfer included in rates.
To Gay Bars: None. All bars on island are friendly.
Rooms: 16 rooms with double, queen or king beds.
Bathrooms: All private shower/toilets.

Meals: Full American breakfast.
Vegetarian: Available upon request.
Complimentary: Welcome drink.
Dates Open: All year.
High Season: Feb-Apr.
Rates: Summer $95-$150, extra person $25. Winter $115-$170, extra person $35, includes tax & service fee.
Discounts: For stays of 3 or more nights, group packages. Off-season discounts for groups.

Credit Cards: Visa, MC, Amex, Discover.
Rsv'tns: Required. Walk-ins based on availability.
To Reserve: Travel agent or call direct.
Parking: Ample free off-street parking.
In-Room: Balcony & maid service. Some rooms with AC, color cable TV, ceiling fans, refrigerator.
On-Premises: Conference center, Carnival Museum.
Exercise/Health: Nearby gym.

Swimming: Pool on premises. Nearby ocean.
Sunbathing: At poolside.
Smoking: Permitted.
Pets: Permitted with advance approval.
Handicap Access: 1 room accessible.
Children: Welcome.
Languages: English, Dutch, Papiamento & Spanish.
Your Host: Richard.

IGLTA

Embassy Guest House - Condado

Q-NET Gay/Lesbian ♀♂

Welcome to the *Embassy Guest House-Condado* in the center of Condado, only steps to the beach in San Juan. Awaken to aqua-colored waters off Condado Beach. Relax under a coco palm. Dine at Panaché, our beachfront restaurant and bar. Or, enjoy nearby water and jet skiing, scuba diving, fishing, tennis, golf etc. The San Juan night, with casinos, discos, and shows, is nearby, as is shopping in Old San Juan. The *Embassy* staff helps you enjoy your stay, so come see why Puerto Rico is called the "Shining Star of the Caribbean."

Address: 1126 Calle Seaview-Condado, San Juan, PR 00907
Tel: (787) 725-8284 or (787) 724-7440, **Fax:** (787) 725-2400.

Type: Guesthouse with restaurant & bar on the beach.
Clientele: Mainly gay/lesbian with some straight clientele
Transportation: Taxi or limo from airport, approx $15. 15-min drive.
To Gay Bars: On premises, others 4 blocks away.
Rooms: 1 suite, 7 doubles, 7 quads.
Bathrooms: All private.

Vegetarian: Upon request in Panache Restaurant.
Complimentary: Coffee, tea.
Dates Open: All year.
High Season: Dec 1-May 1.
Rates: $65-$145 Dec 15 to Apr 30, $45-$85 May 1 to Dec 14.
Discounts: 10% on weekly stays during off-season.
Credit Cards: MC, Visa, Amex.

Rsv'tns: Recommended.
To Reserve: Travel agent or call direct.
Minimum Stay: 2 days on holidays & in season.
Parking: Ample, free on-street parking.
In-Room: Maid & room service, color TV, AC, ceiling fans, refrigerators & coffeemakers.
On-Premises: Restaurant, bar, TV lounge & public telephones.

Swimming: Ocean beach.
Sunbathing: On beach or sun decks.
Smoking: Permitted without restrictions.
Pets: Not permitted.
Handicap Access: Yes.
Children: Permitted, no infants, please.
Languages: Spanish, English, French.

IGLTA

Numero Uno Guest House

Q-NET Gay-Friendly 50/50 ♀♂

We Get Rave Reviews!

Among the many accolades our Caribbean guesthouse has received over the years are: "*Numero Uno*...our home away from home..." — *The Washington Post*, October 1995; "*Numero Uno:* With a name like that there's little doubt which of Ocean Park's flower-fringed guesthouses is the most stylish." — *Diversion*, July 1996; "...wonderfully relaxing..." — *The Washington Post*, January 1996.

In its Sunday, February 27, 1994 article the *San Francisco Examiner* quoted our guests' comments as follows: "On our recent trip to Puerto Rico, we were fortunate enough to have stayed at the **Numero Uno**. This charming guest house is located between Isla Verde and Condado and is ideally situated between the San Juan airport (15 minutes) and Old San Juan (10 minutes). Before we had even checked into our rooms, our hosts, Esther and Chris, served us a cold drink from the complete bar by the pool.

continued next page

INN PLACES® 1998

Chris was trained as a chef in New York and offers his culinary skills each night for those wanting to have dinner there. We took advantage of this our first night: fresh seafood kebabs (swordfish, scallops and shrimp), rice pilaf, tossed salad, fresh baby asparagus, homemade chocolate cheesecake and coffee. Even if you can't get a room here, it's worth it just to eat here. Dinner is served by the pool, and reservations are required. ***Numero Uno Guest House*** has been renovated over the past two years, and all of the rooms are spacious, with either double or king-sized beds and private baths, and include a continental breakfast. Rooms fronting the ocean are booked far in advance." — Sue I. and John T., Foster City

Address: Calle Santa Ana #1, Ocean Park, San Juan, PR 00911
Tel: (787) 726-5010, **Fax:** (787) 727-5482.

Type: Guesthouse with restaurant & bar.
Clientele: 50% gay & lesbian & 50% straight clientele
Transportation: Taxi, 10 minutes from airport, fixed $12 price.
To Gay Bars: 4-6 blocks to gay bars.
Rooms: 12 rooms with double, queen or king beds.
Bathrooms: All rooms have private bath/toilets or shower/toilets.

Meals: Expanded continental breakfast.
Vegetarian: We have several vegetarian options on our menu. Several health food stores & restaurants nearby.
Dates Open: All year.
High Season: We book up in advance for December thru April.
Rates: Low season (May-Nov): $75-$110; high season (Dec-Apr): $95-$145.
Discounts: Inquire.

Credit Cards: MC, Visa, Amex.
Rsv'tns: Required.
To Reserve: Travel agent or call direct.
Minimum Stay: 3 days during high season.
Parking: Adequate on-street parking.
In-Room: AC, ceiling fans, maid service.
Exercise/Health: Massage. Nearby gym, weights, Jacuzzi, sauna, steam, massage.

Swimming: Pool & ocean on premises.
Sunbathing: Poolside, on patio, at beach.
Smoking: Permitted, no non-smoking rooms available.
Pets: Permitted with some restrictions. Please call for details.
Handicap Access: Yes.
Children: Welcome.
Languages: Spanish, English.

IGLTA

Ocean Walk Guest House
Where Europe Meets the Caribbean

Gay/Lesbian ♀♂

Formerly a series of Spanish-style homes located directly on the best part of San Juan's beach, ***Ocean Walk*** is now a very casual resort complex with 40 comfortable rooms in a beautiful courtyard setting, with pool, bar and grill. On the large, elevated sun deck, you can enjoy a piña colada, while the sun sets, in a spectacular display of colors, on the horizon. After midnight, all is quiet, and you will hear only the gentle pounding of the surf. Yet, the fast-paced nightlife and the casinos are within walking distance.

Address: Calle Atlantic No 1, Ocean Park, San Juan, PR 00911
Tel: (787) 728-0855 or (800) 468-0615, **Fax:** (787) 728-6434.

Type: Guesthouse with restaurant & bar.
Clientele: Mainly gay & lesbian with some hetero clientele
Transportation: Taxi or rental car from San Juan Int'l Airport approx $12.
To Gay Bars: 10 min walk or short taxi ride.
Rooms: 40 rooms & 5 apartments with single, double & king beds.
Bathrooms: 34 private shower/toilets. 6 rooms share bath/shower/toilet.
Meals: Breakfast & lunch.
Vegetarian: Available upon request.
Complimentary: Coffee, tea, muffins, fruit on the patio (mornings until 11:00).
Dates Open: All year.
High Season: Dec 15-Apr 15.
Rates: US $40-$85 in summer. US $55-$130 in winter.
Discounts: 10% airline discounts, weekly rates for minimum 2 weeks.
Credit Cards: MC, Visa, Amex, Discover, Eurocard.
Rsv'tns: Recommended.
To Reserve: Travel agent or call direct.
Minimum Stay: 4 nights, Dec 16-March 1, if Sat or Sun is involved.
Parking: Adequate on-street parking.
In-Room: Color cable TV, ceiling fans & maid service. Some rooms have AC.
On-Premises: Telephones.
Swimming: At pool on premises or ocean beach.
Sunbathing: At poolside, on beach & common sun decks.
Smoking: Permitted.
Pets: Special permission required.
Handicap Access: Yes. Limited & with assistance.
Children: Welcomed with prior approval.
Languages: English, Spanish, French & German.

IGLTA

Cooper Island Beach Club

Gay-Friendly ♀♂

A Casual Caribbean Beachfront Resort

SEE SPECIAL PAGE 11 COLOR SECTION

Cooper Island Beach Club is a small resort on a 1 1/2-mile by 1/2-mile island, where there are no roads, nightclubs, malls or fast-food outlets. Apart from the Beach Club and its staff, there is one local family, five holiday houses and many goats on the island. Our beachfront restaurant and bar offer one of the best sunset views in the islands. Sheltered from the sun, you can enjoy a cool drink with the Caribbean Sea lapping the sand only a few feet away. In addition, we have built a reputation for serving quality meals in an informal setting, at a reasonable price.

Our twelve guest rooms were built in 1992 and 1996, and have an open-plan bedroom/living room/kitchen, plus balcony, bathroom, a shower that is almost outdoors, and a magnificent view of the Sir Francis Drake channel and several other islands. They are all on the beach, just a few steps from the warm, clear ocean where there is wonderful snorkelling.

Photo by Jim & Odile Scheiner

Your principal activities on Cooper Island will consist of sunbathing, swimming, reading, writing, enjoying relaxing meals in the restaurant and conversation in the bar. If you wish to be more active, you can hike around the island (it's too small to get lost!), and we can arrange day sails and boat trips to other islands. For the SCUBA diver, novice or experienced, we have a fully equipped PADI dive shop on the property where we offer basic and advanced SCUBA instruction, and can take you on a variety of dive tours, including the wreck of the RMS Rhone, a Royal Mail steamship sunk in 1867, which is only 15 minutes by boat from our dock. **Guest Comment:** "There are not enough words to do justice to the immense beauty, tranquility and serenity to be found here."

continued next page

Address: Cooper Island, British VI,
USA office: PO Box 512, Turners Falls, MA 01376
Tel: (413) 863-3162, (800) 542-4624 (USA office)
Fax: (413) 863-3662.
E-mail: info@cooper-island.com **URL:** http://www.cooper-island.com

Type: Beach resort with restaurant, bar, & scuba dive shop.
Clientele: Mainly straight with gay & lesbian following
Transportation: Pick up from ferry dock, no charge on scheduled trips.
Rooms: 12 rooms with queen beds.
Bathrooms: All private shower/toilets.
Vegetarian: Available for lunch & dinner with prior notice.
Dates Open: All year.
High Season: December 15th to April 15th.
Rates: Per night for 2: US $95 (Jun 1-Oct 30); US $155 (Dec 15-Apr 15); US $115 (Apr 15-May 31 & Nov 1-Dec 14). Meal and/or dive packages available.
Discounts: Weekly discounts available.
Credit Cards: MC, Visa, with 5% handling charge.
Rsv'tns: Required.
To Reserve: Travel agent or call direct.
Parking: Boat moorings available.
In-Room: Ceiling fans, kitchen, refrigerator & maid service.
Exercise/Health: Full scuba facilities & watersports.
Swimming: In the ocean.
Sunbathing: On the beach.
Pets: Not permitted.
Handicap Access: No.
Children: Permitted, preferably over 10 yrs old.
Languages: English.
Your Host: Chris.

Fort Recovery Estate

Gay-Friendly

"A Bit of Britain in the Sun"

A great place for a romantic getaway, **Fort Recovery Estate** boasts its own private beach, fresh-water swimming pool and 17th-century Dutch fort. The luxury three- to four-bedroom house on the beach and the one- and two-bedroom seaside and penthouse villas afford spectacular Caribbean views of six islands. All accommodations include daily continental breakfast, air-conditioning, cable TV, kitchen and housekeeping service. Each stay of seven nights includes one dinner, served by waiter service in the privacy of your villa, and a half-day snorkeling trip, per guest. Massages and yoga classes are available, by arrangement, on premises.

Address: Box 239, Road Town, TortolaBVI.
Tel: (284) 495-4354, (800) 367-8455 (wait for ring), **Fax:** (284) 495-4036.
E-mail: FTRHOTEL@caribsurf.com **URL:** www.fortrecovery.com

Type: Bed & breakfast hotel & villa resort with chef on premises.
Clientele: Mostly straight clientele with a gay/lesbian following
Transportation: Taxi.
Rooms: 17 villas with king beds.
Bathrooms: All private shower/toilets.
Meals: Continental breakfast.
Vegetarian: Menu has vegetarian choices. There are lots of vegetarian foods on the island.
Complimentary: One welcome dinner per guest for each 7-night stay.
Dates Open: All year.
High Season: November-June.
Rates: Daily rates $135-$640.
Credit Cards: MC, Visa, Amex.
Rsv'tns: Required.
To Reserve: Travel agent or call direct.
Parking: Adequate free parking.
In-Room: AC, ceiling fans, color cable TV, kitchen, refrigerator, maid & room service.
On-Premises: Meeting rooms, E-mail, fax, phone, typing.
Exercise/Health: Massage & yoga classes. Nearby gym, weights.
Swimming: Pool & the Caribbean.
Sunbathing: Poolside, at beach, on private patio.
Nudity: Please inquire.
Pets: Not permitted.
Handicap Access: No.
Children: Welcome.
Languages: English, Spanish.

IGLTA

On The Beach

Q-NET Gay/Lesbian ♀♂

The Virgin Island's Only Gay-Owned Beachfront Hotel — Our 20th Year!

"In my travels throughout the world, there are but a few most highly recommended places and *On the Beach* is one of these," said Bobby Stevens, *The Guide*, Jan. 1995. "For warmth, comfort, and tranquility, it is unsurpassed."

The hotel provides attractive and immaculate accommodations, two beachfront patios, two fresh water pools and a wonderful beachfront bar. For guests who desire the best, we are pleased to announce our new luxury beachfront villas. Beautifully appointed for true island living, each villa consists of a spacious bedroom, a bathroom, a complete kitchen, dining and living room, and is tiled throughout with Mexican terra-cotta. Amenities include air conditioning, ceiling fans, microwave, as well as an entertainment center with television, stereo and VCR. The villas are in a private, breezy, lushly landscaped tropical setting with sun deck and vine-covered shade patio directly on the beach.

Explore unspoiled and secluded beaches, swim, snorkel, sail, bask in the Caribbean sun or spend romantic evenings viewing breathtaking sunsets. *"On the Beach* on the tiny island of St. Croix is magical. It was the best vacation I've ever taken." — *Frances Stevens, Curve Magazine, Feb. 1995.* **Guest Comment:** "My 12th visit ...I can't imagine staying anywhere else. [The host's] personal attention to every detail is obvious." — Curt K., Virginia Beach, VA

Address: 127 Smithfield, Frederiksted, St. Croix, USVI 00840
Tel: (340) 772-1205 or (800) 524-2018 (Toll-free reservations),
Fax: (340) 772-1757.

Type: Beachfront hotel.
Clientele: Gay & lesbian, good mix of men & women
Transportation: Taxi from airport $10 for 2.
To Gay Bars: Guest bar poolside. "Last Hurrah" gay bar & disco in Frederiksted.
Rooms: 8 rooms, 6 suites & 6 apartments with queen & king beds.
Bathrooms: All have private shower & toilet.
Meals: All rates include continental breakfast. Lunch service available.

Vegetarian: Available in nearby restaurant.
Complimentary: Bottle of rum, weekly cocktail hour, coffee, rolls, juice.
Dates Open: All year.
High Season: Dec 19-Mar 30.
Rates: Low-season $65-$150, shoulder $75-$185, high-season $100-$250.
Discounts: Special off-season packages.
Credit Cards: MC, Visa, Discover.
Rsv'tns: Required.

To Reserve: Travel agent or call direct.
Minimum Stay: Low-season 3 nights, high season 1 week.
Parking: Ample free off-street parking.
In-Room: AC, ceiling fans, cable TV, coffee/tea-making facilities, kitchen, refrigerator & daily maid service.
Exercise/Health: Massage.
Swimming: 2 pools on premises or ocean beach.
Sunbathing: At poolside & on ocean beach or common sun decks.

Nudity: Permitted on nearby isolated beaches & at 1 of our 2 pools.
Smoking: Permitted without restrictions.
Pets: Permitted with prior approval.
Handicap Access: No.
Children: Permitted with prior approval.
Languages: English, Spanish.
Your Host: Bill, Irma & Dan.

IGLTA

CARIBBEAN

VIRGIN ISLANDS - US • SAINT CROIX

INN PLACES® 1998

CARIBBEAN

SAINT THOMAS • VIRGIN ISLANDS - US

Blackbeard's Castle

Gay-Friendly 50/50

The tower at *Blackbeard's Castle*, built in 1679 to scan the Caribbean for pirates and enemy ships, is a national historic site. It provides a spectacular backdrop for the oversized fresh water pool and terrace. The views are exceptional! Spacious and quiet guest rooms provide all the expected amenities. It is an intimate inn whose management team offers all the personal touches that make a vacation memorable. Accolades include: *VOGUE:* "...remarkable view...an excellent restaurant." *AMEX:* "A first-class hotel and restaurant." *PRACTICAL GOURMET:* "...best restaurant on St. Thomas."

Address: PO Box 6041, St Thomas, USVI 00804
Tel: (809) 776-1234, (800) 344-5771, **Fax:** (809) 776-4321.

Type: Hotel with restaurant, bar, & lounge.
Clientele: 50% gay & lesbian & 50% straight clientele
Transportation: Taxi is best from airport.
To Gay Bars: 5-minute drive to gay/lesbian bars.
Rooms: 12 doubles, 4 junior suites, & 4 apartment suites.
Bathrooms: All private.
Meals: Continental breakfast.
Vegetarian: Available upon request.
Dates Open: All year.
High Season: Dec 15-Apr 30.
Rates: Summer $65-$95. Winter $110-$150.
Credit Cards: MC, Visa, Amex, Discover, Diners.
Rsv'tns: Required.
To Reserve: Travel agent or call direct.
Minimum Stay: 3 days during high season.
Parking: Free adequate off-street parking.
In-Room: Cable color TV, AC, direct dial telephones, safes, daily maid service & kitchens in apartment suites.
On-Premises: Gardens.
Exercise/Health: Massage by appointment.
Swimming: In 2 swimming pools.
Sunbathing: At poolside.
Smoking: Permitted without restrictions.
Pets: Not permitted.
Handicap Access: No.
Children: Permitted, over 16.
Languages: English, Spanish & French.
Your Host: David.

IGLTA

JAMAICA • WEST INDIES

Hotel Mocking Bird Hill

Q-NET Gay-Friendly

Where Your Heart Will Sing & Your Soul Will Fly

The breathtaking mountain views and ocean vistas at *Hotel Mocking Bird Hill* will refresh your spirit. This elegant, charming retreat nestled in 6.5, lush, tropical acres has spacious, airy rooms with original art, while the hotel's gallery offers insight into Jamaican art and culture. The clientele is international and the cuisine is creative, using only fresh local produce, some from the hotel's own gardens. This intimate hotel with warm hospitality and personal

Hotel Mocking Bird Hill
Port Antonio, Jamaica.
Tel:876-993-7134/7267 FAX: 876-993-7133, E-MAIL: mockbrd@toj.com

198   FERRARI GUIDES™

touches from the innkeepers is also environmentally friendly. Nearby are rainforests, mountains, and numerous waterfalls, romantic coves, and beautiful beaches.

Address: PO Box 254, Port Antonio, Jamaica, West Indies.
Tel: (876) 993-7267, (876) 993-7134, **Fax:** (876) 993-7133.
E-mail: mockbrd@toj.com

Type: Private, intimate hotel with restaurant, bar, gallery.
Clientele: Straight clientele with a gay & lesbian following
Transportation: From Kingston: car rental or taxi. From Montego Bay: Inland flight to Port Antonio airport with free transfer to hotel.
Rooms: 10 rooms with single, queen or king beds.
Bathrooms: 7 en suite shower/toilets, 3 en suite bath/toilet/showers.
Meals: Additional charge for meals.
Vegetarian: Meals included in menu.
Complimentary: Welcome cocktail. Fresh fruit & flowers in room, small gift.
Dates Open: All year.
High Season: Dec 15-Apr 30.
Rates: For double room: Summer '98 US $95-$110. Winter '97/98 US $130-$150.
Discounts: Group rates (10 or more people), long stays, repeat guests. Call/fax for off-season specials. Jan 6-Feb 28 & May 1-June 30.
Credit Cards: MC, Visa, Eurocard, Amex.
Rsv'tns: Recommended. Walk-ins welcome.
To Reserve: Travel agent or call/fax direct.
Parking: Ample free off-street parking.
In-Room: Ceiling fans, safe, laundry service, balcony with ocean view.
On-Premises: TV lounge, telephone, special tours & hikes arranged.
Exercise/Health: Walking/jogging trail, horseback riding, hiking. Massage with prior appointment.
Swimming: Pool, ocean, rivers, waterfalls.
Sunbathing: At poolside, beach or in the garden.
Smoking: Permitted. Non-smoking rooms available.
Pets: Not permitted. Dogs & cats on premises.
Handicap Access: Yes. Limited, with no special facilities.
Children: Welcome, but not encouraged.
Languages: English, German & French.
Your Host: Barbara & Shireen.

Lighthouse Park

Gay-Friendly ♀♂

Rustic, Peaceful Caribbean Ambiance

Lighthouse Park is situated on 1-1/2 acres of seaside cliff property. We take pride in ensuring a relaxed, rustic, yet comfortable and hospitable atmosphere. Cabanas, A-frame cottages, a lovely stone villa and camping sites provide varied accommodations. All units are set amongst tropical foliage and flowers. Snorkeling and swimming are excellent, and there are clothing-optional areas. Local transport, both to town and to white sand beaches, is easy and bike rentals are available.

Address: PO Box 3, Negril, Jamaica, West Indies.
Tel: (876) 957-0252.

Type: Seaside cabanas, a stone house & tent spaces.
Clientele: Mostly straight clientele with a gay/lesbian following of 40% gay artist & musician types
Transportation: Airport bus US $25 per person 1 way, private taxi US $60. 1-1/2 hr (approx 45 min) scenic drive.
To Gay Bars: No gay bars in Jamaica.
Rooms: 10 doubles.
Bathrooms: 3 private, others share.
Campsites: 8-9 tent sites (bring your own tents).
Vegetarian: Fresh fruit & vegetables available in town & vegetarian plate available at most restaurants.
Dates Open: All year.
High Season: Dec 15th-May 1st.
Rates: Low season US $15-$105, high season US $20-$175 & 15% tax.
Discounts: 10% on stays of 14 days or longer.
Credit Cards: MC, Visa, Amex.
Rsv'tns: Required with 3-day deposit (certified check or money order).
To Reserve: Travel agent or call direct.
Minimum Stay: 3 days during high season.
Parking: Adequate off-street security parking.
In-Room: Stone house has kitchen privileges & maid service. A communal kitchen is available.
Exercise/Health: Snorkeling on premises. Sun deck carved into rocks has ladder to deep water.
Swimming: Deep-sea swimming off cliff on premises. 4 miles to white sandy beach.
Sunbathing: On beach or common sun decks.
Nudity: Permitted in sea-access areas & on sun decks.
Smoking: Permitted.
Handicap Access: No.
Children: Not recommended under 12 years (30-40-ft cliffs).
Languages: English.
Your Host: Sharon.

Seagrape Villas

Home Away From Home With Your Own Cook & Maid

Rent a whole house for a Caribbean escape. Enjoy daily adventures as you explore Jamaica's beaches, its history, sights, activities and landmarks. *Seagrape Villas* are 3 lovely houses right on the sea. Each has 4 bedrooms, 4 baths, a private pool and its own cook and maid. For two guests or groups up to 24, *Seagrape Villas* offer privacy and the opportunity to get to know the island and its people firsthand. Plan your own delectable menu and shop with the cook, discovering local produce and cuisine. Rent a car to go to different places each day, exploring this friendly island.

Address: Ocho Rios, Jamaica, West Indies.
Tel: (773) 693-6884, (800) 637-3608, **Fax:** (847) 297-6882.

Type: 3 four-bedroom villas each with cook & maid.
Clientele: Everyone welcome
Transportation: Car is best.
Rooms: 3 villas, each with 4 bedrooms and single beds.
Bathrooms: A private bath for each bedroom.

Vegetarian: Always available.
Dates Open: All year.
High Season: December-April (Xmas-Easter).
Rates: $2500 per villa per week high season, $1800 low season.
Discounts: Available. Call for details.
Rsv'tns: Required.

To Reserve: Travel agent or call direct.
Minimum Stay: 1 week.
Parking: Ample off-street parking.
In-Room: AC, ceiling fans, laundry service & maid service.
Swimming: Each villa has a private pool. Ocean on premises.

Sunbathing: At poolside.
Nudity: Permitted poolside.
Smoking: Permitted anywhere.
Pets: Permitted.
Handicap Access: Yes, but not specially equipped.
Children: Children welcomed.
Languages: English.

Hotel Casa Blanca de Manuel Antonio S.A.

Q-NET Gay/Lesbian

Admittedly, our Hotel is Definitely NOT the Main Attraction Here...

...because we are within 15 minute's walking distance to Playita, the one and only gay beach in the whole country. *Hotel Casa Blanca* guesthouse is on a hillside overlooking the beaches. A steady ocean wind makes your stay comfortable and our private atmosphere makes you feel at home. Relax in our tropical garden, 2 pools, or on the sun deck. If you like action, we can arrange beach or mountain horseback riding, boat trips into the mangroves, guided tours to Manuel Antonio National Park, multiday excursions to untouched tropical islands, and any number of water adventures. Nearby Quepos provides ample nightlife with discos and casinos.

HOTEL CASA BLANCA DE ML. ANT. S.A.

Address: Apdo 194, Quepos-Manuel Antonio 6350 Costa Rica.
Tel: (506) 777-0253 (Tel/Fax). (From USA, dial 011 before area code)
E-mail: cblanca@sol.racsa.co.cr
URL: http://bertha.pomona.edu/cblanca/

Type: Hotel guesthouse.
Clientele: Exclusively for gay & lesbian guests, their relatives & friends
Transportation: Pick up provided by Sansa (400 Colones per person), TravelAir ($4 dollars per person) & Directo (free).
To Gay Bars: 3 mins by car or cab to gay/lesbian bar & gay/lesbian bar & restaurant.
Rooms: 4 rooms, 2 suites & 4 apartments with single, double or king beds.
Bathrooms: All private.
Meals: Breakfast at additional charge of $5 plus tax.
Vegetarian: Available upon request on premises & at nearby restaurants.
Complimentary: Tea & coffee.
Dates Open: All year.
High Season: November-April.
Rates: USD, tax not included. Double: Low $40-high $70. Apt: Low-$50-high $90. Suites: Low $90-high $140, $10 per extra bed.
Credit Cards: Visa, MC, Amex & Eurocard.
Rsv'tns: Required.
To Reserve: Travel agent or call direct.
Parking: Adequate free off-street parking. Guarded private parking lot.
In-Room: All with ceiling fans & laundry service. Suites with kitchenette. Apartments with kitchenette, refrigerator & panoramic views.
On-Premises: Refrigerators & freezers outside of rooms. Laundry facilities, phone, tropical garden, flight & hotel reservation services.
Exercise/Health: Massage upon request. Gym, weights & massage in downtown Quepos.
Swimming: Pool on premises, gay beach within walking distance. Nearby pool & river.
Sunbathing: At poolside, in the garden, on common sun decks & at the beach.
Nudity: Permitted poolside, in the pool, in the garden & on the sun deck.
Smoking: Permitted without restrictions.
Pets: Permitted. Must have entered country legally & have all the paperwork.
Handicap Access: Yes. No stairs for suites, 4 rooms, garden & poolside.
Children: Not especially welcome.
Languages: Management: Spanish, English & German. Cleaning staff: Spanish, little English.
Your Host: Harald & Rainer.

IGLTA

INN PLACES® 1998

Hotel La Mariposa

Q-NET Gay-Friendly 50/50 ♀♂

An Astounding Pacific Paradise

Hotel La Mariposa is located on the Pacific Coast of Costa Rica. We offer villa suites and deluxe rooms, most with air conditioning and private in-room Jacuzzi. The Spanish arches and gardens add to the elegance and charm of this tropical paradise. Our split-level villas accommodate up to four adults, and all rooms overlook the panorama of Manuel Antonio National Park, with stunning mountain and ocean views. Pristine, palm-fringed beaches await you, with the luxuriance of the rainforest a few short minutes away. Other features include room service, pool, lounge and bar. Our beautiful open-air restaurant serves all day with a French twist.

Address: PO Box 4, Manuel Antonio Beach, Quepos, Costa Rica.
Tel: in US: (352) 379-5980, (800) 416-2747, **Fax:** (352) 379-5940.
Direct: (506) 777-0355 or (506) 777-0456, Fax: (506) 777-0050.
(From USA, dial 011 before area code)
E-mail: htlmariposa@msn.com **URL:** www.lamariposa.com

Type: Hotel with restaurant, bar & gift shop.
Clientele: 50% gay & lesbian & 50% straight clientele
Transportation: Air from San Jose on Travel Air or Sansa. Inquire about pick up from Quepos airport. Pick up from San Jose $120 each way.
Rooms: 22 rooms with double, queen or king beds.
Bathrooms: All private bath/shower/toilets. Deluxe rooms with Jacuzzi.
Meals: Full breakfast.
Vegetarian: Available nearby.
Complimentary: Coffee.
Dates Open: All year.
High Season: Dec-Apr.
Rates: Low season US $90-US $135. High season US $120-US $180.
Discounts: Inquire about special rates.
Credit Cards: MC, Visa.
Rsv'tns: Required.
To Reserve: Travel agent or call direct.
Parking: Free parking.
In-Room: Telephone, AC, ceiling fans, maid, room & laundry service.
On-Premises: Video tape library, walkways, Pacific Ocean views.
Exercise/Health: Jacuzzi, massage. Nearby gym, weights.
Swimming: Pool on premises. Ocean nearby.
Sunbathing: Poolside, on common sun decks, at beach.
Nudity: Beach at Manuel Antonio.
Smoking: Permitted.
Pets: Not permitted.
Handicap Access: Not at present time, we are working on this.
Children: On request. Mostly adult clientele.
Languages: Spanish, Italian, English, French.
Your Host: Carlos.

Hotel Colours - The Guest Residence San Jose

Gay/Lesbian ♀♂

Experience Not Just a Place, But a State of Mind

You and your friends are invited to experience our newly expanded and completely renovated resort in San José, Costa Rica. ***Colours***, the premier guesthouse of Costa Rica, is of Spanish-style architecture with unique and stylish finishing touches. Now, all accommodations feature vibrant tropical "colours" and private, tiled baths. Our exciting new pool, Jacuzzi and garden areas truly make our property the BEST the capital city has to offer. We are pleased to present an atmosphere of total enjoyment, from lounging poolside doing absolutely nothing... to lively conversation during happy hours at the bar in Marcel's — our own restaurant/bar. We want you to have the opportunity to squeeze every drop of pleasure from your well-deserved vacation. Our location is conveniently set in an exclusive residential district, a few minutes from the new Plaza Mayor Mall, the US Embassy and several neighborhood parks. From here, it's just a 10-minute ride to central San José, but only one block to pharmacies, grocery store, liquor stores, bars, restaurants and a weekly farmers' market.

Upon arrival and settling in, an orientation is offered covering currency exchange, what's where in the neighborhood, massage, city access for shopping, sightseeing, restaurants and nightlife. Our multilingual staff will advise guests of guided day excursions to attractions within and outside of San José, such as volcanoes, biological reserves, island boat cruises, whitewater river rafting, and others. From the main balcony of the poolside house, you look out over the enclosed garden and pool/Jacuzzi area, with a view in the distance of the mountain ranges surrounding the city. Take some time for sunning beside the solar-heated pool and have your complimentary tropical breakfast there or at Marcel's — an exciting new experience in dining, featuring international cuisine evenings prepared by our chef, Renate. Our facility features various room types to suit your taste and personal budget, with Bahamian paddle fans, CD-

continued next page

INN PLACES® 1998 203

clock radios and free security boxes. Also on property are three large social rooms, one of which features English-speaking cable and movie channels.

Beaches of Nosara — Province of Guanacaste

Also available is our own *Colours - The Lodge - Nosara...* In the selva (jungle/woods), with ocean views to the Pacific, this rustic lodge retreat is a special destination for individuals wanting beaches, wildlife and more... Truly a unique experience in an intense nature setting for up to six guests.

Speak to our friendly reservation representative at 1-800-ARRIVAL about these two locations with complete tour and travel planning throughout Costa Rica. We will assist you in planning your entire personal holiday. Remember our other distinctive lodging affiliates — *Colours - The Guest Mansion* in romantic Key West, and *Colours at New Penguin Resort and Mantell Plaza* in exciting South Miami Beach, Florida.

Address: c/o Colours Destinations, 255 W 24th St, Miami Beach, FL 33140 USA. **Tel:** (800) ARRIVAL (277-4825), (305) 532-9341, **Fax:** (305) 534-0362. Local San Jose **Tel:**(506) 296 1880. (From USA, dial 011 before area code 506) **E-mail:** newcolours@aol.com **URL:** www.travelbase.com/colours IGLTA

Hotel Kekoldi

Q-NET Gay-Friendly ♀♂

Unique in Costa Rica — Young and Informal

The staff of *Hotel Kekoldi* is young and easygoing like you are. The historic building is uniquely styled, reflecting the colorful atmosphere of the sunny Caribbean islands, and is decorated with sensational paintings by famous English artist Helen Etis. The hotel is located in the historic Barrio Amón, only minutes by foot to the center and all touristic points of interest, as well as to restaurants, bars, discos and cinemas. There are 14 large rooms with king-sized beds, private bathrooms with hot water, telephones, and breakfast, bar and laundry services.

Address: Avenida 9, Calle 3 Bis, across from INVU, San José Costa Rica. **Tel:** (506) 223-3244, **Fax:** (506) 257-5476.(From USA, dial 011 before area code) **E-mail:** kekoldi@sol.racsa.co.cr **URL:** www.costaricainfo.com/kekoldi.html

Type: Hotel with bar & breakfast restaurant.
Clientele: Mostly hetero with a gay/lesbian following
Transportation: Bus or taxi from airport, approx. $10.
To Gay Bars: 2 blocks, an 8-min walk.
Rooms: 14 rooms with single or king beds.
Bathrooms: 14 private shower/toilets.
Vegetarian: Avail. nearby.
Dates Open: All year.
High Season: Dec-Apr.
Rates: Single $24-$32, double $34-$45.
Disc.: On extended stays.
Credit Cards: MC, Visa.
Rsv'tns: Suggested.
To Reserve: Travel agent or call direct.
Parking: Adequate on-street pay parking.
In-Room: Telephone, ceiling fans, maid & laundry service.
On-Premises: TV lounge, video tape library.
Sunbathing: At beach, accessible by bus.
Smoking: Permitted.
Pets: Permitted, inquire in advance.
Handicap Access: No.
Children: Welcome.
Languages: Spanish, English, German.
Your Host: Edgar.

IGLTA

Joluva Guesthouse

Gay/Lesbian ♂

Stay at the Right Place...At the Right Price!

The friendliness of our all-gay, bilingual (Spanish and English) crew at *Joluva Guesthouse* creates a relaxing and welcoming atmosphere. Our rates are friendly, too, and include a continental breakfast with tropical fruits. Our rooms are clean and spacious and have beds with luxury orthopedic mattresses. We're always ready to assist you with vacation plans, arranging tours or trips, or local information. All gay activities and cultural attractions are within walking distance. Special for our guests: San Jose walking tours with gay guide. We serve breakfast each morning.

Address: Calle 3B, between avenues 9 and 11 #936, San Jose & Manuel Antonio Beach Costa Rica. **Tel:** (506) 223 7961, **Fax:** (506) 257 7668. (From USA, dial 011 before area code) USA reservations & info (800) 298-2418.
E-mail: joluva@sol.racsa.co.cr **URL:** www.hotels.co.cr/joluva.html

Type: Bed & breakfast.
Clientele: Mostly men with women welcome
Transportation: Bus or taxi from airport or pick up for extra fee of approx $20.
To Gay Bars: 3 blocks or 10 minutes by foot.
Rooms: 8 rooms with single or double beds.
Baths: 6 private, 2 shared.
Meals: Continental breakfast with tropical fruits.

Vegetarian: We can direct you to these establishments.
Comp.: Coffee all day.
Dates Open: All year.
High Season: Dec-May.
Rates: USD $15-$40 (add $5 per extra person).
Discounts: 10% for 7 nights stay, 15% for 14 nights or more.
Credit Cards: MC, Visa, Amex.
Rsv'tns: Required.

To Reserve: Travel agent or call direct.
Parking: Limited on-street parking or guarded pay lots which we strongly recommend.
In-Room: Color cable TV.
On-Premises: VCR available at $3.00 for 24 hours. Includes all selections from our video library.
Swimming: At the beach.
Sunbathing: At the beach.

Nudity: Gay nude beach at La Playita Manuel Antonio.
Smoking: Permitted but strongly discouraged.
Pets: Not permitted.
Handicap Access: No special provisions. Please inquire.
Children: Not welcomed.
Languages: English, Spanish & Polish.
Your Host: Peter.

La Concha Beach Resort
Gay-Friendly ♀♂

A Hidden Jewel in the Sea of Cortez

Long white sandy beaches, calm blue-green waters, breathtaking sunsets, an abundance of water sports... Where is this haven? *La Concha Beach Resort* in La Paz. It's the perfect destination for vacationers and business travelers. This modern city offers so much: whale watching, world-class scuba diving, sea kayaking, snorkeling with sea lions, sport fishing, exploring deserted islands, great shopping, and fine dining. Just two miles from downtown La Paz in a secluded setting, this resort has 107 air-conditioned rooms, suites and condominiums, a full-service restaurant, two bars, and an outdoor pool overlooking the sea.

Address: Kilómetro 5 Carretera a Pichilingue, La Paz, BCS CP 23010 Mexico.
Tel: In USA: (619) 260-0991, **Fax:** (619) 294-7366 or (800) 999-BAJA (2252).

continued next page

Type: Hotel with restaurant & gift shop.
Clientele: Mostly hetero clientele
Transportation: Airport to La Paz, then airport shuttle. Airport pick up US $16 roundtrip per person (outside service). Transfers to & from town.
To Gay Bars: 3 miles, a 5-minute drive.
Rooms: 103 rooms, 2 suites, 11 condominiums with single or king beds.
Bathrooms: All private shower/toilets.
Campsites: Avail., inquire.
Meals: Inquire about breakfast, lunch & dinner.
Vegetarian: Available at hotel restaurant.
Dates Open: All year.
High Season: Jul-Aug.
Rates: US $65-US $89 for standard rooms.
Discounts: AAA.
Credit Cards: MC, Visa, Amex.
To Reserve: Travel agent or call direct.
Parking: Ample free off-street parking.
In-Room: Color cable TV, telephone, refrigerator, AC, maid, room & laundry service. Condos have kitchen.
On-Premises: Meeting rooms, 2 oceanside bars.
Exercise/Health: 2 Jacuzzis.
Swimming: Pool & ocean on premises.
Sunbathing: At poolside & at beach.
Smoking: Permitted. Non-smoking rooms available.
Children: Welcome.
Languages: Spanish, English.

Casa Aurora
Gay/Lesbian ♀♂

Study Spanish in the City of Eternal Spring

Cuernavaca, the city of the Eternal Spring, is a one hour's drive from Mexico City, on the road to Acapulco. The city's many attractions include the Palace of Cortes, a 16th-century cathedral, the Borda Gardens (once the summer home of Emperor Maximillian and Charlotte), the Brady Museum, the San Anton waterfall, Siqueiros Workshop (named for the famed muralist) and its Spanish-language schools. CETLALIC is the only gay-friendly language school. It offers a three-week lesbian program and a three-week gay program every summer. One of our guest's comments: *"Casa Aurora* is a restored Colonial home, downtown near everything. Once inside, you find an oasis where you can relax, take a siesta in one of the hammocks or listen to fascinating stories of Mexico's history told by your host..."

Address: Arista No. 12, Centro, Cuernavaca, Mor. 62000 Mexico.
Tel: (52 73) 18 63 94.

Type: Bed & breakfast or guesthouse.
Clientele: Mostly gay & lesbian with some hetero clientele
Transportation: Plane or bus from Mexico City. Taxi from bus station to house.
To Gay Bars: 10 blocks to Shadee disco/bar. A 15 min walk, a 5 min drive.
Rooms: 3 rooms with single, double or king bed.
Bathrooms: 1 private bath/ toilet/shower, 1 shared bath/toilet/shower.
Meals: Continental breakfast or 3 meals.
Vegetarian: Owner only cooks vegetarian.
Dates Open: All year.
High Season: Summer (May-August).
Rates: B&B: US $18. Three meals: US $24.
Discounts: For 2 guests in same room: B&B US $32; Three meals: US $42.
Rsv'tns: Preferred.
To Reserve: Call direct.
Minimum Stay: No, but prefer longer stays and students of Spanish.
Parking: Adequate pay parking, parking lot around the corner.
In-Room: Each room has a terrace with a hammock.
On-Premises: Small garden, laundry facilities.
Swimming: Nearby pool. 1 hour to Las Estacas resort.
Sunbathing: In garden.
Smoking: Owner doesn't smoke, but smoking permitted in terraces, garden & in rooms.
Pets: Not permitted.
Handicap Access: Yes. Rooms are all in one floor or on ground floor.
Children: No.
Languages: Spanish, English, French.
Your Host: Antonio.

Arco Iris
Q-NET Gay-Owned & -Operated ♀♂

Feel the Breezes, Get Lost in the Views!

Arco Iris ("rainbow" in Spanish) is set atop the highest point of the exclusive Conchas Chinas neighborhood in Puerto Vallarta. Designed by noted Mexico City architect, Raul Espinoza, this unique hotel is surrounded by lush tropical vegetation, many tropical fruit trees, flowers and herbs. Come, feel the breezes and lose yourself in the views. You will see that the property has been designed to capture every breeze and every possible glimpse of Bahia de Banderas, Los Arcos, the Sierra Madres, and the violet and tangerine sunsets that dip into the blue Pacific ocean.

Enjoy the service of our trained staff who understand that you are taking a well-deserved vacation. Mornings, you will be served a complimentary tropical breakfast at your private pool terrace or dining room, and at day's end, join us on the upper terrace for complimentary sunset margaritas. When planning your Puerto Vallarta activities, ask us for anything that might make your day more relaxing and fun. We are happy to make reservations or give directions to gay-owned shops and restaurants, gay cruises, water sports, massage in your room, jungle tours, whale watching, sunset cruises, dinner reservations, or arrangements for dinner in your dining room or poolside.

Arco Iris offers rooms with views, television, long-distance telephone and air conditioning. We can also offer a three-bedroom, three-bath casita with private pool, a two-bedroom apartment, or a one-bedroom apartment with Jacuzzi. Prices depend on the type of room and the season. Discounts are offered on stays of eight, fourteen and thirty days or more, and there are also special long-term rates during the summer months. Because Puerto Vallarta has become such a popular gay travel destination, advance reservations are necessary.

Address: 115 Paseo de los Delfines, Fracc. Conchas Chinas, Puerto Vallarta, JAL 48390 Mexico.
Tel: (52-322) 15579, **Fax:** (52-322) 15586. In US or Canada: (800) 682-9974.
E-mail: arcoiris@pvnet.com.mx

Type: Bed & breakfast with house & apt. rentals.
Clientele: Mostly gay/lesbian with some hetero clientele
Transportation: Taxi from airport & ferry.
To Gay Bars: 10 blks, 1 mi., a 15-min walk, a 5-min drive.
Rooms: 19 rooms, 4 apts. & 4 3-br houses with single, double, queen or king beds.
Bathrooms: Private: 1 bath/shower/toilet, 10 shower/toilets. Shared: 8 bath/shower/toilets.
Meals: Full tropical break.
Vegetarian: Meat not served with breakfast. 2 vegetarian rest's. nearby.

Complimentary: Sunset margaritas & flavored waters on common terrace. Bottled water, coffee, filters & ice in kitchens.
Dates Open: All year.
High Season: Mid-Oct thru mid-Apr.
Rates: Summer: US $40-US $160, winter: US $60-US $290, spring & fall: US $50-US $195. Prices in US$, can accept pesos at current exchange rate.
Discounts: 5% off stays of 8+ nights; 7.5% off stays of 14+ nights; 10% off stays of 30+ nights; 30% off for long-term summer month stays.
Credit Cards: MC, Visa.
Rsv'tns: Requested.
To Reserve: Travel agent or call direct.
Parking: Ample free on-street parking, security.
In-Room: Phone with long-distance access, ceiling fans, kitchen, refrigerator, coffee & tea-making facilities, maid & laundry service, limited room service. Some rooms have AC, color cable TV, VCR.
On-Premises: Video tape library, fax, internet, e-mail.

Exercise/Health: Jacuzzi, massage. Nearby gym, weights, Jacuzzi, sauna, steam, massage.
Swimming: 4 small swimming pools on premises. Ocean & waterfalls nearby.
Sunbathing: Poolside, on private & common sun decks, patio & at beach.
Nudity: Permitted on private pool terraces.
Smoking: Permitted everywhere.
Pets: Please inquire.
Children: Please inquire.
Languages: Spanish, English.
Your Host: Thom & Ran.

LATIN AMERICA • MEXICO • PUERTO VALLARTA

Casa de los Arcos
Q-NET Gay/Lesbian ♀♂

A Very Hospitable & Private Place Overlooking Puerto Vallarta

Our vacation villa commands an incredible vista of Vallarta and the Pacific Ocean, and from your bedroom you can see Los Muertos and El Dorado beaches. Jungle foliage bordering our back garden provides a backdrop for a changing display of colorful tropical birds. *Casa de los Arcos* accommodates up to eight guests in two totally equipped one- or two-bedroom suites. We can arrange for a cook to come into your suite and prepare dinner for you. So, after a day at the beach, you can return to afternoon drinks and a sumptuous supper with friends.

Address: PO Box 239BB, Puerto Vallarta, Jalisco 48300 Mexico.
Tel: (52-322) 259 90 (Tel/Fax). In USA: (800) 424-3434, ext. 277, ask for Ron.
E-mail: csarcos@tag.acnet.net

Type: Vacation villa.
Clientele: Mostly gay & lesbian with some straight clientele
Transportation: Free airport pick up included in service.
To Gay Bars: 15 min walk, 5 min drive.
Rooms: 2 1600-sq-ft, self-contained, 1- to 2-bedroom suites with king or double beds.
Bathrooms: Private.
Meals: Meals not included in daily rate. Cook avail. for small extra fee, plus food cost. Hosts will help prepare menus & shop. Cook can cater small cocktail parties.
Vegetarian: Cook can prepare vegetarian items.
Complimentary: Welcome margaritas & snacks.
Dates Open: All year.
High Season: Dec-Apr.
Rates: Per-night rates. High season: Suite #1 USD $200, Suite #2 USD $100. Low season: Suite #1 USD $150, Suite #2 USD $75 (if over 2 guests, add USD $25 pp/pn).
Discounts: 10% if over 2 weeks.
Credit Cards: Major credit cards accepted when booking thru USA 800 number.
Rsv'tns: Required.
To Reserve: Travel agent or call direct.
Minimum Stay: 4 days during high season.
Parking: Ample free parking.
In-Room: AC, ceiling fans, telephone, fully equipped kitchen, maid. TV & laundry service upon request.
On-Premises: Terraces, tropical gardens, living room & sitting areas, dining rooms, laundry facilities.
Exercise/Health: Registered masseurs make house calls, short walk to gym.
Swimming: Pool on premises. Ocean a 10 min walk, 5 min drive.
Sunbathing: Poolside & on private sun terraces.
Smoking: Permitted outside, but we prefer that people not smoke in bedrooms.
Pets: No.
Handicap Access: No.
Children: No.
Languages: Spanish, English.
Your Host: Susan & Chris.

Casa Fantasía
Q-NET Gay/Lesbian ♂

Where Your Dreams Become Reality

A jewel in the heart of Puerto Vallarta's gay district awaits. Situated behind tall brick walls to ensure guest privacy, *Casa Fantasía* consists of three separate houses — traditional Old-World-style Mexican haciendas totaling 10,000 square feet of luxury accommodations. The elegant yet informal common areas include sunken living rooms, covered terraces and intimate conversation areas. Eight large bedrooms each contain a private full bath, and guests may choose from twin or king-sized beds. The houses are filled with antique furnishings, limited edition prints and original oil paintings, as well as hundreds of curios and objets d'art which can hold one's attention for hours. All rooms, both common and guest, have plants and/or fresh flowers daily. Outside, the terrace provides a relaxing, regenerating environment with a staffed bar for guests and their friends adjacent to the swimming pool, along with chaise lounges, lounge chairs and tables.

Located in Colonia Emiliano Zapata, Puerto Vallarta's gay district, *Casa Fantasía* is just a block from the beach and a short five-to-ten-minute beach walk to the famous "blue chairs." Vallarta's premier disco, Club Paco Paco, is but two blocks away and the other popular bars, Los Balcones and Zótano, are a leisurely five-minute stroll over the new bridge into downtown. Within a ten-minute walk one can find world-class restaurants, more modest dining, craft and curio shops, museums, clothing stores, a gym and much, much more. The staff at *Casa Fantasía* can also arrange tickets for Vallarta's many paid diversions — day-long excursions to Yelapa, evening dinner cruises, jungle tours, horseback riding, deep-sea fishing, snorkeling, parasailing and the like.

So come, let your new friends at *Casa Fantasía* pamper you in a style to which you will quickly become accustomed. Call or write for our brochure. *Casa Fantasía:* a new standard in Puerto Vallarta!

Address: Apartado Postal #387 Centro, Puerto Vallarta, Jalisco CP 48300 Mexico.
Tel: (52-322) 2 19 04, **Fax:** (52-322) 2 19 23. Toll-free in USA: (888) 636-2539.
E-mail: nenalex@aol.com

Type: Bed & breakfast guesthouse.
Clientele: Mostly men with women welcome. Some straight clientele
Transportation: Airport taxi to B&B.
To Gay Bars: 2 blocks, 1/4 mile, a 5 minute walk, a 2 minute drive.
Rooms: 6 rooms with single or king beds.
Bathrooms: 6 private bath/toilet/showers.

Meals: Full or buffet breakfast. Selection alternates, there is no menu.
Vegetarian: By request and available nearby.
Complimentary: Afternoon beverages (wine, sherry, etc), welcome fruit basket, always something on pillow.
Dates Open: All year.
High Season: Mid-November to mid-April.
Rates: Low season: USD $30-USD $75; High season: USD $52-USD $95.

Rsv'tns: Required.
To Reserve: Travel agent or call direct.
Minimum Stay: 3 days.
Parking: Ample on-street parking.
In-Room: Ceiling fans, laundry & maid service.
On-Premises: TV lounge, video tape library, fax, phone, computer, Internet.
Exercise/Health: Massage. Nearby gym, weights, massage.

Swimming: Pool on premises. Nearby ocean & river.
Sunbathing: Poolside, on patio, at beach.
Smoking: Permitted in all areas & in all rooms.
Pets: Not permitted.
Handicap Access: No.
Children: No.
Languages: Spanish, English.
Your Host: Daniel & Luis.

Casa Panorámica

Q-NET Gay/Lesbian ♀♂

Dramatically-situated on a hillside, *Casa Panorámica* is a 11,000-square-foot villa on 5 levels with spectacular and breathtaking views of the Bahia de Banderas and the town below. While remaining convenient to both beach and downtown, the villa's lofty vantage point catches the cool cross breezes from the mountains. Four separate dining areas, two large terraces for swimming and dining and a small terrace with BBQ provide a variety of relaxing environments. The villa accommodates 12 people comfortably, with complete housekeeping services provided.

Address: Apdo. Postal 114, Puerto Vallarta, Jalisco 48300 Mexico.
Tel: (800) 745-7805, **Fax:** (808) 324-1302 in USA. Or call direct (52-322) 23656.
E-mail: CasaPano@pvnet.com.mx

Type: Bed & breakfast in a private 7 bedroom villa.
Clientele: 75% men & 25% women
Transportation: Airport combi vans.
To Gay Bars: 1-12 blocks to gay bars.
Rooms: 7 rooms with double, queen & king beds.
Bathrooms: All private.
Meals: Full breakfast.
Vegetarian: Upon request.

Complimentary: Coffee, tea.
Dates Open: Closed in August.
High Season: November thru May.
Rates: $85-$95 Nov-May, $65-$75 June-Oct.
Discounts: On stays over two weeks.
Credit Cards: MC, Visa.
Rsv'tns: Recommended 30 days in advance.
To Reserve: Travel agent or call direct.
Minimum Stay: During Christmas.
Parking: Adequate, free, off-street parking.
In-Room: Maid & laundry service, ceiling fans.
On-Premises: Laundry facilities.
Exercise/Health: 7 blocks to new fully-equipped gym.
Swimming: Pool on premises, ocean beach 3 blocks.

Sunbathing: At poolside, on patio, common sun decks or beach.
Smoking: Permitted without restrictions.
Pets: Not permitted.
Handicap Access: Not accessible.
Children: Ages 6 and up permitted.
Languages: Spanish, English.
Your Host: Brian.

Doin' It Right — in Puerto Vallarta

Gay/Lesbian ♀♂

Vallarta is Tropical, Affordable, Gay-Friendly and CLOSE!

MAGICAL Puerto Vallarta, is at the same latitude as Hawaii, but 1 ½ hours closer and more affordable. There are 1 ½ gay beaches, 5 clubs, gay hotels/B&Bs, excursions (hot springs, snorkeling cruises), restaurants rivaling NY and SF at much lower prices, friendly locals, cobblestone streets, shopping. Doin' It Right is the only "family" agency with its own legit "family" land operator, Boana, for airport greets, mini-tours, air tickets, realty, etc. We have over 175 villas and condos (from moderate to the BEST), and gay-friendly hotels & B&Bs. We work ONLY with honestly gay-friendly businesses.

Address: 1010 University Ave #C113-741, San Diego, CA 92103
Tel: (619) 297-3646, (800) 936-3646, **Fax:** (619) 297-3642.

Holly's Mexico

Q-NET Woman-Owned & -Operated ♀

Yes!! Now There's A Holly's in Mexico!

Experience the culture, beauty and lifestyle of Mexico at *Holly's Mexico*, about 35 to 45 minutes north of Puerto Vallarta's airport, in the small, quaint fishing village of Sayulit. The view is awesome from the casa on the hillside and there's a wonderful ocean breeze. The cottage has a fully furnished kitchen, private and shared baths, and is only a few minutes' walk through the village to the beach.

Staying here is like taking a step back in time... You can kayak, surf, ride horses on the beach, take quiet walks, sit on the beach and watch the sunset with a margarita and your favorite Mexican appetizers. Or, you can visit the busy city of Puerto Vallarta with its wonderful culture, food shopping and nightlife. *Holly's* in beautiful Sayulit is perfect because it's far away, yet close enough to do it all... except ski... and if you want that you can come stay at Holly's Lake Tahoe.

A SPECIAL PLACE FOR EVERYONE South of The Border

LATIN AMERICA • MEXICO • PUERTO VALLARTA

Address: Mail to: PO Box 13197, South Lake Tahoe, CA 96151 USA.
Tel: (530) 544-7040, (800) 745-7041.
E-mail: hollys@oakweb.com **URL:** hollysplace.com

Type: Cottage.
Clientele: Mostly women with men welcome
Transportation: Car is best. Pick up from airport $20.
To Gay Bars: 45 miles to gay bars in Puerto Vallarta.
Rooms: 2 cottages with queen beds.
Bathrooms: 1 private & 2 shared bath/shower/toilets.
Vegetarian: Available in village.

Complimentary: Coffeemaker & gourmet coffee, tea, kisses on pillows.
Dates Open: All year.
High Season: Dec 1-Mar 1.
Rates: Lowest summer off-season $40-$50/nt; highest winter (Xmas/New Year) $85-$100/nt.
Discounts: Midweek off-season summer.
Rsv'tns: Required.
To Reserve: Travel agent or call direct.

Minimum Stay: 1 week.
Parking: Limited free off-street parking.
In-Room: Ceiling fans, color TV, VCR, kitchen, refrigerator, coffee & tea-making facilities, maid & laundry service.
On-Premises: Video tape library, books.
Swimming: Nearby ocean beach.

Sunbathing: At beach, on patio & private sun decks.
Smoking: No smoking inside anywhere. Non-smoking rooms available.
Pets: Permitted.
Handicap Access: No.
Children: Any and all children welcome if supervised.
Languages: Spanish, English.
Your Host: Holly.

Mission San Francisco
Your Private Casa Overlooking the Bay

Q-NET Gay-Friendly ♀♂

Allow yourself to experience the extraordinary *Mission San Francisco* and its panoramic bay view. From your private luxurious home, you'll view the bay, tropical hillsides, margarita sunsets, nighttime city lights and palm studded village. Relax under the dome of the master bedroom suite or sun yourself on the very private rooftop terrace. *Mission San Francisco* is in the heart of the village, within walking distance of the gay beach, Mexican bazaar, supermarket, bars and restaurants. Included are 3 bedrooms and 2 baths, with additional rooms available. Weekly and monthly rates. NOTE: Also available in Mexico City, in the very heart of the Zona Rosa, is our one-bedroom rooftop apartment "Casita del Cielo," renting at only $800 per month.

Tel: (916) 933-0370 (Tel/Fax).
E-mail: mpizza@quiknet.com

Type: Two rental homes.
Clientele: Mostly hetero with a gay & lesbian following
Transportation: Airport taxi to home approximately $5.
To Gay Bars: 6 blocks or a 10-minute walk.
Rooms: 1 3-bedroom, 2 bath home & 1 5-bedroom, 4 bath home with single, double & king beds.
Bathrooms: Private bath/toilets.
Complimentary: Refrigerator stocked with beer & soft drinks upon arrival.
Dates Open: All year.
Rates: $295-$495 per week, per home (not per person).
Discounts: 4th week free.
Rsv'tns: Required.
To Reserve: Call direct.
Minimum Stay: Rates are by the week.
Parking: Ample on-street parking.
In-Room: Completely furnished homes with ceiling fans, color cable TV & full kitchens.
Exercise/Health: Nearby gym.
Swimming: 6 block walk to gay beach.
Sunbathing: On private sun decks or nearby beach.
Smoking: Permitted.
Pets: Not permitted.
Handicap Access: No.
Children: Welcome.
Languages: Spanish, English.
Your Host: Mike.

Palapas in Yelapa

Gay-Friendly 50/50 ♀♂

Our *Palapas in Yelapa* are comfortable, simple cabin accommodations in tropical surroundings with spectacular ocean views. All of our palapas (cabins) have gas stoves, cooking utensils, silverware, bathrooms with showers, kerosene lamps, mosquito nets, hammocks, tables, chairs and beds with linens. In town, there are restaurants, shops and a doctor.

Yelapa is hidden in a crescent cove where blue-green waters roll on white sands. Thatched roofs dot the shore and disappear into the dense jungle hillside. A rolling river flows down the palm-covered mountains and gently fills the peaceful bay. The tropical secluded village has many exotic birds, lagoons, waterfalls and colorful flowering trees. Combined with balmy breezes and spectacular reddish-orange sunsets, Yelapa is a paradise hideaway.

Address: c/o Antonio & Lucinda Saldaña, Apartado Postal 2-43, Puerto Vallarta, Jalisco Mexico.
Tel: (52-322) 491 97.

Type: Palapas (cabins).
Clientele: 50% gay & lesbian & 50% straight clientele
Transportation: Plane to Puerto Vallarta, then boat ride to Yelapa.
Rooms: 5 cabins accommodating 2-6 people.
Bathrooms: All private showers & toilets.

Dates Open: All year.
High Season: Nov-Apr.
Rates: USD $15-$35 per night, per cabin.
Discounts: Stays over a week or a month, also group rates.
Rsv'tns: Required, plus 50% deposit.
To Reserve: Call direct.
Minimum Stay: 1 week

usually required with 50% deposit (flexible).
In-Room: Gas stoves, cooking utensils, silverware, beds/linens, kerosene lamps, mosquito nets, tables, chairs & hammocks.
Swimming: Ocean & river a 5-minute walk.
Sunbathing: On ocean beach.

Nudity: On private decks.
Smoking: Permitted.
Pets: Permitted.
Handicap Access: No.
Children: Welcome.
Languages: Spanish & English.
Your Host: Antonio & Lucinda.

Quinta Maria Cortez

Gay-Friendly 50/50 ♀♂

Sumptuously Romantic — Beautifully Baroque

Quinta Maria Cortez is a beautiful beachfront retreat in Puerto Vallarta, complemented by sunny terraces and spectacular views of the ocean. This "Mexaterranean Villa" is especially appealing for those who appreciate a unique ambiance along with a bit of whimsical antiquity by the sea. The inn consists of six suites on seven levels, rising above the white-sand beach. The large-suite/junior-suite accommodations feature eclectic European-style decor with private bath and phone. Most include a kitchenette and balcony. Mid-level at the inn is a common area with a sitting room, fireplace, terrace and palapa-roofed dining area — all with gorgeous ocean views. One level down is the swimming pool and sun terrace.

Address: 132 Calle Sagitario, Playa Conchas Chinas. US reservations: PO Box 1799, Salt Lake City, UT 84110 USA.
Tel: in USA: (801) 531-8100, (888) 640-8100,
Fax: (801) 531-1633.
E-mail: res@quinta-maria.com

Type: Inn.
Clientele: 50% gay & lesbian & 50% straight clientele
Transportation: Taxi is best, or airport transfer.
To Gay Bars: 1 1/2 miles.
Rooms: 3 rooms, 3 suites with single, double, queen or king beds.
Bathrooms: Private: 4 bath/shower/toilets, 1 bath/toilet, 1 shower/toilet.

Meals: Continental breakfast.
Vegetarian: Stores nearby.
Dates Open: All year. Closed for add-on/update May-Sept '98.
High Season: Dec-Apr.
Rates: US $100-US $175.
Discounts: Off-season discounts, subject to availability.
Credit Cards: MC, Visa, Amex.

Rsv'tns: Required.
To Reserve: Travel agent or call direct.
Minimum Stay: 3 nights.
Parking: Limited on-street parking.
In-Room: Telephone, ceiling fans, kitchen, refrigerator, coffee & tea-making facilities, maid service.
Exercise/Health: Nearby gym, weights, massage.

Swimming: Pool & ocean on premises.
Sunbathing: Poolside, on roof, common sun decks & at beach.
Smoking: Permitted. Open-air hotel & rooms.
Pets: Not permitted.
Handicap Access: No.
Children: No.
Languages: Spanish, English.

UNITED STATES

ANCHORAGE • ALASKA

Aurora Winds, An Exceptional B&B Resort

Q-NET Gay/Lesbian ♀♂

Only One Thing Is Missing — YOU!

Far exceeding the standards expected by today's most discriminating traveler, the 5,200-square foot *Aurora Winds* has five sumptuous guest suites, each with its own private bathroom on two secluded acres overlooking Anchorage. The professionally decorated and furnished B&B has an atmosphere of quiet elegance and a contemporary style with an Alaskan home ambiance. Each of the nonsmoking guest rooms is furnished with queen-sized beds, televisions, VCRs, phones, and private sitting areas. Mornings, you have your choice of breakfast selections. Either a full complement of culinary delights or an expanded continental breakfast is available in the dining room or, if you prefer, in bed.

You will be pleasantly surprised by the many amenities the *Aurora Winds* has to offer, including a 10-person Jacuzzi where you can visit with other guests and enjoy a glass of wine following your workout in the exercise room. You might wish to relax in the sauna, play a game of billiards, watch a video on the 52-inch surround sound TV, or just curl up with your best friend in front of one of the four fireplaces.

As your hosts, we strive to provide you with all the services you may need. The *Aurora Winds* is less than 20 minutes from many local attractions. In addition to the unlimited natural wonders that you will find in Anchorage, there are also three gay bars, five bookstores, and a thriving gay community. We look forward to providing you with the special type of hospitality that only Alaskans can offer.

Address: 7501 Upper O'Malley, Anchorage, AK 99516 **Tel:** (907) 346-2533, (800) 642-9640, **Fax:** (907) 346-3192. **E-mail:** awbnb@alaska.net

Type: Bed & breakfast.
Clientele: Good mix of gay men & women with some straight clientele
Transportation: Car is best & advised. Pick up available with prior arrangement.
To Gay Bars: About 15 minutes.
Rooms: 5 suites with twin or queen beds.
Bathrooms: All private.
Meals: Expanded continental breakfast or full breakfast available.
Vegetarian: Available with advance notice.
Complimentary: Coffee, tea, sodas, mineral waters, & evening nightcap.
Dates Open: All year.
High Season: May 15-September 15.
Rates: Winter $65-$125 & summer $85-$165.
Discounts: For longer stays. Inquire for others.
Credit Cards: MC, Visa, Amex.
Rsv'tns: Recommended, especially during high season.
To Reserve: Travel agent or call direct.
Parking: Ample free off-street parking.
In-Room: Telephone & color TV. Fireplaces in 3 rooms.
On-Premises: Meeting rooms, billiards room, TV lounge, theatre room, laundry facilities, & kitchen privileges.
Exercise/Health: Jacuzzi in 4 rooms. Exercise room, free weights, sauna & 10-person Jacuzzi.
Swimming: 3 minutes to year-round Olympic indoor pool.
Sunbathing: On the common sun deck.
Nudity: Permitted in the hot tub.
Smoking: In designated areas only. All sleeping & common areas are non-smoking.
Pets: Permitted, on approval.
Handicap Access: Partial.
Children: Permitted on approval only.
Languages: English. Emergency translator available.
Your Host: Bill & James

IGLTA

Cheney Lake Bed & Breakfast

Gay-Friendly ♀♂

Cheney Lake Bed & Breakfast is located on Cheney Lake in a quiet residential neighborhood. We have a great view of the mountains from the living and dining rooms, while the lake can be viewed from each bedroom and the deck. Curl up beside the fireplace, watch videos, soak in the hot tub, or chat with your hosts who are long-time Alaskans and can offer numerous suggestions on how to enjoy the beauty and adventure of Anchorage and Alaska.

Address: 6333 Colgate Dr, Anchorage, AK 99504
Tel: (907) 337-4391, **Fax:** (907) 338-1023. **E-mail:** cheneybb@alaska.net

Type: Bed & breakfast.
Clientele: Mostly straight with a gay/lesbian following.
Transportation: Car is best.
To Gay Bars: 10-15 minute drive to 3 bars.
Rooms: 3 rooms with king beds.
Bathrooms: Private: 2 bath/toilet/showers, 1 shower/toilet.
Meals: Continental breakfast.
Vegetarian: Available upon request.
Complimentary: Coffee, tea, sodas, beer, wine, juice. Candy & nuts in room.
Dates Open: All year.
Rates: Summer $85, winter $50.
Credit Cards: MC, Visa.
Rsv'tns: Preferred.
To Reserve: Travel agent or call direct.
Parking: Ample free on- & off-street parking.
In-Room: Color TV, VCR, phone, ceiling fans, maid service.
On-Premises: Laundry facilities, TV lounge, video tape library, fax, copier, computer.
Exercise/Health: Nearby gym with weights.
Smoking: Permitted on outside deck. Non-smoking home.
Pets: Not permitted.
Handicap Access: No.
Children: No.
Languages: English.
Your Host: Mary & Janetta.

Alta's Bed and Breakfast

Q-NET Gay/Lesbian ♀♂

This log home with modern amenities in a wilderness setting, only twenty miles from downtown Fairbanks, makes *Alta's Bed & Breakfast* a piece of Alaska's interior to be experienced. In summer, you can fish, hike, soak in the hot tub and enjoy the midnight sun. In winter you can rent snowmobiles, ski or watch the Northern Lights from the solarium. Plan your stay for the Alaska Women's Festival, Solstice Party or even the Winter Carnival in March.

Address: PO Box 82290, Fairbanks, AK 99708
Tel: (907) 389-2582. **E-mail:** picaro@mosquitonet.com

Type: Bed & breakfast.
Clientele: Mostly gay & lesbian with some straight clientele
Transportation: Free pick up from airport, train & bus can be arranged.
To Gay Bars: Fairbanks, Fri & Sat late evenings at the Palace Saloon.
Rooms: 1 single & 1 king.
Bathrooms: 1 private shower/toilet & 1 shared bath/shower/toilet.
Campsites: 2 RV parking only.
Meals: Full breakfast.
Vegetarian: Available upon request.
Complimentary: Soda, coffee, tea & juices.
Dates Open: All year.
Rates: $50-$75.
Credit Cards: MC & VISA through Triangle Tours, Anchorage.
Rsv'tns: Preferred.
To Reserve: Travel agent or call direct.
Parking: Ample free parking. Heated garage for rental cars in winter.
In-Room: Maid service upon request.
On-Premises: TV lounge, laundry facilities & solarium dining room.
Exercise/Health: Hiking, cross-country skiing & snowmobiling.
Sunbathing: On common sun decks.
Nudity: Clothing optional on deck.
Smoking: Permitted outside only. All rooms are non-smoking.
Pets: Not permitted.
Handicap Access: No.
Children: Permitted.
Languages: English, Spanish, Russian.
Your Host: Pete.

Fairbanks Hotel

Woman-Owned & -Operated ♀♂

The newly renovated *Fairbanks Hotel* is so charming and quaint, it fells like a bed and breakfast. Chat with the owners over your morning coffee and plan an enjoyable day of sightseeing, shopping, fishing, or just relaxing. This unique hotel is the oldest hotel in Fairbanks and has been restored in the Art Deco style. As a matter of fact, many guests say that they're reminded of South Beach when they see the hotel for the first time. Some rooms have a private bath, others share down the hall — but each room has a beautiful pedestal-style sink, brass headboard and antique dresser. Transportation to and from the airport is provided free of charge.

Address: 517 Third Ave, Fairbanks, AK **Tel:** (907) 456-6411, (888) 329-4685, **Fax:** (907) 456-1792. **E-mail:** fbxhotl@alaska.net

Type: Hotel.
Clientele: Mostly straight clientele with a gay/lesbian following
Transportation: Car, taxi or hotel suttle from airport or train station. Free pick up from airport or train.
To Gay Bars: 2 miles, a 3 min drive, a 20 min walk.
Rooms: 36 rooms with single, double or queen beds.

Bathrooms: Private: 10 bath/shower/toilets, 26 sinks only. Shared: 4 showers only, 7 WCs only.
Vegetarian: Walking distance to nearby restaurants & grocery store.
Complimentary: Morning coffee & tea.
Dates Open: All year.
High Season: Jun-Aug.
Rates: Summer $60-$89, winter $40-$55.

Discounts: AAA, in winter only.
Credit Cards: MC, Visa, Discover, Amex.
Rsv'tns: Highly recommended in summer season.
To Reserve: Travel agent or call direct.
Parking: Limited on-street pay parking.
In-Room: Telephone, color TV, maid service.

On-Premises: TV lounge.
Sunbathing: Not too common in AK, but we do have a private fenced-in area!
Smoking: Smoking & non-smoking rooms available.
Pets: Not permitted.
Handicap Access: No.
Children: No.
Languages: English, Spanish.
Your Host: Doris & Theresa.

Island Watch B&B

Gay-friendly ♀♂

"A Room With a View"

Situated in a quiet location, five minutes from Homer, *Island Watch B&B* provides a rural feeling within the city limits. Our spacious, cozy accommodations feature views of Kachemak Bay and the Kenai Mountain Range. We offer four units, two of which are ideal for guests who want a very private space. One of our units is made for the physically-challenged. Breakfasts are served family-style in the main house. Nearby walking trails and picnic areas are at your disposal and there are bikes for rent.

Address: PO Box 1394, Homer, AK 99603
Tel: (907) 235-2265. **E-mail:** kyle@xyz.net

Type: Bed & breakfast.
Clientele: Mostly straight clientele with a 30% gay & lesbian following
Rooms: 2 rooms, 1 suite & 1 cabin.
Bathrooms: All private.

Meals: Full breakfast with fresh eggs, fruit & grains.
Vegetarian: No meat served.
Dates Open: Year round.
High Season: June-Aug.
Rates: $80-$110 per

couple, $50 single.
Credit Cards: Discover, MC, Visa.
Rsv'tns: Held with deposit.
Parking: On premises.
Exercise/Health: Bikes for rent, hiking trails.

Smoking: Permitted outside.
Pets: No.
Handicap Access: Yes. 1 room.
Children: Welcome.
Languages: English.

Chalet in the Pines

Gay/Lesbian ♂

A Chalet in the Pines, 15 Miles from Flagstaff, Arizona

Nestled in the mountains of northern Arizona, at Pinewood Country Club in Munds Park, Arizona, is cozy *Chalet in the Pines*. The chalet is surrounded by national forest with over 200 miles of logging trails to hike, cross-country ski or just explore. The chalet has a large fireplace, vaulted ceilings, entertainment center and large redwood deck, as well as formal dining and catering available for those special occasions. Country club facilities are available, including golf, tennis, pool and dining. Whether you are by yourself or with a special friend, you'll find the atmosphere here relaxing, quiet and enjoyable.

A 2-1/2 hour drive to the Flagstaff area from Phoenix takes you through a variety of landscapes which change as the elevation gets higher. When you arrive in Flagstaff, you are definitely in the pines. The city is presided over by the rather stately presence of the San Francisco Peaks, two ancient volcanic mountains which stay snow-covered till very late each spring. Flagstaff's Snow Bowl has downhill skiing, and there are lots of crosscountry skiing trails in the area. Another two hours north lies the Grand Canyon. It's an easy day trip to the Petrified Forest, where you can see and touch giant trees that were turned to stone eons ago and see a movie depicting the wetter, warmer environs that once characterized the area. Even closer to Flagstaff is the Meteor Crater. Its huge size will amaze you even more when you tour its museum and find out how small was the meteor which created it. Another nice day trip takes you winding down the mountains along Oak Creek to Sedona. The scenery is incredible, and dining choices abound.

Address: PO Box 25640, Munds Park, AZ 86017 **Tel:** (520) 286-2417.

Type: Bed & breakfast at a country club.
Clientele: Mostly men with women welcome
Transportation: Car is best (15 mi from Flagstaff, 110 mi from Phoenix).
To Gay Bars: 15 miles to gay bars in Flagstaff.
Rooms: 4 bedrooms (1 suite, 1 studio, 2 large bedrooms).
Bathrooms: 2 private full baths, 1 shared full bath.
Meals: Expanded continental & full breakfast. Dinner available.
Complimentary: Tea, coffee, cocktails, set up service.
Dates Open: All year.
High Season: July-August.
Rates: Single $75, double $110-$125.
Discounts: Weekly 10%.
Rsv'tns: Preferred.
To Reserve: Call direct.
Parking: Ample off-street parking.
In-Room: Color cable TV, VCR, telephone, maid service.
On-Premises: Laundry facilities, video tape library, fireplace.
Exercise/Health: Jacuzzi. Nearby sauna & country club.
Swimming: Nearby country club pool.
Sunbathing: On common sun decks at chalet & poolside at country club.
Smoking: Permitted on the deck.
Pets: Permitted with owner's approval.
Handicap Access: No.
Children: No.
Languages: English.
Your Host: Mike & Steve.

UNITED STATES — FLAGSTAFF • ARIZONA

Hotel Monte Vista

Q-NET Gay-Friendly ♀♂

Experience Yesteryear

Located on what was once the well-known Route 66, the *Hotel Monte Vista* has been a social and business center for Flagstaff since its inception in 1927. Today the hotel has been restored to its original splendor with antique reproductions, ceiling fans, brass, and plush carpeting. The renovation has created a unique atmosphere designed to make your stay a pleasant one. Notables including Clark Gable, John Wayne, Walter Brennan, Jane Russell, Spencer Tracey, Carol Lombard and Gary Cooper have, in years gone by, enjoyed the ambiance and comforts of Flagstaff's finest full-service hotel.

Address: 100 North San Francisco St, Flagstaff, AZ 86001
Tel: (520) 779-6971, (800) 545-3068, **Fax:** (520) 779-2904.

Type: Hotel with restaurant, bar, English Pub, and shops.
Clientele: Mostly straight clientele with a gay & lesbian following.
Transportation: Car is best. Free pick up from train. 2 blocks from Amtrak, 1 mile from Greyhound & 3 miles from airport.
To Gay Bars: 2 blocks.

Rooms: 50 rooms with single, double, queen, king or bunk beds.
Bathrooms: All private.
Vegetarian: Available in the hotel coffeeshop.
Dates Open: All year.
High Season: May-October.
Rates: $25-$90.
Credit Cards: MC, Visa, Amex, Discover.

Rsv'tns: Required, if possible. Walk-ins are welcome.
To Reserve: Travel agent or call direct.
Parking: Adequate free off-street & on-street parking. We have our own lot.
In-Room: Color cable TV, telephone, ceiling fans & maid service.
On-Premises: Fax, copier & laundry facilities.

Swimming: 15 miles to Oak Creek Canyon.
Sunbathing: On the roof.
Smoking: Permitted inside some of the rooms.
Pets: No wolf hybrids, otherwise OK.
Handicap Access: No.
Children: Welcome.
Languages: English, Spanish.
Your Host: Jimmy.

PHOENIX

Arizona Royal Villa

Men ♂

Enjoy Palm Springs-style accommodations in downtown Phoenix. Accommodations are available for long or short stays, ranging from one day to several months. The walled complex is totally private, with keyed entry. Rooms range from small hotel rooms to furnished one-bedroom apartments. The pool and Jacuzzi are open year-round. *The Arizona Royal Villa* is popular, because of the amenities, competitive rates and strategic location to all the bars. Book early to avoid disappointment! Day passes available for $10.

Address: 1110 E Turney Ave, Phoenix, AZ 85014
Tel: (602) 266-6883 (Tel/Fax), toll free: (888) 266-6884.
E-mail: azroyalvil@aol.com **URL:** http://www.swlink.net/~goodtime

Type: Bed & breakfast motel.
Clientele: Men only
Transportation: Car is best. $10 for pick up from airport.
To Gay Bars: Walking distance to 1 local gay bar & restaurant, others 1 mile away.
Rooms: 3 rooms, 3 suites & 3 apartments with queen beds.

Bathrooms: All private.
Meals: Continental breakfast.
Dates Open: All year.
High Season: October-May.
Rates: High season (Oct-May) from $59.95. Low season (Jun-Sep) from $45.95.
Credit Cards: MC, Visa, Amex.
Rsv'tns: Recommended.

To Reserve: Travel agent or call direct.
Minimum Stay: Two nights on holiday weekends.
Parking: Adequate free parking.
In-Room: Color cable TV, AC, coffee & tea-making facilities, kitchen, refrigerator.
On-Premises: Laundry facilities.
Exercise/Health: Jacuzzi, weights.

Swimming: Heated pool on premises (in season only).
Sunbathing: At poolside.
Nudity: Permitted.
Smoking: Permitted.
Pets: Not permitted.
Handicap Access: No.
Children: Not permitted.
Languages: English, some French, Italian, Spanish.

Arizona Sunburst Inn

Men ♂

"A Man's Resort" in the Heart of Phoenix

The *Arizona Sunburst Inn* provides a unique setting that is totally private, yet right in the heart of Phoenix. A tropical-like garden is complete with a large heated pool, hot tub, shaded patios and a mist system. Our all-male, clothing-optional resort is highly recommended by over 5000 past guests. We offer spacious rooms with queen-sized beds, cable TV and maid service. We're only blocks away from gay bars and great restaurants.

Address: 6245 N 12th Place, Phoenix, AZ 85014
Tel: (602) 274-1474, (800) 974-1474.

Type: Bed & breakfast resort.
Clientele: Men only.
To Gay Bars: 6 blocks.
Rooms: Seven rooms with queen beds.
Bathrooms: Private & shared.
Meals: Expanded continental breakfast.

Dates Open: All year.
High Season: Oct to May.
Rates: $69 and up.
Credit Cards: MC, Visa, Amex.
Rsv'tns: Required.
To Reserve: Call direct.
Parking: Ample off-street & on-street parking.
In-Room: Color cable TV,

AC, coffee/tea-making facilities & maid service.
On-Premises: Kitchen.
Exercise/Health: Hot tub & massage on premises. Nearby gym, weights, sauna & steam.
Swimming: Pool on premises.
Sunbathing: On the patio

area around the pool.
Nudity: Clothing optional.
Smoking: Permitted on patio. No smoking in rooms.
Pets: Not permitted.
Handicap Access: No.
Children: No.
Languages: English.
Your Host: Bill & Wayne.

Casa De Mis Padres

Q-NET Gay-Owned & -Operated ♀♂

Your Oasis in the Desert

SEE SPECIAL PAGE 12 COLOR SECTION

Guests who seek an intimate Southwest atmosphere in the spirit and style of Arizona need look no further — *Casa De Mis Padres* is your oasis in the desert. This private and exclusive retreat was originally built in 1950, expanded in 1980, and restored in 1995. The 8000-square-foot Santa Barbara-style home is surrounded by mature palm trees, fragrant citrus, and lawn areas for year-round outdoor recreation such as croquet or badminton. Mexican paved patios and fireplaces embrace the pool, which is heated in winter. During the lazy summer months, relax poolside under a blanket of refreshingly cool mist as you take in the warm southern sun. You may enjoy an expanded continental breakfast and cocktail hour each day in the main residence or, weather permitting, poolside, served by your warm and responsive hosts.

Impeccable decor and fine art are only part of your experience. Great care and attention to detail have been given to our two unique resort-style accommodations. The *Pool Casita* has two king suites and is set up for

continued next page

INN PLACES® 1998

longer stays for couples traveling together. There is also a full kitchen with separate dining and living rooms open to the pool patio, bar-be-cue and outside wet bar. The three-room *Library Suite* features a home theatre system and an extensive collection of books and magazines. We are minutes away from golf, tennis, shopping and fine dining of Old Town Scottsdale. Arrive as a guest and leave as a friend who is already looking forward to coming home again.

Address: 5965 E Orange Blossom Lane, Phoenix, AZ 85018
Tel: (602) 675-0247, **Fax:** (602) 675-9476.
E-mail: casadmp@aol.com

Type: Bed & breakfast in a private home.
Clientele: Mostly men with women welcome, straight-friendly
Transportation: Car or a short taxi drive.
To Gay Bars: 2 miles, a 5 min drive.
Rooms: 2 suites, 1 cottage with king beds.
Bathrooms: All private: 1 bath/shower/toilet, 2 shower/toliets.
Meals: Expanded continental breakfast.

Vegetarian: Always available, no meat served.
Complimentary: Welcome champagne tray with snacks, evening cocktail hour, in-room tea & coffees.
Dates Open: All year.
High Season: Late Oct-May.
Rates: $150-$250.
Discounts: 5 nights or more 10% off.
Credit Cards: MC, Visa, Amex, Discover.
Rsv'tns: Required.

To Reserve: Travel agent or call direct.
Minimum Stay: 2 nights. 3 nights on holiday weekends.
Parking: Ample free off-street parking.
In-Room: Telephone, AC, ceiling fans, color cable TV, VCR, coffee & tea-making facilities, maid service. Cottage has kitchen. Library suite has refrigerator.
On-Premises: Video tape library.

Swimming: Pool on premises, heated in winter.
Sunbathing: Poolside & on patio.
Smoking: Permitted outside. All non-smoking rooms.
Pets: Not permitted.
Handicap Access: No.
Children: No, not set up for children.
Languages: English.
Your Host: Brian.

Larry's B & B

Gay/Lesbian ♂

A Gay Place to Stay

At *Larry's B & B*, our large private home offers three guest rooms, with shared bath or private bath, living and family rooms, all at economical rates. Guests enjoy the beauty of Phoenix's weather in the privacy of our pool area, surrounded by walls and tropical vegetation. We are near both golf and tennis facilities. Full breakfast is included, lunch and dinner are available by arrangement. Pickup at Sky Harbor Airport is $10.00.

Address: 502 W Claremont Ave, Phoenix, AZ 85013-2974
Tel: (602) 249-2974.

Type: A true bed & breakfast in our home.
Clientele: Mostly gay men with women welcome. Some straight clientele such as relatives or friends
Transportation: Pick up from bus, airport or train for $10.
To Gay Bars: 5 minutes to gay/lesbian bars.
Rooms: 3 rooms with queen or king beds.
Bathrooms: 1 private bath/ toilet, 1 shared full bath.
Meals: Full breakfast, lunch & dinner by arrangement.
Vegetarian: Upon request.
Complimentary: Tea, coffee & soft drinks. Wine or hard drinks with meals.
Dates Open: All year.
High Season: January through April.
Rates: Singles $50-$55 daily, $300-$335 weekly. Doubles $60-$70 daily, $375-$410 weekly.
Discounts: $5 off 2nd to 6th day per room on daily rate.
Rsv'tns: Preferred.
To Reserve: Call direct.
Parking: Ample free off-street parking.
In-Room: Telephone, color TV & ceiling fans, AC.
On-Premises: Central AC/ heat, TV lounge, laundry facilities & use of refrigerators.
Exercise/Health: Jacuzzi.
Swimming: Pool, not heated in winter.
Sunbathing: At poolside, on patio & common sun decks.
Nudity: Permitted in backyard, please inquire.
Smoking: Permitted on outside patio only.
Pets: Permitted.
Handicap Access: Yes.
Children: Permitted.
Languages: English, limited Japanese, Spanish.
Your Host: Larry & Jim.

The Mary Claire II

Gay/Lesbian ♀♂

Our lovely 1,800-square-foot, Southwest-style townhome offers one private guest bedroom, a private guest bath, and two great hostess/cooks. The bed and breakfast is located ten minutes from the airport, making it a convenient place to stay for tourists or business travelers. Numerous golf courses are nearby, the Phoenix downtown is 15 minutes away, and we're just one mile from downtown Tempe. If you're visiting Phoenix for the Fiesta Bowl, the Phoenix Open, the Ping/ Standard Register LPGA, or for an escape from winter, *The Mary Claire II* is the perfect place to stay!

Address: 303 E Patrician Dr, Tempe, AZ 85282
Tel: (602) 967-2767.

Type: Bed & breakfast.
Clientele: Gay & lesbian. Good mix of men & women
Transportation: Car. Free pick up from airport.
Rooms: 1 rooms with double bed.
Bathrooms: 1 private bath/ shower/toilet.
Meals: Full breakfast.
Vegetarian: Available upon request. Several vegetarian restaurants within 1-2 miles.
Dates Open: All year.
High Season: Winter.
Rates: $50-$65.
Rsv'tns: Required.
To Reserve: Call direct.
Parking: Adequate covered parking.
In-Room: Telephone, AC, ceiling fans, color cable TV, VCR, kitchen, refrigerator.
On-Premises: Laundry facilities.
Exercise/Health: Jacuzzi. Nearby gym, weights, Jacuzzi, sauna, steam, massage.
Swimming: Pool on premises & nearby.
Sunbathing: Poolside & on patio.
Nudity: Permitted on patio.
Smoking: Permitted on patio only.
Pets: Permitted (only dogs allowed are working dogs), very sociable cats in residence.
Handicap Access: No.
Children: No.
Languages: English.
Your Host: Lisa & Marianna.

Southwest Inn at Eagle Mountain

Q-NET Gay-Friendly ♀♂

Relax in Complete Privacy, While Enjoying Total Luxury

The *Southwest Inn at Eagle Mountain*, a combination of small luxury hotel and large bed and breakfast, borders the 18th fairway of the Eagle Mountain Golf Course. Our custom-designed guestrooms feature Southwest decor, high ceilings and bold Southwest prints and graphics. Three deluxe room types are available, each designed and decorated to get a "WOW" from our guests when they enter their room. King rooms feature roomy California King-sized beds, a sleeper-sofa and a comfortable sitting area. The sitting areas in our Dual-Queen rooms are in their own special alcove, near kiva-style fireplaces, and our large suites have both a living room with queen-sized sleeper-sofa, and a separate bedroom with a king-sized bed. Bathrooms have solid-granite vanity tops with two sinks, and the suites' bathrooms boast a romantic six-foot whirlpool tub with a private window and a 50-mile view.

In addition, rooms offer a large work area with excellent task lighting, a modem jack on a separate phone line, and a convenient electrical outlet for your laptop. Your room can also have its own outside 7-digit phone number so you can have a fax line or answering machine, in addition to your normal room phone. You can even retrieve your room's voice mail messages from outside the resort with any touch-tone phone. Of course, if you prefer, our hotel voice mail system will handle your calls for you.

Deluxe continental breakfasts are served in the lodge building's breakfast room which overlooks the 18th green. A typical breakfast consists of fresh-baked bagels with a variety of cream cheeses, muffins, fruits, juices, coffee and tea, as well as other appetizing surprises. Make the *Southwest Inn at Eagle Mountain* your weekend getaway from the hustle and bustle of the Phoenix metropolitan area. We're only 15 minutes from the heart of Scottsdale. **TO OPEN FEBRUARY, 1998:** We're now accepting reservations for arrivals after Feb.1, 1998. Please call our Sedona hotel at (800) 992-8083.

Address: 9800 N. Summer Hill Blvd, Fountain Hills, AZ 85268
Tel: (602) 816-3000, (800) 992-8083, **Fax:** (602) 816-3090.
E-mail: eminfo@swinn.com

Type: Bed & breakfast hotel resort with gift shop.
Clientele: Mostly straight clientele with a gay/lesbian following
Transportation: Car is best.
To Gay Bars: 30-45 min drive to Scottsdale & Phoenix gay bars.
Rooms: 31 rooms, 11 suites with dual queen or king beds.
Bathrooms: 42 private bath/shower/toilets.
Meals: Expanded continental breakfast.
Vegetarian: Breakfast is vegetarian.
Complimentary: Tea & coffee.
Dates Open: All year.
High Season: Jan-May.
Rates: Please inquire.
Discounts: We open Feb 1 '98, ask about opening special rates.
Credit Cards: MC, Visa, Discover, Amex.
Rsv'tns: Required.
To Reserve: Travel agent or call direct.
Minimum Stay: 2 nights on holiday weekends.
Parking: Ample free off-street parking near rooms.

In-Room: Telephone, AC, ceiling fans, color cable TV, VCR, refrigerator, coffee & tea-making facilities, maid service.
On-Premises: Meeting rooms.

Exercise/Health: Gym, weights, Jacuzzi, 18-hole golf course. Nearby steam, massage.
Swimming: Pool on premises. Lake nearby.

Sunbathing: Poolside & on private sun decks.
Smoking: All non-smoking. Designated outside smoking areas.
Pets: Not permitted.
Handicap Access: Yes,

ramps, rails in bathroom, wide doors, TTY.
Children: All ages welcome when accompanied by parents.
Languages: English.
Your Host: Joel & Sheila.

Stewart's B&B
Men ♂

A Leather-Friendly B&B

Located in North Central Phoenix, *Stewart's B&B* offers a taste of the Southwest with a masculine touch. Nudity is encouraged — so get butt-naked, enjoy, play and sunbathe on the secluded, very private patio with its moss-covered fountain, beehive fireplace and hot tub/spa. Sling available. Hike in the nearby Phoenix Mountain Preserve, bike the canals, sightsee the Valley of the Sun and sample the menus at the nearby world-renowned resorts. The owner is a member of Trust, APEX, Water Boys and R.H.S.D.

Address: 1319 E. Hayward, Phoenix, AZ 85020
Tel: (602) 861-2500, **Fax:** (602) 861-0242. **E-mail:** stewphx@aol.com

Type: Bed & breakfast.
Clientele: Men only. Especially leather-friendly
Transportation: $10 pick up from airport by arrangement.
To Gay Bars: 6 miles, a 5-minute drive.
Rooms: 3 rooms with double or queen beds.
Bathrooms: Shared bath/shower/toilet.
Meals: Expanded continental breakfast.

Vegetarian: Available on special request, if possible to accommodate.
Complimentary: Coffee, tea, pop.
Dates Open: All year.
Rates: Double $55, Queen $75, $10 extra per person per night.
Discounts: 20% discount after 4th night.
Credit Cards: MC, Visa.
Rsv'tns: Required.

To Reserve: Call direct.
Parking: Ample free off-street parking. Trailer parking possible.
In-Room: AC/air cooler, telephone.
On-Premises: TV lounge, video tape library, laundry facilities, fax, e-mail, computer, copy machine.
Exercise/Health: Weights/ workout machine, spa/hot tub.

Sunbathing: On patio.
Nudity: Permitted throughout house & on patio.
Smoking: Permitted outside only. House non-smoking.
Pets: Permitted if small, well-trained & friendly.
Handicap Access: No.
Children: No.
Languages: English, some German & Spanish.
Your Host: Stewart.

Windsor Cottage
Gay/Lesbian ♂

Where Everyone Is Treated Like Royalty

Feel like a king or queen when you stay at *Windsor Cottage*, two English Tudor-style cottages with full baths, living areas, sleeping areas and fresh flowers. French doors open to the pool surrounded by beautiful gardens where breakfast is served. Located in the heart of Phoenix, *Windsor Cottage* is central to the very best that Phoenix has to offer. Only minutes away from museums, theaters, symphonies, sports,

continued next page

restaurants, shops, parks, and the bars, it is nestled in the Willow Historic District of Central Phoenix. Bikes are available for explorers.

Address: 62 West Windsor, Phoenix, AZ 85003 Tel: (602) 264-6309.

Type: Bed & breakfast guesthouse cottages.
Clientele: Mostly men with women welcome
Transportation: Car, airport Super Shuttle ($7), pick up from airport or train by arrangement, $10.
To Gay Bars: 2 miles.
Rooms: 2 cottages with queen beds.
Bathrooms: Private shower/toilet.
Meals: Expanded continental breakfast.
Vegetarian: Please inquire.
Complimentary: Soda, bottled water.
Dates Open: All year.
High Season: Oct-May.
Rates: $55-$125.
Credit Cards: MC, Visa, Amex.
Rsv'tns: Required.
To Reserve: Travel agent or call direct.
Minimum Stay: Required.
Parking: Ample free off-street parking.
In-Room: Color cable TV, phone, ceiling fans, AC, coffee/tea-making facilities, refrigerator, microwave, laundry service.
On-Premises: Laundry facilities.
Exercise/Health: Massage, bikes on premises.
Swimming: Pool on premises.
Sunbathing: At poolside.
Nudity: Permitted at poolside.
Smoking: Permitted outdoors & at poolside only.
Pets: Not permitted.
Handicap Access: Yes.
Children: No.
Languages: English.
Your Host: Greg.

Apple Orchard Inn of Sedona

Gay-Friendly ♀♂

Sedona's Best-Kept Secret

Experience the *Apple Orchard Inn's* natural beauty on nearly two acres of wooded splendor, overlooking Wilson Mountain and Steamboat Rock. In the heart of Sedona, on the site of the historic Jordan Apple Farm, our totally renovated inn is a short walk to world-renowned galleries, fine dining and shopping in "uptown" Sedona. Our custom-designed rooms flavored with the Old West, offer modern luxuries such as Jacuzzi tubs and private patios. Romance is always in the air in Sedona, and ours is the prefect setting for a special occasion.

Address: 656 Jordan Road, Sedona, AZ 86336
Tel: (520) 282-5328, (800) 663-6968, Fax: (520) 204-0044.
E-mail: appleorc@sedona.net URL: www.appleorchardbb.com

Type: Bed & breakfast inn.
Clientele: Mostly straight clientele with a gay/lesbian following
Transportation: Car is best from Phoenix Int'l Airport or Flagstaff. Free pick up from Sedona airport.
Rooms: 7 rooms with king or queen beds.
Bathrooms: Private bath/shower/toilets or bath/toilets. 6 baths have Jacuzzi.
Meals: Full breakfast.
Vegetarian: We do special meals for vegetarians. 1 mile to vegetarian & health food stores.
Complimentary: Mini-fridges in-room with soft drinks, water & juice. Turn-down service has chocolate coyotes & saguaro cactus on pillows. Coffee served all day, cookies at night.
Dates Open: All year.
High Season: Apr-Jun & Aug-Oct.
Rates: $135-$195.
Discounts: 10% AAA, 20% off in summer & winter.
Credit Cards: MC, Visa, Amex.
To Reserve: Call direct.
Parking: Ample free parking.
In-Room: Telephone, AC, ceiling fans, color cable TV, VCR, refrigerator, maid service. 2 suites have fireplaces.
On-Premises: Video tape library, laundry facilities.
Exercise/Health: Jacuzzi, massage. Nearby gym, weights, sauna, steam, massage.
Swimming: River nearby.
Sunbathing: On patio, at river.
Smoking: Non-smoking facility.
Pets: Not permitted. Pet hotel nearby.
Handicap Access: Yes, ramps, rails in bathroom, wide doors.
Children: We're an adult getaway. Children over 10 years old welcome.
Languages: English, some German.
Your Host: Bob & Paula.

Cozy Cactus

Q-NET Gay-Friendly ♀♂

Magical Red Rock Vistas & a Healthy Dose of Old-Fashioned Hospitality

Overlooking the valley between Sedona's red rock cliffs and one of John Wayne's favorite movie locations, Wild Horse Mesa, we invite you to share the sunsets from our patio, as they play across the nearby red cliffs. *Cozy Cactus* is a ranch-style home, comfortably furnished with family heirlooms and theatrical memorabilia from our professional careers. Each guest room has large windows and private bath. Each pair of bedrooms share a sitting room with fireplace and small kitchen, perfect for two couples traveling together.

Address: 80 Canyon Circle Dr, Sedona, AZ 86351
Tel: (520) 284-0082, (800) 788-2082, **Fax:** (520) 284-4210.

Type: Studio & 1-BR cabins & some rooms
Clientele: Mostly straight clientele with a gay & lesbian following
Transportation: Car is best.
To Gay Bars: 120 miles to Phoenix.
Rooms: 5 rooms with single, queen or king beds.
Bathrooms: All private bath/toilets.

Meals: Full breakfast.
Vegetarian: Available.
Complimentary: Refreshments available in the afternoon.
Dates Open: All year.
High Season: Mar-May & Sept-Nov.
Rates: $95-$115 for 2 people.
Discounts: Special weekly rates. AAA & Senior discount 10%.

Credit Cards: MC, Visa, Amex, Discover.
Rsv'tns: Recommended.
To Reserve: Travel agent or call direct.
Parking: Ample free off-street parking.
In-Room: AC, refrigerator, & maid service. Fireplace in sitting area.
On-Premises: TV lounge & laundry facilities.
Exercise/Health: 3 major golf courses in town.
Swimming: 10 minutes to community pool. 15 minutes to swimming hole at Slide Rock.
Sunbathing: On the patio.
Smoking: Permitted on patios only.
Pets: Not permitted.
Handicap Access: Yes.
Children: Welcome.
Languages: English, Italian & ASL.

The Huff 'n Puff Straw Bale Inn   Gay/Lesbian ♀♂'

Do the following things tickle your fancy? Canoeing the Verde River while being followed by great blue heron... Wading in Wet Beaver Creek and then sunbathing on huge red boulders... Spotting roadrunners and quail on your return to the inn... Scouting Indian ruins and seeing petroglyphs (tours to Indian ruins can be arranged)... If so, then make your reservation now at *The Huff 'n Puff Straw Bale Inn,* just 19 miles from Sedona. Your woman host also encourages male guests. Please note that this is a non-toxic home.

Address: 4320 E Beaver Creek Rd, Rimrock, AZ 86335 **Tel:** (520) 567-9066.

Type: Inn.
Clientele: Mostly gay & lesbian with some straight clientele
Transportation: Car is best or airport shuttle ($10) to Camp Verde. Pickup from Camp Verde.
Rooms: 2 rooms with queen beds.
Bathrooms: All private.

Meals: Continental breakfast.
Vegetarian: Available (cooked) for lunch & dinner, $10 per person per meal.
Complimentary: Tea & coffee.
Dates Open: All year.
Rates: $60-$70.
Discounts: Up to 1/2 fee is work exchangeable.

To Reserve: Travel agent or call direct.
Minimum Stay: Not required, but $5 extra for stays of only 1 night.
Parking: Ample free off-street parking.
In-Room: AC, color satellite TV.
Exercise/Health: Massage.
Swimming: In nearby creek.
Sunbathing: In yard.
Smoking: Smoking permitted outdoors.
Pets: Permitted, must be on leash.
Handicap Access: Yes. Wheelchair ramp, handicap shower, non-toxic home.
Children: Welcome.
Languages: English.
Your Host: Susan.

Paradise by the Creek B&B   Women ♀
Serenity Awaits You at Our Red Rock Hideaway

Nestled in a green valley amidst red rock canyons, our cozy ranch home sits on a quiet lane surrounded by willows and cottonwoods. You can swim in the creek or laze on its banks and watch the sun set orange on spectacular Cathedral Rock. *Paradise by the Creek's* two guest rooms with shared bath are perfect for two couples travelling together, but if it's just a getaway for the two of you, then the whole suite is yours. Wait till you see the stars in the Sedona sky!

continued next page

Address: 215 Disney Lane, Sedona, AZ
Tel: (520) 282-7107, **Fax:** (520) 282-3586. **E-mail:** canyonct@sedona.net

Type: Bed & breakfast.
Clientele: Mostly women with men welcome
Transportation: Car is best. We're 2 hours north of Phoenix.
To Gay Bars: 120 miles. None in Sedona.
Rooms: 2 rooms with double or queen beds.
Bathrooms: 1 private bath/toilet/shower, 1 shared bath/shower/toilet.
Campsites: RV parking only, electric hook up only.
Meals: Continental breakfast.
Vegetarian: Vegetarian restaurants in Sedona township, 3 miles away.
Complimentary: Fresh fruit, juices, pastries, cereals, milk, tea, coffee, beer & wine.
Dates Open: All year.
Rates: $75-$120.
Rsv'tns: Required.
To Reserve: Call direct.
Parking: Ample free off-street parking.
In-Room: Cooler, telephone, TV, ceiling fans, refrigerator, coffee & tea-making facilities.
Exercise/Health: Nearby massage, floats, healings, psychic readings.
Swimming: Creek nearby.
Sunbathing: In private garden.
Smoking: Permitted outside, rooms are non-smoking.
Pets: Not permitted.
Handicap Access: Able to accommodate special needs on individual basis.
Children: Welcome. There are pets, farm animals, creek & trees for them to explore.
Languages: English.
Your Host: Cheryl & Debbie.

Paradise Ranch   Women ♀

If you are looking for a quiet place to relax from your daily routine or are interested in bringing someone special to a beautiful retreat, *Paradise Ranch* offers a guesthouse for women who want to experience the beauty of Sedona in a safe environment. Fill your lungs with our perfect clean air and bubble your cares away in the privacy of our hot tub, surrounded by beautiful trees and clear blue sky. Get in touch with your soul in our sweat lodge. Let yourself be pampered at *Paradise Ranch*, the area that the Yavapi Indians called the home of the Great Mother.

Address: 135 Kachina Dr, Sedona, AZ 86336 **Tel:** (520) 282-9769.

Type: Guesthouse.
Clientele: Women only
Transportation: Car is best.
Rooms: 1 cottage with double bed.
Bathrooms: 1 private.
Complimentary: Tea & coffee.
Dates Open: All year.
Rates: $85 to $125 per night.
Rsv'tns: Required.
To Reserve: Call direct.
Parking: Ample free parking.
In-Room: Color TV, evap cooler, kitchen, refrigerator, laundry service.
On-Premises: Meeting rooms.
Exercise/Health: Jacuzzi, massage, sweat lodge, life readings, life force transfusions, crystal healings.
Swimming: Creek.
Nudity: Permitted in Jacuzzi & while sunbathing.
Smoking: Not permitted.
Pets: Not permitted.
Handicap Access: No.
Children: Not permitted.
Languages: English, some German, some Spanish.

Sappho's Oasis   Women ♀

An Oasis in the High Desert

Sappho's Choice offers travelers a great hot tub, a strong cup of coffee and a comfortable bed. This charming guesthouse oasis with its spectacular views of Cathedral Rock, is a private, special and affordable place. Just outside our front door are opportunities for magical hikes leading to the National Forest Service, as well as scenic walks to the creek. Sedona's many shops and fine dining are also close by. We welcome lesbians and gay men and look forward to seeing you soon!

Address: PO Box 1863, Sedona, AZ 86339
Tel: (520) 282-5679. **E-mail:** Oasis42773@aol.com

Type: Bed & breakfast.
Clientele: Mostly women with men welcome
Transportation: Car is best, free pickup from shuttle.
Rooms: 1 suite, 1 cottage with double bed.
Bathrooms: Private: 1 shower/toilet, 1 bath/shower/toilet.
Meals: Continental breakfast.
Vegetarian: On request.
Dates Open: All year.
High Season: Mar-Nov.
Rates: $65-$75 per night.
Discounts: Sliding scale & work exchange available.
Rsv'tns: Required.
To Reserve: Call direct.
Parking: Ample off-street parking.

In-Room: AC, ceiling fans, telephone.	private & common sun decks.	non-smoking. Smoking permitted outside in designated areas.	**Children:** No. **Languages:** English, some French.
Exercise/Health: Jacuzzi.	**Nudity:** Permitted on sun decks.	**Pets:** Not permitted.	**IGLTA**
Swimming: Nearby river.	**Smoking:** All rooms are	**Handicap Access:** No.	
Sunbathing: On patio & on			

Southwest Inn at Sedona

Q-NET Gay-Friendly ♀♂

Sedona's "Inn Place" to Stay

The magic of the incredible Red Rocks, the ancient Anasazi and Sinagua Indian ruins with their pictograph and petroglyph sites, and the famous "Vortexes" make Sedona the new adventure capital of Arizona... and the perfect place to spend a fabulous honeymoon. Sedona's 4,500-foot elevation produces an almost perfect climate year-round — the air is clean and the lifestyle is wonderful.

Recipient of the AAA Four Diamond award, *Southwest Inn at Sedona*, with its beautiful, large rooms and fantastic customer service, is a unique combination of small luxury hotel and top-quality bed & breakfast. Guestrooms feature king- and dual-queen beds, 25" televisions, refrigerators, coffee makers, telephones (with free local calls, as well as 800# calls) and wonderful Southwest decor. Each room has a fireplace and its own patio or deck facing Sedona's magnificent red rock views. Two-room suites are also available. A deluxe continental breakfast with fresh-baked bagels, muffins, fruit, cereal, juices, etc. is included in the room rate.

Southwest Inn is "THE" place to stay in Sedona. Our property is three years old, entirely non-smoking, and offers a pool and spa which are perfect spots from which to enjoy the area's ambiance. We are located near all of the area's varied activities which include horseback riding, hiking, jeep rentals and tours, ballooning, restaurants, theaters and galleries. A concierge service, located in our luxurious lobby, is at your disposal to help you plan your activities and make dinner and tour reservations. Special rates on weeknight stays are offered for Internet browsers. Call us for reservations or for information on our honeymoon/anniversary packages and our Verde Canyon Railroad combo packages.

Address: 3250 W., Highway 89A, Sedona, AZ 86336
Tel: (520) 282-3344, (800) 483-7422, **Fax:** (520) 282-0267.
E-mail: jg@sedona.net **URL:** http://www.swinn.com

continued next page

UNITED STATES • TUCSON • ARIZONA

Type: Bed & breakfast inn & motel.
Clientele: Mostly straight clientele with a gay/lesbian following
Transportation: Car is best.
Rooms: 24 rooms, 4 suites with king & dual queen beds.
Bathrooms: All private.
Meals: Expanded continental breakfast.
Vegetarian: At Sage vegetarian restaurant, other local restaurants have some veg. dishes.
Complimentary: Iced tea in lobby, coffee makers in rooms.
Dates Open: All year.
High Season: Mar-May, Oct & holiday periods.
Rates: High season: $135-$165, suites $195. Low season: $99-$135, suites $125-$175.
Discounts: Internet specials $99, see website.
Credit Cards: MC, Visa, Amex, Discover.
Rsv'tns: Not required, but we often sell out.
To Reserve: Travel agent or call direct.
Minimum Stay: 2 nights on in-season weekends (Fri-Sat or Sat-Sun).
Parking: Ample free off-street parking.
In-Room: Telephone, AC, ceiling fans, color cable TV, VCR, refrigerator coffee & tea-making facilities, maid service.
On-Premises: Breakfast room.
Exercise/Health: Jacuzzi. Nearby gym, weights, sauna, steam, massage.
Swimming: Pool on premises.
Sunbathing: Poolside.
Smoking: No smoking in rooms, on decks, patios or in pool areas.
Pets: Not permitted.
Handicap Access: Yes. Ramps, rails in bathroom, wide doors.
Children: Welcome. Free up to 12 yrs old.
Languages: English.
Your Host: Joel, Sheila, Conna & Kirsten.

Adobe Rose Inn Bed & Breakfast   Gay-Friendly ♀♂'

"What is More Agreeable Than One's Home?" — Cicero

Casual comfort best describes the atmoshpere of *The Adobe Rose Inn*, a beautifully restored 1933 adobe home located in the historic Sam Hughes neighborhood, just two blocks from the university. There are three charming lodgepole-furnished rooms in the main house, two of which have cozy, beehive fireplaces and stained-glass windows. There are also two private cottages that are ideally suited for longer stays. All rooms have cable television and private baths, as well as access to the very private bougainvillea-draped swimming pool and hot tub. The property is gated and surrounded by six-foot adobe walls, providing privacy and enhancing the quiet of this prestigious neighborhood.

Address: 940 N Olsen Ave, Tucson, AZ 85719
Tel: (520) 318-4644, (800) 328-4122, **Fax:** (520) 325-0055.
E-mail: aroseinn@aol.com

Type: Bed & breakfast.
Clientele: Mostly straight clientele with a gay/lesbian following
Transportation: Rental car, taxi or shuttle.
To Gay Bars: 2 miles, a 5-minute drive.
Rooms: 3 rooms, 2 cottages with single, queen or king beds.
Bathrooms: 5 private.
Meals: Full breakfast.
Vegetarian: Always available (meat always served on the side), special diet meals with advance notice.
Complimentary: Cookies, lemonade.
Dates Open: All year.
High Season: Mid Dec-May.
Rates: Summer $45-$60, Sept-Dec $75-$90, Jan-May $95-$125.
Discounts: Senior (65+) discounts.
Credit Cards: MC, Visa, Eurocard, Discover.
Rsv'tns: Reservations suggested, walk-ins welcome.
To Reserve: Travel agent or call direct.
Minimum Stay: Required at certain times of the year.
Parking: Ample on- & off-street parking.
In-Room: Maid service, kitchen, refrigerator, ceiling fans, phone, AC, color cable TV, VCR, coffee/tea-making facilities.
Exercise/Health: Hot tub on premises. Nearby gym, weights, Jacuzzi, sauna, steam, massage.
Swimming: Pool on premises.
Sunbathing: Poolside, on common sundecks, on patio.
Smoking: Permitted outside only, all rooms are non-smoking.
Pets: Not permitted.
Handicap Access: No.
Children: No.
Languages: English.

228   FERRARI GUIDES™

Casa Alegre Bed & Breakfast Inn

Q-NET Gay-Friendly ♀♂

Warmth & Happiness of a Bygone Era

Our charming, 1915 craftsman-style bungalow is just minutes from the University of Arizona and downtown Tucson. At *Casa Alegre,* each guest room has private bath and TV, and its decor reflects an aspect of Tucson's history, such as the mining industry or the Indian Nation. The Arizona sitting room opens onto the inn's serene patio and pool area. A scrumptious full breakfast is served in the sun room, formal dining room or outside on the patio. Shopping, dining and entertainment are all within walking distance.

Address: 316 East Speedway Blvd, Tucson, AZ 85705
Tel: (520) 628-1800, (800) 628-5654, **Fax:** (520) 792-1880.

Type: Bed & breakfast.
Clientele: Mostly straight with a gay & lesbian following.
Transportation: Car is best. Shuttle service from airport $15 maximum.
To Gay Bars: 3 blocks.
Rooms: 5 rooms with queen or king beds.
Bathrooms: All private bath/toilets.
Meals: Full breakfast.
Vegetarian: Available upon request.
Complimentary: Cool soft drinks & snacks by pool in summer, tea & goodies in front of fireplace in winter.
Dates Open: All year.
High Season: September 1 through May 31.
Rates: Summer $60-$75, rest of year $80-$105.
Discounts: 10% senior, corporate, week or longer stays.
Credit Cards: MC, Visa, Discover.
Rsv'tns: Preferred.
To Reserve: Travel agent or call direct.
Parking: Ample free on-street & off-street covered parking.
In-Room: AC, ceiling fans, maid service.
On-Premises: Meeting rooms, guests' refrigerator on covered patio.
Exercise/Health: Spa on premises. Nearby gym, weights, sauna, steam & massage.
Swimming: Pool on premises.
Sunbathing: At poolside or on patio.
Smoking: Permitted outside only.
Pets: No facilities available for pets.
Handicap Access: No.
Children: Permitted under close supervision of parents because of antiques & pool.
Languages: English.

Casa Tierra Adobe Bed & Breakfast Inn

Gay-Friendly ♀♂

The Quintessential Desert Experience

Casa Tierra is located on five acres of beautiful Sonoran desert, fifteen miles west of Tucson and minutes from The Desert Museum and Saguaro National Park. This area is famous for its unique Saguaro cacti, spectacular mountain views and brilliant sunsets. Our rustic adobe home with vaulted brick ceilings, interior arched courtyard and Mexican furnishings, recalls haciendas found in old Mexico. Each guest room has a private bath, queen-sized bed, microwave oven, small refrigerator, private entrance and a patio overlooking the desert landscape. After a day of sightseeing, hiking or birding, enjoy the Jacuzzi or just relax with us in the quiet of the desert.

Address: 11155 West Calle Pima, Tucson, AZ 85743
Tel: (520) 578-3058 (Tel/Fax).

Type: Bed & breakfast inn.
Clientele: Mostly straight with a gay & lesbian following.
Transportation: Car is necessary.
To Gay Bars: 15 miles or 25 minutes.
Rooms: 3 rooms with queen beds.
Bathrooms: 2 private bath/shower/toilets & 1 private shower/toilet.
Meals: Full breakfast.
Vegetarian: Always.
Complimentary: Tea & coffee self-serve bar, fruit in room.
Dates Open: Sept 1-May 31.
High Season: Feb, Mar, Apr & holidays.
Rates: $85-$95. $10 extra for single night stay, $10 for a third person. Weekly house rental available.
Discounts: 10% for 7 or more days.
Rsv'tns: Suggested.
To Reserve: Call direct.
Minimum Stay: Two nights or $10 extra.
Parking: Ample free off-street parking.
In-Room: Telephone, ceiling fans, evaporative coolers, microwave & refrigerator.
Exercise/Health: Jacuzzi.
Massage by appointment.
Sunbathing: On the patio.
Nudity: Permitted in the Jacuzzi with discretion.
Smoking: Permitted on outside private patios only.
Pets: Not permitted.
Handicap Access: No.
Children: Welcomed, age 3 and older.
Languages: English & small amounts of Spanish.
Your Host: Karen & Lyle.

Hills of Gold Bed & Breakfast

Q-NET Lesbian-Owned & -Operated ♀

We are the Gold at the End of the Rainbow

Experience the Southwest at *Hills of Gold* in a single private suite on four acres of Sonoran desert, only 10 minutes from downtown Tucson. Hike Sabino Canyon, visit the Desert Museum, explore Kitt Peak Observatory, or relax right here. Your suite has a bedroom, sitting area, bath and private deck with mountain views. Enjoy the shared areas of our home-covered porches, hot tub, pool gas grill and library. Your choice of a hearty Southwestern or expanded continental breakfast is included, and box lunches and dinners can be arranged. TO OPEN FEBRUARY, 1998.

Address: 3650 W. Hills of Gold, Tucson, AZ 85745
Tel: (520) 743-4229 (Tel/Fax).
E-mail: hillsgold@theriver.com

Type: Bed & breakfast.
Clientele: Women only
Transportation: Car is best.
To Gay Bars: 15 min drive.
Rooms: 1 suite with queen & sofa bed, can accommodate 4 people.
Bathrooms: Private shower/toilet.
Meals: Full breakfast.
Vegetarian: Available by arrangement & nearby.
Complimentary: Tea, coffee, bottled water.
Dates Open: All year.
Rates: $80.
Discounts: 10% discount for 4 or more nights.
Rsv'tns: Required.
To Reserve: Travel agent or call direct.
Parking: Ample off-street parking.
In-Room: AC, ceiling fans, color cable TV, VCR, refrigerator, coffee & tea-making facilities, microwave. Laundry service by arrangement.
On-Premises: Video tape & book libraries.
Exercise/Health: Jacuzzi. Massage by arrangement.
Swimming: Pool on premises.
Sunbathing: Poolside.
Nudity: Permitted poolside.
Smoking: Permitted only on private deck. Room is non-smoking.
Pets: Not permitted.
Handicap Access: No.
Children: All ages welcome, have pool toys & books for children.
Languages: English.
Your Host: Terry & Melissa.

Montecito House
Women ♀

Mom, I'm Home!

Experience the friendly, relaxed atmosphere of *Montecito House*, my home, not a business. My B & B is a hobby, a way to meet people from around the world. Discussions at breakfast over fresh grapefruit juice from the tree in my yard are usual. Many guests meet here once and establish friendships that grow each year. Returning guests often mention the feeling of coming home again.

Address: PO Box 42352, Tucson, AZ 85733 **Tel:** (520) 795-7592.

Type: Bed & breakfast.
Clientele: Mostly lesbian with men welcome. Some straight clientele.
Transportation: Car is best, pick up from airport or bus available, prices vary.
To Gay Bars: 2 miles.
Rooms: 2 rooms with double beds.
Bathrooms: 1 private bath/toilet & 1 shared bath/shower/toilet.
Campsites: RV parking with electric only, share inside bathroom.
Meals: Continental breakfast.
Vegetarian: Available upon prior arrangement.
Complimentary: Tea, soda, coffee, juices, fresh fruit, nuts, crackers.
Dates Open: All year.
High Season: February.
Rates: Summer $35-$40, winter $40-$45.
Discounts: On weekly rates with reservation.
Rsv'tns: Recommended.
To Reserve: Call direct.
Minimum Stay: $10 surcharge for 1-night stay.
Parking: Ample, free off-street & on-street parking.
In-Room: Color TV, AC, telephone, maid service.
On-Premises: TV lounge, pinball, laundry facilities, use of kitchen if pre-arranged.
Exercise/Health: Nearby Jacuzzi/spa, massage, golf, tennis.
Swimming: In nearby pool.
Sunbathing: At poolside or on patio.
Nudity: Permitted in the house with consent of other guests.
Smoking: Permitted on outside front porch only.
Pets: Not permitted, cat & dog in residence.
Handicap Access: Baths not accessible.
Children: Not encouraged, but call to discuss.
Languages: English.
Your Host: Fran.

Santuario Inn Tucson
Gay-Owned & -Operated ♀♂

Leave the World Behind

A new kind of experience awaits at *Santuario Inn Tucson*. Your hosts welcome you with open arms and invite you to forget your troubles as you enter the haven they have created. Escape from the outside world in bedrooms full of luxurious amenities designed to pamper your senses. Indulge in a private bath where your inner gardens are sure to blossom, or let your mind go free and your body

continued next page

and soul rest as you stroll through the greenery and quiet of secluded gardens. On premises is the Kuriyama relaxation therapy center where, for an additional fee, patrons can embark on a journey of self-discovery and relaxation through Reiki, meditation and precious aromatics.

Address: PO Box 57538, Tucson, AZ **Tel:** (520) 519-0390, **Fax:** (520) 519-1374.

Type: Retreat with Kuriyama relaxation therapy center.
Clientele: Mostly gay & lesbian with some straight clientele
Transportation: Car is best. There are no business signs, directions to inn are mailed with confirmation receipt. Arizona Stagecoach $18.
To Gay Bars: 6 miles, a 12 min drive.
Rooms: 2 rooms, 1 suite with queen beds.
Bathrooms: Private: 1 bath/shower/toilet, 1 shower/toilet.
Meals: Full breakfast.
Vegetarian: At breakfast, if requested. At dinners at a fee.
Complimentary: Tea, coffee, juices, waters, mints on pillow, snack basket.
Dates Open: All year.
High Season: Feb-May.
Rates: $215-$265.
Discounts: No charge for 7th consecutive night.
Credit Cards: MC, Visa, Amex.
Rsv'tns: Required 2 weeks prior to check in.
To Reserve: Travel agent or call direct.
Minimum Stay: 2 nights on weekends & holidays.
Parking: Ample free off-street parking.
In-Room: Telephone, AC, ceiling fans, color cable TV, VCR, maid service.
On-Premises: Meeting rooms, fax, video tape library.
Exercise/Health: Jacuzzi, sauna, steam, massage, reiki. Nearby hair salon, gym, weights, Jacuzzi, sauna, steam.
Swimming: Nearby pool.
Sunbathing: On patio.
Smoking: Premises is all non-smoking.
Pets: Not permitted.
Handicap Access: No, single-level property with small steps.
Children: No.
Languages: English, Spanish.

Tortuga Roja Bed & Breakfast

Q-NET Gay/Lesbian ♀♂

Come, Share Our Mountain Views

SEE SPECIAL PAGE 14 COLOR SECTION

Tortuga Roja Bed & Breakfast is a 4-acre cozy retreat at the base of the Santa Catalinas, whose windows look out on an open landscape of natural high-desert vegetation. A bicycle and running path along the Rillito River right behind our house can be followed for four miles on either side. Our location is close to upscale shopping and dining and numerous hiking trails. It's an easy drive to the university, local bars and most tourist attractions. Some of our accommodations have fireplaces and kitchens.

Address: 2800 E River Rd, Tucson, AZ 85718
Tel: (520) 577-6822, (800) 467-6822.

Type: Bed & breakfast.
Clientele: Good mix of gays & lesbians
Transportation: Car is best.
To Gay Bars: 10-minute drive.
Rooms: 2 rooms & 1 cottage with queen beds.
Bathrooms: All private.
Meals: Expanded continental breakfast.
Dates Open: All year.
High Season: September-May.
Rates: Please call for rates.
Discounts: For weekly & monthly stays.
Credit Cards: Discover, MC, Visa.
Rsv'tns: Often essential.
To Reserve: Travel agent or call direct.
Minimum Stay: 2 nights on holiday weekends.
Parking: Ample free off-street parking.
In-Room: Color TV, VCR, AC, ceiling fan, radio & telephone. Cottage has kitchen.

FERRARI GUIDES™

On-Premises: Laundry facilities & kitchen privileges.
Swimming: Pool & hot tub on premises.
Sunbathing: At poolside & on the patio.
Nudity: Permitted poolside & in hot tub.
Smoking: Permitted outdoors only.
Pets: Not permitted.
Handicap Access: Limited. Not wheelchair accessible.
Children: Permitted in guest cottage only.
Languages: English.

IGLTA

Arbour Glen B&B Victorian Inn & Guesthouse

Q-NET Gay-Friendly 50/50 ♀♂

Kindle Your Romance in Old-World Elegance!

The Arbour Glen, circa 1896, sits on a hillside overlooking the Eureka Springs historical district. Our tree-covered hollow is the perfect picturesque setting for relaxation and enjoyment and is home to hummingbirds, deer, and rare birds. *The Arbour Glen* has been completely restored with comfort in mind but retains its old world charm and elegance. Each guest room is decorated with antiques, handmade quilts, brass and iron bedsteads, and fresh flowers. We serve a full gourmet breakfast, with china, silver and fanciful linen, on the veranda overlooking the hollow.

Our guests enjoy sipping coffee, while watching the deer and the birds. Though only steps away from downtown shops and restaurants, our location provides a secluded setting, very private and relaxing and comfortable. Spacious, shady verandas with swings overlook the rock and flower garden, complete with fish pond and fountain. There is a nearby nature trail for walking. Accommodations have hardwood floors with hand-hooked area rugs; clawfoot tubs; deluxe, in-bath, brass-trimmed Jacuzzis for two; and color cable TV with remote and VCR, all hidden in armoires. The house has heirloom antiques throughout and queen-sized Victorian beds. At Christmas, we feature a Victorian Christmas display.

Located on the Historic Loop and Trolley Route, *The Arbour Glen White Street Guesthouse* is adjacent to Ermillio's Fine Italian Restaurant, with art galleries, coffee shop, bookstore and horse-drawn carriage rides only steps away. Adding to the luxury are country club privileges that are available at nearby Holiday Island for you to swim, golf, or enjoy a game of tennis. Eureka Springs is a real Victorian village, nestled in the Ozark Mountains of Arkansas. The narrow, winding streets, hand-cut limestone walls and hillside parks and homes take advantage of the natural Ozark Mountain setting. One can discover shops and galleries filled with unique items not found anywhere else, many of which are lovingly and patiently handcrafted. Your stay here will definitely be an unforgettable experience. Come see for yourself!

Address: 7 Lema, Eureka Springs, AR 72632
Tel: (501) 253-9010, (800) 515-GLEN(4536). **E-mail:** arbglen@ipa.net

continued next page

UNITED STATES • ARKANSAS • EUREKA SPRINGS

Type: Bed & breakfast.
Clientele: 50% gay & lesbian & 50% straight clientele.
Transportation: Car is best. Pick up from airport.
To Gay Bars: 5 blocks. An 8-minute walk or 3-minute drive.
Rooms: 5 suites with double or queen beds.
Bathrooms: All private.
Meals: Full gourmet breakfast.
Vegetarian: Available with prior notification.
Complimentary: Mints, tea, coffee, soft drinks & afternoon desserts upon request.
Dates Open: All year.
High Season: April through October & holidays.
Rates: Low season $65-$115, high season $75-$125.
Discounts: On reservations for more than 3 nights. Honeymoon packages available.
Credit Cards: MC, Discover, Visa, Amex.
Rsv'tns: Required.
To Reserve: Travel agent or call direct.
Minimum Stay: 2 nights on weekends, 3 nights on holiday & festival weekends.
Parking: Ample free off-street parking.
In-Room: Color cable TV, VCR, AC, ceiling fans, refrigerator, coffee & tea-making facilities, fireplaces, Jacuzzis for two & maid service.
On-Premises: Nature trail.
Exercise/Health: Jacuzzi & nature trail.
Swimming: In nearby river, lake & country club.
Sunbathing: On the premises or at nearby lakes.
Smoking: Permitted outside on verandas only.
Pets: Not permitted.
Handicap Access: No.
Children: Not especially welcome.
Languages: English.
Your Host: Jeffrey.

Greenwood Hollow Ridge

Gay/Lesbian ♀♂

It's Gay in the Ozarks!

Greenwood Hollow Ridge is a country home located on 5 heavily-wooded acres in Eureka Springs, the little Switzerland of the Ozarks. We are the only EXCLUSIVE lodging in the area, a live-and-let-live community that charms every visitor. The entire downtown shopping district is listed on the National Register of Historic Places. Popular attractions include the Passion Play, arts & crafts fairs, music festivals, the Vintage Train Ride and watersports. Our guests have country club privileges for golf and tennis. Come and be gentled in the privacy of our quiet, country setting in the woods.

Address: Rte 4, Box 155, Eureka Springs, AR 72632 **Tel:** (501) 253-5283.

Type: Bed & breakfast.
Clientele: Exclusively gay! Good mix of gay men & women
Transportation: Car is a must! Free pickup from airport.
To Gay Bars: 2 miles to gay/lesbian bar.
Rooms: 3 rooms & 1 apartment with single, double & king beds.
Bathrooms: 1 private bath/toilet, 1 private shower/toilet, shared full bath.
Campsites: RV parking only.
Meals: Full breakfast.
Vegetarian: Available on request.
Complimentary: Welcome wine.
Dates Open: Closed February.
High Season: May through October.
Rates: Summer $45-$65, winter $35-$45.
Rsv'tns: Encouraged.
To Reserve: Travel agent or call direct.
Parking: 5 acres of parking.
In-Room: Color TV, ceiling fans, AC & kitchen.
On-Premises: Meeting rooms.
Exercise/Health: Jacuzzi & exercycle.
Swimming: 15-minute drive to lake.
Sunbathing: On patio or private sun deck.
Nudity: Permitted at spa.
Pets: Small pets OK.
Handicap Access: Yes, ramps.
Children: Not welcomed.
Languages: English & Spanish.

Pond Mountain Lodge & Resort

Gay-Friendly 50/50 ♀♂

Get the Peak Experience...

Mountain breezes, panoramic views, and thoughtful hospitality await at historic Eureka Springs' *Pond Mountain Lodge & Resort*. Both a bed & breakfast and resort, casually elegant *Pond Mountain* is located just two miles south of Eureka Springs at the county's highest elevation. Guests enjoy fishing ponds, heated swimming pool, horseback riding, Jacuzzi suites and cabin, TV/VCRs, billiards room, refrigerators, microwaves, gourmet coffee service, complimentary champagne and hearty breakfasts each morning. Warm and unintrusive hosting, and the serenity and beauty of 150 acres of mountain wonder make this the ideal respite.

Address: Rt 1 Box 50, Eureka Springs, AR 72632
Tel: (501) 253-5577, (800) 583-8043.
URL: www.eureka-usa.com/pondmtn/

Type: B&B resort with riding stables. Cabin with spa room.
Clientele: 50% gay & lesbian & 50% straight clientele
Transportation: Car is best.
Rooms: 5 suites with queen or king beds. 2-bedroom cabin.
Bathrooms: All private.
Meals: Full buffet breakfast (except cabin).
Vegetarian: Breakfast on request. Several excellent restaurants nearby.
Complimentary: Champagne, non-alcoholic sparkling cider, popcorn. Gourmet coffee, candy in room. Winter: sherry.
Dates Open: All year.
High Season: Apr 15-Nov 5.
Rates: Double occupancy: high season $100-$160, winter $85-$140. Cabin $140 year-round.
Discounts: 10% on stays of more than 3 days, rental of more than 3 units, or "family" AARP. 5% AARP.
Credit Cards: MC, Visa, Discover.
Rsv'tns: Recommended for weekends for Jacuzzi suites.
To Reserve: Travel agent or call direct.
Minimum Stay: 2 nights for special events.
Parking: Ample free off-street parking.
In-Room: Color TV, VCR, video tape library, AC, coffee/tea-making facilities, refrigerator, kitchen. Some ceiling fans, most have fireplace. Telephone in guest house.
On-Premises: Meeting room.
Exercise/Health: Jacuzzi in suites, massage by appointment. Hiking on 150 acres, fishing in private ponds. Horseback riding add'l fee.
Swimming: Heated pool on premises. Nearby river & lake.
Sunbathing: At poolside & on common sun decks.
Smoking: Permitted on outside covered verandah only. All rooms non-smoking.
Pets: Not permitted.
Handicap Access: Yes, cabin.
Children: Welcome. Separate building has family units which accommodate children.
Languages: English.
Your Host: Judy.

Country Comfort Bed & Breakfast

Gay/Lesbian ♀♂

Country Comfort, City Sights!

Gay and lesbian travelers to the Orange County area will find themselves right at home here! We are only 7 miles from Disneyland and the Anaheim Convention Center, 5 miles from the *new* Anaheim Pond and the Anaheim Stadium, all of them on the same street leading to our B&B! Beaches are within 20 miles and you'll enjoy our solar-heated pool and Jacuzzi, too. Other nearby attractions include Knott's Berry Farm, the Orange County Performing Arts Center, the Los Angeles Theater District, Universal Studios, Magic Mountain, the Queen Mary, Catalina, Sea World, San Diego Zoo and the Wild Animal Park. In case you are looking for a few "wild animals" of a different sort, dance or dine at 11 local gay and lesbian clubs and bars!

We offer guests country-style hospitality in a quiet residential neighborhood in Orange. Our home is noted for its unique glass architecture looking out onto the Orange Hills. Private rooms are decorated for your comfort and pleasure, including bathrobes, cable TV, telephone, antiques and ceiling fan. The *Blue Room* has a private atrium entrance, perfect for relaxing by yourself or with a friend. Everyone is welcome to relax in the family room with super-screen TV, VCR and laser-disks. For the person with special needs, the home is handicap-accessible with adaptive equipment available on prior notice. Exercise equipment for the fitness buff is also available.

Breakfast is bountiful, tailored to satisfy your individual needs. Our stuffed French toast has a reputation all its own, served country style. Early birds can enjoy their juice and cappuccino by the pool.

It's *your* holiday! We invite you to spend your time with us...in *Country Comfort.*

Address: 5104 E Valencia Drive, Orange, CA 92869-1217
Tel: (714) 532-4010, **Fax:** (714) 997-1921. **E-mail:** gerilopker@aol.com

Type: Bed & breakfast.
Clientele: Gay & lesbian, good mix of men & women.
Transportation: Car is best. Pick up from Disneyland Hotel, airport shuttle stop or Anaheim Amtrack station (small charge may apply).
To Gay Bars: 10 miles by car.
Rooms: 2 rooms with trundle, queen or king bed.
Bathrooms: 1 private bath/ toilets & 1 private shower/ toilet.
Meals: Full breakfast.

Vegetarian: Upon request, many local restaurants.
Complimentary: Tea, coffee, soft drinks, wine, beer.
Dates Open: All year.
Rates: $75.
Discounts: For extended stays (over 5 days).
Credit Cards: None.
Rsv'tns: Recommended 1-2 weeks in advance. Occasional last-minute rooms available. Call first.
To Reserve: Travel agent or call direct.
Minimum Stay: Prefer 2 nights.

Parking: Ample free on-street parking.
In-Room: Cable color TV, telephone, ceiling fans, maid service, refrigerator.
On-Premises: TV lounge, laundry facilities, copier, fax, computer rental.
Exercise/Health: Jacuzzi, treadmill, exercise bike, mini-trampoline. Nearby gym, massage.
Swimming: Pool on premises, 15 miles to ocean. Hydrotherapy spa now available.
Sunbathing: At poolside, on common sun decks, patio or nearby beach.
Smoking: Permitted outdoors on patio, atrium & sun deck.
Pets: Not permitted.
Handicap Access: Yes, 1 story no barriers. Bath equip. available with prior arrangement.
Children: Permitted when the stay is private (no other booked guests).
Languages: English, Signing.
Your Host: Joanne & Geri.

Smoketree Resort

Q-NET Gay-Friendly ♀♂

Smoketree Resort was originally built in the late 40's and early 50's and was frequented by movie stars over the years. All of our rooms have been recently upgraded. Our location is in the San Bernardino Mountains is on three acres close to Big Bear Lake and a national forest. The main lodge house has five suites with bath and fireplace. There are also 25 cabins for two or for up to eight people. We are close to the village. You can walk to shopping and restaurants. Skiing, mountain biking, hiking and boating are only a few minutes away.

Address: 40154 Big Bear Blvd, PO Box 2801, Big Bear Lake, CA 92315
Tel: (909) 866-2415 or (800) 352-8581.

Type: Bed & breakfast & cabins in Big Bear ski resort area.
Clientele: Mostly straight with 10% gay & lesbian following
Transportation: Car is best. Free pick up from Big Bear Airport.
To Gay Bars: San Bernardino, 1 hour & 30 minutes.
Rooms: 10 cabins.
Bathrooms: All private.
Complimentary: Coffee, tea & hot chocolate in room.
Dates Open: All year.
Rates: Low season $49-$150, High season $59-$220.
Credit Cards: MC, Visa, Amex, Discover.
Rsv'tns: Suggested.
To Reserve: Travel agent or call direct.
Minimum Stay: Required in high season.
Parking: Ample free off-street parking.
In-Room: Color TV, telephone, maid service. Cabins have kitchens.
Exercise/Health: Jacuzzi & massage.
Swimming: Heated pool on premises, 5 minutes to lake.
Sunbathing: At poolside.
Smoking: No smoking in office.
Pets: Small pets, $10 per night. May not be left unattended.
Handicap Access: No.
Children: Permitted.
Languages: English.
Your Host: Joseph & Russell.

Sea Breeze Resort

Gay-Friendly ♀♂

Glistening Water, Tree-Covered Mountains, Clear Blue Skies

Sea Breeze is a lakefront resort on California's largest natural lake. Enjoy swimming, boating and fishing just steps away from your tastefully-decorated, impeccably-clean cottage with fully-equipped kitchen. Relax and enjoy our beautifully-landscaped grounds, and picturesque lake and mountain views. Exclusively for our guests are a covered lighted pier, boat slips/mooring, launching ramp, beach, swim float, picnic tables, chaise lounges and Weber barbecues. For those seeking more arduous activities, boat and jet ski rentals, parasailing, glider rides and top name entertainment are a short distance away.

Address: 9595 Harbor Dr, (Mail: PO Box 653), Glenhaven, CA 95443
Tel: (707) 998-3327.

Type: Resort with cottages.
Clientele: Mostly straight clientele with a gay & lesbian following.
Transportation: Car is best.
Rooms: 6 cottages with full kitchens, 1 room with refrigerator. Single, double, queen or king beds.
Bathrooms: All private
bath/toilet/showers.
Vegetarian: Available at nearby restaurants.
Complimentary: Coffee, tea, hot cocoa & ice.
Dates Open: Apr 1-Oct 31.
High Season: June-Sep.
Rates: $60-$90.
Credit Cards: MC, Visa.
To Reserve: Call direct.
Minimum Stay: 3-night minimum on holidays.
Parking: Ample free off-street parking. Ample parking for boat trailers on-site
In-Room: Color cable TV, AC, ceiling fans, coffee/tea-making facilities, kitchen & refrigerator.
On-Premises: Large enclosed rumpus/club room.
Swimming: Lake on premises.
Sunbathing: At the beach & on the lawns.
Smoking: Permitted without restrictions.
Pets: Not permitted.
Handicap Access: No.
Children: Well-disciplined children welcome.
Languages: English.
Your Host: Phil & Steve.

UNITED STATES
EUREKA • CALIFORNIA

Abigail's Elegant Victorian Mansion B&B Lodging Accommodations
Gay-Friendly ♀♂

A Passion for Quality, Service & the Extra-Ordinary

A designer's showcase, **Abigail's Elegant Victorian Mansion B&B Lodging Accommodations** is an award-winning 1888 National Historic Landmark of opulence, grace and grandeur. Exclusively for the non-smoking traveler, the "Elegant Victorian" is a living-history house-museum for the discriminating connoisseur of authentic Victorian decor. This designer's showcase is recommended by AAA, Frommers, Fodor's, Mobile and Michelin, and is rated "4-Star" by the prestigious international group Chambres d'Hotes - Auberges. With "the most stunningly spectacular interiors in the state," *World Traveler* magazine calls the inn "One of America's most extra-ordinary accommodations."

Address: 1406 C Street, Eureka, CA 95501
Tel: (707) 444-3144, **Fax:** (707) 442-5594.

Type: Bed & breakfast.
Clientele: Mostly hetero clientele with a gay & lesbian following.
Transportation: Car is best. Free pick up from bus, train, ferry dock. Pick up from airport $20.
To Gay Bars: 13 blocks, a 5 min drive.
Rooms: 4 doubles, 1 triple.
Bathrooms: Suite has private bath. 3 other rooms have access to 3 addt'l baths & Finnish sauna.
Meals: Full breakfast.
Vegetarian: At any time,

upon request at check-in or earlier.
Complimentary: Afternoon & evening hot drinks & snacks. Turn-down service includes Belgian chocolate truffles. Guest fridge filled with complimentary drinks, snacks.
Dates Open: All year.
High Season: June-Sept, holidays & special events.
Rates: Winter $95-$165, summer $120-$185.
Discounts: 10% if Inn Places is mentioned & discount requested at time of reservation.

Credit Cards: MC, Visa.
Rsv'tns: Required.
To Reserve: Call direct.
Parking: Ample free off-street parking. On-site security parking behind locked gates.
In-Room: Telephone, AC, b/w TV, maid & laundry service.
On-Premises: TV lounge, meeting rooms, laundry facilities, horseless-carriage tours.
Exercise/Health: Croquet, sauna, massage.

Swimming: Nearby ocean beach & river.
Sunbathing: On private sun decks, at beach & river.
Nudity: Permitted in sauna areas, private yard space & at nearby beach.
Smoking: Exclusively non-smoking inn. At no time is smoking permitted anywhere on premises.
Pets: Not permitted.
Handicap Access: No.
Children: Permitted ages 14 & older.
Languages: English, French, Dutch, German.

IDYLLWILD

The Pine Cove Inn
Gay-Friendly ♀♂

Picture yourself in one of the nine A-frame chalet units at *The Pine Cove Inn*, surrounded by natural landscaping and enjoying the clear, crisp mountain air. You're up at 6,200 feet, and the views are nothing less than incredible. Your individually-decorated room has private bath, fridge and microwave oven. Each of our seven rooms has a fireplace, one unit has a full kitchen and a television, and three have larger private decks with magnificent mountain views. In winter, our toboggan run will carry you down a mountain of fun.

Address: 23481 Hwy 243, Idyllwild, CA 92549
Tel: (909) 659-5033, toll-free (888) 659-5033, **Fax:** (909) 659-5034.

Type: Bed & breakfast & conference center.
Clientele: 25% gay & lesbian & 75% straight clientele.
Transportation: Car is best.
To Gay Bars: 1 hour to

Palm Springs' gay/lesbian bars.
Rooms: 10 units (1 apartment unit is above the lodge).
Bathrooms: All private.
Meals: Full breakfast.
Vegetarian: Just let us

know when you make your reservation.
Complimentary: Tea & coffee in room.
Dates Open: All year.
Rates: $70-$100 plus 10% tax.
Discounts: On mid-week stays (Sun-Thurs).

Credit Cards: MC, Visa, Amex.
Rsv'tns: Recommended.
To Reserve: Travel agent or call direct.
Minimum Stay: 2 nights on weekends, 3 nights on holiday weekends.

Parking: Ample, free, off-street parking.
In-Room: Fridge, microwave oven. 1 unit has full kitchen & TV.
On-Premises: TV lounge, meeting rooms, lodge with fireplace, books, games, puzzles.
Sunbathing: On private sun decks.
Smoking: Some rooms non-smoking. Smoking permitted outdoors, in TV lounge & lodge.
Pets: Not permitted.
Handicap Access: Limited accessibility.
Children: Permitted, $10 extra 12 years and older.
Languages: English.
Your Host: Bob & Michelle.

Casa Laguna Bed & Breakfast Inn

Q-NET Gay-Friendly ♀♂

Sun, Sand & Sea

SEE SPECIAL PAGE 15 COLOR SECTION

Casa Laguna is a unique, 20-room country inn on a terraced hillside, overlooking the Pacific Ocean. Its towering palms hover over meandering paths and flower-splashed patios, swimming pool, aviary and fountains, making this intimate, mission-style inn a visual delight. Many rooms and suites have sweeping views. A cottage, set on its own, has private garden, sun decks and ocean views. The mission house, itself, has two bedrooms and two fireplaces. Laguna Beach combines art, seaside casualness and colorful landscapes for an ideal retreat.

Address: 2510 South Coast Hwy, Laguna Beach, CA 92651
Tel: (714) 494-2996, (800) 233-0449, **Fax:** (714) 494-5009.

Type: Bed & breakfast inn.
Clientele: Mostly straight clientele with a gay & lesbian following
Transportation: Car is best. Jitney service from Orange County Airport, about $20.
To Gay Bars: One mile to nearest one. There are others in Laguna Beach.
Rooms: 15 rooms, 4 suites & 2 cottages. Single, double or king beds.
Bathrooms: All private shower/toilets.
Meals: Expanded continental breakfast.
Vegetarian: Fruit, cereals & breads available at breakfast.
Complimentary: Wine, cheese, snacks, tea & coffee are served each afternoon in the library.
Dates Open: All year.
High Season: July until Labor Day.
Rates: Winter $79-$175, summer $90-$225.
Discounts: Winter & midweek discounts.
Credit Cards: MC, Visa, Amex, Diners, Bancard, Eurocard & Discover.
Rsv'tns: Required, but walk-ins accepted.
To Reserve: Travel agent or call direct.
Minimum Stay: Only on national holidays.
Parking: Ample free off-street parking.
In-Room: Color cable TV, telephone, ceiling fans & maid service. Some rooms with refrigerators. Kitchens in the 4 suites & 2 private homes.
On-Premises: Meeting rooms & TV lounge/library.
Swimming: Pool.
Sunbathing: At poolside, on the patio & common sun decks.
Smoking: Permitted. Non-smoking rooms available.
Pets: Small pets permitted with prior arrangements.
Handicap Access: No.
Children: Permitted, but must be attended by an adult at all times.
Languages: English, Spanish.

INN PLACES® 1998

UNITED STATES • CALIFORNIA • LAGUNA BEACH

239

UNITED STATES · LAGUNA BEACH · CALIFORNIA

Coast Inn

Q-NET Gay/Lesbian ♂

The *Coast Inn* is the oldest and most popular gay resort in America, providing year-round fun right on the Pacific Ocean, with the world's most beautiful beaches. All rooms have color TV, phones, private baths, and a sun deck or balcony overlooking the bathing beach. We are also home to the world famous "Boom Boom Room," with dancing to the hottest and latest music til 2 am. We are 2 minutes from the West Street gay beach and 15 minutes from San Onofre nude beach. Dana Point Harbor is only five miles away and provides some of the finest surfing, windsurfing, sailing, fishing, snorkling, and scuba diving in Southern California. Disneyland is 30 miles away. Laguna Beach itself has an abundance of fine shopping and dining and is home of The Pageant of the Masters.

Address: 1401 S Coast Hwy, Laguna Beach, CA 92651
Tel: (714) 494-7588, (800) 653-2697, **Fax:** (714) 494-1735.
E-mail: coastinn@msn.com **URL:** http://www.boomboomroom.com

Type: Resort hotel with restaurant & "Boom Boom Room" bar & disco.
Clientele: Mostly men with women welcome.
Transportation: Rental car from LAX or San Diego Airport or John Wayne Airport, 12 mi north.
To Gay Bars: World famous "Boom Boom Room" on the premises. 3 other bars in walking distance.

Rooms: 23 rooms
Bathrooms: Each room has a private bath & sun deck or balcony.
Vegetarian: We have a full menu in the restaurant with some vegetarian food available.
Dates Open: All year.
High Season: Apr-Oct.
Rates: $60-$160.
Discounts: Stay 6 nights & get the 7th night free.

Credit Cards: MC, Visa, Amex, Diners, Discover.
Rsv'tns: Strongly suggested.
To Reserve: Travel agent or call direct.
Minimum Stay: 2-nights on weekends.
Parking: Limited free off-street parking.
In-Room: Color cable TV, telephone, maid service, & room service.

Swimming: In the ocean.
Sunbathing: On the beach & on private common sun decks.
Nudity: Permitted on sun decks.
Smoking: Permitted everywhere.
Pets: Not permitted.
Handicap Access: No.
Children: Not permitted.
Languages: English.

The Bavarian House

Q-NET Gay/Lesbian ♀♂

Breathe the Pine-Scented Mountain Air Year-Round

Amidst the pristine beauty of the Sierra Nevada is *The Bavarian House*, a spacious bed and breakfast nestled on a mountainside on the south shore of Lake Tahoe. In summer, enjoy hiking, biking, swimming, horseback riding, or exploring the exquisite granite peaks, lakes, and forestland. Return home and take in the cool pine-scented mountain air and breathtaking views from one of the large decks. Winter is the time for skiing (Heavenly Valley, Tahoe's largest ski resort is just four blocks away), snowmobiling, horse-drawn sleigh rides, roaring fires, hot cider, and watching the snow quietly fall. Casinos and restaurants are close by for year-round entertainment.

The Bavarian House has three generous guest rooms (for a maximum of six guests), each with a private bath, king-sized bed, and TV/VCR and rustic mountain decor. Rates include daily maid service, a hearty breakfast and access to a large video library. The greatroom, with its large river rock fireplace and vaulted, beamed ceilings, is a comfortable place to talk with friends, sample some wine and cheese, or just relax in front of a cozy fire. The loft, overlooking the greatroom, has game tables, a reading lounge, and a piano. A separate, three-bedroom chalet is also available — perfect for couples or groups. Join your hosts, Jerry and Kevin, and you'll understand why guests return again and again.

Address: PO Box 624507, Lake Tahoe, CA 96154
Tel: (800) 431-4411, (530) 544-4411.

Type: Bed & breakfast guesthouse.
Clientele: Good mix of gays & lesbians
Transportation: Shuttle or rental car from Reno airport (1 hr), or taxi from South Lake Tahoe Airport (15-min drive).
To Gay Bars: 10 minutes by car.

Rooms: 3 rooms with king beds.
Bathrooms: All private bath/toilets.
Meals: Full breakfast.
Vegetarian: Available with advance notice.
Complimentary: Wine & cheese upon arrival. Set-ups, coffee, tea & juices.
Dates Open: All year.

Rates: $95-$130.
Rsv'tns: Required.
To Reserve: Call direct.
Minimum Stay: $15 premium for 1-night stay.
Parking: Adequate free off-street parking.
In-Room: Color cable TV, VCR, video tape library & maid service.
Swimming: At nearby lake.

Sunbathing: On common sun decks or nearby beach.
Nudity: 30-minute drive to nude beach.
Smoking: Permitted outside.
Pets: Not permitted.
Handicap Access: Not wheelchair accessible.
Children: Not permitted.
Languages: English.

Inn Essence
A Special Place for You!

Gay/Lesbian ♀♂

Nestled in the mountains at Lake Tahoe, amidst the world famous ski resorts and casinos, is *Inn Essence*. Gourmet chef for the stars and interior designer, Patrick Finn opens his home to you. The beautifully appointed rooms are just waiting to pamper you. Enjoy an aromatherapy spa after a day of hiking, skiing, snowmobiling, swimming, sunbathing and more. Then snuggle in by the fire or enjoy an exciting show at the casinos. Our picturesque garden setting, complete with swimming pool, is perfect for poolside ceremonies. *Inn Essence* will truly be "a special place for you"!

Address: 865 Lake Tahoe Blvd, South Lake Tahoe, CA 96150
Tel: (530) 577-0339, **Fax:** (530) 577-0118, (800) 57 TAHOE.
E-mail: innessence@aol.com

Type: Bed & breakfast guesthouse.
Clientele: Gay & lesbian clientele.
Transportation: Car or plane.
To Gay Bars: 9 miles.
Rooms: 2 rooms with king or queen beds.
Bathrooms: 1 shared bath/shower toilet with spa tub & essential oils.
Meals: Full gourmet breakfast. Lunch, dinner & catering available.
Vegetarian: Always available.
Complimentary: Tea, coffee, morning newspapers, gourmet treats, mints on pillow.
Dates Open: All year.
Rates: $89-$129.
Discounts: Available for extended stays. Book both rooms for concurrent stay for 10% disocunt.
Rsv'tns: Required.
To Reserve: Call direct.
Minimum Stay: Inquire.
Parking: Ample free off-street & on-street parking.
In-Room: Color cable TV, VCR, video library, telephone, maid & laundry service, private entrances.
On-Premises: TV lounge, laundry facilities.
Exercise/Health: Jacuzzi.
Swimming: Pool in summer season. River & lake nearby.
Sunbathing: On common sun decks, poolside or at the beach.
Nudity: Permitted at gay nude beach.
Smoking: Permitted in smoking areas outside. Non-smoking rooms.
Pets: Not permitted.
Handicap Access: No.
Languages: English.
Your Host: Patrick.

Lakeside B 'n B Tahoe

Gay/Lesbian ♀♂

Romantic, Exciting, Right on the Water!

Lakeside B 'n B Tahoe, a private home smack-dab on the water, has antiques, plants and magnificent views of Lake Tahoe and mountains from all three guest rooms. There is a steam room, Jacuzzi, grand piano, fireplace, library, lakeside deck and parklike grounds. Fresh-baked bread and gargantuan gourmet breakfasts are served from a printed, personalized menu with many choices. Fabulous skiing in winter, swimming, boating and nude sunbathing in summer, and 24-hour Nevada gaming action are minutes away. On the quiet Nevada side of North Lake Tahoe, the B&B is 4 hours from San Francisco and 45 minutes from Reno.

Address: Box 1756, Crystal Bay, NV 89402
Tel: (702) 831-8281, **Fax:** (702) 831-7FAX (7329).
E-mail: TahoeBnB@aol.com

Type: Bed & breakfast.
Clientele: Gay & lesbian, good mix of men & women
Transportation: Car is best. Carry chains in winter.
To Gay Bars: About 1/2 hr drive to Faces in South Lake Tahoe or 45 min to Reno bars.
Rooms: 3 rooms with queen beds.
Bathrooms: 1 private & 1 shared.
Meals: Full breakfast from printed menu with many choices, daily gourmet special & fresh-baked bread.
Vegetarian: Available whenever a guest wants it.
Complimentary: Wine, coffee, other goodies, breakfast in bed if desired.
Dates Open: All year.
High Season: Dec-Apr (skiing season) & Jun-Oct.
Rates: $75-$165.
Rsv'tns: Required.
To Reserve: Call direct.
Minimum Stay: $15 premium for one-night stays.
Parking: Ample free off-street parking.
In-Room: Color cable TV, VCR & huge video tape library (1100+ titles).
On-Premises: Library, giant screen TV, fireplace, bearskin rug, grand piano, many musical instruments, laundry facilities & lakeside decks with dramatic views of Lake Tahoe.
Exercise/Health: Jacuzzi & steam room in suite. Communal hot tub & sauna available in 1998. Swim, boat, ski, horseback ride, hike, nearby health club.
Swimming: In lake.
Sunbathing: At lakeside, on private & common sun decks. Nude beach nearby.
Nudity: Permitted if OK with other guests.
Smoking: Outside only.
Pets: Permitted if well behaved, must get along with my pets.
Handicap Access: No. Steep steps & steep access to lake.
Children: Welcomed (up to 12 yrs free).
Languages: English, some French & Spanish.
Your Host: Steven.

SierraWood Guest House

Q-NET Gay/Lesbian

The Privacy Is a Luxury in Itself

SierraWood is a romantic, cozy chalet in the woods, where you've dreamed of taking a special friend for an exciting vacation together or getting away by yourself for relaxation and renewal. Here, beside a rippling stream, we're surrounded by U.S. Forest preserve. For those who want to balance the peace and privacy of the wooded chalet, the glittering allure of Lake Tahoe's gaming casinos, superstar entertainers, clubs, restaurants and nightlife is only a few miles away. In summer, you can charter *SierraWood's* own 25-foot *Lancer* for an exciting day on the waters of Lake Tahoe. Your hosts will serve cocktails and lunch, while you soak in the sun and the sights. On another day, try hiking through flowering meadows to the pristine alpine lakes nearby. The winter delight is downhill and cross-country skiing at one of three major ski resorts.

The chalet is an inviting, 6-bedroom, 4-bath home whose unique architecture incorporates open-beam cathedral ceilings, pine paneling and both a rock fireplace and an antique potbelly stove. There are bay windows, floor-to-ceiling windows, and skylights, plus an outdoor redwood hot tub with a view of the river, white fir and aspen woods. Our convivial cocktail hour begins with a soak in the hot tub. Then we join in the warm glow of a sumptuous dining table, sparkling with candlelight, Waterford crystal and the laughter and good conversation of happy company. A healthy breakfast is also included in the daily fare.

Address: PO Box 11194, Tahoe Paradise, CA 96155-0194
Tel: (530) 577-6073, (800) 700-3802.

Type: Bed & breakfast guesthouse with dinner included.
Clientele: Good mix of gay men & women
Transportation: Car is best. Free pick up from airport & bus.
To Gay Bars: 12 miles to gay/lesbian bar & the casinos.
Rooms: 4 rooms with double, queen or king beds.
Bathrooms: 1 private bath, 2 private sinks, 2 shared bath/shower/toilets.
Meals: Full breakfast & dinner.
Vegetarian: Available with 3 days' notice.
Complimentary: BYOB, setups provided, tea & coffee, beverages, mints on pillow, wine with dinner.
Dates Open: All year.
Rates: Single $80, double $115-$130. Holidays $90-$150.
Rsv'tns: Preferred 2 days in advance.
To Reserve: Travel agent or call direct.
Minimum Stay: 2 days on holidays.
Parking: Ample free parking.
In-Room: Telephone, VCR, maid, room & laundry service.
On-Premises: Fireplace, lounge with color TV, laundry facilities.
Exercise/Health: Weights & hot tub with Jacuzzi.
Swimming: River on premises, lake nearby, nude beach 45 min.
Sunbathing: On beach or common sun decks.
Nudity: On decks & in hot tub.
Smoking: Permitted without restrictions.
Pets: Small pets permitted, if housebroken.
Handicap Access: No.
Children: Not permitted.
Languages: English.
Your Host: David & LeRoy.

The Grove Guest House

Gay/Lesbian ♀♂

Luxury and Privacy — Perfect Central Location!

The first choice for your stay in Los Angeles, the unique *Grove Guest House* provides you with your own private, luxurious villa with a separate bedroom, kitchen and spacious living room. Located in a quiet, historical district, you can walk to West Hollywood fun. It features a glamorous black-bottom pool and party spa amidst lush tropical landscaping. You can even suntan nude, if you like. Leather furniture, VCR, cable TV, private phone with free local calls, and a refrigerator stocked with goodies are just some of the amenities. Enjoy!

Address: 1325 N Orange Grove Ave, Los Angeles - West Hollywood, CA 90046
Tel: (213) 876-7778, **Fax:** (213) 876-3170.

Type: Guesthouse.
Clientele: Gay & lesbian
Transportation: Car is best, taxi or LAX super shuttle.
To Gay Bars: 1 block. A 5-minute walk or 2-minute drive.
Rooms: 1 large villa with separate bedroom.
Bathrooms: Private shower/toilet.
Meals: Continental breakfast & snacks.

Vegetarian: Lots of vegetarian food nearby.
Complimentary: Kitchen is well stocked with a range of food & goodies.
Dates Open: All year.
Rates: $135 per day for 2 people. Additional people & selected dates slightly higher.
Discounts: On extended stays.
Rsv'tns: Required.
To Reserve: Travel agent or call direct.

Parking: Ample free parking.
In-Room: Eat-in kitchen, color cable TV, VCR, video tape & book library, AC, ceiling fans, phone, refrigerator, microwave, coffee & tea-making facilities.
Exercise/Health: Jacuzzi on premises. Nearby gyms offer discounts to our guests.
Swimming: Pool on premises. Nearby pool & ocean.

Sunbathing: At poolside.
Nudity: Permitted by pool & spa.
Smoking: Permitted, but not in bedroom, please.
Pets: Not permitted.
Handicap Access: No.
Children: Not especially welcome.
Languages: English, French.
Your Host: Oliver.

Holloway Motel

Gay/Lesbian ♀♂

The Holloway is a 22-unit motel centrally located in West Hollywood. This Southern California-style wooden stucco structure has traditional furnishings, very reasonable rates, and a warm, friendly feeling. Each room has color cable TV, air conditioning, phone, shower, toilet, and maid service. *The Holloway* is adjacent to restaurants and close to several gay and lesbian bars. We are also near Hollywood, Beverly Hills, and Sunset Strip, and under 30 minutes from most major Southern California attractions.

Address: 8465 Santa Monica Blvd, West Hollywood, CA 90069
Tel: (213) 654-2454, (888) 654-6400, **Fax:** (213) 848-7161.

Type: Motel.
Clientele: Mostly gay & lesbian with some straight clientele.
Transportation: Car, taxi or LAX super shuttle.
To Gay Bars: 4 blocks.
Rooms: 20 rooms & 2 suites with single or queen beds.

Bathrooms: Each room has its own shower & toilet.
Vegetarian: Available nearby.
Dates Open: All year.
Rates: $55/night including tax, Sun-Thurs; $65, Fri-Sat & holidays. Studios add $10-$20/night. Higher on holidays. Prices subject to change.

Discounts: Available for advance payment & extended stay.
Credit Cards: MC, Visa.
Rsv'tns: Recommended.
To Reserve: Call direct.
Parking: Free off-street parking.
In-Room: Color cable TV, AC, telephone, maid service.

Exercise/Health: Several gyms down the street.
Smoking: Permitted. Non-smoking rooms available.
Pets: Not permitted.
Handicap Access: No.
Children: Permitted.
Languages: English & Spanish.
Your Host: Rudy & Dave.

Le Montrose Suite Hotel De Gran Luxe

Q-NET Gay-Friendly ♂

Indulge Yourself...Stay With Us at Le Montrose

Nestled in a quiet, residential area two blocks from the world-famous Sunset Strip, **Le Montrose** is a most pleasant alternative, offering 128 charming suites, friendly, personalized service, and attention to details with the special grace of a European-style hotel. Each suite includes sunken living room, cozy fireplace, refrigerator, color TV with VCR and twice-daily maid service. If you need to be in constant touch with your office, you'll value the state-of-the-art, multiline telephone with dataport, fax machines, and voice mail services in each suite. Most suites at **Le Montrose** include a kitchenette, and many offer private balconies with a breathtaking city view.

You can enjoy suite service dining in your suite or on the rooftop terrace, with a panoramic view of the west side. Superb dining indoors is available at the intimate Library Restaurant. Relax in the heated pool and spa, or catch a game of tennis on the lighted court. Both are located on the rooftop. Complimentary bicycles are available for exploring the surrounding West Hollywood area. Among the many attractions within a 7-mile radius of the hotel are Universal Studios, Mann's Chinese Theater, Pacific Design Center, Rodeo Drive, Cedars Sinai Medical Center and the Beverly Center. Ask about the Salon Room, which has 1,300 square feet of function space for small meetings or receptions. Other hotel services include valet laundry service, on-property laundry facilities, underground valet parking, in suite movies with Nintendo, currency exchange, full concierge and business services and a new, state-of-the-art fitness center with on-call private trainer and masseuse.

Address: 900 Hammond St, West Hollywood, CA 90069
Tel: (310) 855-1115, (800) 776-0666, **Fax:** (310) 657-9192.

Type: Hotel with restaurant.
Clientele: Mostly straight clientele with a gay male following
Transportation: Car is best.
To Gay Bars: 2 blocks or a 10-minute walk.
Rooms: 128 suites. 13 1-bedroom & 60 executive suites with kitchens. 36 junior suites with refrigerator (no kitchen). Double, queen or king beds.
Bathrooms: All private.
Vegetarian: Available upon request of guest.
Complimentary: Welcome fresh fruit. Departure, cookies & milk.
Dates Open: All year.
Rates: $190-$475.
Discounts: 35% discount if you ask for Ferrari Rate.
Credit Cards: MC, VISA, Amex, Diners & others.
Rsv'tns: Required. Call (800) 776-0666.
To Reserve: Travel agent or call direct.
Parking: Ample covered pay parking.
In-Room: Color cable TV, VCR, premier movies & Nintendo, fax machines, AC, telephones (3 per suite), fireplaces, kitchen, refrigerator, coffee/tea-makers, room & laundry service, and maid service twice daily.
On-Premises: Meeting rooms & laundry facilities.
Exercise/Health: Full service fitness center. Free tennis & free bicycles for guest use. Rooftop terrace with Jacuzzi.
Swimming: Heated pool on premises. 10 miles to beaches.
Sunbathing: At poolside or on the roof.
Smoking: Permitted. Non-smoking rooms are available.
Pets: Permitted with deposit.
Handicap Access: Yes.
Children: Permitted.
Languages: English, Spanish, French, German, Japanese, Chinese & Romanian.

IGLTA

Le Parc Hotel

Q-NET Gay-Friendly ♀♂

West Hollywood's Great Little Hotel

For those who prefer their luxury hotel to be more of a refuge from LA's fast lane than a tribute to it, we suggest *Le Parc Hotel*. Gracefully set in one of West Hollywood's most peaceful residential neighborhoods, you'll feel like you are miles away from the action, when in reality you are conveniently right in the middle of it. *Le Parc Hotel* offers elegant seclusion within walking distance of the bars, restaurants, sports clubs and businesses that make West Hollywood a world-renowned gay destination. Whether traveling for business (Pacific Design Center, The Beverly Center, Melrose's art galleries or antique shops) or pleasure (Revolver, Mickys, Rage, Trunks, The Palms) your destination is just a short walk away.

Our 154 luxury suites provide a living room with fireplace, balcony, kitchenette, video cassette player, Nintendo, multiline phones, walk-in closets and complimentary cable TV. As a truly full-service hotel, we offer morning and evening maid service, room service, free morning newspaper, and Cafe Le Parc, a private restaurant exclusively for guests of the hotel.

Casual and comfortable, with the feeling of an exclusive country club, *Le Parc* is a haven when your hectic day is over. While West Hollywood's best health clubs, World Gym and Bally's Sports Connection are just around the corner, the hotel has its own facilities exclusively for guests' use, including a well-equipped gym and sauna, as well as a rooftop pool, jacuzzi and tennis and basketball courts. *Le Parc Hotel* not only requests, but respects your business and community, and is committed to giving back to the gay and lesbian community via philanthropic endeavors. From the private guests-only restaurant, to the hotel's meeting and banquet rooms to the friendly service and amenities, *Le Parc Hotel* specializes in the fine art of casual elegance.

Address: 733 N. West Knoll Dr, West Hollywood, CA 90069
Tel: (310) 855-8888 , Reservations USA only: (800) 578-4837, **Fax:** (310) 659-7812.

Type: Hotel with restaurant and bar.
Clientele: Mostly straight clientele with a gay and lesbian following
Transportation: Car is best.
To Gay Bars: 1-3 blocks.
Rooms: 154 suites with single, double & king beds.
Bathrooms: All private.
Vegetarian: Two restaurants & health food store nearby

Complimentary: Welcome fresh fruit basket, limousine service.
Dates Open: All year.
Rates: Deluxe suite $225; One-bedroom suite $275; Premier Suite $250.
Discounts: 30% discount if you mention Inn Places.
Credit Cards: MC, VISA, Amex, Diners, JCB.
Rsv'tns: Required.
To Reserve: Travel agent or call direct.

Parking: Adequate covered off-street pay parking (either valet or self-park).
In-Room: Color cable TV, Nintendo, AC, telephone, kitchen, refrigerator, microwave, coffee & tea-making facilities, maid, room, & laundry service.
On-Premises: Meeting rooms, coin laundry facilities.
Exercise/Health: Gym, weights, Jacuzzi, sauna, massage.

Swimming: Heated pool on premises.
Sunbathing: On rooftop.
Smoking: Permitted, non-smoking rooms available.
Pets: Permitted in deluxe suites only with $50 fee.
Handicap Access: Yes.
Children: Permitted, under 17 stay free with parent.
Languages: English, Spanish, Arabic, French.
Your Host: Dona & Josh.

IGLTA

Ramada Hotel West Hollywood

Q-NET Gay-Friendly 50/50 ♀♂

Affordable Luxury in the Heart of Gay Los Angeles

Located between Beverly Hills and Hollywood, the *Ramada West Hollywood* is within walking distance to all of the area's popular cafes, restaurants, bars and nightclubs. Universal Studios and most tourist attractions are located within 10 minutes. Built in 1989 and renovated in 1995, the hotel has 175 rooms and suites, an outdoor pool, discount healthclub memberships and Enterprise car rental. There is also a clothing boutique and a food court which includes Starbucks Coffee, Pizzeria Uno's, Baja Buds Mexican Restuarant, Wok Deli — Chinese, Bagel Bakery and Juice Shop.

Address: 8585 Santa Monica Blvd, West Hollywood, CA 90069
Tel: (310) 652-6400, (800) 845-8585, **Fax:** (310) 652-2135.

Type: Hotel with restaurant, food court, clothing store & car rental agency.
Clientele: 50% gay & lesbian & 50% straight clientele
Transportation: From LAX airport: shuttle $12 per person each way, taxi $25 each way.
To Gay Bars: 4 blocks, 1/2 mile, a 10-minute walk, a 5-minute drive.
Rooms: 135 rooms, 40 suites with double, queen or king beds.
Bathrooms: All private bath/toilet/showers.

Vegetarian: Available at hotel restaurant, 2 vegetarian restaurants nearby.
Complimentary: Daily newspaper, afternoon & evening coffee.
Dates Open: All year.
High Season: Apr 30-Sept 30.
Rates: Summer $99-$259, winter $89-$209.
Discounts: AAA, AARP, government, entertainment card. 15% off when mentioning the Ferrari Guides. All accepted upon availability.

Credit Cards: MC, Visa, Amex, Diners, Discover.
Rsv'tns: Reservations suggested, walk-ins welcome.
To Reserve: Travel agent or call direct.
Minimum Stay: Required during special events.
Parking: Ample on-street & covered pay parking ($8 per day).
In-Room: Color cable TV, AC, telephone, coffee/tea-making facilities, maid, room & laundry service.
On-Premises: Laundry facilities.

Exercise/Health: Nearby gym, weights, Jacuzzi, sauna, steam.
Swimming: Pool on premises.
Sunbathing: At poolside.
Smoking: Permitted by the pool area & in smoking rooms.
Pets: Not permitted.
Handicap Access: Yes.
Children: Welcome.
Languages: English, Spanish, French.
Your Host: David.

IGLTA

Saharan Motor Hotel

Q-NET Gay-Friendly ♂

An Oasis in Los Angeles

The *Saharan Motor Hotel* is conveniently located in the heart of Hollywood. We're surrounded by famous restaurants, night clubs, theaters and shopping centers, not to mention many of the most popular gay night spots. Minutes from downtown LA, Universal Studios, Dodger Stadium, the Hollywood Bowl, the Chinese Theater and the Farmers' Market, the *Saharan* is equally convenient for both the business and the vacation traveler.

Address: 7212 Sunset Blvd, Los Angeles, CA 90046
Tel: (213) 874-6700, **Fax:** (213) 874-5163.

Type: Motel.
Clientele: Mostly straight clientele with a 20%-30% gay male following.
Transportation: Super shuttle from LAX.
To Gay Bars: 4 blocks to men's bars.
Rooms: 54 rooms & 8 suites with double, queen or king beds.

Bathrooms: All private.
Complimentary: Coffee all day.
Dates Open: All year.
High Season: May-September.
Rates: Summer $40-$75, rest of year $36-$70.
Credit Cards: MC, Visa, Amex, Diners.
Rsv'tns: Recommended.

To Reserve: Travel agent or call direct.
Parking: Adequate free parking.
In-Room: Maid service, satellite color TV, telephones & AC.
Swimming: Pool on premises or 20 minutes to ocean beach.

Sunbathing: At poolside or on beach.
Smoking: Permitted without restrictions.
Pets: Not permitted.
Handicap Access: No.
Children: Permitted.
Languages: English, Spanish, Japanese & Chinese.

San Vicente Inn & Resort

Q-NET Gay/Lesbian ♂

A Resort Paradise in West Hollywood

With all the careful attention of an inn and the superior amenities of a resort, the *San Vicente Inn & Resort* is the only gay-owned and -operated guesthouse in West Hollywood. The resort, which has been designated a historical landmark, features a variety of accommodations, from self-contained cottages (complete with refrigerator, microwave, sitting area and a private bath), to suites and rooms with both private and shared baths. Each room comes with cable television, private phone lines with answering machines, and most have air conditioning and VCRs.

Clothing is optional on the fine redwood sun deck, and the large solar-heated swimming pool offers a chance to cool off or cool down surrounded by sprays of colorful tropical flowers. The inn's comfortable environment and intimate atmosphere are reflected in the friendly, helpful management and staff. You can sit with other guests or find a secluded spot among the leafy foliage. And, for those who prefer to sightsee, there is always a band of hunky local boys frequenting the pool and clothing-optional sun decks. New to the complex is a hot tub and mini-gym to keep you fit and stress-free on your vacation. Continental breakfast is served daily on the garden patio.

Located minutes away from the heart of West Hollywood, we are just a few miles from Beverly Hills, Hollywood, Silverlake and Century City. Santa Monica Boulevard (Gay Street USA) is only steps away with its dozens of restaurants, cafes, bars, dance clubs, gymnasiums, shops and boutiques. Famous Sunset Strip and Sunset Plaza are two blocks from us, and the trendy Melrose district, the Pacific Design Center and Avenues of Design are all within walking distance. For gay movie buffs, there are hundreds of sites celebrating the Golden Years of Hollywood. On awarding us the Editor's Choice Award for the third consecutive year, Out & About said, "...a perfect in-town location, attentive management and a Key West-resort feel."

Address: 845 San Vicente Blvd, West Hollywood, CA 90069
Tel: (310) 854-6915, **Fax:** (310) 289-5929.

Type: Bed & breakfast guesthouse resort.
Clientele: Mostly men with women welcome
Transportation: Shuttle service from the airport or rental car.
To Gay Bars: 1 block.
Rooms: Suites: 2 penthouse, 2 executive, 4 poolside. 3 cottages, 5 bedrooms, 12 units.
Bathrooms: Private & shared.
Meals: Expanded continental breakfast.
Vegetarian: 5-minute walk.
Complimentary: Tea, coffee, juice.
Dates Open: All year.
Rates: $69-$199 plus tax.
Credit Cards: MC, Visa, Amex, Diners, Discover.
Rsv'tns: Required, but walk-ins OK.
To Reserve: Travel agent or call direct.
Parking: Parking on property & on street.
In-Room: Color TV, AC, telephones, kitchen, refrigerator, coffee/tea-making facilities & maid service.
Exercise/Health: Jacuzzi, mini-gym.
Swimming: Pool on premises.
Sunbathing: At poolside or on common sun decks.
Nudity: Permitted poolside.
Smoking: Permitted outside.
Pets: Not permitted.
Handicap Access: No.
Children: Not especially welcome.
Languages: English & Spanish.
Your Host: Terry & Rocky.

MENDOCINO COUNTY • CALIFORNIA — UNITED STATES

The Inn at Schoolhouse Creek

Q-NET Gay-Friendly ♀♂

This Country Environment is Relaxation at its Best

Facing the Pacific Ocean like a small, rural community, **The Inn at Schoolhouse Creek** has offered lodging to coastal visitors since the 1930's. Separate cottages and rooms in small buildings all have ocean views and private baths, and most have fireplaces. The inn offers a relaxed and comfortable atmosphere where you can enjoy your vacation on your own schedule. The charming, historic village of Mendocino with its many fine galleries and shops is only three miles away. The surrounding area offers rivers, harbors, beaches and spectacular state parks, as well as wine tasting in the nearby Anderson valley.

Address: 7051 N Highway One, Little River, CA 95456
Tel: (707) 937-5525, (800) 731-5525, **Fax:** (707) 937-2012.
E-mail: al@binnb.com **URL:** www.binnb.com

Type: Cottage inn.
Clientele: Mostly straight clientele with a gay & lesbian following
Transportation: Car is best.
Rooms: 7 rooms & 6 cottages with double or queen beds.
Bathrooms: Private: 5 bath & toilets, 8 shower & toilets.

Meals: Enhanced continental breakfast.
Complimentary: Tea & coffee in rooms. Snacks & beverages in ranch house
Dates Open: All year.
High Season: May-Sept.
Rates: Summer $65-$95, winter $75-$150.
Credit Cards: MC, Visa.
Rsv'tns: Suggested.

To Reserve: Call direct.
Minimum Stay: Required.
Parking: Ample off-street parking.
In-Room: Kitchen, refrigerator, coffee & tea-making facilities.
On-Premises: Lounge.
Exercise/Health: Hot tub, canoe, mountain bikes.

Swimming: Ocean nearby.
Sunbathing: At beach & on private sun decks.
Smoking: Permitted outside only.
Pets: Limited.
Handicap Access: No.
Children: Yes.
Languages: English.
Your Host: Al & Penny.

Sallie & Eileen's Place

Q-NET Women ♀

Sallie & Eileen's Place offers a safe and comfortable place for women near Mendocino, state parks, beaches, hiking, biking, horseback riding, river canoeing and a large women's community. The A-frame is a studio with fireplace and rockers, double bed and a large private bathroom with sunken tub. The cabin has lots of windows, and is wonderful in the rain. It also has a private yard and deck, a woodburning stove, and a loft bedroom with queen bed.

Address: Box 409, Mendocino, CA 95460
Tel: (707) 937-2028

Type: Studio cottage and a guesthouse.
Clientele: Women only
Transportation: Car.
To Gay Bars: 3 1/2 hours by car.
Rooms: 2 cottages with double or queen beds.
Bathrooms: All private bath/toilets.
Complimentary: Mints, special blend of coffee, regular & decaf.

Dates Open: All year.
High Season: Spring break, summer & Christmas.
Rates: A-frame $65, cabin $80 for 1-2, $15 each add'l woman, plus county tax.
Discounts: Weekly rates, mid-week specials during fall & winter.
Rsv'tns: Required.
To Reserve: Call direct.
Minimum Stay: 2 nights, 3-4 on holiday weekends.

Parking: Ample free off-street parking.
In-Room: Kitchen, refrigerator & coffee/tea-makers. Fireplace in A-frame. Ceiling fans in cabin.
Exercise/Health: Hot tub $5 a day per person.
Swimming: 3 miles to ocean and river beaches.
Sunbathing: A-frame has private sun deck. Cabin has sun deck and its own yard.

Nudity: Permitted anywhere on the land.
Smoking: Not permitted in A-frame, permitted in cabin.
Pets: Dogs in cabin only, $5 per day per dog.
Handicap Access: No.
Children: Permitted in cabin only. $10 to age 12. No boy children over 10.
Languages: English, Spanish & French.
Your Host: Sallie & Eileen.

Alexander Resort

Men ♂

Chill Out in Beautiful Palm Springs

Epitomizing the serenity of the casual Palm Springs lifestyle is *Alexander Resort*. Its spacious, mist-cooled grounds have fountain, pool, spa and a fabulous mountain view. Guests enjoy hospitality that is both gracious and friendly. Rooms are furnished in desert hues, with direct-dial phones, refrigerators and remote color TV with adult videos. Use our bikes to explore many bike paths or enjoy Village Fest every Thursday evening nearby. Complimentary breakfast and light lunch are served at poolside daily, with parties on major holidays.

Address: 598 Grenfall Rd, Palm Springs, CA 92264
Tel: (760) 327-6911 or (800) 448-6197.

Type: Garden court guesthouse.
Clientele: Men only.
Transportation: Car is best but bus & cabs are available. Free pick up from airport or bus.
To Gay Bars: 5-minute drive to gay bars, clubs & restaurants.
Rooms: 3 rooms, 3 studios with kitchens & 2 deluxe studios with kitchens & private patios. Twin or king beds in studios.
Bathrooms: 6 private bath/toilets & 2 private shower/toilets.

Meals: Expanded continental breakfast & light lunch.
Vegetarian: Available on request.
Complimentary: Fruit & in-room coffee & tea. Iced tea poolside.
Dates Open: All year.
High Season: December-June.
Rates: $79-$99 in season. Specials off season.
Discounts: 10% for 7 days, 15% for 14 days & 20% for 30 days. More for longer stays and off season.
Credit Cards: MC, VISA, Discover & Amex.

Rsv'tns: Strongly recommended!
To Reserve: Travel agent or call direct.
Minimum Stay: 2 nights on weekends in season. Longer for holiday periods.
Parking: Ample free off-street parking.
In-Room: Maid service, color TV, male video channel, VCR, telephone, AC/heat, kitchen, refrigerator, shower massage & coffee/tea service.
On-Premises: Laundry facilities, gas BBQ, & video library.

Exercise/Health: Jacuzzi, bicycles. Masseurs available at extra charge. Large gym nearby (passes available).
Swimming: In the pool.
Sunbathing: At poolside or on the patio.
Nudity: Permitted in all outside areas.
Smoking: Permitted without restrictions.
Pets: Not permitted.
Handicap Access: All facilities are at ground level.
Children: Not permitted.
Languages: English.
Your Host: Bud & Chuck.

Atrium/Vista Grande/Mirage

Q-NET Men ♂

If You Don't Stay at the Mirage, You'll Wish You Had!

Palm Springs's unique exotic male playground, *Atrium/Vista Grande/Mirage*, is set in a multi-level tropical environment. The giant, contoured boulders on which you can sunbathe nude, overlook the 18-man Jacuzzi and the waterfall grotto with its ring of fire. Two pools, a second Jacuzzi, outdoor mist system, gym, fire pit, bar, large natural stone BBQ, botanical gardens, open-beam ceilings and private patios are worth the trip.

Address: 574 Warm Sands Dr, Palm Springs, CA 92264
Tel: (760) 322-2404 or (800) 669-1069. **Fax:** (760) 320-1667.
E-mail: mirage4men@aol.com

continued next page

UNITED STATES — PALM SPRINGS · CALIFORNIA

Type: Private male resort.
Clientele: Men only
Transportation: Free pick up from the airport & bus.
To Gay Bars: Close to gay bars & restaurants.
Bathrooms: All private.
Complimentary: Coffee maker, fresh coffee, tea, cream, & sugar.
Dates Open: All year.
High Season: All year.
Rates: $79-$165.
Discounts: Airline personnel.
Credit Cards: All credit cards.
Rsv'tns: Recommended.
To Reserve: Travel agent or call direct.
Minimum Stay: 3 days on weekends.
Parking: Adequate, free, off-street parking.
In-Room: Color TV, VCR, laundry & maid service, AC, telephone, & kitchen.
On-Premises: Laundry facilities (free).
Exercise/Health: 2 Jacuzzis & micro-cool outdoor mist.
Swimming: 2 pools on premises.
Sunbathing: At poolside or on the sun decks.
Nudity: Permitted everywhere.
Smoking: Permitted without restrictions.
Pets: Not permitted.
Handicap Access: No.
Children: Not permitted.
Languages: English, German, Dutch, limited French.
Your Host: Bob & Alvin.

IGLTA

Avanti Resort Hotel   Men ♂

Hot Days, Hot Nights, Hot Men!!!

Avanti is a secluded resort at the foot of the San Jacinto Mountains and set in an environment of lush gardens, with large heated pool and spa, and an outdoor Kool Mist system. Fully-equipped kitchens, VCRs and microwaves are just a few of the many amenities offered. The resort is within walking distance of downtown Palm Springs, where guests can explore Palm Canyon Drive, a panoply of shops, restaurants and galleries, theatres and many gay establishments. Please join us for a memorable vacation.

Address: 715 San Lorenzo Rd, Palm Springs, CA 92264
Tel: (760) 325-9723, (800) 572-2779, **Fax:** (760) 325-4357.

Type: Hotel.
Clientele: Men only
Transportation: Car is best, bus, taxi.
To Gay Bars: 3 blocks or a 5-minute walk.
Rooms: 5 rooms & 9 suites with queen or king beds.
Bathrooms: All private bath/toilets.
Meals: Continental breakfast served daily.
Vegetarian: 10-min. walk.
Complimentary: Coffee, iced tea & popcorn.
Dates Open: All year.
High Season: October to June.
Rates: $49-$129 per night per room.
Discounts: Stay 7 nights for reduced rate.
Credit Cards: MC, Visa, Amex, Discover.
Rsv'tns: Required or recommended.
To Reserve: Travel agent or call direct.
Minimum Stay: 2 days on weekends, 3 days on holidays.
Parking: Adequate off-street parking.
In-Room: Color cable TV, VCR, video tape library, AC, telephone, ceiling fans, kitchen, refrigerator, coffee & tea-making facilities, maid service.
Exercise/Health: Gold's Gym 3 miles, local gym 4 blocks.
Swimming: Heated pool.
Sunbathing: At poolside, on patio.
Nudity: Permitted everywhere.
Pets: Not permitted.
Handicap Access: Mostly.
Children: Not permitted.
Languages: English.

Bee Charmer Inn   Q-NET Women ♀

The Palm Springs Private Hotel for Women

Created exclusively for women in 1993, the *Bee Charmer Inn* takes pride in providing an atmosphere of comfort and privacy. Soft, southwestern pastels accent your room, while deep colors of the desert landscape surround you at poolside. Restau-

252   FERRARI GUIDES™

rants and nightclubs that fit your lifestyle, unlimited shopping opportunities, hiking in the Indian canyons, tennis and golf are a few of the many attractions located minutes from the inn. An occasional holiday BBQ or cocktail hors d'oeuvres create a chance to make friends from all over the world.

Address: 1600 E Palm Canyon Dr, Palm Springs, CA 92264
Tel: (760) 778-5883. **E-mail:** beecharmps@aol.com

Type: Private women's resort.
Clientele: Women only
Transportation: Rental car from Palm Springs Regional Airport (approx 3 miles), taxi, bus.
To Gay Bars: 1/2 mile walk to 10 min drive to gay bars & restaurants.
Rooms: 14 rooms with queen or king beds, sleeper sofas.
Bathrooms: All private.
Meals: Expanded continental breakfast.
Dates Open: All year.
High Season: Sept 1-July 5.
Rates: $75-$99 high season, $55-$79 low season.
Discounts: On extended stays, please inquire.
Credit Cards: All major credit cards accepted.
Rsv'tns: Recommended.
To Reserve: Travel agent or call direct.
Minimum Stay: During holidays & special events.
Parking: Free on-site parking.
In-Room: Color cable TV, telephone, AC, refrigerator, micowave, maid service.
Swimming: Pool on premises.
Sunbathing: Poolside.
Nudity: Tops optional.
Smoking: Permitted outside only.
Languages: English.
Your Host: Denise.

Canyon Club Hotel   Men ♂

Palm Springs' Largest Exclusively Gay Hotel

Canyon Club is large enough to be exciting, quiet enough to be relaxing, but private enough to be clothing optional. With 32 rooms, there are enough people around to make for friendly camaraderie day and night. Recently renovated, the rooms are clean, comfortable, and uncluttered. With air conditioning (not evaporative coolers); remote-controlled, color, cable TV; telephone; and refrigerator, the rooms are highly appealing. There are also several 24-hour, in-house, all-male video channels. Some rooms are available with full kitchens and some have private patios. Ample common areas, including a large lobby with a cozy fireplace for cool fall and winter evenings, await those times that you'd prefer to spend in the company of your fellow guests.

The 50-foot pool is surrounded by a private, spacious, sunny courtyard, where you can relax the day away, meet the other guests, read, relax, and enjoy the views. You can work on the perfect tan — with or without tan lines; the entire facility (except the lobby) is clothing optional. Both the sauna and steam room are especially invigorating on cool fall and winter evenings or after a hard day around the pool. The 16-man capacity spa is among the largest of any gay hotel in Palm Springs, and a full gym is available so you'll be sure not to miss your workout.

In the evening, take a short walk to the center of downtown Palm Springs where you're sure to find restaurants or shops to your liking. *Canyon Club* is

continued next page

within five to 15 minutes drive of all the gay restaurants and nightspots of Palm Springs and adjacent cities, and is about a one-hour drive from Ontario International Airport and a two-hour drive from Los Angeles or San Diego. http://www.tenpct.com/canyonclub

Address: 960 N Palm Canyon Dr, Palm Springs, CA 92262
Tel: (760) 322-4367 or (800) 295-2582, **Fax:** (760) 322-4024.
E-mail: CanyonClub@tenpct.com

Type: Hotel.
Clientele: Men only
Transportation: Car is best, one mile from airport.
To Gay Bars: 5-10 minute drive.
Rooms: 32 rooms with double, queen or king beds.
Bathrooms: 30 private bath/toilet/showers, 2 private shower/toilets.
Meals: Continental breakfast.

Dates Open: All year.
High Season: Spring & fall.
Rates: $59-$99.
Discounts: On stay of 5 nights.
Credit Cards: MC, Visa, Amex, Discover.
Rsv'tns: Recommended.
To Reserve: Call direct.
Minimum Stay: Most weekends & holidays.
Parking: Ample free off-street parking.

In-Room: Color cable TV, AC, telephone, refrigerators & maid service. Some have full kitchens & private patios. Two in-house video channels.
On-Premises: Lobby with fireplace.
Exercise/Health: Full gym, Jacuzzi, dry sauna & steam room. Gym passes available.

Swimming: Large pool on premises.
Sunbathing: At poolside & on the patio.
Nudity: Clothing optional everywhere except lobby.
Smoking: Permitted. No non-smoking rooms.
Pets: Not permitted.
Handicap Access: No.
Children: Not welcome.
Languages: English.

Chestnutz

Q-NET Men ♂

The Luxury of Fantasy

Each morning begins with a continental or full breakfast made to order which you may enjoy either poolside or in the privacy of your shaded patio. Later, you can choose to nude sunbathe beneath our cooling outdoor mist, take a refreshing swim, enjoy a video or book from our private library, or engage a new friend in a board or card game. If a home-cooked meal is in your plans, you will appreciate our fully appointed gas kitchen units with microwaves or BBQ grills — and you can dine in your suite or out on your private patio in the shadow of the spectacular mountain sunset.

Centrally located in the heart of the "HOT" San Lorenzo district, *Chestnutz* is a short walk to downtown Palm Springs where famous restaurants and shopping await you. Stroll through an array of antique shops, sip espresso at a sidewalk cafe, or try your luck at the new Spa Casino. If it's a more high-energy workout you're looking for, grab a pass to Golds Gym, or bike or roller-blade down the newly completed bike path to Cathedral City. A five-minute drive will take you to the gay nightlife in Palm Springs, or to the hiking and exploring adventures found in the historical Indian Canyons. And what better way to top off a long day than in our large tiled Jacuzzi under the bright desert stars, comparing notes with other guests. As the newest and finest in private resorts, *Chestnutz* offers its guests all of the amenities and comforts you have come to expect. Escape reality to the luxury of fantasy at *Chestnutz*.

Address: 641 San Lorenzo Rd, Palm Springs, CA 92264
Tel: (760) 325-5269, (800) 621-6973, **Fax:** (760) 320-9535.
E-mail: chestnutz1@aol.com

Type: Resort.
Clientele: Men only
Transportation: Car is best. Free pick up at airport or bus.
To Gay Bars: 6 blocks to 1 mile, a 15-min walk, a 5-min bike ride.
Rooms: 6 queen & 6 king rooms, 2-BR suites.
Bathrooms: All private.
Meals: Full & continental breakfast. Sunday brunch.
Vegetarian: Available on request.

Complimentary: Morning newspaper, assorted cold beverages & fresh fruit poolside, 24-hr coffee/tea station, evening hors d'oeuvres
Dates Open: Year round.
High Season: Jan-May.
Rates: Summer $49-$69. Winter $89-$119.
Discounts: 7 days or longer & VIP guests.
Credit Cards: MC, Visa, Amex, Discover.
Rsv'tns: Preferred.

Minimum Stay: 2 nights on weekends & 3-4 nights on holidays.
Parking: Ample off-street parking.
In-Room: Color cable TV, VCR, AC, telephone, ceiling fans, refrigerator, maid service. King rooms & 2-BR suites have kitchens.
On-Premises: Video/book/game library.
Exercise/Health: Large Jacuzzi (gym & steam planned for 1998). Bikes by

reservation.
Swimming: Large heated pool on premises.
Sunbathing: Everywhere.
Nudity: Clothing tolerated.
Smoking: Permitted.
Pets: By pre-arrangement, pet-rent applies per visit.
Handicap Access: Full access except in bedrooms.
Children: Not permitted.
Languages: English.
Your Host: Paul & Jim.

IGLTA

Columns Resort

Men ♂

A Man's Private Paradise

The *Columns* provides a relaxing, comfortable setting to enjoy in solitude or with new friends. Our newly-decorated rooms surround a large, heated pool and spa, in a tropical courtyard. Clothing is optional at all times, and our Cool Mist and air conditioning ensure your total comfort while you enjoy our mountain views. Each spacious room includes a kitchen and dining area, coffee maker, private bath, phone, color cable TV, VCR and firm, queen-sized bed. Our large tape collection is available at your leisure. We pride ourselves on our tranquil, sharing environment and cleanliness. Come, relax with us.

Address: 537 Grenfall Rd, Palm Springs, CA 92264
Tel: (760) 325-0655, (800) 798-0655, **Fax:** (760) 322-1436.
E-mail: rescolumns@aol.com

Type: Private resort hotel.
Clientele: Men only
Transportation: Car is best. Free pick up from airport, train or bus with prior

arrangement.
To Gay Bars: 3-4 blocks to men's bars.
Rooms: 7 studios with queen beds & kitchens.

Bathrooms: All private shower/toilets.
Meals: Expanded continental breakfast provided daily.
Complimentary: Coffee/

cream/sugar in rooms. Soft drinks, iced tea, lemonade & snacks available. Icebreakers 1/2x wk

continued next page

UNITED STATES

Dates Open: All year.
High Season: Jan-Jun.
Rates: $65-$95.
Discounts: 10% on 6 days & to repeat guests. 1 day free for 7 or more nights.
Credit Cards: MC, Visa, Amex, Discover.
Rsv'tns: Highly recommended!

To Reserve: Travel agent or call direct.
Minimum Stay: 2 nights on weekends, longer on some holidays.
Parking: Ample, free, off-street parking.
In-Room: Maid service, AC, remote color cable TV & VCR, kitchen, refrigerator, coffee/tea-making facilities,

telephone, ceiling fans, video tape library.
On-Premises: Barbeque, bicycles, fax/copier, modem, lap counter at pool.
Exercise/Health: Jacuzzi, bicycles, micro-cool outdoor mist, add'l charge for massage. Gym passes available.
Swimming: Pool on pre-

mises.
Sunbathing: At poolside.
Nudity: Permitted inside compound.
Smoking: Permitted without restrictions.
Pets: Not permitted.
Handicap Access: No.
Children: Not permitted.
Languages: English.
Your Host: Jack & Blaine.

PALM SPRINGS • CALIFORNIA

Desert Paradise Hotel

Q-NET Men ♂

An Ambiance of Style & Sophistication

Lush garden settings and majestic mountain views create the mood at *Desert Paradise Hotel.* Our attention to detail and dedication to service afford each guest a truly memorable experience. Stylish accommodations include private bath, telephone, color TV, VCR, air conditioning and kitchens. Exotic grounds, a poolside mix of music and laughter, and proximity to the excitement of Palm Springs combine to meet your every expectation. This is a gentleman's resort of the highest caliber, representing the best the desert has to offer!

Address: 615 Warm Sands Dr, Palm Springs, CA 92264
Tel: (760) 320-5650, (800) 342-7635, **Fax:** (760) 320-0273.

Type: Hotel.
Clientele: Men only
Transportation: Car or taxi. 5 minute taxi ride to hotel.
To Gay Bars: 5 minutes by car to bars.
Rooms: 10 rooms & 2 suites with queen or king beds.
Bathrooms: All private shower/toilets.
Meals: Fresh fruit expanded continental breakfast.

Vegetarian: Available upon request.
Complimentary: Snacks, beverages. Beverages available with breakfast.
Dates Open: All year.
High Season: Oct-Jun.
Rates: $75-$135, subject to change.
Discounts: Weekly rates, please inquire.
Credit Cards: All major cards including MC, VISA, Amex, Diners & Discover.
Rsv'tns: Preferable to as-

sure availability.
To Reserve: Travel agent or call direct.
Minimum Stay: 2 nights on weekends, longer on some holidays.
Parking: Ample free off-street parking.
In-Room: Color cable TV, VCR, film library, AC, maid service, telephone, kitchen, microwave, refrigerator.
On-Premises: Fax, laundry facility for guests, large poolside patio area, lush garden settings.

Exercise/Health: Spa, nearby gym.
Swimming: Pool on premises.
Sunbathing: At poolside.
Nudity: Permitted everywhere.
Smoking: Permitted except in lobby.
Pets: Small pets permitted with restrictions. Inquire first.
Handicap Access: No.
Children: No children.
Languages: English.
Your Host: Basil & Larry.

FERRARI GUIDES™

El Mirasol Villas

Gay/Lesbian ♀♂

Over 20 Years as One of Palm Springs' Premier Gay Resorts

Returning again and again to the villas built by Howard Hughes in the 1940s, our established multi-national clientele enjoy reserve, class, the finest service and a pleasant ambiance behind the walls and gates of *El Mirasol*. Guests will find our uniformed staff dedicated to a high level of service. That's why *El Mirasol Villas* has been considered one of Palm Springs' premier gay resorts. Join us poolside for breakfast and lunch. The fact that two thirds of our guests are repeat visitors and one third are by enthusiastic referral, speaks for itself.

Address: 525 Warm Sands Dr,, Palm Springs, CA 92264
Tel: (760) 327-5913, (800) 327-2985, **Fax:** (760) 325-8931.
E-mail: mirasol@mail.gte.net **URL:** http://home1.gte.net/mirasol

Type: Resort hotel.
Clientele: Gay men, lesbians & bisexuals
Transportation: Drive. Fly to: Palm Springs Regional Airport (free pick up), Ontario or Los Angeles airports.
To Gay Bars: A few blocks to major nightclub & neighborhood bars.
Rooms: 12 king & queen studios, 1- & 2-bedroom suites.
Bathrooms: All private.
Meals: Continental breakfast & lunch.
Vegetarian: By arrangement.
Complimentary: Lemonade, iced tea, bottled spring water.
Dates Open: All year.
Rates: $95-$275.
Discounts: On extended stays.
Credit Cards: All major credit cards.
Rsv'tns: Recommended.
To Reserve: Travel agent or direct.
Minimum Stay: Required at times.
Parking: Ample, free off-street parking.
In-Room: Color cable TVs & VCRs in bed- & living rooms. AC, telephone, some kitchens (at least fridge & microwave), maid service. Some studios have private patios.
On-Premises: Laundry facilities, video library, fax, copier. Fireplace, library, games & jigsaw puzzles in Common Room.
Exercise/Health: Jacuzzi, bicycles, discounted passes to gyms. Massage by appointment.
Swimming: 2 pools on premises.
Sunbathing: At poolside, on private sun decks or on patio.
Nudity: Permitted in & around 1 of the pools.
Smoking: Permitted.
Pets: Welcomed, fee.
Children: Not permitted.
Languages: English, French.
Your Host: Hugh.

IGLTA

Inn Exile

Men ♂

Where Being Gay Is a Way of Life

Close your eyes and fantasize about a place where the open air calls you to the sparkling pool in the desert sun. Breathe in the dramatic view of towering mountains, while being refreshed by our outdoor mist cooling system. At *Inn Exile*, clothing is always optional. There's no need to miss your workout...our gymnasium is here for you. Call or write for brochure.

Address: 545 Warm Sands Drive, Palm Springs, CA 92264
Tel: (760) 327-6413, (800) 962-0186, **Fax:** (760) 320-5745.
E-mail: innexile@earthlink.net **URL:** http://www.innexile.com

Type: Resort.
Clientele: Men only
Transportation: Car is best.
To Gay Bars: Three minutes by car, a 10 minute-walk.
Rooms: 26 rooms with king beds.
Bathrooms: All private full baths.
Dates Open: All year.
Rates: $85-$115.
Discounts: For 7 nights or more.
Credit Cards: MC, Visa, Amex, Discover, Diners, Carte Blanche.
Rsv'tns: Required.
To Reserve: Travel agent or call direct.
Minimum Stay: Required at times. Please inquire.
Parking: Adequate, free off-street and on-street parking.
In-Room: Color TV, VCR, video tape library, AC, houseman service, telephone & refrigerator.
On-Premises: TV lounge.
Exercise/Health: Gym, weights, Jacuzzi, steam room.
Swimming: Pools on premises.
Sunbathing: At poolside.
Nudity: Permitted without restriction.
Smoking: Permitted without restriction.
Pets: Not permitted.
Handicap Access: Yes.
Children: Not permitted.
Languages: English.
Your Host: John & Carter.

IGLTA

INNdulge Palm Springs

Men ♂

Warm Sands' Newest Playground for Men

Pamper, pleasure, and gratify yourself at Warm Sands' newest resort for gay men. *INNdulge*, located in Palm Springs' premier gay area of 15 gay resorts, has 20 large rooms surrounding a secluded, private courtyard with an expansive 24-hour heated pool and a large whirlpool spa. Of course, clothing is forever optional! Spoil yourself with a complimentary Euro-breakfast of croissants, juice, breads, and coffee and daily afternoon "vins et fromages" by the pool. Inquire about the weekday specials — and summer rates, which can be up to 50% off.

Address: 601 Grenfall Rd, Palm Springs, CA 92264
Tel: (760) 327-1408, (800) 833-5675, **Fax:** (760) 327-7273.
URL: http://www.inndulge.com

Type: Inn.
Clientele: Men only
Transportation: Car is best. Free pick up from airport (5 blocks away).
To Gay Bars: 5 blocks, a 10-min. walk, a 3-min. drive.
Rooms: 18 rooms & 2 suites with king beds.
Bathrooms: 20 private shower/toilets.
Meals: Continental breakfast.
Vegetarian: None available.

Complimentary: Afternoon poolside wine & cheese service 5:00pm-6:00pm.
Dates Open: All year.
High Season: January-May.
Rates: Winter $85-$125, summer $59-$99.
Discounts: Summer discounts up to 50%.
Credit Cards: MC, Visa, Amex, Discover.
To Reserve: Travel agent or call direct.

Parking: Ample free off-street parking.
In-Room: Color cable TV, VCR, AC, coffee/tea-making facilities, telephone, refrigerator, maid & laundry service. Some rooms with kitchen.
On-Premises: Video tape library, laundry facilities.
Exercise/Health: Nearby gym, weights.
Swimming: Pool on premises.

Sunbathing: At poolside.
Nudity: Permitted throughout pool area & courtyard.
Smoking: Permitted.
Pets: Small, well-trained pets permitted.
Handicap Access: No.
Children: No.
Languages: English, French.
Your Host: John & Jean-Guy.

IGLTA

InnTrigue

Men ♂

The Two Worlds of InnTrigue Await You

You'll be intrigued by these two deluxe adjoining properties in the heart of Palm Springs. They have spacious, colorfully landscaped courtyards and magnificent mountain vistas. Relax around the totally private, CLOTHING OPTIONAL sparkling pools and secluded spas of *InnTrigue*. The poolside one- and two-bedroom suites have private patios, fully equipped kitchens, king-sized beds, remote cable TV with VCR, and an extensive video library. Complimentary Gold's Gym passes are available. Out & About Editor's Choice Award.

Address: 526 Warm Sands Dr, Palm Springs, CA 92264
Tel: (760) 323-7505, (800) 798-8781, **Fax:** (760) 323-1055.
URL: www.gaytraveling.com/inntrigue

Type: Private male resort.
Clientele: Men only.
Transportation: Car is best. Free pick up from the airport or bus station.
To Gay Bars: Within walking distance of gay bars & restaurants.
Rooms: 28 rooms.
Bathrooms: All private.
Meals: Continental breakfast & evening social gathering.
Complimentary: Coffee & tea. Occasional cookouts, large cocktail parties & holiday dinners.
Dates Open: All year.
Rates: $75-$135.
Discounts: For extended stays. Please inquire.
Credit Cards: All major credit cards.
Rsv'tns: Recommended.
To Reserve: Travel agent or call direct.
Minimum Stay: 2 nights on weekends.
Parking: Adequate free off-street parking.
In-Room: Color cable TV, VCR, male video tape library, AC, phone, kitchen, refrigerator, coffee/tea-makers, houseman service.
On-Premises: Laundry facilities, cool-mist system, security access gate.
Exercise/Health: 2 Jacuzzis, pool table. Complimentary Gold's Gym day passes, massage by appt., bicycles.
Swimming: 2 pools on premises.
Sunbathing: At poolside & on patios.
Nudity: Permitted everywhere.
Smoking: Permitted without restrictions.
Pets: Inquire.
Handicap Access: Yes.
Children: Not permitted.
Languages: English.
Your Host: Michael, Terry & Don.

IGLTA

La Posada de Las Palmas

Men ♂

Return in Style to Old Palm Springs

SEE SPECIAL PAGE 16 COLOR SECTION

Desert home of many Hollywood stars, the Las Palmas area of Palm Springs is also home to *La Posada de Las Palmas,* an Old Palm Springs-style hotel reflecting the area's Spanish Colonial, Mediterranean and Old California heritage. Nine studios and rooms surround a large pool and landscaped patio and, thanks to nearby Mt. Jacinto, many have dramatic mountain views. All studios and suites have direct-dial phones, color TV, coffee-makers, refrigerators and most have full kitchens. Continental breakfast is served poolside or in the comfortable reception area. Private and quiet, we're walking distance to restaurants, bars, shopping, and the center of Palm Springs village.

Address: 120 W. Vereda Sur, Palm Springs, CA 92262
Tel: (760) 323-1402, (888) 411-4949,
Fax: (760) 416-3337.

Type: Hotel inn.
Clientele: Men only
Transportation: Car is best. Free pick up from airport.
To Gay Bars: 15 blocks, 1 mile, a 15 min walk, a 6 min drive.
Rooms: 3 rooms, 6 studios with king or queen beds.
Bathrooms: All private bath/shower/toilets.
Meals: Expanded continental breakfast.
Vegetarian: Available by request. Restaurants serving vegetarian food are nearby.
Complimentary: Bottled water, iced tea available all day. Weekend cocktail happy hour.
Dates Open: All year.
High Season: Oct-May.
Rates: High season: $79-$129, low season: $49-$89.
Discounts: Ask about 7th night free on 6-night stay. Call for extended stay rates & Grand Opening specials.
Credit Cards: MC, Visa, Amex, Bancard.
Rsv'tns: Required.
To Reserve: Travel agent or call direct.
Minimum Stay: 2 nights, 3 nights on some holidays. Call for single night availability.

continued next page

INN PLACES® 1998

259

Parking: Ample off-street parking.	**On-Premises:** TV lounge, laundry facilities, fax.	**Sunbathing:** Poolside.	pets welcome with prior arrangement.
In-Room: Telephone, AC, color cable TV, refrigerator, coffee & tea-making facilities, maid & laundry service. VCR available, some rooms have kitchen.	**Exercise/Health:** Bicycles. Nearby hiking, tennis, gym, weights, Jacuzzi, massage. Gym passes available. **Swimming:** Large, heated pool on premises.	**Nudity:** Permitted in pool area. **Smoking:** Permitted in all outside areas. Non-smoking rooms available. **Pets:** Small, well-behaved	**Handicap Access:** No. **Children:** No. **Languages:** English. **Your Host:** Thom & Rob. IGLTA

Sago Palms   Men ♂

Your Home in the Desert

A private, clothing-optional resort in the Warm Sands area, the *Sago Palms* offers peaceful and secluded surroundings for total relaxation. Step through our gates and find lush tropical gardens with statuary and beautiful flowering plants shaded by tall palm trees.

Our units surround a rectangular full-sized swimming pool with a misting system to lower temperatures on those really hot days. Off to the side in its own shaded tropical setting is our Jacuzzi/spa where you can relax and enjoy the heated and soothing bubbling waters. Choose from either our one-bedroom batchelor unit, studios, or suites. Our two-bedroom unit is perfect for couples travelling together who might want to share a bath to save on expenses. Our rooms have all the amenities of home — king-sized beds, TV/VCRs, telephones and full baths. The studios come with a full kitchen and the suites have separate bedrooms and living rooms with fireplaces. Each unit is equipped with its own air conditioning and heating, and most units have semi-private rear patios.

The complex includes a weight/workout area and we also provide free day passes to the local gym. Bicycles are also available for exploring Palm Springs. An extensive continental breakfast is provided each morning by the pool. Our tremendous library of movies is here for your enjoyment, including many of classics, new releases and, of course, an extensive library of adult movies, as well. Unique among the Palm Springs resorts, we are small enough to get to know our guests and we have many repeat customers. Many of them tell us that they consider this their "home in the desert." We are proud to have made many lasting friendships from all over the world. Come, join the Sago Palms family.

Address: 595 Thornhill Rd, Palm Springs, CA 92264
Tel: (800) 626-SAGO (7246), (760) 323-0224, **Fax:** (760) 320-3200.
E-mail: sagopalmca@aol.com **URL:** www.webworksps.com/sago/

Type: Guesthouse.
Clientele: Men only
Transportation: Car is best. Free pickup from airport or bus.
To Gay Bars: 1 mile, a 10 min walk to gay bars & restaurants.
Rooms: 6 suites with king beds.
Bathrooms: All private bath/toilets.
Meals: Continental breakfast.
Vegetarian: 2 natural food restaurants nearby. We have had vegan couples stay here with no problem.
Complimentary: Small chocolates or treats in rooms occasionally.
Dates Open: All year.
High Season: Oct-May.
Rates: High season $79-$149, low season $59-$109.
Discounts: Midweek & on extended stays.
Credit Cards: MC, Visa, Amex, Bancard, Discover.
Rsv'tns: Required.
To Reserve: Call direct.
Minimum Stay: 2 nights, 5 nights on holidays.
Parking: Ample off-street parking.
In-Room: Phone, color cable TV, VCR, AC, ceiling fans, refrigerator, coffee/tea-making facilities & maid service. 5 suites have kitchens, 1 suite has microwave & small fridge.
On-Premises: Laundry facilities, video tape library.
Exercise/Health: Gym, weights, Jacuzzi, massage.
Swimming: Pool on premises. Nearby pool & water park.
Sunbathing: At poolside.
Nudity: Permitted in the compound.
Smoking: Permitted anywhere outside. All rooms are non-smoking.
Pets: Permitted on case by case basis.
Handicap Access: Yes.
Children: No.
Languages: English, Spanish.
Your Host: David & Ben.

Santiago Resort

Men ♂

Palm Springs' Most Spectacular Private Men's Resort

We're winner's of Out & About's 1997 Editor's Choice Award for "exceptionally notable & distinctive gay lodging...a men's guesthouse that reflects stylish sophistication," and *Genre Magazine* says we're "...one of Palm Spring's most refined gay resorts," voting us "the most elegant men's guesthouse." Exotically landscaped, secluded grounds provide a peaceful enclave for the discriminating traveller. Enjoy magnificent mountain views from our terrace level, while an oversized diving pool, a 12-man spa and an outdoor cooling mist system complete the setting. Our poolside, courtyard or terrace suites and studios, featuring king-sized beds with feather duvet covers, superior quality towels and linens and shower massages, set the *Santiago's* standard of excellence and luxury. And clothing is forever optional...

Address: 650 San Lorenzo Rd, Palm Springs, CA 92264-8108
Tel: (760) 322-1300, (800) 710-7729, **Fax:** (760) 416-0347.
E-mail: santiagops@earthlink.net **URL:** www.prinet.com/santiago

Type: Hotel resort.
Clientele: Men only
Transportation: Car is best. Free pick up from airport or bus.
To Gay Bars: A 10-minute walk or a 3-minute drive.
Rooms: 10 rooms, 13 suites with king beds.
Bathrooms: Private: 19 shower/toilets, 4 bath/toilet/showers.
Meals: Expanded continental breakfast, lunch.
Vegetarian: Available.
Complimentary: Courtyard luncheon, Gold's gym passes.
Dates Open: All year.
High Season: Jan-May.
Rates: $99-$129.

continued next page

UNITED STATES

Discounts: On extended stays.
Credit Cards: MC, Visa, Amex, Discover.
Rsv'tns: Recommended.
To Reserve: Travel agent or call direct.
Minimum Stay: Required at times, please inquire.
Parking: Ample free off-street parking.
In-Room: Color cable TV, VCR, AC, telephone, refrigerator, microwave, houseman service.
On-Premises: Video tape library, fax, photocopier, laundry facilities.
Exercise/Health: Jacuzzi, nearby gym.
Swimming: Diving pool on premises.
Sunbathing: At poolside.
Nudity: Permitted without restriction.
Smoking: Permitted without restriction.
Pets: Not permitted.
Handicap Access: Yes.
Children: No.
Languages: English, French.

Triangle Inn   Men ♂

Everything... Except Ordinary!

PALM SPRINGS • CALIFORNIA

Finally... a secluded resort geared to the gay male traveler that will exceed your expectations. As you pass through the gate to our sun-drenched tropical gardens, you will be allured by the refreshing, sparkling pool and soothing Jacuzzi.

You can select from our studios, junior, one- and two-bedroom suites. For your added pleasure, our rooms include all the modern conveniences of today: remote color TV & VCR, stereo with CD & tape players, private telephones, large private baths, complete with oversized fluffy towels and blow dryers. All rooms also have central air conditioning, offering refrigerated air, evaporative cooling and heat systems. The junior, one- and two-bedroom suites come with fully-equipped kitchens and the studios offer a kitchenette. All just steps from our sparkling, heated pool and soothing Jacuzzi... where swimsuits are optional. Enjoy our own daily "Palm Springs" breakfast buffet served poolside. Call for a free color brochure.

The *Triangle Inn* is an experience well worth repeating again and again. It is a delightful feast for the eyes and a soothing embrace for the troubled spirit, a place where one can make new friends or surrender to peace and solitude. Either way, there is always something here to remind us that life is worth living. Visitors return home with recharged batteries, ready once more to face the challenges of everyday life. The *Triangle Inn* is an experience that will linger on long after the end of the vacation.

Address: 555 San Lorenzo, Palm Springs, CA 92264
Tel: (760) 322-7993, (800) 732-7455, **Fax:** (760) 322-0784.

Type: Inn.
Clientele: Men only.
Transportation: Free pick up from Palm Springs airport.
To Gay Bars: 5- to 10-minute drive to all gay bars.
Rooms: 3 rooms & 6 suites with queen or king beds.
Bathrooms: All private bath/toilets.
Meals: Expanded continental breakfast.
Dates Open: All year.
High Season: October 1- June 21.
Rates: $89-$199. Inquire for summer value rates.
Discounts: Inquire.
Credit Cards: MC, Visa, Amex.
Rsv'tns: Required.
To Reserve: Travel agent or call direct.
Minimum Stay: Inquire for specific minimums.
Parking: Ample free off-street parking.

In-Room: AC, maid service, telephone, stereo, CD, color TV, VCR, kitchen & refrigerator.
On-Premises: Video tape library.
Exercise/Health: Jacuzzi,

massage by appointment & bicycles.
Swimming: Pool on premises.
Sunbathing: At poolside with microcool outdoor cooling system.

Nudity: Permitted at poolside.
Smoking: Permitted without restrictions.
Pets: Not permitted.
Handicap Access: Inquire.

Children: Not permitted.
Languages: English.
Your Host: Kevin & Matthew.

IGLTA

The Villa
Men ♂

Stay Where the Fun Never Sets!

Stay where the fun is at the desert's "favorite party hotel." Always popular, *The Villa* is Palm Springs' largest full-service resort, with 45 rooms spread bungalow-style over 2.5 acres of lush gardens and palms. Dine alfresco or inside our landmark hacienda at our acclaimed restaurant. Enjoy the Sunday T-dance and live entertainment at our poolside bar, or just enjoy the view of Palm Springs' hottest men. The pool, 10-man spa and sauna are open all night. Our new 2.5-acre playgorund opens in 1998.

Address: 67-670 Carey Rd, Cathedral City, CA 92234
Tel: (760) 328-7211. Reservations (800) VILLA OK, **Fax:** (760) 321-1463.
E-mail: reservations@thevilla.com **URL:** http://thevilla.com

Type: Resort with pool bar, restaurant, Sunday T-dance.
Clientele: Men only
Transportation: Car or cab.
To Gay Bars: 1/2 mile by car to men's bars.
Rooms: 45 rooms with double or queen beds.
Bathrooms: All private.
Meals: Continental breakfast.

Dates Open: All year.
High Season: Jan-July 4.
Rates: Off season $45-$85, in season $49-$99, holidays $100-$120.
Discounts: Off season: 1 night free on 2-night stay. In season: Tue, Wed, Thurs free with 2 prior nights stay.
Credit Cards: MC, VISA & Amex.
Rsv'tns: Recommended.
To Reserve: Travel agent or call direct.

Minimum Stay: 2-4 days on holidays.
Parking: Ample off-street parking.
In-Room: Separate entrances, remote control color TV/radio, direct-dial phone, maid services, refrigerators, microwaves, AC.
On-Premises: Meeting room, fireplace dining room, public telephone.
Exercise/Health: Sauna, Jacuzzi, massage.
Swimming: Pool on premises.
Sunbathing: At poolside or on lawn.
Smoking: Permitted. Non-smoking rooms available.
Pets: Not permitted.
Handicap Access: Please inquire.
Children: Not permitted.
Languages: English, limited Spanish.

Applewood Inn and Restaurant

Q-NET Gay-Friendly

SEE SPECIAL PAGE 17 COLOR SECTION

Russian River's Preeminent B&B

Once a mission-style retreat in the redwoods, *Applewood* has been transformed into an elegant country inn and restaurant that has become the darling of food critics and editors steering their readers to romantic getaways. "If you can't spend the night — *Applewood* is truly one of the finest inns in the wine country — dinner is the next best excuse for a visit," noted *The Press Democrat* in August, 1997. The beauty of the redwoods, apple trees and vineyards...the relaxing pool and Jacuzzi...the stylish rooms with European down comforters...the pleasure of sitting by the fire or reading in the library...the marvelous food in a firelit dining room...your willing hosts and two tail-wagging dogs...all await your arrival at this contemporary Eden.

Address: 13555 Hwy 116, Guerneville, CA 95446
Tel: (707) 869-9093, (800) 555-8509.
E-mail: stay@applewoodinn.com **URL:** http://applewoodinn.com

Type: Inn with restaurant serving 4-course dinners.
Clientele: Mostly straight clientele with a gay & lesbian following
Transportation: Car is best. Free pick up from Santa Rosa airport.
To Gay Bars: 5-minute drive to men's/women's bars.
Rooms: 10 rooms & 6 suites with queen beds.
Bathrooms: All private.
Meals: Full breakfast included, dinner offered to guests & public Tuesdays thru Saturdays.
Vegetarian: Upon request with 1-day notice.
Complimentary: Chocolates on pillows, coffee and tea all day.
Dates Open: All year.
High Season: Apr-Nov.
Rates: Doubles $145-$250.
Credit Cards: MC, Visa, Amex, Discover.
Rsv'tns: Recommended. Essential for dinner.
To Reserve: Travel agent or call direct.
Minimum Stay: 1 night midweek, 2 nights on weekends, 3 nights on holiday weekends.
Parking: Ample, free off-street parking.
In-Room: Color TV, phone & maid service. Suites also have showers for two or Jacuzzi baths, fireplaces & private patios or verandas.
On-Premises: Meeting rooms, private dining rooms, public telephone, laundry facilities & fax.
Exercise/Health: Jacuzzi, massage. Jacuzzi baths in suites.
Swimming: Heated pool on premises, river nearby. 10 minutes to ocean.
Sunbathing: At poolside & on private verandas with suites.
Smoking: Not permitted.
Pets: Not permitted.
Handicap Access: Yes, ramps, wide doors, grab bars.
Children: Not permitted.
Languages: English.
Your Host: Darryl & Jim.

Fern Falls

Q-NET Gay/Lesbian ♀♂

SEE SPECIAL PAGE 18 COLOR SECTION

Romance Amidst the Redwoods

Fern Falls is a hillside habitat in a captivating canyon of Cazadero, whose cascading creeks merge with the languid waters of the Russian River. The custom-designed curved deck of the main house looks over the creek and ravine, and an ozonator spa sits above the waterfall on a hill nestled below a giant boulder amidst beautiful gardens. Nearby you can try wine tasting at the Korbel Winery, horseback riding, a soothing enzyme bath and massage at Osmosis, canoeing on the Russian River, or hiking in the redwood forests.

Address: 5701 Austin Creek Rd, PO Box 228, Cazadero, CA 95421
Tel: (707) 632-6108, **Fax:** (707) 632-6216.

Type: Guesthouse & cottages.
Clientele: Gay & lesbian. Good mix of men & women.
Transportation: Car is best.
To Gay Bars: 12 miles to bars in Guerneville.
Rooms: 1 suite & 3 cottages with double or queen beds.
Bathrooms: Private.
Dates Open: All year.
High Season: May-October.
Rates: $75-$150.
Discounts: Weekly rates.
Rsv'tns: Required.
To Reserve: Travel agent or call direct.
Minimum Stay: 2 nights on weekends in season.
Parking: Adequate free parking.
In-Room: Color cable TV, VCR, coffee/tea-making facilities, kitchen, refrigerator. Cabins have fireplaces.
On-Premises: Video tape library, fax, phone, laundry facilities.
Exercise/Health: Jacuzzi. Nearby gym, massage.
Swimming: Creek on premises. Nearby ocean, river & waterfall.
Sunbathing: On private & common sun decks.
Nudity: Permitted on decks, in garden & at creek.
Smoking: Permitted outside on decks.
Pets: Permitted in cottages if well-behaved.
Handicap Access: No. Terrain is hilly & steep.
Children: Permitted, must be supervised & well-behaved.
Languages: English.
Your Host: Darrel & Peter.

Highland Dell Inn Bed & Breakfast

Gay-Friendly 50/50 ♀♂

Exceptional Service in a Spectacular Setting

The landmark *Highland Dell Inn Bed & Breakfast,* with its vista of the Russian River, captures the serenity of a more gentle era. Rich, stained glass windows, a gigantic lobby fireplace, heirloom antiques and a collection of historical photos set the tone for arriving guests. The large pool is under the redwoods. The area offers ca-

continued next page

INN PLACES® 1998   265

noeing, swimming, fishing, backpacking, nature trails, horseback riding, cross-country cycling, enzyme baths, and even hot-air ballooning. One of our guests comments, *"The warmth of your hospitality, the charm of this beautiful B&B, delicious food, the view...a perfect getaway. Lady (dog) certainly lives up to her name."*

Address: 21050 River Blvd, Box 370, Monte Rio, CA 95462-0370
Tel: (707) 865-1759, (800) 767-1759.
E-mail: highland@netdex.com

Type: Bed & breakfast inn.
Clientele: 50% gay & lesbian & 50% straight clientele. Sometimes more gay than straight
Transportation: Car is best.
To Gay Bars: 5-minute drive to most gay venues.
Rooms: 4 rooms & 4 suites with queen or king beds.
Bathrooms: 8 private bath/toilet/showers.
Meals: Full breakfast. Restaurant on premises.
Vegetarian: Available upon request.
Complimentary: Tea & coffee. Candies throughout.
Dates Open: Open all year except for Jan 2-Feb 1.
High Season: May-Oct.
Rates: Summer $90-$160 & winter $75-$160.
Discounts: Inquire.
Credit Cards: MC, Visa, Amex, Discover, Eurocard, JCB.
Rsv'tns: Required.
To Reserve: Travel agent or call direct.
Minimum Stay: 2 nights on weekends. 3 nights some holidays.
Parking: Ample, free off-street parking.
In-Room: Maid service, color cable TV, telephone. Suites also have VCR, refrigerator.
On-Premises: Meeting rooms, video tape library, fax & copy service.
Exercise/Health: Massage. Nearby gym, weights.
Swimming: Seasonal pool on premises. 6 miles to ocean beach & river nearby.
Sunbathing: At poolside or on the beach.
Smoking: All rooms are non-smoking.
Pets: Pets up to 40 pounds with pet deposit in 1st floor rooms only + $10.
Handicap Access: Yes, with assistance to building.
Children: No.
Languages: English.
Your Host: Glenn & Anthony.

Highlands Resort
Gay/Lesbian ♀♂

Experience the Magic of the Redwoods!

Built in the 1940s, the classic bungalows and rooms of *Highlands Resort* reflect the casual comfort of that era. The grounds of our contry resort cover three acres and are lush with mature redwood trees and gardens. The pool area has the ambiance of a private home and the spa tub sits out under the redwood trees. Both the pool and spa areas are clothing-optional. Make new friends in our lounge over breakfast, or enjoy a game of Scrabble by the pool. We are just a short walk to the bars, restaurants and shops in Guerneville, and a short drive to the area's wineries.

Address: PO Box 346, 14000 Woodland Dr, Guerneville, CA 95446
Tel: (707) 869-0333, **Fax:** (707) 869-0370.
E-mail: highlands@wclynx.com **URL:** www.travel.org/HighlandsResort

Type: Inn and campground.
Clientele: Good mix of gay men & women.
Transportation: Car is best.
To Gay Bars: 2 blocks to men's/women's bars. A 5-minute walk or 2-minute drive.
Rooms: 10 rooms, 1 suite & 6 cottages with double, queen or king beds.
Bathrooms: 10 private, others share.
Campsites: 20 tent sites with 3 showers & 2 restrooms.
Meals: Continental breakfast on weekends.
Dates Open: All year.
High Season: April-October.
Rates: Summer $45-$125, winter $40-$90.
Credit Cards: MC, Visa, Amex, Discover.
Rsv'tns: Recommended.
To Reserve: Travel agent or call direct.
Minimum Stay: 2 nights over weekends.
Parking: Ample free parking.
In-Room: Maid service, 2 kitchens.
On-Premises: TV lounge.
Exercise/Health: Hot tub.
Swimming: Pool on premises.
Sunbathing: At poolside or on the patio.
Nudity: Permitted around pool & hot tub.
Smoking: Permitted in designated areas.
Pets: Permitted by special arrangement.
Handicap Access: No.
Children: Not especially welcome.
Languages: English.
Your Host: Lynette & Kenneth.

Huckleberry Springs

Q-NET Gay-Friendly 50/50 ♀♂

A Sonoma Wine Country Inn

Located on 56 wooded acres, **Huckleberry Springs** offers private cottage accommodations in an intimate and peaceful setting. Four modern cottages offer guests all amenities, including VCR, queen beds, skylights and wood-burning stoves. The lodge boasts dramatic views from its mountaintop location and is a cozy spot to sit, read or relax. Guests sunbathe on the pool decks or on the large deck. Breakfast and dinner are served in the lodge. Massage is available on premises and canoeing, hiking, bicycling, golf, tennis, wineries and the ocean are nearby.

Address: PO Box 400, Monte Rio, CA 95462
Tel: (707) 865-2683, (800) 822-2683. **E-mail:** hucksprings@netdex.com

Type: Cottages & B&B on 56 acres one mile from the river.
Clientele: 50% gay & lesbian & 50% straight clientele
Transportation: Rental car is best.
To Gay Bars: 6 miles.
Rooms: 4 cottages with queen beds.
Bathrooms: All private.
Meals: Full breakfast. Dinner by reservation.
Vegetarian: With advance notice upon reservation.
Complimentary: Tea, coffee & spring water.
Dates Open: Mar 2-Dec 14.
High Season: May-Sep.
Rates: $145 double occupancy. Full breakfast included in rate.
Credit Cards: MC, Visa, Amex.
Rsv'tns: Required.
To Reserve: Travel agent or call direct.
Minimum Stay: 2 days.
Parking: Ample free parking.
In-Room: Ceiling fans, hairdryers, woodstoves, refrigerator, VCR, stereos, coffee & tea-making facilities.
On-Premises: Catering, kitchen with advance request, meeting rooms & TV lounge.
Exercise/Health: Jacuzzi-massage cottage by appointment.
Swimming: Pool on premises, river nearby.
Sunbathing: Poolside, private & common sun decks, at nearby ocean, riverside beaches.
Nudity: Permitted in the hot tub.
Smoking: No smoking on property.
Pets: Not permitted.
Handicap Access: Only the lodge.
Children: Not permitted.
Languages: English & Spanish.
Your Host: Rebecca & Suzanne.

IGLTA

Jacques' Cottage

Q-NET Gay/Lesbian ♂

The Ultimate in Privacy

Amidst oaks, redwoods, and fruit trees, *Jacques' Cottage* is located in the heart of California wine country, only minutes from the wineries and fine restaurants that made Sonoma County famous. Many gay clubs and restaurants are 10 minutes away. Fishing, canoeing, or swim-

continued next page

INN PLACES® 1998

UNITED STATES — RUSSIAN RIVER • CALIFORNIA

ming at the gay beach (five minutes from the cottage) are possible in the tranquil Russian River. At *Jacques' Cottage,* enjoy a hot tub under the stars, lounge by the pool, or have a glass of wine on your private deck overlooking the vineyards.

Address: 6471 Old Trenton Road, Forestville, CA 95436
Tel: (707) 575-1033, (800) 246-1033, **Fax:** (707) 573-8911.
E-mail: jacques@wco.com **URL:** www.wco.com/~jacques

Type: Large, private guest cottage.
Clientele: Mostly men with women welcome
Transportation: Car is best.
To Gay Bars: 8 miles to all the bars.
Rooms: 1 cottage with 2 queen beds.
Bathrooms: Private bath/toilet/shower.
Complimentary: Coffee & coffee-maker in cottage.
Dates Open: All year.
High Season: May-end of Oct.
Rates: $100-$125.
Discounts: Weekly rates available.
Rsv'tns: Required.
To Reserve: Travel agent or call direct.
Minimum Stay: 2 nights.
Parking: Ample, free off-street parking.
In-Room: Color TV, VCR, video tape library, laundry service, private phone line, bathrobes, kitchen, refrigerator, coffee & tea-making facilities, CD.
On-Premises: Sun deck.
Exercise/Health: Free weights poolside, Jacuzzi on premises. Nearby gym, massage.
Swimming: Pool on premises. River with gay beach 2 miles, or lake 35 miles away.
Sunbathing: At poolside or on private sun deck.
Nudity: Permitted.
Smoking: Permitted.
Pets: Permitted.
Handicap Access: No.
Children: Permitted.
Languages: English.
Your Host: Jacques.

Mountain Lodge Resort
Gay-Friendly 50/50 ♀♂

Discover *Mountain Lodge Resort,* one of the Russian River's best-kept secrets. Explore the possibilities! Peaceful gardens and secluded decks nestle into the artfully landscaped grounds. The pool and hot tubs overlook the Russian River. Gay bars of the area are a short distance away.

Address: PO Box 169, 16350 1st St, Guerneville, CA 95446
Tel: (707) 869-3722, **Fax:** (707) 869-0556.

Type: Condo-style ground level units.
Clientele: 50% gay & lesbian & 50% straight clientele
Transportation: Car is best from San Francisco.
To Gay Bars: 2-minute walk to gay & lesbian bars.
Rooms: 27 apartments with queen beds.
Bathrooms: All private baths.
Dates Open: All year.
Weekly/monthly rentals based on availability.
High Season: May through September.
Rates: Summer $49-$150. Winter $40-$95. Based on double occupancy.
Discounts: For stays of three nights or more Sunday-Thursday or for a week or more.
Credit Cards: MC, Visa, Amex, Discover.
To Reserve: Travel agent or call direct.
Minimum Stay: On holiday weekends.
Parking: Ample off-street parking. Gated security at night, key access only.
In-Room: Color cable TV, kitchen, refrigerator, coffee & tea-making facilities & maid service.
On-Premises: Laundry facilities.
Exercise/Health: Jacuzzi. Steam in one resort room.
Swimming: Pool & river on premises.
Sunbathing: At poolside, on the beach, or on private & common sun decks.
Nudity: Permitted in spas after dark with discretion.
Smoking: Permitted without restrictions.
Pets: Not permitted.
Children: Permitted. Small children at pool between 3 & 6 pm only.
Languages: English.

Rio Villa Beach Resort
Gay-Friendly 50/50 ♀♂

Rio Villa is a cluster of resort cabins, units and suites surrounded by spacious decks, abundant gardens and lush lawns, sheltered by the redwoods. Decor reflects the warmth of old-world charm. Newly-remodeled rooms have kitchens, private baths, sofas, king and queen beds, color TV, outdoor BBQs and private sun decks. A stroll through the old-fashioned herb and flower gardens along the river leaves one refreshed and grateful. Weekends, a buffet breakfast of homemade coffee cakes, muffins, fresh fruit, juices and coffee is served on the redwood patio.

Address: 20292 Hwy 116, Monte Rio, CA 95462
Tel: (707) 865-1143, **Fax:** (707) 865-0115.
E-mail: riovilla@sonic.net **URL:** http://sonic.net/~riovilla

Type: Beach resort.
Clientele: 50% gay & lesbian & 50% straight clientele
Transportation: Car is best.
To Gay Bars: 10 minutes to men's/women's bars.
Rooms: 10 rooms, 2 suites & 2 cottages with double, queen & king beds.
Bathrooms: Private: 12 shower/toilets, 1 full bath & 1 sink. 1 shared shower, some spa tubs.
Meals: Continental breakfast on weekends.
Complimentary: Tea & coffee in all kitchen units.
Dates Open: All year.
High Season: May-September.
Rates: High season $69-$179. Low season $65-$150.
Discounts: Multiple-day packages available. Off-season bargains.
Credit Cards: MC, Visa, Amex & Discover.
Rsv'tns: Preferred.
To Reserve: Call direct.
Minimum Stay: High season weekends & holidays.
Parking: Ample, free, off-street parking.
In-Room: Color cable TV, kitchen, refrigerator & maid service.
Exercise/Health: Nearby Jacuzzi & massage.
Swimming: River on the premises, ocean beach nearby.
Sunbathing: On beach, private & common sun decks & patio.
Smoking: Permitted.
Pets: Not permitted.
Children: Permitted but not encouraged.
Languages: English.

The Willows

Q-NET Gay/Lesbian

Where Tourists Are Treated Just Like Home Folk!

A GUESTHOUSE ON THE RUSSIAN RIVER
15905 RIVER ROAD • P.O. BOX 365
GUERNEVILLE, CA 95446 • (707) 869-2824

The Willows guesthouse offers a country home vacation on five spectacular acres overlooking the Russian River. In the main lodge, there are thirteen private, cozy bedrooms, some with fireplaces and color TVs, all with direct-dial telephones. Nine bedrooms have private baths. In the spacious living room, you will enjoy a large stone fireplace, extensive library and grand piano. A sun deck with hot tub and sauna extends the length of the lodge. On the rambling, well-tended property, ideal for tent camping, you'll find quiet, wooded seclusion and sunny, landscaped lawns, which slope down to the private dock on the river. Use of the canoes is provided at no additional charge. Guests at *The Willows* are served a complimentary breakfast of fresh fruit, pastries, juice and coffee, and are welcome to make use of the community kitchen and outdoor barbecues. Many excellent restaurants are a short walk away. At *The Willows*, you'll find a relaxed, intimate, and friendly atmosphere, where you can get away from it all, yet be in the heart of the maddening fun on the Russian River.

Address: PO Box 465, 15905 River Rd, Guerneville, CA 95446
Tel: (707) 869-2824, (800) 953-2828, **Fax:** (707) 869-2764.

Type: Riverfront guesthouse inn with tent camping.
Clientele: Good mix of gay men & women
Transportation: Car is best.
To Gay Bars: 2 blocks (1/4 mi). 10-minute walk or 1-minute drive.
Rooms: 13 rooms with queen beds.
Bathrooms: 9 private, 4 shared.
Campsites: Can accommodate 120 tent campers. RV access, no hook-ups. Full toilet & shower facilities, 4 showers for men, 2 showers for women, 2 toilets for each.
Meals: Expanded continental breakfast.
Vegetarian: At nearby restaurants.
Complimentary: Tea & coffee served all day.
Dates Open: All year.
High Season: May thru September.

continued next page

UNITED STATES — SACRAMENTO · CALIFORNIA

Rates: Rooms $59-$129, special weekday rates.
Credit Cards: MC, Visa, Amex, Discover.
Rsv'tns: Required.
To Reserve: Travel agent or call direct.
Minimum Stay: 2 nights on weekends (rooms only during peak season).
Parking: Ample free on- & off-street parking.
In-Room: Color cable TV, VCRs, video tape library, telephone, ceiling fans, maid service.
On-Premises: Large community kitchen. Private dock with canoes & kayaks on river.
Exercise/Health: Hot tub, sauna & massage. Gym in town.
Swimming: In the river.
Sunbathing: On the beach or common sun deck, 5 acres of park-like grounds.
Nudity: Permitted in designated areas.
Smoking: Permitted outside the lodge. All rooms non-smoking.
Pets: Not permitted.
Handicap Access: No.
Children: Not permitted.
Languages: English.

Hartley House Inn

Q-NET Gay-Friendly 50/50 ♀♂

A New Standard of Excellence

Hartley House is a stunning turn-of-the-century mansion with the sophisticated elegance of a small European hotel. The home's stately character is preserved in original inlaid hardwood floors, stained woodwork, leaded and stained glass windows, and original brass light fixtures. Authentic antique furnishings, period artworks, and collectibles decorate the parlor, dining room, and guest rooms. Mornings, savor generous breakfasts of freshly baked muffins, fresh fruit, coffees, teas, and a variety of home made specialties. The elegant decor, relaxed atmosphere and convenient location are all qualities that bring guests back time and time again.

Address: 700 Twenty-Second St, Sacramento, CA 95816-4012
Tel: (916) 447-7829, (800) 831-5806, **Fax:** (916) 447-1820.
E-mail: randy@hartleyhouse.com **URL:** http://www.hartleyhouse.com

Type: Bed & breakfast.
Clientele: 50% gay & lesbian & 50% straight clientele
Transportation: Car is best, airporter to door approx $10.
To Gay Bars: 5 blocks to gay/lesbian bars.
Rooms: 5 rooms with double, queen or king beds.
Bathrooms: All private.
Meals: Full breakfast.
Vegetarian: Always available. Extensive menu, cooked to order.

Complimentary: Cookies, beverages, turndown service with mints on pillow.
Dates Open: All year.
High Season: Spring through fall.
Rates: $95-$160.
Discounts: Corporate discounts available.
Credit Cards: MC, Visa, Amex, Discover, Carte Blanche, Diners, JCB, ATM cards.
Rsv'tns: Recommended.
To Reserve: Travel agent or call direct.

Minimum Stay: On holiday weekends only.
Parking: Ample, free on- & off-street parking.
In-Room: Maid, room & laundry service, color cable TV, stereo/cassette clock radios, AC, ceiling fans, robes, soaps, shampoos, multi-line phones & modem ports (no charge for local calls or long distance access).
On-Premises: Meeting room, dining room, library, fax & copy facilities.

Exercise/Health: Massage on premises with appointment. Discount at nearby local health club.
Swimming: In lake, river or nearby pool.
Sunbathing: On beach or courtyard.
Smoking: Permitted outdoors.
Pets: Not permitted.
Handicap Access: No.
Children: Permitted if older and by prior arrangement.
Languages: English & Spanish.
Your Host: Randy.

FERRARI GUIDES™

Balboa Park Inn
More Than You'll Pay For...

Q-NET Gay/Lesbian ♀♂

UNITED STATES — CALIFORNIA • SAN DIEGO

Balboa Park Inn is a collection of 26 distinctive, immaculate and beautifully-appointed suites, located in the heart of San Diego's gay community. We're just footsteps (1-1/2 blocks) from Balboa Park and the world famous San Diego Zoo. Nearby are the numerous cafes, shops, restaurants and nightclubs of Hillcrest, the city's gayest area of town. A short drive will find you at the Pacific's doorstep, including Black's Beach, a favorite spot for nude sunbathing. Rent a car to see the sights, or use our comprehensive public transportation system. We're just minutes from the airport, train station and bus terminal downtown, and only 20 miles from Tijuana, Mexico, the world's most visited city.

The **Balboa Park Inn** is your affordable, "family"-oriented destination in San Diego. Stay with us. We promise that you'll always get more than you paid for!

Address: 3402 Park Blvd, San Diego, CA 92103
Tel: (619) 298-0823, (800) 938-8181, **Fax:** (619) 294-8070.
URL: www.balboaparkinn.com

Type: Bed & breakfast inn.
Clientele: Good mix of gay men & women, with some straight clientele
Transportation: Car is best or taxi from airport.
To Gay Bars: 6 blocks to men's, 3 blocks to women's bar. A 15-minute walk or 5-minute drive.
Rooms: 19 suites & 7 rooms with single, queen or king beds.
Bathrooms: All private.

Meals: Expanded continental breakfast.
Complimentary: Coffee, tea or hot chocolate in suite.
Dates Open: All year.
High Season: Summer.
Rates: $80-$200 plus tax.
Discounts: For established business accounts.
Credit Cards: MC, Visa, Amex, Diner's, Carte Blanche, Discover.
Rsv'tns: Required 3-4 wks. ahead in summer.

To Reserve: Travel agent or call direct.
Minimum Stay: 3 days on holiday weekends.
Parking: Ample, free, on-street parking.
In-Room: Color cable TV, telephone, AC, refrigerator, coffee/tea-making facilities, ceiling fans, room, laundry & maid service.
On-Premises: Maids do laundry.
Swimming: Pool nearby, 10-15-min drive to ocean beach, 30-min drive to Black's Beach.
Sunbathing: On private and common sun decks.
Smoking: Permitted without restrictions.
Pets: Not permitted.
Handicap Access: Yes, one room.
Children: Permitted.
Languages: English, Spanish.

IGLTA

INN PLACES® 1998

Banker's Hill Bed & Breakfast

Gay-Owned & -Operated ♀♂

Located in San Diego's historic Banker's Hill neighborhood, *Banker's Hill Bed & Breakfast* combines the elegance of days gone by with the amenities of today. Open year-round, this historic 1912 Craftsman home with fully restored Victorian interior and all-new bathrooms, features seven bedrooms, each distinguished with unique faux-finish walls and furnishings. Telephone, voice mail and fax capabilities, color televisions, cable and VCRs are also in all of the rooms. Our bed and breakfast also features a newly built swimming pool and hot tub, a billiard table, suntan bed, workout room and laundry facilities.

Conveniently situated, *Banker's Hill Bed & Breakfast* is adjacent to the many shops, restaurants, gyms and gay and lesbian clubs of Hillcrest. We're only four blocks from Balboa Park's museums, its Olympic-sized swimming pool, tennis courts, golf course and the world-famous San Diego Zoo. Services available to our guests include massage, videos and safer-sex supplies.

Address: 3315 Second Ave, San Diego, CA
Tel: (619) 260-0673, (800) 338-3748, **Fax:** (619) 260-0674.
E-mail: BHBB@INREACH.COM **URL:** http://home.inreach.com/BHBB/

Type: Bed & breakfast.
Clientele: Gay & lesbian. Good mix of men & women
Transport.: Car or taxi.
To Gay Bars: 4 blocks, a 5 min walk, a 3 min drive.
Rooms: 6 rooms (2 suites) with single, queen or king beds.
Bathrooms: Private: 2 bath/shower/toilets. Shared: 1 bath/shower/toilet, 1 shower only.
Meals: Expanded continental breakfast.
Vegetarian: No meats at breakfast. 5 blocks to vegetarian restaurants.
Dates Open: All year.
Rates: $85-$200.
Discounts: 10% on stays of 5 or more days (possibly more if longer).
Credit Cards: MC, Visa, Amex.
Rsv'tns: Required.
To Reserve: Travel agent or call direct.
Minimum Stay: 2 nights on weekends.
Parking: Ample on-street parking.
In-Room: AC, ceiling fans, telephone, color cable TV, VCR, maid service.
On-Premises: TV lounge, video tape library, laundry facilities.
Exercise/Health: Gym, weights, Jacuzzi, steam, massage, tanning bed, pool table. Nearby gym, weights, Jacuzzi, sauna, massage.
Swimming: Pool on premises. Ocean & lake nearby.
Sunbathing: Poolside & at beach.
Smoking: Non-smoking house, smoking permitted outside.
Pets: Not permitted.
Handicap Access: No.
Children: No.
Languages: English.
Your Host: James & Thom.

IGLTA

The Beach Place
Gay/Lesbian ♂

Minutes from downtown, Hillcrest and most tourist attractions, the Ocean Beach section of San Diego retains the charm of a small town. No high-rise hotels block the view or prevent access to the beach. At *The Beach Place,* you enjoy the privacy of your own apartment with deck, small garden, full kitchen with microwave, bedroom with queen bed and living room with color TV and adult films. The central courtyard has a gazebo with a huge hot tub, as well as a patio for sunbathing.

Address: 2158 Sunset Cliffs Blvd, San Diego, CA 92107 **Tel:** (619) 225-0746.

Type: Guesthouse.
Clientele: Mostly men with women welcome
Transportation: Car is best.
To Gay Bars: 10-minute drive to numerous bars in Hillcrest, Pacific Beach & Point Loma.
Rooms: 4 suites with queen beds.
Bathrooms: All private.

Complimentary: Tea, coffee, sugar, salt, pepper & utensils.
Dates Open: All year.
Rates: $60 per night or $350 per week for 2 people. $15 per night per additional guest.
Rsv'tns: Required.
To Reserve: Travel agent or call direct.
Minimum Stay: 2 days.

Parking: Adequate off-street covered parking.
In-Room: Kitchen with microwave & refrigerator, color cable TV, ceiling fans & maid service.
On-Premises: Gas barbeque available in the courtyard.
Exercise/Health: Jacuzzi.
Swimming: 4 blocks to ocean beach.

Sunbathing: On the patio & private sun decks.
Nudity: Permitted on sun decks.
Pets: Sometimes with prior arrangement.
Children: Permitted at times with prior arrangement.
Languages: English

IGLTA

Dmitri's Guesthouse
Gay/Lesbian ♂

Overlooking downtown in one of San Diego's historic turn-of-the-century neighborhoods, *Dmitri's* is minutes from the convention center, Gaslamp entertainment area, Horton Plaza shopping, Balboa Park, our famous zoo, the Old Globe Theatre, the Aerospace Museum, Old Town, the bays and beaches, and just blocks from the stops for bright red trolleys that go to Tijuana, Mexico. A variety of accommodations with private baths include continental breakfast served at poolside.

Address: 931 21st St, San Diego, CA 92102
Tel: (619) 238-5547.

Type: Guest house.
Clientele: Mostly men with women welcome
Transportation: Pickup from airport, bus or train, $10.
To Gay Bars: 6 blocks to gay/lesbian bars.
Rooms: 5 doubles with queen beds, or 1-2 double beds.

Bathrooms: 3 private, 2 shared.
Meals: Continental breakfast.
Complimentary: Tea & coffee.
Dates Open: All year.
High Season: Jul-Sept.
Rates: 2 people $55-$85, $15 per extra person.
Discounts: Weekly rates available.

Credit Cards: MC, Visa.
Rsv'tns: Required.
To Reserve: Travel agent or call direct.
Minimum Stay: 2 nights on weekends.
Parking: Adequate free on-street parking.
In-Room: Maid service, color TV, kitchen.
On-Premises: Telephone, TV lounge.

Exercise/Health: Hot tub.
Swimming: Pool.
Sunbathing: At poolside or on common sundecks.
Nudity: Permitted.
Smoking: Permitted outdoors.
Pets: Not permitted.
Handicap Access: No.
Children: Not permitted.
Languages: English, limited Spanish.

The Hillcrest Inn

Gay/Lesbian ♀♂

Good Value In the Heart of Gay Hillcrest

The Hillcrest Inn is one of San Diego's newer hotels, a 45-room establishment in the midst of the city's favorite restaurant, bar and shopping neighborhood. Each room is clean and comfortable and has a private bath and telephone. The building has security gates and a beautiful new Jacuzzi and sunning patio. The downtown business district and the harbor are directly to the south. Balboa Park, with its zoo, museums, galleries and restaurants, is immediately to the east. Mission Bay, Sea World and Pacific beaches are a short drive to the north.

Address: 3754 5th Ave, San Diego, CA 92103
Tel: (619) 293-7078, (800) 258-2280, **Fax:** (619) 293-3861.

Type: Hotel.
Clientele: Mostly gay & lesbian, with some straight clientele.
Transportation: Auto, city bus or taxi.
To Gay Bars: 6 bars within a 2 block radius.
Rooms: 45 rooms with twin, double & queen beds.
Bathrooms: All private bath/shower/toilets.
Complimentary: Coffee 8am to closing.
Dates Open: All year.

Rates: $49-$55.
Discounts: Week-long reservations, pay for 5 nights, get 2 free. Repeat customer discount.
Credit Cards: MC, Visa, Amex, Diners, Optima, Carte Blanche.
Rsv'tns: Recommended.
To Reserve: Travel agent or call direct.
Minimum Stay: 2 nights on holidays, special events.
Parking: Limited, free off-street parking & adjacent pay lot.
In-Room: Color TV, telephone, ceiling fans, maid service, kitchen, refrigerator, microwave, voice mail, data ports.
On-Premises: Laundry facilities, snack machines, tour desk.
Exercise/Health: Jacuzzi.
Swimming: Ocean beach 15 min by car.
Sunbathing: On private sunning patio.

Smoking: Permitted without restrictions. Non-smoking rooms available.
Pets: Not permitted.
Handicap Access: Yes, ramps & special bathroom facilities.
Children: Not permitted.
Languages: English, some Spanish, French & Japanese.
Your Host: Mark.

IGLTA

Keating House

Gay-Friendly 50/50 ♀♂

This Is No Addam's Family Victorian!

Keating House is a bright, sunny bed and breakfast overflowing with light, color and flowering plants. Over 100 years old, it has retained the charm and glamour of the turn-of-the-century. But this is no museum! We're a take-your-shoes-off relax-and-stay-awhile kind of place. Touring "America's finest city" can be exhausting, but not when you start and end your day with us. Have the time of your life, then, we'll return you to your world refreshed, relaxed and rejuvenated.

Address: 2331 Second Ave, San Diego, CA 92101-1505
Tel: (619) 239-8585, (800) 995-8644, **Fax:** (619) 239-5774.

Type: Bed & breakfast inn.
Clientele: 50% gay & lesbian & 50% straight clientele
Transportation: Bus, taxi, or car.
To Gay Bars: Short drive or cab ride to men's & women's clubs.
Rooms: 8 rooms with double or queen beds.
Bathrooms: 2 private bath/toilets & 3 shared bath/showers.
Meals: Full, sumptuous breakfast served every morning.
Complimentary: Beverages.
Dates Open: All year.
Rates: Rooms $60-$85 per night. Third person $25.
Discounts: 10% for 5 days or more.
Credit Cards: MC, VISA, Amex & Discover.
Rsv'tns: Required.
To Reserve: Travel agent or call direct.
Minimum Stay: 2 nights on holidays & Valentine's weekend.
Parking: Unlimited, free on-street parking.
On-Premises: Large front porch. 2 lush sun & shade gardens.
Swimming: 10 minutes to ocean beaches. 15 minutes to Coronado Island.
Sunbathing: In the sun garden.
Smoking: Permitted outside only.
Pets: Not permitted.
Handicap Access: No.
Children: Permitted.
Languages: English, French, limited Spanish.

IGLTA

Park Manor Suites Hotel

Gay/Lesbian

"San Francisco Charm" in Gay Hillcrest

At *Park Manor Suites Hotel* we pride ourselves on our friendly staff and hospitality. Eighty elegantly appointed suites boast full kitchens, dining areas and baths, as well as cable and color TV. Enjoy incredible views while lunching at the Top of the Park Penthouse. Its Monday-Friday lunch menu consists of daily specials to please every palate at reasonable prices. Evening dining at Inn at the Park restaurant features dishes prepared by our chef who is specially trained in European-style cuisine. Located adjacent to Balboa Park at Sixth Avenue and Spruce Street, we are within walking distance to all gay restaurants and bars.

Address: 525 Spruce St, San Diego, CA 92103
Tel: (619) 291-0999, (800) 874-2649, **Fax:** (619) 291-8844.

Type: Hotel with restaurant & bar.
Clientele: 60% gay & lesbian & 40% straight clientele
Transportation: Car or taxi.
To Gay Bars: On premises & 1 block walking distance.
Rooms: 80 single, double & triple suites.

Bathrooms: All private.
Meals: Continental breakfast. Optional lunch & dinner.
Dates Open: All year.
Rates: $79-$169.
Discounts: Senior citizens 10%.
Credit Cards: MC, Visa, Amex, Discover.
To Reserve: Travel agent or call direct.

Parking: Free parking.
In-Room: Color TV, ceiling fans, telephone, voice mail, kitchen, refrigerator, coffeemaker, maid & room service.
On-Premises: Meeting rooms, laundry facilities, catering.
Sunbathing: On rooftop sun deck or across street at Balboa Park.

Smoking: Non-smoking suites available.
Pets: Permitted with $30 cleaning fee.
Handicap Access: Yes.
Children: Permitted with no restrictions.
Languages: English, Spanish, French & German.

IGLTA

Atherton Hotel

Gay-Friendly

European Charm in the Heart of San Francisco

Constructed in 1927, the *Atherton Hotel* was renovated in 1996 to enhance its "Old San Francisco" feel. The lobby's original marble floor, molded ceiling and etched glass project the ambiance of an intimate European inn. The Atherton Grill, serving continental cuisine, breakfast and Sunday champagne brunch, also offers dinner mid-May through October. Our English-style pub, The Abbey room, decorated with

continued next page

INN PLACES® 1998

antique abbey altar panels, offers a full bar from 5 pm. The hotel is walking distance to the Cable Cars, Union Square and theaters. With intimate charm and friendly service, we have proudly served our community for over 16 years.

Address: 685 Ellis St, San Francisco, CA 94109
Tel: (415) 474-5720, (800) 474-5720, **Fax:** (415) 474-8256.

Type: Hotel with restaurant and bar.
Clientele: Mostly straight clientele with a gay & lesbian following
Transportation: Shuttle from airport about $10, taxi maximum $30. All major public transportation lines nearby.
To Gay Bars: 1 block to men's bars on Polk Street, 10 minutes' drive to Castro (3 metro stops).
Rooms: 75 rooms with twin, queen or king beds.
Bathrooms: All private baths.
Complimentary: Coffee from 7:30am-2pm, weekdays lobby newspapers.
Dates Open: All year.
High Season: June-October.
Rates: US $79-$129.
Discounts: AAA, senior. Inn Places rate $69.
Credit Cards: MC, Visa, Amex, Diners, Discover.
Rsv'tns: Required.
To Reserve: Travel agent or call direct.
Minimum Stay: 2 nights during Gay Pride & Folsom St. Fair.
Parking: Adequate on-street pay parking.
In-Room: Color satellite TV, telephone & maid service.
On-Premises: Private dining room.
Exercise/Health: Nearby gym.
Swimming: In nearby ocean.
Smoking: Not permitted in lobby. Non-smoking rooms available.
Pets: Not permitted.
Handicap Access: No.
Children: Children under 12 with accompanying parents stay free.
Languages: English, German, Spanish, Italian, French, Tagalog.
Your Host: Antonio & Garey.

IGLTA

Beck's Motor Lodge

Gay-Friendly 50/50 ♀♂

If you've searched for a hotel with moderately-priced, comfortable accommodations in a picturesque neighborhood setting, discover *Beck's Motor Lodge* on world-famous Market St. In the midst of the Castro area and convenient to everything, it is surrounded by tree-lined streets, quaint shops and Victorian homes. It's easy to relax with special touches like in-room fresh coffee service, refrigerators, parking, color cable TV and our private sun deck with lovely views of the city. Our staff is friendly and accommodating.

Address: 2222 Market St, San Francisco, CA 94114
Tel: (415) 621-8212, (800) 227-4360, **Fax:** (415) 241-0435.

Type: Motel.
Clientele: 50% gay & lesbian & 50% straight clientele.
Transportation: Airport shuttles.
To Gay Bars: 1 block.
Rooms: 57 rooms with queen or king beds.
Bathrooms: All private.
Vegetarian: Amazing Grace is 1 block away.
Complimentary: Coffee in room.
Dates Open: All year.
High Season: May-Oct.
Rates: $75-$125.
Discounts: Senior citizen & AAA 10%.
Credit Cards: Visa, MC, Amex, Diners & Discover.
Rsv'tns: Required.
To Reserve: Travel agent or call direct.
Parking: Adequate free off-street parking.
In-Room: Color cable TV, telephone, refrigerator, maid service & coffee & tea-making facilities. 10 rooms have AC.
On-Premises: Laundry facilities for guests.
Exercise/Health: Gym & weights nearby.
Swimming: 3-1/2 miles to ocean beach.
Sunbathing: On common sun decks.
Smoking: 24 non-smoking & 33 smoking rooms.
Pets: Not permitted.
Handicap Access: No ramps, but doors are wide.
Children: Welcomed.
Languages: English, Spanish, French & Tagalog.
Your Host: Irene.

Bock's Bed & Breakfast

Q-NET Gay/Lesbian ♀♂

In Operation Since 1980

Bock's is a lovely 1906 Edwardian residence in the Parnassus Heights area of San Francisco with beautiful views of the city. Golden Gate Park is two blocks away and public transportation is nearby. Host, Laura Bock, has restored the original virgin redwood walls of the dining and entry rooms as well as the mahogany inlaid oak floors of the latter. The latest renovation project was completed with the addition of a new bathroom & the restoration of two original pocket doors on the main floor. Laura's enthusiasm and touring tips about her native city are enjoyed by an international clientele.

Address: 1448 Willard St, San Francisco, CA 94117
Tel: (415) 664-6842, Fax: (415) 664-1109.

Type: Bed & breakfast.
Clientele: Mostly gay & lesbian with some straight clientele
Transportation: From airport take one of the van shuttles outside the 2nd level.
To Gay Bars: 1 mile to gay/lesbian bars.
Rooms: 3 rooms with single, double or queen beds.
Bathrooms: 1 private, 1 private sink, others share full bath.
Meals: Expanded continental breakfast.
Vegetarian: I can accommodate special needs & there is vegetarian food nearby.
Complimentary: Coffee, tea, hot chocolate service in rooms. Small, shared guest refrigerator.
Dates Open: All year.
High Season: May through October.
Rates: $45-$80 plus tax. $10 each add'l person, plus tax.
Credit Cards: None.
Rsv'tns: Recommended.
To Reserve: Call direct.
Minimum Stay: 2 nights.
Parking: On-street parking. Inexpensive lot 2 blocks away.
In-Room: Color TV, telephone, electric hot pot, radios, coffee/tea-making facilities. Private balcony in 1 room.
On-Premises: Deck off of living room, laundry facilities, guest refrigerator.
Swimming: Pool nearby, ocean beach 3 miles away.
Sunbathing: On private or common sun decks.
Smoking: Non-smokers only.
Pets: Not permitted.
Handicap Access: No.
Children: Permitted.
Languages: English, smattering of French.
Your Host: Laura

Carl Street Unicorn House
Women ♀

Carl Street Unicorn House is a small Victorian house located near San Francisco's Golden Gate Park within walking distance of great restaurants and cafes, the aquarium, museums, and a variety of interesting shops. There is a collection of over 200 ethnic dolls, many pieces of artwork and antiques befitting a Victorian home. Your host resides on the top floor, while guests occupy the ground floor.

Address: 156 Carl St, San Francisco, CA 94117
Tel: (415) 753-5194.

Type: Bed & breakfast.
Clientele: Mostly women with men welcome, some straight clientele.
Transportation: Airport shuttle van to door.
To Gay Bars: 5-10 minutes' drive to gay/lesbian bars.
Rooms: 2 rooms with double beds.
Bathrooms: 1 shared bath/shower/toilet.
Meals: Continental breakfast.
Complimentary: Tea & coffee.
Dates Open: All year.
High Season: Summer.
Rates: $40-$50, $5 extra for 1 night stay.
Discounts: 10% on stays of 7 days or more.
Rsv'tns: Required.
To Reserve: Call direct.
Minimum Stay: Required on weekends.
Parking: On-street parking.
On-Premises: TV lounge.
Swimming: 5 min drive to pool.
Sunbathing: On the patio.
Smoking: Not permitted.
Handicap Access: No.
Children: Permitted if over 6 years.
Languages: English.

Castillo Inn
Gay/Lesbian ♂

Your Home Away from Home

The *Castillo Inn* is a short five-minute walk to Market and Castro Streets and one block to major public transportation. The inn has four rooms that are very clean and share a bath. Three of the rooms have queen-sized beds and one room has a double bed. A deluxe continental breakfast is included, and a voice mail answering service, a telephone and fax are available for guests. The *Castillo Inn* is a non-smoking establishment and our rates range from $55 to $75. Ask us about our two-bedroom suite.

Address: 48 Henry St, San Francisco, CA 94114
Tel: (415) 864-5111, (800) 865-5112, Fax: (415) 641-1321.

continued next page

Type: Bed & breakfast.
Clientele: Mostly men with women welcome
Transportation: Shuttle, taxi, other public transportation.
To Gay Bars: 2 blocks, a 2-5 min walk.
Rooms: 4 rooms, 1 apartment with double or queen beds.
Meals: Expanded continental breakfast.
Vegetarian: Available nearby.
Dates Open: All year.
High Season: July-October.
Rates: $55-$75.
Discounts: Please inquire.
Credit Cards: MC, Visa, Amex.
Rsv'tns: Required.
To Reserve: By travel agent or direct call Jan-Mar. Call direct other times.
Minimum Stay: Sometimes required.
Smoking: Permitted outside, non-smoking rooms available.
Pets: Not permitted.
Handicap Access: No.
Languages: English, Spanish.

Chateau Tivoli
Gay-Friendly 50/50

The Greatest Painted Lady In the World

Chateau Tivoli under new management since early 1997, is an authentic period restoration of a Victorian mansion built in 1892. The book *Painted Ladies Revisited* calls it "...the greatest Painted Lady in the world." Fully licensed as a hotel Bed & Breakfast, the residence features eight guest bedrooms. The building exterior has become a San Francisco landmark, painted in twenty-two different colors, and highlighted with brilliant gold leafing. The roof is multi-colored slate tile, mounted in a special diamond pattern and surrounded by fabulous iron grill work. The interior is resplendent with hardwood floors, stately columns and numerous stained glass windows. There are four woodburning fireplaces. The walls and ceilings in bedrooms and hallways are covered in Bradbury & Bradbury wallpaper and accented by gold leaf and various faux treatments.

The mansion has been so faithfully restored that guests experience the sensation of a timetravel journey back to San Francisco's romantic golden age of opulence. Here, they are surrounded by genuine antiques and art from the estates of Cornelius Vanderbilt, Charles de Gaulle, J. Paul Getty, the Countess of Richelieu and the famous San Francisco madame, Sally Stanford. Spacious and grand, the rooms and suites feature elegant canopy beds and marble baths, balconies and views, fireplaces and stained glass, towers and turrets, each facet contributing to the atmosphere that makes *Chateau Tivoli* a truly unforgettable experience.

Address: 1057 Steiner St, San Francisco, CA 94115
Tel: (415) 776-5462, (800) 228-1647, **Fax:** (415) 776-0505.
URL: www.citysearch.com/sfo/chateautivoli

Type: Bed & breakfast.
Clientele: 50% gay & lesbian & 50% straight clientele
Transportation: Shuttle or taxi from airport.
To Gay Bars: Ten minutes to gay & lesbian bars.
Rooms: 5 doubles, 4 suites (2 with 2 bedrooms).
Bathrooms: 5 private, others share with only one other room.
Meals: Expanded continental breakfast Mon-Fri, champagne brunch available Sat & Sun.
Complimentary: Afternoon wine tasting, coffee, tea, herb tea, juice, etc.
Dates Open: All year.
High Season: Mar-Oct.
Rates: $90-$220.
Discounts: For 4 or more days.
Credit Cards: MC, Visa, Amex.
Rsv'tns: Required.
To Reserve: Travel agent or call direct.
Minimum Stay: 2 days on weekends.
Parking: Ample, on-street parking in residential neighborhood.
In-Room: Maid service, telephone.
On-Premises: Meeting rooms.
Smoking: Permitted outside on patio.
Pets: Special permission required.
Children: Welcome.
Languages: English.
Your Host: Chris, Sonny & Victoria.

The Essex Hotel

Q-NET Gay-Friendly ♀♂

The Essex Hotel, totally renovated in recent years, is centrally located and within walking distance of all major points, including Cable Car line, Union Square, Chinatown, theaters and many fine restaurants. Polk Street is only a block away and gay men's bars are two blocks away. The Airporter shuttle to our front door is only $12. The hotel has a European atmosphere, pleasant, comfortable double rooms with high-quality furnishings, color TV, maid service, and direct dial phones. Most rooms have private baths.

Address: 684 Ellis St, San Francisco, CA 94109
Tel: (415) 474-4664, (800) 453-7739, **Fax:** (415) 441-1800.
In CA (800) 443-7739.

Type: Hotel.
Clientele: Mostly straight clientele with a gay & lesbian following
Transportation: Airporter shuttle $12.
To Gay Bars: 2 blocks to men's bars.
Rooms: 100 rooms with single or queen beds.

Bathrooms: 50 private bath/toilets, others share. 100 private sinks.
Complimentary: Coffee.
Dates Open: All year.
Rates: Single $69, double $79.
Discounts: 10% to holders of Inn Places, subject to room availability.

Credit Cards: MC, Visa, Amex.
Rsv'tns: Suggested.
To Reserve: Travel agent or call direct.
Parking: Adequate on-street pay parking.
In-Room: Color TV, direct dial phone, maid service.
On-Premises: Public telephone, central heat.
Smoking: Permitted without restrictions.
Pets: Not permitted.
Handicap Access: No.
Children: Permitted.
Languages: English, French, German.

IGLTA

Inn At The Opera

Q-NET Gay-Friendly ♀♂

"The Most Civilized Oasis in Town," Gourmet 8/93.

Built in 1927, five years before the San Francisco Opera first performed at the War Memorial, the *Inn At The Opera* has long been a convenient address for visiting patrons and artists. Within a two-block radius are, not only the Opera House, Davies Symphony Hall and the San Francisco Ballet, but also the Civic Auditorium, site of many entertainment

continued next page

INN PLACES® 1998   279

productions, Herbst Auditorium, home to numerous lecture series and small music presentations, and the Museum of Modern Art.

Twenty-nine guest rooms and 18 suites occupy six floors, each decorated in pastel colors with queen-sized canopy beds and oversized pillows. Guests enjoy twice-daily maid service, daily valet and room service. A complimentary breakfast is served daily in the Inn's restaurant, Ovation at the Opera. Fresh homemade muffins and scones, cheeses and Italian meats, fruits and fresh-squeezed juices are bountifully displayed on the buffet. The intimate dining room with Belgian tapestries and a quiet Mozart quartet playing in the background, is truly the most civilized way to greet the morning in San Francisco.

In the evening, Ovation at the Opera is transformed into an elegant club-like setting, where people sit in coversational clusters of cushy chairs and sofas, drinking flutes of champagne and aperitifs. A wonderful dining experience is complemented by a pianist and a subtle glow from the fireplace. Although the Inn is in a very beautiful setting, it is our personalized service that we are most proud of. Our staff is very knowledgeable of restaurants, shopping, galleries and activities. We look forward to welcoming you to the *Inn At The Opera* on your next visit to San Francisco.

Address: 333 Fulton St, San Francisco, CA 94102
Tel: (415) 863-8400, (800) 325-2708, **Fax:** (415) 861-0821.

Type: Hotel with restaurant & bar.
Clientele: Mostly straight clientele with a gay & lesbian following
To Gay Bars: 5-minute drive to men's bar.
Rooms: 29 queens, 18 suites.

Bathrooms: All private.
Meals: Continental breakfast.
Dates Open: All year.
Rates: $125-$265.
Credit Cards: MC, Vsia, Amex, Diners Club.
Rsv'tns: Required.

To Reserve: Travel agent or call direct.
Parking: Adequate pay parking.
In-Room: Color TV, maid, room & laundry service, telephone, kitchen, refrigerator.

Smoking: Permitted, non-smoking rooms available.
Pets: Not permitted.
Languages: English, Spanish, French, Chinese interpreter available.

IGLTA

Inn 1890

Q-NET Gay-Owned 50/50 ♀♂

A "Very San Francisco" Queen Anne Victorian

When the Queen Anne Victorian at 1890 Page Street was built in 1890, it towered over a neighborhood of few houses and mostly empty lots. The "neighborhood" was then a sparsely populated weekend recreational area, but stories are told of the home being once inhabited by a famous San Francisco gold-rush family and, later, by a physician who provided illegal medical services. Designed by prominent architect Samuel Newsom, and built at the princely cost of $10,050, its beauty and significance are still noted by the many neighborhood tours that walk by.

Newly refurbished, *Inn 1890* graciously blends Victorian elegance with modern conveniences for your complete comfort. Most rooms have expansive bay windows, twelve-foot ceilings, hardwood floors and Oriental rugs. Brass or iron queen-sized beds with plush down and feather comforters will keep you warm and rested. Our luxurious bathrobes and slippers are especially cozy when curling up in front of one of the original wood fireplaces. Your private telephone has its own telephone number and message center, and offers free unlimited local calls and free long-distance access. Also for your convenience, kitchenettes are provided in each room and are great for light cooking and warming leftovers from the many local restaurants.

Inn 1890 is in a quiet residential neighborhood in the geographic center of the city. Minutes away is Buena Vista Park and the famous and historical Castro District. One block west is Golden Gate Park, which houses a variety of museums and world-renowned gardens, including the Japanese Tea Garden and the Strybing Arboretum. Walking and biking paths throughout the park lead to the beach and stunning vistas of the Pacific coastline. Walk to the health club, University of California at San Francisco and the University of San Francisco. A variety of public transportation options are very nearby.

Address: 1890 Page St, San Francisco, CA 94117
Tel: (415) 386-0486, (888) INN-1890 (466-1890), **Fax:** (415) 386-3626.
E-mail: inn1890@worldnet.att.net **URL:** http://adamsnet.com/inn1890

Type: Bed & breakfast inn.
Clientele: 50% gay & lesbian & 50% straight clientele
Transportation: Airport van or shuttle to front door. Free pick up from local bus.
To Gay Bars: 4 blocks, a 10 min walk.
Rooms: 7 rooms, 1 apartment with single, double or queen beds.
Bathrooms: Private: 3 shower/toilets. Shared: 3 showers only, 1 shower/toilet, 3 WCs only.

Meals: Expanded continental breakfast.
Vegetarian: Available nearby.
Complimentary: 24-hour cookies, nuts, mints, coffee & tea, cereal, fruit, jam, jelly, hot chocolate, juice.
Dates Open: All year.
High Season: May-Oct.
Rates: Summer $69-$79 +hotel tax; Winter $59-$69 +hotel tax; Apartment $115 +hotel tax.
Discounts: On stays of 1 week or more.

Credit Cards: MC, Visa.
Rsv'tns: Required.
To Reserve: Travel agent or call direct.
Minimum Stay: 2 nights.
Parking: Limited, covered, off-street pay parking ($5/night).
In-Room: Telephone, color TV, coffee & tea-making facilities, kitchenette with refrigerator, microwave, sink, dishes.
On-Premises: Book library, board games, fax, modem,

laundry facilities, garden & patio.
Exercise/Health: Nearby gym, weights.
Swimming: Nearby pool & ocean.
Sunbathing: On patio, at beach & Golden Gate Park.
Smoking: Permitted outside on patio. Non-smoking rooms available.
Pets: Permitted with prior permission.
Handicap Access: No.
Children: Welcome.
Languages: English.

UNITED STATES • SAN FRANCISCO • CALIFORNIA

Inn On Castro

Q-NET Gay/Lesbian ♀♂

The innkeepers invite you into a colorful and comfortable environment filled with modern art and exotic plants. All rooms vary in size and have private baths. Meet fellow travelers from all over the world for a memorable breakfast. The *Inn On Castro's* location is unique, just 100 yards north of the intersection of Market and Castro, where you are in a quiet neighborhood, yet only a stone's throw away from the Castro Theater, plus dozens of bars, restaurants and shops. With the *Underground* almost virtually adjacent to the *Inn*, big-name store shopping and cable car, etc. are just a few minutes away. There is literally something for everyone.

SEE SPECIAL PAGE 18 COLOR SECTION

Address: 321 Castro St,
San Francisco, CA 94114
Tel: (415) 861-0321.

Type: Bed & breakfast.
Clientele: Good mix of gay men & women
Transportation: Supershuttle from airport approx $11 per person.
To Gay Bars: Less than 1-minute walk to men's/women's bars.
Rooms: 6 rooms & 2 suites with double, queen or king beds, self-catering apartment.
Bathrooms: All private.

Meals: Full breakfast.
Vegetarian: Available with advance notice.
Complimentary: Afternoon wine, brandy night cap, tea, coffee, juices.
Dates Open: All year.
High Season: May-October.
Rates: Rooms $85-$160.
Credit Cards: MC, Visa, Amex.
Rsv'tns: Recommended 1 month in advance.
To Reserve: Call direct.

Minimum Stay: 2 days on weekends, 3 on holidays, 4 days Folsom Fair, Castro Fair & Gay Lib days.
Parking: Adequate on-street parking.
In-Room: Color TV on request, telephone, maid service, refrigerator.
On-Premises: Lounge & dining room.
Exercise/Health: Gym, weights, jacuzzi, sauna, steam & massage across the street.

Swimming: Nearby pool.
Sunbathing: On private sun decks.
Smoking: Permitted on patio, front porch, rear deck.
Pets: Not permitted.
Handicap Access: Patio suite is handicap-accessible.
Children: Permitted but not encouraged.
Languages: English, French, German & Dutch.

The Inn San Francisco

Q-NET Gay-Friendly ♀♂

Distinctly San Franciscan Warmth & Hospitality

Feel the years slip away, as you step through the massive, wooden doors of the *Inn San Francisco*. Each of the guest rooms is individually decorated with antique furnishings, fresh flowers, marble sinks, polished brass fixtures and exquisite finishing touches. All are extraordinarily beautiful and the feeling of classic, old-world elegance and grandeur is carried throughout. In the garden, under the shade of an old fig tree, an enchanting gazebo shelters the inviting hot tub.

Address: 943 S Van Ness Ave, San Francisco, CA 94110
Tel: (415) 641-0188, (800) 359-0913, **Fax:** (415) 641-1701.

FERRARI GUIDES™

Type: Bed & breakfast inn.
Clientele: Mixed, straight clientele with very strong gay/lesbian following
Transportation: Airport Shuttle $10 per person.
To Gay Bars: 8 blocks to men's & women's bars.
Rooms: 13 rooms, 7 luxury suites & 1 apartment with single, double or queen beds.
Bathrooms: 19 private bath/shower/toilets, 2 share.
Meals: Full buffet breakfast.

Vegetarian: Our breakfast includes a huge array of fresh fruits, granola, home-made breads or muffins & a cheese plate.
Complimentary: Coffee, tea, sherry complimentary in parlor, truffles in room.
Dates Open: All year.
Rates: Rooms $85-$225.
Discounts: Stays of 1 week or longer.
Credit Cards: Visa, MC, Amex, Diners, Carte Blanche, Discover.

Rsv'tns: Required.
To Reserve: Call direct.
Minimum Stay: Weekends, particularly on holidays, require a 2 night stay, but we are flexible. Call.
Parking: Several covered garages w/electric door openers, parking $10/night.
In-Room: Maid & laundry service, color TV, telephone, refrigerator.
On-Premises: Laundry facilities.

Exercise/Health: Redwood hot tub in tropical gazebo.
Sunbathing: On private & common sun decks, patios & on rooftop.
Smoking: Not permitted in parlor.
Pets: Not permitted.
Handicap Access: No.
Children: Permitted.
Languages: English, Spanish, Chinese, limited French.

IGLTA

The Lombard Central, A Super 8 Hotel
Gay-Friendly ♀♂

Old-World Charm and Today's Hospitality

SEE SPECIAL PAGE 19 COLOR SECTION

The Lombard Central, reminiscent of old San Francisco with an intimate lobby featuring marble floors, etched glass, mahogany columns, and a grand piano, offers guests old-world charm and Super 8 hospitality. At the 100-room hotel, you'll find the attention to detail and personal service exceptional. From making reservations at the hotel's famous Faces Cafe Restaurant to arranging special tours of the city and beyond, the staff is eager to make your stay perfect. We are conveniently located in the heart of downtown San Francisco's performing arts and civic center district, and are only five blocks from the famous cable cars.

Address: 1015 Geary Blvd,
San Francisco, CA 94109
Tel: (415) 673-5232, (800) 777-3210,
Fax: (415) 885-2802.

Type: Hotel with breakfast cafe.
Clientele: Mostly straight clientele with a gay/lesbian following
Transportation: From airport, car or airport shuttle is best.
To Gay Bars: 2 blocks, a 5-minute walk.
Rooms: 100 rooms with single, double, queen or king beds.
Bathrooms: All private bath/shower/toilets.
Vegetarian: Available at

breakfast & at nearby restaurants.
Complimentary: 24-hr coffee & tea, complimentary wine hour weekdays 5:30 pm-6:30 pm.
Dates Open: All year.
High Season: Jul-Aug.
Rates: $74-$99.88.
Discounts: Weekend & midweek specials, senior rates. All special rates subject to availability.
Credit Cards: Visa, Amex, Discover, MC, Diners.
Rsv'tns: Recommended in high season.

To Reserve: Travel agent or call direct.
Parking: Adequate pay parking.
In-Room: Color TV, telephone, ceiling fans, maid & laundry service.
On-Premises: Meeting rooms, fax available.

Exercise/Health: Nearby gym.
Smoking: Permitted in smoking rooms. Non-smoking rooms available.
Pets: Not permitted.
Handicap Access: No.
Children: Welcome.
Languages: English, Spanish, German.

The Metro Hotel

Gay-Friendly 50/50 ♀♂

A Great Discovery

A small, affordable hotel with 24 rooms on two floors, **The Metro Hotel** is situated in a historic district of San Francisco, walking distance to The Castro, The Haight and Golden Gate Park. We have new interiors with private baths, as well as the convenience of delicious food at The Metro Cafe. Let us make your stay in San Francisco a memorable event with our friendly atmosphere, secluded enchanted garden, and cafe. Our convenient location is only 10 minutes by bus from downtown San Francisco, and 8 blocks from the Castro District.

Address: 319 Divisadero St, San Francisco, CA 94117
Tel: (415) 861-5364, **Fax:** (415) 863-1970.

Type: Hotel.
Clientele: 50% gay & lesbian & 50% straight clientele.
Transportation: Car or airport shuttle.
To Gay Bars: 8 blocks to men's bars.
Rooms: 24 rooms & 2 suites, double or queen beds.

Bathrooms: All private.
Meals: Metro Cafe on premises for breakfast or lunch.
Vegetarian: Available at The Metro Cafe on premises.
Dates Open: All year.
High Season: Summer.
Rates: $55-$104.
Discounts: Call to see what is available at the time.
Credit Cards: MC, Visa, Amex, Discover.
Rsv'tns: Required. 48-hour cancellation notice also required.
To Reserve: Call direct or travel agent.
Parking: Free parking 6pm-9am.

In-Room: Cable color TV, telephone, modem, maid service.
Sunbathing: On patio or in garden.
Smoking: Permitted.
Pets: Not permitted.
Handicap Access: No.
Children: Permitted.
Languages: English & Spanish.
Your Host: Dean.

The Parker House

Q-NET Gay/Lesbian ♂

Castro Convenience in a Country-Like Setting

Castro's newest, most beautiful guesthouse, **The Parker House**, is a renovated 1909 Edwardian mini-mansion with expansive gardens and lawn areas, fern dens, statues, fountains and walking paths. The home offers a relaxing library/front room with fireplace and piano, an ornate formal dining room/meeting room, all-glass sun/breakfast room and sunning decks. Rooms feature private baths, cable TV, modem ports, voice mail, king- or queen-sized beds and expanded continental breakfast. We're steps away from bars, cafes, restaurants, Dolores Park and streetcars. Traveling alone or in a group, for business or pleasure... you won't be disappointed. Hosts Bob and Bill will take care of everything! Call toll-free for more information.

Address: 520 Church St, San Francisco, CA 94114
Tel: (415) 621-3222, toll-free: (888) 520-PARK (7275).
E-mail: parkerhse@aol.com
URL: http://members.aol.com/PARKERHSE/sf.html

Type: Guesthouse.
Clientele: Mostly men with women welcome
Transportation: Airport shuttle.
To Gay Bars: 2 blocks.
Rooms: 5 rooms, 2 suites with king or queen beds.
Bathrooms: 5 private bath/toilet/showers.
Meals: Expanded continental breakfast.
Vegetarian: Partial vegetarian breakfast. Great vegetarian restaurants nearby.
Complimentary: Afternoon tea & coffee in garden.
Dates Open: All year.
High Season: All year.
Rates: $99-$169.
Credit Cards: MC, Visa.
Rsv'tns: Suggested.
To Reserve: Travel agent or call direct.
Minimum Stay: Required only on holiday & event weekends.
Parking: Adequate pay parking.
In-Room: Color cable TV, telephone, voice mail, modem ports, maid service.
On-Premises: Meeting rooms, fax, voice mail, modem ports, laundry facilities.
Exercise/Health: Nearby gym, weights, Jacuzzi, sauna, steam, massage.
Swimming: Nearby pool & ocean.
Sunbathing: On common sun decks, in garden area, at beach.
Smoking: Permitted in designated common areas. No smoking in rooms.
Pets: Not permitted.
Handicap Access: No.
Children: No.
Languages: English, Spanish, a little German.
Your Host: Bob & Bill.

IGLTA

Renoir Hotel

Gay-Friendly ♀♂

See Special PAGE 19 Color Section

San Francisco's Newest First Class Downtown Hotel

The *Renoir Hotel* is a newly-renovated historical landmark building, just three blocks from Folsom Street, Polk Street, and three subway stations from the Castro. It is the best bargain in downtown San Francisco, providing charming European ambiance with classical music throughout. The ornate interior includes an original Renard in the reception area and Renoir prints placed tastefully throughout the hotel. The Royal Delight Restaurant serves breakfast, lunch and dinner. Also available are the lounge and lobby cafe and room service. *Inn Places* discount to $79 available most dates.

Address: 45 McAllister St,
San Francisco, CA 94102
Tel: (415) 626-5200, (800) 576-3388,
Fax: (415) 626-0916
URL: www.renoirhotel.com

Type: Hotel with restaurant, bar, espresso bar & gift shop.
Clientele: Mostly straight with a gay & lesbian following
Transportation: BART subway from Oakland airport to Civic Center Station. Shuttle van from SF Airport to hotel.
To Gay Bars: 2 blocks. About 10 gay bars within 5 blocks.
Rooms: 123 rooms & 3 suites with twin, double, queen & king beds.
Bathrooms: All private.
Vegetarian: Vegetarian items on restaurant & cafe menus.
Dates Open: All year.
High Season: May 15-Nov 15.
Rates: High season $99-$150, low season $79-$150.
Discounts: Inn Places rate: $79.
Credit Cards: All major credit cards.
Rsv'tns: Required.
To Reserve: Travel agent or call direct.
Minimum Stay: Gay Day Parade weekends & some sold-out periods, for last minute reservations.
Parking: Valet parking $14 day.
In-Room: Color TV, telephone, maid, room & laundry service.
On-Premises: Meeting rooms. Executive level offers modem hookups for computers.
Exercise/Health: YMCA 1 block from hotel with 7 floors of facilities. Non-member admission $13 per day.
Swimming: At nearby YMCA pool.
Nudity: 7 miles to nude beaches.
Smoking: Permitted in half the rooms & the bar. Non-smoking rooms available.
Pets: Not permitted.
Handicap Access: Yes. 3 handicap rooms. Ramp provided upon request.
Children: Welcome.
Languages: English, German, French, Russian, Spanish/Portuguese, Cantonese/Mandarin/Tagalog
Your Host: Steve.

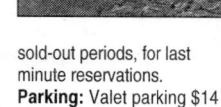

Twenty-Four Henry Guesthouse

Q-NET Gay/Lesbian ♀♂

An Intimate Guesthouse in the Heart of the Castro

24 Henry Guesthouse is a serene, non-smoking environment in San Francisco's gay Castro district. Within a block or two of the house are scores of cafes, shops, bars, and public transportation. Each beautifully appointed guest room has a private phone with answering machine. Our Victorian parlour/lounge is the setting for an extended continental buffet every morning where you may meet travelers from other parts of the globe. Also, consider our Apartment/Suite for a romantic or business getaway.

Address: 24 Henry St, San Francisco, CA 94114
Tel: (800) 900-5686, (415) 864-5686, **Fax:** (415) 864-0406.
E-mail: walterian@aol.com

Type: Guesthouse.
Clientele: Everyone is welcome
Transportation: Shuttle from airport to our door.
To Gay Bars: 2 blocks.
Rooms: 1 single, 5 doubles with queen beds.
Bathrooms: 2 private, 4 shared.

Meals: Extended continental buffet.
Vegetarian: Available upon request.
Complimentary: Hosts will help with travel planning.
Dates Open: All year.
Rates: Rooms $55-$95.
Credit Cards: MC, Visa, Amex.
Rsv'tns: Advised, preferably 2-3 weeks in advance.
To Reserve: Travel agent or call direct.
Minimum Stay: 2 days.
Parking: Adequate on-street parking.
In-Room: Individual phone lines with answering machines, no charge for local calls.
On-Premises: TV lounge, library.

Smoking: Non-smoking guesthouse.
Pets: Not permitted.
Handicap Access: No.
Children: Permitted.
Languages: English, Spanish.
Your Host: Walter.

IGLTA

UNITED STATES
SAN FRANCISCO • CALIFORNIA

The Villa

Gay/Lesbian ♀♂

Spectacular Views of San Francisco

SEE SPECIAL PAGE 20 COLOR SECTION

The Villa is the flagship guesthouse of San Francisco Views rental services. Located atop one of the Castro's legendary hills, we offer magnificent views of the city from our double rooms and suites. Guests have the use of our fireplace lounge, complete kitchen and dining area overlooking our decks and swimming pool. Suites are equipped with TV, VCR and telephone with answering machine. We are minutes from the financial and shopping districts of downtown San Francisco, three blocks from the heart of the Castro and are open all year. Short- or long-term rentals available.

Address: 379 Collingwood, San Francisco, CA 94114
Tel: (415) 282-1367, (800) 358-0123, **Fax:** (415) 821-3995.
E-mail: sfviews@aol.com

Type: Guesthouse.
Clientele: Good mix of gays & lesbians
Transportation: Easily accessible by car, or shuttle from airport.
To Gay Bars: 3 blocks or a 5-minute walk.
Rooms: 4 rooms, 3 suites & 4 apartments with single, double, queen or king beds.
Bathrooms: Rooms: private & shared. Apartments have private baths.
Meals: Continental breakfast.
Vegetarian: Restaurants nearby.
Dates Open: All year.
High Season: Summer & Fall.
Rates: Daily from $80, weekly $500, monthly rates available.
Discounts: Please inquire.
Credit Cards: MC, Visa, Amex.
Rsv'tns: Recommended.
To Reserve: Call direct.
Minimum Stay: 2 days.
Parking: Free off-street & on-street parking.
In-Room: Color cable TV, VCR, telephone, kitchen, refrigerator & maid service.
On-Premises: TV lounge, laundry facilities & shared kitchen on each floor.
Swimming: Pool on premises, ocean nearby.
Sunbathing: At poolside & on common sun decks.
Smoking: Permitted inside the rooms. Non-smoking rooms available upon request.
Pets: Not permitted.
Handicap Access: No.
Children: Permitted, but not especially welcome.
Languages: English & Spanish.

INN PLACES® 1998

The Willows

Q-NET Gay/Lesbian ♀♂

Your Haven Within The Castro

Housed in a 1904 Edwardian, *The Willows* derives its name from the handcrafted bentwood willow furnishings which grace each room. Complementing these unique pieces are antique dressers and armoires, plantation shutters, cozy comforters and fine English wallpaper borders. Each of our twelve guest bedrooms also has the country freshness of flowers, potted plants and dried floral arrangements. As an added comfort to each room, we provide direct dial telephones, alarm clock radios, kimono bathrobes, and fine Crabtree & Evelyn soaps.

The Willows is noted for its homey atmosphere and personal, friendly service. In the morning, wake up to a newspaper at your door followed by the pampered touch of breakfast served in bed. To help you plan your day's activities, our innkeepers are always available with helpful suggestions and directions. The sitting room welcomes guests to gather in the evening for cheese and conversation. Upon returning to the Inn at night, guests will appreciate the touch of a turned-down bed softly illuminated by the warmth of a glowing table lamp and a port nightcap, our classic finish to another day at *The Willows*. At the crossroads to the city's efficient transportation system, each of San Francisco's unique neighborhoods, attractions and convention sites are easily accessible. Dotting our neighborhood are a wide range of fine restaurants, specialty and second hand shops, gyms, bars and a vintage '30s movie palace.

Address: 710 14th St, San Francisco, CA 94114
Tel: (415) 431-4770, **Fax:** (415) 431-5295.
E-mail: Vacation@WillowsSF.com **URL:** www.WillowsSF.com

Type: Bed & breakfast inn.
Clientele: Gay & lesbian. Good mix of men & women
Transportation: Airport shuttle to the inn $10.
To Gay Bars: 1/2 block to men's bar, 3 to women's.
Rooms: 10 1-BR rooms, 1 2-BR room, 1 2-BR suite.
Bathrooms: 4 separate water closets, 4 separate showers, sinks in all rooms.
Meals: Expanded continental breakfast.

Vegetarian: Vegetarian-only restaurant (Amazing Grace) 1/2 block away.
Complimentary: Sherry nightcap with chocolate truffle.
Dates Open: All year.
High Season: June 15th-November 15th.
Rates: $64-$125.
Discounts: Midweek off season.
Credit Cards: MC, VISA, Discover, Amex.

Rsv'tns: Recommended 2 weeks in advance.
To Reserve: Call direct.
Minimum Stay: 2 nights on weekends.
Parking: Adequate on-street, limited off-street pay parking.
In-Room: TV on request, direct dial telephone, computer modem jacks, alarm clock radios, maid & room service, refrigerator in some rooms.

On-Premises: TV lounge area, refrigerator in pantry, iron/ironing board, beach towels.
Exercise/Health: Co-ed & women's gyms 1 block.
Swimming: Nearby pool & ocean.
Smoking: Permitted without restrictions.
Pets: Not permitted.
Handicap Access: No.
Children: Not permitted.
Languages: English, German.

Glenborough Inn

Q-NET Gay-Friendly ♀♂

Have Breakfast in Bed in a Romantic B&B

You step into the past, where life was quieter and the pace relaxed. Your room is fresh, immaculate, old-fashioned, with plants, fresh flowers and antiques. You might meet others around the fireplace, or in the gardens for hors d'oeuvres, or indulge yourself in the enclosed garden hot tub for private use. Pamper yourself with a gourmet breakfast delivered to your room. Leave your car, and take the shuttle to the beach or around town. The *Glenborough Inn* is Santa Barbara's most romantic gay-owned, gay-friendly B&B.

Address: 1327 Bath St, Santa Barbara, CA 93101
Tel: (805) 966-0589, (800) 962-0589, **Fax:** (805) 564-8610.
E-mail: glenboro@silcom.com

Type: Bed & breakfast inn.
Clientele: Mostly straight clientele with a gay/lesbian following
Transportation: Taxi from airport or train station.
To Gay Bars: 5 minutes by car to gay bars.
Rooms: 7 rooms & 4 suites with king, queen & full beds.
Bathrooms: 11 private bath/shower/toilets.
Meals: Full gourmet breakfast brought to room.
Vegetarian: No meat is served at the inn. Special diets accommodated with continental breakfast.
Complimentary: Evening refreshments & hors d'oeuvres, hot drinks & cookies nightly.
Dates Open: All year.
High Season: Jun-Oct.
Rates: $100-$250.
Discounts: Midweek corporate rates for guests on business.
Credit Cards: MC, Visa, Amex, Diners, Discover.
Rsv'tns: Recommended (not usually needed midweek).
To Reserve: Travel agent for Mon-Thurs stays or call direct.
Minimum Stay: 2 nights on weekends & 3 nights for 3-day holidays.
Parking: Ample free off- and on-street parking.
In-Room: Telephones & maid service.
On-Premises: Parlour, gardens, guest refrigerator & fax.
Exercise/Health: Outdoor enclosed (garden) Jacuzzi on sign-up basis.
Swimming: At nearby ocean beach.
Sunbathing: In gardens & at nearby beach.
Nudity: Nude beach nearby.
Smoking: ALL rooms are non-smoking; smoking permitted in gardens & patios.
Pets: Not permitted.
Handicap Access: No.
Children: Not especially welcomed.
Languages: English, Spanish & sign language.
Your Host: Michael, Steve.

Organic Gardens B&B

Q-NET Gay-Friendly ♀♂

A Way of Gentle Living

Five miles from Sequoia National Park is a peaceful retreat known as *Organic Gardens*. Surrounding the B&B are raised bed gardens where the innkeepers grow food organically, as well as a young fruit orchard. Each of our tiled rooms has a solarium, private entrance and bath, and a secluded hot tub is situated next to the studio/gallery.

Weather permitting, an organic vegetarian breakfast is served on our deck with panoramic river and mountain views. Specialties include homemade bread, crepes, granola, fried potatoes and organic seasonal fruit. Special diets are accommodated and, in winter, breakfast is served indoors next to the woodburning stove.

Address: 44095 Dinely Dr, Three Rivers, CA 93271
Tel: (209) 561-0916, **Fax:** (209) 561-1017.
E-mail: eggplant@theworks.com **URL:** http://www.theworks.com/~eggplant

Type: Bed & breakfast with photo & weaving gallery.
Clientele: Mostly straight with a gay & lesbian following
Transportation: Car is best.
Rooms: 2 rooms with queen bed.
Bathrooms: 2 private shower/toilets.
Meals: Full breakfast.
Vegetarian: All food is vegetarian, non-dairy available on request upon arrival.
Dates Open: All year.
High Season: May-Aug.
Rates: $95 per night, dbl occupancy. $20 extra per extra person, per room.
Credit Cards: MC, Visa.
Rsv'tns: Recommended during busy season.
Minimum Stay: 2 nights on weekends.
Parking: Ample off-street parking.

continued next page

INN PLACES® 1998

In-Room: Private entrances, ceiling fans, evaporative cooler, cast-iron stove.
Exercise/Health: Hot tub.
Sunbathing: On common sun decks.
Nudity: Permitted at the hot tub.
Smoking: Non-smoking B&B, smoking permitted off property only.
Pets: Not permitted.
Handicap Access: Bathrooms have 1 step up & are not large.
Children: No, 2nd floor deck where breakfast is served may be dangerous.
Languages: English, Tagalog, Chinese.

Sonoma Chalet B&B   Gay-Friendly ♀♂
A Wine Country Getaway

One of the first bed and breakfast inns established in Sonoma, our Swiss-style farmhouse and country cottages are situated on three acres, blocks from Sonoma's historic square. Relax in *Sonoma Chalet's* uniquely decorated rooms with fireplace or wood-burning stove, antiques, quilts and collectibles. Cross a wooden bridge to the popular fairy-tale-like Honeymoon Cottage. Complimentary bicycles are available for the more ambitious, or simply relax in the outdoor Jacuzzi. Enjoy a delightful continental breakfast served in your cottage or on the deck overlooking a 200-acre ranch.

Address: 18935 Fifth St West, Sonoma, CA 95476
Tel: (707) 938-3129, (800) 938-3129.

Type: Bed & breakfast.
Clientele: Mostly straight clientele with gays & lesbians welcome
Transportation: Car is best.
To Gay Bars: 1-hour drive to San Francisco & Russian River resorts.
Rooms: 2 rooms, 1 suite & 3 cottages with double or queen beds.
Bathrooms: 5 private & 1 shared.
Meals: Expanded continental breakfast.
Complimentary: Tea & coffee. Sherry in room.
Dates Open: All year.
High Season: Apr-Oct.
Rates: $85-$65.
Credit Cards: MC, Visa, Amex.
Rsv'tns: Required.
To Reserve: Travel agent or call direct.
Minimum Stay: 2 nights on weekends & holidays during high season.
Parking: Ample free parking.
In-Room: Ceiling fans, refrigerator, coffee & tea-making facilities.
Exercise/Health: Free use of bicycles, Jacuzzi on premises. Nearby gym, weights & massage.
Smoking: Permitted outside only.
Pets: Not permitted.
Handicap Access: No.
Children: By prior arrangement.
Languages: English.
Your Host: Joe.

Asti Ranch   Q-NET Women ♀

Asti Ranch is a charming one-bedroom cottage, with full kitchen, in a rural wine growing region 1-1/2 hours north of San Francisco. The ranch has eight sheep, two llamas, as well as ducks and geese on the pond. It is close to the premium wineries of Sonoma and Napa counties and only 1/2 hour from a major lesbian/gay resort. Fish, swim or canoe in the Russian river. Excellent restaurants and shopping are close by and it is only 45 minutes to the Pacific Ocean.

Address: 25750 River Rd, Cloverdale, CA 95425
Tel: (707) 894-5960, **Fax:** (707) 894-5658.

Type: Cottage.
Clientele: Women only.
Transportation: San Francisco Airport, then 2 hours north. Airport shuttle available to Santa Rosa.
To Gay Bars: 1/2 hour drive.
Rooms: 1 cottage with queen bed & double futon.
Bathrooms: Private bath/shower/toilet.
Complimentary: Tea, coffee & 1 bottle of wine en suite.
Rates: Week $500-$750, weekend $200-$300.
Rsv'tns: Required.
To Reserve: Call direct.
Minimum Stay: 2 nights.
Parking: Ample off-street parking.
In-Room: Ceiling fans, kitchen, refrigerator, coffee & tea-making facilities.
Exercise/Health: Nearby gym, Jacuzzi & massage.
Swimming: Nearby river & lake.
Sunbathing: On the patio or by the pond.
Smoking: Not permitted.
Pets: Not permitted.
Handicap Access: Yes.
Children: Not especially welcome.
Languages: English.

Whispering Pines B&B

Q-NET Gay-Friendly 50/50 ♀♂

Relax and Vacation in Peaceful Surroundings

A ranch-style home in a peaceful wooded area, *Whispering Pines B&B* is located in the middle of the Sonoma/Napa wine country. What a perfect place in which to relax away from city life, enjoy the sounds of nature and gaze at myriad stars while soaking in the hot tub at night! Full breakfast is served in the dining room or on the deck. We are close to wineries, balloon and glider rides, mud baths and massage, restaurants and more. Your congenial hostesses have many ideas of enjoyable things to do.

Address: 5950 Erland Rd, Santa Rosa, CA 95404
Tel: (707) 539-0198 (Tel/Fax).

Type: Bed & breakfast.
Clientele: 50% gay & lesbian & 50% straight clientele
Transportation: Car is best.
To Gay Bars: 10 miles, a 15 min drive.
Rooms: 2 rooms with double or queen beds.
Bathrooms: 2 private bath/toilets, 2 private shower/toilets.
Campsites: Room for tent, trailer or motor home.
Meals: Full breakfast.
Vegetarian: Available on request.
Complimentary: Wine & fruit in room.
Dates Open: All year.
High Season: May-Oct.
Rates: $125 year round.
Discounts: On stays of 2 nights or more.
Rsv'tns: Recommended.
To Reserve: Call direct.
Parking: Ample off-street parking.
In-Room: AC, ceiling fans, VCR, woodstove.
On-Premises: Phone, fax, video tape library, garden seating, picnic area.
Exercise/Health: Exercycle, Jacuzzi.
Swimming: Pool.
Sunbathing: Poolside.
Smoking: Permitted outside. All rooms are non-smoking.
Pets: Permitted in outside kennel.
Children: Inquire.
Languages: English.
Your Host: Sharon & Jeannie.

UNITED STATES • CALIFORNIA • SONOMA COUNTY

UNITED STATES — ASPEN • COLORADO

Hotel Aspen
Best Way to Stay in Aspen

Q·NET Gay-Friendly ♀♂

This striking, contemporary 45-room hotel on Main Street has large, beautifully-appointed rooms with king or queen beds, wet bars, cable TV, air conditioning, in-room safes, refrigerators, and private baths. Most rooms open onto terraces or balconies and some have private Jacuzzis. Guests relax year-round under beautiful mountain skies on our patio courtyard with its heated swimming pool and two Jacuzzis. In the lounge, take in incredible panoramic views while enjoying a complimentary mountain breakfast or afternoon wine and cheese in the lounge.

Hotel Aspen is the perfect home base from which to enjoy what the spirited town of Aspen has to offer. In winter, there is world-class skiing. Summer sports include golf, tennis, swimming, hiking, biking, river rafting and trout fishing. For the culturally-minded, there are daily concerts, dance and theater. And whatever the season, there are numerous shops, galleries and restaurants.

From the moment you arrive, our professional staff caters to your needs, ensuring a vacation that goes beyond expectation. *Hotel Aspen* is centrally located, just a short stroll from everything, and is convenient to free public transportation. The airport is only three miles from town and the city of Denver is a scenic 3-1/2 hour drive from Aspen.

Address: 110 W Main St, Aspen, CO 81611
Tel: (970) 925-3441, (800) 527-7369, **Fax:** (970) 920-1379.
E-mail: aspengroup@rof.net **URL:** http://www.aspen.com/ha/

Type: Hotel with breakfast & meeting room.
Clientele: Mainly straight with a gay & lesbian following
Transportation: Car. City provides shuttle transport from airport. Amtrak from Denver to Glenwood Springs.
To Gay Bars: About 3 blocks.
Rooms: 40 rooms & 5 suites with double, queen or king beds.
Bathrooms: All private.
Meals: Expanded continental buffet breakfast. We call it a Mountain Breakfast.

Vegetarian: At almost all restaurants. Best in Aspen, Explore Booksellers & Coffeehouse, is only 2 blocks away.
Complimentary: Apres-ski receptions in season.
Dates Open: All year.
High Season: Ski season: Xmas thru New Year, 2nd wk of Feb thru 3rd wk of Mar, July 4th.
Rates: Summer, $59-$160 per night; winter $69-$295 per night.
Discounts: Inquire. Mention ^IInn PlacesI^ for an instant 10% discount.
Credit Cards: MC, Visa, Amex, Diners & Discover.
Rsv'tns: Strongly suggested.
To Reserve: Travel agent or call direct.
Minimum Stay: At certain times. Inquire.
Parking: Ample free off-street & on-street parking.
In-Room: Cable color TV, AC, telephone, refrigerator, coffee/tea-maker & maid service. 4 rooms with Jacuzzi.
On-Premises: Meeting rooms, valet service, & helpful front desk staff.
Exercise/Health: Gym & outside Jacuzzi. Day passes available at the Aspen Athletic Club.
Swimming: On premises large outdoor heated pool. 25 miles to Reudi Reservoir.
Sunbathing: At poolside or on private sun decks.
Smoking: Permitted in rooms, but not in common areas.
Pets: Dogs permitted in some rooms.
Handicap Access: Yes. All 1st-floor rooms.
Children: Permitted.
Languages: English, Spanish, German, French & Australian.

292   FERRARI GUIDES™

Pikes Peak Paradise B&B

Q-NET Gay-Friendly 50/50 ♀♂

We're So Happy, You Might Even Say We're...Gay!

Take: A Southern mansion and hospitality and an unexcelled view of Pikes Peak. Mix with: Romantic atmosphere and privacy, a fireplace, queen- and king-sized beds with fresh sheets, and a gourmet breakfast. Add: Friendly hosts eager to make you feel at home and a pinch of good conversation. Fold in: A basketful of dreams yet-to-be, a plentiful supply of "glad-to-be-gay." Shake and bake with: Enjoyment. It will yield: A large bundle of unforgettable moments and memories at *Pikes Peak Paradise*.

Address: PO Box 5760, Woodland Park, CO 80866
Tel: (719) 687-7112, (800) 354-0989, **Fax:** (719) 687-9008.
E-mail: ppp@cyber-bbs.com

Type: Bed & breakfast.
Clientele: 50% gay & lesbian & 50% straight clientele
Transportation: Car.
To Gay Bars: 25 minutes to Colorado Springs gay/lesbian bars.
Rooms: 5 rooms with queen & king beds.
Bathrooms: 3 private bath/toilets & 2 private shower/toilets.
Meals: Full gourmet breakfast. Breakfast in bed available.

Vegetarian: Available upon request.
Complimentary: Tea, coffee, peanuts, soft drinks, mints on pillows.
Dates Open: All year.
High Season: May-October.
Rates: $95-$195.
Discounts: Sun-Thurs: 2 nights for price of 1, year round.
Credit Cards: MC, Visa, Amex, Discover.
Rsv'tns: Requested.

To Reserve: Travel agent or call direct.
Parking: Ample free off-street parking.
In-Room: Ceiling fans, refrigerator, fireplace, hot tub.
On-Premises: Public telephones & living room.
Exercise/Health: Massage $50/hour. Jacuzzi.
Swimming: 10 miles to public pool.
Sunbathing: On patio. 3 rooms have private deck.

Nudity: Permitted on private deck & in hot tub.
Smoking: Permitted outdoors.
Pets: Toy breed dogs & declawed cats by prior arrangement.
Handicap Access: Yes, 1 deluxe room with Jacuzzi tub.
Children: Permitted if over 12 yrs.
Languages: English.
Your Host: Tim, Martin & Priscilla.

The House at Peregrine's Perspective

Q-NET Gay-Owned & -Operated ♂

A Secluded B&B-style Mountain Retreat

Near Denver, *The House at Peregrine's Perspective* offers an escape to the country for a private retreat, romantic getaway, or a vacation in spectacular scenery close to ski slopes, hike and bike trails, lakes and whitewater rivers, sport and recreation areas. Home to *White Crane: A Journal of Gay Men's Spirituality*, the house is a large, honey-colored log cabin lodge beautifully appointed with antique fixtures and comfortable furnishings, nestled in an aspen grove on the sunny side of an evergreen-wooded mountain with a view of snow-capped peaks.

Address: PO Box 1018, Conifer, CO 80433-1018
Tel: (303) 697-0558. **E-mail:** editor@whitecranejournal.com
URL: http://www.whitecranejournal.com

continued next page

UNITED STATES — DENVER • COLORADO

Type: Bed & breakfast, 45 min from downtown Denver.
Clientele: Mostly men with women welcome.
Transportation: Car is best.
To Gay Bars: 45 min to Denver gay bars.
Rooms: 4 rooms with single, double or queen beds.
Bathrooms: Private: 1 sink.
Shared: 3 bath/shower/toilets.
Meals: Expanded continental breakfast.
Vegetarian: Available upon request.
Complimentary: Sweets in room, afternoon beverages & snacks.
Dates Open: All year.
High Season: May-Oct.
Rates: $75.
Discounts: On extended stays.
Credit Cards: MC, Visa.
Rsv'tns: Required.
To Reserve: Call direct.
Parking: Ample free off-street parking.
On-Premises: TV lounge, Great Room with huge stone fireplace, den & library.
Exercise/Health: Weights, Jacuzzi.
Sunbathing: On patio with hot tub.
Nudity: Permitted in hot tub area.
Smoking: Permitted on patio & in smoking lounge.
Pets: Not permitted.
Handicap Access: No.
Children: By prior arrangement only.
Languages: English.
Your Host: Kip & Toby.

Bobby's Bed/Breakfast
Home Away from Home

Men ♂

Bobby's Bed/Breakfast offers contemporary lodging at reasonable rates, with king-sized bed, private bath, color TV, VCR, bar refrigerator, air-conditioning, phone, breakfast, a library, video selections, laundry facilities, massage, and discount coupons. *Bobby's* is in a lovely, centrally located, Spanish-style complex in the heart of the gay area, near Cheesman Park. It is only one block to buses. Clubs, bars, and eateries are nearby. Your host will be glad to assist you with information about places to go and things to do. Please kick off your shoes, relax, and enjoy my home, while you're away from yours! NOTE: Owner may be moving, please call B&B for updated information.

Tel: (303) 831-8266 or (800) 513-7827.

Type: In home stay.
Clientele: Exclusively men
To Gay Bars: 4 blocks.
Rooms: 1 room with king bed. 2nd room available, please inquire.
Bathrooms: 1 private tub/shower/toilet.
Meals: Expanded continental breakfast.
Complimentary: Set-up service, tea, coffee, pop.
Dates Open: All year.
Rates: $50-$70, subject to change.
Discounts: Special weekly rate available.
Rsv'tns: Preferred.
To Reserve: Travel agent or call direct.
Minimum Stay: Prefer 2 nights.
Parking: Ample off-street parking.
In-Room: Color TV, VCR, video tape library, telephone & refrigerator.
On-Premises: Laundry facilities.
Exercise/Health: Massage on premises. Year-round sauna & Jacuzzi.
Swimming: Pool in summer.
Sunbathing: On the patio or poolside.
Nudity: Please inquire.
Smoking: Permitted outside only.
Pets: Not permitted.
Handicap Access: No.
Children: Not permitted.
Languages: English.
Your Host: Bob.

Twin Maples Bed & Breakfast
Your Accommodation of Choice in Denver

Gay/Lesbian ♀♂

This prominent residence, dating from 1906, still features original Tiffany light fixtures, wood-mantel fireplace, hardwood appointments and lead-glass windows are reminiscent of a by-gone era. *Twin Maples* is ideally located in the historic Congress Park area, close to sightseeing, excellent dining, a lively nightlife, and offers easy access to public transportation. Our rooms are spacious and richly appointed with period antiques and Queen Anne furnishings. In the European tradition, our ultra-firm beds are dressed with colorful linens and feather pillows. You will find that our cozy living room welcomes you to relax, read or chat with new friends in front of the warm fire. And for the musically talented, the baby grand piano awaits your touch in the adjoining music room. Above all, you can expect our friendly personal assistance will ensure you a memorable stay.

Address: 1401 Madison St., Denver, CO 80206
Tel: (303) 393-1832, toll free: (888) 835-5738, **Fax:** (303) 394-4776.
E-mail: twinmaples@boytoy.com

Type: Bed & breakfast.
Clientele: Mostly gay & lesbian with some straight clientele
Transportation: Air Porter, North Denver Shuttle.
To Gay Bars: 4 blocks, a 5 minute walk, a 5 min. drive.
Rooms: 3 rooms, 2 suites with queen or king beds.

Bathrooms: Private: 1 bath & toilet, 1 bath/shower/toilet. Shared: 3 bath/shower/toilets.
Meals: Expanded continental breakfast.
Complimentary: Coffee, tea, mints on pillows.
Dates Open: All year.
Rates: $85-$160.

Discounts: 6th night free.
Credit Cards: MC, Visa, Amex.
Rsv'tns: Required.
To Reserve: Travel agent or call direct.
Parking: Adequate off & off-street parking.
In-Room: Telephone, ceiling fans, maid service.

On-Premises: TV lounge, fax.
Sunbathing: On patio.
Smoking: Permitted outside on patio or porch. House is non-smoking.
Pets: Not permitted.
Handicap Access: No.
Children: No.
Languages: English.

Victoria Oaks Inn

Q-NET Gay/Lesbian

The warmth and hospitality of *Victoria Oaks Inn* is apparent the moment you enter this historical, restored 1896 mansion. Elegant, original oak woodwork, tile fireplaces and dramatic hanging staircase replete with ornate brass chandelier, set the mood for a delightful visit. The nine guest rooms are finished with stylish, restored antiques from the turn-of-the-century and have panoramic views through leaded glass windows and soft colors throughout. The individual character and appointments of *Victoria Oaks Inn* are designed for your personal comforts in your home-away-from-home. Whether your visit is for business or pleasure, *Victoria Oaks* is conveniently located near Denver's bustling business and financial district, numerous shopping areas and varied tourist attractions.

The mansion is quietly nestled blocks from many of Denver's finest restaurants and close to major traffic arteries, providing quick access for any excursion. The historic Capitol Hill district offers special attractions, including the Unsinkable Molly Brown House, Botanic Gardens and the domed State Capitol Building. Within walking distance are the city park, the zoo, the Museum of Natural History and Imax Theatre. As a home you'd love to come home to, whether for a night or for the week, *Victoria Oaks* stands proudly apart. As a small inn, we offer personalized services not often available at larger hotels. Begin each morning with an inspiring continental breakfast, including freshly-squeezed orange juice, blended coffee and teas and a choice of fresh pastries, croissants, bagels and fresh fruits with the morning paper. Start your evening with a complimentary glass of wine from our wine cellar.

Address: 1575 Race St, Denver, CO 80206
Tel: (303) 355-1818, (800) 662-OAKS (6257), **Fax:** (303) 331-1095.
E-mail: vicoaksinn@aol.com

continued next page

Type: Bed & breakfast.
Clientele: Mostly gay & lesbian with some straight clientele
Transportation: Taxi.
To Gay Bars: 4 blks to gay/lesbian bars.
Rooms: 9 doubles.
Bathrooms: 7 private, 2 share.
Meals: Expanded continental breakfast.
Complimentary: Tea, coffee, juices, beer, wine & sodas.
Dates Open: All year.
High Season: June-August.
Rates: $50-$85.
Discounts: Weekly and group rates.
Credit Cards: MC, Visa, Amex, Diners & Discover.
Rsv'tns: Recommended 2 weeks in advance.
To Reserve: Travel agent or call direct.
Parking: Adequate free off-street parking.
In-Room: Maid & laundry service & telephone.
On-Premises: Meeting rooms, private dining rooms, TV lounge & laundry facilities.
Sunbathing: In the backyard.
Smoking: Permitted without restrictions.
Pets: Not permitted.
Handicap Access: No.
Children: Permitted if well-behaved.
Languages: English.
Your Host: Clyde.

Butternut Farm
Gay-Friendly ♀♂

Bed & Breakfast in the 18th Century

Everywhere you look at *Butternut Farm*, you'll find an 18th-century treasure: a cherry highboy, a gateleg table, banister-back chairs, and English delft. Outside there are tulips in the spring, herb gardens, and Adirondack chairs on a stone patio. On two wooded and landscaped acres, "Everything about this amazing place — from the lovingly restored old house and farm buildings to the antique furnishings and exotic animals, from the homemade breakfast jams to the bedtime sherry — conspires to make a couple of nights and breakfasts quite unforgettable" said one guest.

Address: 1654 Main St, Glastonbury, CT 06033
Tel: (860) 633-7197, **Fax:** (860) 659-1758.

Type: Bed & breakfast 10 minutes outside Hartford.
Clientele: Mostly straight clientele with a gay/lesbian following.
Transportation: Car is best.
To Gay Bars: 10 miles or a 10-15 minute drive.
Rooms: 3 rooms, 1 suite, 1 apartment with single or double beds.
Bathrooms: 3 private bath/toilets, 2 private shower/toilets.
Meals: Full breakfast.
Vegetarian: Available nearby, breakfast is vegetarian.
Complimentary: Wine, beer, setup service, tea, coffee, mints, chocolates. Sherry in room.
Dates Open: All year.
Rates: $70-$90.
Discounts: On longer stays.
Credit Cards: Amex.
Rsv'tns: Preferred.
To Reserve: Call direct.
Parking: Ample free off-street parking.
In-Room: Color TV, VCR, AC, phone. Apartment: coffee & tea-making facilities, refrigerator.
On-Premises: TV lounge, video tape library, fax.
Exercise/Health: Nearby gym with weights & massage.
Swimming: Nearby pool, river.
Smoking: Permitted outside only.
Pets: Not permitted.
Handicap Access: No.
Children: Welcome.
Languages: English, French, some German & Italian.
Your Host: Don.

The Adams House
Gay-Friendly ♀♂

"Quaint & Cozy...Friendly...Beautiful...& Relaxing"

Adams House is a 1790's-era house on a full acre of lush greenery and flower gardens, offering a homey colonial atmosphere featuring old fashioned fireplaces in the dining room and two bedrooms. Guests can choose between the main house and the *Garden Cottage*, a self-contained building just far enough away to ensure total privacy. Breakfast is a delicious medley of fresh fruit, homemade muffins and hot entrées with fabulous coffee. Guests' comments: "Quaint, cozy, fun, relaxing." "A perfect getaway." "Friendly, beautiful." "A blessing."

Address: 382 Cow Hill Rd, Mystic, CT 06355
Tel: (860) 572-9551.

Type: Bed & Breakfast.
Clientele: Mostly straight clientele with gays & lesbians welcome
Transportation: Plane to Groton, taxi, train or ferry to New London, then taxi. Free pick up (usually) from Mystic train station.
To Gay Bars: 9 miles to New London.
Rooms: 6 rooms with queen beds & 1 room with double sofabed & queen bed.
Bathrooms: 7 private.

Meals: Full breakfast.
Vegetarian: Always available.
Complimentary: Hot or iced tea on arrival or request.
Dates Open: All year.
High Season: Memorial Day to Labor Day.
Rates: $95-$175. Off-season rates available.
Discounts: Sun-Thur nights, 3rd night half price. November through April negotiable.

Credit Cards: MC, Visa, Amex, Discover.
Rsv'tns: Recommended for weekends & Jun-Sep.
To Reserve: Call direct.
Minimum Stay: 2 nights on weekends & holidays.
Parking: Ample free off-street parking.
In-Room: AC & maid service. Garden Cottage has color cable TV, refrigerator.
On-Premises: TV lounge.
Exercise/Health: Sauna in Garden Cottage.
Swimming: 20-30 minutes by car to several beaches, 1 nude.
Sunbathing: On the lawn or at the beaches.
Nudity: At nude beach.
Smoking: Permitted in yard only.
Pets: Not permitted.
Handicap Access: Garden Cottage accessible, 2 steps.
Children: Welcome in Garden Cottage.
Languages: English.
Your Host: Mary Lou & Greg.

Honeysuckle

Women ♀

Victorian Inn & Adjoining Houses near the Delaware Beaches

Come to *Honeysuckle* and enjoy the easygoing atmosphere at our popular Victorian inn and adjoining houses, Wisteria and Larkspur, near the Delaware beaches. Women feel at home in the comfortable spaces that our houses provide. Our sauna and outdoor hot tubs are year-round favorites. In summer, stroll our porches, decks and gardens to the large in-ground pool with privacy fencing. Snuggle by the fireside in winter. VCRs, stereos, games, a canoe and our library of women's books and music will keep you busy between trips to the beaches, restaurants and outlet malls. Now celebrating our 10th year.

Address: 330 Union St, Milton, DE 19968 **Tel:** (302) 684-3284.

Type: Inn & 2 adjoining houses.
Clientele: Women only
Transportation: Car is best.
To Gay Bars: 12 miles to Rehoboth gay/lesbian bars.
Rooms: 4 rooms & 2 private rental houses with double or queen beds. Each private house accommodates up to 6 people.
Bathrooms: 2 private bath/ whirlpool tubs. Others shared. Outdoor shower by pool.

Meals: Full breakfast for inn guests only.
Vegetarian: Upon request.
Complimentary: Coffee and teas.
Dates Open: All year.
High Season: Summer (June through September).
Rates: $85-$175.
Discounts: 10% for 7 days or more.
Credit Cards: MC, Visa.
Rsv'tns: Required.
To Reserve: Travel agent or call direct.

Minimum Stay: On holiday weekends only.
Parking: Ample free off-street parking.
In-Room: Inn: self-controlled AC/heat & one room with whirlpool in bath. Houses: AC/heat, private hot tub, whirlpool/massage room.
On-Premises: TV lounge & kitchens.
Exercise/Health: Sauna, outdoor hot tub & whirlpool in private baths. Massage available.

Swimming: Pool on premises.
Sunbathing: At poolside or on the beaches.
Nudity: Permitted poolside.
Smoking: Permitted outdoors.
Pets: Not permitted, excellent kennel nearby.
Handicap Access: 1 house available with 1st-floor bedroom/bath.
Children: Not permitted.
Languages: English.
Your Host: Mary Ann & Julie.

Cabana Gardens Bed & Breakfast

Gay-Owned & -Operated ♀♂

Luxury Guesthouse with Spacious, Contemporary Design

Built in 1995, *Cabana Gardens Bed & Breakfast* is the newest luxury guesthouse in Rehoboth Beach. You will delight in the home's spacious, contemporary design. Featured are three levels of plant-filled decks, including decks which overlook downtown Lake Gerar and the ocean, as well as an enormous roof-top deck. The bed & breakfast has three sitting areas for socializing with other guests and our guest rooms have private baths, decks and great views! We are centrally located, only three blocks from the many shops and restaurants of Baltimore Avenue and Rehoboth Avenue.

Address: 20 Lake Avenue, Rehoboth Beach, DE 19971
Tel: (302) 227-5429, **Fax:** (302) 227-5380. **E-mail:** cabanagardens@ce.net

Type: Bed & breakfast.
Clientele: Gay & lesbian. Good mix of men & women
Transportation: Car is best, free pick up from bus.
To Gay Bars: 1 block to Cloud Nine & Blue Moon.
Rooms: 8 rooms with double or queen beds.
Bathrooms: All private bath/shower/toilets.
Meals: Continental breakfast.

Dates Open: All year.
High Season: June-Sept.
Rates: Summer: weekends $115-$160, Mon-Thurs $85-$85. Winter: $50-$75.
Discounts: Stay 7 nights, get 1 weekday free.
Credit Cards: MC, Visa, Discover.
Rsv'tns: Suggested.
To Reserve: Travel agent or call direct.

Minimum Stay: 2 nights in season.
Parking: Ample free off-street parking.
In-Room: AC, ceiling fans, color cable TV, kitchen, refrigerator, maid service.
On-Premises: Private decks with lake views, enormous rooftop deck, shared kitchen area & wet bar, meeting rooms, TV lounge.

Swimming: Ocean nearby.
Sunbathing: On roof, private & common sun decks, at beach.
Smoking: Permitted in outside areas only.
Pets: Not permitted.
Handicap Access: Ground-floor rooms available with a 2-step access.
Children: No.
Languages: English.
Your Host: Gary.

The Mallard Guest Houses

Gay/Lesbian ♀♂

Newly Renovated

The Mallard Guest Houses provide comfortable accommodations in this quaint Atlantic seashore community nestled just south of Delaware Bay. Our in-town location is very convenient to bars, fine restaurants and shopping. The inn is decorated in fine furnishings. Enjoy a warm afternoon at the beach or visit our town's many attractions. Enjoy the best of Rehoboth, while staying at the best in Rehoboth.

Address: 60 Baltimore Ave, Rehoboth Beach, DE 19971
Tel: (302) 226-3448.

Type: Guesthouses. Three locations in Rehoboth.
Clientele: Gay & lesbian. Good mix of men & women
Trans.: Car is best.
To Gay Bars: Adjacent to bars.
Rooms: 20 rooms.
Bathrooms: All private.
Meals: Cont. breakfast.
Complimentary: Coffee & tea.

Dates Open: All year.
High Season: Memorial Day-Labor Day.
Rates: $65-$175.
Discounts: Inquire for special packages.
Credit Cards: MC, Visa.
Rsv'tns: Required.
To Reserve: Travel agent or call direct.

Parking: Adequate off-street parking.
In-Room: TV & Jacuzzi tubs.
On-Premises: TV lounge.
Exercise/Health: Jacuzzi tubs in some locations & outdoor spa.
Swimming: 2 blocks to ocean beach.

Sunbathing: On private sun decks & at the beach.
Smoking: Permitted in designated areas. All rooms are non-smoking.
Pets: Sometimes in off season.
Handicap Access: Not fully accessible.
Children: Inquire.
Languages: English.

The Rams Head

Q-NET Men ♂

European Hospitality in a Masculine Environment

Not far from the madding crowd lies a private haven, protected from intruding eyes by its surrounding walls and lush gardens. We call this place *The Rams Head*. Unique in the Rehoboth Beach area, it is bordered by fields and forests, yet is only minutes from the beach, bars, restaurants, tax-free outlet malls, and shops. According to the *Washington Post*, "The Rams Head is an upscale retreat for gay men in an area that seems to have more gay or gay-friendly establishments than Munich has beer halls."

The Rams Head is proud to be the only exclusively all-male bed and breakfast resort in the Rehoboth Beach area. Discover relaxed and comfortable European hospitality in a distinctly East Coast seashore setting. We are a totally enclosed compound, complete with heated pool, gymnasium with universal equipment, free weights & ten-man sauna, enclosed private hot tub/spa, and an outdoor poolside cabana — where we host full breakfast in the morning and complimentary open bar in the afternoon. Comfortably-appointed accommodations are bright, spacious and individually decorated in traditional style. Each bedroom has a queen-sized bed, private bath, color TV, VCR, hair dryers, central air, and refrigerator. Pamper yourself in a man-to-man environment. Alternate e-mail: TwoRams4_1@ce.net.

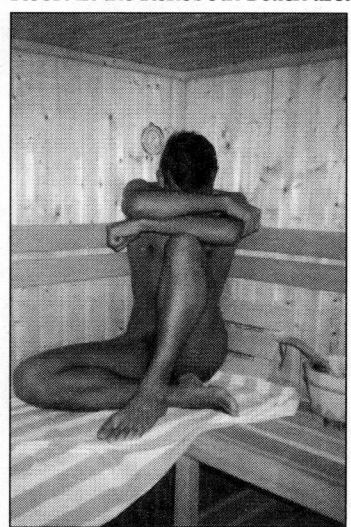

Address: RD 2 Box 509, Rehoboth Beach, DE 19971-9702
Tel: (302) 226-9171.
E-mail: TwoRams41@aol.com
URL: www.theramshead.com

Type: Bed & breakfast.
Clientele: Men only
Transportation: Car is best.
To Gay Bars: 1 mile to dance bar, 2 miles to cruise bars.
Rooms: 2 economy rooms, 5 deluxe rooms & 2 suites, all with queen beds.
Bathrooms: All private.
Meals: Full breakfast.
Complimentary: Non-alcoholic & alcoholic beverages served poolside during day.
Dates Open: May 1-Oct 1.
High Season: May 1-Oct 1.
Rates: $110-$145.
Credit Cards: MC, Visa, Discover, Amex.
Rsv'tns: Required.
To Reserve: Call direct.
Minimum Stay: 2 days in season, 3 days on holidays.
Parking: Ample, free off-street parking.
In-Room: Housekeeping service, color cable TV, VCR, refrigerator, hair dryer.
On-Premises: Library, sitting lounge, cabana with open bar.
Exercise/Health: Full gym with free weights, universal & 10-man sauna, gazebo with hot tub.
Swimming: Heated pool on premises, ocean beach 2 miles.
Sunbathing: At poolside & on the beach.
Nudity: Permitted poolside & in spa & sauna area.
Smoking: Permitted without restriction.
Pets: Not permitted.
Handicap Access: No.
Children: Not permitted.
Languages: English.
Your Host: Jim & Carl.

Rehoboth Guest House

Gay/Lesbian ♀♂

Rehoboth's Oldest Continually Running Gay Guesthouse

Rehoboth Guest House, is a charming Victorian beach house 1-1/2 blocks from the beach on a residential street close to gay shopping & dining. Feel at home in 12 airy, white-washed rooms with large windows and painted floors. Relax over continental breakfast in the sun room or rock on the flower-lined front porch. Enjoy sun decks, gay beaches, outdoor cedar showers, Saturday evening wine and cheese, or nearby shops, restaurants and bars. Whether you are taking a long vacation or grabbing a weekend, you will always feel relaxed and welcome. Newly renovated.

Address: 40 Maryland Ave, Rehoboth, DE 19971
Tel: (302) 227-4117, (800) 564-0493.

Type: Bed & breakfast guesthouse.
Clientele: Mostly gay & lesbian with some hetero clientele
Transportation: Car is best.
To Gay Bars: 1 block.
Rooms: 12 rooms & 1 apartment sleeping 4.
Double, queen & king beds.
Bathrooms: Private & shared baths.
Meals: Continental breakfast.
Complimentary: Wine & cheese in backyard or living room on Sat afternoon.
Dates Open: May-October.
High Season: May-October.
Rates: Pre/post season: $45-$75; in season: $65-$150; Apartment $125-$350.
Discounts: Special rates for Sun thru Thur stays.
Credit Cards: MC, Visa.
Rsv'tns: Required.
To Reserve: Travel agent or call direct.
Minimum Stay: 2 nights weekends, holiday weekends 3 nights.
Parking: Most rooms with free off-street parking, limited free on-street parking.
In-Room: All rooms have AC & ceiling fans.
On-Premises: 2 sun decks, front porch with rockers, 2 picnic tables in backyard, 2 outdoor, enclosed showers/ dressing rooms with hot water.
Exercise/Health: Gym a few blocks away on boardwalk.
Swimming: 1-1/2 blocks to beach, short walk to gay beaches.
Sunbathing: On common sun decks or at the beach.
Smoking: Permitted on porch or decks.
Pets: Not permitted.
Handicap Access: No.
Children: Not permitted.
Languages: English.

Silver Lake

Q-NET Gay/Lesbian ♀♂

"Gem of the Delaware Shore"

Silver Lake Guest House is "the best of the bunch" (Fodor's Gay Guide), "the best option" (Out & About), and "the gem of the Delaware shore" (The Washington Post). Located in a tranquil waterfront setting in the midst of a waterfowl preserve on Rehoboth Beach's most scenic drive, this beautiful home offers its guests much more than a conventional bed and breakfast. It is also the resort's closest guesthouse to gay Poodle Beach.

Completely renovated in 1997, *Silver Lake* provides spectacular lake and ocean views from its sprawling columned veranda, balconies and decks. All of the bedrooms have private baths, cable TV and central air conditioning. Many of the rooms have panoramas of the lake and ocean from private balconies. Guests may enjoy breakfast quietly in their rooms, in the second-floor sunroom, or on the third-floor sun deck where the lake and ocean are on full display. Breakfast includes muffins baked daily, fresh fruit, juice, tea and coffee, along with the daily newspaper.

Behind the main house is the Carriage House with its very private, large two-bedroom apartments. Each has a private entrance, living room, dining area and complete kitchen. *Silver Lake* is about quality of life. Whether for a weekend or extended vacation, guests enjoy an ambience of comfort and relaxation in the midst of nature at its best.

Address: 133 Silver Lake Dr, Rehoboth Beach, DE 19971
Tel: (302) 226-2115, (800) 842-2115.

Type: Bed & breakfast guesthouse.
Clientele: Gay & lesbian. Good mix of men & women
Transportation: Car is best.
To Gay Bars: Walking distance.
Rooms: 14 rooms & 2 two-bedroom apartments with queen or king beds.
Bathrooms: All private.
Meals: Expanded continental breakfast.
Complimentary: Tea, coffee, juices & fruit.
Dates Open: All year.
High Season: Summer.
Rates: In season $80-$300, off season from $60.
Discounts: For longer stays.
Credit Cards: MC, Visa, Amex, Discover
Rsv'tns: Required.
To Reserve: Call direct.
Minimum Stay: 2-3 nights on summer weekends.
Parking: Ample, free off-street parking.
In-Room: Color cable TV, AC, maid service, kitchens in apartments. Some rooms have private decks.
On-Premises: Meeting rooms, guest kitchen, sun room, lounge, BBQ grills, sun decks, beach chairs & towels, ice, sodas, outdoor showers, lake front lawn & gardens.
Exercise/Health: On jogging & biking course. Gym nearby.
Swimming: 5-minute walk to gay ocean beach.
Sunbathing: At beach or on decks.
Smoking: Permitted.
Pets: Permitted in apartments only, by prior arrangement.
Handicap Access: Yes, call for details.
Children: Not permitted except by prior arrangement.
Languages: English.
Your Host: Joe & Mark

The Summer Place
Gay/Lesbian ♀♂

In the Heart of Gay Rehoboth

Summer Place Hotel is located on the ocean block with a sun deck overlooking the Atlantic Ocean. Known for 100 years as "Yellow House," this property was recently remodeled from the foundation up. Each room has a private bath, television, air conditioning, heat and telephone. The one-bedroom condos have a kitchen that includes a dishwasher, microwave, stove and refrigerator. Comfortable, clean and quiet, our hotel is in an excellent location in the heart of gay Rehoboth is just a walk to all bars and restaurants. Open year round.

Address: 30 Olive Ave, Rehoboth Beach, DE 19971
Tel: (302) 226-0766, (800) 815-3925, **Fax:** (302) 226-3350.

Type: Hotel.
Clientele: Mostly gay & lesbian with some straight clientele
Transportation: Car is best.
To Gay Bars: A 1-minute walk.
Rooms: 23 rooms, 5 apartments.
Bathrooms: All private.
Dates Open: All year.
High Season: Jun-Aug.
Rates: Rooms: $40-$165 per day. Apartments: $60-$185 per day.
Credit Cards: Visa, MC, Discover, Amex, Nexus.
Minimum Stay: 1-3 nights.
Parking: Parking pass available.
In-Room: AC, telephone, color cable TV. Apartments also have dishwasher, stove, microwave, refrigerator.
On-Premises: Sun deck overlooking ocean.
Swimming: 1 minute to beach.
Smoking: Smoking & non-smoking rooms available.
Pets: No.
Handicap Access: 1st floor accommodations easy to enter.
Your Host: Dan.

INN PLACES® 1998

UNITED STATES • WASHINGTON • DISTRICT OF COLUMBIA

The Brenton

Q-NET Gay/Lesbian ♂

Your Accommodation of Choice in Washington, DC

Dating from 1891, *The Brenton* is located in the Dupont Circle neighborhood, 12 blocks north of the White House. Rooms are spacious and well-appointed, with antiques, art and Oriental carpets on handsome wood floors. The rooms are air conditioned, have direct-dial phones with answering machines and most have ceiling fans. In the European tradition, the baths are shared, and our beds are ultra-firm. The cozy front parlor welcomes you to relax with new friends and the staff encourages questions about local sights, activities and dining. Make yourself at home, and enjoy Washington as the locals do.

Address: 1708 16th St NW, Washington, DC 20009
Tel: (202) 332-5550, (800) 673-9042, **Fax:** (202) 462-5872.

Type: Guesthouse.
Clientele: Mostly men with women welcome
Transportation: Metro to Dupont Circle, then short walk.
To Gay Bars: 1 block to gay bar.
Rooms: 8 rooms, 1 suite with single, double, queen or king beds.
Bathrooms: 3 shared bath/shower/toilets, 1 shared toilet. Suite has private bath.
Meals: Expanded continental breakfast.
Complimentary: Cocktail hour in evening, coffee, tea, always.
Dates Open: All year.
High Season: March through October.
Rates: $79-$99.
Credit Cards: MC, Visa, Amex, Discover.
Rsv'tns: Recommended.
To Reserve: Travel agent or call direct.
Parking: Limited on-street pay parking. Garage nearby.
In-Room: Maid service, telephone, AC, ceiling fans. Suite has kitchen, sitting area, TV/VCR.
On-Premises: Dining rooms, TV lounge.
Exercise/Health: Nearby gym.
Smoking: Permitted without restrictions.
Pets: Not permitted.
Handicap Access: No.
Children: Not permitted.
Languages: English.
Your Host: Bob.

Capitol Hill Guest House

Gay-Owned 50/50 ♀♂

Capitol Hill Guest House is a Victorian row house with original woodwork and appointments, ideally located in the historic Capitol Hill district. Formerly home to congressional pages, the house has ten moderately-priced rooms. We're a short walk from the Capitol and the mall, close to the Eastern Market, fine restaurants and the Smithsonian Museums. Whether for business or pleasure, the convenience and charm of our house will make your stay comfortable and fun.

Address: 101 Fifth St NE, Washington, DC 20002
Tel: (202) 547-1050 (Tel/Fax), (800) 261-2768.

Type: Bed & breakfast guest house.
Clientele: 50% gay & lesbian & 50% straight clientele
Transportation: Taxi from airport, metro from Union Station.
To Gay Bars: 6-7 blocks to men's or women's bars.
Rooms: 10 rooms with single, double or queen beds.
Bathrooms: Private & shared.
Meals: Continental breakfast.
Vegetarian: Available at nearby restaurants.
Complimentary: Sherry in living room.
Dates Open: All year.
High Season: Spring & fall.
Rates: $45-$125.
Discounts: For senior citizens.
Credit Cards: Visa, MC, Amex (with surcharge), Discover.
Rsv'tns: Recommended.
To Reserve: Travel agent or call direct.
Parking: Adequate, free, on-street parking, permits provided.
In-Room: B&W TV for fee.
On-Premises: Refrigerator in the hall.
Swimming: 6 blocks to indoor public pool.
Smoking: Permitted on porch or in backyard.
Pets: Not permitted.
Handicap Access: No.
Children: Permitted, if over 8 years.
Languages: English, Spanish, Portuguese, American Sign Language.
Your Host: Antonio.

Embassy Inn

Gay-Friendly ♀♂

The **Embassy Inn** is a charming, gay-friendly B&B on historical 16th St. We offer a relaxing, friendly atmosphere and convenience to metro, shops, restaurants, grocery store and nightlife. You'll enjoy personalized service, continental breakfast, and evening sherry, as you relax in the warm lobby with a great selection of books and magazines. Our staff is always happy to help with dining suggestions, tourist information or directions. The inn is a great value and is easily accessible to all of Washington's sights. The neighborhood is quaint and offers something for everyone.

Address: 1627 16th St, Washington, DC
Tel: (202) 234-7800 or (800) 423-9111, **Fax:** (202) 234-3309.

Type: Hotel inn.
Clientele: Mostly straight clientele with a gay & lesbian following
Transportation: Taxi from airport. Metro Red line from Union Station to Dupont Circle, then 4-1/2 blocks to inn.
To Gay Bars: 2 blocks to men's bar, 5 blocks to Dupont Circle gay & lesbian bars.
Rooms: 38 rooms with single & double beds.
Bathrooms: All private shower/toilets.
Meals: Expanded continental breakfast.
Complimentary: Evening sherry year-round, coffee/tea 24 hours.
Dates Open: All year.
High Season: April-May & September-October.
Rates: High season $79-$110, low season $59-$89.
Discounts: On extended stays, weekend rates, government (business) travel, based on availability.
Credit Cards: MC, Visa, Amex, Carte Blanche, Diner's.
Rsv'tns: Preferred. Must be guaranteed with credit card.
To Reserve: Travel agent or call direct.
Parking: Limited on-street parking, 24-hr pay garage 8 blocks away.
In-Room: Telephone, color cable TV, free HBO, AC, maid service.
On-Premises: Dry cleaning service.
Exercise/Health: Facilities within close walking distance.
Swimming: Facilities within close walking distance.
Smoking: Not permitted in main lobby. Non-smoking rooms available. Limited smoking rooms.
Pets: Not permitted.
Handicap Access: No.
Children: Permitted.
Languages: English, Spanish.

The Kalorama Guest House at Kalorama Park

Q-NET Gay-Friendly ♀♂

Your Home in Washington, DC

The Kalorama Guest House is the place to call home when you are in D.C. We are located on a quiet, tree-lined street, only a short walk from two of Washington's most trendy neighborhoods, Dupont Circle and Adams Morgan. You'll be near a potpourri of bars, ethnic restaurants, nightspots, antique shops and the underground metro. After staying in a bedroom decorated tastefully with Victorian antiques and enjoying a continental breakfast, an evening aperitif and our nationally-known hospitality, we're sure you'll make our house your home whenever you visit Washington. If you prefer a smaller, more intimate guesthouse, please inquire about our other property, *The Kalorama Guest House at Woodley Park.*

Address: 1854 Mintwood Pl NW, Washington, DC 20009 **Tel:** (202) 667-6369, Fax: (202) 319-1262.

Type: Bed & breakfast.
Clientele: Gay-friendly establishment. Mostly straight clientele with a gay & lesbian following
Transportation: Taxi or subway are best.
To Gay Bars: 4 blocks to men's bars at Dupont Circle.
Rooms: 29 rooms & 2 suites with double or queen beds.
Bathrooms: 12 private, 19 rooms share (2-3 rooms per bath).
Meals: Continental breakfast.
Complimentary: Sherry in parlor (afternoon aperitif), lemonade in summer.
Dates Open: All year.
High Season: Mar-Jun & Sep-Oct.
Rates: Rooms $50-$95, suites $80-$115.
Discounts: AAA.
Credit Cards: MC, Visa, Amex, Diners.
To Reserve: Travel agent or call direct.
Minimum Stay: 2 nights required occasionally.
Parking: Limited pay parking off-street & limited free on-street parking.
In-Room: AC, maid & laundry service. Some rooms with ceiling fans.
On-Premises: Meeting rooms, TV lounge, guest fridge, laundry facilities.
Exercise/Health: Gym with weights nearby.
Swimming: In nearby pool.
Sunbathing: On landscaped backyard.
Smoking: Discouraged in breakfast room. Non-smoking rooms available.
Pets: Not permitted.
Handicap Access: No.
Children: Prefer those over 10 years old.
Languages: English.
Your Host: Tami.

IGLTA

Morrison House

Q-NET Gay-Friendly ♂

The Romance of Old Europe, The Charm of Early America

SEE SPECIAL PAGE 21 COLOR SECTION

Designed and staffed with the utmost care, ***The Morrison House*** blends the romance of Old Europe with the charm of Early America. Elegantly decorated with authentic Federal Period reproductions, we offer gracious hospitality and uncompromising service. Designed after the grand manors of the Federal Period, our guestrooms evoke the traditional elegance of late-eighteenth century Alexandria with their four-poster mahogany beds, brass chandeliers and sconces, and decorative fireplaces. ***Morrison House*** is centrally located in historic Old Town Alexandria, just minutes from Washington, DC and Washington International Airport. We're a Mobil four-star and AAA four-diamond hotel.

Address: 116 South Alfred Street, Alexandria, VA
Tel: (703) 838-8000, (800) 367-0800, **Fax:** (703) 548-2489.

Type: Inn & hotel with restaurant & bar.
Clientele: Mostly straight clientele with a gay male following
Transportation: Taxi from National Airport. 7 blocks from metro station.
To Gay Bars: 7 miles, a 15 min drive.
Rooms: 42 rooms, 3 suites with single, queen or king beds.
Bathrooms: 45 private bath/shower/toilets.
Meals: Continental breakfast.
Vegetarian: Can be accommodated at all times.
Complimentary: Tea & coffee in mornings, turn-down "treat" (cookies).
Dates Open: All year.
High Season: Apr-Jun & Sept-Nov.
Rates: Jan-Feb & Jul-Aug: $125-$295/nt, Mar-Jun & Sept-Dec: $185-$295/nt.
Credit Cards: MC, Visa, Amex, Diners.
Rsv'tns: Required.
To Reserve: Travel agent or call direct.
Parking: Ample, pay covered parking. Valet parking.
In-Room: Telephone, AC, color cable TV, maid & room service.
On-Premises: Meeting rooms, 2 restaurants.
Exercise/Health: Gym nearby.
Smoking: Permitted in the grill. Smoking & non-smoking rooms available.
Pets: Not permitted.
Handicap Access: Yes, elevator.
Children: Welcome.
Languages: English, Spanish, Japanese, Ethiopian, Arabic, Italian, French.

The William Lewis House

Q-NET Gay-Owned & -Operated ♂

Washington's Finest Bed & Breakfast

You are always welcome at *The William Lewis House*, Washington's finest bed & breakfast. We are conveniently located near Logan Circle, in the heart of the gay community. We are very close to 17th Street, Dupont Circle, Adams Morgan and The Mall. Three different subway lines are within walking distance of the house, the closest of which is the U Street Station on the Green Line. Many of Washington's best restaurants are within a short walk of the house.

Built just after the turn of the century in 1904, this classically inspired house has been painstakingly and faithfully restored to its original grandeur through an intensive and meticulous eleven-year process. It is appointed with antiques, authentic reproduction wall papers and working gas lights. *The William Lewis House* is a warm and charming reflection of the quality of a bygone era. Relax in the gilded parlor or richly paneled dining room in front of one of four working fireplaces. The spacious rooms are appointed with family heirlooms and antique carpets. Each bed has cotton linens, feather mattresses and pillows to add to your comfort. Handmade chocolates are delivered to your bedside each evening by request. A full breakfast is served Saturday, Sunday and Monday. An expanded continental breakfast is served Tuesday through Friday.

In addition to the antique luxuries of a completely restored house, *The William Lewis House* also offers many modern conveniences such as direct-dial telephones with answering machines and ceiling fans in each guest room. A hot tub is located in the garden to help relax you after a long day of touring. Your hosts Theron, Dave and their lovable pup, Winston, will welcome you and try to make you feel as though you are staying with friends. We will provide you with pertinent information about the things that have brought you to Washington, as well helpful suggestions about activities in the community.

Address: 1309 R St NW, Washington, DC
Tel: (202) 462-7574, (800) 465-7574, **Fax:** (202) 462-1608.
E-mail: wlewishous@aol.com **URL:** http://www.wlewishous.com

Type: Bed & breakfast.
Clientele: Mostly gay men, all welcome
Transportation: Taxi. Metro to U St or Dupont Circle, then a short walk.

To Gay Bars: 1-4 blocks. A 5-minute walk.
Rooms: 4 rooms with double or queen bed.
Bathrooms: 2 shared bath/ shower/toilets. 1 shared WC/toilet.
Meals: Expanded continental or full breakfast.
Vegetarian: Many vegetarian restaurants nearby.

Complimentary: Coffee, tea & snacks always. Homemade chocolates at your bedside, by request.
Dates Open: All year.
Rates: $65-$75.

Discounts: On extended stays.
Credit Cards: Visa, MC, Discover, Amex.
Rsv'tns: Required.
To Reserve: Travel agent or call direct.
Parking: Adequate on-street parking.
In-Room: Ceiling fans, direct-dial phone with answering machine, maid service.
On-Premises: Laundry facilities.
Exercise/Health: Hot tub in garden. Nearby gym.
Swimming: Nearby pool.
Sunbathing: In nearby parks.
Smoking: Permitted in garden only.
Pets: Not permitted.
Handicap Access: No.
Languages: English.
Your Host: Theron & Dave.

Windsor Inn

Q-NET Gay-Friendly ♀♂

A Relaxing Oasis in Washington

A relaxed atmosphere and personalized service typify the *Windsor Inn*, a charming art deco-style bed and breakfast on historical 16th Street, convenient to the metro and a variety of restaurants. We're happy to help with dining suggestions, tourist information, etc. Rooms are comfortable and pleasantly decorated. Our nine suites have beautiful ceiling borders and a basket of special soaps and shampoo, extra-thick towels and small refrigerators. The *Windsor* is also close to nightlife and sights. We are a friendly alternative to the larger convention hotels.

Address: 1842 16th St NW, Washington, DC 20009
Tel: (202) 667-0300, (800) 423-9111, **Fax:** (202) 667-4503.

Type: Hotel inn.
Clientele: Mostly straight clientele with a gay & lesbian following
Transportation: Taxi from airport. From Union Station take metro red line to Dupont Circle, then walk 5-1/2 blocks.
To Gay Bars: 3 blocks to men's bars & 5 blocks to gay & lesbian bars.
Rooms: 43 rooms & 2 suites with single, double or queen beds.
Bathrooms: All private.
Meals: Expanded continental breakfast & evening sherry.
Complimentary: Sherry in lobby all year, coffee & tea 24 hours.
Dates Open: All year.
High Season: Apr-May & Sept-Oct.
Rates: High season $79-$150, low season $59-$99.
Discounts: On extended stays, govt. ID, weekend rates (space-available).
Credit Cards: MC, Visa, Amex, Diners, Carte Blanche.
Rsv'tns: Preferred with a credit card guarantee.
To Reserve: Travel agent or call direct.
Parking: On-street parking, some limitations.
In-Room: Maid service, telephone, color cable TV, free HBO, AC, refrigerator in 2 suites & 7 rooms.
On-Premises: Small conference room, same-day laundry service, dry cleaning.
Exercise/Health: Facilities within close walking distance.
Swimming: Facilities within close walking distance.
Smoking: Lobby non-smoking. Most rooms are non-smoking.
Pets: Not permitted.
Handicap Access: No.
Children: Permitted.
Languages: English, limited Spanish & French.

UNITED STATES

AMELIA ISLAND • FLORIDA

Amelia Island Williams House
Q-NET Gay-Friendly ♀♂

A Historic Bed & Breakfast with a Heritage of Elegance

"The most exquisite B&B in Florida and one of the most exquisite B&Bs in the South...the uncontested gem of Amelia Island." "Top Inn of the Year 1995" — *Country Inns magazine* This 1856 ante-bellum mansion is the town's oldest and most historic home, featuring outstanding architectural details and antiques and art dating from the 1500s. Eight guest suites include a regal anniversary suite with original Napoleonic antiques. Breakfast is served in the opulent red and gold dining room. From *The Amelia Island Williams House* enjoy 13 miles of unspoiled beaches, horseback riding, golf, tennis, fishing, and shopping in restored historic downtown.

Address: 103 S 9th St, Amelia Island, FL 32034
Tel: (904) 277-2328, **Fax:** (904) 321-1325. Reservations only: (800) 414-9257.
E-mail: topinn@aol.com **URL:** www.williamshouse.com

Type: Bed & Breakfast.
Clientele: Mainly straight clientele with a gay & lesbian following.
Transportation: Car. 30 minutes from Jacksonville International Airport.
To Gay Bars: 45-minute drive.
Rooms: 8 rooms with king or queen beds.
Bathrooms: All private.
Meals: Full breakfast.
Vegetarian: Vegetarian food available upon request. Will cook for dairy allergies.
Complimentary: Wine & cheese in afternoon.
Dates Open: All year.
High Season: Summer.
Rates: $135-$175 per night.
Credit Cards: MC, Visa.
Rsv'tns: Required.
To Reserve: Travel agent or call direct.
Minimum Stay: Required during special events weekends.
Parking: Ample off-street & on-street parking.
In-Room: Color cable TV, video tape library, VCR, AC, ceiling fans, maid service. 6 rooms have working fireplaces.
On-Premises: Formal English walking garden.
Exercise/Health: 2 rooms have private Jacuzzis. Massage on call.
Swimming: Nearby ocean.
Sunbathing: At the beach.
Smoking: Not permitted in house. Permitted on porch & in courtyard only.
Pets: Not permitted. Pet boarding service available at vet's or in private home.
Handicap Access: Yes.
Children: Not especially welcome. 12 years & up OK.
Languages: English.
Your Host: Dick & Chris.

DAYTONA BEACH

The Villa
Q-NET Gay/Lesbian ♀♂

Live Like Royalty

Live like royalty in our national-register historical Spanish mansion, constructed in 1929 by the finest craftsmen. *The Villa* grandly overlooks two-plus acres of landscaped grounds in the heart of Daytona Beach. The interior, particularly the public areas, continues the Spanish theme of the exterior. The present proprietor has beautifully and authentically furnished the mansion in keeping with the architecture of the period with massive sideboards, carved chairs and art objects from the owner's collection filling the building. The mansion with its impressive moldings and stencilled ceilings, the work of the famous Mizner Studios, is one of the finest examples of Spanish Colonial Revival architecture, rivaling mansions in Palm Beach and Miami.

Guests appreciate the secluded tropical garden, swimming pool and spa, private sun deck and public areas. Stay in guest rooms named for nobility: the King Juan Carlos, Queen Isabella, Marco Polo and Christopher Columbus rooms are decorated with the finest period pieces. *The Villa* is located within walking distance of Daytona's world-famous beach, fine dining, shopping and nightlife. Saint Agustine, America's oldest city, is only 45 minutes away. Orlando, home of Disney World and other theme parks, is just an hour's drive. Cape Canaveral, site of shuttle launches, is less than an hour's drive.

The staff is more than happy to advise guests on a variety of activities, car rentals and special events. Groups may rent the entire villa on a weekly basis and arrangements can be made for cooking, maid service and car and driver. A stay at *The Villa* will take you back to a period of grand living. It is without a doubt one of the finest accommodations catering to the travelling community.

Address: 801 N Peninsula Dr, Daytona Beach, FL 32118
Tel: (904) 248-2020 (Tel/Fax). E-mail: thevillabb@aol.com

Type: Bed & breakfast.
Clientele: Mainly gay & lesbian with some straight clientele
Transportation: Car or taxi. Pick up from airport or train can be arranged.
To Gay Bars: 12 blocks.
Rooms: 4 rooms with queen or king beds.
Bathrooms: All private.
Meals: Expanded continental breakfast.

Complimentary: Tea, coffee & soft drinks.
Dates Open: All year.
Rates: $65-$190.
Credit Cards: MC, Visa, Amex.
Rsv'tns: Required in most cases.
To Reserve: Travel agent or call direct.
Minimum Stay: Required during peak season & special events.

Parking: Ample free off-street parking.
In-Room: Maid service, color TV, AC.
On-Premises: TV lounge, use of refrigerator.
Exercise/Health: Hot spring spa. Nearby gym, weights & tanning salons.
Swimming: Pool on premises, 4 blocks to ocean beach.

Sunbathing: At poolside.
Nudity: Permitted on pool deck only, with approval.
Smoking: Permitted outside only.
Pets: Not permitted.
Handicap Access: No.
Children: Not permitted.
Languages: English.
Your Host: Jim.

IGLTA

The Bahama Hotel
Q-NET Gay-Friendly ♀♂

In the Center of Fort Lauderdale Beach

Comfortable furnished rooms, overlooking the center of Fort Lauderdale Beach and the Atlantic Ocean, will put you in a vacation frame of mind. At *Bahama Hotel*, let yourself relax in a large, heated, fresh-water pool and stretch out for tanning on our patio which gets the warm Florida sun all day long. Refreshments are always close by in our tropical patio bar. Enjoy fine cuisine morning, noon, and evening in our Deck Restaurant overlooking the bright blue waters of the Atlantic.

Address: 401 N Atlantic Blvd (A1A), Fort Lauderdale, FL 33304
Tel: (954) 467-7315, (800) 622-9995, Fax: (954) 467-7319.
E-mail: bahama@bahamahotel.com URL: http://www.bahamahotel.com

Type: Hotel with restaurant & bar.
Clientele: Mostly straight clientele with a small gay following
Transportation: Car or taxi from airport.
To Gay Bars: 5 miles or 10-minute drive.
Rooms: 43 rooms, 1 suite,

23 efficiency cottages with double or king beds.
Bathrooms: Private baths.
Meals: Full breakfast.
Vegetarian: Available upon request.
Complimentary: Coffee in lobby.
Dates Open: All year.
High Season: Dec-Apr.

Rates: Low season $69-$159, high season $95-$275.
Credit Cards: MC, Visa, Amex, Diners, Discover.
Rsv'tns: Required.
To Reserve: Travel agent or call direct.
Minimum Stay: Required

during holidays & special events.
Parking: Adequate free off-street parking.
In-Room: Color cable TV, AC, telephone, kitchen, refrigerator, maid & room service.

continued next page

INN PLACES® 1998 309

UNITED STATES / **FORT LAUDERDALE • FLORIDA**

On-Premises: Laundry facilities.
Exercise/Health: Weights & massage on premises. Gym nearby.
Swimming: Pool on premises. Ocean nearby.
Sunbathing: At poolside, on common sun decks, on ocean beach.
Smoking: Permitted. Non-smoking rooms available.
Pets: Permitted. Dogs under 20 lbs.
Handicap Access: Yes.
Children: Welcome.
Languages: English, French, Spanish, Portuguese.

IGLTA

Gemini House Men ♂

This is THE Place to Get Naked & Relax!

Three houses (we live in one) on an enclosed half acre offer gay male naturist vacation rentals in the B&B tradition. Each house has two individually decorated guestrooms which share one bath, dining room and kitchen. Breakfast doesn't consist of donuts and bottled juice, but a full meal with fresh-squeezed juice and Starbuck's coffee. The enclosed yard is a tropical paradise, where you can enjoy our oversized heated swimming pool, hot tub, or nap in a hammock under towering palm trees! Member: GNI, IMEN, Naturist Society.

Address: Fort Lauderdale, FL 33334
Tel: (954) 568-9791, (800) 552-7415, **Fax:** (954) 568-0617.
E-mail: GeminiHse@aol.com **URL:** http://www.geminihse.com

Type: Vacation rental, guesthouse.
Clientele: Men only
Transportation: Car is best.
To Gay Bars: 6 blocks to gay bars.
Rooms: 4 rooms with single, queen & king beds.
Bathrooms: 2 shared bath/ shower/toilets.
Meals: Full breakfast.
Vegetarian: Available if requested in advance.
Complimentary: Fresh-baked cookies every night in room.
Dates Open: All year.
High Season: Nov-Apr.
Rates: High $90, Low $70.
Discounts: Students & on extended stays.
Rsv'tns: Required.
To Reserve: Call direct.
Minimum Stay: 2 nights.
Parking: Ample off-street parking.
In-Room: AC, color cable TV, VCR, ceiling fans, maid service.
On-Premises: Laundry facilities, book & video tape libraries, full kitchen. Car rental discounts.
Exercise/Health: Gym, Jacuzzi, massage, outdoor tropical shower.
Swimming: Pool on premises. Ocean nearby.
Sunbathing: Poolside.
Nudity: Enitre property is a "no clothing zone."
Smoking: Permitted outside only.
Pets: Not permitted.
Handicap Access: No.
Children: No.
Languages: English.
Your Host: John & Rick.

IGLTA

King Henry Arms Gay/Lesbian ♂

The Best Is Yet to Come: YOU!

King Henry Arms, with its friendly, home-like atmosphere and squeaky-clean accommodations, is just the place for that romantic getaway. Spend your days relaxing amidst the tropical foliage by our pool, or at the ocean beach, just 300 feet away. Enjoy your evenings at the many restaurants and clubs, before returning to the quiet comfort of your accommodations. Truly a jewel by the sea.

Address: 543 Breakers Ave, Ft. Lauderdale, FL 33304-4129
Tel: (954) 561-0039 or (800) 205-KING (5464).

Type: Motel.
Clientele: Mostly men with women welcome
Transportation: Car or taxi from Ft. Lauderdale airport.
To Gay Bars: 2 miles to gay/lesbian bars.
Rooms: 4 rooms, 6 suites & 2 apartments with single, double or king beds.
Bathrooms: All private bath/toilet/showers.
Meals: Continental breakfast.
Vegetarian: Restaurants & stores nearby.
Dates Open: All year.
High Season: Winter months.
Rates: Spring thru fall $49-$66, winter $81-$104.
Discounts: 10% on 8-30 nights, 15% on 31-60 nights and 20% on 61 nights or more, plus summer specials.
Credit Cards: MC, VISA, Amex, Discover, Novus.
Rsv'tns: Prefer 1 month in advance, earlier in season.
To Reserve: Travel agent or call direct.
Minimum Stay: 7 nights in high season.
Parking: Adequate free off-street parking.
In-Room: Maid service, color cable TV, telephone,

AC, safe & refrigerator. Apartments & suites have kitchens.
On-Premises: Laundry facilities.
Exercise/Health: Gym nearby.
Swimming: Pool on premises, ocean beach nearby.
Sunbathing: At poolside, on beach or patio.
Smoking: Permitted without restrictions.
Pets: Not permitted.
Handicap Access: No.
Children: Not especially welcomed.
Languages: English.
Your Host: Don, Roy & Kevin.

IGLTA

La Casa del Mar

Gay/Lesbian ♂

The Only B&B on Fort Lauderdale Beach

Select your room at *La Casa del Mar* from these themes: for romantic getaways, the Stolen Kiss room; for art lovers, the cool colors of the Monet room; for a trip over the rainbow, the Judy Garland room; or for guests who want to experience the early West, the Southwest/American Indian room. Enjoy breakfast with homemade baked goods in the serenity of tropical gardens and fountain.

Address: 3003 Granada St, Ft. Lauderdale, FL 33304-4317
Tel: (954) 467-2037, (800) 739-0009, **Fax:** (954) 467-7439.
URL: www.ssl-online.com/Casa

Type: Bed & breakfast.
Clientele: Mostly men with women welcome
Transportation: Car is best.
To Gay Bars: 10 blocks, 2 miles or a 10-minute drive.
Rooms: 6 rooms & 4 suites with single & double beds.
Bathrooms: Private baths.
Meals: Full American breakfast.
Vegetarian: Special menu available, must be requested when making reservation.
Complimentary: Wine & cheese served poolside Mon-Sat.
Dates Open: All year.
High Season: Dec-Apr.
Rates: May 1-Dec 15 $75-$95, Dec 16-Apr 30 $100-$135.
Discounts: Summer promotions as advertised in Florida gay publications.
Credit Cards: MC, Visa, Amex, Diners Club.
Rsv'tns: Required. Walk-ins welcome, subject to availability.
To Reserve: Travel agent or call direct.
Minimum Stay: 3-day stay in season.
Parking: Ample free parking, 1 parking space per room.
In-Room: Color cable TV, VCR, telephone, refrigerator, ceiling fans, AC, maid service.
On-Premises: Self-service laundry facilities available, video tape library.
Swimming: Pool & ocean.
Sunbathing: At poolside & on ocean beach.
Smoking: Permitted. Non-smoking rooms available.
Pets: Not permitted.
Handicap Access: No.
Children: No.
Languages: English.
Your Host: Lee & Larry.

Orton Terrace

Gay/Lesbian ♀♂

The INN Place for the IN Men

Orton Terrace is located in the Central Beach area only steps from the beach. We offer a quiet, relaxing and friendly atmosphere with the largest apartment accommodations found in the area. The one- and two-bedroom apartments have full-sized kitchens and 27" TVs. All rooms feature phones, cable TVs, safes, refrigerators and microwaves. Videos and VCRs are also available. Our grounds feature pool, BBQ and a quiet tropical courtyard setting.

Address: 606 Orton Ave, Ft. Lauderdale, FL 33304
Tel: (954) 566-5068, **Fax:** (954) 564-8646.
Toll-free in USA, Canada & Caribbean: (800) 323-1142.

Type: Motel.
Clientele: Gay & lesbian
Transportation: Taxi.
To Gay Bars: 3 miles, a 6-min drive, a 45-min walk.
Rooms: 7 guestrooms, 7 2-BR apartments with single, double or queen beds & 7 1-BR apartments.
Bathrooms: All private.
Meals: Continental breakfast.
Dates Open: All year.
High Season: Dec-Feb & Apr.
Rates: Dec-May: $79-208, May-Dec: $54-$148.
Credit Cards: MC, Visa, Amex, Discover.
Rsv'tns: Required.
To Reserve: Travel agent or call direct.
Minimum Stay: Please inquire.
Parking: Adequate free off-street parking.

continued next page

In-Room: AC, ceiling fan, color cable TV, VCR, video tape library, phone, coffee/tea making facilities,
kitchen, refrigerator, maid service.
On-Premises: Laundry facilities.
Swimming: Pool on premises. Ocean nearby.
Sunbathing: Poolside, on patio, at beach.
Nudity: Clothing optional.
Smoking: Permitted.
Pets: Not permitted.
Handicap Access: No.
Children: Please inquire.
Languages: English.
IGLTA

The Palms on Las Olas
Men ♂
Fort Lauderdale's Finest Guest Suites

Affordable luxury in classic fifties style awaits at *The Palms on Las Olas*. Spacious accommodations, ranging from simple hotel rooms to grand one-bedroom suites, include AC, remote control cable TV, telephones and, in season, a full continental breakfast. We're in the heart of "chic" Las Olas Boulevard, one mile from the beach, and close to shops, restaurants and bars. This is the most central, safe location available. Relax by the pool, or take a water taxi from our private dock and explore the canals and waterways of Old Fort Lauderdale.

Address: 1760 E Las Olas Blvd, Ft. Lauderdale, FL 33301
Tel: (954) 462-4178, (800) 550-POLO (7656), **Fax:** (954) 463-8544.

Type: Guesthouse motel.
Clientele: Gay men only
Transportation: Car is best.
To Gay Bars: 5 blocks or 1/2 mile. An 8-minute walk or 2-minute drive.
Rooms: 2 rooms, 5 suites, 6 efficiencies with full-sized, queen or king beds.
Bathrooms: All private.
Meals: Expanded continental breakfast, high season only.
Dates Open: All year.
High Season: Dec-Apr.
Rates: Summer $60-$99, winter $85-$165.
Credit Cards: MC, Visa, Amex.
Rsv'tns: Requested.
To Reserve: Travel agent or call direct.
Minimum Stay: 3 days during high season.
Parking: Ample free off-street parking.
In-Room: Color cable TV, AC, telephones, coffee/tea-making facilities, maid, room & laundry service. Efficiencies & apartments with full kitchens.
On-Premises: Laundry facilities & fax.
Exercise/Health: Nearby gym.
Swimming: Heated pool on premises, ocean nearby.
Sunbathing: At poolside & on common sun decks.
Nudity: Permitted poolside.
Smoking: Permitted.
Pets: Not permitted.
Handicap Access: No.
Children: No.
Languages: English.
IGLTA

The Royal Palms
Men ♂
Five-Star Luxury Beneath Towering Palms

Welcome to the award-winning *Royal Palms*, Fort Lauderdale's only five-star accommodation for the gay traveler. Experience our tropical paradise, where atmosphere, attention to detail and service are unequaled. All accommodations surround the secluded tropical garden, pool and sun deck, where complimentary breakfast is served. We are minutes from shops, bars and restaurants and two blocks from the main Fort Lauderdale beach. *The Royal Palms* was chosen as one of the top three gay accommodations in the United States by Out & About, and received their 1996 Five Palm Award. 1997 Greater Fort Lauderdale Superior Small Lodging Award of Excellence.

Address: 2901 Terramar St, Ft Lauderdale, FL 33304
Tel: (954) 564-6444, Fax: (954) 564-6443.
E-mail: ryalpalms@aol.com URL: http://www.royalpalms.com

Type: Hotel with wine & beer bar.
Clientele: Men only.
Transportation: Car is best, but taxi service very good.
To Gay Bars: 3 miles (10-min drive).
Rooms: 8 rooms, 4 suites with king & queen beds.
Bathrooms: All private.
Meals: Expanded continental breakfast.
Dates Open: All year.

High Season: Mid-December-May.
Rates: Summer $99-$169, winter $140-$210.
Discounts: 3-4 in season.
Credit Cards: MC, Visa & Amex.
Rsv'tns: Strongly recommended.
To Reserve: Travel agent or call direct.
Minimum Stay: 3 days in high season.

Parking: Ample free off-street parking.
In-Room: Color cable TV, VCR, CD players, video tape & CD libraries, AC, ceiling fans, telephone, kitchen, refrigerator, coffee/tea-making facilities, maid service, safes, computer hookup to phone.
Exercise/Health: Nearby gym, weights, Jacuzzi & sauna.
Swimming: Heated pool on premises, nearby ocean beach.
Sunbathing: At poolside, on beach, patio, private sun decks.
Nudity: Permitted.
Smoking: Permitted.
Pets: Not permitted.
Children: Not permitted.
Languages: English, Spanish & French.
Your Host: Richard & Rick.

IGLTA

The Resort on Carefree Boulevard

Q-NET Lesbian-Owned & -Operated ♀

Affordable Luxury Especially For You

Private and secluded, **Resort on Carefree Boulevard** is set on 50 acres of pine land, with two lakes, on Florida's beautiful Gulf Coast. Resort and manufactured homes, which accommodate from two to eight people, are available for weekly or monthly rental. Amenities in these furnished homes include linens, dishes, pots and pans. Rental rates also include electric, water, sewer, local telephone and basic cable. RV sites have compact service pedestals, for convenient hookup, and concrete pad. Our private clubhouse complex, featuring amenities found in major resort hotels, includes the services of an activities director.

Address: 3000 Carefree Blvd, Fort Meyers, FL 33917-7235
Tel: (941) 731-3000, (800) 326-0364,
Fax: (941) 731-3519.
URL: http://www.resortoncb.com

Type: Manufactured homes & RV rental sites, resort community & sports club.
Clientele: Women only
Transportation: Car or SW International Airport.
To Gay Bars: 10 miles.
Rooms: 1- thru 4-BR

manufactured homes with double, queen or king beds.
Bathrooms: Units available with 1 or 2 baths.
Campsites: RV site rentals. Available hookups include electric, water, sewer, basic cable TV.

Vegetarian: Available within 1 mile.
Complimentary: Ted & coffee.
Dates Open: All year.
High Season: Nov 1-Apr 30.

Rates: 1-BR: summer $45-$66, winter $64-$94. 2-BR: summer $70-$91, winter $100-$130. RV: off $17-$23, on $24-$32.

continued next page

INN PLACES® 1998

313

Discounts: Inquire about weekly & monthly discounts. **Credit Cards:** MC, Visa. **Rsv'tns:** Required. **To Reserve:** Call direct. **Minimum Stay:** 3 days. **Parking:** Adequate covered free off-street parking.	**In-Room:** Telephone, AC, ceiling fans, color cable TV, kitchen, refrigerator, coffee & tea-making facilities. VCR in most units. Maid & laundry service available. **On-Premises:** Meeting rooms, TV lounge, fax, copier, video tape library, laundry facilities, billiard	room, arts & crafts room. **Exercise/Health:** Gym, weights, Jacuzzi, putting green, shuffleboard & tennis courts. Clubhouse facilities operated under private club membership. **Swimming:** Pool. Nearby ocean. **Sunbathing:** Poolside.	**Smoking:** Permitted in designated areas. Non-smoking rooms available. **Pets:** Permitted, must be leashed. **Handicap Access:** Yes, ramps. **Children:** No. **Languages:** English, Spanish.

Alexander's Guesthouse

Gay/Lesbian ♂

We Are Key West!

From the moment you arrive at *Alexander's,* you will appreciate our thoughtful service and our attention to detail. Built as a private residence in 1910 in what is now known as Old Town, *Alexander's* was established as a guesthouse in 1981. Our lovely common living areas set the mood. Handsome quarters await you, each one unique and with amenities chosen to anticipate your needs. Our bright, comfortable rooms all have bahama fans, AC, TV, VCRs, phone and refrigerators.

The secluded grounds, radiant throughout the day, are a haven for sun-worshippers. Guests can soak up the sun all day on our multi-level decks, or stroll through the lush, sunny tropical garden surrounding the heated pool. Sunbathe poolside or revel in your sense of freedom on one of our private sun decks above the gardens. If you're in the mood for a swim, frolic in the pool beneath cascading bougainvillaea. Evenings, gather by the pool with fellow guests for the complimentary evening cocktail hour.

Truly representative of Key West at its finest, Fleming Street is replete with classic Conch houses, antique stores, food markets, a ship chandlery, the public library and more. Key West is legendary for its incomparable weather and liberal attitudes. Favored daytime activities range from watersports to gallery hopping. Only a short walk away is Duval Street, where nights of celebration and revelry await you. Its clubs, restaurants and bars offer fun and entertainment lasting until the early morning.

Address: 1118 Fleming St, Key West, FL 33040
Tel: (305) 294-9919 or (800) 654-9919.
E-mail: alexghouse@aol.com

Type: Guesthouse.
Clientele: 75% gay, 25% lesbian
Transportation: Taxi from the airport.
To Gay Bars: 6-7 blocks to men's & women's bars.
Rooms: 12 doubles, 5 quads
Bathrooms: 15 private, 2 shared.
Meals: Expanded continental breakfast.
Complimentary: Daily happy hour.
Dates Open: All year.
High Season: December 15-April 15.
Rates: Winter $130-$275, summer $80-$180.
Credit Cards: MC, Visa, Amex, Discover.
Rsv'tns: Recommended.
To Reserve: Travel agent or call direct.
Minimum Stay: Minimum for most holidays & special events.
Parking: Adequate free on-street parking.
In-Room: Self-controlled AC, VCRs, color TV, free HBO & remote, telephone, hair dryers, maid service, refrigerator & ceiling fans.
Swimming: In pool or at nearby ocean beach.
Sunbathing: On private & common sun decks, on the beach & at poolside.
Nudity: Permitted for sunbathers on 2nd & 3rd floor sun decks.
Smoking: Permitted without restrictions.
Pets: Not permitted.
Handicap Access: No.
Children: Not permitted.
Languages: English.
IGLTA

Atlantic Shores Resort

Q-NET Gay/Lesbian ♀♂

Oceanfront — In the Heart of Old Town

From the moment you arrive at *Atlantic Shores Resort*, our friendly, casual and qualified staff eagerly await to assist you on your fantasy vacation. The grounds of this tropical Art Deco-style hotel are luxurious and manicured, and our oceanfront, clothing-optional pool is a favorite with tourists and locals alike. The popular Pool Bar and Grill boasts a stairway to the sea, water sports accessibility and the legendary "Tea by the Sea." Diner Shores Restaurant offers breakfast and lunch overlooking South Street, with frequent live entertainment. We're located on the sunrise side of Key West, minutes from bars, shops and restaurants.

Address: 510 South St, Key West, FL 33040
Tel: (305) 296-2491, (800) 526-3359, **Fax:** (305) 294-2753.
E-mail: AtlShores@aol.com

Type: Hotel with restaurant, pool bar & grill.
Clientele: Gays, lesbians & liberal adults
Transportation: Airport taxi or car is best.
To Gay Bars: Gay bar on premises.
Rooms: 72 with queen, king or 2 doubles. Efficiencies available.
Bathrooms: All private.
Vegetarian: Available in
Diner Shores & Pool Bar on premises.
Dates Open: All year.
Rates: Summer $80-$125, winter $130-$250.
Discounts: Please inquire, group rates.
Credit Cards: MC, Visa, Amex, Diners, Discover, Carte Blanche, Eurocard, Bancard.
Rsv'tns: Highly recommended.
To Reserve: Travel agent or call direct.
Minimum Stay: On holidays & special events.
Parking: Free parking.
In-Room: Color cable TV, AC, telephone, maid service. Efficiencies have refrigerator, microwave, coffee maker.
On-Premises: Fax, copy machine, laundry facilities, safe deposit boxes.
Exercise/Health: Nearby gym, weights & massage.
Swimming: Pool on premises, also on ocean front.
Sunbathing: At poolside & pier.
Nudity: Permitted in pool area.
Smoking: Permitted.
Pets: Not permitted.
Handicap Access: Limited accessibility. Check availability.
Children: No.
Languages: English, Spanish, Polish.
IGLTA

INN PLACES® 1998   315

Big Ruby's Guesthouse

Gay/Lesbian ♂

On our quiet little lane, in peace and privacy, our three guesthouses, each in traditional historic design, stand secluded behind a tall fence. Inside *Big Ruby's*, luxury touches are everywhere. Immaculate rooms have sumptuous beds with four king-sized pillows and superthick bath sheets for towels. Awaiting you outside are a beautiful lagoon pool, spacious decks and lounge areas in a completely private tropical garden. Full breakfast is served at poolside. Evenings, we gather by the pool for wine and the easy companionability of good conversation. You'll never feel so welcome, so comfortable, so at home.

Address: 409 Applerouth Lane, Key West, FL 33040-6534
Tel: (305) 296-2323 or (800) 477-7829.

Type: Guesthouse.
Clientele: Mostly men with women welcome
Transportation: Fly to Key West, 15 min by cab (less than $12) to guesthouse.
To Gay Bars: Less than 1/2 block.
Rooms: 17 rooms with queen or king beds.
Bathrooms: Private: 12 shower/toilet, 3 full baths. 2 shared full baths.
Meals: Full breakfast every morning. Dinners on Christmas, New Year & Thanksgiving.
Complimentary: Wine served each evening from 6pm-8pm except Sunday.
Dates Open: All year.
High Season: December 21-April 30.
Rates: Winter $125-$210, summer $79-$130.
Discounts: 10% on stays of 7 days or more between 5/1-12/20, excluding holidays.
Credit Cards: MC, Visa, Amex, Discover, Diners Club, Carte Blanche.
Rsv'tns: Recommended.
To Reserve: Travel agent or call direct.
Minimum Stay: On holidays.
Parking: Limited off-street parking.
In-Room: Maid service, color cable TV, AC, Bahama fan, refrigerator, 4 king-sized pillows, huge, thick towels, laundry service, video library. Some rooms with VCR.
On-Premises: TV lounge, public telephone.
Exercise/Health: Rainforest (outdoor tropical shower). Nearby gym & massage.
Swimming: Pool, nearby ocean beach.
Sunbathing: At poolside, on private or common sun decks, ocean beach.
Nudity: Permitted poolside & in sunning yard.
Smoking: Permitted without restrictions. 2 non-smoking rooms available.
Pets: Not permitted.
Handicap Access: Yes.
Children: Not permitted.
Languages: English.
Your Host: George & Frank.

IGLTA

Blue Parrot Inn

Gay-Friendly 50/50 ♀♂

Hatched in 1884 and Still Flying High

The *Blue Parrot*, in the heart of historic Old Town, is a tropical, secluded, quiet and clean retreat near famous Duval Street. Our pool is heated during the cooler months and is delightfully usable year round. Beaches, clubs, restaurants and shops are only a very short walk away. We are just two blocks from famous Duval Street where fine restaurants coexist with a crazy assortment of bars, ranging from elegant garden affairs to funky rock-and-roll joints with peanut-covered floors. All water activities are nearby, including diving, and snorkeling on America's only living coral reef. The atmosphere is relaxed and friendly; the music is usually classical. Brochure available. AAA-approved.

316

FERRARI GUIDES™

Address: 916 Elizabeth St, Key West, FL 33040
Tel: (305) 296-0033, (800) 231-BIRD (2473).
URL: http://www.blueparrotinn.com

Type: Bed & breakfast.
Clientele: 50% gay & lesbian & 50% straight clientele
Transportation: Key West International Airport, then taxi.
To Gay Bars: 4 blocks, a 5 min walk.
Rooms: 10 rooms with single, double or queen beds.
Bathrooms: Private; 7 shower/toilets, 3 bath/toilet/showers.
Meals: Expanded continental breakfast.

Vegetarian: Vegetarian food 1 block.
Dates Open: All year.
High Season: January-April.
Rates: Summer $70-$160, winter $105-$180.
Discounts: AAA, AARP & on stays of 5 nights or longer.
Credit Cards: MC, Visa, Amex, Diners, Eurocard, Discover.
Rsv'tns: Required.
To Reserve: Travel agent or call direct.

Minimum Stay: Required only on weekends, some holidays & special events.
Parking: Adequate free on-street parking.
In-Room: AC, color cable TV, telephone, refrigerator, ceiling fans, maid service.
On-Premises: Fax & photocopy service, bicycle rentals.
Exercise/Health: Massage. Nearby gym, weights, massage.
Swimming: Pool on premises. Ocean nearby.

Sunbathing: Poolside, on private & common sun decks, at beach.
Nudity: Permitted on elevated sun deck with separate entrance.
Smoking: Permitted anywhere.
Pets: Not permitted.
Handicap Access: Yes.
Children: Adults only.
Languages: English.
Your Host: Larry & Frank.

IGLTA

The Brass Key Guesthouse

Gay/Lesbian ♂

The Only Thing Missing is You!

Key West's premier gay and lesbian guesthouse offers attentive service and luxury accommodations in a traditional Conch-style setting of wide verandas, louvered plantation shutters and ceiling fans. Expansive sun decks, a sparkling heated pool and a whirlpool spa glisten within *The Brass Key's* private, hedged compound featuring flowering hibiscus, bougan-villaea, jasmine and seven varieties of exotic palms.

Located on a quiet street in the heart of Old Town's finest neighborhood, *The Brass Key* is surrounded by restored homes, galleries, restaurants and shops and is just minutes from the nightlife of world-famous Duval Street. The harborfront is but two blocks away, offering casual waterside restaurants and salty bars, as well as gay sailing excursions and seaplane adventures.

The sixteen guest rooms and one-bedroom suites at *The Brass Key* are light and airy, featuring handcrafted furniture and traditional antiques, tropical fabrics and local artworks. Each offers king/queen bed, air-conditioning, telephone with voicemail, color television with VCR and videocassette library, hair dryer, Caswell-Massey toiletries, refrigerator and nightly turndown.

While the amenities and service of *The Brass Key* are first-class, the atmosphere is always friendly and laid-back: guests enjoy morning conversation during the breakfast buffet; later, many spend the day relaxing together in the sun chaises surrounding the pool. For the energetic, *The Brass Key* often arranges

continued next page

group charters for an afternoon snorkel cruise or sunset champagne sail. The evening's cocktail hour provides a further chance to share the day's exploits (and the previous night's misdeeds) and to finalize dinner and club plans.

The Brass Key has been featured by *The Advocate, Conde Nast Traveler, Genre,* and was recently awarded *Out & About's* highest rating "Five Stars - Exceptional." Join us soon and let our staff and guests welcome you to the native warmth and exotic verve of the Caribbean.

Address: 412 Frances St, Key West, FL 33040
Tel: (305) 296-4719, (800) 932-9119, **Fax:** (305) 296-1994.

Type: Bed & breakfast guesthouse.
Clientele: Mostly men with women very welcome
Transportation: Airport pick up $10.
To Gay Bars: 5-7 blocks to gay & lesbian bars.
Rooms: 14 rooms & 2 suites with queen or king beds.
Bathrooms: All private.
Meals: Expanded continental breakfast.
Complimentary: Afternoon cocktails.

Dates Open: All year.
High Season: Mid-December - mid-April.
Rates: Winter $145-$280. Summer $75-$165.
Credit Cards: Amex, Discover, MC, Visa.
Rsv'tns: Highly recommended.
To Reserve: Travel agent or call direct.
Minimum Stay: Required holidays, special events.
Parking: Ample free on-street parking.
In-Room: AC, ceiling fan,

phone w/ voicemail, color cable TV, VCR, videocassette library, hair dryer, refrigerator, bathrobes, laundry, maid & turndown service.
On-Premises: Spacious living room with breakfast area.
Exercise/Health: Whirlpool spa on premises & gym nearby. Bicycles at guesthouse.
Swimming: Heated pool on premises. Ocean beach half mile.

Sunbathing: Poolside & on sun decks.
Nudity: Permitted on rooftop sun deck.
Smoking: Non-smoking rooms available.
Pets: Not permitted.
Handicap Access: Yes. Wheelchair ramp. 1 guestroom/bath for the physically challenged.
Children: Not permitted.
Languages: English.

IGLTA

Chelsea House

Q-NET Gay-Friendly 50/50 ♀♂

Chelsea House is a uniquely open, restored 19th-century, two-story home with 18 guestrooms and two-bedroom suite. All rooms (except for one) have semi-private or private balconies. The suite has a full kitchen, living room, hardwood floors and two private balconies. Our acre of land, two blocks from Duval Street, has extensive, tropical gardens, pool and clothing-optional sun deck, and on-property parking. We provide a thorough orientation for guests and are always around to lend friendly advice. Experience the unique ambiance of this historic Old Town, adult-only home and the special attention to individual needs from an informed, experienced staff. Gay-owned and -operated.

Address: 707 Truman Ave, Key West, FL 33040
Tel: (305) 296-2211, USA & Canada: (800) 845-8859, **Fax:** (305) 296-4822.
E-mail: chelseahse@aol.com

Type: Guesthouse.
Clientele: 50% gay & lesbian & 50% straight clientele

Transportation: Fly to Key West International. $16 per person round trip for airport pick up.

FERRARI GUIDES™

To Gay Bars: 2 blocks.
Rooms: 18 rooms & one 2-bedroom suite with double, queen or king beds.
Bathrooms: All private.
Meals: Continental breakfast buffet.
Vegetarian: Available nearby.
Complimentary: Cuban coffee & iced tea all day. Chocolates at nightly turndown.

Dates Open: All year.
High Season: December 15-April 17.
Rates: Summer $79-$115, winter $118-$170, spring $98-$145.
Discounts: 10% for 7 or more days in summer.
Credit Cards: MC, Visa, Discover, Bancard & Eurocard.
Rsv'tns: Preferred.
To Reserve: Travel agent or call direct.

Minimum Stay: On holidays & special events.
Parking: Adequate free off-street parking.
In-Room: Color cable TV, AC, ceiling fans, telephone, safe, hair dryer, refrigerator, coffee/tea-making facilities & maid service.
Exercise/Health: Nearby full-service health facility & water sports.
Swimming: Pool on premises, Gulf of Mexico nearby.
Sunbathing: At poolside or clothing-optional sun deck above pool building.
Nudity: Permitted on clothing-optional sun deck.
Smoking: Permitted.
Pets: Permitted with exception.
Handicap Access: Yes.
Children: Not permitted.
Languages: English, German, French.
Your Host: Gary & Jim.

Coconut Grove for Men

Men ♂

Enjoy unparalleled views of Old Town and the Gulf of Mexico from our rooftop decks at *Coconut Grove Guest House.* The widow's walk provides a private spot to tan, take in the ocean air or experience Key West's sunsets. Friendliest service and largest, best suites in town.

Address: 817 Fleming St, Key West, FL 33040
Tel: (305) 296-5107, (800) 262-6055.

Type: Guesthouse.
Clientele: Men only
Transportation: Taxi.
To Gay Bars: 3 blocks to men's bars.
Rooms: 5 singles, 11 doubles, 2 suites, 4 1-bedroom apartments in annex across the street.
Bathrooms: 20 private, 2 shared.
Meals: Continental breakfast.

Dates Open: All year.
High Season: December 20th-April 15th.
Rates: High season, $85-$200. Low season, $55-$100.
Credit Cards: MC, Visa.
To Reserve: Travel agent or call direct.
Minimum Stay: Required at certain times.
Parking: On-street parking.

In-Room: Maid service, color TV, kitchen, refrigerator & AC.
On-Premises: Meeting rooms, telephone.
Exercise/Health: Gym, weights.
Swimming: Pool.
Sunbathing: At poolside & on common sun decks, or roof.

Nudity: Permitted at the pool & sun decks.
Smoking: Permitted without restrictions.
Pets: Not permitted.
Handicap Access: No.
Children: Not permitted.
Languages: English, German, French, Swedish.

IGLTA

INN PLACES® 1998

UNITED STATES — KEY WEST • FLORIDA

Colours - The Guest Mansion Key West

Gay/Lesbian ♀♂

Experience Not Just a Place, But a State of Mind

With new administration, this historic Victorian mansion, originally built in 1889 in the center of Old Town, has undergone a contemporary conversion and extensive renovation, yet retains its original details, such as chandeliers, 14-foot ceilings and polished wood floors. Accommodations at *Colours - The Guest Mansion Key West* vary from simple sitting rooms to elaborate suites. Amenities include cable TV, paddle fans, air conditioning and balconies with hammocks. Stroll half a block to the shops, restaurants and nightlife entertainment of Duval St. Celebrate colourful sunsets at the secluded tropical and Jacuzzi — the perfect setting in which to relax and unwind.

In addition to *Colours - The Guest Mansion,* we are affiliated wtih other classic Key West properties. One call to our reservation team at 1-800-ARRIVAL does it all! Plan your Key West Get-A-Way today! Ask about our other destinations and distinctive lodgings: Hotel Colours in San José, Costa Rica and Colours at the NEW Penguin Resort and The Mantell Plaza in South Miami Beach.

Address: 410 Fleming St, Key West, FL 33040
Tel: (800) ARRIVAL, (277-4825), (305) 532-9341, **Fax:** (305) 534-0362.
E-mail: newcolours@aol.com **URL:** www.travelbase.com/colours IGLTA

FERRARI GUIDES™

Coral Tree Inn

Men ♂

Coral Tree Inn is a newly renovated resort in the heart of Old Town, across the street from The Oasis, our mother house. Ten suites open onto balconies, with multi-level sun decks cascading from the 3rd level down to the pool, courtyard and whirlpool under the trellis and the coral tree. Tastefully decorated rooms have AC, color cable TV, Bahama fans, refrigerators, hair dryers, coffee-makers, and robes to wear during your visit. Clothes are optional and complete concierge services are available. You will find our hospitality genuine and generous.

Address: 822 Fleming St, Key West, FL
Tel: (305) 296-2131 or (800) 362-7477, **Fax:** (305) 296-9171.

Type: Guesthouse.
Clientele: Men only
Transportation: Taxi from airport.
To Gay Bars: 3-1/2 blocks.
Rooms: 10 rooms with queen beds.
Bathrooms: All private.
Meals: Expanded continental breakfast.
Complimentary: Wine & hors d'oeuvres at sunset for an hour by the pool.

Dates Open: All year.
High Season: December 16-May 1.
Rates: Summer $99-$135, winter $159-$189.
Discounts: Airline flight service.
Credit Cards: MC, Visa, Amex.
Rsv'tns: Strongly advised.
To Reserve: Travel agent or call direct.

Minimum Stay: Required on holidays & special events.
Parking: Limited free on-street parking. Car is not really needed.
In-Room: Color TV, AC, ceiling fans, refrigerator, maid service.
Exercise/Health: Jacuzzi & use of 2 Jacuzzis at The Oasis.

Swimming: Pool & nearby ocean beach. Use of 2 pools at The Oasis.
Sunbathing: At poolside or on common sun decks.
Nudity: Permitted in public areas.
Smoking: Permitted.
Pets: Not permitted.
Handicap Access: No.
Children: Not permitted.
Languages: English, Spanish.

Curry House

Men ♂

Key West's Premiere Guest House for Men

If you find many of your new friends speak with an intriguing accent, it's because the *Curry House* is internationally popular. With only nine rooms, getting to know your fellow guests happens naturally while lounging by our black lagoon pool or at our daily happy hour. As your hosts, we're wholeheartedly at your service. Your room will be immaculate, your bed as comfortable as any you've ever slept in. *Curry House* is a short 3-block stroll from Duval Street, Key West's lively mainstream.

Address: 806 Fleming St, Key West, FL 33040
Tel: (305) 294-6777, (800) 633-7439, **Fax:** (305) 294-5322.

Type: B&B guesthouse.
Clientele: Men only
Transportation: Airport taxi, approx. $6.
To Gay Bars: 4 blocks to men's bars.
Rooms: 9 rooms with double & queen beds.

Bathrooms: 7 private.
Meals: Full breakfast.
Vegetarian: Available nearby.
Complimentary: Free cocktail hour from 4-6 PM.
Dates Open: All year.

High Season: January through May.
Rates: Summer $75-$95, winter $120-$150.
Credit Cards: MC, Visa, Amex.

Rsv'tns: Recommended during in-season (3-6 months in advance).
To Reserve: Call direct or travel agent.

continued next page

INN PLACES® 1998   321

UNITED STATES

Minimum Stay: 3 nights in high season, 1 night on summer weekends.
Parking: Ample free on-street parking.
In-Room: Refrigerator,

maid service, AC, ceiling fans.
On-Premises: Public telephone.
Exercise/Health: Jacuzzi.
Swimming: Pool or ocean beach.

Sunbathing: At poolside or on private or common sun decks.
Nudity: Permitted at poolside and on balconies.
Smoking: Permitted without restrictions.

Pets: Not permitted.
Handicap Access: No.
Children: Not permitted.
Languages: English.

IGLTA

KEY WEST • FLORIDA

Duval House

A Traditional Inn in Paradise

Gay-Friendly 50/50 ♀♂

Outside our front gate lie the galleries, sidewalk cafes and exciting nightlife of Duval Street. Yet, within the *Duval House* compound, seven historic Victorian houses are surrounded by magnificent tropical gardens. Relax under our century-old Banyan tree, swim in our romantic pool, enjoy a free buffet breakfast on a sunny deck. We pride ourselves on being friendly and open to all. Rooms feature wicker and antiques, with ceiling fans, Caribbean colors, and restful porches or balconies for you to enjoy the gentle island tradewinds.

Address: 815 Duval St, Key West, FL 33040
Tel: (305) 294-1666 or (800) 22-DUVAL (38825).

Type: Inn.
Clientele: 50% gay & lesbian & 50% straight clientele
Transportation: Taxi from airport.
To Gay Bars: 1/2 block to men's & 3 blocks to women's bars.
Rooms: 26 rooms & 3 suites with double or queen beds.
Bathrooms: 27 private

shower/toilets & 2 shared showers.
Meals: Expanded continental breakfast.
Dates Open: All year.
High Season: December 22nd thru April 15th.
Rates: High season $120-$190, low season $85-$140.
Discounts: 10% weekly during off-season.
Credit Cards: MC, Visa,

Amex, Discover & Diners.
Rsv'tns: Recommended.
To Reserve: Travel agent or call direct.
Parking: Adequate off-street parking.
In-Room: AC, maid service, suites have kitchen & ceiling fans.
On-Premises: TV lounge.
Exercise/Health: Nearby gym, weights, sauna & steam.

Swimming: Pool on premises, ocean beach nearby.
Sunbathing: At poolside, private sun decks, or on ocean beach.
Smoking: Permitted without restrictions.
Pets: Not permitted.
Handicap Access: No.
Children: Under 16 years discouraged.
Languages: English, German.

Equator

The New Age of Male Accommodation

Men ♂

Equator ushers in a new millennium in Key West men's resorts. Deluxe suites, rooms with private decks, rooms with pocket kitchens and bungalow rooms create a world of whimsy and comfort unlike any other. Our spacious accommodations feature specialty lighting, Italian tile floors, security access, climate control and Florida tropical interiors. Luxuriate in our tropical setting with a black lagoon pool, orchids, sunning decks, fountain pond and monsoon outdoor shower. *Equator*, a place where time stands still... poised on the edge of the 21st century.

Address: 818 Fleming St, Key West, FL 33040
Tel: (305) 294-7775, (800) 278-4552, **Fax:** (305) 296-5765.

Type: Guesthouse.
Clientele: Men only.
Transportation: Taxi from airport.
To Gay Bars: 4 blocks to gay bars.
Rooms: 15 rooms, 1-2 room suite, 3 addt'l suites. King or queen beds, 2 rooms with x-long full beds.
Bathrooms: All private baths.
Meals: Full breakfast.
Vegetarian: Available across the street.

Complimentary: Cocktails, turndown service, room snacks.
Dates Open: All year.
High Season: Mid-Dec thru May.
Rates: High season $115-$185, mid-season $105-$145, summer $90-$125.
Credit Cards: MC, Visa, Amex.
Rsv'tns: Required.
To Reserve: Travel agent or call direct.

Minimum Stay: Required.
Parking: Car not necessary, but on-street parking available.
In-Room: AC, ceiling fans, color cable TV, VCR available, video tape library, phone, refrigerator, maid service. Some rooms have pocket kitchen, 3 have private decks, 4 have street-side balcony.
Exercise/Health: Whirlpool.

Swimming: Pool on premises, ocean nearby.
Sunbathing: Poolside, on private sun deck, at beach.
Nudity: Permitted poolside.
Smoking: Smoking rooms available.
Pets: Sorry, no pets.
Handicap Access: Yes.
Children: No.
Languages: English.
Your Host: Joe & Bill.

IGLTA

Heron House

Q-NET Gay-Friendly

Feel Free...Feel Relaxed...Feel Welcomed

Amidst orchids, bougainvillaea, jasmine and palms, a secluded tropical garden fantasy awaits you. This warm and friendly place to relax and dream is *Heron House*. Spacious sun decks surround a sparkling pool. Our light, airy and spacious rooms are a careful mix of old and new and have a tropical flare with wicker, casual and comfortable furnishings. Luxurious marble bathroom vanities reflect an attention to detail.

Address: 512 Simonton St, Key West, FL 33040
Tel: (305) 294-9227, (888) 676-8654, **Fax:** (305) 294-5692.
E-mail: heronKW@aol.com **URL:** http://www.heronhouse.com

Type: Guesthouse.
Clientele: Mostly straight clientele with a gay & lesbian following
Transportation: Car or airport, then taxi.
To Gay Bars: 1 block to men's bars.
Rooms: 21 rooms with double, queen or king beds.
Bathrooms: All private bath/toilets.

Meals: Deluxe continental breakfast.
Vegetarian: 1 block away.
Dates Open: All year.
High Season: Dec 20-April 30.
Rates: Winter: Dec 20-Apr 30 $149-$249; Shoulder: May 1-30 & Oct 20-Dec 19 $109-$199; Summer: June 1-Oct 19 $99-$179.
Credit Cards: MC, Visa, Amex, Diners.

Rsv'tns: Recommended.
To Reserve: Travel agent or call direct.
Minimum Stay: During holidays and special events.
Parking: Ample on-street parking.
In-Room: Maid service, ceiling fans, AC, color TV, refrigerators, telephones, private entrances.
Exercise/Health: Some rooms have Jacuzzis.

Swimming: Pool, ocean beach.
Sunbathing: At poolside, on roof or on private or common sun decks.
Nudity: Permitted on sun deck.
Smoking: Restricted.
Pets: Not permitted.
Handicap Access: Yes. Ramps.
Children: Not permitted.
Languages: English.

INN PLACES® 1998

The Island Key Courts of Key West Q-NET Gay-Friendly ♀

Go Native in Key West! Best Values! Best Rates!

We are the only Key West accommodation offering a special welcome package for women, and a detailed insider's guide to all Key West activities & attractions of interest to women. We invite you to go native and live like a Key Wester at the *Island Key Courts*. For a price similar to that of a standard room-with-bath accommodation, we offer a charming cottage-style Island Residence — a complete, self-contained apartment suite with the convenience and savings of a fully equipped kitchen and the roomy comfort of a Studio Residence, a One-Bedroom Residence or a Two-Bedroom, Two-Bath Residence. (Our residences sleep 1-9 guests!) A real, laid-back hideaway — and all within easy walking distance of downtown bars, boutiques, restaurants and Atlantic beaches!

With our condo format, you will have total peace and privacy: No crowded lobbies, no miles of hallways — most of our 14 units have a private entrance from the garden. There is no intrusive staff, just meticulous daily maid service and friendly concierges ready to direct you to the best of the insider's Key West.

In addition to our best values and reasonable rates, as a guest of the *Island Key Court II* (817 Catherine St) you will receive a wonderful, free extra — a complimentary membership to the private beach club at a nearby resort, located just a few blocks from us. You will have unlimited access to a private, sandy beach, a sparkling pool, a complete health club with fully equipped gym and spa, two fabulous restaurants and three tropical bars. As a guest of *Island Key Court I* (910 Simonton St) you receive a complimentary pass to Key West's best beach, a local favorite, the Fort Zachary Taylor Beach. There you can swim, snorkel, fish in the sun, or enjoy a picnic or BBQ in the shade of a tropical pine forest. Additionally, "Fort Zach," a national historic landmark, features a fascinating Civil War fort to explore.

Address: 910 Simonton St (office) & 817 Catherine St, Key West, FL 33040
Tel: (305) 296-1148, (800) 296-1148, **Fax:** (305) 292-7924.
E-mail: rayebv@aol.com **URL:** http://www.q-net/islandkeycourts

Type: Apartment suites & guestrooms.
Clientele: Mostly straight clientele with a strong lesbian following
Transportation: Taxi from Key West airport (5-minute drive), car from Miami (3-hour drive).

To Gay Bars: 5 blocks, a 7-minute walk, a 3-minute drive.
Rooms: 14 apartments with single, queen & king beds, rollaways.
Bathrooms: All private: 7 bath/toilets, 7 shower/toilets.

Meals: Many great restaurants nearby.
Vegetarian: Vegetarian restaurants in town.
Dates Open: All year.
High Season: Christmas-Easter.
Rates: Summer $59-$199, winter $99-$299.
Discounts: Various.

Credit Cards: MC, Visa, Amex, Diners.
Rsv'tns: Required.
To Reserve: Call direct or travel agent.
Minimum Stay: Required during holidays & special events.
Parking: Adequate free on-street parking.

In-Room: Color cable TV, AC, phone, ceiling fans, full kitchen, coffee/tea-making facilities, maid service.
Exercise/Health: Jacuzzi at Island Key Courts I. Complimentary membership at nearby private health club.
Swimming: Complimentary membership at same private pool & beach club.
Sunbathing: By the pool & at the beach.
Nudity: Island Key Courts II: Permitted in private garden/porch.
Smoking: OK.
Pets: Not permitted.
Handicap Access: No.
Children: Yes.

La-Te-Da Hotel

Gay/Lesbian ♀♂

A Place of Fantasy and Fun

The fabled La Terraza, known affectionately as *La-Te-Da*, recently reopened after a total restoration. This European-style hotel is set in a compound, arranged around a glorious private pool framed by tropical palms. The main building houses a gourmet restaurant, a disco and a terrace bar, all with an ambiance of romance and charm. Originally built as a private residence, in 1892 the legendary Cuban patriot, Martí, used the balcony of the main house as a rallying place for raising funds for the liberation of Cuba. *La-Te-Da* is within walking distance of all Old Town attractions, as well as beaches, shopping and watersports.

Address: 1125 Duval St, Key West, FL 33040
Tel: (305) 296-6706, (800) 528-3320, **Fax:** (305) 296-0438.

Type: Hotel with restaurant, show bar.
Clientele: Mostly gay & lesbian with some straight clientele
Transportation: Car or taxi.
To Gay Bars: A 2 minute walk to gay bars.
Rooms: 16 rooms with king or queen beds.
Bathrooms: All private.
Vegetarian: Available on property.
Dates Open: All year.
High Season: Christmas thru Easter.
Rates: Summer/fall $59-$95, winter/spring $120-$240.
Credit Cards: MC, Visa, Amex, Discover, Diners.
To Reserve: Travel agent or call direct.
Minimum Stay: Required during holidays.
Parking: Off-street parking available for 1 car per room.
In-Room: AC, color cable TV, ceiling fans, telephone, coffee & tea-making facilities, maid & room service.
On-Premises: Restaurant, show bar, meeting rooms.
Exercise/Health: Nearby gym, weights, Jacuzzi, sauna, massage.
Swimming: Pool on premises, ocean nearby.
Sunbathing: Poolside, private & common sun decks, on patio.
Nudity: Permitted on clothing-optional sun deck.
Smoking: Permitted anywhere. No non-smoking rooms available.
Pets: Not permitted.
Handicap Access: Yes.
Children: No.
Your Host: Jim & Godfrey.

Lavadia

Gay-Owned & -Operated ♀♂

Distinctive Lodging in Paradise

Legend of the island claims that *Lavadia* (view of the sea) was built in 1890 by a Russian sea captain. City records indicate that the estate was occupied in 1906 by Frank J. Roberts, an accountant for Richard Peacon, Jr., the vice president of Tropical Building Investments, who resided in the substantial home until 1923. Today, it

continued next page

INN PLACES® 1998

325

UNITED STATES — KEY WEST • FLORIDA

is a private retreat, enjoyed by families from around the world. Another home of Southernmost Hospitality, it is located on William Street in Old Town Key West, and is within walking distance of local attractions. Boasting typical gingerbread trim on the wrap-around veranda, the home's two-thousand-square-feet of exquisitely appointed furnishings and antiques await the most discriminating tastes.

Within the stately three-story traditional home, the first floor offers a formal parlor, romantic dining room for candle-lit dinners, a gourmet kitchen and a large Florida room with additional bath. The second level features three bedrooms and two bathrooms, all uniquely appointed. Executives will appreciate the writing table with two-line telephone, fax and answering machine. French doors lead you to the heated swimming pool and outdoor deck area with mini bar, barbecue grill and ice maker. A privacy fence ensures all the ingredients for a magical vacation. The third-floor attic apartment has a private entrance from the main home, is ideal for servants' quarters, and can sleep six teenagers. The 700-square-foot apartment is air-conditioned and has skylights, a queen-sized bed and two futons in the living area, a fully equipped kitchen, and a private Jacuzzi in the bathroom. The apartment is not available separately and will only be rented to ensure privacy.

Address: Mail to: Southernmost Hospitality, 524 Eaton St, #150, Key West, FL 33040
Tel: (305) 294-3800, (888) 294-3800, **Fax:** (305) 294-9298.
E-mail: keywestlodging@sprynet

Type: Cottage, guesthouse private rentals.
Clientele: Gay, lesbian & straight clientele
Transportation: Taxi & bicycle.
To Gay Bars: 1 block, a 2 min walk.
Rooms: 3 apartments, 4 cottages, 2 luxury homes with single, double, queen or king beds.
Bathrooms: All private bath/shower/toilets.
Dates Open: All year.
High Season: Jan-Mar.
Rates: $200-$500.
Rsv'tns: Required.
To Reserve: Travel agent or call direct.
Minimum Stay: 7 nights.
Parking: Limited on-street pay parking.
In-Room: Telephone, AC, ceiling fans, color cable TV, VCR, kitchen, refrigerator, coffee & tea-making facilities, maid service.
Swimming: Pool on premises.
Sunbathing: Poolside, on private sun decks, at beach.
Nudity: Permitted.
Smoking: Non-smoking rooms available.
Pets: Not permitted.
Handicap Access: No.
Children: No.

Lighthouse Court   Men ♂

Lighthouse Court is Key West's largest, most private guest compound. A variety of restored conch houses connected by decking, nestled in lush tropical foliage, it combines the charm of days past with contemporary taste and design. Accommodations include rooms, apartments and suites. Rooms have TV, air conditioning and/or Bahama fans, refrigerators, and many have kitchen facilities. Located one block from historic Duval Street, *Lighthouse Court* is a short stroll from shops, galleries, beaches, sailing & snorkeling as well as Key West's famous nite life.

Address: 902 Whitehead St, Key West, FL 33040 **Tel:** (305) 294-9788.

Type: Guesthouse with restaurant, bar & health club.
Clientele: Men only
Transportation: Taxi from airport.
To Gay Bars: 1 block to Duval St bars.
Rooms: 4 singles, 30 doubles, 4 suites & 4 efficiencies.
Bathrooms: 38 private & 4 shared.
Vegetarian: Breakfast & lunch.
Dates Open: All year.
High Season: Jan 20 thru Easter, Fantasy Fest-late October, New Years' Eve.
Rates: $60-$235.
Credit Cards: MC, Visa.
Rsv'tns: Preferred.
To Reserve: Call direct.
Minimum Stay: Required on holidays.
Parking: Ample free on-street parking.
In-Room: Maid & room service, AC, ceiling fans, fridge, telephone & TV.
On-Premises: Meeting rooms, TV lounge, beer-and-wine bar.
Exercise/Health: Jacuzzi, health club on premises, gym, weights, massage.
Swimming: Pool on premises, ocean beach nearby.
Sunbathing: At poolside, on roof, common sun decks, or on beach nearby.
Nudity: Permitted.
Smoking: Permitted without restrictions.
Pets: Not permitted.
Handicap Access: Inquire.
Children: Not permitted.
Languages: English, French.

Mangrove House

Men ♂

Intimate and Friendly in the Key West Tradition

Located in the centre of historic Old Town Key West, this charming "Eyebrow" house offers spacious and comfortable accommodations exclusively for gay men. Nestled in a lush tropical setting, *Mangrove House* is quiet and secluded yet steps away from the heart of Duval Street. All units have private bath, phone, air conditioning and cable TV. Clothing is optional around the beautiful solar-heated pool and hot tub. A copious continental breakfast is served poolside every morning and complimentary refreshments are available throughout the afternoon.

Address: 623 Southard St, Key West, FL
Tel: (800) 294-1866, (305) 294-1866, **Fax:** (305) 294-8757.
E-mail: mangrove@conch.net

Type: Guesthouse.
Clientele: Men only
Transportation: Car, taxi from airport, walk from bus depot.
To Gay Bars: 2 blocks or a 3-minute walk.
Rooms: 2 rooms & 2 apartments with double or queen beds.
Bathrooms: 4 private bath/toilets.
Meals: Continental breakfast.
Complimentary: Refreshments in the afternoon.
Dates Open: All year.
High Season: December-April.
Rates: Off season $75-$115, high season $95-$175. Special rates for Fantasy Fest.
Discounts: 10% for stays of 7 or more nights in high season & during Fantasy Fest.
Credit Cards: MC, Visa, Amex, Discover.
Rsv'tns: Highly recommended.
To Reserve: Travel agent or call direct.
Minimum Stay: 3 nights for holidays, 4 nights for Fantasy Fest.
Parking: Ample on-street parking on safe residential street.
In-Room: Color cable TV, telephone, AC, ceiling fans & maid service. Apartment has kitchen, refrigerator & coffee/tea-making facilities.
Exercise/Health: Jacuzzi & weights on premises. Nearby gym, massage.
Swimming: Pool on premises. Nearby ocean.
Sunbathing: At poolside.
Nudity: Permitted on property.
Smoking: Permitted without restrictions.
Pets: Not permitted.
Handicap Access: No. 4 steps from street to rooms.
Children: Not welcome.
Languages: English, French, German & Italian.

New Orleans House - Key West

Gay-Owned & -Operated ♂

It's Mardi Gras Every Night

Location, location, location... it's all here at Key West's premier gay compound, the New Orleans-style *New Orleans House - Key West*. Our all-modern guestrooms are above the world-famous Bourbon Street Pub and provide queen beds and private-line phones. Some units have kitchenettes. The *New Orleans House - Key West* **will open in January, 1998** to an all-male clientele... you won't be disappointed! Call for reservations — we want you in the bag!

Address: 724 Duval St (2nd floor), Key West, FL 33040
Tel: (305) 293-9800,
Fax: (305) 294-9298.
E-mail: keywestlodging@sprynet

New Orleans House
Key West, Florida

Key West's Premier Gay Complex
opening January 1, 1998

continued next page

UNITED STATES

KEY WEST • FLORIDA

Type: Guesthouse.
Clientele: Men only
Transportation: Taxi, then bike.
To Gay Bars: 1/2 min walk.
Rooms: 8 rooms, 2 cottages with queen beds.
Bathrooms: 8 private bath/shower/toilets, 2 shared bath/shower/toilets.

Meals: Continental breakfast.
Dates Open: All year.
High Season: Jan-Mar.
Rates: $75-$275.
Credit Cards: MC, Visa, Amex.
Rsv'tns: Required.
To Reserve: Travel agent or call direct.

Minimum Stay: 3 nights.
Parking: Limited off-street parking.
In-Room: Telephone, AC, ceiling fans, color cable TV.
On-Premises: TV lounge.
Exercise/Health: Gym, weights, Jacuzzi.

Swimming: Pool on premises.
Sunbathing: Poolside, on common sun decks.
Nudity: Permitted on patio, sun deck & in garden.
Pets: Not permitted.
Handicap Access: Yes.
Children: No.

Newton Street Station
Join Us in Our Corner of Paradise

Men ♂

Newton Street Station, formerly the home of the stationmaster of the Florida East Coast Railway, is an intimate guesthouse in a quiet, residential section of Old Town Key West. Rooms are individually-decorated and breakfast is served on the tropical sun deck. Lounge by the pool, nude, if you like, enjoy the tropical gardens, or work out on the exercise deck. Visit shops and galleries, or enjoy some of the finest water sports in the country. *Newton Street Station* is one of the friendliest, all-men's guesthouses in Key West, where our goal is to make you feel welcome.

328   FERRARI GUIDES™

Address: 1414 Newton St, Key West, FL 33040
Tel: (305) 294-4288, (800) 248-2457, **Fax:** (305) 292-5062.
URL: http://www.travelbase.com/destinations/keywest/newton-street-station

Type: Guesthouse.
Clientele: Men only
Transportation: Inexpensive taxi ride from airport.
To Gay Bars: 5 minutes by car to men's bars.
Rooms: 6 rooms & 1 suite with double beds.
Bathrooms: 4 private, 2 shared & 1 half-bath.
Meals: Continental breakfast.
Dates Open: All year.
High Season: December 15th-April 30th.
Rates: Winter $80-$120, summer $60-$80.
Discounts: 10% for a week or more, or for members of nudist/naturist groups.
Credit Cards: MC, Visa, Amex.
Rsv'tns: Highly recommended.
To Reserve: Travel agent or call direct.
Minimum Stay: During holidays & special events.
Parking: Ample free on-street parking.
In-Room: Maid service, color cable TVs, AC, refrigerator, phone, some ceiling fans.
On-Premises: TV lounge & free local phone calls.
Exercise/Health: Weights & bicycles
Swimming: Pool or nearby ocean.
Sunbathing: At poolside, on private & common sun decks, or patio.
Nudity: Permitted anywhere on premises.
Smoking: Permitted without restrictions.
Pets: Not permitted.
Handicap Access: No.
Children: Not permitted.
Languages: English, limited French & limited German.
Your Host: John.

IGLTA

Oasis, A Guest House
Men ♂

Oasis, A Guest House is Key West's most elegant guesthouse, a magnificently restored 1895 mansion in the historic district, where you capture the true charm and excitement of this idyllic isle. Multi-level sun decks allow secluded sunbathing, plus breathtaking views of town and gulf. Tastefully-appointed rooms have AC, private bath, color TV, Bahama fans and robes to wear during your visit. We have two of the island's largest private pools (one heated) and Forida's largest Jacuzzi. The sun decks and pools are open 24 hours a day, clothes optional. Share the tranquil beauty of our home and experience our genuine and generous hospitality.

Address: 823 Fleming Street, Key West, FL 33040
Tel: (305) 296-2131 or (800) 362-7477, **Fax:** (305) 296-9171.

Type: Guesthouse with beer & wine bar.
Clientele: Men only
Transportation: Taxi from airport.
To Gay Bars: 4 blocks to men's/women's bars.
Rooms: 19 rooms with queen beds.
Bathrooms: 19 private bath/toilets.
Meals: Expanded continental breakfast.
Complimentary: Wine party every evening with hors d'oeuvres by the main pool.
Dates Open: All year.
High Season: January-April.
Rates: Summer $99-$135, winter $159-$189.
Discounts: 10% airline travel agents.
Credit Cards: MC, Visa, Amex.
Rsv'tns: Preferred.
To Reserve: Travel agent or call direct.
Minimum Stay: During holidays & special events.
Parking: Plenty of on-street parking.
In-Room: Maid service, color TV, refrigerator, AC & ceiling fans.
Exercise/Health: Jacuzzi.
Swimming: 2 large pools on premises.
Sunbathing: At poolside or on private sun decks.
Nudity: Permitted.
Smoking: Permitted without restrictions.
Pets: Not permitted.
Handicap Access: No.
Children: Not permitted.
Languages: English, Spanish.
Your Host: Gerry.

IGLTA

Pilot House

Gay-Owned 50/50 ♀♂*

"Another Home of Southernmost Hospitality"

Pilot House is a grand two-story Victorian mansion built, circa 1900, by Julius Otto as his private home. Today the structure stands proud in the center of the Key West historical district known as Old Town. It boasts verandas and porches with hand-milled spindles and gingerbread trim. After the labored restoration in 1990, receiving the prestigious "Excellence Award for Preservation" by the Florida Keys Preservation Board, we opened the doors to the mansion as a guest residence.

Pilot House is appointed with a careful blend of antiques and decorated with tropical furnishings, accommodating the discriminating tastes of experienced travelers. We offer unique lodging accommodations with eight guest rooms to choose from, all with private bath, color cable TV, phone, air conditioning and paddle fans. Newly added to the tropical paradise of the *Pilot House* compound are the brand-new poolside cabana suites, which feature in-room Jacuzzis, mini-bars and modern tropical decor. Each has its own outside entrance and selected "smoking-allowed" suites are also available.

Address: 414 Simonton St, Key West, FL 33040
Tel: (800) 648-3780, (305) 293-6600, **Fax:** (305) 294-9298.
E-mail: pilothousekeywest@sprynet

Type: Guesthouse.
Clientele: 50% gay & lesbian & 50% straight clientele
Transportation: Taxi.
To Gay Bars: 1 block.
Rooms: 14 rooms with pull, queen or king beds.
Bathrooms: All private bath/shower/toilets.
Vegetarian: Several gourmet markets & juice bars in Key West.

Dates Open: All year.
High Season: Jan-Mar.
Rates: Season $175-$250, summer $100-$175.
Discounts: 10% weekly.
Credit Cards: MC, Visa, Amex.
Rsv'tns: Preferred.
To Reserve: Travel agent or call direct.
Minimum Stay: 3 nights.

Parking: Limited on-street or pay parking.
In-Room: Telephone, AC, ceiling fans, color cable TV, kitchenette, refrigerator, coffee & tea-making facilities, maid service.
Exercise/Health: Jacuzzi, bike rentals. Nearby gym, weights, steam, massage.
Swimming: Pool. Ocean nearby.

Sunbathing: Poolside, on private sun decks, at beach.
Nudity: Permitted in pool & spa.
Smoking: Permitted on porches & in cabana rooms.
Pets: Not permitted.
Handicap Access: Yes, ramps, rails in bathroom, wide doors, roll-in shower.
Children: No.
Languages: English.

Rainbow House

Q-NET Women ♀

Welcome to Paradise - We've Expanded!

At the *Rainbow House,* we have everything from a standard room to a deluxe suite. All of our rooms have queen-sized beds, color TV, telephones, air conditioning, as well as Bahama fans and, of course, private bath. We serve an expanded continental breakfast poolside every morning. Enjoy it in our air conditioned pavilion or poolside. It's complimentary to our guests and a wonderful social setting. After breakfast, lounge on one of the sunbathing decks, or sit in the shade while you read a book with the gentle island breezes rustling the palm trees above.

2 Hot Tubs! 2 Swimming Pools! 38 Rooms & Suites!

As relaxing and comfortable as the guesthouse is, you may want to venture out to have fun. We can take care of that, too. We have a full-time concierge to help with snorkeling, scuba, kayaking, parasailing, bike trails, beaches, and, of course, Key West's many different restaurants. Just turn the corner of our street, and start your shopping exodus. Duval Street has everything you can imagine, from art galleries to T-shirts, from jewelers to sushi bars. Of course, while you're in Key West, you'll have to experience one of our fabulous sunsets. They light up the sky and they're always memorable. And why not watch the sunset from Mallory Square, where you'll see jugglers, sword swallowers, tightrope walkers and characters that'll make you say "Only in Key West!"

There's plenty of nightlife, from rock-and-roll to disco, from piano bars to jazz, all within walking distance. As a matter of fact, most of our guests park their cars and leisurely stroll the streets of Old Town Key West. Whatever your vacation needs are...peace and quiet, the laid-back life, sun and fun, romantic or rejuvenating...pamper yourself with the special atmosphere we've created for you at the *Rainbow House.*

Address: 525 United St, Key West, FL 33040
Tel: (305) 292-1450, (800) 74-WOMYN (800 749-6696).

Type: Bed & breakfast guesthouse.
Clientele: Women only
To Gay Bars: 5-minute walk to gay/lesbian bars.
Rooms: 38 rooms & suites.
Bathrooms: All private.
Meals: Expanded continental breakfast.
Dates Open: All year.

High Season: Jan-Apr.
Rates: $69-$189.
Credit Cards: MC, Visa, Discover, Preferred, Amex.
Rsv'tns: Strongly recommended.
To Reserve: Call direct or travel agent.
Minimum Stay: During holidays.

Parking: On-street parking.
In-Room: Maid service, color TV, phones, AC.
Kitchens available.
Exercise/Health: Jacuzzi.
Swimming: 2 pools or 1 block to ocean.
Sunbathing: At poolside, on private sun decks or on ocean beach.

Nudity: Permitted at poolside.
Pets: Not permitted.
Handicap Access: One unit available.
Children: Not permitted.
Languages: English.
Your Host: Marion.

IGLTA

UNITED STATES

FLORIDA • KEY WEST

INN PLACES® 1998

UNITED STATES
KEY WEST • FLORIDA

Sea Isle Resort

Men ♂

What do You Want in Paradise?

The *Sea Isle Resort* is located in the center of Old Town, a short walk from the many attractions that Key West offers gay travelers. We are noted for our friendly, relaxed ambience and, as one of the largest, exclusively gay guesthouses, our guests have ample opportunity to socialize with vacationers from all over the US and abroad. Included among the many features provided to our guests are three sun decks, an air-conditioned gym, free off-street parking, and more. Continental breakfast is served daily and weekend cocktail parties are complimentary.

Address: 915 Windsor Lane, Key West, FL 33040
Tel: (305) 294-5188, (800) 995-4786, **Fax:** (305) 296-7143.
E-mail: seaislefun@aol.com
URL: http://members.aol.com/seaislefun

Type: Resort, compound.
Clientele: Predominantly gay men
Transportation: Taxi from airport.
To Gay Bars: 3 blocks.
Rooms: 17 rooms with queen or king beds, 5 rooms with 2 queen beds & 2 suites.
Bathrooms: All private.
Meals: Expanded continental breakfast.
Complimentary: Weekend cocktail parties.

Dates Open: All year.
High Season: Mid-Dec thru end-Apr.
Rates: Single or double occ: summer $75-$140, winter & holidays $125-$200. $20 extra per person/night for 3rd & 4th person.
Credit Cards: Visa, MC, Novus (Discover).
Rsv'tns: Highly recommended.
To Reserve: Travel agent or call direct.
Minimum Stay: Required holidays, special events & many weekends.

Parking: Free off-street private parking.
In-Room: AC, telephone, color cable TV, VCR, refrigerator, maid service. Coffee makers & hair dryers available.
On-Premises: Covered outdoor Florida room.
Exercise/Health: Large, private whirlpool, air-conditioned gym with Nautilus equipment, Olympic free weights, benches, squat rack.
Swimming: Large, solar-heated pool on premises. Beaches half mile.
Sunbathing: On spacious sun decks (2 ground-level, 1 elevated).
Nudity: Permitted, except during breakfast.
Smoking: Permitted without restrictions.
Pets: Permitted, $10 per pet/night add'l charge.
Handicap Access: Yes, with assistance.
Children: Not permitted.
Languages: English.
Your Host: Randy & Jim.

IGLTA

Sheraton Key West All-Suite Resort

Gay-Friendly ♀♂

Island Suites in the Key West Tradition

Sheraton Key West, an all-suite hotel, is located right across from popular Smathers Beach on the Atlantic Ocean side of the island. Our friendly staff will meet your every need and you'll enjoy the familiar Sheraton service and quality that you have come to depend on. All of our accommodations are comfortable

FERRARI GUIDES™

suites with lots of room and amenities. There is free shuttle service into Old Town and we offer moped rental services. Rooms include a wet bar, microwave and coffee maker. We also offer a fitness center and pool with cascading waterfall.

Address: 2001 S Roosevelt Blvd, Key West, FL 33040
Tel: (305) 292-9800, **Fax:** (305) 294-6009.

Type: Resort with restaurant, shops & bar.
Clientele: Mostly straight clientele with a gay/lesbian following
Transportation: Hotel car or taxi from airport. Pick up from airport.
To Gay Bars: 1.5 miles, a 10-minute drive.
Rooms: 180 suites with double or king beds.
Bathrooms: All private bath/toilets.

Vegetarian: In restaurant on property.
Complimentary: Coffee & tea in all suites.
Dates Open: All year.
High Season: Dec 22-Apr 15.
Rates: High season $200-$450, low season $140-$300.
Discounts: AAA, AARP.
Credit Cards: MC, Visa, Amex, Diners, Eurocard, Discover.
Rsv'tns: Suggested.

To Reserve: Travel agent or call direct.
Parking: Ample free off-street parking.
In-Room: AC, telephone, color cable TV, coffee & tea-making facilities, refrigerator, maid & room service.
On-Premises: Laundry facilities, meeting rooms.
Exercise/Health: Gym, weights, Jacuzzi.
Swimming: Pool. Ocean nearby.
Sunbathing: Poolside, on private sun decks, at beach.
Smoking: Permitted in rooms. Non-smoking rooms available.
Pets: Not permitted.
Handicap Access: Yes.
Children: Welcome. There are poolside activities & toys.
Languages: English, German, Spanish, Portuguese.

IGLTA

Simonton Court Historic Inn & Cottages

Gay-Friendly 50/50 ♀♂

Once You Stay Here, You'll Always Come Back

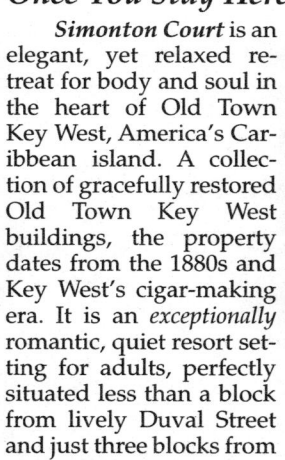

Simonton Court is an elegant, yet relaxed retreat for body and soul in the heart of Old Town Key West, America's Caribbean island. A collection of gracefully restored Old Town Key West buildings, the property dates from the 1880s and Key West's cigar-making era. It is an *exceptionally* romantic, quiet resort setting for adults, perfectly situated less than a block from lively Duval Street and just three blocks from Key West's harbor and Mallory Square. All forms of entertainment — unique shops, excellent restaurants, live theater and a bar for everyone's taste — are only a short walk away. America's only living coral reef makes for some of the finest diving, snorkeling, fishing and boating experiences anywhere in the world.

A lovely private garden compound, with hot tub and three separate pools, brick paths, tin roofs, French doors and lush foliage canopies create the ambiance for three levels of accommodation. An old cigar-makers' factory, now the Inn, and a building called the Manor House, offer charming rooms, each unique and each with either kitchenette or refrigerator. Cottages, with wood floors and wicker furniture, are ideal for 2-6 people, with 2-3 separate sleeping areas and private porches and/or decks. The Mansion, built in the Victorian era, is now the

continued next page

INN PLACES® 1998

property's most elegant accommodation, offering an unsurpassed level of service. Some of the Mansion's suites have outdoor decks, and one has a most private widow's walk for sweeping panoramic views of the city and ocean, with an in-room Jacuzzi — *very* romantic! A few rooms can be combined into suites; two rooms in the Manor House form a private suite with a pool and deck for the exclusive use of the suite when combined.

The staff is friendly and helpful, but low-key, never intrusive. A luscious complimentary continental breakfast is served every morning and can be carried into one of many garden alcoves or porches.

Address: 320 Simonton St, Key West, FL 33040
Tel: (800) 944-2687, (305) 294-6386, **Fax:** (305) 293-8446.

Type: Cottage inn. **Clientele:** 50% gay & lesbian & 50% straight clientele **Transportation:** Taxi or airport shuttle 10 minutes from airport. **To Gay Bars:** 4 blocks to gay & lesbian bars. **Rooms:** 2 rooms, 14 suites & 6 cottages with bunk, double, queen or king beds. **Bathrooms:** All private shower/toilets.	**Meals:** Expanded continental breakfast. **Vegetarian:** Vegetarian food available at several restaurants within 4 blocks. **Dates Open:** All year. **High Season:** Dec 15-May 1 & all national holidays. **Rates:** In season $150-$350, mid season $130-$255, low season $110-$200. **Discounts:** Airline. **Credit Cards:** MC, Visa, Amex, Discover.	**Rsv'tns:** Recommended. **To Reserve:** Travel agent or call direct. **Minimum Stay:** 2 days weekends, 5 days Christmas, New Year, Fantasy Fest, 4 days high season. **Parking:** Ample on-street or pay parking. **In-Room:** Color cable TV, VCR, AC, telephone, ceiling fans, refrigerator, coffee & tea-making facilities & maid service. Some units with kitchens.	**Exercise/Health:** Hot tub. **Swimming:** 4 heated pools. 3 blocks to beach. **Sunbathing:** At poolside or on beach. **Smoking:** Permitted without restrictions. **Pets:** Not permitted. **Handicap Access:** No. **Children:** Not permitted. **Languages:** English. **IGLTA**

Colours at The NEW Penguin Resort & The Mantell Plaza

Q-NET Gay/Lesbian ♀♂

Experience Not Just a Place, But a State of Mind

Close your eyes and imagine white sandy beaches, turquoise waters, warm ocean breezes, the boardwalk, a refreshing late afternoon swim in a secluded tropical pool under swaying palms and clear blue skies, Lincoln Road Mall, the culinary delights of South Beach's finest restaurants, and dancing 'til dawn at the hottest clubs on the planet. All this is possible when you plan your stay with us...

Now, Colours Destinations is located in *The New Penguin Resort* — the best address on Ocean Drive. With new ownership, this historic Art Deco hotel has been renovated and expanded to include a new swimming pool, the Front Porch Cafe, and the additional rooms of the original President Hotel on Collins. Fun, tropical ambiance with that special Art Deco flair... featuring 117 varied rooms with rates ranging from low single of $73, to high double of $178. Directly across Ocean Drive, the hot gay beach scene makes this truly "The Best of SoBe."

Additionally, Colours is affiliated with Island Outpost Properties and other South Beach locations, such as *The Mantell Plaza*. A condo hotel, renovated to feature individually-owned and -appointed kitchenette studios for travelers who prefer more of the comforts of home. A large, stunning swimming pool with gardens, a laundry and a small workout gym are on the property. **Call the reservation line at 1-800-ARRIVAL for information on these and other** Colours' distinctive lodgings: Hotel Colours in San Jose, Costa Rica, and Colours - The Guest Mansion in romantic Key West.

Tel: (800) ARRIVAL (277-4825), (305) 532-9341, **Fax:** (305) 534-0362.
E-mail: newcolours@aol.com **URL:** www.travelbase.com/colours

IGLTA

Island House

Q-NET Men ♂

South Beach's Biggest All-Gay Guesthouse

Award-winning *Island House*, a fully restored historic Art Deco guesthouse, offers comfortably furnished accommodations for men, ranging from rooms to studios and suites. This well-appointed guesthouse with its tropical, eclectic flavor and casual flair is South Beach's biggest all-gay guesthouse. Onehundred percent gay-owned, *Island House* and its friendly staff will

continued next page

INN PLACES® 1998

make you feel right at home. Start the morning off by enjoying a complimentary continental breakfast buffet with your new neighbors, served upstairs in the breakfast room overlooking Collins Avenue. After the beach or before dinner, enjoy complimentary beer and wine for happy hour on the front porch with old and new friends.

Centrally located in the heart of South Beach, we're walking distance to hot sizzling nightlife, cruisy bars, and a variety of restaurants — from outdoor cafes and neighborhood diners, to trendy bistros and elegant restaurants with world-famous cuisine. South Beach serves up what you're hungry for... The fabulous white sandy beaches, the tropical ocean breezes, the swaying coconut palms and the clear, blue ocean water and warm rays from the sun all create a steamy romantic setting. And beaches full of hot, sexy, sweaty men create bountiful social opportunities...

Our original location at 715 82nd Street in Miami Beach is off the beaten track, yet only five minutes to the gay nude beach and 15 minutes to the sizzling nightlife of South Beach. Enjoy our lushly landscaped tropical patio area, gardens and sun deck. Unwind in the Jacuzzi with your new friends. Nude sunbathing is always permitted at this more intimate location.

Address: 1428 Collins Avenue, Miami Beach, FL 33139
Tel: (305) 864-2422, (800) 382-2422, **Fax:** (305) 865-2220.

Type: Guesthouse.
Clientele: Gay men
Transportation: From airport: taxi, Supershuttle. A car is not needed.
To Gay Bars: Walking distance to all bars & restaurants.
Rooms: 20: rooms, standard rooms, deluxe rooms & studios.
Bathrooms: Private.
Meals: Continental breakfast buffet.

Complimentary: Beer & wine for Happy Hour (weekends & holidays).
Dates Open: All year.
High Season: Dec 1-Apr 30 & holidays.
Rates: Off season: $49-$99. Season: $69-$129.
Discounts: For extended stays & airline employees, subject to availability.
Credit Cards: MC, Amex, Visa, Discover, Diners Club.
Rsv'tns: Recommended. However, we will try to accommodate your last minute plans, subject to room availability.
To Reserve: Call direct.
Minimum Stay: Required during holiday periods.
Parking: 1-1/2 blocks to municipal garage. Limited street parking.
In-Room: Color cable TV, room phones, AC, ceiling fans, refrigerator, wet bars, maid service.
Exercise/Health: Masseur on call. Discount gym passes.
Swimming: 1 block to gay beach.
Sunbathing: 1 block to gay beach.
Nudity: 10 min to gay nude beach.
Smoking: Permitted.
Pets: No.
Handicap Access: No.
Languages: English, Spanish, French.

IGLTA

The Jefferson House

Close to Everything, Away from it All

Gay/Lesbian ♀♂

The *Jefferson House* is located in the midst of the historical Art Deco District of South Beach. Famous Miami Beach and exciting Ocean Drive are a few blocks from our door, as are the diverse restaurants and clubs of the area. All of our air conditioned rooms have private baths and queen-sized beds, and are tastefully appointed to add warmth and charm. Enjoy the friendly hospitality of a fine breakfast served on our deck overlooking a lovely tropical garden and pool. Come and experience the camaraderie that *The Jefferson House* has to offer.

Address: 1018 Jefferson Ave, Miami Beach, FL 33139
Tel: (305) 534-5247, **Fax:** (305) 534-5953.
E-mail: sobejhouse@aol.com **URL:** http://www.sobe.com/jhouse

Type: Bed & Breakfast.
Clientele: Mostly gay & lesbian with some straight clientele.
Transportation: Car, taxi, shuttle or bus.
To Gay Bars: 3 blocks. A 5-minute walk or 2-minute drive.
Rooms: 6 rooms & 1 suite with queen beds.
Bathrooms: All private shower/toilets.
Meals: Full breakfast.

Vegetarian: Available upon request.
Complimentary: Coffee all day.
Dates Open: All year.
High Season: Nov 1-Apr 30 & holidays.
Rates: High season $109-$165, mid season $89-$135.
Credit Cards: MC, Visa, Amex.
Rsv'tns: Required.
To Reserve: Travel agent or call direct.

Minimum Stay: Required on weekends & holidays.
Parking: Limited on-street parking.
In-Room: TV, AC, radio, maid service & phones with free local calls.
On-Premises: Laundry facilities, guest refrigerator, deck, tropical garden.
Exercise/Health: Nearby gym, weights, tennis, track & basketball. Special rates for guests.
Swimming: Pool on premises, ocean nearby.

Sunbathing: On deck poolside or at the beach.
Smoking: Permitted anywhere.
Pets: Not permitted.
Handicap Access: No.
Children: Not especially welcome.
Languages: English, Spanish, German.
Your Host: Jonathan & Todd.
IGLTA

Lily Guesthouse
Q-NET Gay/Lesbian ♀♂

An Oasis in the Heart of South Beach

The *Lily Guesthouse* is located in the heart of the Art Deco District in South Beach, half a block from the beach and within walking distance of nightclubs, famous restaurants and shopping. Built in 1936, this historical building was completely remodeled in 1994 by local interior designers. The guesthouse consists of two buildings, separated by an interior patio. The rear building has rooms and suites with private entrances, terraces and a common sun deck. All rooms have cable TV, marble bathrooms and cold kitchens.

Address: 835 Collins Ave, Miami Beach, FL
Tel: (305) 535-9900, (800) 535-9959, **Fax:** (305) 535-0077.

Type: Hotel/Guesthouse.
Clientele: Mostly gay & lesbian with some straight clientele
Transportation: Taxi.
To Gay Bars: 1-2 blocks.
Rooms: 9 rooms & 9 suites with queen beds.
Bathrooms: All private.
Complimentary: Coffee &

doughnuts in lobby.
Dates Open: All year.
High Season: October 1-April 30.
Rates: Low season $80-$95, high season $100-$275.
Credit Cards: MC, Visa, Amex.

To Reserve: Travel agent or call direct.
Parking: Ample on-street pay parking, 1 block to municipal parking, valet parking $16/day.
In-Room: AC, color cable TV, phone, refrigerator.
On-Premises: Sun deck, terraces.

Swimming: Nearby ocean.
Sunbathing: On common sun deck, at nearby beach.
Pets: Not permitted.
Handicap Access: No.
Children: No.
Languages: English, Spanish.
IGLTA

Miami River Inn
Gay-Friendly ♀♂

Enjoy the Charm of the Past Complemented by the Technology of Today

Miami River Inn is located in the ethnically diverse Miami River Neighborhood of East Little Havana. Centrally located across the Miami River from downtown, the inn is an oasis in the heart of Miami. The "compound" consists of five

continued next page

INN PLACES® 1998   337

wooden cottages surrounding a pool and Jacuzzi in a lush tropical setting full of flowers, soaring palms and other native greenery. South Beach, Coconut Grove, Key Biscayne and Coral Gables are all within a 15-minute drive. Downtown & Little Havana are within walking distance.

Address: 118 SW South River Dr, Miami, FL 33130
Tel: (305) 325-0045, (800) HOTEL 89 (468-3589), **Fax:** (305) 325-9227.
E-mail: miami100@ix.netcom.com

Type: Bed & breakfast with furnished apartments.
Clientele: Mostly straight clientele with a gay & lesbian following.
Transportation: Car is best. Taxi or SuperShuttle from airport. Pick up for large parties can be arranged for a fee.
To Gay Bars: 5 miles or a 10-minute drive.
Rooms: 40 rooms & 14 apartments with single, double, queen or king beds.
Bathrooms: All private.
Meals: Expanded continental breakfast.
Vegetarian: Available at nearby restaurants.
Complimentary: Glass of wine at check-in.
Dates Open: All year.
High Season: Nov-Apr.
Rates: Nov 1-Apr 30 $89-$125, May 1-Oct 31 $69-$125.
Discounts: Gov't rate $59, AAA 10%, AARP 10%, Airline & travel 25%.
Credit Cards: MC, Visa, Amex, Diners, Discover, Carte Blanche.
Rsv'tns: Preferred. Necessary during high season.
To Reserve: Call direct.
Parking: Ample free parking in enclosed lot. Locked at night with guest access.
In-Room: Color cable TV, AC, ceiling fans, telephone & maid service.
On-Premises: Lounge, meeting rooms, fax, copier, conference call & laundry facilities (coin operated).
Exercise/Health: Jacuzzi on premises. Nearby gym, Jacuzzi, sauna, steam, massage, walking/running path, tennis & golf.
Swimming: Pool on premises.
Sunbathing: At poolside.
Smoking: Prohibited in rooms & closed public spaces.
Pets: Permitted with reservation.
Handicap Access: Yes. General access & rooms.
Children: Welcome.
Languages: English, Spanish.
Your Host: Sallye, Jane & Raymond.

IGLTA

Normandy South

Q-NET Men ♂

If Gauguin Had Stopped Here, He May Never Have Made it to Tahiti!

Standing on a palm-lined street in a quiet, safe, residential neighborhood close to the convention center, *Normandy South* is a Mediterranean revival home among similar architectural gems dating from Art Deco's heyday, the Roaring 20s. Within easy walking distance of South Beach's ever-expanding choice of gay clubs, trendy restaurants and chic (and funky!) shops, we welcome the sophisticated male traveler who demands a prime location, luxury and elegance without formality and stuffiness.

Guest accommodations are generous, each with a new marble and tile bath en suite, and are poshly furnished with queen- and king-sized beds, exciting, original art and colorful dhurries. In addition to three doubles and three suites (one with its own terrace) in the main house, there are two doubles in the carriage house at the opposite end of the spectacular "Miami Vice" pool.

338

FERRARI GUIDES™

When not out dancing, shopping or cruising the gay beaches, guests are encouraged to lounge poolside, perfecting a no-tan-line tan, socialize in the Jacuzzi or work off those extra piña coladas in the 44-foot lap lane. For a change of pace, one can slip off to the shaded grotto and luxuriate in the hot tub beneath a thatched chickee, or snooze in the oversized hammock. As might be expected in this tropical hideaway, clothing is optional both inside and outside. Should one choose, a freshly-plucked hibiscus or jasmine tucked behind one's ear is raiment enough. What is not optional is smoking. Guests are strictly limited to non-smokers, no exceptions. Here, one is free to enjoy, without interference, the freshly-scented ocean breezes and fragrant blossoms that abound.

Miami Beach, FL **Tel:** (305) 674-1197, **Fax:** (305) 532-9771.

Type: Guesthouse.
Clientele: Men only
Transportation: Super Shuttle or taxi direct from airport to guesthouse.
To Gay Bars: 10 minutes to Warsaw, Westend, Hombre, Twist, Salvation, Loading Zone & others.
Rooms: 5 rooms & 3 suites with queen or king beds.
Bathrooms: All private.
Meals: Tropical continental breakfast.
Dates Open: Nov-May.
High Season: Christmas to Easter
Rates: Nov-Xmas & Easter-May $110-$165; Xmas-Easter $120-$175; May $90-$140. Rates effective thru Nov 98.
Credit Cards: MC, Visa, Amex.
Rsv'tns: Recommended.
To Reserve: Travel agent or call direct.
Minimum Stay: Varies with season & holiday.
Parking: Ample, free off-street parking.
In-Room: Full-range cable TV, central air, maid & complimentary laundry service, refrigerator, VCR w/fun flics, ceiling fans.
Exercise/Health: Gym & Jacuzzi with massage by appointment.
Swimming: Heated pool w/ lap lane on premises. Five minutes to gay beaches.
Sunbathing: At poolside, on private or common sun decks & at public beaches.
Nudity: Clothing optional inside, poolside, on sun decks, in grotto, at nude gay beach.
Smoking: Accommodations are for non-smokers only.
Pets: Permitted with prior arrangement.
Handicap Access: No.
Children: Not permitted.
Your Host: Hank & Bruce.

IGLTA

Richmond Hotel

Gay-Friendly ♂

A Truly Distinctive South Beach Experience

The Richmond represents a return to a gentler era when Miami Beach was the winter capital of North America. Launched prior to the outbreak of World War II, it was the creation of a modern-day Marco Polo whose travels took him from the capitals of Europe to the trade routes of Asia and, finally, to the warm sands of South Florida.

The Richmond was designed by Miami Beach's most famous Art Deco architect, L. Murray Dixon, and was one of the first oceanfront hotels on Collins Avenue. The restoration of this oceanfront Art Deco masterpiece in the heart of South Beach has resulted in the creation of a small luxury hotel offering beautiful accommodation in a fabulous location. Its service is reminiscent of the days when our guests were picked up by our Woody station

continued next page

INN PLACES® 1998   339

wagon at Miami's old FEC railway station and were greeted personally by our parents and grandparents.

As part of our effort to create a truly distinctive South Beach experience, the Verandah dining terrace offers fantastic creations combining the savory tastes of the Old South with great American favorites, all served in South Beach's most romantic setting. Guests enjoy a free, deluxe continental breakfast every morning as the sun begins to rise over the sparkling blue waters of the Atlantic. A wonderful place for a gay or lesbian holiday, its perfect location is a short walk to the gay beach, the pulsating night clubs and world-famous Ocean Drive and Lincoln Road. Shopping, dining, dancing until dawn... all just steps away from the most peaceful oasis in South Beach — *The Richmond*. "Four Palms, highly recommended," Out & About, November, '97.

Address: 1757 Collins Ave, Miami Beach, FL 33139
Tel: (305) 538-2331, (800) 327-3163, **Fax:** (305) 531-9021.
E-mail: richmondmb@aol.com

Type: Hotel with restaurant.
Clientele: Mostly straight with a gay male following
Transportation: From airport: taxi $23 or Super Shuttle $10 per person.
To Gay Bars: 5 blocks, an 8 min walk, a 2 min drive.
Rooms: 99 rooms with queen beds.
Bathrooms: 99 private bath/toilets.
Meals: Continental breakfast.
Complimentary: Condoms & lube.

Dates Open: All year.
High Season: Dec-Apr.
Rates: Winter $160-$355; Summer $140-$280.
Discounts: Corporate rates available.
Credit Cards: MC, Visa, Diners, Amex.
Rsv'tns: Required.
To Reserve: Travel agent or call direct.
Minimum Stay: 3-night minimum required during certain holiday periods.

Parking: Adequate off-street pay parking. Valet only: $12 overnight, unlimited in/out.
In-Room: AC, color cable TV, telephone with voice mail capability, maid, room & laundry service.
On-Premises: Meeting rooms, business services.
Exercise/Health: Gym & Jacuzzi on premises. Nearby weights, sauna, steam, massage.
Swimming: Pool & ocean on premises.

Sunbathing: Poolside, on private sun decks, at beach.
Smoking: Permitted in hotel common areas & guest rooms. Non-smoking rooms available.
Pets: Not permitted.
Handicap Access: Yes.
Children: No.
Languages: English, Portuguese, Spanish, French, Creole.
Your Host: Pat & Allan.

IGLTA

Things Worth Remembering
Gay/Lesbian ♀♂
Movie, Television, Broadway & Sports Memorabilia

Dustin Hoffman's bust from the movie "Hook," Jane Alexander's dress from "The Great White Hope," and Christina Ricci's pajama's from "Mermaids" are among the items for you to view at *Things Worth Remembering*, a B&B decorated with collectibles, memorabilia and autographs. Whether you choose to relax among the collectibles, stroll through our garden with its blooming rose bushes, or simply watch the birds in flight, this will be a vacation you will never forget. Your hosts are business professionals with many interesting inside stories from their years as Disney World employees.

Address: 7338 Cabor Ct, Orlando, FL 32818
Tel: (407) 291-2127 (Tel/Fax, call before faxing), (800) 484-3585 (code 6908).

Type: Bed & breakfast.
Clientele: Gay & lesbian. Good mix of men & women
Transportation: Car is best. Free pick up from airport, train & bus.
To Gay Bars: A 15 min drive to gay bars.

Rooms: 1 room with queen bed.
Bathrooms: Private bath/toilet.
Meals: Continental breakfast.
Vegetarian: Full access to kitchen. Special requests OK.
Complimentary: Guest fridge with drinks, water, snacks.
Dates Open: All year.
High Season: Summer.
Rates: $65-$75.

Discounts: 10% discount if you mention Inn Places ad. Stay 1 week, 7th day free.
Rsv'tns: Required.
To Reserve: Travel agent or call direct.
Parking: Adequate free off-street parking.

In-Room: AC, ceiling fans, telephone, color cable TV, VCR, kitchen, refrigerator, coffee & tea-making facilities.

On-Premises: Video tape library.
Exercise/Health: Nearby gym, weights, Jacuzzi, sauna, steam, massage.

Swimming: Nearby pool, ocean, river, lake & water parks.
Sunbathing: On patio.
Smoking: Permitted outside only.

Pets: Not permitted.
Handicap Access: Please inquire.
Languages: English.
Your Host: James & Lindsey.

Mill House Inn

Q-NET Gay/Lesbian ♂

Exclusively Yours on Scenic Perdido Bay

The Mill House on Perdido Bay was built in the 1870s to serve as housing for local mill workers. After Hurricane Erin in 1995, the house underwent major renovation and now boasts a new upper-level secluded back porch, as well as private entrances to all rooms. There are first- and second-story verandas equipped with ceiling fans, sound system and a magnificent view of Perdido Bay. All rooms are large and have either queen or king bed, ceiling fan, TV, refrigerator and a wonderful view of the bay. We are just 10 minutes from Johnson Beach on Perdido Key.

Address: 9603 Lillian Highway, Pensacola, FL 32506
Tel: (850) 455-3200, toll-free: (888) 999-4575, Fax: (850) 458-6397.
E-mail: TMHBB@aol.com

Type: Bed & breakfast guesthouse.
Clientele: Mostly men with women welcome
Transportation: Car.
To Gay Bars: A 15-minute drive to men's bars, a 5-minute drive to women's bars.
Rooms: 3 rooms with king or queen beds.
Bathrooms: Private & shared.
Meals: Full breakfast.
Vegetarian: If requested at time of reservation. No vegetarian food nearby.

Complimentary: Iced tea always, coffee mornings, mint/candy on pillow. Welcome basket with chips, soda, bottled water, etc.
Dates Open: All year.
High Season: May 1-Oct 1.
Rates: Winter $65, summer $70-$85.
Discounts: Stay 5 nights, 6th free. 10% discount if both upstairs rooms in same party (shared bath).
Credit Cards: MC, Visa, Discover.
Rsv'tns: Required.

To Reserve: Travel agent or call direct.
Minimum Stay: Required on holidays only.
Parking: Ample off-street parking.
In-Room: AC, color TV, ceiling fans, VCR, refrigerator, maid & laundry service.
On-Premises: TV room.
Exercise/Health: Soloflex, large hot springs spa. Massage can be brought on to premises.
Swimming: Bay. Nearby Gulf of Mexico.

Sunbathing: On patio & at beach.
Nudity: Permitted in house, on upstairs sun deck & in spa. Nude beach in Navarre.
Smoking: Permitted outside only. All rooms are non-smoking.
Pets: Not permitted.
Handicap Access: Downstairs king room with private bath is accessible.
Children: No.
Languages: English.
Your Host: Scott.

Sea Oats by the Gulf

Gay-Friendly 50/50 ♀♂

Sea Oats, on lovely Treasure Island, is minutes from St. Petersburg, directly on the Gulf of Mexico. The hotel, with its traditional Key West charm, is modern with beautifully-appointed apartments, efficiencies and studios overlooking the Gulf. Rooms are individually climate controlled, have color cable TV and fully-equipped kitchenette with microwave. Other amenities include a private yard bordered by palm trees and an eight person Jacuzzi. John's Pass, where you can charter boats, go parasailing, take dinner cruises or enjoy many fine restaurants and shops, is one block away. We are AAA approved.

Address: 12625 Sunshine Lane, Treasure Island, FL 33706 **Tel:** (813) 367-7568.

Type: Motel.
Clientele: 50% gay & lesbian & 50% straight clientele.
Transportation: Car is best. Limo from Tampa airport available. $10 each way (40 minute ride).
To Gay Bars: All within 5-20 minutes.

Rooms: 1 room & 10 apartments with double & queen beds.
Bathrooms: 7 private shower/toilets & 4 private

bath/toilet/showers.
Dates Open: All year.
High Season: Jan-May.

continued next page

UNITED STATES

Rates: Low $35-$95, high $50-$110.
Discounts: 2 week or longer stay.
Credit Cards: MC & VISA.
To Reserve: Call direct.
Minimum Stay: Required weekends only, Fri/Sat.

Parking: Adequate free on-street parking.
In-Room: Color cable TV, AC, kitchen, refrigerator, coffee/tea-making facilities, maid & laundry service. Some with ceiling fans.
On-Premises: Laundry facilities.

Exercise/Health: Jacuzzi on premises. Nearby gym.
Swimming: Ocean on the premises & nearby.
Sunbathing: On the patio, in the backyard or at the beach.
Nudity: Permitted in Jacuzzi area if you book it.

Smoking: Permitted.
Pets: Permitted, with fee, on stays of 2 weeks.
Handicap Access: No.
Children: Welcome if well-behaved.
Languages: English.
Your Host: JoAnn & Christie.

SARASOTA • FLORIDA

The Dragon's Den   Gay/Lesbian ♂

A Special Place to Stay in Sarasota

Sarasota is the cultural center of Florida's Gulf Coast, offering beautiful beaches, museums, art galleries and theater galore! Just minutes away from all of this is *The Dragon's Den*, a private guest suite, located in a lovely home in a park-like setting. The suite includes a bedroom, full bath and a sitting room with its own private entrance. After a full day of activity, relax in total privacy in the sparkling pool and adjoining ceramic tile hot tub. Shopping, restaurants and gay bars are nearby. Everyone is welcome here.

Address: Sarasota, FL **Tel:** (941) 923-2646.

Type: B&B guesthouse.
Clientele: Mostly men with women welcome
Transportation: Car is necessary.
To Gay Bars: 3-5 miles, 10-minute drive.
Rooms: 1 suite with double bed.
Bathrooms: Private bath/toilet/shower.
Meals: Continental breakfast.

Vegetarian: Available nearby.
Complimentary: Wine, beer, cocktail on arrival, set-ups available.
Dates Open: All year.
High Season: Dec 15-Apr 15.
Rates: Single $30, double $50.
Discounts: 7th day free.
Rsv'tns: Required with 1st night's deposit.

To Reserve: Call direct.
Parking: Ample off-street parking.
In-Room: Color cable TV, AC, ceiling fans, reading material, refrigerator, coffee & tea-making facilities, maid & laundry service.
On-Premises: Phone, large, screened lanai, grill privileges.
Exercise/Health: Jacuzzi, massage. Nearby gym with weights, sauna & steam.

Swimming: Pool on premises. Beaches nearby.
Sunbathing: At poolside.
Nudity: Permitted poolside.
Smoking: Permitted poolside only.
Pets: Not permitted.
Handicap Access: No.
Children: No.
Languages: English.
Your Host: Steven.

TAMPA

Gram's Place Bed/Breakfast & Music   Gay/Lesbian ♀♂

A Casual Taste of Amsterdam & Key West in the Center of Tampa

Gram's Place is a relaxing, laid-back eclectic Key West-style B&B, featuring the music of Jazz, Blues, Folk Country, Rock & Roll, etc. The cottages were named in honor of legendary singer/songwriter Gram Parsons (1946-1973). There are three rooms with shared baths (private sinks in the rooms) and three rooms with private baths, queen-sized beds, and hardwood floors. Each house has a kitchen and dining area. The neighborhood is located two miles NW of downtown Tampa and historic Ybor City. You'll find *Gram's Place* most comfortable with the feel of a faraway island.

Address: 3109 N Ola Ave, Tampa, FL 33603
Tel: (813) 221-0596 (Tel/Fax), **Pager:** 292-1415.
E-mail: GramsPl@aol.com **URL:** http://members.aol.com/gramspl/index.html

Type: Bed & breakfast cottages.

Clientele: 70% gay/lesbian & 30% straight clientele.

Transportation: We offer personal shuttle service, for half the price of cab fare, to bars, restaurants, airport,

train & bus.
To Gay Bars: 1/2 mile & 2 blocks to restaurant, bar & disco.
Rooms: 7 rooms with 2 kitchens & 2 dining rooms.
Bathrooms: 4 private, others share.
Meals: Continental breakfast.
Complimentary: Coffee, orange juice, Coca Cola machine on premises.
Dates Open: All year, but please inquire.
High Season: Dec-Apr.
Rates: In-season: pvt bath $95, shared bath $75. Off-season: pvt bath $80, shared bath $65.
Discounts: Weekly & off season discounted rates available.
Credit Cards: MC, Visa, Amex.
To Reserve: Call direct or travel agent.
Parking: Ample on- & off-street free parking in a well-lit area.
In-Room: Color HBO & cable TV, AC, ceiling fans, telephone & maid service.
On-Premises: TV lounge, laundry facilities, kitchen privileges, BYOB pub. Occasional live music in courtyard.
Exercise/Health: Jacuzzi & outside shower/toilet facilities, waterfalls.
Swimming: Public pools nearby. 30 minutes to ocean beach.
Sunbathing: On the private sun deck by the Jacuzzi.
Nudity: Permitted if other guests do not mind.
Smoking: Prefer outside smoking, but not mandatory.
Pets: Permitted, with restrictions.
Handicap Access: No.
Children: Permitted over 5.
Languages: English.
Your Host: Mark.

UNITED STATES

FLORIDA • TAMPA

Sawmill Campground

Gay-Owned & -Operated ♀♂

Peaceful Camping, 38 Miles North of Tampa

Camp along the winding Withlacoochee River and enjoy nature in a peaceful setting, where mankind and nature communicate. Among the old cypress trees are hawks, singing birds and our favorite visitor, the owl. *Sawmill Campground* facilities include 42 private acres with nature trails, large wooded sites, seasonal sites, group camping, clean showers, rec hall, general store, and a boat ramp. Activities include canoe rentals, pot-luck dinners, bingo, theme weekends, fishing, horseshoes, shuffleboard, basketball, and weekend bonfires. A half a mile away are 47 miles of state biking and hiking trails. Orlando, Disney and Tampa are all less than an hour away.

Address: 21710 US Hwy 98, Dade City, FL 33523
Tel: (352) 583-0664, **Fax:** (352) 583-0661. **E-mail:** flsawmill@aol.com

Type: Campground with convenience store.
Clientele: Gay & lesbian. Good mix of men & women
Transportation: Car or train. Free pick up from train.
To Gay Bars: 29 miles, a 30 min drive.
Rooms: Cottages & cabins available in 1998.
Bathrooms: Shared bath/shower/toilet. Bathouse for men & women.
Campsites: 174 RV & campsites (24 tent sites, 33 electric & water only, 117 electric, sewer & water). Group tent campsites available
Dates Open: All year.
High Season: All year.
Rates: $15-$30.
Discounts: Weekly, monthly & seasonal rates.
Rsv'tns: Suggested on weekends.
To Reserve: Call direct.
Minimum Stay: Required on holiday weekends.
Parking: Ample free off-street parking.
On-Premises: Meeting rooms, TV lounge, video tape library, laundry facilities, copies, fax, notary.
Exercise/Health: Canoe & tube rentals, fishing, horseshoes, shuffleboard. Half mile to 47 miles of bike,
hike, blade & horse trails.
Swimming: Pool & river on premises. Lake nearby.
Sunbathing: Poolside.
Nudity: Permitted poolside.
Smoking: No smoking in common building.
Pets: Permitted if leashed.
Handicap Access: No.
Children: No.
Languages: English.
Your Host: Joe, Don, Jim, John & Ron.

Hibiscus House B&B

Gay/Lesbian ♀♂

Tropical Elegance at Its Best

Recapture early Florida at the *Hibiscus House B&B*. Originally built as the mayor's mansion, the house has seven guest rooms individually decorated with antiques, all with private baths and private terraces. The suite has a terrace, living room, bedroom and bath. The poolside cottage sleeps 6 and has a kitchen. Relax with a complimentary cocktail by the tropical pool or take our bikes and explore

WEST PALM BEACH

continued next page

INN PLACES® 1998   343

UNITED STATES — WEST PALM BEACH • FLORIDA

Palm Beach in leisurely fashion. Your hosts, Raleigh & Colin, are always accessible. Our clientele come as guests and leave as friends!

Address: 501 30th St, West Palm Beach, FL 33407
Tel: (561) 863-5633 (Tel/Fax), (800) 203-4927.
URL: http://www.hibiscushouse.com

Type: Bed & breakfast.
Clientele: Mainly gay & lesbian with some straight clientele.
Transportation: Pick up service available from airport, bus, train, port, rental car advised.
To Gay Bars: 10-minute drive.
Rooms: 5 rooms, 1 suite & 1 cottage with queen beds.
Bathrooms: 2 private bath/toilets & 5 private shower/toilets.
Meals: Full breakfast.
Vegetarian: Available with advance notice.
Complimentary: Cocktails, tea, coffee, soda, chocolates on pillow.
Dates Open: All year.
High Season: December through April.
Rates: Low season $65-$130, high season $85-$175.
Discounts: For long-term stays.
Credit Cards: MC, Visa, Amex, DC.
Rsv'tns: Required.
To Reserve: Travel agent or call direct.
Parking: Ample, free off-street parking.
In-Room: Maid service, color TV, telephone, AC & ceiling fans.
On-Premises: Laundry facilities & kitchen privileges.
Swimming: In pool on premises or 15 minutes to ocean.
Sunbathing: At poolside or on patios & private sun decks.
Nudity: Permitted with discretion.
Smoking: Permitted with restrictions.
Pets: Small pets permitted.
Handicap Access: No.
Children: Not permitted.
Languages: English.
Your Host: Raleigh & Colin.

Tropical Gardens Bed & Breakfast Gay/Lesbian ♀♂

Tropical Gardens Bed & Breakfast (formerly known as West Palm Beach B&B), an enchanting house built in the 1930s, has private baths, AC, paddle fans, and cable TV, all set in a private Key West-style compound. Your hosts have retained the charm of old-world Florida with white wicker furniture in a colorful Caribbean decor. Tan by the poolside or on private sun decks secluded by lush tropical foliage. Tour the area on complimentary bicycles, or just relax and kick off your sandals! We are centrally located, one block from the waterway, minutes to beaches or the town of Palm Beach. We look forward to making your stay an enjoyable and memorable one!

Address: 419 32nd St, Old Northwood Historic District,
West Palm Beach, FL 33407-4809
Tel: (561) 848-4064, (800) 736-4064, **Fax:** (561) 848-2422.

Type: Bed & breakfast guesthouse with cottages.
Clientele: Good mix of gays & lesbians
Transportation: Complimentary pickup from airport, bus, train, Port of Palm Beach. Rental car advised.
To Gay Bars: 1-1/2 miles to downtown gay nightclub.
Rooms: 2 rooms, 2 poolside cottages with queen beds.
Bathrooms: 1 private bath/toilet & 2 private shower/toilets.
Meals: Expanded continental breakfast.
Vegetarian: Available upon request.
Complimentary: Iced tea, wine, beer, soft drinks.
Dates Open: All year.
High Season: Dec-Apr.
Rates: Summer $55-$85, winter $65-$125.
Discounts: Weekly, mid-week & off-season rates.
Credit Cards: MC, Visa, Amex, Diners.
Rsv'tns: Required.
To Reserve: Travel agent or call direct.
Minimum Stay: 2 nights on holidays.
Parking: Ample, free, well-lit, off-street parking & on-street parking.
In-Room: Color cable TV, VCR, maid service, AC, ceiling fans, kitchen, refrigerator, coffee & tea-making facilities.
On-Premises: TV lounge.
Exercise/Health: Jogging trail by waterway, bicycle path (complimentary bicycles available), nearby public tennis & golf.
Swimming: Pool on premises. Nearby ocean, including MacArthur Beach (gay).
Sunbathing: At poolside, on patio & common sun decks & at the beaches.
Nudity: Permitted on sun decks & poolside with discretion.
Smoking: Permitted outdoors, all rooms non-smoking.
Pets: Not permitted.
Handicap Access: No.
Children: No.
Languages: English, Spanish.
Your Host: Robert & Skip.

The Bonaventure

Enchantment in the Heart of the City

Gay-Friendly 50/50 ♀♂

Experience the comfort, irresistible charm and funky elegance of this exquisitely restored Victorian home set in a fragrant grove of dogwoods, azaleas and magnolias. Formerly home to the Griffith School of Music, **The Bonaventure** is soon to be listed on the National Historic Registry. Carefully chosen Victorian and Art Deco furnishings complement the original art glass light fixtures, burnished wood moulding, pocket doors and hand-carved stairwell. Four light-filled bedrooms, each with its own working fireplace, have comfortable beds (two feather-beds) with fine cotton linens. The Violet Suite, with private bath, features a separate sunroom with sofa and chairs, overlooking the southern gardens and goldfish pond.

Wander the lovely grounds to discover the wisteria-draped archway which leads to the goldfish pond and turtle spa. Or, if guests' schedules permit, complimentary wine and hors d'oeuvres are served evenings on the veranda or in the parlour. Breakfast may include freshly baked croissants, scones and pastries, quiche, French toast, freshly squeezed juices, excellent coffees and teas, plus a variety fresh fruit daily.

Many of Atlanta's better restaurants are just blocks away in the vibrant midtown/Virginia Highland neighborhood: Babettes, Harvest, Surin, Terra Cotta, among others. The Carter Presidential Library is three blocks away. There is also an eclectic mix of blues and jazz clubs, bars, boutiques, art galleries, antique shops and unusual coffee shops within easy walking distance.

Address: 650 Bonaventure Ave, Atlanta, GA 30306
Tel: (404) 817-7024, **Fax:** (404) 249-9988. **E-mail:** bonaventure@mindspring.com
URL: http://www.mindspring.com/~friedato

Type: Bed & breakfast guesthouse.
Clientele: 50% gay & lesbian & 50% straight clientele
Transportation: MARTA to North Ave stn, then taxi; MARTA to N. Ave Stn, #2 Ponce de Leon bus to Bonaventure Ave, then 1/2 block to B&B. Free pick up from MARTA when available.
To Gay Bars: 2 blocks, 1/4 mile, 3 min walk, 1 min drive.
Rooms: 3 rooms, 1 suite.

Bathrooms: Private: 1 bath/toilet, 1 shower/toilet, 1 bath/shower/toilet. Shared: 1 bath/shower/toilet, 1 WC only.
Meals: Expanded continental breakfast.
Vegetarian: Vegetarian breakfast always available. Numerous restaurants nearby.
Complimentary: Sherry, coffee, tea, cocoa, fresh juices, mineral water. Cheese platter with wine optional at cocktail hour.
Dates Open: All year.

Rates: $85-$125.
Discounts: 10% discount for artists & musicians.
Credit Cards: All major credit cards accepted.
Rsv'tns: Required.
To Reserve: Travel agent or call direct.
Parking: Ample free secured off-street parking.
In-Room: AC, maid & room service, bottled water. Cordless telephone available.
On-Premises: Laundry facilities, TV lounge, video tape library, fax & computer available, music, lovely private gardens with fish pond.
Exercise/Health: Nearby gym & weights.
Sunbathing: By the pond.
Smoking: Permitted on veranda & in garden. All rooms are non-smoking.
Pets: Not permitted.
Handicap Access: No.
Children: Not especially welcome. Well-behaved children ages 12 & up are tolerated.
Languages: English, French.
Your Host: Mary Beth.

UNITED STATES • GEORGIA • ATLANTA

Caruso Manor

Gay/Lesbian ♂

Comfort of a Hotel and the Warmth of a Private Home

From the *Caruso Manor* in Atlanta's National Historic District, you can stroll the treelined streets to nearby shops and restaurants. This Georgian two-story home, like other homes in the in-town neighborhood of Virginia-Highland, was built in the early 1900s and has been lovingly restored in recent years. Your host, John, uses fresh produce from the local farmers' market to prepare an expanded continental breakfast.

Address: Atlanta, GA **Tel:** (404) 875-1706, **Fax:** (404) 875-4227.

Type: Bed & breakfast.
Clientele: Mostly men with women welcome.
Transportation: MARTA or taxi.
To Gay Bars: 2 miles.
Rooms: 2 rooms with double or queen bed.

Bathrooms: Private & shared.
Meals: Continental breakfast.
Complimentary: Fresh fruit basket in room.
Dates Open: All year.
Rates: Single $65, double $75.

Rsv'tns: Required.
To Reserve: Call direct.
Minimum Stay: 2 nights on weekends.
Parking: Adequate free on-street parking.
In-Room: AC, telephone, maid service.

Smoking: Permitted outside only. Non-smoking rooms available.
Pets: Not permitted.
Handicap Access: No.
Children: No.
Languages: English.
Your Host: John & Mel.

Nine Twelve Barnard Bed & Breakfast

Gay/Lesbian ♀♂

A Victorian B&B in the Hostess City of the South

Don and Kevin warmly welcome you to *912 Barnard,* a restored double house in the heart of Savannah's Victorian district. Our home is within walking distance of shops, restaurants, museums and beautiful Forsyth Park, the crown-jewel of Savannah's historic squares. Antique furnishings and four original fireplaces set the decor. On the first floor is the double parlor living room-dining room, full kitchen and laundry facilities. Upstairs, two graciously appointed guest rooms await. We serve continental breakfast, complimentary beverages and, of course, plenty of assistance for sightseeing, shopping or dining.

Address: 912 Barnard St, Savannah, GA 31401 **Tel:** (912) 234-9121.

Type: Bed & breakfast.
Clientele: Exclusively gay & lesbian.
Transportation: Car, bus or taxi.
To Gay Bars: 12 blocks, a 5-minute drive.
Rooms: 1 shared bath/shower/toilet & one 1/2 bath.
Meals: Expanded continental breakfast.
Vegetarian: Available upon prior request & at nearby deli.

Complimentary: Coffee, tea, soft drinks.
Dates Open: All year.
High Season: Mar-Sept.
Rates: $79 per night.
Discounts: $5 for cash payment.
Rsv'tns: Required.
To Reserve: Call direct.
Minimum Stay: 2 nights on weekends.

Parking: Adequate free on-street parking.
In-Room: Color TV, VCR, phone, ceiling fans, fireplaces, AC, maid service.
On-Premises: Laundry facilities, video tape library.
Exercise/Health: 1 block to tennis courts, walking & running paths.
Swimming: 15 minutes to ocean & Tybee Beach, gay beach nearby.

Sunbathing: On common sundecks, at beach.
Nudity: Inquire.
Smoking: Permitted outside only, rooms are non-smoking.
Pets: Not permitted.
Handicap Access: No.
Children: No.
Languages: English.
Your Host: Kevin & Don.

Park Avenue Manor B&B

Gay-Owned & -Operated ♀♂

Retaining the True Ambiance of Graceful Southern Living

Our pristine inn with its lace-upon-lace draperies, fine furnishings, angel ceiling borders and double staircases, greets you with charm upon entering our two formal parlors. *Park Avenue Manor B&B's* five suites feature four-poster beds, antique furniture, silk carpets, period prints, porcelains, working fireplaces and private baths (some with original claw-foot tubs). The Dining Room for your full, formal breakfast, has the air of the Old South, with its stately portraits, stained glass and working fireplace. To pamper our guests, we offer a full breakfast, televisions, turndown service, afternoon tea, cordials, and more.

Address: 107-109 West Park Avenue, Savannah, GA
Tel: (912) 233-0352.
E-mail: pkavemanor@aol.com **URL:** www.bbonline.com/ga/parkavenue

Type: Bed & breakfast.
Clientele: Mostly gay & lesbian with some gay-friendly straight clientele
Transportation: Car is best.
To Gay Bars: 1 mile to gay bar owned by B&B, a 12 min walk, a 1 min drive.
Rooms: 5 rooms with single, double or queen beds.
Bathrooms: 5 private bath/shower/toilets.

Meals: Full breakfast.
Vegetarian: 1 block to vegetarian restaurant, a 1 min walk.
Complimentary: Set ups, sherry in parlors, tea & coffee.
Dates Open: All year.
High Season: Apr-May.
Rates: $85-$110.
Discounts: Corporate $69, ARRP 10%. Ask about special rates.

Credit Cards: MC, Visa, Amex.
Rsv'tns: Required.
To Reserve: Call direct.
Parking: Ample, free off-street parking.
In-Room: Telephone, AC, color cable TV, maid, room & laundry service.
On-Premises: Laundry facilities, private phone jacks for business computers.
Exercise/Health: Nearby gym, weights, Jacuzzi, sauna, steam, massage.
Swimming: Nearby pool, ocean.
Sunbathing: On patio & private sun decks, at beach.
Smoking: Permitted on decks. No non-smoking rooms available.
Pets: Not permitted.
Handicap Access: No.
Children: No.
Languages: English, Spanish.
Your Host: Jonathan.

Hale Aloha Guest Ranch

Q-NET GayILesbian ♀♂

Find the Real Spirit of Aloha at a Hillside Hideaway

Discover the "house of welcome and love" with its spacious lanais and spectacular ocean views. *Hale Aloha* is nestled at 1,500 feet in the lush South Kona hillside. Guests will enjoy the peace and tranquillity of the five-acre park-like citrus and macadamia nut plantation which borders a state forest preserve. Stroll, get a massage, relax in the Jacuzzi, sunbathe, or be more adventurous and bike and snorkel. The City of Refuge and Kealakekua Bay (famous for its tropical fish, sea turtles and often-present dolphins) are right down below, and Volcano National Park is a scenic 68 miles away.

Address: 84-4780 Mamalahoa Hwy, Captain Cook, HI 96704
Tel: (808) 328-8955 (Tel/Fax), (800) 897-3188.
E-mail: halealoha@aol.com **URL:** http://members.aol.com/halealoha

Type: B&B guest ranch.
Clientele: Gay & lesbian
Transportation: Car is best.
To Gay Bars: A 25-minute drive to Kona gay bar.

Rooms: 3 rooms, 1 suite, 1 studio apartment with king, queen or double beds.
Bathrooms: Master suite: private double shower/Jacuzzi, bath/toilet. Apartment: private shower/toilet, 3 rooms share bath/toilet.
Meals: Full breakfast.
Vegetarian: Available at breakfast & at local stores & restaurants.

Complimentary: Refreshments on arrival, Kona coffee, iced tea.

continued next page

UNITED STATES

Dates Open: All year.
High Season: Holidays.
Rates: $60-$100.
Discounts: 10% on stays of 4 nights.
Credit Cards: MC, Visa, Diners, Discover, JCB.
Rsv'tns: Required.
To Reserve: Travel agent or call direct.

Minimum Stay: 2 nights on weekends & holidays.
Parking: Ample free off-street parking.
In-Room: Maid service, 3 rooms share kitchen. Apartment has own kitchen.
On-Premises: Video tape library, kitchenette, color TV & VCR, coffee & tea-making facilities.

Exercise/Health: Jacuzzi, massage, mountain bikes, snorkel gear, boogie boards.
Swimming: Nearby ocean.
Sunbathing: On common sun decks, on private areas throughout 5-acre property, at beach.
Nudity: Permitted while sunbathing, in Jacuzzi & at nude beach near Kona.
Smoking: Permitted outside. All rooms are non-smoking.
Pets: Not permitted.
Children: Please inquire.
Languages: English, German.
Your Host: Johann & Lennart.

IGLTA

Hale Kipa 'O Pele

Q-NET Gay/Lesbian ♀♂*

Romance Flows Where Lava Glows!

HAWAII - BIG ISLAND • HAWAII

Hale Kipa 'O Pele bed and breakfast is named for the sacred spirit, Madame Pele, goddess of fire, ruler of Hawaii's volcanoes and protector of the forest. It is believed that Pele's spirit guards the property even today! Situated on the volcanic slopes of Mt. Hualalai, above the sunny southern Kona coast, the tropical estate and plantation-style home are distinctly unique. A majestic volcanic dome graces the entrance drive. The house surrounds an open-air atrium with lava rock waterfall, koi pond and a tiled walkway providing a private entrance to each room-suite.

The *Maile* is a corner room with spacious sitting area, private bath and intimate covered patio. The *Ginger* has a large walk-in closet, private bath with sunken tub and sliding glass doors that access the wooden deck and provide a view of the gardens. The expansive *Pele Bungalow* has a cozy bedroom, full bath, living room, mini-kitchen and a large private covered patio overlooking the fruit tree grove.

A covered wooden lanai wraps around the entire front of the home, providing full panoramic views of the lush landscape. Enjoy a buffet-style tropical continental breakfast at YOUR leisure on the lanai or in the dining room. After a day of activities, relax in the garden Jacuzzi or enjoy movies on the Pro-Logic Surround Sound(tm) system.

Hale Kipa 'O Pele is a close 5 miles to the beach and all activities. Guests can enjoy scuba diving, para-sailing, deep sea fishing, helicopter tours, or walk along the scenic shores and quaint village-style shops of old Kona Town. We cater to both singles and couples seeking the true "ALOHA" spirit and a serene and romantic atmosphere that only a tropical-style bed and breakfast can offer! Our guests will be rejuvenated by exotic Hawaii, and the enthusiasm of both hosts who truly cherish this small part of the world known as PARADISE!

Address: PO Box 5252, Kailua-Kona, HI 96745
Tel: (800) LAVAGLO, (808) 329-8676.
E-mail: halekipa@gte.net. **URL:** http://home1.gte.net/halekipa/

Type: Bed & breakfast & bungalow.
Clientele: Good mix of gays & lesbians
Transportation: Rental car is best. Airport courtesy pick up for travel industry employees.
To Gay Bars: 6 miles.
Rooms: 2 suites with queen beds, 1 bungalow with 1 queen bed & 2 twin beds.
Bathrooms: All private bath/shower/toilets.

Meals: Tropical island-style continental breakfast.
Complimentary: Refreshments upon arrival, wine & cheese at sunset.
Dates Open: All year.
Rates: $65-$115 plus room & state taxes.
Discounts: 10% for 7 nights.
Credit Cards: MC, Visa, Amex.
Rsv'tns: Required.
To Reserve: Travel agent or call direct.

Minimum Stay: Usually 2 nights.
Parking: Adequate free off-street parking.
In-Room: Ceiling fans & maid service. Bungalow has mini-kitchen, cable TV & VCR.
On-Premises: TV lounge with theatre sound & video tape library. Expansive covered decks.
Exercise/Health: Jacuzzi on premises. Gym & racquetball nearby.

Swimming: Nearby ocean.
Sunbathing: On Jacuzzi sun deck, at beach, on the lawn.
Nudity: Permitted in the Jacuzzi & at nearby nude beach.
Smoking: Permitted outside & on covered decks.
Pets: Not permitted.
Handicap Access: No.
Children: Not especially welcome.
Languages: English.

IGLTA

Hale Ohia Cottages

Q-NET Gay-Friendly 50/50 ♀♂

Volcano Magic Unleashed

There are many special places in Hawaii, but few rival the serenity and magic of *Hale Ohia*, the historic Dillingham summer estate located on several acres of exquisitely landscaped grounds. It is across Highway 11 from the village of Volcano and one mile from Hawaii Volcanoes National Park. Built in 1931, *Hale Ohia* is comprised of a main residence, a guest cottage, a gardener's cottage and numerous support structures. *Hale Ohia Cottage*, once a gardener's cottage, has three bedrooms, a large living room, fully furnished kitchen, covered lanai and covered parking. *Hale Lehua Cottage*, the oldest of the cottages, was originally built as a private study. This one-bedroom cottage is graced by a lava rock fireplace and has limited cooking facilities and a covered lanai with garden views. The *Iiwi* and *Camellia* suites each have private entrances and private bath with leaded glass windows and comfortable sitting and reading areas. The two-bedroom *Dillingham Suite* in the main residence offers the quiet elegance of a 1930's kamaaina home. Under the sugi trees is *Ihilani Cottage*, our deluxe private cottage under the sugi trees, featuring a private fountained garden, fireplace, kitchenette and antique leaded windows.

Nestled in a botanical garden setting, our complex affords guests a unique view of Hawaii's past. The gardens were developed over thirty years by a resident Japanese gardener who left the natural volcanic terrain untouched while gently grooming it into the most beautiful botanical garden in Volcano. While staying at *Hale Ohia,* discover the mystique of Volcano. Walk through lush fern forests, see newly created lands and feel the energy and magic of Kilauea, the most active volcano on earth and home to Pele, the goddess of fire. After a day of hiking, enjoy a book under a wisteria-covered gazebo or relax in the heated Japanese soaking tub

continued next page

under huge sugi pines. We have been featured in *The New York Times* "Sophisticated Traveler" and *National Geographic Traveler Magazine,* December 1994, and *Travel & Leisure,* January 1996.

Address: PO Box 758, Volcano, HI 96785
Tel: (800) 455-3803 or (808) 967-7986, **Fax:** (808) 967-8610.
E-mail: haleohia@bigisland.com

Type: Bed & breakfast & cottages.
Clientele: 50% gay & lesbian & 50% straight clientele
Transportation: Car is best.
To Gay Bars: 26 miles.
Rooms: 4 suites & 3 cottages with single, double or queen beds.
Bathrooms: All private shower/toilets.

Meals: Continental breakfast.
Vegetarian: Vegetarian health food store nearby.
Complimentary: Tea & coffee.
Dates Open: All year.
High Season: Nov 15-Jan 15 & June 15-Sep 5.
Rates: $75-$115.
Discounts: Travel agents, ASU, Kamaaina. 2 or more nights.

Credit Cards: MC, Visa.
Rsv'tns: Suggested.
To Reserve: Travel agent or call direct.
Parking: Ample free off-street covered parking.
In-Room: Kitchen, refrigerator, coffee/tea-maker, maid & laundry service.
On-Premises: Meeting rooms.
Exercise/Health: Steam, massage & heated Japanese furo.
Swimming: In nearby ocean.
Sunbathing: In private sun area.
Smoking: Smoking permitted outside only.
Pets: Not permitted.
Handicap Access: Yes. One unit is barrier free.
Languages: English.
Your Host: Michael & Vito.

IGLTA

Kalani Oceanside Retreat

Soulful, Sensual & Natural Hawaii

Q-NET Gay/Lesbian ♀♂

Kalani Oceanside Retreat is the only coastal lodging facility within Hawaii's largest conservation area. Here, you are treated to Hawaii's real aloha comfort, traditional culture, healthful cuisine and extraordinary adventures: thermal springs, a naturist dolphin beach, snorkel pools, kayaking, waterfalls, crater lake and spectacular Volcanoes National Park. Come for an anytime getaway or for one of several annual week-long events: Gay Spirit, Pacific Men, Hula Heritage, Adventure Camp, Body Electric, Dance & Music Festivals, Healing Arts and massage academy. Our international, native, gay and lesbian staff welcome you!

Address: Box 4500-IP, Pahoa, HI 96778-9724
Tel: (800) 800-6886, (808) 965-7828,
Fax: (808) 965-9613.
E-mail: kh@ILHawaii.net
URL: http://randm.com/kh.html

Type: Retreat with restaurant & native gift shops.
Clientele: 70% gay & lesbian & 30% straight clientele.
Transportation: Rental car is best, taxi service.

To Gay Bars: 15 miles, 15-min drive.
Rooms: 35 lodge rooms & 7 cottage units with single, double, queen or king beds.
Bathrooms: 14 private & 20 shared.

Campsites: 20 tent sites with convenient hot showers & restrooms.
Meals: Breakfast, lunch, dinner served daily.
Vegetarian: Always available.

Complimentary: Tea, coffee, juices.
Dates Open: All year.
Rates: Rooms $45-$110, cottages $90-$130. With meal plan $70-$180. Campsites $20-$25 per person.

350   FERRARI GUIDES™

Week-long adventures & events $570-$1,140. **Discounts:** 10-20% to senior citizens, island natives, vacation (long-term) rentals. **Credit Cards:** MC, Visa, Amex. **Rsv'tns:** Preferred. **To Reserve:** Travel agent or call direct.	**Parking:** Ample, free off-street parking. **In-Room:** Cottages with fridge, partial maid service. **On-Premises:** Meeting rooms, kitchens, dance studio, 113 acres of tropical beauty. **Exercise/Health:** Weights, Jacuzzi, sauna & massage.	**Swimming:** Olympic pool on premises. Ocean beach, river, lake & snorkel tidal pools nearby. **Sunbathing:** At poolside, oceanfront & on beach. **Nudity:** Permitted anytime oceanfront at ocean beach or after 7pm at pool & spa. **Smoking:** Permitted outdoors.	**Pets:** Not permitted. **Handicap Access:** Yes. **Children:** Permitted. **Languages:** English, Spanish, French, German & Japanese. **Your Host:** Richard, Delton & Carol. **IGLTA**

Our Place Papaikou's B&B

Q·NET Gay-Friendly 50/50 ♀♂

A Private, Lush, Tropical Retreat

Four miles north of Hilo, in the village of Papaikou, *Our Place Papaikou's B&B* is a charming place to stay close to the town of Hilo. Our lovely cedar home overlooks Ka'ie'ie Stream and is set amid a tropical garden with fragrant flowers and tropical fruit trees (all ORGANICALLY grown). The "Great Room," splendid with its cathedral ceiling, has a library, fireplace, grand piano, and cable TV, all of which guests are invited to enjoy. The guestrooms share a common lanai that overlooks Ka'ie'ie Stream. There are two doubles (Early American full bed & Oriental queen bed), a master bedroom with king bed and private bath, and a loft "Tree House" (for groups). Breakfast is organic tropical fruit from the garden and orchard, Kona coffee or tea, granola, tropical fruit juice and breads.

Nearby attractions include shore fishing, surfing, ocean kayaking and snorkeling at beaches and ocean parks (anywhere from 1/4 to 34 miles away). It's two miles to the Hawaii Tropical Botanical Garden, 7 miles to the Nani Mau Gardens, 10 miles to Akaka Falls, 6 miles to Rainbow Falls, and Hawaii Volcanoes National Park is 34 miles from us. Your hosts are Ouida and Sharon. Ouida is a retired MD who is now practicing as a licensed acupuncturist and herbalist. She is trained in traditional Chinese medicine and is president of the Traditional Chinese Medical College of Hawaii, located in Waimea. Her hobby is gardening. The gardens at *Our Place* are Ouida's design. Sharon is a Rolfer and is also interested in lapidary. (Notice for rockhounds: Sharon and Ouida would like to trade for rough cutting material.)

Address: PO Box 469, Papaikou, HI 96781
Tel: (808) 964-5250, (800) 245-5250.
E-mail: rplace@aloha.net **URL:** http://www.best.com/~ourplace

Type: B&B with rolfer & licensed acupuncturist. **Clientele:** 50% gay & lesbian & 50% straight	clientele **Transportation:** Car is best. **Rooms:** 4 rooms with king,	queen & double beds. **Bathrooms:** 1 private bath/toilet/shower, 1 shared bath/shower/toilet.	**Meals:** Expanded continental breakfast. **Vegetarian:** Breakfast is

continued next page

UNITED STATES

vegetarian.
Dates Open: All year.
High Season: Dec-Apr.
Rates: $55-$100.
Discounts: 10% senior & weekly discount.
Credit Cards: Visa, MC.
Rsv'tns: Required.
To Reserve: Travel agent or call direct.
Minimum Stay: 2 nights.
Parking: Ample free off-street parking.
In-Room: Master bedroom has color cable TV, phone, ceiling fan, maid service.
On-Premises: Refrigerator, microwave, Great Room with cable TV.
Exercise/Health: Nearby gym with weights & Jacuzzi.
Swimming: River on premises, ocean nearby.
Sunbathing: At nearby beach.
Smoking: Permitted on covered lanai.
Pets: Not permitted.
Handicap Access: No.
Children: Welcome over 12 years of age.
Languages: English.
Your Host: Ouida & Sharon.

HAWAII - BIG ISLAND • HAWAII

Pamalu

Q-NET Gay/Lesbian ♀♂

An Island Within an Island

"A home away from home. I feel like I've been in a different world," is how one guest described the Hawaiian country house *Pamalu*, situated on five private acres in sunny Kapoho. Relax on the screened lanai with vaulted ceiling overlooking colorful landscaping and lawns surrounding a 40-foot pool and pavilion with BBQ where you can listen to doves and trade winds in the palms. It's an easy walk to snorkeling with colorful reef fish among underwater coral gardens. Nearby is a lagoon warmed by volcanic vents, a surfing area, and a black sand, clothing-optional beach. Volcano National Park with many hiking trails is an hour's drive.

Address: RR 2, Box 4023, Pahoa, HI
Tel: (808) 965-0830, **Fax:** (808) 965-6198.

Type: B&B country retreat, 10 minutes from Pahoa town.
Clientele: Mostly gay & lesbian with some straight clientele
Transportation: Car is best (rental car from Hilo airport, a 40-minute drive).
Rooms: 3 rooms & 1 suite, all with queen beds
Bathrooms: Private: 1 shower/toilet, 3 bath/toilet/showers.
Meals: Expanded continental breakfast.
Vegetarian: Vegetarian store a 10-minute drive.
Complimentary: Tea, coffee, juice.
Dates Open: All year.
Rates: $60-$100.
Discounts: 10% for stay of 1 week.
Rsv'tns: Required.
To Reserve: Travel agent or call direct.
Minimum Stay: 2 nights.
Parking: Ample free off-street parking.
In-Room: Computer phone jack.
On-Premises: TV lounge, video tape library.
Exercise/Health: Nearby gym, weights, massage, acupuncture.
Swimming: Pool on premises, nearby lagoon,
20-min drive to black sand beach.
Sunbathing: At poolside, on patio, at beach.
Nudity: Permitted IN pool & at beach (20-25 minutes away).
Smoking: Permitted outside & at poolside pavilion.
Pets: Not permitted.
Handicap Access: Inquire.
Children: Please inquire.
Languages: English.

R.B.R. Farms

Gay/Lesbian ♂

R.B.R. Farms is, to this day, a working macadamia nut and coffee plantation. The old plantation home has been totally renovated and a swimming pool added. The house is secluded, accessed only by an unimproved 3/4-mile-long drive. R.B.R. Farms is privately-owned and -managed, so it retains the personal touch and attention to detail that sets us apart among outstanding bed and breakfasts in the world. R.B.R. Farms... a place to come, to stay, to remember, to return.

Address: PO Box 930, Captain Cook, HI 96704
Tel: (800) 328-9212, **Tel/Fax:** (808) 328-9212. **E-mail:** rbrfarms@gte.net

Type: Bed & breakfast.
Clientele: Mostly men with women welcome, few straight clientele
Transportation: Rental car is best.
To Gay Bars: Kona has a gay bar.
Rooms: 4 rooms & 1 cottage with single, queen or king beds.
Bathrooms: 1 private bath/toilet, 4 shared bath/shower/toilets.
Meals: Full breakfast.
Vegetarian: Available upon request.
Complimentary: Soft drinks, iced tea daytimes at pool, mints on pillow.
Dates Open: All year.
Rates: $60-$150.
Credit Cards: MC, VISA.
Rsv'tns: Required.
To Reserve: Travel agent or call direct.
Minimum Stay: Usually two nights.
Parking: Ample free parking.
In-Room: Color cable TV, VCR, ceiling fans & maid service.
On-Premises: Public telephones.
Exercise/Health: Jacuzzi & massage.
Swimming: Pool on premises, ocean beach nearby.
Sunbathing: At poolside, on common sun decks & on the beach.
Nudity: Permitted at poolside & on private decks.
Smoking: Not permitted in rooms. Permitted on grounds & common areas.
Pets: Not permitted.
Handicap Access: No.
Children: Not permitted.
Languages: English.
Your Host: Bob & Jane.

The Samurai

Gay/Lesbian ♀♂

A Unique Blend of Japanese and Hawaiian Culture

The Samurai is an authentic Japanese warrior-class dwelling imported from Japan and reconstructed in Captain Cook, Hawaii. The trickling waterfall and koi ponds nestled in temple grass form an intimate Japanese entry garden recreating a moment in Old Japan. Upon entering the house, exposed cypress beams, shoji screens, fusuma doors, and tatami mats further emphasize the unique Japanese flavor of this old inn. Sitting on a promontory overlooking majestic Kealakekua Bay, and a breathtaking view of the southern Kona Coast, it is not hard to understand why The Samurai is renowned to Hawaii's gay visitors.

For a Zen experience of simple luxury, honorable guests may choose the Tatami Room, situated in the original historic part of the house and furnished in old Japanese style (with the exception of a

continued next page

"western" king-sized bed). It features an adjoining indoor/outdoor living and dining lanai — where one can sunbathe, watch the incredible sunsets or read in complete privacy. For a more traditional, yet equally beautiful accommodation, one may choose the Shogun Room — a studio apartment, beautifully furnished in a mission oak and Japanese antique blend. Both accommodations have full kitchens and private baths. The more modest Kimono Room offers a private lanai, refrigerator and a private, unattached bath. All rooms have lanai from which to enjoy the dazzling views and access to the hot tub.

Your host, Douglass, who has lived in the area for 10 years, restored and opened the inn in 1989. He holds an M. Ed. in counseling and, in addition to appreciating the Japanese aesthetic, has a deep reverence for Hawaiian values and culture. He will be delighted to share his knowledge and Aloha with you.

Address: 82-5929 Mamalahoa Hwy, Captain Cook, HI 96704
Tel: (808) 328-9210, **Fax:** (808) 328-8615. **E-mail:** shibui@aloha.net

Type: Bed & breakfast.
Clientele: Mostly gay/lesbian with some friendly straights
Transportation: Rental cars are necessary on the big island.
To Gay Bars: 20 minutes.
Rooms: 3 doubles & 1 apartment.
Bathrooms: 3 private. 2 of the rooms share 1 bath.

Meals: Continental tropical breakfast.
Complimentary: Tea, coffee, & juice.
Dates Open: All year.
High Season: Winter & late summer.
Rates: $55-$85 all year.
Discounts: On stays longer than a week.
Credit Cards: MC, Visa.
Rsv'tns: Required.
To Reserve: Travel agent or call direct.

Parking: Free off-street parking.
In-Room: Color TV, VCR, refrigerator. 2 rooms have kitchen.
On-Premises: TV lounge, meeting rooms, & laundry facilities.
Exercise/Health: Hot tub.
Swimming: 15-minute drive to ocean beach.
Sunbathing: On private decks.

Nudity: Permitted on private decks. 30-minute drive to gay nude beach.
Smoking: Permitted on the lanais.
Pets: Not permitted.
Handicap Access: Accessibility to one room on the 1st floor.
Children: Permitted.
Languages: English & American Sign Language.
Your Host: Douglass.

Tropical Tune-Ups

Lesbian-Owned & -Operated ♀

Deluxe Tropical Getaways for Women

Designed for two or more women, *Tropical Tune-Ups'* deluxe retreat packages include your own private home in a five-star resort area, rental car, massage, guided excursions, private yoga sessions, airport lei greeting and a welcome basket. Our houses on the Big Island's sunny Kona Coast are either oceanfront homes, or they have ocean views and are a short walk to the beach. Attractively furnished, they include linens, kitchen, television, VCR, washer/dryer and microwave. Our Romantic Tropical Escape package includes the items mentioned above, plus couples massage and a catered dinner with an optional commitment ceremony. Customized retreats are also availble.

Address: PO Box 4488, Waikoloa, HI 96738
Tel: (808) 882-7355 (Tel/Fax), (800) 587-0405.
E-mail: vacations@tropicaltuneups.com **URL:** http://tropicaltuneups.com

Type: Private rental house.
Clientele: Women only
Transportation: Airport pick up service included in package.

Vegetarian: Healthfood stores & vegetarian restaurants nearby.
Dates Open: All year.
Credit Cards: MC, Visa.
Rsv'tns: Required.

Minimum Stay: 5 nights.
In-Room: Telephone, color TV, VCR, kitchen, washer/dryer.

Exercise/Health: Nearby gym, weights, Jacuzzi/spa, sauna, massage, golf.
Swimming: Nearby ocean.
Languages: English.

Wood Valley B&B Inn

Q-NET Women ♀

Off the Tourist Track, But Close to Power Spots

Glimpse old Hawaii at our secluded plantation home on twelve acres of pasture and gardens near Volcano National Park and beaches of green or black sand. From *Wood Valley Bed & Breakfast* one can see the ocean, watch the weather change and experience the serene seclusion of one of the Big Island's more mystical and enchanted places. We serve a home-grown breakfast each morning which features fruit from the orchard, eggs from the coop and Kona coffee. Lomi Lomi massage is available, and you can relax in our outdoor hot tub or steam bath. Our clientele is mostly women, with men welcome.

Address: PO Box 37, Pahala, HI 96777
Tel: (808) 928-8212, (800) 854-6754, **Fax:** (808) 928-9400.
E-mail: jessie@aloha.net **URL:** http://civic.net/webmarket/hawaii/jessie

Type: Bed & breakfast with a farm atmosphere.
Clientele: Mostly women with men welcome
Transportation: Rent a car and arrive in daylight hours. Car is essential.
To Gay Bars: 60 miles to Kona gay bars.
Rooms: 1 single, 2 doubles.
Bathrooms: Unique outdoor bathing & indoor shared toilet.
Campsites: Tent sites, toilet & shower.

Meals: Full breakfast, food options are limited, please call ahead. Kitchen privileges.
Vegetarian: All vegetarian cuisine.
Complimentary: Welcome to graze in orchard & garden.
Dates Open: All year.
High Season: November-March.
Rates: Single $35, double $55 with 10% tax.

Discounts: 11th day free. Work exchange available, please inquire.
Credit Cards: None.
Rsv'tns: Recommended, with deposit.
To Reserve: Call direct.
Parking: Ample free off-street parking.
In-Room: Telephone.
On-Premises: Satellite TV, laundry facilities, shared lanai, kitchen, dining room & VCR with tapes of local interest.

Exercise/Health: Walking trails, steam bath, massage available.
Swimming: Ocean beach is 15 miles away.
Sunbathing: On the beach, in the backyard.
Nudity: Clothing is optional.
Smoking: Permitted outdoors.
Pets: Not permitted.
Handicap Access: No.
Children: Permitted with prior arrangement.
Languages: English.

Aloha Kauai Bed & Breakfast

Q-NET Gay/Lesbian ♀♂

Seclusion and Hawaiian Hospitality

Above the lazy Wailua River in *Aloha Kauai,* Hawaii speaks in the soft murmur of wind chimes, the sweet smell of tropical flowers, and the shimmery water of the pool. Close to Kapaa town beaches and Donkey Beach, this B&B is a hideaway conveniently located within minutes of restaurants, shops, and scenic attractions. It is close to spectacular Opaekaa Falls, hiking trails in the forests of Sleeping Giant, and freshwater spots at the Wailua Reservoir. Choose from four rooms: the Hibiscus Room, the Bamboo Room, the Orchid Suite, or the Pool House.

Address: 156 Lihau St, Kapaa, HI 96746 **Tel:** (808) 822-6966, (800) 262-4652.

Type: Bed & breakfast.
Clientele: Gay & lesbian. Good mix of men & women.
Transportation: Car is best.
To Gay Bars: 5 miles or a 5-minute drive.
Rooms: 4 rooms with single, queen or king beds.
Bathrooms: Private & shared.
Meals: Full breakfast.

Vegetarian: Available upon request.
Complimentary: Sunset refreshments (cocktails, sodas, etc.).
Dates Open: All year.
Rates: $60-$85.
Rsv'tns: Required.
To Reserve: Travel agent or call direct.
Parking: Ample off-street parking.

In-Room: Color cable TV, VCR, ceiling fans, maid service.
On-Premises: Meeting rooms, TV lounge.
Exercise/Health: Nearby gym with weights, Jacuzzi, sauna, steam, massage.
Swimming: Pool on premises. Nearby pool, ocean, river.

Sunbathing: At poolside, on patio & at beach.
Smoking: Permitted on patios & other outside areas.
Pets: Not permitted.
Handicap Access: Yes.
Children: No.
Languages: English.
Your Host: Dan & Charlie.

IGLTA

INN PLACES® 1998

Anuenue Plantation B&B

Gay-Owned & -Operated ♂

Your Paradise Plantation

Above Kauai's Coconut Coast and midway between awesome Waimea Canyon and the famous Na Pali Coast, is *Anuenue Plantation*. In the quiet of this modern estate, surrounded by ocean and mountain views, you'll relax while watching the ever-changing rainbows, clouds, waterfalls, sunsets and stars. Explore surrounding beaches, jungle trails, galleries, restaurants, gardens and shops. Mornings, you will be treated to a full tropical breakfast. At the end of the day, visit on the lanais and, occasionally, there are dances, concerts and seminars on-site in the ballroom.

Address: PO Box 226, Kapaa, HI
Tel: (808) 821-0390, **Fax:** (808) 821-0693. **E-mail:** BnB@anuenue.com

Type: Bed & breakfast & cottage.
Clientele: Mostly men with women welcome
Transportation: Car rental necessary.
Rooms: 3 rooms & 1 cottage with queen or king beds.
Bathrooms: 4 private bath/shower/toilets.
Meals: Full breakfast.
Vegetarian: Vegetarian breakfast served, also available island-wide.
Dates Open: All year.
Rates: $75-$95.
Discounts: 10% weekly.
Rsv'tns: Required.
To Reserve: Travel agent or call direct.
Parking: Ample off-street parking.
In-Room: Telephone, ceiling fans.
On-Premises: TV lounge, video tape library.
Exercise/Health: Nearby gym, weights, massage.
Swimming: Nearby pool, ocean.
Sunbathing: At beach.
Smoking: Permitted outdoors only.
Pets: Not permitted.
Handicap Access: No.
Children: No.
Languages: English.
Your Host: Fred & Harry.

Hale Kahawai

Q-NET Gay/Lesbian ♀♂

Gay-owned & -operated (Don't Settle for Straight Imitations!)

Across Kuamoo Road from Opaekaa Falls, *Hale Kahawai* overlooks the Wailua River gorge, a short stroll from one of Kauai's largest sacred temples. A serene garden surrounds the three guest rooms and one studio, with cable TV, bath, kitchenettte and ceiling fans. Enjoy tropical breakfasts in the dining lounge or on the lanai, overlooking the bamboo-shaded sun deck, koi and waterlily pond, and Mounts Waialeale and Kawaikini. Relax in the evenings in the garden hot tub, illuminated by Tiki torches. Outdoor activities include helicopter tours, horseback riding, golf and snorkeling. Secluded beaches, fine dining and shopping are close by.

Address: 185 Kahawai Place, Kapaa, HI 96746
Tel: (808) 822-1031, **Fax:** (808) 823-8220.
E-mail: BandBKauai@aol.com

Type: Bed & breakfast.
Clientele: Gay & lesbian. Good mix of men & women
Transportation: Rental car from airport.
To Gay Bars: 5 miles, a 10-minute drive.
Rooms: 3 rooms & 1 apartment with queen or king beds.
Bathrooms: 2 private bath/toilet/shower, 2 shared bath/shower/toilet.

Meals: Expanded continental breakfast.
Vegetarian: On request.
Complimentary: Tea, coffee, juice & soda.
Dates Open: All year.
High Season: Dec-Mar.
Rates: Rooms $60-$80, Apt. $90. Plus 10% tax.
Discounts: On stays of 7 nights or longer.
Rsv'tns: Required.
To Reserve: Travel agent or call direct.

Minimum Stay: 2 nights.
Parking: Ample free off-street parking.
In-Room: Apartment has kitchen, coffee & tea-making facilities, color cable TV, refrigerator. All rooms have ceiling fans.
On-Premises: TV lounge & video tape library.
Exercise/Health: Jacuzzi, massage. Nearby gym.
Swimming: Nearby ocean & river.

Sunbathing: On private sun decks, at beach.
Nudity: Permitted in Jacuzzi & on sun deck.
Smoking: Permitted on lanai or in garden.
Pets: Not permitted.
Handicap Access: No.
Children: No.
Languages: English.
Your Host: Arthur & Thomas.

Kalihiwai Jungle Home

Gay-Friendly 50/50 ♀♂

Be Tarzan or Jane in Our Jungle Home

Spectacular waterfall, jungle and mountain views await you at *Kalihiwai*, a beautiful rental on the Northshore of the Garden Island of Kauai. Beautifully furnished, this *luxury* rental is decorated with antique Hawaiian art and has a marble bathroom with Jacuzzi bathtub, marble fireplace, and a hammock for two on a balcony overlooking the jungle and waterfall. Ideally located, it is the perfect place for a dream vacation. *Kalihiwai* is situated on half an acre of tropical splendor, affording spectacular glassed-in panoramic views from each room.

Address: PO Box 717, Kilauea, HI 96754
Tel: (808) 828-1626, **Fax:** (808) 828-2014. **E-mail:** thomasw@aloha.net
URL: http://www.hshawaii.com/kvp/jungle/

Type: Vacation rental.
Clientele: 50% gay & lesbian & 50% straight clientele.
Transportation: Car is best. Airport less than 1 mile from home.
To Gay Bars: 15 miles or a 30-minute drive.
Rooms: 1 bedroom with queen bed.
Bathrooms: Private bath with Jacuzzi bathtub.
Vegetarian: Vegetarian

health food restaurants nearby.
Complimentary: Papayas & bananas on arrival.
Dates Open: All year.
Rates: $100-$150 per day, depending on length of stay.
Discounts: For longer stays of 1-4 weeks & for a single person.
Rsv'tns: Required.
To Reserve: Travel agent or call direct.
Minimum Stay: Required.

Parking: Adequate free parking on premises.
In-Room: Telephone, ceiling fans, private full kitchen, coffee/tea-making facilities, laundry service, color TV, VCR, marble fireplace. Maid service extra.
On-Premises: Laundry facilities, fax & private phone.
Exercise/Health: Jungle walk to beach. Nearby gym, weights, Jacuzzi, sauna, steam, massage, facial.
Swimming: Nearby Olym-

pic-sized lap pool, ocean, river & lake.
Sunbathing: On the patio & beach.
Nudity: Permitted in house, on balcony, at nearby secret beach.
Smoking: No smokers permitted.
Pets: Not permitted.
Handicap Access: No, upstairs unit.
Children: Welcome.
Languages: English.
Your Host: Thomas & Doug.

INN PLACES® 1998

UNITED STATES • HAWAII • KAUAI

UNITED STATES • KAUAI • HAWAII

Mohala Ke Ola B&B Retreat

Q-NET Gay-Friendly ♀♂

Escape to Paradise

Leave the cares and stresses of civilization behind. Enjoy a Hawaiian lomi-lomi massage or rejuvenate with one of the other body treatments available, including shiatsu, acupuncture and Reiki. ***Mohala Ke Ola B&B Retreat*** is situated high above the lush Wailua River Valley and is surrounded by magical mountain and waterfall views. It provides an ideal location from which to explore the island. We'll gladly share our insights on the best hikes, scenic lookouts, secret beaches, tropical gardens, helicopter and boat tours.

Address: 5663 Ohelo Rd, Kapaa, Kauai, HI 96746
Tel: (808) 823-6398 (Tel/Fax),
toll-free (888) GO-KAUAI (465-2824).
E-mail: kauaibb@aloha.net
URL: www.waterfallbnb.com

Type: Bed & breakfast.
Clientele: Mostly straight clientele with a gay & lesbian following
Transportation: Car is best.
To Gay Bars: 5 miles or a 10-minute drive to Sideout.
Rooms: 3 rooms with queen beds. 1 room with king bed.
Bathrooms: 3 private, 1 shared.
Meals: Continental breakfast.
Vegetarian: Local Thai & health food store deli.
Complimentary: Coffee & tea.
Dates Open: All year.
High Season: Nov-May.
Rates: $65-$95.
Discounts: Weekly rate 10%.
Rsv'tns: Required.
To Reserve: Travel agent or call direct.
Minimum Stay: Prefer 3 nights minimum.
Parking: Ample free off-street parking.
In-Room: Ceiling fans.
On-Premises: TV lounge, meeting rooms & laundry facilities.
Exercise/Health: Jacuzzi, massage, acupuncture, lomi lomi, shiatsu, Reiki on premises.
Swimming: Pool on premises. Ocean & river nearby.
Sunbathing: At poolside or on the beach.
Nudity: Permitted in hot tub & pool at discretion of other guests. 15 min to nude beach.
Smoking: Permitted outside only. This is a non-smoking environment.
Pets: Not permitted.
Handicap Access: No.
Children: Not especially welcome.
Languages: English, Japanese & German.

Pali Kai

Gay/Lesbian ♀♂

Where Mountains Greet the Sea

Kauai's spectacular North Shore surrounds you at ***Pali Kai***, on a hilltop with views of mountains, valley and ocean. All bedrooms in this beautiful home have queen beds, private baths, TV/VCR, literature about the island, and sweeping ocean views. An inviting hot tub which overlooks the ocean is also available for your relaxation. A luxurious lawn and lush gardens surround the house and a private hiking trail leads to the Kalihiwai River and beach. Swimming and snorkeling beaches, hiking trails and rivers for kayaking are nearby.

FERRARI GUIDES™

Address: PO Box 450, Kilauea, Kauai, HI 96754
Tel: (808) 828-6691, **toll-free:** (888) 828-6691. **E-mail:** palikai@aloha.net

Type: Bed & breakfast with panoramic views of mountains, Kalihiwai Valley & the ocean.
Clientele: Gay & lesbian. Good mix of men & women
Transportation: Car is essential, rent at airport.
To Gay Bars: 20 minutes by car.
Rooms: 1- or 2-bdrm suite, studio, cottage.

Bathrooms: All private.
Meals: Self-catering island-style breakfast.
Dates Open: All year.
Rates: $70 singles, $80 doubles.
Rsv'tns: Required.
To Reserve: Travel agent or call direct.
Parking: Ample off-street parking.

In-Room: Telephone, TV, VCR, CD/cassette player, refrigerator, microwave, ceiling fan, coffee/tea-making facilities & maid service.
On-Premises: BBQ.
Exercise/Health: Jogging path to river & beach, hot tub available to all. Spa, tennis & golf nearby.

Swimming: At nearby ocean beaches.
Sunbathing: At beach & in front yard.
Nudity: In hot tub & at some nearby beaches.
Smoking: Permitted outdoors only.
Languages: English.

IGLTA

Royal Drive Cottages

Gay-Lesbian ♀♂

An Enchanted Tropical Hideaway

Looking for quiet and privacy? Up in the lush green hills of the Eden-like Wailua district, down a private road, you'll find the beautiful *Royal Drive* guest cottages. You look out upon a lush tropical garden, where the temptation to settle under a tree in the garden and never move is strong. Your on-site host is very happy to offer suggestions to help make your stay truly special, guiding you to off-the-beaten-path experiences. From a guest book filled with unsolicited enthusiasm, *Such a wonderful place to rest and heal from life's realities.*

Address: 147 Royal Drive, Wailua, Kauai, HI 96746
Tel: (808) 822-2321 (Tel/Fax).

Type: Private cottages with exceptional garden views.
Clientele: Mainly gay/lesbian with some straight clientele.
Transportation: Car essential, discount rentals with Avis through host.
To Gay Bars: 10 min drive.
Rooms: 2 cottages with king or twin beds.

Bathrooms: All private.
Complimentary: Concierge service, snorkeling & beach gear. Tropical fruit trees for guests' picking in season.
Dates Open: All year.
Rates: $80.
Rsv'tns: Suggested.
To Reserve: Travel agent or call direct.
Parking: Ample free off-street parking.

In-Room: Well-equipped kitchenette in each cottage.
On-Premises: Laundry facilities.
Exercise/Health: Hot tub, massage on premises. Nearby gym, hiking, tennis, golf, all water activities.
Swimming: Ocean beach & river nearby, gay nude beach 15 minutes.
Sunbathing: On sun deck,

lawn & nearby beaches.
Nudity: Permitted in hot tub, on sun deck & some beaches.
Smoking: Permitted outdoors.
Pets: Not permitted.
Handicap Access: 3 stairs up to one cottage, 1 step to the other.
Languages: English.

Andrea & Janet's Maui Vacations

Q-NET Gay-Friendly 50/50 ♀♂

We Provide the Rest!

Andrea & Janet's Maui Vacations offer spacious one- and two-bedroom lesbian-owned oceanfront suites, bed & breakfast, and luxury beachfront homes on the island of Maui, rated year after year as the #1 island in the world! Enjoy amenities like tennis courts, swimming pool, whirlpool spa, world-class beaches and snorkeling. Join Andrea on her turtle and dolphin tours, walks and distance swims and whale watching adventures during whale season. Call now for a free brochure.

Address: Box 424, Puunene, Maui, HI 96784
Tel: (800) 289-1522, **Tel/Fax:** (808) 879-6430.
E-mail: andrea@maui.net **URL:** http://maui.net/~andrea

continued next page

UNITED STATES

Type: Oceanfront suites, luxury homes & B&B.
Clientele: 50% gay & lesbian & 50% straight clientele
Transportation: Car is best.
To Gay Bars: 2 miles.
Rooms: All types available.
Bathrooms: Private.
Dates Open: All year.
Rates: $65 and up.

Credit Cards: MC, Visa, Discover.
Rsv'tns: Required.
To Reserve: Direct or call travel agent.
Minimum Stay: 2 nights.
Parking: Ample parking.
In-Room: Cable TV, VCR, CD player, phone, ceiling fans, full kitchens, washer/dryer, beach gear.
On-Premises: BBQ, breathtaking flowering trees & plants.
Exercise/Health: Whirlpool spa, snorkel lessons, boogie boards, snorkels, beach chairs, coolers, tennis rackets, beach toys, putting green on premises.
Swimming: Pool & ocean on premises.
Sunbathing: Poolside, on lanai & beach.

Nudity: Clothing-optional beach nearby.
Smoking: Not permitted.
Pets: No.
Handicap Access: No.
Children: OK.
Languages: English, some German.
Your Host: Andrea & Janet.

IGLTA

MAUI • HAWAII

Anfora's Dreams

Q-NET Gay-Friendly 50/50 ♀♂

Maui Condos with Your Lifestyle in Mind

Like a jewel piercing the Pacific Ocean, lush, tropical Maui and her magnificent volcanoes rise out of the sea to warmly caress your soul. *Anfora's Dreams*, with both one- and two-bedroom condos, are located in sunny Kihei. Both ocean and park are just across the road. Units are completely furnished in deluxe style, with total comfort in mind, and rooms have beach or ocean views. Take a walk along the beach or a refreshing dip in the pool or Jacuzzi. Here, on Maui, you will learn the true meaning of "Maui No Ka Oi." Maui is the best!

Address: Attn: Dale Jones, PO Box 74030, Los Angeles, CA 90004
Tel: (213) 737-0731, **Reservations:** (800) 788-5046, **Fax:** (818) 224-4312.

Type: Condo.
Clientele: 50% gay & lesbian & 50% straight clientele.
Transportation: Car is best.
To Gay Bars: 15 miles or 20 minutes by car.
Rooms: Singles to suites with queen beds.
Bathrooms: All private bath/toilets.
Vegetarian: Complete kitchens in condos.

Dates Open: All year.
High Season: November 15 through February 15.
Rates: $79-$120.
Credit Cards: MC, Visa.
Rsv'tns: Required, but can do spot bookings on available basis.
To Reserve: Call direct.
Minimum Stay: 4 nights.
Parking: Ample free off-street parking. Assigned space with guest spaces available.

In-Room: Color cable TV, telephone, kitchen, refrigerator, ceiling fans, coffee & tea-making facilities. Some with AC.
On-Premises: Laundry facilities. 2-bedroom, 2-bath has washer/dryer in unit.
Exercise/Health: Jacuzzi, nearby gym.
Swimming: Pool on premises, ocean across the road.

Sunbathing: At poolside, on patio & nearby beach.
Nudity: Nude beach 10 minutes away.
Smoking: Permitted.
Pets: Not permitted on Maui.
Handicap Access: Yes. Single only.
Children: We welcome all guests with open arms.
Languages: English.

Blair's Original Hana Plantation Houses Q-NET Gay-Friendly 50/50 ♀♂

Serenity Defined

Watch the sunrise from cliffs overlooking the rugged coastline. Bathe in secluded pools fed by mountain waterfalls, once known only to ancient Hawaiian kings. Hike through lush tropical jungles and fields of bamboo. Completely escape mainland tensions and enjoy a traditional Hawaiian vacation on 5 superbly landscaped acres on the remote, exclusive windward coast of Maui. This is serenity. This is Hana. These are the *Original Hana Plantation Houses*.

Address: Hana, Maui, Mail: 2957 Kalakaua Ave, Honolulu, HI 96815
Tel: (808) 923-0772, (800) 228-HANA,
Fax: (808) 922-6068.
E-mail: hana@kestrok.com

Type: Guesthouses. 15 private homes (14 in Hana, 2 deluxe on Molokai).
Clientele: 50% gay & lesbian & 50% straight clientele
Transportation: Car from Kahuli Airport, via Hana Hwy or fly directly into Hana.
To Gay Bars: 1.5 hours.
Rooms: 1 studio, 8 homes, 1 apt, 1 guesthouse, 2 deluxe homes on Molokai.
Bathrooms: All private.
Vegetarian: Health food cafe at our Botanical Gardens.
Complimentary: Bananas, avocados, citrus, passion fruit, coffee and coconuts from our plantation.
Dates Open: All year.
High Season: Jan-Mar & Jul-Sept.
Rates: $80-$160 per night, plus tax.
Discounts: 10% for stays longer than 1 week.
Credit Cards: MC, Visa, Amex.
Rsv'tns: Required.
To Reserve: Travel agent or call direct.
Minimum Stay: 2 nights.
Parking: Free off-street parking.
In-Room: Maid service, color TV, telephone, kitchen, refrigerator, ceiling fans.
Exercise/Health: Hot tub, small gym. Massage arranged.
Swimming: Natural pools, waterfalls & ocean beach are nearby.
Sunbathing: On the beach, on private sun decks.
Nudity: Permitted on private lanai. Clothing optional beach, pools nearby.
Smoking: Permitted outdoors.
Pets: Not permitted.
Languages: English.

IGLTA

Golden Bamboo Ranch Q-NET Gay-Friendly 50/50 ♀♂

Tropical Splendor in a Garden Paradise

This private, seven-acre estate is nestled on the lower slopes of upcountry Maui along the spectacular road to Hana. *Golden Bamboo Ranch* is centrally located to all of Maui's bounty—10 minutes from Hookipa windsurfing beach, Twin Falls, with natural

continued next page

INN PLACES® 1998

swimming pools, or the "cowboy" town of Makawao. We have just renovated a cottage and three plantation house suites, all with unobstructed, panoramic ocean views through horse pastures (we have horses) and forests on one side and a tropical garden and lily pond on the other.

Address: 422 Kaupakalua Rd, Haiku, Maui, HI 96780
Tel: (808) 572-7824 (Tel/Fax), (800) 344-1238.
E-mail: golden@maui.net **URL:** www.maui.net/~golden

Type: Cottage & plantation house suites.
Clientele: 50% gay & lesbian & 50% straight clientele.
Transportation: Rental car is best.
To Gay Bars: 30 minutes to Hamburger Mary's in Wailuku.
Rooms: 3 suites & 1 cottage with single, queen or king beds.
Bathrooms: 4 private bath/toilet/showers.
Meals: Expanded continental breakfast left daily in accommodations.
Vegetarian: Available with prior notice. 15-minute drive to 2 vegetarian restaurants & 2 health food stores.
Dates Open: All year.
Rates: $69-$90.
Discounts: For seven or more days.
Credit Cards: MC, Visa, Amex.
Rsv'tns: Required.
To Reserve: Travel agent or call direct.
Parking: Ample free off-street parking.
In-Room: Color TV, telephone, ceiling fans, kitchen, refrigerator, coffee/tea-making facilities & maid service.
On-Premises: Laundry facilities.
Exercise/Health: 5 minutes to Twin Falls hiking path to waterfalls & natural swimming pools.
Swimming: Nearby ocean & natural swimming pools.
Sunbathing: On the patio & at the beach.
Nudity: Permitted on patios & terraces. 30 minutes to super gay nude beach.
Smoking: Permitted on patios & terraces. Non-smoking rooms available.
Pets: Not permitted.
Handicap Access: Yes. Plantation house is ground level.
Children: Not especially welcome.
Languages: English, French & Spanish.
Your Host: Marty & Al.

IGLTA

Hale Huelo

Gay-Owned 50/50 ♀♂

Azure Ocean, Misty Volcano, Verdant Rainforest — Heavenly Hale Huelo

To enter *Hale Huelo* is to truly lose yourself in "Maui Time." The magnificent vistas of craggy volcano and blue Pacific excite the senses, yet somehow soothe the mind. Unwinding is our specialty! Whether swimming in the main pool or relaxing in the secluded hot tub, the tensions of the world seem to drift off into the rainforest below, often startling the rosy cheek parrots living there to take to the air. Indulge yourself in this special place in the Hawaiian jungle paradise.

Address: PO Box 1237, Haiku, HI 96708
Tel: (808) 572-8669;
Fax: (808) 573-8403.
E-mail: halehuel@maui.net

Type: Bed & breakfast.
Clientele: 50% gay & lesbian & 50% straight clientele
Transportation: Car is best. Pick up from airport $20.
To Gay Bars: 25 miles.
Rooms: 3 rooms with queen beds.
Bathrooms: All private shower/toilets.
Meals: Expanded continental breakfast.
Vegetarian: Vegetarian restaurants & grocery stores nearby.
Dates Open: All year.
High Season: Nov-Mar.
Rates: Summer $85-$100; Winter $100-$125; Whole house $2400/week all year.
Discounts: 10% on stays of 7 days or longer.
Rsv'tns: Required.
To Reserve: Travel agent or call direct.
Minimum Stay: 2 nights.
Parking: Ample, free off-street parking.
In-Room: Ceiling fans, color TV, VCR, tea & coffee-maker, refrigerator, microwave.
On-Premises: Phone, fax, IBM computer, book & video tape libraries, laundry facilities.
Exercise/Health: Jacuzzi, massage. Nearby gym, weights, massage.
Swimming: Pool on premises. Nearby ocean, river.
Sunbathing: Poolside, on patio, common sun decks, at beach.
Nudity: Permitted with discretion at pool, on decks & in Jacuzzi.
Smoking: Permitted outside only.
Pets: Not permitted.
Handicap Access: No.
Children: No.
Languages: English.
Your Host: Doug.

Hale Makaleka
Women ♀

Hale Makaleka, a bed and breakfast for women, is situated on the leeward south shore of the island. We have a large, light and airy room with private bath and private entrance overlooking the garden. Tropical breakfast is served on our upstairs deck from where whales can be seen during winter months. Relax in homey, restful seclusion, chat with us about mainland happenings, stories of Maui, sightseeing, shopping and activities in the lesbian community. Resort activities, dining experiences and white sand beaches are within four miles.

Address: Kihei, HI 96753 **Tel:** (808) 879-2971.

Type: Bed & breakfast.
Clientele: Women only.
Transportation: Rental car.
To Gay Bars: 30 minutes to Hamburger Mary's in Wailuku.
Rooms: 1 double with private entrance.
Bathrooms: Private.
Meals: Full tropical breakfast.
Vegetarian: Available upon request.
Dates Open: All year.
High Season: December through April.
Rates: $60 double, $55 single.
Rsv'tns: Required.
To Reserve: Call direct.
Minimum Stay: 2 days.
Parking: Adequate, free off-street parking.
In-Room: Color TV, VCR.
On-Premises: Laundry facilities, refrigerator & telephone.
Exercise/Health: Nearby gyms.
Swimming: One mile to ocean beach.
Sunbathing: In secluded garden, on nearby beach.
Nudity: Permitted in garden & at "Little Beach" 6 miles away.
Smoking: Permitted outside.
Pets: Not permitted.
Handicap Access: No.
Children: Not permitted.
Languages: English.
Your Host: Margaret & Jackie.

Halfway to Hana House
Q-NET Gay-Friendly 50/50 ♀♂

A Refreshing Alternative

This cozy private studio is nestled in lush seclusion, a 20-minute's drive from Paia town on the Hana road. Sparkling clean and airy, with a double bed, mini-kitchen, private bath and entrance, *Halfway to Hana House* features a breakfast

continued next page

patio overlooking a tropical valley with ocean views. There are banana and bamboo groves, citrus and papaya orchards, a pineapple field, tropical flowers, herb gardens and a lily pond. Your host, a long-time Maui resident and avid outdoor enthusiast gives restuarant and adventure tips, and may even invite you to go snorkeling or kayaking on a Sunday morning.

Address: PO Box 675, Haiku, Maui, HI 96708
Tel: (808) 572-1176, **Fax:** (808) 572-3609.
E-mail: gail@maui.net **URL:** www.maui.net/~gailp

Type: Bed & breakfast with champagne, wine, beer available for purchase.
Clientele: 50% gay & lesbian & 50% straight clientele (1 studio ensures complete privacy)
Transportation: Car is best. No public transportation available.
To Gay Bars: 20 miles by car to Wailuku.
Rooms: 1 private studio suite with double bed.
Bathrooms: 1 private shower/toilet.
Meals: Expanded continental breakfast.
Vegetarian: All breakfasts.
Complimentary: Chocolate-covered macadamia nuts, herb teas.
Dates Open: All year.
High Season: Dec-Apr.
Rates: Single $55-$60, double $60-$70.
Discounts: 10% for 7 or more days.
Rsv'tns: Recommended. Walk-ins welcome if space is available.
To Reserve: Travel agent or call direct.
Minimum Stay: 3 nights
(shorter stays with prior arrangement).
Parking: Ample off-street parking area shaded by trees.
In-Room: Coffee/tea-making, mini-kitchen, beach mats, shampoo, razors, toothpaste, color TV, radio, CD/tape player.
On-Premises: Telephone, refrigerator, laundry facilities, covered patio with table & chairs, lounge chair.
Exercise/Health: Nordic track, trampoline, massage.
Swimming: Nearby fresh water pools, ocean beach 15 min away, lap pool 20 mi away.
Sunbathing: At the beach, on private patio & private grounds.
Nudity: Permitted on private patio & in secluded areas on private ground.
Smoking: This is a non-smoking environment.
Pets: Permitted if specific arrangements are made.
Handicap Access: No, pathways are gravel.
Children: Permitted over age of 10.
Languages: English, limited French & Japanese.

Huelo Point Flower Farm B&B

Q-NET Gay-Friendly 50/50 ♀♂

"One of the Most Spectacular — and Romantic — B&Bs in Hawaii"

There is a place of unforgettable beauty, breathtaking views and lush tropical gardens offering the finest in accommodation on Maui's gorgeous North Shore... *The Huelo Point Flower Farm* is a private, secluded 2-acre estate perched at the edge of a 300-foot sea cliff, overlooking Waipio Bay. Choose the glass-walled "Gazebo" cottage at cliff's edge, the spacious Carriage House, the romantic Guest House or the stunning Main House. All offer exquisite views of the ocean and Mt. Haleakala. Guests enjoy our 50-foot swimming pool, our hot tubs, as well as the organic fruits and vegetables from our gardens.

Address: PO Box 1195, Paia, Maui, HI 96779 **Tel:** (808) 572-1850.
E-mail: huelopt@maui.net **URL:** http://www.maui.net/~huelopt

Type: Bed & breakfast & vacation rental homes.
Clientele: 50% gay & lesbian & 50% straight clientele
Transportation: Rental car, 1/2 hour from airport.
To Gay Bars: 40-min drive.
Rooms: Main house for 6: 1 king, 2 queen beds; Cottage for 2: 1 queen; Carriage house for 6: 2 queens, 1 double; Guest house for 4: 1 king, 1 double.
Bathrooms: All private.
Meals: Continental breakfast (cottage only).
Vegetarian: Almost always available.
Complimentary: Tea, coffee, farm-fresh fruits.
Dates Open: All year.
High Season: Dec 15-Jan 15, rates 25% higher.
Rates: Cottage $110/night, carriage house $125/night. Guest house $180/night dbl. occ., Main house $2000/week for up to 4, plus tax.
Discounts: Weekly discount.
Rsv'tns: Required. Walk-ins welcome if space is available.
To Reserve: Call direct.
Minimum Stay: 2 days.
Parking: Ample off-street parking on gated estate.
In-Room: Color TV/VCR, stero receiver, CD player, telephone, kitchen, refrigerator.
On-Premises: Laundry facilities.
Exercise/Health: Jacuzzis, massage.
Swimming: Pool on premises. 20 min drive to ocean beach. 10 min drive to waterfalls & natural pools.
Sunbathing: At poolside & on the patio.
Nudity: Permitted on private patios.
Smoking: Permitted.
Pets: Permitted by request.
Handicap Access: Yes.
Children: Small children could be a problem because of 300 foot cliff.
Languages: English, French, & Russian.
Your Host: Guy & Doug.

Jack & Tom's Maui Condos

Q-NET Gay-Friendly ♀♂

Tropical Sun, Sandy Beaches, Gentle Trade Winds...Maui No Ka Oi (is the best)

Explore the island, play a little tennis, relax by the pools or enjoy the sand and surf of the finest beaches on Maui, including the nude beach at Makena (only minutes away). At the end of your day, return to your private one- or two-bedroom condominium to freshen up for a night out. Or, if you prefer, prepare dinner in your own fully-equipped kitchen and enjoy a quiet evening at home. All units at *Jack & Tom's Maui Condos* have either ocean or garden views, are clean, comfortable and are equipped to make you want to stay a lifetime.

Address: Write: Margaret Norrie Realty, PO Box 365, Kihei, HI 96753
Tel: (800) 800-8608, (808) 874-1048, **Fax:** (808) 879-6932.
E-mail: mauijack@aol.com

Type: Private condominiums within larger complexes.
Clientele: Mostly straight clientele with a gay & lesbian following.
Transportation: Car is a must on Maui. We can arrange car rental.
To Gay Bars: 5 miles & 15 miles.
Rooms: 40 condos with queen or king beds.
Bathrooms: All private.
Dates Open: All year.
High Season: December 15 to April 15.
Rates: Summer $50-$90, winter $50-$125.
Rsv'tns: Required.
To Reserve: Travel agent or call direct.
Minimum Stay: 4 days.
Parking: Ample off-street parking.
In-Room: Color cable TV, AC, ceiling fans, telephone, kitchen & laundry facilities. Some units have VCRs, stereos.
Exercise/Health: Nearby gym.
Swimming: Pool on premises. Ocean beach across the street.
Sunbathing: At poolside or on the beach.
Smoking: Permitted. Non-smoking units available.
Pets: Not permitted.
Handicap Access: Yes.
Languages: English.
Your Host: Jack & Tom.

Kailua Maui Gardens

Q-NET Gay-Friendly 50/50 ♀♂

Stay With Us for a True Tropical Island Experience

Located in the picturesque village of Kailua, **Kailua Maui Gardens** is an undiscovered hideaway on the edge of Maui's vast rainforest. Enchanting pathways and bridges lead you through two acres of fabulous gardens, which surround our well-appointed accommodations, most with ocean views. The house has its own pool, spa and barbecue lanai area. Cottage guests can relax in the garden spa, where they will be surrounded by the lush gardens. Enjoy nearby waterfalls and natural swimming pools. It's an ideal setting for large groups, individuals and couples.

Address: SR Box 9 (Hana Hwy), Haiku, Maui, HI 96708
Tel: (800) 258-8588, (808) 572-9726,
Fax: (808) 572-5934.
E-mail: kmg@maui.net
URL: www.maui.net/~kmg/

Type: Cottage & house rental.
Clientele: 50% gay & lesbian & 50% straight clientele.
Transportation: Rental car is best, $30 for pickup from airport.
To Gay Bars: 40 minutes.
Rooms: 3 cottages, one 3-bdrm house & one 1-bdrm apartment with queen or king beds.
Bathrooms: All private bath/toilets.
Vegetarian: Chef & vegetarian food available with prior notice.
Complimentary: Fresh fruit, tea, coffee & tropical flowers from estate gardens.
Dates Open: All year.
High Season: June-Sept & Dec-March.
Rates: $60-$200 plus tax.
Discounts: For 4 days or longer.
Rsv'tns: Required.
To Reserve: Travel agent or call direct.
Minimum Stay: 2 nights.
Parking: Ample, free off-street parking.
In-Room: Color TV, VCR, stereo/compact disc player, kitchen, telephone, ceiling fans.
On-Premises: Two outside BBQs, covered lanai for house & covered lanai at common area for cottages.
Exercise/Health: Private spa for house & garden spa for cottages.
Swimming: Pool with house, 8 miles to beach, 1/4 mile to waterfall, natural pools.
Sunbathing: At poolside or on private patios.
Nudity: Permitted in pool area & around spas.
Smoking: Permitted outdoors.
Pets: Not permitted.
Handicap Access: Main house is accessible.
Children: Over 12 years permitted.
Languages: English.

IGLTA

Triple Lei/Huelo Point Lookout Cottages

Gay-Friendly 50/50 ♀♂

The Real Hawaii...It's Still There if You Know Where to Look

Where else could you sit and watch rainbows march to your doorstep and slip over your house? Or be able to hike to a 127-foot waterfall and swim in its pools? Come prepared to enjoy the unique peace and beauty as well as the drama and power of Maui's north shore...bananas, red gingers, papayas, a hot tub and

366   FERRARI GUIDES™

shower under the stars. *Triple Lei/Huelo Pt. Lookout Vacation Rentals & B&B* is a private, 2-acre estate ideally located for you to explore the exquisite beauty of the real Hawaii.

Address: PO Box 117, Paia, HI 96779
Tel: (808) 573-0914, (800) 871-8645, **Fax:** (808) 573-0227.
E-mail: dreamers@maui.net **URL:** wwte.com/lookout.htm

Type: 3 cottages & 1 suite.
Clientele: 50% gay & lesbian & 50% straight clientele
Transportation: Car is essential. There is no public transportation.
To Gay Bars: 40 minutes by car.
Rooms: 3 cottages with either king or queen beds.
Bathrooms: Private.
Meals: Expanded continental breakfast.
Vegetarian: Several wonderful vegetarian restaurants & grocery stores available in Paia, a 30-minute drive.
Complimentary: Tea & coffee. We often provide special surprise snacks of fruit, nuts, bread or cookies.
Dates Open: All year.
Rates: $95-$275.
Rsv'tns: Required. Standby sometimes available.
To Reserve: Call direct.
Minimum Stay: 3 days.
Parking: Lots of free parking!
In-Room: Coffee/tea-making facilities, telephone, color TV. Suite: Kitchenette. Cottages: VCR, kitchen, microwave, washer/dryer.
On-Premises: Laundry facilities. We own a video store, so guests have free reign!
Exercise/Health: Jacuzzi. Massage by arrangement. Nearby yoga classes, hiking, riding.
Swimming: Pool on premises. Nearby ocean, waterfalls, pools.
Sunbathing: On private sun decks.
Nudity: Permitted in hot tub & on private sun decks.
Smoking: Permitted outside only.
Pets: Permitted outside only.
Handicap Access: 1 cottage is wheelchair accessible.
Children: Welcome.
Languages: English, some Spanish.
Your Host: Jeff & Sharyn.

Waipio Bay Lookout Lodging   Q-NET Gay/Lesbian ♀♂
On Maui's Scenic North Shore

Our secluded two-acre estate, **Waipio Bay Lookout Lodging**, is perched at the edge of a 300-foot cliff overlooking pristine Waipio Bay on Maui's North Shore. We have two very spacious oceanfront guest rooms in the main house, each offering guests breathtaking views, private entries and private lanais. Each room has a queen-sized bed, comfortable sitting area and a small kitchenette facility which includes a toaster oven, coffeemaker, refrigerator and utensils. A continental breakfast is provided in each room featuring locally grown fresh fruit, juices, muffins and breads, specialty teas and Kona coffee. Our swimming pool and Jacuzzi are available to guests, and waterfalls and natural pools are also nearby.

We are about an hour's drive from Hana, and its nearby black sand beach at Waianapanapa State Park and red sand beach just outside of Hana. The Seven Sacred Pools are another 45-minute drive past Hana. One of Maui's nicest beaches at Makena, 50 minutes from us on the South Shore. It's divided into two beaches: Big Beach and Little Beach (a nude beach just a walk over the rocks from Big Beach). The summit of Haleakala Crater, which can be seen from the front of our house, is

continued next page

UNITED STATES

MAUI • HAWAII

only about 1-1/4 hours away. Various tour companies offer bike excursions down from the summit, and there are hiking trails throughout the crater. Dress warmly as the temperatures at Haleakala are much colder than here. If you're interested in snorkeling, take a boat to Molokini. We can recommend a tour company with a very knowledgable crew. They provide snorkel gear, give you a lesson and offer Snuba for those interested in going a little further down into the ocean.

Address: PO Box 856, Haiku, HI 96708
Tel: (808) 572-4530 (Tel/Fax).
URL: http://www.maui.net/~regal/wb.html

Type: Bed & breakfast.
Clientele: Mostly gay & lesbian with some straight clientele
Transportation: Car.
Rooms: 3 rooms with queen beds.
Bathrooms: Private: 2 bath/shower/toilets, 1 shower/toilet.

Meals: Continental breakfast.
Complimentary: Juice, fruit, coffee, tea.
Dates Open: All year.
Rates: $75-$115, plus 10% tax.
Discounts: 10% on stays over 7 days.
Rsv'tns: Required.
To Reserve: Travel agent or call direct.

Minimum Stay: 2 nights.
Parking: Ample off-street parking.
In-Room: Ceiling fans, refrigerator, coffee & tea-making facilities.
On-Premises: Waterfalls.
Swimming: Pool, river & waterfalls. Ocean nearby.
Sunbathing: Poolside, on common sun decks & patio.

Nudity: Permitted.
Smoking: Permitted outside, not in rooms.
Pets: Not permitted.
Handicap Access: Yes, wide doors.
Children: Welcome over 8 years of age.
Languages: English, French, German, Spanish.
Your Host: Bob & Christa.

OAHU - HONOLULU

A Tropic Paradise

Q-NET Gay-Owned 50/50 ♀♂*

The Heart of Aloha

We look forward to hosting your stay in what we feel is one of this Earth's most serene and beautiful places. *A Tropic Paradise*, our elegant Hawaiian home in the friendly town of Kailua, has large, beautiful rooms with private baths, in-room refrigerator, television and cable. A waterfall whispers beside the tropical pool and spa, and the island's most beautiful beach is steps from your home. We provide beach mats, towels and coolers for guests to use when touring the area's many grottos and waterfalls. Walk our beach at sunrise, or on a moonlit night and touch the Soul of Aloha. Whether it's shopping, Oahu's nightlife, a luau, or Hawaii's thrilling water sports, it's all here for you.

Address: 43 Laiki Place, Kailua, HI
Tel: (808) 261-2299, (888) 362-4488, Fax: (808) 263-0795.
E-mail: darreld@gte.net

Type: Bed & breakfast vacation homes.
Clientele: 50% gay & lesbian & 50% straight clientele
Transportation: Car is best.
To Gay Bars: 8 miles, a 20 min drive.
Rooms: 5 rooms, 1 suite, 1 apartment, 2- & 3-BR home with single, queen or king beds.
Bathrooms: 4 private & 4 shared bath/shower/toilets.
Meals: Expanded continental breakfast.
Vegetarian: Available as requested.
Complimentary: Tea & coffee.
Dates Open: All year.
Rates: B&B rooms $70-$85, weekly rates available. Suites $125-$250/day. 2-3BR homes $200-$400.
Discounts: Weekly & monthly rates available.
Rsv'tns: Required.
To Reserve: Travel agent or call direct.
Minimum Stay: 3 days.
Parking: Ample free off-street parking.
In-Room: Fans, color cable TV, refrigerator, maid service.
On-Premises: TV lounge, laundry facilities.
Exercise/Health: Jacuzzi, massage. Nearby gym, weights, Jacuzzi, sauna, steam, massage.
Swimming: Pool & ocean on premises.
Sunbathing: Poolside, on patio & at beach.
Smoking: Non-smoking home. Permitted in outdoor smoking area.
Pets: Not permitted.
Handicap Access: Yes, ramps.
Children: Welcome. Pool toys for children with parental supervision.
Languages: English, Spanish.
Your Host: Ken & Alex.

Hotel Honolulu
Gay/Lesbian ♀♂

Although it is in the heart of Waikiki, *Hotel Honolulu* has been carefully designed to be different from any other in modern day Hawaii. We are trying to create an oasis in time to take our guests back to the quieter, more gentle and relaxed way of life in these beautiful islands. Large and small studios and suites each have a different theme. All have kitchens, baths and outside lanai. Enjoy the rooftop garden sun deck for relaxation and comfort. We are two blocks from the beach and next door to our best gay clubs and the nicest restaurants and shops in the famed Kuhio district.

Address: 376 Kaiolu St, Honolulu, HI 96815
Tel: (808) 926-2766, (800) 426-2766 (US/CAN), **Fax:** (808) 922-3326.
E-mail: hotelhnl@lava.net **URL:** http://www.lava.net/~hotelhnl

Type: Hotel.
Clientele: Good mix of gay men & women.
Transportation: Pre-arranged airport/Waikiki shuttle, or taxi. 1st class airport shuttle R/T is $25 with lei greeting.
To Gay Bars: The main gay bars are on our block.
Rooms: 15 rooms & 10 suites with king or queen beds.
Bathrooms: All private.
Complimentary: Coffee & tea.
Dates Open: All year.
High Season: Nov-Mar.
Rates: $69-$129.
Credit Cards: MC, Visa, Amex, Diners, Discover, JCB.
Rsv'tns: Preferred.
To Reserve: Call direct or reserve through your travel agent.
Minimum Stay: 4 days from Dec 20 to Jan 6.
Parking: Adequate off-street, covered, pay parking. Least expensive on the island.
In-Room: Color TV, AC, ceiling fans, telephone, kitchen & refrigerator.
On-Premises: Laundry room & garden sun deck.
Exercise/Health: Massage on premises. Nearby gym & sauna.
Swimming: Ocean beach 2 blocks away.
Sunbathing: On beach &
common sun deck (lanai).
Smoking: Permitted without restrictions.
Pets: Small pets permitted if prearranged.
Handicap Access: No. Only on the 1st floor.
Children: Permitted.
Languages: English, Spanish, French, German & Hawaiian.
Your Host: John, Rob, Karen, Guy, Todd, Tami.

IGLTA

Pacific Ocean Holidays
Gay/Lesbian ♀♂
Hawaii Vacations for Gay Men & Women

Pacific Ocean Holidays specializes in Hawaii vacation packages for gay travelers. Choose when to travel, the length of stay, the island or islands to visit, and the price range and type of lodgings desired. We package a selection of gay and gay-friendly bed and breakfast homes, resort hotels, and condominiums. On Oahu, our Waikiki packages include lodging, flower lei greeting, airport transfers and a gay-hosted welcome and orientation meeting. Kauai, Maui, and Hawaii (Big Island) packages include lodging and rental car. All packages also include a per-

continued next page

sonalized itinerary, applicable taxes, and our gay "Pocket Guide to Hawaii." Flights to and between the islands can also be included.

Pacific Ocean Holidays provides a convenient, hassle-free way to arrange the basic components of your Hawaii vacation through one reliable and knowledgable source. In business since 1982, we've earned a reputation for personal, individualized, and friendly service, with attention to detail. *Pacific Ocean Holidays* is licensed by the State of Hawaii and is a charter member of the International Gay & Lesbian Travel Association. Call or write for our free gay Hawaii vacation brochure.

Address: PO Box 88245, Dept IP, Honolulu, HI 96830-8245
Tel: (808) 923-2400, (800) 735-6600, **Fax:** (808) 923-2499.
E-mail: poh@hi.net **URL:** http://gayhawaii.com

| **Type:** Bed & breakfasts, hotels & condos. | **Clientele:** Gay & lesbian
Credit Cards: MC, VISA, Amex, Discover, Novus. | **Rsv'tns:** Required.
To Reserve: Travel agent or call direct. | **Minimum Stay:** 3 nights.
Languages: English. |

Waikiki AA Studios
(Bed & Breakfast Honolulu & Statewide) Q-NET Gay-Friendly ♀♂

One Call Does it All!

Waikiki AA Studios, Hawaii's largest B&B agency has over 350 studios and bed & breakfasts on all of the islands. We also offer good rates on cars and interisland flights. Our volume means lower rates! Fax, E-mail or snail mail us for a free brochure. Then contact us by phone (toll-free USA/Canada), E-mail or fax for a give-and-take which will provide us with a better awareness of your desires. We offer places which are actually open on the dates you want, and more information (dates, places, etc) means better help!

Address: 3242 Kaohinani, Honolulu, HI 96817
Tel: (808) 595-7533, (800) 288-4666, **Fax:** (808) 595-2030.
E-mail: BnBsHI@Aloha.net **URL:** http://planet-hawaii.com/bnb-honolulu

| **Type:** Studios, hosted rentals & statewide bed & breakfast reservation service.
Clientele: Mostly straight clientele with a gay & lesbian following.
To Gay Bars: Some are near men's/women's bars.
Rooms: 9 studio apartments in Waikiki, 390 homestays & studios in | other locations.
Bathrooms: All private in Waikiki, private & shared elsewhere.
Meals: Breakfast in homestays varies with host.
Dates Open: All year.
High Season: Dec 15th-Easter.
Rates: $45-$150.
Discounts: On weekly & monthly stays. | **Credit Cards:** MC, Visa.
Rsv'tns: Recommended.
To Reserve: Travel agent or call direct.
Minimum Stay: 3 days.
Parking: Both free and pay parking.
In-Room: Studios have color TV, telephone, AC, kitchen.
On-Premises: Studios have laundry facilities. | **Swimming:** Studios have pool, ocean is 1-1/2 blocks away.
Sunbathing: At poolside, on beach.
Smoking: No restrictions in studios. 25% of homestays permit smoking.
Pets: Not permitted.
Handicap Access: Some locations are accessible.
Languages: English. |

Fish Creek Lodging

See listing under Jackson, Wyoming.

Aura Soma Lava

Woman-Owned & -Operated ♀♂

Here, "Love" is a Verb

Located along the Portneuf River, *Aura Soma Lava* is two acres of healing energy. With our geothermal bathing, labyrinth, conference center and bookstore, we are dedicated to mind/body healing and soul development. We cater to corporations or private parties. We can cater your event. Or attend one of ours. Small groups of up to 20 can sleep camp-style on sleeping pads which are provided and some cottage space is also available. Our bookstore includes alternative healing books and supporting products, womyn's evolution, sprituality, herbs, aromatherapy, massage products, candles, crystals, and more. We sponsor a women's music festival in September.

Address: 97 N 2nd East, Lava Hot Springs, ID 83246
Tel: (208) 776-5800, (800) 757-1233, **Fax:** (208) 776-5550.
E-mail: asl@micron.net

Type: Guesthouse with small convention center & commercial kitchen.
Clientele: Gay, lesbian & straight clientele
Transportation: Car is best. Small, private airport in Lava, pick up from airport in Pocatello, ID.
To Gay Bars: 30 miles.
Rooms: 1 cottage & convention center with double or queen beds, bunks & floor pads.
Bathrooms: Private: 2 bath/shower/toilets. Shared: 2 bath/shower/toilets, 1 WC only.
Meals: Guests can cook on site.
Complimentary: Guests can bring own spirits on property.
Dates Open: All year.
High Season: Jun-Aug.
Rates: $200-$350 per day, per group not including food. Rates vary according to group size.
Discounts: Group rates.
Credit Cards: MC, Visa.
Rsv'tns: Required.
To Reserve: Travel agent or call direct.
Parking: Ample free off-street parking.
In-Room: Telephone, ceiling fans, color TV, VCR, kitchen, refrigerator, coffee & tea-making facilities, maid & laundry service.
On-Premises: Meeting rooms, laundry facilities, business services, video tape library, alternative healing & living enrichment bookstore.
Exercise/Health: Natural hot springs on premises.
Swimming: Pool & river on premises.
Sunbathing: Poolside & on patio.
Smoking: Permitted outside, non-smoking rooms available.
Pets: Well-mannered pets only.
Handicap Access: Yes, ramps.
Children: Welcome.
Languages: English.
Your Host: Evelee & Cheryl.

The Little House On The Prairie

Gay-Friendly ♀♂

Home of the Stars

The Little House On The Prairie is a Queen Anne Victorian homestead surrounded by acres of woodlands, gardens, swimming pool and pond. "It is a showpiece of a home, full of turn-of-the-century Victorian antiques, wooden parquet floors and theater memorabilia...and it is anything but little." (Mike Monson, *Champaign-Urbana News-Gazette*) Guests at *The Little House On The Prairie* have included many stars who performed at the The Little Theatre On The Square in Sullivan druing the 60s, 70s and 80s. It is in the heart of Amish country, yet only 3 hours from Chicago and 2 hours from St. Louis.

Address: PO Box 525, Sullivan, IL 61951 **Tel:** (217) 728-4727.

Type: Bed & breakfast.
Clientele: Mostly straight clientele with a gay & lesbian following
Transportation: Car is best.
To Gay Bars: 60 miles to Champaign, IL.
Rooms: 4 rooms with single, double & queen beds. 1-BR suite with king bed.
Bathrooms: 3 private shower/toilets, 2 private bath/shower/toilets.
Meals: Full breakfast.
Vegetarian: Available if asked for in advance.
Complimentary: Wine, tea, cheese, crackers & fruit. Mints in room.
Dates Open: April 1-Jan 1.
High Season: Jun-Aug. Usually sold out in advance.
Rates: $55-$125.
Rsv'tns: Required.
To Reserve: Call direct.
Parking: Ample free parking.
In-Room: AC, maid service & video tape library. 1 room with color TV & VCR. Fireplace in suite. Coffee/tea-making facilities available.
On-Premises: Meeting rooms & TV lounge.

continued next page

INN PLACES® 1998

UNITED STATES — CHICAGO · ILLINOIS

Exercise/Health: Jacuzzi in suite. Nearby gym, weights, sauna & massage.
Swimming: Pool on premises. Nearby lake.
Sunbathing: At poolside.
Nudity: Permitted in the wooded area.
Smoking: Permitted in sun room & outdoor areas.
Pets: Not permitted.
Handicap Access: No.
Children: Not especially welcome.
Languages: English, French & Italian.
Your Host: Guy & Kirk.

Best Western Hawthorne Terrace

Gay-Friendly 50/50 ♀♂*

In the tradition of fine old Colonial manors, *Best Western Hawthorne Terrace* offers charming accommodations set in picturesque period architecture, fully restored to modern convenience. Steps away from Lincoln Park and Lake Michigan, *Hawthorne Terrace* is right in the heart of Chicago's gay community, where fine dining, eclectic nightlife, shopping and theatres abound. Wrigley Field, Halsted Street, Lincoln Park Zoo and Chicago's great lakefront beaches are all close by, and it is only ten minutes to the downtown area.

Address: 3434 N Broadway, Chicago, IL 60657
Tel: (773) 244-3434, (888) 675-BEST (2378), **Fax:** (773) 244-3435.

Type: Hotel with exercise facility.
Clientele: 50% gay & lesbian & 50% straight clientele
Transportation: Taxi is best.
To Gay Bars: Across the street.
Rooms: 44 rooms, 15 suites with double or queen beds.
Bathrooms: 59 private bath/shower/toilets.
Meals: Continental breakfast.
Vegetarian: Not available on premises, numerous vegetarian restaurants nearby.
Dates Open: All year.
High Season: May-Oct.
Rates: $89-$119.
Discounts: AAA, AARP, airline, government, corporate (15%) available all year, must mention affiliation at time of reservation to apply.
Credit Cards: MC, Visa, Amex, Diners, Discover.
Rsv'tns: Strongly recommended.
To Reserve: Travel agent or call direct.
Parking: Ample covered, off-street pay parking.
In-Room: Telephone, AC, color cable TV, modem hookups, maid & room service.
On-Premises: Laundry facilities, fax (free incoming, charge for outgoing), copier.
Exercise/Health: Jacuzzi, sauna, cardio-vascular exercise equipment. Nearby gym.
Swimming: Pool at nearby healthclub. Lake nearby.
Sunbathing: On roof & at beach.
Smoking: Permitted, except in non-smoking rooms. Non-smoking rooms available.
Pets: $250 addt'l deposit, small pets in carriers.
Handicap Access: Yes, ramps, CC TVs. Limited wide doors, rails in bathrooms, smoke detectors for the hearing impaired.
Children: Welcome. Under age 12 are free.
Languages: English, Spanish.

City Suites Hotel — Neighborhood Inns of Chicago

Gay-Friendly ♀♂

The City Suites Hotel offers a touch of European style with comfortable and convenient accommodations at affordable rates. Located on Chicago's dynamic near north side, close to famous Halsted St., Wrigley Field and the eclectic Sheffield/Belmont area, we're in the heart of Chicago's gay community. Only steps from our door, you'll find the city's finest dining, shopping, theatres and exciting nightlife. The *City Suites* is truly Chicago's best value!

Address: 933 West Belmont, Chicago, IL 60657
Tel: (773) 404-3400, **Fax:** (773) 404-3405. **Reservations:** (800) CITY-108.

Type: Hotel.
Clientele: Mostly straight, with a gay & lesbian following
Transportation: Taxi.
To Gay Bars: 1 block to gay/lesbian bar.
Rooms: 16 guest rooms & 29 suites.
Bathrooms: All private.
Meals: Continental breakfast.

Complimentary: Newspaper.
Dates Open: All year.
Rates: $95-$109, rates based on single occupancy.
Discounts: Group.
Credit Cards: MC, Visa, Amex, Discover, Diners.
Rsv'tns: Recommended.
To Reserve: Travel agent or call direct.

Parking: Ample, off-street, pay parking.
In-Room: Maid & full room service, telephone, AC, color cable TV.
On-Premises: Laundry facilities.
Exercise/Health: Discounted daily rates at nearby health club with gym & weights.

Swimming: Lake Michigan nearby.
Sunbathing: At the lake.
Smoking: No restrictions.
Pets: Small pets with pre-approval.
Handicap Access: No.
Children: Permitted.
Languages: English.

IGLTA

UNITED STATES • ILLINOIS • CHICAGO

Old Town Bed & Breakfast

Q-NET Gay/Lesbian ♀♂

Old Town Bed & Breakfast is a modern townhouse splendidly furnished and decorated with pictures and art objects from three centuries. A walled garden, library with easy chairs, marble bath with oversized tub, and cherrywood sleighbeds invite rest, reflection and renewal. Lake Michigan, Lincoln Park and an urban village surround. Parking is ample.

Public transportation is best. North Michigan Avenue shopping, Gold Coast mansions and fine restaurants are a five- to 12-minute walk. If you prefer complete privacy, you can have the run of the entire second floor. Just ask us when you make your reservation.

Address: 1451 N North Park Ave, Chicago, IL 60610-1226
Tel: (312) 440-9268.

Type: Bed & breakfast.
Clientele: Mostly gay & lesbian with some straight clientele
Transportation: All transportation is best.
To Gay Bars: 2 blocks.
Rooms: 2 rooms with queen beds.
Bathrooms: 1-1/2 shared or ask for the private bath option.
Meals: Continental breakfast.

Vegetarian: Always available.
Complimentary: Tea, coffee & juice.
Dates Open: All year.
Rates: $90 for all rooms.
Discounts: Extended stays.
Credit Cards: MC, Visa, Amex.
To Reserve: Travel agent or call direct.
Parking: Ample off-street parking.

In-Room: Color cable TV, video tape library, AC, telephone & laundry service.
On-Premises: TV lounge with fireplace, meeting rooms.
Exercise/Health: Nearby gym.
Swimming: Nearby pool & lake.

Sunbathing: In enclosed private garden.
Nudity: Permitted upstairs.
Smoking: Not permitted.
Pets: Not permitted.
Handicap Access: No.
Children: Not permitted.
Languages: English, German, French, Italian & Spanish.
Your Host: Michael.

Park Brompton Inn
— Neighborhood Inns of Chicago

Gay-Friendly ♀♂

English Elegance with the Flair of Chicago Style

In the tradition of fine, old English inns, the *Park Brompton Inn* offers a romantic 19th-century atmosphere on Chicago's bustling North Side. Poster beds and tapestry furnishings lend a hint of Dickensian spirit to finely appointed rooms. Steps away from the park and Lake Michigan, and only ten minutes from downtown via scenic Lake Shore Drive, *Park Brompton Inn* is located in Chicago's largest gay district, where fine dining, shopping and theatres abound. Wrigley Field, Halsted Street, Lincoln Park Zoo and a beautiful lakefront are nearby.

Address: 528 W Brompton, Chicago, IL 60657
Tel: (773) 404-3499, **Fax:** (773) 404-3495. Reservations: (800) PARK-108.

Type: Inn.
Clientele: Mostly straight clientele with a gay/lesbian following
Transportation: Taxi & public transportation. Private cars available.
To Gay Bars: 1 block to gay/lesbian bars.
Rooms: 23 suites, 31 singles.

Bathrooms: All private.
Meals: Continental breakfast.
Vegetarian: Several restaurants nearby.
Complimentary: Newspaper.
Dates Open: All year.
Rates: $85-$119, based on single occupancy.
Discounts: Group.

Credit Cards: MC, Visa, Amex, Discover, Diners.
Rsv'tns: Recommended.
To Reserve: Travel agent or call direct.
Parking: Ample off-street pay parking nearby.
In-Room: Maid & full room service, telephone, AC & color cable TV.
On-Premises: Laundry facilities.

Swimming: Lake Michigan across the street.
Sunbathing: At the lake, Belmont Rocks.
Smoking: No restrictions.
Pets: Small pets permitted with approval.
Handicap Access: No.
Children: Permitted.
Languages: English.

Surf Hotel — Neighborhood Inns of Chicago   Gay-Friendly ♀♂
In the Heart of Chicago's Gay Community

On a quiet, tree-lined street in Lincoln Park, and just 10 minutes from downtown Chicago via scenic Lake Shore Drive, the *Surf Hotel* combines atmosphere with accessibility. This intimate, Parisian-style hotel is steps away from Chicago's beautiful lakefront, the park, the zoo, the city's finest restaurants and Chicago's version of the Off-Broadway theatre district. Built in 1920, the *Surf* offers tastefully appointed rooms and is a truly affordable alternative for discriminating guests who prefer personality and ambiance when choosing lodgings.

Address: 555 W Surf, Chicago, IL 60657
Tel: (773) 528-8400, **Fax:** (773) 528-8483. Reservations: (800) SURF-108.

Type: Hotel.
Clientele: Mainly straight clientele with a gay/lesbian following
Transportation: Taxi & public transportation. Private cars available.
To Gay Bars: 1 block to gay & lesbian bars.
Rooms: 20 singles, 31 doubles & 4 suites.
Bathrooms: All private.

Meals: Continental breakfast.
Vegetarian: Available nearby.
Complimentary: Newspaper.
Dates Open: All year.
Rates: $85-$119, based on single occupancy.
Discounts: Group.
Credit Cards: MC, Visa, Amex, Discover, Diners.

Rsv'tns: Recommended.
To Reserve: Travel agent or call direct.
Parking: Ample, off-street pay parking nearby.
In-Room: Color cable TV, AC, maid & full room service.
On-Premises: Laundry facilities.
Exercise/Health: Discounted daily rates at nearby health club with gym & weights.

Swimming: Lake Michigan & health club pool nearby.
Sunbathing: At the lake, Belmont Rocks.
Smoking: No restrictions.
Pets: Small pets permitted with pre-approval..
Handicap Access: No.
Children: Permitted.
Languages: English.

INN PLACES® 1998

La Corsette Maison Inn & The Sister Inn

Gay-Friendly ♀♂

Two Historical Properties

La Corsette Maison Inn, a Mission-style mansion built in 1909, is acclaimed by historians as one of the finest examples of Arts and Crafts architecture in the Midwest. The original mission oak woodwork, art nouveau windows, and brass light fixtures highlight the decor. Guest rooms are furnished in French country decor, with goose down comforters and pillows. Enjoy a gourmet dinner in the 4-1/2 star restaurant preceded by a history and tour of the inn. *The Sister Inn,* a 140-year-old Federal-style building, features two luxurious bed chambers, both lavishly furnished and designed with privacy in mind. We're a 25-minute drive from Des Moines.

Address: 629 1st Ave E, Newton, IA 50208
Tel: (515) 792-6833, **Fax:** (515) 792-6597.

Type: Two inns, one with restaurant.
Clientele: Mainly straight clientele with a gay & lesbian following.
Transportation: Car is best, free pick up from airport.
To Gay Bars: 25 minutes to Des Moines.
Rooms: 5 doubles, 2 suites with double, queen & king beds.
Bathrooms: All private.

Meals: Full breakfast.
Vegetarian: By prior arrangement.
Complimentary: Tea, coffee, pop & snacks.
Dates Open: All year.
High Season: May through August, December.
Rates: $70-$185.
Discounts: Corporate discount with corporate number.

Credit Cards: MC, Visa, Amex.
To Reserve: Call direct or travel agent.
Minimum Stay: Required at certain peak times.
Parking: Ample off-street parking.
In-Room: Ceiling fans, AC, double whirlpools, fireplaces. Phones & color TV upon request.
On-Premises: Meeting rooms & laundry facilities.

Swimming: At nearby pool.
Smoking: Permitted outside only, all rooms non-smoking.
Pets: Permitted by prior arrangement, but not in rooms.
Handicap Access: No.
Children: Permitted by pre-arrangement.
Languages: English.
Your Host: Kay.

Kentucky Holler House

Lesbian-Owned & -Operated ♀♂

Come to the Country and Stay Awhile

Our brightly painted cottage, **Kentucky Holler House,** is the perfect place to "feel" the country! Our warm and cozy "Nest," a cute, compact attic suite for two has a private entrance, sitting rooms, full bath and deck with a view. The "Pond View" suite features a private entrance, full bath, dining area and decks. Our country location, 30 miles from Fort Knox, is perfect for relaxing and sunning on the decks, reading in the gazebo and exploring nature. Visiting anglers are welcome to fish in the ponds, then grill and eat their catch at one of our picnic spots.

Address: Rt 1 Box 51BB, Harned, KY **Tel:** (502) 547-4507

Type: Bed & breakfast, 30 miles from Ft. Knox.
Clientele: Mostly gay & lesbian with some straight clientele
Transportation: Car is best.
To Gay Bars: 60 miles, a 70 min drive.
Rooms: 2 suites with double beds.
Bathrooms: 2 private bath/shower/toilets.
Meals: Expanded continental breakfast.
Vegetarian: By prior arrangement. Suites have refrigerators, so guests may bring food, 30 miles to vegetarian restaurant.
Complimentary: Beverages in suite refrigerator, coffee & tea in room.
Dates Open: All year.
High Season: Oct-Nov for Fall Foliage.
Rates: $65-$95.
Rsv'tns: Required.
To Reserve: Travel agent or call direct.
Parking: Ample off-street parking.
In-Room: Ceiling fans, refrigerator, coffee & tea-making facilities.
Sunbathing: On private & common sun decks.
Smoking: Permitted outside, both suites are non-smoking.
Pets: Not permitted.
Handicap Access: No.
Children: No.
Languages: English.
Your Host: Sylvia.

Three Forty-Three Beharrell

Gay/Lesbian ♀♂

Gaslights and roses set the tone as you pass through the gate of the picket fence upon arriving at *343 Beharrell.* Our 100-year-old Queen Anne home, with 10-foot ceilings and hardwood floors throughout, provides a quiet and secure accommodation. The deck beckons you to relax and enjoy our huge yard with its striking 200-year-old beech tree and herb garden. We are a direct four-mile and one stop-light drive from downtown Louisville and all of its many cultural and outdoor attractions.

Address: 343 Beharrell Ave, New Albany, IN 47150
Tel: (812) 944-0289, (800) 728-3262.

Type: Bed & breakfast, 2-1/2 miles from Louisville, KY.
Clientele: Gay & lesbian. Good mix of men & women
Transportation: Car is best. Pick up from airport with advance notice, $15 each way.
To Gay Bars: 3 miles, a 10 minute drive.
Rooms: 3 rooms with queen beds.
Bathrooms: 1 private shower/toilet, 2 shared bath/shower/toilet.
Meals: Expanded continental breakfast.
Vegetarian: Available upon request.
Complimentary: Soft drinks, mints on pillows, snacks.
Dates Open: All year.
High Season: May-Aug.
Rates: Low: $65-$75; High: $75-$90.
Rsv'tns: Required.
To Reserve: Travel agent or call direct.
Minimum Stay: 2 nights on weekends.
Parking: Ample, free off-street parking.
In-Room: Ceiling fans, AC, color cable TV, telephone.
On-Premises: Huge gay library. Laundry facilities (slight charge).
Exercise/Health: Weights. Tennis nearby.
Sunbathing: On common sun decks.
Smoking: Permitted on deck only.
Pets: Not permitted.
Handicap Access: No.
Children: No.
Languages: English, French.
Your Host: Collin & Doug.

Bourgoyne Guest House
Gay/Lesbian ♀♂

A Courtyard Retreat on Bourbon Street

The excitement of Bourbon Street, coupled with a courtyard retreat from the hullabaloo, is what *Bourgoyne Guest House* offers visitors to the fabled French Quarter. Fine restaurants, museums, bars, discos...everything you'd want to see in the old section of the city is an easy walk from our central location. Guest accommodations range from cozy studios to spacious one- and two-bedroom suites of unusual style and elegance. All are furnished with antiques and all have private baths, kitchens, air conditioning and telephones.

Address: 839 rue Bourbon, New Orleans, LA 70116
Tel: (504) 524-3621 or (504) 525-3983.

Type: Guesthouse.
Clientele: Mostly gay & lesbian with some straight clientele.
Transportation: Taxi or airport shuttle.
To Gay Bars: 1 block to men's bar, 7 blocks to women's bars.
Rooms: 3 rooms & 2 suites.
Bathrooms: All private.
Dates Open: All year.
Rates: $70-$160.
Credit Cards: MC & VISA.
Rsv'tns: Recommended.
To Reserve: Travel agent or call direct.
Parking: Off-street pay parking nearby.
In-Room: AC, color TV, telephones, complete kitchens, maid & laundry service.
On-Premises: Meeting rooms, laundry facilities, kitchen.
Sunbathing: On the patio.
Smoking: Permitted without restrictions.
Pets: Not permitted.
Handicap Access: No.
Children: Permitted.
Languages: English & French.

Boys On Burgundy
Gay/Lesbian ♂

Boys on Burgundy is located in the heart of the French Quarter, only steps from the bars and famous New Orleans sights and restaurants. This spacious, quiet B&B with friendly, courteous hosts, offers reasonable rates, cable TV, unlimited local calls and large, comfortable rooms that make you feel at home. Everyone is invited to enjoy our large, well-landscaped patio. No standard institutional hotel stay here! Members of Gala Choruses and NOGMC.

Address: 1030 Burgundy St, New Orleans, LA 70116
Tel: (504) 524-2987, (800) 487-8731.

Type: Bed & breakfast.
Clientele: Men
Transportation: Airport shuttle service.
To Gay Bars: 3 blocks.
Rooms: 3 rooms with king beds.
Bathrooms: 1 private bath/shower/toilet, 1 shared bath/shower/toilet.
Meals: Continental breakfast.
Vegetarian: Available nearby.
Dates Open: All year.
High Season: September through May.
Rates: Call for rates.
Credit Cards: MC & VISA.
Rsv'tns: Required.
To Reserve: Call direct.
Minimum Stay: 2 nights, except for certain holidays.
Parking: On-street parking.
In-Room: Color cable TV, AC, telephone.
On-Premises: Kitchen, refrigerator, coffee/tea-making facilities, large, well-landscaped patio.
Exercise/Health: Nearby gym, weights, spa, sauna, steam & massage.
Swimming: Nearby pool.
Sunbathing: On the patio & at private clubs.
Smoking: Permitted on patio only.
Pets: Not permitted.
Handicap Access: No.
Children: Not especially welcome.
Languages: English.

Bywater Bed & Breakfast
Q-NET Gay/Lesbian ♀♂

Bywater Bed & Breakfast is a late Victorian "double shot-gun" cottage in the Bywater neighborhood, a short distance from Faubourg Marigny and the French Quarter and close to tourist attractions. Decorated with contemporary Southern folk art, guest space includes living room, library, dining room, kitchen and enclosed backyard patio. Groups can be accommodated with special prior arrangement. This is a women-owned B&B.

Address: 1026 Clouet St, New Orleans, LA 70117 **Tel:** (504) 944-8438.

Type: Bed & breakfast.
Clientele: Mostly gay & lesbian with some straight clientele
Transportation: Car or taxi.
To Gay Bars: 1 mile or a 5-minute drive.
Rooms: 3 rooms with king or double beds.
Bathrooms: 1 private bath/shower/toilet, 2 private sinks, 2 shared bath/shower/toilets.
Meals: Expanded continental breakfast.
Vegetarian: Request in advance. Vegetarian restaurants nearby.
Complimentary: Coffee & tea.
Dates Open: All year.
High Season: Mardi Gras, Jazz Fest.
Rates: $60-$75. No increase for special events.
Discounts: Negotiable on stays of two weeks or more.
Credit Cards: MC, Visa.
Rsv'tns: Required.
To Reserve: Call direct.
Minimum Stay: 2 nights on weekends, longer during Jazz Fest & Mardi Gras.
Parking: Ample on-street parking.
In-Room: AC, ceiling fans.
On-Premises: TV lounge, laundry facilities, video tape library.
Sunbathing: On the patio.
Smoking: Permitted only outdoors & on rear patio.
Pets: Permitted with advance arrangements.
Handicap Access: No.
Children: Welcome with advance arrangements.
Languages: English.
Your Host: Betty-Carol & Ken.

Bywater Guest House
Gay-Friendly 50/50 ♀♂

A relaxed, comfortable atmosphere in an 1872 Eastlake Victorian home located in the Bywater National Historic District, 2 miles from the French Quarter. Amenities include: served breakfast, afternoon tea and pastries, maid service, comfortable beds with feather mattresses, and a private courtyard — all within a 5-minute drive to the Vieux Carre. Be sure to visit our web site or e-mail us for more information.

Address: 908 Poland Ave, New Orleans, LA
Tel: (504) 949-6381, (888) 615-7498.
E-mail: bywatergh@aol.com **URL:** http://members.aol.com/bywatergh/

Type: Bed & breakfast.
Clientele: 50% gay & lesbian & 50% straight clientele
Transportation: Car is best.
To Gay Bars: 1.5 miles, a 5 minute drive.
Rooms: 3 rooms with queen beds.
Bathrooms: 1 shared bath/shower/toilet, 1 shared WC/toilet only.
Meals: Full breakfast.
Vegetarian: Available upon request. Some vegan restaurants in the city.
Complimentary: Snacks always available, tea & pastries in afternoon, bedtime snack.
Dates Open: All year.
High Season: Mardi Gras, Jazz Fest (dates vary).
Rates: $75-$115.
Discounts: 10% discount for stays of 5 nights or more.
Credit Cards: MC, Visa, Discover.
Rsv'tns: Required.
To Reserve: Call direct.
Parking: Ample, free off-street parking.
In-Room: Maid service.
On-Premises: TV lounge.
Smoking: Permitted in couryard only. No smoking allowed in the building.
Pets: Not permitted.
Handicap Access: No.
Children: No.
Languages: English.
Your Host: Loren & Bill.

Fourteen Twelve Thalia, A Bed and Breakfast
Gay/Lesbian ♀♂

Brant-lee and Terry wish to welcome you into their home, *Fourteen Twelve Thalia, A Bed & Breakfast.* Your spacious, bright and comfortable one-bedroom apartment in this renovated Victorian house has a king-sized bed, private bath, kitchen with microwave, a large living room with queen-sized sofa sleeper, access to laundry facilities, color cable TV and a private entrance. The patio is available for sunbathing and relaxing among the flowers. Our location in the lower Garden District is convenient to the French Quarter, downtown and the art and warehouse districts, the convention center and Super Dome.

Address: 1412 Thalia, New Orleans, LA 70130
Tel: (504) 522-0453. **E-mail:** grisgris@ix.netcom.com

Type: Bed & breakfast.
Clientele: Mostly gay & lesbian with some straight clientele
Transportation: Car, streetcar or taxi.
To Gay Bars: 14 blocks to French Quarter bars. From 5-20 minutes by car, taxi or streetcar.
Rooms: Self-contained apartment with king bed, queen sleeper sofa & private entrance. For 2-4 people.
Bathrooms: Private.
Meals: Breakfast furnishings supplied for self-catering kitchen.
Vegetarian: Available with advance notice.
Complimentary: Tea, coffee, juices & fresh fruit.

continued next page

INN PLACES® 1998

Dates Open: All year.
High Season: Mardi Gras, Jazz Fest, Sugar Bowl/New Years.
Rates: $75-$95 or $125-$175 during special events.
Discounts: For stays of more than 3 nights.
Rsv'tns: Required.
To Reserve: Call direct.
Minimum Stay: 2 nights. Mardi Gras 4 nights, other special events 3 nights.
Parking: Ample on-street parking.
In-Room: Color cable TV, AC, telephone, ceiling fans, kitchen & refrigerator. Washer/dryer available.
On-Premises: Laundry facilities.
Sunbathing: On the patio.
Smoking: Not permitted in the apartment. Permitted on deck or patio.
Pets: Small pets that are crate trained.
Handicap Access: Yes. Low steps, wide doors, accessible bath.
Children: Welcomed but limited to 2.
Languages: English.

Frenchmen Hotel
Gay-Operated 50/50

Experience the personalized attention, romantic feelings and relaxed atmosphere of a guesthouse with the added luxuries of a hotel. Tucked away in the French Quarter, *The Frenchmen* puts the quaint shops, historical homes and fine restaurants of the Quarter and the Faubourg Marigny at your doorstep. Rooms decorated with period furniture surround you with the charm of a bygone era, while assuring your comfort with climate control.

Address: 417 Frenchmen St, New Orleans, LA 70116
Tel: (504) 948-2166, (800) 831-1781.

Type: Bed & breakfast.
Clientele: 50% gay & lesbian & 50% straight clientele
Transportation: Car, airport shuttle or taxi.
To Gay Bars: 1 block.
Rooms: 25 rooms, 2 suites with single, double or queen beds.
Bathrooms: 25 private bath/shower/toilets.
Meals: Continental breakfast.
Dates Open: All year.
Rates: $59-$189.
Credit Cards: MC, Visa, Amex.
Rsv'tns: Required.
To Reserve: Travel agent or call direct.
Parking: Limited free covered off-street parking.
In-Room: Telephone, AC, ceiling fans, color cable TV, maid service.
On-Premises: Fax.
Exercise/Health: Jacuzzi.
Swimming: Pool on premises.
Sunbathing: At poolside & on roof.
Smoking: Non-smoking rooms available.
Pets: Not permitted.
Handicap Access: No.
Children: No.
Languages: English.

Glimmer Inn
Woman-Owned & -Operated

A Gay-Friendly Place To Come Home To

We invite you to experience New Orleans by staying in our home, the *Glimmer Inn*. This 1891 Victorian features grand period elements such as a cypress and mahogany staircase, 13-foot cove ceilings, pocket doors, stained glass and ceiling medallions with crystal chandeliers. A New Orleans theme is carried throughout the inn, with poster art, music, books and memorabilia. Each guestroom is unique and individually appointed with custom fabrics. We're located on the St. Charles streetcar line, across from the Garden District, 15 minutes via streetcar to the French Quarter or uptown attractions.

Address: 1631 7th St, New Orleans, LA 70115 **Tel:** (504) 897-1895.

Type: Bed & breakfast & cottage.
Clientele: Mostly straight clientele with a gay/lesbian following
Transportation: Taxi from airport (1/2 hour, $21 flat rate for 2).
To Gay Bars: 3 miles, a 45 min walk, a 10 min drive.
Rooms: 5 rooms, 1 cottage with single, double, queen or king beds.
Bathrooms: Private: 1 shower/toilet. Shared: 3 bath/shower/toilets.
Meals: Expanded continental breakfast.
Vegetarian: Vegetarian restaurants are up- & down-town from us.
Dates Open: All year.
High Season: Oct-Nov & Mar-May.
Rates: $60-$85; summer $55-$80; special events (Jazzfest, Mardi Gras) $100-$145.
Rsv'tns: Required.
To Reserve: Travel agent or call direct.
Minimum Stay: 2 nights.
Parking: Ample free on-street parking.
In-Room: AC, ceiling fans, color TV, B/W TV, maid service.
On-Premises: TV lounge, video tape library.
Smoking: Permitted everywhere, except in dining room. Sleeping rooms aired between guests, but not restricted.
Pets: Cats allowed in main house & cottage. Dogs in cottage only. Must be quiet & well-behaved.
Handicap Access: No.
Children: Must be well-behaved.
Languages: English.
Your Host: Sharon & Cathy.

Ingram Haus

Gay-Owned & -Operated ♀♂

Minutes from the excitement of the French Quarter, *Ingram Haus*, in historic Faubourg Marigny, is a perfect solution for long-term guests on business or vacation who need a temporary apartment. Each two-bedroom suite has a private entrance, full kitchen, queen-sized beds, private bath, phone, color TV and air conditioning. French Quarter bars and restaurants, Canal Street shops, Aquarium of the Americas and Riverfront Streetcar line are within walking distance. We are also served by five bus lines, all within half a block from our door.

Address: 1012 Elysian Fields, New Orleans, LA
Tel: (504) 949-3110 (Tel/Fax). **URL:** www.andrewjaegers.com/Ingram

Type: Guesthouse.
Clientele: Mostly gay & lesbian with some straight clientele
Transportation: Taxi from airport.
To Gay Bars: 1/2 block to Phoenix Bar, Men's Room & Charlene's.
Rooms: 2 apartments with queen beds.
Bathrooms: 2 private shower/toilets.

Vegetarian: 1/2 block to a small supermarket.
Complimentary: Coffee, tea.
Dates Open: All year.
High Season: Setp-Nov, Mardi Gras, Mar-May.
Rates: Jun 1-Aug 15 $50/night, Aug 16-May 31 $75/night, special events $100-$150/night.
Discounts: Weekly rates (except during special events): Jun 1-Aug 15

$250/wk, Aug 16-May 31 $375/wk. Summer & extended stay rates available.
Rsv'tns: Required.
To Reserve: Call direct.
Minimum Stay: 2 nights (5 nights for some events).
Parking: Adequate on-street parking.
In-Room: Telephone, AC, ceiling fans, color cable TV, kitchen, refrigerator, coffee & tea-making facilities.

On-Premises: Guest laundry facilities.
Swimming: 12 blocks to country club pool.
Sunbathing: On patio.
Smoking: Permitted, no non-smoking rooms available.
Pets: Not permitted.
Handicap Access: No.
Children: No.
Languages: English.
Your Host: Scott.

La Dauphine, Residence des Artistes

Q-NET Gay-Owned & -Operated ♀♂

The "HOT" Place to Stay

Located in the artsy, bohemian Faubourg Marigny gay area, just four blocks from the French Quarter, *La Dauphine* is a hundred-year-old charmingly renovated Victorian — a mellow and relaxing retreat from the legendary, whirling scene of the inner Quarter which sizzles literally twenty-four hours a day. Visitors immediately sense the city's uninhibited, up-lifting attitude. Whether it's soaking up the confetti-strewn atmosphere or the sensation you get from your morning beignets and cafe au lait at Cafe du Monde, you'll find the streets filled with sensuality, mystery and the languid, listless air of the river and the swamps.

La Dauphine offers large, quiet rooms with queen-sized, four-poster beds. Each room has a private bath, either within the room or just outside, ceiling fans, cable TV/VCR and phone. A complimentary gay video tour of the city, produced by your host, and bicycles are provided free of charge to guests. Airport pickup can be arranged for longer stays. Your host, Ray Ruiz, is a native writer/photogra-

continued next page

pher, specializing in gay travel who has written for magazines worldwide: *Our World* — the international travel magazine, *Genre,* Germany's *MÄNNERaktuell* and *Du und Ich,* Holland's *De Gay Krant* Ireland's *Gay Community News,* England's *Rouge,* Denmark's *PAN Bladet,* Sweden's *Reporter,* and *Gay Scotland.* Ray is happy to clue you in to the local scene, especially regarding Creole and Cajun cuisine, art, antiques, architecture and music. The city is alive and pulsating with hundreds of cabarets, gallery happenings and entertainment venues, plus scores of weekend festivals celebrated yearly. *Art News* dubbed the renaissance "Boom Time on the Bayou," as counter-culture, alternative lifestyle, and gay and lesbian vitality fuse and flourish all over town. New Orleans offers the insouciant traveler a rich, exotic and gay history to explore, as well as a diverse nightlife.

Address: 2316 Rue Dauphine, New Orleans, LA 70117 **Tel:** (504) 948-2217, **Fax:** (504) 948-3420. **E-mail:** LaDauphine@aol.com **URL:** http:// www.ladauphine.com

Type: Guesthouse.
Clientele: Mosty gay & lesbian with some straight clientele
Transportation: Call us about airport shuttle. Free pick up from airport, train or bus on stays of over 3 nights.
To Gay Bars: 2 blocks, a 4 min walk, a 1 min drive.
Rooms: 4 rooms, 1 suite with queen or king beds.
Bathrooms: Private: 1 bath/shower/toilet, 4 shower/toilets.
Meals: Continental breakfast.
Vegetarian: Available everywhere.
Complimentary: Coffee & tea.
Dates Open: All year.
Rates: $65-$125 per night, $400/wk 1 person, $500/wk 2 persons.
Discounts: Call for special event rates.
Credit Cards: MC, Visa, Discover, Eurocard.
Rsv'tns: Required.
To Reserve: Travel agent or call direct.
Minimum Stay: 3 nights.
Parking: Ample, on-street parking.
In-Room: Telephone, AC, ceiling fans, color cable TV, VCR.
On-Premises: TV lounge, laundry facilities, fax, computer (PC), video tape library.
Exercise/Health: Weights.
Swimming: Nearby pool, ocean, lake.
Sunbathing: On patio & common sun decks.
Nudity: Inquire about private sunbathing on patio.
Smoking: Rooms & residence are non-smoking. Smoking permitted outside only.
Pets: Not permitted. Host has 2 dogs on premises.
Handicap Access: No.
Children: No.
Languages: English, French.
Your Host: Ray.

IGLTA

Lafitte Guest House
Gay-Friendly 50/50 ♀♂

The French Quarter's Premier Guest House For Over 40 Years

This elegant French manor house, meticulously restored to its original splendor and furnished in fine antiques and reproductions, has all the comforts of home, including air conditioning. Located in the quiet, residential section of famous Bourbon St., *Lafitte Guest House* is just steps from the French Quarter's attractions. Continental breakfast is served in your room, in our tropical courtyard or in our Victorian parlour. Wine and hors d'oeuvres are served each evening at cocktail hour. Parking is available on the premises.

Address: 1003 Bourbon St, New Orleans, LA 70116
Tel: (504) 581-2678, (800) 331-7971, **Fax:** (504) 581-2677.
URL: www.lafitteguesthouse.com

Type: Bed & breakfast guesthouse.
Clientele: 50% gay & lesbian & 50% straight clientele.
Transportation: Limo from airport, $65 for 2. Pick up from airport or train, $21 taxi, airport shuttle $10/person.
To Gay Bars: 1 block.
Rooms: 12 rooms, 2 suites & 3 apartments with double, queen or king beds.
Bathrooms: 7 private bath/ toilets & 7 private shower/ toilets.
Meals: Continental breakfast.
Vegetarian: Vegetarian food nearby.
Complimentary: Wine & hors d'oeuvres.
Dates Open: All year.
High Season: Sept 1st-Dec 1st, Jan 1st-May 31st.
Rates: 1-bdrm $89-$169, 2-bdrm suite $155-$169.

Discounts: AAA 10%.
Credit Cards: MC, Visa, Amex, Discover, Diners Club.
Rsv'tns: Required with deposit.
To Reserve: Travel agent or call direct.
Minimum Stay: 2 days on weekends. Inquire for special events.
Parking: Paid off-street parking.
In-Room: Color TV, AC, telephone & maid service. Some rooms have refrigerators & ceiling fans.
On-Premises: Victorian parlor & courtyard.
Exercise/Health: Nearby gym, weights, Jacuzzi/spa, sauna, steam & massage.
Swimming: Available at two of our off-premises townhouses.
Smoking: Not permitted in house.
Pets: Not permitted.
Handicap Access: No.
Children: Permitted.
Languages: English.
Your Host: Robert & Bobby.

The Lions Inn
Men ♂

The Lions Inn is a handsome, 1840's private home with guest rooms and is located in the historic Faubourg-Marigny area, 5 blocks from the French Quarter. Amenities include central air, private baths, cable TV, VCR & CD, garden, swimming pool and continental breakfast.

Address: 2517 Chartres St, New Orleans, LA 70117
Tel: (504) 945-2339, **Fax:** (504) 949-7321.

Type: Bed & breakfast.
Clientele: Men only
Transportation: Taxi from airport or RR station.
To Gay Bars: 2 blocks or 5 minutes by foot.
Rooms: 4 rooms & 1 suite with queen beds.
Bathrooms: Private & shared.
Meals: Continental breakfast.
Dates Open: All year.
Rates: $50-$100 except special events & holidays.
Discounts: 10% on stays of 4 nights or more.
Credit Cards: MC, VISA.
Rsv'tns: Required.
To Reserve: Call direct.
Minimum Stay: 2 days.
Parking: Ample on-street parking.
In-Room: AC, color cable TV, ceiling fans & telephone.
Exercise/Health: Jacuzzi. Nearby gym.
Swimming: Pool on premises.
Sunbathing: At poolside.
Smoking: Not permitted in rooms.
Pets: Not permitted.
Handicap Access: No.
Children: Not especially welcome.
Languages: English.
Your Host: Jon & Earl.

Macarty Park Guest House
Q-NET Gay/Lesbian ♀♂

A Tropical Paradise in the City

Enjoy beautiful, private poolside cottages, spacious suites and rooms in this Eastlake Victorian guesthouse. Step out of your room into lush, tropical gardens and jump into the sparkling heated pool. Enjoy the tranquility of the cool water on moonlit nights. Rooms are tastefully decorated in antique and reproduction furnishings, and are impeccably clean, each with a private bath. Located in a national historical district, *Macarty Park's* staff is eager to make your stay enjoyable and fun. All this for a fraction of what you would pay elsewhere!

Address: 3820 Burgundy St, New Orleans, LA 70117-5708
Tel: (504) 943-4994, (800) 521-2790, **Fax:** (504) 943-4999.
E-mail: faxmehard@aol.com

continued next page

Type: Bed & breakfast guesthouse with cottages.
Clientele: Mostly gay & lesbian with some straight clientele
Transportation: Cab from airport. Pickup from Amtrak available.
To Gay Bars: A 2-minute drive, 10 blocks.
Rooms: 6 rooms & 2 cottages with king, queen, full or twin beds.
Bathrooms: All private.
Meals: Continental breakfast.
Complimentary: Brewed coffee & tea.
Dates Open: All year.
Rates: Off season $49-$115, In season $59-$115 (except special events).
Credit Cards: MC, Visa, Amex, Discover.
Rsv'tns: Required with deposit.
To Reserve: Travel agent or call direct.
Minimum Stay: 2 days on weekends.
Parking: Ample free off-street parking.
In-Room: Color cable TV, AC, telephone & maid service. Some accommodations have kitchen, refrigerator, ceiling fans, coffee & tea-making facilities.
Exercise/Health: Complete universal gym with rowing machine, free weights, ab machine.
Swimming: In-ground heated pool on premises.
Sunbathing: At poolside, on common sun decks & on patio.
Nudity: Permitted around pool.
Smoking: Permitted without restrictions.
Pets: Not permitted.
Handicap Access: No.
Children: Not especially welcomed.
Languages: English & French.
Your Host: John.

IGLTA

Mentone Bed & Breakfast
Gay/Lesbian ♀♂

Mentone Bed & Breakfast offers a suite in a Victorian home in the Faubourg Marigny district next to the historic French Quarter. The suite is furnished with antiques and Oriental rugs, has thirteen-foot ceilings, a sitting room, and a private entrance. The sound of the paddle wheels on the river and of the horse-drawn carriages in the street below lull guests to sleep in the evenings. Enjoy the solitude of our home and tropical garden, or venture five blocks into the heart of the Quarter for entertainment and nightlife.

Address: 1437 Pauger St, New Orleans, LA 70116 **Tel:** (504) 943-3019.

Type: Bed & breakfast.
Clientele: Mostly gay & lesbian with some straight clientele.
Transportation: Shuttle, taxi or limo from airport at expense.
To Gay Bars: 3-4 blocks.
Rooms: 1 suite with double bed.
Bathrooms: All private shower/toilets.
Meals: Expanded continental breakfast of pastries or bread, fruit bowl.
Complimentary: Champagne, coffee, & tea.
Dates Open: All year except Christmas.
High Season: Sept 1-June 1.
Rates: $100, except for special events.
Discounts: Reduction after 7-night stay.
Rsv'tns: Preferred.
To Reserve: Call direct.
Minimum Stay: On weekends and for special events.
Parking: Adequate free on-street parking or limited off-street free parking.
In-Room: Color TV, AC, ceiling fans, telephone, kitchenette, refrigerator & coffee & tea-making facilities.
Smoking: On the balcony off the suite. Non-smoking room.
Pets: Not permitted.
Handicap Access: No.
Children: Permitted on approval.
Languages: English & limited French.

Pauger House Guest Suites
Gay-Owned & -Operated ♀♂

In historic Faubourg Marigny, three short blocks from the French Quarter and six blocks from Interstate 10, *Pauger House Guest Suites* are a sensible alternative to expensive French Quarter hotels. Here, guests will enjoy privacy and comfort in well-appointed, comfortable rooms with private bath, spacious suites or full apartments. Walk through the Old French Quarter on sultry summer nights, dine on spicy New Orleans cuisine, or plunge into the city's party culture... Whether you want to get away from the winter snow, or take a holiday — whatever time of year — there's always a reason to visit New Orleans!

Address: New Orleans, LA
Tel: (504) 944-2601, (800) 484-8334 (access code: 9834).

Type: Guesthouse & completely furnished apartments.
Clientele: Mostly gay & lesbian with some straight clientele
Transportation: Car or taxi.
To Gay Bars: 3 blocks, a 5 min walk, a 2 min drive.
Rooms: 3 rooms, 7 suites,

2 apartments with single, double, queen or king beds.
Bathrooms: Private: 6 bath/shower/toilets, 3 shower/toilets.
Vegetarian: 1 mile to vegetarian food.
Complimentary: Coffee & tea.

Dates Open: All year.
High Season: Fall, Spring, Mardi Gras.
Rates: Single high season $49-$69, low season $40-$50.
Discounts: 5 & 7 day discounts.
To Reserve: Travel agent or call direct.

Minimum Stay: Required.
Parking: Adequate free off-street parking, auto gate.
In-Room: Telephone, AC, ceiling fans, color cable TV, kitchen, refrigerator, coffee & tea-making facilities.
Exercise/Health: Gym nearby.

Sunbathing: On common sun decks.
Smoking: Permitted in all rooms.
Pets: Not permitted.
Handicap Access: No.
Children: Please inquire.
Languages: English, German.

Rober House
Gay/Lesbian ♀♂

Welcome to America's most fascinating city, whose unique personality was blended from many cultures. New Orleans offers you fun, music, excitement and delicious foods. Come, experience and capture the charm of the French Quarter at *Rober House*. Here, in a quiet, residential location, our one-bedroom, living, kitchen and full-bath condos are fully furnished and have all the amenities, plus courtyard and swimming pool. Three of the apartments can sleep up to 4 people. Great savings only minutes from fabulous restaurants and tourist attractions.

Address: 820 Ursulines St, New Orleans, LA 70116-2422
Tel: (504) 529-4663 or 523-1246, (800) 523-9091.

Type: Guesthouse.
Clientele: Mostly gay & lesbian with some straight clientele
Transportation: Taxi from airport $21. Shuttle bus, $10 per person, stops across the street.
To Gay Bars: Two blocks to 1 bar & three blocks to 4 other bars, all in the same direction.
Rooms: 5 apartments (3 apts. sleep up to 4 people each) with queen beds & queen sofa beds.
Bathrooms: All private.
Vegetarian: Health restaurant nearby.
Complimentary: Coffee.
Dates Open: All year.
High Season: Special events weeks & weekends.
Rates: July 1-Aug 27, $69-$89. Rest of year, $90-$125, except special events periods (call for rates).
Discounts: Weekly rates.
Credit Cards: All accepted.
Rsv'tns: Required.
To Reserve: Travel agent or call direct.
Minimum Stay: 3 days in summer & 2 days rest of year.
Parking: On-street parking & plenty of parking garages near Canal St.
In-Room: Color TV, AC, ceiling fans, telephone & kitchen with refrigerator.
Swimming: Pool.
Sunbathing: At poolside.
Nudity: Permitted poolside if no one else objects.
Smoking: Preferably outside the apartments.
Pets: Not permitted.
Handicap Access: 1 unit is accessible with help.
Children: Welcomed.
Languages: English, German & Danish.

Royal Barracks Guest House
Q-NET Gay/Lesbian ♂

A World of Your Own

In a newly-renovated Victorian home located in a quiet, residential neighborhood, this gay-owned & -operated guesthouse will offer you the hospitality of the historical French Quarter. Within a few blocks are 24-hour restaurants, bars and delicatessens. Rooms at *Royal Barracks* are individually decorated, have private entrances and have all modern conveniences. All open onto our high-walled, private patio with wet bar, refrigerator, ice maker and hot tub. Our avid return customers, many of whom often book a year in advance, consider their accommodations here their own secluded, private hideaway.

Address: 717 Barracks St, New Orleans, LA 70116
Tel: (504) 529-7269, (888) 255-7269, **Fax:** (504) 529-7298.

Type: Guesthouse.
Clientele: Mostly gay
Transportation: $15 per person airport shuttle, taxi $21 flat fee.
To Gay Bars: 1/2 block to men's & 7 blocks to women's bars.
Rooms: 5 rooms & 1 suite with double & queen beds.
Bathrooms: All private.
Meals: Continental breakfast.
Dates Open: All year.
High Season: Oct-May.

continued next page

UNITED STATES

NEW ORLEANS • LOUISIANA

Rates: Jun 15-Sep 15, $65-$100. Winter, $90-$140.
Credit Cards: MC, Visa.
Rsv'tns: Required.
To Reserve: Travel agent or call direct.
Parking: On-street parking, numerous parking lots.
In-Room: Color TV, telephone, ceiling fans, AC & maid service.
On-Premises: Ice machine & refrigerator in the courtyard.
Exercise/Health: Jacuzzi.
Nudity: Permitted.
Smoking: Permitted without restrictions.
Pets: Not permitted.
Handicap Access: No.
Children: No.
Languages: English.
Your Host: Michael & James.

IGLTA

Ursuline Guesthouse

Gay/Lesbian ♀♂

Our guesthouse is located in the midst of the French Quarter, near restaurants, shops, museums and all that makes New Orleans famous. Constructed in the 18th century, *Ursuline Guest House* is today an historical structure enhanced with all the modern amenities desirable to the out-of-town guest.

All rooms have modern bathrooms, air conditioning, color cable TV, carpeting or hardwood floors, are furnished with an eclectic blend of furniture, and some open onto a serene, old French Quarter courtyard with wrought iron furniture and a hot tub. We are confident you will be pleased.

Address: 708 rue des Ursulines, New Orleans, LA 70116
Tel: (504) 525-8509,
reservations: (800) 654-2351,
Fax: (504) 525-8408.

Type: Guesthouse.
Clientele: Mostly gay & lesbian with some straight clientele
Transportation: Airport shuttle $10. Taxi $21 for 1 or 2 people.
To Gay Bars: 3 blocks.

Rooms: 12 rooms with single, double & queen beds.
Bathrooms: All private.
Meals: Continental breakfast.
Vegetarian: Vegetarian restaurant within walking distance.

Complimentary: Coffee. Wine in courtyard each evening.
Dates Open: All year.
High Season: Sept-May.
Rates: $85-$125. Higher on holidays & for special events.
Credit Cards: MC, Visa, Amex.
Rsv'tns: Recommended.
To Reserve: Call direct.
Minimum Stay: Two nights weekends & 3-5 days during special events & holidays.

Parking: Limited off-street parking $10/day.
In-Room: Color TV, AC, direct dial telephone & maid service.
Exercise/Health: Whirlpool in courtyard.
Smoking: 1 non-smoking room available.
Pets: Permitted with restrictions.
Handicap Access: Yes, limited.
Children: Not equipped to handle.
Languages: English.

The Estorge House

Q-NET Lesbian-Owned 50/50 ♀♂

Come Pass a Good Time at the Elegant Old Lady of Market Street

French Louisiana and Southern Hospitality are still alive and well here at *The Estorge House*. Return to a time of genteel elegance with a sincere welcome to our home. Our guest rooms are lavished with fresh flowers, antique furnishings, European and Egyptian linens and claw-foot tubs to create an atmosphere of comfort and relaxation. When you arrive, you are welcomed with an afternoon wine or tea service in our formal parlor or, if you prefer, your wine may be served to you while you enjoy our outdoor hot tub.

We love to pamper our guests, so we turn down the linens, fluff up the pillows, place a rose between the sheets and the rest is up to you! If that's not enough, a bedtime snack of homemade chocolate chip cookies and milk OR popcorn and M&M's is sure to satisfy! We like to ease into the morning with a leisurely breakfast, take time to chat, enjoy the garden view and enjoy an extra cup of Cajun blend.

We all love New Orleans, but there is so much more to experience in Louisiana. Just 2-1/2 hours from New Orleans is Acadiana, rich in Cajun culture, and much more. Here in Opelousas, Louisiana's third-oldest city, we celebrate the Cajun culture with world-famous musicians and Cajun cooking. We are home to the award-winning Cajun fiddler Hadley Castille, the Zydeco Festival, Chef Paul Prudhomme, and Tony Chachere's Creole Foods. Just 20 minutes away is Lafayette, the heart of French-speaking Louisiana, where some of the world's best Cajun restaurants can be experienced, and Mardi Gras is a week-long celebration. Les bon temps roulee!!! (Let the good times roll!!!)

Address: 427 North Market Street, Opelousas, LA
Tel: (318) 942-8151.

Type: Bed & breakfast.
Clientele: 50% gay & lesbian & 50% straight clientele
Transportation: Car is best.
To Gay Bars: 18 miles, a 20 min drive.
Rooms: 2 rooms with double beds.
Bathrooms: 2 private bath/shower/toilets.
Meals: Full breakfast.
Vegetarian: Upon request.
Complimentary: Wine in formal parlor or by outdoor hot tub. Bedtime snacks of chocolate chip cookies & milk OR popcorn & M&Ms. Rose on pillow.
Dates Open: All year.
Rates: $125.
Discounts: Senior citizens, police officers.
To Reserve: Call direct.
Parking: Ample off-street parking.
In-Room: Telephone, AC, color cable TV, maid service.
On-Premises: Laundry facilities, guest library, tour of historical home.
Exercise/Health: Jacuzzi.
Smoking: Permitted outside.
Pets: Not permitted.
Handicap Access: No.
Children: No.
Languages: English, ASL.
Your Host: Sherl & Judith.

Maple Hill Farm B&B Inn

Gay-Friendly ♀♂

Get Away From It All, Yet Be Near It All...

On 62 acres just minutes from Augusta, *Maple Hill Farm* is the only B&B Inn in the Capitol area. Breakfast is hearty country fare, cooked to order from our menu. Guest rooms provide amenities, including private bath and a whirlpool for two! We provide an excellent "base camp" from which to explore Maine. Hike, enjoy the private swimming hole, or relax in front of the fireplace. The coast, lakes, mountains and Freeport shopping are all within an hour's drive. Hallowell, just 3 miles away, is the gay community for this area. Rated "Best bed & breakfast, hands down," *Main Times*.

Address: Outlet Rd, RR1 Box 1145, Hallowell, ME 04347
Tel: (207) 622-2708, (800) 622-2708, **Fax:** (207) 622-0655.
E-mail: maple@mint.net URL: www.mint.net/maple

Type: Bed & breakfast with gallery.
Clientele: Mostly straight clientele with a gay & lesbian following.
Transportation: Car is best. Rentals available at Portland or Augusta airports.
To Gay Bars: 5 miles to P.J.'s in Augusta. 1 hour to Portland bars.
Rooms: 6 rooms & 1 suite with double or queen beds.
Bathrooms: Private: 3 shower/toilets, 1 full bath. 1 shared full bath.
Campsites: Rustic camping adjacent to small spring-fed pond in woods. Very private.

Meals: Full breakfast cooked to order from menu.
Liquor service.
Vegetarian: Cooked to order breakfast. Excellent vegetarian-oriented restaurant nearby.
Complimentary: Evening tea or coffee. Mints in room. Bathroom amenities.
Dates Open: All year.
High Season: July-October (summer & fall foliage).
Rates: Summer $55-$125 winter $45-$100.
Discounts: Government rates available.
Credit Cards: MC, Visa, Amex, Diners, Discover.
Rsv'tns: Recommended.

To Reserve: Travel agent or call direct.
Minimum Stay: Required some peak summer & fall weekends.
Parking: Ample free off-street parking.
In-Room: AC, telephone, color TV, clock radio & maid service. 1 room with Jacuzzi bath.
On-Premises: TV lounge, meeting rooms, fax machine.
Exercise/Health: Jacuzzi in 1 guest room. Nearby gym & massage.
Swimming: Swimming hole in the woods. 1 mile to lake.
Sunbathing: On common sun decks & at the swimming hole.
Nudity: Permitted at swimming hole.
Smoking: Permitted outside or on covered porch only, not inside building or rooms.
Pets: Not permitted.
Handicap Access: Yes. Ramp to 1st floor guest room & fully accessible bathroom.
Children: Well-behaved children over 8 are welcome. Younger children by permission only.
Languages: English, some French.
Your Host: Scott & Vince.

Devilstone Oceanfront Inn

Gay/Lesbian ♀♂

On the Famous Bar Harbor Shorepath, Yet Only a Block from Town

An early neighbor of the Rockefellers and Pulitzers, *Devilstone* was one of the original estates built on the shorepath in 1885, with unusual romantic gardens flowing to the ocean's edge on nearly two acres. Located on Mt. Desert Island, Bar Harbor and Acadia National Park (ANP is five minutes from us) offer biking, golfing, kayaking, sailing, hiking, climbing, whalewatching cruises, etc. Movies and nearly 75 restaurants are all a short walk from the inn. Very quiet, peaceful and beautifully designed, *Devilstone* is the perfect place to relax.

Address: PO Box 801, Bar Harbor, ME 04609
Tel: (207) 288-2933, **Fax:** (207) 288-4388.
E-mail: devilrock@aol.com

Type: Inn.
Clientele: Mostly gay & lesbian with some straight clientele.
Transportation: Car is best.
Rooms: 6 rooms with queen or king beds.
Bathrooms: 6 private bath/tub/shower/toilets.
Meals: Expanded continental breakfast.
Vegetarian: Many restaurants nearby.
Complimentary: Afternoon tea, coffee, cocktail set ups, munchies, mints on pillows.
Dates Open: May 15-October 15.
High Season: Summer.
Rates: $95-$295 per night.
Discounts: On stays of 1 week or more.
Credit Cards: MC, VISA.
Rsv'tns: Required.
To Reserve: Call direct.
Minimum Stay: Please inquire.
Parking: Ample free off-street parking.
In-Room: Beautiful sitting areas, maid service. AC in some rooms.
On-Premises: The beautiful shorepath & ponds.
Exercise/Health: Horseshoes, weights, Jacuzzi. Nearby gym, weights.
Swimming: Ocean on premises. Nearby lake.
Sunbathing: On common sun decks, beach, patio.
Smoking: No smoking.
Pets: Not permitted.
Handicap Access: No.
Children: No.
Languages: English.

IGLTA

Lindenwood Inn
Gay-Friendly

A Quiet Place by the Harbor

Built at the turn of the century, **Lindenwood Inn** derives its name from the stately linden trees that still line the front lawn now, as they did then. Recently remodeled, each room is individually decorated and has a private bath. The inn is filled with an eclectic mix of art and furnishings gathered by the host in his travels. Many rooms feature harbor views from sun-drenched balconies. Relax and unwind in one of the inn's elegant sitting rooms, or on the large, shaded porch, while listening to the sounds of the harbor just a few steps away.

Address: Box 1328, Clark Point Rd, Southwest Harbor, ME 04679
Tel: (207) 244-5335.

Type: Inn.
Clientele: Mostly straight clientele with a gay & lesbian following
Transportation: Car is best.
To Gay Bars: 40 miles or 1 hour by car.
Rooms: 15 rooms, 5 suites & 3 cottages with double or queen beds.
Bathrooms: All private & 3 housekeeping cottages.
Meals: Full breakfast.
Vegetarian: Available upon request.
Complimentary: Tea, coffee & setup service.
Dates Open: Apr-Dec.
High Season: Jul-Oct.
Rates: Jul-Sept: $95-$225; Sept-Oct 15: $85-$195; Oct 16-June 15: $75-$175.
Credit Cards: MC, Visa, Discover.
Rsv'tns: Suggested in the summer.
To Reserve: Call direct.
Minimum Stay: Summer & holidays.
Parking: Ample free off-street parking.
In-Room: Ceiling fans & maid service. Some rooms with fireplaces, TV or balconies.
On-Premises: Meeting room, sitting rooms with fireplaces, balconies, private access to water.
Exercise/Health: Hot tub. Nearby gym, weights, Jacuzzi/spa, sauna, steam & massage.
Swimming: In-ground heated pool on premises. Nearby ocean, river & lake.
Sunbathing: On private sun decks & on nearby beach.
Nudity: Nude beach nearby.
Smoking: Permitted on porches only.
Pets: Not permitted.
Handicap Access: No.
Children: Not especially welcomed.
Languages: English.

Manor House Inn
Gay-Friendly

Bar Harbor's Historic Victorian Inn

The moment you step into the front entry, a romantic Victorian past becomes the present. Our elegant common rooms are decorated with antiques, Victorian wallcoverings, original maple floors and several working fireplaces. Our in-town location on tree-lined West St. lets you enjoy privacy, while staying within easy walking distance of Bar Harbor's fine shops, restaurants, whale watching, schooner rides, bike rentals, and even Bar Island. The spacious suites at **Manor House Inn** are graciously furnished, have working fireplaces, private baths, garden views and king-sized beds.

Address: 106 West St, Bar Harbor, ME 04609
Tel: (207) 288-3759, (800) 437-0088, **Fax:** (207) 288-2974.

continued next page

Type: Bed & breakfast.
Clientele: Mostly straight clientele with a gay/lesbian following.
Transportation: Car is best.
Rooms: 9 rooms & 5 suites with queen or king beds.
Bathrooms: All private baths.
Meals: Full breakfast.
Complimentary: Tea, coffee, lemonade, iced tea & apple cider in season.
Dates Open: May through Oct.
High Season: July-Oct.
Rates: Seasonal $89-175, off season $55-$135.
Credit Cards: MC, Visa.
Rsv'tns: Highly recommended as early as possible.
To Reserve: Call direct.
Minimum Stay: 2 nights July & Aug & holiday weekends.
Parking: Adequate on-street & off-street parking.
In-Room: Maid service. Some rooms have fireplaces, cottages have color cable TV.
On-Premises: TV lounge, veranda & gardens.
Swimming: Beaches at the ocean or nearby lakes.
Sunbathing: On the beach.
Smoking: Not permitted.
Pets: Not permitted.
Children: Permitted (12 years and up).
Languages: English.

Alden House Bed & Breakfast
Q-NET Gay-Owned 50/50 ♀♂

One of the Top Five Culturally Cool Towns in the U.S.

Come to the coast and enjoy an authentic, affordable New England community. The Alden House (c. 1840), located in the heart of the historic district, is graced with a hand-carved cherry staircase and mantel, several marble fireplaces, German silver hardware, a curved pocket door, formal parlors and library. The town has lovely shops, art galleries and restaurants and was named by *USA Today* as one of the top five "culturally cool" towns in the U.S. Activities abound, including antiquing, skiing, biking, hiking, kayaking, the theatre, cruises and train excursions. Commitment ceremonies are welcomed.

Address: 63 Church St, Belfast, ME 04915 **Tel:** (207) 338-2151.
E-mail: Alden@agate.net **URL:** www.bbonline.com/me/alden

Type: Gay-owned & -operated bed & breakfast.
Clientele: 50% gay & lesbian & 50% straight clientele
Transportation: Car, or air to Bangor or Portland, ME.
To Gay Bars: 37 miles, a 40 min drive.
Rooms: 7 rooms with single, double or queen beds.
Bathrooms: 5 private shower/toilets, 2 shared bath/shower/toilets.
Meals: Full breakfast.
Vegetarian: Available upon request, with notice.
Complimentary: Coffee, tea, lemonade, sherry, mid-afternoon snack.
Dates Open: All year.
High Season: July-beginning of October.
Rates: $65-$95.
Discounts: Extended stay discounts.
Credit Cards: MC, Visa, Amex.
To Reserve: Call direct.
Parking: Ample off-street parking.
In-Room: VCR, maid service.
On-Premises: Video tape library.
Exercise/Health: Massage. Nearby gym, weights, Jacuzzi, sauna.
Swimming: Nearby pool & ocean.
Smoking: Permitted on outside porches only.
Pets: Not permitted.
Handicap Access: No. First-floor room has some accessibility.
Children: No.
Languages: English.
Your Host: Jessica & Marla.

The Black Duck Inn on Corea Harbor
Q-NET Gay-Friendly ♀♂

Explore the Real Downeast!

Retreat from the hassles of daily city life on 12 acres in a tranquil, Downeast fishing village. The land is full of rock outcrops (to sit, read, paint, or birdwatch), wild berries, hidden tidal bays, and salt marshes. From *The Black Duck Inn,* enjoy the sight of one of the most picturesque harbors in Maine. The inn is only a few miles from the Schoodic section of Acadia National Park and is close to other wildlife sanctuaries, a fresh water pond, sand beaches, public golf courses, antique shops, and restaurants.

Address: PO Box 39, Crowley Island Rd, Corea, ME 04624
Tel: (207) 963-2689, **Fax:** (207) 963-7495.
E-mail: bduck@acadia.net **URL:** www.blackduck.com

Type: Bed & breakfast.
Clientele: Mostly straight clientele with a gay/lesbian following.
Transportation: Car is best. Free pick up from boat into harbor.
To Gay Bars: 50 miles.
Rooms: 3 rooms, 1 suite, 2 cottages with single, double or queen beds.
Bathrooms: Private: 3 shower/toilets, 1 bath/shower/toilet. 1 shared bath/shower/toilet.
Meals: Full breakfast.
Vegetarian: Vegan by advance request, otherwise fully available. Restaurants nearby in season.
Complimentary: Early coffee (6:30 am).
Dates Open: All year.
High Season: July-September.
Rates: Winter $65-$95, summer $75-$135.
Discounts: On weekly & monthly cottage rentals, without breakfast.
Credit Cards: MC, Visa.
To Reserve: Travel agent or call direct.
Minimum Stay: 3 nights to 1 week in cottages.
Parking: Ample free off-street parking.
In-Room: Maid service.
On-Premises: Meeting rooms, TV lounge, VCR, library, fireplaces, fax.
Exercise/Health: Walking trails on premises.
Swimming: Ocean, nearby lake.
Sunbathing: On patio, at beach.
Smoking: No smoking in house or cottages.
Pets: Not permitted.
Handicap Access: No.
Children: Please inquire.
Languages: English, Danish.
Your Host: Barry & Bob.

Arundel Meadows Inn
Gay-Friendly

A Relaxing Getaway With a Four-Star Breakfast!

Small and personal, this nineteenth-century farmhouse has rooms and suites decorated in art and antiques, with private bathrooms and summer air conditioning. Three rooms have working fireplaces and all have comfortable sitting areas for reading and relaxing. Nearby Kennebunkport has antiques, artists' studios and excellent restaurants. Golf, tennis, fishing and cross-country skiing are readily accessible. At *Arundel Meadows Inn,* guests enjoy spring picnic meadows, summer flower gardens, fall foliage and winter fires in the living room.

Address: PO Box 1129, Kennebunk, ME 04043-1129
Tel: (207) 985-3770.
URL: http://www.biddeford.com/arundel_meadows_inn

Type: Bed & breakfast.
Clientele: Mostly straight clientele, with gays & lesbians welcome.
Transportation: Car is best.
To Gay Bars: 10 miles to Ogunquit, ME, 25 miles to Portland, ME gay bars.
Rooms: Five rooms and two suites with single, double, queen and king beds.
Bathrooms: All private.
Meals: Full breakfast.
Vegetarian: Available upon request.
Complimentary: Afternoon tea.
Dates Open: All year (subject to change).
High Season: Memorial Day through Columbus Day.
Rates: Summer $75-$125, winter $55-$85.
Discounts: 10% on 5 nights or more.
Credit Cards: MC & VISA.
Rsv'tns: Required.
To Reserve: Call direct.
Minimum Stay: 2 days on weekends Memorial Day through Columbus Day.
Parking: Adequate free off-street parking.
In-Room: AC & maid service. 3 rooms have color TV.
Swimming: Ocean beach is nearby.
Sunbathing: At the beach, on the patio, 2 rooms with private sun decks.
Smoking: Not permitted.
Pets: Not permitted.
Handicap Access: Yes.
Children: Not permitted under 12 years of age.
Languages: English.

Lamb's Mill Inn
Q-NET Gay-Friendly

Ewe Hike, Ewe Bike, Ewe Ski, Ewe ZZzzz...

Lamb's Mill Inn is a small country inn nestled among the foothills of the White Mountains in the picturesque village of Naples. Surrounded by two of Maine's largest lakes, Sebago and Long

continued next page

INN PLACES® 1998

Lake, Naples is the hub of summertime water activities in this area. Winter brings cross-country and alpine skiers, snowmobilers and ice fishermen. The spectacular fall foliage invites hikers and bikers to hit the trails. In spring, canoeing the Saco River and nearby ponds is a popular pastime. The inn is a 19th-century farmhouse, newly renovated and abounding with country charm.

Our six rooms offer a romantic atmosphere and feature private baths. You will awaken to the aroma of a full country breakfast served in our two gracious dining rooms. Enjoy the privacy and scenic beauty of twenty acres of field and woods, or a leisurely stroll to the charming village. Browse along the causeway and discover parasailing, aerial sightseeing, watercycling, windsurfing and tours on the Songo River Queen. Play golf and tennis, or visit the many country fairs and flea markets. Dine in gourmet restaurants, or sample local Yankee recipes in small cafes and diners. To end an exciting day, unwind in our hot tub. All this and more is yours at *Lamb's Mill Inn*, an inn for all seasons.

Address: Box 676, Lamb's Mill Rd, Naples, ME 04055 **Tel:** (207) 693-6253.

Type: Bed & breakfast inn.
Clientele: Large gay & lesbian clientele.
Transportation: Car from Portland airport 25 miles away.
To Gay Bars: 25 miles to Portland gay/lesbian bars.
Rooms: 6 rooms with 1 king, 4 queens, 1 full bed.
Bathrooms: All private.
Meals: Full gourmet breakfast.
Vegetarian: Yes.
Complimentary: Ice & munchies available in afternoon as well as tea & coffee.
Dates Open: All year.
High Season: Summer & for fall foliage.
Rates: High peak (May 16-Labor Day) $85-$105; Peak (Sept-Dec 31) $75-$95; Low (Jan-May 15) $65-$85.
Discounts: Sixth consecutive night free. 15% midweek (Mon-Thurs) for 3 night stay.
Credit Cards: MC & VISA.
Rsv'tns: Recommended.
To Reserve: Travel agent or call direct.
Minimum Stay: Two nights on weekends in high season.
Parking: Ample free off-street parking.
In-Room: Color cable TV, maid service, refrigerators.
On-Premises: 2 private dining rooms, 2 TV lounges, stereo, BBQ's, 1 reading & game lounge.
Exercise/Health: Hot tub, treadmill, canoeing, windsurfing, parasailing, boat rides, water cycling, trails, downhill skiing, bicycling.
Swimming: Town beach is at the bottom of our hill on Long Lake.
Sunbathing: On patio, private sun decks or anywhere on 20 acres.
Smoking: Permitted outside.
Pets: Not permitted.
Handicap Access: No.
Children: Not permitted.
Languages: English.

IGLTA

Admiral's Inn & Guesthouse

Q-NET Gay-Owned ♀♂

SEE SPECIAL PAGE 23 COLOR SECTION

Unique in Ogunquit...

The Admiral's Inn is located 65 miles north of Boston in Ogunquit, Maine. Our spacious grounds are within walking distance of the beach and all other village pleasures, and the privacy of our backyard pool is perfect for enjoying a morning or late-night swim, or a quiet afternoon retreat. We are unique in that we offer not only traditional guesthouse accommodations, but also efficiency and motel rooms with refrigerators and private baths. All rooms are air-conditioned and have electic heat and television. *Admiral's Inn* is gay-owned and -operated.

Address: #70 US Rt. 1, PO Box 2241, Ogunquit, ME 03907 Tel: (207) 646-7093.

Type: Bed & breakfast guesthouse & motel.
Clientele: Mostly gay & lesbian clientele. Straight-friendly
Transportation: Car is best.
To Gay Bars: 1/4 mile (a 5 min walk) to men's/women's bars.
Rooms: 3 doubles, 5 efficiencies, 1 apartment, 5 quads.
Bathrooms: 9 private, 8 shared.
Campsites: 6 RV parking (electric & water hookups only), 6 tent spaces.
Meals: Continental breakfast for rooms in guesthouse.
Vegetarian: 1/2 mile to vegetarian restaurant.
Complimentary: Morning coffee.
Dates Open: All year.
High Season: Mid-June thru mid-Sept.
Rates: Summer $45-$108, winter $35-$65.
Credit Cards: MC, Visa, Amex, Discover.
Rsv'tns: Strongly recommended during high season.
To Reserve: Call direct.
Minimum Stay: 2 nights during summer, 3 nights on holidays.
Parking: Ample, free parking, 2 lots on property.
In-Room: Color TV, AC, maid service, some with kitchen, refrigerator.
On-Premises: TV lounge, laundry facilities.
Exercise/Health: Nearby gym, weights, Jacuzzi, sauna, massage.
Swimming: Outdoor pool on premises. 10 min walk to beach.
Sunbathing: At poolside or on the beach.
Nudity: At guest discretion.
Smoking: Permitted outside.
Pets: Not permitted.
Handicap Access: Yes, 2 rooms.
Children: Not encouraged.
Languages: English.
Your Host: David & Garry.

Beauport Inn and Cafe

Gay-Friendly 50/50 ♀♂

Comfortable Elegance

The *Beauport Inn* is a cozy, expanded cape-style home with an attached gourmet cafe. Located on Shore Road on the trolley line, approximately halfway between town center and Perkins Cove, our inn provides a quiet location within easy walking distance to shops, restaurants, the beach, the Playhouse and the Marginal Way walking path. Relax in our pine-panelled living room with piano and fireplace, our comfortable TV area or on our deck overlooking the gardens. Breakfast is served in the dining room or may be enjoyed on the deck.

Address: PO Box 1793, 102 Shore Rd, Ogunquit, ME 03907
Tel: (800) 646-8681, (207) 646-8680.
E-mail: lobster@cybertours.com URL: www.ogun-online.com\beauport

Type: Bed & breakfast with gourmet cafe.
Clientele: 50% gay & lesbian & 50% straight clientele.
Transportation: Car is best.
To Gay Bars: 1/2 mile. A 10-minute walk or 3-minute drive.
Rooms: 6 rooms with twin or queen beds.
Bathrooms: All private.
Meals: Expanded continental breakfast.
Vegetarian: At nearby restaurants.
Dates Open: March 1-Dec 15.
High Season: Jul-Aug.
Rates: Summer $95. Fall & spring $65-$75.
Discounts: 10% for weekly stays.
Credit Cards: MC, Visa.
Rsv'tns: Required.
To Reserve: Call direct.
Minimum Stay: Required.
Parking: Adequate free off-street parking.
In-Room: AC & maid service. 2 rooms have private balconies.
On-Premises: TV lounge.
Exercise/Health: Nearby gym, massage & golf.
Swimming: Nearby ocean.
Sunbathing: On common sun decks & at the beach.
Smoking: Permitted outside only. Entire house is non-smoking.
Pets: Not permitted.
Handicap Access: Cafe is accessible.
Children: Welcome over 10 years of age.
Languages: English, Spanish.

Heritage of Ogunquit

Q-NET Women ♀

"Beautiful Place by the Sea"

Heritage of Ogunquit is a Victorian reproduction in a quiet area which is just an eight-minute walk to the beach, cove and the fabulous Marginal Way floral footpath along the ocean's edge. *The Heritage* features a hot tub, giant cedar deck,

continued next page

INN PLACES® 1998

sitting room with TV and VCR, refrigerator and microwave. Expanded continental breakfast is served overlooking perennial gardens and five acres of woods. Check out the new "kd Lang Loft" occupying the entire third floor, with private entry, deck and more! Lesbian-owned and -operated.

Address: PO Box 1295, Ogunquit, ME 03907 **Tel:** (207) 646-7787.
E-mail: heritageo@cybertours.com
URL: http://www.one-on-onepc.com/heritage

Type: Bed & breakfast.
Clientele: 99% women with gay men welcome
Transportation: Car. Pick up from airport in Portland, ME, $30 roundtrip, from bus in Portsmouth, NH, $25 roundtrip.
To Gay Bars: 5 min walk.
Rooms: 5 rooms with queen beds. 1 room has additional single bed & 2 have double futons.
Bathrooms: 3 private bath/ toilets & 2 rooms share.
Meals: Expanded continental breakfast.
Vegetarian: Nearby restaurant.
Dates Open: All year.
High Season: Jul-Aug.
Rates: $55-$115.
Discounts: Weekly, & weekdays off season.
Credit Cards: MC, Visa.
Rsv'tns: Required.
To Reserve: Call direct.
Minimum Stay: 2 nights on weekends & 3 nights on holiday weekends.
Parking: Ample free off-street parking.
In-Room: Ceiling fans. Loft has AC, microwave, refrigerator, TV, VCR, toaster oven, sitting area. Maid service on request.
On-Premises: Common room with TV, VCR, refrigerator, microwave, toaster oven.
Exercise/Health: Hot tub & mini exercise area with treadmill, free weights & other equipment.
Swimming: 5 min walk to ocean.
Sunbathing: On common sun decks & at the beach.
Smoking: Not permitted indoors.
Pets: Not permitted.
Handicap Access: No.
Children: Welcome.
Languages: English, limited German & Spanish.

THE INN at Two Village Square   Gay/Lesbian ♀♂

Ogunquit, Maine —The Quiet Alternative

Overlooking Ogunquit Square and the Atlantic Ocean, THE INN is an 1886 Victorian home perched on a hillside amidst towering trees. Our heated pool, hot tub and extensive decks provide views far to sea. Our atmoshpere is congenial and relaxed. Deluxe continental breakfast is served in our wicker-filled dining room, and guest rooms have color TV, ceiling fans and air conditioning. You are invited to join our Saturday get-acquainted party, Tuesday poolside barbeque and reserved seating at Ogunquit's Playhouse. Make our "home on the hill" YOUR home in Ogunquit.

Address: 135 US Rte 1, PO Box 864, Ogunquit, ME 03907
Tel: (207) 646-5779, **Fax:** (207) 646-6797.
E-mail: theinntvs@aol.com **URL:** http://www.q-net/theinntvs

Type: Bed & breakfast inn.
Clientele: Good mix of gays & lesbians
Transportation: Car. Free pick up from airport limo or bus in Portsmouth NH.
To Gay Bars: 2-minute walk to gay & lesbian dance bar & piano bar.
Rooms: 18 rooms with double, queen or king beds.
Bathrooms: Private: 14 full baths, 3 sinks. Shared: 1 full bath, 2 toilets.
Meals: Expanded continental breakfast.
Complimentary: Tea/coffee in guest kitchen. In season: Tues pm BBQ; Sat nite get-acquainted party (also holidays).
Dates Open: May-Columbus Day.
High Season: Late June-Labor Day.
Rates: In season $75-$130. Spring & fall $50-$75.

FERRARI GUIDES™

Discounts: Ask about spring & fall specials.
Credit Cards: MC, Visa, Amex, Discover. Debit cards.
Rsv'tns: Strongly recommended in season.
To Reserve: Call direct.
Minimum Stay: On holidays and in season. Short stays as space permits.
Parking: Ample free off-street parking.
In-Room: Color TV, AC, ceiling fans & maid service.
On-Premises: Common sitting rooms, TV lounge, public telephone, & piano. Shared guest kitchen with refrigerator for cold food preparation & serving.
Exercise/Health: Hot tub & bicycles. Massage nearby. Free guest membership in local gym.
Swimming: Heated pool on premises. Gay section of beach a short walk away.
Sunbathing: On poolside deck, sun deck, or nearby public beach.
Smoking: Permitted in outdoor areas.
Pets: Not permitted (facilities for cats & dogs nearby).
Handicap Access: Minimal accessibility.
Languages: English.
Your Host: Bob & Jeff.

Leisure Inn

Gay-Friendly 50/50 ♀♂

The Warm Feelings of Grandmother's House

Capture the feel of coastal village life in Ogunquit, a picturesque resort town by the sea. *Leisure Inn* is traditionally Maine, with uniquely-decorated guest rooms reflecting all the charm of old New England. In summer, there's plenty of fun in the sun, but have you ever known the sensation of walking the beach after the first snow of autumn? Everything in Ogunquit is within walking distance, from fine restaurants, to quaint and interesting shops. We're only a five-minute walk from the beach.

Address: 6 School St, PO Box 2113, Ogunquit, ME 03907
Tel: (207) 646-2737, Fax: (207) 646-2471.
E-mail: ReySaint@aol.com URL: http://members.aol.com/reysaint

Type: Bed & breakfast guesthouse, cottages, apts.
Clientele: 50% gay & lesbian & 50% straight clientele.
Transportation: Car is best.
Rooms: 12 rooms, 3 apartments & 3 cottages with double & queen beds.
Bathrooms: 12 private, others share.
Meals: Continental breakfast.
Dates Open: May-Oct.
Rates: $58-$89.
Credit Cards: MC, Visa.
Rsv'tns: Preferred (and advised for July & Aug).
To Reserve: Call direct.
Minimum Stay: Two days on weekends, 3 on summer holiday weekends.
Parking: Ample, free off-street parking.
In-Room: Room service, most have color TV, AC, some kitchens.
On-Premises: Meeting rooms.
Exercise/Health: Inquire.
Swimming: Short walk to ocean beach.
Sunbathing: At beach, on patio.
Pets: Not permitted.
Languages: English, French.

Moon Over Maine

Gay/Lesbian ♀♂

Tranquility and Romance Await You

Moon Over Maine, built in 1839, has been beautifully restored. Many rooms feature original New England pine floors and gabled ceilings and most have direct access to the multilevel deck, overlooking a wooded yard. It will take you two minutes to walk to Ogunquit's gay nightlife and five minutes to walk to the beach. Spend a relaxing day at the beach and a quiet evening with us. Gaze at the moon as you sit in the hot tub or simply relax with someone you love.

Address: PO Box 1478, 6 Berwick Rd, Ogunquit, ME 03907
Tel: (207) 646-MOON (6666), (800) 851-6837.
E-mail: MoonMaine@aol.com

Type: Bed & breakfast.
Clientele: Mostly gay & lesbian with some straight clientele.
Transportation: Car is best.
To Gay Bars: 1 block to The Club or The Front Porch.
Rooms: 9 rooms with queen beds.
Bathrooms: All private shower/toilets.
Meals: Expanded continental breakfast.
Vegetarian: Breakfast is vegetarian. Most local restaurants have vegetarian entrees.
Complimentary: Soft drinks, candy.

continued next page

Dates Open: April-November.	**Credit Cards:** MC, Visa, Discover.	**In-Room:** Color cable TV, AC, maid service.	sun decks & at beach. **Smoking:** Permitted outside only.
High Season: June-August.	**To Reserve:** Travel agent or call direct.	**Exercise/Health:** Jacuzzi. Nearby gym, weights, massage.	**Pets:** Not permitted. **Handicap Access:** No.
Rates: Summer $69-$120, winter $49-$79.	**Minimum Stay:** July-August: 2 nights on weekends.	**Swimming:** Ocean nearby.	**Children:** No. **Languages:** English.
Discounts: Discounts on weekly stays.	**Parking:** Adequate free off-street parking.	**Sunbathing:** On common	**Your Host:** John.

Ogunquit Beach Inn

Gay-Owned & -Operated ♀♂

Ogunquit's Newest Gay Inn

Ogunquit Beach Inn is unique in offering not only a fine selection of traditional guesthouse accommodations, but also cottages and a three-bedroom carriage house. Our guestrooms feature cable TV and are furnished with an attractive, Main seacoast decor. Our comfortable parlor and library is a perfect place to read or meet new friends. We're a five-minute walk to the white sands of Ogunquit Beach, one of the top-rated beaches in the United States. We're also quite close to Ogunquit's bars, dining and theater. An Indian word meaning "beautiful place by the sea, *Ogunquit* lives up to its name.

Address: 8 School St, Box 1803, Ogunquit, ME 03907
Tel: (207) 646-1112, (888) 97-MAINE (62463), **Fax:** (207) 646-4724.

Type: Bed & breakfast, guesthouse, cottage, inn.	shower/toilets, 3 shared bath/shower/toilets.	stays & mid-week specials. **Credit Cards:** MC, Visa.	gym, weights, massage. **Swimming:** Ocean nearby.
Clientele: Gay & lesbian. Good mix of men & women	**Meals:** Expanded continental breakfast.	**Rsv'tns:** Required. **Minimum Stay:** 2 nights on	**Sunbathing:** On patio & at beach.
Transportation: Car is best.	**Vegetarian:** Available at 3 nearby restaurants.	weekends, 3 nights on holidays.	**Smoking:** Permitted outside.
To Gay Bars: 2 blocks, a 3 min walk. Near Front Porch, across street from Hooch & Holly's.	**Complimentary:** Soft drinks, soda, fruit. **Dates Open:** All year, except Jan.	**Parking:** Adequate free off-street parking. **In-Room:** Color cable TV, maid service.	**Pets:** Permitted in 1 cottage only, facility nearby for dogs & cats. **Children:** Welcome in cottages.
Rooms: 7 rooms, 1 apartment & 2 cottages with double or queen beds.	**High Season:** Jun-Aug (Memorial Day-Labor Day). **Rates:** $45-$110.	**On-Premises:** TV lounge, video tape library. Outside beach shower.	**Languages:** English. **Your Host:** Michael & Gregory.
Bathrooms: 5 private bath/	**Discounts:** Call on weekly	**Exercise/Health:** Nearby	

Ogunquit House

Gay-Friendly 50/50 ♀♂

Originally a schoolhouse in 1880, *Ogunquit House* is now a tastefully-restored bed and breakfast in a country setting at the edge of town. We offer a clean, comfortable, reasonably-priced vacation spot. Guest rooms are spacious, with both private and shared baths. Beach, restaurants, shops, movies and art galleries are all within walking distance. Ogunquit's trolley stops almost at your door to bring you to the Marginal Way, Perkins Cove and The Playhouse.

Address: 3 Glen Ave, Box 1883, Ogunquit, ME 03907 **Tel:** (207) 646-2967.

Type: Bed & breakfast & cottages.	men's/women's bars. **Rooms:** 6 rooms & 4 cottages with single, queen or king beds.	**Vegetarian:** Three nearby restaurants offer vegetarian food.	**Credit Cards:** MC, Visa, Discover.
Clientele: 50% gay & lesbian & 50% straight clientele.			**Rsv'tns:** Recommended.
		Dates Open: Mar 15-Jan 2.	**To Reserve:** Call direct.
Transportation: Car is best.	**Bathrooms:** 8 private, others share.	**High Season:** July through August.	**Minimum Stay:** Summer 2 nights, holidays 3 nights.
To Gay Bars: 2 blocks to	**Meals:** Continental breakfast.	**Rates:** $59-$135 summer, $45-$70 winter.	**Parking:** Ample free off-street parking.

In-Room: Maid service, AC, some have kitchen or refrigerator and color cable TV.
On-Premises: TV lounge.
Swimming: 5-minute walk to ocean beach.
Sunbathing: On beach, patio, or private sun decks.
Smoking: Permitted with restrictions.
Pets: Permitted with restrictions in the cottages.
Handicap Access: No.
Children: Permitted in cottages, over 12 only in the inn.
Languages: English.

Yellow Birch Farm
Gay/Lesbian ♀

An Organic Farm in Downeast Maine

Yellow Birch Farm is a working farm on a peninsula, near wild, unspoiled Cobscook Bay, 20 minutes from historic Eastport and half an hour from New Brunswick, Canada. The area is a nature lover's paradise of particular interest to birdwatchers, hikers and kayakers. In this scenic, serene setting, we raise livestock and organic vegetables. Our seasonal, two-room guest cottage has a full kitchen, woodstove, outdoor hot shower, and outhouse. The spacious, year-round studio features a woodstove, skylights, private entrance, cooking facilities and a full bath.

Address: Young's Cove Road, Pembroke, ME 04666
Tel: (207) 726-5807. **E-mail:** yellowbirchfarm@nemaine.com

Type: B&B or weekly rental in a cottage or large studio.
Clientele: Mostly women with men welcome
Transportation: Car is best.
To Gay Bars: 2-1/2 hours to Bangor.
Rooms: One cottage with bunk beds & queen futon & 1 large studio with queen bed.
Bathrooms: 1 private bath/toilet & 1 private outhouse & outdoor hot shower.
Meals: Expanded continental breakfast.
Vegetarian: Organically raised vegetables available from the farm.
Dates Open: Studio, all year. Cottage, May-Oct.
Rates: $55 double, $15 each additional person.
Discounts: Housekeeping basis. $300 wk double occupancy, $50 per additional guest.
Rsv'tns: Required.
To Reserve: Travel agent or call direct.
Parking: Ample parking.
In-Room: Studio has cooking facilities, color TV & ceiling fan. Cottage has full kitchen.
Swimming: Nearby lakes.
Nudity: Permitted anywhere.
Smoking: Permitted outside.
Pets: Not permitted.
Handicap Access: No.
Children: Please inquire.
Languages: English & French.
Your Host: Bunny.

Parkside Parrot Inn
Lesbian-Owned & -Operated ♀♂

Park Yourself Here at the Parkside Parrot Inn

One block from Portland's most beautiful park and four blocks from the edge of the downtown district, the *Parkside Parrot Inn* offers gay and lesbian travelers a comfortable place to stay in the heart of Portland's most diverse neighborhood. Our 100-year-old home is furnished with country antiques and retains many of its original features. Expanded continental breakfast is served in our beautiful common room, with abundant natural light streaming through the front bay window. It's easy walking distance to L.L. Bean's Factory Store, quaint waterfront shops, fine restaurants, two gay/lesbian bars, and the city's only gay/lesbian gift- & bookstore.

Address: 273 State Street, Portland, ME 04101 **Tel:** (207) 775-0224.

continued next page

Type: Bed & breakast. **Clientele:** Mostly gay & lesbian with some straight clientele **Transportation:** Car is best (1/2 mi from hwy), 5 mi from airport by taxi. Free pickup from airport (weekends only) or bus. **To Gay Bars:** 4 blocks, 1/4 mi, a 5 min walk, a 1 min drive. **Rooms:** 3 rooms with double or queen beds.	**Bathrooms:** 1 private & 1 shared bath/shower/toilet. **Meals:** Expanded continental breakfast. **Vegetarian:** Breakfast foods are vegetarian. Several restaurants nearby serve veg. selections. **Complimentary:** Fruit basket in afternoon in common room. **Dates Open:** All year. **High Season:** May-Sept. **Rates:** $65-$80.	**Discounts:** Weekly discount. **Credit Cards:** MC, Visa. **Rsv'tns:** Required. **To Reserve:** Call direct. **Minimum Stay:** 2 nights on holiday weekends. **Parking:** Adequate free off-street parking. **In-Room:** Maid service. **On-Premises:** TV lounge, video tape library, backyard patio & garden.	**Exercise/Health:** Jacuzzi (for a small fee). Nearby gym, weights, Jacuzzi . **Swimming:** Nearby ocean & lake. **Sunbathing:** On patio. **Smoking:** Permitted in outside designated areas only. **Pets:** Not permitted. **Handicap Access:** No. **Children:** No. **Languages:** English. **Your Host:** Julie & Joan.

The Vicarage by the Sea

Q-NET Lesbian-Owned 50/50 ♀♂

A Piece of Paradise!

The Vicarage by the Sea is a traditional bed and breakfast located on beautiful and private Curtis Cove, where guests can take long, tranquil walks along the stunning Atlantic Ocean, and experience spectacular sunsets and extraordinary star gazing. Come to the beauty of Harpswell and share in the serenity of our bed and breakfast. Surrounded by trees filled with various species of birds, one can sit and listen to the ocean as it caresses the shore. Perhaps you wish to embrace an "authentic" Maine experience by letting us show you how to harvest and prepare mussels or clams. At your request, you may order the "Johanna Special," consisting of a lobster, steamers and shrimp cocktail. We're only five minutes from fine dining, where the most delectable seafood one could ever imagine, much less acquire, awaits you: Maine lobster, fish and shellfish fresh off the boat at low prices. Local boat excursions take you to Admiral Perry's famous Eagle Island, as well as let you witness the grace of the friendly seals.

Inside, *The Vicarage* is decorated with wonderful artwork representing the diverse, artistic capabilities of local artists and is as stunning as its natural surroundings. Sit and relax in the lovely sun room or curl up on the couch and enjoy a good book. We're located thirty minutes from the famous L.L. Bean store and forty minutes from the growing city of Portland, where you will find fine dining, art galleries, and plenty of performing arts. Portland also boasts a fabulous nightlife! *The Vicarage* reflects a simple lifestyle which seeks to live in harmony with the beauty of its surroundings. There are gentle pets, including four resident greyhounds. We invite you to savor our hospitality. Many have said, "The Vicarage truly is a piece of paradise!"

Address: PO Box 368B, Harpswell, ME 04079
Tel: (207) 833-5480 (Tel/Fax). **E-mail:** jmoulton@biddeford.com

Type: Bed & breakfast.
Clientele: 50% gay & lesbian & 50% straight clientele
Transportation: Car is best.
To Gay Bars: A 40 min drive.
Rooms: 3 rooms, 1 suite with single, double or queen beds.
Bathrooms: Private: 1 bath/shower/toilet, 1 shower/toilet. Shared: 1 bath/shower/toilet.
Meals: Full breakfast.
Vegetarian: Vegetarian breakfast on request, owners are vegetarians.
Dates Open: Closed in Feb.
High Season: Jul-Aug.
Rates: Summer $65-$120, winter $45-$100.
Credit Cards: MC, Visa.
Rsv'tns: Required.
To Reserve: Call direct.
Parking: Adequate free parking.
In-Room: Ceiling fans, color TV, VCR, coffee & tea-making facilities.
On-Premises: TV lounge.
Exercise/Health: Canoe rental & kayak accessibility. Nearby gym, weights, Jacuzzi, sauna, steam, massage, tennis, boat cruises & kayak rental.
Swimming: Ocean on premises.
Sunbathing: At beach.
Smoking: Permitted outside. All rooms are non-smoking.
Pets: Well-mannered pets permitted.
Handicap Access: Yes, wide doors.
Children: Welcome.
Languages: English.
Your Host: Johanna & Cheryl.

Wiscasset Place
Gay-Owned 50/50 ♀♂

A Harborside B&B in One of Maine's Best-Known Coastal Villages

Wiscasset Place, an elegant 1927 Colonial Revival home, was built by a local shipbuilder who specialized in the construction of luxury yachts. Our three guest rooms each have a private, full bath, air conditioning, cable television and telephone — unique qualities for B&Bs in the mid-coast region. Two of the rooms boast expansive water views. Guests may make full use of two living rooms (each with a fireplace), a dining room, our solarium which overlooks Wiscasset Harbor, islands and the backcove, and our large yard noted for its collection of unusual antique roses. We're a thirty minute's drive from outlet shopping in Freeport (home of L.L. Bean), and a three hour's drive from Boston.

Address: Ten Middle Street, Box 33, Wiscasset, ME 04578-0033
Tel: (207) 882-7981. **E-mail:** wiscassetplace@clinic.net
URL: http://www.wiscassetplace.com (after Jan 15, '98)

Type: Bed & breakfast.
Clientele: 50% gay & lesbian & 50% straight clientele
Transportation: Car is best. Free pick up from Wiscasset bus station.
To Gay Bars: 24 miles, a 30 min drive.
Rooms: 3 rooms with double or queen beds.
Bathrooms: 3 private bath/shower/toilets.
Meals: Continental breakfast.
Vegetarian: Available on premises & nearby.
Complimentary: Set up service, beer & wine from 5pm-7pm.
Dates Open: All year.
High Season: Jul-Aug.
Rates: Summer $85-$115, winter $55-$75.
Discounts: Multiple day discounts on stays of over 5 days.
Credit Cards: MC, Visa.
Rsv'tns: Requested, but not required.
To Reserve: Call direct.
Parking: Ample, free off-street parking.
In-Room: Telephone, AC, color cable TV, VCR, maid service.
On-Premises: Meeting rooms, TV lounge, video tape library.
Exercise/Health: Nearby gym, weights, massage
Sunbathing: On patio.
Smoking: Permitted outside, no smoking inside.
Pets: Not permitted.
Handicap Access: No.
Children: No.
Languages: English, some French.
Your Host: Alden & Don.

William Page Inn
Gay-Friendly ♀♂

B&B Inn Close to Annapolis Naval Academy

Planning to visit the U.S. Naval Academy? Then why not stay at *The William Page Inn* in the historical district, just 50 yards from the visitor's gate of the academy. Built in 1908, this dark brown, cedar-shingle, wood-frame structure was the local Democratic party clubhouse for more than 50 years. The B&B inn is a handsomely renovated turn-of-the-century home, furnished with genuine antiques and

continued next page

INN PLACES® 1998   399

period reproductions, with a feeling of quiet, hushed, elegance, and Victorian splendor. We are a Mobil & AAA-rated approved establishment.

Address: 8 Martin St, Annapolis, MD 21401
Tel: (410) 626-1506 ext. 7, (800) 364-4160 ext. 7, **Fax:** (410) 263-4841.
E-mail: wmpageinn@aol.com

Type: Bed & breakfast.
Clientele: Mainly straight with gay & lesbian following
Transportation: Car is best. Additional charge for pick up from airport, train or bus.
To Gay Bars: 40 minutes to DC bars/Baltimore bars.
Rooms: 4 rooms & 1 suite with queen beds.
Bathrooms: 3 private bath/ toilet/showers, 2 shared

bath/shower/toilets.
Meals: Full breakfast.
Vegetarian: Available upon request.
Complimentary: Wet bar set up, complimentary sodas.
Dates Open: All year.
High Season: Mar-Nov.
Rates: $105-$200.
Discounts: Mid week, stays of 5 or more days, winter rates.

Credit Cards: MC, Visa.
Rsv'tns: Required, but walk-ins welcome.
To Reserve: Travel agent or call direct.
Minimum Stay: For special events & high season weekends.
Parking: Limited free off-street parking.
In-Room: AC, maid service. Color cable TV in suite.
Exercise/Health: Jacuzzi en suite.

Swimming: Nearby state park beach, 2 hrs to ocean beach.
Sunbathing: At nearby state park beach.
Smoking: Permitted outdoors.
Pets: Not permitted.
Handicap Access: No.
Children: Permitted if 12 yrs, or older.
Languages: English.
Your Host: Robert & Greg.

Abacrombie Badger Bed & Breakfast
Gay-Friendly 50/50 ♀♂

Elegant Lodgings in Baltimore's Cultural Center

Across the street from the Meyerhoff Symphony Hall and two blocks from the Lyric Opera House, the Theater Project, and the beginning of Baltimore's Antique Row sits *Abacrombie Badger*. Music lovers, business people, visitors, and Baltimoreans will find the 12 individually-decorated rooms in this renovated 1880's townhouse a delight. Guests are welcome to relax in the parlor or enjoy a meal at the restaurant. The B&B subscribes to the highest standards of service, comfort, and cleanliness.

Address: 58 W Biddle St, Baltimore, MD 21201 **Tel:** (410) 244-7227, **Fax:** (410) 244-8415.

Type: Bed & breakfast with restaurant & bar.
Clientele: 50% gay & lesbian & 50% straight clientele
Transportation: Car or taxi. Light rail from airport to Cultural Center stop.
To Gay Bars: 1 block, a 1 minute walk.
Rooms: 12 rooms with single & queen beds.

Bathrooms: All private.
Meals: Expanded continental breakfast.
Vegetarian: Fresh fruit & homemade bread with breakfast. Six blocks to vegetarian restaurants.
Complimentary: Chocolates.
Dates Open: All year.
High Season: March-November.

Rates: $79-$165.
Credit Cards: MC, Visa, Amex, Diners, Discover.
Rsv'tns: Required.
To Reserve: Travel agent or call direct.
Minimum Stay: 2 nights on weekends during high season.
Parking: Ample free off-street parking. Parking lot adjoins B&B.

In-Room: Color cable TV, AC, telephone, maid service.
Smoking: Permitted outdoors only.
Pets: Not permitted.
Handicap Access: No.
Children: Well-mannered children over 10 years of age welcome.
Languages: English, French, German, Dutch.
Your Host: Paul & Collin.

Mr. Mole Bed & Breakfast

Gay-Friendly ♀♂

Maryland's Only Four-Star Award B&B (1995-1997 Mobil Travel Guide)

Mr. Mole has renovated his grand 1870 Baltimore row house on historic Bolton Hill, close to downtown, Inner Harbor, the Symphony and Antique Row, to provide gracious accommodations for discriminating guests. The comfortable, English-style decor, with 18th- and 19th-century antiques, adorns five spacious suites with private phones and full baths. Two suites offer a private sitting room and two bedrooms. Garage parking, with automatic door opener, is included, as is a hearty Dutch-style breakfast of homemade bread, cake, meat, cheese and fruit.

Address: 1601 Bolton St, Baltimore, MD 21217
Tel: (410) 728-1179 or **Fax:** (410) 728-3379.

Type: Bed & breakfast.
Clientele: Mostly straight clientele with a gay & lesbian following.
Transportation: Car or taxi.
To Gay Bars: Five minutes by car to gay/lesbian bars.
Rooms: 3 rooms & 2 suites with queen beds.

Bathrooms: All private bath/toilets.
Meals: Expanded continental breakfast.
Complimentary: Chocolates.
Dates Open: All year.
High Season: Mar-Nov.
Rates: $97-$155.
Credit Cards: MC, Visa, Discover, Amex, Diners Club.
Rsv'tns: Required.
To Reserve: Travel agent or call direct.
Minimum Stay: 2 nights on weekends in high season.
Parking: Free parking in garage with automatic opener.

In-Room: Maid service, AC, telephone & clock radio.
Smoking: Permitted outdoors only.
Pets: Not permitted.
Children: Well-mannered children over 10 years welcome.
Languages: English.

Red Lamp Post

Gay/Lesbian ♀♂

We would like to welcome you to *Red Lamp Post*, our living home. Become part of the environment and enjoy the company of your host Kery. Located just 3 miles from historic downtown Cumberland, we are near antique shops, the C&O Canal, the new Allegheny Central Railroad, Early American historic sites, scenic beauty, Rocky Gap State Park, Deep Creek Lake, winter sports, hiking and biking trails. Enjoy homemade breakfast and snacks and refreshments in the evening.

Address: 849 Braddock Rd, Cumberland, MD 21502 **Tel:** (301) 777-3262.

Type: Bed & breakfast.
Clientele: Mostly gay & lesbian with some straight clientele.
Transportation: Car or free pick-up at train or airport from DC or Pittsburgh (commuter from Pittsburgh).
To Gay Bars: New bar in Cumberland, 1-1/2 hours to Hagerstown, Altoona, Morgantown bars.
Rooms: 3 rooms with full or queen beds.
Bathrooms: 1-1/2 shared.

Campsites: Nearby.
Meals: Full breakfast included, dinner available at additional cost.
Vegetarian: Available on request.
Complimentary: Cocktails, refreshments upon arrival.
Dates Open: All year.
High Season: Summer and fall.
Rates: $55 single, $65 double. Inquire about specials.

Discounts: Discount for 3 days or more.
Credit Cards: MC & VISA.
Rsv'tns: Required.
To Reserve: Call direct.
Minimum Stay: Required during special events in the area.
Parking: Adequate free off-street parking.
In-Room: AC, cable TV, electric blanket & ceiling fans.
On-Premises: Living room & TV lounge with fire-

places, sunroom or deck for breakfast.
Exercise/Health: Weights, rowing machine, stationary cycle, spa.
Swimming: 10 minutes by car to lake.
Sunbathing: On patio.
Smoking: Permitted in designated areas.
Pets: Not permitted.
Handicap Access: No.
Children: Not permitted.
Languages: English.
Your Host: Kery.

Ivy House B&B

Gay-Friendly 50/50 ♀♂

In a College Town Four Miles from Northampton

Our colonial cape home, portions of which date from circa 1740, has been handsomely restored with distinctive interiors, exposed beams, fireplace, country kitchen, and new baths. The patio and lovely landscaped grounds add to the atmosphere of this romantic setting. *Ivy House* is close to the Northampton scene, Cummington gay beach, and Vermont, just a block from the U. Mass. Fine Arts Center, and near the homes of Robert Frost and Emily Dickinson. The Five Colleges, Old Deerfield, Brimfield, and the Berkshires, are also convenient. Host John welcomes both men and women.

Address: 1 Sunset Court, Amherst, MA 01002 **Tel:** (413) 549-7554 (Tel/Fax).

Type: Bed & breakfast.
Clientele: 50% gay & lesbian & 50% straight clientele.
Transportation: Car is best. Pick up from Hartford-Springfield airport $25 per person, $5 from Amherst bus or train station.
To Gay Bars: 5 miles.

Rooms: 1 room with queen bed & 1 room with twin beds.
Bathrooms: 2 baths.
Meals: Full breakfast.
Dates Open: All year.
High Season: Mid-May college graduations and fall foliage.
Rates: $60-$80 year-round.
Discounts: For midweek or more than 6 nights.
Rsv'tns: Required.
To Reserve: Travel agent or call direct.
Minimum Stay: 2 nights at peak periods & most Fridays & Saturdays.
Parking: Adequate free off-street parking.
Swimming: Nearby pool, river & lake.
Sunbathing: On the patio.
Smoking: Outside on porch only.
Pets: Not permitted.
Handicap Access: No.
Children: No.
Languages: English, French & Spanish.
Your Host: John.

Amsterdammertje

Gay/Lesbian ♀♂

A Little of Holland in Boston

Amsterdammertje Euro-American B&B is for the discriminating, sophisticated, down-to-earth, value-conscious traveler. This home-away-from-home in a beautiful and quiet setting at the ocean is barely 20 minutes by car from downtown Boston (45 minutes by public transportation). Boston and its surroundings definitely warrant a visit of seven to ten days, depending on your own pace and on how far you wish to travel. Your host, the Flying Dutchman, will provide one personally guided tour, other obligations permitting. Call, write, or fax for a brochure, reservation form, and inn policy.

Address: PO Box 1731, Boston, MA 02205
Tel: (617) 471-8454 (Tel/Fax). **Tel only** (800) 484-6401 (* 1676).
URL: www.usagaynet.com/whoami/massachusetts/wma69.htm

Type: Bed & breakfast.
Clientele: Mostly gay & lesbian with some straight clientele
Transportation: Car or public transportation (subway & bus). Charge for pick up, please inquire.
To Gay Bars: 10 miles, a 12-minute drive.
Rooms: 3 rooms with twin or queen beds.
Bathrooms: 1 private shower/toilet, 2 shared bath/shower/toilets.

Meals: Full breakfast.
Vegetarian: Available.
Complimentary: Welcome snack, house robe, before-bed tea/hot chocolate & cookies.
Dates Open: All year.
High Season: April-October.
Rates: $55-$100, weekly: $340-$640.
Rsv'tns: Required.
To Reserve: Call/fax direct.
Minimum Stay: 3 days. Exceptions possible if/when space is available, $10 surcharge.
Parking: Ample free off-street parking.
On-Premises: In living room & kitchen: color cable TV, VCR, telephone, refrigerator. Charge for fax & laundry service.
Exercise/Health: Skiing 20-minutes to 2 hours away. Gym in downtown Boston with weights, sauna, steam, massage.

Swimming: Nearby pool, ocean, lake.
Sunbathing: On patio. 1-10 mins to beach.
Smoking: No smoking permitted.
Pets: Generally not permitted. Arrangements could be made.
Handicap Access: No.
Children: Preferably 10 years and older.
Languages: English, Dutch, German, French, Italian, Spanish, Polish.

402 FERRARI GUIDES™

Chandler Inn

Gay-Friendly 50/50 ♀♂

Location, Location, Location!

On the edge of historic Back Bay and the wonderfully eclectic South End, Boston's most exciting small hotel offers visitors myriad fringe benefits, great rates and a location just two blocks from the train and bus stations. *The Chandler Inn* is nestled within the diverse neighborhood of the South End. Here, you'll find a lively collection of restaurants, shops and a wide spectrum of social life. All of this is no more than a short walk from fashionable Newbury St., Copley Place, Theater district and the convention center. Our bar, Fritz, serves brunch Saturday and Sunday.

Address: 26 Chandler St, Boston, MA 02116
Tel: (617) 482-3450, (800) 842-3450,
Fax: (617) 542-3428.
E-mail: inn3450@ix.netcom.com
URL: www.chandlerinn-fritz.com

Type: Bed & breakfast hotel with gay bar on premises.
Clientele: 50% gay & lesbian & 50% straight clientele
Transportation: Taxi from airport $15. 2 block walk from Back Bay Amtrak/subway station.
To Gay Bars: Gay/lesbian bar inside building.
Rooms: 56 rooms with double, queen & twin beds.
Bathrooms: All private.

Meals: Continental breakfast.
Dates Open: All year.
High Season: April-November.
Rates: Singles $74-$119. Doubles $84-$129.
Discounts: AARP, off-season.
Credit Cards: All credit cards.
Rsv'tns: Required.
To Reserve: Travel agent or call direct.

Minimum Stay: 2 nights on weekends in season.
Parking: Limited on-street parking. Municipal lots 2 blocks away.
In-Room: Private direct-dial telephone, color Direct TV & AC.
On-Premises: Gay bar.
Exercise/Health: Discount at Metropolitan Health Club 1 block away.
Sunbathing: On Boston's

Esplanade, a ten minute walk from the hotel.
Smoking: Permitted. 16 non-smoking rooms, no smoking in common areas.
Pets: Permitted.
Handicap Access: No.
Children: Permitted.
Languages: English & Spanish.

IGLTA

UNITED STATES • MASSACHUSETTS • BOSTON

INN PLACES® 1998

Four-Sixty-Three Beacon Street Guest House

Gay-Friendly 50/50 ♀♂

Boston's Best Slept Secret

Located in Boston's historic Back Bay, the **463 Beacon Street Guest House** offers a comfortable and affordable hotel alternative. Our turn-of-the-century brownstone-style building includes private baths, kitchenettes, cable TV, air conditioning and complimentary local phone service, Our warm, quiet, residential setting is near public transportation, the Prudential-Hynes Convention Center, colleges, restaurants, and is minutes away from downtown Boston and Cambridge. Discounted weekly & monthly rates and parking available.

Address: 463 Beacon St, Boston, MA 02115
Tel: (617) 536-1302, **Fax:** (617) 247-8876.

Type: Guesthouse.
Clientele: 50% gay & lesbian & 50% straight clientele.
Transportation: Taxi, public transportation, airport shuttle bus.
To Gay Bars: Five minutes by car to gay bars.
Rooms: 20 rooms with double & king beds.
Bathrooms: 16 private bath/toilets, 4 sink/washbasins only.

Meals: Meals not included.
Complimentary: Coffee, tea.
Dates Open: All year.
High Season: May-October.
Rates: $65-$99 per night.
Discounts: Discounts for weekly & monthly stays.
Credit Cards: MC, Visa, Amex.
Rsv'tns: Required.
To Reserve: Travel agent or call direct.

Parking: Limited off-street parking.
In-Room: Color cable TV, telephone, AC, kitchenette with refrigerator.
On-Premises: Laundry facilities.
Sunbathing: 1 unit with private deck.
Smoking: Permitted with some restrictions.
Pets: Not permitted.
Handicap Access: No.
Children: No.
Languages: English, French & Spanish.

Greater Boston Hospitality

Gay-Friendly ♀♂

An Uncommonly Civilized Way to Travel

Greater Boston Hospitality offers superb accommodations in the Boston area in hundreds of friendly, private homes and inns, all of which are carefully screened for comfort, cleanliness and congeniality of hosts. Bed and breakfasts range from Federal to Colonial to Georgian, from cozy to luxury, from city to suburb to country. Neighborhoods throughout Boston are included. Many of our accommodations include parking. All include breakfast and knowledgeable, friendly hosts. Be it for business or pleasure, we'll help you to have a welcoming and wonderful time.

Address: PO Box 1142, Brookline, MA 02146
Tel: (617) 277-5430. **URL:** www.channel1.com/BnB

Type: Reservation service for bed & breakfasts, guesthouses & inns.
Clientele: Good selection of very gay-friendly accommodations.
To Gay Bars: 10 blocks or 1/2 mile from most accommodations.
Rooms: 180 rooms & 10 suites with single, double,

queen or king beds.
Bathrooms: 160 private. Shared 10 bath/shower/toilets & 18 showers only. Most have private baths.
Meals: Expanded continental, continental, or full breakfast.
Vegetarian: Several vegetarian restaurants in the greater Boston area.
Complimentary: Many hosts offer cold &/or hot drinks, candy & flowers.
Dates Open: All year.
High Season: Apr 1-Dec 1.
Rates: $50-$130. Luxury suites to $680.
Discounts: Inquire, discounts vary.
Credit Cards: MC, Visa, Amex (depending on location).
Rsv'tns: Required.
To Reserve: Travel agent or call direct.
Parking: Adequate parking: free, pay, off- & on-street.
In-Room: Color cable TV, AC, telephone & maid service, depending on location.
On-Premises: Libraries, pianos & decks in various locations.
Exercise/Health: Gym, weights, sauna, steam, massage in various locations.
Swimming: Pools on premises & nearby pool, ocean & lake.
Sunbathing: On patios.
Smoking: Generally permitted outside only.
Pets: Not permitted.
Handicap Access: Some are.
Children: Inquire.
Languages: English, French, Italian, Spanish, German.
Your Host: Kelly, Lauren & Jack.

Victorian Bed & Breakfast
Women ♀

TLC in Massive Doses

Our guests say: "Thanks for such friendly hospitality, helpful Boston hints and great food. You two are a delight!" "We feel like we've found a home in the big city." "The best place, the best hosts!" *Victorian Bed & Breakfast* offers elegant and comfortable accommodations just 5 minutes from Boston's Copley Place. All the tourist attractions of the city, plus gay and lesbian bars are nearby. We're sure you'll find your accommodations feel just like home...only better!

Tel: (617) 536-3285.

Type: Bed & breakfast.
Clientele: Women only.
Transportation: Car or taxi from airport, easy subway trip from airport.
To Gay Bars: Close to all gay/lesbian bars.
Rooms: 1 room accommodates up to 4 women with king-sized bed & double couch.
Bathrooms: Private bath/toilet.
Meals: Full breakfast.
Vegetarian: Food to please all tastes and needs.
Complimentary: Soft drinks.
Dates Open: All year.
High Season: All year.
Rates: $60 for 1, $75 for 2, $85 for 3 & $95 for 4.
Rsv'tns: Required.
To Reserve: Call direct.
Minimum Stay: 2 nights on weekends.
Parking: Free off-street parking.
In-Room: Large living room, easy chairs, black & white TV, AC, laundry done by hostess, if stay longer than 4 nights, maid service.
Smoking: Not permitted.
Pets: Not permitted. We have 3 cats in residence.
Handicap Access: No.
Children: Not permitted.
Languages: English.
Your Host: Claire & Lois.

Gateways Inn
Gay-Friendly ♀♂

A Music- & Nature-Lover's Delight in The Berkshires

Gateways Inn, a turn-of-the-century inn in historic Lenox, is steeped in European charm. From the French rose entrance windows to the lobby's gracious, sweeping staircase, guests are transported to another place and time. Dine near the fireplace in our elegant candlelight restaurant, or browse our gift shop featuring silver objects imported from Italy. Each of the 12 guestrooms is individually and tastefully deco-

continued next page

INN PLACES® 1998

405

rated, some with fireplaces and romantic queen- and king-sized canopied or sleigh beds. The sumptuous two-room suite has an Italian-marbled bath with Jacuzzi tub. Located in the heart of the Berkshires, we're close to premier cultural attractions such as Tanglewood, as well as sports activities.

Address: 51 Walker St, Lenox, MA 01240
Tel: (413) 637-2532, (888) 492-9466, **Fax:** (413) 637-1432.
E-mail: gateways@berkshire.net **URL:** www.gatewaysinn.com

Type: Bed & breakfast with restaurant, bar & gift shop with imported Italian silver objects.
Clientele: Mostly straight clientele with a gay/lesbian following
Transportation: Car is best.
Rooms: 11 rooms, 1 suite with double, queen or king beds.
Bathrooms: 12 private bath/shower/toilets.
Meals: Expanded continental breakfast.

Vegetarian: Several dishes in our menu. Special meals prepared upon request.
Complimentary: Tea & coffee.
Dates Open: All year.
High Season: Jul, Aug, Oct.
Rates: High period (Jun 1-Oct 29) & holidays: $100-$380; Low period (Oct 30-Dec 30 & Jan 1-May 31) $75-$305.
Discounts: Up to 20% for corporations with previous agreements.

Credit Cards: MC, Visa, Amex, Diners, Discover.
Rsv'tns: Recommended in high season.
To Reserve: Travel agent or call direct.
Minimum Stay: Summer: 3 nights on weekends, Oct & holidays: 2 nights on weekends.
Parking: Private parking lot with ample, free parking.
In-Room: Telephone, AC, color cable TV. Suite has VCR.

On-Premises: Meeting rooms.
Exercise/Health: Tennis. Nearby gym, weights, sauna, steam, massage.
Swimming: Nearby pool & lake.
Smoking: Entire building is non-smoking.
Pets: Not permitted.
Handicap Access: No.
Children: No.
Languages: English, Italian, Spanish.
Your Host: Fabrizio & Rosemary.

Summer Hill Farm   Gay-Friendly ♀♂

Berkshire Arts and a Country Setting

Enjoy the beauty and culture of the Berkshires at *Summer Hill Farm*, a 200-year-old colonial farmhouse on a 20-acre horse farm. Rooms are pleasantly furnished with English family antiques. Delicious country breakfasts are served family-style in the dining room or on the sunporch. A haybarn has been newly converted to a delightful, spacious, 2-room, all-season guest cottage. We're in the country, yet minutes from Tanglewood, Jacob's Pillow Dance, theatres, fine art galleries, restaurants and shops. Choose from a wide variety of outdoor activities. The countryside is beautiful in all seasons. Come for the fall colors or our winter wonderland.

Address: 950 East St, Lenox, MA 01240 **Tel:** (413) 442-2057, (800) 442-2059.

Type: Bed & breakfast.
Clientele: Mostly straight clientele with a gay & lesbian following.
Transportation: Car is best. No charge for pick up from local bus.
Rooms: 6 rooms with single, double, queen or king beds.
Bathrooms: All private.
Meals: Full home-cooked breakfast. Continental breakfast in cottage.
Vegetarian: Available with special request.

Dates Open: All year.
High Season: Mid June-Labor Day & October.
Rates: Summer & October $90-$190. Winter & spring $65-$135.
Discounts: For groups & stays of a week or more, up to 20% discount; mid-week reductions.
Credit Cards: Visa, MC, Amex.
Rsv'tns: Required.
To Reserve: Call direct.
Minimum Stay: On July,

August, October & holiday weekends.
Parking: Ample free off-street parking.
In-Room: Color cable TV, AC, maid service. 2 rooms with fireplaces, 1 with refrigerator. Cottage: coffee/tea-making facilities, refrigerator, TV, AC, microwave, toaster.
Exercise/Health: Riding by arrangement. Nearby gym, sauna, massage, hiking, biking, canoeing, skiing,

tennis, horseback riding.
Swimming: 5 miles to lake.
Sunbathing: On private or common sun decks & on the lawns.
Smoking: No smoking indoors.
Pets: Not permitted.
Handicap Access: Yes. Cottage only.
Children: Infants, & children 5 & over. Must be well-behaved & closely supervised.
Languages: English.
Your Host: Michael & Sonya.

Walker House

Gay-Friendly ♀♂

A Most Harmonious Place to Visit

Walker House, is an 1804-era federal manor, furnished in antiques, on 3 acres of gardens and woods near the center of the picturesque village of Lenox. Rooms, decorated with a musical theme honoring composers, such as Beethoven and Mozart, have private baths, some with claw-foot tubs and fireplaces. Our library theatre features a large-screen video projection system. Walk to galleries, shops and good restaurants. Tanglewood, Jacob's Pillow and summer theatres are only a short drive.

Address: 64 Walker St, Lenox, MA 01240
Tel: (413) 637-1271, (800) 235-3098, **Fax:** (413) 637-2387.
E-mail: phoudek@vgernet.net
URL: http://www.regionnet.com/colberk/WalkerHouse.html

Type: Bed & breakfast inn.
Clientele: Mainly straight with a gay & lesbian following
Transportation: Car is best. 1 block from New York & Boston buses.
To Gay Bars: 35 miles to Albany & Northampton.
Rooms: 8 rooms with double, queen or king beds.
Bathrooms: All private.
Meals: Expanded continental breakfast.
Vegetarian: Breakfasts have no meat; other vegetarian meals available at restaurants within walking distance.
Complimentary: Bottle of wine in room, afternoon tea or lemonade daily.
Dates Open: All year.
High Season: July, August, October.
Rates: Summer $80-$190, Oct $80-$150, Sept & Nov-Jun $70-$120.
Discounts: 10% off for single persons in rooms depending on availability.
Rsv'tns: Advisable during busy periods.
To Reserve: Call direct.
Minimum Stay: On holidays & summer weekends.
Parking: Ample free on- & off-street parking.
In-Room: AC, maid service.
On-Premises: Meeting rooms, TV lounge, library theatre with large-screen video projection system.
Exercise/Health: Nearby gym, massage.
Swimming: Nearby river & lake.
Sunbathing: On the patio, lawns & garden, at the beach.
Smoking: Non-smoking property.
Pets: Permitted by prior approval at reservation time.
Handicap Access: Yes. 3 1st-floor rooms accessible.
Children: 12 years of age & older welcome.
Languages: English, Spanish, French.

Captain Dexter House of Edgartown

Gay-Friendly ♀♂

Romantic guest rooms, each uniquely different, are distinctively decorated with fine furnishings to create the warmth and ambiance of an elegant private home. Each has its own bathroom. Several have working fireplaces and four-poster beds with white lace canopies. At *Captain Dexter House of Edgartown*, rooms are richly appointed with many amenities, to let you know how special you are to us. Fresh, home-baked breakfast breads are served in our elegant dining room or enchanting flower-filled garden. It's only a short stroll to the town, harbor, shopping and dining.

Address: 35 Pease Point Way, PO Box 2798, Edgartown, MA 02539
Tel: (508) 627-7289, **Fax:** (508) 627-3328.

Type: Bed & breakfast.
Clientele: Mostly straight clientele with a gay & lesbian following.
Transportation: Car to ferry or airport.
To Gay Bars: Gay organization & 1 gay-friendly bar on island.
Rooms: 11 rooms with double or queen beds.
Bathrooms: All private baths.
Meals: Expanded continental breakfast.
Complimentary: Lemonade, sherry.
Dates Open: April through November.
High Season: Mid June through Labor Day.
Rates: Summer $110-$200, winter $65-$175.
Credit Cards: MC, Visa, Amex, Diners.
To Reserve: Travel agent or call direct.
Minimum Stay: Required on high season weekends.
Parking: Ample off-street parking.
In-Room: Maid service, most rooms with AC & ceiling fans.
On-Premises: Meeting rooms, laundry facilities, refrigerator.
Exercise/Health: Nearby aerobics classes & gym.
Swimming: At nearby ocean beach.
Sunbathing: In yards & at nearby ocean beach.
Smoking: Not permitted in all rooms.
Pets: Not permitted.
Handicap Access: No.
Children: Permitted. Prefer 12 years or older.
Languages: English.

Martha's Place

Q-NET Gay-Owned ♀♂

Come Pamper Yourself in Style

Martha's Place is a gay-owned and -operated stately Greek Revival overlooking Vineyard Haven Harbor, two blocks from the ferry, village shops, restaurants and the beach. Rooms boast harbor views and are beautifully decorated with fine antiques, oriental carpets and crystal chandeliers. Other amenities include private baths, bathrobes, fireplaces and Jacuzzi. Breakfast in bed is available and the pampering continues at night with turndown service in wonderful beds dressed in fine Egyptian cotton linens. Afternoon tea and cocktails are served. To enhance your enjoyment of Martha's Vineyard, we have tennis, beach chairs and coolers, bicycles and more! Your host's previous experience as an employee of Ritz Carlton hotels is evident in the style of hospitality at Martha's Place. As a guest at our island escape, your stay will be an especially memorable one.

Address: 114 Main St, PO Box 1182, Vineyard Haven, MA 02658
Tel: (508) 693-0253.

Type: Inn.
Clientele: 60% gay & lesbian clientele
Transportation: Ferry. Taxi is a maximum $10 rate about anywhere on island.
To Gay Bars: 1-1/2 hours to Boston or Provincetown gay bars.
Rooms: 6 rooms with double or queen beds.
Bathrooms: 2 rooms with shower/toilet/sink, 4 rooms with tub/shower/toilet/sink.
Meals: Expanded continental breakfast. Breakfast in bed available.
Vegetarian: Available nearby.
Complimentary: Open bar at tea time in afternoon, liqueur after dinner in room, turndown chocolates & bottled water.
Dates Open: All year.
High Season: Jun-Sept.
Rates: Summer $175-$275, fall $150-$225, winter $125-$225.
Credit Cards: MC, Visa.

Rsv'tns: Required.
To Reserve: Travel agent or call direct.
Minimum Stay: 3 nights on holiday weekends.
Parking: Ample free off-street parking.
In-Room: AC, color cable TV, VCR, room, laundry & maid service.
On-Premises: Meeting rooms, TV lounge, fax, copier.
Exercise/Health: Jacuzzi. Nearby gym, weights, sauna, Jacuzzi, steam, massage.
Swimming: Nearby pool, ocean, lake.
Sunbathing: At beach & side yard.
Nudity: Permitted at beach.
Smoking: Permitted outside. All rooms are non-smoking.
Pets: Not permitted.
Handicap Access: Yes.
Children: No.
Languages: English.
Your Host: Richard & Martin.

IGLTA

Innamorata

Women ♀

For Romance and Relaxation

Northampton, the lesbian mecca, abounds with great food, cultural events and shopping. Nearby are many athletic, historical and cultural activities. With so much to do here, *Innamorata* is your perfect getaway. Our seven-acre, secluded country estate has open lawns surrounded by spectacular woods. Our three spacious pine guest rooms are decorated with flowers and homemade country touches. We have an extensive women's library, a living room with fireplace and a huge sunporch for our guests' relaxation. Bountiful, delicious breakfasts are served in a warm familial atmosphere. Yvonne and Kristen welcome you!

Address: 47 Main St, PO Box 113, Goshen, MA 01032-0113 **Tel:** (413) 268-0300.

Type: Bed & breakfast guesthouse.
Clientele: Mostly women with men welcome.
Transportation: Car is necessary.
To Gay Bars: 12 miles or 20 minutes by car.
Rooms: 3 rooms with queen beds.
Bathrooms: 1 shared bath/shower/toilet.
Meals: Expanded continental breakfast.
Vegetarian: Always available upon request. Many vegetarian choices in Northampton.
Complimentary: Beverage upon arrival.
Dates Open: All year.
High Season: May-Oct.
Rates: $60-$80 per room, double occupancy.
Discounts: 10% on stays of 4 or more days.
Rsv'tns: Required.
To Reserve: Call direct.
Minimum Stay: 2 nights on weekends & holidays.
Parking: Ample free off-street parking, covered if necessary.
On-Premises: TV lounge, living room with fireplace, library & sunporch.
Exercise/Health: Tennis, hiking, cross-country/downhill skiing, biking & canoeing.
Swimming: Lake & river nearby.
Sunbathing: On the lawns.
Nudity: Permitted with discretion on secluded lawns.
Smoking: Permitted outside only.
Pets: Not permitted.
Handicap Access: No, all bedrooms are upstairs.
Children: No. Kids' weekends available. Please inquire.
Languages: English.
Your Host: Kristen & Yvonne.

Tin Roof Bed & Breakfast

Q-NET Women ♀

Visit Lesbianville, USA

Tin Roof is a turn-of-the-century farmhouse in the scenic Connecticut River Valley, five minutes from Northampton. Our peaceful backyard has panoramic views of the Berkshire Hills and gardens galore. Breakfast features home-baked muffins, fruit, yogurt, granola, juice and hot beverage of choice. There's color TV, a lesbian video library and a front porch with porch swing. Whether you're considering moving to the area or just visiting, your long-time resident hosts will give you lots of local information and acclimate you to the area. Friendly felines in residence.

Address: PO Box 296, Hadley, MA 01035 **Tel:** (413) 586-8665.

Type: Bed & breakfast.
Clientele: A women's space where lesbian-friendly men are welcome.
Transportation: From Hartford airport, rent a car or take a bus to Northampton.
To Gay Bars: 10 minutes to gay/lesbian bars.
Rooms: 3 rooms with double beds.
Bathrooms: 1 shared bath/shower/toilet, 1 shared toilet, sink.
Meals: Expanded continental breakfast.
Vegetarian: Upon request.
Dates Open: All year.
Rates: Single $55, $60 for two people.
Discounts: 7th night free.
Rsv'tns: Required.
To Reserve: Call direct.
Minimum Stay: 2 nights on weekends & holidays.
Parking: Ample off-street parking.
On-Premises: Laundry facilities, TV in living room.
Exercise/Health: Nearby health club.
Swimming: In nearby river.
Sunbathing: In the garden.
Smoking: Permitted outside.
Pets: Not permitted.
Handicap Access: No.
Languages: English.
Your Host: Jane & Diane.

Admiral's Landing Guest House

Gay/Lesbian ♀♂

You've Been Waiting a Long Time to Get Away

Admiral's Landing Guest House... One block from the bay beach, shops and restaurants, offering spacious rooms with private baths, parking and a friendly, social atmosphere. Provincetown has miles of sandy beaches and dunes, wonderful shops and restaurants. This is the perfect place to truly relax and be yourself. Call or write for photo brochure, or visit our web site.

Address: 158 Bradford St, Provincetown, MA 02657
Tel: (800) 934-0925, (508) 487-9665, Fax: (508) 487-4437.
E-mail: adm158@capecod.net
URL: http://www.ptown.com/ptown/admiralslanding/

Type: Guesthouse & efficiency studios.
Clientele: Gay men & women
Transportation: Courtesy transportation from airport & ferry with prior arrangement.
To Gay Bars: 3 blocks to men's bar. 5-minutes' walk to women's bar.
Rooms: 6 doubles & 2 efficiencies.
Bathrooms: 4 private & 2 shared. Studio efficiencies have private baths.
Meals: Continental breakfast, afternoon snacks.
Dates Open: All year. Studios May 1-Nov 17 only.
High Season: May-Sept.
Rates: Summer & holidays: $76-$112; winter: $39-$59; spring/fall $46-$82.
Discounts: Group rates.
Credit Cards: MC, Visa.
Rsv'tns: Strongly recommended.
To Reserve: Travel agent or call direct.
Minimum Stay: Holiday weekends & July-August.
Parking: Free off-street parking.
In-Room: TV, VCR, phone, ceiling fans, refrigerator, maid service.
On-Premises: Patio, TV lounge with video library.
Exercise/Health: Gym nearby.
Swimming: Ocean beach nearby.
Sunbathing: On ocean beach or patio.
Smoking: Permitted in studios only.
Pets: Permitted in studios only.
Handicap Access: Studios have limited accessibility.
Children: Not permitted.
Languages: English.
Your Host: Chuck & Peter

Ampersand Guesthouse

Q-NET Gay/Lesbian ♂

A Delightful Home Base in Provincetown

    Ampersand Guesthouse is a fine example of mid-nineteenth century Greek Revival architecture located in the neighborly west end of Provincetown, just a short walk from town center. Each of the bedrooms is unique in its layout, creating a range of accommodations from suites of two to three rooms, to shared baths, to private baths. All are furnished in a careful blend of contemporary appointments and restored antiques, many original to the house. There is also a studio apartment that looks out on both the water and the yard.

    Continental breakfast is served daily in the large, gracious living room, a gathering place for guests throughout the day & evening. It has a fireplace seating arrangement, a gaming table and a dining area for relaxing and socializing. And guests have use of the yard as well as a second-story sun deck which commands a view of the harbor and Commercial Street. You may be looking for a quiet, restful time for meeting new friends, walking or sunbathing on the nearby beaches, and enjoying the singular views of nature around Provincetown. Or you may be seeking the bustle of a resort town famous for its shops, restaurants, and active social life. In either case, *Ampersand Guesthouse* provides a delightful home base both in season and off.

    Address: 6 Cottage St, PO Box 832, Provincetown, MA 02657
    Tel: (508) 487-0959, (800) 574-9645, **Fax:** (508) 487-4365.
    E-mail: ampersan@capecod.net

Type: Guesthouse.
Clientele: Mostly men with women welcome.
Transportation: Take taxi from the airport or walk from town center.
To Gay Bars: 6 blocks to men's bars.
Rooms: 11 rooms & 1 apartment with double or queen beds.
Bathrooms: 9 private bath/toilets & 2 shared bath/shower/toilets.
Meals: Continental breakfast.
Dates Open: All year.
High Season: Memorial Day-Labor Day week.
Rates: $55-$75 off season, $75-$125 high season.
Credit Cards: MC, Visa, Amex.
Rsv'tns: Required.
To Reserve: Call direct.
Minimum Stay: 5 nights in July & Aug, 2 nights on May, June & Sept weekends & off-season holidays.
Parking: Limited free off-street parking.
In-Room: Maid service.
On-Premises: TV lounge.
Swimming: Ocean beach nearby.
Sunbathing: Sun decks.
Smoking: Permitted in rooms. Living room smoke-free.
Pets: Not permitted.
Children: Not permitted.
Languages: English.
Your Host: Bob & Ken.

The Bayberry

Gay-Owned & -Operated ♂

Blue Sky, Sun, Sand & Sea... Come Stay With Me

An award-winning designed home, *The Bayberry* has been renovated with all of the modern conveniences. The decor is a blend of antiques and collectibles which have been carefully selected over the years. The routines you are accustomed to need not be left at home — so, come and enjoy this "home-away-from-home" whose reputation has been built on a standard of cleanliness and a home-like atmosphere not found in larger establishments. We love to cook and entertain and encourage our guests to participate. Our hospitality reunites friends year after year.

Address: 16 Winthrop, Provincetown, MA 02657
Tel: (508) 487-4605 (Tel/Fax), (800) 422-4605.
E-mail: sixteen@capecod.net URL: http://www.capecod.net/bayberry

Type: Bed & breakfast.
Clientele: Mostly men with women welcome. Some straight clientele
Transportation: Car or air from Boston/Providence. Free pick up from airport, bus, ferry dock.
To Gay Bars: 1 block, a 2 min walk.
Rooms: Rooms, suites & apartments with queen beds.
Bathrooms: All private.

Meals: Expanded continental breakfast.
Vegetarian: Guests may fix vegetarian food in common kitchen, if desired.
Complimentary: Wine, sherry, mixers.
Dates Open: Early spring to late fall.
High Season: July-Sept.
Rates: Off season: $55-$135, On season: $95-$175.
Credit Cards: MC, Visa,

Amex, Discover.
Rsv'tns: Required.
To Reserve: Travel agent or call direct.
Minimum Stay: Inquire, depends on time of year.
Parking: Ample, free off-street parking.
In-Room: AC, ceiling fans, color cable TV, VCR, refrigerator, coffee & tea-making facilities, maid, room & laundry service. Some rooms have kitchen.
On-Premises: TV lounge.

Exercise/Health: Nearby gym, weights, Jacuzzi, sauna, steam, massage.
Swimming: Nearby pool & ocean.
Sunbathing: On private & common sun decks, at beach.
Smoking: Non-smoking.
Pets: Not permitted.
Handicap Access: No.
Children: No.
Languages: English.

IGLTA

Bayview Wharf Apartments

Women ♀

Overlooking the Cape's most picturesque harbor, *Bayview Wharf Apartments* is a perfect place to relax and enjoy your holiday in the gayest town in the Northeast. We are located in the center of Provincetown, near all local shops, restaurants, and bars. The beaches are nearby, ideal for swimming and sunbathing. We extend a warm welcome to our guests and hope to see you soon in Provincetown.

Address: 421 Commercial St, Provincetown, MA 02657 Tel: (508) 487-1600.

Type: Apartments.
Clientele: Mostly women with men welcome
Transportation: Car, train or bus.

To Gay Bars: 1/2 block.
Rooms: 15 apartments in 4 locations around P'town, with double or queen beds.
Bathrooms: All private.

Dates Open: All year.
High Season: May 15-Sept 15.
Rates: In season $800-$1600 per week, off season

$650-$1100 per week.
Rsv'tns: Required.
To Reserve: Call direct.
Minimum Stay: 1 week in season, 3 nights off season.

Parking: Adequate free & pay parking within 1/2 block.
In-Room: Color cable TV, full kitchens, coffee/tea-making facilities. Some have AC, telephone, ceiling fans.
Exercise/Health: Nearby gym, weights, Jacuzzi, sauna, steam, massage.
Swimming: All but 2 apts. are directly on the beach.
Sunbathing: On common sun decks, beach.
Smoking: Permitted. Some non-smoking units available.
Pets: Permitted with pet deposit (some units).
Handicap Access: Some units accessible.
Children: Welcome.
Languages: English, German.

The Beaconlight Guest House

Q-NET Gay/Lesbian

"The Kind of House We Wished We Lived In"

Awaken to the aroma of freshly-brewed coffee and home-baked cakes and breads. Relax in the English country house charm of our elegant bedrooms and spacious drawing rooms, complete with open fire, grand piano, and antique furnishings. Multi-level sun decks provide panoramic views of Provincetown. *Beaconlight's* exceptional reputation for pampered comfort and caring service has grown by the word of mouth of our many returning guests. We truly become your home away from home! "The kind of house we wished we lived in. Exceptional 5-Palms Award 1997" — Out & About.

Address: 12 Winthrop St, Provincetown, MA 02657
Tel: (508) 487-9603 (Tel/Fax), (800) 696-9603.
E-mail: beaconlite@capecod.net **URL:** www.capecod.net/beaconlight/

Type: Guesthouse.
Clientele: Mostly men in high season. Good mix of men & women at other times
Transportation: Car, ferry or air from Boston. Free airport/ferry pick up provided if arranged.
To Gay Bars: 2 minutes' walk to gay bars, 1/2 block to tea dance.
Rooms: 10 rooms, 2 suites with double, queen or king beds.
Bathrooms: 2 private bath/toilets & 8 private shower/toilets.

Meals: Gourmet continental breakfast.
Vegetarian: Available in local restaurants.
Complimentary: Coffee & tea.
Dates Open: All year.
High Season: Mid June to mid September.
Rates: High season $80-$200, off-season $45-$140.
Discounts: Off season: 10% for returning guests.
Credit Cards: MC, Visa, Amex.
Rsv'tns: Required.

To Reserve: Call direct or travel agent.
Minimum Stay: 5 to 7 days during high season.
Parking: Free off-street parking, 1 car per room.
In-Room: Color cable TV, VCR, AC, ceiling fan, telephone with voice mail & data port, refrigerator, daily laundry & maid serice.
On-Premises: TV lounge, grand piano, fireplace, laundry services, fax & internet services, cycle storage.
Exercise/Health: Nearby gym, bike hire, massage. In-house massage on season.
Swimming: Nearby pool & ocean.
Sunbathing: On private sun decks.
Smoking: A non-smoking guesthouse, except on outside decks.
Pets: Not permitted.
Handicap Access: No.
Children: Not permitted.
Languages: English.
Your Host: Trevor & Stephen.

IGLTA

INN PLACES® 1998

Boatslip Beach Club

Gay/Lesbian

Simply the Best for Over 25 Years!

The **Boatslip Beach Club**, beginning its 30th season, is a 45-room contemporary resort on Provincetown Harbor. Thirty-three rooms have glass doors opening onto private balconies overlooking our fabulous deck, pool, private beach and the bay. All rooms have either one queen or two double beds, private baths, direct-dial phones and color cable TV. Off-street parking, morning coffee, admission to Tea Dance and sun cots are all complimentary. We offer a full-service restaurant, poolside grille and raw bar and evening entertainment. Call or write your hosts: *Peter Simpson and Jim Carlino* for further information....*YOU OWE IT TO YOURSELF!!!*.

Address: 161 Commercial St Box 393, Provincetown, MA 02657
Tel: (800) 451-SLIP (7547), (508) 487-1669, **Fax:** (508) 487-6021.
E-mail: boatslip@provincetown.com **URL:** www.provincetown.com/boatslip

Type: Hotel with restaurant, bar, disco, card & gift shop, & sportswear boutique.
Clientele: Gay & lesbian. Good mix of men & women
Transportation: Car is best. Walk from ferry.
To Gay Bars: Bar on premises, good mix of men & women. Women's bar 2 blocks away.
Rooms: 30 rooms with double beds & 15 rooms with queen beds.
Bathrooms: All private bath/toilets.

Vegetarian: Available.
Complimentary: Morning coffee, sun cots, admission to Tea Dance.
Dates Open: April thru October.
High Season: June 18th-September 7th.
Rates: Off season $65-$100. In season $130-$185.
Discounts: Group rates available. Call for information.
Credit Cards: MC & VISA.
Rsv'tns: Strongly recommended in season.

To Reserve: Call direct.
Minimum Stay: Three nights by reservation, less if available.
Parking: Ample free covered off-street parking.
In-Room: Color cable TV, direct-dial phones, maid service, limited room service. Ceiling fans in some rooms.
On-Premises: Meeting rooms, public telephone, central heat, restaurant & bar.
Exercise/Health: Nearby gym, weights & massage.
Swimming: Pool or ocean beach.
Sunbathing: On beach, private/common sun decks or poolside.
Smoking: Permitted without restrictions.
Pets: Not permitted.
Handicap Access: No.
Children: Permitted, but not recommended.
Languages: English.
Your Host: Peter & Jim

IGLTA

The Bradford Carver House

Gay/Lesbian ♂

Your Home away from Home — Where There Are No Strangers, Only Friends You Haven't Met!

UNITED STATES

MASSACHUSETTS • PROVINCETOWN

The Bradford Carver House was built in the mid-nineteenth century and is conveniently located in the heart of Provincetown. Experience our warm hospitality and cozy accommodations in a friendly and relaxed atmosphere. Our rooms, all with private baths, are perfect for those who seek the charm of a guesthouse. A complimentary continental breakfast is served each morning on our patio. Come join us at *The Bradford Carver House* and we will make your stay a memorable one.

Address: 70 Bradford St, Provincetown, MA 02657
Tel: (508) 487-4966, (800) 826-9083, **Fax:** (508) 487-7213.
Guest Tel: (508) 487-5699.

Type: Guesthouse.
Clientele: Mostly men with women welcome
Transportation: Bus, car, ferry or plane.
To Gay Bars: Across street, others 1 or 2 blocks.
Rooms: 5 rooms with double, queen & king beds.
Bathrooms: All private.
Meals: Expanded continental breakfast.
Vegetarian: In nearby restaurants.

Dates Open: All year.
High Season: Mid-June thru mid-Sept, Memorial Day weekend.
Rates: Summer $105-$115, fall & spring $49-$79, winter $39-$59.
Discounts: Nov 16-Apr 9. Stay 4 nights pay for 3. Excludes holidays & special events.
Credit Cards: MC, Visa, Amex, Discover.

Rsv'tns: Highly recommended in season.
To Reserve: Call direct or travel agent.
Minimum Stay: Required, varies with dates.
Parking: Free off street parking.
In-Room: AC, ceiling fans, color cable TV, VCR, refrigerator, ceiling fans, maid service.
On-Premises: Guest telephone, TV lounge, large video collection, common patio.
Exercise/Health: Local gym nearby.
Swimming: Nearby pool, bay & ocean.
Sunbathing: On patio.
Pets: No.
Handicap Access: No.
Children: No.
Languages: English, Tagalog (Pilipino).
Your Host: Bill & José.

INN PLACES® 1998   415

The Brass Key Guesthouse

Gay/Lesbian ♂

Unique in Provincetown

The Brass Key Guesthouse is renowned for providing gay and lesbian travelers with the finest in luxury accommodations, attentive service and meticulous housekeeping. In concert with numerous accolades from its guests and from travel writers of the gay media, *The Brass Key* is one of five gay-designated lodgings throughout the United States to receive *Out & About's* coveted Editor's Choice award (1994-1997).

Located on a quiet side street in the heart of town, 30 guest rooms in a collection of restored 19th-century homes and four charming private cottages overlook the heated dip pool, whirlpool spa and landscaped courtyards. All accommodations offer traditional New England architecture enhanced by English and American Country antiques. Yet no two rooms are alike: each presents its own special warmth and personality with details such as a vaulted skylit ceiling, a teddy bear loft, a working fireplace, framed antique quilts or courtyard and harbor views.

Throughout the four seasons, *The Brass Key* presents a private and exclusive retreat. In the early Spring, flowering tulips, forsythia, azalea and rhododendron greet guests. From Memorial Day through September, the action shifts to the sun: while many guests enjoy the seashore beaches, others relax and socialize in the enclosed courtyard. In the Fall, as crisp nights complement the warm days of Indian summer, and later, throughout the quiet of Winter, a blazing fire in the hearth accords the perfect backdrop to savor a bottle of wine and ward off the outside chill.

Guests are offered every amenity: individually-controlled heating and air-conditioning, twin-line telephone with voice mail, color cable televisions with VCR and videocassette library, mini-bar, hair dryer, Crabtree & Evelyn bath toiletries; some deluxe rooms further feature fireplaces, king beds and oversized whirlpool baths. The staff of *The Brass Key* looks forward to the pleasure of your company.

Address: 9 Court St, Provincetown, MA 02657
Tel: (508) 487-9005, (800) 842-9858, **Fax:** (508) 487-9020.

Type: Bed & breakfast guesthouse.
Clientele: Mostly men with women very welcome.
Transportation: Ferry, auto, or plane from Boston. Provincetown airport taxi $5.
To Gay Bars: 2 blocks to gay & lesbian bars.
Rooms: 30 rooms & 4 cottages with queen or king beds.
Bathrooms: All private.
Meals: Expanded continental breakfast.
Complimentary: Afternoon cocktails.
Dates Open: All year.
High Season: Mid-June to mid-September, also holidays, special weekends.
Rates: In season $185-$295 & off season $75-$190.
Credit Cards: Amex, Discover, MC, Visa.
Rsv'tns: Highly recommended.
To Reserve: Travel agent or call direct.
Minimum Stay: Required in season, during holidays & special events.
Parking: Ample free off-street parking.
In-Room: Color cable TV, VCR, Bose stereo, video tape library, AC, telephone, ceiling fan, minibar, fireplace, whirlpool bath, hair dryer, bathrobes. Laundry, maid & turndown service.
On-Premises: Spacious liv-

ing rooms with breakfast area, fireplaces.
Exercise/Health: Whirlpool spa & nearby gym.
Swimming: Heated pool on the premises; also nearby ocean beaches.
Sunbathing: Poolside courtyard & sun decks.
Smoking: Non-smoking rooms available.
Pets: Not permitted.
Handicap Access: Yes. Wheelchair parking & ramp. 2 guestroom/baths for the physically challenged.
Children: Not permitted.
Languages: English.

IGLTA

The Buoy
Gay/Lesbian ♀♂

The Buoy is located conveniently in the center of Provincetown, close to everything that this gay & lesbian resort town has to offer. Near shops and restaurants, the inn is also just a short distance from the beach. Of the nine guestrooms, two have king beds, private baths and cable television. There is also cable TV in the common room for your enjoyment. In the summer, the backyard is perfect for sunning and relaxing your cares away. We offer morning coffee, off-season rates, and parking is also available.

Address: 97 Bradford St, Provincetown, MA 02657
Tel: (508) 487-3082, (800) 648-0364, **Fax:** (508) 487-4887.

Type: Guesthouse.
Clientele: Good mix of gay men & women
To Gay Bars: 1/2 block to major discos.
Rooms: 1 single, 7 doubles, 1 triple.
Bathrooms: 2 private, 3 shared.
Meals: Cont. breakfast.

Dates Open: All year.
High Season: June-August.
Rates: In-season $50-$90, off-season $35-$75.
Credit Cards: MC, Visa.
Rsv'tns: Required with 1/2 deposit within 5 days of booking.

To Reserve: Call direct.
Minimum Stay: 3 nights; 5 nights on holidays.
Parking: 6 spaces off premises.
In-Room: Maid service, rooms with private bath have color cable TV.
On-Premises: Cable TV in common room.

Swimming: Ocean beach nearby.
Sunbathing: On the beach or deck.
Smoking: Permitted without restrictions.
Pets: Not permitted.
Handicap Access: No.
Children: Not permitted.
Languages: English.

Captain's House
Gay/Lesbian ♂

The Captain's House is one of the oldest guesthouses of Provincetown. Built more than a century ago, it represents the typical architecture and simple elegance of a bygone era. Though on busy Commercial St., we're located up a secluded little alley where there is an absence of noise and a lot of unexpected privacy. Our charming little patio is great for morning coffee, cook-outs or sun tanning, and you will find the common room to be most comfortable. Our rooms are charming, immaculate and comfortable, with reasonable rates.

Address: 350-A Commercial St, Provincetown, MA 02657
Tel: (508) 487-9353, **Reservations:** (800) 457-8885.

Type: Guesthouse.
Clientele: Mostly men with women welcome.
Transportation: Taxi from airport 5 min. 2-min. walk from bus, ferry.
To Gay Bars: 5-10 minutes' walk to everything.
Rooms: 1 small single, 8 doubles & 2 rooms with 2 beds.

Bathrooms: 3 private & 2 shared. All rooms have sinks.
Meals: Continental breakfast.
Dates Open: All year.
High Season: Memorial Day-Labor Day.
Rates: $50-$100.
Discounts: By request on stays of 7 days or more.

Credit Cards: MC, VISA, Amex, Discover.
Rsv'tns: Necessary, as soon as possible.
To Reserve: Call direct.
Parking: Free parking.
In-Room: Color TV, maid service, refrigerator, & ceiling or window fans.
On-Premises: TV lounge, public telephone, & central heat.

Swimming: Ocean beach nearby.
Sunbathing: On beach or private patio.
Smoking: Permitted with restrictions.
Pets: Not permitted.
Handicap Access: No.
Children: Not permitted.
Languages: English.
Your Host: David & Bob.

INN PLACES® 1998   417

Carl's Guest House

Q-NET Men ♂

Where Strangers Become Friends

Our house is decorated in the clean, simple manner most suited to a beach vacation. Friendly, decent guys come from around the world to enjoy sea, sun and sand. At *Carl's Guest House,* all guest rooms are private, clean, comfortable and fairly priced. You can kick off your shoes and relax in an inviting living room with stereo, cable TV and a selection of video tapes of all ratings. We have been catering to gay *gentlemen* since 1975.

Address: 68 Bradford St, Provincetown, MA 02657
Tel: (508) 487-1650, brochure/rates tape: (800) 348-CARL.
E-mail: carlptwn@tiac.net **URL:** http://www.tiac.net/users/carlptwn

Type: Guesthouse.
Clientele: Men
Transportation: $1 bus, $5 taxi from airport; short walk from bus stn & boat dock.
Rooms: 14 rooms with single, double or queen beds.
Bathrooms: Private & semi-private.
Meals: Complimentary coffee, tea, soups and ice in lounge service area.
Complimentary: Coffee, tea, etc.
Dates Open: All year.
High Season: Mid-June to mid-September.
Rates: Summer $55-$125, other times $29-$69.
Discounts: For groups, gay business organizations during off season.
Credit Cards: MC, Visa.
To Reserve: Call direct.
Parking: Limited off-street & adequate on-street parking.
In-Room: Color TV, private sun decks, patios, AC, fridge, ceiling fans.
On-Premises: TV lounge with color cable TV & VCR.
Exercise/Health: Nearby gym.
Swimming: One block to ocean beach.
Sunbathing: On beach, private or common sun deck.
Nudity: Permitted on sun decks, in shower rooms.
Smoking: Smoking areas are limited.
Pets: Not permitted.
Handicap Access: No.
Children: Not permitted.
Languages: English.

Check'er Inn Resort

Q-NET Women ♀

Enjoy the Sweetness of Life

Since 1983, the *Check'er Inn Resort* has provided freindly, relaxing hospitality in a private setting, only one block from the world's finest gay and lesbian resort. Recently renovated, all accommodations now offer private entrances, private decks (or patios), in-room phone and color cable TV. All apartments are nicely appointed and include full-sized kitchens. The lawn and gardens invite a friendly game of croquet. You'll find hammocks tucked away for an afternoon in the shade with a good book, and a BBQ for grilling your favorite summer fare. Come see how sweet, spacious and comfortable your vacation can be. Member PBG and WIP.

Address: 25 Winthrop St, Provincetown, MA 02657
Tel: (508) 487-9029, (800) 894-9029.
E-mail: lilith@ptownlib.com **URL:** www.ptownlib.com/checker.html

Type: Suites & apartments.
Clientele: Primarily women
Transportation: 2 miles to airport, 6 blocks to ferry or bus.
To Gay Bars: 1 block to everything.
Rooms: 1 suite, 3 apartments.
Bathrooms: All private.
Dates Open: Apr-Nov.
High Season: Jun-Aug.

Rates: Low $100-$150 per night, high $900-$1,200 per week.
Discounts: 10% on Dotty's birthday in July. Occasional weekend specials in Apr & Sept.
Rsv'tns: Required.
To Reserve: Direct or travel agent.
Minimum Stay: 2 nights off season, longer minimums

during summer & holidays.
Parking: Off-street & on-site parking.
In-Room: Fully equipped apartments with kitchen, TV, phone, etc. Each unit has a private deck or patio.
On-Premises: Large lawn, BBQ.
Exercise/Health: Jacuzzi hot tub.
Swimming: 1 block to bay beach.

Sunbathing: On premises & at beach.
Nudity: Permitted in specified areas.
Smoking: Non-smoking rooms provided, please specify.
Pets: Not permitted.
Languages: English.
Your Host: Dotty, innkeeper.

The Chicago House Gay/Lesbian ♀♂

When in P-Town, Think of Chicago... (House, That Is!)

Chicago House, surrounded by charming gardens, canopied porches, inviting decks and patios, offers guests ten attractive rooms, nearly all with private bath, and four apartments with kitchenettes. Guests return each year, to the two historical Cape Cod homes that make up *Chicago House*, for the delicious homemade muffins and cakes baked daily for continental breakfast. One of the oldest established P-Town guesthouses, we stay open all year, offering a roaring fire in the common room in winter. We're centrally located, but on a quiet side street.

Address: 6 Winslow St, Provincetown, MA 02657
Tel: (508) 487-0537, (800) SEE-PTOWN (733-7869), **Fax:** (508) 487-6212.
E-mail: chihse@aol.com **URL:** http://members.aol.com/ChiHse

Type: Bed & breakfast guesthouse.
Clientele: Good mix of gay men & women.
Transportation: Car or boat from Boston. Free pick up from airport & ferry dock.
To Gay Bars: 1 block or 1 min walk.
Rooms: 10 rooms, 4 apartments with single, double, queen or king beds.
Bathrooms: Private: 1 bath/toilet, 8 shower/toilets.

Others share.
Meals: Continental breakfast.
Vegetarian: Available in restaurants.
Complimentary: Tea, coffee, mints on pillow.
Dates Open: All year.
High Season: July & August.
Rates: Summer $49-175 & winter $35-135.
Credit Cards: MC, Visa, Amex.

Rsv'tns: Suggested.
To Reserve: Call direct.
Minimum Stay: During July & August.
Parking: Adequate, free off-street parking.
In-Room: Color TV, maid service, kitchen & refrigerator.
On-Premises: TV lounge, meeting rooms, courtesy phone & guest refrigerator.
Exercise/Health: Gym & weights nearby.

Swimming: Nearby pool & ocean beach.
Sunbathing: On patio or nearby poolside & ocean beach.
Smoking: Permitted.
Pets: Permitted with advance notice & some restrictions.
Handicap Access: No.
Children: Permitted off season.
Languages: English.
Your Host: Randy.

Dexter's Inn

Gay/Lesbian ♀♂

Come Out to Provincetown & Feel at Home With Us

The experience of a lifetime awaits you in Provincetown. Steeped in history and located in the heart of downtown Provincetown, *Dexter's Inn* is just a short walk to Commercial Street, shops, restaurants, art galleries and clubs. Our unique cluster of rooms allows for private entrance from deck or patio. In-season, enjoy homemade muffins or breads, juice, and coffee each morning on the garden patio or in our cozy Keeping Room. Our spacious sun deck and patio are the perfect places to relax and meet new friends. UNDER NEW OWNERSHIP.

Address: 6 Conwell St, Provincetown, MA 02657
Tel: (508) 487-1911 (Tel/Fax), **toll-free:** (888) 521-1999.

Type: Bed & breakfast guesthouse.
Clientele: Gay & lesbian. Good mix of men & women
Transportation: Car, air, bus & ferry. Free airport pick up available with 1 week's notice.
To Gay Bars: 5-min walk.
Rooms: 15 rooms with double beds, some twin beds for 3 people.
Bathrooms: 12 private, 3 rooms share 1 bath.
Meals: Expanded continental breakfast, in-season & holidays.
Dates Open: All year.
High Season: Jun 15-Sept 15 & holidays.
Rates: $75-$99 in-season & holidays, $50-$60 off-season.
Discounts: Special off-season rates for long stays.
Credit Cards: MC, Visa.
Rsv'tns: Required.
To Reserve: Call direct.
Minimum Stay: Required in-season & holidays.
Parking: Ample on-premises free parking, 1 car per room.
In-Room: Maid service, color cable TV. Ceiling fans or AC in all rooms.
On-Premises: Sun deck, patio, refrigerator & courtesy phone.
Swimming: Ocean beach nearby.
Sunbathing: On ocean beach & sun deck.
Smoking: Non-smoking house. Smoking permitted outdoors.
Pets: Not permitted.
Handicap Access: Limited.
Children: Permitted over 14 years of age.
Languages: English.

Dusty Miller Inn

Q-NET Women ♀

Guests Thrive on the Friendly, Easy Atmosphere!

Making guests feel at home is our specialty at *Dusty Miller Inn*. The pleasant comfort of our porch rocking chairs seems to promote interesting conversations, and friendships are struck there. Our porch rockers also give you a great vantage point for peoplewatching. Expect to feel at ease and in the perfect mood to enjoy the fun of Provincetown. Our rooms are well-appointed and comfortable.

Address: 82 Bradford St, Provincetown, MA 02657 **Tel:** (508) 487-2213.

Type: Guesthouse.
Clientele: Mostly women with men welcome
Transportation: Taxi. Free pick up from airport with at least one week prior arrangement.
To Gay Bars: Across the street.
Rooms: 12 rooms & 1 apartment, all doubles.
Bathrooms: 10 private, others share.
Meals: Morning coffee or tea.
Dates Open: All year.
High Season: Memorial Day to Labor Day.
Rates: In season: $68-$78 double, $115 apt. Off season: $45-$55 double, $80 apartment.

FERRARI GUIDES™

Credit Cards: MC, Visa.
Rsv'tns: Required.
To Reserve: Call direct.
Minimum Stay: Rooms: 2 nights in season (holidays 3 nights). Apts: 2 nights (in season 7 nights).
Parking: 1 space per room on premises or in private lot approximately 1 block away.
In-Room: Maid service, color TV. Ceiling fans, fans, or AC in all rooms. Refrigerators in 7 rooms & apartment. Other rooms have access to refrigerators.
On-Premises: BBQ grills, common room, & desk phone in office.
Swimming: Ocean beach nearby.
Sunbathing: On the beach or in the front yard.
Smoking: Permitted without restrictions.
Pets: Permitted in designated rooms.
Handicap Access: No.
Children: Permitted.
Languages: English.

Elephant Walk Inn

Gay/Lesbian ♀♂

Elephant Walk "Unforgettable"

Elephant Walk Inn was built as a private country home in 1917. The large mission-style house was converted to an inn some years later. Its proximity to the center of town and the then existing railroad made it a favorite stop for early Provincetown visitors.

The decor of the inn recalls the romantic feeling of an Edwardian house of the past. Many of the rooms are decorated with original paintings, prints and antiques. One room has a canopy bed, another a four-poster, while brass and enamel beds grace two others. Old captain's bureaus, antique tables and Oriental carpets are scattered about.

However, to this echo of the past have been added the modern conveniences of the present. Each guest room has its own private bath as well as a remote cable color TV, a small refrigerator, and a ceiling fan. Air-conditioning is also available as an option.

Continental breakfast is served each morning on the glass-enclosed front porch where guests can also find a varied supply of reading material. Some guests enjoy their coffee on the large second floor sun deck which is at the rear of the inn overlooking the landscaped garden. The deck, with its scattering of summer furniture, is a favorite gathering spot for guests to meet and to enjoy a drink after a day at the beach.

Free parking is provided on the premises. Although a car is not necessary for seeing Provincetown with its myriad shops, restaurants and clubs, it is convenient to have one for exploring and finding a secluded beach with windswept dunes. June and September are the perfect times to do that. The days are warm and bright and although everything is open, there are no crowds.

Please call or write for a free brochure.

Address: 156 Bradford St, Provincetown, MA 02657
Tel: (508) 487-2543 or (800) 889-WALK (9255). **Guest phone:** (508) 487-2195.
E-mail: elephant@capecod.net **URL:** http://www.capecod.net/elephantwalk

Type: Bed & breakfast.
Clientele: Good mix of gay men & women.
Transportation: Pick up from airport, ferry or bus available.
To Gay Bars: 5-minute walk to men's, women's bars.
Rooms: 8 rooms with double, queen or king beds.

continued next page

UNITED STATES

Bathrooms: All private shower/toilets.
Meals: Continental breakfast.
Dates Open: Apr 15-Nov 10.
High Season: June 19-Sept 12.
Rates: In season $92-$115, off season $46-$81.
Discounts: 15% discount on stays of 7 days or more Apr 15-Jun 19 & Sept 15-Nov 10.
Credit Cards: MC, Visa, Amex, Diners, Discover.
Rsv'tns: Required 4-8 wks in advance in high season.
To Reserve: Call direct.
Minimum Stay: 3 nights in season, more on weekends, holidays.
Parking: Ample free off-street parking.
In-Room: Maid service, color TV, refrigerator, ceiling fans, phones, some with AC.
On-Premises: Lounge, sun deck. Guest phone in lounge.
Swimming: Ocean beach 1-1/2 blocks.
Sunbathing: On beach or common sun deck.
Smoking: Permitted in rooms, not in lounge.
Pets: Not permitted.
Handicap Access: No.
Children: Usually not permitted. Please inquire.
Languages: English.
Your Host: Len.

PROVINCETOWN • MASSACHUSETTS

Gabriel's   Women ♀

Perhaps There Really are Small Corners of This Earth That Come Close to Heaven

In the Heart of Provincetown • Conference Center •Workshops • Breakfast • Gym • Jacuzzis • Steam Room • Sauna • In-room Phones • Sun Decks • Barbecue • Fireplaces • Bicycles • Parking • Cable TV • Air Conditioning • Business Services • Group Rates Available

Come close to heaven.

Since 1979, *Gabriel's* has welcomed women and their friends to two beautiful old homes graced by antique furnishings, patios and gardens. Each guest room and suite, decorated differently, is distinguished by its own personality. We also offer modern conveniences such as fax, e-mail and copy services; cable TV, VCRs, in-room phones and fully-equipped kitchens.

Whether you take a soothing soak in one of our two hot tubs, unwind in our steam room or sauna, lounge on the sun decks, work out in our exercise area, relax in the common room around a fire, or set out at twilight towards the bright lights of Commercial Street, or the last, purple light of day fading over Herring Cove, you're certain to experience the unique character of Provincetown and the cozy hospitality of *Gabriel's*.

We are also home to *Siren's Workshop Center* offering a variety of classes for body, mind and spirit. Our lovely sky-lit meeting space is available year-round to both individuals and groups for conferences, ceremonies or other special events. Please accept our invitation to join us anytime in the comfortable, safe and heavenly setting of *Gabriel's*. Warmly, *Gabriel Brooke, Innkeeper*

Address: 104 Bradford St, Provincetown, MA 02657
Tel: (800) 9MY-ANGEL, (508) 487-3232, **Fax:** (508) 487-1605.
E-mail: gabriels@provincetown.com
URL: http://www.provincetown.com/gabriels

Type: Guesthouse & workshop center.
Clientele: Mostly women with men welcome
Transportation: Free pick up from airport, bus or ferry dock.
To Gay Bars: 1 block.
Rooms: 10 rooms & 10 apartments with double or queen beds.
Bathrooms: 16 private baths. 4 shared baths.
Meals: Homemade breakfast.
Complimentary: Coffee, tea, juice, fruit, muffins, cereal, chocolates on pillow.
Dates Open: All year.
High Season: Memorial Day to Labor Day week.
Rates: Winter $50-$100, Border season $65-$135, high season $80-$175.
Discounts: Nov 1-Apr 1, 3rd night free with coupon, coupons for repeat guests.
Credit Cards: MC, Visa, Amex, Discover.
Rsv'tns: Recommended.
To Reserve: Travel agent or call direct.
Minimum Stay: 2 nights in season & on weekends off season.
Parking: Reserved parking

422   FERRARI GUIDES™

in a nearby lot for $5 per night. **In-Room:** Cable TV, telephones, housekeeping service, refrigerators, fully equipped kitchens (in apartments). Some rooms with AC, ceiling fans & fireplaces.

On-Premises: TV lounge, conference room, library, games, common kitchen for light meals, two gardens. **Exercise/Health:** Yoga classes, 2 outdoor hot tubs, sauna, steam room, exercise room, discounts on massage. **Swimming:** Nearby ocean beach. **Sunbathing:** On beach and common sun decks. **Nudity:** Permitted on patio in our enclosed yard.

Smoking: Permitted with restrictions, smoke-free rooms available. **Pets:** Usually not permitted, but sometimes we bend. **Handicap Access:** No. **Children:** Permitted. **Languages:** English, French.

The Grandview Inn
Gay/Lesbian ♂

The Grandview Inn, an 1870's renovated captain's home, is ideally located in the picturesque West End, just seconds away from bustling Commercial Street's restaurants, galleries, shops and entertainment. Beaches are also minutes away. Continental breakfast is served daily from our umbrella-festooned decks, known for their panoramic views of the tip of Cape Cod and Provincetown Harbor. Room rates are moderately priced, and parking is also available. Treat the inn as your home, where friends are always welcome!

Address: No. 4 Conant St, Provincetown, MA 02657
Tel: (508) 487-9193. **E-mail:** vanbelle@capecod.net

Type: Guesthouse.
Clientele: 70% men, 30% women
Transportation: Plane from Boston to P'town airport, taxi to inn. Boat 9:30am from Boston, walk to inn.
To Gay Bars: 1 block to nearest bar, 1 min walk to afternoon tea dance.
Rooms: 12 rooms double, queen & king beds.

Bathrooms: Private, semi-private & shared.
Meals: Continental breakfast.
Vegetarian: Health food restaurants nearby.
Complimentary: Coffee & juices available in common room daily in season.
Dates Open: All year.
High Season: May 15-Sept 15.
Rates: High season $60-

$125, low season $40-$85.
Credit Cards: MC, Visa.
Rsv'tns: Required in season.
To Reserve: Call direct.
Minimum Stay: Major holidays during high season.
Parking: Available on a first come, first served basis.
In-Room: Maid service.
On-Premises: TV lounge, common room, kitchen.
Exercise/Health: High-tech

gym a 2-minute walk.
Swimming: Within walking distance.
Sunbathing: On common sun decks & nearby beaches.
Smoking: Permitted in designated outside areas.
Pets: Not permitted.
Handicap Access: No.
Children: No.
Languages: English.
Your Host: Tom & Michael.

Gull Walk Inn
Q-NET Women ♀

The Oldest Women's Guesthouse in Provincetown

Established in 1978, The Gull Walk Inn is the oldest women's guesthouse in Provincetown. The inn is located in the center of town, a block from Town Hall and MacMillan Wharf. This ensures that you'll be near everything and yet be sheltered from the hustle and bustle of town life. *The Gull Walk* is a small inn with five simple and clean guest rooms and two large shared baths. With its two

continued next page

INN PLACES® 1998

porches (one with a distant water view), common room and large private garden, you are welcomed to relax and feel at home.

Address: 300A Commercial St, Provincetown, MA 02657
Tel: (508) 487-9027 (Tel/Fax), (800) 309-4725.

Type: Guesthouse.
Clientele: Women only
To Gay Bars: 2 minutes to women's bar.
Rooms: 2 doubles, 1 single, 2 quads.
Bathrooms: 2 shared.
Meals: Continental breakfast.
Vegetarian: Restaurant 3 houses away, also health food store 4 houses away.
Complimentary: Coffee, tea, muffins.
Dates Open: All year.
High Season: May thru September.
Rates: Oct-Apr $29-$45, May-Sept $49-$72.
Rsv'tns: Required.
To Reserve: Call direct.
Minimum Stay: During holidays & August only.
Parking: Ample free on- & off-street & reserved parking.
On-Premises: TV lounge, refrigerator, microwave, VCR, porches, gardens.
Exercise/Health: Gym & weights 1 block away.
Swimming: Ocean beach.
Sunbathing: On ocean beach, common sundecks or on lawn.
Smoking: Permitted outdoors.
Pets: Not permitted.
Handicap Access: No.
Children: Permitted, if supervised.
Languages: English, French.
Your Host: Kathy & Polly.

Heritage House

Gay/Lesbian ♀♂

Having a Wonderful Time...Wish You Were Here!

Our house, with thirteen rooms on three floors, a large living room, two verandas and views of Cape Cod Bay and the harbor, is next door to the Heritage Museum between Commercial Street and Bradford Street. Some of the best people watching in Provincetown is to be had from the upper and lower verandas of *Heritage House*. Shops, the bay beach and many fine restaurants are just a short walk from our door. Our fluffy towels, fresh and crisp linens, sparkling-clean bathrooms, delicious coffee, homemade muffins and a friendly, comfortable atmosphere will help make your stay a pleasant one. We are committed to providing our guests with all these things and more. As your hosts, we'd like to help you enjoy the magic of Provincetown.

Address: 7 Center St, Provincetown, MA 02657
Tel: (508) 487-3692. **E-mail:** heritageh@capecod.net

Type: Guesthouse.
Clientele: Mostly gay & lesbian with some straight clientele
Transportation: Car or fly into Provincetown Airport from Boston's Logan Airport. Free pick up from airport & ferry wharf.
To Gay Bars: 5-minute walk to women's & men's bars.
Rooms: 13 rooms & 1-bedroom condo with single, double or king beds.
Bathrooms: 4 shared bath/shower/toilets. Condo with private bath.
Meals: Buffet breakfast.
Vegetarian: Breakfast is mostly vegetarian & restaurants featuring vegetarian selections are only a 5-minute walk.
Complimentary: Ice available. Refrigerator on each floor.
Dates Open: All year.
High Season: June through September & holidays weekends.
Rates: In season $50-$115, off season $40-$90.
Discounts: Off-season group rates available.
Credit Cards: MC, Visa, Amex.
Rsv'tns: Preferred.
To Reserve: Call direct.
Minimum Stay: 3 nights on holiday weekends.
Parking: Free off-street parking.
In-Room: Maid service.
On-Premises: Living room has color cable TV & VCR.
Exercise/Health: Gym, weights & massage nearby.
Swimming: In nearby ocean.
Sunbathing: At the beach.
Smoking: Permitted in rooms.
Pets: Not permitted.
Handicap Access: No.
Children: Not especially welcomed.
Languages: English, French.

FERRARI GUIDES™

Hotel Piaf

Q-NET Gay/Lesbian ♀♂

A Very Small, Very French Guesthouse in Provincetown

In the heart of Provincetown, the *Hotel Piaf* is a completely restored 1820 Cape, offering the finest service, luxurious informality, and the greatest attention to detail. The house has three rooms and one suite each with its own private full bath, telephone, and cable TV.

The house, just a minute's walk from Town Hall and the Meeting House, sits in the middle of a large garden with hammocks strung between tall locust trees and Adirondack chairs here and there for an afternoon's lazy read. The inn is furnished with a mix of the owner's family antiques and comfy, overstuffed chairs. Down comforters, terry cloth robes, European bath products, and fresh flowers are just a few of the comforts we've included.

Continental breakfast (included in your room rate) consists of a croissant or brioche, depending on the baker's whim, coffee, tea, espresso or cappucino, and juice. A booklet in each room gives recommendations for local dining and sightseeing. We are happy to make dinner reservations for you, reconfirm your travel plans with the airlines, and take you to the airport or meet your flight if you let us know in advance.

Relax on the deck or take a short walk to the ferry wharf and the Boston boat. We want your stay with us to be as comfortable, special, pampered, and relaxing as we like when we're on vacation. We are small and our facilities are historic and charming not lavish and grand, but we believe our attention to detail and our commitment to your comfort is unparalleled in town.

Address: 3 Prince St, Provincetown, MA 02657
Tel: (508) 487-7458, (800) 340-PIAF, **Fax:** (508) 487-8646.
E-mail: reserve@piaf.com **URL:** http://www.piaf.com

Type: Bed & breakfast.
Clientele: Mostly gay & lesbian with some straight clientele
Transportation: Car, plane, ferry. Free pick up from airport, bus, ferry dock.
To Gay Bars: 1 block, a 4-minute walk.
Rooms: 3 rooms, 1 suite with double or king beds.
Bathrooms: All private bath/toilets.

Meals: Continental breakfast.
Vegetarian: Available nearby.
Complimentary: Cocktails, set-up service, tea & coffee, mints on pillow.
Dates Open: May-Dec.
Rates: $80-$185.
Credit Cards: MC, Visa, Amex.
Rsv'tns: Required.

To Reserve: Travel agent or call direct.
Minimum Stay: Required on holiday weekends.
Parking: Adequate free parking.
In-Room: Color cable TV, VCR, telephone, maid, room & laundry service.
On-Premises: Video tape library, living & dining rooms, garden.

Exercise/Health: Nearby gym, weights, massage.
Swimming: Ocean nearby.
Sunbathing: On common sun decks, in garden.
Smoking: Permitted outside. No non-smoking rooms available.
Pets: Not permitted.
Handicap Access: No.
Children: Welcome.
Languages: English, French.

Lamplighter Inn & Cottage

Q-NET Gay/Lesbian ♂

Gentle Sea Breezes and the Grace and Charm of Yesteryear

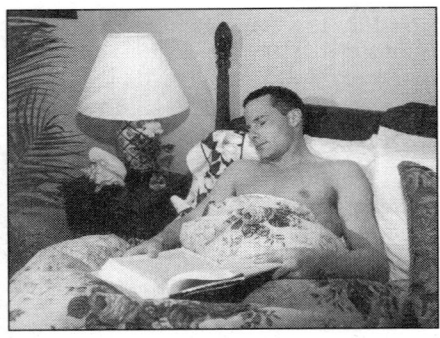

Lamplighter Inn is just a stroll to most beaches and the center of town. Our antique sea captain's home is on one of Provincetown's highest hills, overlooking Cape Cod Bay, and is within walking distance of all restaurants, shops and bars. Our inn is immaculate, and we strive to assure that your stay will always be remembered. Our must-see gardens include a water garden, cacti, rare shrubs and perennials. Come relax and enjoy Provincetown at the *Lamplighter Inn.* Please visit our website at http://www.CapeCodAccess.com/Lamplighter.

Address: 26 Bradford St, Provincetown, MA 02657
Tel: (508) 487-2529, (800) 263-6574, **Fax:** (508) 487-0079.
E-mail: lamplite@lamplite.com
URL: http://www.CapeCodAccess.com/Lamplighter

Type: Bed & breakfast guesthouse & cottage.
Clientele: Mostly men with women very welcome
Transportation: Car, bus. Ferry or Cape Air from Boston. Free pick up from airport, bus, ferry dock.
To Gay Bars: 3 blocks or 1/8 mile, a 5 minute walk.
Rooms: 7 rooms, 2 suites & 1 cottage with double, queen or king beds.
Bathrooms: 8 private baths, 2 semi-private baths.
Meals: Expanded continental breakfast.
Vegetarian: Available at local restaurants, delis & grocery stores. 5-min. walk to A&P.
Complimentary: Turn-down service, ice.
Dates Open: All year.
High Season: Mid-June through mid-September.
Rates: Winter $39-$75, spring & fall $55-$129, summer $89-$179.
Discounts: Off-season specials & discounts on longer stays.
Credit Cards: MC, Visa, Amex.
Rsv'tns: Highly recommended during peak season, holidays & special events.
To Reserve: Call direct or travel agent.
Minimum Stay: 5 nights during high season.
Parking: Free off-street parking, 1 car per room.
In-Room: Color cable TV, VCR, AC, telephones, ceiling fans, maid service, robes, kitchen, refrigerators.
On-Premises: Roof-top sun deck, bicycle rack, patios, BBQ grill, video library, fax machine.
Exercise/Health: Local gym nearby. Weights, massage.
Swimming: At nearby pool, ocean, lake or bay.
Sunbathing: On private roof-top sun deck.
Nudity: Permitted on roof-top deck.
Smoking: Non-smoking rooms. Smoking permitted on sun deck and in outdoor areas.
Pets: Not permitted.
Handicap Access: No.
Children: Not especially welcomed.
Languages: English.
Your Host: Steve & Brent.

IGLTA

Land's End Inn

Gay/Friendly 50/50 ♀♂

Relax in Victorian Comfort

Land's End Inn commands a splendid windswept location with breathtaking views of Provincetown Harbor and the whole of Cape Cod from on high. Built in the late Victorian period, the inn still houses part of the original owner's collection of oriental wood carvings and stained glass. Spacious rooms furnished with antiques provide a lived-in atmo-

A.Blake Gardener, Photographer

426

FERRARI GUIDES™

sphere where the modern world has not entered. Here in the quiet west end, we're close to ocean beaches, restaurants and nightlife.

Address: 22 Commercial St, Provincetown, MA 02657
Tel: (508) 487-0706, (800) 276-7088.

Type: Bed & breakfast guesthouse.
Clientele: 50% gay & lesbian & 50% straight clientele
Transportation: Car is best or fly via Provincetown Airport. Bus & ferry runs from Boston Memorial Day-Labor Day.
To Gay Bars: 15-min walk to men's/women's bars.
Rooms: 13 rooms, 1 suite & 2 apartments with double or queen beds.
Bathrooms: 16 private bath/toilets.
Meals: Continental breakfast.
Dates Open: All year.
High Season: Memorial Day Weekend-Sept 30.
Rates: $90-$295.
Credit Cards: MC, Visa.
Rsv'tns: Recommended.
To Reserve: Call direct.
Minimum Stay: Summer 5-7 days, off-season weekends and some holidays have minimums.
Parking: Ample free off- & on-street parking.
In-Room: Maid service. Some units with kitchens & ceiling fans.
On-Premises: Public telephone, refrigerator, living rooms.
Swimming: Nearby ocean.
Sunbathing: On private sun decks, lawn or nearby beach.
Smoking: Not permitted inside. Permitted on decks, porches & in garden.
Pets: Not permitted.
Handicap Access: No.
Children: Permitted if under 1 year or over 12.
Languages: English.
Your Host: Anthony.

Lotus Guest House

Gay/Lesbian ♀♂

Lotus Guest House is situated in a beautiful Victorian building in the heart of town near beaches, bus, and ferry. The guesthouse has large, spacious rooms with private or shared bath, and a beautiful 2-bedroom suite with a private balcony overlooking Commercial Street. There is a charming common deck where you can enjoy a morning coffee or just relax and socialize. The centralized location of this guesthouse enables you to walk to every restaurant, nightclub, shop, and gallery in town.

Address: 296 Commercial St, Provincetown, MA 02657
Tel: (508) 487-4644.

Type: Guesthouse with boutique.
Clientele: Mostly gay/lesbian
Transportation: Taxi from airport, Boston Ferry & bus lines 1/2 block.
To Gay Bars: 1 block.
Rooms: 12 rooms & 1 suite with double beds.
Bathrooms: 3 private bath/toilets & 2 shared bath/shower/toilets.
Complimentary: Morning coffee.
Dates Open: May-Oct.
High Season: July-Aug.
Rates: In season $55-$110, off season $35-$80.
Discounts: Call about weekly specials.
Credit Cards: MC, Visa, Amex.
Rsv'tns: Recommended.
To Reserve: Travel agent or call direct.
Minimum Stay: 3 nights weekends, 3-7 nights holidays, call.
Parking: Limited on-street parking, Municipal & private lots 1/2 block away.
In-Room: Maid service & ceiling fans.
On-Premises: Large common deck, tables & chairs in garden.
Swimming: Ocean beach.
Sunbathing: On beach & patio.
Smoking: Permitted.
Pets: Not permitted.
Handicap Access: No.
Languages: English.

UNITED STATES • MASSACHUSETTS • PROVINCETOWN

Normandy House

Gay-Owned ♀♂

A Room With More Than Just A View

Awaken each morning to a gentle sea breeze and sweeping ocean views of Provincetown harbor and Cape Cod Bay. Then, join us in our sun-drenched common room for continental breakfast. Rooms have TV, VCR and refrigerator, and all have air conditioning. Furnishings range from contemporary to antiques. Shed the accumulated tensions of urban living by relaxing on the sun deck with panoramic views of the lower cape, or melt those frazzled nerves away in the hot tub! *Normandy House* is your haven by the sea.

Address: 184 Bradford St, Provincetown, MA 02657
Tel: (508) 487-1197 or (800) 487-1197.

Type: Guesthouse.
Clientele: 80% gay & lesbian & 20% straight clientele
To Gay Bars: 10-minute walk to men's/women's bars.
Rooms: 7 rooms, 1 apartment & 2-BR suite with double or queen beds.
Bathrooms: 5 private & 2 shared.
Meals: Continental breakfast.

Complimentary: Ice & mixes.
Dates Open: All year.
High Season: Mid-June to mid-September.
Rates: High season $80-$195, low season $60-$100.
Credit Cards: MC, Visa, Amex.
Rsv'tns: Required.
To Reserve: Call direct.
Minimum Stay: 4 nights on Memorial Day weekend, 7

nights on big holidays & Carnival.
Parking: Limited free off-street parking.
In-Room: Cable color TV, VCR, video tape library, AC, ceiling fans, telephone, kitchen, refrigerator & maid service.
On-Premises: Lovely common rooms w/sun porch, sun deck, Jacuzzi.
Exercise/Health: Jacuzzi.
Swimming: Nearby town beach & National Seashore

beaches.
Sunbathing: On common sun deck, patio & at nearby beaches.
Nudity: On sun deck with discretion.
Smoking: Permitted. Non-smoking room available.
Pets: Not permitted during high season.
Handicap Access: No.
Children: Not permitted during high season.
Languages: English.
Your Host: Dennis.

Pilgrim House Inn

Women ♀

Where the Girls Are in Provincetown

Pilgrim House Inn offers you everything you could want for a perfect Provincetown vacation — from its bright and inviting rooms, to Vixen, the on-premises nightclub and lounge. The inn's unique off-street location is a short stroll down a brick walkway, directly onto Commercial Street with its galleries, shops, clubs and restaurants. Our rooms feature queen- or full-sized beds, private baths, AC, color television and telephones. At night, come in to play at Vixen, our very own nightclub. Enjoy dancing and nightly live shows in the club, or listen to jazz and blues in the lounge.

Address: 336 Commercial St, Provincetown, MA 02657
Tel: (508) 487-6424, **Fax:** (508) 487-6296.

Type: Inn with bar & disco.
Clientele: Mostly women with men welcome
To Gay Bars: Downstairs on premises, others nearby.
Rooms: 17 rooms, 2 suites with double or queen beds.
Bathrooms: All private.

Meals: Continental breakfast.
Dates Open: Apr 1-Jan 15.
High Season: Summer & special weekends.
Rates: $79-$109 per night.
Credit Cards: MC, Visa, Amex.

To Reserve: Travel agent or call direct.
Parking: Adequate pay parking.
In-Room: Telephone, AC, color TV, maid service.
On-Premises: Meeting rooms, TV lounge.

Sunbathing: At beach.
Pets: Not permitted.
Handicap Access: Yes. Ramps, rails in bathroom, wide doors, elevator.
Children: Welcome.

428

FERRARI GUIDES™

The Prince Albert Guest House

Q-NET Gay-Owned & -Operated ♀♂

Fine Lodging on Cape Cod Bay

Built in 1870 for a wealthy Provincetown family, *The Prince Albert Guest House* was constructed during the reign of Queen Victoria and named for her husband, Prince Albert. The home, formerly known as the Casablanca Guesthouse and, most recently as the Four Bay Guesthouse, was entirely renovated, inside and out, during the spring of 1997. This renovation resulted in the addition of three new guestrooms, five new private baths and new brick patios in both the front of the guesthouse and in the fenced-in rear gardens. The guesthouse offers ten guestrooms, eight private baths and two hall baths. All rooms have telephones, air conditioning, ceiling fans, color cable televisions, VCRs and small refrigerators. Throughout the home, the *Prince Albert's* heritage is reflected in the Victorian period furnishings, antiques and the plush Oriental rugs.

The Prince Albert is an ideal spot for your summer vacation. We are situated across from Cape Cod Bay and the popular Boatslip Beach Club with its well-known Tea Dance. Step outside and walk over to Provincetown Harbor, or stroll down Commercial Street — we're just a short walk from Provincetown's renowned restaurants, art galleries, shops and clubs, including the A-House and the Pied Piper. With all of the clubs in town, there is no lack of live shows and entertainment. The Cape Cod National Seashore is a quick bike ride from our front door and Herring Cove Beach is easily accessible by foot, bicycle or town loop bus. With miles of beach and forest cycling trails, there is ample opportunity to visit this beautiful seaside area. If your interests lean more toward water activities, then you will not be disappointed! Provincetown offers whale watching tours, fishing and wind surfing, as well as jet skiing, speed boating and sailing. Many events take place here throughout the year, including Women's Week in October, Men's Singles Week in November and Carnival Week filled with parades, costume balls and contests.

Address: 166 Commercial St, Provincetown, MA 02657
Tel: (508) 487-0859, (800) 992-0859, **Fax:** (508) 487-1533.
E-mail: ohart@capecod.net

Type: Guesthouse.
Clientele: Mostly gay & lesbian with some straight clientele
Transportation: Air direct to P'town, or air to Boston then ferry to P'town.
To Gay Bars: 1 block, a 2 min walk.
Rooms: 10 rooms with double, queen or king beds.

Bathrooms: 8 private bath/shower/toilets. 2 shared bath/shower/toilets.
Meals: Coffee & tea only.
Vegetarian: Several vegetarian restaurants in town.
Complimentary: Tea & coffee.
Dates Open: All year.
High Season: June-Sept.

Rates: Summer $75-$150, winter $70-$85.
Credit Cards: MC, Visa.
Rsv'tns: Required.
To Reserve: Call direct.
Minimum Stay: Required.
Parking: Limited pay parking. 5 spaces off-site, first-come basis.
In-Room: Telephone, AC,

ceiling fans, color cable TV, VCR, refrigerator, maid service.
Sunbathing: On patio.
Smoking: Permitted outside on patios. All guest rooms are non-smoking.
Pets: Not permitted.
Handicap Access: No.
Children: No.
Languages: English.

INN PLACES® 1998

Ravenwood Guestrooms & Apartments
Quiet Accommodation in the Gallery District

Q-NET Women ♀

Originally a sea captain's residence, *Ravenwood* now offers comfortable and inviting guestrooms and apartments to Provincetown visitors. Some rooms have ocean views. Other features are decks, beamed ceilings and Casa Blanca fans. Guests relax in an enclosed backyard with flower gardens, statues and fountain. Each accommodation has its own outside sitting deck or picnic area. We are centrally located, directly across the street from the harbor, near the beach and only a five-minute stroll to the center of town. A Cape Cod cottage is also available for long weekends or by the week.

Address: 462 Commercial St, Provincetown, MA 02657
Tel: (508) 487-3203 (Tel/Fax)

Type: Guest room & year-round apartments, condo & year-round cottage.
Clientele: Women. Men permitted only if accompanied by their women friends.
Transportation: Plane, bus, ferry, car from Boston.
To Gay Bars: 5 blocks to men's/women's bars.
Rooms: 1 room, 3 apartments & 1 cottage.
Bathrooms: All have private shower & toilet.
Vegetarian: Available at many nearby restaurants.
Complimentary: Mints on pillows, private catering of flowers, champagne, balloons, etc can be arranged.

Dates Open: All year.
High Season: Spring whale watching, fall foliage, winter holidays & July & August.
Rates: Summer $80-$125, winter $60-$110.
Discounts: Off season 3rd consecutive night free. Better price on stays of over 2 weeks.
Credit Cards: All major cards accepted for deposit only.
Rsv'tns: Recommended.
To Reserve: Travel agent or call direct.
Minimum Stay: 3 nights holiday wknds, 7 nights July-Aug & Oct Women's Week. Inquire about shorter stays.

Parking: Ample off-street parking. 1 private spot per room. Other parking available.
In-Room: Color cable TV, VCRs, ceiling fans & refrigerators. Apts have kitchens.
On-Premises: Patio, BBQ, private fenced-in yards or private decks. Special arrangements available for commitment ceremonies or domestic partner registration.
Exercise/Health: Complimentary passes to a gym & Jacuzzi 4 blks away. Massage available.

Swimming: At ocean beach.
Sunbathing: On ocean beach, private sun decks & in private garden.
Nudity: Permitted on private decks of apts.
Smoking: Permitted without restrictions. Non-smoking rooms available.
Pets: Not permitted.
Handicap Access: Studios are accessible.
Children: Permitted (age restrictions).
Languages: English, French.
Your Host: Valerie.

Revere House

Q-NET Gay/Lesbian ♂

Home Sweet Home

Revere House is a restored captain's home of the Federal period, circa 1820-1840. The charm and ambiance of this bygone era still prevails throughout the ten antique-filled rooms, which include a comfortable studio with a kitchenette and a private bath. In season, coffee, tea, juice and homemade muffins and breads are served in the common room, which overlooks the garden. It's a short walk to shops, galleries, restaurants and nightclubs, and for those desiring some solitude, the majestic ocean is only minutes away. Free parking is available.

Address: 14 Court St, Provincetown, MA 02657
Tel: (508) 487-2292, (800) 487-2292.
E-mail: reveregh@tiac.net **URL:** www.provincetown.com/revere

Type: Guesthouse.
Clientele: Mostly men with women welcome.
Transportation: Car, bus or boat.
To Gay Bars: 1 block to gay/lesbian bars.
Rooms: 7 rooms & 1 efficiency apartment with double, queen or king beds.
Bathrooms: 1 private shower/toilet, 2 shared bath/shower/toilet & 1 toilet only.
Meals: Cont. breakfast.
Vegetarian: Restaurants within 2 blocks.
Dates Open: April-November.
High Season: June-September.
Rates: In-season $50-$110, off-season $30-$70.
Credit Cards: MC, Visa, Amex.
Rsv'tns: Suggested.
To Reserve: Call or e-mail direct.
Minimum Stay: Holidays 4 days, Jul-Aug 4 days on weekends.
Parking: Ample free off-street parking.
In-Room: Some rooms have color cable TV. 1 has AC.
On-Premises: Common lounge, refrigerator & microwave.
Swimming: Ocean beach.
Sunbathing: On beach or in yard.
Smoking: Permitted with restrictions.
Pets: Not permitted.
Handicap Access: No.
Children: Not permitted.
Languages: English & limited French.

IGLTA

Roomers

Q-NET Gay/Lesbian ♂

Provincetown...the name alone evokes thoughts of a quaint fishing village surrounded by beautiful beaches and untamed sand dunes, fine restaurants and a shopper's paradise. *Roomers* guesthouse maintains the charms of the past, but has the crisp, clean, contemporary feel of today. Each room is decorated with quality antiques and has private bath, queen-sized bed, ceiling fan, TV and refrigerator. Cozy and intimate...that's *Roomers'* style.

Address: 8 Carver St, Provincetown, MA 02657 **Tel:** (508) 487-3532.

Type: Guesthouse.
Clientele: Mostly men with women welcome
Transportation: Free pickup from airport or ferry.
To Gay Bars: Gay bar across the street, others 1-3 blocks.
Rooms: 9 rooms with twin or queen beds.
Bathrooms: All private.
Meals: Cont. breakfast.
Dates Open: Apr-Dec.
High Season: Memorial Day weekend, July, August & Labor Day weekend.
Rates: In-season $105-$140, off-season $65-$105.
Credit Cards: Visa, Amex, MC.
Rsv'tns: Required.
To Reserve: Call direct.
Minimum Stay: 5 days in-season.
Parking: Free off-street parking, 1 space per room.
In-Room: Refrigerator, maid service, color cable TV.
On-Premises: 2 common rooms.
Sunbathing: In side yard.
Smoking: Permitted without restrictions.
Children: Not permitted.
Languages: English.
Your Host: Andrew.

INN PLACES® 1998   431

Sandpiper Beach House

Gay/Lesbian ♀♂

A Beautiful Waterfront Guesthouse

Refurbished in 1997, the *Sandpiper* is a beautiful turreted Victorian guesthouse on the beach next to the world-famous Boatslip. All rooms have private baths, and several have glass doors and balconies overlooking the harbor. Off-street parking and continental breakfast are included in your room rate. Also included is the use of our private beach and the Boatslip's pool, sun cots, and free admission to the Boatslip Tea Dance. We are open year-round and off-season rates are available. Please call toll-free or write for further information.

Address: 165 Commercial St,
PO Box 646, Provincetown, MA 02657
Tel: (508) 487-1928 or (800) 354-8628.
E-mail: sandpiper@provincetown.com
URL: www.provincetown.com/sandpiper

Type: Guesthouse.
Clientele: Gay & lesbian. Good mix of men & women
Transportation: Car is best, or taxi from airport.
To Gay Bars: Next door to men's & 2 blocks to women's bar.
Rooms: 9 rooms with double beds & 4 with queen beds.
Bathrooms: All private shower/toilets.

Meals: Continental breakfast.
Dates Open: All year.
High Season: June 18th-Sept 9th.
Rates: Off-season $75-$100, in-season $115-$185.
Discounts: Off-season rates available.
Credit Cards: MC, Visa.
Rsv'tns: Required in season. Strongly recommended off season.
To Reserve: Call direct.

Minimum Stay: 6 nights in season. Varies off season.
Parking: Adequate free off-street parking.
In-Room: Cable color TV, ceiling fans & maid service. Most have AC, some with refrigerators, all with direct-dial phones.
On-Premises: Common room, large veranda & patio.
Exercise/Health: Nearby gym, weights & massage.

Swimming: Pool next door in season. Ocean beach.
Sunbathing: At poolside, on beach, private sun decks or patio.
Smoking: Permitted.
Pets: Not permitted.
Handicap Access: Limited accessibility.
Children: Permitted, but not recommended.
Languages: English.
Your Host: Fred.

IGLTA

Sea Drift Inn

Q-NET Men ♂

A Guesthouse for Gay Men

Sea Drift is a complex of two guesthouses catering to gay men. We're within walking distance of all restaurants, shops and bars. We provide such amenities as extra beach towels, parking passes, aspirin and items you might forget to pack. Eighteen double rooms with European-style shared baths have daily maid service. A private bar has ice, mixers and limes, stereo, TV/VCR with movies. BBQ facilities for guests are outside, as are a sundeck and expanded garden and patio. We serve continental breakfast and occasionally host cocktail parties.

Address: 80 Bradford St, Provincetown, MA 02657
Tel: (508) 487-3686.

Type: Guesthouse.
Clientele: Men only
Transportation: Free pick up from Provincetown Airport.
To Gay Bars: 1 block to men's bars.
Rooms: 18 rooms with single or double beds.
Bathrooms: 5 shared bath/shower/toilets.
Meals: Continental breakfast.
Complimentary: Set-up service, ice.
Dates Open: All year.
High Season: Jul-Aug.
Rates: $50-$80.
Discounts: 10% on each night after 7 days.
Credit Cards: MC, Visa, Discover.
Rsv'tns: Highly recommended.
To Reserve: Call direct.
Minimum Stay: 2 nights on weekends & 5 on holidays.
Parking: Limited, free, off-street parking.
In-Room: Maid, room & laundry service.
On-Premises: Outside deck.
Swimming: 2 blocks to ocean beach.
Sunbathing: On deck or beach.
Smoking: Permitted without restrictions.
Pets: Not permitted.
Handicap Access: No.
Children: Not permitted.
Languages: English.
Your Host: Dick.

Six Webster Place

Q-NET Gay/Lesbian ♀♂

A 1750's Bed & Breakfast

Six Webster Place is a newly restored 1750's bed and breakfast located on a quiet lane in the heart of historic Provincetown. This historic home is an ideal year-round retreat for guests who seek a small and intimate colonial atmosphere in the spirit and style of Ye Old New England. The architecture, layout and amenities are of a grace and character of a bygone era, recently improved for modern convenience and comfort (yes, indoor plumbing was installed in 1986). In addition to our traditional guest rooms with working fireplaces and private baths, we now offer luxury apartments as well.

Address: 6 Webster Place, Provincetown, MA 02657
Tel: (508) 487-2266, (800) 6 WEBSTER.
URL: http://www.ptown.com/ptown/lodging/sixwebster

Type: Bed & breakfast.
Clientele: Mostly gay & lesbian with some straight clientele
Transportation: Free pickup from airport, bus, ferry.
To Gay Bars: 1 block to men's/women's bars.
Rooms: 7 rooms, 2 suites & 3 apartments with double, queen or king beds.
Bathrooms: Private: 6 shower/toilets, 2 full baths. 2 shared full baths.
Meals: Expanded continental breakfast.
Vegetarian: All vegetarian.
Dates Open: All year.
High Season: June-October.
Rates: Summer $50-$105, winter $35-$85.
Credit Cards: MC, Visa, Amex, Discover.
Rsv'tns: Recommended.
To Reserve: Travel agent or call direct.
Minimum Stay: 5 days in July & August.
Parking: Free off-street parking (1 space per rental).
In-Room: Maid service, color TV/VCR, ceiling fans. Most rooms have fireplaces.
On-Premises: TV lounge.
Exercise/Health: Jacuzzi.
Swimming: Ocean beach, bay beach.
Sunbathing: On beach, common sun decks & patio.
Smoking: Permitted without restrictions.
Pets: Permitted.
Handicap Access: Studio apartment is accessible.
Children: Permitted in off-season.
Languages: English.

IGLTA

INN PLACES® 1998

Sunset Inn

Q-NET Gay/Lesbian ♀♂

You'll Love the Sunsets from The Sunset

The *Sunset Inn* is one of Provincetown's oldest guesthouses. Built in the mid-nineteenth century as a private home, it has been a guesthouse welcoming visitors for more than half a century. If the *Sunset Inn* looks familiar, it may be that you've seen one of the many paintings or photographs depicting the building. Scores of artists have been attracted by the stately elegance and beauty of the inn. Among them renowned local artist Robert Kennedy, whose paintings of the inn can be found in art galleries throughout the country, and American artist Edward Hopper, whose famous painting of the inn entitled *Rooms for Tourist* hangs in the permanent collection at the Yale University Art Gallery in New Haven.

At the *Sunset Inn* you're in the heart of Provincetown, just one block from the center of town and the beach. Stroll down Commercial Street and browse the unique shops and galleries that have made Provincetown famous. Enjoy dinner at one of the many fine restaurants the town has to offer; from hot dogs to haute cuisine, you're sure to find what you crave. And, of course, there is the legendary excitement of the Provincetown nightlife with cabarets, comedy shows, dance clubs and nightclubs — all within walking distance of the inn. For the outdoor types, we are close to the National Seashore bike trails, whale watching, fishing boats, dune rides and airplane sightseeing.

We offer spacious, comfortable guest rooms, each distinct in its decor. You'll find all the modern conveniences, yet we've retained the cozy warmth of a Cape Cod inn. Our sun decks and porches afford spectacular views of Provincetown Harbor and are a perfect vantage point from which to view Provincetown's sunsets. We've carefully created a cordial and informal setting to ensure that your stay with us is comfortable and relaxed.

Address: 142 Bradford St, Provincetown, MA 02657
Tel: (508) 487-9810, (800) 965-1801.
E-mail: sunset1@capecod.net **URL:** www.ptown.com/ptown/sunsetinn

Type: Guesthouse.
Clientele: Mostly gay & lesbian with some straight clientele
Transportation: Car, airplane, ferry from Boston. Free pick up from Provincetown airport.
To Gay Bars: 3 blocks to gay bars.
Rooms: 20 rooms with single, double or queen beds..
Bathrooms: 12 private shower/toilets, 6 shared bath/shower/toilets.
Meals: Continental breakfast.
Vegetarian: Available nearby.
Complimentary: Ice.
Dates Open: Apr 15-Nov 1.
High Season: Mid-Jun to mid-Sept.
Rates: Off season (spring & fall): $44-$75; high season (summer): $59-$120.
Credit Cards: MC, Visa, Discover.
Rsv'tns: Highly suggested.
To Reserve: Travel agent or call direct.
Minimum Stay: 4 nights weekends, 4 nights Memorial Day, 5 nights 4th of July & Labor Day.
Parking: Ample free off-street parking.
In-Room: Maid service, color TV, telephone.
On-Premises: TV lounge.
Exercise/Health: Nearby gym, weights, massage.
Swimming: In nearby ocean & bay.
Sunbathing: On common sun decks, at beach.
Nudity: Permitted on top deck.
Smoking: Permitted in room.
Pets: Not permitted.
Handicap Access: No.
Children: No.
Languages: English.

Three Peaks

Gay/Lesbian ♀♂

... *A Victorian Bed and Breakfast*

Comfort is what is emphasized at *Three Peaks*, an 1870's Victorian house originally built as a summer home for a prominent Midwestern family. Today it is a perfect B&B for guests visiting Provincetown. It is located in the East End where art galleries, shops, restaurants, and entertainment are within a few minutes' walk. Town beaches are a block away, while the National Seashore beaches of Herring Cove and Race Point are within bike or driving distance. In season, the town "Loop" bus provides transportation to all areas. After sightseeing, relax on the patio/deck or on the rockers on the wraparound front porch.

Address: 210 Bradford St, Provincetown, MA 02657
Tel: (508) 487-1717, (800) 286-1715.
E-mail: threepks@capecod.net
URL: www.capecod.net/threepeaks

Type: Bed & breakfast.
Clientele: Good mix of gays & lesbians
Transportation: Free airport, bus or ferry dock "shuttle" service.
To Gay Bars: 10-15 minute walk.
Rooms: 5 rooms with queen or double beds, 2 apartments with double beds.
Bathrooms: All private bath/toilets.
Meals: Continental breakfast.
Complimentary: Juice bar.
Dates Open: All year.
High Season: Memorial Day weekend through Labor Day weekend.
Rates: In-season $90-$125, mid-season $60-$95, off-season $50-$85.
Discounts: 10% on stays of 7 or more nights, mid- & off-season specials.
Credit Cards: MC, Visa, Discover.
Rsv'tns: Recommended for high season.
To Reserve: Call direct.
Minimum Stay: 2-3 nights. 4-5 nights for holidays & special events.
Parking: Ample free off-street parking.
In-Room: Color cable TV & refrigerator. In-season AC or ceiling fans, VCR in apartments.
On-Premises: Common room/reading room, outdoor patio/sun deck, garden areas, bike rack.
Exercise/Health: Nearby gym, tennis, bicycle rental & bicycle trails.
Swimming: One block to bay beach.
Sunbathing: On patio/deck & nearby beach.
Smoking: Smoke-free atmosphere.
Pets: Not permitted.
Handicap Access: No.
Languages: English.
Your Host: Walt & John.

The Tradewinds Inn

Gay-Owned & -Operated ♀♂

One of Provincetown's Finest Guesthouses

Tradewinds Inn is one of the most friendly and gracious inns you'll find. Each room has a special charm, some with poster beds and antiques, others with brass beds or designer wicker furniture. The suite has vaulted ceilings and fridge. Most rooms have private baths, color TV and VCR. We're conveniently located a few steps from Commercial St., with free parking.

Address: 12 Johnson St, Provincetown, MA 02657
Tel: (508) 487-0138, (800) 487-0132, **Fax:** (508) 487-9484.
URL: tradewindsinn.com

continued next page

UNITED STATES

Type: Guesthouse.
Clientele: Gay & lesbian. Good mix of men and women
Transportation: Car is best.
To Gay Bars: 5 blocks, a 5 min walk.
Rooms: 16 rooms with double or queen beds.
Bathrooms: 12 private bath/shower/toilets, 4 shared bath/shower/toilets.
Meals: Continental breakfast.
Vegetarian: Available nearby.
Dates Open: All year.
High Season: Jun-Aug.
Rates: Summer $70-$180, fall $70-$160, winter $65-$130, spring $65-$150.
Credit Cards: MC, Visa, Amex.
Rsv'tns: Required.
To Reserve: Call direct.
Minimum Stay: Required.
Parking: Adequate free parking.
In-Room: Ceiling fans, color cable TV, VCR, refrigerator, maid service.
On-Premises: TV lounge, video tape library.
Exercise/Health: Jacuzzi. Gym nearby.
Swimming: Ocean nearby.
Sunbathing: On ocean beach or patio.
Smoking: Permitted, non-smoking rooms available.
Pets: Not permitted.
Handicap Access: No.
Children: No.
Languages: English.

PROVINCETOWN • MASSACHUSETTS

The Tucker Inn at Twelve Center   Q-NET Gay/Lesbian ♀♂

A Romantic Country Inn by the Sea

The Tucker Inn at Twelve Center, originally a sea captain's home, pays tribute to Provincetown's history and Captain Miles B. Tucker's tradition of gracious hospitality.

There are eight spacious, antique-filled rooms, most with queen-sized beds and private baths, and one fully equipped cottage. The inn is located on a quiet side street in the heart of Provincetown. A complimentary expanded continental breakfast is served daily in the comfortable living room or on a private tree-shaded patio. There is ample on-site parking.

Address: 12 Center St, Provincetown, MA 02657
Tel: (508) 487-0381, **Fax:** (508) 487-6235.
URL: http://www.provincetown.com/tucker

Type: Bed & breakfast inn.
Clientele: Mostly gay & lesbian.
To Gay Bars: A 2-minute walk to gay & lesbian bars.
Rooms: 6 queens & 2 doubles, 1 fully equipped cottage apartment.
Bathrooms: Private baths in queen rooms, semi-private in doubles.
Meals: Expanded continental breakfast (all homemade specialties).
Complimentary: Beach chairs & towels, daily room fresh.
Dates Open: May 1-Nov 1.
Rates: $90-$125 high season, $70-$100 low season.
Credit Cards: Visa, MC.
Rsv'tns: Suggested.
To Reserve: Call direct.
Minimum Stay: 3 nights Jul-Aug, 5 nights holidays & Women's Week.
Parking: Ample parking on premises.
In-Room: Color cable TV, ceiling fans, spacious antique-filled rooms.
On-Premises: Patio & yard for quiet relaxation, bike rack.
Swimming: In nearby bay, 1 block.
Sunbathing: In yard or back patio.
Smoking: Permitted outside.
Pets: Not permitted.

FERRARI GUIDES™

Watership Inn

Gay/Lesbian ♂

Quiet & Conveniently Located

A home to ship captains in the seafaring days of the 1820's, *Watership Inn* is now a comfortable inn. Enjoy the fresh, salt air, clean skies and bright, Cape Cod sunshine. Walk the beaches or cycle the miles of trails through the dunes. *Watership Inn* is half a block from the harbor, right in the center of town, close to everything, yet on a quiet sidestreet.

Address: 7 Winthrop St, Provincetown, MA 02657
Tel: (508) 487-0094, (800) 330-9413.
URL: www.cimarron.net/usa/ma/watership

Type: Bed & breakfast.
Clientele: Mostly men with women welcome
To Gay Bars: 2 blocks to all gay bars.
Rooms: 15 rooms & 2 2-BR apartments with queen or double beds.
Bathrooms: All private.
Meals: Continental breakfast.
Complimentary: Ice & mixers in season.

Dates Open: All year.
High Season: May-Sept.
Rates: Rooms $35-$120, apartment $75-$175 per night.
Discounts: 10% on weekly stays, Nov-Mar 3rd night free.
Credit Cards: MC, Visa, Amex, Discover.
Rsv'tns: Suggested.
To Reserve: Call direct or travel agent.

Minimum Stay: Required on some summer holiday weekends.
Parking: Ample free parking.
In-Room: Maid service, color TVs. All rooms fan-cooled.
On-Premises: Common room with wood stove.
Exercise/Health: Gym nearby.

Swimming: At nearby pool & ocean beach.
Sunbathing: In yard & on private & common sun decks.
Smoking: Permitted without restrictions.
Pets: Not permitted.
Handicap Access: No.
Children: Not permitted.
Languages: English.
Your Host: Rick.

Windamar House

Q-NET Women ♀

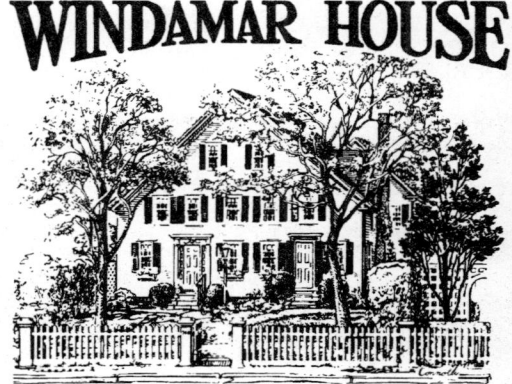

Windamar House is one of Provincetown's most beautiful, historical, seaside properties. It stands on half an acre with colorful English flower gardens and manicured lawns. This mini-estate is directly across from Cape Cod Bay in the quiet east end. From the moment you step into *Windamar's* elegant, two-story entrance hall and take the winding staircase to one of her fine guest rooms, you know that you are in a very special place. Every detail in this stately home, circa 1840, has

continued next page

INN PLACES® 1998

437

been lovingly attended to. Each room has its own unique decor, tastefully wallpapered and filled with antiques and original artwork. The front rooms have water views and the others have views of the gardens. No matter the location of your room, you have a pleasant view of a natural setting. One of the most popular accommodations is the dramatic studio room that features a cathedral ceiling, an entire wall of glass overlooking the gardens and an antique carved bed. The penthouse apartment has expansive water views, skylights, exposed beams and cathedral ceiling...a wonderful mix of old and new. The centrally located common room offers guests a pleasant mingling space and use of refrigerator, microwave and cable TV with VCR. Continental breakfast features fresh-baked muffins and breads. It's only a 15-minute walk through the east end gallery district to the downtown area, just far enough away from the hustle-bustle, but close enough to enjoy the nightlife, restaurants, shops and galleries that Provincetown offers. Provincetown Tennis Club is a 3-minute walk. At low tide, guests can take a romantic stroll on the tidal flats directly across the street and view the town from a totally different vantage point. The clientele is mostly women, with men most welcome. In the off-season, the entire house can be booked for reunions, special events, small conferences or seminars.

Address: 568 Commercial St, Provincetown, MA 02657
Tel: (508) 487-0599, **Fax:** (508) 487-7505.
E-mail: windamar@tiac.net **URL:** www.provincetown.com/windamar/

Type: Bed & breakfast guesthouse.
Clientele: Mostly women with men welcome. Some straight clientele off season
Transportation: Car or plane. Free pick up from airport, bus or ferry dock.
To Gay Bars: 20-minute leisurely walk.
Rooms: 6 rooms & 2 fully equipped apartments with double or queen beds.
Bathrooms: 4 private shower/toilets. 4 rooms share 3 baths.

Meals: Continental breakfast.
Vegetarian: Provincetown has a lot available for vegetarians.
Dates Open: All year.
High Season: Jun 15-Sept 15.
Rates: Summer: rooms $60-$125; apts $775-$885/wk. Off season: $45-$85; apts $85-$95/day. Mid season: $55-$95; apts $650-$750/wk
Discounts: Off season, long stays, or booking the whole house.

Rsv'tns: Required.
To Reserve: Call direct.
Minimum Stay: 5 nights on July 4th & Labor Day, 4 nights Memorial Day.
Parking: Ample free off-street parking. Full private lot at rear of the property.
In-Room: Maid service.
On-Premises: TV/VCR lounge, common room with refrigerator & microwave.
Exercise/Health: 3-minute walk to tennis club. Massage can be arranged.
Swimming: Cape Cod Bay

300 feet directly across the street. Nearby ocean beach.
Sunbathing: On Windamar's exceptional estate-like grounds or at the beach.
Smoking: No.
Pets: Not permitted.
Handicap Access: No.
Children: Not permitted.
Languages: English & French.
Your Host: Bette.

IGLTA

Campit

Gay/Lesbian ♂

Where Friendly People Camp

When visiting Saugatuck, gay & lesbian campers can stay in an all gay-operated, all gay and lesbian campground located just 7 miles from Saugatuck's gay beach and 6 miles from the gay bars. *Campit* features all the usual amenities, such as mini-store with ice and soft drinks, modern bath and shower facilities and a game room. We're also near a supermarket, so it's easy to make a run for that one item you forgot to pack.

Address: 6635 118th Ave, Fennville, MI 49408 Tel: (616) 543-4335.

Type: Campground.
Clientele: Mostly men with women welcome.
Transportation: Car is best.
To Gay Bars: 10 minutes to men's/women's bars in Saugatuck.
Rooms: 60 campsites.
Campsites: 37 hookups

(electric only), 30 tent sites & 30 RV parking spaces with modern toilets & showers, also "Portajohns" throughout the park.
Dates Open: May 1st-Nov 1st.
Rates: $10 per person, $3 per night for electric. Rates slightly higher on holidays.

Discounts: Group rates.
Rsv'tns: Required on holiday weekends.
To Reserve: Call direct.
Minimum Stay: 3 nights on holidays.
Parking: Plenty of off-street parking.
On-Premises: TV lounge & laundry facilities.

Exercise/Health: Free weights.
Swimming: At the lake in Saugatuck.
Pets: Permitted, if on leashes.
Handicap Access: No, steps up to restrooms.
Children: Not permitted.
Languages: English.

Deerpath Lodge

Women ♀

Deerpath offers a healing habitat, secluded from the world by 45 wooded acres and the Kalamazoo River. A Native American motif pervades the lodge and rooms are spacious and handsomely decorated with Mission-style furniture. All rooms feature private baths and king-sized beds. A kitchenette is available, as is a greatroom with fireplace and an outdoor, four-season hot tub. Come, explore our meadow wildflowers and cruise the river in our kayaks or canoe. The lodge is near Lake Michigan beaches, marina, golf, galleries, cross-country ski trails and all of the delights of Saugatuck.

Address: PO Box 849, Saugatuck, MI 49453
Tel: (616) 857-DEER (3337), **toll-free** (888) DEERPATH.

Type: Guesthouse.
Clientele: Women only
Transportation: Auto. Free pick up from bus.
To Gay Bars: 6 miles.
Bathrooms: All private.
Complimentary: Organic coffee & accompaniments.
Dates Open: All year.
High Season: Jun-Aug & Oct.
Rates: $90-$100.

Discounts: Early prepayment, winter bonus nights.
Rsv'tns: Required.
To Reserve: Call direct.
Minimum Stay: 2 nights, longer on holiday weekends.
Parking: Ample off-street parking.
In-Room: AC. 1 kitchenette with refrigerator & coffee/tea-making facilities.

On-Premises: Meeting rooms.
Exercise/Health: Kayaks, canoe, hot tub, hiking & skiing trails.
Swimming: Near Lake Michigan.
Sunbathing: Riverside or at the beach.
Nudity: Nude beach nearby.
Smoking: Permitted outside. Non-smoking rooms available.
Pets: Not permitted.
Handicap Access: Yes. Main floor suite w/assistance. Bathroom not wheelchair accessible.
Children: Welcome only if carefully supervised.
Languages: English.
Your Host: Linda & Dianne.

Douglas Dunes Resort

Q-NET Gay/Lesbian ♀♂

A Deluxe Resort Complex

Douglas Dunes Resort is located in the Saugatuck/Douglas area, along the Lake Michigan shoreline. Accommodations range from deluxe motel rooms and cottage suites to steam bath-style rooms. Guests can lounge at our large heated

continued next page

pool with bar service, dine at our award-winning *Magnolia Grill*, dance the evening away in our disco, enjoy entertainment in the cabaret, or just relax in our bistro bar or garden deck. In winter, enjoy cross-country skiing or snowmobiling.

Address: 333 Blue Star Highway, Douglas, MI 49406
Tel: (616) 857-1401, **Fax:** (616) 857-4052.

Type: Motel with restaurant, bar & disco.
Clientele: Good mix of gay men & women
Transportation: Car is best. Bus, Amtrak, airport in Grand Rapids.
To Gay Bars: On premises.
Rooms: 23 rooms, 23 steam bath-style rooms, 3 suites & 10 cottages with double or king beds.
Bathrooms: 36 private bath/toilets. Steam bath-style have showers, share baths.
Vegetarian: Available upon request.
Dates Open: All year.
High Season: Summer.
Rates: Winter $48, summer $25-$125.
Credit Cards: MC, Visa, Amex, Diners, Discover.
Rsv'tns: Required.
To Reserve: Travel agent or call direct.
Minimum Stay: Weekend packages.
Parking: Ample off-street parking.
In-Room: Color TV, AC, telephone, ceiling fans, maid & room service.
On-Premises: Meeting rooms, TV lounge.
Exercise/Health: Nearby gym.
Swimming: Pool on premises, 1/2 mi to lake.
Sunbathing: At poolside.
Smoking: Permitted.
Pets: Permitted with deposit & not left alone.
Handicap Access: Yes.
Children: Permitted.
Languages: English.

IGLTA

The Kirby House

Gay/Lesbian ♀♂

A beautifully-restored 105-year-old Victorian manor on the state historical registry, *The Kirby House* is known for its comfortable elegance, warm hospitality and sumptuous breakfast/brunch buffets. Entirely furnished with turn-of-the-century antiques, the house becomes an adventure into days gone by. The establishment offers a beautiful, secluded pool, hot tub and sunning decks overlooking acres of woodland. *The Kirby House* is more than a place to stay, it's a place to linger.

Address: PO Box 1174, Saugatuck, MI 49453
Tel: (616) 857-2904 (Tel/Fax), (800) 521-6473.
E-mail: kirbyhse@aol.com **URL:** www.bbonline.com/mi/kirby

Type: Bed & breakfast.
Clientele: Mostly gay & lesbian with some straight clientele
Transportation: Car is best. Free pick up from Amtrak, bus and airport.
To Gay Bars: 4 blocks to gay bars.
Rooms: 8 rooms with single, double or queen beds, 2 apts, 1 cottage (sleeps 6).
Bathrooms: 9 private & 2 share.
Meals: Full breakfast buffet.
Vegetarian: Available upon request.
Dates Open: All year.
High Season: June through October.
Rates: $85-$125.
Discounts: 10% on extended stays and vacation packages. Sun-Thurs package-5 nights for price of 4.
Credit Cards: MC, Visa, Amex & Discover.
Rsv'tns: Required.
To Reserve: Travel agent or call direct.
Minimum Stay: 3 nights July & August wknds. 2 nights other wknds.
Parking: Ample off-street parking.
In-Room: Maid service, ceiling fans, AC.
On-Premises: Courtesy telephone, kitchen privileges, ice, gas BBQ.
Exercise/Health: Bicycles, Jacuzzi.
Swimming: Pool or lake.
Sunbathing: At poolside, lakeside or on common sun decks.
Nudity: 2 miles to nude beach.
Smoking: Permitted in common areas.
Pets: Permitted with restrictions.
Handicap Access: No.
Children: Permitted weekdays with prior arrangement.
Languages: English.
Your Host: Loren & Marsha.

Moore's Creek Inn

Gay/Lesbian ♀♂

Where Friendships Are Formed

Saugatuck is a quaint, little village 3 hours from Detroit and 2 1/2 from Chicago. It's known as a popular beach resort for gays and lesbians and as an artistic haven, and it has a large selection of specialty shops. *Moore's Creek Inn* is an old-fashioned farmhouse, over 100 years old. Rooms are decorated in different themes: The Erte Elegance room is filled with Erte prints. Walt's Woom has Disney paraphernalia. The Teddy Bear Den features small and large stuffed bears. Two gathering rooms have grand piano, movie library and a 50-inch TV.

Address: 820 Holland St, Saugatuck, MI 49453
Tel: (616) 857-2411, (800) 838-5864.

Type: Bed & breakfast.
Clientele: Mainly gay & lesbian with some straight clientele
Transportation: Car is best. Free pick up from airport.
To Gay Bars: 3 miles or ten-minute drive.
Rooms: 4 rooms with double, queen or king beds.
Bathrooms: 4 private shower/toilets.
Meals: Full breakfast.
Vegetarian: Cold or hot cereals, fruit & cheese.
Complimentary: Tea, coffee, mixes for cocktails (no alcohol). Evening wine & cheese tasting.
Dates Open: All year.
High Season: May-September.
Rates: Summer $75-$95, winter $65-$85.
Discounts: Four or more days, 10% off, full occupancy party 10% off.
Credit Cards: MC, Visa, Amex.
Rsv'tns: Required.
To Reserve: Travel agent or call direct.
Minimum Stay: 2 days in season.
Parking: Ample off-street parking.
In-Room: Ceiling fans, window fans.
On-Premises: Meeting rooms, TV lounge.
Exercise/Health: Massage at nearby salon.
Swimming: At nearby lake.
Sunbathing: On the beach.
Smoking: Permitted in 1st floor gathering rooms only, not in bedrooms.
Pets: Not permitted.
Handicap Access: No.
Children: Not encouraged.
Languages: English.
Your Host: Clif & Fred.

Newnham SunCatcher Inn

Gay/Lesbian ♀♂

Newnham SunCatcher Inn is on a secluded lot in the heart of Saugatuck's business district, close to shops, restaurants, recreation and the lake beaches. The turn-of-the-century home with wraparound porch, complete with gingerbread carvings, has been carefully restored to the grandeur of its day. Period furniture once again graces its 5 bedrooms. Behind the main house, a two-cottage suite provides more private accommodations. Features are a large sun deck, hot tub and swimming pool.

Address: 131 Griffith, Box 1106, Saugatuck, MI 49453
Tel: (616) 857-4249.
URL: http://wwwbbonline.com/mi/suncatcher/index.html

Type: Bed & breakfast.
Clientele: Mostly gay & lesbian with some straight clientele.
Transportation: Free pick up from airport, train.
To Gay Bars: 3-minute drive to gay/lesbian bars.
Rooms: 5 doubles, 2-cottage suite (cottage is a guest house with complete facilities).
Bathrooms: 3 private, others share.
Meals: Full breakfast.
Vegetarian: Available on request.
Complimentary: Tea, coffee, juices, mints on pillow.

continued next page

UNITED STATES

Dates Open: All year.
High Season: May-October.
Rates: Rooms $65-$85 weekdays & off-season weekends, $75-$100 summer weekends; call for cottage rates.
Discounts: During off-season.

Credit Cards: MC, VISA.
Rsv'tns: Required.
To Reserve: Call direct.
Minimum Stay: 2 nights on weekends.
Parking: Ample free off-street parking.
In-Room: AC.
On-Premises: Common room, meeting room, fireplace, TV lounge, telephone, kitchen available.
Exercise/Health: Jacuzzi.
Swimming: In-ground heated swimming pool.
Sunbathing: At poolside or on private sun decks.

Nudity: 3 mi to nude beach.
Smoking: Permitted on outside deck only.
Pets: Not permitted.
Handicap Access: No.
Children: Permitted weekdays only.
Languages: English.

DULUTH • MINNESOTA

Stanford Inn
Q-NET Gay/Lesbian ♀♂

The *Stanford Inn*, celebrating its 10th anniversary, is Minnesota's first gay-owned bed & breakfast. This elegant Victorian home was built in 1886 and features natural woodwork and hardwood floors throughout, as well as an entrance is graced by a hand-carved oak staircase and an eight-foot stained glass window. The 4 bedrooms are all charmingly decorated with period antiques, the suite has a private bath, and all accommodations include complete gourmet breakfast and room service coffee. We are located two blocks from Leif Erickson Park, the Rose Garden, Lake Superior, and within walking distance of shops and restaurants.

Address: 1415 E Superior St, Duluth, MN 55805
Tel: (218) 724-3044. URL: http://www.visitduluth.com/stanford

Type: Bed & breakfast.
Clientele: Mostly gay & lesbian with a following of straight clientele
Transportation: Car is best.
Rooms: 3 rooms & 1 suite.
Bathrooms: 1 private & 2 shared.
Meals: Full gourmet breakfast & room service coffee.

Vegetarian: Available upon request.
Complimentary: Coffee, tea, & juices.
Dates Open: All year.
High Season: May-Oct.
Rates: $75-$115.
Discounts: For weekdays (Sun-Thur), groups, also corporate & single rates.
Credit Cards: MC, Visa, Amex, Discover.

Rsv'tns: Required.
To Reserve: Call direct.
Parking: Adequate off-street & on-street parking.
In-Room: Room service.
On-Premises: TV lounge.
Exercise/Health: Sauna.
Swimming: Lake 2 blocks.
Sunbathing: On the beach.

Nudity: Permitted at creek, 1 mile away. Directions on request.
Smoking: Permitted on the porch.
Pets: Permitted with restrictions.
Handicap Access: No.
Children: OK with prior arrangement.
Languages: English.

KENYON

Dancing Winds B&B Retreat
Gay-Friendly 50/50 ♀♂

Quiet Your Mind & Refresh Your Spirit

Dancing Winds B&B/Retreat is refreshingly different from most other accommodations — you can be as sociable or as private as you want! Enjoy the haven of our recently renovated guestwing, with a spacious, yet cozy living room and well-equipped kitchen. Upstairs is your large bedroom and full bath. We can easily accommodate up to four adults with two children. Your refrigerator comes fully stocked with locally produced foods, including our milk, eggs, and award-winning cheeses. This allows guests the freedom to start their day at their own pace. Participate in farm activities, enjoy the goats and/or explore our beautiful countryside!

Address: 6863 Co. #12 Blvd, Kenyon, MN
Tel: (507) 789-6306, Fax: (507) 789-5233.
E-mail: dancingwinds@juno.com

Type: B&B/retreat, campground with licensed cheesery on farmstead.
Clientele: Men & women, 50% straight clientele

Transportation: Car is best.
To Gay Bars: 60 miles to Minneapolis & 40 miles to Rochester gay/lesbian bars.

Rooms: Deluxe guestwing sleeps up to 4 adults or 4 adults & 2 children.
Bathrooms: Private full bath.

Campsites: 3 tent sites with shower & toilet available. Evening bonfires upon request, weather permitting.

FERRARI GUIDES™

Complimentary: Fully stocked refrigerator with locally produced foods featuring fresh goat's milk, eggs & cheese from farm.
Dates Open: All year.
High Season: Winter for skiing, fall for Fall Colors season.
Rates: $70 per night, 2 persons; $25 per addt'l adult.

$15 per addt'l child. Camping (2 persons/site) $10, b'fast extra.
Discounts: On stays of 3+ nights. Work exchange available, when possible.
Credit Cards: MC, Visa.
Rsv'tns: Required at most times.
To Reserve: Call direct.
Parking: Ample, free off-street parking.

In-Room: Heat, ceiling fans, kitchen, living room with patio & deck.
On-Premises: TV/VCR, games, library, music.
Laundry facilities at extra charge.
Exercise/Health: Plenty of work to do: throwing hay bales, fencing, milking goats & goat wrangling in general!
Swimming: River & pool nearby.
Sunbathing: In yard.
Smoking: Not permitted.
Pets: Not permitted.
Children: Permitted.
Languages: English, limited French.
Your Host: Mary.

Be Yourself Inn — Twin Cities
Gay/Lesbian ♂

Jon and Phillip invite you to relax and be yourself in their spacious, 4-level, 4,200 sq. ft. executive home. We're 10-20 minutes from the airport, the Mall of America, gay bars and downtown. The fully-enclosed grounds have an expansive deck that's great for natural sunning. In winter, enjoy the living room's fire place, vaulted beamed ceilings and views of snow-covered evergreens. A delicious breakfast, Happy Hour, and a large, mirrored, queen sized bedroom are just some of the extra touches that will truly make *Be Yourself Inn — Twin Cities* your home away from home.

Address: 1093 Snelling Ave South, St. Paul, MN 55116
Tel: (612) 698-3571 or **Fax:** (612) 699-3840.
E-mail: fullcrum@mn.uswest.net

Type: Bed & breakfast.
Clientele: Men.
To Gay Bars: 8 min drive.
Rooms: 2 rooms with queen beds.
Bathrooms: All private.
Meals: Full breakfast.
Vegetarian: Available daily.
Complimentary: Coffee, tea, soft drinks, mineral water & beer at all times.

Happy Hour drinks 5-6:30pm daily.
Dates Open: All year.
Rates: $65-$70 per night.
Discounts: One coupon per stay for 10% off next total bill for one stay. Good for one year.
Credit Cards: MC, Visa.
Rsv'tns: Required.
To Reserve: Travel agent or call direct.

Parking: Ample free off-street parking.
In-Room: Color TV/VCR.
On-Premises: Meeting rooms, TV lounge, AC, laundry facilities for guests, use of complete lower level kitchen.
Swimming: Walk to pool, 10 min drive to Mississippi River & Twin City Lakes.
Sunbathing: On private sun deck.
Nudity: Permitted on private deck.
Smoking: Not permitted.
Pets: Not permitted.
Handicap Access: No.
Children: Not permitted.
Languages: English, Spanish.
Your Host: Jon & Phillip

The Doanleigh Inn
Gay-Friendly ♀♂

Casual Elegance Where All Your Needs are Attended to

European and American antiques enhance the Georgian architecture of *The Doanleigh Inn*, centrally located between the famed Country Club Plaza and Hallmark Crown Center. A delicious, full, gourmet breakfast awaits both leisure and business travelers each morning; the butler's pantry is always stocked with sodas, juices, and snack foods. Enjoy a room with fireplace, deck or whirlpool tub, and pamper yourself by curling up in luxurious robes. And if you must work during your stay, the guest office center provides free local phone and faxes, as well as computer modem access.

Address: 217 East 37th St, Kansas City, MO 64111
Tel: (816) 753-2667, **Fax:** (816) 531-5185.

Type: Bed & breakfast.
Clientele: Mostly straight clientele with a gay & lesbian following.

Transportation: Car is best, airport shuttle.
To Gay Bars: 2 blocks to nearest gay/lesbian bar. 5

minutes by foot or car to others.
Rooms: 5 rooms with queen or king beds.

Bathrooms: All private. Some with Jacuzzi.

continued next page

INN PLACES® 1998   443

UNITED STATES

Meals: Full gourmet breakfast, evening wine & hors d'oeuvres.
Vegetarian: Always available.
Complimentary: Homemade cookies, fruit juices, soda, snacks, coffee, tea, weekend wine & cheese, local newspaper.
Dates Open: All year.

Rates: $95-$150.
Discounts: Corporate rates available Sun-Thurs.
Credit Cards: MC, Visa, Amex, Discover.
Rsv'tns: Required.
To Reserve: Travel agent or call direct.
Minimum Stay: 2 nights some holiday weekends.
Parking: Ample free off-street parking.

In-Room: Maid service, color cable TV, speaker phone, AC, computer hookup. Some rooms with fireplace, deck or whirlpool tub.
On-Premises: Grand piano, meeting rooms, TV lounge, laundry facilities, fax.

Exercise/Health: 5-minute drive to Golds gym, tennis courts, walking paths.
Smoking: Permitted on outdoor porches.
Pets: Not permitted.
Handicap Access: No.
Children: Permitted, please inquire.
Languages: English.
Your Host: Terry & Cynthia.

ST. LOUIS • MISSOURI

A St. Louis Guesthouse in Historic Soulard   Q-NET Gay/Lesbian ♂

ST. LOUIS GUESTHOUSE In Historic Soulard

St. Louis Mo.

Come Home to St. Louis

A St. Louis Guesthouse, in historical Soulard, is tucked between downtown, Busch Stadium, the Anheuser Busch Brewery and the Farmers Market. A gay bar and restaurant are next door. Of the eight apartments in the building, three are available as guest suites. Each has two large rooms, phone, a private bath, AC, wet bar with refrigerator and a private entrance opening onto a pleasant courtyard with hot tub. If your visit to St. Louis is for business or pleasure, please consider *A St. Louis Guesthouse* your home away from home.

Address: 1032-38 Allen Ave, St Louis, MO 63104
Tel: (314) 773-1016.

Type: Guesthouse.
Clientele: Mostly men with women welcome.
Transportation: Car is best. Free pick up from airport, bus or train.
To Gay Bars: Next door.
Rooms: 3 suites with double or queen beds.
Bathrooms: All private shower/toilets.

Complimentary: Coffee, tea & hot chocolate always available.
Dates Open: All year.
Rates: $65.
Discounts: Weekly rate.
Credit Cards: Amex, Discover, Visa, MC, Diners.
Rsv'tns: Required.
To Reserve: Call direct.
Minimum Stay: 2 nights on weekends.

Parking: Ample free off-street & on-street parking.
In-Room: Color cable TV, ceiling fans, refrigerator, coffee/tea-maker, telephone (free local calls), maid service & laundry service, AC.
On-Premises: Laundry facilities, BBQ, hot tub in courtyard.
Exercise/Health: Non-sexual massage is $40.
Sunbathing: In courtyard.
Nudity: In hot tub & courtyard.
Smoking: Permitted.
Pets: Not permitted.
Handicap Access: No.
Children: Not permitted.
Languages: English.
Your Host: Garry & Billy.

Brewers House Bed & Breakfast   Gay/Lesbian ♀♂

Brewers House is a Civil War-vintage home, whose location amidst several breweries, is minutes from downtown and only blocks from bars, restaurants and shops. Some rooms feature fireplaces and unusual items. The hot tub in the intimate garden area offers total privacy. Enjoy a view of downtown from the deck. Visit the Soulard Market, a colorful open-air market established in 1790, or Anheuser-Busch, home of the world's largest brewery (free tours include the Clydesdales and beer tasting), or take a ride to the top of the Gateway Arch.

Address: 1829 Lami Street, St. Louis, MO 63104
Tel: (314) 771-1542.

Type: Bed & breakfast.
Clientele: Good mix of gays & lesbians.
Transportation: Car is best or cab from Transit Station. Free pick up from train.
To Gay Bars: 7 blocks or 1/2 mile. 15 minutes by foot, 5 minutes by car.
Rooms: 3 with double or king beds.
Bathrooms: 1 private bath/toilet, 1 private sink & 1 shared bath/shower/toilet.
Meals: Expanded continental breakfast.
Vegetarian: Available upon request. Restaurant nearby.
Complimentary: Coffee always available.
Dates Open: All year.
Rates: $60-$65.
Discounts: 7th day free.
Credit Cards: MC, Visa.
Rsv'tns: Recommended.
To Reserve: Travel agent or call direct.
Parking: Ample parking.
In-Room: Color cable TV, AC, ceiling fans, maid service & laundry service.
On-Premises: TV lounge.
Exercise/Health: Jacuzzi.
Sunbathing: On common sun decks.
Nudity: Permitted in Jacuzzi in secluded garden.
Smoking: Permitted.
Pets: Permitted, but call ahead.
Handicap Access: No.
Children: Permitted.
Languages: English.

Lafayette House Bed & Breakfast
Lesbian-Owned & -Operated ♀♀♂

An 1876 Queen Anne Mansion in Historic Lafayette Square

From the moment you arrive, you'll be surrounded by **Lafayette House Bed & Breakfast's** unique personality! Located minutes from downtown St. Louis, the house is furnished comfortably with antiques and traditional furniture, and the third-floor suite has a private bath and kitchen. Our Victorian Room with its fireplace and Jacuzzi, is designed for a more romantic getaway. Mornings, Annelise will treat you to a full gourmet breakfast which may include homemade breads, muffins, crab-stuffed quiche or Belgian waffles with warm blueberry compote. We're ABBA-inspected and -approved, and have resident cats.

Address: 2156 Lafayette Ave, St Louis, MO
Tel: (314) 772-4429, (800) 641-8763, Fax: (314) 664-2156.
URL: http://www.bbonline.com/mo/lafayette/

Type: Bed & breakfast.
Clientele: Mostly straight clientele with a gay/lesbian following
Transportation: Car or public transportation. Metro link to Union Station, then taxi.
To Gay Bars: 3-5 miles, a 5-7 min drive.
Rooms: 5 rooms, 1 suite with double or queen beds.
Bathrooms: 3 private bath/shower/toilets. 3 rooms share a large common bath/shower/toilet.
Meals: Full breakfast.
Vegetarian: Available with advance notice.
Complimentary: Cookies in afternoon, soda.
Dates Open: All year.
High Season: May-Oct.
Rates: $60-$150.
Discounts: Corporate 10% discount, extended stay.
Credit Cards: MC, Visa, Amex, Diners, Discover.
Rsv'tns: Required.
To Reserve: Travel agent or call direct.
Parking: Ample, free on-street parking.
In-Room: Telephone, AC, ceiling fans, color cable TV, VCR, kitchen, refrigerator, coffee & tea-making facilities.
On-Premises: Meeting rooms, TV lounge, fax.
Exercise/Health: Jacuzzi. Nearby massage.
Smoking: Permitted outside on deck.
Pets: No. Resident cats.
Handicap Access: No.
Children: Welcome.
Languages: English.
Your Host: Annelise & Nancy.

Napoleon's Retreat Bed & Breakfast
Gay-Friendly 50/50 ♀♀♂

Follow Napoleon...Retreat in Style!

Napoleon's Retreat, an elegantly-appointed French second-empire townhouse dating to the 1880s, is in St. Louis' Lafayette Square, one of the nation's oldest historical districts. In our four spacious bedrooms, guests enjoy the elegant ambiance of antiques along with conveniences such as color TVs and telephones. Conveniently close to St. Louis' Union Station shopping and entertainment complex, Busch Stadium and Brewery, Gateway Arch and riverfront park, Cherokee St. Antique Row and world-renowned Missouri Botanical Gardens, as well as excellent dining and shopping. The perfect retreat for business or pleasure.

Address: 1815 Lafayette Ave, St Louis, MO 63104
Tel: (314) 772-6979, (800) 700-9980.

continued next page

UNITED STATES

Type: Bed & breakfast guesthouse.
Clientele: 50% gay & lesbian & 50% straight clientele.
Transportation: Car. From airport 20 minutes on Hwy 70. 1 mile to MetroLink station.
To Gay Bars: 5 blocks or 1 mile. 20-minute walk or 5-minute drive.
Rooms: 4 rooms with queen beds.
Bathrooms: All private.
Meals: Full breakfast.
Vegetarian: Can easily accommodate special diets.
Complimentary: Tea, coffee, juices, sodas, sherry, homemade chocolate chip cookies.
Dates Open: All year.
Rates: $65-$95.
Credit Cards: MC, Visa, Amex, Discover.
Rsv'tns: Required.
To Reserve: Travel agent or call direct.
Minimum Stay: 2-night for 3-day weekend holidays (Memorial Day, July 4th, Labor Day, Thanksgiving).
Parking: Ample on-street parking.
In-Room: Color cable TV, AC, ceiling fans, telephone, clock radio & maid service.
On-Premises: Meeting rooms, fax.
Exercise/Health: 2 miles to YMCA with gym, weights, Jacuzzi, sauna, steam & massage.
Swimming: Pool at YMCA.
Sunbathing: In patio area.
Smoking: Permitted outside only.
Pets: Not permitted.
Handicap Access: No.
Children: Permitted.
Languages: English.
Your Host: Michael & Jeff.

BOZEMAN • MONTANA

Lehrkind Mansion Bed & Breakfast Gay-Friendly ♀♂

Not Just a Room For the Night — An Experience

Listed in the National Register of Historic Places, the *Lehrkind Mansion* reflects the ambiance of Montana's Victorian past. Built in 1897, this Queen Anne home's spectacular features include gables, overhangs, porches, bays and a large corner tower. Relax in overstuffed chairs and enjoy the unique, rare period antiques and original woodwork. The mansion is known for its music parlor and library, with its rare, seven-foot-tall 1897 Regina music box — Montana's largest. From our filling gourmet breakfasts to beds smothered in thick down comforters, at *Lehrkind Mansion* quality is of the highest concern.

Address: 719 North Wallace Ave, Bozeman, MT 59715
Tel: (406) 585-6932 (Tel/Fax) call before faxing, (800) 992-6932.
E-mail: lehrkindmansion@imt.net
URL: http://www.imt.net/~lehrkindmansion/index.htm

YELLOWSTONE NATIONAL PARK AREA

Type: Bed & breakfast with wedding & meeting facilities.
Clientele: Mostly straight clientele with a gay/lesbian following
Transportation: Car is best, taxi from airport.
Rooms: 4 rooms, 1 suite with double or queen beds.
Bathrooms: 3 private bath/shower/toilets, 1 shared bath/shower/toilet.
Meals: Full breakfast.
Vegetarian: Vegetarian & vegan breakfasts available. Local co-op carries vegetarian food items.
Complimentary: Lemonade & cookies, evening tea, mints on pillow with turndown.
Dates Open: All year. **High Season:** June 1-Oct 1 & Dec 15-Apr 1.
Rates: $65, $165 year round.
Credit Cards: MC, Visa, Amex, Discover.
Rsv'tns: Required, walk-ins OK.
To Reserve: Travel agent or call direct.
Minimum Stay: 2 nights on weekends.
Parking: Ample free on- & off-street parking.
In-Room: Maid service.
On-Premises: Meeting rooms, TV lounge, video tape library, large yard & gardens.
Exercise/Health: Large therapeutic hot tub, massage, mountain bikes. Nearby gym, weights, Jacuzzi, sauna, massage.
Swimming: At nearby pool.
Sunbathing: On patio & common sun decks.
Nudity: Permitted in hot tub with discretion & consideration of other guests.
Smoking: No smoking inside. Smoking available outside, save butts!
Pets: Not permitted.
Handicap Access: Lower floor only, wide doors.
Children: Welcome if well-behaved & watched by parents.
Languages: English & German.
Your Host: Jon & Christopher.

Yellowstone Riverview Lodge B&B Gay-Owned & -Operated ♀♂

Welcome to a Little Bit of Paradise

The *Yellowstone Riverview Lodge B&B*, a beautiful hand-hewn log home, is located in the heart of the Paradise Valley, one of Montana's most spectacular areas. Surrounded by the majestic Absaroka and Gallatin Mountains, the lodge overlooks the serene Yellowstone River, famous for its blue-ribbon fly fishing.

Yellowstone National Park is only minutes away. Our location offers endless year-round activity, such as horseback riding, river rafting, fishing, hiking and cross-country skiing. With great food and breathtaking views, this truly is a little bit of paradise.

Address: 186 East River Road, Emigrant, MT 59027
Tel: (406) 848-2156, (888) 848-2350.
E-mail: riverview@imt.net **URL:** http://www.wtp.net/go/riverview

Type: Bed & breakfast.
Clientele: Mostly straight clientele with a gay/lesbian following
Transportation: Car is best.
Rooms: 4 rooms with twin, double or queen beds.
Bathrooms: 2 private shower/toilets, 2 shared bath/shower/toilets.
Campsites: 1 teepee. Use of shared bathroom & all communal spaces, breakfast included with night's stay.
Meals: Full breakfast. Pack lunches & 3- & single-course dinners available on request.
Vegetarian: Available by request & at restaurant 12 miles away.
Complimentary: Evening cookies & chocolates in room, coffee, tea, soft drinks, microwave popcorn.
Dates Open: All year.
High Season: Jun-Aug.
Rates: High season $80-$105, off season $65-$90.
Discounts: 1 night free if booking 1 full week. 15% off if booking all 4 rooms.
Credit Cards: MC, Visa.
Rsv'tns: Encouraged.
To Reserve: Call direct.
Parking: Ample free off-street parking.
In-Room: Ceiling fans, maid service.
On-Premises: Phone, TV lounge, video tape library. Dining/kitchenette area w/ refrigerator, dishwasher, microwave. Reading & games library, coffee & tea-making facilities, outside patio & deck.
Exercise/Health: Weights, cadiovascular equip, spinning bike, slide board & steps. Nearby gym, weights, Jacuzzi, sauna, steam, massage.
Swimming: Pool & river nearby.
Sunbathing: On common sun decks, patio.
Smoking: Permitted outside only.
Pets: Permitted with advance notice & permission.
Handicap Access: No.
Children: Welcomed if supervised & well-behaved.
Languages: English.
Your Host: Steve & Bill.

Las Vegas Private Bed & Breakfast

Q-NET Gay/Lesbian ♂

Lucky You!

My home, *Las Vegas Private Bed & Breakfast*, features a unique, European decor with lots of amenities. Outside are tropical plants and trees around the pool area. Further back are the aviaries, with tropical birds and parrots. Las Vegas has 24-hour entertainment. Other activities: desert sightseeing, water sports on Lake Mead, private sailboats with catered dining, Grand Canyon tours in a private plane, Laughlin excursions, alpine mountain tours, winter skiing, and hiking to hot springs along the Colorado River.

Address: Las Vegas, NV **Tel:** (702) 384-1129 (Tel/Fax).

Type: Bed & breakfast.
Clientele: Mostly men with women welcome
Transportation: Pick up from airport at minimal charge.
To Gay Bars: 5-block walk to gay bars.
Rooms: 3 rooms & 1 suite with queen or king beds.
Bathrooms: 2 shared full bathrooms, one with whirlpool. Outside hot/cold shower.
Meals: Full breakfast & evening snack, other meals by request.
Vegetarian: Available upon request.
Complimentary: Cocktail, etc.
Dates Open: All year.
High Season: Spring & late summer, holidays.
Rates: One person $59, double $79, triple $12 add'l.
Discounts: 25% after 7-day stay.
Rsv'tns: Required. Cancellation policy: 1 week in advance, fee of 50% of deposit.
To Reserve: Travel agent or call direct.
Minimum Stay: Weekend 2 nights, Saturday arrival OK.
Parking: On-street parking.
In-Room: Color cable TV, VCR, AC, ceiling fans, room service & laundry service.
On-Premises: Meeting rooms, laundry facilities.
Exercise/Health: Jacuzzi, sauna & hot tub.
Swimming: Pool on premises.
Sunbathing: At poolside or on the patio.
Nudity: Permitted without restrictions.
Smoking: Permitted outdoors in most areas.
Pets: Permitted with prearrangement.
Handicap Access: No, not wheelchair accessible.
Children: Not permitted.
Languages: English, German, French, Danish, Swedish & Norwegian.
Your Host: Ole.

INN PLACES® 1998

Country Options

Gay-Friendly 50/50 ♀♂

Our location in the foothills of the White Mountains makes *Country Options* an easily accessible getaway destination. We're just two hours from Boston and visitors are assured abundant natural beauty and diverse outdoor activities year-round. We are on the main street of a busy little village with shops, restaurants and a bike rental/repair shop nearby. The area offers a challenging golf course and unspoiled Squam Lake, where *On Golden Pond* was filmed. The inn offers a comfortable, relaxed atmosphere, antique decorations and newly-decorated common areas and bathrooms.

Address: 27-29 N Main St, Ashland, NH 03217 **Tel:** (603) 968-7958.

Type: Bed & breakfast.
Clientele: 50% gay & lesbian & 50% straight clientele
Transportation: Car is best. We will pick up from bus station in Plymouth.
To Gay Bars: 1 hour to Manchester gay/lesbian bars.

Rooms: 5 rooms with double beds.
Bathrooms: 2 shared bath/shower/toilets.
Meals: Full breakfast.
Vegetarian: Upon request.
Dates Open: All year.
High Season: Fall foliage.
Rates: Singles $35, doubles $45-$55.

Rsv'tns: Recommended.
To Reserve: Call direct.
Minimum Stay: 2 nights on holiday weekends.
Parking: Adequate free off-street parking.
In-Room: Self-controlled heat.
On-Premises: TV lounge.
Swimming: River, lake or nearby indoor pool.

Sunbathing: On nearby beach or in small backyard area at the inn.
Smoking: No smoking.
Pets: Not permitted.
Handicap Access: No.
Children: Permitted, but infants not encouraged.
Languages: English.

The Highlands Inn

Q-NET Women ♀

A Lesbian Paradise!

Surrounded by 100 scenic mountain acres, *The Highlands Inn* is a 200-year-old lovingly restored farmhouse that has operated as a country inn for more than 100 years. Fifteen miles of trails, for walking hand-in-hand or cross-country skiing in winter, grace the property. An enormous heated pool with sun deck is a gathering place for swimmers and sunworshippers alike. Sunsets at the inn are spectacular.

Our 20 rooms are individually decorated in comfortable antiques, with lots of special touches. All have good views and most have private baths. Spacious, comfortable common areas include: an enormous fireplaced living room, a library, a tremendous, sunny breakfast room, TV/VCRs with an excellent gay & lesbian video collection, an enclosed wicker-filled sunporch, and a private whirlpool spa.

Commitment ceremonies, honeymoon packages and special events are available. Join us for spectacular fall colors, super winter skiing, lush mountain springtime and all summer sports. We're here for you year round — a lesbian paradise! The inn is conveniently located just 2-1/2 hours from Boston and the Maine coast, 4-1/2 hours from Provincetown, and three hours from Montreal. 1995-1997 Out & About Editor's Choice Award.

Address: Box 118 (IP), Bethlehem, NH 03574 **Tel:** (603) 869-3978.

Type: Bed & breakfast inn.
Clientele: A women-only lesbian paradise
Transportation: Car is best. Closest major airport: Manchester, NH 1-1/2 hrs. Free pick up from bus.
To Gay Bars: 1-1/2 hours to gay/lesbian bars.
Rooms: 19 rooms & 1 cottage with double or queen beds.
Bathrooms: 14 private bath/toilets. Shared: 2 bath/shower/toilets, 1 toilet only.
Meals: Full breakfast.
Vegetarian: Breakfasts don't include meat. Vegetarian options at most local restaurants.

Complimentary: Lemonade, cider, popcorn, pretzels, coffee & tea.
Dates Open: All year.
High Season: Summer, fall & winter weekends.
Rates: Rooms $55-$110.
Discounts: For longer stays varying seasonally (ex. 15-20% off 7-night stay year-round, except holidays).
Credit Cards: MC, Visa.
Rsv'tns: Recommended. (For added privacy our sign always says No Vacancy, so ignore it if driving by without reservations).
To Reserve: Call direct or travel agent.

Minimum Stay: On in-season weekends 2 nights. Longer on holidays.
Parking: Ample free parking.
In-Room: Self-controlled heat & maid service. Some rooms have kitchens available & some have TVs/VCRs. Video tape library, refrigerator, coffee & tea-making facilties, microwave.
On-Premises: TV lounge, VCRs, use of the farmhouse's full kitchen, library, piano, BBQ grills, stereo & boardgames.
Exercise/Health: Hot tub, Jacuzzi & lawn games. 15 miles of hiking & skiing trails. Massage can be arranged.
Swimming: Heated pool, nearby rivers & lakes.
Sunbathing: On common sun deck or at poolside.
Nudity: Topless sunbathing fine.
Smoking: Permitted in smoking area. Most areas & all rooms are smoke-free.
Pets: Permitted in certain rooms, with prior arrangement.
Handicap Access: Yes.
Children: Permitted with a gay parent.
Languages: English.
Your Host: Grace.

IGLTA

Red Hill Inn

Q·NET Gay-Friendly ♀♂

Quiet, Peaceful and Secluded, Yet Close to Everything...

The *Red Hill Inn* is a restored estate on sixty acres overlooking the White Mountains and Squam Lake. In the heart of the Lakes Region, two hours north of Boston, our guest rooms offer beautiful views of fields, woods or mountains. All rooms have private baths and telephones and are decorated with beautiful antiques. Many rooms have fireplaces, some have Jacuzzis and some suites also feature sitting rooms. The inn boasts a wonderful restaurant, where everything is made from scratch, and a small lounge where we have a fireplace and weekend entertainment. Come see the beautiful New Hampshire countryside and experience an authentic country inn!

Address: RFD #1, Box 99M, Centre Harbor, NH 03226
Tel: (603) 279-7001. **E-mail:** info@redhill.com **URL:** www.redhill.com

Type: Inn with bar and restaurant, cross-country ski trails.
Clientele: Mostly straight clientele with a gay/lesbian following
Transportation: Car is best. Free pick up from airport or bus.

To Gay Bars: 90-minute drive to Manchester gay/lesbian bars.
Rooms: 20 rooms, 3 suites & 1 cottage with single, double, queen or king beds.
Bathrooms: All private.
Meals: Full breakfast.
Vegetarian: On our menu nightly.

Dates Open: All year.
High Season: Mid-June through Nov 1.
Rates: $78-$175.
Discounts: For longer stays.
Credit Cards: MC, Visa, Amex, Diners, Carte Blanche, Discover.
Rsv'tns: Helpful.
To Reserve: Travel agent or call direct.
Minimum Stay: 2 nights on weekends in season.
Parking: Ample free parking.

continued next page

INN PLACES® 1998

| In-Room: Telephone & maid service. 5 rooms have Jacuzzis & 13 have fireplaces. On-Premises: Private dining rooms, meeting rooms, TV lounge, public telephone & central heat. Exercise/Health: 5 rooms have Jacuzzis. | Swimming: At nearby lake. Sunbathing: On beach. Smoking: Permitted without restrictions. Pets: Not permitted. | Handicap Access: No. Children: Well-behaved only! Languages: English. IGLTA |

White Rabbit Inn & Catering

Q-NET Gay-Owned 50/50 ♀♂

Personally Exquisite

The stately, circa 1760 *White Rabbit Inn*, provides true privacy, complemented by attentive hospitality. Delicious aromas wafting from the huge, modern and immaculate kitchen remind you that your host, Executive Chef Gregory Martin, has an exclusive, first-class international culinary background. This classic brick mansion is a joy to behold. Open year round, it offers several formal conference rooms, dining rooms, an atrium and patio, and four very private guestrooms in over 6,000-square-feet. Its solid brick, marble and hardwood construction, tall ceilings and spacious hallways, beautiful ornate wood paneling, extravagant fireplaces and lavish moldings contribute to the serene and secluded atmosphere. The lovely, sunny Victorian Bridal Suite overlooks expansive landscape and features a classic marble bath. Two other rooms feature queen-sized beds, while the fourth has twins. Private in-room sinks, lighted walk-in closets and tasteful antiquarian decor add to the pampering during your visit.

Gregory Martin's experience as Catering Services Manager with Playboy Resorts of New Jersey, his education in food service management, and his degree in culinary arts amply complement his life's ambition — to be the best in "personally exquisite" hospitality. "I live to please people," asserts Chef Martin. "For me, there is no greater pleasure than helping someone's dream come true... For example, at some point before my guests turn in, I ask them for their personal menu requests for breakfast... I want each guest to have exactly what they wish to start their morning off right." The *White Rabbit Inn and Catering* is a splendid choice whether you are planning a shopping trip, an outing to your favorite ski resort, or just want to get away for a couple of days, you'll love your time with us.

Directions: From the Portsmouth/Seacoast/Boston area, I-93, Rte 101 East, to Exit 1, follow Rte 28 Bypass North 8 mi., bear left on Pleasant St., follow 1 mi. to 62 Main St. The inn is on the left, at the end of a long, climbing brick wall.

Address: 62 Main St, Allenstown, NH 03275
Tel: (603) 485-9494, (888) 216-9485, **Fax:** (603) 485-9522.
E-mail: scott@whtrabbit.com **URL:** www.whtrabbit.com

Type: Bed & breakfast inn.
Clientele: 50% gay & lesbian & 50% straight clientele
Transportation: Car is best.
To Gay Bars: 10 miles, a 15-20 min drive.
Rooms: 4 rooms with twin or queen beds.
Bathrooms: 1 private bath/shower/toilet, 1 private sink only. Others share 1 bath/shower/toilet.
Meals: Expanded or full continental breakfast.
Vegetarian: Available.
Complimentary: Tea & coffee, mints on pillow.
Dates Open: All year.
High Season: Summer, autumn, Oct fall foliage.
Rates: $75-$90 PB +tax.
Credit Cards: All major credit cards.
Rsv'tns: Inquire.
To Reserve: Travel agent or call direct.
Parking: Ample free off-street parking.
In-Room: Telephone, color cable TV, VCR, maid service.
On-Premises: Meeting rooms, business services.
Exercise/Health: Jacuzzi.
Swimming: Pool. Nearby river & lake.
Sunbathing: Poolside & on patio.
Pets: Not permitted.
Handicap Access: No.
Children: No.
Your Host: Gregory.

Bungay Jar

Q-NET Gay-Friendly ♀

Conducive to Romance & Quiet Pleasures

Built from an 18th-century barn, the *Bungay Jar* and its exuberant gardens have been featured on the covers of national magazines. The seven large guest rooms and suites with mountain or woodland views include such welcoming touches as lavish linens, handmade quilts, ornate beds, and comfortable chairs or a desk. Breakfast specialties include oatmeal pancakes, popovers, and fresh fruit salads. Stroll through an enchanted wood to a hidden river, star gaze on a private balcony, enjoy a fireside chat, and awaken to mountain air, and wild blueberry pancakes.

Address: PO Box 15, Easton Valley Rd, Franconia, NH 03580
Tel: (603) 823-7775, (800) 421-0701, **Fax:** (603) 444-0100.
E-mail: info@bungayjar.com **URL:** www.bungayjar.com

Type: Bed & breakfast.
Clientele: Mostly straight. Strong lesbian following, especially in winter, men always welcome
Transportation: Car is best.
To Gay Bars: 15 min from Highland Inn.
Rooms: 7 rooms, single, double, queen or king beds.
Bathrooms: Private: 3 bath/toilets, 2 shower/toilets. 1 shared shower/toilet/sink.
Meals: Full breakfast & afternoon tea & snacks.
Vegetarian: All breakfasts (meat served separately). Please inform us of dairy product intolerance.
Complimentary: Afternoon snack with tea.
Dates Open: All year.
High Season: July-October.
Rates: Fall foliage $120-$195, all other seasons: $95-$160.
Discounts: Inquire.
Credit Cards: MC, Visa, Discover, Amex.
Rsv'tns: Advised.
To Reserve: Call direct.
Minimum Stay: 2 nights some weekends & foliage season.
Parking: Ample, off-street parking (15 acres).
In-Room: Maid service.
On-Premises: Fireplaces, common area, telephone.
Exercise/Health: Sauna, hiking trails. Massage by appointment.
Swimming: At nearby pool, river, lake, swimming hole.
Sunbathing: On many porches & hammock.
Nudity: Permitted in private, 2-person sauna.
Smoking: Not permitted.
Pets: Not permitted.
Handicap Access: No.
Children: Permitted over age 6.
Languages: English.

The Horse & Hound Inn

Q-NET Gay-Friendly ♂

Off the beaten path at the base of Franconia's Cannon Mountain and adjacent to White Mountains National Forest and the Franconia Notch State Park is one of New England's finest traditional inns. Visitors to *The Horse &*

continued next page

Hound Inn are treated to a quiet, relaxed atmosphere of pine paneling, three cozy fireplaces and comfortable guest rooms. The area supports plenty of activities such as hiking, boating, cross-country skiing, antiquing, and sightseeing. There are also bluegrass festivals, chamber music concerts, craft demonstrations, and museums.

Address: 205 Wells Rd, Franconia, NH 03580 **Tel:** (603) 823-5501, (800) 450-5501.

Type: Bed & breakfast inn with restaurant & lounge.
Clientele: Mostly straight clientele with a gay male following
Transportation: Car is best.
To Gay Bars: 1-1/2 hrs to Manchester, NH, 2-1/2 hrs to Boston, MA.
Rooms: 8 rooms & 2 suites with double, queen or king beds.
Bathrooms: Private: 7 bath/toilets, 1 shower/toilet.

2 shared bath/shower/toilets.
Meals: Full breakfast & dinner with map.
Vegetarian: Always available.
Dates Open: Closed April-early May & November till Thanksgiving.
High Season: Fall foliage Sep 15-Oct 15 & ski time Dec 26-Mar 31.
Rates: $79.95 double, $67.45 single.
Discounts: Mention *Inn*

Places for 20% discount Sun-Thur, 10% Fri-Sat.
Credit Cards: MC, Visa, Amex, Diners & Discover.
Rsv'tns: Preferred.
To Reserve: Travel agent or call direct.
Parking: Ample free off-street parking.
In-Room: Window fans & maid service.
On-Premises: TV lounge, VCR in lobby & laundry facilities.
Exercise/Health: Gym with

nautilus 12 miles.
Swimming: 1-1/2 mi to lake, $2.50 fee.
Sunbathing: On grassy backyard.
Smoking: Permitted except in dining room & lobby.
Pets: Permitted, $10 charge.
Handicap Access: No.
Children: Permitted, additional charge.
Languages: English.
Your Host: Bill & Jim.

The Notchland Inn
Gay-Friendly ♀♂

A Magical Location...Naturally Secluded

Get away from it all, relax and rejuvenate at our comfortable 1862 granite mansion located on 400 acres in the midst of beautiful mountain vistas. *The Notchland Inn* rests atop a knoll at the base of Mount Bemis and looks out upon Mounts Hope and Crawford.

Within *The Notchland Inn*, experience the comforts and pleasures of attentive and friendly hospitality! Settle in to one of our seven guest rooms or five spacious suites, each individually appointed and all with woodburning fireplaces and private baths. The front parlor is a perfect place to sit by the fire and read or to visit with other guests. The music room draws guests to the piano, or to the stereo to listen to music they personally select. The sun room offers a great place to sip your coffee and read a novel or just enjoy the great views.

In the evening, *Notchland's* wonderful 5-course dinner is served in a romantic, fireplaced dining room looking out to the gazebo by our pond. Our Chef creates a new menu each day, her elegant flair respecting the traditional while exploring the excitement of international cuisines. Morning brings a bountiful country breakfast to fuel you for the adventures of the day.

Nature's wonders abound at *Notchland* and include 8,000 feet of Saco River frontage and two of the area's best swimming holes. The Davis Path hiking trail starts just across the road from the Inn. Other activities to enjoy are mountain biking, cross-country skiing, snowshoeing, fishing, or soaking in the wood-fired hot tub which sits in a gazebo by the pond. For animal lovers there's a Burnese Mountain dog, a Belgian draft horse, miniature horses and two llamas. Nearby attractions include: Crawford Notch, ski areas, shopping at North Conway's antiques, arts & crafts, and factory outlet stores, and the Mount Washington Auto Road & Cog Railway.

Address: Hart's Location, NH 03812-9999
Tel: Reservations: (800) 866-6131 or (603) 374-6131, **Fax:** (603) 374-6168.
E-mail: notchland@aol.com

Type: Inn with restaurant with full liquor license.
Clientele: Mostly straight clientele with a gay & lesbian following.
Transportation: Car is best. Free pick up from bus.
To Gay Bars: 2 hours to Manchester, NH. 2+ hours to Portland, ME.
Rooms: 7 rooms & 5 suites with single, queen or king beds.
Bathrooms: 6 private shower/toilets & 6 private bath/shower/toilets.
Meals: Full breakfast & dinner.

Vegetarian: Available with advance notice (dinners by reservation, prepared to order). All dietary restrictions considered.
Complimentary: Various treats at various times.
Dates Open: All year.
High Season: Foliage (Sep 15-Oct 20) & Christmas to New Year (Dec 23-Jan 1).
Rates: Per person per night MAP double occupancy: $90-$112.50, Holiday & foliage $105-$132.50.
Discounts: 2, 3, 4 & 5 night mid-week packages (per person per package, MAP,

double occupancy) $165-$465.
Credit Cards: MC, Visa, Amex, Discover.
Rsv'tns: Subject to prior booking.
To Reserve: Travel agent or call direct.
Minimum Stay: Required at times.
Parking: Ample free off-street parking.
In-Room: Maid service, ceiling fans, some rooms have AC.
On-Premises: Meeting rooms.
Exercise/Health: Spa,

massage by appointment. Nearby gym, weights, Jacuzzi, steam, massage, skiing, sleigh & carriage rides.
Swimming: River on premises. Nearby pool, river & lake.
Sunbathing: On patio, lawns or at the beach.
Smoking: Non-smoking environment.
Pets: Not permitted.
Handicap Access: No.
Children: Mature children only. No TV. Many animals & outdoor activities.
Languages: English.
Your Host: Les & Ed.

Post and Beam Bed & Breakfast

Gay-Friendly ♀♂

"There Are No Strangers — Only Friends We Haven't Met"

The Monadnock Region, known for its New England charm and "Currier & Ives" appeal, is home to *The Post and Beam Bed & Breakfast*, a 1797 restored Colonial farmstead. Guests love the quiet, cozy romantic atmosphere, and marvel at the posts and beams, wide pine floors and fireplaces. Nearby are hiking trails, biking, golfing, fishing, cross-country skiing, swimming and gorgeous fall foliage. The region is also rich in art galleries, music, theater, covered bridges and great shopping. Your friendly innkeepers will make your stay comfortable and relaxing, and serve you bountiful homemade breakfasts. Groups are welcome.

Address: HCR 33, Box 380, Centre St, Sullivan, NH 03445
Tel: (603) 847-3330, (888) 3 ROMANCE, **Fax:** (603) 847-3306.
E-mail: postandbeam@top.monad.net
URL: http://www.nhweb.com/postandbeam/

continued next page

Type: Bed & breakfast. **Clientele:** Mostly straight clientele with a gay & lesbian following **Transportation:** Car is best. Closest major airport: Manchester, NH (1 hr). Free pick up from bus in Keene. **To Gay Bars:** A 1-hour drive to Manchester gay bars. 2 hours to Boston, MA bars. **Rooms:** 7 rooms with single, queen or king beds. **Bathrooms:** Private: 2 shower/toilets, 1 WC only. 5 shared bath/shower/toilets. **Meals:** Full or continental breakfast. **Vegetarian:** Vegetarian breakfast available. Please inform us of dairy product intolerance. **Complimentary:** Afternoon tea, cookies, snacks, apples. **Dates Open:** All year. **High Season:** Mid-June thru Nov 1. **Rates:** High season $60-$85, low season $45-$75. **Discounts:** Mention Inn Places for 10% discount. Seniors 10% discount. **Credit Cards:** MC, Visa, Discover, Amex. **Rsv'tns:** Preferred. **To Reserve:** Call direct. **Minimum Stay:** 2 nights during fall foliage & holiday weekends. **Parking:** Ample free off-street parking. **In-Room:** Window fans. Some rooms have AC, gas fireplaces. **On-Premises:** TV lounge, video tape & book libraries, telephone. Flower & herb gardens, apple trees, arbor with swing, large gazebo. **Exercise/Health:** Nearby gym, massage. **Swimming:** Nearby river, lake. **Sunbathing:** On grounds. **Smoking:** Permitted only in designated areas. No smoking in bedrooms. **Pets:** Not permitted. **Handicap Access:** Yes. **Children:** Must be at least 5 years old. **Languages:** English, French. **Your Host:** Darcy & Priscilla.

The Inn at Bowman a B&B

Gay-Owned 50/50 ♀♂

Gracing the White Mountains

Tall columns, reminiscent of a Southern-style plantation, grace the front porch of *The Inn at Bowman*. Originally built in 1948 as a private summer residence, the inn has been completely renovated, graciously combining twentieth-century comfort with luxury, charm and a friendly ambience. Rooms and suites feature fresh flowers, flannel sheets in winter, plush towels and either private or shared baths. A bountiful continental breakfast is served in the dining room where guests meet to socialize. This area is a traveler's dream with inspiring mountain views and a wide variety of outdoor activities. Many parks are within an hour's drive, and tax-free shopping is six miles away in the town of Gorham.

Address: Rte 2, Randolph, NH 03570 **Tel:** (603) 466-5006.

Type: Bed & breakfast guesthouse inn. **Clientele:** 50% gay & lesbian & 50% straight clientele **Transportation:** Car. Free pick up from bus. **To Gay Bars:** 20 miles, a 25 min drive. **Rooms:** 5 rooms & suites with single, double or queen beds. **Bathrooms:** 2 private bath/shower/toilets & sinks only. 3 shared bath/shower/toilet. **Campsites:** Tent sites. Full deluxe bathhouse. **Meals:** Expanded continental or buffet breakfast. **Vegetarian:** Available nearby. **Complimentary:** Tea & coffee, mints on pillow, set up service, soft drinks. **Dates Open:** All year. **High Season:** Fall foliage, winter skiing, spring hiking, summer mtn. biking. **Rates:** Off season: $79-$149; Holidays & Ski Week: $99-$179. **Discounts:** Stay 3 nights, 4th night free. **Credit Cards:** MC, Visa, Amex, Diners, Bancard. **Discover. Rsv'tns:** Recommended. **To Reserve:** Call direct. **Minimum Stay:** 2 nights on holiday weekends. **Parking:** Ample free off-street parking. **In-Room:** Some rooms have color cable TV w/ satellite, AC, ceiling fans, kitchen, maid & room service. **On-Premises:** 2 pianos, TV lounge, sun room. **Exercise/Health:** Jacuzzi (104 degrees). 8 miles to gym. **Swimming:** Pool on premises (heated to 90 degrees, summer only). **Sunbathing:** Poolside & on private sun decks. **Nudity:** Permitted when sunbathing & in hot tub area. **Smoking:** Permitted on porches & in pool area. **Pets:** Not permitted. **Handicap Access:** One step up to facility. **Children:** No. **Languages:** English & French. **Your Host:** Jerry & Rich.

Surfside Resort Hotel

Gay/Lesbian ♂

A Complete Gay Destination in Atlantic City

SEE SPECIAL PAGE 26 COLOR SECTION

The Surfside Resort Hotel is a complete destination right in the heart of Atlantic City. Our boutique-style hotel features 50 individually decorated rooms offering accommodations from single to king beds; from affordable to deluxe. Our expansive pool and sun deck are surrounded on all sides to form a private space for your relaxation and enjoyment. You can sun yourself all day by our heated swimming pool with the convenience of cool drinks from the bar and snacks to dinner from the grill. Our current expansion has doubled the size of the hotel and added a grand new lobby, complete with a fireplace and continental breakfast bar. The hotel now offers phones in every room and electronic locks that use magnetic stripe cards in place of keys.

Always a popular destination, there's something happening 24 hours a day, 365 days a year in Atlantic City. Enjoy the world-famous beach and boardwalk. Dine in world-class restaurants and incredible all-you-can-eat buffets. Test your luck gambling at Atlantic City's famous casinos. See the biggest names in entertainment, plus cabarets and review shows. STUDIO SIX, New Jersey's hottest dance club specializing in the very best dance music and featuring a dazzling light, sound and video spectacular, is right next door. Doors open at 10 pm and don't close until dawn. The Brass Rail Tavern is open 24 hours, offering draft beer and friendly atmosphere. The Surfside Sun Deck bar is open seasonally. Enjoy a cool drink while catching some sun, or gaze at the stars at night. The Surfside Grill and the Brass Rail Grill offer breakfast, lunch, dinner and snacks. There's something for everyone, and there's always something to do. We're 1-1/2 blocks from the beach and boardwalk, and 1/2 block from the Sands, Ballys and Claridge casinos.

Address: 10-18 S. Mt. Vernon Avenue, Atlantic City, NJ 08401
Tel: (609) 347-SURF (7873), (888) 277-SURF (7873).

Type: Resort complex with restaurant, grill, bars, cabaret, dance club & sun deck.
Clientele: Mostly men with women welcome
Transportation: Bus, train & air. Pick up available.
To Gay Bars: 3 gay bars
on premises, others 2 blocks.
Rooms: 50 rooms with single, double & king beds.
Bathrooms: Most are private, others share.

continued next page

INN PLACES® 1998   455

UNITED STATES

Complimentary: VIP membership to Studio Six during stay.
Dates Open: All year.
High Season: May-Oct.
Rates: High season $65-$145, winter $49-$125.
Discounts: 7th night free. Special packages available.
Credit Cards: MC, Visa,

**MAC, Amex, Discover.
Rsv'tns:** Preferred.
To Reserve: Travel agent or call direct.
Minimum Stay: 2 nights on weekends. Some holidays 3 nights.
Parking: Off-street parking.
In-Room: AC, color TV, maid service, refrigerator, deluxe rooms offer wet bar.

On-Premises: Restaurant, grill, sun deck, bar & dance club.
Exercise/Health: Jacuzzi.
Swimming: Heated pool on premises.
Sunbathing: On large sun deck & bar. Ocean beach.
Smoking: Permitted without restrictions.

Pets: Not permitted.
Handicap Access: No. One flight of stairs to main entrance.
Children: Not recommended.
Languages: English, Spanish.

IGLTA

PLAINFIELD • NEW JERSEY

The Pillars of Plainfield
Bed & Breakfast

Q-NET Gay-Friendly 50/50 ♀♂*

Sylvan Seclusion With Easy Access to Manhattan

The Pillars is a lovingly-restored Victorian/Georgian mansion. Relax by the Music Room fire, read a book from the living room library, play the organ, listen to the stereo, watch a video. Swedish breakfast at *The Pillars* is expanded continental, served at your convenience, but you may wish to cook your own in the huge kitchen. We have over 20 years' experience in the hospitality industry and are eager to offer a quality experience to our guests. Plainfield is a beautiful town with easy access to Manhattan by commuter train. It's a town where rainbow flags and windsocks can be seen on local houses and is fast becoming the "Gay Capital of New Jersey."

Address: 922 Central Ave, Plainfield, NJ 07060-2311
Tel: (908) 753-0922 (Tel/Fax), (888) PILLARS (745-5277).
E-mail: Pillars2@juno.com **URL:** http://bestinns.net/usa/nj/rdpillars.html

Type: Bed & breakfast.
Clientele: 50% gay & lesbian & 50% straight clientele
Transportation: Train or bus to Plainfield, car or taxi to house.
To Gay Bars: 1/2 mile. 8 miles to the famous "Den" at Rutgers University.
Rooms: 4 suites with twin or queen beds.
Bathrooms: All private bath/shower/toilets.
Campsites: Parking for self-contained RV with electric & water hookup.

Meals: Expanded continental breakfast.
Vegetarian: Facilities to prepare your own vegetarian meals.
Complimentary: Coffee, tea. Beverages afternoon & evening.
Dates Open: All year.
Rates: $60-$115.
Discounts: Call for discounts.
Credit Cards: Visa, MC, Amex.
Rsv'tns: Required.
To Reserve: Travel agent or call direct.

Parking: Ample off-street parking.
In-Room: AC, coffee/tea-making facilities, maid & room service.
On-Premises: Meeting rooms, TV lounge, VCR, stereo, organ, laundry & kitchen facilities, library & fireplace.
Exercise/Health: Health clubs in the area.
Swimming: Outstanding gay nude beach at nearby Sandy Hook.
Sunbathing: In secluded backyard.

Smoking: Permitted only on the sun porch in inclement weather.
Pets: Well-behaved dogs permitted with prior arrangement. We have a Cairn Terrier.
Handicap Access: No.
Children: Welcome under 2 years old & over 12 years old. Crib, playpen & cots available.
Languages: English.
Your Host: Chuck & Tom.

IGLTA

---

456 FERRARI GUIDES™

Brittania and W.E. Mauger Estate B&B

Gay-Friendly 50/50

Linda Ronstadt Slept Here!

From this great inn in the heart of Albuquerque you can walk to the convention center, historic Old Town, museums, the BioPark, shops and restaurants. This 1897 restored Victorian B&B on the National Register of Historic Places has three floors with eight elegant rooms, all complete with private baths. Guests enjoy a full gourmet breakfast, evening treats, complimentary beverages and ample parking. The *Brittania and W.E. Mauger Estate B&B* has a three-star rating by Mobil and a three-diamond rating by AAA.

Address: 701 Roma Ave NW, Albuquerque, NM 87102
Tel: (505) 242-8755, (800) 719-9189, **Fax:** (505) 842-8835.
URL: http://www.thuntek.net/tc_arts/mauger

Type: Bed & breakfast.
Clientele: 50% gay & lesbian & 50% straight clientele
Transportation: Car is best or taxi.
To Gay Bars: 3 miles by car.
Rooms: 7 rooms & 1 suite with single, double, queen or king beds.
Bathrooms: All private baths with showers.

Meals: Full breakfast.
Vegetarian: Available if pre ordered.
Complimentary: Wine, cheese, juice, cookies, brownies, chips, fruit, candy & coffee.
Dates Open: All year.
High Season: Mar thru Oct.
Rates: $69-$149.
Discounts: AAA.
Credit Cards: MC, Visa, Amex, Diners, Discover.
Rsv'tns: Required.
To Reserve: Call direct or travel agent.
Minimum Stay: 2 nights for special events.
Parking: Ample, free, off-street parking, private lot, will accept RV.
In-Room: Color TV, maid & room service, AC, ceiling fans, coffee/tea-making facilities & refrigerator.

On-Premises: TV lounge, meeting rooms, catering for special occasions.
Exercise/Health: Walking distance to downtown fitness center.
Sunbathing: On patio.
Smoking: Permitted in designated outside areas.
Pets: Call to inquire.
Handicap Access: No.
Children: Call to inquire.
Languages: English.

The Casitas at Old Town

Gay/Lesbian

A Glimpse of the Past Beneath a Sea of Sky

Enjoy the hospitable warmth and comfort of New Mexico's classic adobe dwellings on the secluded edge of Albuquerque's oldest historical area. *Casitas at Old Town* are early dwellings restored to modern comfort with fireplace, kitchen area, bedroom, bath and patio, all furnished with authentic New Mexico pieces. Stroll into the plaza of nearby Old Town with its adjacent museums, drive an hour to Santa Fe, or just relax in absolute privacy...with one foot in the past.

Address: 1604 Old Town Rd NW, Albuquerque, NM **Tel:** (505) 843-7479.

Type: Suites with private entrances.
Clientele: Mostly gay & lesbian with some straight clientele
Transportation: Car is best.
To Gay Bars: A 15-minute drive to men's & women's bars.
Rooms: 2 suites with double or queen bed.
Bathrooms: 2 private shower/toilets.
Vegetarian: 1 block to vegetarian food.
Complimentary: Tea & coffee makings in each suite.

continued next page

UNITED STATES — ALBUQUERQUE • NEW MEXICO

Dates Open: All year.
Rates: $85 all year.
Discounts: On extended stays.
Rsv'tns: Preferred.
To Reserve: Travel agent or call direct.

Parking: Ample off-street parking.
In-Room: AC, kitchen, refrigerator, coffee & tea-making facilities.

Exercise/Health: Nearby gym.
Sunbathing: On the patio.
Nudity: Permitted on patios.
Smoking: Not permitted.

Pets: Not permitted.
Handicap Access: No.
Children: Not especially welcome.
Languages: English, minimal Spanish.

Golden Guesthouses Gay/Lesbian ♀♂

Peace, Privacy & Southwestern Flair

Come to the *Golden Guesthouses* where we offer that "country-in-the-city" feeling. Our charming, spacious one-bedroom casitas will make you feel right at home. Each house offers a front porch, private patio, living room, kitchen area and private bath. The guesthouses are located in the North Valley near the Rio Grande River, a quick block from the Rio Grande Nature Center and minutes from museums, restaurants, bars and Old Town Plaza. We are happy to offer directions, make suggestions, or leave you absolutely alone with the hope that your stay with us will be a memorable experience.

Address: 2645 Decker NW, Albuquerque, NM 87107
Tel: (888) 513-GOLD (513-4653), (505) 344-9205, **Fax:** (505) 344-3434.
E-mail: GoldenGH@aol.com **URL:** http://www.highfiber.com/~goldengh/

Type: 2 guesthouses.
Clientele: Mostly gay & lesbian with some straight clientele
Transportation: Car is best.
To Gay Bars: 3 miles to gay bars.
Rooms: 1 house with full bed, 1 house with queen bed.

Bathrooms: Private shower/toilet.
Meals: Continental breakfast.
Vegetarian: Available upon request.
Complimentary: Beer, wine, champagne upon request, sodas, juice, bottled water, bagels, snacks.
Dates Open: All year.
Rates: $85 daily, $420 weekly.

Discounts: Ask for Inn Places discount price of $69 daily.
Rsv'tns: Recommended or take a chance.
Parking: Ample free off-street parking.
In-Room: AC, ceiling fans, coffee & tea-making facilities, refrigerator, kitchen area.

Exercise/Health: Nearby gym, massage, mountain bicycle rental (will deliver).
Sunbathing: On patio.
Nudity: Permitted on private patio.
Smoking: No cigarette smoking.
Pets: Not permitted.
Handicap Access: No.
Children: Welcome.
Languages: English.

Hacienda Antigua Bed and Breakfast

Q-NET Gay-Friendly ♀♂

Secluded, Serene and Romantic — Featured on TLC's "Great Country Inns"

Walk through the massive carved gates of *Hacienda Antigua* and step back in time. The gentle courtyard with its big cottonwood tree and abundance of flowers is the heart of this 200-year-old adobe hacienda. In summer, relax on the peaceful portal or bask in the sun by the large swimming pool. In winter enjoy a crackling piñon fire in your own kiva fireplace. Enjoy the outdoor Jacuzzi year-round. Visitors linger, not wanting to leave the warm Southwestern hospitality, full breakfasts, and splendid rooms comfortably furnished with antiques. Member New Mexico & Albuquerque B&B Associations.

Address: 6708 Tierra Dr NW, Albuquerque, NM 87107
Tel: (505) 345-5399, (800) 201-2986.
URL: www.haciendantigua.com/bnb/

Type: Bed & breakfast.
Clientele: Mostly straight clientele with gays & lesbians welcome
Transportation: Car is best.
To Gay Bars: 1-5 miles.
Rooms: 4 rooms & 1 suite with single, queen or king beds.
Bathrooms: All private.
Meals: Full breakfast.
Vegetarian: Served upon request. Our breakfasts are ample & we will accommodate any dietary request.
Complimentary: Glass of wine. Chocolates in the room.
Dates Open: All year.
High Season: Aug-Oct.
Rates: $95-$150.
Credit Cards: MC, Visa, Amex, Discover.
Rsv'tns: Required.
To Reserve: Travel agent or call direct.
Parking: Ample free off-street parking.
In-Room: AC, ceiling fans & fireplaces.
On-Premises: TV lounge.
Exercise/Health: Jacuzzi on premises. Gym & weights nearby.
Swimming: Pool on premises.
Sunbathing: At poolside or on the patio.
Smoking: Permitted outside.
Pets: Not permitted.
Handicap Access: No.
Children: Limited acceptance.
Languages: English, Italian.

Hateful Missy & Granny Butch's Boudoir & Manure Emporium

Gay/Lesbian ♀

A Rather Queer Bed & Breakfast — The Gravy May be Lumpy, But the Beds Ain't

Yippy-Ki-Yay! *Hateful Missy & Granny Butch* have relocated to a 24-acre ranch south of Albuquerque in the Rio Grande Valley and we are definitely "for the birds." Located close to two major bird and wildlife sanctuaries, our stunning two-story adobe home boasts beamed ceilings, brick floors, wood-burning stoves, a luxurious Jacuzzi tub, huge picture windows for all sorts of bird watching (ho-ho!), cable TV, VCRs and selected videos.

Relax, hike, mountain bike to the river for a romantic picnic, punch a dogie, slap a hog, get bitten by a red ant, shoot pool, or go to Albu*queer*qe for even more excitement. Then, come home to terrific food, prepared, whenever possible, with Missy's home-grown organic veggies. Granny Butch's mean cuisine "a la New Mexico" will leave you breathless. Be tortured by our canine coordinator, Rotten Long-Young. Remember! The gravy may be lumpy, but the beds ain't. Call soon. Operators must be standing by somewhere.

Address: PO Box 556, Veguita, NM 87062 **Tel:** (800) 397-2482, (505) 861-3328.

Type: Bed & breakfast with Granny Butch's Genital Store & Art Gallery
Clientele: Mostly women with men very welcome
Transportation: Car is necessary, poor public transportation. 1 free round-trip pick up, if absolutely necessary, from airport, bus, train. $25 round-trip charge thereafter.
To Gay Bars: 45 miles. 45 minutes by car.
Rooms: 3 rooms, 1 suite with 1 king & 3 queen beds.
Bathrooms: 3 bath/shower/toilet rooms, suite has Jacuzzi. Only at full capacity does anyone share.
Campsites: 2 RV parking spaces only.

Meals: Full breakfast. Other meals, picnic or box lunches available at nominal price.
Vegetarian: Simply indicate your need.
Complimentary: Wine or sparkling cider, cheese, cracker basket, fruit juices, fruit, snacks, X-rated candy on pillows.
Dates Open: All year.
High Season: September-March.
Rates: $85-$125. During holidays & special events (balloon fiesta, etc) $100-$150.
Discounts: Weekly rates except during holidays & special events.
Rsv'tns: Preferred.

To Reserve: Travel agent or call direct.
Minimum Stay: Required during holidays & special events.
Parking: Ample free parking. Some covered parking.
In-Room: Color cable TV, VCR, ceiling fans, refrigerator, coffee & tea-making facilities, room, maid & laundry service. Telephone in 2 rooms.
On-Premises: TV lounge, video tape library, video & parlour games, jigsaw puzzles, pool table, etc. Computer, fax, laundry facilities.
Exercise/Health: Massage by appointment, Jacuzzi & outdoor hot tub, mountain bikes, hiking, bird watching at 2 huge bird & wildlife sanctuaries. Waterskiing, boating & fishing at nearby lake.
Swimming: At huge nearby man-made lake.
Sunbathing: Everywhere on premises & on patio.
Nudity: Permitted everywhere on premises.
Smoking: We are a non-smoking facility. Outdoor smoking is fine.
Pets: Permitted, must be well-mannered, sociable & housebroken.
Handicap Access: No.
Children: We accept no children.
Languages: English, some French, Spanish, Japanese.
Your Host: Butch & Rita.

The Rainbow Lodge Bed & Breakfast

Gay-Friendly 50/50

Sweeping Vistas, Southwest Elegance, and a Hot Tub with Mountain Views

Escape to the Land of Enchantment and to the *Rainbow Lodge*. We are conveniently located on the historic Turquoise Trail in the Sandia Mountains, between Albuquerque and Santa Fe, just 25 minutes from the Albuquerque airport. The *Rainbow Lodge* provides panoramic views, sweeping vistas and Southwest-style elegance. Occupying over 6,000 square feet, the lodge has beamed ceilings, flagstone and wooden floors, seven fireplaces, a hot tub overlooking the mountains, an expansive brick-covered terrace, an adobe-walled courtyard, a water fountain, and even miniature donkeys to entertain you.

Colorful and unique suites await you at the *Rainbow Lodge*, including private bathrooms, queen-sized beds, sitting areas, color TVs and beautiful mountain views. Some of our suites offer a kitchen, fireplace, VCR and CD player. Guests are treated to a delicious breakfast, including New Mexico specialties, homemade muffins, freshly baked breads, seasonal fruit, gourmet coffees, teas and juices. A plate of homemade cookies awaits all guests upon arrival.

The entertainment in New Mexico is limited only by your imagination. Enjoy striking contrasts in seasons with golden autumns, dazzling white winters, clear blue springs and sun-drenched summers. Day trips include hiking, skiing, mountain biking, horseback riding, hot air ballooning, horse racing and river rafting. There are also Native American pueblo tours, ancient ruins, spectacular restaurants, as well as endless art galleries and gift shops which capture the spirit of the Southwest. At the end of the day, pamper yourself in our steaming hot tub and relax while gazing at the Sandia skies and the star-filled nights. If you need the ultimate ESCAPE, New Mexico and the *Rainbow Lodge* can be your place to renew worn spirits, rekindle a romance, or be your home base for all of the enchanting excitement that New Mexico has to offer.

Address: 115 Frost Rd, Sandia Park, NM 87047
Tel: (505) 281-7100. **E-mail:** rainbowbed@aol.com

Type: Bed & breakfast.
Clientele: 50% gay & lesbian & 50% straight clientele
Transportation: Car is best, 25 miles from airport.
To Gay Bars: 16 miles.
Rooms: 4 suites with queen beds.
Bathrooms: Private.
Meals: Full breakfast.
Vegetarian: Available upon request.
Complimentary: Gourmet cookies, coffee, herbal tea, soda, fully stocked non-alcoholic wet bar with snacks.
Dates Open: All year.
High Season: Summer & fall.
Rates: $70-$100.
Discounts: Discounts for week-long stays.
Credit Cards: MC, Visa, Amex, Discover.
Rsv'tns: Highly recommended.
To Reserve: Travel agent or call direct.
Minimum Stay: 2 nights on weekends.
Parking: Ample free parking on site.
In-Room: Color TV, VCR, CD stereo, ceiling fan, fireplace, kitchen, coffee/tea-making facilities, refrigerator, laundry & room service.
On-Premises: Meeting rooms, laundry facilities.
Exercise/Health: Hiking, biking, skiing. Outdoor hot tub.
Sunbathing: On common sun decks.
Nudity: Permitted in hot tub, with discretion.
Smoking: Permitted on terrace. All rooms non-smoking.
Pets: Permitted in available on-site kennels.
Handicap Access: No.
Children: Not especially welcomed.
Languages: English.
Your Host: Rusty, Jody & Sue.

Rio Grande House

Gay-Friendly ♀♂

This landmark adobe residence, *Rio Grande House*, is located near historic Old Town, major museums and the Rio Grande nature center. Southwestern charm is reflected throughout with beamed ceilings, brick floors, Kiva fireplaces and museum-quality antiques. Collectibles from East Africa, Nepal, Pakistan and Yemen are used to decorate each room.

Address: 3100 Rio Grande Blvd NW, Albuquerque, NM 87107
Tel: (505) 345-0120 or (505) 344-9463. **E-mail:** nmypinon@aol.com

Type: Bed & breakfast.
Clientele: Mostly straight clientele with a gay & lesbian following.
Transportation: Car is best.
To Gay Bars: 15-minute drive.
Rooms: 5 rooms with double, queen or king beds.
Bathrooms: All private shower/toilets.
Meals: Full breakfast.
Vegetarian: Available upon request.
Dates Open: All year.
High Season: Jun-Oct.
Rates: $60-$75 (Balloon Fiesta $100)
Discounts: Mid-week & seniors.
Rsv'tns: Required.
To Reserve: Call direct.
Parking: Ample off-street parking.
In-Room: Color TV, AC, telephone, fireplaces, wet bar, private entrance.
On-Premises: Laundry facilities.
Sunbathing: On patio.
Smoking: Permitted. Non-smoking rooms available.
Pets: Permitted with approval.
Handicap Access: No.
Children: Not permitted.
Languages: English.
Your Host: Jim & Craig.

The W.J. Marsh House Victorian B&B

Gay-Friendly 50/50 ♀♂

We Even Have A Ghost!

The *W.J. Marsh House Victorian Bed & Breakfast*, built in 1892, is on the National Register of Historical Places and is located in Albuquerque's old *Railroad Town* historic district. The six unique guest rooms are brimming with antiques. Two female ghosts, dressed in turn-of-the-century gowns, are often seen in the Rose Room. We're five minutes from the airport, walking distance from UNM and the convention center downtown. Old Town, the zoo and nature center, museums, the Indian Pueblo Cultural Center, the aquarium, botanical gardens and the world's longest, highest tramway are a short drive away.

Address: 301 Edith SE, Albuquerque, NM 87102-3532
Tel: (505) 247-1001, **Toll-free:** (888) WJ MARSH (956-2774).

Type: Bed & breakfast inn with separate Victorian cottage.
Clientele: 50% gay & lesbian & 50% straight clientele.
Transportation: Car is best. Cab from airport less than $10 one way.
To Gay Bars: 2-3 miles to gay & lesbian bars.
Rooms: 6 rooms, 1 cottage with single, double or queen beds.
Bathrooms: 2 private toilets with shared shower & 2 shared bath/shower/toilets.
Meals: Full gourmet breakfast in house. Full kitchen in cottage (breakfast not provided).
Vegetarian: Available with prior notice. Many vegetarian restaurants nearby.
Complimentary: Depends on time of year & mood of the Innkeeper. Alcohol is not provided.
Dates Open: All year.
High Season: First week of Oct (International Balloon Fiesta). Make reservations by July.
Rates: Single $65-$115, double $95-$125. Cottage $400 per week for 2, $500 per week for 3 or 4.
Discounts: Stays of one week or more.
Credit Cards: Visa, MC.
Rsv'tns: Preferred. Same-day calls accepted IF space is available.
To Reserve: Call direct.
Minimum Stay: During Balloon Fiesta: 3 nights weekends, 2 nights during the week.
Parking: Ample free off-street & on-street parking. Well-lit walkways to entrances.
In-Room: AC & maid service. Color cable TV, ceiling fans & kitchen in cottage. Laundry service on request.
On-Premises: Meeting room, laundry facilities & phone.
Exercise/Health: Self-guided walking tours. Nearby gym, Jacuzzi, sauna, steam & massage.
Swimming: Nearby pools, river & lakes.
Smoking: Not permitted anywhere, not even on the grounds!
Pets: Not permitted.
Handicap Access: No, sorry.
Children: Permitted in cottage only. Permitted in main house if 12 or older.
Languages: English, Spanish, French.

The Inn of La Mesilla

Gay-Friendly 50/50 ♀♂

The Essence of Northern New Mexico

The Inn of La Mesilla is a private residence bordering the Santa Clara Indian Reservation. The Hoemann's invite you to enjoy two private bedrooms, each with private bath. Our pueblo-style home has Mexican tile throughout. The Inn has a new hot tub with large, festive deck for sunning or enjoying views. The Inn is minutes from Chimayo, Puye Cliffs, Santa Fe, Taos and eight northern Indian pueblos. A full breakfast is served, and afternoon snacks are available from 5:00-6:00 pm. Two Springer Spaniels, Pork Chop and Te-Bone, reside in home.

Address: Rt 1, Box 368A, Española, NM 87532 **Tel:** (505) 753-5368.

Type: Bed & breakfast.
Clientele: 50% gay & lesbian & 50% straight clientele
Transportation: Car is best.
To Gay Bars: 30 minutes to Santa Fe.
Rooms: 2 rooms with queen or king bed.
Bathrooms: All private bath/ showers.
Campsites: RV parking.
Meals: Continental-plus breakfast & afternoon refreshments.
Vegetarian: Special veggie dishes for breakfast if requested in advance.
Complimentary: Afternoon snacks between 5pm-6pm.
Dates Open: All year.
Rates: $90.
Discounts: 10% to senior citizens.
Rsv'tns: Required.
To Reserve: Travel agent or call direct.
Parking: Ample free parking.
In-Room: Color cable TV & ceiling fans.
On-Premises: TV lounge, baby grand piano & use of refrigerator for sodas & such.
Exercise/Health: Hot tub on premises. Nearby gym, hot springs & massage.
Sunbathing: On hot tub deck.
Smoking: Permitted outside only.
Pets: Not permitted. Kennel 5 minutes away.
Handicap Access: No.
Children: Not permitted.
Languages: English, some Spanish.

Saltamontes Retreat — Grasshopper Hill

Lesbian-Owned & -Operated ♀

Mountain Solace & Inspiration for Writers, Artists & Adventurers

Geared towards writers, artists and explorers, this practical, low-budget lodging is located half an hour northeast of Santa Fe. Enjoy the tranquility and inspiration of *Saltamontes Retreat — Grasshopper Hill* while soaking in the hot tub under a starry sky, or taking in the mountain vistas of Pecos and Santa Fe National Wilderness Peak. Local activities range from fishing, hiking and swimming, to mountain biking, cross-country skiing and backpacking along the creeks and tributaries of the Pecos River Basin. Guests must not be allergic to pets as there are resident dogs, cats, ducks and geese. The lodge owner lives on premises.

Address: Old Colonias Rd, 2 Llanitos Ln, E. Pecos,
Mail to: PO Box 374, Pecos, NM 87552 **Tel:** (505) 757-2528.

Type: B&B inn. Rural residence with guest lodgings.
Clientele: Mostly women with some hetero clientele
Transportation: Car. In winter, front- or 4-WD vehicle if recent snow.
To Gay Bars: 26 miles, a 30 min drive.
Rooms: 3 rooms with single or double beds.
Bathrooms: 2 shared bath/ shower/toilets.
Meals: Communal kitchen,
guests can shop & cook.
Vegetarian: Summer garden produce.
Complimentary: Herb tea, coffee.
Dates Open: All year.
High Season: Apr-Nov.
Rates: $40-$55/nt, $225-$250/wk, $475-$550/month.
Discounts: Weekly & monthly discounts.
Rsv'tns: Required. Overnight travelers welcome.
Parking: Ample free on-street parking, driveway.
In-Room: Maid & laundry service.
On-Premises: Meeting rooms, TV lounge, laundry facilities, study, Mac Plus, desk, phone service w/ credit card.
Exercise/Health: Jacuzzi.
Swimming: River nearby.
Sunbathing: On patio & common sun decks.
Nudity: Permitted in hot tub, deck.
Smoking: Permitted outside only, non-smoking rooms available.
Pets: Short term only if spayed, neutered. Pets on premises.
Handicap Access: No.
Children: Permitted wtih short-term, enroute travelers.
Languages: English, Spanish.
Your Host: Pamela.

Arius Compound

Q-NET Gay-Friendly ♀♂

Experience Adobe Living...

...in your own authentic Santa Fe *Casita*, ideally located on Canyon Road, the heart of Santa Fe's historic East Side with charming shops, galleries and fine restaurants. Up a quiet lane, surrounded by high adobe walls filled with gardens, patios, fruit trees and our ever-hot redwood tub, each *Casita* has 1 or 2 bedrooms, fully-equipped kitchen, living room with corner Kiva fireplace (wood provided), private bath or shower, private patio and loads of Southwest style. Don't be a visitor. Live here, at *Arius Compound*, if only for a few days.

Address: PO Box 1111, 1018-1/2 Canyon Rd, Santa Fe, NM 87504-1111
Tel: Out of Town: (800) 735-8453,
Local: (505) 982-2621, **Fax:** (505) 989-8280.
E-mail: len@ariuscompound.com

Type: Cottages.
Clientele: 60% straight & 40% gay & lesbian clientele
Transportation: Car is best.
Rooms: 3 cottages (two 1-br & one 2-br) with single, double or queen beds. Futon sleepers in living rooms.
Bathrooms: 2 private shower/toilets & 1 private bath/shower/toilet.
Dates Open: All year.
High Season: July-August.
Rates: 1-bedrm: low $80, high $115. 2-bedrm: low $135, high $175.
Credit Cards: MC, Visa, Amex, Discover.
Rsv'tns: Not required, but usually sold out without reservations.
To Reserve: Call direct.
Parking: Adequate off-street parking.
In-Room: Color cable TV, telephone, ceiling fans, kitchen, refrigerator, coffee & tea-making facilities.
Exercise/Health: Jacuzzi.
Swimming: Nearby pool.
Sunbathing: On private & common sun decks & patio.
Smoking: Permitted outside. Non-smoking rooms available.
Pets: Permitted. Check first.
Handicap Access: No.
Children: Welcome.
Languages: English.
Your Host: Len & Robbie.

Four Kachinas Inn Bed & Breakfast

Q-NET Gay-Friendly ♀♂

Our Breakfasts Will Win Your Acclaim

On a quiet street, built around a private courtyard, *Four Kachinas Inn* is a short walk from the historic Santa Fe Plaza via the Old Santa Fe Trail. Rooms have private baths, private entrances and southwestern furnishings which include antique Navajo rugs, Hopi kachina dolls, handcrafted wooden furniture and saltillo tile floors. A continental-plus breakfast, prepared by our award-winning baker, is served in your room. Rated 3 diamonds by AAA. **Guest Comments:** "I was born in New Mexico, and this B&B felt like home....Great breakfasts here, too." -Felix, Berkeley, CA

Address: 512 Webber St, Santa Fe, NM 87501
Tel: (505) 982-2550, (800) 397-2564, **Fax:** (505) 989-1323.
E-mail: 4kachinas@swcp.com **URL:** http://www.4kachinas.com/bbinn/

Type: Bed & breakfast.
Clientele: Mostly straight clientele with gays & lesbians welcome.
Transportation: Car is best.
To Gay Bars: 7 blocks. A 15-minute walk or 5-minute drive.
Rooms: 6 rooms with single, queen or king beds.
Bathrooms: All private.
Meals: Generous continental breakfast.
Vegetarian: Available.

Complimentary: Tea, soft drinks & cookies every afternoon in guest lounge.
Dates Open: Feb 1st through Jan 4th.
High Season: May 1-Oct 31 & major holidays.
Rates: High season $73-$130. Low season $60-$110.
Credit Cards: MC, Visa, Discover.
Rsv'tns: Required.
To Reserve: Travel agent or call direct.

Minimum Stay: 3 nights high season weekends, 2 nights low season wknds. 3-5 nights certain holidays & special events.
Parking: Adequate free off-street parking.
In-Room: Color cable TV, ceiling fans, telephone & maid service.
On-Premises: Guest lounge (no TV).
Exercise/Health: Nearby gym, weights, Jacuzzi, tennis, golf, steam & massage.

Swimming: Nearby pool.
Sunbathing: On the patio.
Smoking: Permitted outside only. All rooms are non-smoking.
Pets: Not permitted.
Handicap Access: Yes. 1 room & guest lounge are wheelchair accessible.
Children: Not especially welcome.
Languages: English, Spanish, some French.
Your Host: Andrew & John.

Heart Seed B&B and Spa

Q-NET Gay-Friendly 50/50

Capture the Spirit of the Land of Enchantment

Heart Seed B&B and Spa is located on 100 acres in a spectacular mountain setting 25 miles south of Santa Fe near the historic village of Los Cerrillos and the popular artist's colony of Madrid. Stay in Santa Fe-style B&B rooms, retreat rooms or a three-bedroom mountain chalet. Retreat rooms provide fully equipped kitchenettes to accommodate longer stays. Enjoy the common room/library, massage and full-day spa. The grounds also include a shaded deck, outdoor hot tub, meditation garden, labyrinth, and hiking and biking trails.

Address: PO Box 6019, Santa Fe, NM 87502-6019
Tel: (505) 471-7206.
E-mail: hrtseed@nets.com **URL:** http://www.nets.com/heartseed

Type: Bed & breakfast and spa & mountain chalet.
Clientele: 50% gay & lesbian & 50% straight clientele
Transportation: Individual car.
To Gay Bars: 25 miles to Santa Fe bars.
Rooms: 2 rooms & 2 apartments with queen beds & a 3-bdrm mountain chalet.
Bathrooms: Private baths.

Meals: Full gourmet breakfast.
Vegetarian: Generally available.
Complimentary: Tea, coffee & snacks.
Dates Open: All year.
High Season: Currently Apr-Oct.
Rates: $79-$89.
Discounts: All year for stays of 4 or more days.
Credit Cards: MC, Visa, Amex.

Rsv'tns: Required.
To Reserve: Call direct.
Parking: Ample free covered parking.
In-Room: Some fully equipped kitchenettes.
On-Premises: TV lounge, VCR, meeting rooms, library with books, tapes & CDs, huge deck, meditation garden.
Exercise/Health: Full-day spa, hot tub, massage, herbal wraps, salt glows &

hiking. Mountain biking & horseback riding nearby.
Sunbathing: On private & common sun decks.
Smoking: Permitted in designated outdoor areas only.
Pets: Not permitted.
Children: Well-behaved children welcome. No special arrangements for children.
Languages: English.
Your Host: Judith & Gayle Dawn.

INN PLACES® 1998   465

Inn of the Turquoise Bear

Q-NET Gay/Lesbian

Where the Action Is... Stay Gay in Santa Fe!

The *Inn of the Turquoise Bear* occupies the home of Witter Bynner (1881-1968), a prominent gay citizen of Santa Fe, active in cultural and political affairs. A noted poet, essayist and translator, Bynner was a staunch advocate of human rights (supporting the suffrage movement and the rights of Native Americans and other minorities) and a vocal opponent of censorship.

Bynner's rambling adobe villa, built in Spanish-Pueblo Revival style from a core of rooms dating to the mid 1800's, is one of Santa Fe's most important historic estates. With its signature portico, tall pines, magnificent rock terraces, meandering paths, and flower gardens, the inn offers guests a romantic retreat close to the center of Santa Fe. As the only gay-oriented bed & breakfast in downtown Santa Fe, the *Turquoise Bear* is the perfect choice for both couples and individuals traveling alone.

Bynner and Robert Hunt, his lover of more than 30 years, were famous for the riotous parties they hosted in this house, referred to by Ansel Adams, a frequent visitor, as "Bynner's Bashes." Their home was the gathering place for the creative and fun-loving elite of Santa Fe and guests from around the world. Their celebrity guests included D.H. & Frieda Lawrence, Igor Stravinsky, Willa Cather, Errol Flynn, Martha Graham, Christopher Isherwood, Georgia O'Keeffe, Rita Hayworth, Thornton Wilder, Robert Frost — and many others.

Ralph and Robert, the new owners of the Witter Bynner Estate, reside on the property. Their goals are to rekindle the spirit of excitement, creativity, freedom and hospitality for which this remarkable home was renowned; to protect, restore and extend the legacy of its famous gay creator; and to provide their guests with the experience of a unique setting that captures the essence of traditional Santa Fe. Whether you are coming to New Mexico for the opera, the art scene, the museums, skiing, hiking, exploring Native American and Hispanic cultures, or just to relax away from it all, the *Inn of the Turquoise Bear* is the place to stay in Santa Fe. Robert and Ralph look forward to the privilege of serving as your hosts during your visit.

Address: 342 E Buena Vista Street, Santa Fe, NM 87501
Tel: (505) 983-0789, (800) 396-4104, **Fax:** (505) 988-4225.
E-mail: bluebear@roadrunner.com

Type: Bed & breakfast inn.
Clientele: 70% gay & lesbian and 30% straight clientele
Transportation: Car is best, shuttle bus from Albuquerque airport.
To Gay Bars: 8 blocks, 1 mile, a 15 min walk, a 2 min drive.
Rooms: 9 rooms, 2 suites with double, queen or king beds.
Bathrooms: Private: 1 bath/toilet, 4 shower/toilets, 4 bath/shower/toilets. Shared: 1 shower only.
Meals: Expanded continental breakfast.

Vegetarian: Available nearby.
Complimentary: Tea, coffee & fruit all day. Wine & cheese in afternoon. Sherry & brandy in common room.
Dates Open: All year.
High Season: April-October & December.
Rates: Per room, double occupancy: high season $95-$250, low season $90-$210.
Discounts: 10% for AAA, AARP. Weekly rate: 10% discount.
Credit Cards: MC, Visa, Amex, Discover.
Rsv'tns: Required, but we accept late inquiries.
To Reserve: Travel agent or call direct.
Minimum Stay: Required during certain holidays.
Parking: Ample free, walled & gated off-street parking.
In-Room: Color cable TV, VCR, fans, telephone, maid service. Some rooms have refrigerators.
On-Premises: Meeting rooms, video tape & book libraries, fax (sending & receiving).
Exercise/Health: Jacuzzi planned. Nearby gym, weights, Jacuzzi, sauna, steam, massage.
Swimming: Pool nearby.
Sunbathing: On patios.
Nudity: Permitted in various patio areas.
Smoking: Permitted on patios, not in rooms or public rooms.
Pets: Small pets OK in some rooms.
Handicap Access: One guest room accessible, but no access to rest of the building.
Children: Over 12 years OK, but children discouraged.
Languages: English, Spanish, French, Norwegian, German.
Your Host: Ralph & Robert.

IGLTA

Open Sky B&B
Gay-Friendly 50/50 ♀♂

An Endless Open Vista

Want to get away from it all? *Open Sky B&B* is a spacious and serene adobe with spectacular open views of Jamez, the Sangre de Cristo and Ortiz Mountains, and Santa Fe. Located off the historical Turquoise Trail in the countryside of Santa Fe, this B&B offers privacy and peace to enjoy the natural beauty that has made this area popular. Three rooms furnished in southwest decor have king- or queen-sized beds and private baths. A breakfast of fresh breads and fruit is served at individual tables outside the rooms.

Address: 134 Turquoise Trail, Santa Fe, NM 87505
Tel: (505) 471-3475, (800) 244-3475. **E-mail:** skymiller@aol.com

Type: Bed & breakfast.
Clientele: 50% gay & lesbian & 50% straight clientele
Transportation: Car is best, shuttlejack from airport.
To Gay Bars: 16 miles.
Rooms: 3 rooms with queen or king beds.
Bathrooms: All private
Meals: Expanded continental breakfast.
Vegetarian: Available upon request.
Complimentary: Gourmet coffee, herbal teas, fresh flowers!
Dates Open: All year.
High Season: Summer & holidays.
Rates: $70-$120.
Discounts: 10% for over 7 nights.
Credit Cards: Visa, MC, Discover, Amex.
Rsv'tns: Preferred for guaranteed availability.
To Reserve: Call direct or travel agent.
Parking: Ample off-street SAFE parking.
In-Room: Color TV, telephone, refrigerator.
On-Premises: Large 600 sq. ft. living room with fireplace.
Exercise/Health: Jacuzzi, cross-country skiing, hiking, bicycling & massage.
Swimming: At nearby river & lake.
Sunbathing: On the patio.
Smoking: Permitted outside only. Entire B&B is smoke-free.
Pets: Please inquire.
Handicap Access: Yes.
Children: Permitted with restrictions.
Languages: English & German.

The Triangle Inn-Santa Fe

Gay/Lesbian ♀♂

Internationally Acclaimed... Exclusively Lesbian & Gay

Santa Fe is one of the world's most desirable destinations, offering the visitor an extraordinary range of vacationing opportunities. *The Triangle Inn* is Santa Fe's sole exclusively lesbian and gay property and is the perfect retreat from which to explore all that Northern New Mexico offers.

The Inn is a rustic adobe compound, dating from the turn of the century, located on an acre of pinon- and juniper-studded land. It offers nine very distinct private casitas, ranging from studios to a two-bedroom house. Each is furnished in Southwestern style with Mexican and handmade furniture and has living and sleeping areas, kitchenettes and private baths. Most have kiva fireplaces and private patios. Special attention has been paid to details — the rooms are appointed with TV/VCRs, stereo/CD players, air conditioning, telephones, and down comforters. Further amenities include gourmet teas, coffees and cocoas, bath robes and spa towels. A scrumptious heavy continental breakfast is provided to you, in your casita, each day.

The Triangle Inn has two large courtyards. The Hacienda Courtyard boasts a stunning free-standing portal with an outdoor fireplace and guest gathering areas. Afternoon refreshments are provided in this delightful setting, which is also frequently used for commitment ceremonies and other functions. The Main Courtyard, around which most of the casitas are situated, has extensive plantings, a large hot tub, deck and sunbathing areas.

Although Santa Fe is not a gay resort, our visitors always find themselves comfortable in this small but sophisticated artist colony. The region offers more opportunities than most — world-class opera, a famed art market, 260 restaurants, miles of hiking and skiing trails, native American pueblos and ruins, Spanish and Mexican culture, and, of course, our world-renowned views. Come to *The Triangle Inn — Santa Fe* and discover the real Southwest!

Address: PO Box 3235, Santa Fe, NM 87501
Tel: (505) 455-3275 (Tel/Fax).
E-mail: TriangleSF@aol.com **URL:** http://www.roadrunner.com/~triangle/

Type: Inn.
Clientele: Good mix of gays & lesbians.
Transportation: Car is best.
To Gay Bars: 12 miles to gay/lesbian bars.
Rooms: 9 cottages with queen & king beds & kitchenettes.
Bathrooms: All private.

Meals: Expanded continental breakfast & fully equipped kitchen.
Vegetarian: All breakfasts are vegetarian.
Complimentary: Gourmet coffee, herbal teas, juices, snacks & afternoon cocktail gatherings.
Dates Open: All year.
High Season: April-Octo-

ber, Thanksgiving & Christmas.
Rates: Low season $70-$120. High season $80-$140.
Discounts: On weekly stays & for NM residents.
Credit Cards: MC, Visa, Eurocard.
Rsv'tns: Recommended.
To Reserve: Travel agent

or call direct.
Minimum Stay: 3 days during holidays.
Parking: Ample, free, off-street parking.
In-Room: TV/VCR, stereo/CD player, AC, telephone, ceiling fans, robes, spa towels, kitchenettes, refrigerator, coffee/tea-mak-

ing facilities & maid service. Some rooms have fireplaces.
On-Premises: 2 common courtyards (1 with covered portal & outdoor fireplace, 1 with hot tub & sun deck),
VCR tape library, games, fax.
Exercise/Health: Jacuzzi on premises. Nearby gym, weights, sauna, steam & massage.
Swimming: Nearby pool.
Sunbathing: On private & common sun decks.
Smoking: Non-smoking rooms available.
Pets: Permitted with advance notice ($5 per day).
Handicap Access: Yes.
Children: Children of all ages welcome.
Languages: English & Spanish.
Your Host: Sarah & Karan.

The Ruby Slipper

Q-NET Gay/Lesbian

SEE SPECIAL PAGE 28 COLOR SECTION

A Perfect Balance of Privacy & Personal Attention

At *The Ruby Slipper,* our guest rooms, individually decorated with handmade furniture, have private baths and fireplace or woodstove. Breakfast specialties include scrumptious breakfast burritos, omelettes and banana pancakes. Our lovely grounds are complete with an outdoor hot tub. A vacation in Taos might include hiking, horseback riding, world-class skiing, gallery viewing, shopping or visiting Taos Pueblo. *The Ruby Slipper* is Northern New Mexico's most popular and relaxing gay-friendly bed and breakfast. Come see what everybody's talking about!

Address: PO Box 2069, Taos, NM 87571 **Tel:** (505) 758-0613.

Type: Bed & breakfast.
Clientele: Mostly gay/lesbian with some straight clientele.
Transportation: Car is best. 2-1/2 hours from Albuquerque by car. Taxi from bus stop to Ruby Slipper, $5.
To Gay Bars: 1-1/4 hours to Santa Fe gay & lesbian bars.
Rooms: 7 rooms with double, queen or king beds.
Bathrooms: All private.
Meals: Full breakfast.
Vegetarian: Available.

Complimentary: In-room coffee-maker with fresh ground coffee & assorted teas.
Dates Open: All year.
High Season: Summer, holidays and ski season.
Rates: $79-$104 per night for two, $94-$119 for Xmas holidays.
Discounts: On weekly stays, if booked directly.
Credit Cards: MC, Visa, Amex, Discover.
Rsv'tns: Recommended.
To Reserve: Travel agent or call direct.
Minimum Stay: 2-3 days on holidays, 2 days some weekends.
Parking: Adequate free off-street parking.
In-Room: Maid service, ceiling fans, coffee & tea-making facilities. All rooms have fireplace or woodstove.
On-Premises: Telephone, common room for guests, refrigerator stocked with items for purchase.
Exercise/Health: Hot tub on the premises, health club in town.
Swimming: 10 minutes to pool, 20 to Rio Grande.
Sunbathing: On hot tub deck or patio.
Nudity: Permitted in the hot tub.
Smoking: Permitted outdoors.
Pets: Not permitted.
Handicap Access: Yes, call for details.
Children: Permitted.
Languages: English.

IGLTA

UNITED STATES • NEW MEXICO • TAOS

UNITED STATES — ANGELICA • NEW YORK

Jones Pond Campground
Men ♂

Jones Pond Campground is an all-male, adult retreat on 119 rustic acres with two large natural trails and 135 sites. All trailer and RV sites have electric & water hookups, picnic tables and fireplaces. Many tent sites have picnic tables and fireplaces, and some have water and electric. The camp store has basic supplies and grocery items. There is a two-story recreation hall, a large pond, a 65-foot swimming pool, volleyball and basketball courts, and a baseball diamond. Events include variety & craft shows, Leather weekends, Christmas in July, pool/pizza parties, and Fantasy weekends.

Address: 9835 Old State Rd, Angelica, NY 14709-9729
Tel: (716) 567-8100, Fax: (716) 567-4518.
E-mail: jonespond-dorin@worldnet.att.net

Type: Campground.
Clientele: Men only
Transportation: Car is best.
To Gay Bars: 1-1/2 hr to Buffalo or Rochester.
Rooms: Trailers for rent (supply your own bedding & utensils).
Bathrooms: 2 shower/toilet facilities with 4 showers each.

Campsites: Tent & trailer sites, 135 with electric & water.
Dates Open: May 1-Oct 4.
High Season: July-September.
Rates: Rates vary, call for brochure.
Discounts: For weekly & monthly stays.
Credit Cards: Visa, MC, Discover, Novus.

Rsv'tns: Required, with a $20 deposit.
To Reserve: Call direct.
Parking: Ample free parking.
On-Premises: TV lounge, exercise area, gathering room, dance room with DJ.
Exercise/Health: Weights.
Swimming: Pool on premises.

Sunbathing: At poolside.
Nudity: Permitted at the pool & in nonrestricted areas.
Smoking: Permitted.
Pets: Permitted on leash.
Handicap Access: Yes.
Children: Not permitted.
Languages: English.
Your Host: Wayne & Roger.

CATSKILL MOUNTAINS

Bradstan Country Hotel
Gay-Friendly ♀♂

That Uptown Feeling in Upstate N.Y.

After a 21 month, painstaking renovation, *Bradstan Country Hotel* was awarded The First Sullivan County Board of Realtors Award for Architectural Excellence. In addition to our large comfortable rooms, the *Bradstan* also features a 70-foot private deck and a 60-foot front porch overlooking beautiful White Lake, where your favorite water activities are at your beck and call. At the end of the day, order up your favorite cocktail and enjoy the live cabaret entertainment in *Bradstan's* own piano bar lounge. All this just 2 hours from NYC. Ask us about hosting your special affair or meeting at our inn.

Address: Route 17B, PO Box 312, White Lake, NY 12786
Tel: (914) 583-4114 (Tel/Fax).

Type: Bed & breakfast inn with cottages & bar.
Clientele: Mainly straight clientele with a gay & lesbian following.
Transportation: Car is best, no charge for pick up, prior arrangement required.
To Gay Bars: Piano bar on premises with mixed crowd.
Rooms: 2 rooms, 3 suites & 2 cottages with queen beds.
Bathrooms: All private.

Meals: Expanded continental breakfast.
Vegetarian: Our breakfast is acceptable for vegetarians.
Dates Open: Open weekends all year & 7 days a week from 4/1 to 8/31.
High Season: Memorial Day to Labor Day.
Rates: $105-$115 summer, $75-$85 winter.
Discounts: Discounts available to groups & stays of 5 nights or more.

Credit Cards: MC, VISA, Discover, Amex.
Rsv'tns: Recommended.
To Reserve: Call direct.
Minimum Stay: 2 night minimum stay on weekends from Memorial Day to 10/31.
Parking: Free adequate on-street & off-street parking.
In-Room: B&B: AC, maid service, ceiling fans. Year-round cottages have color cable TV, full kitchens.

On-Premises: Piano lounge, meeting rooms.
Swimming: At private lake.
Sunbathing: On sun deck or private lake front.
Smoking: Permitted.
Pets: Not permitted.
Handicap Access: No.
Children: Permitted with prior arrangement, over the age of 8.
Languages: English.
Your Host: Scott & Edward.

Palenville House

Gay-Owned 50/50 ⚥

A magnificent, turn-of-the-century Victorian home, *Palenville House* is named after this quaint hamlet which was home to the legendary Rip Van Winkle. We are within walking distance of hiking trails, swimming holes, the Rip Van Winkle Golf Course, the Palenville Interarts Colony, as well as parks, ski areas and shopping galore. Our romantic suite features breathtaking mountain views, a sleeping loft, woodburning stove with open fire, deck, cable TV, VCR and Jacuzzi. We also have a new 10-person hot tub. Our full country breakfast includes fruit, fresh-baked muffins, juice, and French toast, pancakes, waffles or omelets.

Address: Jct Rts 23A & 32A, PO Box 465, Palenville, NY 12463-0465
Tel: (518) 678-5649, Fax: (518) 678-9038.
E-mail: palenville@aol.com URL: http://members.aol.com/palenville

Type: Bed & breakfast.
Clientele: 50% gay & lesbian & 50% hetero clientele
Transportation: Car is best. Free pick up from bus.
To Gay Bars: 30 miles, a 30 min drive.
Rooms: 4 rooms & 1 suite with single, double or queen beds.
Bathrooms: Private & shared.
Meals: Full breakfast.
Vegetarian: On request.
Complimentary: Coffee, tea, hot chocolate, soda.
Dates Open: All year.
High Season: January.
Rates: $60-$125.
Discounts: 10% discount on multiple-night stays.
Credit Cards: Discover.
To Reserve: Travel agent or call direct.
Minimum Stay: Required on holidays.
Parking: Ample free parking.
In-Room: Color cable TV, VCR.
On-Premises: TV lounge.
Exercise/Health: Jacuzzi.
Swimming: Lake & creek nearby.
Sunbathing: In backyard.
Smoking: No smoking, except on enclosed porch.
Pets: Not permitted.
Handicap Access: No.
Children: No.
Languages: English & Spanish.
Your Host: Jim & Jim.

Stonewall Acres

Gay/Lesbian ⚥

A Bit of Norman Rockwell Americana...Village Voice

Get away from it all just ninety miles from New York City in our two charming, cozy cottages full of collectibles. We have 12 1/2 acres of lovely grounds with lawn and woods, flower gardens, an in-ground Esther Williams pool, a private pond. One cottage is seasonal and one is fully winterized. We're located 20 minutes from the original Woodstock site, on a country road, minutes from downhill skiing, horseback riding and convention centers. You have hundreds of options to be busy — or just kick back and hang out in the hammock or the pool. The *New York Press* says "*Stonewall Acres* is a pretty place, has a rejuvenating atmosphere and a congenial owner." Call for details.

Address: PO Box 556, Rock Hill, NY 12775
Tel: (914) 791-9474, in NYC Metro area: (800) 336-4208.

Type: 2 cottages, one fully winterized.
Clientele: Mostly gay/lesbian with some straight clientele
Transportation: Car is best.
To Gay Bars: 25-minute drive to gay/lesbian bar.
Rooms: 2 rooms with double beds. 2 cottages,
one with double & one with queen bed.
Bathrooms: All private.
Meals: Cook in cottages.
Complimentary: Tea, coffee.
Dates Open: All year.
High Season: July-August.
Rates: Weekends $74, weekdays $55.
Discounts: Full week & monthly discounts.
Credit Cards: Amex.
Rsv'tns: Preferred.
To Reserve: Call direct or travel agent.
Parking: Ample off-street parking.
In-Room: Kitchens in the cottages.
On-Premises: Each cottage has its own BBQ picnic area.
Exercise/Health: Fishing,
walking trails on 12 1/2 acres.
Swimming: Pool on premises (seasonal, June 15-Labor Day).
Sunbathing: At poolside.
Smoking: Permitted.
Pets: Especially welcome.
Handicap Access: No.
Children: Permitted.
Languages: English.
Your Host: Bill & David.

Rufus Tanner House

Q-NET Gay-Friendly 50/50 ♀♂

Wonderful antiques help retain the charm of our 1864 Greek Revival farmhouse's tastefully and comfortably updated interior. The four guestrooms at the *Rufus Tanner House* are air-conditioned and have private baths. And each one offers something special — a fireplace, sitting area, or Jacuzzi. Enjoy a stroll on our two-plus acres of lawn and orchard or spend a quiet evening in front of the living room fireplace. Stay with us just 1 or 2 nights or enjoy our winery Weekend Package. You'll never run out of things to do here! In any event, we look forward to seeing you soon!

Address: 60 Sagetown Rd, Pine City, NY 14871-9502
Tel: (607) 732-0213, **Fax:** (607) 735-0620. **E-mail:** RufusTan@servtech.com

Type: Bed & breakfast.
Clientele: 50% gay & lesbian & 50% straight clientele.
Transportation: Car is best. Free pick up from airport or bus.
To Gay Bars: 15 minutes to David & The Body Shop in Elmira, 45 minutes to Common Ground in Ithaca.
Rooms: 3 rooms with doubles & 1 queen bed.
Bathrooms: All private & 1 with Jacuzzi.
Meals: Full breakfast.
Vegetarian: Available upon request.
Complimentary: Tea, juice, soda.
Dates Open: All year.
High Season: May 1-November 1.
Rates: $55-$105 per night for two, $5 each extra guest.
Discounts: Special honeymoon & weekend packages & long-term stays of 4 or more nights.
Credit Cards: MC, Visa.
Rsv'tns: Preferred.
To Reserve: Travel agent or call direct.
Parking: Ample free off-street parking.
In-Room: AC, maid & room service. One room has fireplace.
On-Premises: Baby grand piano, CDs, color cable TV, VCR, small video tape library, telephone, refrigerator, laundry facilities for long-term guests.
Exercise/Health: Weight machine, treadmill, running areas, outdoor hot tub.
Jacuzzi in one room & nearby full service fitness center.
Swimming: Nearby creek. 15 min to public pool, 45 min to Cayuga & Seneca Lakes.
Sunbathing: On common sun decks.
Smoking: Not permitted.
Pets: Not permitted.
Handicap Access: No.
Children: Permitted if well-behaved.
Languages: English.
Your Host: Bill & John.

Belvedere

Men ♂

For magnificent terrace views over 100 miles of water, with superb sunsets, stay at *Belvedere*. Many of our rooms have terraces because this old mansion was built in the tradition of a Venetian palace, complete with towers, domes, statuary and fountains. There are also sun decks, a hot tub, a Roman swimming pool and an extensive gym. Though our rooms are not large, they have frescoed ceilings, antiques, Oriental rugs and crystal chandeliers. Most have private baths.

Address: Box 4026, Cherry Grove, Fire Island, NY 11782
Tel: (516) 597-6448, **Fax:** (516) 597-9391.

Type: Guesthouse and cottages.
Clientele: Men only
Transportation: Car, Long Island RR or air.
To Gay Bars: 2 blocks or a 5-minute walk.
Rooms: 30 rooms, 5 suites & 30 cottages with single, double & king beds.
Bathrooms: 20 private bath/toilets & 10 private sink/washbasins. Others share.
Meals: Continental breakfast weekends & holidays.
Complimentary: Coffee always available & cocktail parties on holiday weekends.
Dates Open: May 1st-Oct 15th.
Rates: Rooms $80-$200 weekdays, $300-$500 weekends.
Credit Cards: MC, Visa, Amex.
Rsv'tns: Required.
To Reserve: Call direct.
Parking: Ample pay parking at ferry terminal on mainland.
In-Room: Refrigerator & ceiling fans. Some color TVs & VCRs.
On-Premises: TV lounge & coffee/tea-making facilities.
Exercise/Health: Gym, weights & Jacuzzi.
Swimming: Pool & 5 minutes to ocean beach.
Sunbathing: At poolside, beach, patio, roof, private and common sun decks.
Nudity: Permitted in all sunbathing areas.
Pets: Not permitted.
Handicap Access: Yes.
Children: Not permitted.
Languages: English & French.

IGLTA

Cherry Grove Beach Hotel
Gay/Lesbian ♀♂

Cherry Grove Beach Hotel, Fire Island's largest hotel, is located in the heart of town, only steps from the beach, restaurants, shops and bars. Choose between our economy and deluxe room with refrigerator, microwave, air conditioning, television/VCRs and telephones. Ask about reserving a room and receiving additional nights for only $19.98! It is home to the Ice Palace, offering New York's top DJs, drag shows, guest entertainers and theme parties. Lounge by our 30' by 60' pool or roam freely with deer on the finest natural beach in the world!

Address: PO Box 537, Sayville, NY 11782-0537
Tel: (516) 597-6600, **Fax:** (516) 597-6651.
E-mail: grovehotel@aol.com **URL:** www.grovehotel.com

Type: Hotel with bar & disco.
Clientele: Good mix of gay men & women.
Transportation: Ferry.
To Gay Bars: Within 200 feet of 5 gay bars.
Rooms: 64 studio apartments with high rise sleep sofas for 2.
Bathrooms: All private.
Vegetarian: 3 restaurants have vegetarian alternatives.
Dates Open: May 1-Oct 1.
High Season: Memorial Day-Labor Day.
Rates: Off season $39-$299 & in season $69-$399.
Discounts: Group & midweek. Ask about additional nights at $19.98.
Credit Cards: MC, Visa, Amex, Discover.
Rsv'tns: Required.
To Reserve: Call direct.
Minimum Stay: Two nights on weekends.
Parking: At ferry terminal on the other side.
In-Room: Color TV, AC, maid service, telephone, ceiling fans, kitchen & refrigerator.
Swimming: In the 30' x 60' pool or at nearby ocean beach.
Sunbathing: At poolside or on the beach.
Nudity: Permitted on the beach.
Smoking: Permitted. Non-smoking rooms are available.
Pets: Not permitted.
Handicap Access: Yes. Rooms available.
Children: Not permitted.
Languages: English.
Your Host: Isaac.

Pleasant Grove B&B
Gay-Friendly 60/40 ♀♂

Ithaca and the Finger Lakes Wine Country

Pleasant Grove is a comfortable country home from the 1930s above the west shore of Cayuga Lake in the Finger Lakes wine country. Panoramic views from the deck make afternoon tea and morning breakfast special times. Hike, birdwatch and cross-country ski in our fields and woods.

continued next page

INN PLACES® 1998

Taughannock Falls State Park provides swimming and boating on Cayuga Lake. Four golf courses are minutes away. Wineries, antique shops and fine restaurants make a visit memorable. Both Cornell University and Ithaca College are fifteen minutes away.

Address: 1779 Trumansburg Rd (Rte 96), Jacksonville, NY 14854-0009
Tel: (607) 387-5420, (800) 398-3963. **E-mail:** jlg4@cornell.edu.

Type: Bed & breakfast.
Clientele: 60% gay & lesbian & 40% straight clientele.
Transportation: Car.
To Gay Bars: 10 miles from gay/lesbian bar.
Rooms: 2 rooms with queen beds.
Bathrooms: 2 private.
Meals: Full breakfast.

Vegetarian: Always available.
Complimentary: Afternoon tea, coffee.
Dates Open: All year.
High Season: May-October.
Rates: $65-$80.
Rsv'tns: Preferred.
To Reserve: Call direct.
Minimum Stay: During major university & college weekends.

Parking: Ample, free off-street parking.
Exercise/Health: Cross-country skiing, hiking & birdwatching. Golf courses nearby.
Swimming: Cayuga Lake & streams nearby.
Sunbathing: Common sun decks.

Smoking: Not permitted in the house.
Pets: Not permitted.
Handicap Access: No.
Children: Permitted over 12 years old by prior arrangement.
Languages: English & German.
Your Host: James & Robert.

One Thirty-Two North Main
Gay/Lesbian ♂

The Hot Place to be COOL This Summer

To make each guest feel like a personal friend visiting has been the primary objective at *One Thirty-Two North Main* for 26 summers. On two tranquil acres, just steps from quaint village shops and trendy restaurants, we offer fifteen accommodations in various locations, including the main house, the annex, the cottage and the cabana, and an unusually inviting large and secluded swimming pool surrounded by a "jungle" of trees. From *One Thirty-Two*, it's a 5-minute drive or bike ride to one of the world's most beautiful beaches.

Address: 132 N Main St, East Hampton, NY 11937
Tel: (516) 324-2246 or (516) 324-9771.

Type: Mini-resort.
Clientele: Mostly men with women welcome.
Transportation: Car, train or bus. Short walk from Long Island RR station, Hampton Jitney & Hamptons on My Mind bus stops.
To Gay Bars: 4 miles to bar, disco & restaurant.
Rooms: 13 rooms with single, double, queen or king beds, 1 apartment & 1 cottage.
Bathrooms: 5 private

shower/toilets & 8 shared bath/shower/toilets.
Meals: Continental breakfast.
Dates Open: May-Sept.
High Season: All weekends from July 4th to Labor Day.
Rates: $80-$225.
Discounts: On stays including 5 weekdays.
Credit Cards: MC, Visa, Amex.
Rsv'tns: Required.
To Reserve: Travel agent or call direct.

Minimum Stay: 2 nights on weekends in July & August.
Parking: Ample free off-street parking.
In-Room: Maid service, refrigerator, ceiling fans. Some accommodations have AC.
On-Premises: TV lounge.
Exercise/Health: Nearby gym, weights, steam & massage.
Swimming: 20 ft by 50 ft pool on premises, 1 mile to ocean beach.
Sunbathing: At poolside,

on patio or ocean beach.
Nudity: Permitted at poolside.
Smoking: Permitted without restrictions.
Pets: Permitted in cabana.
Handicap Access: Yes, very small step at back entrance.
Children: Permitted in annex or cabana.
Languages: English, Italian.
Your Host: Tony

IGLTA

The Inn at Applewood
Gay-Friendly 50/50 ♀♂

Great Food, Friendly Service & Comfortable Surroundings

Guests come to *The Inn at Applewood* for relaxation and a taste of the country, and leave raving about their dining experience at The Would Restaurant. Co-owner and awardwinning chef, Claire Winslow, creates exotic menus, making use

474   FERRARI GUIDES™

of fresh herbs and vegetables grown by partner Debra Dooley in the inn's own garden. Guests frequently say that dining by a crackling fire with white linen tablecloths, candlelight and fresh flowers, in the Applewood's old-resort atmosphere relaxes them and takes them back to slower days. The Would has an awardwinning wine selection and its own bakery.

Address: 120 North Rd, Highland, NY
Tel: (914) 691-2516, **Fax:** (914) 691-7607.
E-mail: thewould@aol.com **URL:** thewould.com

Type: Inn with restaurant.
Clientele: 50% gay & lesbian & 50% straight clientele
Transportation: Car or train. Free pick up from train.
To Gay Bars: 3 blocks, a 5 min walk.
Rooms: 5 rooms with queen or king beds.

Bathrooms: All private bath/shower/toilets.
Meals: Full breakfast.
Vegetarian: Available.
Complimentary: $10 off dinner check.
Dates Open: All year.
Rates: $90 per night, 2 people max.
Credit Cards: MC, Visa, Amex.

Rsv'tns: Required.
To Reserve: Call direct.
Parking: Ample free parking.
In-Room: AC, ceiling fans, color TV, refrigerator, coffee & tea-making facilities, maid service.
On-Premises: Meeting rooms, laundry facilities, fax.

Swimming: Nearby river, lake.
Smoking: Non-smoking rooms available.
Pets: Not permitted.
Handicap Access: Restaurant, yes; rooms, no.
Children: No.
Your Host: Debra & Claire.

A Greenwich Village Habitué
Gay-Friendly 50/50 ♀♂

Your Perfect Home Away From Home

A Greenwich Village Habitué has fully-appointed apartments available in an owner-occupied 1830's Federal brownstone in the historic West Village. Antique filled apartments come complete with living room, sleeping alcove, dining alcove, fully-equipped kitchen and full bath. The apartments overlook a formal English garden. They are perfect for both business or tourism and are only a short distance from the Convention Center. *As Quoted by Mimi Reed of Food and Wine Magazine:* "It was to our delight, an immaculate, graciously stocked and elegantly furnished apartment (with a mahogany sleigh bed) in a brownstone. It seemed a great bargain."

Address: New York's West Village, **Tel:** (212) 243-6495.

Type: Private, fully-equipped apartments.
Clientele: Sophisticated, well-traveled persons, some of whom are gay & lesbian.
Transportation: Taxi or Cary bus.
To Gay Bars: Walking distance to most gay & lesbian bars.
Rooms: 2 fully-appointed

private apartments with queen beds.
Bathrooms: Private.
Vegetarian: Complete vegetarian/health food center nearby.
Dates Open: All year.
Rates: $145 plus taxes (single or double occupancy).
Rsv'tns: Advance reservation required.

To Reserve: Call direct.
Minimum Stay: 3 nights.
Parking: Limited on-street pay parking.
In-Room: AC, color TV, telephone, answering machine, full kitchen, refrigerator, coffee & tea-making facilities. Daily maid service available for additional charge.

Exercise/Health: Nearby gym.
Smoking: Not permitted.
Pets: No.
Handicap Access: No.
Children: No.
Languages: English, Spanish.
Your Host: Matthew & Lewis.

Abode, Ltd
Gay-Friendly ♀♂

Privacy & Luxury in a NYC Brownstone or Apartment

Have your heart set on staying in one of those delightful, restored brownstones? Or how about a contemporary luxury apartment in the heart of Manhattan? *Abode* selects hosts with great care, and all homes are personally inspected to ensure the highest standards of cleanliness, attractiveness and hospitality. All the attractions of New York City—theatres, museums, galleries, restaurants, parks and shopping—are within easy reach. Select an unhosted contemporary luxury apartment or a private apartment, with country inn ambiance, in an owner-occupied brownstone.

Address: PO Box 20022, New York, NY 10021
Tel: (212) 472-2000, (800) 835-8880.

Type: Reservation service.
Clientele: Mostly straight clientele-gay/lesbian following
Transportation: Taxi.
To Gay Bars: Within a few blocks in most Manhattan neighborhoods.
Rooms: 40 apartments with queen, double, & king beds.
Bathrooms: All private.
Meals: Self-serve continental breakfast in most.
Dates Open: All year.
Rates: $120-$400/night.
Discounts: Special rates for extended stays.
Credit Cards: Amex.
Rsv'tns: Required.
To Reserve: Call direct.
Minimum Stay: 4 nights.
Park: Ample pay parking.
In-Room: Color/color cable TV, VCR, AC, telephone, answering machine, kitchen, refrigerator, coffee & tea-making facilities. Daily maid service can be arranged at guests' expense.
On-Premises: Laundry facilities at some locations.
Smoking: Smoking & non-smoking available.
Children: Over 12 years permitted in some apartments. Please inquire.
Languages: English.

Chelsea Mews Guesthouse
Gay ♂

Friendly, Private & Affordable

Ours is an old fashioned atmosphere, with Victorian garden. Guestrooms are furnished with antiques, and there is even an antique shop on the ground floor. You'll find the location of *Chelsea Mews* very convenient to all attractions, transportation and shopping. Advance reservations are advised.

Address: 344 W 15th St, New York, NY 10011 **Tel:** (212) 255-9174.

Type: Guesthouse.
Clientele: All male
Transportation: Any city transportation.
To Gay Bars: 1-1/2 blocks.
Rooms: 8 rooms with single or double beds.
Bathrooms: 1 private bath/toilet, others share bath/shower/toilet, 2 semi-private baths.
Meals: Continental breakfast of coffee.
Dates Open: All year.
Rates: $75-$150.
Rsv'tns: Required.
To Reserve: Call direct.
Parking: Ample on-street pay parking.
In-Room: Color TV, AC, telephone, refrigerator, coffee-making facilities & maid service.
On-Premises: Garden.
Smoking: All rooms non-smoking.
Pets: Not permitted.
Handicap Access: No.
Children: Not especially welcomed.
Languages: English.

Chelsea Pines Inn

Q-NET Gay/Lesbian ♂

Your Passport to Gay New York

Fodor's Gay Guide USA calls us "The best-known gay accommodation in the city... equidistant from the Village and Chelsea attractions... this 1850 town house is run by a helpful staff... pleasantly furnished rooms... it's a great deal!" Bordering Greenwich Village and Chelsea, two of the most colorful and interesting gay areas of New York City, the *Chelsea Pines Inn* is the ideal place from which tourists can explore the city. A short walk away are restaurants, shops, clubs, and bars. The famous Christopher Street area is just 10 minutes away by foot. Both subway and bus stops at the corner make the entire city easily accessible.

The inn has newly decorated rooms, guest areas, and hallways; new carpeting; new lighting; and new colors. Charmingly decorated with vintage movie posters, the rooms have full- or queen-sized beds, direct-dial phones, air conditioning and central heating, color cable TVs with free HBO, refrigerators, hair dryers and washing facilities. Daily maid service and a fax service is also available. And, despite its recent renovation, the inn still has modest rates. A complimentary, expanded continental breakfast includes fresh fruit, homemade bread and Krispy Kreme donuts, New York's newest sensation, delivered fresh to our door. Breakfast is available in the outdoor garden when the weather permits, or in our breakfast room or new year-round greenhouse. The inn is centrally located for airline travelers — JFK Airport is 45-60 minutes away, La Guardia Airport is 25-30 minutes away, and Newark Airport is 30-45 minutes from the inn.

Address: 317 W 14th St, New York, NY 10014
Tel: (212) 929-1023, **Fax:** (212) 620-5646. **E-mail:** cpiny@aol.com

Type: Bed & breakfast inn.
Clientele: Mostly men with women welcome
Transportation: Car service to inn or bus to Manhattan, then taxi or subway.
To Gay Bars: 1/2 block to men's, 5-minute walk to women's bars.
Rooms: 25 rooms with double or queen beds.
Bathrooms: 11 private & 8 semi-private, others share. Sink in every room.
Meals: Expanded continental breakfast with homemade bread.
Vegetarian: Vegetarian restaurant nearby.
Complimentary: Coffee, cookies & Krispy Kreme donuts all day.
Dates Open: All year.
High Season: Spring, summer & fall.
Rates: $79-$109 plus taxes.
Credit Cards: All major cards.
Rsv'tns: Recommended.
To Reserve: Call/fax direct, or travel agent.
Minimum Stay: 3 nights on weekends, 4 nights on holidays.
Parking: Paid parking in lot or garage (1 block).
In-Room: Maid service, color cable TV with free HBO, AC, phone & refrigerator.
On-Premises: Garden.
Exercise/Health: 1 block to gym.
Smoking: Permitted.
Pets: Not permitted.
Handicap Access: No.
Children: Not permitted.
Languages: English.
Your Host: Al, Jay & Tom.

IGLTA

INN PLACES® 1998 477

Colonial House Inn

Q-NET Gay/Lesbian ♀♂

Being Gay Is Only Part of Our Charm

Colonial House is like a European hotel. The inn, on a quiet street in Chelsea, has 20 modern and impeccably clean rooms. All have color cable TV, radio and air conditioning, sinks and direct-dial phone. Some rooms have private baths and fireplaces. Most have refrigerators. The roof sun deck and homemade muffins at breakfast round out the amenities, but the real attraction here is service, including a 24-hour concierge. If you have any trepidation about the Big Apple, this is the place to stay. Winner of Out & About 1994-'97 Editor's Choice Award.

Address: 318 W 22nd St, New York, NY 10011
Tel: (212) 243-9669, (800) 689-3779, **Fax:** (212) 633-1612.
URL: www.colonialhouseinn.com

Type: Bed & breakfast inn.
Clientele: Good mix of gays & lesbians
Transportation: Airport bus to city, then taxi. Self-pay car service. Will arrange pick up from airport.
To Gay Bars: 1/2 block to several men's, 10-minute walk to women's bars.
Rooms: 20 rooms.
Bathrooms: 12 shared baths & 8 private. All rooms have washing facilities.
Meals: Continental breakfast. Fresh-baked homemade muffins, bagels, special house-blend coffee, assorted juices daily, fresh fruit & cereal.
Complimentary: Tea, coffee & mints.
Dates Open: All year.
Rates: $65-$99 daily, $420-$665 weekly, plus tax.
Discounts: Weekly rates available.
Credit Cards: Not accepted.
Rsv'tns: Recommended.
To Reserve: Travel agent or call direct.
Parking: On-street parking or 1/2 block to off-street pay parking.
In-Room: Maid service, color cable TV, AC, direct dial phones, radios, alarm clocks, some with refrigerators or fireplaces.
On-Premises: TV lounge.
Exercise/Health: Weights on premises. Gym & massage nearby.
Sunbathing: On common sun deck or rooftop.
Nudity: Permitted on sun deck.
Smoking: Permitted in rooms.
Pets: Not permitted.
Handicap Access: No.
Children: Mature children permitted.
Languages: English, Spanish, Italian, French, German.

IGLTA

East Village Bed & Breakfast

Q-NET Women ♀

East Village Bed & Breakfast is situated in a tasteful second-floor apartment located in an urban, multi-cultural, multi-ethnic neighborhood close to shops, galleries and affordable restaurants. Greenwich Village, SoHo, Chinatown and other areas of interest are within easy reach. The kitchen comes complete with items for preparing your own continental breakfast. You are usually on your own in your own apartment.

Address: 244 E 7th St #6, New York, NY 10009 **Tel:** (212) 260-1865.

Type: Bed & breakfast.
Clientele: Women only
Transportation: Airport bus to Grand Central Station or Port Authority in Manhattan. Then taxi or bus.
To Gay Bars: Twenty minute bus ride or a little longer walk.
Rooms: 2 rooms with single or double bed.
Bathrooms: 1 shared bath/shower/toilet.
Meals: Self-service continental breakfast.
Complimentary: Coffee, tea, juices & snacks.
Dates Open: All year.
Rates: $50-$75 per day for 1 or 2 people.
Rsv'tns: Required.
To Reserve: Call direct.
Minimum Stay: 2 nights on weekends.
Parking: Adequate free on-street parking.
In-Room: AC & telephone.
On-Premises: Guests may use kitchen, refrigerator & watch TV.
Smoking: Not permitted.
Pets: Usually permitted but call in advance.
Handicap Access: No.
Children: Permitted.
Languages: English.

The New York Bed & Breakfast Reservation Center

Q-NET Gay ♂

Perfect Accommodations in New York, San Francisco, South Beach, Loire Valley & Paris

Having started out as the host of a Manhattan bed and breakfast, I know that potential guests appreciate getting a clear and honest description of the accommodations and of the surrounding neighborhood before they book. I know they appreciate dealing with a person who is not only interested in booking once, but looking down the road for repeat business.

The New York Bed & Breakfast Reservation Center offers a wide variety of bed and breakfast accommodations in New York City at prices ranging from $60 to $90 per night. Several are within a few blocks of major Midtown hotels and theatres. We also have private studios and apartments for people who wish to be on their own. Unhosted facilities start at $100 per night, some less. Apartments are also available by the month. Our clients are not only tourists, but corporations who are trying to cut down on their corporate travel expenses.

Our hosts are New Yorkers who make their guest rooms or apartments available for paying guests. Our hosted accommodations include continental breakfast.

All accommodations are personally inspected. I turn down an average of seven out of ten inquiries to join our center, although many have been doing bed and breakfast for years. I prefer to turn down a property, rather than to place someone in an accommodation that is not satisfactory. We can suggest reasonably-priced airport pick up to facilitate getting into New York. Aside from finding the most appropriate accommodations for our guests, we try to enhance their stay in New York by assisting in every way possible. And now, you can also call us for accommodations in Paris, the Loire Valley, London and South Beach, Miami.

Tel: (212) 977-3512, (800) 747-0868.

Type: Bed & breakfast & apartments.
Clientele: Gay
Transportation: Taxi is best. Charge for pick up from public transportation stations.
To Gay Bars: Walking distance to most, depending on the accommodation.
Rooms: 25 rooms, 10 suites & 15 apartments.
Bathrooms: Most are private, but some are shared.
Meals: Continental breakfast at hosted accommodations.
Complimentary: Tea & coffee.
Dates Open: All year.
Rates: $60-$90 & up hosted or $100-$150 & up unhosted private apartments.
Credit Cards: Amex.
Rsv'tns: Required.
To Reserve: Travel agent or call direct.
Minimum Stay: 2 days.
Parking: Variety of adequate parking conditions. On-street pay parking.
In-Room: Color TV, AC, ceiling fans, telephone, kitchen, & refrigerator.
On-Premises: Doorman & concierge service with secured buildings.
Sunbathing: On private sun decks when available.
Smoking: Permitted sometimes.
Pets: Permitted sometimes.
Handicap Access: Some are accessible.
Children: Permitted.
Languages: English, Spanish & French.

IGLTA

INN PLACES® 1998

Three Thirty-Three West 88th Associates
Gay/Lesbian ♀♂

Beautifully-Furnished Apartments in Manhattan

For visits to New York, consider these exceptional one-bedroom apartments, just restored, in an 1890's brownstone on the west side of Manhattan, directly across the park from the Metropolitan Museum of Art. From *333 West 88th's* safe and advantageous location, it's an easy trip, via subway or bus, to the theater district, the World Trade Center and the ferry to the Statue of Liberty. You can walk to Lincoln Center. Riverside Park, whose handsome promenade overlooks the Hudson, is 200 feet from the door. Apartments are unhosted, giving guests maximum independence. Coffee and tea are provided, and nearby groceries are open 24 hours a day.

Address: 333 West 88th St, New York, NY 10024
Tel: (212) 724-9818, (800) 724-9888, **Fax:** (212) 769-2686.
E-mail: albertmc@mail.idt.net **URL:** http://www.idt.net/~albertmc

Type: Bed & breakfast. **Clientele:** Mostly gay & lesbian with some straight clientele **Transportation:** Taxi from airports. #1 subway line to 86th St Station. **To Gay Bars:** 8 blocks.	**Rooms:** Unhosted B&B apartments & hosted B&B rooms. **Bathrooms:** All private. **Complimentary:** Coffee & tea set-up. **Dates Open:** All year. **Rates:** $420-$709 weekly.	**Discounts:** Jan & Feb 20% off. **Rsv'tns:** Required with deposit. **To Reserve:** Call direct. **Minimum Stay:** 2 to 4 days. **Parking:** Limited free on-street parking. Nearby garages suggested.	**In-Room:** Color TV, AC, telephone, kitchen & HiFi. **Smoking:** Permitted. **Pets:** Not permitted. **Handicap Access:** No. **Children:** Welcome. **Languages:** English. **Your Host:** Albert.

Guion House
Gay-Friendly ♀♂

In the Heart of the Finger Lakes

The *Guion House Bed & breakfast* is a beautiful 1876 Second Empire home located in the historic district of Seneca Falls. Most of the home's original woodwork and wonderful ceiling rosettes still exist. Start your day with our bountiful breakfast of Belgian waffles, assorted breads and muffins, seasonal fruit and breakfast beverages. No matter what the season, there is plenty to see and do. We are one block from downtown, shops, museums and Women's Rights National Park.

Address: 32 Cayuga St, Seneca Falls, NY 13148
Tel: (315) 568-8129, (800) 631-8919. **URL:** www.flare.net/guionhouse

Type: Bed & breakfast. **Clientele:** Mostly straight clientele with a gay/lesbian following.	**Transportation:** Car is best. **To Gay Bars:** 1 hour to Syracuse or Rochester gay	& lesbian bars. **Rooms:** 2 queens, 1 full, 1 room with 2 twin beds, rollaways available.	**Bathrooms:** 2 private, 1 shared. **Meals:** Full candlelight breakfast.

FERRARI GUIDES™

Vegetarian: Available upon request.
Dates Open: Year round.
High Season: July, August, September, October.
Rates: $65-$75.
Discounts: For 4 or more days.
Credit Cards: MC, Visa.
Rsv'tns: Suggested.
To Reserve: Call direct.
Parking: Free off-street parking on premises.
In-Room: AC, maid service.
On-Premises: Library, double parlor.
Exercise/Health: Hiking at state parks, 5 minutes.
Swimming: 5 minutes to state park & lake.
Smoking: Permitted outdoors.
Pets: Not permitted.
Handicap Access: No.
Children: Children over 12 welcome.
Languages: English.

River Run Bed & Breakfast Inn

Q-NET Gay-Owned ♀♂

A Century of Welcome

Our exquisite 1887 Queen Anne "cottage" is surrounded by the Catskill Forest Preserve, with its magnificent hiking trails, splendid foliage and superb skiing. Our eclectic Victorian village features tennis, swimming, theatre, museum, antiques, a weekly country auction, horseback riding, and a variety of restaurants. Rejuvenate yourself on our delightful wraparound porch or in our book-filled parlor, complete with piano and fireplace. Step into the oak-floored dining room, bathed in the colors of the inn's signature stained-glass windows, and enjoy homemade breakfasts and refreshments. At *River Run*, all are welcome, and all are made comfortable.

Address: Main St, Fleischmanns, NY 12430 **Tel:** (914) 254-4884.

Type: Bed & breakfast, 35 min. from Woodstock, NY.
Clientele: Mostly straight clientele with a significant gay & lesbian following
Transportation: Car is best. 2 1/2 hours from NYC. Trailways bus stops at our front door, direct from NYC.
To Gay Bars: 35 miles or a 50-min drive to Kingston.
Rooms: 8 rooms & 1 apartment with single, double, queen or king beds.
Bathrooms: Private: 3 shower/toilets, 3 bath/shower/toilets. 2 shared full baths.
Meals: Deluxe continental breakfast.
Vegetarian: Available upon request. Most diets accommodated.
Complimentary: Afternoon refreshments.
Dates Open: All year.
High Season: Memorial Day-Labor Day, Sep-Oct (foliage), Dec-Mar (skiing).
Rates: $55-$105.
Discounts: 10% for single & 4 or more night stays.
Credit Cards: MC, Visa.
Rsv'tns: Strongly recommended. Walk-ins accommodated if space is available.
To Reserve: Travel agent or call direct.
Minimum Stay: 2 nights weekends, 3 nights holiday weekends.
Parking: Ample free on-street parking.
In-Room: Color & B/W TV, maid service. Kitchen in apartment.
On-Premises: TV lounge, VCR, tea-making facilities, fireplace & piano.
Exercise/Health: Massage. Nearby gym.
Swimming: Stream on premises. Nearby pool, river & lake.
Sunbathing: On private grounds & at nearby pool.
Smoking: Inn is non-smoking except for apartment accommodation.
Pets: Well-behaved, fully-trained, well-socialized pets permitted.
Handicap Access: Yes. Apartment is on ground level.
Children: Welcome. Rollaway, crib available.
Languages: English, French, German.
Your Host: Larry.

Camp Pleiades
A Mountain Resort for Women

Q-NET Women ♀

Slow your pace and enjoy a new appreciation of nature at private, heavily wooded *Camp Pleiades*, a 67-acre mountain resort with stream-fed swimming pond and hiking trails leading into the Appalachian Trail. Activities include swimming, hiking, mountain biking, sports, arts and crafts, nature studies, bird watching, gardening, and general relaxation. Tennis, horseback riding and whitewater rafting are nearby. Special events such as festivals, foliage weekends and Family Camp, are scheduled throughout the season. Private and group cabins are available, some with bath. The central shower house has hot showers and flush toilets. Three family-style meals are served daily.

Address: Route 2, Box 250, Hughes Gap Rd, Bakersville, NC 28705
Tel: summer (704) 688-9201, **Fax:** (704) 688-3549. **Winter call** (904) 241-3050, **Fax:** (904) 241-3628. **E-mail:** starcamp@aol.com

Type: Mountain resort with clothing shop.
Clientele: Women, with men welcome for Family Camp, group bookings, Fall Foliage
Transportation: All major highway access or by air to Asheville or Tri-cities airport, TN. Fee for airport pickup.
To Gay Bars: 35 miles to Johnson City, TN.
Rooms: 12 cabins with single, double or queen beds.
Bathrooms: Private: 2 shower/toilets, 1 WC only. Shower house: 6 private showers, flush toilets & sinks, 1 tub, hot/cold H2O.
Campsites: Yes.
Meals: American Plan, picnic lunches for hikers & day trippers.
Vegetarian: Available.
Complimentary: Coffee, tea, cocoa, lemonade, snacks.
Dates Open: Memorial Day-Labor Day.
High Season: Jul-Aug, holiday weekends.
Rates: Daily $45-$85, weekly $285-$535. Special rates for special events.
Discounts: 10% for groups of 6 or more in 1 cabin.
Credit Cards: MC, Visa, Amex.
Rsv'tns: Required.
To Reserve: Call direct.
Minimum Stay: 2-day minimum.
Parking: Ample free off-street parking.
On-Premises: Meeting space, TV lounge with VCR & videos, library, board games, hammocks.
Exercise/Health: Hiking, sports.
Swimming: Pond on premises. Nearby pool, river & lakes.
Sunbathing: At pond & in open glens around property.
Smoking: Permitted in designated areas only. All buildings are non-smoking.
Pets: No pets.
Handicap Access: No. Sign language interpreters available with advance notice.
Children: Welcome with adult supervision & during annual Family Camp.
Languages: English.
Your Host: Barbara & Jacque.

Emy's Nook

Women ♀

Emy's Nook, an 80-year-old house in the Grove Park area of Asheville, is just north of downtown in an area of lovely old homes, some of which are on the Historic Register. Our guesthouse provides a spacious, comfortable room with a queen-sized bed and a small sitting area. Cool, shady and inviting, the spacious backyard has a swing, sitting chairs and a creek. The community is an active walking, jogging and cycling area with a nearby park for rest and relaxation. Access to downtown activities, businesses and shopping is quick and easy, and there are many nearby shops, galleries and recreational facilities.

Address: 6 Edwin Place, Asheville, NC 28801 **Tel:** (704) 281-4122 (Tel/Fax).

Type: Guesthouse.
Clientele: Women only
Transportation: Car is best. We're on downtown bus line. Free pick up from bus, train. Pick up from airport $10 (pre-arranged, if possible).
To Gay Bars: Close by, a 5-min drive.
Rooms: 2 rooms with queen bed.
Bathrooms: One shared bath/shower/toilet.
Meals: Light continental breakfast.
Vegetarian: Many vegetarian possibilities nearby.
Complimentary: Tea & coffee.
Dates Open: All year.
High Season: April-Christmas.
Rates: $45 per night, 1 or 2 people.
Discounts: 5% on stays of 4 or more nights.
Rsv'tns: Required.
To Reserve: Travel agent or call direct.
Minimum Stay: 2 nights.
Parking: Ample free on- or off-street parking.
In-Room: B&W or color TV, ceiling fans, coffee & tea-making facilities.
On-Premises: Laundry facilities.
Exercise/Health: Nearby gym, weights, massage.
Swimming: Nearby river & lake, YWCA & YMCA.
Sunbathing: In private yard.
Smoking: Permitted on patio. All rooms are non-smoking.
Pets: Not permitted.
Handicap Access: No.
Children: No.
Languages: English.

Mountain Laurel B&B
Lesbian-Owned ♀♂

Distinctive, Classy Comfort in a Secluded, Mountain Setting

Mountain Laurel is in a new, contemporary home nestled into a ridge surrounded by mountain views, a secluded, private cove and 13 wooded acres. Gourmet breakfasts are a specialty, featuring such items as Eggs Benedict, blueberry pancakes, pecan waffles, french omelettes accompanied by orange juice, fresh fruit, homemade jams and plenty of coffee. Though there are many fine restaurants in nearby Asheville, you may choose to dine at the B&B. There's plenty to do, from whitewater rafting or hiking to the many diversions Asheville has to offer. Give *Mountain Laurel* a try. You won't be disappointed.

Address: 139 Lee Dotson Rd, Fairview, NC 28730 **Tel:** (704) 628-9903.

Type: Bed & breakfast.
Clientele: Gay & lesbian
Transportation: Air to Asheville, then rent car or drive your own car.
To Gay Bars: 30 minutes to Asheville & 3 gay bars.
Rooms: 3 rooms with queen or king beds.
Bathrooms: All private full baths.
Meals: Full gourmet breakfast from a menu. Dinner with advance notice at additional charge. Gourmet menu.
Vegetarian: Available upon request. Vegetarian entrees on dinner menu.
Complimentary: Mints on pillows & cocktail set-ups.
Dates Open: All year.
Rates: $80 per night, single or double occupancy.
Discounts: Coupon specials in off season. Will trade accommodations with other B&B proprietors.
Credit Cards: Visa, MC.
Rsv'tns: Required 2 weeks in advance.
To Reserve: Call direct.
Minimum Stay: 2 nights July 1-Nov 1.
Parking: Ample free off-street parking.
In-Room: Ceiling fans, color TV & VCR. CD player in one room.
On-Premises: TV lounge, pool table, game room, piano, laundry facilities & refrigerator space.
Exercise/Health: 6-person hot tub, excercise equipment. Jacuzzi in 1 room. Hiking trails. Tubing & rafting 1 hour away in mountains.
Swimming: In Lake Lure 20 minutes away.
Sunbathing: On private & common sun decks.
Nudity: Permitted in 6-person hot tub under the stars or for sunbathing on decks.
Smoking: No smoking in house. Smokers are respected.
Pets: Not permitted.
Handicap Access: No. Could make some arrangements. Inquire.
Children: Not permitted.
Languages: English.

Sophie's Comfort
Women ♀

Escape from Your Busy World to Sophie's Mountain Bliss

At *Sophie's Comfort* enjoy a private upstairs area consisting of bedroom, bath and a morning room. Cuddle up and enjoy the view of the spectacular Blue Ridge Mountains from your windows. We are located ten minutes from the village of Black Mountain where you will find unique shops, delicious casual dining, crafts and antiques. Asheville restaurants, bars and dancing, the Biltmore Estate, arts

continued next page

and entertainment are just 20 minutes away. Front door hiking trails, outdoor activities and the Blue Ridge Parkway are special features of *Sophie's Comfort*.

Tel: (803) 787-5777 (Reservations).

Type: Bed & breakfast.
Clientele: Women only
Transportation: Car is best.
To Gay Bars: A 30 minute drive.
Rooms: 1 suite with single or double beds.
Bathrooms: Private bath/toilet/shower.
Campsites: Parking is by side of house on a private road. Special arrangements must be made for van & RV parking.
Meals: Vegetarian continental breakfast. No meat served.
Vegetarian: 1 vegetarian restaurant in Black Mountain, several in Asheville.
Complimentary: Tea & coffee.
Dates Open: March 1-November 31.
High Season: May-October.
Rates: $45-$55.
Rsv'tns: Required.
To Reserve: Call direct.
Minimum Stay: 2 days & nights.
Parking: Limited on-street parking. Van & RV parking by special arrangement.
In-Room: Ceiling fans, coffee & tea-making facilities, CD/tape player radio.
Smoking: Permitted outside only.
Pets: Not permitted.
Handicap Access: No.
Children: No.

Twenty-Seven Blake Street
Women ♀

Romantic Elegance, Private Gardens, Warm Hospitality

Be with that special person in charming, romantic Victorian (c. 1897) surroundings. Enjoy our own beautiful, judged gardens and antique furnishings. *Twenty-Seven Blake Street* also offers cable TV, private bath, a private entrance and off-street parking. We are convenient to quaint shops, mountain trails, waterfalls, the Biltmore Estate and the Blue Ridge Parkway. We welcome you to our women-only accommodation in this very gay-friendly town.

Tel: (704) 252-7390.

Type: Bed (no breakfast).
Clientele: Women
Transportation: Easy walk to downtown. Car is best for exploring countryside.
To Gay Bars: Three minutes to 4 bars.
Rooms: 1 room with double bed.
Bathrooms: 1 private.
Meals: Fine coffees in room.
Vegetarian: Close to fine restaurants.
Complimentary: Fine coffee & tea.
Dates Open: Usually all year.
High Season: May-Oct.
Rates: $65.
Rsv'tns: Appreciated.
To Reserve: Call direct.
Minimum Stay: 2 nights on weekends.
Parking: Off-street parking in garden area.
In-Room: Color cable TV, AC, small refrigerator.
Exercise/Health: Hiking trails, rafting, gyms, tennis courts all nearby.
Swimming: Nearby pool, river, lake, waterfalls & mountain streams with sliding rock.
Smoking: Outside, please. Smoke-free home.
Pets: Not permitted.
Handicap Access: No.
Children: Not permitted.
Languages: English.

Old Mill B&B
Gay/Lesbian ♀♂

Come, be lulled to sleep on the banks of a rushing mountain stream in spectacular Hickory Nut Gorge. *Old Mill B&B* provides rustic comfort in rooms overlooking the river and hearty breakfasts of eggs benedict or soda-water pancakes with sausage and homemade apple sauce to fortify you for days of hiking, tubing, rafting, canoeing, tennis or golf. Shopping and dining are all close by, as is Asheville, Biltmore House, the Blue Ridge Parkway, Chimney Rock Park, Lake Lure, Flat Rock Playhouse, and the Carl Sandburg Home.

Address: Hwy 64/74-A/9, Lake Lure Hwy, Box 252, Bat Cave, NC 28710
Tel: (704) 625-4256.

Type: Bed & breakfast with gift shop.
Clientele: Mostly gay & lesbian with some straight clientele
Transportation: Car is best.
To Gay Bars: 20 miles to Asheville gay/lesbian bars.
Rooms: 4 rooms.
Bathrooms: All private.
Meals: Full breakfast.
Complimentary: Drinks on arrival.
Dates Open: All year.
Rates: $35-$85.
Discounts: 10% for INN
Places readers.
Credit Cards: MC, Visa, Amex, Discover.
Rsv'tns: Recommended.
To Reserve: Travel agent or call direct.

484

FERRARI GUIDES™

Minimum Stay: 2 nights on weekends.
Parking: Ample free on-street parking.
In-Room: Maid service, ceiling fans, & sitting areas.
3 rooms have color TV.
On-Premises: TV lounge with VCR.
Exercise/Health: Soloflex & hot tub.
Swimming: River out back
with tubing.
Sunbathing: Sun decks.
Smoking: Permitted without restrictions.
Pets: Permitted with restrictions.
Handicap Access: Limited accessibility.
Children: Please call.
Languages: English & limited Spanish.
Your Host: Walt.

Stone Pillar B&B
Q-NET Gay-Friendly ♀♂

A Mountain Getaway for You & a Special Friend

Visit *Stone Pillar B&B* for a homey atmosphere in a friendly, scenic mountain community on the Blue Ridge Parkway. *Stone Pillar* provides easy access to a quaint village and antique, craft, and specialty shops, fine restaurants, summer theatre, hiking, cross-country ski trails, seven ski slopes and some of the most beautiful scenery in the Blue Ridge Mtns. Relax in the rock garden or in front of a warm fire. Your hosts, George and Ron, can help you plan a variety of activities and events to make your visit to Blowing Rock a memorable one.

Address: PO Box 1881, 144 Pine St, Blowing Rock, NC 28605
Tel: (704) 295-4121, (800) 962-9371. E-mail: stonepillar@blowingrock.com
URL: http:www.blowingrock.com/northcarolina/stonepillar

Type: Bed & breakfast.
Clientele: Mostly straight clientele with a gay & lesbian following.
Transportation: Private auto is best.
To Gay Bars: 30 miles to Hickory, NC, gay bars.
Rooms: 6 rooms with single, double or queen beds.
Bathrooms: All private.

Meals: Full breakfast.
Vegetarian: Available with 24 hrs notice.
Dates Open: All year.
High Season: May 1-Nov 1.
Rates: Summer $70-$110, winter $60-$95.
Discounts: 10% on stays of 4 nights, 10% for group taking the entire house.
Credit Cards: MC, Visa.
Rsv'tns: Advisable 4 weeks ahead in peak season.

To Reserve: Call direct.
Minimum Stay: 2 nights on weekends, high season, & holidays.
Parking: Ample, off-street parking.
In-Room: Alarms, radios, ceiling fans.
On-Premises: Living & dining areas with fireplace.
Exercise/Health: All degrees of hiking trails nearby, whitewater rafting.
Swimming: 2 blocks to town pool.
Smoking: Permitted outdoors.
Pets: Not permitted.
Handicap Access: 1 room is handicap accessible.
Children: Not encouraged.
Languages: English.
Your Host: George & Ron.

Joan's Place
Q-NET Women ♀

Joan's Place is a B&B for women in my home, offering a rustic setting, secluded among trees, with a serene and picturesque environment. I have 2 bedrooms, one large with double bed, one smaller with double bed. There is a shared, full bath across the hall. Guests have access to my living room, with TV and stereo, ping-pong room downstairs, and large deck overlooking the trees. I am 2 miles south of Chapel Hill and UNC Campus, with easy access to Raleigh, Durham and Research Triangle Park.

Address: c/o M. Joan Stiven, 1443 Poinsett Dr, Chapel Hill, NC 27514
Tel: (919) 942-5621.

Type: Bed & breakfast.
Clientele: Women only
Transportation: Personal car only.
To Gay Bars: About 10 miles to Durham gay bar.
Rooms: 2 rooms with double beds.
Bathrooms: 1 shared bath/shower/toilet.

Meals: Continental breakfast.
Vegetarian: Available upon request. 2 vegetarian stores & vegetarian restaurants nearby.
Complimentary: Tea, coffee & juices.
Dates Open: All year.

High Season: Spring, summer and fall.
Rates: $50-$55 per night.
Discounts: Weekly rates.
Rsv'tns: Preferred.
To Reserve: Call direct.
Parking: Ample, free off-street parking.
In-Room: AC & telephone.

On-Premises: TV lounge.
Smoking: Permitted outdoors.
Pets: Not permitted.
Handicap Access: No.
Children: Not permitted.
Languages: English.
Your Host: Joan.

INN PLACES® 1998 485

William & Garland Motel

Gay-Friendly ♀♂

Simple Accommodations in an Oceanside Setting

William & Garland Motel, a small family business, is oceanside with a lovely nature trail walkway to the beach. There are no phones and no pool. The rooms are clean and comfortable and guests who are quiet and who come to relax and enjoy a peaceful atmosphere are appreciated. The beach is located on a 20-acre plot called the Salter Path Dunes Natural Area. It is not crowded and is great for sunning, swimming, and fishing. Very good seafood restaurants — some with lounges — are within walking distance.

Address: PO Box 204, Hwy #58, Salter Path, NC 28575 **Tel:** (919) 247-3733.

Type: Motel with beach access & kitchen facilities.
Clientele: Mostly straight clientele with a gay/lesbian following.
Transportation: Car is best.
Rooms: 8 rooms & 3 mobile homes with double beds.
Bathrooms: Private: 8 shower/toilets, 3 bath/shower/toilets.
Meals: Restaurants nearby.
Vegetarian: Possibly available at nearby restaurant.
Dates Open: April 1-Nov 30.
High Season: Memorial Day weekend-Labor Day.
Rates: $45-$65.
Discounts: 10% discount for paid stay of 7 nights.
Credit Cards: MC, Visa.
Discover.
Rsv'tns: It's a good idea.
To Reserve: Call direct.
Minimum Stay: Required.
Parking: Adequate free parking.
In-Room: Color cable TV, AC, coffee/tea-making facilities, kitchen, refrigerator.
Exercise/Health: Nearby fishing, amusement park.
Swimming: At nearby ocean.
Sunbathing: At beach.
Smoking: Permitted. No non-smoking rooms.
Pets: Permitted, 25 lbs & smaller.
Handicap Access: No.
Children: Permitted if quiet & well-behaved.
Languages: English.

Mineral Springs Inn

Gay/Lesbian ♂

Southern Hospitality with Modern Amentities

The *Mineral Springs Inn*, located in the heart of the Raleigh/Durham/Chapel Hill triangle, offers an easygoing getaway from the business bustle of the Research Triangle Park, just ten minutes away. This authentic 1890's North Carolina farmhouse has been modernized and offers five thematically decorated guestrooms and a full Southern breakfast. We are minutes from Duke University, the University of North Carolina and North Carolina State. It is also an easy ride to the Blue Ridge Mountains and Atlantic beaches.

Address: 718 South Mineral Springs Rd, Durham, NC 27703
Tel: (919) 596-2162 (Tel/Fax), (888) 833-6900. **E-mail:** boucvalt@ix.netcom.com
URL: http://pw2.netcom.com/~boucvalt/main.html

Type: Inn.
Clientele: Mostly men with women welcome
Transportation: Car or taxi.
Rooms: 5 rooms with double or queen beds.
Bathrooms: Private: 3 shower/toilets, Shared: 2 bath/shower/toilets.
Meals: Full breakfast.
Vegetarian: Available upon request. Chinese & Mexican vegetarian available nearby.
Complimentary: Coffee, tea & wine in late afternoon.
Dates Open: All year.
Rates: $100-$120.
Discounts: 10% discount on weekly rental.
Credit Cards: MC, Visa, Amex.
Rsv'tns: Required.
To Reserve: Travel agent or call direct.
Parking: Limited free off-street parking.
In-Room: AC, color cable TV, telephone, maid service.
On-Premises: Fax.
Exercise/Health: Jacuzzi, free weights & machine.
Swimming: Pool in spring of 1998.
Sunbathing: Poolside.
Nudity: Permitted in Jacuzzi & pool.
Smoking: Permitted outside only.
Pets: Not permitted.
Handicap Access: No.
Children: No.
Languages: English.
Your Host: John & Mike.

Phoenix Nest
Lesbian-Owned &-Operated ♀♂

Mysical Mountain Cottage

A perfect romantic hideout, **Phoenix Nest** is a quiet, peaceful, magical cottage tucked away in the woods at the top of a mountain. Experience "ambiance plus" in this very private, fully furnished cabin with wood-burning stove and one bedroom with double bed, a queen-sized futon and a double sleeper sofa. Linens, towels and kitchen utensils are provided. The private deck affords a ripping mountain view! Nearby amusements include whitewater rafting, hiking, horseback riding, mountain biking, gem mining, golf, casinos, fishing and quaint towns with unique shopping opportunities.

Address: 1228 Lowery Lane, Franklin, NC 32734
Tel: (850) 421-1984. **E-mail:** tippy@nettally.com

Type: Cottage, mountain cabin.
Clientele: Mostly gay & lesbian with some straight clientele
Transportation: Private car is best.
To Gay Bars: 70 miles to Asheville gay & lesbian bars.
Rooms: 1 cottage with double bed, queen futon, double sofa sleeper.

Bathrooms: 1 private bath/shower/toilet.
Complimentary: Tea & coffee.
Dates Open: All year.
High Season: May-Nov.
Rates: $350/week, $85/night.
Discounts: For longer stays & repeat visitors.
Credit Cards: MC, Visa.
Rsv'tns: Recommended.

To Reserve: Call direct.
Parking: Ample off-street parking.
In-Room: Telephone, ceiling fans, color TV, VCR, kitchen, refrigerator, coffee- & tea-making facilities, laundry service. Full kitchen in cabin.
On-Premises: Books.
Swimming: River & lake nearby.

Sunbathing: On private sun decks.
Nudity: Permitted. Secluded cabin, nudity is your call.
Smoking: Permitted only outside & on deck.
Pets: Not permitted.
Handicap Access: Partially, ramps.
Languages: English.

Rainbow Acres (Honey's),
Women ♀

Great for a romantic getaway, **Rainbow Acres (Honey's)** is a quiet, peaceful and mystical mountain retreat. The cozy, fully furnished, fully equipped guesthouse is available year-round for individual rentals, mini-festivals and reunions. Kitchen privileges are available in the fully furnished kitchen and our private decks offer "knock-your-socks-off" views.

Address: Mail: PO Box 1367, Franklin, NC 28734
Tel: (704) 369-5162. For weekly rentals: (800) 442-6400 (ask for Caren).

Type: Guesthouse.
Clientele: Women-only
Transportation: Private car is best.
To Gay Bars: 72 miles to Asheville, 2 hours to Atlanta.
Rooms: 5 doubles.
Bathrooms: 1 private, 3 shared.
Meals: Kitchen privileges in guesthouse.

Complimentary: Coffee & tea.
Dates Open: All year.
High Season: May through October.
Rates: $60-$75 per room; whole house rentals available.
Discounts: For longer stays.

Rsv'tns: Required.
To Reserve: Call direct.
Parking: Adequate parking.
In-Room: Guest rooms have ceiling fans, 2 rooms have color TV.
On-Premises: TV lounge, public telephone.
Exercise/Health: Mountain roads for hiking or running.

Swimming: Lake & river nearby.
Sunbathing: Common sun decks.
Smoking: Permitted outdoors.
Pets: Not permitted.
Children: With prior arrangement.
Languages: English.

Prospect Hill B&B

Gay-Owned 50/50 ♀♂

The Perfect Country Retreat in the City

We invite you to join us at the **Prospect Hill Bed & Breakfast,** an elegantly-restored 1867 Italianate townhouse with spectacular views of downtown Cincinnati. We're nestled into a wooded hillside in the Prospect Hill National Historical District, within a mile of most gay bars and restaurants, and only 15 blocks from the convention center. Your comfort is assured in our spacious rooms. A large six-person hot tub, antiques and wood-burning fireplaces compliment your romantic getaway. *"Thanks for making me feel like I was on vacation even though I was not."*

Address: 408 Boal St, Cincinnati, OH 45210 Tel: (513) 421-4408.

Type: Bed & breakfast.
Clientele: 50% straight & 50% gay & lesbian clientele.
Transportation: Car is best.
To Gay Bars: 8 blocks to gay/lesbian bar & restaurant.
Rooms: 4 rooms with double or queen beds.
Bathrooms: 2 private & 1 shared bath/shower/toilet.
Meals: Breakfast buffet.

Vegetarian: Available upon request.
Complimentary: Mints on pillows, tea, coffee, soft drinks, cookies, fruit basket.
Dates Open: All year.
Rates: $89-$129.
Discounts: 10% for 1 week or more.
Credit Cards: MC, VISA, Amex, Discover.
Rsv'tns: Recommended.
To Reserve: Call direct.

Minimum Stay: 2 nights certain weekends. Not required otherwise.
Parking: Ample, free off-street parking.
In-Room: Color TV, central AC.
On-Premises: Woodburning fireplace, telephone, refrigerator, coffee/tea-maker, large side deck, shade trees.
Exercise/Health: Jacuzzi on premises. Gym, weights,

Jacuzzi, sauna, steam nearby.
Swimming: Nearby pool.
Sunbathing: On common sun decks.
Smoking: Permitted outside.
Pets: Not permitted.
Handicap Access: No.
Children: Permitted if 12 years or older.
Languages: English.
Your Host: Gary & Tony.

Zelkova Country Manor

Gay-Friendly 50/50 ♀♂

A World of Country Elegance

A tree-lined drive welcomes you to a world of country elegance and manor life. Tucked into Ohio's pastoral countryside is **Zelkova Country Manor,** a romantic country retreat where goosedown pillows are still filled for guests and pure cotton sheets carry the faint scent of flowers from nearby perennials. Our menus are inspired by the fresh fruits and vegetables harvested from the Manor's bountiful gardens. A classic Georgian Revival manor with a hillside view, the manor rests on 27 acres of sprawling green lawns, country gardens, lush woodland and wetlands.

Address: 2348 S. County Rd 19, Tiffin, OH
Tel: (419) 447-4043, Fax: (419) 447-6473. E-mail: zelkova@bpsom.com

Type: Inn with spa, restaurant & bar, 30 mi south of Toledo & 60 mi north of Columbus.
Clientele: 50% gay & lesbian & 50% straight clientele
Transportation: Only by car.
To Gay Bars: 30 miles, a 30 min drive.
Rooms: 8 suites with queen or king beds.
Bathrooms: 8 private bath/shower/toilets.
Meals: Full breakfast.
Vegetarian: Always available from menu.
Complimentary: Tea, coffee, soft drinks, candies, fruit, cookies.
Dates Open: All year.
Rates: $75-$195.
Credit Cards: MC, Visa, Amex, Discover.

Rsv'tns: Required.
To Reserve: Travel agent or call direct.
Parking: Adequate off-street parking.
In-Room: Telephone, AC, color cable TV.
On-Premises: Meeting rooms, TV lounge, video tape library, laundry facilities.
Exercise/Health: Spa, aromatherapy, massage

therapy & esthetic services.
Swimming: Pool.
Sunbathing: Poolside.
Smoking: Permitted in library only. All rooms are non-smoking.
Pets: Not permitted.
Handicap Access: 1 guest room is accessible.
Children: No.
Languages: English.
Your Host: Michael.

America's Crossroads
Men ♂

Private Homestays in Oklahoma City

America's Crossroads is the reservation service for a network of homes in the metropolitan Oklahoma City area. Since 1994, Les and Michael have offered the traditional European-style bed & breakast they love. All homestays include a full breakfast on request, and most homes in our network can accommodate up to four people at one time. We are geared to the gay traveler and provide a selection of gay-owned and -operated homes. With I-35, I-40 and I-44 all passing through the metro area, this is an ideal stopover for the cross-country traveler, putting you at America's Crossroads.

Address: PO Box 270642, Oklahoma City, OK 73137
Tel: (405) 495-1111, **Fax:** (405) 787-5332. **E-mail:** LesMike91@aol.com **URL:** http://members.aol.com/LesMike91/acbb.htm

Type: Private homestays.
Clientele: Men only
Transportation: Private car best.
To Gay Bars: 5-15 min.
Rooms: 3 homes, each with 2 rooms with queen beds.
Bathrooms: Private & shared.

Meals: Full breakfast upon request.
Vegetarian: Available with advance notice.
Dates Open: All year.
Rates: Per night rates from $30 (single) & $35 (double).
Rsv'tns: Minimum 1 week advance.
To Reserve: Call direct.

Minimum Stay: No minimum.
Parking: On- & off-street parking.
In-Room: Telephone, radio, AC.
Exercise/Health: Free weights & exercise bicycle. Jacuzzi, hot tub available.
Swimming: Pool at some locations.

Sunbathing: On patios.
Nudity: Permitted in hot tubs only.
Smoking: Permitted in some locations, please inquire.
Pets: Not permitted.
Handicap Access: No.
Children: No.
Languages: English.
Your Host: Les & Michael.

Habana Inn
Gay/Lesbian ♂

The Heart of Gay Nightlife in One Complex

The *Habana Inn* complex is the hub of gay nightlife in Oklahoma City, within walking distance of a unique gay area with many gay businesses. This 200-room hotel, with two large heated swimming pools, has everything: Gusher's Restaurant is open daily with reasonably priced, excellent food; The Copa Club and the Finishline, a country western bar; and Jungle Red, a large pride store. Plan your next convention or vacation at the *Habana Inn*.

Address: 2200 NW 39th Expwy, Oklahoma City, OK 73112
Tel: (405) 528-2221, (800) 988-2221.

Type: Motel, bar, restaurant & gift shop.
Clientele: Mostly men with women welcome
Transportation: Airport shuttle or car.
To Gay Bars: On premises.
Rooms: 175 singles, doubles & some suites.
Bathrooms: All private.

Meals: Restaurant on premises.
Dates Open: All year.
High Season: June-August.
Rates: $34.95-$130.
Discounts: Weekly rates available.
Credit Cards: MC, Visa, Amex, Discover.

Rsv'tns: Recommended for holidays & weekends.
To Reserve: Call direct.
Minimum Stay: 3 nights on holidays.
Parking: Ample free on-site parking.
In-Room: Maid service, color cable TV, telephone, AC.

Swimming: 2 heated pools.
Sunbathing: At poolside.
Smoking: Permitted without restrictions.
Pets: Permitted with prior arrangement.
Handicap Access: Yes.
Children: Permitted but not encouraged.
Languages: English.

ASHLAND • OREGON / **UNITED STATES**

Will's Reste
Gay/Lesbian ♀♂

Shakespeare's Neighbor

Will's Reste, our small, intimate, friendly and well-located cottage, offers comfortable accommodations three blocks from the Oregon Shakespeare Festival Theatres, Lithia Park and some of Oregon's finest restaurants. Set between the Siskiyou and Cascade Mountains, at 2000 feet, Ashland offers unsurpassed views, cross-country and downhill skiing, many internationally-known cultural events and almost every type of outdoor recreation. Enjoy the peace and serenity of Ashland, a welcome respite from today's frantic lifestyle. So park your car, forget it, and enjoy one of the West's favorite destinations.

Address: 298 Hargadine St, Ashland, OR 97520
Tel: (541) 482-4394.
URL: http://members.aol.com/llinmarin/willsreste/index.htm

Type: Traveller's accommodations.
Clientele: Mainly gay & lesbian with some straight clientele.
Transportation: Car is best, shuttle from airport $10.
Rooms: Self-contained guest house with queen bed.
Bathrooms: Private.

Dates Open: All year.
High Season: June, Sept & ski season.
Rates: $75-$95 plus 7% tax.
Discounts: Weekly rates available.
Rsv'tns: Recommended.
To Reserve: Travel agent or call direct.
Parking: Adequate free on-street parking.

In-Room: AC, telephone, coffee/tea-making facilities, kitchen, refrigerator.
Exercise/Health: Hot tub and outdoor shower, nearby mineral baths & gym. Cycling, hiking trails, whitewater rafting.
Swimming: Nearby pool and lake, river 30 miles.
Sunbathing: On patio or private sun decks.

Nudity: Permitted in hot tub at discretion of other guests.
Smoking: Permitted outdoors only.
Pets: No, resident cat.
Handicap Access: Please inquire.
Children: Please inquire.
Languages: English, Spanish.
Your Host: Gary.

South Coast Inn Bed & Breakfast
Q-NET Gay-Friendly 50/50 ♀♂

Charm & Comfort on Oregon's Rugged, Unspoiled Southern Coast

Surrender yourself to turn-of-the-century hospitality. Enjoy coffee in front of the stone fireplace. Relax in the spa or sauna, or bask in the warmth of beautiful antiques. Wake up to a gourmet breakfast and a beautiful ocean view. *South Coast Inn* is centrally located in Brookings, on the southern Oregon coast. Built in 1917, and designed by Bernard Maybeck, the inn exhibits the grace and charm of a spacious craftsman-style home. AAA-approved member of PAII.

Address: 516 Redwood St, Brookings, OR 97415
Tel: (800) 525-9273, (541) 469-5557, **Fax:** 469-2615. **E-mail:** scoastin@wave.net

Type: Bed & breakfast.
Clientele: 50% gay & lesbian & 50% straight clientele.
Transportation: Car is best.
Rooms: 3 rooms with queen beds. 1 cottage.
Bathrooms: 1 private bath/toilet & 3 private shower/toilets.

Meals: Full breakfast.
Dates Open: All year.
High Season: Memorial Day-Sep.
Rates: $79-$89.
Discounts: 10% senior.
Credit Cards: MC, Visa, Amex, Discover.
Rsv'tns: Suggested.
To Reserve: Travel agent or call direct.

Parking: Ample free off-street parking.
In-Room: Color cable TV, VCRs & ceiling fans. Cottage has kitchenette.
Exercise/Health: Indoor Jacuzzi & sauna, Universal gym.
Swimming: Nearby pool, river & ocean.
Sunbathing: On the patio,

common sun decks & at the beach.
Smoking: Permitted outside only.
Pets: Not permitted.
Handicap Access: No.
Children: Welcomed if 12 or over.
Languages: English.
Your Host: Ken & Keith.

Bontemps Motel

Gay-Friendly 50/50 ♀♂

Vintage Charm, Comfort & Reasonable Rates

Bontemps Motel offers suites, kitchenettes and studios with cable TV & HBO, in-room phones and twin, double or queen beds. Smoking and non-smoking rooms are available and children and pets are always welcome. Located about 130 miles southeast of Bend, OR, we are in a natural paradise, close to the Malheur Wildlife Refuge, as well as a variety of hunting and fishing areas. For a real "Western adventure," trail riding is nearby (by the hour, half day or overnight), and rock hounds will be as close to "rock heaven" here as they can possible get.

Address: 74 West Monroe, Burns, OR 97720
Tel: (541) 573-2037, (800) 229-1394, **Fax:** (541) 573-2577.

Type: Motel.
Clientele: 50% gay & lesbian & 50% straight clientele
Transportation: Car is best, taxi, or chartered flights into Burns Airport.
To Gay Bars: 187 miles to Boise, ID gay bars.
Rooms: Suites, kitchennettes & studios with twin, double or queen beds.
Bathrooms: Private.

Vegetarian: Available nearby.
Complimentary: Mints, coffee, shampoos & lotions.
Dates Open: All year.
High Season: May-Oct.
Rates: $27-$65.
Discounts: Inquire about winter discount.
Credit Cards: MC, Visa, Diners, Discover, Amex.
Rsv'tns: Required.

To Reserve: Travel agent or call direct.
Parking: Ample free, covered, off-street parking.
In-Room: AC, color cable TV, HBO, telephone, kitchen, refrigerator, microwaves, coffee & tea-making facilities, maid, room & laundry service.
On-Premises: Laundry facilities, fax, Fedex.
Exercise/Health: Facilities

3 blocks away.
Swimming: Nearby public pool, river & lake.
Nudity: Please inquire.
Smoking: Permitted in rooms & on patio. Non-smoking rooms available.
Pets: Permitted.
Handicap Access: Please inquire.
Children: Welcome.
Languages: English, ASL.
Your Host: Dave & Zach.

Ocean Gardens Inn

Gay-Friendly 50/50 ♀♂

For a Restful Stay on Pacific Beaches

Ocean Gardens Inn rests on a bluff above the Pacific Ocean, nestled in a quiet residential area of Lincoln City among shrub, bulb and perennial gardens. Each oceanfront unit is tastefully decorated with original works of art and photography, and the beds are adorned with quilts and comforters. Our hot tub overlooks the ocean. In addition to taking a quiet walk

continued next page

INN PLACES® 1998

491

on the beach, nearby activities include kite flying, tidepooling, surfing, horseback riding, golfing, gambling at Chinook Winds Casino, boating at Devils Lake, or whale watching.

Address: 2735 NW Inlet, Lincoln City, OR 97367
Tel: (541) 994-5007, (800) 866-9925. Guest line (541) 994-3069.

Type: Oceanfront inn.
Clientele: 50% gay & lesbian & 50% straight clientele
Rooms: 5 suites, 2 motel rooms.
Bathrooms: All private.
Complimentary: Tea & coffee.
Dates Open: All year.
High Season: Memorial Day thru mid-Oct.

Rates: Seasonal, $55-$150, based on double occupancy.
Discounts: 10% AARP, senior, or Canadian resident w/ 2-night minimum, 10% 7 nights or longer.
Credit Cards: MC, Visa, Discover.
Rsv'tns: Guaranteed reservations required, 72-hour cancellation policy.

To Reserve: Travel agent or call direct.
Minimum Stay: July-Sept 2 nights on weekends; 3 nights on holiday weekends.
Parking: Free outside off-street parking.
In-Room: Fresh flowers, cable TV, phones, coffee makers, refrigerators, maid service, separate entrances.

Exercise/Health: Hot tub.
Swimming: Ocean nearby.
Sunbathing: At hot tub.
Smoking: All units non-smoking. Permitted outdoors only.
Pets: Not permitted.
Handicap Access: No.
Children: Welcome over age of 12.
Languages: English.

MacMaster House circa 1895
Gay-Friendly ♀♂

Location—FABULOUS!

Adjacent to Portland's scenic Washington Park and the beautiful Japanese and Rose Test Gardens, this historic Colonial mansion is perfect for those who want to be near downtown nestled in a quiet neighborhood. Popular hiking trails are nearby, as well as the fashionable 23rd Avenue cafe/boutique district. Spacious bedrooms are furnished with European antiques and have their own small library, desk, dressing table and reading chair. Seven fireplaces cozy things up, and a full breakfast is served in the elegant dining room. Seven guest rooms are available, some with private bath and fireplace.

Address: 1041 SW Vista Ave, Portland, OR 97205
Tel: (503) 223-7362, reservations: (800) 774-9523. **URL:** www.macmaster.com

Type: Bed & breakfast with antique shop.
Clientele: Mostly straight clientele with a gay & lesbian following
Transportation: Super Shuttle door-to-door (800) RIDE-PDX. Car is ok.
To Gay Bars: 15-20 minutes by foot.
Rooms: 7 rooms & 2 suites

with double or queen beds.
Bathrooms: 2 private, others share.
Meals: Acclaimed full breakfast.
Complimentary: Red & white wine, local ale, sodas & fruit juices in guest's refrigerator.
Dates Open: All year.
High Season: May-Oct.

Rates: $75-$120 plus lodging tax.
Credit Cards: MC, Visa, Amex, Discover.
Rsv'tns: Advisable.
To Reserve: Call direct.
Parking: Limited on-street parking.
In-Room: Color TV, AC.
Exercise/Health: Facilities nearby.
Swimming: At nearby pool.

Sunbathing: 15 min to Sauvie Island.
Smoking: Permitted on veranda only.
Pets: Dog in residence.
Handicap Access: No.
Children: Not especially welcomed. Permitted over 14 years old.
Languages: English, French.

Middle Creek Run Bed & Breakfast

Q-NET Gay-Owned 50/50

Old-World Comfort in Oregon's Willamette Valley

In the rolling hills of the Willamette Valley lies **Middle Creek Run,** a rural 1902 Queen Anne Victorian. After eight years of careful renovation, the proprietors have designed their home around their collection of art and antiques. Guestrooms offer a comfortable ambiance in a period setting of antique furnishings, while perennial gardens and farmlands grace each window view. Our meals, an exuberant hodgepodge of culinary delights are prepared from recipes created in-house and collected over the years. Vineyards, antique shops, galleries, golf and the Spirit Mountain Gaming Casino are in the area.

Address: 25400 Harmony Rd, Sheridan, OR **Tel:** (503) 843-7606, (800) 843-7606.

Type: Bed & breakfast, 1 hr from Portland, 1/2 hr from Salem.
Clientele: 50% gay & lesbian & 50% straight clientele
Transportation: Car is best. About 1 hr from Portland airport.
To Gay Bars: 50 miles, a 1 hr drive.
Rooms: 4 rooms, 1 suite with double beds.

Bathrooms: 3 shared bath/shower/toilets.
Meals: Full breakfast.
Vegetarian: Available with 1 week's advance notice & nearby.
Complimentary: Coffee, tea, snacks, truffles on pillow.
Dates Open: All year.
Rates: $75-$125.
Rsv'tns: Required.
To Reserve: Call direct.

Minimum Stay: 2 nights on holiday weekends.
Parking: Ample, free off-street parking.
In-Room: Maid & turn-down service.
On-Premises: Meeting rooms, library, piano, perennial gardens.
Exercise/Health: Gym nearby.
Swimming: River on premises.

Sunbathing: On common sun decks, at river.
Nudity: Permitted at river.
Smoking: Permitted on porches & decks. All rooms non-smoking.
Pets: Not permitted.
Handicap Access: No.
Children: No.
Languages: English, some Spanish.
Your Host: John & Marc.

Sullivan's Gulch Bed & Breakfast

Q-NET Gay/Lesbian

Western Hospitality Celebrating Diversity

Sullivan's Gulch Bed & Breakfast, a lovely 1904 home, decorated with Western art and Native American art & artifacts, is in the charming, quiet area of NE Portland known as Sullivan's Gulch. Near the famed Lloyd Center shopping mall and cinemas, the Convention Center and the Coliseum, we're also two blocks from NE Broadway's shops, microbreweries and restaurants, and

continued next page

INN PLACES® 1998

minutes from downtown. We serve an expanded continental breakfast that celebrates our local bakeries and the natural abundance of the Pacific Northwest.

Address: 1744 NE Clackamas Street, Portland, OR 97232
Tel: (503) 331-1104, **Fax:** (503) 331-1575.
E-mail: thegulch@teleport.com **URL:** www.teleport.com/~thegulch/

Type: Bed & breakfast.
Clientele: Mostly gay & lesbian with gay-friendly straight folk welcome
Transportation: Car is best. Public transportation nearby. We offer free pick up service from all terminals.
To Gay Bars: 5 blocks.
Rooms: 3 rooms with queen beds.
Bathrooms: 2 private, 1 shared.

Meals: Expanded continental breakfast, special requests honored.
Vegetarian: Special requests honored.
Complimentary: Coffee & tea available all day.
Dates Open: All year.
High Season: Summer.
Rates: $70-$85 plus tax, double occupancy.
Discounts: Available for extended stays.

Credit Cards: Visa, MC, Amex.
Rsv'tns: Required.
To Reserve: Travel agent or call direct.
Parking: Adequate free off-street & on-street parking.
In-Room: Cable TV, ceiling fans. Breakfast served in room upon request.
Exercise/Health: Gyms nearby.
Sunbathing: On common sun deck.

Nudity: 20 minutes to nude beach.
Smoking: Not permitted.
Pets: Resident dog. Well-behaved dogs permitted.
Handicap Access: No. Many steps.
Children: Lesbian & gay families welcome.
Languages: English.
Your Host: Skip & Jack.

IGLTA

Whispering Pines Bed & Breakfast/Retreat Gay/Lesbian ♀♂

Peace & Quiet & Country Comfort

Cradled in the Cascade foothills of Southern Oregon, just 15 minutes off Interstate 5, peace and solitude abound on the 32 acres of pine and pasture that make up *Whispering Pines Bed & Breakfast/Retreat*. In summer, swim in our pool, or enjoy river rafting, fishing, hiking, biking and nearby cultural activities such as the Oregon Shakespeare Festival and the Britt Music Festival. In winter, ski your cares away, then return to our steamy hot tub. Or just sit back, relax, and enjoy the quiet of our rural setting.

Address: 9188 W. Evans Creek Rd, Rogue River, OR 97537
Tel: (541) 582-1757, (800) 788-1757. **E-mail:** whispering_pines@hotmail.com

Type: Bed & breakfast.
Clientele: Mainly gay/lesbian with some straight clientele.
Transportation: Car is best. Pick up from bus or Medford airport, fee or free depends on length of stay. Small charge for other trips.
Rooms: 2 rooms with queen beds, 1 bunkhouse with 3 doubles (sleeps 6).

Bathrooms: Rooms share 1 bath. Bunkhouse has shower & composting toilet.
Campsites: RV's & camping available.
Meals: Full country breakfast.
Vegetarian: Available upon request.
Dates Open: All year.
High Season: May-October.

Rates: Rooms $65-$75 double occupancy.
Discounts: 10% for 3 or more nights (loft excluded).
Rsv'tns: Preferred.
To Reserve: Call direct.
Parking: Ample, free off-street parking.
In-Room: AC.
On-Premises: TV lounge.
Exercise/Health: Hot tub.
Swimming: Pool on premises, river nearby.

Sunbathing: At poolside or on private & common sun decks.
Nudity: Permitted.
Smoking: Permitted in a very limited outside location only.
Pets: Not permitted.
Handicap Access: No.
Children: Permitted by special arrangement.
Languages: English.
Your Host: Lorna & Karen.

The Oregon House

Q-NET Gay-Friendly ♀♂

See the Coast From Our Point of View

High on a cliff above the Pacific Ocean, *Oregon House* is like no other property on the Oregon coast. Surrounding the complex are 3 1/2 acres of forest, lawn and wooded trails, a creek crossed by arched wooden bridges, a lighted trail down the cliff to the beach. The beach is ideal for bonfires and picnics, tidepooling, mussel gathering, kite flying and collecting sand dollars. Lodgings, decorated in country inn style, are sited across the property. Five have fireplaces, three have Jacuzzi tubs, one has a private hot tub and fireplace, nine have kitchens and all have private baths.

Address: 94288 Hwy 101, Yachats, OR 97498
Tel: (541) 547-3329. **E-mail:** orehouse@aol.com

Type: Inn with small gift shop.
Clientele: Mostly straight with a gay & lesbian following
Transportation: Car is best.
To Gay Bars: 1-1/2 hrs or 80 miles to Eugene.
Rooms: 2 rooms, 7 suites & 1 cottage with single, queen or king beds.

Bathrooms: All private bath/toilets.
Dates Open: All year.
High Season: May 15-October 15, every weekend, holiday & school break.
Rates: High season $50-$110 plus tax, low season $40-$95 plus tax.
Credit Cards: MC, Visa, Diners, Discover.
Rsv'tns: Recommended.
To Reserve: Call direct.

Minimum Stay: 3 nights July, August & some holidays & 2 night weekends some holidays & high season.
Parking: Adequate free off-street parking.
In-Room: Ceiling fans, kitchen, refrigerator & coffee/tea-making facilities.
On-Premises: Telephone.
Exercise/Health: Jacuzzi in 3 rooms, hot tub in 1 room.

Swimming: Ocean beach for the hardy.
Sunbathing: On the beach, patio & private sun decks.
Smoking: Permitted outside only.
Pets: Not permitted.
Handicap Access: One room.
Children: Permitted if well-behaved.
Languages: English.
Your Host: Bob & Joyce.

See Vue

Gay-Friendly 50/50 ♀♂

Lodging Where the Mountains Meet the Sea

A coastal landmark since 1945, the *See Vue*, with its spectacular ocean view, is nestled between the breathtaking Coast Mountains and the everchanging Pacific Ocean. Room motifs range from the quaint Granny's Rooms to the northwest American Indian Salish Room. Fireplaces, antiques and flourishing indoor plants contribute to the homey and restful serenity. There is easy access to miles of hiking trails, tidepools, Heceta Head Lighthouse, Sea Lion Caves, restaurants and coastal shopping.

Address: 95590 Hwy 101, Yachats, OR 97498 **Tel:** (541) 547-3227.

Type: Motel.
Clientele: 50% gay & lesbian & 50% straight clientele
Transportation: Car is best.
To Gay Bars: 1-1/2 hours to gay bars in Eugene, OR.
Rooms: 6 rooms, 3 suites & 1 cottage with single or double beds.

Bathrooms: All private.
Dates Open: All year.
High Season: May 16-Oct 15.
Rates: Summer $45-$70, winter $42-$65.
Credit Cards: MC, Visa.
Rsv'tns: Recommended at least 3 weeks in advance.
To Reserve: Call direct.
Minimum Stay: On rooms with kitchen or fireplace, 2 nights on weekends or in high season.
Parking: Ample off-street parking.
In-Room: Color TV, some kitchens & fireplaces.
Swimming: In the ocean, if you are brave (cold water!).
Sunbathing: On ocean beach.

Smoking: Permitted with restrictions; some non-smoking rooms.
Pets: Permitted if not left unattended. $5 per pet, per night charge.
Handicap Access: No.
Children: Permitted.
Languages: English.
Your Host: Renee, Julie, Ila Suzanne.

Grim's Manor

At the Edge of Pennsylvania Dutch Country

Q-NET Gay/Lesbian

The 200-year-old *Grim's Manor* site, at the edge of Pennsylvania Dutch country, includes a historic stone farmhouse on five secluded acres of land. Step back in time, experiencing the history of this home and its laid-back, noncommercial atmosphere, while enjoying all modern comforts. The property includes a huge restored barn, complete with hex signs. The manor is near the city of Reading, antique shops, Doe Mountain skiing, Hawk Mountain birdwatching, the Clove Hill Winery, Crystal Cave, Dorney Park and Wildwater Kingdom.

Address: 10 Kern Road, Kutztown, PA 19530 **Tel:** (610) 683-7089.

Type: Bed & breakfast.
Clientele: Mostly gay & lesbian with some straight clientele.
Transportation: Car is best, free pick up from Allentown or Reading Airport or Bieber Bus Tours in Kutztown from NYC.
To Gay Bars: 1/2 hr to Reading/Allentown, PA, 1-1/4 hrs to Philadelphia, 2 hrs to NYC.
Rooms: 4 rooms with queen beds (3 with fireplaces).
Bathrooms: All private shower/toilets.
Meals: Full breakfast, served all-you-can-eat homestyle.
Vegetarian: Available upon request.
Complimentary: Light refreshments upon arrival, bedside snack, soft drinks, morning coffee tray.
Dates Open: All year.
High Season: Kutztown, PA German Festival—July 4th week.
Rates: $65.
Rsv'tns: Required.
To Reserve: Call direct.
Parking: Ample free off-street parking.
In-Room: Color TV, AC, ceiling fans & maid service. Some rooms with fireplaces, VCR.
On-Premises: TV lounge, VCR, laundry facilities, kitchen & indoor spa.
Swimming: At nearby pool or Dorney Park & Wildwater Kingdom.
Sunbathing: On the lawn.
Smoking: Permitted outside or with consideration for others.
Pets: Not permitted.
Handicap Access: No.
Children: Permitted with consideration for others.
Languages: English.

Fox & Hound B&B of New Hope

Gay-Friendly 50/50

On two beautiful acres of park-like, formal grounds stands *Fox & Hound B&B*, a fully-restored historic 1850's stone manor. Full gourmet breakfasts are served on our outside patio or in our spacious dining room. Our ample guest rooms, all with private baths and four-poster canopy beds, are furnished with a fine blend of period antiques and are air-conditioned for your comfort. Guest rooms with 2 beds are available, and some feature fireplaces and Jacuzzis. We're within walking distance of the center of New Hope. AAA 3-Diamond & Mobil Guide-approved.

Address: 246 W Bridge St, New Hope, PA 18938
Tel: (215) 862-5082 or (800) 862-5082 (outside of PA).
URL: http://www.visitbucks.com/foxandhound

Type: Bed & breakfast.
Clientele: 50% gay & lesbian & 50% straight clientele.
Transportation: Car is best. Trans Bridge Bus lines from New Jersey & Port Authority NYC. Pick up from bus.
To Gay Bars: One block walking distance (4 minutes).
Rooms: 8 rooms with twin, double, queen & king beds.
Bathrooms: All private.
Meals: Continental breakfast Mon-Fri, full breakfast Sat & Sun.
Vegetarian: Available upon request.
Dates Open: All year.
High Season: October.
Rates: Summer, spring, fall, Sun-Thurs $65-$115, Fri, Sat, $115-$165, winter specials.
Discounts: Corporate & long term.
Credit Cards: MC, Visa, Amex.
Rsv'tns: Required, especially on weekends. In high season required 2-3 weeks in advance.
To Reserve: Call direct.
Minimum Stay: Call for details.
Parking: Ample, free off-street parking.
In-Room: Maid service, AC, ceiling fans, fireplaces, TV upon request.
On-Premises: Use of kitchen on limited basis.
Exercise/Health: Jacuzzis.
Tubing & canoeing at nearby river, tennis & fitness passes available.
Swimming: Pool within walking distance, Delaware river 1/4 mile.
Sunbathing: At poolside.
Smoking: Permitted throughout house.
Pets: Not permitted.
Handicap Access: No.
Children: Permitted if 14 or older.
Languages: English.

The York Street House B&B
Lesbian-Owned 50/50 ♀♂

Gracious & Elegant Inn-Town Accommodations

Built in 1909 by industrialist George Massey, **York Street House**, with its all-modern conveniences was featured in 1911 as *House and Garden* magazine's "Home of the Year." Today, this designer showcase delights guests with its antique Waterford crystal sconces and chandelier, cut-glass doorknobs, original tile and clawfoot master bath, and a winding staircase which leads to six gracious guestrooms. Gourmet breakfast is served in our oak-trimmed dining room. Antique shops, art galleries and fine restaurants are two blocks away, or walk to New Hope, PA with its own entertainment, theatre and gay clubs.

Address: 42 York Street, Lambertville, NJ 08530
Tel: (609) 397-3007, Fax: (609) 397-9677. E-mail: nferg@msn.com

Type: Bed & breakfast.
Clientele: 50% gay & lesbian & 50% straight clientele
Transportation: Car is best. Bus from Port Authority in NYC.
To Gay Bars: 1 mile, a 20 min walk, a 5 min drive.
Rooms: 4 rooms, 1 suite with double or queen beds. Some canopy beds.
Bathrooms: All private.
Meals: Full breakfast.
Vegetarian: Available by prior arrangement, all special diets accommodated. Restaurants nearby.
Complimentary: Coffee & tea service, homemade cookies, soda, mineral waters.
Dates Open: All year.
High Season: Apr-Dec.
Rates: $100-$200 all year.
Discounts: On extended stays & whole house rental.
Credit Cards: MC, Visa, Discover, Amex.
Rsv'tns: Required.
To Reserve: Travel agent or call direct.
Minimum Stay: Generally 2 nights on weekends, 3 nights holiday wknds. Occasional single nights available.
Parking: Ample free off-street parking.
In-Room: AC, ceiling fans, color cable TV, refrigerator, coffee & tea-making facilities, maid service. VCR available.
On-Premises: Video tape library.
Exercise/Health: Nearby gym, massage.
Swimming: Nearby pool & river.
Smoking: Smoking permitted outside house only. All rooms non-smoking, $100 fine for violations.
Pets: Not permitted. You may indulge ours.
Handicap Access: No.
Children: No.
Languages: English.

IGLTA

Oneida Campground and Lodge
Gay/Lesbian ♂

Oneida Camp offers 100 wooded and meadowed acres with well-spaced campsites. Cottages and campsites use the bath house, which has hot showers and modern facilities. We are also a spiritual retreat where you can experience comradeship as you commune with new friends. There is a show on Saturday night, volleyball and a nature trail. Our disco features a DJ. Beverages are sometimes supplied on weekends at the disco. There is occasional leadership at the meditation center. Nudity is permitted. Call for directions to the campground.

Address: PO Box 537, New Milford, PA 18834
Tel: (717) 465-7011 or (717) 853-3503.

continued next page

Type: Campground & lodge with clubhouse, sauna, disco, rental cottage & 2 guesthouses.
Clientele: Mostly men with women present occasionally
Transportation: Small charge for pick up ($10 one way) from Binghamton bus or airport.
To Gay Bars: 20 miles to Binghamton, NY gay bars.
Rooms: 14 rooms & 2 cottages with single & double beds.
Bathrooms: Shared: 2 tubs, 5 showers & 9 bath/shower/toilets.
Campsites: 40 tent sites & 20 sites with electric, water & dump station.
Meals: Coffee hour 11am Sun, restaurants are 3 miles away.
Complimentary: Fri & Sat night disco.
Dates Open: Open Mar 25-Nov 10. Seasonals May 1-Oct 15. Call ahead for off season camping or lodge.
High Season: Jun-Aug.
Rates: Reasonable & vary according to days & number accommodated.
Rsv'tns: Advisable for holiday weekends.
To Reserve: Call direct.
Minimum Stay: No minimum...even day camping ok.
Parking: Ample free parking.
In-Room: Color TV, refrigerator, stove, light housekeeping in general area outside room.
On-Premises: TV lounge, library, meditation center, fitness center, pool table room, use of kitchen.
Exercise/Health: Sauna.
Swimming: Spring-fed lake or swim pond. Planning in-ground heated pool for year 2000.
Sunbathing: On the patio & at poolside.
Nudity: Permitted on the grounds.
Smoking: Permitted in most areas unless posted.
Pets: Permitted, but must be controlled or leashed.
Handicap Access: Not recommended for wheelchairs.
Children: Not normally allowed, call ahead.
Languages: English, A.S.L.

Antique Row Bed & Breakfast

Gay-Friendly 50/50 ♀♂

Perfectly Positioned for the Gay/Lesbian Communities

Antique Row B&B is centrally located for business and tourism, only a few blocks from the convention center. We're a small European-style B&B with mixed clientele. Rooms in this 180-year-old townhouse are attractively furnished with comfortable beds, down comforters, designer linens and sufficient pillows for watching TV and reading in bed. The color cable TV has Bravo, CineMax and Showtime. A more spacious fully furnished flat for added privacy is available, as well as an additional accommodation across the street.

Address: 341 South 12th St, Philadelphia, PA 19107
Tel: (215) 592-7802, **Fax:** (215) 592-9692.

Type: Bed & breakfast & fully furnished flat.
Clientele: 50% gay & lesbian & 50% straight clientele
Transportation: Easy access for all forms of transportation.
To Gay Bars: Within a few blocks of most gay & lesbian bars.
Rooms: 5 rooms & 1 apartment with double or queen beds.
Bathrooms: 2 private shower/toilets & 2 shared bath/shower/toilets.
Meals: Full breakfast.
Vegetarian: Within walking distance to several vegetarian restaurants.
Dates Open: All year.
High Season: April-October.
Rates: $40-$100.
Discounts: Extended stays.
Rsv'tns: Recommended.
To Reserve: Call direct.
Parking: Off-street pay parking ($5.75 for 24 hours). Recommended for safety.
In-Room: Color cable TV & AC. Apartment has telephone, kitchen, refrigerator & coffee & tea-making facilities.
Smoking: Permitted.
Pets: Not permitted.
Handicap Access: No.
Children: Case-by-case depending on child's age, season & available accommodations.
Languages: English, a little Spanish & a little German.

Gaskill House

Gay/Lesbian ♀♂

The Comfort & Privacy of Home — The Gracious Service of a European Luxury Hotel

Gaskill House is located in the heart of Philadelphia's Society Hill Historic District, and is listed with the National Registry of Historic Homes. A private residence since 1828, the townhouse has been fully restored and furnished to reflect the graciousness of the early eighteenth century — with the comforts and modern amenities of the 1990s. With only four guestrooms, visitors to *Gaskill House* receive pampering and personal attention. Your hosts live on premises and work to anticipate your needs. The large, elegantly furnished rooms, each with private bath and fireplace ensure luxury and comfort after days of sightseeing or business.

Address: 312 Gaskill St, Philadelphia, PA 19147
Tel: (215) 413- 2887 or (215) 413-0669. **E-mail:** erosphilly@aol.com

Type: B&B guesthouse.	**Vegetarian:** Available upon prior request.	**Parking:** Ample, covered, on- & off-street pay parking.	sauna, steam, massage.
Clientele: Mostly gay & lesbian with some straight clientele	**Complimentary:** Mints on pillow.	**In-Room:** AC, ceiling fans, fireplaces, color cable TV, VCR, coffee & tea-making facilities, maid & room service.	**Swimming:** Pool nearby.
Sunbathing: On patio.
Smoking: Permitted on garden patio.
Pets: Not permitted.
Transportation: Car, taxi.
To Gay Bars: 2 blocks, a 3 min walk.
Rooms: 2 rooms with queen beds.
Bathrooms: All private.
Meals: Full breakfast.	**Dates Open:** All year.
High Season: All year.
Rates: $100-$140.
Discounts: Negotiable for weeknights & extended stays.
Rsv'tns: Required.
To Reserve: Call direct.	**On-Premises:** TV lounge, video tape library, laundry facilities.
Exercise/Health: Nearby gym, weights, Jacuzzi,	**Handicap Access:** No.
Children: Welcome.
Languages: English, Spanish.
Your Host: Chris & Guy.

Glen Isle Farm Country Inn

Q-NET Gay-Friendly 50/50 ♀♂

Historic Hospitality

Come and experience, as did George Washington on June 3, 1773, the "historic hospitality" of *Glen Isle Farm*. At that time, the farm was known as the Ship Inn. Other guests have included James Buchanan, before he became the fifteenth president of the United States, as well as the United States Continental Congress, while on its way to York. During The Civil War, *Glen Isle Farm* was a stop on the underground railroad, thus it has an important place in civil rights history. Today, the farm is a secluded 8-acre gentleman's estate. The approach is down a long, heavily-wooded drive and across a small stone bridge. The drive circles up to the imposing front entrance, leading you up granite steps and across a broad checkerboard porch of black slate, white marble and red brick, through a glass vestibule and to the wide front door. Once inside, you can feel the wonderful sense of history present in this 268-year-old home.

On your visit, you might enjoy a cool autumn afternoon in the upstairs sunroom, sipping a cappuccino or glass of sherry. Watch the fall colors and the shadows, as they gently cross the walled garden. Play a tune on the grand piano in the music room or just curl up with a good book from the selection in the library. If you are the more active type, you may want to take one of the many day trips available. Visit historic Valley Forge. Take the train to Philadelphia, the nation's first capital. Go antiquing, or visit beautiful Longwood Gardens and the Brandywine River Museum, the home of the Wyeth school and collection. You may want to take a bike ride or go hiking on the many nearby roads and trails. Maybe you've come in May to attend the Devon Horse Show, or to see some of the nearby Amish country, and enjoy a slice of Shoofly Pie. Come and experience the "historic hospitality" that is *Glen Isle Farm*.

Address: Downingtown, PA 19335-2239
Tel: (610) 269-9100, Reservations/Info: (800) 269-1730,
Fax: (610) 269-9191.

continued next page

Type: Bed & breakfast inn.
Clientele: 50% gay & lesbian & 50% straight clientele.
Transportation: Car or train. Free pick up from train or airport shuttle.
To Gay Bars: 30 miles, or 40 minutes by car, to Norristown or Philadelphia.
Rooms: 4 rooms with queen or king beds.
Bathrooms: 2 private, 2 shared.
Meals: Full breakfast, other meals by arrangement. Our restaurant is licensed by the county.
Vegetarian: Available with prior arrangement.
Dates Open: All year.
High Season: April through October.
Rates: $60-$90 + tax.
Discounts: 10% on stays of 7 or more nights. Seniors 10%.
Credit Cards: MC, Visa, Discover.
Rsv'tns: Required.
To Reserve: Travel agent or call direct.
Parking: Ample off-street parking.
On-Premises: TV lounge. Weddings, reunions & business meeting space available.
Swimming: Nearby river & lake.
Sunbathing: On the patio or in the gardens.
Smoking: Permitted outdoors only.
Pets: Not permitted. Dogs in residence.
Handicap Access: Limited.
Children: By arrangement.
Languages: English.
Your Host: Glenn & Tim.

The Inn on the Mexican War Streets

In the Historic Old Allegheny District...

Gay/Lesbian ♂

Come experience the adventure and convenience of inner-city living in a gentrified way, just minutes from downtown shopping, nightlife and other attractions. Staying at the *Inn on the Mexican War Streets,* in an historic district of Victorian-era row houses in Pittsburgh's Northside, puts you in the heart of what used to be the city of Allegheny. While at the inn, relax and experience the tranquillity of the rear courtyard, listen to the fountain or sit by the fireplace and enjoy some refreshments. Whichever room you choose, each will radiate a character and charm of its own...and the hospitality that is truly Pittsburgh.

Address: 1606 Buena Vista St, Pittsburgh, PA 15212 **Tel:** (412) 231-6544.

Type: Inn.
Clientele: Mostly men with women welcome
Transportation: Airport taxi or airport bus to town, then taxi. $10 pick up from airport, train or bus.
To Gay Bars: 8 blocks, a 15-minute walk, a 5-minute drive.
Rooms: 3 rooms, 12 apartments, bunkhouse with single, queen, king or bunk beds.
Bathrooms: Private: 1 shower/toilet, 12 bath/shower/toilets. Shared: 1 bath/shower/toilet.
Meals: Expanded continental breakfast.
Complimentary: Fresh fruit on arrival, homemade cookies at night, mints.
Dates Open: All year.
Rates: $65-$85.
Discounts: On stays of 5 days or longer.
Credit Cards: VISA.
Rsv'tns: Required.
To Reserve: Call direct.
Parking: Ample, on- & off-street parking.
In-Room: AC, color cable TV, VCR, video tape library, phone, kitchen, refrigerator, ceiling fans, coffee/tea-making facilities, maid & laundry service.
On-Premises: TV lounge, laundry facilities, landscaped courtyard.
Exercise/Health: Nearby gym, sauna, weights, steam, sauna.
Swimming: Nearby pool.
Sunbathing: On private sun decks, in courtyard.
Smoking: Permitted in rooms or outside. Not permitted in common areas.
Pets: Not permitted.
Handicap Access: No.
Children: No.
Your Host: Jeffery & Karl.

Blueberry Ridge

Women ♀

For That Romantic Country Feeling

Pat and Greta, of *Blueberry Ridge*, offer you friendship and warmth in the company of women. In a beautiful, secluded cedar house, you'll relax in the hot tub or by the wood-burning stove while enjoying a panoramic view of the Delaware Water Gap. Stroll the woods or go out for a romantic dinner. Winter brings skiing, ice skating, sleigh riding. Summer offers canoeing, whitewater rafting, riding, hiking, golf, tennis. Year-round interests include auctions, antique & candle shopping.

Address: Mail to: McCarrick/Moran, RR 1 Box 67, Scotrun, PA 18355
Tel: (717) 629-5036 or (516) 473-6701.

Type: Bed & breakfast guesthouse.
Clientele: Women only.
Transportation: Car is best.
To Gay Bars: 10 miles or 20 minutes by car to Rainbow Mountain Disco.
Rooms: 4 rooms with double, queen & king beds.

Bathrooms: 1 private, others shared
Meals: Full country breakfast. Holiday weekend specials include breakfasts & 1 dinner.
Complimentary: Baked goods, tea & coffee.
Dates Open: All year.
Rates: Rooms $55-$75.
Rsv'tns: Required.

To Reserve: Call direct.
Parking: Ample off-street parking.
In-Room: TV, ceiling fan & VCRs.
On-Premises: TV lounge, videos, kitchen.
Exercise/Health: Outdoor hot tub.
Swimming: River is 5 miles away.

Sunbathing: On common sun decks.
Nudity: Permitted in the hot tub.
Smoking: Permitted outdoors.
Pets: Not permitted.
Handicap Access: No.
Children: Permitted.
Languages: English, Spanish.

Rainbow Mountain Resort

Gay/Lesbian ♀♂

Our Finest Amenity: "Enjoying The Freedom To Be Yourself"

Rainbow Mountain Resort has a style and setting like no other resort of its kind. You will find us nestled high atop a Pocono mountainside on 85 private, wooded acres with a spectacular view of the surrounding mountains. Welcoming both men and women, we are open year-round, and have a friendly, courteous staff to serve you.

Dine on fabulous four-course gourmet meals and full American breakfasts, join the crowd in the Dance Club or relax in the Lizard Lounge. Our Olympic-sized outdoor pool is just what the doctor ordered for the summer. Take in a day of antique shopping, or hike the many beautiful trails in the fall. Ski some of the best mountains in Pennsylvania during the winter. Take a romantic horseback ride or canoe

continued next page

POCONOS • PENNSYLVANIA — **UNITED STATES**

down the Delaware River in the spring. Come to *Rainbow Mountain Resort* to play, to celebrate, to get a good night's sleep. Choose from one of our 46 lovely, antique-filled rooms or cabins. There is always something to do in this four-season resort area. But remember, our finest amenity will always be *"Enjoying The Freedom To Be Yourself."*

Address: 210 Mt. Nebo Rd., East Stroudsburg, PA 18301 **Tel:** (717) 223-8484.
E-mail: mountain@ptdprolog.net **URL:** http://www.rainbowmountain.com

Type: Resort with dance club, piano bar, patio dining, pool bar & restaurant.
Clientele: Good mix of gay men & women
Transportation: Car is best or bus to Stroudsburg, then taxi.
To Gay Bars: Gay & lesbian bar on premises.
Rooms: 30 rooms & 16 cottages with double & queen beds. Cottages are seasonal, May-October.
Bathrooms: 36 private & 2 shared in lodge.
Meals: Full breakfast & dinner.
Vegetarian: Limited availability on menu.
Dates Open: All year.
High Season: 4-season resort area.
Rates: From $60, includes breakfast & dinner.
Discounts: For groups over 25 people, except some holidays.
Credit Cards: MC, Visa, Amex, Discover.
Rsv'tns: Recommended two weeks in advance.
To Reserve: Travel agent or call direct.
Minimum Stay: 2 nights on weekends. 3 nights on holidays.
Parking: Ample free off-street parking.
In-Room: Maid service, color TV, ceiling fans & AC.
On-Premises: Meeting room.
Exercise/Health: Tennis, volleyball, badminton, horseshoes, hiking, basketball, paddle & row boats, & skiing.
Swimming: Outdoor Olympic-sized pool with pool bar.
Sunbathing: At poolside.
Smoking: Permitted. Smoking & non-smoking dining area.
Pets: Not permitted.
Handicap Access: No.
Children: Adult-oriented resort.
Languages: English.
Your Host: Georgeann & Laura.

Stoney Ridge
Women ♀

For a respite from the city, stay at *Stoney Ridge,* our charming new cedar log home in the secluded Pocono Mountains of Pennsylvania. The house is beautifully furnished with antiques to give it that warm country feeling, while providing all the modern conveniences. Within 10 miles of here, you can enjoy restaurants, skiing, canoeing, hiking, trout fishing, dancing, antiquing, etc.

Address: mail to: P. McCarrick, RR 1 Box 67, Scotrun, PA 18355
Tel: (717) 629-5036 or (516) 473-6701.

Type: Cedar log home with 2 bedrooms, stone fireplace.
Clientele: Women only
Transportation: Car is best.
To Gay Bars: 10-minute drive to Rainbow Mountain disco/restaurant.
Rooms: Cabin with 2 double bedrooms.
Bathrooms: 1-1/2 baths.
Dates Open: All year.
Rates: $100/$250/$550, by mid-week night, weekend, week.
Rsv'tns: Required.
To Reserve: Call direct.
Parking: Ample off-street parking.
In-Room: Telephone.
On-Premises: TV lounge with VCR.
Swimming: River & lake nearby.
Smoking: Permitted without restrictions.
Pets: Permitted.
Children: Permitted.
Languages: English & Spanish.

Hillside Campgrounds

Men ♂

Hillside is a men-only campground, in the mountains of NE Pennsylvania on over 176 acres of private woodlands (45 of which are a very private play area) with nudity permitted throughout. We have RV hookups, parking and tent sites, 2 sites for groups of 50 or more, rental cabins, two large, clean bathhouses, flush toilets, and showers. There's a pool, volleyball and a rec hall with occasional impromptu amateur entertainment and get-togethers. There are nature trails, small streams, Friday and Saturday disco and a Saturday evening bonfire. We're halfway between Binghamton, NY and Scranton, PA, just off I-81. Call for directions.

Address: Mail to: PO Box 726, Binghamton, NY 13902 **Tel:** (717) 756-2007.

Type: Campground with disco, snack bar, & camping supplies.
Clientele: Men only
Transportation: Private automobile is best.
To Gay Bars: 30 miles.
Campsites: 200+ sites. Most have electric & water. 2 bath houses.
Dates Open: May 1st-Oct 15th.

Rates: From $30 to $56 for 2 nights weekends. Weeknights $15.
Discounts: For longer stays.
Rsv'tns: Required.
To Reserve: Call direct.
Minimum Stay: On weekends & holidays.
Parking: Ample off-street parking.

On-Premises: Rec room with DJ and disco on weekends. Different theme weekends all summer.
Exercise/Health: Volleyball court & free weights.
Swimming: Pool on premises.
Sunbathing: At poolside.
Nudity: Permitted anywhere on our 176-plus acres.

Smoking: Permitted without restrictions.
Pets: Permitted. No dogs at pool. Pick up excrement. Dogs must not disturb guests.
Handicap Access: Yes.
Children: Not permitted.
Languages: English.
Your Host: Dave & Dan

Brinley Victorian Inn

Gay-Friendly ♀♂

Romantically decorated with fine antiques, Trompe l'Oeil period wallpapers and satin-and-lace window treatments, *Brinley Victorian Inn* is a haven of peace in this city by the sea. In the heart of Newport's historic district, the *Brinley* is within walking distance of historic sites, including the oldest Episcopal church and America's first synagogue. Close by are the *gilded era* mansions of the 19th century, hundreds of 17th-century colonials, the famed America's Cup waterfront, unique shops and restaurants, magnificent beaches and two gay bars.

Address: 23 Brinley St, Newport, RI 02840
Tel: (401) 849-7645, (800) 999-8523, **Fax:** (401) 845-9634.

Type: Bed & breakfast inn.
Clientele: Mostly straight clientele with a gay/lesbian following
Transportation: By car.
To Gay Bars: Within walking distance to gay/lesbian bars.
Rooms: 16, including 1 suite.
Bathrooms: 14 private, 2 share 1 bathroom.
Meals: Expanded continental breakfast.

Complimentary: Bottle of champagne for special occasions.
Dates Open: All year.
High Season: May 23-Oct 1.
Rates: Please call for current rates.
Discounts: Mid-week & longer stays, multiple reservations (5 rooms).
Credit Cards: MC, Visa, Amex.
Rsv'tns: Recommended.

To Reserve: Travel agent or call direct.
Minimum Stay: 2 nights on in-season weekends, 3 on holiday weekends.
Parking: Adequate, free on- and off-street parking.
In-Room: Maid service, AC, ceiling fans, refrigerators (some rooms). Suite has fireplace.
On-Premises: 2 porches, 2 parlors, library & patio courtyard.

Exercise/Health: Jacuzzi in suite.
Swimming: Ocean beach or bay.
Sunbathing: On beach and in private courtyard.
Smoking: No smoking.
Pets: Not permitted.
Handicap Access: No.
Children: 8 years & older, at owner's discretion.
Languages: English.

INN PLACES® 1998

Captain James Preston House

Q-NET Gay-Friendly ♀♂

A Charming Victorian Inn in the Heart of Historic Newport

This delightful B&B, located in a large Victorian home, includes two cozy sitting rooms, a dining room and a sunny breakfast porch. It's an easy walk to all of Newport's unique attractions — the harbor, mansions, Cliff Walk, beaches and shopping. There's even ample off-street parking. Comfortably furnished accommodations at the *Captain James Preston House* include two doubles, one single and two queens. The inn's namesake, Captain Preston, served in the English Navy during the 18th century. His descendent, Paul Preston, also a captain, enjoys hosting guests year round and has excellent contacts for local sporting, entertainment and outdoor activities.

Address: 378 Spring St, Newport, RI 02840
Tel: (401) 847-4386, **Fax:** (401) 847-1093.
E-mail: EEXK82A@prodigy.com **URL:** http://pages.prodigy.com/EEXK82A

Type: Bed & breakfast.
Clientele: Mostly straight with a gay/lesbian following
Transportation: From airport by shuttle. From train by bus (local bus line) or taxi. Bus station a 10 min walk to inn. Ask about pick up.
To Gay Bars: A 5 minute walk.
Rooms: 5 rooms with single, double or queen beds.
Bathrooms: 1 private shower/toilet. 2 shared bath/shower/toilets.
Meals: Expanded continental breakfast.
Vegetarian: Available with prior notice.
Complimentary: Tea in afternoon, if requested.
Dates Open: All year.
High Season: Summer.
Rates: Summer $100-$150, winter $60-$100.
Discounts: Inquire about extended stays.
Rsv'tns: Recommended.
To Reserve: Travel agent or call direct.
Parking: Ample free off-street parking.
In-Room: Ceiling fans, maid service.
On-Premises: TV lounge, meeting rooms, business services, laundry facilities.
Exercise/Health: Nearby gym, tennis, kayaking, sailing.
Swimming: Nearby pool & ocean.
Sunbathing: At beach & on patio.
Smoking: Permitted on porches. All non-smoking rooms.
Pets: OK if crated.
Handicap Access: Yes.
Children: No.
Languages: English, French.
Your Host: Paul, Martin Preston.

Hydrangea House Inn

Q-NET Gay-Friendly 50/50 ♀♂

Quiet Sophistication in the "City by the Sea"

During the "gilded" period of Newport, when America's wealthy families were building lavish summer homes and bringing with them every luxury, a little luxury found its way to the natives of Newport, themselves. Gardeners who worked on the mansion grounds, it is said, took home cuttings of the exotic plants they cared for, among them the hydrangea, and grew them in their own gardens. We have taken our name from the hydrangea, which blooms all over Newport, because we, like the gardeners, have brought a little luxury home, and we would love to share that feeling of old, luxurious Newport with you.

Built in 1876, this Victorian townhouse has been carefully transformed, and its 6 guest rooms, each with its own sumptuous personality, is elegantly decorated with antiques. Plush carpeting, thick cozy towels, crystal water glasses, long-stemmed goblets for your wine setups, and afternoon refreshments all help make your stay a real luxury. Your day will start with our gratifying hot buffet breakfast served in the contemporary fine art gallery. For your enjoyment we will serve our special blend of *Hydrangea House* coffee, fresh squeezed juice, home-baked bread and granola, and perhaps raspberry pancakes or seasoned scrambled eggs. The gallery may also serve as a unique setting for small conferences and business meetings.

Our location is right on Bellevue Avenue just 1/4 mile from the mansions and in the center of Newport's "Walking District," within steps of antique shops, clothing stores, galleries, ocean beaches and historical points of interest. Your hosts will be happy to recommend restaurants and popular night spots. Buses and the airport shuttle stop outside our door. We know you'll love it here: In 1989, the **Boston Globe** said of the inn, *"In a city renowned for its lodging, the Hydrangea House is not to be missed!"* We're not a mansion, just a special place that's home away from home, with our welcome mat out for new friends.

Address: 16 Bellevue Ave, Newport, RI 02840
Tel: (401) 846-4235, (800) 945-4667, **Fax:** (401) 846-6602.
E-mail: bandbinn@ids.net

Type: Bed & breakfast with contemporary art gallery.
Clientele: 50% gay & lesbian & 50% straight
Transportation: Car is best. Pick up from airport by shuttle $16 per person. Bus station 5-min walk to inn. Local bus line, taxi.
To Gay Bars: 5-minute walk to gay/lesbian bars.
Rooms: 6 rooms with double, queen, king beds.
Bathrooms: All private bath/toilets.

Meals: Full breakfast.
Vegetarian: Available upon request.
Complimentary: Homemade chocolate chip cookies, afternoon tea & lemonade.
Dates Open: All year.
High Season: May-October.
Rates: Summer $125-$165, Suite $280. Off season $75-$125, Suite $195.
Discounts: 2-4-1 second night free Nov-Apr with Sun-Wed check-in.
Credit Cards: MC, Visa.

Rsv'tns: Required, but walk-ins based on availability.
To Reserve: Travel agent or call direct.
Minimum Stay: 2 days June-Sept & weekends all year. 3 days on holidays.
Parking: Ample free off-street parking on site.
In-Room: AC, refrigerator & maid service.
On-Premises: Meeting rooms.
Exercise/Health: Massage by appt. Gym with weights, exercise room, aerobic class, $8-$12 day 5 min away.
Swimming: 5-minute walk to ocean beach.
Sunbathing: On beach or common sun decks.
Smoking: Permitted outdoors ONLY.
Pets: Not permitted.
Handicap Access: No.
Children: Permitted.
Languages: English.

Melville House Inn

Q-NET Gay-Friendly ♀♂

Where the Past Is Present

Staying at the *Melville House Inn* is like a step back into the past. Built c. 1750, the house is located in the heart of the historical Hill section of Newport, where the streets are still lit by gas. The French General, Rochambeau, quartered some of his troops here when they fought in the Revolutionary War under George Washington. The house where Washington and his envoy, Major General Marquis de Lafayette, met Rochambeau is across the street.

continued next page

Although the *Melville House Inn* is on one of Newport's quietest streets, it is only one block from Thames Street and the harborfront, and many of the city's finest restaurants, antique shops and galleries. We're within walking distance of many places of worship, such as Touro Synagogue (the oldest in the U.S.), Trinity Church (c. 1726) and St. Mary's (where President Kennedy married Jacqueline). The Tennis Hall of Fame; the famous and lavish mansions of the Vanderbilts, Astors and Belmonts; The Naval War College; and Newport's finest ocean beaches are just a very short drive.

The seven rooms, furnished in traditional Colonial style, are available with both private and shared baths. A romantic fireplace suite is available during the cold months. Guests in the suite are greeted with champagne upon arrival, treated to after-dinner drinks and served breakfast in bed the next day. The full breakfast features homemade granola, muffins and various other baked breads, such as buttermilk biscuits, bagels, scones, Yankee cornbread and Rhode Island Johnnycakes. Afternoon tea is served daily. Guests enjoy a cup of tea or our special Melville House Blend coffee, a glass of sherry and biscotti, as we discuss the day's activities and our favorite places for dinner. Your hosts, Vince and David, will share with you their Newport experiences and will do their best to make your visit as pleasant as possible. Stay at the *Melville House Inn*, "Where the Past is Present."

Address: 39 Clarke St, Newport, RI 02840
Tel: (401) 847-0640, (800) 711-7184, **Fax:** (404) 847-0956.
E-mail: innkeeper@ids.net

Type: Bed & breakfast.
Clientele: Mostly straight clientele with a gay & lesbian following
Transportation: Car is best. Short walk from bus station. Limo from Providence Airport.
To Gay Bars: 2 blocks.
Rooms: 7 rooms with single, double or king beds. 1 fireplace suite available in winter.
Bathrooms: 5 private shower/toilets & 2 shared

bath/shower/toilets.
Meals: Full breakfast.
Vegetarian: Served every day.
Complimentary: Tea & sherry at 4pm with refreshments & homemade biscotti. Hot soup in winter.
Dates Open: All year.
High Season: Memorial Day through Columbus Day.
Rates: Summer $115-$145 & winter $85-$125. Fire-

place suite $165.
Discounts: On stays of 3 or more nights.
Credit Cards: MC, Visa, Amex, Discover.
Rsv'tns: Suggested for weekends & holidays.
To Reserve: Travel agent or call direct.
Minimum Stay: 2 nights on weekends & 3 nights on holidays & special events.
Parking: Ample free off-street parking.

In-Room: AC & maid service.
Exercise/Health: Health club nearby.
Swimming: In nearby ocean.
Sunbathing: At the beach.
Smoking: Not permitted.
Pets: Dewey and Spike, the feline innkeepers, do not want to share their affections.
Handicap Access: No.
Languages: English.
IGLTA

Prospect Hill Guest House
Gay-Owned ♀♂

In the Heart of the Harbor District

Newly renovated, *Prospect Hill Guest House* offers four beautifully appointed second-floor guest rooms, each with private bath and kitchenette. While the decor of each room differs, all have Oriental rugs, antique furniture, original art and ceiling fans. Originally built as a carriage and sailmaker's loft, the guesthouse has maintained its unique historic integrity, including the large barn doors on the front of the building. The building is registered with the Newport National Historic Register District. On the first floor is one of Newport's hidden treasures — a large, eclectic art gallery that is worth your time to stop in and browse through.

Address: 32 Prospect Hill St, Newport, RI
Tel: (401) 847-7405 or (401) 847-7383.

Type: Guesthouse with art gallery.
Clientele: Mostly gay & lesbian with some straight clientele
Transportation: Car is best.
To Gay Bars: David's bar next door.
Rooms: 4 suites with queen & king beds.
Bathrooms: Private: 2 bath/toilets & 2 shower/toilets.
Meals: Continental breakfast.
Complimentary: Rooms have small fridge with water, juice & soda.
Dates Open: All year.
High Season: Jun-Oct.
Rates: $85-$175.
Credit Cards: MC, Visa.
Rsv'tns: Suggested in summer & holiday seasons.
To Reserve: Travel agent or call direct.
Minimum Stay: 2 nights in Jul & Aug.
Parking: Limited free off-street parking (1 space per room).
In-Room: Color TV, VCR, AC, ceiling fans, coffee & tea-making facilities, kitchen, refrigerator, maid & laundry service.
Exercise/Health: Nearby gym, weights, Jacuzzi.
Swimming: Ocean nearby.
Sunbathing: At beach.
Smoking: No smoking in guesthouse.
Pets: Not permitted.
Handicap Access: No.
Children: No.

IGLTA

The Villa

Gay-Friendly ♀♂

An Oasis of Privacy & Luxury

Indulge in the lush, perfumed gardens, Italian fountains, and majestic porticos and verandas of *The Villa*. After sunning, you can splash and frolic in our sparkling sapphire pool and unwind in the outdoor hot tub. When winter approaches, *The Villa* transforms into a warm and cozy nest where you can escape to your own fireplace or the hot waters of your private Jacuzzi. Just five minutes from beaches, we're located at the crossroads of historic Westerly and the quaint seaside village of Watch Hill, close to Mystic, Misquamicut Beach, and the Foxwoods Resort and Casino.

Address: 190 Shore Road, Westerly, RI 02891
Tel: (401) 596-1054, (800) 722-9240, **Fax:** (401) 596-6268.
URL: www.thevillaatwesterly.com

Type: Bed & breakfast.
Clientele: Mainly straight with gay/lesbian following
Transportation: Train. Van service from Amtrak (Westerly) Station is free.
To Gay Bars: 1/2 hr drive to New London, CT.
Rooms: 2 rooms & 5 suites with full, queen or king beds.
Bathrooms: All private.
Meals: Expanded continental breakfast.
Vegetarian: Available upon request.
Dates Open: All year.
High Season: Memorial Day to Labor Day.
Rates: Summer $95-$195, winter $65-$155.
Discounts: Off season, mid-week.
Credit Cards: MC, Visa, Amex.
To Reserve: Travel agent or call direct.
Minimum Stay: Peak weekends only.
Parking: Ample, free off-street parking.
In-Room: Color cable TV, AC, maid service, telephone, ceiling fans & refrigerator.
Exercise/Health: Jacuzzi.
Swimming: Pool on premises & nearby ocean beach.
Sunbathing: At poolside & beach.
Nudity: Nearby nude ocean beach.
Smoking: Permitted in rooms but not in common areas.
Pets: Well-behaved pets welcomed, prior approval & $25 fee required.
Handicap Access: No.
Children: Accepted, but not encouraged.
Languages: English & Italian.
Your Host: Jerry, Rose.

INN PLACES® 1998

Twosuns Inn Bed & Breakfast

Q-NET Gay-Friendly ♂

A Prince of an Inn in an Antebellum Brigadoon!

Enjoy the charm of a small, resident host B&B in one of the South's most beautiful coastal towns, located about midway between Charleston, SC (65 miles) and Savannah, GA (45 miles). Since 1990, *TwoSuns* has offered well over 10,000 guests a casually elegant atmosphere in a restored 1917 grand home on the Bay, balanced with modern baths, individually appointed guestrooms, a daily "Tea & Toddy Hour," comfortable beds and sumptuous breakfasts. The setting and bayview are idyllic, the hosts are friendly and fun, and the suns rise at *TwoSuns*.

Address: 1705 Bay Street, Beaufort, SC 29902
Tel: (803) 522-1122 (Tel/Fax), (800) 532-4244.
Area code changing to (843) in March, 1998.
E-mail: twosuns@islc.net **URL:** twosunsinn.com

Type: B&B with TwoSuns Handwovens gift area on premises.
Clientele: Mostly straight with a small gay male following
Transportation: Car, airport transport. from Savannah, GA (45 mi) or Charleston, SC (65 mi). Free pick up from private airpt on Lady's Island & downtown marina.
To Gay Bars: 7 blocks, 1/4 mile, a 12 min walk, a 3 min drive.
Rooms: 6 rooms with king, queen or twin beds.
Bathrooms: Private: 2 bath/shower/toilets, 4 shower/toilets.
Meals: Full breakfast.
Vegetarian: We accommodate vegetarian diners.
Complimentary: Tea & Toddy hour with snacks, hors d'oeuvres, cheese & crackers, etc, candy.
Dates Open: All year.
High Season: Mar-Nov.
Rates: Mar-Nov: $105 single, $135 double; Dec-Feb (except Christmas holiday season): $85 sgl, $105 dbl.
Discounts: AAA, AARP, CAA, seniors 10%; 4+ nights 10%. Corp. rate Sun-Thurs $85 sgl, $100 dbl.
Credit Cards: MC, Visa, Amex, Diners, Discover.
Rsv'tns: Required.
To Reserve: Travel agent or call direct.
Parking: Adequate free off-street parking.
In-Room: Telephone, AC, ceiling fans, maid service. Room service & color cable TV available. Skylight Room has TV/VCR, fridge.
On-Premises: Meeting room, TV lounge area, video tape library. Fax, display materials, easel, flip chart, limited use of computer, copier services, small mtg. refreshements.
Exercise/Health: Nearby gym, massage.
Swimming: Ocean nearby.
Sunbathing: At beach.
Smoking: Permitted outside on verandah, screened porch & library.
Pets: Not permitted.
Handicap Access: Yes. Ramps, rails in bathroom, wide doors, handicap shower. 1 handicap accessible room on 1st fl.
Children: OK, ages 12 & over.
Languages: English.
Your Host: Carroll & Ron.

Charleston Beach B&B

Q-NET Gay/Lesbian ♀♂

Ten miles from Charleston's historical district, facing the Atlantic Ocean on a picturesque barrier island is *Charleston Beach B&B*. Our 22-room Dutch Colonial home has been extensively remodeled and imaginatively decorated with four-poster beds and antiques. Rooms are equipped with refrigerators, fresh flowers and robes and are attractively priced. Browse our extensive library, play volleyball in the pool, sunbathe on decks surrounded by lush gardens, or unwind in the spa. At our popular social hour with open bar, guests discuss the day's activities and make plans for dinner at Charleston's many fine restaurants.

Address: PO Box 41, Folly Beach, SC 29439 **Tel:** (803) 588-9443.

Type: Guesthouse.
Clientele: Good mix of gay men & women
To Gay Bars: 15 minutes to Charleston's gay bars.
Rooms: 8 rooms & 1 suite with bunk & queen beds.
Bathrooms: 2 private bath/toilets & 3 shared bath/shower/toilets.
Meals: Continental breakfast.
Complimentary: Open bar for social hour, juices, tea & coffee.
Dates Open: All year.
High Season: Apr-Sept.
Rates: $45-$99.
Discounts: 10% for 7 days.
Credit Cards: MC, Visa, Discover.
Rsv'tns: Recommended.
To Reserve: Travel agent or call direct.
Minimum Stay: 2 days on the weekends, 3 on holidays.
Parking: Adequate free off-street parking.
In-Room: Maid service, AC, ceiling fans & refrigerator.
On-Premises: TV lounge.
Exercise/Health: Jacuzzi & seasonal massage.
Swimming: Pool on premises. Beach is 2 blocks away.
Sunbathing: At poolside & on common sun decks.
Nudity: Permitted in Jacuzzi and in deck area.
Smoking: Permitted except in bed.
Pets: Not permitted.
Children: Off-season.
Languages: English.
Your Host: Betty, Butch & Michael.

Calhoun House
(Formerly Charleston Columns Guesthouse)

Gay/Lesbian ♀♂

The Charleston Experience: Ultimate Charm and Warm Hospitality

To the residents of Charleston, life in the Historic District is like stepping back into history and sharing timeless charm and majestic beauty on a daily basis. Charleston offers a serene reflection of a lifestyle that has all but vanished. When you come to visit, you will want to stay in accommodations befitting the "Charleston Experience." From the moment you arrive at *Calhoun House*, you feel the charm and hospitality for which Charleston is renown. Every effort is made to make your stay memorable.

Begin your day with a healthy continental breakfast, and experience the warm, friendly hospitality that you naturally expect of "The Old South." Information on tours and entertainment, restaurant recommendations, and complimentary maps are cheerfully provided upon request. When you are ready to "do Charleston," staff members will gladly arrange a tour of antebellum homes, a horse-drawn carriage ride around the city, a harbor tour, a guided walking tour or even bicycle rentals.

Like the beautiful city of Charleston, the guesthouse is elegant. Built as a private residence in 1910, the house features suites, guest rooms and public rooms graced with 19th- and early 20th-century period-style furnishings and antiques, designer linens, Oriental rugs and ceiling fans (although the entire house is air conditioned). The stately living room, dining room and porches provide a comfortable setting for relaxation and congenial entertainment.

Calhoun House is located in the Historic District of downtown Charleston, an easy walk to historic sites, great shopping and exciting nightlife. The people of

continued next page

Charleston have been welcoming guests for over 300 years, and they know how to make you feel welcome and right at home. Come see for yourself!

Address: 273 Calhoun St, Charleston, SC 29401
Tel: (803) 722-7341. **E-mail:** CHS65@AOL.COM

Type: Guesthouse.
Clientele: Good mix of gays & lesbians
Transportation: Car is best.
To Gay Bars: 7 blocks or a 10-min. walk, 5 min. drive.
Rooms: 5 rooms.
Bathrooms: 4 private, 1 shared.
Meals: Continental breakfast. Gourmet coffee, tea, juices, fresh fruit, yogurt, cereals, pastries.
Dates Open: All year.
High Season: Mar-Nov.
Rates: $95-135. $25 add'l person. Tax included.
Discounts: One night free for 7-night stay.
Rsv'tns: Recommended.
To Reserve: Travel agent or call direct.
Parking: Adequate free off-street parking.
In-Room: Color cable TV, AC, ceiling fans, maid & laundry service.
On-Premises: TV lounge, laundry facilities for guests.
Swimming: 7 miles to gay beach.
Smoking: Permitted in kitchen & on porches.
Pets: Not permitted.
Handicap Access: No.
Languages: English.
Your Host: Frank & Jim.

Eighteen Fifty-Four Bed & Breakfast   Gay/Lesbian ♀♂

A Tropical Retreat in the Heart of Charleston

Centrally located in Harleston Village, one of the premier restored areas of Charleston's renowned National Register historical district, *1854* is sited in an unusual antebellum edifice of distinctive Italianate design. Both suites are charmingly decorated with an eclectic mix of antique and modern furnishings, original art and sculpture. They have private entrance and access to a rear garden nestled in a lush grove of banana trees and other tropical plantings. The city's best restaurants, gay bars and shopping are a short walk away.

Address: 34 Montagu Street, Charleston, SC 29401 **Tel:** (803) 723-4789.

Type: Bed & breakfast.
Clientele: Mostly gay & lesbian with some straight clientele
Transportation: Car is best.
To Gay Bars: Four blocks or ten minutes to all local gay bars.
Rooms: 2 full suites with double beds.
Bathrooms: All private bath/toilets.
Meals: Continental breakfast.
Vegetarian: Available with advance notice.
Dates Open: All year.
Rates: $95-$115. Rates may vary seasonally.
Discounts: 10% discount for stays of 3 or more nights.
Rsv'tns: Required, but will accept late call-ins.
To Reserve: Travel agent or call direct.
Parking: Ample free on-street parking.
In-Room: Kitchen, refrigerator, AC, color TV, maid service & private outdoor garden area.
On-Premises: Lush tropical garden.
Swimming: 10-15 miles from all Charleston beaches, including Folly Beach gay area.
Smoking: Permitted.
Pets: Not permitted.
Handicap Access: No.
Children: Permitted with advance notice only. No infants.
Languages: English.

Camp Michael B&B   Gay/Lesbian ♀♂

Out and About in the Black Hills

Situated about 12 miles from Rapid City, *Camp Michael* is surrounded by the beautiful and serene atmosphere of the Black Hills of South Dakota. Our guests always comment on the absolute quiet of our place. Tourist attractions such as Mt. Rushmore, Devils Tower, the Badlands, Custer State Park and Deadwood are all within easy access. We give you a farm-style breakfast that you'll think Grandma made. You'll also have your own living room, private entrance and verandah. A great place to stay for a great price.

Address: 13051 Bogus Jim Rd, Rapid City, SD 57702
Tel: (605) 342-5590.
E-mail: campmike@rapidnet.com **URL:** www.campmike.com

Type: Bed & breakfast 12 miles outside Rapid City, 15 minutes from Mt. Rushmore.
Clientele: Gay & lesbian. Good mix of men & women
Transportation: Car is best.
Rooms: 3 rooms with double, queen or king beds.
Bathrooms: 2 shared bath/shower/toilets.
Meals: Full farm-style breakfast. Supper, if you arrive in time.
Vegetarian: Upon request.
Complimentary: Tea & coffee.
Dates Open: All year.
High Season: May-September.
Rates: $55-$75.
Discounts: Weekly rates.
Rsv'tns: Preferred.
To Reserve: Call direct.
Parking: Ample free off-street parking.
In-Room: Ceiling fans, color TV, VCR, coffee & tea-making facilities, kitchen, refrigerator, maid & laundry service.
On-Premises: TV lounge, video tape & reading libraries, laundry facilities, wet bar, refrigerator, microwave.
Exercise/Health: Power Rider, walking, hiking. Sauna & hot tub coming.
Sunbathing: On grounds.
Nudity: Open for discussion & depends on clientele.
Smoking: Permitted on verandah & in smoking room.
Pets: Permitted (dogs, cats, horses).
Handicap Access: No.
Children: Welcome.
Languages: English, sign language.
Your Host: Michael & Mike.

Belvedere Heights B&B

Gay-Friendly ♀♂

Appalachian Beauty on the Virginia-Tennessee Border

In an area famous for its beautiful mountain scenery, **Belvedere Heights B&B** is a wonderful setting for your Appalachian getaway! The spacious rooms of our stately 1930s mansion are furnished with your comfort in mind with either queen or double beds, air conditioning, refrigerators and color TVs. In the dining areas, sumptuous breakfasts can be enjoyed between 8 A.M. and 10 A.M. Come join us for a fun-filled stay or just a relaxing weekend in the Smokey Mountains — you're in the middle of it all for great day trips, hiking, biking, canoeing and skiing.

Address: 100 Belvedere Heights, Bristol, TN **Tel:** (423) 764-3860 (Tel/Fax).

Type: Bed & breakfast.
Clientele: Mostly straight clientele with a gay/lesbian following
Transportation: Car is best, 20 min to Tri-City Airport.
To Gay Bars: 20 miles, a 25 min drive to gay bars in Johnson City, TN.
Rooms: 2 rooms, 1 suite with queen beds.
Bathrooms: 3 private bath/toilet/showers.
Meals: Full breakfast.
Vegetarian: Available upon request.
Complimentary: Juice, soft drinks, tea & coffee.
Dates Open: All year.
Rates: $100-$150.
Credit Cards: MC, Visa.
Rsv'tns: Required.
To Reserve: Travel agent or call direct.
Minimum Stay: 3 nights during Nascar weekends in Apr & Aug.
Parking: Ample free off-street parking.
In-Room: AC, telephone, color cable TV, refrigerator, maid service.
Swimming: Nearby river & lake.
Sunbathing: On common sun decks.
Smoking: Permitted in common areas & on grounds. Non-smoking rooms available.
Pets: Not permitted.
Handicap Access: No.
Children: No.
Languages: English.
Your Host: Ben & Phil.

Christopher Place

Q-NET Gay-Owned 50/50 ♀♂

We're Easy to Find, but Hard to Forget

Surrounded by expansive mountain views, this premiere bed & breakfast includes over 200 acres to explore, a pool, tennis court and sauna. Relax by the marble fireplace in the library, retreat to the game room, or enjoy a hearty mountain meal in our restaurant. Romantic rooms are available with a hot tub or fireplace. Off I-40 at exit 435, *Christopher Place* is just 32 scenic miles from Gatlinburg and Pigeon Forge. Perfect for special occasions and gatherings. Rated 4 diamonds by AAA.

Address: 1500 Pinnacles Way, Newport, TN 37821
Tel: (423) 623-6555, (800) 595-9441 (for brochure), **Fax:** (423) 613-4771.
E-mail: thebestinn@aol.com

Type: Gay-owned & -operated inn with restaurant.
Clientele: 50% gay & lesbian clientele
Transportation: Car is best. $25 for pick up from airport.
To Gay Bars: 40 miles or an hour drive.
Rooms: 9 rooms & 1 suite with double, queen or king beds.
Bathrooms: Private: 2 bath/toilets, 4 shower/toilets & 4 bath/shower/toilets.

Meals: Full breakfast.
Vegetarian: Available with 24-hour notice.
Complimentary: Afternoon tea & lemonade.
Dates Open: All year.
High Season: Jul-Oct.
Rates: $150-$300.
Discounts: Special gift to Inn Places readers.
Credit Cards: MC, Visa, Amex.
Rsv'tns: Recommended.
To Reserve: Travel agent or call direct.

Minimum Stay: Some holidays or special weekends.
Parking: Ample free off-street parking.
In-Room: AC, ceiling fans & maid service. Some rooms with hot tubs & fireplaces.
On-Premises: TV lounge, VCR, video tape library, meeting rooms, game room, tanning bed, fax, copy, word processing equipment.
Exercise/Health: Sauna & weights.

Swimming: Pool on premises.
Sunbathing: At poolside.
Nudity: Permitted in sauna.
Smoking: Permitted in game room & on porches.
Pets: Not permitted.
Handicap Access: Yes.
Children: Ages 12 & over welcomed.
Languages: English.
Your Host: Drew.

IGLTA

Timberfell Lodge

Men ♂

Impeccable Accommodations, Inspired Cuisine & Courteous Staff

Timberfell is a fully self-contained gay men's resort, including two lodging facilities, *The Lodge* and *The Poolhouse Annex Building*. *The Lodge* is a beautiful three-story stone and log guesthouse nestled in a lush, wooded hollow, with 250 acres of mountain trails and springs and an oak barn, surrounded by grassy meadowland. *The Lodge*, decorated with a lovely, eclectic collection of antiques and Oriental rugs, overlooks a pond and a picturesque willow tree. Guests enjoy a charming living room with a ceiling fan, a large stone fireplace, wide screen TV, VCR, a full video library and a stereo. *The Poolhouse Annex building*, the newest lodging facility at *Timberfell*, is highlighted by the *Corral Room*. This beautiful room is the largest guest room. It comes complete with a large sitting area, a king-sized bed, TV, VCR, stocked bar refrigerator, private sink, private bath and a veranda with a great view. Also, there are the new *Roommate Rooms*, with two double beds in each room. A full gourmet breakfast, hors d'oeuvres, and dinner are included for all guests, for example, French omelets or buckwheat waffles served with blueberries, pure maple syrup and whipped cream. All gourmet dinners are prepared with the highest-quality ingredients, right down to our homemade desserts and fresh-ground café Angelica. Our chef studied under French President Mitterrand's former personal chef. The chef and his accomplished sous-chef are on duty daily to create the finest of gourmet dining experiences. All of the deluxe rooms are furnished with king- or queen-sized beds, TV, VCR, down pillows and handmade quilts. Nearby attractions include Dollywood, Biltmore Estates, the Appalachian Trail, whitewater rafting and historical Jonesborough, Tennessee.

Address: 2240 Van Hill Rd, Greeneville, TN 37745
Tel: (423) 234-0833, (800) 437-0118, (888) TIMBERFELL.
URL: www.gaytraveling.com/timberfell

Type: Resort.
Clientele: Men only, levi/leather & naturists welcome.
Transportation: Pick up from airport & bus.
To Gay Bars: 30 miles or a half-hour drive.
Rooms: 15 rooms with bunk, double, queen or king beds.
Bathrooms: 4 private shower/toilets, 2 private sinks. Others share.
Campsites: 4 RV parking spaces & 50 tent sites. Campers have full bath house clean-up facilities. Electric, sewer & water.

Meals: Modified American Plan: full breakfast, appetizer trays, full dinner with wine.
Vegetarian: Available upon request.
Complimentary: Toiletry baskets & terry cloth robes.
Dates Open: All year.
High Season: April through October.
Rates: $94-$169 single occupancy ($60 for additional person). $94 bunkroom. Campsites $35 with lodge privileges extra.
Discounts: 7th night free on stay of 7 days or more.

Credit Cards: MC, VISA, Amex & Discover.
Rsv'tns: Required.
To Reserve: Travel agent or call direct.
Minimum Stay: 2 nights on holidays.
Parking: Free off-street secured parking.
In-Room: Color TV, housekeeping & laundry service. Deluxe rooms have VCR, bar refrigerators & coffee pots.
On-Premises: Central AC, living room with entertainment center & 24-person dining room.
Exercise/Health: 20-person sauna, 8-person

Jacuzzi, massages, bikes, bench press, gravity inversion, fishing & hiking trails & canoe.
Swimming: 20 x 40 foot heated pool on premises.
Sunbathing: At poolside, pond, on common sun deck or in backyard.
Nudity: Permitted inside lodge and on all 250 acres.
Smoking: A smoking area is set aside for winter.
Pets: Call ahead.
Handicap Access: No.
Children: Not permitted.
Languages: English.

IGLTA

Park Lane Guesthouse

Gay/Lesbian ♀♂

Discover the Live Music Capital of the World

Entertainment and natural beauty abound year-round in Austin. **Park Lane Guesthouse,** a restored traditional Texas home, is five minutes from shops and restaurants and only one mile to the lively downtown entertainment district, gay

continued next page

INN PLACES® 1998 513

bars, the river, parks, and hike and bike trails. Located in historic Travis Heights neighborhood, the spacious private cottage surrounded by gardens and ancient live oaks has a full kitchen. There is a cozy guest room with private bath in the main house. Come discover friendly Austin with us.

Address: 221 Park Lane, Austin, TX 78704 **Tel:** (512) 447-7460, (800) 492-8827.

Type: Cottage & guesthouse.
Clientele: Mostly gay & lesbian with some straight clientele
Transportation: Car or taxi from airport, or call for pick up from airport, train, bus ($10 each way).
To Gay Bars: 10 blocks, a 20-minute walk, a 5-minute drive.
Rooms: 1 room in house, 3 rooms in cottage with double or queen beds.
Bathrooms: Private shower/toilet. 2-person tiled shower in cottage.
Meals: Expanded continental breakfast.
Vegetarian: Breakfast is vegetarian, 3-5 block to 5 restaurants.
Complimentary: Tea, coffee always available.
Dates Open: All year.
High Season: October-May.
Rates: Guestroom in main house: single $75, double $85. Cottage (accommodates 4): $110 double ($18 each addt'l person).
Discounts: 1 night free with full week's stay.
Rsv'tns: Required.
To Reserve: Call direct.
Parking: Ample off-street.
In-Room: AC, maid service, coffee/tea-making facilities, ceiling fans. Cottage: color TV, VCR, kitchen, refrigerator, ceiling fans.
Exercise/Health: Massage on premises & nearby.
Swimming: Nearby pool, river, lake.
Sunbathing: On common sun decks.
Smoking: Permitted outside only. All rooms are non-smoking.
Pets: Permitted with prior notice & pet deposit.
Handicap Access: Cottage is accessible.
Children: Welcome, but there are no special facilities.
Languages: English.

Summit House
Gay/Lesbian ♀♂

Best Breakfast in Texas!

Located on an old Indian campground above the Colorado River, the house and herb gardens nestled under 100-year-old oak trees give the feeling of a secluded hideaway. The guesthouse is close to the heartbeat of Austin, just minutes from downtown, quaint shopping and dining. We have a very down-home atmosphere at the *Summit House*. Your host, David, will be helpful in letting you know what is going on in the Live Music Capital of the World. He also conducts shopping and gourmet tours of Austin, as well as a variety of sightseeing tours of the city, including the gay nightlife. Come experience the true feeling of Texas!

Address: 1204 Summit St, Austin, TX 78741-1158 **Tel:** (512) 445-5304.

Type: Guesthouse.
Clientele: Gay & lesbian, straight-friendly. Bears are especially welcome.
Transportation: Car, taxi, bus.
To Gay Bars: 15 minute walk, a 5 minute drive.
Rooms: 3 suites with queen beds, 1 single with a 3/4 bed.
Bathrooms: 1 private, 1 shared & 1 outdoor shower garden.
Meals: Full down-home breakfast.
Vegetarian: Available. Vegetarian markets & restaurants nearby.
Complimentary: Wine, beer, iced tea, coffee, juice, home-baked goodies & fresh fruit.
Dates Open: All year.
High Season: Oct-May.
Rates: Single or double $49-$99.
Discounts: Stay 5 nights, 6th night is free.
Rsv'tns: Recommended
To Reserve: Call direct.
Parking: Off-street parking.
In-Room: Central AC & heat, ceiling fans, sitting area, color TV, phone service, large windows, natural fabrics, flowers from garden.
On-Premises: Great trees, natural garden setting, lots of birds and wildlife.
Exercise/Health: Massage, weights, nearby hike & bike trail.
Swimming: Nearby public pools. 2 miles to Barton Springs, one of the world's best swimming holes.
Sunbathing: On patio.
Nudity: Permitted in private sunning area.
Smoking: Permitted outside only.
Pets: Permitted.
Handicap Access: No.
Children: Over the age of 13 permitted.
Languages: English.
Your Host: David.

Ziller House

Q-NET Gay-Owned 50/50 ♀♂

An Exclusive Alternative to Austin's Premium Hotels

SEE SPECIAL PAGE 28 COLOR SECTION

This exquisitely renovated 1930s Mediterranean-style estate is nestled among giant oaks on a secluded bluff above the south shore of Town Lake. Private, yet centrally located, *Ziller House* evokes the feeling of an Italianate villa of the '30s with a blend of antique and contemporary appointments. Five large bedrooms offer elegant alternatives to Austin's premium hotels. Enjoy a game of pool in the oak-paneled billards room, or, after a jog along the neighborhood hike-and-bike trail, relax in the natural-stone swimming pool and spa with views of Austin's skyline. Austin's live music and entertainment district, gay bars, restaurants and shopping are minutes away.

Address: 800 Edgecliff Terrace, Austin, TX 78704
Tel: (512) 462-0100, (800) 949-5446, **Fax:** (512) 462-9166.

Type: Bed & breakfast.
Clientele: 50% gay & lesbian & 50% straight clientele
Transportation: Car is best.
To Gay Bars: 1 1/2 miles, a 30 min walk, a 5 min drive.
Rooms: 3 rooms, 1 suite, 1 cottage with queen or king beds.
Bathrooms: 5 private bath/shower/toilets.

Meals: Expanded or full breakfast.
Vegetarian: Available in restaurant 1.5 miles away & at whole foods market. Not available at the house.
Complimentary: Tea, coffee, sodas, juice, bottled water, chocolates.
Dates Open: All year.
Rates: $120-$200.

Credit Cards: MC, Visa, Amex.
Rsv'tns: Required.
To Reserve: Call direct.
Parking: Adequate free off-street parking.
In-Room: Telephone, AC, color cable TV, refrigerator, coffee & tea-making facilities, microwave, maid service.
On-Premises: Billards room.

Exercise/Health: Jacuzzi.
Swimming: Pool on premises.
Sunbathing: Poolside.
Smoking: Permitted outside only. All rooms are non-smoking.
Pets: Not permitted.
Handicap Access: No.
Children: No.
Languages: English, Italian.

Bello Vista

Gay-Owned & -Operated ♀♂

Let the Wimberley Way Weave its Magic & Win Your Heart

Bello Vista is a beautiful new home in the Texas hill country, 30 miles from Austin and 40 miles from San Antonio. This custom-designed home offers unlimited views of the valley and hills surrounding the artsy village of Wimberley. Enjoy the nightlife in nearby Austin or San Antonio, shop Wimberley Market Days, tube the river below or in New Braunfels, shop in Fredericksburg, or simply watch the sunsets and feed the deer from your patio. Let the Wimberley Way and the Texas hill country captivate your hearts as it has many others. TO OPEN NOVEMBER, 1997.

Address: 2121 Hilltop, Wimberley, TX **Tel:** (512) 847-6425.

continued next page

UNITED STATES

Type: Bed & breakfast.
Clientele: Mostly gay & lesbian with some straight clientele
Transportation: Car is best.
To Gay Bars: 30 mi to Austin & 40 mi to San Antonio gay bars.
Rooms: 2 rooms with queen or king beds.

Bathrooms: 2 private bath/shower/toilets.
Meals: Continental breakfast.
Vegetarian: Available nearby.
Complimentary: Set up service, wine in room.
Dates Open: All year.
High Season: May-Sept.
Rates: Summer $95-$125, winter $75-$100.

Rsv'tns: Required.
To Reserve: Call direct.
Parking: Ample off-street parking.
In-Room: Telephone, AC, ceiling fans, color cable TV, VCR, reifrigerator, coffee & tea-making facilities, maid & laundry service.
On-Premises: Laundry facilities, microwave.

Swimming: River nearby.
Sunbathing: On patio.
Smoking: Non-smoking home.
Pets: Permitted under 25 lbs.
Handicap Access: Yes, wide doors.
Children: No.
Languages: English.
Your Host: John & Max.

CORPUS CHRISTI • TEXAS

Anthony's by the Sea
Gay/Lesbian ♀♂

A few minutes from Padre Island National Seashore, *Anthony's by the Sea* is hidden by live oaks on two thirds of an acre with pool and therapy spa and spacious lawn. Choose from four bedrooms (some with private baths and seating areas) or two guest cottages, which have private baths, living rooms, dining areas, and fully-equipped kitchens with dishwasher and microwave. The lanai is covered and carpeted, with chandeliers, BBQ, and fountains. Gourmet breakfasts are served in an open dining area or on the patio where guests can watch hummingbirds, butterflies, squirrels, and geckos.

Address: 732 S Pearl, Rockport, TX 78382 **Tel:** (512) 729-6100, (800) 460-2557.

Type: Bed & breakfast.
Clientele: Mostly gay & lesbian with some straight clientele.
Transportation: Car is best.
To Gay Bars: 30 miles to Corpus Christi bars.
Rooms: 5 rooms & 1 cottage. 740 sq ft Spanish Suite w/wet bar, large living area & king bed.
Bathrooms: 4 private & 1 shared.

Meals: Full gourmet breakfast.
Vegetarian: Available upon request.
Complimentary: Juices, iced tea, coffee, lemonade, & an afternoon snack.
Dates Open: All year.
Rates: $60-$95.
Discounts: 7th day free.
Credit Cards: MC, Visa.
Rsv'tns: Requested.
To Reserve: Travel agent or call direct.

Parking: Carports.
In-Room: Color TV, VCR, AC, ceiling fans, refrigerator & maid service.
On-Premises: TV lounge, laundry facilities, telephone & full, covered lanai with fans & chandeliers.
Exercise/Health: Jacuzzi.
Swimming: Pool on premises. 5 blocks to beach.
Sunbathing: On common

sun decks & at the beach 5 blocks away.
Nudity: Permitted by the pool with restrictions. Private deck available.
Smoking: Permitted with restrictions.
Pets: On approval.
Handicap Access: No.
Children: Permitted in the cottage, suites.
Languages: English & Spanish.
Your Host: Tony & Denis

DALLAS

Courtyard on the Trail
Gay/Lesbian ♀♂

Maximum Comfort, Privacy and Convenience

Enter through arched gates into a relaxing and memorable experience at *Courtyard on the Trail*. While close to downtown and North Dallas, we are far enough removed to afford guests a country setting in which to kick back and relax. The B&B is decorated with elegant antique and modern furnishings, fine linens and art. Your bed-

516   FERRARI GUIDES™

room has direct access to the pool and courtyard through French doors, affording you maximum comfort, privacy and convenience. Luxuriate in your marble bathroom's extra-large bathtub while contemplating the beautiful clouds painted on a blue sky overhead. Whether you are in town for business or celebrating a special occasion, your host will ensure a personalized, first-class stay.

Address: 8045 Forest Trail, Dallas, TX 75238
Tel: (214) 553-9270 (Tel/Fax), (800) 484-6260 pin #0465.
E-mail: akrubs4u@aol.com

Type: Bed & breakfast.
Clientele: Mostly gay & lesbian with some straight clientele
Transportation: Car.
To Gay Bars: 6 miles, a 15 minute drive.
Rooms: 3 rooms with king or queen beds.
Bathrooms: 3 private bath/toilet/showers.
Meals: Full gourmet breakfast.
Vegetarian: Available if prearranged. Vegetarian cuisine within 1 mile.
Complimentary: Wine & delectables upon arrival & each day thereafter. Mints each night.
Dates Open: All year.
High Season: All year.
Rates: $95-$125.
Discounts: Extended stays over 3 days 10%. All repeat customers 10%.
Credit Cards: MC, Visa.
Rsv'tns: Required.
To Reserve: Travel agent or call direct.
Minimum Stay: Required on holidays.
Parking: Ample off-street parking.
In-Room: AC, color cable TV, VCR, telephone, laundry service.
On-Premises: Meeting rooms, fax & computer, video tape library, private garden.
Exercise/Health: Massage.
Swimming: Pool on premises.
Sunbathing: Poolside, in hammock in private garden.
Nudity: Permitted poolside with discretion.
Smoking: Permitted outside only.
Pets: Not permitted.
Handicap Access: No.
Children: No.
Languages: English.
Your Host: Alan.

Inn on Fairmount

Gay/Lesbian ♀♂

The Ambiance of an Inn, the Luxury of a Fine Hotel

The *Inn on Fairmount* is located in the heart of the Oak Lawn/Turtle Creek area, minutes from restaurants, clubs and the Dallas Market Center. There are seven finely-furnished bedrooms and suites with private baths, a beautifully decorated lounge and a Jacuzzi. Coffee is placed outside your door each morning. Continental breakfast is served in the lounge as is evening wine and cheese. For the ambiance of an inn and the luxury of a fine hotel, spend a night or two with us and experience the style and good taste which is the *Inn on Fairmount!*

Address: 3701 Fairmount, Dallas, TX 75219
Tel: (214) 522-2800 or Fax: (214) 522-2898. URL: innonfairmount-dallas.com

Type: Bed & breakfast inn.
Clientele: Mostly gay & lesbian with some straight clientele
Transportation: Car or airport super shuttle.
To Gay Bars: 2-1/2 blocks.
Rooms: 7 rooms with twin, queen & king beds.
Bathrooms: All private.
Meals: Continental breakfast.
Dates Open: All year.
Rates: Per night: rooms $90, mini-suites $105, 2-room suite $130.
Discounts: On longer stays.
Credit Cards: MC, Visa, Discover.
Rsv'tns: Recommended, especially on weekends.
To Reserve: Travel agent or call direct.
Parking: Ample free off-street parking.
In-Room: Color TV, VCR, AC, telephone, maid service. Some rooms with ceiling fans.
On-Premises: Fax machine, video tape library.
Exercise/Health: Jacuzzi.
Sunbathing: On common sun decks.
Smoking: Not permitted in lobby.
Pets: Not permitted.
Handicap Access: 1 room with widened doors.
Children: Not especially welcome.
Languages: English, Spanish.
Your Host: Michael.

Symphony House

Q-NET Gay-Owned & -Operated ♀♂

Personal Houseman Ensures Satisfaction

Symphony House, a fully furnished luxury four-bedroom, two-bath home, is conveniently located six miles east of downtown Dallas on I-30. All the comforts of home are at your fingertips, including ample linens, towels, dishes and cooking

continued next page

utensils. In addition, there is a pool, spa, cabana with bar, ceiling fans, and a three-quarter acre backyard. Owner, Greg, and his dog, Sadie, live on the property in a separate apartment. Greg has had over 15 years experience in the luxury hotel business and will act as your concierge and personal houseman.

Address: 6327 Symphony Lane, Dallas, TX 75227-1737
Tel: (214) 388-9123. **E-mail:** SymphonyHouse@webtv.net

Type: Gay vacation & party rental house.
Clientele: Mostly gay & lesbian with some straight clientele
Transportation: Car is best or taxi from airport. Car rental agency 1 block from house.
To Gay Bars: 3 miles, a 5 min drive.
Rooms: 4 rooms with queen beds.
Bathrooms: 2 shared bath/shower/toilets.
Vegetarian: Vegetable tray as hors d'oeuvre upon request.
Complimentary: Guests prepare & serve themselves: welcome wine, beer & hors d'oeuvres stocked in refrigerator, coffee & tea.
Dates Open: All year.
Rates: $175-$250 per night. $1,050-$1,500 per week.
Discounts: For singles & couples using only 2 bedrooms & 1 bath (other br & bath will be closed off).
Credit Cards: MC, Visa, Amex.
Rsv'tns: Recommended.
To Reserve: Travel agent or call direct.
Parking: Ample, free off-street parking. Gated driveway holds 6 cars, wide street with sidewalks.
In-Room: House has telephone, AC, color cable TV, VCR, kitchen, refrigerator, coffee & tea-making facilities, laundry service. Daily maid service in living areas & kitchen only.
On-Premises: Book library, 2 living areas, 2 dining areas, kitchen utility w/ washer & dryer. House can accommodate parties up to 100 people. Bartender & waitstaff available at extra charge.
Exercise/Health: Jacuzzi.
Swimming: Pool on premises.
Sunbathing: Poolside & on patio.
Nudity: Permitted throughout house & in pool area.
Smoking: Permitted everywhere, but preferably in living areas only.
Pets: Permitted. Must be sociable & housetrained or stay in backyard. 1 well-trained dog on premises.
Handicap Access: No.
Children: Welcome.
Languages: English.
Your Host: Greg.

IGLTA

Gar-Den Suites
Gay/Lesbian ♂

Affordable Lodging In the Center of Montrose

In the center of the Montrose area, walking distance to several clubs, restaurants and shopping is the *Gar-Den Suites* bed and breakfast. Our location is close to museums, parks, the zoo, the Astrodome and theaters. Each two-room suite is adjacent to quiet, private sun decks and features a full bath, refrigerator, microwave, TV/VCR combination and a central video library. Telephone and fax are available on premises. Neighborhood travel is commonly done on foot, bicycle, taxi or metro bus, so no rental car is needed. Airport shuttles are available.

Address: 2702 Crocker St, Houston, TX 77006
Tel: (713) 528-2302, (800) 484-1036 (code 2669).

Type: Bed & breakfast.
Clientele: Mostly men with women welcome
Transportation: Car. Airport, then shuttle bus, pickup from airport $20-$30.
To Gay Bars: 1 block, 1/2 mile, a 5 min walk.
Rooms: 2 suites with double beds.
Bathrooms: Private: 1 bath/toilet, 1 shower/toilet.
Meals: Continental breakfast.
Vegetarian: Available nearby.
Complimentary: Cheese & crackers, fruit.
Dates Open: All year.
Rates: $60-$90.
Discounts: 10% stays of 1 week or more.
Credit Cards: MC, Visa, Amex, Discover.
Rsv'tns: Required.
To Reserve: Call direct.
Parking: Adequate free off-street parking.
In-Room: AC, color TV, VCR, video tape library, refrigerator, coffee & tea-making facilities, kitchen, maid service.
On-Premises: Laundry facilities.
Exercise/Health: Nearby gym, weights, Jacuzzi, sauna, steam, massage.
Swimming: Pool nearby.
Sunbathing: On common sun decks.
Nudity: Permitted on sun deck.
Smoking: Permitted outside only.
Pets: Limited, pets under 20 lbs will be considered.
Handicap Access: No.
Children: No.
Languages: English.
Your Host: Dennis & Gary.

The Lovett Inn

Gay/Lesbian ♀♂

You'll Love It at the Lovett!

A distinctive bed and breakfast located in Houston's Montrose/Museum district, *The Lovett Inn* was built in 1924 as the home of former mayor Judge Joseph Hutcheson, who lived here until his death in 1973. Tom Fricke, the current owner, bought the home in 1989 with the purpose of creating an inn. Located on elegant, tree-lined Lovett Boulevard, the inn is reminiscent of an earlier time and continues to be maintained in the traditional style of the era in which it was built. Many of the same amenities offered in larger hotels can be found here. Rooms are available with microwaves, wet bars and coffeemakers. And what better way to relax after a day of meetings or shopping than to enjoy the landscaped grounds, swimming pool and Jacuzzi?

Many of Houston's finest restaurants are within a short walk of *The Lovett*, while others are only a short drive away. We are situated in the heart of Houston, with easy access to downtown, the Galleria, the medical center and the museum district. Houston's theater district, home to the opera, ballet and symphony, is only ten minutes from the inn. We are also within walking distance of a number of museums, such as The Museum of Fine Arts, the Menil Collection, the Contemporary Arts Museum and the Holocaust Museum. The Imax Theater, Hermann Park, the University of St. Thomas and Rice University are equally close. Montrose is the heart of Houston's gay and lesbian community, featuring bars, coffee houses, bookstores and eclectic shops catering to the community. We look forward to having the opportunity to host you at *The Lovett Inn*. Please feel free to call our toll-free number for reservations and information.

Address: 501 Lovett Blvd, Houston, TX 77006
Tel: (713) 522-5224, **Fax:** 528-6708, (800) 779-5224.

Type: Inn.
Clientele: 75% gay & 25% straight clientele.
Transportation: Airport shuttle to downtown Hyatt, then taxi.
To Gay Bars: 1/2 block to gay/lesbian bars.
Rooms: 3 rooms, 3 suites, 1 apartment & 1 cottage with double, queen or king beds.
Bathrooms: All private. 3 with whirlpool baths.

Meals: Continental breakfast.
Vegetarian: Available.
Complimentary: Tea, coffee, candy in rooms.
Dates Open: All year.
Rates: $85-$145.
Discounts: Group and long-term rates.
Credit Cards: MC, Visa, Amex, Discover.
Rsv'tns: Suggested.
To Reserve: Call direct.
Minimum Stay: Required at peak times.

Parking: Ample, free parking.
In-Room: Color cable TV, VCR, kitchen, coffee & tea-making facilities & laundry service.
On-Premises: Meeting rooms & TV lounge. Laundry available.
Exercise/Health: Jacuzzi. Nearby gym, weights, Jacuzzi, sauna, steam & massage.

Swimming: Pool on premises, 30-60 minutes to ocean beach, lake.
Sunbathing: At poolside or on private sun decks.
Smoking: Permitted in public areas & in some smoke-friendly rooms.
Pets: Permitted on approval.
Handicap Access: No.
Children: Permitted on approval.
Languages: English.

IGLTA

Montrose Inn
Gay-Owned & -Operated ♂

Basic & Butch

The *Montrose Inn* is an all-male gay bed and breakfast situated in the middle of gay Houston, within walking distance of a dozen gay bars. Our slogan, "Basic & Butch" means just that — we have no antique furniture, no sauna and no swimming pool. What we DO have are clean, modern, private, comfortable rooms with color TV, VCR, phone and firm queen-sized beds... and the price is right. Rooms offer access to a full kitchen and free laundry. If you're a gay man coming to Houston to party, cruise and experience local gay nightlife, then we're definitely the place to stay — right in the middle of gay Houston!

Address: 408 Avondale, Houston, TX 77006 **Tel:** (713) 520-0206, (800) 357-1228.

Type: Bed & breakfast.
Clientele: Men only
Transportation: Airport bus to downtown, then taxi.
To Gay Bars: 3 blocks.
Rooms: 7 rooms with queen beds.
Bathrooms: Private: 1 bath/toilet/shower, 1 shower/toilet. Shared: 2 bath/shower/toilets.
Meals: Full breakfast.
Complimentary: Coffee, tea & soft drinks 24 hrs.
Dates Open: All year.
Rates: $59-$99.
Credit Cards: MC, Visa, Amex, Diners, Discover.
To Reserve: Travel agent or call direct.
Parking: Adequate, free off-street parking.
In-Room: Telephone, AC, color TV, VCR, maid & laundry service.
On-Premises: Laundry facilities, video tape library.
Smoking: Smoking & non-smoking rooms available.
Pets: Permitted if well-behaved.
Handicap Access: No.
Children: No.
Languages: English.

IGLTA

Adelynne's Summit Haus & Summit Haus II
Q-NET Gay/Lesbian ♀♂

Welcome, Wilkommen, Bienvenidos, Bienvenue, Benvenuto, C'mon Over, Stay Awhile...

Adelynne's Summit Haus & Summit Haus II are two elegant 1920's bed and breakfast accommodations. Just minutes north of San Antonio's downtown historical, multicultural attractions, they offer luxury, comfort and privacy for less than most hotels. Furnishings include rare Biedermeier antiques, crystal, porcelain, Persian and Oriental rugs and French and English antiques. The adjacent 2000-square-foot cottage is beautifully-furnished with all the comforts of elegant accommodations in our tradition of Texas hospitality.

Address: 427 W Summit, San Antonio, TX 78212
Tel: (800) 972-7266, (210) 736-6272, (210) 828-3045, **Fax:** (210) 737-8244.

Type: Bed & breakfast.
Clientele: Gay & lesbian. Good mix of men & women.
Transportation: Car.
To Gay Bars: 1 mile or 5 minutes by car.
Rooms: 2 rooms, 1 suite & 1 cottage with double, queen or king beds.
Bathrooms: 3 private bath/ toilets & 1 private shower/ toilet.
Meals: Full breakfast.
Complimentary: Brandy, cognac, soft drinks & beer.
Dates Open: All year.
Rates: $75-$160.
Credit Cards: MC, Visa, Amex.
Rsv'tns: Required.
To Reserve: Call direct.
Minimum Stay: 2 nights on weekends.
Parking: Ample free off-street parking.
In-Room: Color TV, AC, telephone, ceiling fans, refrigerator, coffee & tea-making facilities.
On-Premises: Meeting rooms & laundry facilities.
Sunbathing: In the backyard & on common sun decks.
Smoking: Outside on the decks. All other areas non-smoking.
Pets: Not permitted.
Handicap Access: No.
Children: Will accept children over 10 years of age.
Languages: English & German.

FERRARI GUIDES™

Arbor House Inn & Suites

Q-NET Gay-Owned ♀♂

The Best-Kept Secret in Downtown San Antonio

The *Arbor House Inn* invites you to the most unique all-suites inn in San Antonio. Although it looks like a B&B, the five buildings, built in 1903, have central AC/heat, state-of-the-art phone and messaging systems, private baths and furnishings unlike any hotel you have ever visited. The location is convenient to the Riverwalk and downtown, but you won't have to fight the crowds to "get away from it all" — just relax in our formal gardens under the grape arbor. Come see for yourself — you will be forever grateful that you found us.

Address: 540 South St. Mary's St, San Antonio, TX 78205
Tel: (210) 472-2005, **Toll-free:** (888) 272-6700, **Fax:** (210) 472-2007.

Type: Hotel.
Clientele: Mostly straight clientele. Looking to increase gay & lesbian clientele
Transportation: Airport limo or taxi.
To Gay Bars: 2 blocks, a 5 min. walk, a 2 min. drive.
Rooms: 11 suites with king or double beds.
Bathrooms: Private: 3 shower/toilets, 8 bath/shower/toilets.

Meals: Continental breakfast.
Vegetarian: Inquire. Available nearby.
Complimentary: Coffeemaker in all suites.
Dates Open: All year.
Rates: High season (Oct-May): $140-$250; Low season (Jun-Sept): $95-$250.
Credit Cards: MC, Visa, Amex, Discover.
Rsv'tns: Required.

To Reserve: Travel agent or call direct.
Minimum Stay: Required on holiday weekends.
Parking: Adequate free off-street parking.
In-Room: AC, color cable TV, telephone, coffee & tea-making facilities, maid service. Some rooms have refrigerators & ceiling fans.
Exercise/Health: 1 block to Riverwalk, nearby weights, Jacuzzi, sauna, massage.

Swimming: Pool nearby.
Sunbathing: Poolside & on patio.
Smoking: Permitted outside, on porch & on balcony. All suites are non-smoking.
Pets: Small-medium dogs permitted (under 25 lbs), $15 charge per night.
Handicap Access: No.
Children: Welcome.
Languages: English.
Your Host: Reg & Dale.

The Garden Cottage

Gay/Lesbian ♀♂

Come to *The Garden Cottage* in San Antonio. There's no place like it! We offer privacy and a country-style atmosphere, yet we're minutes from downtown, shopping, restaurants, museums, and public gardens. Our cozy cottage, shaded by Texas pecan trees in a quiet residential neighborhood, is conveniently located near San Antonio's historic and cultural attractions. San Antonio is home to the Alamo, River Walk, and its five Spanish missions are part of the National Park System.

Address: San Antonio, TX
Tel: (210) 828-7815, (800) 235-7215, **Fax:** (210) 828-4539. **E-mail:** juma@texas.net

Type: Cottage adjacent to the San Antonio Botanical Gardens.
Clientele: Mainly gay/lesbian with some straight clientele.

Transportation: Taxi, rental car, or bus.
To Gay Bars: 6 blocks to gay bar, 15-20 min to lesbian bars.

Rooms: 1 cottage with double beds.
Bathrooms: 1 private shower/toilet.
Complimentary: Drinks, snacks, fruit, popcorn.

Dates Open: All year.
High Season: March-May & Sept-Nov.
Rates: $50-$80.

continued next page

INN PLACES® 1998   521

Discounts: Weekly rate $250-$350.
Rsv'tns: Required.
To Reserve: Call direct.
Minimum Stay: 2 nights.
Parking: Ample, free off-street parking.

In-Room: Color cable TV, VCR, AC, telephone, ceiling fans, kitchen, refrigerator, coffee & tea-making facilities.
On-Premises: Laundry facilities upon request.

Exercise/Health: Massage $30-$40.
Swimming: 15 min to public pool, 1 hr to river, lake, 2 hrs to ocean beach.
Sunbathing: On patio.
Smoking: Permitted on porch.

Pets: Not permitted.
Handicap Access: Not wheelchair accessible.
Children: No.
Languages: English, German.

Mt. Peale Bed & Breakfast Country Inn
Gay-Owned 50/50 ♀♂

A Mountain Paradise in Southeastern Utah

A short 35 miles southeast of Moab, *Mt. Peale Bed & Breakfast* rests at the base of Southeastern Utah's greatest peaks, the La Sal Mountains. Each guestroom is individually decorated, representing the natural diversity of the area. The Garden Nook represents the wildflowers & birds of Mt. Peale; The Timber Trek illuminates the unforgettable terrain and wildlife of the La Sal Mountains; and The Sea Cove reflects the innkeepers' love of the sea. A nutritious breakfast is served daily inside or outdoors on the deck. The area's summer and winter activities include hiking, four-wheeling, biking, fishing, skiing, snowmobiling and snow shoeing.

Address: PO Box 366, LaSal, UT 84530
Tel: (801) 686-2284 (Tel/Fax), (888) 687-3253, **mobile:** (801) 260-1305.
URL: www.moab-canyonlands.com/mtpeale

Type: Bed & breakfast & cottages.
Clientele: 50% gay & lesbian & 50% straight clientele
Transportation: Car, 4-wheel drive helpful, airport in Moab. Free pickup from Moab airport or Monticello airstrip with Inn Places ad.
To Gay Bars: 150 miles to gay bars.
Rooms: 3 rooms, 1 cottage with double (extended), queen or single beds.
Bathrooms: 2 rooms

Meals: Buffet breakfast, family-style dinner, picnic available.
Vegetarian: Available, specify when making reservation.
Complimentary: Fruit drinks, wine set-ups, cocktails, tea & coffee.
Dates Open: All year.
High Season: Apr-Jul & Sept-Nov.
Rates: $65-$120.
Discounts: 10%-15% weekdays during low season.

Credit Cards: MC, Visa.
Rsv'tns: Required, walk-ins accepted.
To Reserve: Travel agent or call direct.
Minimum Stay: Required Dec 25-Jan 1 & any festival wknd. 2 nights holiday wknds.
Parking: Adequate free parking.
In-Room: Maid, room & laundry service, portable phone.
On-Premises: Meeting rooms, TV lounge, fax,

phone, modem, laundry service ($3 per load).
Exercise/Health: Volleyball, basketball, horseshoes, Jacuzzi, massage by appointment when making reservation.
Swimming: Nearby river, lakes.
Sunbathing: On common sun decks, on hot tub deck.
Smoking: Permitted outside.
Pets: Please inquire.
Handicap Access: No.
Children: Welcome.

Anton Boxrud B&B
Gay-Friendly ♀♂

Salt Lake's Closest B&B to Downtown

When looking for a warm homebase from which to explore Salt Lake City and the Wasatch mountains, we invite you to relax in the casual elegance of our historic home, *Anton Boxrud B&B*. Half a block from the Governor's Mansion, we are the closest B&B to downtown, just a 15-minute walk. In the evenings, enjoy complimentary beverages and snacks. The hot tub can provide liquid refreshment of a different kind. We serve full breakfasts featuring Grandma Glady's freshly baked cinnamon buns.

Address: 57 South 600 East, Salt Lake City, UT 84102
Tel: (801) 363-8035, (800) 524-5511, **Fax:** (801) 596-1316.

Type: Bed & breakfast.
Clientele: Mostly straight clientele with a gay & lesbian following.
Transportation: Car or taxi.
To Gay Bars: 8 blocks.
Rooms: 6 rooms & 1 suite with single, queen or king beds.
Bathrooms: Private: 2 shower/toilets, 3 full baths. Shared: 1 full bath, 1 shower.

Meals: Full breakfast.
Complimentary: Evening snacks, beverages, coffee & tea.
Dates Open: All year.
High Season: Jun-Oct (summer) & Jan-Mar (ski season).
Rates: $64-$134.
Credit Cards: MC, Visa, Amex, Diners, Discover.
Rsv'tns: Recommended.
To Reserve: Call direct.

Minimum Stay: 2 nights on weekends.
Parking: Ample on-street & off-street covered parking.
In-Room: AC, mints, terrycloth robes, flowers, shampoo & soap, maid service.
On-Premises: TV lounge, meeting rooms.
Exercise/Health: Jacuzzi on premises. Nearby gym, weights, Jacuzzi, sauna, steam & massage.
Swimming: Nearby pool & lake.
Sunbathing: At the beach.
Smoking: Permitted outside only.
Pets: Not permitted.
Handicap Access: No.
Children: Welcome.
Languages: English, French.
Your Host: Jane & Jerome.

Red Rock Inn
Gay-Friendly ♀♂

Experience the spectacular red rock cliffs of Zion National Park in relaxed comfort at *Red Rock Inn*. Each of our five rooms is individually decorated to offer a unique flavor and ambiance. They all have patios with a view and private baths (4 rooms feature jetted tubs, suite has outdoor hot tub). Enjoy your complimentary breakfast (delivered in a basket to your door each morning) in the shade of an old pecan tree as you plan your day in one of the world's most beautiful and inspiring natural wonders.

Address: 998 Zion Park Blvd, PO Box 273, Springdale, UT 84767
Tel: (801) 772-3139. **E-mail:** rrinn@infowest.com

Type: Intimate bed & breakfast cottages.
Clientele: Mostly straight clientele with a gay & lesbian following.
Transportation: Car is the only way.
To Gay Bars: 150 miles to Las Vegas.
Rooms: 3 rooms with queen beds, 1 with king bed, 1 2-room suite.

Bathrooms: Private: 4 whirlpool bath/shower/toilet, 1 full bath.
Meals: Full breakfast.
Vegetarian: Available with prior arrangements.
Dates Open: All year.
High Season: May-Sept.
Rates: $60-$140.
Credit Cards: MC, Visa, Amex, Discover.

Rsv'tns: Required in high season.
To Reserve: Call direct.
Minimum Stay: 2 nights on holidays.
Parking: Adequate free off-street parking.
In-Room: Color cable TV, AC, ceiling fans & maid service. Suite has VCR.
Exercise/Health: Massage available by appointment.

Swimming: Nearby pool & river.
Sunbathing: On private sun decks & patios, common patio & lawn.
Smoking: Not permitted.
Pets: Not permitted.
Handicap Access: Yes.
Children: Allowed with special arrangements.
Languages: English.

The Inn at HighView

Q-NET Gay-Friendly ♀♂

Vermont the Way You Always Dreamed It Would Be...

...but the way you've never found it, until now. Everyone who arrives at *The Inn at HighView* has the same breathless reaction to the serenity of the surrounding hills. The inn's hilltop location offers incredible peace, tranquility and seclusion, yet is convenient to all the activities that bring you to Vermont, such as skiing, golf, tennis and antiquing. Ski cross-country or hike our 72 acres. Swim in our unique rock garden pool. Enjoy our gourmet dinner, relax by a blazing fire, snuggle under a down comforter in a canopy bed, or gaze 50 miles over pristine mountains.

Address: RR 1, Box 201A, East Hill Road, Andover, VT 05143
Tel: (802) 875-2724, **Fax:** (802) 875-4021. **E-mail:** hiview@aol.com

Type: Inn with restaurant for Inn guests only.
Clientele: Mostly straight with a gay & lesbian following
Transportation: Car is best. Amtrak to Bellows Falls, VT (19 mi), Rutland (Killington) 30 mi. Taxi from Bellows Falls $20. Car rental from Rutland.
To Gay Bars: 40 min by car. Proximity to a bar is NOT the reason to come here!
Rooms: 6 rooms & 2 suites with single, double, queen or king beds.
Bathrooms: All private.
Meals: Full breakfast with dinner available on most weekend nights at a prix fixe rate.

Vegetarian: We specialize in Italian cuisine and have many pasta dishes without meat.
Complimentary: Sherry in room & turn-down service. Tea & coffee always. Conferences receive coffee service, snacks.
Dates Open: All year except for 2 weeks in November & 2 weeks in April.
High Season: Sep 15 through Oct 25, Christmas holiday week, & all of February.
Rates: Fall/Winter: $95-$145 double occupancy. $20 per extra person in suite. Summer: $99 mid-week double occupancy.
Discounts: For mid-week stays in winter & for longer than 2 days on weekends when no 3-night minimum is in effect.
Credit Cards: MC, Visa.
Rsv'tns: Required.
To Reserve: Travel agent or call direct.
Minimum Stay: 3 nights on holiday weekends & week between Christmas & New Year.
Parking: Ample free off-street parking.
In-Room: Maid & laundry service. 1 room with fireplace, 3 with canopy beds, 7 with private balconies & entrances, 2 with AC.
On-Premises: Meeting rooms, TV lounge, laundry facilities, gazebo with view, BBQ picnic area, game room, huge fireplace with comfortable couches in living room, library & CD player.
Swimming: Pool on premises.
Sunbathing: At poolside.
Smoking: Permitted outside only.
Pets: Small pets sometimes permitted depending on how full we are. Please inquire.
Handicap Access: 1 room accessible, but doorway is narrow.
Children: Permitted in suites only except during peak season. Please inquire.
Languages: English, Italian & Spanish.
Your Host: Greg & Sal.

Candlelight Motel

Gay-Friendly ♀♂

Four Spectacular Seasons to Explore Vermont

In the charming village of Arlington, Vermont, once the home of Norman Rockwell, **Candlelight Motel** is nestled in a valley with magnificent mountain views. Your room has a comfortable bed, private bath, air conditioning and color cable TV. Join us for continental breakfast by the fireplace. Good restaurants are nearby. Vermont has brilliant red and gold foliage in autumn, nearby skiing in winter, and crystal clear days and cool nights in the spring. Four seasons of activities include fishing, hiking, biking, canoeing and skiing. AAA & Mobil rated.

Address: Rt 7A, PO Box 97, Arlington, VT 05250
Tel: (802) 375-6647, (800) 348-5294.

Type: Motel with fireside lounge.
Clientele: Mostly straight clientele with a gay & lesbian following.
Transportation: Car.
To Gay Bars: 1-hr drive to bar in Brattleboro area. 1-1/4 hr drive to gay & lesbian bars in Albany, NY.
Rooms: 17 rooms with double or queen beds.

Bathrooms: All private bath/toilets.
Meals: Continental breakfast.
Complimentary: Coffee, tea & juices.
Dates Open: All year.
High Season: Fall foliage.
Rates: $45-$75.
Discounts: Group bookings & ski packages.
Credit Cards: MC, VISA & Amex.

Rsv'tns: Recommended.
To Reserve: Call direct.
Minimum Stay: On holiday weekends.
Parking: Ample free off-street parking.
In-Room: Color cable TV, AC, telephone & maid service. Refrigerators in 14 rooms.
On-Premises: Fireside guest area.

Swimming: Pool on premises.
Sunbathing: At poolside.
Smoking: Permitted. Non-smoking rooms available. Fireside guest area is non-smoking.
Pets: Not permitted.
Handicap Access: No.
Children: Permitted with restrictions.
Languages: English.

IGLTA

Howden Cottage

Gay-Friendly ♀♂

Howden Cottage offers cozy lodging and warm hospitality in the atmosphere of an artist's home. We're located in downtown Burlington, convenient to The Marketplace Shopping Mall, Lake Champlain, cinemas, night spots, churches, great restaurants, theatre, concerts, the U. of Vermont and the Fletcher Allen Health Center. The Shelburne Museum is a short drive away, as are five major ski areas and Vermont's spectacular fall foliage. Breakfast is served in our solarium. Owner-occupied & -run.

Address: 32 N Champlain St, Burlington, VT 05401-4320
Tel: (802) 864-7198, **Fax:** (802) 658-1556.

Type: Bed & breakfast.
Clientele: Mostly straight clientele with a gay/lesbian following.
Transportation: Bus stop is one block away.
To Gay Bars: 2-1/2 blocks to gay/lesbian bar.
Rooms: 2 rooms & 1 suite with single, double or queen beds.

Bathrooms: 1 private shower/toilet, 2 sinks & 1 shared bath/shower/toilet.
Meals: Continental breakfast.
Dates Open: All year.
High Season: July-Oct.
Rates: $44-$89.
Credit Cards: MC, Visa.
Rsv'tns: Suggested.

To Reserve: Call direct.
Parking: Adequate off-street & on-street parking.
In-Room: Telephone, sinks in room, AC/heat.
Exercise/Health: Nearby gym, weights, Jacuzzi, sauna, steam, massage.
Swimming: In the lake or at the YMCA or nearby river.

Sunbathing: Lakeside.
Nudity: Permitted at nearby river & quarry.
Smoking: Not permitted.
Pets: Not permitted.
Handicap Access: No.
Children: Permitted with prior arrangement.
Languages: English.
Your Host: Bruce.

INN PLACES® 1998

Phineas Swann B&B

Gay-Friendly 50/50 ♀♂

A Light-hearted, Premier Bed & Breakfast

Located at the base of the Jay Peak Ski Resort, 35 miles from north of Stowe, is our light-hearted B&B, *Phineas Swann*. The four guest rooms are filled with Vermont country antiques and feature canopy and carved-wood beds, and we serve gourmet breakfasts and afternoon teas that are simply amazing! Right out back is the Trout River and within walking distance are natural waterfalls and a swimming hole. *Country Living*, *The Boston Phoenix* and *Out Magazine* have all written about us — we're everything a Vermont bed and breakfast should be... and more. Call us today for a free brochure.

Address: PO Box 43, The Main Street,, Montgomery Center, VT 05471
Tel: (802) 326-4306.

Type: Bed & breakfast.
Clientele: 50% gay & lesbian & 50% straight clientele
Transportation: Car is best. Pick up from airport.
To Gay Bars: 1 hour to gay bars in Burlington, VT & 1-1/2 hours to Montreal.
Rooms: 4 rooms with queen & double beds.

Bathrooms: 2 private baths, 1 shared full bath.
Meals: Full gourmet breakfast & afternoon tea.
Vegetarian: Available.
Complimentary: 4pm tea with home-baked surprises. Mints & chocolates in room.
Dates Open: All year.
High Season: July, August, February & March.
Rates: $50-$79.

Credit Cards: MC, VISA & Discover.
Rsv'tns: Recommended.
To Reserve: Call direct.
Parking: Free covered parking.
In-Room: Ceiling fans & maid service.
On-Premises: TV lounge, VCR, game boards & meeting rooms.

Exercise/Health: Snowmobile paths, skiing, tennis, hiking, fishing & golf.
Swimming: Swimming hole with mountain water & river.
Smoking: Not permitted.
Pets: Not permitted.
Handicap Access: No.
Children: Not especially welcome.
Languages: English.
Your Host: Michael & Glen.

Country Cousin

Gay/Lesbian ♀♂

Experience Vermont's Gay Bed & Breakfast

Located on 15 beautifully landscaped acres, *Country Cousin* is a truly traditional bed and breakfast housed in an 1824 Greek Revival farmhouse. It is nestled in a valley between the West Mountains and the Green Mountains of Southwestern Vermont, just north of Bennington. *Country Cousin* is surrounded by Vermont's year-round activities.

Three major downhill ski areas are within 30 minutes and you can cross-country ski right from the front door. Enjoy biking, canoeing or horseback riding through the Green Mountains. Antiquing and sightseeing along historic Route 7A, exploring Vermont's quaint hamlets, or enjoying the outlet stores and gourmet dining of nearby Manchester are other popular activities. You may, however, just prefer to curl up next to the fireplace with a good book or relax in the sun and enjoy the company of our friendly guests and staff.

The spacious farmhouse offers two common areas for guests: a quiet antique-filled living room with views of Mt. Equinox and a magnificent post and beam music room with cathedral ceilings, stained-glass, grand piano and a 25-foot natural stone fireplace. The music room leads to a large sunning deck complete with wooden tub. The rolling lawns beyond take you to two large spring-fed ponds, perfect for nude swimming and sunbathing, with clothing being optional. Our inn offers four uniquely decorated guest rooms, some with feather beds, down comforters, or patchwork quilts. Warm robes are provided and guests are encouraged to enjoy the public areas in comfort. A full country breakfast is served daily after morning coffee in front of the fireplace. Afternoon tea, snacks and conversation are also a part of our hospitality. We are sure you will enjoy our country retreat and return again and again, as so many of our guests have!

Address: RR 1, Box 212 Old Depot Rd, Shaftsbury, VT 05262
Tel: (802) 375-6985 or (800) 479-6985.

Type: Bed & breakfast.
Clientele: Gay & lesbian
To Gay Bars: 1 hr to Brattleboro, VT & 1-1/4 hours by car to Albany, NY.
Rooms: 5 rooms with double or queen beds.
Bathrooms: All private.
Meals: Full breakfast.
Vegetarian: Available on request.

Complimentary: Tea, coffee, juices, snacks.
Dates Open: All year.
High Season: Fall.
Rates: $70-$85 (surcharge: $10/night for holidays, $20/night for fall foliage).
Discounts: Weekly rates.
Credit Cards: MC, Visa.
Rsv'tns: Recommended.
To Reserve: Travel agent or call direct.

Minimum Stay: 2 days on weekends preferred, but not essential.
Parking: Adequate off-street parking.
On-Premises: Music room with stone fireplace & great room, partial AC.
Exercise/Health: Wooden hot tub.
Swimming: 2 ponds on premises.

Sunbathing: On sun deck.
Nudity: Permitted on deck, in spa & pond areas.
Smoking: Permitted outdoors.
Pets: Permitted with prearrangement.
Handicap Access: Yes, with some restrictions.
Children: With prearrangement.
Languages: English.

Fitch Hill Inn

Gay-Friendly ♀♂

SEE SPECIAL PAGE 29 COLOR SECTION

Elegant, But Not Stuffy

Historic *Fitch Hill Inn,* c. 1797, occupies a hill overlooking the magnificent Green Mountains. Its location, central to Vermont's all-season vacation country, offers a special opportunity to enjoy the true Vermont experience. This is the town in which Charles Kuralt said he would like to settle. Antique-decorated guest rooms all have spectacular views. Breakfasts and, by arrangement, gourmet dinners, are prepared by the innkeeper. The library has video tapes, books, and an atmosphere of comfort and ease. The newly-renovated 18th century living room is wonderful for music, reading, and sitting by the fireside.

Address: RR 2 Box 1879,
Fitch Hill Rd,
Hyde Park, VT 05655
Tel: (802) 888-3834,
(800) 639-2903,
Fax: (802) 888-7789.

continued next page

INN PLACES® 1998 527

UNITED STATES — STOWE • VERMONT

Type: Bed & breakfast inn with restaurant for guests only.
Clientele: Mostly straight with a gay & lesbian following.
Transportation: Car is best. We do not pick up from Burlington International Airport except for those on extended stays.
To Gay Bars: 40 miles to Burlington.
Rooms: 4 rooms with 3 queens & 1 double, 1 suite with 2 single beds & 1 double bed. 1 efficiency apt with queen bed.
Bathrooms: All private.

Meals: Full breakfast.
Vegetarian: Available with reservation & prior arrangement.
Complimentary: Tea, sherry, snacks, bathrobes, bottled water. Maple syrup & candy in rooms.
Dates Open: All year.
High Season: Dec 25-Jan 3, Sept 15-Oct 15 & Feb.
Rates: $85-$95; suite/apt: $120-$160.
Discounts: On stays over 2 days (except during high season), 10% for AAA.
Credit Cards: MC, Visa, Amex.

Rsv'tns: Suggested.
To Reserve: Travel agent or call direct.
Minimum Stay: 2 nights during high seasons.
Parking: Ample off-street parking.
In-Room: Maid & laundry service, color TV, VCR, telephone, ceiling fans, 300+ video library. Suite & apt have fireplaces. Suite: AC, color cable TV, living room.
On-Premises: Meeting rooms, TV lounge, VCR library. Kitchen & refrigerator privileges available.

Exercise/Health: Hot tub, skiing, hiking, biking, horseback riding, golf & canoeing.
Swimming: Lake & river nearby.
Sunbathing: On the beach.
Smoking: Not permitted inside. Permitted on 3 outdoor porches.
Pets: Not permitted.
Handicap Access: No.
Children: Permitted over 10.
Languages: English, Spanish & some French.
Your Host: Richard & Stanley.

Honeywood Country Lodge
Q-NET Gay-Friendly ♀♂

Experience Vermont Hospitality at Its Best

Experience the ambiance and luxury of a country inn with the privacy of a motel. At *Honeywood Country Lodge* we're famous for early-morning baking and continental-plus breakfasts. Our large tastefully decorated rooms have cathedral ceilings and patio doors leading to a common balcony and our four acres of land. The rooms feature double, queen and king brass or canopy beds with hand-made quilts. Enjoy mountain views or dabble your feet in the brook which runs behind our property. In winter, cross-country ski from your door. We are the closest AAA Three-Diamond lodging to the slopes at Stowe Mountain Resort.

Address: 4527 Mountain Rd, Stowe, VT 05672
Tel: (802) 253-4124, (800) 659-6289, **Fax:** (802) 253-7050.
E-mail: honeywd@aol.com

Type: Bed & breakfast motel.
Clientele: Mostly straght clientele with a gay & lesbian following
Transportation: Pick up from airport, train, bus & ferry dock. We use a local taxi service which usually charges $20-$50.

To Gay Bars: 30 miles to Burlington gay bars.
Rooms: 12 rooms, 1 suite with single, double, queen or king beds.
Bathrooms: Private: 1 shower/toilet, 12 bath/toilet/showers.
Meals: Expanded continental breakfast.

Vegetarian: Available nearby.
Complimentary: Afternoon hors d'oeuvres & refreshments.
Dates Open: All year.
High Season: Sept 18-Oct 19, Dec 24-Jan 2, Feb 13-20.
Rates: Summer $62-$99,

winter $66-$129, high season $79-$179.
Discounts: Seniors & multi-day discounts 3 days or more, midweek Sun-Thurs stays pay 4 days. Not available during peak periods.
Credit Cards: MC, Visa, Amex, Discover.

528 FERRARI GUIDES™

Rsv'tns: Recommended in regular & high season.
To Reserve: Travel agent or call direct.
Minimum Stay: 2 nights on weekends, 3-4 nights high season.
Parking: Ample free off-street parking.

In-Room: AC, color cable TV, telephone, ceiling fans, refrigerator, maid service. Some rooms have fire-places & efficiencies.
Exercise/Health: Jacuzzi. Nearby gym, weights, Jacuzzi, sauna, steam, massage.

Swimming: Pool, river on premises. Nearby river & lake.
Sunbathing: Poolside & on grass near rooms or pool.
Smoking: Permitted outside or in smoking rooms. Non-smoking rooms available.

Pets: Not permitted.
Handicap Access: Yes, 1 room handicap-equipped with some restrictions.
Children: We accommodate families with 1 or 2 well-behaved children.
Languages: English.
Your Host: Carolyn & Bill.

Grünberg Haus Bed & Breakfast

Gay-Friendly ♀♂

Spontaneous Personal Attention in a Handbuilt Austrian Chalet

Our romantic Austrian inn, *Grünberg Haus*, rests on a quiet hillside in Vermont's Green Mountains, perfect for trips to Stowe, Montpelier, Waterbury and Burlington. Choose guest rooms with wonderful views from carved wood balconies, secluded cabins hidden along wooded trails or a spectacular carriage house with skywindows, balconies and modern kitchen. Relax by the fire or warm-weather Jacuzzi, ski or walk our cross-country trails, gather fresh eggs or enjoy the grand piano as you savor your imaginative, memorable breakfast. Explore Vermont.

Address: RR2, Box 1595 IP, Route 100 South, Waterbury-Stowe, VT 05676-9621
Tel: (802) 244-7726, (800) 800-7760. E-mail: grunhaus@aol.com

Type: Bed & breakfast guesthouse & cabins.
Clientele: Mostly straight clientele with a gay & lesbian following.
Transportation: Car is best, pick up from airport $25, bus $5, ferry dock $25, train $5.
To Gay Bars: 25 miles to Pearl's in Burlington, VT.
Rooms: 10 rooms, 1 suite & 2 cottages with single, double or queen beds.
Bathrooms: 9 private shower/toilets & others share shower/toilets.

Meals: Full, musical breakfast.
Vegetarian: Breakfast always vegetarian.
Complimentary: Set-ups, soft drinks, coffee & tea, cordials & snacks. BYOB OK.
Dates Open: All year.
High Season: Feb & March, July-October & Christmas.
Rates: $55-$140.
Discounts: 10% for seniors & stays of 4 or more days.
Credit Cards: MC, Visa, En Route, Discover.

Rsv'tns: Suggested.
To Reserve: Travel agent or call direct.
Parking: Ample free off-street parking.
In-Room: Maid service, fans & balcony. One kitchen unit.
On-Premises: Tennis court, Steinway grand piano, library, fireplace, chickens, BYOB pub. Groomed cross-country ski center.
Exercise/Health: Jacuzzi, sauna, 40 acres for hiking.

Swimming: Pool, river or lake nearby.
Sunbathing: At poolside, by river or lake or on common sun decks.
Nudity: Clothing-optional swimming areas nearby.
Smoking: Permitted outside.
Pets: Not permitted. Pick up & delivery of pets at registered kennel is available.
Handicap Access: No.
Children: Permitted.
Languages: English.
Your Host: Chris & Mark.

INN PLACES® 1998   529

Wilson-Lee House Bed & Breakfast

Gay-Owned & -Operated ♀♂

Relaxation as it Should Be in the Land That Time Forgot

On Virginia's Eastern Shore in historic Cape Charles, life moves at a deliciously slower pace. The *Wilson-Lee House Bed & Breakfast*, furnished with heirloom antiques and modern classics, offers six luxurious rooms, each with private bath. The James W. Lee Room features a splendid whirlpool. Mornings, full gourmet breakfasts are served and, after dark, the nightlife in Norfolk awaits just 45 minutes across the Chesapeake Bay Bridge Tunnel. With the beach only steps away, sunset sails can be arranged at your request. Pamper yourself — you deserve it.

Address: 403 Tazewell Ave, Cape Charles, VA 23310-3217
Tel: (757) 331-1954, **Fax:** (757) 331-8133.
E-mail: WLHBnB@aol.com. **URL:** www.accomack.com / WLHBnB

Type: Bed & breakfast, 45 min from Norfolk.
Clientele: Mostly straight clientele
Transportation: Car is best, Norfolk Int'l airport.
To Gay Bars: 40 miles, a 50 minute drive.
Rooms: 6 rooms with queen beds.
Bathrooms: All private. One with whirlpool & 1 private bath across hall.

Meals: Full breakfast.
Vegetarian: Can be arranged with advance notice.
Complimentary: Welcome mint on pillow, setups provided, soda, ice, BYOB.
Dates Open: All year.
High Season: Late Apr to mid-Nov.
Rates: High season $85-$120, low season $50-$75.
Credit Cards: MC, Visa, Amex.

Rsv'tns: Required.
To Reserve: Travel agent or call direct.
Parking: Ample free off-street parking.
In-Room: AC, AM/FM clock radio & stereo CD player. Color cable TV available.
On-Premises: Meeting rooms, video tape & CD libraries. Refrigerator for guest use.
Swimming: 5-10 minute

walk to Chesapeake Bay beach, drive to ocean.
Sunbathing: At beach.
Smoking: Permitted only on NON-enclosed portion of porch.
Pets: Not permitted.
Handicap Access: No.
Children: Only children over 12 years of age.
Languages: English.
Your Host: David, Leon.

IGLTA

The Mark Addy

Gay-Friendly ♀♂

Lodging in an Elegant Tradition

The Mark Addy is conveniently located between the beautiful Blue Ridge Mountains and Thomas Jefferson's Charlottesville. This beautifully restored and lovingly appointed country inn dates back to 1884, offering all who stay here the richness of a bygone era. The charming rooms and luxurious suites have private bathrooms with either a double whirlpool bath, double shower, or an antique claw-foot tub with shower. Much of what we know about gracious living and warm welcomes we learned from our family. It is with considerable pride and affection that this historic home bears their names.

Address: 56 Rodes Farm Dr, Nellysford, VA 22958
Tel: (804) 361-1101, (800) 278-2154. **E-mail:** markaddy@symweb.com
URL: www.symweb.com / rockfish / mark.html

Type: Country inn.
Clientele: Mostly straight with a gay & lesbian following
Transportation: Airport or Amtrak pick up available at extra charge.
To Gay Bars: 30 minutes to gay bars.
Rooms: Rooms & suites.

Bathrooms: All private. Double whirlpool bath, double shower or tub with shower.
Meals: Bountiful breakfast. Dinner. Catering available.
Vegetarian: Upon request.
Complimentary: In guest kitchen: beer, soda, juice,

iced tea, VA peanuts, homemade cookies.
Dates Open: All year.
Rates: $90-$135.
Discounts: Some available Sun-Thurs or for extended stays.
Credit Cards: MC, Visa.
Rsv'tns: Required.

To Reserve: Travel agent or call direct.
Minimum Stay: 2 nights in Oct, Feb, Apr-June & holidays.
In-Room: Down comforters, liqueur decanters, local goat's milk skin products, central AC.

530 FERRARI GUIDES™

On-Premises: 5 porches. Catering, including commitment ceremonies.
Exercise/Health: Excercise
facilities nearby.
Swimming: Swimming nearby.
Smoking: Permitted on porches only.
Pets: Not permitted.
Handicap Access: 1 room totally wheelchair accessible.
Children: Permitted age 12 & over.
Languages: English, German.
Your Host: John & Saverio.

A Touch of Country
Gay-Friendly 50/50 ♀♂

Daydream on the Porch Swings...

...or stroll through town, stopping at antique and gift shops, sampling savory fare at local restaurants. There's no need for detailed itineraries, for you've come to relax at *A Touch of Country*, our restored 1870's Shenandoah Valley home in historic New Market. We've gone to great lengths to create a warm, friendly atmosphere for your stay, setting the tone with antiques and country collectibles. Come morning, a down-home country breakfast fortifies you for visiting the Blue Ridge Mtns., New Market Battlefield, caverns and other points of interest.

Address: 9329 Congress St, New Market, VA 22844 **Tel:** (540) 740-8030.

Type: Bed & breakfast.
Clientele: 50% gay & lesbian & 50% straight clientele
Transportation: Car.
To Gay Bars: 1-1/2 hrs to gay bar in Charlottesville or 2 hours to DC.
Rooms: 6 rooms with double or queen beds.
Bathrooms: All private shower/sink/toilets.
Meals: Full breakfast.
Vegetarian: Available with advance request.
Complimentary: Soda available upon arrival.
Dates Open: All year.
High Season: September-November.
Rates: $60-$75, plus tax.
Discounts: For longer stays.
Credit Cards: MC, VISA, Discover, Amex.
Rsv'tns: Recommended.
To Reserve: Travel agent or call direct.
Minimum Stay: 2 days on holiday weekends & October-November weekends.
Parking: Adequate free off-street parking.
In-Room: Self-controlled AC.
On-Premises: TV lounge.
Swimming: At nearby pool.
Smoking: Not permitted.
Pets: Not permitted.
Handicap Access: No.
Children: Permitted if well-behaved and over 12 years old.
Languages: English.
Your Host: Jean & Dawn.

Bellmont Manor Bed & Breakfast
Gay-Friendly 50/50 ♀♂

Thrill Your Taste Buds and Your Appetite for History

Having a country gourmet breakfast arrive at your door with silver service is indeed special, and it is yours for the asking at *Bellmont Manor*, where gracious Southern hospitality is accented by great food. The house and its four bedrooms have been filled with an eclectic array of furniture, pictures, glass, brass, and china, including antiques and Virginia heirlooms. Only 20 minutes from downtown Richmond, VA, *Bellmont Manor* is surrounded by a treasure-trove of historic sites and museums for guests to visit.

Address: 6600 Belmont Rd, Chesterfield, VA 23832
Tel: (804) 745-0106. **E-mail:** bellmont@aol.com

continued next page

UNITED STATES

Type: Bed & breakfast.
Clientele: 50% gay & lesbian & 50% straight clientele
Transportation: Car is best. Pick up from airport & train station, $20 charge.
To Gay Bars: 5 miles or a 15-min drive.
Rooms: 4 rooms with single, double or queen beds.

Bathrooms: Private & shared.
Meals: Full breakfast.
Vegetarian: Available by prior arrangement.
Complimentary: Wine, tea, coffee, hors d'oeuvres.
Dates Open: All year.
Rates: $55-$125, plus tax.
Discounts: 10% on stays of 3 nights or more.
Credit Cards: MC, Visa, Discover, Amex.
Rsv'tns: Required.
To Reserve: Travel agent or call direct.
Minimum Stay: 2 nights on weekends.
Parking: Ample free off-street parking.
In-Room: AC, TV, ceiling fans, phone.
On-Premises: TV lounge.
Exercise/Health: Gym nearby.

Swimming: Pool & river nearby.
Sunbathing: On patio.
Smoking: Permitted outside only.
Pets: Not permitted. Dogs on premises.
Handicap Access: No.
Children: No.
Languages: English.
Your Host: Uly & Worth.

Marc-James Manor

Q-NET Gay/Lesbian ♀♂

Marc-James Manor B&B is a contemporary interpretation of an English manor house, situated on nearly two acres in the Highland Heights district of Bellingham. The guest suite has a private entrance off a semi-secluded courtyard, queen-sized bed, wet bar, wood-burning fireplace, and private bath. Guests can choose between a continental breakfast served in their room or on the patio, or, if preferred, a late morning brunch served in the main hall. The B&B is located one hour south of Vancouver and 90 minutes north of Seattle, close to museums, shopping, and the general arts community.

Address: 2925 Vining St, Bellingham, WA 98226 **Tel:** (360) 738-4919.

Type: Bed & breakfast.
Clientele: Mostly gay & lesbian with some straight clientele
Transportation: Car is best. $5 pick up charge from airport, train, ferry dock.
To Gay Bars: A 15-minute drive.
Rooms: 1 suite with queen bed.
Bathrooms: Private bath/toilet.
Meals: Full breakfast or tray.

Vegetarian: Always available.
Complimentary: Tea on day of arrival, chocolate on pillow, sherry & port in room. Tea from 4:30pm-5:30pm.
Dates Open: All year.
High Season: April-Oct.
Rates: $95-$125. Special packages available.
Discounts: Special rate for relocaters $75.
Rsv'tns: Required.
To Reserve: Call direct.

Minimum Stay: 2 days on weekends during high season.
Parking: Adequate free off-street parking.
In-Room: Coffee/tea-making facilities, refrigerator.
On-Premises: Meeting rooms, TV lounge, solarium, laundry facilities. Commitment ceremonies & receptions for up to 35 guests, includes china, crystal, silver, linen. Inquire about caterers.

Exercise/Health: Jacuzzi, sauna.
Swimming: Nearby lake.
Sunbathing: On patio.
Nudity: Permitted in solarium hot tub, not protected from hosts' view.
Smoking: Not permitted. 3 dogs & 2 cats in residence.
Handicap Access: No.
Children: Facility not designed for children.
Languages: English.
Your Host: Marc & Jim.

FERRARI GUIDES™

Mary Kay's Romantic Whaley Mansion Inn Q-NET Gay-Friendly ♀♂

Take Someone You Love to Mary Kay's

Slip off your shoes, sink into our soft carpets, snuggle into our satin sheets, sip your own champagne and enjoy our superb coffee and our own hand-dipped truffles. *Mary Kay's Romantic Whaley Mansion Inn* is listed by AAA as a 4-diamond B&B. We specialize in romantic rendezvous, birthdays, anniversaries, honeymoons, retreats and marriage encounters. We have six elegant bedrooms with private baths in a historical Victorian mansion. The candlelit breakfast is presented on crystal and sterling silver in the formal dining room. All rooms have VCR, color TV, refrigerators, and free movies.

Address: 415 Third St, Chelan, WA 98816
Tel: (509) 682-5735, (800) 729-2408 (USA & Canada), **Fax:** (509) 682-5385.
E-mail: whaley@televar.com **URL:** http://www.lakechelan.com/whaley.htm

Type: Bed & breakfast.
Clientele: Mostly straight clientele with a gay/lesbian following
Transportation: Car is best. Free pick up from bus or airport in Chelan.
To Gay Bars: 175 miles from Seattle gay/lesbian bars.
Rooms: 6 rooms with double, queen or king beds.
Bathrooms: All private.
Meals: 5-course candlelight breakfast.

Vegetarian: Always available.
Complimentary: Chocolates & truffles.
Dates Open: All year.
High Season: May 15-Sept 15
Rates: $115-$135 summer, $85-$105 winter.
Discounts: Off-season specials. 1st night regular price, 2nd night 1/2 price.
Credit Cards: MC, Visa.
Rsv'tns: Required. 72-hour cancellation policy.

To Reserve: Call direct.
Minimum Stay: 2 days on weekends, 3 days on holidays (summer).
Parking: Ample off-street parking.
In-Room: Color TV, VCR, AC, ceiling fans, refrigerators, maid service & free movies.
On-Premises: Meeting rooms, TV lounge, laundry facilities, & player piano.
Exercise/Health: Cross-country skiing, boating,

tennis courts, hiking & walking trails. Nearby fitness center.
Swimming: At Lake Chelan.
Sunbathing: On common sun decks.
Smoking: Permitted outdoors.
Pets: Not permitted.
Handicap Access: No.
Children: Not permitted, unless renting whole house.
Languages: English.
Your Host: Mary Kay & Carol.

Wild Lily Ranch Gay/Lesbian ♀♂

A Rustic Forest Retreat under Towering Cedars & Firs

In the Cascade Mountains one hour from Seattle, near the gay-friendly town of Index, are several cozy cabins made of cedar logs and cobblestones known as *Wild Lily Ranch*. Each cabin has a woodstove or fireplace and loft with skylights. They also have large picture windows with mini-blinds, dutch doors, small rustic porches looking out over the Skykomish River, nicely-finished hardwood floors, and spectacular views from every window. Among the many local activities available to guests are whitewater rafting, horseback riding and cross-country and downhill skiing. Luxury camping is available in two tents, each with double beds on wooden platforms with linens provided. A buffet breakfast is served in the picnic area each morning.

Address: PO Box 313, Index, WA 98256 **Tel:** (360) 793-2103.

continued next page

Type: Bed & breakfast with luxury camping available in 2 tents.
Clientele: Mainly gay & lesbian with some straight clientele
To Gay Bars: Gay-friendly bars in Index.
Rooms: Small log cabins.
Bathrooms: Modern, shared, centrally located bath house with bath/shower/toilets.

Campsites: 2-room tents already set up on the beach also with double beds & linens provided.
Meals: Continental breakfast.
Dates Open: All year.
High Season: June, July, August, September.
Rates: $65 all year, $10 for each additional person.
Discounts: 5 days or more 10% off.

Rsv'tns: Required.
To Reserve: Call direct.
Minimum Stay: 2-days on weekends.
Parking: Ample free parking.
In-Room: Refrigerator, fireplaces, cable color TV in cabins.
Exercise/Health: Recreational building has Jacuzzi, sauna, Health Rider & tropical plants.

Swimming: In river on premises.
Sunbathing: On the beach.
Nudity: Permitted on the beach with discretion.
Smoking: Permitted outside only.
Pets: Permitted with $10 daily pet fee.
Handicap Access: No.
Children: Not permitted.
Languages: English.
Your Host: Mike.

White Swan Guest House

Gay-Friendly ♀♂

The Best-Kept Secret in La Conner

Welcome to the *White Swan Guest House,* an 1890's farmhouse with wicker chairs on the porch, piles of books and a platter of homemade chocolate chip cookies on the sideboard, English-style gardens, fruit trees and acres of farmland. Country breakfast is served in our sunny yellow dining room. The Garden Cottage is a perfect romantic hideaway, with private bath, kitchen and sun deck. Visit nearby La Conner, a charming waterfront village. *White Swan* is ninety miles from Vancouver, BC, one hour north of Seattle and close to the San Juan Islands' and Victoria ferries.

Address: 1388 Moore Rd, Mt Vernon, WA 98273
Tel: (360) 445-6805. **URL:** www.cnw.com/~wswan/

Type: Bed & breakfast guesthouse.
Clientele: Mostly straight clientele with a gay/lesbian following
Rooms: 3 rooms & one large cottage for up to 4 persons. Queen & king beds.
Bathrooms: 2 shared in older home, 1 private in cottage.

Meals: Expanded country continental breakfast, with muffins, fruit, coffee.
Vegetarian: Only vegetarian food is served.
Complimentary: Fresh chocolate chip cookies always available.
Dates Open: All year.
High Season: Jul-Aug & Apr (Tulip time).

Rates: Single $65, double $80, cottage $125-$185.
Credit Cards: MC, Visa.
Rsv'tns: Preferred.
To Reserve: Call direct.
Parking: Ample off-street parking.
In-Room: Maid & laundry service, kitchen available in cottage.
On-Premises: Kitchen.

lounge, gorgeous flower garden, sun deck.
Sunbathing: On lawn or on cottage's private sun deck.
Smoking: Permitted outdoors only.
Pets: Not permitted.
Handicap Access: No.
Children: Welcome in garden cottage.
Languages: English.
Your Host: Peter.

Inn At Swifts Bay

Gay-Owned ♀♂

A Small Inn with a National Reputation

Since 1988, **The Inn At Swifts Bay** has gained national recognition as one of the finest accommodations in the beautiful San Juan Islands of Washington State. This elegant country home sits on three wooded acres with a private beach nearby. The inn has five quiet and romantic guest rooms, three with private baths and fireplaces. The living room also has a fireplace and the den has over 300 videos to choose from. After a workout and sauna in the exercise studio, relax in the hot tub located at the edge of the woods — we provide robes and slippers. Here's what others say about the inn.

"The most memorable part of the trip...a stay at Inn At Swifts Bay...the setting is beautiful and serene, the accommodations excellent, and the food of gourmet quality!" — *San Francisco Sunday Chronicle-Examiner*

"Stateroom elegant." — *Vogue*

"Entrust yourself to the warm hospitality of the Inn At Swifts Bay. In the morning, one of the greatest pleasures of your stay awaits, a breakfast that is famous island-wide!" — *Brides Magazine*

"Those who appreciate luxury and superb cuisine will find the Inn At Swifts Bay to their liking. The Tudor-style inn is classy, stylish and oh, so comfortable...a breakfast that is nothing short of sensational!" — *West Coast Bed & Breakfast Guide*

Inn Places Reader Commment: "The inn is impeccably and tastefully decorated. Everything is done with warmth and quality. All of your needs and desires are met before you know what you want. The inn has a sense of class I have dreamed about, but have never found."

Address: Lopez Island,, WA 98261
Tel: (360) 468-3636, **Fax:** (360) 468-3637.
E-mail: inn@swiftsbay.com **URL:** www.swiftsbay.com

Type: Bed & breakfast inn.
Clientele: Mostly straight clientele with a gay/lesbian following
Transportation: By car ferry from Anacortes or daily plane from Seattle or Anacortes. Pick up from airport, ferry dock, or marina.
To Gay Bars: Drive 1 hr to Bellingham or Everett. 1-1/2 hrs to Seattle bars.
Rooms: 2 rooms, 3 suites with queen beds.
Bathrooms: 3 private shower/toilets & 1 shared bath/shower/toilet.
Meals: Full gourmet breakfast.
Vegetarian: Dietary restrictions accommodated.
Complimentary: Sherry in living room. Fridge with mineral waters, microwave popcorn, tea & apples.
Dates Open: All year.
High Season: May-Oct.
Rates: $95-$175.
Credit Cards: MC, Visa, Discover, Amex.
Rsv'tns: Preferred.
To Reserve: Travel agent or call direct.
Minimum Stay: Only on holiday weekends.
Parking: Ample free off-street parking.
In-Room: Maid service. Room 5 has TV, VCR & stereo.
On-Premises: Telephone in library, VCR with film library, fax, refrigerator with ice & mineral water.
Exercise/Health: Hot tub & massage (by appointment only), exercise studio & sauna
Swimming: Ocean or lake (very cold!).
Sunbathing: On beach, patio or lawn.
Nudity: Permitted in the hot tub.
Smoking: Not permitted inside.
Pets: Not permitted.
Handicap Access: No.
Children: Not permitted.
Languages: English.
Your Host: Rob, Mark & Dan.

IGLTA

INN PLACES® 1998

535

Equinox Inn

Gay/Lesbian ♀♂

Equinox Inn is situated on 2-1/2 acres in a serene natural wooded setting on the Tulilap Indian reservation. This two-bedroom Northwest-style inn features contemporary furnishings mixed with antiques. Sleep in The Wizard's Nook under the eves or in The Beltane, a sunny spacious room with luxury bath, aromatherapy and candlelight. The local area is great for canoeing in sheltered waters or try your hand at pier fishing or, in season, crabbing and clamming. Nearby attractions include the Tulilap tribal center, while shopping, dining and the Tulilap Casino are a 15-30 minute's drive from the inn.

Address: 13522 12th Ave NW, Marysville, WA **Tel:** (360) 652-1198.

Type: Bed & breakfast.
Clientele: Mostly gay & lesbian with some straight clientele
Transportation: Car is best. Pick up available, please inquire.
To Gay Bars: A 30 minute drive.
Rooms: 2 rooms with double or king beds.

Bathrooms: Private bath/toilets.
Meals: Full breakfast. Picnic lunch or Medieval supper at extra cost.
Vegetarian: Available upon request.
Complimentary: Before-dinner wine.
Dates Open: All year.
High Season: Jun-Aug.

Rates: $85-$95.
Credit Cards: Visa, MC, Discover.
Rsv'tns: Required.
To Reserve: Call direct.
Parking: Ample on-street parking.
In-Room: Black & white TV.
On-Premises: TV lounge, meeting rooms.

Exercise/Health: Massage (can be booked at time of reservation).
Swimming: Puget Sound & lake on premises, lake nearby.
Sunbathing: On common sun decks.
Smoking: Permitted on deck.

Shakti Cove Cottages

Q-NET Gay/Lesbian ♀♂

Experience the Peacefulness of Shakti Cove

Though much of the Long Beach peninsula is heavily touristed, you'll find Ocean Park much quieter. *Shakti Cove Cottages* are secluded on three wooded acres. They're rustic, but have all the amenities you'll require. Don't expect chic, but DO expect quiet, privacy and the sound of the ocean. It's a five-minute walk over a footpath to the beach. Stroll in search of sand dollars, go hiking in a wildlife refuge, or browse the many antique shops nearby. An easy drive from Seattle or Portland, it's a good place to kick back and relax.

Address: PO Box 385, Ocean Park, WA 98640 **Tel:** (360) 665-4000.

Type: Cottages.
Clientele: Mainly gay & lesbian with some straight clientele
Transportation: Car is best.
To Gay Bars: 2-1/2 hours to Portland, Oregon.
Rooms: 10 cottages with

queen beds.
Bathrooms: All private.
Dates Open: All year.
High Season: June, July, August.
Rates: $60-$70.
Discounts: October-March 3 nights for 2.
Credit Cards: MC, Visa.

Rsv'tns: Suggested.
To Reserve: Call direct.
Minimum Stay: Required during holidays.
Parking: Ample free covered parking.
In-Room: Color TV, kitchen, refrigerator.

Swimming: 5 min walk to ocean beach.
Sunbathing: On the beach.
Smoking: Permitted.
Pets: Permitted.
Handicap Access: No.
Children: Permitted.
Languages: English.
Your Host: Liz & Celia.

Oyster Bay

Q-NET Gay-Owned & -Operated ♀♂

We Don't Mind if You're Straight, As Long As You Act Gay in Public

Parade through the tunnel of trees to *Oyster Bay*, a spectacular custom log home in serene, park-like surroundings. Our home boasts 364 feet of waterfront and overlooks Totten Inlet and the Black Hills. Built from handcrafted logs, the house also features a carved stairway, a 35-foot stone fireplace and decks galore! *Oyster Bay's* beautiful rooms are furnished with queen-sized beds and down comforters. We offer complete privacy, combined with a casual air, to ensure our guests' ultimate comfort, and we look forward to your special requests, whether it's dinner, flowers, or champagne. While relaxing in a hot bath choose from our complimentary selection of bath oils and soak and massage creams, then lounge on the private decks in our Turkish robes, followed by a wonderful gourmet meal from our resident executive chef.

Oyster Bay is great for couples or groups of friends who just want to get away. While staying at *Oyster Bay*, trail ride on our beautiful Arabian horses (weather permitting), or just visit the barn and play with the babies. Boating, kayaking, fishing, biking and hiking are all within a 20-minute drive. Many other outdoor options are available, including ocean beaches and Hood Canal (40 minutes from us by car), or exploring the beautiful Olympic Peninsula with its mountains and rainforests. The Little Creek Casino is five minutes away. We're one hour from Seattle or Portland — let us chauffer you to either city for the ultimate shopping experience. Please call us for specials and discount rates.

Address: 2830 Bloomfield Rd, Shelton, WA **Tel:** (360) 427-7643.

Type: Bed & breakfast.
Clientele: Mostly gay & lesbian with some straight clientele
Transportation: Car is best.
To Gay Bars: 20 min drive.
Rooms: 3 rooms with single or queen beds.
Bathrooms: 2 shared bath/shower/toilets.
Meals: Expanded continental breakfast.
Vegetarian: Available upon request.

Complimentary: Sherry in room, tea, coffee, imported chocolates, bath oils, soaks, massage creams.
Dates Open: All year.
High Season: May/Sept.
Rates: $85-$140.
Discounts: Call for specials & discount rates.
Rsv'tns: Recommended.
To Reserve: Call direct.
Parking: Ample, free off-street parking.

In-Room: Maid service.
On-Premises: Telephone, fireplace, private decks, TV lounge w/ satellite TV, video tape, reading & music libraries, foosball table, board games, picnic area, kitchen, executive chef on premises.
Exercise/Health: Hot tub & garden room by Spring '98. Arabian horses & riding instruction.
Swimming: Puget Sound nearby.

Sunbathing: On private sun decks.
Nudity: Permitted under certain conditions, see manager.
Smoking: Permitted on decks & porches.
Pets: Not permitted.
Handicap Access: No.
Children: No.
Languages: English, Italian.
Your Host: Chet & Ingrid.

INN PLACES® 1998

UNITED STATES

WASHINGTON • OLYMPIA

537

Foxglove Cottage

Woman-Owned & -Operated ♀♂

...an island within an island

Timelessness, peace and solitude distinguish this tasteful one-bedroom cottage in a tranquil cedar grove on Orcas Island's beautiful northern shore, built from turn-of-the-century timbers from the old Island Church. From under plump quilts, you might see deer grazing just outside your window as you lazily awaken to the forest's melodious welcome. *Foxglove Cottage* combines the dual advantages of complete privacy and self-sufficiency with easy, walking-distance proximity to spectacular beach sunsets and the unhurried seaside rhythms of quaint Eastsound village. Come for sustenance, rejuvenation and sanctuary.

Address: Rt 1, Box 1238, Eastsound, WA 98245 **Tel:** (360) 376-5444 (Tel/Fax). **E-mail:** shull@fidalgo.net

Type: Guesthouse cottage.
Clientele: Gay & lesbian. Good mix of men & women
Transportation: Car is best. Free pick up from airport.
Rooms: 1 cottage with single or queen beds.
Bathrooms: Private bath/shower/toilet.
Vegetarian: 1 mile to organic food store & several restaurants with vegetarian fare.
Complimentary: Tea & coffee. Full kitchen stocked with condiments & other basics.
Dates Open: All year.
High Season: Jun-Sept.
Rates: $85 per night.
Discounts: Weekly rate 10% off on 7 night stay.
Rsv'tns: Required. Book early, fills quickly in summer.
To Reserve: Call direct.
Minimum Stay: 2 nights weekends, 3 nights holiday weekends.
Parking: Ample off-street parking.
In-Room: Color cable TV, telephone. Full kitchen with all appliances, coffeemaker, microwave, etc.
Exercise/Health: Nearby gym, weights, Jacuzzi, sauna, massage.
Sunbathing: On private deck & grounds. Quiet pebble beach nearby.
Smoking: Permitted outside only.
Pets: Not permitted.
Handicap Access: No.
Children: Not especially welcome.
Languages: English & Spanish.

Rose Cottage

Women ♀

Orcas Island, Gem of the San Juans

Rose Cottage is a cozy, private waterfront sanctuary for two on Orcas Island. It has a spectacular sunrise view of Mount Baker, a sunny deck and a long, private pebble beach. Situated above an artist's studio, it nestles among old firs and looks over fragrant vegetable and flower gardens and meandering lawns that end down at the beach. Orcas has excellent kayaking, biking, fishing, hiking and freshwater swimming. Moran State Park is within five miles. The local village, Eastsound, handy for groceries, restaurants and theater, is just under two miles away.

Address: Rt 2, Box 951, Eastsound, WA 98245 **Tel:** (360) 376-2076.
E-mail: lal@fidalgo.net **URL:** www.pacificws.com/rosecottage

Type: Guesthouse.
Clientele: Mostly women with men welcome.
Transportation: Car is best. Free pick up from airport.
To Gay Bars: 80 miles north to Vancouver, BC or 80 miles south to Seattle, WA.
Rooms: 1 cottage with double feather bed.
Bathrooms: Private shower/toilet.
Vegetarian: Organic food store & several restaurants with vegetarian meals 2 miles away.
Complimentary: Tea, coffee, cookies & flowers. (Fresh eggs when the hens are laying!)
Dates Open: All year.
High Season: Jun through Sept.
Rates: Summer $85 per night. Winter $75 per night.
Discounts: Weekly rates 10% discount.
Rsv'tns: Required.
To Reserve: Travel agent or call direct.
Minimum Stay: 2 nights weekends & 3 nights holiday weekends.
Parking: Off-street parking for one car.
In-Room: Kitchen, refrigerator & coffee/tea-making facilities.
On-Premises: Deck.
Exercise/Health: Gym, weights, sauna, steam & massage nearby.
Swimming: Ocean beach on premises. Pool & lake nearby.
Sunbathing: At the beach & on private sun deck.
Nudity: Permitted on private deck with discretion.
Smoking: Not permitted.
Pets: Not permitted.
Handicap Access: No.
Children: Not permitted.
Languages: English, French & Italian.

Maple Rose Inn

Q-NET Gay-Owned & -Operated ♀♂

Triple-"A"-Rated: Alternative, Affirming, Aire

On the Olympic Peninsula in northwest Washington State, *The Maple Rose Inn* is your gateway to spectacular Olympic National Park and its rainforest, Washington's Pacific Ocean beaches and to Canada, via Victoria and Vancouver, BC. Our contemporary country inn is serenely set in the Olympic Mountain foothills. We offer spacious common areas in which to relax with a book or view a movie. Take tea in the solarium, use the exercise facilities, soak in the hot tub, or unwind on the deck, perhaps catching a glimpse of the deer that frequent our "backyard."

Address: 112 Reservoir Rd, Port Angeles, WA 98363
Tel: (360) 457-ROSE (7673), (800) 570-2007.
E-mail: maplerose@tenforward.com   **URL:** www.northolympic.com/maplerose

Type: Bed & breakfast.
Clientele: Mostly straight with a gay/lesbian following
Transportation: Car is best, pick up from ferry dock.
To Gay Bars: Nearest gay bars in Seattle or Victoria.
Rooms: 2 rooms, 3 suites with single, double, queen or king beds.
Bathrooms: 5 private bath/shower/toilet.
Meals: Expanded or full continental breakfasts.

Vegetarian: Vegan available on request & nearby.
Complimentary: Fresh coffee & tea in room, soft drinks.
Dates Open: All year.
High Season: Memorial Day-Labor Day.
Rates: Summer $79-$147, winter $69-$127.
Discounts: 3rd night, 1/2 off.
Credit Cards: MC, Visa, Amex.
To Reserve: Travel agent or call direct.

Parking: Ample off-street parking.
In-Room: Telephone, ceiling fans, color cable TV, VCR, kitchen, refrigerator, coffee & tea-making facilities, maid & laundry service.
On-Premises: Meeting rooms, TV lounge, video tape library.
Exercise/Health: Jacuzzi, massage, exercise equipment.
Swimming: Nearby pool, ocean, river, lake.

Sunbathing: Ample deck space.
Smoking: Permitted outside & on ample covered porch space.
Pets: 1 room allows a dog. Kennel available $15/day.
Handicap Access: No.
Children: Welcome if well-behaved & supervised at all times.
Languages: English, a little Spanish.
Your Host: Geoff & Darryl.

IGLTA

Ravenscroft Inn

Gay-Friendly ♀♂

SEE SPECIAL PAGE 32 COLOR SECTION

Take a Short Trip to Far Away...

One of the most romantic hideaways in the Pacific Northwest is located high on a bluff overlooking historic Port Townsend, the Olympic Peninsula's Victorian seaport. The *Ravenscroft Inn* is noted for its colonial style, a replication of a historic Charleston single house.

The Inn offers a unique combination of colonial hospitality, mixed with a casual air that spells comfort to its guests. The hosts take great pleasure in looking after their guests' special requests, whether it's dinner, theatre, concert reservations, or arranging for flowers or champagne, all are carried out with ease and alacrity.

continued next page

INN PLACES® 1998

539

While staying at the *Ravenscroft Inn,* you can explore the Olympic National Park, walk the seven mile sand spit at Dungeness or hike through North America's only rainforest. Port Townsend and its environs meets all your vacation requirements offering scenic beauty, theatre, unparalleled dining, boating, biking, fishing, kayaking and hiking. Top this off with a delectable breakfast and fresh roasted gourmet coffee, served each morning. **Guest Comment:** "There was never a detail left unattended."

Address: 533 Quincy St, Port Townsend, WA 98368
Tel: (360) 385-2784, (800) 782-2691, **Fax:** (360) 385-6724.

Type: Bed & breakfast.
Clientele: Mainly straight with a gay & lesbian following
Transportation: Car is best. Free pick up from Port Townsend Airport (from Seattle via Port Townsend Airways).
To Gay Bars: 2 hrs by car.
Rooms: 8 rooms & 2 suites with single, queen or king beds.
Bathrooms: 4 private bath/shower/toilets & 5 private shower/toilets.

Meals: Full breakfast.
Vegetarian: Available on request. When making reservation, all dietary restrictions addressed.
Complimentary: Sherry, coffee, tea, set-up service, juices.
Dates Open: All year.
High Season: May 15-Oct 15.
Rates: $68-$175 May 15-Oct 15, $65-$145 Oct 16-May 14.

Discounts: Single discount.
Credit Cards: MC, Visa, Amex, Discover.
Rsv'tns: Required.
To Reserve: Call direct.
Minimum Stay: Some weekends, special holidays & special events.
Parking: Ample free off-street parking.
In-Room: Color TV on request, maid service.
On-Premises: Meeting room, library, great room.

Exercise/Health: Soaking tub in suite, gym available, weights, Jacuzzi, sauna, steam & massage at nearby Athletic Club.
Swimming: At local school pool.
Sunbathing: On common sun decks & at beach.
Smoking: Permitted on outdoor balconies only.
Pets: Not permitted.
Children: Permitted over 12 years of age.
Languages: English.

Bacon Mansion
Gay-Friendly ♀♂

Seattle's Finest B&B for Sun (and Rain!) Lovers!

The Bacon Mansion is an elegant English Tudor house in the Harvard-Belmont Historical District. Here in Capitol Hill, one of Seattle's most exciting neighborhoods, dining, sightseeing, nightlife and boutiques are just a few blocks away. A variety of well-appointed accommodations, from moderate rooms to suites and even a carriage house, warmly welcome every guest. Eight rooms have private baths. We have immense, beautifully decorated day rooms and a large, private, partially-covered patio for sun (and rain!) lovers. Don't miss it!

Address: 959 Broadway East, Seattle, WA 98102
Tel: (206) 329-1864, (800) 240-1864, **Fax:** (206) 860-9025.
URL: http://www.site-works.com/bacon

Type: Bed & breakfast guesthouse.
Clientele: 40% gay & lesbian & 60% straight clientele.
Transportation: Shuttle

Express from airport, taxi from train.
To Gay Bars: Two blocks to famous Elite Tavern on Broadway.
Rooms: 7 rooms & 3 suites with double or queen beds.

Bathrooms: Private: 4 shower/toilet, 4 full baths. 2 shared full baths.
Meals: Buffet breakfast.
Vegetarian: Always available.

Complimentary: Tea, coffee, mints on pillow.
Dates Open: All year.
High Season: May through October.
Rates: Summer $84-$134, winter $72-$124.

Discounts: 10% on stays of over 6 nights, winter only.
Credit Cards: MC, Visa, Amex, Discover.
Rsv'tns: Required.
To Reserve: Call direct.
Minimum Stay: Required.
Parking: Ample, off-street parking.
In-Room: Color TV, telephone & maid service.
On-Premises: Meeting rooms, refrigerator & fax.
Exercise/Health: Nearby gym, weights & massage.
Swimming: At nearby pool & lake.
Sunbathing: On patio & common sun deck.
Smoking: Permitted outside only.
Pets: Not permitted.
Handicap Access: One suite accessible.
Children: Permitted in some rooms only.
Languages: English.
Your Host: Daryl.

Bed & Breakfast on Broadway

Gay-Friendly 50/50 ♀♂

Gleaming chandeliers, antiques and Oriental rugs grace the interior of *Bed & Breakfast on Broadway*. This distinctive 1901 Pacific Northwest-style house is filled with antiques and art objects. Original paintings and contemporary works of art by Northwest artists, as well as our own resident artist, Russ Lyons, are on display throughout the house. Our quiet and intimate B&B features four charming guest rooms with private bath, and a scrumptious continental breakfast is served daily. We're withing walking distance of the area's restaurants & shops.

Address: 722 Broadway E., Seattle, WA 98102
Tel: (206) 329-8933,
Toll-free: (888) 329-8933,
Fax: (206) 726-0918.

Type: Bed & breakfast.
Clientele: 50% gay & lesbian & 50% straight clientele
Transportation: Car, taxi or Super Shuttle.
To Gay Bars: 1 block.
Rooms: 4 rooms with queen beds.
Bathrooms: 4 private bath/toilets.
Meals: Expanded continental breakfast.
Vegetarian: Available upon request.
Dates Open: All year.
High Season: May-Sept.
Rates: Summer $95-$115, winter $85-$105.
Credit Cards: All major credit cards.
Rsv'tns: Recommended 2-3 weeks in advance.
To Reserve: Call direct.
Minimum Stay: 2 nights on weekends, 3 nights on holidays.
Parking: Limited off-street parking.
In-Room: Color cable TV, maid service. 2 rooms with private deck.
Exercise/Health: Nearby gym, weights.
Swimming: Nearby pool, ocean, lake.
Smoking: Smoke-free.
Pets: Not permitted.
Handicap Access: No.
Children: No.
Languages: English.
Your Host: Don & Russ.

Capitol Hill Inn

Gay-Friendly 50/50 ♀♂

You Can't Be Any Closer

Capitol Hill Inn, an elegantly restored 1903 Queen Anne, delights guests with treasures from a bygone era. Elaborate restoration details include custom-designed wall coverings, period chandeliers, and original, intricately carved wood mouldings. Rooms are lavishly furnished with European antiques, brass beds and down comforters, which are especially cozy on crisp, Seattle nights. A sumptuous

continued next page

INN PLACES® 1998 541

breakfast includes such items as blintzes, lox and bagels, quiche and fresh fruit. There are issues of *NY Times*, books, and magazines in the parlor and AAA has given us a 3 diamond rating. We're six blocks from the Convention Center. Recommended: AAA 3 diamonds, Best Places Pacific Northwest, Best Places to Kiss. Member: Seattle Visitors & Convention Bureau, Seattle B&B Assn.

Address: 1713 Belmont Ave, Seattle, WA 98122
Tel: (206) 323-1955, **Fax:** (206) 322-3809. **URL:** www.capitolhillinn.com

Type: Bed & breakfast.
Clientele: 50% gay & lesbian & 50% straight clientele
Transportation: Airport shuttle $14 per person or taxi approx. $30.
To Gay Bars: 1 block.
Rooms: 6 rooms with single, double, queen or king beds.

Bathrooms: All private bathrooms, 2 rooms have private 1/2 baths & shared hall shower.
Meals: Full breakfast.
Vegetarian: Available upon request.
Dates Open: All year.
Rates: $89-$160.
Discounts: 10% in off-season, winter only.

Credit Cards: MC, Visa, Amex.
Rsv'tns: Recommended.
To Reserve: Call direct.
Parking: Free parking.
In-Room: Maid service. Americana & Sherlock Holmes suites have fireplace, Jacuzzi & queen beds.
On-Premises: Parlors, living room, public telephone.

Exercise/Health: Jacuzzis in two suites.
Swimming: At downtown health club.
Smoking: Permitted on the porch or outdoors.
Pets: Not permitted.
Handicap Access: No, stairs.
Children: Not permitted.
Languages: English.
Your Host: Katie & Joanne.

Chambered Nautilus Bed & Breakfast Inn   Gay-Friendly ♀♂

A Classic Seattle-style Inn

Welcome to *Chambered Nautilus*, a classic Seattle-style B&B inn combining the warmth of a country inn with excellent access to the city's theaters, bars, restaurants and shopping. An elegant 1915 Georgian mansion, it has fine views of the Cascade Mountains and is perched on a peaceful hill in Seattle's University district. Guest rooms are large, airy and comfortably furnished with American and English antiques. A full breakfast completes your stay with fresh fruit, juice, granola, a wide array of entrees and plenty of fresh-roasted Seattle coffee! We welcome guests to share the comfortable, gracious ambiance of this classic inn.

Address: 5005 22nd Ave NE, Seattle, WA 98105
Tel: (800) 545-8459, (206) 522-2536, **Fax:** (206) 528-0898.

Type: Bed & breakfast inn.
Clientele: 80%/20%, mainly straight with a gay & lesbian following
Transportation: Your own car or airport shuttle or taxi to our front door.

To Gay Bars: Less than 10 minutes' drive or 20 minutes' by bus to gay/lesbian bars.
Rooms: 6 rooms.
Bathrooms: All private baths.

Meals: Full breakfast.
Vegetarian: On request.
Complimentary: Afternoon & evening tea and home-made cookies.
Dates Open: All year.
High Season: May-Oct.

Rates: $79-$109.
Discounts: Winter rates available. Discounts available to U. of Washington visiting faculty, off-season only.

FERRARI GUIDES™

Credit Cards: MC, Visa, Amex.
Rsv'tns: Strongly recommended (6-8 weeks in season), 1 week cancellation policy.
To Reserve: Call direct.
Minimum Stay: 3 days on holiday weekends, 2 on summer weekends.

Parking: Adequate free on-street parking.
In-Room: Maid service, clock radio, down comforters, bathrobes, bottled water & resident teddy bears. 4 rooms have porches.
On-Premises: Meeting rooms, living room w/ fireplace, sun porch, large yard & garden, library, guest refrigerator, phone & fax available.
Exercise/Health: Spa & gym nearby.
Swimming: Lake swimming nearby.
Sunbathing: On room porches with discretion.

Smoking: No smoking in the inn. Permitted outside in garden only.
Pets: Not permitted.
Handicap Access: No.
Children: Over 8 years of age & only by prior arrangement.
Languages: English & French.
Your Host: Joyce & Steve.

Gaslight Inn

Q-NET Gay/Lesbian ♀♂

SEE SPECIAL PAGE 31 COLOR SECTION

Welcome to *Gaslight Inn,* a Seattle four-square house built in 1906. In restoring the inn, we have brought out the home's original turn-of-the-century ambiance and warmth, while keeping in mind the additional conveniences and contemporary style needed by travelers in the nineties. The interior is appointed in exacting detail, with strikingly rich, dark colors, oak paneling, and an enormous entryway and staircase.

Gaslight Inn's comfortable and unique rooms and suites are furnished with quality double or queen-sized beds, refrigerator and television. Additional features for your special needs, such as private bath and phone service, are available in some rooms. Some rooms also have decks with fabulous views or fireplaces. The living room, with its large oak fireplace, is always an inviting room, as is the library. Through the late spring and summer, we encourage you to relax and unwind at poolside with a glass of wine after a long, busy day. This private, in-ground, heated pool with several decks and interesting plant arrangements, is found at the back of the inn.

Gaslight Inn is convenient to central Seattle's every attraction: Volunteer Park, City Center, and to a plethora of gay and lesbian bars, restaurants and retail stores in the Broadway district. All of us at *Gaslight Inn* send you a warm advance welcome to Seattle.

Address: 1727 15th Ave, Seattle, WA 98122 **Tel:** (206) 325-3654, **Fax:** (206) 328-4803.
E-mail: innkeepr@gaslight-inn.com
URL: www.gaslight-inn.com

continued next page

INN PLACES® 1998

UNITED STATES — **SEATTLE • WASHINGTON**

Type: Guesthouse.
Clientele: Mostly gay/lesbian with some straight clientele
Transportation: Shuttle Express from airport $15. (206) 286-4800 to reserve ride.
To Gay Bars: 2 blocks to men's bars, 3 blocks to women's bars.
Rooms: 9 doubles, 7 suites.
Bathrooms: 11 private, others share.
Meals: Expanded continental breakfast.
Complimentary: Coffee, tea & juices, fresh fruit, pastries.
Dates Open: All year.
High Season: Summer.
Rates: $68-$158.
Credit Cards: MC, Visa, Amex.
Rsv'tns: Recommended at least 2 weeks in advance.
To Reserve: Call direct.
Minimum Stay: 2 days on weekends, 3 days on holidays.
Parking: Ample on-street & off-street parking.
In-Room: Color TV, maid service & refrigerator.
On-Premises: Meeting rooms, living room, library, public telephone.
Swimming: Seasonal heated pool.
Sunbathing: On private or common sun decks or at poolside.
Smoking: Permitted on decks & porches only.
Pets: Not permitted.
Handicap Access: No.
Children: Not permitted.
Languages: English.
Your Host: Trevor, Stephen & John.

IGLTA

Landes House

Gay/Lesbian ♀♂

Landes House is an historic turn-of-the-century home a short walk from the shops and restaurants of the popular Broadway district. It is named for Bertha Landes, Seattle's only woman mayor, who was elected in 1926. The house has a warm and inviting ambiance, large gracious day rooms, elaborate woodwork and a private garden courtyard with hot tub. Most rooms have private baths, and several have private decks with views of Seattle's skyline, Puget Sound and the Olympic Mtns.

Address: 712 11th Ave E, Seattle, WA 98102
Tel: (206) 329-8781, (888) 329-8781,
Fax: (206) 324-0934.

Type: Bed & breakfast.
Clientele: Mostly gay/lesbian with some straight clientele
Transportation: For airport shuttle, call 622-1424 or (800) 942-0711.
To Gay Bars: 2-10 blocks to most men's & women's bars.
Rooms: 10 rooms & 1 apartment with queen or king beds.
Bathrooms: 9 private, others share.
Meals: Expanded continental breakfast.
Vegetarian: Always available, 3 blocks to The Gravity Bar.
Complimentary: Coffee, tea, summer beverages.
Dates Open: All year.
High Season: April-October.
Rates: Winter $68-$180, summer $70-$180.
Discounts: 7th night free.
Credit Cards: MC, Visa.
Rsv'tns: Strongly suggested (6-8 weeks in season).
To Reserve: Call direct.
Minimum Stay: 2 nights on weekends, 3 on holidays.
Parking: Adequate free off-street parking.
In-Room: Color TV, telephone, maid service, ceiling fans.
On-Premises: Laundry facilities.
Exercise/Health: Hot tub.
Swimming: Lake & beach nearby.
Sunbathing: On private & common sun decks.
Nudity: Permitted in hot tub.
Smoking: Permitted (Non-smoking rooms available).
Pets: Not permitted.
Handicap Access: No.
Children: Not permitted.
Languages: English.
Your Host: Tom, Dave & Jim.

Enchanted Blue Wave Bed & Breakfast

Q-NET Lesbian-Owned & -Operated ♀

Celebrating Our 15th Year Filled With Women!

Come be pampered at *The Wave*, a luxurious Victorian oceanfront mansion. Our amenities include an Italian marble fireplace, antique furnishings and a Baldwin concert grand piano. There is also a games room with pool table and big-screen TV, VCR and movies, a fitness room, as well as an outdoor spa with private deck and an English garden sun deck with BBQ. Scrumptious breakfasts are served, and we offer complimentary champagne or sparkling juice for your celebrations. Visit our website for a list of local events. Discover what thousands of women all over the world have — an elegant place of our own, a decadent haven for traveling women.

Address: PO Box 147, 1004 41st Place, Seaview, WA 98644
Tel: (360) 642-3471, **Fax:** (360) 533-5371.
E-mail: bluewave@mailexcite.com **URL:** www.enchantedbluewave.com

Type: Bed & breakfast guesthouse inn.
Clientele: Women only
Transportation: Car.
To Gay Bars: 100 miles to Seattle & Portland gay bars.
Rooms: Rooms with single, double, queen or king beds.
Bathrooms: Private: 1 bath/toilet. Shared: 2 bath/shower/toliets, 2 WCs only.
Meals: Expanded continental breakfast.
Vegetarian: Always available on request.
Complimentary: Bottle of champagne or sparkling juice, tea, coffee, cocoa.
Dates Open: All year.
High Season: Jun-Oct.
Rates: Winter $60-$85, summer $60-$95.
Discounts: Winter weekdays stay 2 nights, get 3rd night free.
Credit Cards: MC, Visa.
Rsv'tns: Required, but walk-ins welcome.
To Reserve: Call direct.
Minimum Stay: 2 nights weekends, 3 nights holiday weekends.
Parking: Ample free parking.
On-Premises: Telephone, TV lounge, color cable TV, VCR, sound system, video tape library, games room, kitchen, refrigerator, coffee & tea-making facilities.
Exercise/Health: Gym, Jacuzzi.
Swimming: Ocean on premises.
Sunbathing: Poolside, on private & common sun decks, on patio & at beach.
Nudity: Permitted in outdoor hot tub with private deck.
Smoking: Permitted outdoors on decks, 3 rooms are non-smoking.
Pets: No.
Handicap Access: Stairs required outdoors. 1 ground floor guestroom.
Children: Well-behaved younger girls welcome, but place is set up for women.
Languages: English.

The Gallery Suite

Gay-Friendly 50/50 ♀♂

Art by the Sea

Escape to Langley for a quiet, romantic weekend. Enjoy our regional contemporary art collection and the island's beautiful sunsets. This quaint Victorian town has three fine restaurants, art galleries, shopping, antique shops and many nearby beaches. Come to *The Gallery Suite* for a stay in an artfully-appointed waterfront suite with an unobstructed view of Saratoga Passage and Camano Head. Breathe sea air from the spacious deck. Picturesque, seaside Langley is just outside your door.

Address: PO Box 458, Langley, WA 98260 **Tel:** (360) 221-2978.

Type: Bed & breakfast with art gallery.
Clientele: 50% gay & lesbian & 50% straight clientele.
Transportation: Car, airport shuttle, ferry boat. Pick up from ferry dock.
To Gay Bars: 1 hour to gay/lesbian bars.
Rooms: 1 suite with queen bed.
Bathrooms: 1 private.
Meals: Continental breakfast.
Complimentary: Swiss chocolates, beverages, fruit & cheese.
Dates Open: All year.
High Season: Memorial Day-Labor Day.
Rates: $110 1st night, $90 2nd night & $90 for 3rd & subsequent nights.
Credit Cards: MC, Visa, Amex, Discover.
Rsv'tns: Required, 1 week cancellation policy.
To Reserve: Travel agent or call direct.

continued next page

INN PLACES® 1998

Roseland Guest House & Campground Q-NET Gay-Owned & -Operated ♂

Kick Back & Relax in the West Virginia Mountains

In the northern panhandle of West Virginia, 32 miles south of Wheeling, *Roseland Guest House & Campground* is one mile off a country road at the end of a lane. Our private, secluded mountain location is on 222 acres of rolling mountains and meadows. Clothing is optional throughout and a locked gate at the end of the property ensures your privacy. While retaining many original features, our 19th-century guesthouse features modern conveniences as well as a 42-foot-long Great Room with cathedral ceiling, loft, dining area, kitchen and stunning mountain views. Numerous campsites are scattered throughout and are available for both tenting and campers.

Address: RD 1, Box 185B, Proctor, WV 26055-9703
Tel: (304) 455-3838. **E-mail:** roseland@rcvideo.com

Minimum Stay: 2 nights on holidays, weekends.
Parking: Ample free off-street parking.
In-Room: Maid service, refrigerator, coffee pot, kitchen.
Exercise/Health: Local gym nearby, massage available.
Swimming: Lake & saltwater passage 1/2 hour drive.
Sunbathing: On private sun decks or patio.
Smoking: Permitted on outside deck only.
Pets: Permitted with special permission.
Handicap Access: No.
Children: Not permitted.
Languages: English.

Type: B&B guesthouse & campground with food service, dancing, theme weekends.
Clientele: Men only
Transportation: Car is best.
To Gay Bars: 32 miles.
Rooms: 3 rooms, barracks with single, double or queen beds
Bathrooms: Shared: 2 bath/shower/toilets, 2 outdoor showers for campers.
Campsites: Tent sites, 10
RV parking only, some w/ electric & water.
Meals: Full breakfast, dinner for guesthouse & barracks only.
Vegetarian: Upon request. Advise of any special dietary needs.
Complimentary: Sodas & mixers available.
Dates Open: All year.
High Season: June-Oct with theme weekends.
Rates: Summer $40-$90, winter 10% off.
Discounts: 10% to groups.
Credit Cards: MC, Visa.
Rsv'tns: Preferred 1 week in advance.
To Reserve: Travel agent or call direct.
Minimum Stay: 2 nights on holidays.
Parking: Ample off-street parking.
In-Room: Ceiling fans.
On-Premises: Meeting rooms, TV lounge, video tape library, kitchen.
Exercise/Health: Weights,
Jacuzzi, horseshoes, volleyball, hiking.
Swimming: Pool & pond on premises.
Sunbathing: Poolside & in yard.
Nudity: Permitted throughout facility.
Smoking: Permitted outside only.
Pets: Permitted, must be good around people.
Handicap Access: No.
Children: No.
Languages: English.
Your Host: Daniel.

The Allyn Mansion Inn Gay-Friendly ♀♂

"Inside...the Year is Always 1885" — Country Living Magazine

Grand Prize winner of the Great American Home Awards presented by the National Trust for Historic Preservation and recipient of the Wisconsin Historical Society's Certificate of Commendation for Historic Preservation because of its "exceptionally thorough and meticulous restoration," the *Allyn Mansion* ranks as one of the finest restoration efforts in the nation. Along with walnut woodwork, frescoed ceilings, ten marble fireplaces and other original features, the mansion is completely furnished in authentic Victorian antiques. Guests enjoy the use of three formal parlors and two grand pianos.

Address: 511 E Walworth Ave, Delavan, WI 53115
Tel: (414) 728-9090, **Fax:** (414) 728-0201.
E-mail: joeron@allynmansion.com **URL:** www.allynmansion.com

Type: Bed & breakfast with gift & antique shop.
Clientele: Mostly straight clientele with a gay & lesbian following.
Transportation: Car is best. Airport bus from Chicago or Milwaukee. Pick up from bus.
To Gay Bars: 35 miles.
Rooms: 8 rooms with queen beds.
Bathrooms: 5 private (showers), 3 share 4 baths

(2 showers, 2 tubs).
Meals: Full breakfast.
Vegetarian: Available upon request.
Complimentary: Wine & cheese at 6 pm.
Dates Open: All year.
High Season: May-Feb.
Rates: $125 (2nd floor, queen beds, private bath, fireplace). $100 (3rd floor, queen beds, share 4 baths)
Discounts: 30% 1-person rate weekdays, 20% senior (60+) rate Wed & Thurs.

Credit Cards: MC, Visa.
Rsv'tns: Required.
To Reserve: Call direct. (Travel agents weekdays only.)
Minimum Stay: No Saturday night-only stays (Fri-Sat or Sat-Sun minimum).
Parking: Ample free off-street parking.
In-Room: AC. Some rooms with working fireplace.
On-Premises: Fax & meeting space.

Exercise/Health: Nearby gym, weights, Jacuzzi, sauna, steam & massage.
Swimming: Nearby pool & lake.
Smoking: Strictly forbidden anywhere in the house.
Pets: Not permitted.
Handicap Access: No.
Children: Not especially welcome.
Languages: English & French.
Your Host: Ron & Joe.

Eleven Gables Inn on the Lake Gay-Friendly ♀♂

A Harbour Village Holiday on Lake Geneva

Eleven Gables Inn on the Lake, a quaint lakeside 1847 Carpenter's Gothic inn, offers privacy in a prime resort area, a short lakefront stroll to fine dining, boutiques and entertainment. Fringed by multimillion-dollar estates, this "Newport of the Midwest" lake area is busy in all seasons. Activities include golf, tennis, equestrian activities, huntclubs and stock theatre, as well as magnificent autumn-color tours, biking, hiking, and colder sports during the pristine white snows of winter. Breakfast is served overlooking the lake in the warmer months and before the front drawing room fireplace in winter.

Address: 493 Wrigley Dr, Lake Geneva, WI 53147
Tel: (414) 248-8393, (800) 362-0395.

Type: Bed & breakfast.
Clientele: Mostly straight with a gay/lesbian following
Transportation: Car is best. Limo charter from Milwaukee or O'Hare Airport.
To Gay Bars: 40 miles, a 45-minute drive.
Rooms: 12 (bedrooms,

bridal chamber and 2- & 3-bedroom country cottages).
Bathrooms: All private.
Meals: Sun-Thurs: expanded continental breakfast. Weekends/holidays: full breakfast.

Vegetarian: Limited menus in most restaurants.
Complimentary: Cocktail set ups.
Dates Open: All year.
High Season: June 15-Labor Day.

Rates: $42.50-$110 per person, double occupancy.
Discounts: Sun-Thurs (multiple night discounts) Labor Day-June 15.

continued next page

INN PLACES® 1998   547

Credit Cards: MC, Visa, Amex, Diners, Discover.
Rsv'tns: Required.
To Reserve: Travel agent or call direct.
Minimum Stay: 2-3 nights weekends & holidays year-round.
Parking: Limited off-street parking, 1 car per unit.

In-Room: Fireplaces, down comforters, wet-bar, kitchenettes, TV/VCRs, whirlpools, AC, ceiling fans, courtyard & balcony, private entrances.
On-Premises: Meeting rooms, fax, copy machine, BBQ, bike rental, courtesy phone, private pier, boating,

hiking, fishing.
Exercise/Health: Nearby gym, weights, Jacuzzi, sauna, steam, massage.
Swimming: Lake on premises.
Sunbathing: On private & common sun decks, patio, private pier, at beach.
Smoking: Permitted in pri-

vate courtyards, balconies, pier & in some rooms. Non-smoking rooms available.
Pets: Not permitted.
Handicap Access: Country Cottage is accessible.
Children: Limited occupancy, no cots, rollaways or sleeping bags permitted.
Languages: English.

Chase On The Hill Bed & Breakfast   Gay-Friendly 50/50 ♀♂

Escape to the Country!

The rolling hills of southern Wisconsin are the setting for *Chase On The Hill*, an 1846 farmhouse B&B offering charming accommodations and convenient access to the area's many attractions. Guest rooms are decorated with country antique furnishings, and the master bedroom features skylights, queen bed and a private bath. There are numerous gardens, benches and swings outdoors, along with farm animals on the premises and cats in residence. The surrounding area is rich in bird-watching, fishing, hiking and biking opportunities. We welcome you to our comfortable retreat, easily accessible from Madison, MIlwaukee and Chicago.

Address: 11624 State Road 26, Milton, WI 53563
Tel: (608) 868-6646. **E-mail:** mchase@jvlnet.com

Type: Bed & breakfast.
Clientele: 50% gay & lesbian & 50% straight clientele.
Transportation: Car is best. Free pick up from bus.
To Gay Bars: 35 miles to Madison.
Rooms: 3 rooms with queen, double or trundle beds.

Bathrooms: 1 private bath/ toilet, 1 shared bath/ shower/toilet.
Meals: Full breakfast.
Vegetarian: Vegetarian breakfast served with advance notice.
Complimentary: Afternoon beverages, chocolates on nightstand.
Dates Open: All year.

High Season: Summer.
Rates: $50-$75 all year.
Discounts: For single occupancy.
Credit Cards: MC, Visa, Discover.
Rsv'tns: Required.
To Reserve: Call direct.
Parking: Ample free off-street parking.
On-Premises: AC, meeting rooms, TV lounge.

Swimming: Lakes nearby.
Sunbathing: On the patios.
Smoking: Permitted outdoors only.
Pets: Not permitted.
Handicap Access: No.
Children: Welcome if over 12 years old.
Languages: English, Spanish, elementary German.
Your Host: Michael.

Chanticleer Guesthouse   Q-NET Gay-Friendly 50/50 ♀♂

A Romantic Country Inn Nestled Among the Orchards of Door County

SEE SPECIAL PAGE 32 COLOR SECTION

Welcome to the *Chanticleer*, situated on 30 private acres in picturesque Door County, WI. With over 250 miles of shoreline, 12 lighthouses, 5 state parks and countless antique and gift shops, you're not far from unlimited fun and adventure. The *Chanticleer's* majes-

548   FERRARI GUIDES™

tic maples and delicate fields of wild flowers are a grand sight as you stroll on our nature trail. After your walk, tour our beautiful gardens, lounge poolside or relax on your private terrace overlooking the *Chanticleer's* serene countryside. All deluxe suites include double whirlpools, fireplaces and breakfast delivered to your room.

Address: 4072 Cherry Rd, Sturgeon Bay, WI 54235
Tel: (920) 746-0334.

Type: Bed & breakfast.
Clientele: 50% gay & lesbian & 50% straight clientele.
Transportation: Car.
To Gay Bars: 45 miles or a 50-minute drive to 5 bars in Green Bay.
Rooms: 8 suites (6 with queen & 2 with king beds).
Bathrooms: All private bath/toilet/showers.
Meals: Expanded continental breakfast.
Vegetarian: Our breakfast is vegetarian. Vegetarian restaurants nearby.

Complimentary: Tea, coffee, juice, cookies, fresh fruit & candy.
Dates Open: All year.
High Season: Jun-Oct for summer festivals, fall & pumpkin festivals. Feb-Mar for ski season.
Rates: $115-$175.
Discounts: 10% summer 5 or more days. 10% winter 3 or more days (Sun-Thurs). Weekday specials.
Credit Cards: MC, Visa, Discover.
Rsv'tns: Required. Walk-ins welcome if rooms available.
To Reserve: Call direct.
Minimum Stay: 2 nights on weekends.
Parking: Ample free off-street parking in paved lot.
In-Room: Color TV, VCR, CD & cassette stereo, AC, coffee/tea-making facilities, ceiling fans, refrigerator, fireplace, double whirlpool tub, room & maid service.
On-Premises: Meeting rooms.
Exercise/Health: Sauna on premises. Nearby gym & weights.
Swimming: Heated pool on premises, nearby lake.
Sunbathing: At poolside, on patio & private & common sun decks.
Smoking: Permitted with restrictions. Non-smoking sleeping rooms available.
Pets: Not permitted.
Handicap Access: Yes.
Children: Not especially welcome.
Languages: English.
Your Host: Bryon & Darrin.

Bar H Ranch

Women ♀

The Undiscovered Side of the Grand Tetons

In addition to regularly planned trail riding and horsepacking trips, **Bar H Ranch** offers loft accommodation to guests scheduling their own activities. The newly-remodeled barn loft is quite luxurious with lodgepole pine walls and ceilings, wall-to-wall carpet, and oak floors in kitchen and bath. The modern kitchen is fully-equipped with Jenn Aire range and breakfast bar. The bathroom sports a bathtub with claw feet. Sun yourself on the large deck, use the picnic table and chairs, BBQ, or relax and enjoy the fabulous views. Yellowstone and Grand Teton Nat'l Parks and Jackson Hole are all easy drives from the ranch.

Address: Box 297, Driggs, ID 83422
Tel: (208) 354-2906, (800) 247-1444.

Type: Self-contained, private ranch accommodation on a working cattle ranch.
Clientele: Mostly women with men welcome
Transportation: Car is best. Rental cars available from Jackson Hole or Salt Lake City airports.
Rooms: Loft, tipi or B&B in main house.
Bathrooms: Private bath.

Meals: Full breakfast for B&B only.
Vegetarian: Vegetarian food nearby.
Dates Open: Spring-fall. Closed in winter.
Rates: Loft $90/night, $580/wk. Tipi $50/night, $300/wk. B&B $90/night.
Rsv'tns: Highly recommended.
To Reserve: Call direct.
Minimum Stay: 2 nights in loft.

Parking: Ample off-street parking on ranch.
In-Room: Color TV, VCR, telephone, fully-equipped kitchen, dishwasher, Jenn Aire range with oven, refrigerator.
On-Premises: Deck & BBQ.
Exercise/Health: Horseback riding, hiking, fly fishing, cycling.
Swimming: Nearby river,
lake and public natural hot water pool.
Sunbathing: On private sun deck.
Smoking: Permitted on deck.
Pets: Cat with prior permission, dog may be acceptable.
Handicap Access: No.
Children: Inquire.
Languages: English.
Your Host: Edie & Gloria.

INN PLACES® 1998 549

Fish Creek Lodging

Gay/Lesbian ♀♂

Have it All — While You Get Away from it All

Nestled in the foothills of the Teton Mountain Range, a secluded log cabin offers solitude and natural beauty for a truly peaceful getaway. Enjoy hiking, fishing, skiing, viewing wildlife or just relax. Visit nearby Yellowstone National Park, Grand Teton National Park and Jackson Hole, Wyoming. Fish the Henry's Fork of the Snake River and Warm River, or ski from your doorstep across the rolling meadows and surrounding forests. *Fish Creek Lodging*, a newly remodeled cabin, is fully furnished with everything you need for a perfect vacation.

Address: Warm River, PO Box 833, Ashton, ID 83420-0833 **Tel:** (208) 652-7566.

Type: Log cabin.
Clientele: Gay & lesbian. Good mix of men & women.
Transportation: Rental cars available from Jackson Hole & Idaho Falls, ID airports.
Rooms: Cabin with queen beds.
Bathrooms: All private.

Dates Open: All year.
High Season: Summer & fall.
Rates: Summer $75-$90 per night. Winter $90-$115 per night for 2 people.
Discounts: Weekly & monthly rates.
Rsv'tns: Highly recommended.

To Reserve: Call direct.
Minimum Stay: 2 nights.
Parking: Acres of off-street parking, some covered.
In-Room: All conveniences, full kitchen, TV/VCR, woodstove.
Swimming: Nearby rivers & lakes.

Sunbathing: On patio, private sun decks & 20 acres.
Smoking: Smoking outside only.
Pets: With prior permission.
Handicap Access: No.
Children: Permitted, but not especially welcome.
Languages: English.

Redmond Guest House

Gay-Friendly 50/50 ♀♂

The *Redmond Guest House* is situated on a quiet, residential street, five blocks from Jackson's town square. Guests enjoy privacy in the back garden with barbecue and outdoor furniture. The guest house features lodgepole-pine furniture, a large brick fireplace, color TV and private bath with a queen-sized bed. Guests prepare their own breakfasts. The beautiful Jackson valley has long been a premier vacation destination. Even the Northern Plains Indians journeyed here in summer to gather healing herbs and hunt.

Address: Box 616, Jackson, WY 83001 **Tel:** (307) 733-4003.

Type: Guesthouse.
Clientele: 50% gay & lesbian & 50% straight clientele.
Transportation: Car is best. Free pick up from airport.
Rooms: 1 apartment with single & queen bed.
Bathrooms: Private.

Dates Open: May 1st-September 15th.
High Season: June through September.
Rates: Per night: $110.
Discounts: 10% discount if you mention Inn Places, 10% senior citizen discount.
Rsv'tns: Preferred.
To Reserve: Call direct.

Minimum Stay: 2 nights on weekends, 3 nights on holidays.
Parking: Ample off-street parking.
In-Room: Color cable TV, kitchen, refrigerator, coffee & tea-making facilities.
On-Premises: BBQ & outdoor furniture.

Sunbathing: On the patio.
Smoking: Permitted outside only.
Pets: May be permitted, please inquire.
Handicap Access: No.
Children: Permitted.
Languages: English.
Your Host: Sue Ann

RV & CAMPING INDEX

EUROPE

■ **FRANCE**
DOMME
La Dordogne Camping de
Femmes 46
SOUTHWEST FRANCE - RURAL
Mondès 52
Pitau 53
Roussa 54
Saouis 54
■ **IRELAND**
CORK
Amazonia 63

AUSTRALIA

■ **NEW SOUTH WALES**
BERRY
Tara Country Retreat 133
BINGARA
Hill Nudist Retreat, The 134
■ **QUEENSLAND**
CAIRNS
Witchencroft 150

CARIBBEAN

■ **WEST INDIES**
JAMAICA
Lighthouse Park 199

LATIN AMERICA

■ **MEXICO**
BAJA CALIFORNIA SUR
La Concha Beach Resort 205

CANADA

■ **ONTARIO**
HAMILTON
Cedars Tent & Trailer Park 179
NIAGARA FALLS
Fairbanks House Bed & Breakfast 180

USA

■ **ALASKA**
FAIRBANKS
Alta's Bed and Breakfast 215
■ **ARIZONA**
SEDONA
Paradise by the Creek B&B 225
TUCSON
Montecito House 231
■ **ARKANSAS**
EUREKA SPRINGS
Greenwood Hollow Ridge 234
■ **CALIFORNIA**
RUSSIAN RIVER
Highlands Resort 266
Willows, The 269
SONOMA COUNTY
Whispering Pines B&B 291
■ **FLORIDA**
FORT MYERS
Resort on Carefree Boulevard, The 313
TAMPA
Sawmill Campground 343
■ **HAWAII**
HAWAII - BIG ISLAND
Kalani Oceanside Retreat 350
Wood Valley B&B Inn 355
■ **MAINE**
AUGUSTA
Maple Hill Farm B&B Inn 388
OGUNQUIT
Admiral's Inn & Guesthouse 23
■ **MICHIGAN**
SAUGATUCK
Campit 439
■ **MINNESOTA**
KENYON
Dancing Winds B&B Retreat 442
■ **MONTANA**
YELLOWSTONE NATIONAL PARK AREA
Yellowstone Riverview Lodge B&B 446
■ **NEW HAMPSHIRE**
RANDOLPH
Inn at Bowman a B&B, The 454
■ **NEW JERSEY**
PLAINFIELD
Pillars of Plainfield Bed & Breakfast, The 456
■ **NEW MEXICO**
ALBUQUERQUE
Hateful Missy & Granny Butch's
Boudoir & Manure Emporium 460

INN PLACES® 1998   551

- **NEW YORK**
  ANGELICA
    Jones Pond Campground 470
- **NORTH CAROLINA**
  ASHEVILLE
    Camp Pleiades 482
- **OREGON**
  ROGUE RIVER
    Whispering Pines B & B Retreat 494
- **PENNSYLVANIA**
  NEW MILFORD
  Oneida
    Campground and Lodge 497
  SCRANTON
    Hillside Campgrounds 503

- **TENNESSEE**
  GREENEVILLE
    Timberfell Lodge 512
- **WASHINGTON**
  INDEX
    Wild Lily Ranch 533
- **WEST VIRGINIA**
  WHEELING
    Roseland Guest House & Campground 546

WOMEN'S INDEX

AFRICA
- **SOUTH AFRICA**
  CAPE TOWN
    Owl and the Pussycat, The 33

EUROPE
- **BELGIUM**
  ANTWERP
    Kris's Antwerp Women's B&B 38
- **FRANCE**
  BRITTANY
    Chez Jacqueline 44
  DOMME
    La Dordogne Camping de Femmes 46
  SOUTHWEST FRANCE - RURAL
    Hilltop Cantegrive Farmhouses 51
    Mondès 52
    Roussa 54
    Saouis 54
- **GERMANY**
  BERLIN
    Artemisia, Women Only Hotel 56
  NORTH-RHINE WESTPHALIA AREA
    Berkhöfel 59
  OSTFRIESLAND
    Frauenferienhof Ostfriesland 59
- **IRELAND**
  CORK
    Amazonia 63
- **ITALY**
  ACQUI TERME
    La Filanda Guesthouse 67
  ISOLA D'ELBA
    Casa Scala 68

- **NETHERLANDS**
  AMSTERDAM
    Liliane's Home; GH for Women Only 82
- **UK - ENGLAND**
  BRIGHTON
    Bannings Guest House 102
  ISLE OF WIGHT
    Ridge Cottage 113
- **UK - WALES**
  AMMANFORD - DYFED
    Apple Cottage 130
  SNOWDONIA NATIONAL PARK
    Dewis Cyfarfod 131

AUSTRALIA
- **NEW SOUTH WALES**
  SYDNEY
    Helen's Hideaway 140
- **QUEENSLAND**
  CAIRNS
    Witchencroft1 150

NEW ZEALAND
- **NORTH ISLAND**
  WELLINGTON
    Mermaid, The 162
- **SOUTH ISLAND**
  CHRISTCHURCH
    Bushline Lodge 163

LATIN AMERICA

■ **MEXICO**
PUERTO VALLARTA
Holly's Mexico 211

CANADA

■ **BRITISH COLUMBIA**
VANCOUVER
Hawks Avenue Bed & Breakfast 171
■ **QUEBEC**
MONTREAL
La Douillette 187
Pension Vallières 189

UNITED STATES

■ **ARIZONA**
SEDONA
Paradise by the Creek B&B 225
Paradise Ranch 226
Sappho's Oasis 226
TUCSON
Hills of Gold Bed & Breakfast 230
Montecito House 231
■ **CALIFORNIA**
MENDOCINO COUNTY
Sallie & Eileen's Place 250
PALM SPRINGS
Bee Charmer Inn 252
SAN FRANCISCO
Carl Street Unicorn House 277
SONOMA COUNTY
Asti Ranch 290
■ **DELAWARE**
MILTON
Honeysuckle 297
■ **FLORIDA**
FORT MYERS
Resort on Carefree Boulevard, The 313
KEY WEST
Island Key Courts of Key West, The 324
Rainbow House 22
■ **HAWAII**
HAWAII - BIG ISLAND
Tropical Tune-Ups 354
Wood Valley B&B Inn 355
MAUI
Hale Makaleka 363
■ **LOUISIANA**
NEW ORLEANS
Bywater Bed & Breakfast 378
■ **MAINE**
OGUNQUIT
Heritage of Ogunquit 393
PEMBROKE

Yellow Birch Farm 397
■ **MASSACHUSETTS**
BOSTON
Victorian Bed & Breakfast 405
NORTHAMPTON
Innamorata 409
Tin Roof Bed & Breakfast 409
PROVINCETOWN
Bayview Wharf Apartments 412
Check'er Inn Resort 418
Dusty Miller Inn 420
Gabriel's 422
Gull Walk Inn 423
Pilgrim House Inn 428
Ravenwood Guestrooms & Apartments 430
Windamar House 437
■ **MICHIGAN**
SAUGATUCK
Deerpath Lodge 439
■ **NEW HAMPSHIRE**
BETHLEHEM
Highlands Inn, The 448
FRANCONIA
Bungay Jar 451
■ **NEW MEXICO**
ALBUQUERQUE
Hateful Missy & Granny Butch's
Boudoir & Manure Emporium 460
■ **NEW YORK**
NEW YORK
East Village Bed & Breakfast 478
■ **NORTH CAROLINA**
ASHEVILLE
Camp Pleiades 482
Emy's Nook 482
Mountain Laurel B&B 483
Sophie's Comfort 483
Twenty-Seven Blake Street 484
CHAPEL HILL
Joan's Place 485
FRANKLIN
Rainbow Acres (Honey's) 487
■ **PENNSYLVANIA**
POCONOS
Blueberry Ridge 501
Stoney Ridge 502
■ **WASHINGTON**
ORCAS ISLAND
Rose Cottage 538
SEAVIEW
Enchanted Blue Wave Bed & Breakfast 545
■ **WYOMING**
JACKSON
Bar H Ranch 549

INN PLACES® 1998   **553**

INDEX TO ACCOMMODATIONS

ABC

A Greenwich Village Habitué	475
A St. Louis Guesthouse in Historic Soulard	444
A Touch of Country	531
A Tropic Paradise	368
Abacrombie Badger Bed & Breakfast	400
Abigail's Elegant Victorian Mansion B&B Lodging Ac	238
Abode, Ltd	476
Adams House, The	296
Adelynne's Summit Haus & Summit Haus II	520
Admiral's Inn & Guesthouse	23, 392
Admiral's Landing Guest House	24, 410
Adobe Rose Inn Bed & Breakfast	228
Alden House Bed & Breakfast	390
Alexander Resort	251
Alexander's Guesthouse	314
Allyn Mansion Inn, The	546
Aloha Kauai Bed & Breakfast	355
Alpha Lodge Private Hotel	101
Alta's Bed and Breakfast	215
Amaryllis Guest House, The	127
Amazonia	63
Amelia Island Williams House	308
America's Crossroads	489
Ampersand Guesthouse	411
Amsterdam House BV	72
Amsterdam Toff's	73
Amsterdammertje	402
Anco Hotel-Bar	74
Andrea & Janet's Maui Vacations	359
Anfora's Dreams	360
Anthony's by the Sea	516
Antique Row Bed & Breakfast	498
Anton Boxrud B&B	522
Anuenue Plantation B&B	356
Apple Cottage	130
Apple Orchard Inn of Sedona	224
Applewood Inn and Restaurant	17, 264
Arbor House Inn & Suites	521
Arbour Glen B&B Victorian Inn & Guesthouse	233
ARCO Hotel — Norddeutscher Hof	56
Arco Iris	206
Ardmory House Hotel	129
Aries Guest House	128
Arius Compound	464
Arizona Royal Villa	218
Arizona Sunburst Inn	219
Armadillo Guest House, The	128
Artemisia, Women Only Hotel	56
Arundel Meadows Inn	391
Aspen Lodge	159
Asti Ranch	290
Atherton Hotel	275
Atlantic Shores Resort	315
Atrium/Vista Grande/Mirage	251
Auchendean Lodge Hotel	127
Aura Soma Lava	371
Aurora Winds, An Exceptional B&B Resort	214
Aux Berges	184
Avanti Resort Hotel	252
Bacon Mansion	540
Bahama Hotel, The	309
Balboa Park Inn	271
Balconies, The	155
Bales Mead	123
Banker's Hill Bed & Breakfast	272
Bannings Guest House	102
Banting House	181
Bar H Ranch	549
Barrington's Private Hotel	103
Bathley Guest House	122
Bavarian House, The	241
Bayberry, The	412
Bayview Wharf Apartments	412
Be Yourself Inn — Twin Cities	443
Beach House, The	177
Beach Place, The	273
Beaconlight Guest House, The	24, 413
Beauport Inn and Cafe	393
Beck's Motor Lodge	276
Bed & Breakfast on Broadway	541
Bee Charmer Inn	252
Beech Crescent	99
Bellmont Manor Bed & Breakfast	531
Bello Vista	515
Belvedere	472
Belvedere Heights B&B	511
Berkhöfel	59
Best Western Hawthorne Terrace	372
Big Ruby's Guesthouse	316
Black Duck Inn on Corea Harbor, The	390
Black Tulip Guesthouse	75
Blackbeard's Castle	198
Blair's Original Hana Plantation Houses	361
Bliss Flatlits	33
Blue Parrot Inn	316
Blueberry Ridge	501
Boatslip Beach Club	25, 414
Bobby's Bed/Breakfast	294
Bock's Bed & Breakfast	276
Bonavente, The	345
Bontemps Motel	491
Bourgoyne Guest House	378
Boys On Burgundy	378
Bradford Carver House, The	415
Bradstat Country Hotel	470
Brass Key Guesthouse, The (Key West)	317
Brass Key Guesthouse, The (Provincetown)	416
Brenton, The	302
Brewers House Bed & Breakfast	444
Briars	121
Brickfield Hill Bed & Breakfast Inn	136
Brickfields Terrace	154
Brinley Victorian Inn	503
Brittania and W.E. Mauger Estate B&B	457
Bromptons Guesthouse	115
Bull Lodge	125
Bungalow 't Staaksken	38
Bungay Jar	451
Buoy, The	417

FERRARI GUIDES™

Burnside	180	Cliff House Hotel at the Beach	123
Bushline Lodge	163	Coast Inn	240
Butternut Farm	296	Coconut Grove for Men	319
Bygone Beautys Cottages	135	Colibri Bed & Breakfast	170
Bywater Bed & Breakfast	378	Colonial House Inn	478
Bywater Guest House	379	Colours - The Guest Mansion Key West	320
C&G Bed & Breakfast House	76	Colours at The NEW Penguin Resort & The Mantell Pl	334
Cabana Gardens Bed & Breakfast	298	Columbia Cottage Guest House	170
Calgary Westways Guest House	166	Columns Resort	255
Calhoun House	509	Cooper Island Beach Club	11, 195
Camp Michael B&B	510	Coral Tree Inn	321
Camp Pleiades	482	Corinda's Cottages	153
Campit	439	Cottages, The	34
Candlelight Motel	525	Country Comfort Bed & Breakfast	236
Canyon Club Hotel	253	Country Cousin	526
Cape Schanck Lodge Bed & Breakfast	156	Country Options	448
Capitol Hill Guest House	302	Courtfield Hotel	131
Capitol Hill Inn	541	Courtyard on the Trail	516
Captain Dexter House of Edgartown	407	Coward's Guest House	104
Captain James Preston House	504	Cozy Cactus	224
Captain's House	417	Creffield, The	100
Captain's Quarters	10, 192	Crestow House	109
Carl Street Unicorn House	277	Curry House	321
Carl's Guest House	418		
Carlton Hotel	120		
Caruso Manor	346	**DEF**	
Casa Alegre Bed & Breakfast Inn	229		
Casa Alexio	90	Dancing Winds B&B Retreat	442
Casa Amigos	88	Danner House Bed & Breakfast	179
Casa Aurora	206	Deerpath Lodge	439
Casa de los Arcos	208	Desert Paradise Hotel	256
Casa De Mis Padres	12, 219	Devilstone Oceanfront Inn	388
Casa Fantasia	208	Dewis Cyfarfod	131
Casa Laguna Bed & Breakfast Inn	15, 239	Dexter's Inn	420
Casa Marhaba	89	Divine Lake Nature's Sport & Spa Resort	182
Casa Panorámica	210	Dmitri's Guesthouse	273
Casa Pequena	89	Doanleigh Inn, The	443
Casa Scala	68	Doin' It Right — in Puerto Vallarta	210
Casa Tierra Adobe Bed & Breakfast Inn	230	Dorchester Inn	137
Casitas at Old Town, The	457	Douglas Dunes Resort	439
Castillo Inn	277	Dragon's Den, The	342
Catnaps 1892 Downtown Guesthouse	181	Dunsany Bed & Breakfast	64
Catnaps Private Guest House	103	Dusty Miller Inn	420
Cedars Tent & Trailer Park	179	Duval House	322
Centre Apartments Amsterdam	77	East Village Bed & Breakfast	478
Chalet in the Pines	217	Edgecliffe Hotel, The	112
Chambered Nautilus Bed & Breakfast Inn	542	Edward Hotel	98
Chandler Inn	403	Edward Lodge	147
Chanticleer Guesthouse	32, 548	Eighteen Fifty-Four Bed & Breakfast	510
Charleston Beach B&B	508	Eighteen Twenty-Four James	148
Chase On The Hill Bed & Breakfast	548	El Mirasol Villas	257
Château Cherrier B&B	185	Elephant Springs Hotel	36
Chateau Tivoli	278	Elephant Walk Inn	421
Check'er Inn Resort	418	Eleven Gables Inn on the Lake	547
Chelsea House	318	Ellesmere House	125
Chelsea Mews Guesthouse	476	Embassy Guest House - Condado	193
Chelsea Pines Inn	477	Embassy Inn	303
Cheney Lake Bed & Breakfast	215	Emy's Nook	482
Cherry Grove Beach Hotel	473	Enchanted Blue Wave Bed & Breakfast	545
Chestnutz	254	Equator	322
Cheviot View Guest House	120	Equinox Inn	536
Chez Jacqueline	44	Essex Hotel, The	279
Chicago House, The	419	Estorge House, The	387
Chico Guest House	78	Fairbanks Hotel	216
Christopher Place	512	Fairbanks House Bed & Breakfast	180
City Suites Hotel — Neighborhood Inns of Chicago	373	Fairfield Lodge	64
Claddagh House Bed & Breakfast	174	Fern Falls	18, 265
		Fernie Westways Guest House	167

INN PLACES® 1998

Finns Hotel Pension	42	Hill Nudist Retreat, The	134
Fish Creek Lodging	550	Hillcrest Inn, The	274
Fitch Hill Inn	29, 527	Hills of Gold Bed & Breakfast	230
Fort Recovery Estate	196	Hillside Campgrounds	503
Fountain Inn, The	97	Hilltop Cantegrive Farmhouses	51
Four Kachinas Inn Bed & Breakfast	464	Hodgkinson's Hotel & Restaurant	110
Four-Sixty-Three Beacon Street Guest House	404	Holloway Motel	245
Fourteen Twelve Thalia, A Bed and Breakfast	379	Holly Park House	114
Fox & Hound B&B of New Hope	496	Holly's Mexico	211
Foxglove Cottage	538	Honeysuckle	297
Foxwood Bed & Breakfast, The	166	Honeywood Country Lodge	528
Frankies Guesthouse	65	Horse & Hound Inn, The	451
Frauenferienhof Ostfriesland	59	Hotel Acon	57
Frenchmen Hotel	380	Hotel Aero	78
Furama Hotel Central	137	Hotel Aspen	292
Furama Hotel Darling Harbour	138	Hotel Casa Blanca de Manuel Antonio S.A.	201
		Hotel Celeste Residence	68
		Hotel Central Marais	48

GHI

		Hotel Colours - The Guest Residence San Jose	203
		Hotel de France	44
Gabriel's	422	Hotel des Nations	48
Gallery Suite, The	545	Hotel Elysium	61
Gar-Den Suites	518	Hotel Goldenes Schwert	94
Garden Cottage, The	521	Hotel Honolulu	369
Gaskill House	498	Hotel Kekoldi	204
Gaslight Inn	31, 543	Hotel La Mariposa	202
Gateways Inn	405	Hotel Louxor	49
Gemini House	310	Hotel Mocking Bird Hill	198
George IV Hotel	104	Hotel Monte Vista	218
Gingerbread House Bed & Breakfast	186	Hotel New York	79
Glen Isle Farm Country Inn	499	Hotel Orfeo	80
Glenborough Inn	289	Hotel Piaf	425
Glimmer Inn	380	Hotel Romàntic i La Renaixença	92
Golden Bamboo Ranch	361	Hotel Rosamar	91
Golden Guesthouses	458	Hotel Scalinata di Spagna	69
Governors on Fitzroy B&B	139	Hotel Sonnenhof	60
Gram's Place Bed/Breakfast & Music	342	Hotel the Golden Bear	80
Grandview Inn, The	423	Hotel "The Village"	81
Greater Boston Hospitality	404	Hotel Villa Schuler	70
Green Rose at Scott Point	168	Hotel Wilhelmina	81
Greenways Apartments	152	Hotel Windsor	42
Greenwood Hollow Ridge	234	House at Peregrine's Perspective, The	293
Grim's Manor	496	House on McGill, The	182
Grove Guest House, The	245	Howden Cottage	525
Grünberg Haus Bed & Breakfast	529	Huckleberry Springs	267
Guion House	480	Hudsons Guest House	105
Gull Walk Inn	423	Huelo Point Flower Farm B&B	364
Habana Inn	489	Huff 'n Puff Straw Bale Inn, The	225
Hacienda Antigua Bed and Breakfast	459	Hydrangea House Inn	504
Hale Aloha Guest Ranch	347	Ingram Haus	381
Hale Huelo	362	Inn 1890	280
Hale Kahawai	356	Inn at Applewood, The	474
Hale Kipa 'O Pele	348	Inn at Bowman a B&B, The	454
Hale Makaleka	363	Inn at HighView, The	29, 524
Hale Ohia Cottages	349	Inn at Schoolhouse Creek, The	250
Halfway to Hana House	363	Inn At Swifts Bay	30, 535
Hartley House Inn	270	Inn At The Opera	279
Hateful Missy & Granny Butch's Boudoir & Manure E..	460	INN at Two Village Square, THE	23, 394
Hawks Avenue Bed & Breakfast	171	Inn Essence	242
Heart Seed B&B and Spa	465	Inn Exile	257
Helen's Hideaway	140	Inn of La Mesilla, The	463
Heritage House	424	Inn of the Turquoise Bear	27, 466
Heritage of Ogunquit	393	Inn On Castro	18, 282
Heron House	323	Inn on Fairmount	517
Hibiscus House B&B	343	Inn on the Mexican War Streets, The	500
Highland Dell Inn Bed & Breakfast	265	Inn San Francisco, The	282
Highlands Inn, The	448	Innamorata	409
Highlands Resort	266		

556 FERRARI GUIDES™

INNdulge Palm Springs 258
InnTrigue 258
Interludes 126
Island House 335
Island Key Courts of Key West, The 324
Island Watch B&B 216
Ivy House B&B 402

JKL

Jack & Tom's Maui Condos 365
Jacques' Cottage 267
Jefferson House, The 336
Joan's Place 485
Joluva Guesthouse 204
Jones Pond Campground 470
Kailua Maui Gardens 366
Kalani Oceanside Retreat 350
Kalihiwai Jungle Home 357
Kalorama Guest House at Kalorama Park, The 304
Keating House 274
Kennard Hotel, The 95
Kentucky Holler House 377
King Henry Arms 310
Kingsmead Guest House 98
Kirby House, The 440
Kris's Antwerp Women's B&B 38
Künstler-Pension Sarah Petersen 58
La Casa del Mar 311
La Concha Beach Resort 205
La Conciergerie Guest House 9, 186
La Corsette Maison Inn & The Sister Inn 376
La Dauphine, Residence des Artistes 381
La Dordogne Camping de Femmes 46
La Douillette 187
La Filanda Guesthouse 67
La Posada de Las Palmas 16, 259
La Salamandre 45
La-Te-Da Hotel 325
Lafayette House Bed & Breakfast 445
Lafitte Guest House 382
Lakes Holiday Apartments, The 151
Lakeside B 'n B Tahoe 16, 243
Lamb's Mill Inn 391
Lamplighter Inn & Cottage 426
Landes House 544
Land's End Inn 426
Larry's B & B 221
Las Vegas Private Bed & Breakfast 447
Lavadia 325
Lawley on Guildford, The 157
Le Coureur des Bois 190
Le Montrose Suite Hotel De Gran Luxe 246
Le Parc Hotel 247
Le St. Christophe Bed & Breakfast 188
Le Traversin 189
Lehrkind Mansion Bed & Breakfast 446
Leicester Grange 101
Leigh House 96
Leisure Inn 395
Lighthouse Court 326
Lighthouse Park 199
Liliane's Home; Guesthouse for Women Only 82
Lily Guesthouse 337
Lindenwood Inn 389
Lions Inn, The 383
Little House On The Prairie, The 371

Lodge and The Keep, The 95
Lombard Central, A Super 8 Hotel, The 19, 283
Lotus Guest House 427
Lotus Hotel 37
Lovett Inn, The 519
Lugger Bay Beach Resort 149

MNO

Macarty Park Guest House 383
MacMaster House circa 1895 492
Maes B&B 83
Mallard Guest Houses, The 298
Mangrove House 327
Manor House Boutique Hotel 140
Manor House Inn 389
Mansfield House 129
Maple Hill Farm B&B Inn 388
Maple Rose Inn 539
Marc-James Manor 532
Mark Addy, The 530
Martha's Place 408
Mary Claire II, The 221
Mary Kay's Romantic Whaley Mansion Inn 533
Mas La Bonoty Hotel & Restaurant 43
Mayfair Hotel & Ye Olde Cottage Inne 111
Medina Executive Apartments 141
Medusa Hotel 8, 142
Melville House Inn 505
Mengyuan 147
Mentone Bed & Breakfast 384
Mermaid, The 162
Metro Hotel, The 284
Miami River Inn 337
Middle Creek Run Bed & Breakfast 493
Mill House Inn 341
Mineral Springs Inn 486
Mission San Francisco 212
Mohala Ke Ola B&B Retreat 358
Mondès 52
Montecito House 231
Montrose Inn 520
Moon Over Maine 395
Moore's Creek Inn 441
Morandi alla Crocetta 67
Morrison House 21, 305
Mountain Laurel B&B 483
Mountain Lodge Resort 268
Mr. Mole Bed & Breakfast 401
Mt. Peale Bed & Breakfast Country Inn 522
Napoleon's Retreat Bed & Breakfast 445
Nelson House 171
New Hotel de Lives 40
New Orleans House - Key West 327
New York Bed & Breakfast Reservation Center, The ... 479
New York Hotel, The 115
Newnham SunCatcher Inn 441
Newton Street Station 328
Nine Twelve Barnard Bed & Breakfast 346
Noosa Cove 151
Normandy House 428
Normandy South 338
Notchland Inn, The 452
Noupoort Guest Farm 35
Number Seven Guesthouse 116
Numero Uno Guest House 193
O Canada House 172

Oak Bay Guest House	175	Prospect Hill B&B	488
Oasis, A Guest House	329	Prospect Hill Guest House	506
Ocean Gardens Inn	491	Quinta Maria Cortez	213
Ocean View Villas	191		
Ocean Walk Guest House	194		
Ocean Wilderness	176		

RST

Ogunquit Beach Inn	396	R.B.R. Farms	353
Ogunquit House	396	Rainbow Acres (Honey's),	487
Old Fisher House B&B, The	178	Rainbow House (FL)	22, 331
Old Mill B&B	484	Rainbow House (NZ)	163
Old Town Bed & Breakfast	374	Rainbow Lodge Bed & Breakfast, The	461
On The Beach	197	Rainbow Mountain Resort	501
One Sixty-Three Drummond Street	155	Ramada Hotel West Hollywood	248
One Thirty-Two North Main	474	Rams Head, The	299
Oneida Campground and Lodge	497	Ravenscroft Inn	32, 539
Open Sky B&B	467	Ravenswood Hotel	124
Oregon House, The	495	Ravenwood Guestrooms & Apartments	430
Organic Gardens B&B	289	Red Hill Inn	449
Orongo Bay Homestead	160	Red Lamp Post	401
Orton Terrace	311	Red Rock Inn	523
Our Place Papaikou's B&B	351	Red Squirrel Lodge	124
Owl and the Pussycat, The	33	Redmond Guest House	550
Oyster Bay	537	Regis House	129
		Rehoboth Guest House	300
		Renoir Hotel	19, 285

PQ

		Residence Linareva	165
Pacific Ocean Holidays	369	Resort on Carefree Boulevard, The	313
Palapas in Yelapa	212	Revere House	431
Palenville House	471	Richmond Hotel	339
Pali Kai	358	Ridge Cottage	113
Palm Court Bed & Breakfast	156	Rio Grande House	462
Palms on Las Olas, The	312	Rio Villa Beach Resort	268
Pamalu	352	River Run Bed & Breakfast Inn	481
Paradise by the Creek B&B	225	Riverside Apartments	84
Paradise Ranch	226	Rober House	385
Park Avenue Manor B&B	346	Rochdale	153
Park Brompton Inn — Neighborhood Inns of Chicago	374	Room With a View	62
Park Central The Darlinghurst	160	Roomers	431
Park Lane Guesthouse	513	Rose Cottage	538
Park Lodge Hotel	143	Rosehill in the Fern	108
Park Manor Suites Hotel	275	Roseland Guest House & Campground	546
Parker House, The	284	Roussa	54
Parkside Parrot Inn	397	Royal Barracks Guest House	385
Pauger House Guest Suites	384	Royal Drive Cottages	359
Pennant Hall	132	Royal Hotel	173
Penryn House	107	Royal Palms, The	312
Pension Niebuhr	57	Rubens Bed & Breakfast	85
Pension Vallières	189	Ruby Slipper, The	28, 469
Penzion David Hotel	41	Rufus Tanner House	472
Phineas Swann B&B	526	Rural Roots Bed and Breakfast	174
Phoenix Nest	487	Sago Palms	260
Pikes Peak Paradise B&B	293	Saharan Motor Hotel	248
Pilgrim House Inn	428	Sallie & Eileen's Place	250
Pillars of Plainfield Bed & Breakfast, The	456	Saltamontes Retreat — Grasshopper Hill	463
Pilot House	330	Samurai, The	353
Pine Cove Inn, The	238	San Vicente Inn & Resort	249
Pitau	53	Sandpiper Beach House	432
Pleasant Grove B&B	473	Sandy's on the Strand	152
Pond Mountain Lodge & Resort	235	Santa Fe Luxury Bed & Breakfast	136
Post and Beam Bed & Breakfast	453	Santiago Resort	17, 261
Prague Home Stay	41	Santuario Inn Tucson	231
Priello Bed & Breakfast	71	Saouis	54
Primrose Hotel, The	99	Sappho's Oasis	226
Prince Albert Guest House, The	429	Sawmill Campground	343
Private Chateau Accommodations	47	Sea Breeze Resort	237
Private London Accommodations	117	Sea Drift Inn	432
Private Paris Accommodations	50	Sea Isle Resort	332

558   FERRARI GUIDES™

Sea Oats by the Gulf	341
Seagrape Villas	200
See Vue	495
Shakti Cove Cottages	536
Shalimar Hotel	105
Shangri-La Country Lodge	34
Sheraton Key West All-Suite Resort	332
SierraWood Guest House	244
Silver Lake	300
Simonton Court Historic Inn & Cottages	333
Sinclairs Guest House	106
Singel Suite — The Bed & Breakfast Suites	86
Six Webster Place	433
Smoketree Resort	237
Soho Guestrooms	118
Sonoma Chalet B&B	290
Sophie's Comfort	483
South Coast Inn Bed & Breakfast	490
Southwest Inn at Eagle Mountain	222
Southwest Inn at Sedona	227
Spring Valley Guest Ranch	190
Stanford Inn	442
Stewart's B&B	223
Stone Pillar B&B	485
Stonewall Acres	471
Stoney Ridge	502
Stoneybroke House	66
Stratford Lodge	121
Sullivan's Gulch Bed & Breakfast	493
Sullivans Hotel	9, 144
Summer Hill Farm	406
Summer Place, The	301
Summerhill Guest House	168
Summit House	514
Sunhead of 1617	87
Sunridge Hotel, The	111
Sunset Inn	434
Surf Hotel — Neighborhood Inns of Chicago	375
Surfside Resort Hotel	26, 455
Swanbourne Guest House	158
Sydney Star Accommodation	145
Symphony House	517
Tara Country Retreat	133
Te Puna Wai Lodge	164
Te Puru Coast View Lodge	161
Ten Cawthra Square B&B & Cawthra Square GH	183
Things Worth Remembering	340
Three Forty-Three Beharrell	377
Three Peaks	435
Three Thirty-Three West 88th Associates	480
Timberfell Lodge	512
Tin Roof Bed & Breakfast	409
Tortuga Roja Bed & Breakfast	14, 232
Touring Hotel	46
Tradewinds Inn, The	435
Triangle Inn	262
Triangle Inn-Santa Fe, The	468
Triple Lei/Huelo Point Lookout Cottages	366
Tropical Gardens Bed & Breakfast	344
Tropical Tune-Ups	354
Troutbeck	161
Tucker Inn at Twelve Center, The	25, 436
Turtle Cove Resort Cairns	149
Twenty-Four Henry Guesthouse	286
Twenty-Seven Blake Street	484
Twin Maples Bed & Breakfast	294
TwoSuns Inn Bed & Breakfast	508
Tybesta Tolfrue	130

UVW

Ursuline Guesthouse	386
Vicarage by the Sea, The	398
Victoria Court Sydney	146
Victoria Oaks Inn	295
Victorian Bed & Breakfast	405
Villa Konstantin	62
Villa Roumégous	55
Villa, The (Palm Springs)	263
Villa, The (SF)	20, 287
Villa, The (FL)	308
Villa, The (RI)	507
W.J. Marsh House Victorian B&B, The	462
Waikiki AA Studios (Bed & Breakfast Honolulu & Sta	370
Waipio Bay Lookout Lodging	367
Walker House	407
Warham Old Post Office Cottage	122
Watership Inn	437
Weekender Bed & Breakfast, The	176
West Wind Guest House, The	169
Westend Hotel & Cosmo Bar	88
West's Motor Inn, The	165
Whispering Pines B&B	291
Whispering Pines Bed & Breakfast/Retreat	494
Whistler Retreat, The	178
White Horse Hotel	93
White House Hotel, The	107
White Rabbit Inn & Catering	450
White Swan Guest House	534
Wild Lily Ranch	533
William & Garland Motel	486
William Lewis House, The	306
William Page Inn	399
Willows, The (Russian River)	269
Willows, The (SF)	288
Will's Reste	490
Wilson-Lee House Bed & Breakfast	530
Winchester Guest House (formerly Sapho's Choice)	184
Windamar House	437
Windsor Cottage	223
Windsor Inn	307
Wiscasset Place	399
Witchencroft	150
Wood Valley B&B Inn	355
Woodbine Villa	109

XYZ

Yellow Birch Farm	397
Yellowstone Riverview Lodge B&B	446
York Street House B&B, The	497
Zelkova Country Manor	488
Ziller House	28, 515

INN PLACES® 1998 559

FERRARI GUIDES
ORDER FORM

Please Send The Following Ferrari Guides To:

NAME

ADDRESS

CITY/STATE (PROVINCE)

ZIP/POSTAL CODE   COUNTRY

ITEM	PRICE/BK	QUANTITY	TOTAL
SUBSCRIPTION TO FERRARI GUIDES			
3-BOOK SET FOR MEN (Includes Shipping in US/CANADA)	$42.95		
3-BOOK SET FOR WOMEN (Includes Shipping in US/CANADA)	$41.95		
SINGLE COPIES			
Ferrari Guides' Gay Travel A to Z™	$16.00		
Ferrari Guides' Men's Travel in Your Pocket™	$16.00		
Ferrari Guides' Women's Travel in Your Pocket™	$14.00		
Ferrari Guides' Inn Places®	$16.00		
Ferrari Guides' Gay Paris	$17.95		
Ferrari Guides' Gay Mexico	$17.95		
SHIPPING: USA CANADA ONE BOOK $5.00 $10.00 TWO BOOKS $6.00 $12.50 THREE BOOKS $7.00 $15.00 FOUR BOOKS $8.00 $17.50			
PLEASE ENCLOSE THIS AMOUNT			

All prices are in US dollars. Prices good for US & Canada only.
All other countries: Please fax/phone/e-mail for additional shipping cost.

SEND TO:
Ferrari International Publishing, Inc.
P.O. Box 37887, Phoenix, AZ 85069 USA
Tel: (602) 863-2408 Fax: (602) 439-3952
E-mail: ferrari@q-net.com
Internet Orders: http://www.q-net.com